**Critical Acclaim for
Ron Chernow's *The House of Morgan*,
WINNER OF THE 1990 NATIONAL BOOK AWARD FOR NON-FICTION:**

"*The House of Morgan* offers a long look at how the contemporary financial landscape came into being. . . . A panoramic and well-researched look at the most powerful family of banks in America over the last century . . . Chernow has a supple, refined style." —*The Washington Post Book World*

"Chernow presents fresh portraits of the Morgans and the brilliant senior partners who made the bank an international powerhouse. . . . He dishes up enough scandal, tragedy, and intrigue for a TV miniseries." —*USA Today*

"A brilliant, generation-spanning history of the Morgan banking empire, which offers a wealth of social and political as well as economic perspectives. . . . He writes in a lively, definite fashion that could make the exhaustively documented account the standard reference for specialists as well as lay readers." —*Kirkus Reviews* (starred review)

"Entertaining and meticulously researched . . . pulls aside the cloak of mystery that has long surrounded this powerful American institution . . . that wielded far more power than most Americans ever imagined, even in their most fevered nightmares." —*Dallas Times Herald*

"Packed with revelations, Chernow's mammoth history demystifies the inner workings of the secretive Morgan banking empire." —*Publisher's Weekly*

"Brilliantly researched and written, *The House of Morgan* is to . . . *Liar's Poker* what *War and Peace* is to a Judith Krantz novel. . . . To a potentially dry and certainly difficult subject—the influence of high finance on modern life—Chernow brings a lively style and the endurance of a trouper." —*The Wall Street Journal*

"Long, ambitions, but highly readable . . . Chernow highlights the degree to which the Morgan bank symbolized an era of Anglo-American hegemony and the growing shift of financial power from London to New York. . . . The book is as much about the characters of Morgan as about its history." —*The Economist*

"Chernow vividly portrays the influence that the Morgan banks have had on the history of the Western economy since the late-eighteenth century. . . . Epic . . . An important book." —*Library Jounral* (starred review)

THE HOUSE OF
MORGAN

An American Banking
Dynasty and the Rise of
Modern Finance

RON CHERNOW

GROVE PRESS
New York

For Valerie and Israel and Ruth

·

Published simultaneously in Canada
Printed in the United States of America

Library of Congress Cataloging-in-Publication Data

Chernow, Ron.
      The house of Morgan: an American Banking dynasty and
the
   rise of modern finance / by Ron Chernow.

      ISBN 978-0-8021-4465-2
      eISBN 978-0-8021-9813-6

      1. Morgan Guaranty Trust Company of New York—
History.
      2. Banks and banking—United States—History. I. Title.

      HG2613.N54M6613 1990 332.1'2'097471—dc20   89-
17542

DESIGN BY JOYCE C. WESTON

Grove Press
an imprint of Grove Atlantic
154 West 14th Street
New York, NY 10011

Distributed by Publishers Group West
groveatlantic.com

22 23 24 25   16 15 14 13 12

It is necessarily part of the business
of a banker to profess a conventional respectability
which is more than human. Life-long practices of
this kind make them the most romantic and
the least realistic of men.

—*John Maynard Keynes*

CONTENTS

"THE HOUSE OF MORGAN"
20TH ANNIVERSARY EDITION

Like many first books, *The House of Morgan* was something of a happy accident in the author's life when it was published twenty years ago. After years toiling in the vineyard of freelance magazine work, I decided to take a breather from that hectic world in the mid 1980s and landed a job in a public policy foundation called The Twentieth Century Fund, where I was put in charge of financial policy studies. During this heyday of the bull market that roared through Ronald Reagan's presidency, huge numbers of people were swept into the financial world for the first time, whether as foot soldiers in investment banks or small investors dabbling in common stocks, and they had little historic perspective on the new world they inhabited.

As I dipped into the rich literature of financial history, I was struck that the old Wall Street—elite, clubby, and dominated by small, mysterious partnerships—bore scant resemblance to the universe of faceless conglomerates springing up across the globe. It dawned on me that the hordes of financial novices might be ripe for a history that would chronicle how the old Wall Street evolved into the new. A straight history, I knew, would be a tedious task for readers and do small justice to the turbulent pageant of heroes and scoundrels I was unearthing. So I posed the question: was there a single family or firm whose saga could serve as a prism through which to view the panoramic saga of Anglo-American finance? There were relatively few dynasties in financial history and, hence, few suitable candidates. Some names, such as Rothschild, had long since passed the zenith of their glory, while others had a contemporary resonance with only shallow roots in the past. Only one firm, one family, one name rather gloriously spanned the entire century and a half that I wanted to cover: J.P. Morgan. To reconstruct the Morgan story, I realized, would be a daunting enterprise, for I would have to narrate the intricate stories of four interlocking firms: J.P. Morgan and Morgan Stanley in New York, Morgan Grenfell in London, and Morgan et Compagnie in Paris.

As an old English major and novelist *manque*, I had no training in historical methods, nobody to steer me in the right direction, as I bumbled about in my early research. I had naively assumed that, within its august walls, J.P. Morgan & Co. housed a comprehensive set of historical papers and that it would be my task to lay my hands on it. For six months, I lunched with two affable bank representatives as they and their associates debated whether to cooperate with my project. Then one day, I made a startling discovery: the papers of Thomas W. Lamont, senior partner of the Morgan bank during the inter-war years, resided at the Harvard Business School Library. During my first day of research there, I pored over correspondence between Lamont and Franklin Roosevelt, Benito Mussolini, Charles Lindbergh, and Nancy Astor. These papers threw open a window on the hermetically sealed world of Morgan partners.

Aside from the grace and clarity of these letters—old-school bankers tended to be surprisingly literate—they were detailed and gripping beyond my wildest imaginings. When Lamont spoke on the telephone with President Herbert Hoover, for instance, a dutiful amanuensis took down a verbatim transcript. Suddenly, the opaque Morgan world had turned transparent. Soon I uncovered papers of other Morgan partners at Amherst, Yale, Columbia, the University of Virginia, and, of course, the Morgan Library in New York. Sometimes I felt as if I could trail the Morgan partners around the bank on an almost hourly basis. Curiously enough, nobody at J.P. Morgan & Co. had ever noticed the disappearance of tens, perhaps hundreds, of thousands of internal documents. So much for the vaunted Morgan reputation for secrecy!

When I signed the contract for *The House of Morgan*, I had worried about a shortage of original documents and now had to contend with the embarrassment of riches. My advance, if generous for a first book, could scarcely cover years of leisurely research, so I had to cram a gigantic amount of work into a brief span. Somehow I managed to research and write an eight hundred-page book in two-and-a-half years—a feat I could never duplicate today. I was sustained by the sheer excitement of my findings, the knowledge that I had luckily stumbled upon the foremost drama in financial history. I also coasted on the pent-up energy of a young writer who had finally secured his first book contract after many failed efforts. Whenever I think of the time spent on the book, I remember the headlong pace, the frantic reading into the night, the exhausting attempt to squeeze the epic story of finance between two covers. It is therefore with a sense of miraculous good fortune that I now open the book and find lucid, coherent prose that shows, at least to my eyes, little of the sweat and haste of its creation.

R.C.
BROOKLYN, NEW YORK
SEPTEMBER 2009

PROLOGUE

This book is about the rise, fall, and resurrection of an American banking empire—the House of Morgan. Perhaps no other institution has been so encrusted with legend, so ripe with mystery, or exposed to such bitter polemics. Until 1989, J. P. Morgan and Company solemnly presided over American finance from the "Corner" of Broad and Wall. Flanked by the New York Stock Exchange and Federal Hall, the short building at 23 Wall Street, with its unmarked, catercorner entrance, exhibited a patrician aloofness. Much of our story revolves around this chiseled marble building and the presidents and prime ministers, moguls and millionaires who marched up its steps. With the records now available, we can follow them inside the world's most secretive bank.

The old pre-1935 House of Morgan was probably the most formidable financial combine in history. Started by an American banker, George Peabody, in London in 1838, it was inherited by the Morgan family and transplanted to New York to famous effect. In the popular mind, the two most familiar Morgans—J. P. Morgan, Sr. (1837–1913), and J. P. Morgan, Jr. (1867–1943)—are rolled into a composite beast, J. P. Morgan, that somehow endured for more than a century. Their striking physical resemblance—the bald pate, the bulbous nose, the pear-shaped frame—has only fed confusion. For admirers, these two J. P. Morgans typified the sound, old-fashioned banker whose word was his bond and who sealed his deals with a handshake. Detractors saw them as hypocritical tyrants who bullied companies, conspired with foreign powers, and coaxed America into war for profit. Nobody was ever neutral about the Morgans.

Before the Depression, 23 Wall was headquarters of an empire with several foreign outposts. Seated behind rolltop desks on the Broad Street side, the New York partners were allied with three other partnerships— Morgan Grenfell in London, Morgan et Compagnie in Paris, and Drexel and Company, the so-called Philadelphia branch of J. P. Morgan. Of these, Morgan Grenfell was easily the most powerful, forming the central London–New York axis of the Morgan empire. It was a transatlantic post office for British and American state secrets. Before the New Deal, the term "House of Morgan" applied either to J. P. Morgan and Com-

xi

pany in New York or, more broadly, to the whole shadowy web of partnerships.

The old House of Morgan spawned a thousand conspiracy theories and busied generations of muckrakers. As the most mandarin of banks, it catered to many prominent families, including the Astors, Guggenheims, du Ponts, and Vanderbilts. It shunned dealings with lesser mortals, thus breeding popular suspicion. Since it financed many industrial giants, including U.S. Steel, General Electric, General Motors, Du Pont, and American Telephone and Telegraph, it entered into their councils and aroused fear of undue banker power. The early House of Morgan was something of a cross between a central bank and a private bank. It stopped panics, saved the gold standard, rescued New York City three times, and arbitrated financial disputes. If its concerns transcended an exclusive desire for profit, it also had a peculiar knack for making good works pay.

What gave the House of Morgan its tantalizing mystery was its government links. Much like the old Rothschilds and Barings, it seemed insinuated into the power structure of many countries, especially the United States, England, and France, and, to a lesser degree, Italy, Belgium, and Japan. As an instrument of U.S. power abroad, its actions were often endowed with broad significance in terms of foreign policy. At a time when a parochial America looked inward, the bank's ties abroad, especially those with the British Crown, gave it an ambiguous character and raised questions about its national loyalties. The old Morgan partners were financial ambassadors whose daily business was often closely intertwined with affairs of state. Even today, J. P. Morgan and Company is probably closer to the world's central banks than any other bank.

This empire was shattered by the Glass-Steagall Act of 1933, which erected a high wall between commercial banking (making loans and accepting deposits) and investment banking (issuing stocks and bonds). In 1935, J. P. Morgan and Company chose to remain a commercial bank and spun off Morgan Stanley, an investment house. Seeded with J. P. Morgan capital and personnel, Morgan Stanley for decades clearly exhibited common ancestry with its Morgan brother down the block. They shared many clients and kept alive a family feeling no less potent for its informality. Glass-Steagall didn't bar J. P. Morgan from holding a minority stake in an *overseas* securities house, however. Until 1981, it kept a one-third interest in Morgan Grenfell. As our story will show, the three Morgan houses functioned as a *de facto* House of Morgan long after the New Deal ended and in the early 1970s even contemplated reunion. Today for the first time, the three houses lack formal links and are engaged in fierce rivalry. As deregulation in London and New York has dismantled old regulatory barriers, the three increasingly clash as they sell competing services.

While people know the Morgan houses by name, they are often mystified by their business. They practice a brand of banking that has little resemblance to standard retail banking. These banks have no teller cages, issue no consumer loans, and grant no mortgages. Rather, they perpetuate an ancient European tradition of wholesale banking, serving governments, large corporations, and rich individuals. As practitioners of high finance, they cultivate a discreet style. They avoid branches, seldom hang out signposts, and (until recently) wouldn't advertise. Their strategy was to make clients feel accepted into a private club, as if a Morgan account were a membership card to the aristocracy.

The truest heir to the old House of Morgan is J. P. Morgan and Company, also known by the name of its bank subsidiary, Morgan Guaranty Trust. A universe away from the coarse bustle of Chase Manhattan or Citibank, it seduces the rich with leather armchairs, grandfather clocks, and polished brass lamps. In private dining rooms, anniversaries of accounts are celebrated, with customers receiving engraved menus as souvenirs. The bank won't soil its white gloves with just anybody's cash, and many depositors bring along corporate connections. Although the bank is bashful about revealing precise figures, it prefers personal accounts of at least $5 million and will occasionally stoop as low as $2 million—as a favor. The Morgan bank is the foremost repository of old American money.

While private accounts give Morgan its glamorous cachet, they generate only a small fraction of the profits. The bank concentrates on blue-chip corporations and governments, organizing large credits and securities issues and trading foreign exchange and other instruments. The Morgan bank used to boast that ninety-six of America's one hundred largest corporations were clients and hinted that in two of the remaining cases, it had blackballed the companies as unfit. As with personal accounts, it never wanted to appear too eager for business. Instead of setting up offices hither and yon, it preferred to have clients make pilgrimages to it. This rule applied to its outposts abroad as well: a Lyons businessman would travel to Paris, a Midlands businessman to London, to see his Morgan banker. Even in today's far more competitive world, there is seldom more than one J. P. Morgan office in a country.

For more than a century, this traditional formula, reworked many times, has paid off handsomely. On the eve of the 1987 crash, J. P.

Morgan and Company was America's most expensive bank, even though only the fourth largest. Based on its share price, it would have cost $8.5 billion to buy, or more than Citicorp. Although beleaguered by over $4 billion of Latin American debt, J. P. Morgan's subsidiary bank, Morgan Guaranty, was America's only major bank to boast a triple-A rating. For most of the 1980s, it had the highest return on equity of any bank, often ranking second in profits only to Citicorp and with only *half* its assets. As the nation's premier trust bank, it managed $65 billion in securities on Black Monday 1987. It has been praised as "first in quality by about any measure you can think of" and "for many the perfect bank."[1] Although a fair share of blunders and isolated scandals have undercut the hyperbole, the judgments remain generally valid.

At least until it swept into hostile takeovers in the late 1980s, Morgan Guaranty best retained the historic Morgan culture of gentlemanly propriety and conservative dealings. As confidant of the Federal Reserve and other central banks, it still exhibits vestiges of its old statesman's role. Morgan Stanley, in contrast, has wandered furthest from its roots. From 1935 through the 1970s, it enjoyed a reign such as no investment bank will ever match. Its clients included six of the seven-sister oil companies (Gulf Oil being the exception) and seven of America's ten largest companies. Such success led to storied arrogance, a comic vanity. When one partner left for First Boston in the mid-1970s, he was congratulated by another: "That's really exciting. Now you'll be dealing with the *second*-best list of clients."[2] Indeed, the client rosters of any two competitors together couldn't have touched Morgan Stanley's. When the firm started advertising in the 1970s, an agency created a sketch of a thunderbolt piercing a cloud, with the caption, "IF GOD WANTED TO DO A FINANCING, HE WOULD CALL MORGAN STANLEY." For Morgan Stanley partners, this neatly summarized their place in the cosmos. Asked at the 1988 annual meeting about the firm's policy of serving on nonclient boards, Chairman S. Parker Gilbert paused thoughtfully and replied, "We have no non-clients."[3]

Once nicknamed the house of Blood, Brains, and Money, Morgan Stanley fussily demanded exclusive relations with companies. If clients dared to consult another house, they were advised to look elsewhere for a banker. Wall Street grumbled about these "golden handcuffs," but neither it nor the Justice Department could ever break the shackles; far from feeling imprisoned, companies craved this association with the Morgan mystique and gloried in their servitude. In floating stocks or bonds, Morgan Stanley insisted on being sole manager, its name engraved in solitary splendor atop the "tombstone ads" that announce offerings. This pomposity was clever advertising, helping to make Morgan Stanley the "Rolls Royce of investment bankers."[4]

Today Morgan Stanley occupies sixteen floors of the Exxon Building in New York City. Its odyssey from a small, genteel underwriting house to a razzle-dazzle financial conglomerate traces the rise of modern Wall Street itself. It has been the perfect bellwether of postwar finance. Long regarded as uncommonly successful but stuffy, it underwent a startling metamorphosis in the 1970s, from which it emerged in unrecognizably aggressive form. Once Wall Street's most conservative firm, it violated taboos it had conscientiously upheld and made respectable a far rougher style of finance. In 1974, it carried out the first hostile raid of the modern era, then dominated that rambunctious world. (In early 1989, it was still America's top merger adviser, claiming $60 billion in deals during the year's first half.) In the 1980s, it gentrified junk bonds and amassed a huge two-billion-dollar war chest for leveraged buyouts, the decade's riskiest innovation. After shocking Wall Street by siding with corporate raiders, it became a raider itself, acquiring stakes in forty companies. For more than a decade, an incredulous business press has exclaimed, "*This* is Morgan Stanley?" All the while, with its 30-percent return on equity, it has consistently rated as the most profitable of publicly traded securities firms. It has had unerring strategic judgment.

To complete the family album, we note Morgan Grenfell, one of London's most prestigious merchant banks. Throughout its history, it has exuded an aura of Eton, country houses, gentleman's clubs, and Savile Row tailoring. Tucked away at an angle on L-shaped Great Winchester Street in the City—London's equivalent of Wall Street—it stands unmarked behind a tall, pedimented portal and gauzy curtains. Inside, it has the winding, intimate passageways of a private mansion, lined with small conference rooms named after deceased partners.

In the early postwar years, Morgan Grenfell was run by a clutch of rather tired, apathetic old peers and was derisively termed the House of Lords by Morgan Guaranty people. (It still has several knights and lords on its blue-ribbon board.) Through much of the 1950s and 1960s, it mostly issued securities for venerable industrial clients and battled against a lethargy bred by success. Then, like Morgan Stanley, it cast off its sloth and turned into the City's most marauding firm, specializing in aggressive takeovers. Like Morgan Stanley, it used its prestige to stretch the limits of acceptable behavior and became the gentleman pirate of the City. As the star of London's takeover scene in the 1980s, it shattered the sedate world of British finance it had once exemplified.

Throughout the decade, it regularly ranked first in London takeovers and by 1985 was managing four of the six largest acquisitions in the City. Then its dandified raiders, with their swaggering style, led the firm straight into the share-price manipulation of the Guinness scandal. Prime Minister Margaret Thatcher would personally demand the heads of two Morgan Grenfell executives in what was regarded as the City's worst scandal of the century.

The story of the three Morgan banks is nothing less than the history of Anglo-American finance itself. For 150 years, they have stood at the center of every panic, boom, and crash on Wall Street or in the City. They have weathered wars and depressions, scandals and hearings, bomb blasts and attempted assassinations. No other financial dynasty in modern times has so steadily maintained its preeminence. Its chronicle holds up a mirror in which we can study the changes in the style, ethics, and etiquette of high finance. To order this vast panorama, we will divide our saga into three periods. This framework applies principally to the Morgan houses but also has, I think, more general relevance to other banks.

During the pre-1913 Baronial Age of Pierpont Morgan, bankers were masters of the economy, or "lords of creation," in author Frederick Lewis Allen's phrase. They financed canals and railroads, steel mills and shipping lines, supplying the capital for a nascent industrial society. In this age of savagely unruly competition, bankers settled disputes among companies and organized trusts to tame competition. As the major intermediaries between users and providers of capital, they oversaw massive industrial development. Because they rationed scarce capital, they were often more powerful than the companies they financed and acquired increasing control over them. This produced a generation of headstrong bankers who rolled up fabled fortunes, aroused terror in the populace, and finally prompted a political campaign to curb their hypertrophied influence.

In the Diplomatic Age of J. P. Morgan, Jr., bounded by the two world wars, private bankers served as adjuncts of government, performing covert missions and operating as co-equals of central banks. Morgan bankers were now power brokers and unofficial representatives of governments at global conferences. As confidants of kings, presidents, and popes, they operated under the close supervision of Washington or Whitehall in foreign dealings. To the outside world, they often seemed the visible face of government policy. At home, they remained "traditional banker" to companies that, if still loyal, decreasingly needed the patronage of a strong banker. Maintaining exclusive relations with clients, the Morgan partners enjoyed the luxury of a world that seems enviably graceful and unhurried by modern standards.

In the postwar Casino Age, bankers have lost control over clients in the fierce, anonymous competition of global markets. Multinational corporations now tower over bankers and rival them in terms of capital and financial expertise. Institutional investors, such as insurance companies, mutual funds, and pension funds, present new countervailing sources of power. With companies and governments able to raise money in many currencies and countries, the power balance has tilted dramatically away from the bankers. This sounds paradoxical in an age dominated by daily news stories of flashy billion-dollar deals. Yet as the Morgan story shows, this new style of financial aggression is really a symptom of the bankers' weakness. As their old clients have been liberated, gentleman bankers have had to hustle for business and search for new niches. They have found these niches in a ruthless world of corporate takeovers that has rescued them but endangered the economy. In this bruising new age of finance, bankers have jettisoned traditions that had ruled Anglo-American finance since Victorian times.

This book's thesis is that there will never be another bank as powerful, mysterious, or opulent as the old House of Morgan. What the Rothschilds represented in the nineteenth century and the Morgans in the twentieth won't be replicated by any firm in the next century. The banker no longer enjoys a monopoly on large pools of money. As world finance has matured, power has become dispersed among many institutions and financial centers. So our story looks back at a banking world fast vanishing from sight—one of vast estates, art collections, and ocean-going yachts, of bankers who hobnobbed with heads of state and fancied themselves ersatz royalty. Contrary to the usual law of perspective, the Morgans seem to grow larger as they recede in time.

BROOKLYN, NEW YORK
JULY 1989

Simplified Chronology of the Morgan Empire

London	New York	Paris
1838 Peabody, Riggs and Company	**1861** J. P. Morgan and Company	**1868** Drexel, Harjes and Company
1843 George Peabody	**1864** Dabney, Morgan and Company	**1895** Morgan, Harjes and Company
1851 George Peabody and Company	**1871** Drexel, Morgan and Company	**1926** Morgan et Compagnie
1854 Junius Morgan becomes a partner of George Peabody.	**1895** J. P. Morgan and Company	**1940** Morgan et Compagnie, Société Anonyme, approved as Paris branch of J. P. Morgan and Company.
1864 J. S. Morgan and Company	**1935** Morgan Stanley and Company (investment bank)	**1962** Creation of Morgan et Compagnie, Société Anonyme (Euromarket underwriting operation of Morgan Guaranty Trust and Morgan Grenfell). Morgan Guaranty continues its Paris branch as a parallel operation.
1910 Morgan Grenfell and Company	**1935** J. P. Morgan and Company (commercial bank)	
1934 Morgan Grenfell and Company Limited (J. P. Morgan and Company stake reduced to one-third; remaining third sold in 1981–82)	**1940** J. P. Morgan and Company, Incorporated	
1981 Creation of Morgan Grenfell Incorporated, an investment banking	**1942** J. P. Morgan and Company sells shares to the public for first time.	
	1959 Merger with Guaranty Trust to form Morgan	
	1970 Partial incorporation	
	1975 Full incorporation	
	1977 Creation of Morgan Stanley International in London	
	1986 Morgan Stanley sells shares to public for first time.	

subsidiary in New York.

1986 Morgan Grenfell sells shares to the public for first time.

1989 Deutsche Bank buys Morgan Grenfell.

Guaranty Trust Company of New York

1969 Creation of J. P. Morgan and Company Incorporated (one-bank holding company for Morgan Guaranty Trust)

1979 Creation of Morgan Guaranty Ltd in London (name changed to J. P. Morgan Securities Ltd. in 1988)

1988 J. P. Morgan becomes worldwide marketing name for J. P. Morgan and Company, Inc., and for Morgan Guaranty Trust Company.

1967 Morgan et Compagnie International (Morgan Stanley buys a two-thirds stake)

1975 Morgan Stanley buys remaining one-third stake in Morgan et Compagnie International from Morgan Guaranty and Morgan Grenfell.

PART ONE

The Internal Age

The Baronial Age
1838-1913

CHAPTER ONE

SCROOGE

• •

•

W H E N Baltimore merchant George Peabody sailed for London in 1835, the world was in the throes of a debt crisis. The defaulting governments weren't obscure Balkan nations or South American republics but American states. The United States had succumbed to a craze for building railroads, canals, and turnpikes, all backed by state credit. Now Maryland legislators, with the bravado of the ruined, threatened to join other states in skipping interest payments on their bonds, which were largely marketed in London. As one of three state commissioners assigned to renegotiate the debt, Peabody urged officials to tone down their rhetoric and placate British bankers. But American legislators found it easier to pander to the hatred of foreign bankers rather than to raise new taxes to service debt.

London was the sun in the financial solar system. Only Britain had a huge surplus of funds in a capital-short world, and sterling was the currency of world trade; its official use dated back to William the Conqueror. In the afterglow of the Napoleonic Wars, bankers of the City—London's financial district—were self-styled potentates, often with access to more money than the governments and companies they financed. Firms such as Barings and Rothschilds maintained an imperial reserve, omitting their names from doorways and letterheads, refusing to solicit business or open branches, and demanding exclusive client relations. Statesmen from Europe and Latin America trooped humbly to their doorsteps. One observer remarked, "to be asked for lunch was like being received in audience by a king."[1]

Though intensely patriotic, the forty-year-old Peabody identified with the British creditors. When the other Maryland commissioners returned home in despair, Peabody threw a glittering dinner for a dozen bankers to persuade them that Americans weren't all rustic swindlers. He argued that only new loans could guarantee repayment of the old—a convenient line to be echoed by many future debtor states. Far from cutting off Maryland's credit, the bankers advanced another $8 million. As his friend the English political leader George Owen said of Peabody, "He borrowed the money on his face."[2] To mitigate British prejudice against "venal" Americans, he boldly waived his $60,000 commission from Maryland.

Peabody, a good talker, was not prepossessing. Over six feet tall with light blue eyes and dark brown hair, he had a rumpled face, with knobby chin, bulbous nose, side whiskers, and heavy-lidded eyes. That this homely man would found the House of Morgan—later a white-glove affair with high-society partners famous for good looks and stylish dress—is ironic. He carried the scars of early poverty and was quick to feel slights and perceive enemies. Like many who have overcome early hardship by brute force, he was proud but insecure, always at war with the world and counting his injuries.

Born in Danvers, Massachusetts, he had only a few years of schooling. When he was a teenager, his father died, and Peabody worked in his brother's shop to support his widowed mother and six siblings. When he later prospered in a Baltimore dry-goods business with a rich older partner, Elisha Riggs, he remained haunted by his past. "I have never forgotten and never can forget the great privations of my early years," he later said.[3] He hoarded his money, worked incessantly, and retained a lonely air.

In 1837, Peabody moved to London. A year later he opened a merchant house at 31 Moorgate in London, furnishing it with a mahogany counter, a safe, and some desks. He joined a select group of merchant bankers who traded in dry goods and also financed such trade; hence, their businesses became known as merchant banks. They developed a form of wholesale banking remote from the prosaic world of bank books, teller windows, and checking accounts. Their specialty was "high finance"—serving only governments, large companies, and rich individuals. They financed overseas trade, issued stocks and bonds, and dealt in commodities. Ordinary people could no more do business with George Peabody than they can today place a deposit with Morgan Guaranty, Morgan Grenfell, or Morgan Stanley.

In setting up in London, Peabody planted the American flag in alien territory. The United States relied on British capital to finance development and often resented that its economic fate was decided abroad. As one congressman said in 1833, "the barometer of the American money market hangs up at the stock exchange in London."[4] Peabody, hoping to tap this transatlantic money flow, became a leading dealer of American state bonds in London, reversing a contemporary trend in which London banks sent representatives to America. The House of Baring—which bankrolled the Louisiana Purchase and always had an American on its board—employed Thomas Ward as its American agent, while the Rothschilds, who were ambivalent about America, posted August Belmont, Sr., to New York.

Instead of blending into his British milieu, Peabody shrewdly flaunted his Americanism, wrapping himself in the flag and boosting American products. He declared that George Peabody and Company would be "an American house," and that he wanted to give it "an American atmosphere—to furnish it with American journals—to make it a centre for American news, and an agreeable place for my American friends visiting London."[5] Yet amid the patriotic pride lurked a colonial mentality, possibly a sense of his own inferiority, a constant need to impress the British. He hoped to refute what had "almost become a byword among the English that no American House in London could long sustain their credit."[6]

Beneath a genial air, Peabody was a solitary miser. He lived in furnished rooms in a Regent Street hotel and aside from taking occasional fishing trips, worked nonstop. During one twelve-year period, he never took off two consecutive days and spent an average of ten hours per day at work. Notwithstanding his stirring speeches about America's destiny, he didn't return home for twenty years, and during that time his personality darkened along with the dismal performance of American state bonds. During the severe depression of the early 1840s—a decade dubbed the Hungry Forties—state debt plunged to fifty cents on the dollar. The worst came when five American states—Pennsylvania, Mississippi, Indiana, Arkansas, and Michigan—and the Florida territory defaulted on their interest payments. In an early debtors' cartel, some American governors banded together to favor debt repudiation. To this day, the reprobate Mississippi remains in unashamed default.

British investors cursed America as a land of cheats, rascals, and ingrates. State defaults also tainted federal credit, and when Washington sent Treasury agents to Europe in 1842, James de Rothschild thundered, "Tell them you have seen the man who is at the head of the finances of Europe, and that he has told you that they cannot borrow a dollar. Not a dollar."[7] Clergyman Sydney Smith sneered at the American "mob" and said that whenever he met a Pennsylvanian at a London dinner, he felt "a disposition to seize and divide him. . . . How such a man can set himself down at an English table without feeling that he owes two or three pounds to every man in the company, I am at a loss to conceive; he has no more right to eat with honest men than a leper has to eat with clean men."[8] Even Charles Dickens couldn't resist a jab, portraying a nightmare in which Scrooge's solid British assets are transformed into "a mere United States' security."[9]

When his beloved Maryland defaulted, Peabody's own nightmare was complete. Whenever he met a British investor, he said, he felt shame. The British were especially incensed over Maryland and Pennsylvania because those states were settled by Anglo-Saxon stock and therefore should have known better. Having marketed about half of Maryland's securities to individual investors in Europe, Peabody was victimized by his own success. The brouhaha had direct repercussions, and he became *persona non grata* around London. The London *Times* noted that while Peabody was an "American gentleman of the most unblemished character," the Reform Club had blackballed him for being a citizen of a country that reneged on its debts.[10] Gloomily he wrote a friend, "You and I will, I trust, see that happy day, when as formerly, we can own ourselves Americans in Europe, without a blush for the character of our Country."[11]

A hallmark of merchant bankers was that they vouched for the securities they sponsored. At first, Peabody merely sent letters to Baltimore friends, scolding them about the need for Maryland to resume interest payments. Then he tired of persuasion and rewarded reporters with small gratuities for favorable articles about the state. At last, in 1845 he conspired with Barings to push Maryland into resuming payment. They set up a political slush fund to spread propaganda for debt resumption and to elect sympathetic legislators; they even drafted the clergy into giving sermons on the sanctity of contracts. By means of a secret account, the two firms transferred £1,000 to Baltimore, 90 percent from Barings and 10 percent from Peabody—a strategy Barings duplicated in Pennsylvania. Most shocking of all, Barings bribed Daniel Webster, the orator and statesman, to make speeches for debt repayment. The bankers conducted this shabby campaign with a skulking sense of guilt; it wasn't their preferred style. "Your payment to Mr. Webster would not appear very well if it should get out," Joshua Bates, the senior Baring partner, warned Thomas Ward, American bagman for the operation.[12] Bates, a sober, diligent Bostonian, cringed at what they were doing: "I have a sort of instinctive horror of doing one thing to effect another, or using any sort of subterfuge or reserve," he confessed to Ward.[13]

Whatever their scruples, the conspiracy thrived: pro-resumption

Whigs were elected in both Maryland and Pennsylvania, and London bankers again received payments from both states.[14] Peabody, never one to forget an injury, excluded the most persistent debtors, Florida and Mississippi, from his later philanthropies. Even altruism had its limits.

When the depreciated state bonds Peabody had bought up in the early 1840s paid interest again, he reaped a fortune. Then, as revolution swept across the Continent in 1848, American securities seemed a safe haven in comparison with Europe. And as the California gold rush and Mexican War wiped away the last vestiges of depression by the late 1840s, Peabody took new pride in his native roots. Now he fancied himself the ambassador of American culture in London and dispensed barrels full of American apples, Boston crackers, and hominy grits.

On July 4, 1851, he hosted the first of his Independence Day dinners, featuring the elderly duke of Wellington as guest of honor. Beneath a portrait of Queen Victoria and a Gilbert Stuart of George Washington, the British minister in Washington and the American minister in London drained an oak loving cup and toasted the start of the Great Exhibition in London's new Crystal Palace. Because Congress wouldn't finance American exhibitors, Peabody played the impresario, paying to display Cyrus McCormick's reaper and Samuel Colt's revolvers. But not all of Peabody's July Fourth pageants of Anglo-American friendship followed the desired script. In 1854, when Peabody toasted Queen Victoria before President Pierce—an act Washington thought arch heresy—James Buchanan, the U.S. ambassador in London and later President, indignantly stormed from the room.

As banker and cicerone for Americans in London—once, in a single week, he dined eighty visiting Americans and took thirty-five to the opera—Peabody was constantly exposed to the fierce snobbery of British aristocrats toward the American commercial class. This condescension was particularly flagrant during Commodore Vanderbilt's trip to London in 1853. The Commodore—vulgar, profane, and lecherous—wanted to show London society the full splendor of America's richest man. With his wife and twelve children, he had sailed to England aboard his ornate, two-thousand-ton North Star, equipped with caterer, doctor, and chaplain. Peabody squired the Vanderbilts about Hyde Park and installed them in his box at Covent Garden; meanwhile, the court ostracized the ostentatious Commodore.

Peabody amassed a $20-million fortune in the 1850s as he financed everything from the silk trade with China to iron rail exports to America. Although he built a lyceum and library for his native Danvers in the early 1850s, he mostly hoarded his money in preparation for the next panic. His insecurities only worsened as he had more to lose. He told a friend in 1852, "My capital is . . . ample (certainly nearer 400,000 pounds than 300,000) . . . but I have passed too many money panics, unscathed, not to have seen how often large Capitals are swept away, and that even with my own I must use caution."[15]

Junius Morgan, who became Peabody's partner in 1854, later told how he found him one morning at the countinghouse looking sickly and rheumatic. The miserly Peabody didn't own a carriage but came to work by public horsecar. "Mr. Peabody, with that cold you ought not to stick here," Morgan said. Taking hat and umbrella, Peabody agreed to go home. Twenty minutes later, on his way to the Royal Exchange, Morgan found Peabody standing in the rain. "Mr. Peabody, I thought you were going home," the younger man said. "Well, I am, Morgan," Peabody replied, "but there's only been a twopenny bus come along as yet and I am waiting for a penny one."[16] By this time, Peabody's bank account bulged with over £1 million.

Enjoying the clerk's revenge, Thomas Perman, Peabody's assistant, handed down a trove of nasty stories that tarnish the halo Peabody acquired as a result of his benevolence. He told how his boss, who ate lunch at his desk each day from a small leather lunch box, would dispatch an office boy to buy him an apple. These apples cost one pence halfpenny, and Peabody would give the boy twopence; although the boy dreamed of keeping the halfpenny change as a tip, Peabody always demanded it back.

By the early 1850s, Peabody was approaching sixty and plagued by gout and rheumatism. His annual savings were staggering: he spent only about $3,000 of a total annual income of $300,000.[17] With such wealth and such stinginess, he was ripe for spiritual conversion. As he later said, "When aches and pains came upon me, I realized I was not immortal . . . I found that there were men in life just as anxious to help the poor and destitute as I was to make money."[18]

Wanting to dedicate himself to philanthropy, Peabody had only one problem. As an autocratic banker, he had never shared authority and only reluctantly made his office manager, Charles C. Gooch, a junior partner in 1851, so that someone could act in his absence. Gooch was a sad-faced Bob Cratchit who addressed Peabody like a trembling clerk; in fact, he had started as head clerk. He started one letter to his boss by writing, "Dear Sir, I do not often trouble you with letters, for I know you do not like the trouble of reading them, & mine are on subjects not over agreeable."[19] Gooch was being groomed for a career of permanent subordination and forelock tugging.

Ordinarily, Peabody would have chosen a son or nephew to take over the business. Most merchant banks were family partnerships with a few talented outsiders. But as a bachelor, Peabody was in the unusual position of having to shop for an heir and bequeath his empire to a stranger. He was, however, no stranger to the company of women. While he didn't smoke or drink, he resorted to the shadowy world of illicit pleasures. The tale-bearing Perman regaled the Morgans with the story of Peabody's mistress in Brighton, whom he liberally favored with advances of £2,000. He excluded this woman and her illegitimate daughter from his will, and for years after his death, Peabody's daughter Mrs. Thomas would materialize and badger the Morgans for money. In the late 1890s, the Morgans received an appeal from her two sons—one training to be a barrister, the other at Oxford or Cambridge. The aging Perman was dispatched to verify their Peabody genes. When he returned, he breathed with amazement, "Both of them have the old man's nose to a dot."[20]

We don't know why Peabody relegated love to the dim corners of his life. In general, he specialized in what Dickens called telescopic philanthropy—bountiful love for abstract humanity combined with extreme stinginess toward the individuals he knew personally. He would enjoy a reputation for generosity throughout the Victorian world—everywhere, in fact, but among his unacknowledged family and employees.

Peabody had definite requirements for his successor: he wanted a sociable American with a family and experience in foreign trade. His Boston associate, James Beebe, recommended his junior partner, Junius Spencer Morgan. Junius had been with J. M. Beebe, Morgan for three years. In May 1853, he visited London with his family, bringing along his high-spirited but sickly son, John Pierpont, then recovering from rheumatic fever. Pierpont was boyishly thrilled with his first exposure to British culture. He visited Buckingham Palace and Westminster Abbey, excitedly handled a million pounds of bullion at the Bank of England, and listened to a Sunday sermon at Saint Paul's. Meanwhile, his father talked business with Peabody, whom Pierpont found "pleasant but smoky."[21] In general, Pierpont found Peabody a queer, likable old buzzard.

Junius Spencer Morgan was tall with sloping shoulders and the thickening midriff of a strong but sedentary man. He had a wide face, light blue eyes, a prominent nose, and a firm mouth. He was witty and genial, but a deep reserve and watchfulness lay behind the charm. Junius Morgan always had a gravely mature air. His skeptical eyes gave him a hooded gaze, a banker's air of vigilance. Big and brooding, he was the sort of prematurely middle-aged young man old financiers found consoling. A contemporary writer called him grim-mouthed; indeed, it is hard to imagine him young or carefree. He was solemn and businesslike and always master of his emotions.

Peabody asked Morgan to be his partner and receive his empire on a silver platter. Junius's grandson, J. P. Morgan, Jr., later recounted their exchange:

"You know," said Peabody, "I shall not want to go on much longer but, if you will come as a partner for ten years, I shall retire at the end of them, and at that time shall be willing to leave my name, and, if you have not accumulated a reasonable amount of capital in the concern, some of my money also, and you can go ahead as the head of it."

"Well, Mr. Peabody," replied Morgan, "that sounds like a very good offer, but there are many things to be considered, and I could not think of giving an answer until I have looked over the books of the firm and have some idea of the business and of the methods by which it is done."[22]

It is revealing that Morgan didn't leap at the fortune but responded with cool self-control. Evidently he was mightily pleased by the books—capital of £450,000, a caliber of business only one rung below the houses of Baring and Rothschild. So in October 1854, he was admitted into partnership, and he settled into new walnut-paneled headquarters at 22 Old Broad Street. The partnership document stipulated that the firm would buy and sell stocks, engage in foreign exchange, extend banking credits, and broker railroad iron and other commodities. To entertain American visitors, Peabody gave Morgan an expense account of £2,500 per year. A fortune had been deeded over—or so it seemed at the time. A decade later, as Peabody was being canonized for his philanthropy, Junius Morgan would bitterly recall the promises Peabody had made to him. And he would join the ranks of those spurned during George Peabody's ascent to sainthood.

WHEN Morgan moved to London in 1854, it was a more auspicious time for an American banker than it had been when Peabody was flogging the hated Maryland bonds in the 1830s. American grain prices soared during the Crimean War, and western railroads that transported grain boomed as well, creating a mania for their shares. Railroads devoured vast amounts of capital, and in the decade before the Civil War, investors poured $1 billion into their development, triple any former commitment. As a leading London dealer of American railroad securities, George Peabody and Company was well placed to exploit this latest craze.

Yet, as the decade passed, Junius Morgan must have doubted the wisdom of transplanting his family to England. Peabody was a trying partner, and no real warmth existed between the two, as shown by their correspondence when the junior partner visited America each year. Their letters are formal and correct but notably lacking even in pleasantries. Morgan would make obligatory inquiries about Peabody's health—always apt to please his hypochondriacal partner—but addressed him as "Dear Sir" and signed each letter with frosty respect—"J. S. Morgan." Morgan found Peabody petty and vindictive and told how his partner once spent half the afternoon hauling some poor cab driver down to the police station for overcharging him.

Then, in 1857, it looked as if Morgan would be denied his promised fortune. Wheat prices tumbled with the end of the Crimean War, causing hardship for American banks and railroads. By October, New York banks stopped gold payments, preventing American correspondents from transferring funds to Peabody in London. He was suddenly overextended on his American bills. At the same time, London investors sold American securities, siphoning more funds from Peabody and provoking a serious cash squeeze. Rumors raced through London that George Peabody and Company was about to fail, a prospect heartily relished by rivals, who disliked the old American. Morgan had also earned the displeasure of Barings by aggressively cutting prices on American securities and trying to steal their accounts.

Now the major London houses told Morgan they would bail out the firm—but only if Peabody shut down the bank within a year. When Morgan relayed this patent blackmail to Peabody, the older man reacted "like a wounded lion."[23] Defiant, he dared them to bring down his firm. George Peabody and Company was saved by an emergency credit line of £800,000 from the Bank of England, with Barings a guarantor of the loan. The vengeful Peabody, who felt Barings had mercilessly pressed him to pay outstanding bills, asked that the name of the firm be stricken from a published list of banks rescuing his firm. For Peabody, who had just made a resplendent return to America after a twenty-year absence, the incident confirmed his innate pessimism. "It is not yet three months since I parted from you, and left the country prosperous and the people happy," he wrote his niece. "Now all is gloom and affliction."[24]

The 1857 panic made a deep impression on Morgan's twenty-year-old son, Pierpont, who had just started on Wall Street as an unsalaried apprentice at Duncan, Sherman and Company, New York agent for Peabody. Tutored by partner Charles Dabney, an excellent accountant, Pierpont learned to evaluate ledgers and fathom the mysteries of the chaotic American banking system. Ever since Andrew Jackson killed the second Bank of the United States in 1832, the United States lacked a uniform currency. Each state had a separate banking system, and in many places debts could be settled in foreign currency. Pierpont, new to Wall Street, was vexed by rumors of his father's pending default and heard about the Bank of England rescue while visiting Cyrus Field's office. His later tolerance for the proposed Federal Reserve System has often been traced to this early Bank of England bailout of his father's firm.

It was a baptism by fire for the Morgan family. Shaken, the elder Morgan became a more cautious and skeptical banker. He now demanded to see statements from correspondent banks in America, even if it meant offending them. And he began to lecture his son, often at wearisome length, on the need for conservative business practice; the 1857 panic would be the text of many sermons. "You are commencing upon your business career at an eventful time," he wrote. "Let what you now witness make an impression not to be eradicated . . . *slow* & *sure* should be the motto of every young man."[25] Junius Morgan developed a lofty disdain for price competition and adopted the royal passivity of the Rothschilds and the Barings, who refused to offer cut-rate terms: "If we cannot keep the account on such a basis we must be content to let others outbid us."[26]

Another disaster soon followed. Like the French *banques d'affaires* or the universal German banks, London merchant banks took equity stakes in ventures. For instance, George Peabody and Company had helped to bankroll Sir John Franklin's expedition in search of the Northwest Passage. But its most farsighted bet was a £100,000 investment in Cyrus Field's transatlantic cable, which would unite Wall Street and the City. The scheme looked inspired on August 16, 1858, when Queen Victoria made the first cable call, to President James Buchanan. In a burst of national pride, New York City engaged in two weeks of fireworks and euphoric celebration. Peabody dizzily wrote to Field, "Your reflections must be like those of Columbus after the discovery of America."[27] He spoke too soon, however: in September, the cable snapped, the venture's share prices plummeted, and Peabody and Junius Morgan absorbed steep losses. Eight years would pass before full service was restored.

Although Peabody was nominal head until 1864, Junius Morgan assumed control of George Peabody and Company in 1859. In increasingly poor health, Peabody took his first European vacation in twenty-one years. After the outbreak of the American Civil War, Morgan traded Union bonds, which seesawed with the outcome of each battle. After the Union army was routed at Bull Run, bonds plunged, then rebounded sharply when Union troops stopped the Confederate advance at Antietam Creek. Sending a telegram via Nova Scotia, Pierpont alerted his father to Vicksburg's fall in July 1863—in time for the elder Morgan to profit from a sudden rise in American securities. Such calamity trading wasn't thought bloodthirsty or reprehensible among merchant bankers but had an honored place in their mythology. As one Rothschild boasted, "When the streets of Paris are running with blood, I buy."[28]

Despite his Yankee sympathies, Morgan was stymied in undertaking Union financing. After southern banks drained their deposits from the North, Lincoln cast about for new sources of funds. With Lancashire textile mills closely allied with southern cotton plantations, the City was cool to any large-scale operation for the North. To finance the war debt, the president turned to Philadelphia banker Jay Cooke—later dubbed a financial P. T. Barnum—whose agents fanned out across America to sell war bonds in the first mass-market securities operation in the country's history. Among the buyers in London were George Peabody and Junius Morgan. Yet the Civil War was the one major military conflict in which the Morgans were handicapped by political circumstances: it was a bonanza for German-Jewish bankers on Wall Street, who raised loans from the numerous Union sympathizers in Germany. In future, the Morgans' political impulses would mesh perfectly with profitable opportunities.

THE Civil War years saw the metamorphosis of George Peabody from Scrooge to Santa Claus. He had been a prototypical heartless banker, a one-dimensional hoarder. As a contemporary said, "Uncle George, as Americans . . . call him—was one of the dullest men in the world: he had positively no gift, except that of making money."[29] Yet this dour man suddenly became prodigal in his gifts; his philanthropy was as immoderate as his earlier greed. He found it hard to break his miserly habits. "It is not easy to part with the wealth we have accumulated after years of hard work and difficulty," he confessed.[30] Now a lifetime of hoarding was disgorged in one compensatory binge, cleansing his Yankee conscience. Perhaps as a young man Peabody had worked too much for others and as an adult too much for himself. In any event, he could do nothing by halves and again went to extremes.

By 1857, he had begun to endow a Peabody Institute in Baltimore. (Unlike later Morgan benefactions, often anonymous and discreet, Peabody wanted his name plastered on every library, fund, or museum he endowed.) In 1862, he began to transfer £150,000 to a trust fund to build housing projects for London's poor. These Peabody Estates, with gas lamps and running water, would be a vast improvement over the medieval poorhouses of Victorian London, and they still dot the city. He deeded a five-thousand-share block of the Hudson's Bay Company to finance the operation. For this revolutionary act of generosity, he became the first American to receive the Freedom of the City of London. "From a full and grateful heart," he declared at a Mansion House dinner, "I say that this day has repaid me for the care and anxiety of fifty years of commercial life."[31] Peabody's openhandedness became so proverbial that he was soon besieged with a thousand begging letters a month.

During Peabody's last years, the scope of his charity grew dazzling. He endowed a natural history museum at Yale University, an archaeology and ethnology museum at Harvard, and an educational fund for emancipated southern blacks. For this last, he handed over a $1-million batch of defaulted Mississippi and Florida bonds, hoping these states would someday resume payment and enrich the fund. There were further bequests for the housing projects, finally amounting to £500,000. As Peabody turned into a one-man welfare state, admirers saw celestial virtues in this former skinflint. Victor Hugo remarked, "On this earth there are men of hate and men of love. Peabody was one of the latter. It is on the face of these men that we see the smile of God."[32] Gladstone said that he "taught men how to use money and how not to be its slave."[33] Queen Victoria tried to honor him with a baronetcy or a knighthood, but Peabody—as if a stranger to worldly pleasures—declined this one. Instead, the queen dashed off a fulsome personal note from Windsor Castle, praising Peabody's "princely munificence" to London's poor and enclosing a miniature portrait of herself, wearing the Koh-i-noor diamond and the decoration of the Order of the Garter.[34]

Throughout this apotheosis, Peabody never extended his charity to Junius Morgan. In 1864, their ten-year agreement expired, and Peabody retired. At this point, according to the promise Peabody had made to lure Morgan to London, the junior partner was to receive the use of his name and possibly his capital. Instead, Peabody decided to pull both his name and his capital from the concern. Perhaps in his new sanctity he wanted to erase his name from the financial map and enshrine it in the world of good works. But to Morgan, as later recorded by his grandson, "it was, at that time, the bitterest disappointment of [his] life that Peabody refused to allow the old firm name to be continued."[35] Junius reluctantly renamed the firm J. S. Morgan and Company (its name until Morgan Grenfell was formed in 1910). Peabody also forced Morgan to buy the office lease at 22 Old Broad Street on onerous terms. J. P. Morgan, Jr., wrote, "My Grandfather always used to say that Mr. Peabody had been very hard on him as to the price of the lease."[36] Of course, Junius Morgan's anger toward Peabody was tempered by the extraordinary profits they had divided—over £444,000 earned in a ten-year period. And he *had* inherited the chief American bank in London.

When Peabody died, in 1869 at age seventy-four, the British government dug a grave for him in Westminster Abbey, but his deathbed words, "Danvers—Danvers, don't forget" deprived London of his remains. The Prince of Wales, later Edward VII, unveiled a statue of Peabody behind the Royal Exchange—a rare honor, considering the scarce space in the City. Even in death, Peabody managed to foster Anglo-American harmony. The British had just built a forbidding warship, the *Monarch,* whose sheer size caused consternation in America and scare talk of the vessel's being used to demand tribute from American cities. The young Andrew Carnegie sent an anonymous cable to the British cabinet: "First and best service possible for *Monarch,* bringing home body Peabody."[37] Whether this was the genesis of the idea or not, Queen Victoria shipped Peabody's corpse to America aboard the ironclad. The ship rigged up a maudlin funeral chapel, with tall candles burning above a black-draped coffin. In America, the ship was met by Admiral Farragut's squadron. Pierpont Morgan, in charge of funeral arrangements, devised a tribute of martial splendor, with British and American soldiers marching together behind the financier's coffin.

Before leaving Peabody, we might note an exchange about him within the House of Morgan in 1946. Thomas W. Lamont, chairman of J. P. Morgan and Company, asked Lord Bicester, senior partner of Morgan Grenfell, for a photostat of Queen Victoria's letter thanking Peabody for aiding London's poor. Two years from his death, Lamont was in a nostalgic mood, but Lord Bicester enjoyed shocking the unsuspecting:

> I have always understood that Mr. Peabody, though known as a great philanthropist, was one of the meanest men that ever walked. I do not know if you ever saw the statue of him sitting on a chair behind the Royal Exchange. Old Mr. Burns told me once that when subscriptions were invited in the City to erect a statue there was so

little enthusiasm that there was not sufficient money to pay for the chair, and Mr. Peabody had to pay for it himself. When I first came here the head of our office was Mr. Perman, and I remember when he had been here sixty years Teddy [Grenfell] and I gave all the staff a dinner at the Saucy, and we took them to a Music hall afterwards, and old Mr. Perman was at his desk at nine o'clock the next morning. He knew George Peabody's form well and used to tell Jack [Morgan] many stories . . . indicative of his meanness. I always understood that when he retired he announced he was leaving his money in the business—and at once proceeded to take it out. I believe he left several illegitimate children totally unprovided for.[38]

CHAPTER TWO

POLONIUS

· ·

·

I F Emerson was correct that "an institution is the lengthened shadow of a man," then the shadow-caster of the House of Morgan was Junius Spencer Morgan. Pounded into his son, Pierpont, his precepts codified Morgan philosophy for a century. He was a fussbudget father, fretting over son and bank, a figure so massive and willful that only his son, retrospectively, could reduce him to merely the "father of J. Pierpont Morgan." As one journalist said, "The Morgans always believed in absolute monarchy. While Junius Morgan lived, he ruled the family and the business—his son and his partners."[1] Until Junius died, in 1890, his massive shadow dominated his son's life.

Junius was cool and steady and seldom showed his hand. He had a dry wit and a genial manner and employed iron discipline. His friend George Smalley praised his "grave, strong beauty" and his "eyes full of light" but noticed the face ended "in an immovable jaw, all will." Sometimes the stone facade broke down, but imperceptibly. "Once or twice I have seen him angry, and he showed his anger by a sudden restraint of speech and of manner."[2] That was as far as Junius betrayed emotion.

Where George Peabody bore the scars of early poverty, Junius Morgan had the smooth manners and poise of inherited wealth. Among the possessors of great American fortunes, the Morgans boasted a uniquely pampered lineage. They didn't claw their way up from poverty or legitimize a bloody frontier fortune with later respectability. By the early nineteenth century, they were well-to-do, enjoying a cushion of security generations thick. Affluent and well-bred, they weren't rejected by European aristocracy, as were the Vanderbilts. One finds it hard to track down those poor, benighted Morgans whose early suffering made later wealth glorious. By no accident, the family produced defenders of the social order whose vices sprang from too much comfort and too little exposure to ordinary human misery.

The first Morgan in America was Miles, who emigrated from Wales to Springfield, Massachusetts, sixteen years after the *Mayflower* landed at Plymouth. He prospered as a farmer and fighter of Indians, spawning generations of land-owning Morgans. His descendant Joseph Morgan fought with Washington's army during the American Revolution. In 1817, Joseph sold his farm in West Springfield, Massachusetts, and moved to Hartford, Connecticut, which would become the Morgans' ancestral home. Joseph had a refined air, a straight, delicate nose, and coolly discerning eyes. Like later Morgans, he was a hymn-singer and Bible-thumper and subscribed to the Wadsworth Atheneum, the city's new art museum. As a businessman, he strikingly resembled his progeny: he bought a stagecoach line and the Exchange Coffee House, on whose premises he helped to organize the Aetna Fire Insurance Company. In irrepressible Morgan style, he added the City Hotel, invested in canal and steamboat companies, directed a bank, and helped finance the Hartford and New Haven Railroad, whose grisly train wrecks would haunt his descendants. Joseph made his great windfall in December 1835, when a fire in the Wall Street area destroyed over six hundred buildings. As an Aetna founder, he insisted that the firm pay customers promptly and even bought up Aetna stakes from investors who hesitated to pay. Joseph Morgan's quick action made the firm's reputation on Wall Street and later enabled it to triple its premiums.

To Joseph's wife, Sarah, the Morgans owe those strange eyes—fearful, querulous, and burning—that shone with such famous intensity in the face of young Pierpont. Sarah had a fleshy chin and bulbous nose, adding a peasant roundness to the patrician Morgan face.

In 1836, Joseph bought his son, Junius, a partnership in the Hartford dry-goods house of Howe and Mather. That same year, Junius married Juliet Pierpont, daughter of the Reverend John Pierpont of Boston, pastor of the Old Hollis Street Church. This union of Morgan and Pierpont joined together in their infant son, John Pierpont, born in 1837, a wildly improbable set of genes. A poet and preacher, the Reverend John Pierpont was a fiery abolitionist and friend of William Lloyd Garrison and Henry Ward Beecher. With craggy face and tousled hair, he spurned the Morgans' Yankee trader values. He was a failed merchant from an old New England family and had a romantic temperament and a crusading spirit. He engaged in a bitter public row with his Boston parishioners and was charged with "moral impurity" for speaking the word "whore."[3]

With the church cellar rented to a local rum merchant, the congregation found his views on temperance subversive. It was said that in the heat of argument, the Reverend Pierpont's prominent nose became inflamed—as would his grandson's. To Rev. Pierpont, the Morgans probably owe the streak of repressed romanticism and moralism in their later history. Not by chance would the House of Morgan fancy itself Wall Street's conscience and attract many sons of preachers and teachers.

When Joseph died, in 1847, he left an estate of more than $1 million. Four years later, Junius cashed in his stake in Howe and Mather for an estimated $600,000 and moved to Boston to hunt bigger game. As partner in the restyled J. M. Beebe, Morgan and Company—the city's largest mercantile house—he operated on a global scale, exporting and financing cotton and other goods carried by clipper ships from Boston harbor. It was here that he came to George Peabody's attention.

By this point, Junius's son Pierpont already seemed quite contradictory. One side of him was pure *homo economicus.* As a small boy, he was restricted to a twenty-five-cent weekly allowance and minutely noted candy and orange purchases in a ledger. At twelve, he charged admission to a viewing of his diorama of Columbus's landing. As an adolescent, he was ardent and high-spirited but also petulant and prone to sudden mood swings. He was afflicted with facial rashes, which made him morbidly self-conscious, and his childhood was marred by constant headaches, scarlet fever, and ailments of mysterious provenance. Perhaps the contrast between his own steady nature and Pierpont's unruly temper made Junius fret unduly about his boy. With granite will, he began to mold Pierpont, instructing him to associate with those of his grammar-school classmates "as are of the right stamp & whose influence over you will be good."[4] This Polonius-like voice would drone on for decades.

When his father moved the family to Boston, Pierpont enrolled in the English High School there, from which he graduated in 1854. While there, he suffered a severe bout of inflammatory rheumatism and in 1852 spent several months recuperating in the Azores; the illness left one leg shorter than the other. For the rest of his life, assorted ailments would confine Pierpont to bed several days each month. He was a curious study in contrasts, sometimes sickly, sometimes capable of great bursts of energy that would exhaust him and send him back to bed.

Early on, Pierpont figured in his father's business plans. Junius knew that the houses of Baring and Rothschild operated largely as family enterprises, grooming sons to inherit their respective businesses. In fact, the Rothschild insignia of five arrows commemorated five sons dispatched to five European capitals. The British economist and journalist Walter Bagehot noted, "The banker's calling is hereditary; the credit of the bank descends from father to son; this inherited wealth brings inherited refinement."[5] Since merchant bankers financed foreign trade, their bills had to be honored on sight in distant places, so their names had to inspire instant trust. As a twentieth-century Hambros Bank chairman would put it, "Our job is to breed wisely."[6] The family structure also guaranteed the preservation of the bank's capital.

Besides his three sisters—Sarah, Mary, and Juliet—Pierpont had a younger brother, Junius, Jr., fondly nicknamed "the Doctor," who died in 1858 at age twelve. So it was onto Pierpont, the lone surviving male heir, that Junius Morgan projected his imperial ambitions, in preparation for which he provided him with a gentlemanly education. To allow him to attain fluency in foreign languages and to season him for global business, Junius in 1854 sent Pierpont to the Institut Sillig, a boarding school on Lake Geneva. This was followed by a stint at the German university in Göttingen in 1856, where Pierpont enjoyed the bluff camaraderie of student clubs. He was a dashing, foppish boy, partial to polkadot vests, bright cravats, and checkered pants. Already self-conscious about his skin eruptions, he shied away from the popular student duels that might disfigure his face.

Throughout his life, Pierpont had little intellectual curiosity or aptitude for theorizing, and at Göttingen he excelled most at math. Beneath a rough boyish swagger, he was sensitive to art. He also collected autographs of presidents and famous figures and broken shards of stained glass found in cathedral closes. In later years, these fragments would be embedded in the windows of the West Room of his famous library.

Junius Morgan feared his son's hot temper and moaned to friends, "I don't know what in the world I'm going to do with Pierpont."[7] He said the boy needed "restraining" and tried to inculcate a strong sense of responsibility.[8] When Pierpont was twenty-one, Junius told him he was "the only one [the family] could look to for counsel and direction should I be taken from them . . . I wish to impress upon you the necessity of preparation for such responsibilities—have them ever in view, be ready to assume & fulfill them whenever they shall be laid upon you."[9] Weighty injunctions for a young man.

After Pierpont started work at Duncan, Sherman during the panic year of 1857, he displayed awesome but unsettling precocity. While visiting New Orleans in 1859, he entered into a rash, unauthorized speculation. He gambled the firm's capital on a boatload of Brazilian coffee that had arrived in port without a buyer. He bought the entire shipment and resold it at a quick profit. This first proof of his supreme confidence petrified the gray men of Duncan, Sherman. It was probably on the basis of this incident that the firm refused to make Pierpont a partner. In 1861, he struck off on his own, forming J. P. Morgan and Company at 54 Exchange Place with his cousin James J. Goodwin. At age twenty-four, he was now New York agent for George Peabody and Company. (This J. P. Morgan and Company would be short-lived. The name would be revived in 1895.) A photo of Pierpont from this period shows he had lost his look of teenage frivolity. He was now burly and handsome, with handlebar mustache, full lips, and an intense gaze. Unlike his father's composed look, his already seemed restless.

An important part of Pierpont's duties in New York was supplying his father with political and financial intelligence. Merchant banks required news about government financings or the credit of client companies and placed a premium on such information. The Rothschilds had a celebrated covey of carrier pigeons and courier boats at Folkestone. In a famous lament, Talleyrand sighed, "The English ministry is always informed of everything by Rothschilds ten to twelve hours before Lord Stuart's dispatches arrive."[10]

Pierpont began drafting lengthy letters to his father, outlining political and economic conditions in America and posting them on Nassau Street. He reserved Tuesday and Friday evenings for these reports. For thirty-three years, Junius not only digested them but bound them, like sacred relics, and set them on his shelf. Whether less sentimental than Junius—or else aghast at their contents—Pierpont burned the collection in 1911, twenty-one years after his father's death.

For these thirty-three years, Junius and Pierpont had an intense relationship, despite the geographical distance. They managed to spend an enormous amount of time together: in the fall of each year, Junius made an annual trip to the United States of up to three months, and in the spring Pierpont made his ritual London pilgrimage. But their separation at other times of the year only heightened Junius's anxiety that he couldn't tame his son's wayward nature. He pumped the poor boy full of endless advice and was full of maxims. No aspect of Pierpont's life was too trivial to be overlooked. "You are altogether too rapid in disposing of your meals," he told him. "You can have no health if you go on in this way."[11]

During the Civil War, Pierpont confirmed his father's fears concerning his rashness. Amid a mad rush of Wall Street profiteering, Pierpont financed a deal in 1861 that, if not unscrupulous, showed a decided lack of judgment. One Arthur M. Eastman purchased five thousand obsolete

Hall carbines, then stored at a government armory in New York, for $3.50 apiece. Pierpont loaned $20,000 to a Simon Stevens, who bought them for $11.50 each. By "rifling" these smooth-bore weapons, Stevens increased their range and accuracy. He resold them to Major General John C. Frémont, then commander of the Union forces in Missouri, for $22 each. Within a three-month period, the government had bought back its own, now altered, rifles at six times their original price. And it was all financed by J. Pierpont Morgan.

The extent of Pierpont's culpability in the Hall carbine affair has been endlessly debated. The unarguable point is that he saw the Civil War as an occasion for profit, not service—though he had an alternative role model in his grandfather, the Reverend Pierpont, who served as a chaplain for the Union army when it was camped on the Potomac. Like other well-to-do young men, Pierpont paid a stand-in $300 to take his place when he was drafted after Gettysburg—a common, if inequitable, practice that contributed to draft riots in July 1863. (A future president, Grover Cleveland, also hired a stand-in, although he had a widowed mother to support.) In later years, Pierpont would humorously refer to his proxy as "the other Pierpont Morgan," and he subsidized the man. During the war, he also leapt into wild speculation in the infamous "gold room" at the corner of William Street and Exchange Place. Prices would gyrate with each new victory or defeat for the Union army. Pierpont and an associate tried to rig the market by shipping out a large amount of gold on a steamer and earned $160,000 in the process.

If Pierpont seemed corrupted by rowdy wartime Wall Street, he could also be unexpectedly tenderhearted. In 1861, the year of the Hall Carbine Affair, Pierpont, then twenty-four years old, had a quixotic love affair with Amelia Sturges, a frail girl with oval face and hair parted down the middle whom Pierpont had known for two years. Her father was a patron of the Hudson River school of artists, and her mother was an excellent pianist. When Pierpont wed Mimi in the parlor of her family's East Fourteenth Street townhouse, she already had a terminal case of tuberculosis. Pierpont had to carry Mimi downstairs and prop her up during the ceremony. Guests watched this vignette from a distance, through an open door. After the ceremony, Pierpont carried his bride to a waiting carriage.

They had a touching if bizarre honeymoon, Pierpont toting Mimi around the warm Mediterranean ports and hoping to restore her health. When she died in Nice four months later, Pierpont was inconsolable, and his pious adoration for her never ceased. When he afterwards bought his first painting, it was of a young fey woman, and he hung it in an honored place over his mantle. The experience with Mimi may have taught Pierpont the wrong lessons—a fear of his best impulses, a need to stifle his deep-seated romanticism. Beneath their straitlaced exteriors, the Morgans would always be a sentimental clan, their public reserve often warring with powerful private emotions. Over fifty years later, Pierpont in his will bequeathed $100,000 to endow a rest home for consumptives, called the Amelia Sturges Morgan Memorial. Even his son, Jack, would regard the memory of Mimi as sacred and to be discussed only in hushed tones.

Observing his son's reckless dealings and startling choice of a wife, Junius decided to take Pierpont's life in hand. Between Pierpont and Junius Morgan, there would be total loyalty but also a fierce contest of wills. In 1864, Junius orchestrated an alliance between Pierpont, then twenty-seven, and Charles H. Dabney, thirty years his elder, to form the new firm of Dabney, Morgan and Company. Bolstered by capital from Junius, it would serve as his New York agent. He would retain final control over the credits it issued and the clients it selected. Dabney was expected to exert a steadying influence on Pierpont, and for the next twenty-six years Junius kept a moderating father figure near his son.

In his private life, too, Pierpont fell into line. In May 1865, he married Frances Louisa Tracy—Fanny, as she was known—daughter of a successful lawyer, Charles Tracy, who later performed legal work for Pierpont. She was tall and pretty, with a rosebud mouth. She had a taste for elegant gloves and earrings and seemed thoroughly safe and respectable. If Mimi was a temporary madness, Frances was a return to sanity. Yet it was Mimi whose memory Pierpont would cherish, while the "practical" marriage to Fanny would prove the fiasco, causing terrible pain to them both. Pierpont's unrequited romantic longings would only grow over the years until they later found other—and notoriously varied—outlets.

THE father-son team of Junius and Pierpont Morgan came on the world banking scene at a time of phenomenal expansion of banking power. We shall call it the Baronial Age. It coincided with the rise of railroads and heavy industry, new businesses requiring capital far beyond the resources of even the wealthiest individuals or families. Yet, despite these tremendous needs for capital, financial markets were provincial and limited in scope. The banker allocated the economy's scarce credit. His imprimatur alone reassured investors that unknown companies were sound—there were no government agencies to regulate securities issues or prospectuses—and he became integral to their operation. Companies would come to be associated with their bankers. The New York Central Railroad, for instance, would later be called a Morgan road.

In this phase of the Industrial Revolution, companies were dynamic but extremely unstable. In an atmosphere of feverish growth, many businesses fell into the hands of unscrupulous promoters, charlatans, and stock manipulators. Even visionary entrepreneurs often lacked the managerial skills necessary to convert their inspirations into national industries, and no cadre of professional managers yet existed. Bankers had to vouch for securities and often ended up running companies if they defaulted. As the Baronial Age progressed, the line between finance and commerce would blur until much of industry passed under the control of the bankers.

With such leverage over companies, the leading bankers developed a superior style, behaving like barons to whom clients paid tribute. They operated according to a set of customs that we will call the Gentleman Banker's Code. The House of Morgan would not only transplant this code from London to New York but would honor it until well into the twentieth century. Under this code, banks did not try to scout out business or seek new clients but waited for clients to arrive with proper introductions. They didn't open branch offices and refused to take on new companies unless the move was first cleared with their former banker. The idea was not to compete, at least not too openly. This meant no advertising, no price competition, and no raiding of other firms' clients. Such an arrangement worked to the advantage of established banks and kept clients in an abject, dependent position. But it was a stylized competition—a world of sheathed rapiers—not a cartel, as it often seemed. The elegance of the surface often blinded critics to the vicious underlying relations among the banks.

No less than to industry, bankers dictated terms to sovereign states, and countries, like companies, had their "traditional bankers." Benjamin Disraeli wrote of "the mighty loan-mongers on whose fiat the fate of kings and empires sometimes depended."[12] Byron's witty couplet claimed their "every loan . . . seats a Nation or upsets a Throne."[13] The bankers acquired such power because many governments in wartime lacked the sophisticated tax machinery to sustain the fighting. Merchant banks functioned as their ersatz treasury departments or central banks before economic management was established as a government responsibility. The London banks didn't lend their own funds but would organize large-scale bond issues. Through conspiring closely with governments, they acquired a quasi-official aura. Joseph Wechsberg has referred to merchant banks operating "in the twilight zone between politics and economics."[14] This was turf the Morgans would later claim as their own. It was also very lucrative turf, for bankers to sovereign states might also handle their foreign-exchange transactions and pay out dividends on their bonds.

Every London house could unfurl a scroll of illustrious state loans. From their Saint Swithin's Lane townhouse, the Rothschilds financed Wellington's peninsular campaign and the Crimean War. A familiar adage said that the wealth of the Rothschilds consisted of the bankruptcy of nations. In 1875, Lionel Rothschild would arrange the £4-million financing that permitted Britain to wrest control of the Suez Canal from France. Disraeli laughingly confided to Queen Victoria, "I am of the opinion, Madame, that there never can be too many Rothschilds."[15]

Besides bankrolling the Louisiana Purchase, Barings financed the French indemnity payment after Waterloo, prompting a lapidary tribute from the duc de Richelieu: "There are six great powers in Europe: England, France, Prussia, Austria, Russia, and Baring Brothers."[16] After the failure of Ireland's potato crop in 1845, the Peel government used Barings to buy American corn and Indian meal to relieve the famine—so-called Peel's brimstone. By the time of the Civil War, Barings was the agent bank for Russia, Norway, Austria, Chile, Argentina, Canada, Australia, and the United States. For their trouble, the grandees at 8 Bishopsgate were awarded with four peerages by the close of the nineteenth century—Ashburton, Northbrook, Revelstoke, and Cromer.

Why this perfect mesh between merchant banks and statecraft? As private partnerships, these small banks were free of prying depositors or shareholders and could indulge their political biases. They didn't have to submit to outside examination, and their naturally discreet style made them ideal channels for diplomacy. Because they financed overseas trade, they were far more internationalist in outlook than the High Street bankers who financed British industry and dealt largely with shopkeepers.

The rarefied world of the Rothschilds and the Barings was the one Junius Morgan aspired to—a world hitherto barred to Americans. After Peabody's death, he needed some dazzling derring-do with which to leap into the top ranks of Victorian finance. Only so much glory could be gained from trading Chinese tea or Peruvian guano or selling iron rails to Commodore Vanderbilt. Now in his late fifties, Junius had grown stout with wealth. He was an imposing six-foot figure, with high forehead, beetling brow, and watchful eyes. As an early American patron of Savile Row's "bespoke" tailors, he dressed in suits conservatively tailored by Poole's.

With Peabody gone, he urgently needed to replenish his capital base, which was still meager compared to the Rothschilds and the Barings. Yet he was extremely selective about the business he did and had learned the need for caution. As he lectured Pierpont, "Never under any circumstances do an action which could be called in question if known to the world."[17]

Junius's big chance for a state financing came in 1870, when the Prussians crushed French troops at Sedan in September, seized the emperor, Napoléon III, and laid siege to Paris. After a republic was proclaimed, French officials retreated to Tours and set up a provisional government. Otto von Bismarck, the Prussian chancellor, tried to isolate the French diplomatically. When they approached London for financing, he conducted a propaganda campaign, blustering that a victorious Germany would make France repudiate its debt.

A rare opportunity opened up for an enterprising banker. This was one of the few times in the century that financially self-sufficient France needed to raise money abroad. Barings had floated Prussian loans and didn't wish to upset delicate relations by dealing with France; the Rothschilds dismissed the French cause as hopeless. The City had lately been rocked by defaults in Mexico and Venezuela, and nobody was in a particularly venturesome mood for foreign loans. Enter Junius, who decided to float a syndicated issue for France of £10 million, or $50 million. The French hoped that by using an American banker, they might also be better positioned to purchase American arms.

The French loan showed that he hid a riverboat gambler's flair behind the steely air. This would be Junius's signature deal, complete with that obligatory Rothschild touch—carrier pigeons. In backing France, he had to contend with Bismarck, who was privy to his moves. It later turned out that the private secretary of the French finance minister was a German spy and was feeding Bismarck daily reports on their dealings. Because Junius couldn't speak French and wouldn't take anything on faith, he brought over from France his son-in-law and later partner Walter Hayes Burns to act as translator. Junius insisted that every French document be accompanied by a certified translation.

An innovation in European finance was then enhancing the bankers' power—the syndicate, elite groups of banks that practiced what the French called *haute banque.* Instead of floating bond issues alone, the banks pooled their capital to share the risk of underwriting. Reflecting the extraordinary risks of the French loan, a Morgan-led syndicate offered the bonds at 85. This was 15 points below par—the value at which the bonds could later be redeemed. This sharp discount was designed to coax a skittish public into buying. The French felt blackmailed by these degrading terms, which they thought suitable for a Peru or Turkey. Yet Junius hadn't exaggerated the risks. After Paris fell in January 1871, followed by the Paris Commune, the bonds dropped from 80 to 55, and Junius desperately bought them to prop up the price, nearly wiping himself out. This was all very strange for a man who had urged caution on Pierpont: he was betting the future of his firm on one roll of the dice.

Whatever the risks, it must have been a heady experience for an American to be swaggering like a Rothschild and playing with gigantic sums. The loan had its full complement of theatrics. A brief Morgan Guaranty history still pulsates with the excitement of the episode: "Some communications between Paris and London were implemented by the use of a fleet of carrier pigeons. Several of them, bearing capsules filled with text on tissue paper, actually completed their journeys. One particularly bulky package of documents was sent from Paris to London by balloon!"[18] Some pigeons were apparently shot down and gobbled up by starving Parisians. This left French politicians in the dark during critical moments in the bargaining.

When the war ended, the defeated French didn't renege on the loan, as Bismarck predicted. Instead, they prepaid the bonds in 1873, bringing them up to par, or 100. As with Peabody and his Maryland bonds, Junius pocketed a fortune from this sudden windfall. The loan netted him a whopping £1.5 million. This vastly augmented his firm's capital and propelled him into the upper ranks of government financing. Now the name J. S. Morgan and Company would appear frequently in "tombstone ads" (apparently so called because of their rectangular shape and placement on newspaper obituary pages) announcing underwriting syndicates.

George Smalley said that with the 1870 French loan, his friend Junius went from being a successful man to a power in the City. His impressions of Junius at this moment are telling. On the one hand, he was modest and breezily dismissive about his triumph. He said he had researched the history of twelve French governments since 1789, and "not one of these governments had ever repudiated or questioned the validity of any financial obligation contracted by any other. The continuing financial solidarity of France was unbroken." But Smalley wasn't fooled by such nonchalance. He noted "a fire in his eyes as he spoke which showed he was not insensible to the triumph he had won. Why should he be? It was considered, and has ever since been considered, an event in the history of English finance."[19]

As Junius developed into the wealthiest American banker in London, he acquired the trappings of magnificence. He lived in a Knightsbridge mansion, 13 Princes Gate, a five-story building of neoclassic design facing the south side of Hyde Park. The Morgan household was very dignified. Attended by butlers, the family dressed formally for dinner, which concluded with claret and Havana cigars. It was also a pious place, with Junius lining up the servants each morning for prayers. Following merchant-banking tradition, Junius dabbled in art collecting and often visited galleries with Pierpont when his son was in town. Junius's friends said his home resembled a museum, with sixteenth-century Spanish embroidery on the walls, silver-filled vaults, and an excellent collection of paintings by Reynolds, Romney, and Gainsborough.

Seven miles away, in the London suburb of Roehampton, Junius purchased Dover House, a ninety-two-acre estate with rolling lawns that swept down to the Thames. It was a miniature kingdom. Its dairy flowed with fresh milk and cream, its hothouses yielded blooms, gardeners tended strawberry beds, and children played on playground swings. Dover House was rustic in a formal way, with well-spaced trees and trimmed lawns. In a photograph from 1876, Junius is playing tennis dressed in bowler hat and a three-piece suit and is clutching his racket like a club; he looks incongruous in a recreational setting. Periodically he performed his patrician duty and shot pheasants on a moor.

Junius—tall, sociable, self-confident—and his wife, Juliet Pierpont Morgan, made an odd pair. She was a short, plain, buxom woman who grew increasingly sickly and hypochondriacal. Often homesick, she frequently sailed to New York to stay with Pierpont. While her husband blossomed into one of London's magnificoes and was blessed with robust health, Juliet became more feeble and withdrawn. In her later years, she was an invalid, often closeted in an upstairs bedroom. She seems to have suffered some form of premature senility. This pattern of the sickly wife and the autocratic, headstrong husband would be repeated in the life of their son Pierpont. It also set a pattern of private grief and loneliness that would come to haunt the spectacularly successful Morgan family.

CHAPTER THREE

PRINCE

．　．

．

As Junius Morgan's Wall Street agent for thirty years, Pierpont moved with the massed power of British capital behind him. A Wall Street jest said that his yacht, the *Corsair*, flew the Jolly Roger above the Stars and Stripes, and the Union Jack above both. (Throughout his life, Pierpont would slyly hint at descent from the pirate Henry Morgan.) The young Morgan resembled a burly roughneck with a coat of British polish. Broad-shouldered and barrel-chested, he had dark hair and a pugilist's hands. Over six feet tall, he was something of a dandy, now given to checkered vests. Where Junius had a hard and impenetrable stare, Pierpont's hazel eyes were sad and cloudy. Where his father had unfailing composure, Pierpont was mercurial. In early pictures, he looks edgy, as if spoiling for a fight.

There was plenty to fight about in the rough-and-tumble of the postwar railroad boom. Everybody had a sense of immense enterprise ahead. "We are going some day to show ourselves to be the richest country in the world in natural resources," Pierpont predicted during the Civil War. The railroads would unlock the resources in the American wilderness. Perhaps no business has ever blossomed so spectacularly: within eight years of the war's end, railroad trackage doubled to seventy thousand miles, a spree fed by tens of millions of acres in federal land grants. More than just isolated businesses, railroads were the scaffolding on which new worlds would be built. As Anthony Trollope noted during an American visit, railroads "were in fact companies combined for the purchase of land" whose value they hoped to increase by opening a road. Towns sprang up along the tracks, settled by European immigrants imported by the railroads.[1]

As speculation in rail shares grew frenzied, European investors were stumbling about in the dark. Between Kansas and the Rocky Mountains, schoolboy maps showed a blank space dubbed the great American desert.[2] Europeans relied on their American agents to guide them through this financial wilderness, and American bankers had to keep posted on developments. Soon after completion of the first transcontinental railroad, in May 1869, Pierpont and Fanny Morgan made an extended rail journey across the country, stopping to see Mormon leader Brigham Young in Utah. A competition was already underway on Wall Street between Jewish bankers, such as Joseph Seligman, who wooed German investors with railroad shares, and Yankee bankers, such as Pierpont Morgan, who drew on London money.

From the outset, railways were in a chaotic state as they covered the country in a crazy-quilt expansion that frequently produced more roads than traffic. Because of their exorbitant fixed costs, they should have been public utilities. But this was impossible in an age of free-booting individualism. As a result, assorted hucksters and rogues threw up twice the trackage actually needed. What appeared to be solid investment one moment was revealed as so much watered stock the next. In Henry Adams's judgment, "The generation between 1865 and 1895 was already mortgaged to the railways and no one knew it better than the generation itself."[3]

Such anarchy could easily fire a moralistic young banker like Pierpont Morgan. In his early years, he was exposed to many incorrigible Wall Street rascals, including Daniel Drew, the rustic sharpster who sold Erie stock short while sitting on the railroad's own board (he was called the speculative director), and Jay Gould, the small, swarthy, full-bearded financier who prodigally bribed legislators as he vied for control of the Erie and other railroads.[4] This was the infamous era of the Tweed Ring, Jay Gould's 1869 attempt to corner the gold market, and other acts of larceny on a scale never before imagined. While Junius inhabited the white-glove world of the City, Pierpont had to deal with Wall Street squalor and found it alternately seductive and repellent. Confronted by corruption, he saw himself as a proxy for honorable European and American investors, a tool of transcendent purpose representing the sound men on Wall Street and in the City. But what he saw as a moral crusade others might regard simply as competing self-interest. In his early years, at least, he wasn't always clearly distinguishable from the robber barons he was supposedly contesting.

In 1869, Pierpont, aged thirty-two, was enlisted in a dispute over a small upstate New York railroad that would establish his reputation as a self-assured young banker, unafraid to dirty his hands. This corporate fight would dramatize the transition of the American banker from a passive figure issuing shares for companies to a strong, active force in managing their affairs. The line in question, the 143-mile Albany and Susquehanna, was small and inconsequential. It had only 17 locomotives and 214 cars and ran through the sparsely populated Catskill Mountains between Albany and Binghamton, New York. Yet it became a battleground for competing powers when Jay Gould decided it could advance the fortunes of his Erie Railroad, the so-called Scarlet Woman of Wall Street. Through this road, Gould hoped to sell Pennsylvania coal to New England and also vie with the New York Central for freight from the Great Lakes.

To this end, Gould bought up a block of A&S stock, made an alliance with a dissident wing of directors, and had his pet judge, George C. Barnard, suspend the railroad's founder, Joseph H. Ramsey, from the board. Ramsey countered by having several Gould partisans judicially suspended in turn. In these early days, corporate warfare was no mere euphemism, and the Ramsey and Gould forces sometimes slugged it out directly rather than filing suits and obtaining injunctions. In the Battle of the Susquehanna, Jim Fisk, a former circus roustabout and Gould's chief lieutenant, and his Bowery boys—thugs scraped off New York's streets and operating as Gould's stooges—piled onto a train heading east from Binghamton, their army numbering about 800 men. The Ramsey forces loaded about 450 fighters onto a train heading west from Albany. In a cinematic finale, the two trains crashed head-on at the Long Tunnel near Binghamton. Their headlights were smashed, one locomotive was partly derailed, and eight or ten people were shot before the Gould forces fled. Governor Toots Hoffman summoned the state militia to stop the bloodshed.

On September 7, 1869, momentarily putting down their weapons, the Gould and Ramsey forces converged on the annual board meeting of the A&S. Ramsey—"a little, grey-headed, sallow faced gentleman, weighing about 115 pounds, with a very bright eye"—had recruited the husky Pierpont, who had just returned from his western trip; Pierpont bought six hundred shares of stock in the road for Dabney, Morgan.[5] Pierpont's son-in-law Herbert L. Satterlee later claimed that at the September 7 meeting, Pierpont hurled chubby Jim Fisk down a flight of stairs. The story may be apocryphal. But the meeting was so tense that Ramsey, who had hidden the subscription books in an Albany cemetery, had the documents lowered into the room from a back window to keep them from the hands of the Gould forces. In the end, the meeting was stale-mated by competing injunctions, with each side again claiming control of the road based on two separate elections.

Under Pierpont's tutelage, the Ramsey forces found a friendly judge in the upstate town of Delhi, New York, who obligingly ousted the Erie slate. Pierpont then advised the Ramsey forces, now back in control, to merge their railroad with the friendly Delaware and Hudson line, which they accomplished in February 1870. In settling the dispute, Pierpont made a move that marked his subsequent financial maneuvers: he took payment, not simply in money, but in power, becoming a director of the newly merged railroad. This first board seat was a sign of things to come, starting an era in which bankers sat on corporate boards and gradually came to rule them. Board membership would become a warning flag to other bankers to stay away from a captive company. During the 1870s, Pierpont began to style himself as far more than a mere provider of money to companies: he wanted to be their lawyer, high priest, and confidant. This wedding of certain companies to certain banks—"rela-tionship banking"—would be a cardinal feature of private banking for the next century. It came about not because bankers were strong but because companies were still weak.

PIERPONT'S life was now prosperous and settled. He was making the gigantic salary of $75,000 a year. He and Fanny lived in a brownstone at 6 East Fortieth Street, just across Fifth Avenue from the Croton Reservoir, which arose like a vast Egyptian tomb on the site of today's New York Public Library. The Morgan home was comfortable and clut-tered, furnished with rugs, heavy mahogany furniture, and gilt-framed pictures crowding one on top of the other. In 1872, Pierpont bought Cragston, a country retreat on the Hudson River near West Point. A three-story white Victorian house with rambling porches, its grounds comprised several hundred acres of spectacular river scenery and was Pierpont's answer to Junius's Dover House. There were horse stables, a dairy, tennis courts, and kennels for breeding collies. (When the collies got boisterous, he switched to breeding blooded cattle.) From April to October, Pierpont commuted to Wall Street, crossing the river on his steam launch, the *Louisa*, which seated about eight people. Then he took the train into Manhattan. The Morgans now had three children, Louisa, born in 1866, John Pierpont, Jr., or Jack, born in 1867, and Juliet, born in 1870. Before long, they would add another daughter, Anne.

Behind the aura of comfort and precocity, Pierpont was a troubled young man. He continued to be bedeviled by headaches, fainting spells, and skin flare-ups. In 1871, his partner, Charles Dabney, retired and their partnership was dissolved. Not for the last time, Pierpont contemplated retirement. As if unable to stop his own ambition, he would assume tremendous responsibility, then feel oppressed. He never seemed to take great pleasure in his accomplishments, and for the rest of his life, he craved a restful but elusive peace.

With Dabney retiring, Junius needed to find a partner for Pierpont. He also wanted to broaden the House of Morgan beyond its New York–London axis and strengthen its international securities business. Although we think of global finance as a modern invention, Victorian merchant banks were already multinational in structure and cosmopolitan in orientation. Instead of branch offices, they set up interlocking partnerships in foreign capitals—precisely what Junius now decided to do. In January 1871, he was approached in London by Anthony J. Drexel regarding an affiliation between his Philadelphia bank and the Morgans. Among the Philadelphia banks, Drexel's was second only to Jay Cooke's in government finance. Junius was already Drexel's London correspondent. As when George Peabody approached him, a financial fortune was being laid at Junius's feet. He was not only the ablest American banker of his day; he was also the luckiest.

Son of Francis M. Drexel, an itinerant Austrian portrait painter turned financier, Tony Drexel at forty-five was slim and refined with a smooth forehead, domed head, mild eyes, and handlebar mustache. At the time, Wall Street was shaping up as a provider as well as importer of capital as financial power gravitated from Philadelphia and Boston to New York. Sensing this seismic shift, the influential Drexel wished to fortify his New York operations. As before with Charles Dabney, Junius hoped to hedge the young Pierpont with safeguards and place him under the protective tutelage of an older man. So he suggested to Drexel that he take on Pierpont as his chief partner in New York.

However prodigious Pierpont's gifts, he was still clay modeled by his father's hands. Junius urged him to respond to any invitation from Drexel. Hence in May he dutifully traveled to Philadelphia, dined with Drexel, and chatted with him after dinner. He returned to New York with a partnership agreement scribbled on an envelope. According to the deal, Pierpont would become a partner of Drexel and Company in Philadelphia and Drexel, Harjes in Paris. He would also manage a New York partnership called Drexel, Morgan and Company. The order of the names reflected the importance of the partners. Tony Drexel and his two brothers, Francis and Joseph, were worth about $7 million, while Pierpont had a puny $350,000. To even the score, however, Junius pumped in $5 million. Pierpont always acknowledged his debt to his father—he never pretended to be self-made—and later told New York governor Grover Cleveland, "If I have been able to succeed in the station of life in which I have been cast, I attribute it more than anything to the endorsement of my father's friends."[6] The new Drexel, Morgan was the forerunner of J. P. Morgan and Company.

Before signing the deal, Pierpont laid down a curious condition—that he delay working on the new partnership. Far from itching to start, he felt a need to recuperate from emotional and physical travail. Apparently he was on the edge of a nervous breakdown. Under doctor's orders, he took a fifteen-month vacation, traveling to Vienna and Rome and sailing up the Nile. At work, Pierpont could never relax and developed a powerful urge for escape. He would vacation three months each year and joked that he could perform twelve months of work in just nine months. His son-in-law Herbert Satterlee later wrote, "He seemed to feel better when he was actually travelling than when they settled down anywhere."[7] In the late 1870s, when Pierpont tried to flee work by taking a vacation in Saratoga, New York, a blizzard of business letters and telegrams trailed after him. "There is only one way of getting real rest," he told Junius, "and that is to get on board of a steamer."[8]

Two years after its debut, in 1873, Drexel, Morgan moved to the corner of Wall and Broad streets. It would be the most celebrated address in banking, the financial crossroads of America. Tony Drexel had bought a parcel of land across the street from the New York Stock Exchange for $349 a square foot, which stood as a record for the next thirty years. He built a heavily ribbed marble building with mansard roof, dormer windows, and ornate facade and allegorical figures above the doorway; the six-story building was one of the city's first with an elevator. Splendidly symbolic, its unusual catercorner entrance simultaneously faced the Subtreasury Building on Nassau Street (the most important branch of the U.S. Treasury system) and the Stock Exchange on Wall Street. Appropriately, Drexel, Morgan would specialize in both railroad and government finance and occupy a pivotal place between Wall Street and Washington.

From a personal standpoint, the Drexel-Morgan match wasn't smooth. Pierpont was already gruff and difficult and insisted on having his own way. Joseph Seligman saw him as "a rough, uncouth fellow, continually quarreling with Drexel in the office."[9] But the merger worked just as Junius had planned in terms of tempering Pierpont's xcesses. An early Dun and Company report said, "This young man is ,mart and is perhaps the most venturesome member of the firm but he is kept in check by the Drexels."[10]

The merger with the Drexels gave the Morgans new international breadth. In 1868, Drexel had sent John J. Harjes of Philadelphia to set up a Paris partnership, which performed with élan during the Paris Commune, switching operations to Switzerland to service American travelers and businessmen. (This wartime role would later be quintessentially Morgan's.) As social butterflies who married into many prominent Philadelphia families, the Drexels also added a high-society image to the Morgan bank, and the Philadelphia house would always be a glamorous corner of the emerging empire. Through their interlocking partnerships, the Morgans now had footholds in New York, Philadelphia, London, and Paris. These would remain the brightest stars of the Morgan constellation for a century.

SOON after the Drexel-Morgan merger came an event that catapulted Pierpont Morgan, age thirty-six, into the empyrean of American finance. In 1873, Washington decided to refund, at lower interest rates, the $300 million in bonded debt remaining from the Civil War. Until then, Jay Cooke—Tony Drexel's main Philadelphia rival—reigned as the white-bearded emperor of federal finance. The self-made Cooke had started out as a bank clerk with a quick eye for counterfeit money. At a time when government bonds were the exclusive province of rich men and European banks, he marketed them to the masses. During the Civil War, he pioneered in retail distribution, sending twenty-five hundred "minute-man" agents to peddle Union bonds across America and winning Lincoln's gratitude. With his riches, Cooke built a fifty-two-room castle outside Philadelphia. In the early 1870s, the phrase "rich as Jay Cooke" had the same magic resonance as "rich as Rockefeller" would have in a later day.

Cooke seemed invincible to competitors—at least until he financed the Northern Pacific Railroad in 1869. His promotion for $100 million in Northern Pacific bonds was liberally spiced with invention, fraudulence, and political bribery. To lure European settlers to towns serviced by the railroad, he created a tissue of brazenly surreal lies. Colorful ads depicted fruit groves flourishing along its Great Plains tracks—fantastic claims that won the railroad the nickname of Jay Cooke's Banana Republic. Cow towns were puffed up into vast metropolises, and Duluth, Minnesota, was trumpeted to European immigrants as the "Zenith City of the Unsalted Seas."[11] When grain prices fell after the Franco-Prussian war, the fortunes of the Northern Pacific and other railroads fell along with them. Thus began Jay Cooke's undoing. His vulnerability in relation to the Northern Pacific would provide an opening for Drexel, Morgan to usurp his exalted place in government finance.

In 1873, Cooke teamed up with two Jewish houses—Seligman's on Wall Street and the Rothschilds' in Europe—to obtain the $300 million refunding issue against a vigorous challenge from Drexel, Morgan; J. S. Morgan and Company; Morton, Bliss; and Baring Brothers. Large-scale finance was increasingly shaping up as a contest between powerful syndicates; the sums—and the risks—were now too large for single houses to shoulder alone. The Drexel, Morgan group contested the Cooke monopoly and also circulated insidious rumors that Cooke needed victory in the refunding issue to recoup his Northern Pacific losses. Tony Drexel, a close friend of President Grant, proselytized through his partial ownership of the Philadelphia *Public Ledger.* Bowing to intense pressure from the Drexel, Morgan group, the secretary of the treasury awarded half of the issue to each syndicate, although the status-conscious Junius was disturbed by Cooke's name preceding theirs on the contract. The prominence of American banks in this display of federal financing reflected the new postwar power of Wall Street.

The year 1873 was one of panicky markets that allowed the Morgans to leave behind their reputation as relative outsiders and achieve a commanding position in federal finance. Financial markets were at first unsettled by the scandal of the Crédit Mobilier, builder of the Union Pacific Railroad, and exposed as a giant sinkhole of fraud and corruption. The scandal tarred the reputation of many congressmen holding the ephemeral company's stock. By August 1873, London investors wouldn't touch American bonds, one reporter said, "even if signed by an angel of Heaven."[12] Then, debilitated by the Northern Pacific, the mighty house of Jay Cooke failed on Black Thursday, September 18, 1873.

The failure ignited a full-blown Wall Street panic. For the first time since its formation, the New York Stock Exchange shut its doors for ten days. The corner outside the exchange became a wailing wall of ruined men. Diarist George Templeton Strong noted that "the central focus of excitement was, of course, at the corner of Broad and Wall Streets. People [were] swarming on the Treasury steps looking down on the seething mob that filled Broad Street."[13] Pierpont called in his loans and cabled Junius: "Affairs continue unprecedentedly bad."[14] Five thousand commercial firms and fifty-seven Stock Exchange firms were dragged down in Cooke's maelstrom, a cataclysmic experience for a generation of Americans. "To my parents and to the outside world," financial journalist Alexander Dana Noyes would later recall, "the financial crash of September 1873 had been as memorable a landmark as, to the community of half a century later, was the panic of October 1929."[15]

By today's standards, Wall Street looked almost pastoral: Trinity Church was the tallest structure, and street lamps on the cobblestone streets stood higher than many buildings. The six-story Drexel Building soared above its neighbors. Yet after Jay Cooke's failure, it was popularly seen as the street of sin, a place responsible for corrupting the manners and morals of a pristine frontier nation. Not for the last time, America turned against Wall Street with puritanical outrage and a sense of offended innocence. Thomas Nast's cartoons in *Harper's Weekly* showed heaps of slaughtered animals in front of Trinity Church, the church itself scowling, with the words MORAL, I TOLD YOU SO emblazoned on its steeple. Wall Street already had a way of being renounced once the party was over.

In much the same way as the Morgan bank would in 1929, Pierpont managed a handy profit in the panic year of 1873. He made over $1 million, boasting to Junius: "I don't believe there is another concern in the country [that] can begin to show such a result."[16] With Jay Cooke conveniently wiped off the map, Drexel, Morgan stood, with miraculous suddenness, at the apex of American government finance. Never again would Pierpont Morgan be an outsider, and before long he would be the chief arbiter of the establishment. Drexel, Morgan couldn't immediately capitalize on its fame, however, since the 1873 panic ushered in a period of extended deflation and depression, during which it became hard to credit Junius's injunction to "remember one thing always. . . . Always be a 'bull' on America."[17]

The House of Morgan's future approach to business was shaped in the gloomy days of 1873. The panic was a disaster for European investors, who lost $600 million in American railroad stocks. Stung by all the railroad bankruptcies, Pierpont decided to limit his future dealings to elite companies. He became the sort of tycoon who hated risk and wanted only sure things. "I have come to the conclusion that neither my firm nor myself will have anything to do, hereafter, directly or indirectly, with the negotiation of securities of any undertaking not entirely completed; and whose status, by experience, would not prove it entitled to a credit in every respect unassailable."[18] Another time, he said, "The kind of Bonds which I want to be connected with are those which can be recommended without a shadow of doubt, and without the least subsequent anxiety, as to payment of interest, as it matures."[19]

This encapsulated future Morgan strategy—dealing only with the strongest companies and shying away from speculative ventures.

Under the Gentleman Banker's Code, bankers held themselves responsible for bonds they sold and felt obligated to intervene when things went awry. And the railroads were going awry. Even before the 1873 panic, a new way of dealing with railroad rascality had appeared, devised, improbably, by Jay Gould. When investors boycotted an Erie bond issue in 1871, he proposed to bring in outside coal, railway, and banking interests to run the railroad as "voting trustees" who would control a majority of Erie stock. To placate the conservative side of Wall Street and the City, he proposed Junius Morgan as one trustee. The plan was stillborn but later was revived. By mid-decade, Junius was warning the president of the Baltimore and Ohio Railroad that rate wars among railroads were undermining investors' confidence.[20] The following year, when the Erie went bankrupt, the irate bondholders shackled the road with a "voting trust" that would run the operation. It was a pivotal moment—the revenge of the creditors against the debtors, the bankers against the railwaymen. Later, in Pierpont's hands, the simple device of the voting trust would convert Morgan into America's most powerful man, placing much of the country's railway system under his personal control. Through such trusts, he would convert financiers from servants to masters of their clients.

The story of Pierpont Morgan is that of a young moralist turned despot, one who believed implicitly in the correctness of his views. Strong-willed and opinionated, he had an unshakable faith in his own impulses—a quality that later made him appear as a force of nature, a child of the *Zeitgeist,* making snap decisions that were often eerily right. He differed from most of the Gilded Age robber barons in that their rapacity stemmed from pure greed or lust for power while his included some strange admixture of idealism. As he confronted an economy that offended his sense of business propriety, his very conservatism gave him a revolutionary zeal. He believed, quite arrogantly, that he knew how the economy should be ordered and how people should behave. By no coincidence, he was active in the Young Men's Christian Association, which discouraged gambling among the working class. He also sponsored revival meetings at Madison Square Garden and backed the moral policeman Anthony Comstock, who favored the covering up of nude statues.

Pierpont developed a reputation for snappishness and barking at people, a propensity that grew with his fame. Even in letters to his father as early as the 1870s, he seemed committed to his own way of doing things and wrote less as a servile son than as a highly confident business partner. In 1881, a report by R. G. Dun and Company referred to Pierpont's "peculiar brusqueness of manner" and said it had "made him and his house unpopular with many."[21] He sat behind a glass partition in the mahogany partners' room at 23 Wall Street, chewing on a big cigar and growling out "yes" or "no" when given offers on foreign exchange. He wouldn't haggle and presented his bids for foreign exchange on a take-it-or-leave-it basis. He had a way of letting people cool their heels and knew all the silent tricks of authority. With his clear-cut sense of right and wrong, he quickly became accustomed to exercising leadership.

Not surprisingly, he had trouble delegating authority and low regard for the intelligence of other people. He agonized over finding new partners, and people never measured up to his inflated standards. To find suitable candidates in 1875, he pored over business directories from New York, Philadelphia, and Boston—in vain. "The longer I live the more apparent becomes the absence of brains—particularly soundly balanced brains," he told Junius.[22] Once again, Pierpont flirted with the notion of quitting banking and casting off the oppressive weight of business. In 1876, when Joseph Drexel left the firm, Pierpont wanted to follow him, but he held back, awaiting word of Junius's plans. He was chained to his bank by a sense of mission that never abandoned him. Perhaps never in financial history has anybody else amassed so much power so reluctantly. J. Pierpont Morgan was more exhausted than exhilarated by success. He didn't enjoy responsibility and never learned to cope with it.

Pierpont was a natural leader on Wall Street. Whatever the general public might think of the Morgans, businessmen respected them for their honest dealings. August Belmont, Sr., thought Pierpont "brusque but fair."[23] Andrew Carnegie, who raised the money for his first rolling mill by brokering bonds to Junius, told the story of how during the 1873 panic the Morgans sold his interest in a railroad for $10,000. He already had $50,000 on deposit with Pierpont, and when he showed up to claim his $60,000, Pierpont handed him $70,000 instead. Pierpont said that they had underestimated his account and insisted he accept the additional $10,000. Carnegie didn't want to take the money. "Will you please accept these ten thousand with my best wishes?" Carnegie asked him. "No, thank you," Pierpont replied. "I cannot do it."[24] Carnegie decided that in future he would never harm the Morgans. Interestingly, Carnegie venerated Junius as the model of the sound, old-fashioned banker, but there was always friction between him and Pierpont. After one 1876 meeting with Carnegie, Pierpont bluntly chastised him—"You used language very offensive in its character"—and proceeded to rebut Carnegie's statements about his firm's role in a lawsuit.

The standing of Drexel, Morgan rose steadily through the 1870s. In 1877, a congressional dispute held up payment due the army of General Miles, then fighting the Nez Percé Indians out West. In a flamboyant gesture, Drexel, Morgan volunteered to cash the army's pay vouchers for a 1-percent commission—which made Pierpont very popular with the soldiers. By 1879, the ascendant Morgans were joining with August Belmont and the Rothschilds to market the last Civil War refunding loan. The United States resumed specie payment that year—that is, government notes were payable in silver or gold—and the issue was a great success.

Far from being thrilled by this new parity with the Rothschilds, Pierpont was offended by the supposed high-handedness of his partners. The more conciliatory Junius insisted that the Rothschilds share in any syndicate, but Pierpont's enormous ego brooked no condescension. As he wrote his brother-in-law Walter Burns, now Junius's partner in London: "I need scarcely tell you that having anything to do with Rothschilds & Belmont in this matter is extremely unpalatable to us and I would give almost anything if they were out. The whole treatment of Rothschild's to all the party, from Father downwards is such, as to my mind, no one should stand."[25] In fact, the Rothschilds had badly miscalculated America's importance to the future of world finance, and it would prove an irremediable blunder. Their representative, August Belmont, bemoaned their "utter want of appreciation of the importance of American business."[26] Now the Morgan star was on the rise, and within a generation it would outshine that of both the Rothschilds and the Barings.

THE financial writer John Moody said that until 1879 Pierpont Morgan was "merely the son of his grim-mouthed father."[27] Junius, all business, found it hard to give up his all-consuming work. Now portly like "an East Indian merchant prince in an old English play," he appears slightly bent in photographs, sedentary, heavy with care, gazing from beneath shaggy eyebrows.[28] The airy elegance of youth has settled into a craggy look of suspicion. In 1873, when he reached sixty, Pierpont was already urging him to cut back his schedule. He wrote, "It occurs to me to suggest that *you* need rest as much as I do, & I do not quite see why you cannot also take two days away from office per week."[29] Junius wasn't as rigidly attached to the office as Peabody, but he was domineering and at times had only one partner.

The elder Morgan now began to reap the honors of a semiretirement. On November 8, 1877, he enjoyed a last hurrah in his native country with a New York dinner at Delmonico's in his honor, sponsored by the city's business community. This impressive gathering of more than a hundred people numbered John Jacob Astor and the elder Theodore Roosevelt among its dignitaries. Breaking a self-imposed ban on public appearances, Samuel J. Tilden, a former governor of New York and just-defeated presidential candidate, presided. Toasting Junius as America's preeminent banker in London, Tilden lauded Junius for "upholding unsullied the honor of America in the tabernacle of the Old World."[30] As in Peabody's day, American businessmen believed they had to prove their worth in London. In reply, Junius said his lifelong crusade was that no evil should be spoken of America. Nobody in those days talked of British obligations or of nascent American power—only of how Americans should please British creditors. Under Pierpont, the financial position of the two countries would be strikingly reversed.

Pierpont's relationship with his father was the most important in his life. Junius was the sort of punishing father who built character by stinting on praise and setting exacting standards, keeping up psychic pressure and always making Pierpont prove himself. Tough and demanding, he produced a son who lashed himself into ever greater exertion, only to lapse into sickness, fatigue, or depression. Junius strengthened those already relentless impulses in Pierpont's nature— his overmastering need to achieve, his inordinate sense of responsibility, his hatred of disorder. Yet the patriarchal Morgan clan permitted no rebellion, only veneration of Father. Whatever fear and resentment Pierpont felt were transmuted into exaggerated love, and such filial worship would be equally apparent in Pierpont's own children and grandchildren.

Under his sometimes stern facade, Junius clearly adored Pierpont; the obsessive grooming was a tacit acknowledgment of his son's gifts. In 1876, he decided to buy Pierpont a princely gift—Gainsborough's portrait of the duchess of Devonshire, possibly the world's most popular painting at the time. The Rothschilds had already bid for it, and Junius was prepared to top them by paying Agnew's of Bond Street $50,000. Before the sale was consummated, however, the painting was stolen from Agnew's. Even a £1,000 reward couldn't coax it back. Interestingly, when the painting resurfaced in 1901, Pierpont rushed to buy it for £30,000, or $150,000. "If the truth came out," he conceded regarding the staggering price, "I might be considered a candidate for the lunatic asylum."[31] It was a deeply sentimental homage to his father. At 13 Princes Gate, the London townhouse he inherited from Junius, he hung the painting in the cherished spot over the mantelpiece.

In 1879, Pierpont began to emerge from his father's shadow and take charge of major deals. He was picked to market the largest block of stock ever publicly offered—250,000 shares of New York Central. It was a landmark event for the Vanderbilts, who owned the railroad.

Commodore Cornelius Vanderbilt had died two years before, at eighty-three, leaving a fortune of about $100 million. Though he rejected champagne as too expensive in his last days, he probably ranked as America's richest man. Crude and tobacco chewing, a white-haired, red-cheeked rogue, he chased pretty maids to the end. In his dotage, he fell under the influence of spiritualists and held business talks with the late Jim Fisk, the tough whom Pierpont bested over the Albany and Susquehanna, later killed by a rival suitor to his mistress.

Commodore Vanderbilt's death was a pivotal moment in the shift of business from family to public ownership—a transition rich in possibilities for Pierpont Morgan. To keep his railroad empire intact, the Commodore bequeathed to his oldest son, William Henry, 87 percent of New York Central stock. William was a homely, torpid, thick-set man then in his late fifties whom the Commodore had thought a dunce, berated freely, and exiled to a rude farm on Staten Island. William certainly wasn't groomed to manage the New York Central, which the rough-hewn Commodore ran from a cigar box full of records.

The Commodore had merged eleven small railroads to form the forty-five-hundred-mile New York Central. It branched north from New York City to Albany and then swept west to the Great Lakes, opening the interior to eastern ports. That such power would pass to William Vanderbilt appalled many people. As William Gladstone wrote the Vanderbilt's lawyer, Chauncey M. Depew, "I understand you have a man in your country who is worth $100,000,000, and it is all in property which he can convert at will into cash. The government ought to take it away from him, as it is too dangerous a power for any one man to have."[32] William didn't help to reassure the public, and talked his way into the history books with his retort: "The public be damned; I am working for my stockholders."[33] The scope of Vanderbilt wealth spread fear and led to new calls for public accountability.

What finally induced William Henry to reduce his New York Central stake was publicity generated by New York State Assembly hearings in 1879, chaired by A. Barton Hepburn. This investigating committee exposed secret deals made by the New York Central, which gave preferential rates to oil refiners. As the railroad's chief executive and star witness, William Henry seemed ignorant or evasive about the clandestine maneuvering; to counter bad publicity, he approached Morgan, probably steered to him by Chauncey Depew. New York State was beginning to levy punitive taxes against the New York Central, and it was hoped that by having William Henry sell a huge chunk of stock, thus making him a minority shareowner, the state legislature might relent.

That Vanderbilt chose the forty-two-year-old Pierpont to carry out this delicate operation probably stemmed from the House of Morgan's Anglo-American structure. The principal concern was how to liquidate up to 250,000 shares without collapsing the stock's price. The Morgan-led syndicate demanded that the Vanderbilts refrain from further sales for a year or until all syndicate shares were placed. Another technique to mask the high-volume sale was to sell shares abroad, and J. S. Morgan and Company took an initial 50,000-share block. Junius could act with a discretion impossible on Wall Street. But it was no easy sales job: British investors were still getting mauled by American railroads, and dozens more foundered that year. The world economy was still depressed, with a deep slump in foreign lending. And in the largely unregulated Baronial Age, stock prospectuses were comically skimpy. The New York Central prospectus, for instance, was grandly evasive: "The credit and status of the company are so well known, that it is scarcely necessary to make any public statement."[34] With so little information about a company, the reputation of the sponsoring bank was critically important.

The New York Central deal had an unstated agenda. The syndicate allotted 20,000 shares to Jay Gould, 15,000 to Russell Sage, and 10,000 to Cyrus Field. The inclusion of the odious Gould was part of a truce between Vanderbilt's New York Central and Gould's Wabash, which had been feuding. At first, Vanderbilt wasn't thrilled about this, but Gould effectively blackmailed his way into the syndicate by threatening to deprive the New York Central of Wabash traffic. Gould also felt this association with the Morgans might cloak him in a new respectability and perhaps entitle him to better credit in the future.

When Pierpont announced that he had mysteriously sold the huge block of New York Central shares, much of it abroad, the financial world gaped with wonder. The commission was a colossal $3 million. As he had during the feud over the Albany and Susquehanna, Pierpont demanded a seat on the railroad's board of directors. As Junius told a partner, Pierpont was "to represent the London interest"—that is, he would vote their proxies.[35] Having long chafed at American railroad brigands—even organizing a $300,000 defense committee to protect their stake in Gould's Scarlet Woman—European investors now exacted their revenge. They were tired of railroad shenanigans—bankruptcy, skipped dividends, poor management. So Pierpont Morgan would be their blunt instrument with which to bludgeon American railroads into responsible behavior. He had just the right clubman's pedigree to inspire their trust. Once he chastised a railroad president by exclaiming, "Your roads! Your roads belong to my clients!"[36] Because railroads required constant capital and exhausted the resources of lone entrepreneurs, they were ripe for such banker domination.

As intended, the sale of William Vanderbilt's stock dispersed ownership and New York State slackened its assault against the road. But what the legislators didn't reckon on was that Pierpont would take those scattered shares and effectively recreate their combined power in himself. He began placing his golden manacles on the road. Besides voting all the London proxies, he insisted that the New York Central maintain its $8 dividend for five years, with the House of Morgan acting as fiscal agent to disburse those dividends in New York and London. Before long, the New York Central would be a Morgan road and the company whose shares were recommended most frequently by the Morgan family.

In standing up foursquare for British creditors, Pierpont took the risky step of identifying himself with a foreign power, creating confusion in the popular mind as to his political loyalties. From this time on, he would often be criticized as a mere appendage of London bankers, "a sort of colonial administrator; a representative in America of the financial might of Britain."[37] This ambiguity regarding the bank's Anglo-American character would not only foster considerable paranoia in the American heartland but would also create an identity crisis within the Morgan empire itself.

In the meantime, while Wall Street buzzed over the New York Central affair, Pierpont seemed to derive little joy from it. Far from puffing up with pride, he sounded frazzled and dispirited. Yet again he contemplated giving up business. An 1880 letter to his cousin Jim Goodwin shows how explicitly he began to view himself as an instrument of larger purpose, the representative of masses of investors. He wrote in part,

> I am pressed beyond measure. I never have had such a winter—and although my health has been better than I have had for many winters, still, so far as time is concerned, I have had no leisure whatever. If it were simply my own affairs that were concerned, I would very soon settle the question, and give it up; but with the large interests of others on my shoulders, it cannot be done—and I do not suppose there is any reason why it should, except that I often think it would be very desirable if I could have more time for outside matters.[38]

Several commentators have noted Pierpont's "savior complex," as seen in his private life by his marriage to the tubercular Mimi and in his business life by his crusades for the "London interests." In his own mind, he often acted to benefit others, not simply for self-aggrandizement. This pronounced sense of martyrdom made him extremely sensitive to criticism and also shielded him from true self-knowledge. In more extreme moments, it could invite megalomania. It was too easy to camouflage selfish impulses by invoking a higher cause as the real cause. At the same time, he wasn't motivated by purely selfish motives and had larger concerns than most bankers of his day. In future years, Morgan partisans would praise the bank's high ethical standards and reputation for fairness, while critics would see the self-congratulatory rhetoric as sanctimonious and hypocritical. And both sides would prove right.

CHAPTER FOUR

CORSAIR

. .

.

I N 1882, Pierpont was making half a million dollars a year, and the power balance within the Morgan empire began to tip from London to New York. To mark their new financial status, Pierpont and Fanny sold their high-stooped house on East Fortieth Street and bought a brownstone formerly owned by Isaac N. Phelps (of Phelps, Dodge copper fame) at 219 Madison Avenue at the northeast corner of Thirty-sixth Street, still in Manhattan's Murray Hill neighborhood. In this less crowded New York, the East River was still visible from the house. At a time of sybaritic indulgence, when businessmen wallowed in luxury and showy greed was all the rage, the Morgan home was imposing but unadorned. Its entryway was flanked by Ionic columns, and a bay window overlooked Madison Avenue. Heavy wood furniture and bric-a-brac filled the rooms. In his high-ceilinged library, paneled in Santo Domingan mahogany, Pierpont set his massive desk; it stood in the middle of the room as if the library were the partners' room of a merchant bank. This library was a place of such forbidding gloom that the staff of twelve servants called it the "black library."[1]

A novel feature of the Morgan household was electricity: it was New York's first electrically lighted private residence. Pierpont's interest in the newly harnessed source of energy stemmed from a business deal: in 1878, Thomas Alva Edison had secured capital from the Morgan partners and other financiers to establish the Edison Electric Illuminating Company. Unfortunately, the infernal racket of the electrical generator was the bane of the Morgans' neighbors. Downtown, Drexel, Morgan hosted early meetings of the Edison company and in 1882 became the first Wall Street office to draw electricity from Edison's generating station at Pearl Street. Edison himself, in a Prince Albert coat, attended the debut of electric power at 23 Wall Street, and he kept his personal account at the bank.

The decision to stay in Murray Hill said much about the Morgans, who scorned the *nouveaux riches.* When they opted for that neighborhood, the "quality" were already moving uptown. Along Fifth Avenue, exhibitionist moguls built gaudy palaces, their styles plundered from European châteaus. From Fifty-first to Fifty-second streets, in elephantine splendor, rose William Henry Vanderbilt's mansion. Between Fifty-seventh and Fifty-eighth streets, Cornelius Vanderbilt II, son of William Henry, built another palace on the present site of Bergdorf Goodman.

Matthew Josephson has offered an unforgettable portrait of Gilded Age vulgarity:

> At Delmonico's the Silver, Gold and Diamond dinners of the socially prominent succeeded each other unfailingly. At one, each lady present, opening her napkin, found a gold bracelet with the monogram of the host. At another, cigarettes rolled in hundred-dollar bills were passed around after coffee and consumed with an authentic thrill. . . . One man gave a dinner to his dog, and presented him with a diamond collar worth $15,000. At another dinner, costing $20,000, each guest discovered in one of his oysters a magnificent black pearl. Another distracted individual longing for diversion had little holes bored into his teeth, into which a tooth expert inserted twin rows of diamonds; when he walked abroad his smile flashed and sparkled in the sunlight. . . ."[2]

A cross between Connecticut Yankees and London aristocrats, the Morgans shrank from extravagance and shielded their lives from the newspapers. Like European *haute banque* families, the Morgans were very private. Pierpont was fanatic about his privacy and created an enduring image of a top-hatted tycoon snarling and brandishing a stick at photographers. He belonged to nineteen private clubs, most of the sort restricted to Anglo-Saxon Christian men, and liked to mingle with old money. Unlike most members, he preferred building clubs to using them. When some friends were blackballed from the Union Club, he had Stanford White design the Metropolitan Club, which acquired the tag of the Millionaire's Club. Morgan was the first president. He was never a champion of social justice or equality. When Theodore Seligman, son of one of New York's most prominent Jewish bankers, was blackballed from the Union League Club in 1893, Pierpont didn't protest the exclusion.

For Pierpont, a gentleman wasn't a rich man but a member of a social caste. He is associated with two statements about yachting that sum up his philosophy. The first is that "you can do business with anyone but you can only sail a boat with a gentleman,"[3] and the second (perhaps apocryphal) that anyone who asked about the cost of maintaining a yacht shouldn't buy one. He had no time for bounders or upstarts and despised the rich idle young men about town who pursued women in clubs and cafés. The Morgans would always be strong believers in the work ethic and the duties of the rich. They shunned the snobbish version of high society embodied by Mrs. Astor and Ward McAllister's "Four Hundred"—supposedly the *crème de la crème* of New York society. In bluff, manly style, Pierpont would have thought their balls prissy or vulgar.

A stuffed shirt, Pierpont liked to play chess or whist in the company of older, settled men. He believed in convention and always wore social uniforms suitable to the occasion—a bowler in winter, a Panama hat in summer, for instance. Even when he toured Egypt in 1877 he wore knickerbockers, watch chain, and pith helmet—the approved dress for the imperial tourist. "Physically and intellectually, Morgan reproduced the traditional old-time London banker," said Alexander Dana Noyes.[4] At the office, sitting at his rolltop desk, he wore stiff winged collars, ascots, and heavily starched shirts—trademarks of the serious banker. Only on sweltering days would he peel off his coat in the clublike atmosphere. Like his father, he called himself a merchant and his firm a countinghouse.

The early 1880s saw Pierpont's metamorphosis from a dashing, muscular young man into the portly tycoon with fierce visage and blown-up nose. Now in his forties, he had graying hair and eyebrows and still sported a handlebar mustache. The acne rosacea that had troubled him since adolescence took root in his nose, enlarging and inflaming it until it became Wall Street's most talked-about protuberance. Over the years, it would take on a cauliflower texture. Many people would notice a link between the nose and Pierpont's fiery temper. The nose certainly contributed to an insecurity and lack of social ease that were thinly masked by a barking voice and tyrannical manner. The blustery tone warned the world not to stare at the face. The nose must have been a terrible handicap for a shy, self-conscious man with a tremendous need for female admiration.

The body swelled with the face. In the 1880s, a generation of Wall

Street bankers was doomed by the wisdom of one William Evarts, who credited his longevity to "never under any circumstance having taken exercise."[5] Pierpont usually played cards at a club after work rather than join in a game of tennis. He occasionally lifted dumbbells, but in the late 1880s a medical sage advised him to "stop exercise in every form. Never even walk when you can take a cab."[6] Pierpont loyally followed doctor's orders, doing so while smoking Havana cigars so big and black that they were dubbed Hercules' clubs.[7] A teetotaler by day—the Morgan banks, by tradition, never served alcohol at lunch—he compensated for this abstinence at night, progressing from predinner cocktails to sherry or claret with meals and then to brandy or port afterward. More than husky, he began to develop the sleek girth that symbolized contemporary tycoons.

Although a retiring person beneath his bossy manner, Pierpont maintained an acquaintance with an extensive number of people. As a merchant banker, he had to cultivate clients, and his business life was necessarily social. As a later Baring Brothers chairman remarked of the business, "One of the facets of the art is that if you do not get on with the people you are trying to advise, then you find yourselves out the door."[8] And Pierpont engaged in a constant whirl of dinners and civic functions.

These social pressures took their toll on his marriage, which had already begun to turn into a cold, empty charade. Fanny Morgan was bashful and lacked all relish for the social duties incumbent upon a merchant banker's wife. Sad and anxious, sweet and pious, she preferred reading, gossiping with friends, talking about religion, and discussing social questions. She would be more popular with both their children and their grandchildren than would the dagger-eyed Pierpont. As his world grew larger, Fanny's spirit was either not large enough or not willing enough to fill that space with him. One also suspects that the couple clashed as a result of their very similarity. Both were sensitive and high-strung and too melancholic to provide much solace for the other. Fanny wasn't a tonic to Pierpont's habitual moodiness, and he was doubtless much too busy to attend to her needs. The practical marriage, the supposed antidote to the Mimi affair, turned out to be dangerously impractical.

When Junius returned to London after his 1877 dinner, Pierpont followed. It was the first Christmas he spent away from his children. The next year, Fanny didn't join him for the annual spring trip abroad, and he thereafter developed the habit of traveling to Europe with one of his daughters, spending months apart from his wife each year. These trips combined business and pleasure, and provided cover for infidelity. As a high Victorian, he was proper and respectful toward Fanny in public, even as their separations lengthened. Over time, she would become morose and something of an invalid, pouring her heart out, to her son Jack, among others.

Pierpont wasn't the sort to suffer a loveless marriage lightly. As revealed by his love for Mimi, he was highly romantic. He made pilgrimages to Mimi's grave in Fairfield, Connecticut, traveling there on the anniversary of their wedding or of her death.[9] His eyes cloudy and troubled, he had the soul of a voluptuary beneath a banker's custom-made suit. Even as he scared people away, he was a lonely man, carrying around a vast despair that he couldn't share with anyone. His unhappy marriage probably plunged him deeper into business while also denying him the pleasure of his triumphs.

PIERPONT'S connections in the realm of charity were almost as extensive as his business interests. He preferred to give to religious, cultural, and educational causes, not to social welfare agencies. He never tried to solve the problem of poverty. He wanted to build institutions that were private and elite. He was an original patron of the Metropolitan Museum of Art and the American Museum of Natural History, had a box within the Metropolitan Opera's Golden Horseshoe (he liked romantic, florid operas, especially *Il Trovatore*), and was a major contributor to Saint Luke's Hospital. After Junius took in S. Endicott Peabody (a distant relative of George's) as a partner in London, Pierpont helped his son, the Reverend Endicott Peabody, to buy ninety acres north of Boston for a new prep school, Groton. Modeled after Rugby, it was supposed to develop a good, manly, Christian character in its pupils. Ironically, it spawned that arch enemy of the House of Morgan— Franklin Delano Roosevelt.

Through his friend and personal physician, Dr. James W. Markoe, Pierpont gave one of his rare gifts to the immigrant masses then streaming into New York's Lower East Side. In 1893, Markoe told him of an operation he had performed in a tenement kitchen to save an immigrant mother and her baby. Pierpont counted out three hundred-dollar bills. "See that she gets the proper care," he said, handing the money to the doctor.[10] Eventually Dr. Markoe persuaded him to contribute over $1 million to erect a new building for the New York Lying-In Hospital, where nurses would provide poor pregnant women with food, milk, and prenatal care. Dr. Markoe became the director. As Pierpont became more of a philanderer, his concern for unwed mothers would be the subject of wisecracks about town, as well as stories of doctors at the hospital who married Pierpont's mistresses.

But the institution that most absorbed Pierpont was the Episcopal church, which was part of the Anglican Communion. Religion united his values—beauty, order, hierarchical relationships, veneration of the past, pageantry and pomp. As New York's most influential Episcopal layman, he attended the church's triennial conventions and participated in its abstruse debates. Religion logically accompanied the moralism that drove him at work and lay at the bottom of his indignation at American business practices. His maternal grandfather was a preacher, his paternal grandfather a lusty hymn-singer, and his father's banking maxims were phrased in the epigrammatic style of sermons. Junius often sounded like a frustrated clergyman: "Self-approbation and a feeling that God approves will bring a far greater happiness than all the wealth the world can give."[11] And Pierpont himself was wont to pontificate at 23 Wall Street.

For Pierpont and Fanny, Sundays were devoted to religion. They attended Saint George's Church on Stuyvesant Square, where Pierpont had been a vestryman since 1868, and spent Sunday evenings singing hymns. To gratify Fanny, Pierpont also attended Wednesday evening sessions of the Mendelssohn Club, a choral group. In his early years, he had a strongly prudish streak. In general, his religious interests weren't tied to codes of earthly conduct. Religion moved him on a more primitive level. Whether roaring out hymns at revival meetings or sitting alone in Saint George's, savoring organ music in semidarkness, he seemed mesmerized by ritual and lapsed into reveries of mystic depth.

Approaching Scripture with the literalism of a fundamentalist, Pierpont was as credulous as a child. In 1882, he visited Palestine. Deeply moved, he wrote Fanny about the sensations he experienced before the doorway of Christ's sepulcher: "There is the slab on which He was laid. Impelled by an impulse impossible to resist you fall on your knees before that shrine."[12] In later years, he told his librarian, Belle da Costa Greene, that he believed every word in the Bible, including the account of Jonah and the whale. Once traveling down the Nile with Bishop William Lawrence, he pointed out the precise spot where Moses was plucked from the bulrushes and insisted it happened exactly as set forth in the Bible. In view of this credulity, it is not surprising that Pierpont was fascinated by the occult. For years, he commissioned the astrologer Evangeline Adams to read his horoscope, asking her to study his stars on everything from politics to the stock market. When his son, Jack, was born, the infant's horoscope showed a cardinal cross, associated with depressions—an apt prophecy for the Morgan who steered the bank through 1929.

In 1883, the thirty-three-year-old Rev. William S. Rainsford took over as Saint George's rector. He was a handsome young Irishman with a Cambridge education. Having bankrolled the church's activity, Pierpont had a hand in his appointment. As a social reformer and fiery exponent of the "social gospel," Rainsford told Morgan he would take the job only if the church were democratic and open to the poor. "Done," said Morgan, who agreed to make up the church's deficits.[13] And Rainsford indeed welcomed the poor into Saint George's now-free pews. Eventually the two men became so close that they had breakfast together every Monday morning at 219 Madison Avenue, and Morgan built several new church buildings.

Dr. Rainsford later ran into trouble when he tried to enlarge and democratize the vestry, which met in Morgan's "black library." This went against the grain of Pierpont's arm's-length philanthropy, and he bluntly retorted: "I do not want the vestry democratized. I want it to remain a body of gentlemen whom I can ask to meet me in my study— gentlemen who would feel at home and who could make up deficits out of their pockets."[14] He sent a letter to Rainsford, resigning his post as senior warden; the young rector stubbornly refused to accept it. For several weeks, the two men continued their Monday breakfasts, both eating in silence. During these meals, Pierpont may have recalled the rich men who hounded his reformer grandfather, the Reverend Pierpont. After several weeks of this standoff, Morgan invited Rainsford to see him set sail for Europe. Alone with Rainsford in his stateroom, Pierpont threw his arms around him and exclaimed, "Rainsford, pray for me, pray for me."[15] The feud ended with this melodramatic display of contrition.

Rainsford has left interesting impressions of Pierpont's religious faith: "His beliefs were to him precious heirlooms. He bowed before them as the Russian bows to the 'ikon' before he salutes the master of the house."[16] He saw that for Pierpont the Church wasn't an active, reforming spirit, but a repository of ancient beauty, powerful because it was archaic and unchanging. Rainsford also credited Pierpont with intense loyalty and forthright honesty: "When he said a thing, and looked full at you as he said it, to doubt him was impossible."[17] It was the same look that transfixed two generations of railroad presidents and industrial moguls.

ALTHOUGH the business life of Pierpont Morgan was bound up with the railroads, Pierpont felt more keenly the allure of the sea. At a time when private railroad cars were common showpieces among tycoons, Pierpont never owned one and took private cars, as needed, from the railroads he directed. By midlife, the sea was his best remedy for depression, the place where he escaped from the perpetual strain of the office and was liberated from care. When a yacht-owning fad swept fashionable New York in the 1880s, he needed little inducement to participate. In 1882, he bought the first of a series of enormous yachts, named *Corsair,* and joined the New York Yacht Club. This black-hulled steam yacht—165 feet long and the second largest in the club's fleet—marked a new Morgan magnificence.

It was probably no coincidence that Pierpont bought the *Corsair* soon after it first became apparent that his marriage was disintegrating. The boat was more than a showy bauble. It gave him a social setting beyond Fanny and the children and would later figure in many stories of secret revelry. It permitted an outlaw life beyond the stuffy Victorian bounds of his early married days. He created a group of friends known as the Corsair Club, which provided the camouflage needed to smuggle women on board. The ship was also a second home, particularly when Fanny and the children retreated up the Hudson to Cragston for the summer. Often, Pierpont would dine on the ship and spend the night as it lay at anchor off Manhattan.

Purchase of the *Corsair* coincided with a new phase in Pierpont's career, in which he became an arbiter as well as a financier of railroads. The boat was useful as a meeting place to settle disputes, a secret clubhouse beyond spying eyes. Pierpont had an actor's talent for creating dramatic backdrops for his exploits, and the *Corsair* allowed his business life to take on an aura of operatic flamboyance. This was never truer than in the 1885 dispute between the Pennsylvania Railroad and the New York Central over a railroad called the West Shore.

Pierpont's involvement had a personal dimension. One day in 1881, he saw a peddler leading a pair of donkeys up Broad Street; delighted by their resemblance to small donkeys he had seen in Egypt, he sent a clerk out to buy them. Christened Beelzebub and Apollyon, they were favorites of the Morgan children at Cragston. The following year, his children felt menaced by Irish ruffians building a new railroad below his house on the Hudson's west bank, and Pierpont forbade them to ride unaccompanied by an adult. At the same time, blasts of explosives from the construction of this new West Shore road rattled Cragston's windows, invading the tranquil Morgan hideaway.

The West Shore was that railroad bane of the period—the blackmail line. Extortion artists would lay down parallel lines just to be bought out by an established road. Since railroads were natural monopolies and couldn't survive much direct competition, they could be easily threatened by small competitors. The West Shore ran up the west side of the Hudson, parallel to the New York Central on the opposite bank, then tracked the Central to Buffalo. It was widely believed the powerful Pennsylvania Railroad stood behind the West Shore. So in retaliation, the New York Central broke ground on a South Pennsylvania road to compete with the Pennsylvania from Philadelphia to Pittsburgh.

A fierce rate war between the West Shore and the New York Central hammered down stock and bond prices for both companies, confirming Pierpont's growing hatred of competition. It came at a precarious time for railroad bankers. During a stock market plunge in 1883, there was a near-panic in American rail stocks in London, producing a rising clamor for a financial czar who could arbitrarily settle such disputes. Cyrus Field cabled Junius, "Many of our business men seem to have lost their heads. What we want is some cool-headed strong man to lead."[18] As fiscal agent for the road, Junius watched with alarm as New York Central stock fell below par for the first time; its dividend was halved. In early 1885, Pierpont went to London to consult with Junius and fumed over the "absurd struggle for preeminence" plunging America's railroads into internecine warfare.[19] By the spring of 1885, the West Shore had gone into the hands of a receiver, while the hard-pressed New York Central deferred critical maintenance.

It seems anomalous that America's most famous financier was a sworn foe of free markets. Yet it followed logically from the anarchy of late nineteenth-century railroads, with their rate wars, blackmail, lines, and lack of standardized gauges. To destroy competing lines, railroads could simply refuse to transfer freight to roads that abutted theirs. From an engineering standpoint, Pierpont knew little about railroads. What he did know was that they required steady revenues to cover their fixed interest costs on bonds marketed in New York and London. In the mid-1880s, freight rates were declining sharply under the pressure of savage price-cutting. Pierpont decided that "the principal thing was to secure a harmony between the Pennsylvania and New York Central."[20]

On the sultry morning of July 20, 1885, with an impresario's flair, Pierpont staged a reconciliation between America's two largest railroads. After picking up the New York Central's president, Chauncey Depew, he crossed to a New Jersey pier and took aboard George H. Roberts, president, and Frank Thomson, vice-president, of the Pennsylvania Railroad. Pierpont always denied his yacht was chosen for the sake of secrecy. "I do not know that that was a part of the consideration," he later testified. "It might have been."[21]

Before bringing both parties on board, he worked out the broad outlines of a truce. While the *Corsair* sailed up and down the Hudson, he sat under the rear awning, flanked by the railroad chiefs and smoking his nightmarishly huge black cigar. He stressed the displeasure of European investors with American railroads, but mostly let the railway men debate among themselves. In general, he used two negotiating ploys. He would create a "no-exit" situation and add to it threats that his rivals faced a deadline—a way of building tension and softening up the parties. Also, by saying little, he underscored his position as honest broker and permitted the antagonists to vent their anger. Pierpont was, by nature, a laconic man. He had no gift for sustained analysis; his genius was in the brief, sudden brainstorm. As one lawyer said of him, "Morgan has one chief mental asset—a tremendous five minutes' concentration of thought."[22] By the time the railroad presidents were deposited on their respective shores at seven o'clock that evening, they had agreed to buy out each other's lines and desist from their mutually destructive warfare. Years later, the tunnels and embankments from the abandoned South Pennsylvania line would be incorporated into the Pennsylvania Turnpike. And as the New York Central's business expanded, it enlisted the West Shore tracks for a second line along the Hudson River.

The newspapers lionized the author of this Great Railroad Treaty of 1885, also known as the Corsair Compact.[23] Pierpont had pulled off such a masterly feat that even Junius—so stingy with compliments—told Fanny, "Pierpont handled the West Shore affair better than I could have done it myself."[24] Pierpont was forty-eight when Junius voiced this unprecedented compliment. Once again, Pierpont had performed the kind of task of industrial arbitration that would later be left to courts and public commissions. In the rough-and-tumble of the Baronial Age, competition was naked and brutal, and businessmen lacked trade groups in which they could discuss common problems. Bankers could intervene as neutral parties, particularly where, as with Drexel, Morgan, they had performed work for both companies. Over the years, Pierpont would employ the sharpest lawyers, yet his preferred style was more British— informal deals, handshakes over brandy and cigars, cordial clubroom chats among bankers as they stood in frock coats and stiff collars. The Morgans were never litigious. During one railroad battle, Junius wrote Pierpont, "I hope you will not be tempted into litigation. Life is too short for that."[25]

Bloodletting among railroads intensified in the 1880s. Several railroads skirted bankruptcy. In 1886, Drexel, Morgan reorganized the big Philadelphia and Reading Railroad. This involved issuing new bonds with lower interest rates and assessing shareholders to lighten the burden on the line. The revived railroad was then taken over by a Morgan antagonist named A. Archibald McLeod, who later declared, "I would rather run a peanut-stand than be dictated to by J. P. Morgan."[26] He freely defied Morgan and invaded the territory of his other railroads. The experience would convince Pierpont not to release his grip on reorganized companies.

The basic weakness with America's railroad system was overbuilding, which forced the roads into endless rounds of rate cuts and wage cuts to service debt. At the same time, the massive power of their largest consumers—notably Rockefeller in oil and Carnegie in steel—forced them to grant preferential rebates to big shippers, enraging small western farmers and businessmen and stimulating calls for government regulation. For Pierpont, the leading symbol of railway monopoly, pure competition was never an option. Years later, he said, "The American public seems to be unwilling to admit . . . that it has a choice between regulated legal agreements and unregulated extralegal agreements. We should have cast away more than 50 years ago the impossible doctrine of protection of the public by railway competition."[27] As we shall see repeatedly, the House of Morgan always favored government planning over private competition, but private planning over either.

In 1887, Congress passed the Interstate Commerce Act, the first regulatory commission, which enshrined competition as its guiding principle and eliminated the controversial rebates. Supporters of the act formed a diverse constituency, ranging from small shippers to the railroads themselves; the latter accepted the inevitability of regulation and hoped that in the proper form it might provide some sorely needed stability. But within six months of the creation of the Interstate Commerce Commission, the rebates reappeared. Hence, in 1888 the railroad chieftains decided to graft their own form of self-regulation on the ICC framework under the aegis of Pierpont Morgan.

That December, newspaper readers were regaled with accounts of mysterious doings at Morgan's Murray Hill home. As reporters staked out the house, they saw a procession of western railroad presidents and bankers disappear inside. Those arriving included Charles Francis Adams of the Union Pacific and a ghastly sick Jay Gould representing the Missouri Pacific. The Morgan house was under siege: reporters kept ringing the doorbell and fixed opera glasses on the windows. Inside, at the head of his library table, Pierpont opened the discussion with these words: "The purpose of this meeting is to cause the members of this association to no longer take the law into their own hands when they suspect they have been wronged, as has been too much the practice heretofore. . . . This is not elsewhere customary in civilized communities, and no good reason exists why such a practice should continue among railroads."[28] Clearly, Pierpont's European experience formed his frame of reference.

Backed by representatives of Barings and Brown Brothers, Pierpont offered the railroad presidents a deal: if they refrained from rate-cutting and cutthroat competition, the financiers would stop underwriting competing railways. It was a clever move, for while Wall Street accused the railroads of irresponsible behavior, the railroads blamed Wall Street for floating too many securities and creating the overexpansion that led to price wars. Morgan himself was accused of sponsoring overcapitalized lines that couldn't weather recessions because of their heavy debt load. The December 1888 meetings produced a gentleman's agreement to maintain rates for sixty days; then the group would reassemble at Morgan's house.

A similar gathering took place at Pierpont's "black library" in January 1889. This one yielded plans for a huge centralized group to regulate the entire rail system—the Interstate Commerce Railway Association. This behemoth would set rates, arbitrate disputes, and mete out fines to offending railroads. Pierpont was to head the cartel. The New York *Sun* called the new group "nothing short of a revolution in railroad methods."[29] But the new group soon fell apart under the pressure of western rate wars.

Pierpont's last stab at establishing railroad stability took place at a meeting on December 15, 1890. Besides the earlier luminaries, this gathering drew Stuyvesant Fish of the Illinois Central, James J. Hill of the Great Northern, and T. F. Oakes of the Northern Pacific. Pierpont presented a plan for a Western Traffic Association, which would include one director from each railroad and would set uniform rates; any railroad that cheated would be discharged. He was mightily pleased with his plan. In a rare burst of public candor, he exulted to a reporter, "Think of it—all the competing traffic of the roads west of Chicago and Saint Louis placed in the control of about 30 men!"[30] The statement is splendidly innocent, yet perilously blind. Pierpont believed so implicitly in his own fairness and good judgment that he saw no harm in a large section of America's economy coming under his personal dominion. The *New York Herald* blared, "RAILROAD KINGS FORM A GIGANTIC TRUST."[31] Before too long, this plan, too, would crumble.

In the last analysis, the gentleman's agreements suffered the historic fate of cartels. They couldn't control small outside competitors, who cut rates, outflanked larger rivals, and won new business. With surreptitious cheating and lack of discipline, deals soon collapsed. Even the now-immense authority of Pierpont Morgan couldn't solve the structural problems caused by too many railroads chasing too few passengers and owing too much money. As scores of railroads went bankrupt during the 1893 panic, Pierpont would reorganize many of them and use controversial new techniques to bring about order.

This phase of Pierpont's life shows that his real vice was not money but power. This was not power of a pathological sort, not power to bully men and bask in glory—though there was some of that—but power to take what he saw as a topsy-turvy financial world and set it right. Among robber barons, he was unique in suffering an excess of morality. He believed that he could master the problems of his era at a time when others were confused by the sheer dynamism and speed of economic change.

As this new power accrued to the House of Morgan, making it the premier American bank, excruciating responsibility fell on Pierpont's shoulders. Yet his office staff was slim, with only eighty employees. Pierpont didn't even have a permanent secretary. Junius continued to warn his son against exhausting immersion in business. At the same time, his secretive merchant-banker's sensibility was shocked when Pierpont appointed a clerk to open incoming mail. In the late 1880s, in a final volley of advice, Junius wrote that "no body, however strong & well he may be, can stand such strain upon his physical and mental powers as you have had for the last 2 years without paying sooner or later the penalty unless he gives them a *real rest* & gives it to them *in* season."[32] Yet Junius never saw how much his own unbending style and unrealistically high standards had contributed to Pierpont's slavish dedication to work.

BY the 1880s, as his health was fading, Junius Morgan slowly eased out of business. The Iron Duke of the Morgan saga had become the most influential American banker in London, a peer of Barings and Rothschilds, his firm participating in an international smorgasbord of loans—for the Egyptian national bank, Russian railways, Brazilian provincial governments, and Argentinean public works. Whatever his health problems, he gave an impression of rock-solid durability; the London *Times* declared him "a hale and vigorous man, for his years."[33]

In 1884, Junius's wife, Juliet, died at the age of sixty-eight. Surrounded by her favorite collection of china dogs, she had been, as the Morgan family tactfully phrased it, "confused" in her later years and confined to an upstairs room much of the time. Thus, she had been unable to share in her husband's life. After her death, Junius's solitude was relieved by twice-weekly letters from Pierpont and visits from his grandchildren. J. P. Morgan, Jr., whom the family called Jack, worshiped his grandfather and particularly liked the English formality at 13 Princes Gate, including the way the servants treated him as "heir apparent."[34] Junius was as attached as ever to Pierpont. After a visit from him in the south of France, he wrote, "Pierpont & family left today—House very lonely—miss them dreadfully."[35]

These visits were Junius's main pleasure at the end. A photograph of him taken in 1890 shows the firm mouth and steady gaze of earlier years. His hair was snow-white, his eyebrows white and tufty, and the top of his head was bald. He spent winters at the Villa Henriette in Monte Carlo, which had a beautiful view of the Mediterranean. Leading an orderly, bourgeois life, he dined with friends and took afternoon carriage drives. During one excursion on the afternoon of April 3, 1890, the horses were startled by an onrushing train. Junius jumped up to see whether his coachman could master the team. At that instant, the carriage ran against a heap of stones and flung him violently against a wall, breaking his wrist and causing a brain concussion. For five days, he lay unconscious. Then the flow of maxims ceased forever. Perhaps it was appropriate that Junius's death was dealt by one stunning blow in his seventy-seventh year rather than by a dribbling away of strength; in its obituary notice, the London *Times* remarked that he had hardly been ill in his life.[36] Certainly there was mysterious symbolism in the fact that a train's sudden roar, upsetting a pastoral landscape, had killed one of London's foremost railroad bankers.

Junius was buried in the Cedar Hill Cemetery in Hartford. As he had for Peabody, Pierpont devised a funeral suitable for an illustrious warrior-hero. Hartford shopkeepers along the funeral route closed their businesses for the occasion, while flags flew at half-mast over the state capitol. Pierpont's inscription to Junius for the Morgan Memorial Building at the Wadsworth Atheneum said much about their common identification with London's merchant-banking tradition: "In loving memory of Junius Spencer Morgan, a native of Massachusetts, a merchant of Hartford . . . afterwards a merchant of London."[37]

Did Pierpont resent his father's domination? Or was his admiration as unmixed as he claimed? Whatever anger or ambivalence he felt was buried beneath gigantic monuments. He honored Junius like Hamlet mourning the dead king. For twelve years, he gathered up land around Hartford's Wadsworth Atheneum in order to create the Morgan Memorial, a $1.4-million pink marble building in English Renaissance style that doubled the museum's size. Years later—glancing impatiently at his pocket watch all the while—he surveyed blueprints and rapidly picked out three new buildings for the Harvard Medical School, again to certify a son's love. And upon the red damask wall of the West Room of his own library, Junius's portrait would hold pride of place, ringed by Umbrian Madonnas and infant Saviors—the powerful patriarch surrounded by loving children and ethereal females. After a small fire at his Madison Avenue townhouse, Pierpont was asked which treasure he would have rescued first. "My father's portrait," he said without hesitation.

An American magazine had recently listed Pierpont and Junius as among America's richest men. Now Pierpont inherited an estate of $12.4 million, and his personal fortune doubled overnight. Ten million dollars would stay in the bank. He was bequeathed control of a banking empire and assumed his father's position in the City. Like his father, he stood astride that flow of capital from Britain to America and would profit as it reversed direction in the new century.

After Junius's death, some shackle was lifted from Pierpont's spirit. A new grandiosity flowered and he self-consciously became J. Pierpont Morgan, mogul, pirate, patron of the arts. Before Junius's death, Pierpont's collections were modest; in 1888, he had bought his first literary manuscript, a Thackeray. Now he embarked on a buying spree that would eventually produce the world's largest art collection in private hands. To trumpet the new J. P. Morgan, he also enlisted his friend J. Frederic Tams to design *Corsair II*. Tams was given blank Drexel, Morgan checks and told to forget about expense; the only restriction was that the boat be able to turn around in the Hudson River near Cragston. A dark, sleek ship with a glamorous black hull and yellow smokestack, this new *Corsair* measured over two hundred and forty-one feet in length and aggressively laid claim to the title of the largest pleasure vessel afloat. In time, the mere appearance of the *Corsair II* in foreign harbors would alarm the populace, as if warning of an impending invasion of American capital.

THE men in the Morgan family might have been far happier had not each of three consecutive generations produced only one son to survive to adulthood. In merchant-banking families, the whole weight of the dynasty was at once placed on the male infants. Unlike publicly traded companies, which have a corporate life of their own, private merchant-bank partnerships often relied upon the name, capital, and reputation of a single family. If the male heir(s) refused to go into the family business, it might have to be wound up. Thus, Morgan expectations were lodged first by Junius in Pierpont, then by Pierpont in Jack. In both cases, business pressures would tremendously intensify the typical father-son tensions.

From the outset, Pierpont's relationship with Jack differed from his own with Junius. If Pierpont suffered from Junius's sometimes smothering attention, Jack suffered the curse of neglect. He craved the love of a father who seemed too remote and too self-absorbed to attend to his boyish needs. Between Jack and his father there would always be some distance, some nameless discomfort, that was very different from the intense, manly mutual fascination between Junius and Pierpont. Both Pierpont and Jack were shy and clumsy and steeped in New England formality. It was difficult for the delicate, insecure Jack to cope with the great flashing, roaring engine of a famous father.

Unlike Pierpont, who had been a wild, headstrong boy requiring a firm hand, Jack needed a father to buck up his faltering courage—which Pierpont didn't do. Jack was gentle and sedentary, lacking fire. He attended Saint Paul's School in Concord, New Hampshire, where rich adolescent boys were exposed to Spartan Yankee routines. They had to write weekly letters home but couldn't receive presents and had to seek pocket money from the rector. Where Pierpont wrote boyhood essays in praise of Napoléon, Jack seemed more protective of the weak. Explaining why one teacher was his favorite, he confessed: "I suppose that it is partly because I feel sorrier for him than any of the others—the boys do plague him so."[38] In 1880, at thirteen, he cried upon reading *Dombey and Son*, Dickens's novel about a stern magnate father and his sensitive son. Like his own father, Jack suffered migraine headaches that lasted for days. Big, awkward, and docile, Jack liked well-bred boys, not ruffians, and already sounded middle-aged at twelve, telling Fanny he refrained from marbles because "it doesn't pay for the wear and tear and chapping of the knuckles."[39]

Jack lacked the nerve to contest his terrifying, distant father. Where Pierpont had the fortitude to confront Junius, Jack silently hoped for approval and leaned on his mother for emotional support. He found his father a man of violent and mercurial moods. His anxiety grew especially acute about money, a subject invested with many family taboos.

Like the young Pierpont, Jack kept strict accounts of his expenses. We find him recording ten cents for a library fine at school and charging expenses against his "Christmas money" or "grandpa money."[40] Whenever the subjects of Pierpont and money coincided, Jack trembled: "You see I don't mean to do anything about money that Papa wouldn't like," he told his mother. "Papa hates so to have me come to him about money matters that I did not mean in any way to hint that he ought to pay the bill."[41] Such sentiments abound in his boyhood letters.

Jack's letters to his mother form the most complete record of Morgan family life; unfortunately, no account from Fanny's side remains. It is clear, however, that Jack was passionately attached to his mother. Sensitive to each other's melancholy, they shared the great enigma of J. Pierpont Morgan and consoled each other for forty years. Later on, we shall see Jack Morgan as a bitter old man, yet here he was as an ardent boy, bursting with affection, telling his mother: "Dear, I love you as you know and just now I am full of comfort thinking I am going to see you in less than a week."[42] Even as a teenager, he felt protective toward Fanny and sometimes sounded more like parent than child. As Fanny became depressed and bedridden— there are many references to her invalidism in Jack's letters—he tried to cheer her up. In 1889, he wrote, "As to your blues,– -I can only say, what every one else does, do take care enough not to overtire yourself, and watch against them all you know how."[43] As a teenager, he was slightly puzzled when a friend's mother described Fanny as "calm cold unenthusiastic."[44] Yet the episode suggests that Fanny may have been aloof in the outside world and showed her emotions only in private.

While Pierpont had a smattering of university education at Göttingen, Jack was the first Morgan to obtain a college degree, graduating from Harvard in 1889. He had a broad, smooth face, with dark hair flattened on top, and a mustache. His Harvard years, which coincided with his father's gentleman's agreements, were free of rebellion. While Pierpont knocked heads with railroad satraps in New York, Jack loafed, smoked pipes, and took a gentleman's C, spending his senior year studying the properties of seaweed. It was symptomatic of Jack's humility and his insecurity that when he made an exciting discovery in his laboratory, he chalked it off it to luck.

Like his mother, Jack enjoyed literature, but seemed unsettled by dark worldviews. Proper and squeamish, he was disturbed by *Faust*'s tragic ending and found *La dame aux camélias* depressing. There would be no tubercular Mimi or tear-stained adventures in Jack's young life. Sailing to Europe in 1887, he wrote, "There is only one girl on board who could be called a belle and I have kept very clear of her because she struck me as being very *common*."[45] He flirted with no dangerous doctrines and was already impatient with meddlesome people who stirred up trouble. "I don't know why so many people . . . seem to look upon business as if it were the general sewer in which all ambition and intelligence disappear. I must confess I don't see any harm myself in making a little money, provided that it can be done honestly and reasonably."[46] He was also quite religious. Where other young men hotly debated the justice of the social order, Jack worried about whether gambling should be openly denounced from the pulpit.

Jack has left a melancholy record of the emotional chasm that separated him from his father. He told one satiric story that also said much about Pierpont's self-absorption. He had invited a Harvard classmate to visit him at Cragston, and the young man rode up on the *Corsair* with Pierpont. After introductions, Pierpont promptly buried himself in the newspaper. When they landed, he said to Jack about the classmate, "That is one of the nicest young fellows I've met."[47]

Pierpont apparently found Jack soft and rather passive, lacking the sort of gumption he had as a young man. In 1884 and 1885, he arranged for his son to take a hunting trip in the Rockies with William Rainsford, the rector of Saint George's, who was a great sportsman. Jack shot a bighorn sheep and slept in a snowbound cabin—manly pursuits Pierpont hoped would toughen the young man up. Meanwhile, Jack's intimate life remained confined to his mother.

In 1889, Jack graduated from Harvard and met Jane Norton Grew, daughter of Boston banker and mill owner Henry Sturgis Grew. Descended from several prominent families, including the Sturgises and the Wigglesworths, Jessie, as Jane was called, had a proper Bostonian pedigree. Yet before approving the match, the Morgans and the Grews circled around each other and sniffed for a while. Jack passed along Jessie's genealogy to the snobbish Pierpont and kept requesting a chance to discuss their possible marriage. Finally Pierpont consented to talk with his son during his next trip to Boston. In a letter both angry and wistful, Jack told Fanny what happened:

> On Saturday Papa telegraphed me he should be in Boston a few hours and hoped to see me. He was to arrive at 6:40 and go back at midnight, with a party of twelve for a *Corsair* dinner. I expected to be nearly an hour with him, instead of which his train was delayed and instead of seeing him I waited under a railroad bridge in the rain

for an hour, and had the delightful opportunity of driving from the Station to the Club with him in the same carriage with Mr. Bowdoin [Pierpont's partner] and Mr. Depew [then president of the New York Central]. As he had not sent me on a single one of your telegrams, and had not told me anything about Rainsford's plans or even if he himself was certain to sail on Wednesday the visit was somewhat unsatisfactory. There certainly are some drawbacks to belonging to a busy man no matter how fine he may be as I believe you have sometimes found out.[48]

Most revealing is how the letter ends—with Jack portraying himself and Fanny as common victims of Pierpont. A month later, anxious and trembling, Jack blurted out the facts of the situation with Jessie. Pierpont responded that in the spring he and Fanny would consider the matter. Frightened of his father, Jack was always relieved and grateful when he received sympathetic attention. After a subsequent meeting, he told his mother, "It would be hard for me to exaggerate my thankfulness for the way in which Papa received my confidences, and the satisfaction I feel in having spoken to him. It has made me less blue than I have been for months."[49] On December 11, 1890, Jack and Jessie were wed in Boston's Arlington Street Church, a marriage that made the front page of the *New York Times*.

The oral history that has come down through the Morgan family contends that Jack wanted to be a doctor and became a banker only when his father made it a matter of family honor.[50] In 1892, at the age of twenty-five, Jack became a partner in the Morgan banks in New York, Philadelphia, and Paris. During a twenty-year business association, Jack would remain a close observer of his father, charting his manic-depressive moods and giving him more generous sympathy than he received in return, although the relationship would become somewhat more equal toward the end of Pierpont's life.

Jack entered the Morgan empire at a critical time. In June 1893, Tony Drexel died while visiting the Austro-Hungarian health resort of Karlsbad, leaving an estate said to be worth between $25 and $30 million. While giving Pierpont managerial control in New York, the Drexel family had retained control of Drexel and Company in Philadelphia and Drexel, Harjes in Paris. In October 1893, Anthony Drexel, Jr., decided to retire and devote himself to society pleasures, thus enabling Pierpont to strengthen his hold over the interlocking partnerships in New York, Philadelphia, Paris, and London. At a dinner meeting at the Metropolitan Club—the sole time in Morgan history that the New York and Philadelphia partners sat in one room—he announced a new plan for centralized control.

In the 1895 reorganization, Drexel, Morgan was rechristened J. P. Morgan and Company, while the Paris office became Morgan, Harjes. The Philadelphia house remained Drexel and Company, but the Drexel family passed from the scene, and Pierpont tapped Edward T. Stotesbury, son of a Philadelphia sugar refiner, to head the Philadelphia office. J. S. Morgan and Company in London would soon undergo a major reorganization of personnel. Among the four Morgan partnerships, the only common denominator would be Pierpont's position as all-powerful senior partner; his associates, in contrast, might be partners in some, but not all the firms. Pierpont would take 35 percent of the profits of the combined houses. Power had now passed from London to New York, which would remain the command post of the Morgan empire. Despite its multinational veneer, the Morgan empire would be American-based, with partners at 23 Wall wielding disproportionate power. Where Junius had dispatched Pierpont to New York as the lesser financial center, so Pierpont would dispatch Jack to London, soon to be eclipsed by New York. On the eve of an unprecedented industrial boom in America, which would see the creation of vast trusts, the House of Morgan had opportunely shifted its center of gravity westward across the Atlantic.

PIERPONT Morgan's thunderous presence at 23 Wall Street could be observed by visitors as soon as they entered his glass-enclosed, wood-paneled offices. (The concept was copied from Junius's office.) Seated in a swivel chair before a rolltop desk on the Broad Street side, a coal fire behind him in winter, he would rise, stroll over, and question his partners as he needed to. Lincoln Steffens recalled how he sat in a back room with glass sides and the door open. This sense of access was illusory, however, for his imperious stare could reduce interlopers to jelly. He unnerved those who overstayed a visit by simply writing and not looking up. Steffens recalled that "his partners did not go near him unless he sent for them; and then they looked alarmed and darted in like office boys."[51] Even his partners called him Mr. Morgan, or the Senior. So there he sat, displayed like a carnival waxwork, the man Bernard Baruch termed "the greatest financial genius this country has ever known."[52] He invited intimacy but then rebuffed it; his aura was so fearsome that crowds parted before him on the pavement. Once, when an Episcopal bishop visited Cragston, Pierpont was able to flag down a West Shore train in the middle of the night so the prelate could make his way back to Manhattan.

There are many stories of Pierpont's brusque impatience and his economy of self-expression. He had a short attention span and sometimes worked only from eleven o'clock to three or four in the afternoon, pausing for a sandwich, pie, and coffee at his desk. After saving one merchant's business, he interrupted the man's grateful blubbering to say, "No, it is a busy day. There's no time for that. Good morning."[53] Few were privy to his thoughts, and he often had his own unstated agenda. Journalist Clarence W. Barron tells the story of a young Boston financier, F. H. Prince, who went to Pierpont for investment advice. Prince confessed, "I shook Mr. Morgan's hand and thanked him warmly for the great interest he was taking in me as a young man and said I should never forget his advice. I knew at this time that he was doing everything he could to ruin me."[54]

After Junius's death, Pierpont needed to loosen his autocratic grip, as the sheer volume of work outgrew his need for domination. He had long bewailed his inability to delegate authority—"It is my nature and I cannot help it"—and held no formal meeting of his partners until after the 1907 panic.[55] Despite the scope of his vision, Pierpont was extremely attentive to details and took pride in the knowledge that he could perform any job in the bank: "I can sit down at any clerk's desk, take up his work where he left it and go on with it. . . . I don't like being at any man's mercy."[56] He never entirely renounced the founder's itch to know the most minute details of the business. He examined the cash balance daily, boasted he could pay off all debts in two hours, had a deadeye for fake figures in scanning a ledger, and personally audited the books each New Year's Day. When he found an error, the effect could be memorable for the responsible employee. "He was a perfectly huge man and he had a voice like a bull," said Leonhard A. Keyes, then an office boy who wound the gold Tiffany clock on his desk.[57]

Pierpont Morgan's power flourished during the steep industrial recession that began in 1893. Over fifteen thousand commercial firms failed in a contraction that led to class warfare and quasi-revolutionary strife in many parts of the United States. The bloody rout of steel workers in the Homestead strike of 1892 gave way to the government's merciless crushing of the 1894 Pullman strike. Over six hundred banks failed during this period, and cash grew so scarce as a result of hoarding that brokers traded it on Wall Street curbs. Every company that failed and was reorganized by a bank ended up the bank's captive client. In 1892,

General Electric had been formed through a consolidation of the Edison General Electric Company and Thomson-Houston Electric. When the new company failed the next year, Pierpont rescued it and thus insured GE's future loyalty to the House of Morgan.

Oppressed by debt and overbuilding, more than a third of the country's railway trackage fell into receivership, and English investors exhorted Pierpont to bring order to the industry. Thwarted by gentleman's agreements, Pierpont now tried another approach to forming railway cartels: he would reorganize bankrupt roads and transfer control to himself. Then he wouldn't be at the whim of government or feuding railway chiefs. In reorganizing railways, he ascended to a new plateau of power, beyond what any other private businessman had yet achieved. The lengthy catalogue of railroads that fell under his control included the Erie, Chesapeake and Ohio, Philadelphia and Reading, Santa Fe, Northern Pacific, Great Northern, New York Central, Lehigh Valley, Jersey Central, and the Southern Railway. Virtually every bankrupt road east of the Mississippi eventually passed through such reorganization, or morganization, as it was called. Some thirty-three thousand miles of railroad—one-sixth of the country's trackage—were morganized. The companies' combined revenues approached an amount equal to half of the U.S. government's annual receipts.

It is hard to exaggerate the power that Pierpont accrued. Railroads then comprised 60 percent of all issues on the New York Stock Exchange. Utility and industrial stocks were rated as too speculative for insurance companies and savings institutions, putting railroads in a blue-chip category by themselves. Also, by issuing free passes to politicians, the railroads exercised a giant, corrupting influence on state legislatures. As his bank became a gigantic mill for bankrupt railroads, Pierpont routinely picked up $1-million fees.

With morganization, fixed railway costs were slimmed, and creditors were forced to swap their bonds for ones with lower interest rates, enabling roads to resume debt service. Pierpont would also put a lien on the railroads' vast land and mineral holdings, so that money couldn't be diverted to other enterprises. A court case nearly a hundred years later would show how binding these arrangements were. In 1987, the Burlington Northern Railroad tried to free itself from covenants Pierpont had imposed on the bonds of its predecessor, the Northern Pacific, which fell into receivership in 1893. He had put a lien on 1.9 million acres of land and 2.4 million acres of mineral rights, stipulating that all proceeds should go to improving the road. Analysts estimated that coal, oil, gas, and other minerals on the affected lands were worth billions of dollars. From beyond the grave, Pierpont stood up foursquare for creditors.

As a further guarantee that the roads would never again squander money, a majority of their stock was transferred to "voting trusts." These were usually a euphemism for Pierpont and three or four of his cronies, who ran the railroads, typically for a five-year period. It was an extension of Pierpont's old trick of trading money for power, and it usurped commercial power on a scale unprecedented in banking history. No longer would the banker just finance and advise his clients; now he would intervene directly in running the companies. The distinction between finance and industry was eroding dangerously.

Why would tens of thousands of shareholders yield their shares to this Wall Street pope in exchange for so-called trust certificates? The answer lies in a peculiarity of nineteenth-century finance: when companies lost money, shareholders in bankrupted companies could be dunned for assessments. So investors rushed to give up their shares and avoid the threatened penalties. Pierpont was now an altogether new species of robber baron—not nakedly voracious, not a Rockefeller snuffing out troublesome competitors, but a gruff, well-tailored banker with a legal, if highly controversial, system.

Within the bank, morganization was viewed benignly as the exercise of fiduciary responsibility to shareholders. Pierpont didn't seem to operate by any grand scheme—he was too instinctive for that. A later Morgan partner, Tom Lamont, remarked that he "never knew of a man who addressed himself more exclusively than Mr. Morgan to the ad hoc situation and the ad hoc job that lay before him. All this talk about his devising or building up systems is perfect tosh."[58] Pierpont didn't spin webs or plot paths to power. Rather, he had a messianic faith in his ability to reorder businesses. If he could tidy up America better than anyone else, so be it. He took the technique of the voting trust and endlessly multiplied his power. As Sereno S. Pratt, an editor of the *Wall Street Journal*, later said of him, "His power is not to be found in the number of his own millions, but in the billions of which he was the trustee."[59]

If there was nothing devious about the voting trusts, they created a frightening concentration of Wall Street power. Before the morganization period, more than two-thirds of American railroads had offices outside New York; afterward, most were headquartered there. By 1900, the nation's railroads were consolidated into six huge systems controlled by Wall Street bankers, principally J. P. Morgan and Company and Kuhn, Loeb. In this perpetual-motion machine, Pierpont not only reorganized roads but locked up their future financing. By acting as their trustee or holding a large block of their stock, he ensured bondage to 23 Wall. The banker was strong because the railroads were weak, and however much Pierpont deplored railroad instability, he thrived on such chaos.

Pierpont alone could never have carried out the exhausting work of morganization. Hence the importance, then and later, of Morgan partners. In history books, they are often portrayed as mice scurrying in the background. Yet many were towering figures in their own right, the shadow cabinet of the Morgan government. The railroad reorganizations were carried out by a staff of fewer than 150 employees. This was at a time when old-fashioned banks, such as the House of Morgan, frowned upon typewriters as newfangled. Visitors always marveled at the discrepancy between the bank's power and its size. In 1905, Dr. Hjalmar Schacht, later Hitler's finance minister, recorded this impression: "The entire office was contained in a single room on the ground floor in which were dozens of desks where the employees worked. . . . No question of visitors being formally announced, no waiting, or anterooms. Anyone who saw that a principal was disengaged could walk right up to his desk. Relations between heads and employees were very informal and free-and-easy without thereby lacking in respect."[60]

Pierpont selected partners not by wealth or to fortify the bank's capital but based on brains and talent. If the Morgan style was royal, its hiring practices were meritocratic. The bank had many first-rate technicians. Pierpont's transportation man, Samuel Spencer, was said to know better than anyone in America every detail of railroading "from the cost of a car brake to the estimate for a terminal."[61] Most impressive was Charles Coster, a pale man with neatly brushed hair, pensive eyes, and handlebar mustache. As a young man, Coster had published a history of stamps, and his compulsion to organize and classify never left him. He was the obscure wizard of morganization. Jack Morgan said of him, "His mastery of detail was complete, his grasp of a problem immediate and comprehensive and his power of work astonishing."[62] Wall Street caught fleeting glances of this sedentary genius: "Men saw him by day—a white-faced, nervous figure, hurrying from directors' meeting to directors' meeting; at evening carrying home his portfolio of corporate problems for the night."[63] Yet Coster was no downtrodden clerk: thanks to the wonders of voting trusts, he sat on the boards of fifty-nine corporations!

The House of Morgan would have a contradictory reputation as both a gentleman's club and a posh sweatshop. During the morganization period, lights burned at the bank long after the rest of Wall Street was dark. The partners shouldered unbearable tasks. One journalist remarked that "the House of Morgan was always known as a partner-killer," and the body count mounted steadily. One day in 1894, while waiting for an elevated train after the business day, partner J. Hood Wright dropped dead at the age of fifty-eight. The most shocking death was Coster's, in March 1900, at age forty-eight. He contracted flu or pneumonia and died within a week. Mixing sympathy with outrage, the *New York Times* charged that the tasks piled upon Coster had grown "far heavier than any one man ought to bear, or could bear with safety." Naming Morgan partners who died from overwork by 1900, John Moody said they had "succumbed to the gigantic, nerve-racking business and pressure of the Morgan methods and the strain involved in the care of the railroad capital of America. 'Jupiter' Morgan had alone come through that soul-crushing mill of business, retaining his health, vigor, and energy."[64]

In choosing partners, Pierpont wouldn't tolerate a refusal. He was shameless enough to recruit Coster's successor, railroad lawyer Charles Steele, at Coster's funeral! As the cortege moved along, Pierpont presented a partnership to Steele as a *fait accompli.* "Charles," he said, "it looks as if the Lord had taken charge of this question, and I am going ahead to make the partnership agreement."[65] The courtly Steele later accumulated thirty-six corporate directorships, including those of United States Steel and General Electric, and his wealth would rival Jack Morgan's.

Even as the exhausting pace of work created scandals, a Morgan partnership became the most coveted financial post. Judge Elbert H. Gary, a chairman of United States Steel, said of Pierpont's partners, "He made them all wealthy beyond their dreams."[66] Indeed, in exchange for exquisite torture, a Morgan partner received a guarantee of riches and a seat on the high council of American finance.

CHAPTER FIVE

CORNER

• •

•

I N 1895, Pierpont Morgan engineered his most dazzling feat: he saved the gold standard and briefly managed to control the flow of gold into and out of the United States. The concept behind the gold standard was simple. Ever since January 1879, the government had pledged to redeem dollars for gold, thus insuring the value of the currency. To make this more than an empty boast and reassure worried investors, Washington had a policy of keeping on hand at least $100 million in gold coin and bullion.

In the early 1890s, huge amounts of gold began to flow from New York to Europe. In the circuitous way of world finance, the trouble started in Argentina. In the 1880s, the City of London was swept by a craze for Argentinean securities, which attracted almost half of British money invested abroad. The principal conduit was Baring Brothers, which shared a good deal of Argentinean business with Junius Morgan. Then the Argentinean wheat crop failed and was followed by a coup in Buenos Aires. The prospect of default hurt the Morgan bank in London but nearly collapsed the august Barings, which lost heavily on its Argentinean bonds.

To save Barings from bankruptcy in 1890, the Bank of England organized a rescue fund, to which J. S. Morgan and Company and other rivals contributed. The old Baring partnership was liquidated; the reorganized firm would never regain its former power, and a major Morgan rival was weakened. Before long, Barings shared supremacy in Argentina with the Morgans. Meanwhile, with a stigma attached to foreign holdings, British investors retrenched and drained gold from America. This exodus of metal was greatly accelerated by the 1893 panic, with its bank failures and railroad bankruptcies.

Adding to European jitters were American attempts to tamper with the U.S. currency. Under the Sherman Silver Purchase Act of 1890, the U.S. Treasury had to buy 4.5 million ounces of silver monthly and issue certificates redeemable in gold or silver. This effectively put America on a bimetal basis—that is, money was backed by both gold and silver— expanding the money supply. For the hard-money men of Europe, this looked as if it were an effort by American debtors to debauch the currency and repay loans in cheaper dollars. These creditors venerated the gold standard as their safeguard against such backdoor default. So European bankers redeemed their dollars for gold and shipped the gold back to Europe. For Pierpont Morgan, this was an alarming throwback to the days when George Peabody had to prove that Americans honored their debt. The Silver Act was repealed in 1893 under pressure from Morgan and other bankers. But wary Europeans feared that Populist forces might yet wreck the gold standard and force them to accept unwanted silver for dollars.

Among the indebted farmers of the South and West, the gold standard generated fanatic hatred. The United States was still an agrarian debtor nation, and poor, rural debtors far outnumbered big city bondholders. These farmers had many legitimate grievances, for they contended with the curse of steadily falling prices in the late nineteenth century. Deflation meant they had to repay debt in dearer money—a recipe for ruin. There was no central bank to expand credit during hard times. At the same time, because of tariffs and industrial trusts, the prices of finished goods didn't fall as fast as the price of food. (Thanks to Pierpont and the railway barons, freight rates actually rose.) So farmers welcomed inflation—specifically, higher prices for their own produce—as the only way to remain equal in the contest against bankers and industrialists.

This discontent made bankers the favorite bogeymen in rural political demonology. So venomous was the mood that several western states outlawed bankers, and Texas banned them altogether until 1904.[1] This pervasive anger in the hinterlands crystallized around the House of Morgan, which was seen as a mouthpiece for European finance. A popular, grass-roots mythology claimed that the Bank of England and New York bankers had suborned Congress into enacting the gold standard. For decades, William Jennings Bryan rallied the Populist faithful by inveighing against America's "financial servitude" to British capital.[2] From this period dates the folklore of the House of Morgan as heartless moneymen, traitors in the pay of British gold, glorying in the ruin of American farmers.

The nineteenth-century inflationary nostrums that make for tedious

study today—greenbacks, free silver coinage, bimetallism, and so on—
were attempts by indebted farmers to lighten their debt load. As the
1893 panic worsened, agrarian populists asked the government to mint
silver coins and create cheap money, a move supported by the new
silver-producing states. Farming districts scoffed at the notion that any
damage might be done by going off gold. The *Atlanta Constitution*
remarked that "the people of this country, outside the hotbeds of gold-
buggery and Shylockism, don't care how soon gold payments are suspended."[3] For Pierpont, however, destruction of the gold standard
would subvert European faith in American securities and destroy his
life's work. As he later said, his aim in 1895 was "to build up such
relations of confidence between the United States and the money markets of Europe, that capital from there could be secured in large sums
for our needs."[4]

During 1894, the U.S. gold reserve dipped below the $100-million
floor. Bad money (silver) was driving good money (gold) out of circulation. By January 1895, gold was fleeing New York at a frightening pace.
One could watch this "flight capital" in action as gold bullion was
loaded onto ships in New York harbor, bound for Europe. At fashionable
Manhattan restaurants, sporting men placed wagers as to when America
would go bust and declare its inability to redeem dollars for gold.

The beleaguered president, Grover Cleveland, was a friend of the
House of Morgan and a staunch advocate of the gold standard. During
the four years he spent on Wall Street between his two presidential
terms, Cleveland worked in the law offices of Bangs, Stetson, Tracy, and
MacVeagh. This was the law firm of Pierpont's father-in-law, Charles
Tracy, located next door to the Morgan bank, at 15 Broad Street. Cleve-
land had been good friends with the shrewd Francis Lynde Stetson,
Pierpont's lawyer for the railroad reorganizations and known on Wall
Street as Morgan's attorney general. He also befriended many Wall
Street people and was one of the twelve pallbearers at the funeral of
August Belmont, Sr., in 1890. Although Pierpont was a Republican, he
wasn't antagonistic toward the Democratic Cleveland. In 1884, he cast
his lone Democratic vote for Cleveland precisely because the candidate
endorsed sound money.

As the gold reserve dipped, Cleveland faced a hostile Republican
Congress, which favored free coinage instead of gold; many prairie Democrats concurred. Amid this gloomy deathwatch, Congress refused to
grant President Cleveland the authority to replenish the gold reserve
through a public bond offering. At the same time, Populist fury made
resorting to private bankers like Morgan unthinkable. Cleveland sat

paralyzed. By January 24, 1895, gold reserves had declined to $68 million, and gold coin was especially scarce at the nine Subtreasuries around the country, including that in New York, across Wall Street from the Morgan bank. As a crisis approached, Cleveland turned to the Rothschilds in London, perhaps to deflect charges of being in Wall Street's pocket. When approached by Rothschilds about a bond issue, J. S. Morgan and Company agreed to participate only if Pierpont handled the American end with the Rothschild representative, August Belmont, Jr. On January 31, Pierpont and Belmont met at the New York Subtreasury with William E. Curtis, the assistant secretary of the Treasury. Although no action was taken, the report of the meeting relieved skittish investors, and $9 million in gold on ships in the harbor was returned to land overnight. For Populists, news of the Morgan-Belmont-Curtis meeting confirmed suspicions of a Wall Street–Washington conspiracy.

In the cables he sent to the London partners during this period, Pierpont affords a glimpse into his deepest ideological impulses—his contempt for politics, his regard for European opinion, his allegiance to neoclassic economics, and his disdain for certain Jewish firms. Referring to one leading Jewish house, he said, "we should dislike see business largely in the hands of Speyer & Co. & similar houses." His identification with the London creditors was patent: "We all have large interests dependent upon maintenance sound currency U.S. Important use every exertion . . . success negotiations . . . greater factor is European absorption even temporarily of bonds."[5] His dispatches were often fervent and even melodramatic in tone.

By early February, the New York Subtreasury was losing gold rapidly. Default seemed imminent. Yet the Treasury Secretary John G. Carlisle informed Morgan and Belmont that the Cabinet had flatly rejected their proposed private bond issue. So on Monday, February 4, Belmont set off for Washington, followed by Morgan. Aware of Francis Stetson's friendship with Cleveland, Morgan told him, "There may be papers to be drawn and I want you," and brought him along with a new Morgan partner, the handsome young Robert Bacon.[6] Pierpont told his London partners that the United States was on "the brink of the abyss of financial chaos" and that he wanted to help the U.S. government avert calamity.[7]

Morgan, Bacon, and Stetson took a private railroad car down to Washington, hitched up to the Congressional Limited. When they arrived, they were greeted by Secretary of War Daniel Lamont, who said that the president had decided against a private syndicate and refused to see the party. Pierpont said magisterially, "I have come down to see the president, and I am going to stay here until I see him."[8] While Stetson tried to lobby Cleveland, Bacon applied his charms to Attorney General Richard Olney. That night, in a technique he used to steady his nerves, Pierpont played solitaire—a game called Miss Milliken—until the early hours. After breakfast at the Arlington Hotel, he crossed a snowy Lafayette Square to the White House. One pictures the famous stride, described by a biographer as "elemental, jungle-like."[9]

Pierpont was often taciturn in meetings. At the White House, obedient as a schoolboy, he sat wordless while Cleveland, Attorney General Olney, and Treasury Secretary Carlisle debated the issue. Edgy, he crushed an unlighted cigar, leaving a pile of tobacco on his pants. Cleveland still clung to the hope of a public bond issue, which would spare him congressional obloquy. Not until a clerk informed Carlisle that only $9 million in gold coin remained in government vaults on Wall Street did Pierpont pipe up, saying he knew of a $10-million draft about to be presented. "If that $10-million draft is presented, you can't meet it," Pierpont said. "It will be all over before 3 o'clock." "What suggestions have you to make, Mr. Morgan?" replied the president.[10]

Pierpont laid out an audacious scheme. The Morgan and Rothschild houses in New York and London would gather 3.5 million ounces of gold, at least half from Europe, in exchange for about $65 million worth of thirty-year gold bonds. He also promised that gold obtained by the government wouldn't flow out again. This was the showstopper that mystified the financial world—a promise to rig, temporarily, the gold market. There was some question as to the legality of the proposed issue, and either Morgan or Carlisle dusted off an 1862 statute that granted the Lincoln administration emergency powers to buy gold during the Civil War. When the deal was concluded, Cleveland gave Pierpont a fresh cigar to replace the one he had nervously ground up. Pierpont's blood was now at full boil. He wired London, "We consider situation critical, politicians appear to have absolute control. If fail & European negotiations abandoned, it is impossible overestimate what will be result U.S."[11]

Populist pressure still demanded a public bond issue. As a practical matter, Cleveland awaited congressional action on the Springer Bill, which would have allowed the Treasury to sell long-term bonds; if Congress defeated it, Cleveland thought, he could then resort to Wall Street bankers with far less popular abuse. At the Tuesday-morning meeting, it was agreed that Morgan and Belmont should return when the Springer Bill was killed. By the time it was defeated on Thursday evening, Pierpont was already *en route* to Washington, arriving in a blizzard.

News of the Morgan-Rothschild operation was a sedative for the financial markets. When the syndicate bonds were offered, on February 20, 1895, they sold out in two hours in London, in only twenty-two minutes in New York. Pierpont was jubilant and exhausted: "You cannot appreciate the relief to everybody's mind for the dangers were so great scarcely anyone dared whisper them."[12] Yet the syndicate was a victim of its success. It took up the bonds at 104½, then sold them at an opening price of 112¼; they quickly soared to 119. For the cynical, this sudden appreciation proved the syndicate had cheated the government and underpriced the issue. The interest rate of 3¾ was thought extremely harsh. In just twenty-two minutes, the bankers had booked $6 or $7 million in profits. Morgan would later claim these figures were vastly exaggerated and that the syndicate had earned less than a 5 percent return. Even commentators such as Allan Nevins and Alexander Dana Noyes, otherwise sympathetic to the operation, condemned the stiff terms. Nonetheless, the bankers believed that they themselves had induced the confidence that had led to the higher prices.

The Populist uproar was furious and laced with anti-Semitism because of the Rothschild participation. Populist rabble-rouser Mary Lease called President Cleveland a tool "of Jewish bankers and British gold."[13] The New York *World* described the syndicate as a pack of "bloodsucking Jews and aliens." In his vehement denunciation in Congress, William Jennings Bryan asked the clerk to read Shylock's bond from *The Merchant of Venice.* Bryan always denied that his attacks pandered to anti-Semitism. Campaigning in 1896, he told Jewish Democrats in Chicago, "Our opponents have sometimes tried to make it appear that we are attacking a race when we denounced the financial policy of the Rothschilds. But we are not; we are as much opposed to the financial policy of J. Pierpont Morgan as we are to the financial policy of the Rothschilds."[14]

The gold syndicate, alas, was just a temporary victory: even Pierpont could dam up the gold supply for only so long. By the summer, gold again left the Treasury in large amounts. When a new loan was raised in early 1896, Pierpont had a fresh scheme for a global syndicate which would include the National City Bank of New York, Deutsche Bank of Berlin, and Morgan, Harjes of Paris. (Perhaps to appease the anti-Semites, it was a syndicate of Christian bankers.) But Cleveland didn't want to incite Populist wrath a second time and decided on a public loan, with Morgan taking only about half of a $67-million bond issue.

Despite his venality, the gold operation had been a *tour de force* for Pierpont. He had functioned as America's central bank, stepping into the historic breach between Andrew Jackson's 1832 veto of the second Bank of the United States and passage of the Federal Reserve Act in 1913. So long as governments were financially weak, with primitive monetary methods and small budgets, they had to rely on private bankers. For his part, Grover Cleveland never regretted his decision, praising the "lightning-like rapidity" with which Pierpont Morgan reached his decision and extolling him as a man "of clear-sighted, far-seeing patriotism."[15] By stubbornly adhering to principle, Cleveland alienated small-town farm elements in his own party. In 1896, the Democrats rejected him in favor of William Jennings Bryan. For Bryan, Morgan was a Pontius Pilate who nailed starving farmers to a cross of gold. The sheer savagery of these attacks contributed to the secretive, cautious style of the Morgan bank, which, in turn, further fed popular fantasy about its power.

During the 1896 presidential campaign, Pierpont lobbied for a gold-standard plank in the Republican party platform. He entertained Mark Hanna, Ohio banker and chairman of the Republican National Committee, aboard the *Corsair II.* Generous contributions by Morgan and other bankers to the campaign of William McKinley—23 Wall Street was hung with banners in his support—were thought instrumental in persuading him to champion the gold standard, and in 1900 he signed a law bestowing upon it new legal status. The farmer-banker conflict subsided somewhat when a European wheat famine pushed up farm prices. Also, the Yukon gold rush and gold strikes in South Africa and Australia helped expand the U.S. money supply and led to higher prices. The bitter deflationary politics of the late nineteenth century subsided.

In the 1890s, Pierpont Morgan represented a fact unpalatable to Americans—that America was still financially dependent on Europe. As a debtor nation, the United States had to placate its creditors abroad. England exerted much the same influence over American economic policy as Japan would nearly a century later, when it financed much of the U.S. budget deficit in the 1980s. Like Japan, England was criticized for curbing homegrown American excesses. As Keynes noted, "A debtor nation does not love its creditor, and it is fruitless to expect feelings of goodwill."[16] The ill will descended upon the House of Morgan.

Tutored in London finance, Pierpont knew that British bankers con-

sidered the pound's stability the basis of British wealth. In the nineteenth century, it was the currency every investor wanted to hold.
Pierpont adopted the same attitude toward the dollar. Sound monetary
policy in the United States would be a precondition of America's rise
as the chief creditor nation. In the 1920s, by one of those ironies so
abundant in Morgan annals, the bank would put England itself back on
the gold standard, forcing a later British prime minister to suffer the
same repudiation by his own party as Grover Cleveland experienced in
1895.

I N Pierpont Morgan's career, success often bred more controversy than
acclaim, so the twentieth century was his time of bittersweet triumph.
Sleek and portly in top hat and black overcoat, gray slacks reaching the
tops of shiny shoes, and a watch chain stretched across his paunch, he
personified the new tycoon and the industrial gigantism threatening
pastoral America. His exploits were rendered in mythic terminology.
Life magazine produced a lasting catechism: "Q. Who made the world,
Charles? A. God made the world in 4004 B.C., but it was reorganized in
1901 by James J. Hill, J. Pierpont Morgan and John D. Rockefeller."[17]
Finley Peter Dunne's character Mr. Dooley pictured Morgan this way:
"Pierpont Morgan calls in wan iv his office boys, th' prisidint iv a
national bank, an' says he, 'James,' he says, 'take some change out iv th'
damper an' r-run out an' buy Europe f'r me,' he says. 'I intind to reorganize it an' put it on a paying basis.' "[18] When Pierpont was quoted as
saying "America is good enough for me," William Jennings Bryan's
Commoner snapped back, "Whenever he doesn't like it, he can give it
back."[19] Editorial writers competed to mint Morgan titles—king of
trusts, morganizer of the world, financial titan, Napoléon of finance, or,
more simply, Zeus or Jupiter.

For a republican country lacking a feudal tradition, Morgan and other
robber barons were ersatz aristocrats, their feats avidly chronicled by the
press. The public reacted with fear and resentment but also with some
vicarious pleasure. When Pierpont brusquely ordered his chauffeur to
bypass traffic and drive up on a curb, the public was shocked by his
arrogance but admiring of his implacable will. When Wall Street broker
Henry Clews said of Morgan, "He has the driving power of a locomotive," he suggested something brutish and uncontrollable, but also
something of superhuman strength.[20]

Now the world's most powerful private banker, Pierpont regarded
himself as a peer of royalty. With regal munificence, he dispensed benefactions to the masses. Regretting the dark interior of Saint Paul's Cathe-

dral in London, he underwrote the expense of electric lighting. He visited the kaiser aboard his yacht and advised King Leopold of Belgium on his finances. In 1901, Jack reported to his mother how his father and London partner Sir Clinton Dawkins went down to Gravesend "and dined with the King of the Belgians who wanted to see them about some business and brought his yacht over because Father would not go to Brussels."[21] Pierpont did business on his own territory, even if it sometimes meant treating a king as a commoner.

In 1906, Pierpont vouchsafed a private tour of his art collection at 13 Princes Gate, the townhouse he inherited from his father, to King Edward VII. He had given the king financial advice, and the two often met at European watering holes. Gazing at Sir Thomas Lawrence's famous portrait of the countess of Derby, the king said the ceiling was too low for the picture. "Why do you hang it there?" he asked. "Because I like it there, sir," said Pierpont tersely, feeling no need to elaborate. His son-in-law Herbert Satterlee noted a perfect equality between king and banker: "They were just two friends together and seemed quite content to sit in silence sometimes and not try to entertain each other."[22] As a coronation gift, Pierpont had given the king a $500,000 tapestry, which set off a long-lasting relationship between the House of Morgan and British royalty.

Pierpont also pleased Italian royalty. In 1904, he was honored by Italy for returning a treasured cope that turned out to have been stolen from the Cathedral of Ascoli. King Victor Emmanuel conferred upon him the Great Cordon of Saints Mauritius and Lazarus, making him a cousin of His Majesty whenever he set foot on Italian soil.

Even as Pierpont aspired to heaven, he made religious men think in earthly terms. After a 1905 audience, Pope Pius X breathed with regret: "What a pity I did not think of asking Mr. Morgan to give us some advice about our finances!"[23] The House of Morgan would later advise the papacy on its purchases of American stocks.

As a rule, Pierpont didn't assemble palatial homes. In business as well, he showed surprisingly scant interest in real estate, which produced so many fortunes among his contemporaries. He would say laughingly that he only needed "a place to live in and a lot in the cemetery," and his son, Jack, proudly confessed himself an ignoramus about land.[24] Instead of grand estates, Pierpont had his solid but unpretentious Madison Avenue townhouse and his Hudson River retreat, Cragston, with its kennels, dairies, and gardens.

The splendid exception was Camp Uncas, in the Adirondack Mountains of upstate New York, and that came to him only by accident. In

1898, a friend, architect William West Durant, defaulted on a loan and signed over the rustic camp as payment. Deep in the woods, Camp Uncas crouched beneath wooded cliffs that were thick with evergreens. It covered more than a thousand acres and required a year-round staff of thirty to care for the main lodge and dozens of outlying buildings. Durant had popularized such millionaire retreats in wilderness areas, producing the most lavish log cabins ever made. They had thick wooden posts, walk-in fireplaces, and heavy exposed beams. To lend a rustic, woodland atmosphere, the furniture was nicked with ax scars, and bark was left on the pine logs. Wool Indian blankets, moose heads, and prize fish decorated the walls. When Pierpont threw parties there, he would bring up a private railroad car full of friends, and a baggage car loaded with racks of vintage champagne would rattle along behind them.

With his vagabond nature, Pierpont was too restless to be a member of the landed gentry. His splendor shone most fully at sea. As commodore of the New York Yacht Club, he offered Morgan Cups for races and helped finance the *Columbia,* which defended the America's Cup. He even provided land for the yacht club's new headquarters, on West Forty-fourth Street.

Pierpont's boats, more impressive than his homes, were the real monuments to his wealth. In 1898, over his heated protest, the navy conscripted *Corsair II* for use in the Spanish-American War. The Morgans had opposed the war, and Jack (later labeled a warmonger for his role in World War I) lamented the "needless waste of life & property."[25] The navy paid Pierpont $225,000 for the ship and transformed it into the gunboat *Gloucester.* It saw action in the Battle of Santiago and was damaged by a Spanish shell. Pierpont kept a piece of the ship's splintered mast as a memento.

Corsair III was an even more megalomaniacal affair, a modern pharoah's tomb. Like a lover mourning his dead mistress, Pierpont had reproduced, at fantastic expense, the carpeting and other details of *Corsair II.* Measuring over three hundred feet at the waterline and requiring a crew of seventy, this black-hulled oceangoing ship was built on an altogether new and more garish scale. Among its many details was a special humidor to freshen Pierpont's black eight-inch Meridiana Kohinoor cigars. He reveled in nautical spectacle. When he returned by liner from Europe, the *Corsair* would steam out to greet him as he waved his handkerchief from the larger ship's deck. By transferring to the *Corsair,* he could slip through quarantine without having to mingle with the liner's steerage passengers.

Pierpont often slept aboard his yacht and took clients for sunset cruises. Sometimes, after entertaining friends at Cragston for the weekend, they would all steam back to Manhattan on a Sunday evening, sleep on board, and then awake to a plentiful breakfast before disembarking. The *Corsair* was a therapeutic, if expensive, toy for Pierpont. He continued to slip into depressions that he couldn't shake, and his triumphs seemed only to deepen his gloom. The sea alone would lighten his mood. As Jack told his mother of one 1898 ocean voyage, "JPM has been so worried and bothered by the number of things on his mind and this annoyance of war rumor that it will be a great thing for him to have this voyage. Then if things calm down . . . he will come back for his Aix cure and get 2 more voyages. Those are the only things which really seem to do him any good."[26] Though this may have been partly a cover story—Jack's way of shielding his mother from his father's growing number of affairs—it was also true that for Pierpont Morgan the sea was always his sovereign remedy.

THE dawning of the new century was accompanied by the first great wave of mergers in American history. Spurred by the telephone and telegraph and better transportation, local markets were newly interlaced in regional and national markets. And with American victory in the Spanish-American War, the attention of business also shifted from internal expansion to a global quest for markets. Driven by such changes in the economy, the number of mergers jumped from a modest sixty-nine in 1897 to over twelve hundred by 1899.

So long as markets were local, industry seldom required large-scale financing, and there was a Wall Street and City bias against manufacturers as small-time businessmen. The Morgans had been mostly associated with railroad securities. (As late as 1911, the second Baron Revelstoke of Barings could snobbishly protest, "I confess that personally I have a horror of all industrial companies."[27]) Now, as the great merger wave gathered pace, the focus of elite Wall Street banks shifted from railroads to industrial trusts. In a trust, stockholders would trade their shares in constituent companies for the "trust certificates" of a super holding company. After enacting a law that permitted one company to own another, New Jersey became the preferred state for trust incorporation. By 1901, these new corporate leviathans dominated a long list of industries—sugar, lead, whiskey, plate glass, wire nails, smelting, and coal.

Wall Street bankers effected many of these industrial transformations, and their power swelled in tandem with their creations. Often, trusts were cobbled together from family-owned or closely held firms that had a visceral contempt for competitors' joining the same trust; the bankers were the honest brokers who arbitrated the disputes among them. Since the bankers appraised the value of participating companies, they had to be fair; since this appraisal was seldom accepted by everyone, they had to be stern. Most of all, they had to be trusted. The populace might dread the power of Pierpont Morgan, but he paid his bills promptly, always stuck by his word, and was almost universally respected among businessmen. He also saw competition as a destructive, inefficient force and instinctively favored large-scale combination as the cure. Once, when the manager of the Moët and Chandon wine company complained about industry problems, Pierpont blithely suggested he buy up the entire champagne country.[28]

In William McKinley, the business community had a Republican president who approved of consolidation and didn't interpose any bothersome antitrust obstacles. The genesis of United States Steel in 1901 was inseparable from this permissive regulatory mood, which followed the 1900 GOP landslide. With the defeat of William Jennings Bryan and his anti-imperialist, trust-busting supporters, the business community felt emboldened to try bigger things. A few weeks after the GOP's massive victory, Vice-President Theodore Roosevelt invited Elihu Root, the secretary of war, to attend a dinner in honor of Pierpont Morgan. "I hope you can come to my dinner to J. Pierpont Morgan," he wrote. "You see, it represents an effort on my part to become a conservative man in touch with the influential classes and I think I deserve encouragement."[29]

This dinner preceded by a week the first discussions about U.S. Steel and must have reassured Pierpont that the McKinley administration would be supine in its attitude toward trusts. The inception of the steel trust is still debated. The more colorful versions attribute the idea to steelman John W. "Bet-a-Million" Gates, who allegedly came up with it while shooting pool at the Waldorf-Astoria Hotel, then on Fifth Avenue at Thirty-fourth Street. A former barbed-wire salesman and stock market plunger, Gates was a stout, raffish-looking character, with a derby always tipped back on his head and a big cigar stuck in the corner of his mouth. He used to bet on the speed of raindrops running down a train window and won his nickname from an enormous wager he once made on an English thoroughbred. Not content with an American steel trust, Gates wanted to include German manufacturers and attempt a global cartel.

The more sober versions of U.S. Steel trace the trust to a looming collision between Andrew Carnegie's steel company and two of Pierpont's steel creations, Federal Steel and National Tube. As the top manufacturer of crude steel, Carnegie decided in July 1900 to branch out into finished products, such as pipe and wire. As head of the second largest steel group, Pierpont feared a replication of the railroad chaos, with overbuilding and price wars. He growled that Carnegie would "demoralize" the entire industry through competition. Bracing for a grim battle, he had his makers of finished products prepare to meet Carnegie head-on in crude steel.

On December 12, 1900, a week after he was feted by Teddy Roosevelt, Pierpont attended a famous dinner held for Charles M. Schwab at the University Club in Manhattan. A handsome young man with a long, smooth face, dark hair, and clear brow, Schwab was a faithful lieutenant of Andrew Carnegie's. Morgan sat at Schwab's right and stared at his plate as the young man delivered his after-dinner address. A mellifluous orator and self-dramatizing individual, he evoked for Morgan and the eighty other financiers present a vision of a steel trust which would handle all phases of the business, from mining ore to marketing steel products; the Carnegie and Morgan steel enterprises would be the trust's obvious nucleus. The steel trust was to be a superior sort of conspiracy. Through economies of scale, it would attempt to lower prices and compete in burgeoning world markets. It was a form of national industrial policy, albeit conducted by businessmen for private gain.

After the dinner, Morgan, intrigued, conferred with Schwab for half an hour. As Morgan partner Robert Bacon later said, "It was apparent that [Morgan] had seen a new light."[30] It has never been clear whether Schwab acted at Carnegie's behest or whether he planned to recruit Pierpont first, then take the proposal to Carnegie. In any event, within three weeks, Morgan, Bacon, Gates, and Schwab worked out a proposal in an all-night session at Morgan's "black library." The proposed trust would control more than half the steel business. Besides Carnegie Steel and Morgan's Federal Steel, it would include American Tin Plate, American Steel Hoop, American Sheet Steel, American Bridge, American Steel and Wire, National Tube, National Steel, Shelby Steel Tube, and Lake Superior Consolidated Mines.

In forging U.S. Steel, Pierpont had to deal with two industrialists who represented very different aspects of American business—Andrew Carnegie and John D. Rockefeller. Both were hard-bitten individualists, scornful of bankers, who preferred to finance their operations from retained earnings. Rockefeller entered the deal through his ownership of ore mines and shipping companies on Lake Superior. Pierpont considered both men too crude for his stuffily refined tastes; they saw him as pompous and overbearing. The prudish Carnegie also disapproved of

Pierpont's adulterous escapades. "Carnegie frowned on anything savoring of the flesh and the devil," Schwab said.[31]

After the meeting in the "black library," Schwab sounded out Carnegie on his willingness to sell his steel company to the trust. After a game of golf at Saint Andrews Golf Club in Westchester, Carnegie ruminated, then penciled his selling price, $480 million, on a scrap of paper. He wanted payment in bonds, not watered stock. When Schwab delivered the slip of paper to Morgan, the banker stared at it and said promptly, "I accept this price."[32] In the hurly-burly, Pierpont didn't formalize the deal with a signature and weeks later had to send a lawyer uptown with a contract. Despite his veneration of Junius Morgan, Carnegie enjoyed petty jousting with Pierpont. When Pierpont invited him to 23 Wall Street, Carnegie insisted that Morgan come to his own Fifty-first Street office instead. After a cool fifteen-minute chat, Morgan said in parting, "Mr. Carnegie, I want to congratulate you on being the richest man in the world."[33]

Thin-skinned and vindictive, Carnegie gloated over the deal: "Pierpont feels that he can do anything because he has always got the best of the Jews in Wall Street. . . . It takes a Yankee to beat a Jew, and it takes a Scot to beat a Yankee."[34] Carnegie celebrated too quickly. He later admitted to Morgan that he had sold out too cheap, by $100 million. Not about to spare the industrialist's feelings, Morgan replied, "Very likely, Andrew."[35]

In trying to coax recalcitrant companies into the steel trust, Pierpont showed his ringmaster's flair for cracking the whip. He was irate with those who tried to extract undue advantage. During negotiations at 23 Wall, one major holdout was Bet-a-Million Gates and his American Steel and Wire. To break a deadlock, Pierpont materialized like the wrath of God and thumped a desk. "Gentlemen, I am going to leave this building in 10 minutes. If by that time you have not accepted our offer, the matter will be closed. We will build our own wire plant."[36] His bluff called, Gates capitulated and sold out. Pierpont then went home, boyishly elated.

The House of Morgan generally didn't sponsor new companies and abhorred stock speculation. Junius Morgan had long ago advised his son, "I would recommend your forming a resolution never to buy any stock on speculation."[37] So Pierpont's promotion of U.S. Steel in early 1901 lent "old money" cachet to the rage for trusts. The year 1901 was not unlike 1929 or 1987: the stock market was on everybody's lips. Daily share volume tripled. Wall Street seers babbled of a new age, and newspapers recounted tales of hotel waiters, business clerks, doormen, and dressmakers who made fortunes on Wall Street.[38]

U.S. Steel stoked the bonfire of speculation. At a time when million-dollar issues were considered large, the new corporation was capitalized at a whopping $1.4 billion ($23 billion in 1989 dollars)—the first billion-dollar corporation in history. At the time, all U.S. manufacturing combined had only $9 billion in capitalization. To manage the flood of bonds and stock that financed the deal, Pierpont mustered a monster syndicate of three hundred underwriters. He appointed ace stock manipulator James R. Keene—a sharp-faced man with a pointed beard, known as the Silver Fox of Wall Street—to make a market in the shares. By simultaneously buying and selling shares, Keene created steadily rising prices and the illusion of tremendous volume. Despite predictions that so much stock would saturate the market, the issue's success confirmed the boast of Morgan partner George W. Perkins that a Morgan issue "from the desert of Sahara" would find buyers.[39] For its services, the syndicate took in $57.5 million in stock (nearly $1 billion in 1989 dollars). The U.S. Steel promotion made explicit the marriage of finance and industry that marked the Baronial Age; when four Morgan partners joined the new trust's board, the marriage was consummated.

For many observers, the sheer size of U.S. Steel seemed sinister and unnatural. Even the *Wall Street Journal* admitted to "uneasiness over the magnitude of the affair."[40] Among others, Yale president Arthur Hadley, a noted economist, saw a new need for federal control of large corporations. Ray Stannard Baker, later Woodrow Wilson's biographer, pointed out that the new corporation would have revenues and expenses exceeding the budgets of all but a few world governments.[41] Yet Wall Street was heedless of the critics and celebrated with a record volume of trading. In January 1901, the Big Board traded a record two million shares in one day; after the launching of U.S. Steel that spring, volume reached three million shares. Wall Street was so awash in shares that the Stock Exchange declared a special holiday just to catch up on paperwork.

An unending controversy would surround U.S. Steel: was it Pierpont's greatest deal, as he believed, or a giant scam? The share flotation made multi-millionaires of dozens of steelmen, and the spectacle of so much sudden wealth appalled the public. In 1905, Charles Schwab, U.S. Steel's first president, built a seventy-five-room mansion on Manhattan's Riverside Drive, complete with a pipe organ, art gallery, bowling alley, private chapel, and sixty-foot swimming pool. Gaudy mansions went up all over Pittsburgh with the new steel money, symbolizing a new class of *nouveaux riches* industrialists.

Later the U.S. Bureau of Corporations, a federal agency set up by Teddy Roosevelt, would value U.S. Steel at only half its $1.4-billion selling price, suggesting that investors had purchased an enormous bag of hope, at least half of it hot air. From Vanderbilt, Morgan had learned the trick of basing value not on current assets but on projected earnings. U.S. Steel's subsequent history provided evidence for both detractors and admirers. From an opening price of 38, its stock zoomed to 55, only to skid to less than 9 during the "rich man's panic" of 1903. By January 1904, U.S. Steel couldn't even cover its dividends. Yet it is fair to say that in time the enterprise expanded to the contours of Morgan's vision, becoming America's foremost steel company. It amply rewarded its investors—at least, the patient ones.

BEHIND the growing pomp of Pierpont Morgan lay an ever-present vulnerability. If tragedy, as Aristotle said, has the power to arouse fear and pity, then Pierpont wore a tragic mask. In 1903, Pierpont sat for two minutes as Edward Steichen snapped the famous photograph of him: from deep shadow and gripping the blade-like chair, Pierpont stares out, a tense crease between his brows, his collar stiff, his eyes pitiless points of lights, the gaze legendary in its terror. Steichen tried to make him turn, but Pierpont, self-conscious about his nose, stared straight ahead. The photographer snapped him bristling with anger. Pierpont hated the photo and tore up the first prints. Yet there was sadness as well as fire in the eyes—volcanic energy and despair. The photograph captured the man whole. When Pierpont later relented and offered to pay a stratospheric $5,000 for the photo, the wounded Steichen took two years to deliver copies.

The blazing eyes were linked to the grotesque nose. As the years went by, the acne rosacea made Pierpont's nose monstrous in size and hideous in shape. The nose was invariably touched up in official photographs, perhaps adding to the shock of those who saw him in person. Of his initial encounter with Wall Street's Cyrano, art dealer Joseph Duveen wrote, "No nose in caricature ever assumed such gigantic proportions or presented such appalling excrescences. If I did not gasp, I might have changed color. Morgan noticed this, and his small, piercing eyes transfixed me with a malicious stare."[42] Many anecdotes link Morgan's nose with his short temper—an old story of the vanity of the mighty. He would furiously avenge taunts, and one writer said he never recovered from the phrase "a ruby-visaged magnate."[43] When Bet-a-Million Gates dubbed him Livernose, the jest proved costly: Pierpont blackballed Gates from the Union League and New York Yacht clubs. About his nose, Pierpont could be more sensitive than he was about his trusts. After the newspapers of clubmate Joseph Pulitzer attacked his business dealings, Pierpont complained to the newspaperman not about the allegations, but about the prominence of his nose in the papers' cartoons, which he thought very unfair.

Everybody came to terms with the nose differently. Lady Victoria Sackville-West, probably Pierpont's last mistress, recorded in her diary in 1912, "I have never met anyone so attractive. One forgets his nose entirely after a few minutes."[44] Perhaps intimates did, but not rival businessmen. And children found it scarily hypnotic. When a later partner, Dwight Morrow, brought Pierpont to his home, his wife Betty—having warned the children not to mention the nose—asked the tycoon, "Do you like nose in your tea, Mr. Morgan?"[45]

Pierpont tried everything to cure it, including an electrical remedy recommended by England's Queen Alexandra. But it persisted, like nature's revenge, reminding him of his humanity. In philosophic moments, he converted it into a mark of pride. When the Russian minister of finance, Count Witte, suggested surgery, he replied, "Everybody knows my nose. It would be impossible for me to appear on the streets of New York without it."[46] Still more grandly, he said his nose "was part of the American business structure."[47]

It was probably the nose that made Pierpont eager to hire handsome young men, and he often sent pedigreed collie puppies as a sign of impending partnerships. Over time, the early reputation of Morgan partners as harried technicians caught in the grinding machinery of railroad reorganizations gave way to another equally pronounced tradition: the Morgan partner as elegant fashion plate, suave member of the Social Register catering to rich clients. "A homely man had no chance of being selected a Morgan partner," wrote an early Pierpont biographer. The same could be said, with a few exceptions, of the bank under his son, Jack.[48]

The prototype was Robert Bacon, taken on as partner in 1894 after J. Hood Wright died suddenly. As soon as Bacon was hired, his former boss, Major Henry Lee Higginson, warned him, "Don't overwork like Coster just because you can and like to do it. He is wonderful—and unwise—to do so."[49] Trim and athletic with a strong, wide face and debonair mustache, Bacon was called the Greek God on Wall Street. As a Harvard undergraduate (and classmate of Teddy Roosevelt's), he boxed, ran the hundred-yard dash, captained the football team, was president of the Glee Club, and was number seven on the university crew team and Model Man of his class; his presence at the Corner of Broad and Wall inaugurated a new image for the Morgan partners. With Bacon in mind, a novelist wrote, "When the angels of God took unto themselves wives among the daughters of men, the result was the Morgan partners."[50] Pierpont doted on Bacon and wanted him constantly by his side. It was said Morgan had "fallen in love" with Bacon and "rejoiced in his presence."[51]

Bacon's elevation in the bank signaled a problem with the Morgan empire: Bacon, a charming lightweight, reflected Pierpont's fear of hiring commanding figures. That Bacon was second in command spoke poorly of his boss's managerial judgment. Art critic Roger Fry saw Morgan as a vain, insecure despot who "likes to be in a position of being surrounded by people he has in his power to make and unmake."[52] The most talented early partners—the apostles of Pierpontifex Maximus, or Jupiter's Ganymedes, as they were called—might have been legal and financial wizards, but they were not leaders. Since they were few in number—New York had six partners in the 1890s; the Philadelphia office, four—they had to pull enormous weight.

The danger of Pierpont's despotism was glaringly exposed during the so-called Northern Pacific corner of 1901, perhaps the most controversial takeover fight in American history. After U.S. Steel was successfully launched, Pierpont had sailed to France, where he entertained a dark French countess on the Riviera, leaving the firm in Bacon's hands. Since Coster's death the year before, Bacon knew he was in over his head and reeled under the responsibility. "My life is simply engrossed in this maelstrom," he told his wife.[53] He was soon blindsided by the most powerful Wall Street combination outside that of the Morgan firms—an amalgam of Edward H. Harriman, William Rockefeller, the National City Bank, and Kuhn, Loeb. It was a ganging up of Pierpont's most determined enemies.

A battle had been brewing since 1895, when Pierpont decided not to reorganize the bankrupt Union Pacific, which he scoffed at as "two streaks of iron rust across the plains."[54] His willingness to write off America's southwestern states provided an opening for outsiders. Edward Harriman took up the Union Pacific and merged it with the Southern Pacific. He and his bankers, the Jewish house of Kuhn, Loeb, dominated the southwestern roads as invincibly as Morgan did those of the East and the Northwest. The Northern Pacific corner was the thun-

derous, head-on crash of the railroad systems under the personal dominion of Harriman and Morgan.

Harriman was a very different type from Pierpont. He was short and
bandy-legged, had shifty eyes, and wore wire-rimmed spectacles, an
unkempt mustache, and a peevish expression. Like many on Wall
Street, he was the son of a poor clergyman and an unabashed social
climber. A crack shot, he had a taste for blood sport and played tough
on the stock exchange as well. Where Pierpont preferred back-room
deals sealed with a handshake, Harriman was a market operator—more
a raider than a deal maker. Where Pierpont usually served as proxy for
bondholders, Harriman preferred to buy common stock and exert direct
control. Finally, where Morgan was the establishment figure, Harriman
was an embittered outsider who showed the damage that could be done
by a bright man barred from Pierpont's club. If bankers proved they
could dominate companies through voting trusts and other devices,
Harriman showed that the stock raider could dominate both the bankers
and their companies.

Harriman's banker was the German-born Jacob Schiff, the unbending,
white-bearded patriarch of Kuhn, Loeb who was second only to Pierpont
as a financial railroad overlord. Schiff was such a grandee that one
private Pullman car was seldom enough for him when he traveled.[55] He
was stiff and formal and as haughty as Pierpont Morgan himself.

Like the London merchant bankers, the early Jewish bankers on Wall
Street had started out as dry-goods merchants: the Lehmans began as
Alabama cotton brokers; Goldman, as the owner of a Pennsylvania
clothing store; Kuhn and Loeb, as Cincinnati clothiers; and Lazard, in
a New Orleans dry-goods business. These firms were dynastic, with only
blood or marriage securing partnerships. They worked in the interstices
left by the big Christian houses and dealt more directly in markets than
the Morgans did. Markets were considered coarse by fancy gentile bankers. So Goldman, Sachs specialized in commercial paper, Lehman in
commodity trading. Around 1900, they began underwriting shares for
companies that were spurned by the gentile firms as too lowly—retail
stores and textile manufacturers, for instance. Among them was Sears,
Roebuck, introduced by Goldman, Sachs and Lehman Brothers in 1906.
Of such relatively small issues, the gentile firms would sniff, "Let the
Jews have that one"—snobbery for which they paid dearly in the twentieth century.[56]

Schiff didn't want to settle for the scraps left to the Jews. Alone among
the Jewish bankers he had the gumption to play the grand game and

contest Morgan in government issues and railroad financing. He funneled German and French money into American shares no less expertly than Pierpont did with British money. Much of Kuhn, Loeb's exceptional power derived from the fact that it voted stock shares in American railroads as proxy for legions of German investors.

Morgan referred to Schiff dismissively as "that foreigner."[57] Schiff, in turn, professed to admire Morgan, but his compliments sometimes had a slightly hollow, envious ring. After Pierpont's heroic role in the 1907 panic, Schiff said, "Probably no one could have got the banks to act together . . . as he did, in his autocratic way."[58]

Political, ethnic, and religious differences among bankers permeated Wall Street in the early 1900s. The Yankee-Jewish banking split was the most important fault line in American high finance. And since the two groups would come to dominate American investment banking, their feuds form a recurring theme in the Morgan banking saga. Pierpont's anti-Semitism was well known. Said an early biographer: "He had a deep-seated anti-Semitic prejudice and on more than one occasion needlessly antagonized great Jewish banking firms."[59] His dislike of Jews may have been sharpened by dealings with the Rothschilds. The Jewish tycoon Joseph Seligman noted Pierpont's "freeze-and-thaw attitude" toward him, which he attributed to his discomfort with Jews.[60] During thaws, the two men collaborated on issues, and when Seligman was barred from a fashionable Saratoga hotel, the Morgan bank signed an advertisement protesting the exclusion. In addition, Kuhn, Loeb, in particular, managed many syndicates with the Morgans. The strain of anti-Semitism running through the Morgan story is fascinating precisely because it had to be so carefully suppressed.

The group making common cause with Harriman and Schiff against Morgan in 1901 was the Rockefellers. In 1881, John D. Rockefeller had financed the Standard Oil trust from its huge cash reserves, staying free of Wall Street. As the 1880s progressed, Standard Oil was generating so much cash that the Rockefellers looked about for a financial repository. They chose the National City Bank—the forerunner of today's Citibank—and pumped in so much money that by 1893 it ranked as New York's largest bank. It was a significant development: at a time when bankers tightened their grip on industry, here was an industrial empire fastening its grip on banking. National City became known as the oil bank, much as J. P. Morgan and Company would be called the steel bank. National City Bank's president, James Stillman, with his coldly alert and penetrating eyes, would oppose Pierpont in the Northern Pacific battle but become a close ally later on. Two of Stillman's daughters married two of William Rockefeller's sons, sealing the union of the Rockefellers with the National City Bank.

The Northern Pacific quarrel began when northwestern railroad magnate James J. Hill decided to buy a midwestern road called the Chicago, Burlington, and Quincy. Hill was a garrulous man with a bushy, white untamed beard, shoulder-length hair, and a troll's face. With Morgan's help, he had consolidated the Great Northern and Northern Pacific into a railroad system that dominated transport in the northwestern United States. The purchase of the CB&Q, Harriman feared, would provide Hill with an entrée into Chicago and a possible connection for a transatlantic line; it might even link up with Morgan's New York Central.

Schiff and Harriman pleaded with Hill and Morgan for a stake in the road but were rebuffed. Harriman said implacably, "Very well, it is a hostile act and you must take the consequences."[61] In a manner that anticipated mergers of the 1980s, Schiff and Harriman decided to swallow the railroad that had swallowed the CB&Q—the Northern Pacific. The Northern Pacific ran west from Wisconsin through North Dakota and Montana, terminating in Seattle, Washington. Schiff, torn between dreams of glory and dread of Morgan, passed a sleepless night before acceding to Harriman's plan. It was an extraordinary act of *lèse-majesté*, because the House of Morgan had a substantial stake in the Northern Pacific and wouldn't tolerate such an attack.

The raiders went into the market secretly, buying up $78 million in Northern Pacific shares—at the time, the largest such market operation in history. As share prices rose in April 1901, Pierpont credited it to the bullish tone of stocks set by the launching of U.S. Steel. Schiff cunningly circulated rumors that the rise reflected Northern Pacific's enhanced value after the CB&Q purchase. When a block of shares came into Robert Bacon's hands, he gladly sold. Even the railroad's board sold. It was a masterly con job by Harriman's forces, camouflaged by the ebullient financial markets that followed McKinley's reelection. The newspapers noted that many young men-about-town with newfound stock market fortunes were now calling themselves financiers. At the same time, many investors, apprehensive about the giddy market activity, predicted a general panic.

Then, in May, Northern Pacific stock shot up so fast it seemed to levitate. Hill, who had been beguiled by Bacon's beauty, was troubled by bad dreams. Asleep in his private railroad car in Seattle, he was visited by "a dark-complected angel" who warned of trouble in New York. Hill raced clear across America to Wall Street. On Saturday, May 4, he alerted Bacon to what he saw as a catastrophe in the making.

They cabled Pierpont, now in Aix-les-Bains, and awaited instructions.

At this point, the Harriman-Schiff forces were 40,000 shares short of majority control of the Northern Pacific. That Saturday morning, Harriman ordered Kuhn, Loeb to buy the needed stock, but Jacob Schiff was attending services at Temple Emanu-El, and the order never got executed. The lapse was fateful, for the next day Pierpont told Bacon to purchase 150,000 shares at any price. That Monday morning, Morgan brokers fanned out across the Exchange floor, and insane trading in Northern Pacific ensued.

The jumps in the stock were staggering. On Tuesday, May 7, the stock closed at over 143—a gain of 70 points in three days. The next day, it shot up to 200. This was a corner, a bloody trap for speculators. Speculators kept "shorting" the stock—that is, selling borrowed shares in the belief that the bubble would pop and enable them to buy back the shares at a cheaper price. Instead, the Northern Pacific geyser kept rising, forcing them to liquidate shares of other companies to pay for their borrowed Northern Pacific shares. Hence, the problem was generalized to the entire stock market.

By Wednesday, almost every stock on the Exchange was crashing, with money sucked from the rest of the list to feed the spectacularly surging Northern Pacific. Then came Thursday, May 9, and the biggest market crash in a century. Northern Pacific zoomed up as much as 200 or 300 points per trade, finally hitting 1,000. Then it dropped 400 points on a single trade. The Exchange was a scene of wild pandemonium as speculators found it impossible to locate certificates to cover short sales. The *New York Times* reported: "Brokers acted like insane men. . . . Big men lightly threw little men aside, and the little men, fairly crying with indignation, jumped anew into the fray, using hands and arms, elbows, feet—anything to gain their point. . . . To the spectators in the distant gallery of the Produce Exchange it was something incomprehensible, almost demonic—this struggle, this Babel of voices, these wild-eyed excited brokers, selling and buying, buying and selling."[62]

When brokers appeared with Northern Pacific certificates, they were clawed at by men who feared they would be ruined without them. One broker hired a train from Albany just to deliver one certificate of five hundred shares. Amid this free-for-all, Pierpont Morgan regained control of the Northern Pacific, but at the price of a full-blown panic. It was the madly destructive act of an egotist bent on winning at any cost. The carnage ended when a new Morgan partner, George Perkins, acting with Schiff and Harriman, announced that short sellers would be allowed to buy up shares at only $150 a share. Had the action not been taken, more than half the brokerage houses on Wall Street might have gone belly-up. It had been a pageant of extreme cupidity, one that sparked public apprehension about the omnipotent new financial magnates. The *New York Herald* banner headline of May 9, 1901, summed up the popular view: "GIANTS OF WALL STREET, IN FIERCE BATTLE FOR MASTERY, PRECIPITATE CRASH THAT BRINGS RUIN TO HORDE OF PYGMIES."[63]

The devil-angel nature of Pierpont Morgan was such that he alone started and stopped panics. He often appeared to be two different people of identical appearance but contrasting personalities. Comically, at the panic's height, a *New York Times* reporter found a forlorn investor named Jefferson M. Levy at the Waldorf-Astoria; Levy sighed, "If Mr. Morgan had been here this never would have happened."[64]

Pierpont brooked no criticism of his role in the Northern Pacific. Appearing at the Morgan, Harjes offices in Paris, he said with baronial bluntness, "I owe the public nothing."[65] The closest he ever came to an explanation was a reiteration of the Gentleman Banker's Code: "I feel bound in honor when I reorganize a property and am morally responsible for its management to protect it, and I generally do protect it."[66] Yet his power on Wall Street was now such that like a female elephant charging to protect her young, he couldn't help but crush innocent bystanders. He was too large for the flimsy regulatory structures that encased him; he had outgrown his age. Coming after the U.S. Steel promotion, the Northern Pacific corner reinforced the view that the public was being held hostage by the stock manipulations of a few Wall Street moguls.

For the most part, President McKinley was deaf to such outrage. Then, on September 6, 1901, he was shot by an anarchist named Leon Czolgosz as he stood in the Temple of Music at the Pan-American Exposition in Buffalo. We have graphic descriptions of Pierpont's reaction to the news. He was about to leave 23 Wall Street for the evening and already had on his silk hat when a *New York Times* reporter rushed in with the report. "What?" said Pierpont, seizing the man's arm. He stared into his eyes, overcome with amazement. Then he slumped into a desk chair, awaiting the confirmation that soon came by telephone. "This is sad, sad, very sad news," he told the *Times* reporter.[67] Other accounts describe him as red-faced and almost reeling with shock.

McKinley's assassination would be a turning point in Pierpont Morgan's life, for it installed in the presidency forty-two-year-old Theodore Roosevelt, a man whose view of big business was far more ambivalent than his predecessor's. Jack Morgan was mildly hopeful about the new president, although TR's noisy chatter had grated on

him after the March inauguration. "What I fear is that he may perhaps talk too much which would be very undesirable," he said.[68] In
fact, the presidency of Teddy Roosevelt would mark the start of peri-
odic warfare between the White House and the House of Morgan, warfare that would rage through three straight presidencies—those of
Roosevelt, Taft, and Wilson.

Two months after McKinley's assassination, the feuding parties of the
Northern Pacific corner made their peace. They set up a holding company, the Northern Securities Co., which merged the Northern Pacific,
Great Northern, and CB&Q lines. Both Hill and Harriman were given
seats on the board. If this brought peace between the two most important groups on Wall Street, it also heightened public alarm that a railroad monopoly had taken hold west of the Mississippi. "And it will be
much easier for them to obtain the second half than it was the first,"
said one newspaper editor, foreseeing a subsequent eastern rail monopoly. "One railroad after another will slide gently into their grasp until
any passenger anywhere who objects to traveling on their lines can take
a trolley car or walk."[69] The dreams of the architects of Northern
Securities went beyond the most vivid Populist fear. After tying up
transcontinental railroads, they planned to link them with steamship
lines to Asia—a vision that later would culminate in Edward Harriman's
plans for an around-the-world transportation network. Pierpont, meanwhile, meditated on a rail-ship monopoly of the North Atlantic, extending his domain beyond the borders of the United States. Wall Street
increasingly gazed abroad.

Besides bankrupting thousands of investors, the Northern Pacific corner claimed a last casualty—Morgan partner Robert Bacon. Although he
remained at 23 Wall for another year and a half, his nerves were shot
by the strain. On doctor's orders, he rode to hounds for two years—a
very Morgan form of therapy. When he returned to the United States
from his travel abroad, he occupied a series of positions—assistant secretary of state, secretary of state, and ambassador to France—of a far less
taxing nature than being chief lieutenant to J. Pierpont Morgan.

CHAPTER SIX

TRUST

. .

.

ASSIGNED to J. S. Morgan and Company in London in 1898, Jack Morgan, now thirty-one, was a lonely prince in exile. Tall and broad-shouldered, he was a husky young man with a broad face, a direct gaze, a black mustache, and prominent nose that never assumed the gross proportions of his father's. From afar, Jack watched the epochal events unfolding in New York—the formation of U.S. Steel and the cornering of Northern Pacific—with a vague yearning. He may have felt his date with destiny had been continually rescheduled. While conceding London's pleasures, he complained to his mother, "when I think of home the time does seem a bit long."[1] He grumbled how "profoundest peace" reigned at 22 Old Broad Street, while everything was "jumping about" at 23 Wall Street.[2] Worst of all, he had to watch Pierpont turn the spotlight of his favor on Robert Bacon.

At first, Jack's stay in London was meant to be temporary, but it took a few years before tangled personnel problems at J. S. Morgan and Company were straightened out. In 1897, Pierpont's brother-in-law Walter Hayes Burns died and was replaced by Jack's cousin Walter Spencer Morgan Burns. The senior Burns's death left the London bank short of experienced hands. Young Walter's sister Mary married Lewis Harcourt, the first Viscount Harcourt, spawning a branch of "British Morgans" who were lineal descendants of Junius Morgan. From this blue-blooded lineage would spring Lord William Harcourt, a postwar Morgan Grenfell chairman. A photograph of Pierpont at a house party at the Harcourt estate, Nuneham Park, in 1902 shows Mary Harcourt seated next to King Edward VII.

During his London exile, which lasted until 1905, Jack often seemed embarrassed by his remoteness from Pierpont. To inquiries as to whether Pierpont would attend Edward VII's coronation, he confessed sheepishly, "He is not easy to keep track of and I have almost given up."[3] (In the end, Teddy Roosevelt made Jack a special attaché to the Westminster Abbey coronation.) Once when Jack wished to join his father for a naval pageant at Spithead, he lamented that Pierpont "will probably not think of asking us."[4] He was often excluded from business deals and had to read about the U.S. Steel trust in the newspapers.

Pierpont liked Jack but found him lacking in fire and grit, which only accentuated Jack's insecurities. When Pierpont sailed from London in 1899, Jack wrote his mother how things couldn't proceed in New York in Pierpont's absence. He added, "I only hope it will never come to that with me. Probably it won't owing to the fact that things always will move on without me."[5] The scope of Pierpont's business ventures was too vast to allow for a son's self-doubt to be of concern, and the problem was exacerbated by Jack's not being as bright or as forceful as his father.

Another son might have rebelled. Jack sulked and pined, waiting for approval. Like Junius, he worried perpetually about Pierpont's work binges and "imprudent" appetite and was steadily watchful of him. He described with whimsical humor the sight of his father playing dominoes with Mary Burns: "It is too funny to see Father and Aunt Mary gravely sitting down to play that imbecile game."[6] He also saw his father's vanity, noting how after one good deed he was "simply too pleased with himself."[7] Jack also spied Pierpont's inner pain, his secret well of loneliness: "He is very well and jolly by bits but sometimes I see he feels as lonely as I do and he looks as glum as if he hadn't a friend in the world."[8] Considering that Jack was also cheering up his mother—a partially deaf, sickly woman abandoned by Pierpont for months at a time—one finds admirable his capacity for evenhanded empathy and tender solicitude toward both parents.

Jack's fatalistic acceptance of the London years was eased somewhat by a show of generosity from Pierpont. When Jack arrived in 1898, his father gave him and his wife, Jessie, the use of 13 Princes Gate. Pierpont added 14 Princes Gate to the property and joined the two townhouses. The original house now had the magnificence of a great museum and was resplendent with oils by Velázquez, Rubens, Rembrandt, and Turner—export duties kept Pierpont from taking the collection to America. Jack also used Dover House, Junius's country estate at Roehampton, with its jersey cattle and old-fashioned dairy. Ecstatic at this fatherly attention, Jack told his mother, "He has been dear to us ever since we landed, most thoughtful of everything and immensely interested in Jessie's social *career!* I know he has much enjoyed our being in the house, for it must have been very lonely for him with no one there and we have not hampered him at all, or bothered him with responsibilities."⁹ In 1901, Pierpont gave Jack a Christmas gift—an amount of money so large that he bought a portrait by Sir Joshua Reynolds with just part of it.

Yet Jack and his family found life amid such splendor a shade overwhelming. Every evening—whether Pierpont was in Europe or not—the domestic staff would place periodicals and warm milk beside the master's bed and adjust his reading lamp. And with the townhouse full of so many fragile masterpieces, the housekeeper just didn't dust on days when she felt jittery. Jessie took pride that nothing was broken, but the Morgan children, who now numbered two boys and two girls, found the need for self-control in their play stifling. Later the children recalled family prayers, reading Thackeray and Trollope, strolling in Hyde Park—everything but fun at Princes Gate.

In 1901, Jack rented Aldenham Abbey, a three-hundred-acre country estate in Hertfordshire stocked with pheasant and Southdown sheep said to rival the king's in quality. Jack had a British gentleman's taste for solid country comforts. After buying the abbey in 1910, he restored its original name, Wall Hall. Landscaped by Humphrey Repton, the estate included a turreted house with fake ruins, a conservatory full of tropical plants, and a library that resembled a college chapel. In the Anglophile Morgan world, Pierpont's Dover House staff would meet Jack's Wall Hall crew for cricket matches. The Morgans counterbalanced this Britishness with American touches—for instance, by shipping New York State pippin apples to the London partners.

For Jack, the London years were passed in a gilded cage. He had many friends from merchant-banking families and worked out at Sandow's gym with Eric Hambro. As neighbors there were Earl Grey and Florence Nightingale; for occasional dinner companions, Rudyard Kipling, Henry James, Sir James Barrie, and Mark Twain. Most of all, he had Jessie, a beautiful round-faced woman with pale golden hair, a fair complexion, and smoky blue eyes. Although she had gone to England grudgingly, its society soon reminded her of Boston's, and she became a confirmed Anglophile. She hoped that one of her two sons—Junius Spencer, Jr., born in 1892, or Henry Sturgis, born in London in 1900—would marry an American and the other a British woman; they both ended up marrying Americans.

Jessie Morgan didn't believe in an outside education for girls, and her daughters, Jane and Frances, were tutored at Wall Hall; they never set foot in a formal schoolroom. Jack held that a university education reduced a young woman's femininity, so college was also out of the question. The girls weren't allowed to talk to strangers on steamers or in public places and later saw their upbringing as a suffocating round of social duties.

Jessie and Jack Morgan's marriage was so all-encompassing and so absorbing as to exclude their own children at times. Jessie would not only rule Jack's estates with crisp, managerial efficiency, but she would guide her husband, advise him, and support him emotionally. Having watched the chill descend upon his parents' marriage and been conditioned by a confessional intimacy with his mother, Jack established a marriage that would be the exact opposite of his father's; philandering, for instance, was one Morgan tradition he would not perpetuate.

Jack's London stay had immense advantages for the House of Morgan. England would be Jack's second home, and he grew as tearfully patriotic as any British subject. In 1900, after watching Queen Victoria ride by, he said, "That wonderful little old woman in black and sables with the big spectacles means so much to so many—she represents in a current form so much of the past that it is very thrilling to see her driving through the crowd."[10] During the Boer War, he stood in a cheering throng before the Mansion House after Ladysmith, under siege by the Boers for four months, had been relieved by British troops. Amid a fanfare of silver trumpets, he heard the new King Edward VII proclaimed at Saint James's Palace. He always loved British pageantry.

Jack and Jessie were received into social circles that were closed to most American industrialists of the era. On February 21, 1898, Jack trooped along in sword and cocked hat as Jessie was presented in the throne room of Buckingham Palace. Bedecked in glittering jewels and black robes, Queen Victoria presided in solemn state while Jessie came forward in diamond tiara and obligatory ostrich feathers—the London *Daily Mail* later gushed in describing her beauty and her white satin train trimmed with blue velvet and pink roses. The Morgans also befriended the vivacious Lady Sybil Smith and her husband, Vivian Hugh Smith. Lady Sibyl took them to Windsor Castle to meet her mother, Lady Antrim, a lady-in-waiting, who gave them a private showing of the queen's Holbein and Leonardo drawings. Almost without realizing it, Jack was forging connections that would provide the Morgans with a unique entrée into the society of British nobility and politicians.

As a microcosm of the Anglo-American alliance, the House of Morgan would faithfully reflect its internal power shifts. If the New York office basked in London's glory after the Civil War, the situation was reversed in the new century, with J. S. Morgan and Company participating increasingly in issues that originated in New York. Much of the London capital came from Pierpont, who by the early 1900s was pocketing anywhere from one half to three-quarters of the annual profits booked at 22 Old Broad Street. The London house reflected some of Pierpont's rambunctious spirit. Pierpont's first biographer, Carl Hovey, wrote, "Inside the office there is always a marked amount of bustle and confusion, contrasting with the sedate atmosphere of the typical London institutions surrounding it."[11] Pierpont was just egalitarian enough to stop the practice of clerks bowing in his presence.

Although the Morgans were the darlings of the British establishment, the relationship would always be fraught with tension—less a love affair than a tense jockeying for power. The British could never figure out whether Pierpont and Company were allies or the first wave of a barbarian horde. Wall Street was gaining on the City in the fight for financial supremacy, with the Morgans overtaking the Barings and Rothschilds. "In London, the resuscitated Barings are the only people nearly in the same rank with us," said Sir Clinton Dawkins, a new partner of J. S. Morgan and Company, in 1901. "In the US they are nowhere now, a mere cipher, and the US is going to dominate in most ways."[12] To combat the Yankee upstarts, Barings and Rothschilds, the great nineteenth-century rivals, became less antagonistic toward each other.

During the Boer War, the British government, its gold depleted, turned to Rothschilds in London and Morgans in New York to raise Exchequer bonds. When Pierpont initially balked, the British treasury brought in Barings as well, adding to his displeasure. Sir Clinton Dawkins called the chancellor, Hicks-Beach, "notoriously stupid and most unbusinesslike."[13] The Boer War financing of 1900 had disquieting effects in the City. J. S. Morgan's new office manager, Edward C. Grenfell, noted dismay in London when half of the issue was scheduled for New York. Where Junius had accommodated the Rothschilds, Pierpont defied them, secretly demanding a higher commission on the issue—blackmail to which Britain reluctantly acceded. On the 1902 issue, the Rothschilds unsuccessfully tried to freeze Morgan from the syndicate. From then on, Grenfell, with grim triumph, would note in his journal the mounting ascendancy of the House of Morgan over the House of Rothschild.

With the 1901 creation of U.S. Steel, British financiers were unnerved by Pierpont's daring. The *New York Times* said they were "appalled by the magnitude of the American Steel combination," and the London *Chronicle* termed the trust "little less than a menace to the commerce of the civilized world."[14] Among other things, formation of the trust heralded an export boom of U.S. products to Europe, which would sharpen commercial rivalry between the two.

Around this time, too, Pierpont took a controversial interest in proposals to electrify underground and surface rail lines in London. New tube lines were being built as inner-city congestion required new building in London's outskirts. Pierpont competed to finance an underground line running from Hammersmith through Piccadilly, and into the City. By taking over tube financing, Pierpont also hoped to generate business for two companies in which he had a stake—British Thomson-Houston and Siemens Brothers. Eventually he lost the underground financing to a syndicate headed by Chicago tycoon Charles Tyson Yerkes, the Traction King, best known as the model for Theodore Dreiser's ruthless Frank Cowperwood, protagonist of *The Financier, The Titan,* and *The Stoic.* Despite his rare loss, Pierpont's involvement kindled fears that he would steamroller the English economy, and the London County Council warned that the metropolis was being handed over to the two Americans.

There was now enormous British ambivalence toward Pierpont. On the streets of London, peddlers sold penny sheets entitled "License to Stay on the Earth" and signed "J. Pierpont Morgan."[15] A 1901 cartoon in the New York *World* showed Pierpont asking John Bull, the personified Englishman, "What else have you for sale?"[16] Yet however much the British were distressed by Pierpont's bravado, they relied upon him in American financial matters. In 1901, to safeguard their American investments, London financiers insured his life at Lloyd's for $2 million, placing him, as Jack said, "in the same category with Queen Victoria and other rulers on this side of the Atlantic."[17]

No Morgan move could have aroused more primordial British fears than the one Pierpont made in 1902—the formation of a shipping trust to monopolize the North Atlantic. This was a natural extension of America's new export orientation. Soon after he had formed U.S. Steel, Pierpont was asked by a shipping executive whether it was possible to put North Atlantic steamships under common ownership. "It ought to be," he replied.[18] The shipping scene was then reminiscent of an earlier railroad era—too many ships and destructive rate wars. The Germans threatened British naval superiority, while Americans believed they should profit more from the immigrant traffic, as well as the new vogue among rich Americans for making luxurious transatlantic crossings.

Nakedly asserting American interests, Pierpont assembled a plan for an American-owned shipping trust that would transpose his "community of interest" principle—cooperation among competitors in a given industry—to a global plane. He created an Anglo-American fleet of over 120 steamships—the world's largest under private ownership, dwarfing even the French merchant marine. From a political standpoint, his critical conquests were the Belfast shipyard of Harland and Wolff and the White Star line. In the new trust, Lord Pirrie of Harland and Wolff saw a captive market for his ships, but J. Bruce Ismay, whose father had co-founded White Star, balked at the deal. Pierpont offered White Star shareholders such a rich premium—ten times over the high 1900 earnings—that Ismay not only stayed on as White Star chairman but was coaxed by Pierpont into becoming president of the trust itself, to be called the International Mercantile Marine. Through the White Star purchase and his hiring of Ismay, Pierpont would become ensnared in the *Titanic* catastrophe ten years later.

It was imperative that Pierpont bring the Germans, newly dominant in the North Atlantic, into his trust. Their jumbo transatlantic liners—multitiered wonders of wedding cake extravagance—were setting speed records for Atlantic crossings. An important architect of the shipping trust was Albert Ballin, whose Hamburg-Amerika Steamship Line, with hundreds of vessels, was the world's largest shipping company. In a secret 1901 report, Ballin sketched out the scope of Morgan's ambitions:

It is no secret that Morgan is pursuing his far-reaching plans as the head of a syndicate which comprises a number of the most important and the most enterprising business men in the United States and that railway interests are particularly well represented in it. Morgan himself, during his stay in London a few months ago, stated to some British shipping men that, according to his estimates, nearly 70 percent of the goods which are shipped to Europe from the North Atlantic ports are carried to the latter by the railroads on Through Bills of Lading, and that their further transport is entrusted to foreign shipping companies. He and his friends, Morgan added, did not see any reason why the railroad companies should leave it to foreign-owned companies to carry those American goods across the Atlantic. It would be much more logical to bring about an amalgamation of the American railroad and shipping interests for the purpose of securing the whole profits for American capital.[19]

In late 1901, Morgan struck a deal with Ballin for carving up the North Atlantic traffic: the Morgan syndicate wouldn't inaugurate service to German harbors without express permission from the Germans, while they, in turn, vowed not to expand their service to Britain or Belgium. The partners in the shipping trust would also pool profits and jointly acquire the Holland-America Line.

After meeting with Morgan in London, Ballin, the court Jew of his day, went to Kaiser Wilhelm's Berlin hunting lodge and briefed him on the pact. At first, the kaiser feared American financial trickery. But Ballin pointed out that while the British companies were being swallowed whole, the Germans would remain independent partners. Impressed, the kaiser sat down on his bed and read the agreement, making changes and insisting on the inclusion of North German Lloyd in the cartel. Later, when the kaiser came aboard *Corsair III* at Kiel, Pierpont strolled the deck with him. But in inviting the kaiser to sit down, he committed a serious *faux pas;* Wilhelm, however, accepted the offer from the royal Morgan.

As news of the German agreement leaked out, the public was shocked that consolidation had reared its head on a global scale. In an editorial entitled "Incredible," the *New York Times* said, "If dispatches from Paris should tell us that Mr. Morgan had . . . cabled orders to his home office to take out all the telephones, discharging the stenographers and typewriters and smash the ticker, no man, woman, or child in New York would believe the yarn. Neither will intelligent persons accept as true the story about the terms of the agreement with the German lines."[20] The *Times* saw this restraint of competition as outmoded and inefficient—a line of reasoning now gaining new adherents as revulsion from the trust kings increased.

The British were especially edgy about Pierpont's shipping cartel. They feared that International Mercantile Marine ships might exclusively transport to Europe those goods that originated in the American interior and traveled on Morgan railroads to East Coast ports. Morgan partner George Perkins confirmed this when he exulted that the shipping trust would "practically result in stretching our railroad terminals across the Atlantic."[21] It seemed as if Pierpont Morgan were spinning a seamless web around the world.

Pierpont had to contend with a single holdout, Britain's Cunard Line, whose exclusion Ballin thought might wreck the trust. (There may have been some personal pique here: once detained by a strike of Cunard workers at Liverpool, Pierpont had sworn, on the spot, never to use the line again.) Now, with near-panic in British shipping circles and a popular clamor for Parliament to "save" the seas for Britain, a cabinet committee pressed Cunard not to sell. The British admiralty wanted transatlantic liners available as warships in an emergency and feared having Cunard in foreign hands. To woo the line, the British government granted it lavish subsidies to build two new ships, the *Mauretania* and the *Lusitania*, which would be the world's biggest steamships. In exchange, Cunard agreed to stay in British hands and keep its fleet at the government's disposal.

In crafting a trust, Pierpont had never before had to contend with foreign governments. But as finance became increasingly international and affected sovereign interests, it took on a more political coloring. To temper British fears, Pierpont lobbied Colonial Secretary Joseph Chamberlain, a vocal critic, and resorted to a ruse familiar to modern multinationals: he camouflaged American ownership, first with the trust's very name, the International Mercantile Marine. Pierpont also agreed to man his British ships with British crews, fill their boards with British directors, and have them fly the Union Jack. Finally, his British ships would be in the reserves of the British navy and could be conscripted in case of war. Yet the IMM's five-man voting trust would have an American majority, with Pierpont and his partner Charles Steele joined by P. A. B. Widener, along with Ismay and Lord Pirrie.

The IMM would become a famous Pierpont Morgan flop. When shipping traffic slackened after the Boer War, the Morgan combine and Cunard exhausted each other in debilitating rate wars. From its inception in April 1902, the Morgan syndicate struggled to unload the IMM's unwanted securities. The stock had so much water—that is, inflated value—that it couldn't get a New York Stock Exchange listing. In 1906, the underwriters still held nearly 80 percent of the shares. As the *Wall Street Journal* concluded in a postmortem on Pierpont's shipping trust, "The ocean was too big for the old man."[22]

The British revulsion toward Pierpont probably changed the complexion of his London partnership, J. S. Morgan and Company. Not only had the bulk of its capital been his, but its mostly American partners had largely been recruited from among family members. In the new century, more partners would be British, and the choices more political, as Pierpont spent lavishly to build up the London house. In 1900, he signed up as a partner Sir Clinton E. Dawkins, a distinguished civil servant who had just completed a tour of duty in Egypt and was about to become a finance minister in India. The press saw fresh plans to expand the Morgan domain into Asia.

It was dissatisfaction with Dawkins, apparently, that led Pierpont into merger talks with Barings in 1904. He also feared his new rivals on Wall Street. Lord Revelstoke of Barings, in recalling his meeting with Pierpont on the subject, wrote, "He inveighed bitterly against the growing power of the Jews and of the Rockefeller crowd, and said more than once that our firm and his were the only two composed of white men in New York."[23] The two firms had long identified with each other as the leading Protestant houses in their respective cities.

The proposed merger centered on a plan for the House of Baring to handle the London side, the House of Morgan the New York side; J. S. Morgan and Company would disappear. The talks foundered for two reasons, according to Lord Revelstoke: Pierpont was afraid of disappointing Dawkins by merging the London house; and with Jack Morgan spending so much time in London, his position in the merged firm would be a ticklish affair. "I expect there is little sympathy and less confidence between father and son," said Revelstoke, who was also afraid of being smothered by Pierpont.[24] Soon after these talks collapsed in 1905, Dawkins had a heart attack and died. Jack was then entrusted with the sensitive assignment of recruiting well-connected British partners for the firm of J. S. Morgan and Company. Now the Morgans would buy some expensive British bloodlines.

In 1904, Edward Grenfell was elevated to partner; he became a Bank of England director a year later. A cool, dapper young bachelor who wore smart clothes and had a sharp tongue, Grenfell was snobbish and conservative and possessed a penetrating intellect. He also had a taste for practical jokes. Educated at Harrow and Trinity College, Cambridge, he had eminent ancestors, both his father and grandfather having been directors of the Bank of England and members of Parliament. Even as a young man, he peered at the world unsentimentally and spied out the fraudulent and hypocritical in people. Grenfell would become the London firm's political fixer and ace diplomat, its main contact with the British Treasury and the Bank of England.

In 1905, Grenfell brought in his cousin and Jack Morgan's friend, Vivian Hugh Smith, then working in a family business that managed wharves. A tall, handsome redhead and a charming raconteur, he had gone to Eton and Trinity Hall, Cambridge. He more than Grenfell was in Pierpont's mold. He was a business go-getter, with his hand in many deals. He invested in Caucasian copper and African goldfields and in other Rhodesian enterprises. Smith's father had been a Bank of England governor, and he was a member of the most prolific banking family England has produced, the so-called City Smiths, descended from a seventeenth-century Nottingham banker. (Grenfell wasn't a Smith; he and Vivian were related through their mothers.) Charting the power of this prodigious brood in 1959, Anthony Sampson estimated that seventeen Smith descendants in the City controlled eighty-seven director-ships in seventy-five companies and were chairmen of six companies. The Martin Smiths would intermarry with the Hambros, strengthening that banking alliance. Vivian Smith married the tall, slender, flaxen-haired Lady Sybil, the mischievous, high-spirited only daughter of the sixth earl of Antrim, who owned Glenarm Castle and several square miles of land in Ulster and whose mother had been a lady-in-waiting to Queen Victoria. Gradually, then, the London bank shed its character as an American colony in the City. When Jack returned to New York in 1905, Grenfell and Smith were in charge. When the firm was restyled Morgan, Grenfell in 1910, it was the first time it had ever carried a British name. The Morgans had built their Trojan horse well.

DURING Theodore Roosevelt's presidency, Pierpont Morgan received his most pronounced comeuppance for his role in the American scene. He was now so grand and cloud-wreathed that only a president could chop him down to mortal scale. The public revulsion from him was easy to explain. Wall Street had flourished with the trusts: many were head-quartered in New York and enjoyed closer relations with Wall Street bankers than with the companies from which they were compounded. Teddy Roosevelt wanted to correct the imbalance between government and corporate power, and in so doing he inevitably collided with Pier-pont Morgan.

Although he had created great industrial combines, Pierpont couldn't allow commensurate power to accrue to labor and government. Despite his reverence for the past, patent in the religious and Renaissance art he collected, he was a radical force, unsettling to small-town America, with its agrarian traditions and faith in its own innocence. However much businessmen might respect him, he was now an ogre in the popular press. One Broadway hit show depicted devils blowing across a fiery seat as they sang in unison, "This seat's reserved for Morgan, the great financial Gorgon."[25]

Soon after President McKinley was shot, the House of Morgan tested his successor. Pierpont's new lieutenant, the smooth, insinuating George W. Perkins, cabled the new president, "The country's only consolation at this time is that it has an honest, fearless, loyal American to assume its world wide burdens.[26] A few weeks later, Perkins and Robert Bacon, a former classmate of TR's at Harvard, visited the White House to urge caution and scout out Roosevelt's intentions. The presi-dent said he wanted reform and afterward described Perkins and Bacon "arguing like attorneys for a bad case, and at the bottom of their hearts each would know this if . . . he were not the representative of so strong and dominant a character as Pierpont Morgan."[27]

As much a showman as Pierpont, TR would endlessly manipulate the Morgan symbolism. With the public appalled by the Northern Pacific corner, Roosevelt saw the political wisdom of filing an antitrust suit against the Northern Securities Company, whose formation had marked the Morgan-Harriman truce. Attorney General Philander C. Knox announced the suit after the stock market's close on February 19, 1902. The news caught Morgan by surprise at a dinner. Clearly, *this* White House wouldn't automatically succumb to Morgan pressure. The subsequent confrontations between TR and Morgan showed the tycoon in all his sublime arrogance. The two men shared membership in New York's aristocracy; Pierpont and TR's father were both founders of the American Museum of Natural History. This common background perhaps gave their feud a special rancor—a pattern that would repeat itself with Jack and another notable "class traitor," Franklin Roosevelt.

At a White House meeting that included Attorney General Knox, Morgan expressed indignation that he hadn't received advance word of the Northern Securities suit. In what history has engraved as the ultimate hauteur, he suggested to Roosevelt that Knox and his lawyers meet privately. "If we have done anything wrong," said Pierpont, "send your man to my man and they can fix it up."[28] Knox said testily that they didn't want to fix the merger, but stop it. Worried about U.S. Steel, his favorite stepchild, Morgan asked Roosevelt if he planned to "attack my other interests." Not "unless we find out . . . they have done something we regard as wrong," Roosevelt replied.[29]

In Roosevelt's reaction to the meeting, there was the keen relish and cynicism of the well-bred rebel. He told Knox how Morgan "could not help regarding me as a big rival operator, who either intended to ruin all his interests or else could be induced to come to an agreement to ruin none."[30] Back at 23 Wall, Pierpont dashed off an angry letter to the president, but cooler associates dissuaded him from sending it. In 1903, a court in Saint Paul, Minnesota, backed the government in dissolving the Northern Securities Company and the Supreme Court narrowly upheld the decision a year later. The Sherman Antitrust Act, moribund under McKinley, suddenly took on new life with TR.

Although the Roosevelt-Morgan relationship is sometimes caricatured as that of trust buster versus trust king, it was far more complex than that. The public wrangling obscured deeper ideological affinities, as first demonstrated in the anthracite miners strike of May 1902. The principal coal companies were owned by railroads, such as the Reading, Lehigh Valley, Erie, and others close to the House of Morgan. They wanted to avenge a 10-percent wage increase granted the miners in 1900—a deal that Pierpont had helped to broker—and reacted to the strikers with feudal ferocity. By the fall of 1902, schools were shut in New York for lack of coal, and the Republicans feared retribution in the elections. On October 11, 1902, Elihu Root, the secretary of war, met with Pierpont aboard *Corsair III* in the Hudson River. Roosevelt was ready to run the mines with soldiers and wanted Morgan's support for an arbitration committee. TR was taking an enlightened stand for a president—strikebreaking had been the more typical presidential response.

The approach appealed to Morgan, who liked order and negotiation. He and Root went straight to the Union Club to meet with some railroad presidents. Paternalistic in his own bank, he was more conciliatory toward the miners than the railroad presidents were. At a White House meeting on October 3, the railroad men angrily abused John Mitchell, the young president of the United Mine Workers of America, who reacted with commendable dignity. Two days later, Roosevelt sent Robert Bacon a letter designed to enlist Pierpont's further help. The president said of Mitchell, "He made no threats and resorted to no abuse. The proposition he made seemed to me eminently fair. The operators refused even to consider it; used insolent and abusive language about him, and in at least 2 cases assumed an attitude toward me which was one of insolence."[31] While sympathetic to Roosevelt's plea, Morgan lacked the total power over the railroad men popularly attributed to him, and Roosevelt complained to Henry Cabot Lodge that Morgan hadn't been able to "do much with those wooden-headed gentry."[32]

The crisis climaxed on October 15, 1902, when Perkins and Bacon visited the White House and stayed up close to midnight with Roosevelt, trying to find a way out of the impasse. Roosevelt again saw the two Morgan partners as melodramatic, even slightly ridiculous. As the night wore on, he said, they "grew more and more hysterical, and not merely admitted but insisted that failure to agree would result in violence and possible social war."[33] Roosevelt finally hit upon a way that would allow the operators to save face: they would place the labor representative on the board in a seat reserved for an "eminent sociologist." In the end, the arbitration board granted the miners a 10-percent wage increase but no union recognition. Roosevelt glowingly wrote Morgan, "If it had not been for your going in the matter, I do not see how the strike could have been settled at this time, and the consequences that might have followed . . . are . . . very dreadful to contemplate."[34]

Even on the trust issue, Roosevelt and Morgan were far from antithetical. Roosevelt saw trusts as natural, organic outgrowths of economic development. Stopping them, he said, was like trying to dam the Mississippi River. Both TR and Morgan disliked the rugged, individualistic economy of the nineteenth century and favored big business; they wanted to promote U. S. entry into world markets. But whereas Roosevelt thought economic giantism warranted an equivalent growth in government regulation, Morgan saw no need for countervailing powers. A Victorian gentleman banker at bottom, Pierpont saw trust, honor, and self-regulation among businessmen as providing the needed checks and balances.

That Roosevelt and Morgan were secret blood brothers can be seen in the strange odyssey of Morgan partner George W. Perkins, who ended up a lieutenant to both. He was a handsome, highly imaginative man, with roguish, heavy-lidded gambler's eyes and a sinister baby face behind a handlebar mustache. His father had founded a missionary slum school in Chicago, and George grew up on the grounds of a reform school that his father ran. Before he joined the bank in 1901, he was already an empire-building executive at New York Life Insurance. A voluble, glad-handing deal maker, he was an experiment on Pierpont's part—more chief than Indian—and showed Morgan's knack for picking bright people. He had come to the Corner to solicit a donation for preserving the Palisades, the high cliffs on the western bank of the Hudson. Pierpont gave $25,000 of a requested $125,000, then said to Perkins as he was leaving, "I will give you the whole $125,000 if you will do something for me." When Perkins asked what, Pierpont motioned toward the partners' area. "Take that desk over there."[35]

Morgan gave Perkins a day to decide. President McKinley warned him against the killing regime of a Morgan partner, but the cocky Perkins accepted. Things were stormy from the start. J. P. Morgan and Company employed men for secretarial positions, and Perkins wanted to bring his female secretary from New York Life. "I will not have a damned woman in the place," Pierpont roared, and poor Mary Kihm was stashed away in a bank building around the corner.[36] Later, Perkins moved her over to 23 Wall, but with the proviso that she remain upstairs and never appear on the banking floor.

Flamboyant and outgoing, George Perkins stands out among early partners because he wrote about trusts even as he created them. He challenged the mores of tight-lipped bankers of the Baronial Age. In

August 1902, he pulled off a deal that put him in Pierpont's league. For a $3-million fee, he merged the McCormick Harvesting Machine Company and the Deering Harvester Company plus three smaller companies into International Harvester. This new trust had an 85-percent share of the farm-equipment market. Perkins chose the name International Harvester because he foresaw the rise of global corporations and hoped the new trust would "comply with the laws of various countries and be at home everywhere."[37] Because of the popularity of McCormick Harvesting among farmers, International Harvester was spared the trust-busting fervor that was directed against U.S. Steel.

As the Deering and McCormick families vied to control International Harvester, Perkins came up with an ingenious solution: the House of Morgan would control it. Perkins boasted to Pierpont, "The new company is to be organized by us; its name chosen by us; the state in which it shall be incorporated is left to us; the Board of Directors, the Officers, and the whole outfit left to us—nobody has any right to question in any way any choice we make."[38] Cyrus Hall McCormick, Jr., later called Perkins the most brilliant negotiator he had ever known.[39] When International Harvester was listed on the Stock Exchange, Perkins proudly sent its first report to Roosevelt, writing that "so far as I know, this is the first instance on record that a corporation, on offering its securities to the public, has given to the public complete information as to its affairs."[40]

Perkins's advent came at an auspicious time for Pierpont Morgan. The trusts had thrust Wall Street into the national spotlight and brought about growing federal scrutiny of high finance. Pierpont was still mired in a nineteenth-century businessman's contempt for government— when a fellow vestryman at Saint George's Church, William Jay Schieffelin, the son-in-law of Dr. Markoe, came one day to talk to him about a civil service reform movement, Pierpont thundered, "What do I care about civil service reform!"[41] To worsen matters, Pierpont had a ferocious attitude toward the press, rarely granted interviews, violently refused to be photographed, and warned employees to withhold information from reporters.

The slick, cool George Perkins, with his natty gray alpaca suits and ingratiating manner, enjoyed the smoke-filled rooms. He was the House of Morgan's first real power broker and high-level lobbyist. His later antagonist in the struggle for Theodore Roosevelt's soul, the Kansas Progressive William Allen White, has left some marvelous impressions of Perkins as a silver-tongued devil. White became fascinated with Perkins after Senator Albert J. Beveridge urged White to go into the Senate and said that Perkins, who liked him, could arrange it. White observed that Perkins "made quick decisions, spoke in a soft voice, smiled ingratiatingly, easily." He wrote, "I used to watch him fishing for men with a certain pride in his skill, which I greatly admired." He also declared that "he exuded pleasantly the odor of great power that came from the Morgan connection." At the Bull Moose National Convention in 1912, White saw a "smiling, simpering" Perkins, "spick-n-span, oiled and curled like an Assyrian bull, and a young one, trim and virile."[42]

From his days at New York Life, Perkins would always carry a faint spice of scandal and a reputation as a master manipulator. In 1905, the New York State legislature held sensational hearings regarding the life-insurance industry. They were named after Senator William Armstrong and they made the reputation of chief counsel Charles Evans Hughes, later secretary of state and chief justice of the Supreme Court. The committee showed how rapacious insurance executives poured money into trust companies in which they held stock and squandered policyholders' money on fancy balls. There were stories about a racy house of mirth in Albany and other devices used by New York Life and other insurance companies to sway legislators. Perkins had been in too high a position at New York Life to get off scot-free. Against Pierpont's advice, he had retained his New York Life position and Hughes pummeled him with conflict-of-interest issues. Perkins was charged with illegal campaign contributions and falsifying company records related to the sale of railroad securities. Although the indictments were later thrown out, he had to resign from New York Life.

Where Pierpont's theorizing was largely nonexistent, Perkins's was sophisticated. He gave speeches and published pamphlets on every conceivable subject. He was an oddity at the world's most cryptic bank. He preached a gospel of industrial cooperation, contending that small-scale business depressed wages and retarded technological advance. Not Wall Street, he said, but steam engines and telephones produced trusts. "What is the difference," he proclaimed, "between the U.S. Steel Corporation, as it was organized by Mr. Morgan, and a Department of Steel as it might be organized by the Government?"[43] He drew a parallel Pierpont wouldn't admit to—that trusts, with their centralized production and distribution, were a form of private socialism. And unlike Pierpont, he saw that they had acquired a public character, and he favored government licensing of interstate companies and extended worker benefits, including profit sharing, social insurance, and old-age pensions. This, he boasted, would be "socialism of the highest, best, and most ideal sort."[44] Although Teddy Roosevelt sometimes wondered whether Perkins simply rationalized a selfish Morgan agenda, there was a striking likeness between their views.

That a Morgan partner should advocate socialism is not so startling. After all, Pierpont, starting with his railway associations of the late 1880s, espoused industrial cooperation instead of competition. He liked his capitalism neat, tidy, and under bankers' control. The House of Morgan was banker to established enterprises—the great industrial planning systems that favored stability over innovation, predictability over experimentation, and were threatened by upstart companies; so the bank had a heavy stake in the status quo. Perkins wasn't the only one in the Morgan camp to applaud moves toward a planned, integrated economy. Later on, Judge Elbert Gary of U.S. Steel, who held private dinners to fix prices in the steel industry, testified: "I would be very glad if we had some place where we could go, to a responsible governmental authority, and say to them, 'Here are our facts and figures, here is our property, here our cost of production; now you tell us what we have the right to do and what prices we have the right to charge.'"[45]

As we shall see, the mortal attacks on the House of Morgan came not from socialists but from such trustbusters as Louis D. Brandeis, Felix Frankfurter, and William O. Douglas, who favored small economic units and sharp competition. This tradition would lambaste the Morgan Money Trust as the biggest and most dangerous trust of all. Because the House of Morgan preached socialism for the rich, it always had a partial affinity for those who preached it for the poor.

Yet another dimension of the Pierpont Morgan–Teddy Roosevelt relationship may be seen in the Panama Canal affair. Even as TR fulminated against excessive financial power at home, he gratefully exploited it abroad. In 1902, Congress authorized Roosevelt to pay $40 million to France to buy its uncompleted assets in the Isthmus of Panama for the construction of a canal. Two years later, Pierpont carried out the financing for this largest real estate transaction in history. He traveled to France to oversee the shipment of gold bullion and paid the rest in foreign exchange to the Banque de France. After receiving payment from the United States, the new state of Panama—which TR helped to pry loose from Colombia—named J. P. Morgan and Company its fiscal agent on Wall Street, with exclusive rights to receive its U.S. government payments. The House of Morgan also handled Panama's single biggest investment: $6 million of first mortgages on New York City real estate. So integral was Pierpont in the whole shady Panama Canal affair that one biographer has dubbed him "Roosevelt's bagman in the taking of the Panama Canal."[46]

Thus, in the sparring between Roosevelt and Morgan there was always a certain amount of shadow play, a pretense of greater animosity than actually existed. In the 1904 campaign, the Morgan bank gave $150,000 toward Roosevelt's reelection. In return, Pierpont was sternly lectured by TR at a 1907 dinner of the Gridiron Club, the president wagging his finger at Morgan and Standard Oil's Henry Rogers and thundering for business reform. "And if you don't let us do this," he insisted, "those who will come after us will rise and bring you to ruin."[47] When TR enunciated the famous phrase about "malefactors of great wealth," reporters thought he glanced in Morgan's direction.[48]

Nevertheless, some of the most eloquent encomiums of Pierpont came from TR himself, who "was struck by his very great power and his truthfulness. Any kind of meanness and smallness were alike wholly alien to his nature."[49] Morgan was less forgiving. When Roosevelt went on an African safari, Pierpont declared that he hoped the first lion he met would do its duty.

BADGERED by trustbusters, Pierpont turned with relief to other matters in his later years. By the 1900s, in his early sixties, he was often an absentee boss. Cabling instructions to Wall Street two or three times daily from vacation haunts, he never loosened his grip. He was a restless, frustrated man. He didn't gloat over the stupendous sums he earned, and one doesn't picture him counting up his net worth in the dead of night. He never mistook business for the whole of life. His real passions and temptations were women, art, and religion.

Pierpont tried to suppress press gossip about his escapades, but the Morgan estrangement was no secret. Husband and wife had little in common, and Fanny remained aloof from the social rigors required of a famous man's wife. In a 1902 photograph, she still looks tall, refined, and handsome, with her wavy hair swept up. Yet she was frail and sickly and sometimes lacked the strength to travel. By the early 1900s, she had become rather deaf and used an enormous ear trumpet; she was a semi-invalid and ate alone upstairs when the family gathered for Sunday breakfast.

Despite the tensions between Pierpont and Fanny, the Morgans were family-oriented. In 1904, Pierpont bought Jack a big Victorian brownstone at the corner of Madison Avenue and Thirty-seventh Street, almost a twin of his own. Unexpectedly light and spacious inside, it had forty-five rooms, twenty-two fireplaces, and a dozen bathrooms. By tearing down an intervening house, Jack and his father lived as next-door neighbors, with a common garden in between, from 1905 until Pierpont's death, in 1913.

Jack continued to manage emotional acrobatics, propping up his mother's failing spirits while retaining his father's love. In later years, he functioned as a post office, informing his mother of Pierpont's movements abroad and reporting to his father on his mother's whereabouts. It was formal and awkward, yet Pierpont and Fanny never turned their children against one other. A thoroughgoing Victorian, Pierpont would inquire respectfully after Fanny and try to minimize Jack's discomfort.

In letters often heavy with piety, Jack preached resignation to Fanny. Life, he argued, was simply a matter of bowing to eternal verities. Hadn't he dealt with his father by accepting the inevitable? In the stuffy, patriarchal Morgan world, Fanny's options were terribly limited. In one 1900 letter, he congratulated her for her better health, then said, "Do keep hold of it now it's come at last and don't squander your health on things which seem a necessity to you because they would be a pleasure to others. Keep on letting people do things without you, you'll be better able to do things for them later on. Here endeth the sermon—and there is no collection."[50]

Fanny never achieved such holy resignation and suffered terrible anguish. In 1901, when she visited Rome, Jack wrote her a letter that poignantly stated his conviction that she had to submit to her fate. Although Pierpont isn't mentioned, his ghost hovers in the air:

> Your letter from Rome struck me as distinctly blue. . . . I know there are lots of things in your circumstances which you and others would like to have differently but one must accept the inevitable as a thing which is not in one's own hands, as one does a death or a great anxiety. Nothing one could ever have done and left undone would make two and two into five—if the four is unpleasant there is a moral and religious necessity for accepting the fact and believing in the eternal love which lies behind the troubles.[51]

It seems doubtful that any woman could have wholly gratified Pierpont's appetites. There were two Pierponts—the proper banker and the sensualist—yoked together under extreme pressure; Pierpont could never integrate the two. His attitude toward women was characterized by the common double standard. At the bank, he was stoutly opposed to women employees, and he didn't discuss business with women, whom he saw as inhabiting a separate realm. Once a year, on New Year's Day, Fanny lunched at the Corner—the only time women were invited. At home, however, he was a different man. A female visitor to 219 Madison Avenue once teased Pierpont, saying that while he was charming at home, she heard of the fear he inspired at work. Pierpont blushed, began to protest, then said, "I'm afraid you are right."[52]

For Pierpont, marriage required discretion, not fidelity. It was a matter of paying homage to convention. In January 1902, Charles Schwab, now president of U.S. Steel, motored to Monte Carlo with Baron Henri Rothschild; their scandalous escapades at roulette made the front pages of New York papers. Disgusted with the "wicked" Schwab, Andrew Carnegie wrote Pierpont, "Of course he never could have fallen so low with us. His resignation would have been called for instanter had he done so."[53] George Perkins cabled Schwab that the incident hadn't scandalized Pierpont and that Schwab should go ahead "and have a bully good time."[54] When he returned to New York, Schwab defended himself, telling Morgan he hadn't resorted to closed doors. "That's what doors are for," snapped Morgan.[55] There's no question he possessed a wide streak of cynicism. He once told an associate, "A man always has two reasons for the things he does—a good one and the real one."[56] A revealing comment from a man who styled himself Wall Street's conscience.

In matters of art, Pierpont's standards were puritanical. As a member of the board of the Metropolitan Opera, he was instrumental in canceling production of Richard Strauss's *Salome*. The first-night audience had found the story of the crazed princess who wanted John the Baptist's head too daring for its tastes. Also, rehearsals had been held on Sunday mornings, which infuriated the local clergy. The production was spiked. In embarrassment, another board member, Otto Kahn, wrote to Strauss that "the responsibility for the *Salome* veto must be shared by the clumsiness and the honestly felt, but in this case, totally inappropriate religiosity of Morgan."[57]

While protecting public morals, Pierpont conducted amorous escapades aboard his yachts, in private railroad cars, and at European spas. Wall Street wits said he collected old masters and old mistresses. "Few women could withstand his leonine love-making," insisted an early Pierpont biographer.[58] In his larks can be seen the familiar comedy of the older man suddenly unbuttoned—he could be a jovial Santa Claus. In Paris, he would squire mistresses to a jeweler on the rue de la Paix and invite them to indulge themselves. Once, in Cairo, he tossed a handful of gold jewelry on a hotel table and cried to the ladies, "Now, help yourselves!"[59] (The party included a bishop: did he join in the merriment?) During one Seattle outing, everyone was given a fur. A New York joke of the early 1900s apparently referred to Pierpont's florid face and generosity. One chorus girl says to another, "I got a pearl out of a fresh oyster at Shankley's." "That's nothing," replies her friend. "I got a whole diamond necklace out of an old lobster."[60]

Given Pierpont's theatrical approach to business, it is fitting that he preferred the company of actresses. He gravitated toward women who were free and independent, sassy and high-spirited. Rumors had him competing with Diamond Jim Brady for the affections of Lillian Russell. His most celebrated affair involved the tall, voluptuous Maxine Elliott. She was a stately woman with dark eyes, a long neck, and an imposing presence. She had a provocative tongue—something that always seemed to attract Morgan. "Why, you men in Wall Street are like a lot of cannibals," she taunted him. "You devour anything that comes along— if it is edible."[61] She made such withering comments about the design of *Corsair III*—especially Pierpont's having placed the cabins below-decks—that he shifted the arrangements.

Maxine Elliott was the first woman to build a Broadway theater, purchasing the needed lot two months after the 1907 panic. Scandal-mongers attributed the financing to Morgan. When he and Maxine returned from Europe aboard the same ship in 1908—a rare lapse in Morgan discretion—reporters asked him if he had a stake in the theater. "The only interest I have in Maxine Elliott's Theatre is that I'd like to get a free ticket on opening night," he said.[62] Legend claims he shared her favors with King Edward VII, whom she met at Marienbad in 1908.

These larks, concentrated in Pierpont's later life, were not without Falstaffian pathos. Yet Pierpont could also be a courtly, old-fashioned lover. His last mistress seems to have been Lady Victoria Sackville-West, the daughter of a former British ambassador to Washington. She re-corded how the portly old banker, randy as a schoolboy, suddenly crushed her in his embrace. She wrote in her diary in 1912, "He holds my hand with much affection and says he would never care for me in any way I would not approve of, that he was sorry to be so old, but I was the one woman he loved and he would never change."[63] For a financial god, how tenderly apologetic!

Even at the end of his life, Pierpont had a craving for romance that had probably not been satisfied since his brief marriage to Mimi Sturges fifty years before. Some spot inside him was left untouched by the storied maneuvers on Wall Street, some emptiness that his giant ex-ploits couldn't fill. Even after Pierpont's death, his family would track his liaisons as *objets d'art* he had owned mysteriously surfaced in the collections of other families. In 1936, a German wrote to Jack claiming to be a bastard from Pierpont's student days at Göttingen. Jack wasn't sure the whole thing was a hoax until he established that the man hadn't been born until after his father had left the university. Yet years after his father's death, Jack didn't dismiss the notion out of hand.

In spite of their number, these affairs consumed less of Pierpont's time and interest than his true aphrodisiac—art collecting. When Junius died, Pierpont had a Thackeray manuscript and a few Egyptian antiquities. Then his collecting blossomed along with his banks' profits. At first, he concentrated on books and manuscripts and letters of British royalty, storing them in his Madison Avenue basement. Soon they were heaped upon chairs, and he couldn't keep track of them. Other works gathered dust in 23 Wall's vaults and in a warehouse on East Forty-second Street.

In 1900, he bought property adjoining his house, on East Thirty-sixth Street and drafted architect Charles F. McKim to design a library for his collection. McKim created an Italian Renaissance palace of a coldly remote and balanced beauty. Its marble blocks were so perfectly fitted they required no binding material—a method McKim copied, at considerable expense, from the Greeks. When he settled into the library in 1906, Pierpont took for his office the magnificent West Room, with its walls of crimson damask from the Chigi palace in Rome. A door in the corner opened into the vault. Junius's portrait hung above the mantel. The library was nicknamed the Uptown Branch of J. P. Morgan and Company.

To catalogue the collection, Pierpont in 1905 hired a pretty young woman named Belle da Costa Greene. Only twenty-two, she had impressed Pierpont's nephew with her knowledge of rare books at Princeton's library. She was the product of a broken marriage—she grew up in New Jersey with her mother, who was a music teacher—and had no college education. Dark and enchanting, with green eyes, she had a complexion so dusky that she referred fancifully to her "Portuguese origins," and she was probably part black. Belle Greene had a ferocious wit and remarkable self-confidence. She became more than Pierpont's librarian: she was his confidante, soul mate, and possibly mistress. She read Dickens and the Bible to him and would even attend him at the all-night library session during the 1907 panic.

If the financier liked saucy women, Belle Greene surpassed all rivals. When a lumber magnate proposed to her, she cabled back "All proposals will be considered alphabetically after my fiftieth birthday."[64] She daringly posed nude for drawings and enjoyed a Bohemian freedom. Also the toast of the Harrimans and the Rockefellers, she stayed at Claridge's in London and the Ritz in Paris when on Morgan missions. She could be a buccaneer as well; she once told an assistant, "If a person is a worm, you step on him."[65] Even when she became famous as the director of the Pierpont Morgan Library, she was as mysterious as her mentor and never lectured in public or accepted any honorary awards. Like Pierpont, she burned her letters and diaries before she died in 1950.

In Belle Greene, Pierpont's infatuation with women and art converged. There was some sexual element to the relationship. When she had a four-year affair with connoisseur Bernard Berenson, she insisted that he keep it secret, so as not to awaken Pierpont's jealousy. She flowered in her role as doyenne of the library, presiding in Renaissance gowns, gesturing with a green silk handkerchief, and personally representing Pierpont at art auctions. The forty-six-year age difference between tycoon and librarian didn't seem to matter. "He was almost a father to me," she said after Pierpont died. "His never-failing sympathy, his understanding, and his great confidence and trust in me bridged all the difference in age, wealth, and position."[66] She would be an important figure for many members of the Morgan family and would later appeal to Jack no less than to his father.

Eventually Pierpont put together the largest art collection of any private individual of his day, perhaps of any day. It had Napoléon's watch, Leonardo da Vinci's notebooks, Catherine the Great's snuff box, jewelry of the Medici family, Shakespeare first folios, a five-page letter of George Washington's, Roman coins showing the heads of all twelve Caesars save one. Oblivious to Impressionists and modern American artists, he favored objects with long, romantic histories, European art sanctified by age. The banker of old money did prefer old masters, and valued exquisite craftsmanship and costly materials. Yet paintings accounted for a scant 5 percent of his collection. He preferred tapestries, jewel-encrusted books, gilded altarpieces, illuminated manuscripts, gold and silver cups, porcelains, and ivory. In stressing decorative arts, he followed in the footsteps of the Rothschilds, the Medicis, and other merchant princes. He was proud of his holdings and printed up private catalogues of his collection, which he distributed to the royal households of Europe.

Morgan the collector was recognizably the same man as Morgan the banker. He hated to haggle. He would come to terms by asking a dealer what he had paid and then tacking on 10 or 15 percent; one recalls Pierpont barking bids for foreign exchange on a take-it-or-leave-it basis.

In art and finance, he relied on the deal maker as much as the deal. Francis Henry Taylor, who studied Morgan's habits as a collector, wrote, "He was accused of not looking at the objects when in reality he was looking into the eye of the man who was trying to sell it to him. It was, after all, how he had reached the summit in finance and it had paid off well."[67] To protect himself, he would buy a picture conditionally and leave it on a chair, gathering the free comments of other dealers before completing the purchase. Once, to test art dealer Joseph Duveen's knowledge of Chinese ceramics, he set out five on display. "Only three of them are genuine," he said. "Now tell me which they are." Duveen smashed the two fakes with his cane.[68]

The godfather of U.S. Steel knew that to create a *big* collection he had to buy art in huge batches and purchase entire collections. He roared tenaciously through art history like a freight train shunting from one track to the next. "I have done with the Greek antiquities," he wrote his sister Mary Burns. "I am at the Egyptian."[69] His determination was awesome. Wanting manuscripts owned by one of Lord Byron's relatives in Greece, he stationed an agent there, armed with a letter of credit. For several years, this lonely sentinel bought Byron manuscripts as they came on the market until the collection was complete.

Pierpont could also be childishly impulsive. He loved to hear the stories behind works of art, which he would commit to memory. This genuine interest served him better than the feigned sophistication of insecure millionaires who bought "fine art" and ended up with high-priced junk. When one art dealer appeared with a Vermeer, Pierpont asked, "Who is Vermeer?" After being told, he peered at the $100,000 painting again. "I'll take it," he said. The story may be apocryphal— Morgan had visited European museums for decades and would have seen Vermeers—yet it captures his enthusiasm. In the last analysis, Pierpont relied on his own fallible judgment. In 1911, Jack excitedly reported that a dealer had offered $176,000 for an original 1530 Copernicus manuscript, the basis of modern astronomy. In a huff, Pierpont cabled back: "Do not care for Copernicus, certainly not at such absurd price."[70]

And Pierpont could be disarmed by sentiment. One dealer tried to sell him a manuscript collection that included Poe's *Tamerlane* and Hawthorne's *Blithedale Romance*. When Morgan wouldn't budge, the dealer played his trump card. He noted a Longfellow poem about his grandchildren that, the dealer said, reminded him of Pierpont and *his* grandchildren. "Let me see it," replied Morgan. He put on his spectacles, read the poem, then pounded the table. "I'll take the collection."[71]

The scale of Pierpont's collection was so outsize—it included 225 works of ivory, 140 pieces of majolica, 150 works of Continental silver, and so on—that vanity alone cannot explain it. Rather, it was founded in an impulse that paralleled his banking ambition—to put America on a par with the European civilization he so admired. As in banking, he honored Old World traditions even as he ransacked them. It was said he wished to acquire a collection so huge that Americans wouldn't have to travel to Europe for culture. After 1897, he gave steadily to the Metropolitan Museum of Art and became its board president in 1904. The board of trustees often met in his house. To mount a patriotic assault on European masterpieces, he packed the board with millionaire friends—Frick, Harkness, Rogers, and other industrial captains. In 1905, he brought Sir Purdon Clarke from the South Kensington Museum to direct the museum and then Bloomsbury art critic, Roger Fry, as its curator of paintings. Fry would later taunt Pierpont for his "perfect insensibility" and "crude historical imagination."[72] But the high quality of the Morgan collection would be proof against Fry's petty gibes.

In 1904, after acquiring the townhouse next-door to 13 Princes Gate, he considered converting the two buildings into a museum as a memorial to his father. He also hoped to create memorials to Junius in the four cities in which he had lived—Holyoke, Massachusetts, Hartford, Boston, and London. After deciding that the enlarged London house still couldn't encompass his collection, he commemorated Junius by building the $1.4-million Morgan Memorial in Hartford, doubling the size of that city's art museum, the Wadsworth Atheneum. This single bequest, Pierpont's largest, surpassed the $1 million he had given to the Harvard Medical School in 1901 to honor his father.

A final note on Pierpont's collection concerns the rashness with which he financed it. Usually buying art during the summer, he would postpone payment until early the next year—extraordinary to think of the world's foremost banker buying art on credit! As early as 1902, Teddy Grenfell noted in his journal "vague and disquieting rumors" in the City about the Morgan banks' financial soundness as a result of the whirlwind art collecting.[73] He also noted the tension when the time came to settle these purchases at the London or Paris offices. The sums weren't trivial. At Pierpont's death, the collection was valued at an estimated $50 million, or nearly half his entire fortune.

This nonstop buying posed a potential threat to Pierpont's banking capital. This was especially serious because he chose partners for their talent, not to inject fresh capital into the business. It was one of the House of Morgan's glories that poor boys could join its exclusive club.

Yet Pierpont didn't always husband his capital. Years later, Morgan partner Russell C. Leffingwell passed along the insider stories about the problems created by the art sprees. "The notion that the elder Morgan bought pictures and tapestries partly to make money is certainly contrary to the fact," he told a colleague. "It was a self-indulgence on a magnificent scale, and a source of great anxiety and at times weakness to his firm, which could well have used the money as capital in the business if he had not spent it so lavishly."[74] In the last analysis, the collector's impulse to spend won out over the banker's impulse to save.

CHAPTER SEVEN

PANIC

. .

.

T HE folk wisdom of Wall Street says that if a crash is widely expected, it won't occur, for a saving fear will filter through the
marketplace. This was refuted in 1907, when Wall Street spent a cliff-
hanging year awaiting the crash that *came*. On March 25, panic selling
roiled the Stock Exchange. The financial powers—Henry Clay Frick,
Edward H. Harriman, William Rockefeller, and Jacob Schiff—assembled
at the Corner for a secret meeting. They wanted a $25-million pool to
steady prices. Jack cabled Pierpont in London, saying Schiff "thought
amount of money really needed would be very small, as moral effect of
concerted action on part of large interests heretofore antagonistic would
be sufficient without actual purchases."[1] While Jack favored cooperation, Pierpont fired back a hostile cable, saying such an action "would
be unwise, entirely at variance with all the policies we have ever adopted
being at the head of a declared Stock Exchange manipulation."[2] The
next day, the market rallied—partly on the basis of incorrect reports
that Pierpont had joined relief efforts—and the plan was scrapped. All
spring, as Pierpont cruised around Europe, his partners wired him that
a serious autumn drop appeared likely.

At age seventy, Pierpont was often in low spirits. In photographs, his
eyes look slightly unfocused, as if telling of inner turmoil. The October
1907 panic found him at the Episcopal Convention in Richmond, Virginia. As a lay delegate from New York, he would attend these conventions in opulent style, bringing bishops down by private railroad car and
throwing parties catered by Louis Sherry. Nothing pleased him more
than recondite controversies over prayer-book revisions and other matters remote from the material world. At the same time, the contradictory
Pierpont brought with him a lady friend, Mrs. John Markoe of Philadel-

phia, a relative of his personal physician, Dr. James Markoe, and often mentioned as a possible mistress.

As the Richmond convention progressed, emergency telegrams came in thick and fast from 23 Wall Street. Morgan's friend Bishop William Lawrence noted in his diary how Morgan would study the telegrams, place his palms on the table, then stare fixedly ahead. Though Pierpont was needed on Wall Street, his partners feared a premature return might itself touch off a panic. By Saturday, October 19, he decided to rush back by private railroad car to deal with a spreading bank crisis. "They are in trouble in New York," he told Bishop Lawrence. "They do not know what to do, and I don't know what to do, but I am going back."[3]

The 1907 panic was Pierpont's last hurrah. Although semiretired, reporting to work periodically for only an hour or two, he suddenly functioned as America's central bank. Within two week's time, he saved several trust companies and a leading brokerage house, bailed out New York City, and rescued the Stock Exchange. His victory was Pyrrhic, however, as America decided that never again would one man wield such power. The 1907 panic would be the last time that bankers loomed so much larger than regulators in a crisis. Afterward, the pendulum would swing decidedly toward government financial management.

The panic was blamed on many factors—tight money, Roosevelt's Gridiron Club speech attacking the "malefactors of great wealth," and excessive speculation in copper, mining, and railroad stocks. The immediate weakness arose from the recklessness of the trust companies. In the early 1900s, national and most state-chartered banks couldn't take trust accounts (wills, estates, and so on) but directed customers to trusts. Traditionally, these had been synonymous with safe investment. By 1907, however, they had exploited enough legal loopholes to become highly speculative. To draw money for risky ventures, they paid exorbitant interest rates, and trust executives operated like stock market plungers. They loaned out so much against stocks and bonds that by October 1907 as much as half the bank loans in New York were backed by securities as collateral—an extremely shaky base for the system. The trusts also didn't keep the high cash reserves of commercial banks and were vulnerable to sudden runs.

That Pierpont rescued the trusts was ironic, for they were anathema to the Wall Street establishment. As George Perkins said, "Indeed, we hadn't any use for their management and knew that they ought to be closed, but we fought to keep them open in order not to have runs on other concerns."[4] When J. P. Morgan and other prestigious houses referred clients to them for trust work, the unscrupulous trusts tried to steal the nontrust business of these clients. Two young bankers, Henry Pomeroy Davison of the First National Bank and Thomas W. Lamont of Liberty Bank, were among those who in 1903 set up a "captive" trust called Bankers Trust. Although commercial banks couldn't do trust business, they could own trusts, and they pooled their money to set up the new bank. The idea was that the House of Morgan and its allies would refer trust business to Bankers Trust, which would politely return the customers once their trust business was complete. By no accident, the Morgan bank would stare vigilantly at Bankers Trust across the Corner of Broad and Wall.

On Monday, October 21, the day after Pierpont returned from Richmond, a collapse in copper shares undermined the trusts. There were fears of a copper glut, spurred partly by news that the Morgans would join the Guggenheims in developing new Alaskan copper mines. When an attempt to corner United Copper burst, its stock skidded 35 points in just two hours, spreading ruin and dragging stocks to levels unseen since the 1893 depression. Charles T. Barney, president of Knickerbocker Trust, was associated with F. Augustus Heinze and other speculators who had cornered United Copper. So the stock's fall alarmed the Knickerbocker's eighteen thousand depositors. At its new main office at Thirty-fourth Street and Fifth Avenue, customers lined up on Tuesday morning to empty their accounts.

As panic spread to other trusts around town, Pierpont took charge of the rescue operation. Emergencies seemed to fortify his confidence even as they introduced doubt or terror in others. He formed a committee of young bankers, including Henry Pomeroy Davison of the First National Bank and Benjamin Strong of Bankers Trust. He sent them to audit the Knickerbocker's books. Later, as all-powerful governor of the New York Federal Reserve Bank, Strong would recall peering out at grim depositors from the bank's back room. "The consternation of the faces of the people in the line, many of them I knew, I shall never forget. I know that Harry left the building with a sense of dejection and defeat which it is quite impossible for me to describe." Pierpont wrote off the Knickerbocker as hopeless and it failed on Tuesday afternoon, October 22.[5] "I can't go on being everybody's goat," he said. "I've got to stop somewhere."[6] A few weeks later, refused admission to see Pierpont, Charles Barney of the Knickerbocker shot himself, an act that produced a wave of suicides among the bank's depositors.

On Tuesday night, Pierpont and other bankers met at a Manhattan hotel with Treasury Secretary George B. Cortelyou, who pledged cooperation. The next day, Cortelyou put $25 million in government funds at

Pierpont's disposal. It was an extraordinary transference of power to a private banker and further proof of Teddy Roosevelt's high regard for Morgan.

The Knickerbocker's failure triggered runs on other trusts, especially the Trust Company of America, which was just down Wall Street from the Morgan bank. On Wednesday, October 23, Pierpont summoned the trust presidents and tried to prod them into a rescue pool. It turned out they didn't know one another, making it difficult for them to band together in a crisis. The situation illustrated why bankers believed implicitly in their old-boy networks. After Ben Strong delivered a favorable report on the Trust Company of America, Pierpont made his *ex cathedra* pronouncement: "This is the place to stop the trouble, then."[7] Morgan, George F. Baker of First National Bank, and James Stillman of National City Bank provided $3 million to save the Trust Company of America.

For two weeks, Morgan and his associates stood fast against a spreading typhoon. As panic increased, depositors thronged banks across the city. People sat overnight in camp chairs, bringing food and waiting for the banks to open in the morning. New York police distributed numbers to people to save their places; in other cases, exhausted depositors paid enterprising standees to wait for them. (A later Wall Street eminence, Sidney Weinberg of Goldman, Sachs, earned $10 a day holding down places in line.) To reduce withdrawals and avert the need for shutdowns, trust tellers counted out the money in slow motion, like people in a trance.

Strapped for cash, the trusts called in margin loans from stock market speculators. The price of call money—that is, the interest rate on margin loans to buy stocks—zoomed to 150 percent. Nevertheless, there remained a shortage of ready funds. Perkins cabled Jack, who was in London: "At all times during the day there were frantic men and women in our offices, in every way giving evidence of the tremendous strain they were under."[8] Pierpont was accosted by hundreds of distraught brokers who faced ruin and pleaded for help. Photographs of the Corner show dense throngs of men in derbies and dark coats, solidly massed along Wall Street in somber ranks. For these terrified men, Morgan emerged as the Redeemer, the one man who could save them. In a human wave, they surged right to the door of 23 Wall, where "the struggling mob fought their way on, all looking up at the windows of J. P. Morgan & Co."[9]

On Thursday, October 24, with stock trading virtually halted, New York Stock Exchange president Ransom H. Thomas crossed Broad Street and told Morgan that unless $25 million were raised immediately, at least fifty brokerage firms might fail. Thomas wanted to shut the Exchange. "At what time do you usually close it?" Morgan asked—though the Stock Exchange was twenty paces from his office, Pierpont didn't know its hours: stock trading was vulgar. "Why, at three o'clock," said Thomas. Pierpont wagged an admonitory finger. "It must not close one minute before that hour today."[10] At two o'clock, Morgan summoned the bank presidents and warned that dozens of brokerage houses might fail unless they mustered $25 million within ten or twelve minutes. By 2:16, the money was pledged. Morgan then dispatched a team to the Stock Exchange floor to announce that call money would be available at as low as 10 percent. One team member, Amory Hodges, had his waistcoat torn off in the violent tumult. Then a blessed moment occurred in Morgan annals: as news of the rescue circulated through the Exchange, Pierpont heard a mighty roar across the street. Looking up, he asked the cause: he was being given an ovation by the jubilant floor traders.

The next day, call money soared again to extortionate rates. Eight banks and trust companies had already failed during the week. Pierpont went to the New York Clearing House, the banker's trade group for clearing checks, and got it to issue scrip as a temporary emergency currency to relieve the serious cash shortage. Herbert L. Satterlee has left a wonderful vignette of his father-in-law returning to 23 Wall. It shows why contemporaries saw Morgan as the incarnation of pure will:

Anyone who saw Mr. Morgan going from the Clearing House back to his office that day will never forget the picture. With his coat unbuttoned and flying open, a piece of white paper clutched tightly in his right hand, he walked fast down Nassau Street. His flat-topped black derby hat was set firmly down on his head. Between his teeth he held the paper cigar holder in which was one of his long cigars, half smoked. His eyes were fixed straight ahead. He swung his arms as he walked and took no notice of anyone. He did not seem to see the throngs in the street, so intent was his mind on the thing that he was doing. Everyone knew him, and people made way for him, except some who were equally intent on their own affairs; and these he brushed aside. The thing that made his progress different from that of all the other people on the street was that he did not dodge, or walk in and out, or halt or slacken his pace. He simply barged along, as if he had been the only man going down Nassau Street hill past the Subtreasury. He was the embodiment of power and purpose.[11]

That Friday night, Pierpont called in city religious leaders and asked them to preach calm in their Sunday sermons. Archbishop Farley held a special Sunday mass for businessmen. Grappling with a bad cold that had dogged him for days, Pierpont went up to Cragston for the weekend. On Monday, October 28, New York City mayor George B. McClellan came to the Morgan Library with another serious brush fire to extinguish. Alarmed by events on Wall Street, European investors were withdrawing money from America, and the city couldn't place its warrants abroad. The city needed $30 million to cover its obligations, McClellan said. Morgan, Baker, and Stillman agreed to provide the needed money—the first of four Morgan-led rescues of New York City in this century. In a bravura performance, the seventy-year-old Pierpont extemporaneously drafted a letter-perfect contract on Morgan Library stationery. He also demanded a bankers' committee to monitor the city's bookkeeping practices, a feature of later New York City crises as well.

For a seventy-year-old man with a bad cold, Pierpont handled the 1907 panic like a virtuoso. He sucked lozenges and worked nineteen-hour days. He said that he missed Jack. At moments, his physician, Dr. Markoe, plied his throat with sprays and gargles, as if the banker were an aging boxing champ being resuscitated between rounds. The doctor also extracted a pledge that Pierpont would cut down his cigar consumption to only twenty a day! When he dozed during an emergency meeting, nobody dared disturb the royal snooze. One banker "reached forward and lifted from the relaxed fingers, as one might take a rattle from a baby, the big cigar that was scorching the varnish on the table."[12] For a half hour, he was fast asleep as bankers discussed a $10-million loan.

During the 1907 panic, Pierpont proved that American finance could aspire to high drama. In an elaborate finale on Saturday night, November 2, he devised a rescue for the still-shaky Trust Company of America, for Lincoln Trust, and for Moore and Schley, a speculative brokerage house that was $25 million in debt. This last company held a gigantic majority stake in the Tennessee Coal and Iron Company as collateral against loans. If it had to liquidate that stake, it might collapse the stock market. If Moore and Schley, in turn, collapsed, it might topple other houses as well.

Like an impresario creating his theatrical masterpiece, Pierpont gathered the city's bankers at his library. He settled commercial bankers in the East Room, beneath signs of the zodiac and a tapestry of the seven deadly sins, while in the West Room trust-company presidents sank into deep red couches and armchairs beneath the gaze of saints and Madonnas. In between, like Jupiter above the fray, Pierpont played solitaire in Belle Greene's office.

One spectator was Tom Lamont, now a vice-president of Bankers Trust. Then only an "experienced errand boy," as he said, he was entranced by the pageantry. Of Pierpont's successors, only Lamont would possess the flair to stage such events. He recalled: "A more incongruous meeting place for anxious bankers could hardly be imagined. In one room were lofty, magnificent tapestries hanging on the walls, rare Bibles and illuminated manuscripts of the Middle Ages filling the cases; in another, that collection of the Early Renaissance masters—Castagno, Ghirlandaio, Perugino, to mention only a few—the huge open fire, the door just ajar to the holy of holies where the original manuscripts were guarded."[13]

To save Moore and Schley, Pierpont wanted some payoff for himself. With his usual sense of martyrdom, he felt it was his due. With his peculiar bifocal vision, he saw the panic as a time for both statesmanship and personal gain. At this point, he told friends that he had done enough and wanted some *quid pro quo.* He now took an appropriately big fee.

Pierpont hatched a scheme that would save Moore & Schley, avert its need to sell the Tennessee Coal and Iron block in the open market, and benefit his favorite creation, U.S. Steel. He knew U.S. Steel could profit from Tennessee Coal's huge iron ore and coal holdings in Tennessee, Alabama, and Georgia. For antitrust reasons, it was a prize unattainable under ordinary circumstances. So he struck a deal: U.S. Steel would buy Tennessee Coal stock from Moore and Schley *if* the hesitant trust-company presidents assembled a $25-million pool to protect the weaker trusts. What a characteristic mix of high and low motives!

Ben Strong noticed that Pierpont had locked the enormous bronze doors and pocketed the key. He was up to his old tricks—confinement of adversaries, a deadline, the abrupt appearance of the menacing host after long hours of bargaining. At a quarter to five in the morning, Pierpont pushed a gold pen into the hand of Edward King, leader of the trust presidents. "Here's the place, King. And here's the pen."[14] Beaten down by all-night bargaining, King and the other trust company presidents agreed to contribute to the $25-million pool.

On Sunday night, Henry Clay Frick and Judge Elbert Gary of U.S. Steel sped down to Washington on a midnight train. They traveled in a single Pullman car specially hitched up to a locomotive. They had to secure Roosevelt's approval for U.S. Steel's takeover of Tennessee Coal and Iron before the stock market opened on Monday morning. They ended up interrupting Roosevelt in the middle of his breakfast; mindful of the panic, TR said it was "no public duty of his to interpose any objections."[15] In other words, the Sherman Antitrust Act wouldn't be used against U.S. Steel. Five minutes before the stock market opened at 10:00 A.M., Gary called 23 Wall Street from the White House and told George Perkins that the president had agreed to the plan. The stock market rallied on the news.

Immediately, there were charges that Pierpont had duped Roosevelt into scuttling his antitrust policy and sanctioning, under duress, an anticompetitive steel merger. Wisconsin senator Robert La Follette even said the bankers had rigged up the panic for their own profit. Certainly the $45-million distress sale price of Tennessee Coal and Iron was a steal. Financial analyst John Moody later said that the company's property had a potential value of about $1 billion. Grant B. Schley, head of Moore and Schley, also admitted later that his firm could have been rescued by an outright cash infusion rather than the purchase of the Tennessee Coal stock. So there was far more than altruism at work in the famous all-night rescue of the firm.

Despite this controversy, Pierpont reached the zenith of his influence with the 1907 panic. As his biographer Frederick Lewis Allen wrote, "Where there had been many principalities, there was now one kingdom, and it was Morgan's."[16] Pierpont was suddenly not a pirate but a sage. Woodrow Wilson, then president of Princeton University, said the nation should be advised on its future by a panel of intellectuals, and he recommended Pierpont Morgan as its chairman.[17] The tributes, nonetheless, coincided with new concern about America's financial system. U.S. financial panics recurred with worrisome regularity, every ten years. The 1907 panic exposed many systemic defects. As people hoarded money and banks called in loans, there was no central bank to instill confidence or offset the sudden credit contraction. Sharp drops in the money supply then led to severe recessions. The country needed an elastic currency and a permanent lender of last resort.

From the ashes of 1907 arose the Federal Reserve System: everybody saw that thrilling rescues by corpulent old tycoons were a tenuous prop for the banking system. Senator Nelson W. Aldrich declared, "Something has got to be done. We may not always have Pierpont Morgan with us to meet a banking crisis."[18] By confirming his storied powers, Pierpont also inadvertently fostered talk of an omnipotent Wall Street money trust. President Roosevelt now recommended federal regulation of the stock exchanges, while New York governor Charles Evans Hughes wanted margin requirements raised from 10 to 20 percent. If these suggestions had been enacted, the country might have been spared some of the lurid excesses of the 1929 crash.

The one direct consequence of the 1907 panic was a universal clamor for banking reform. In 1908, Congress passed the Aldrich-Vreeland Currency Act, which created the National Monetary Commission to study changes in the banking system. The commission was chaired by Senator Aldrich of Rhode Island, and the House of Morgan quickly moved to exert influence on it. Perkins cabled Pierpont in London that he and George F. Baker, the walrus-mustached head of the First National Bank, had stayed away from Washington, lest the new legislation be seen as a Wall Street plot. At the same time, Perkins sent a coded cable saying that Harry Davison, Baker's young protégé, would be Aldrich's adviser: "It is understood that Davison is to represent our views and will be particularly close to Senator Aldrich."[19] Davison had been Pierpont's cool lieutenant during the 1907 panic and had greatly impressed him. When the Aldrich commission was about to depart for a tour of Europe's central banks, Davison went ahead to confer with Pierpont, who wanted a private central bank on the Bank of England model. Davison would be the only banker to accompany the senators and congressmen on their mission.

A central bank was by no means supported by all Democrats. William Jennings Bryan and the Populists feared that a central bank would be dominated by the same hard-money men who ran Wall Street. They saw it as an institution that would slay the silverites. In many ways, the concept was associated more with conservative, hard-money men. Pierpont was amenable to central banks so long as they were private and had boards composed of bankers. As Pierpont's man on the commission, Davison reflected his mentor's uncompromising preference for banker rather than politician control of a central bank. He also expected such a bank to introduce a "level playing field" and end the competitive advantage of the trusts.

In November 1910, in what was billed to the press as a "duck-shooting holiday," Davison (now a Morgan partner) and other Wall Street bankers met secretly at the Jekyll Island Club, a palm-shaded seaside compound of turreted buildings off the Georgia coast and a favorite Morgan hideaway. Known as the resort of the one hundred millionaires, Jekyll Island claimed among its organizers Pierpont's chum George F. Baker. Pierpont kept an apartment in its San Souci building. The Jekyll Island meeting would be the fountain of a thousand conspiracy theories. Here Wall Street bankers worked out their plan for a central bank under private aegis, a system of regional reserve banks topped by a governing board of commercial bankers. Davison, an architect of the meeting, not only got a suspicious stationmaster in Brunswick, Georgia, to keep quiet about his suspicions, but often led the discussion. As Paul M. Warburg of Kuhn, Loeb, one of the key theoreticians at the meeting, later said, "Davison had an uncanny gift in sensing the proper moment for changing the topic, for giving the discussion a timely new turn, thus avoiding a clash or deadlock."[20]

When Senator Aldrich presented his bill for a central bank to Congress in 1910, the Democrats blocked it. In 1913, Congressman Carter Glass, a Virginia Democrat, used it as the basis for the Federal Reserve Act, although making extensive modifications. President Wilson successfully demanded that the system of twelve private regional reserve banks be placed under a central political authority, a Washington board that would include the Treasury secretary and presidential appointees. Progressives hoped the Federal Reserve would reduce the House of Morgan's unique power. As we shall see, the truth was far more complex, for the bank would skillfully harness the Fed and use it to amplify its powers. In an ironic outcome unforeseen by reformers, it would become the private bank of choice for central banks throughout the world, giving it an incalculable new advantage.

WHEN the Republican president William Howard Taft took office in 1909, the wily George Perkins flattered himself, thinking that he had already wormed his way into its inner council. Taft sent him a confidential draft of his inaugural address, which was "in all respects conciliatory and harmonizing in tone," Perkins reported to Pierpont.[21] He felt convinced Taft would water down the troublesome Sherman Antitrust Act. In coded cables to Morgan, who was vacationing in Egypt, Perkins made it sound as if he alone had picked the new cabinet. "Acting on suggestion made solely by me 2 weeks ago Franklin Mac-Veagh Chicago has been selected for Secretary of Treasury. Wickersham will be Attorney General and other places are filled to our entire satisfaction."[22]

Yet the one-term Taft administration would be deeply ambivalent toward the House of Morgan. On the surface, it would seem even more hostile than Roosevelt's and surprisingly aggressive in battling the trusts. It filed antitrust suits against two cherished Morgan progeny—U.S. Steel and International Harvester. The Taft years also saw the dismemberment of John D. Rockefeller's Standard Oil trust and James B. Duke's American Tobacco trust. For all his windy attacks on the trusts, Teddy Roosevelt had been far more circumspect about translating his words into tough action.

Yet there was more to the Taft-Morgan relationship than a progressive crusade against a Wall Street cabal. If trust-busting made good political theater, the deeper story was one of foreign collaboration. Even as Washington chastised the banks at home, it was forging them into foreign-loan syndicates in a new age of dollar diplomacy. With the U.S. defeat of Spain and the colonization of the Philippines and Puerto Rico, the country had acquired a new taste for imperialist adventure, and the House of Morgan would be one of its main instruments.

Henceforth, much of the Morgan saga revolves around incestuous dealings between the Morgan banks in New York and London and their respective governments, intrigue that would drape them in mysterious new raiment. The Baronial Age was one of unbridled *laissez-faire*, marked by often unqualified hostility on the part of bankers toward government. But in the dawning Diplomatic Age, there would be an explicit fusion of financial and government power. In time, it would become hard to disentangle the House of Morgan from various aspects of Anglo-American policy. Yet there would also be spectacular instances in which Morgan policy would take on a clandestine life of its own, diverging from official dictates.

The new alliance was mutually advantageous. Washington wanted to harness the new financial power to coerce foreign governments into opening their markets to American goods or adopting pro-American policies. The banks, in turn, needed levers to force debt repayment and welcomed the government's police powers in distant places. The threat of military intervention was an excellent means by which to speed loan repayment. When Kuhn, Loeb considered a loan to the Dominican Republic, backed by customs receipts, Jacob Schiff inquired of his London associate Sir Ernest Cassel, "If they do not pay, who will collect these customs duties?" Cassel replied, "Your marines and ours."[23]

During its first year, the Taft administration recruited the House of Morgan in a scheme to create a financial protectorate over Honduras and bail out British bondholders at the same time. As part of a debt settlement, the bank would buy up old Honduran bonds, which were selling at a steep discount in London. Secretary of State Philander Knox would then impose an American lien on Honduran custom-house receipts and sell new Honduran bonds through a Morgan syndicate. The scheme would be backed up by American military might. Although Senator William Alden Smith, for one, was irate that the State Department supported the Morgan scheme, the bank had actually been dragooned by the government. Serving only prime government clients, the House of Morgan had a supercilious attitude toward small, backward countries. As Jack said in a cable to the London office, "Negotiations only undertaken because U.S. Government anxious get Honduras settled."[24] He and Harry Davison refused to proceed without a treaty that provided ironclad guarantees for the bonds. After enraged mobs besieged the Honduran assembly, protesting threats to their sovereignty, the U.S. Senate vetoed the deal, and the operation was scrapped.

The new era was most vividly adumbrated in China. As with Honduras, the House of Morgan had no great relish for such a foreign operation. Backward and sprawling, lacking a central army and modern budgeting, *fin-de-siècle* China had proved exasperating for foreign bankers. Its officials excelled in playing off one group of foreign creditors against another. (The bankers were accused of exploiting the same strategy with Chinese officials.) This not only bred resentment among bankers but fostered a decided Wall Street prejudice in favor of China's ancient enemy, Japan.

The French, Germans, and British were already well entrenched in China, controlling their own spheres of influence. The European bankers had entered the picture in the late nineteenth century, when provincial Chinese merchants lacked the necessary capital to build railroads. In 1899, Secretary of State John Hay had declared an "open door" policy toward China that was supposed to guarantee unrestricted foreign access. Under Taft, however, the open door was converted into a blunt U.S. demand for inclusion in China on an equal basis with the European powers.

In 1909, the State Department prodded a reluctant Wall Street to undertake Chinese business. A consortium of British, French, and German banks had nearly completed negotiations for a $25-million loan for the Hukuang Railway, which ran from Shanghai to Canton. Much to the European's dismay, the State Department demanded an equal share for U.S. bankers. As Herbert Croly wrote, "The majority of these bankers had gone into the Group not because they were seeking Chinese investments but in order to oblige the administration."[25]

The State Department placed the House of Morgan at the head of an American Bankers Group that included Kuhn, Loeb, the National City Bank, and the First National Bank. Only a few years before, these firms had viciously quarreled during the Northern Pacific corner. Now Washington was welding them into an instrument of national purpose, believing that banker unity would magnify American influence abroad. When

Jack cabled his father in London about the arrangement, Pierpont couldn't suppress his competitive instincts. "Strikes me favorably," he responded, "but, strictly confidential and for your own use only, important J. P. M. & Co. take lead and name mentioned first. Suppose fact already recognized but must not be overlooked."[26]

The American Group met at 23 Wall Street, with Harry Davison in the chair but the State Department pulling the strings. Ordinarily commanding and good-humored, Davison chafed at the controls. He instructed Teddy Grenfell in London, "Think it would be very wise if you would casually but firmly point out to those with whom you come in contact that this is a proposition of the Government and not of the Bankers."[27] The popular press applauded the latest salvo in the Morgan–White House wars and fancied that trustbusters now had bankers on the run. Meanwhile, Davison moaned: "Continue to be governed entirely by wishes of State Department."[28] For bankers who had prided themselves in their fierce independence from government, this new straitjacket was hard to tolerate.

Teddy Grenfell, partner in J. S. Morgan and Company (soon to be Morgan Grenfell) represented the American group in its dealings with the British, French, and German banker groups of the China consortium. Now and in the future, he would be an important intermediary between 23 Wall Street and the British government. Bolted together internally, the Morgan banks acted autonomously in many matters. It was a tricky situation, fraught with conflicts, for the New York and London houses were always sensitive to requests from their respective governments. In 1908, for example, J. S. Morgan and Company withheld a Turkish loan at the Foreign Office's behest, then extended it the following year when bureaucratic winds shifted. So long as British and American interests coincided, this situation posed no problem. But a conflict was buried here that would later tear apart the Anglo-American Morgan empire. However much it might camouflage it, the House of Morgan wasn't a multinational bank but an American bank with partnerships abroad. Many times, it would be impossible to appease both the United States and Britain.

From 1909 to 1913, the American Group served as a conduit for all Morgan dealings with China. Its representative in China was the most dashing, adventurous agent in Morgan history—Willard Dickerman Straight. Straight's life reads like a spy thriller. Fresh out of Cornell, he worked for the Imperial Maritime Customs Service in Peking and studied Mandarin. In 1904, he went to Japan to report on the Russo-Japanese War for Reuters and the Associated Press. A friend in those years described him as "tall, slim, with reddish-brown hair, of unusual frankness and charm of manner."[29] While reporting from Seoul, Korea, he met Edward H. Harriman at a dinner, an experience that transformed his life. Harriman then controlled the Union Pacific Railroad and the Pacific Mail steamship line, which he saw as the first two legs of a round-the-world transportation system. He recruited the enthusiastic Straight to win the critical China rail link. Then, in 1906, Teddy Roosevelt invited Straight to the White House, saying he was signing up bright young Ivy Leaguers to join the Foreign Service and drum up business for American companies abroad. To assist Harriman's venture, Roosevelt assigned Straight—then only in his twenties—to be the U.S. consul general in Mukden, a bustling rail center in Manchuria. He would be the sole State Department representative north of the Great Wall.

In those days, Manchuria was colorfully described as the cockpit of Asia, the place where Russian and Japanese imperial interests clashed and European powers vied for influence. Nobody could have savored this romantic crossroads more than Willard Straight. He was an improbable mix of frank imperialist and young idealist, viewing American bankers as a buffer against Japanese and Russian encroachment in Manchuria. Cloaking dollar diplomacy in a mantle of altruism, he thought unity among foreign bankers would prevent any single country from exploiting China. This argument would eventually be exposed as a self-serving American delusion. But Straight was young and ardent and easily convinced himself of his mission of salvation.

An intimate of mandarins in the Manchu court, he had a poetic sensibility, sketching watercolors of queued street vendors and illustrating a book about China. He sang Kiplingesque lyrics as he strummed his guitar and loved the themes of imperial conquest. His letters were spiced with vivid, exotic imagery, describing China as "the storm center of world politics," a place "where everyone more or less is spying on everyone else."[30] In 1909, he met one of America's richest heiresses, Dorothy Whitney, and they became engaged two years later. She was the orphaned daughter of William C. Whitney, a former navy secretary who had made a fortune in tobacco, traction, automobiles, and stock market speculation, and she had inherited $7 million. Recently president of the Junior League in New York, she was touring China when she met Straight. She had a wild, romantic sensibility that matched his own. In Peking, she recalled, they "walked along the city wall at sunset time and watched the soft glow of the distant purple hills."[31] Dorothy and Willard Straight would pass through the turbulence of revolutionary

China with the cool insouciance of a couple in an elegant Hollywood farce.

In 1909, Straight was appointed representative of the American Bankers Group. He had enough youthful idealism to be disturbed by much of what he saw within the group. During the summer of 1910, he worked at 23 Wall Street—he thought the address a good omen, because the street number was the same as Dorothy's birthday—and was appalled at the way the House of Morgan bossed around the State Department. Davison might chafe at government control, but Straight saw things quite differently. When Pierpont instructed Davison, "You might as well make it clear that when we want to discuss things with the U.S. Government we want [the secretary of state] and not [the assistant secretary],"[32] Straight commented sardonically, "It was not difficult to see where the real power lies in this country."[33] Pierpont might have been so imperious because the secretary of state was Philander C. Knox, who, as attorney general under Roosevelt, had filed the suit against the Northern Securities Company. Knox dutifully came to 23 Wall whenever he wished to speak to the American Group.

In 1910, the China enterprise expanded beyond the railway loan to include a massive $50-million loan to China for currency reform. Willard rhapsodized about the new loan to Dorothy: "It's history . . . and big history at that—the game for an empire."[34] The Chinese objected to a provision that required a Western adviser as a new overseer of Chinese finances. As a compromise, a Dutchman was unobtrusively slipped into the post. In 1911, Straight and representatives from England, France, and Germany signed the loan with Chinese officials. Willard wrote excitedly to Dorothy, "We've arranged it so that we can practically dictate the terms of China's currency reform. When you think of holding the whip hand in formulating the first real sound financial basis for a country of 400 million, it's quite a proposition."[35]

The loan generated worldwide publicity and made Straight an instant hero. Along with his prestigious association with the House of Morgan, the China loan helped reconcile Dorothy's family to her marrying beneath her social station. Teddy Roosevelt interceded to plead Willard's cause. Dorothy belonged to the polo-playing set of Locust Valley and Westbury, two Long Island communities rich in Morgan partners. Robert Bacon and his wife had been almost substitute parents after her own parents died, and she knew Pierpont as well. "Dear Mr. J.P. he's such a sweetie underneath the sternness," she wrote to Willard.[36] In fact,

Straight may have clung to the Morgan position longer than he wanted to because of its social utility.

Straight's naive hopes about the China loan were soon to be dashed by geopolitical realities. He and the bankers had cast their lot with the corrupt Manchu dynasty, which was oblivious to turmoil beyond the palace walls. Straight himself grew disillusioned with the "selfish, narrow-minded bigotry" of the Chinese officials. Yet he wanted to perpetuate the Manchu dynasty to save the loan. He was caught up with the wrong issues; he was worrying about the composition of banking syndicates and missed the popular revulsion from *all* foreign bankers. At a Paris conference on China's finances in 1912, the Japanese and Russians demanded—and obtained—inclusion in the China consortium. This was Straight's nightmare: the group now included China's traditional enemies. Bankers, he saw, couldn't operate in a void but were enmeshed in larger political forces. Gloomily he foresaw "the inevitable day when China's finances will be administered like Egypt's—by an international board. Another dream shattered!"[37]

In 1911, a nationalist revolution in China, fueled partly by resentment of foreign bankers, ousted the Manchu dynasty and declared a republic. The liberal, activist Dorothy Straight was sympathetic to the revolutionaries. In January 1912, Sun Yat-sen became provisional president, heading a movement seeking to unify China and stop foreign meddling. Willard and Dorothy witnessed the panicky exodus of Manchu nobles from a Peking aflutter with radical banners. Willard slept with a loaded revolver by his side. The imaginative Dorothy thrived on the danger, writing, "It would be rather exciting to be attacked by a wild mob in the night."[38]

One evening as the Straights were getting ready to dine with a British neighbor, shooting did erupt nearby. As Willard recalled, "The pop, pop, popping continued and our roof lines stood out sharply against the glow of the first fire. I told Dorothy that it looked like trouble. She didn't mind a bit, but went on dressing for dinner, calm as you please, and objected strenuously when I advised her to get into street dress in order that, if necessary, we could clear out to the Legation."[39] During a pause in the fighting, they made it over to the neighbor's for dinner. But then soldiers began smashing and looting stores nearby. After gathering up their maid and proper clothing, they fled for the safety of the legation but were trapped by rioters on a dead-end street. Finally they were rescued by a contingent of American marines. Piling into a rickshaw, bags strapped to the back, Dorothy and Willard managed to thread their way through pillaging mobs to the legation.[40]

This Morgan foray into China ended with Woodrow Wilson's election and the elevation of that Morgan *bête noire*, William Jennings Bryan, to secretary of state. On March 10, 1913, Harry Davison and Willard Straight visited the new secretary of state in Washington. (Unlike Knox, Bryan would never deign to travel to 23 Wall Street.) Bryan asked them flat out what the group expected from Washington if China defaulted. Davison didn't mince words and said the government might "be called upon to utilize both its military and naval forces to protect the interests of the lenders."[41] Neither Bryan nor Wilson sympathized with such foreign meddling. A week later, Wilson denounced the loan as "obnoxious to the principles upon which the government of our people rests."[42] The government was obviously withdrawing its support.

The next day, the American Bankers Group was effectively disbanded. As a creature of Washington, it couldn't survive without its blessing. Most bankers were relieved, for they had come to doubt China's willingness to repay the loan. The end of the China business wasn't mourned within the House of Morgan, either. As Teddy Grenfell, who had been consumed by it, wrote to Jack, "I think that all of us will have 'China' written on our hearts when we die, with several uncomplimentary epithets after it.' "[43] Yet the experience had bridged differences among big Wall Street banks and made them accustomed to working together abroad. Morgans, National City, and First National arrived at an understanding for participating together in all Latin lending. This Big Three agreement would vastly magnify Morgan power. (Kuhn, Loeb often formed a fourth member of their syndicates.) These same banks, ironically, would shortly be hauled before the Pujo Committee as the abominable Money Trust. What the public wouldn't know was that the Money Trust had been forged, in part, by Washington itself in its quest for foreign influence.

The new age of banker-government collaboration mellowed even the vehemently antigovernment Jack Morgan. After wrangling with Washington over a Honduran loan in 1912, he cabled Grenfell, "You will understand we do not wish accuse our own Government too loudly in view of necessary relations with them other foreign matters."[44] No less ideologically hostile to government than his father, Jack saw the need to mute his public anger. The days of brusque individualism were dead.

Willard Straight returned to work at 23 Wall, but never fit into a mundane office setting. In the 1912 election, he and Dorothy supported their friend from Oyster Bay, Teddy Roosevelt—an act that must have savored of subversive tendencies among the Morgan partners. They also secretly read Louis Brandeis's attacks against Morgan's handling of the

New Haven Railroad. In 1914, they were the financial angels for a new political weekly, *The New Republic,* which initially had a strongly pro-Roosevelt slant. Harry Davison and other partners spurned the chance to participate, and only Thomas Lamont joined them. Restless and adventurous, Willard found it hard to submit to a banker's discipline and chafed at not being made a Morgan partner. He was always concocting new schemes, such as the creation of India House on New York's Hanover Square, a club dedicated to foreign trade, which he outfitted with model ships and antiques. In the end, even the spacious universe of J. P. Morgan and Company would be too confining for the large, venturesome spirit of Willard Straight. He would last only another two years at the bank.

CHAPTER EIGHT

TITANIC

· ·

·

MOROSE and fatalistic in his last years, Pierpont felt misunderstood by the public and angered by the uproar over his trusts. He
shook his cane menacingly at reporters, a murderous gleam in his eyes.
He wouldn't admit to legitimate public curiosity about his affairs. At
Dover House in 1911, he burned the bound letters he had sent to Junius
for thirty-three years, destroying perhaps the most important chronicle
of Anglo-American finance in the late nineteenth century. He craved a
privacy impossible for the world's most famous banker. Like a ghost, he
brooded in the West Room of his library, beneath stained-glass windows
and thick draperies that muffled the sounds of a changing world.

He spent much of his time in Europe, escaping the din of Progressive
politics. His *wanderlust* never deserted him. From European spas, he
would notify Jack of the next stop on his itinerary, adding those ever
awkward words, "advise mother." He felt at home in many places. Once
asked to name his favorite spots, he replied, "New York, because it is
my home; London, because it is my second home; Rome and Khargeh."[1]

Egypt, in particular, held a mystical charm for him, and he visited it
three times in his last three years and helped to bankroll the Metropolitan Museum's Egyptian excavations. (One 1909 photograph shows an
oversize Pierpont on a small donkey galloping into the desert ahead of
his flabbergasted guides.) The excavations at Khargeh, four hundred
miles southwest of Cairo, so intrigued him that he asked Thomas Cook
and Sons to construct a steel Nile steamer named the *Khargeh*. From
this paddle-wheel boat, he would pitch coins into the water, which were
fished up by boys diving from the Nile's bank.

Pierpont was a lonely man, and fame probably only deepened his
isolation. His first biographer, Carl Hovey, wrote, "It is said there are

scarcely fifty men in the financial district who have a speaking acquaintance with Morgan."[2] Pierpont had a wide business acquaintance, but few associates knew him well. Hence, he relied on his family for emotional sustenance. This made especially bruising a feud with his youngest child, Anne Tracy, who was six years Jack's junior. Pierpont Morgan could conquer the world but not his daughter Anne. She was an athletic, spirited girl who liked golf and tennis and rebelled against her formal upbringing. Of all Pierpont's children, Anne most resembled him temperamentally: she was bright, stubborn, imperious, and highly opinionated. Elizabeth Drexel, later the wife of socialite Harry Lehr, recalled her as a "thin lanky child with an elfin face and penetrating eyes" but with "a personality and a will as strong as [Pierpont's] own and a disconcerting habit of putting her elders in the wrong."[3] Once, at a dinner party with Pierpont's cronies, her father peered down the table and asked her what she planned to be when she grew up. "Something better than a rich fool, anyway," she snapped.[4] Despite these gibes, she was close to her father and often accompanied him to Europe aboard *Corsair III*. Once, she served as host to the kaiser aboard the yacht.

By the early 1900s, Anne, now in her early thirties, had grown into a tall young woman with short hair swept back on the sides, a strong nose, dark eyebrows, and her father's intense gaze. She had his executive talents and childlike simplicity and hated cartoonists who mocked her father's nose. She was big and somewhat matronly but also stylish in dress. In 1903, Daisy Harriman, a famous Washington hostess, brought her in as a founder of the Colony Club, the first American ladies' club, patterned after a British gentlemen's club. At Thirtieth Street and Madison Avenue, it was designed by Stanford White and had a marble swimming pool and Turkish baths. Rules forbade men above the first floor. Pierpont had no sympathy for the project and lectured the ladies that "a woman's best and safest club is her own home."[5] Predictably, Dorothy Whitney was an early member.

During the founding of this project, Anne met two older women who would change her life. One was the stoutly mannish Bessie Marbury, the American theatrical agent for George Bernard Shaw and Oscar Wilde; the other was Elsie de Wolfe, the voguish former society girl and actress, now a famed interior designer for her work on the Colony Club. In 1908, Anne, thirty-five, entered into a *ménage à trois* with these two women at their Villa Trianon in Versailles. With its formal gardens, topiary, and trimmed lawns, the Villa Trianon was an incongruously aristocratic setting for such a daring arrangement. De Wolfe designed a dressing room that fit Anne's contradictory nature; on its formal mantelpiece were both a French bust and a leopard-skin velvet rug.

Over the years, these three patrician ladies pioneered in many cultural areas. They opened a Broadway dance hall and sponsored Cole Porter's first musical. They also took up many liberal and feminist causes. Anne supported the strike by women shirtwaist-workers, a largely Jewish group, inspected the sanitary conditions in factories, opened a temperance restaurant in Brooklyn, started a thrift association and vacation fund for young working women, and championed women's suffrage. On December 31, 1908, she lunched at the White House to discuss social welfare with Teddy Roosevelt, who may well have savored the idea of Pierpont's extreme discomfiture. Anne's exposure to her father's business friends bred considerable cynicism in her. When Lincoln Steffens once told her he liked Judge Gary of U.S. Steel, she said impatiently, "Oh, he's too plausible. He has taken you in as he does others."[6]

Pierpont was outraged by Anne's liberal, unconventional behavior. If the three women were discreet about their private affairs—even de Wolfe's biographer shrinks from using the word *lesbian*—they threw gala parties that attracted attention. Bernard Berenson attended their gatherings, as did Pierpont's mistress, Maxine Elliott, who had acted with de Wolfe. The chain-smoking Anne was in an agonizing situation. As one of the world's richest young women, she was relentlessly courted by titled Europeans. Scandal sheets frequently reported her upcoming engagement to the French count Boni de Castellane, which never came about. All the while, she dove deeper into causes and took stands that aligned her with her father's critics.

The facts of the rift between Pierpont and Anne are fragmentary. De Wolfe's biographer Jane S. Smith says Pierpont thought that Bessie Marbury had poisoned Anne's mind against him. She apparently told Anne that Pierpont used her to cover up his trysts with mistresses when Anne accompanied him to Europe on *Corsair III.* Pierpont's other children violently disagreed with this interpretation. Pierpont's middle daughter, Juliet, bristled at references to de Wolfe, while Jack was deeply upset by Anne's behavior. In her memoirs, Marbury handled the controversy tactfully: "Mr. Morgan was patriarchal in his views. The emancipated woman enjoyed no favor in his eyes, therefore as his daughter, she grew up determined that she must think for herself."[7] She also said of him, "To acknowledge defeat was foreign to his temperament. He was always loyal to his mistakes."[8]

Pierpont was wounded by the estrangement. "It broke her father's heart when she elected to part from him," one of Anne's friends told Clarence Barron.[9] As we have seen, Pierpont could be grimly implacable when crossed, and he blamed Bessie Marbury for stealing away his daughter. Hence, he found an ingenious way to torture her. Marbury coveted the French Legion of Honor and believed she deserved it for her work in officially representing French dramatists in the English-speaking world. By chance, in 1909, Robert Bacon, the ex–Greek God of Wall Street, was named ambassador to France. Bowing to Pierpont's wishes, he made sure she was denied the honor. Knowing that the House of Morgan objected prevented Bessie Marbury from ever receiving the government award—even after she spent years raising money for France and donated her Versailles home as a hospital during World War I. De Wolfe won the Croix de Guerre, and Anne was decorated as a commander of the Legion of Honor for running an ambulance corps and performing relief work. But Marbury—notwithstanding letters of praise from former presidents Roosevelt and Taft—couldn't overcome the French fears of offending Morgan interests. Even beyond his grave, Pierpont Morgan would not be thwarted.

PIERPONT'S relationship with Jack improved in his last years, perhaps in reaction to his troubles with Anne and Fanny. Nobody doubted that Jack would take over at the Corner, if only because the bank needed the Morgan name and money. Jack was no slouch and ably handled affairs in his father's absence. Yet he didn't have Pierpont's gargantuan ego. Since boyhood, he had been plagued by secret doubts about himself—it wasn't clear to him whether he had the intestinal fortitude to head a banking empire. In 1910, he had a collapse that was diagnosed as strain and fatigue. So for a number of reasons, he wanted a strong lieutenant, a powerful regent to take charge of the bank on a day-to-day basis. He preferred the role of constitutional monarch, shaping policy and delegating authority.

Two people competed for the position—Harry Davison and George Perkins. Perkins carried several liabilities. He was always shadowed by the insurance scandal from his years at New York Life. But the cause of Perkins's downfall would be that he saw himself as a king in his own right, not simply a Morgan vassal. At his Riverdale estate, he had nine servants, a swimming pool, a ballroom, and a bowling alley. In 1906, he bought the world's largest custom-made car—an eleven-foot French monstrosity with ebony woodwork, a writing desk, and a washstand-table. His worst sin may have been not showing due deference to the

Morgans. He sneered at Jack and thought he was more highly qualified to run the bank. He sometimes made decisions without consulting the Morgans. In 1910, Pierpont told Harry Davison in London that Perkins had defied his wishes on a financing arrangement for the Studebaker Company, news that Davison passed along to Perkins. Perkins then wrote to Pierpont saying, "I am very deeply disturbed by one remark that Davison made, viz., that you felt I had gone ahead and deliberately disregarded an understanding with you and concluded the business to suit myself."[10] Six months later, Perkins left the bank. He was apparently forced out. Tom Lamont later said that Perkins "didn't leave of his own accord. Morgan thought he had been a little second-rate on some deals."[11] When he resigned, Perkins took $5.5 million of his own securities out of the bank—one of many fortunes harvested at the House of Morgan.

For those skilled at reading the tea leaves, it grew clear that Henry Pomeroy Davison would become chief operating executive. After he became a partner in January 1909, he seemed to have almost exclusive access to Pierpont in his library. As was clear in the 1907 panic, the handsome Davison had star quality, a square-jawed toughness noticed by everyone on Wall Street. He had grown up in a small Pennsylvania town, the son of a farm-tools dealer and poor relation in a family of bankers. He skipped college when Harvard denied his scholarship application. He had a steely, distinguished look—long eyebrows, hair parted down the middle, and a wide, firm mouth.

Davison started out working for a bank in Bridgeport, Connecticut. One bank director was P. T. Barnum, who liked him and invited him to join a weekly whist game. In 1893, Davison married Kate Trubee, and they moved to New York so Harry could start work at the Astor Trust Company. One day, a crank appeared at his teller's window, pointed a gun at Davison, and passed him a $1-million check he wanted to cash, payable to "The Almighty." The cool, quick-witted Davison figured out a way to foil the holdup. He doled out the money in small bills and kept saying in a loud, reverential voice, "A million dollars for the Almighty."[12] This gave a bank guard time to notify the police, who arrested the man.

Davison rose quickly as a protégé of George F. Baker, Pierpont's jowly, side-whiskered chum and head of the First National Bank. He moved from the Astor Trust to another Baker bank, the Liberty. Then Baker said, "Davison, I think you'd better move your desk up here with us," and he became a First National vice-president. While there, he organized Bankers Trust in 1903, assisted in the 1907 panic negotiations, and represented Wall Street on Senator Aldrich's National Monetary Commission. These exploits won the attention of Pierpont, who later said, "I always believe everything Mr. Davison tells me."[13]

Anecdotes about Davison convey vigor, geniality, and self-confidence. Manly and decisive, he shot moose in Maine and elephant, buffalo, rhino, hippos, and antelope during a shooting trip up the White Nile. Once he dreamed he was a small-town Pennsylvania bank clerk. In a sweat, he couldn't balance the books. When he awoke, his wife asked what had happened. "I finally solved the problem; I bought the bank," he replied.[14] Immensely sociable, he seldom sat down to dine at his North Shore estate, Peacock Point, with fewer than twenty guests. Taking people under his wing, he had a way of guiding them, sometimes brusquely and a bit intrusively. He was the great talent scout in Morgan history and brought Tom Lamont, Dwight Morrow, Ben Strong, and John Davis into the bank's orbit.

Tom Lamont said that to young bankers on Wall Street, Davison "was not simply a leader. He was a king, an idol, if you please."[15] Lamont was Davison's most important find. After college, he had worked for two years as a reporter on the *New York Tribune.* (Later he would brilliantly parlay this fleeting experience into an image of himself as an old newspaperman.) After salvaging a failing import-export house through clever newspaper advertisements, he renamed it Lamont, Corliss and Company. On Wall Street, he acquired a reputation for straightening out troubled companies. This caught the attention of Harry Davison, his neighbor in Englewood, New Jersey.

Tom Lamont never pushed or clawed his way to the top. He did everything easily, jauntily, effortlessly. In 1903, at the age of thirty-three, he was returning home on the commuter train to Englewood when Harry Davison took his life in hand. As he entered the car, Davison was musing about choices for a secretary-treasurer post at the new Bankers Trust. When Lamont appeared, Davison saw his man. Lamont laughed at the offer. "But I don't know the first thing about banking. All my brief business life I have been borrowing money—not lending it." "Fine," said Davison, "that's just why we want you. A fearless borrower like you ought to make a prudent lender."[16] It was a momentous intuition.

Lamont followed in Davison's footsteps, taking his spot as vice-president at First National Bank in 1909. In late 1910, Pierpont summoned him. "You see that room over there? It's vacant," he said. "Beginning next Monday, I want you to occupy it."[17] Lamont professed bewilderment. "But what can I do for you that is worth while?" he asked. "Oh, you'll find plenty to keep you busy, just do whatever you see before you that needs to be done."[18] Was Lamont's reluctance simple candor—or splendid calculation?

Interestingly, with both Davison and Pierpont, Lamont refused the crown being proffered. He told Pierpont he had a dream of traveling three months each year. Far from being put off, Pierpont said, "Why, of course, take off as much time as you like. That is entirely in your hands."[19] He advised Lamont to take a cruise down the Nile, bringing along a couple of nurses for his children. There was again a certain guile in Lamont's handling of the offer. He must have known that Pierpont spent months abroad each year. Was he holding up a mirror to the old tycoon, saying tacitly, "Look here, don't I remind you of yourself in younger days?" Behind Lamont's urbane charm stood a man of exceptional talent, the more winning for its being presented with such apparent modesty.

To complete preparations for the succession, Pierpont made his final disposition of J. S. Morgan and Company in London. Stipulating that it survive for only a generation, or as long as Pierpont lived, Junius had permitted his name to be used posthumously. Now the twenty years was about to elapse. Jack explained that "as we approached 1910, Father said, 'You will have trouble enough when I die without having to think of a new name for this firm, and I suggest that we should now change it to Morgan Grenfell & Co., and make J. P. Morgan & Co. partners in it, they to keep one million pounds in capital.' "[20]

On January 1, 1910, Morgan Grenfell was born. If it bore, for the first time, a British name, its prestige was guaranteed by its New York money and connections. While Teddy Grenfell's name lent a protective British coloring in the City, the capital remained largely American. Before 1910, Pierpont and Jack had been partners of J. S. Morgan and Company. Under the new dispensation, J. P. Morgan and Company itself would be a partner in London and draw half its profits along with Drexel and Company in Philadelphia. Significantly, this arrangement never worked in reverse. Partners at Morgan Grenfell in London or Morgan, Harjes in Paris would thus hold second-class citizenship within the Morgan universe. The Morgan dynasty was always carefully arranged so that 23 Wall Street remained *primum inter pares.*

DURING Pierpont's last year, he was beset by calamities, as if the gods were punishing him on a scale worthy of his grandeur. His shipping trust, the International Mercantile Marine, faced stiff competition from the Cunard Line, which had built the swift and luxurious *Mauretania* and *Lusitania* with British government subsidies. To counter Cunard, J. Bruce Ismay, president of the IMM, and Lord Pirrie, the shipbuilder, decided to build a pair of mammoth ships. Pierpont, always partial to grandiose ventures, approved the plan. The ships were White Star's *Titanic* and *Olympic.* The House of Morgan even lobbied the New York Harbor Board for a hundred-foot extension of a Hudson River pier so it could receive the twin ships.

In May 1911, Pierpont attended the Belfast christening of the *Titanic* and studied the spot on B deck where his personal suite would be. It would contain a parlor and promenade deck, with timbered walls in Tudor style, and there would be special cigar holders in the bathroom. Though Pierpont and Vivian Smith of Morgan Grenfell both booked spots for the April 1912 maiden voyage, both had to cancel.

Reports of a North Atlantic disaster reached Pierpont in France on the eve of his seventy-fifth birthday. "Have just heard fearful rumor about Titanic with iceberg," he wired New York. "Without any particulars. Hope for God sake not true."[21] As the news spread, European reporters tried to track Pierpont down. When he was finally located in a French château, he seemed devastated. "Think of the lives that have been mowed down and of the terrible deaths," he said.[22]

Over fifteen hundred people perished, including John Jacob Astor IV, George Widener, the son of P. A. B. Widener, and Benjamin Guggenheim. Survivors were picked up by the Cunard Line's *Carpathia.* It was a crowning disaster for the shipping trust, unleashing denunciations against both White Star and Morgan himself. The British-run but American-owned ship was charged with many deficiencies—an insufficient number of lifeboats, a crew who ignored warnings of icebergs, a poorly organized rescue, even failure to put binoculars in the crow's nest. Newspapers depicted luxurious staterooms laid out for Pierpont and others as proof of a misplaced emphasis on winning the carriage trade from Cunard rather than on safety.

Though the Morgan partners had long regarded White Star chairman Bruce Ismay as abrupt and ill-mannered—he had often threatened to quit—they stuck by him at first. Jack deplored the public drubbing that Ismay took, cabling the message that "from telegraphic accounts his treatment New York infernally brutal."[23] Later, Jack and Pierpont insisted he resign his post. The *Titanic* was the last nail in the coffin of the shipping trust. Although the cartel enjoyed a brief revival as Morgan's Export Department sent war supplies to the Allies during World

War I, that wasn't enough to keep it afloat. In October 1914, Jack Morgan decided it had to default on its bonds. Almost four years after the *Titanic* went down, White Star conceded responsibility in court, paying out $2.5 million in damages.

IN 1912, the crusade against the trusts had already reached a thunderous crescendo as much of the presidential campaign revolved around Pierpont and his enterprises. Morgan represented everything that had bothered Americans for a generation—factories thrown up helter-skelter across the landscape, brutal mergers, a carnival atmosphere on Wall Street that produced boomlets and busts in crazy, unending succession. A newspaper cartoon from 1912 shows Pierpont jovially sitting atop a heap of gold coins and dollar bills, clutching industrial plants and office buildings in his fist; the legend reads: "I have not the slightest power."[24] Indeed, the Morgans saw themselves not as financial pirates but as public benefactors. When Harry Morgan was born in 1900, Jack noted a resemblance to Pierpont and said he only hoped his son would help as many people in his lifetime as Pierpont had in his. This sense of virtue contrasted with the reality of their being the target of public calumny, leaving the Morgan family angry and bewildered.

Progressive Democrats criticized the trusts as cruel and inefficient and destructive of the entrepreneurial spirit. Bellwether of the new mood was Woodrow Wilson, then governor of New Jersey. He accused Republican-supported tariffs of shielding the trusts from foreign competition. In January 1910, while still president of Princeton, he had lectured an audience of New York bankers, including Pierpont and George F. Baker, on their duties, saying banking was "founded on a moral basis and not on a financial basis" and chiding them for penalizing small businesses.[25] As Wilson spoke, Pierpont gloomily puffed on his cigar; afterward, injured, he told Wilson the remarks seemed directed at him. Wilson, saying he meant no offense, contended that he spoke merely of principles.

That the Democrats attacked Morgan wasn't surprising. Far more telling was how he became a divisive issue among Republicans and helped to split the party in 1912 over several issues. One involved a Morgan syndicate formed with the Guggenheims in 1906 to exploit the copper of the Kennecott Glacier in Alaska. This "Morganheim" group, as it was dubbed, had launched a veritable financial invasion of the state, buying up steamship lines, coal fields, and canneries and investing $20 million in a railroad to carry copper ore to Prince William Sound on the coast. The press lampooned this "second purchase of Alaska," and one cartoonist introduced a composite monster called Guggenmorgan.

Such wholesale development of Alaska became a test case of the government's attitude toward wilderness areas. It pitted Gifford Pinchot, director of the U.S. Forest Service and a Teddy Roosevelt holdover, against Secretary of the Interior Richard Ballinger, a Taft appointee. Pinchot wanted to preserve the Alaskan wilderness for posterity, while Ballinger thought only the Guggenheim-Morgan combination could finance development in such a remote, costly spot. After public feuding between Pinchot and Ballinger, Taft dismissed Pinchot. When Teddy Roosevelt, on an African safari, heard about this, it fed his sense of having been betrayed by Taft.

Toward the end of his second term, Roosevelt had decided not to file an antitrust suit against the Morgan farm-equipment trust, International Harvester. In 1911, Taft not only filed such a suit, but later released papers purportedly showing that George W. Perkins had blocked an antitrust suit against Harvester back in 1907 by lobbying the head of the U.S. Bureau of Corporations, who warned Roosevelt not to antagonize the Morgan interests without any proof of major wrongdoing.

In October 1911, the Taft administration lodged a suit against U.S. Steel in a further rebuff to the Morgans. "Am horrified at character of bill which beyond everything I thought possible," Harry Davison wrote to the London partners.[26] To the Paris partners, he denounced the "cheap political methods of Taft and his associates."[27] What made this especially galling to both Morgan and Roosevelt was the stress on U.S. Steel's acquisition of Tennessee Coal and Iron during the 1907 panic. This was the deal that Judge Gary and Henry Frick had gotten TR to approve during his breakfast. The former president was hypersensitive to allegations of having been hoodwinked. Defending his actions, Roosevelt said that the suit against U.S. Steel "has brought vividly before our people the need for reducing to order our chaotic Government policy as regards business."[28] The combination of the Pinchot firing and the U.S. Steel and International Harvester suit helped convince Roosevelt to bolt from the Republicans in 1912 and run as presidential candidate of the Progressive, or Bull Moose, party.

The issue of Morgan influence still dogged Roosevelt because of the prominence in his campaign of ex-Morgan partner George W. Perkins. Perkins was furious about Taft's trust-busting. He urged Roosevelt to run, covered many of his preconvention expenses, stage-managed the convention, and chaired the new party's executive committee. It was said he traveled so often to Oyster Bay to see Roosevelt that his chauffeur "knew every pebble in the road, even in the dark."[29] Among Roosevelt's Progressive followers, there lurked residual fear that Pierpont had planted Perkins in the campaign. But Perkins had left the bank on bad terms, and this seems unlikely. The 1912 split between Taft and Roosevelt brought to power the man who had lectured Pierpont on his moral duty: Woodrow Wilson. Meanwhile, the U.S. Steel suit miscarried, and International Harvester had to divest only three small subsidiaries.

The intellectual and political leap most damaging to the House of Morgan was a spreading notion that a Wall Street trust had created the industrial trusts and governed their subsequent destiny. Minnesota congressman Charles A. Lindbergh, Sr., father of the future aviator, coined the title Money Trust, describing it as the most sinister trust of all. Senator George Norris later said of Lindbergh's attack on the Money Trust that "the gentleman from Minnesota is entitled to more credit than any other member."[30] The *Wall Street Journal* correctly noted that the Money Trust was just a code name for Morgan. Legions of young muckraking reporters fanned out across Wall Street and rooted out insidious banking connections. Aided by his young assistant, Walter Lippmann, Lincoln Steffens exposed a web of links among ostensibly competitive New York banks. His exposés in *Everybody's* magazine termed Pierpont "the boss of the United States."

During the summer of 1912, swollen Wall Street power was a hot issue at the Democratic National Convention. In a hell-raising speech, William Jennings Bryan introduced a resolution stating opposition "to the nomination of any candidate for president who is the representative or under obligation to J. Pierpont Morgan, Thomas F. Ryan, August Belmont, or any other member of the privilege-hunting and favor-seeking class."[31] Wilson was more circumspect. While refusing contributions from Morgan, Belmont, and Ryan, he made exceptions for such financial notables as Jacob Schiff and Bernard Baruch. In accepting the nomination, Wilson said, "A concentration of the control of credit . . . may at any time become infinitely dangerous to free enterprise."[32] That summer, he was tutored in economics by lawyer Louis Brandeis, who had combated Morgan control of the New Haven Railroad for several years. Financial reform would form a major part of Wilson's campaign.

Congressman Lindbergh introduced a resolution in the House calling for a congressional probe into the concentration of power on Wall Street. The resulting 1912 hearings of the House Banking and Currency Committee were commonly known by the name of subcommittee chairman Arsène Pujo, a Louisiana Democrat, and they got into high gear after Wilson's victory in November 1912. Pierpont Morgan and his friends, colleagues, and partners were to be the star witnesses.

The Pujo hearings are always portrayed as Pierpont's martyrdom, the public confrontation that led to his death. Of equal relevance to our story is their haunting effect on Jack Morgan. He had coped with the fear of his overpowering father by resorting to awe-struck worship. As Pierpont returned the affection in later years, Jack's gratitude contained an extra element of relief, and he deeply resented the blistering political attacks against his father. A new bitterness, a darker shading, crept into his letters: "As to attacks on the Senior," he wrote Vivian Smith, ". . . owing to a laborious and prolonged press attack . . . in the public mind J.P.M. is no longer a benefactor, or a citizen who would be a credit to any country, but is an ogre lying in the background, and always ready to devour."[33] "The politicians that run our two countries appear to have been seized with a madness," he told Grenfell. "Our country is full of hatred and bitterness and talk."[34]

At first, Jack regarded the Pujo investigation as a "nuisance." He took heart from the opinion of Morgan lawyer, Francis Stetson, that as a private bank they could withhold their books and refuse testimony. Jack even fancied Pierpont might lay out some constructive measures for Pujo's consideration. But in late April 1912, the committee chose as its counsel Samuel Untermyer, a rich, shrewd New York trial lawyer whose pedigree collies had once beaten Pierpont's in competition. Untermyer had already railed against the Money Trust, and Jack was aghast: "Investigation will probably proceed now on as unpleasant lines as can be arranged," he cabled his father.[35] The hearings would sharpen Jack's hostility toward Jews, reporters, Democrats, reformers—all those troublemakers who stirred up the populace. Scarred by the experience, he would grow disenchanted with democracy and what he referred to as America's "amateur Government."[36]

The hearings occurred in December 1912, just as Pierpont hoped to wash his hands of worldly cares. The money kept rolling in—he was making about $5 million a year—and the bank under Jack and Davison almost ran itself. Pierpont was probably more *au courant* on Egyptian excavations than on Wall Street underwritings. At first, he brusquely said he would testify alone in Washington. But on this cusp of the Diplomatic Age, a new accountability was expected, and bankers had to tend their images more prudently. The new team at 23 Wall adopted an aggressive attitude toward public relations dramatically at odds with historical reticence.

Silence was Wall Street's golden rule of conduct. Its leading exemplar was Pierpont's pal George F. Baker of the First National Bank, whose mutton-chop whiskers and gold watch chain across his paunch made him a prototypical Victorian banker. His bank was as mysterious as 23 Wall itself. Known as the Sphinx of Wall Street, Baker was director of more than forty companies. He gave his first newspaper interview in 1863 and not another until 1923, when a young woman said she was promised a job if she gained access to the reclusive Baker. Breaking his silence, he said, "Businessmen of America should reduce their talk two-thirds. Everyone should reduce his talk. There is rarely ever a reason enough for anybody to talk."[37] By then, Baker's fortune was estimated at between $100 and $300 million. He would richly endow the Harvard Business School, in part through the intercession of Tom Lamont.

As a private merchant, Pierpont felt no obligation to inform the public and never hired a publicist. Now a new generation of Morgan partners took charge of a public relations offensive. Not only was Pierpont coached for the hearings by Davison and Lamont, but the bank hired its first publicist. It was the ideal moment for that quintessential banker of the new age, round-faced smiling Tom Lamont. He laid out a secret plan, approved by Pierpont, that would govern Morgan public relations for a generation. To improve the bank's image, Morgan partners would meet with selected reporters, stay in touch with publishers, monitor newspapers, contribute articles, and privately protest critical articles to editors.

Lamont's publicity operation for the Pujo hearings went beyond the lone publicist usually mentioned. An associate of his named Brainerd bought the big Maclures Newspaper Syndicate, which sold material to newspapers across America; this would be their vehicle for countering Pujo. "Our idea is for Brainerd to continue this strictly sub rosa," Lamont cabled Davison, who replied, "Much pleased learn of Brainerd's purchase. Find Senior and others here much impressed with the importance of doing something promptly. We all agreed it is most important have publicity man put to work sub rosa at once on money trust investigation."[38] This flowered into a full-blown scheme for entering publishing. Along with Wall Street friends, the Morgan partners planned to buy papers in major cities—Washington, Chicago, and New York—and purchase two newspaper groups that sold inserts to papers around the country. This part of the campaign apparently lapsed, as did negotiations to buy the *Washington Post*. But the moves reflected a new wish to shape opinion and emerge from the old Morgan cocoon of secrecy.

Instead of going alone to Washington, as he first hoped, Pierpont headed a sixteen-person entourage. The morning of the hearings, he emerged from a big, high-topped limousine and marched up the steps of the Capitol in striped pants, a velvet-collared coat, and silk top hat, grasping a cane. An immense crowd ringed the block: Pierpont was the most famous banker on earth. He was flanked by his daughter Louisa, her hands stuffed deep in a fur muff and her mouth tight with prim disapproval, and Jack, who wore a derby hat, his black mustache flecked with gray. As Pierpont sat in the hearing room, he wore the tragic mask of an old clown, his head mostly hairless, his nose bulbous and grotesquely gnarled, his posture erect and stubbornly proud.

The Pujo hearings are celebrated for Pierpont's triumphant retorts and spirited defense of his business honor; in a moment, we shall hear the well-worn phrases. But let us first note the awesome Morgan power that was revealed, lest the Money Trust theorists seem malcontents. Some 78 major corporations, including many of the country's most powerful holding companies, banked at Morgans. Pierpont and his partners, in turn, held 72 directorships in 112 corporations, spanning the worlds of finance, railroads, transportation, and public utilities. In this era of relationship banking, board seats often meant a monopoly on a company's business. During the previous decade, the House of Morgan had floated almost $2 billion in securities—an astronomical figure for the time.

The Money Trust hysteria stemmed from a wave of bank mergers; Wall Street was snowballing into one big, Morgan-dominated institution. In December 1909, Pierpont had bought a majority stake in the Equitable Life Assurance Society from Thomas Fortune Ryan. This gave him strong influence over America's three biggest insurance companies—Mutual Life, Equitable, and New York Life. Although he subsequently "mutualized" the Equitable and sold it to policyholders, the potential for abuse seemed terrifying.

Pierpont also controlled several New York City trusts through that old trick from railroad days, the voting trust. His Bankers Trust had taken over three other banks. In 1909, he had gained control of Guaranty Trust, which through a series of mergers he converted into America's largest trust; it had two Morgan partners on its voting trust. As a director of both Bankers Trust and Guaranty Trust, Harry Davison blithely claimed that Morgans had no more control over the two banks than over the Pujo Committee itself. But Morgan records reveal a distinctly proprietary tone toward the banks. When Davison vacationed, for instance, Lamont dashed off such memos as "Banking matters— everything running along smoothly and successfully at the Bankers. . . . At the Guaranty Trust things are in good shape."[39] Besides these Morgan-controlled trust companies, the core Money Trust group included J. P. Morgan and Company, First National Bank, and National City Bank. Over the National Bank of Commerce, America's second biggest, Pierpont had such influence that it was styled "J. Pierpont Morgan's bank."[40]

Wall Street bankers incestuously swapped seats on each other's boards. Some banks had so many overlapping directors it was hard to separate them. Five of nine Chase directors were also First National directors, giving George F. Baker control over Chase. The banks also shared large equity stakes in each other. Pierpont was the biggest outside shareholder in Baker's First National Bank. After the 1907 panic, Pierpont also took a large block of National City stock and put Jack on its board. The public could be forgiven for suspecting that these "Morgan banks" avoided competition and exercised veto power over new entrants to the capital markets.

In part, the new financial giants resulted from the stupendous scale of industrial financing. Business gravitated to New York as companies became national in scope. For instance, in 1906 J. P. Morgan and Company captured American Telephone and Telegraph's business from Boston's Kidder, Peabody, which had marketed AT&T bonds in New England but couldn't handle its new need for national financing. Banks had to grow with their customers, and the industrial trusts created a Money Trust as much as the other way around. Similarly, with large-scale foreign financing in China, Latin America, and elsewhere, Washington had forged Wall Street banks into an instrument of statecraft but was then dismayed when they cooperated at home.

Why didn't banks just merge instead of carrying out the charade of swapping shares and board members? Most were private partnerships or closely held banks and could have done so. The answer harked back to traditional American antipathy against concentrated financial power. The Morgan–First National–National City trio feared public retribution if it openly declared its allegiance. In 1911, the group thought of merging the Bank of Commerce and Chase National Bank, but the move was vetoed by National City president James Stillman. As Jack had cabled Pierpont, "His objection arises from his feeling that it is better at present not to call attention to the great power of trio, which might increase public sentiment against that power throughout United States. . . . None of the trio wishes further large investment in bank stocks for long period."[41]

At the Pujo hearings, Pierpont faced a crafty adversary. Short, sharp-nosed, and mustachioed, Samuel Untermyer was no scruffy radical but an affluent lawyer who sported fresh orchids in his lapel. A close student of trusts—he had investigated Equitable Life Assurance and Standard Oil—he had a suave, insinuating style. Pierpont, by contrast, was rough and uncouth in public. At this moment of supreme crisis, he reverted to those precepts that Junius had pounded into his head—the Gentlemen Banker's Code of the City. The famous exchange went as follows:

> *Untermyer:* Is not commercial credit based primarily upon money or property?
> *Morgan:* No, sir, the first thing is character.
> *Untermyer:* Before money or property?
> *Morgan:* Before money or anything else. Money cannot buy it. . . . Because a man I do not trust could not get money from me on all the bonds in Christendom.[42]

Spectators applauded, and businessmen across America stood rapt by this eloquence. The usually taciturn Pierpont had ennobled banking in an unexpected way. On Wall Street, banker Henry Seligman said, stock prices leapt 5 to 10 points on the strength of this testimony.[43] Pierpont phrased the point more colorfully: "I have known a man to come into my office, and I have given him a check for a million dollars when I knew that they had not a cent in the world."[44]

However much financiers might cheer such sentiments, to outsiders the statements sounded like cant preached to dupes. Yet, as we have seen, early merchant bankers used character and class as crude forms of credit screening; ever since the Medicis and Fuggers, it was a practical way for private bankers to protect their precious capital base. Pierpont's statement was neither as cynical as critics thought nor as noble as friends imagined. It was a workable business strategy.

In the history books, Pierpont's epigrammatic sayings stand out. In the transcript of the Pujo hearings, however, they appear against an arid backdrop of denials and monosyllabic grunts, as if he wouldn't concede the hearing's legitimacy. Stamping his cane, Pierpont grew bullheaded and snorted like some angry god held hostage by heathens. Grudging in his explanations, he was led by Untermyer into some absurd statements. For instance, Untermyer got Pierpont to state his rationale for the one-man control of the railroads he sponsored:

> *Untermyer:* But what I mean is that the banking house assumes no legal responsibility for the value of the bonds, does it?
> *Morgan:* No, sir, but it assumes something else that is still more important, and that is the moral responsibility which has to be defended so long as you live.[45]

This was Pierpont in a nutshell: he represented the bondholders and expressed their wrath against irresponsible management. But Untermyer saw more than passive surveillance at stake in the directorships and voting trusts. Besides representing bondholders, the House of Morgan represented itself to ensure a steady flow of business. It could intervene to protect its own interests. Because Pierpont wouldn't admit this, he spouted gibberish:

> *Untermyer:* You do not think you have any power in any department or industry in this country, do you?
> *Morgan:* I do not.
> *Untermyer:* Not the slightest?
> *Morgan:* Not the slightest.[46]

One senses that Untermyer, far from being displeased, gladly used such intransigence to showcase Pierpont's arrogance.

> *Untermyer:* Your firm is run by you, is it not?
> *Morgan:* No, sir.
> *Untermyer:* It is not?
> *Morgan:* No, sir.
> *Untermyer:* You are the final authority, are you not?
> *Morgan:* No, sir.[47]

Despite a mass of circumstantial evidence, the Pujo committee never proved a Money Trust in a strict conspiratorial sense. Rather, it found a "community of interest" that concentrated "the control of credit and money in the hands of a few men, of which J.P. Morgan & Co. are the recognized leaders."[48] It said that six houses—J.P. Morgan and Company, First National, National City, and Kuhn, Loeb along with Boston's Lee, Higginson and Kidder, Peabody—acted in concert in sponsoring securities of prime corporations and governments. It was hard for large companies to market bonds without this group or for rivals to take business away from them.

The Pujo Committee documented the gentlemanly rules of conduct among old-line Wall Street banks. They competed, but in a manner as formal and ritualized as a minuet. They wouldn't bid against each other for bond issues. Rather, a single house would privately negotiate a deal and then assign syndicate allotments to other firms. Over time, these allotments tended to be unvarying for a particular company. As Jacob Schiff told Pujo, "It was not good form to create unreasonable interference of competition. Good practices did not justify competition for security issues."[49] Whether this was a barefaced plot to bar outsiders or just a natural response to market conditions would be debated for the next forty years. The issue would not be settled until the Medina trial of the early 1950s, when the House of Morgan would again be branded the kingpin of the conspiracy.

The Pujo hearings had one immediate consequence that seemed to threaten Morgan power. In December 1913, President Wilson signed the Federal Reserve Act, providing the government with a central bank and freeing it of reliance on the House of Morgan in emergencies; the new Federal Reserve System was a hybrid institution, with private regional reserve banks and a public Federal Reserve Board in Washington. Yet the House of Morgan moved so artfully to form an alliance with the Federal Reserve Bank of New York that for the next twenty years it would actually gain power from the new financial system. The bankers had not yet been tamed.

AFTER the Pujo hearings, Jack and his sister Louisa sat with their father in a private railroad car as he recovered from the strain of his testimony. As soon as servants had brought their luggage from the hotel, they all returned to New York. Jack lauded his father's testimony—thought him "perfectly frank, very helpful to situation"—but developed a visceral loathing for Untermyer, whom he tagged the Beast.[50] He thought the Pujo hearings a blatant assault on the Morgan bank, with other bankers only drawn in as a smokescreen. From Yankee pride, both father and son professed to be immune to the whinings of such little men. Striking a brave tone, Jack said, "We have all here maintained the note which [Pierpont] struck so well in Washington that he was much too big to be annoyed by miserable little things like that."[51] The reality, however, was that Senior never recuperated from the ordeal of this public inquisition.

Pierpont was too thin-skinned to be philosophical about political attacks and didn't recognize himself as the ogre of the newspaper cartoons. He thought himself a generous, paternalistic boss and an avuncular grandfather, not a bloodthirsty monster. He was baffled by the new public scrutiny of businessmen and predicted that "the time is coming when all business will have to be done with glass pockets."[52] He thought Jack might fare better in the new environment. In his last months, Pierpont possessed a melancholy sense of history as having passed him by. He told a visitor in 1913, "When you see Mr. Wilson, tell him for me that if there should ever come a time when he thinks any influence or resources that I have can be used for the country, they are wholly at his disposal."[53] Such a time never came.

Fleeing up the Nile with Louisa, Pierpont could find no respite from his troubles. As always, his ailments were a mass of amorphous symptoms rather than a definable illness. Louisa privately reported to Jack on his digestive upsets, depression, insomnia, and nervous attacks. "Bilious attack practically overcome but result months of strain very apparent now," she cabled as they sailed to Luxor.[54] Jack—always in the wrong place, always full of yearning—now wished to join Pierpont. But theirs was no ordinary father-son relationship. A political succession—no less momentous than a presidential transition—was underway, and Louisa reported that executive power was being placed in his hands. "Your suggestion coming yourself has touched and pleased him, but he is anxious you should remember how much depends upon your being on the spot in New York—how many interests are in your hands. He is too weak make decision; he wishes leave it you."[55] It was the first time Pierpont had ever explicitly delegated top authority to his son.

As Pierpont weakened, fresh doctors were shipped out from New York. The corpulent banker fancied that fresh butter and cream from Cragston might restore him and asked Jack to send some. The final siege came in a $500-a-day suite of Rome's Grand Hotel. News of Pierpont's terminal illness rattled the art world, which braced for a general collapse of prices. The ground floor of the Grand Hotel teemed with art dealers, antiquarians, foppish noblemen, shabby peddlers—all trying to unload a last painting or statue on the dying financier. So zealous were their assaults that the New York Times described them as being "repulsed with the regularity of surf on the beach."[56] Meanwhile, Pierpont's condition required that politics and business not be mentioned. He was groggy but sleepless. Even grains of morphine couldn't soothe his tormented mind or slow his racing pulse. On the night of March 31, he grew delirious and mumbled about his boyhood. Imagining himself back at school in Hartford or Switzerland, he praised "a fine lot of boys" in his class. Before he died, he said, "I've got to go up the hill."[57] He died shortly after midnight. Within twelve hours, the pope and 3,697 other people had telegraphed their regrets to the Grand Hotel.

The Morgan partners attributed the death to Pujo. The charge may be overstated. Pierpont was seventy-five when he died. Almost twenty years before, worried doctors wouldn't approve a life insurance policy in his name. He smoked dozens of cigars daily, stowed away huge breakfasts, drank heavily, and refused to exercise. If Jack lost weight, Pierpont would grow alarmed. When Jack began playing squash regularly, Pierpont said, "Rather he than I."[58] From boyhood, he had been chronically sick, often spending several days in bed each month. Hardly a period of his life was free of illness and depression. That he lasted until seventy-five, with his myriad ailments and resolutely bad habits, is close to miraculous, testimony to a powerful constitution. Then, in his last years, there were numerous disappointments—the *Titanic*, the U.S. Steel and International Harvester suits, Woodrow Wilson's attacks on the Money Trust, and so on—that may have created unbearable stress.

But at Morgans, everybody *knew* Untermyer was the murderous scoundrel. As Lamont told historian Henry Steele Commager, "Within three or four months, out of a seemingly clear sky, his health failed and after a two weeks' illness, from no particular malady, he died."[59] Certainly, the hearings hastened Pierpont's death, but who can say they caused it? Nevertheless, the belief was widespread at the bank and only hardened partners' feelings toward politicians and reformers. Jack began to follow Untermyer's affairs with a morbid curiosity. When a senator attacked the lawyer in 1914, he fairly gloated: "I enjoyed reading every account of it . . . and the more I see him caught in the machinery of his evil deeds, the better pleased I am."[60]

How much had Pierpont amassed? Apart from his art collection, his estate came to $68.3 million, of which about $30 million represented his share in the New York and Philadelphia banks. (Pierpont's $68.3 million estate would be equivalent to $802 million in 1989 dollars.) The value of his art collection was estimated by the Duveens at $50 million. It was testimony to Pierpont's Olympian standing that the release of the figures occasioned some disbelief, even some pity. Andrew Carnegie was truly saddened by the revelation of poor Pierpont's poverty. "And to think he was not a rich man," he sighed.[61] Pierpont's fortune didn't approach those of the great industrialists—Carnegie, Rockefeller, Ford, or Harriman—and he didn't quite edge out Jay Gould. One magazine writer even saw the paltry estate as proof that Pierpont hadn't profited from inside information at his disposal.

When Pierpont's will was disclosed, it contained many surprises. Overflowing with religious fervor, it had a florid opening, in which he committed his soul into the hands of Jesus Christ. He distributed money with great liberality. Besides the Morgan bank capital, Jack was bequeathed $3 million outright, the *Corsair*, the property at Princes Gate and Dover House, and that inestimable jewel, the Morgan collection. Daughters Louisa Satterlee and Juliet Hamilton received $1 million apiece, with an extra million thrown in for their husbands. The long-suffering Fanny received Cragston, the Madison Avenue house, a $100,-000 guaranteed annuity, and a $1-million trust fund. She survived until 1924, faithfully attended by Jack. There was friction in the family regarding Anne Morgan's award of $3 million. Since she would have no children and planned to donate the money to philanthropic activities, some thought she should have received much less.

For Morgan retainers, it was a red-letter day, fulfilling their most delirious dreams. Librarian Belle da Costa Greene got her first Morgan bequest of $50,000—Jack would later match it—plus a guarantee of continued employment at the library. Dr. James Markoe, who pumped Pierpont with medication during the 1907 panic, received a $25,000 annuity, which was to revert to his pretty wife, Annette, should she outlive him. (This bequest, along with legends claiming that doctors at the Lying-In Hospital married Pierpont's former mistresses, kept alive rumors that Annette Markoe had been a mistress of Pierpont's.) Even Pierpont's sailing master, Captain W. B. Porter, received $15,000. In the most astounding act of paternalism, every J. P. Morgan and Company and Morgan Grenfell employee received a free year's salary. (When the bill came due, Jack paid out $373,000.) There was close to $10 million in charitable bequests, including $1.35 million to Dr. Markoe's New York Lying-In Hospital, $1 million to Harvard, $560,000 to Saint George's Church, and $500,000 for the Cathedral of Saint John the Divine in New York City.

By no coincidence, Pierpont's last rites resembled the Anglo-American tribute he had arranged for Junius. He turned his own funeral into a last act of father worship. As Jack said, Pierpont had "left full instructions in regard to funeral which is to be as like his Father's as possible."[62] Again, the mourning was transatlantic, with Pierpont honored by both a memorial service at Westminster Abbey and the closing of the New York Stock Exchange. At sea, flags of the shipping trust flew at half-mast. Back in New York, his body lay in state at the Morgan Library. For the funeral service at Saint George's, a full complement of Episcopal bishops—one each from New York, Connecticut, and Massachusetts—came in response to a summons in Pierpont's will. Harry T. Burleigh, a black baritone, the grandson of an escaped slave, and a favorite of Pierpont's, sang the hymns. Pierpont was buried in the family mausoleum at Hartford's Cedar Hill Cemetery, according to his wishes: "opposite the place where my father's remains are interred."[63]

Perhaps no other event of the year 1913 received as many lines of newspaper copy as Pierpont Morgan's death. Momentarily the critical drumbeat—which had grown so loud and insistent with the Pujo hearings—was silenced. In lengthy obituaries, no analogy was too large to encompass the personage who had just died. The *Economist* called Pierpont "the Napoléon of Wall Street."[64] The *Wall Street Journal* said, "Such men have no successors. . . . There were no successors to Napoléon, Bismarck, Cecil Rhodes or E. H. Harriman, and their authority was not perpetuated."[65] These articles suggested that the last titan had died, and the world of banking would never again see a figure of such scope.

From our later perspective, Pierpont Morgan seems large because of certain characteristics of the Baronial Age. The companies Pierpont Morgan controlled were weak and primitive by today's standards, without a vast, highly trained managerial corps. Many firms had just graduated from the regional to the national level and needed Wall Street bankers in order to obtain broader financing. Even the governments Pierpont lent money to were relatively unsophisticated and lacked the central banks, systems of taxation, and large treasuries of today. Despite the multinational reach of Pierpont's empire, his great exploits—the 1895 rescue of the gold standard, the creation of U.S. Steel, the cornering of Northern Pacific, the negotiations in the 1907 panic—were exclusively American in character.

After Pierpont Morgan's death, the House of Morgan would become less autocratic, less identified with a single individual. Power would be diffused among several partners, although Jack Morgan would remain as figurehead. In the new Diplomatic Age, the bank's influence would not diminish. Rather, it would break from its domestic shackles and become a global power, sharing financial leadership with central banks and governments and profiting in unexpected ways from the partnership. What nobody could have foreseen in 1913 was that Jack Morgan—shy, awkward, shambling Jack who had cowered in the corners of Pierpont's life—would preside over an institution of perhaps even larger power than the one ruled by his willful, rambunctious father.

PART TWO

The Diplomatic Age
1913-1948

CHAPTER NINE

METAMORPHOSIS

• •

•

I N early 1912, the House of Morgan bought 23 Wall Street and its property from Elizabeth Drexel. The hallowed soil fetched the highest price per square foot ever recorded for a real estate deal. A month after Pierpont's death, wrecking crews demolished the old brownish-gray Drexel Building to clear the way for a new marble palace. Never ones to stint, the Morgan partners bought a quarry of Tennessee marble to guarantee a supply of high-quality construction material.

Pierpont had insisted the new building retain a catercorner entrance, facing both Broad and Wall streets. On his last trip to Rome, he had planned to bring home triumphal columns to frame the entrance. Although he never set eyes on the Italian Renaissance building, designed by Trowbridge and Livingston, it preserved his spirit. On December 30, 1913, Jack set the cornerstone, which contained a special copper box. Sealed inside, like saintly relics, were Pierpont's will, a copy of his Pujo testimony, the articles of partnership, and an appropriate merchant-banking touch—the form used for letters of credit. It was a homage to the past even as the firm moved ahead.

Oddly, the angular building, completed in 1914, was smaller than its predecessor. "I wonder what people will think in 300 years or less as to the progress made by Morgans in 35 years," Teddy Grenfell said slyly to Lamont. In shrinking the building's size, the firm expelled other tenants, keeping the Corner to itself. Dwarfed by skyscrapers, the short building made extravagant use of such precious land, as if the bank wished to flaunt its immunity to everyday concerns of cost.

The new building was compact and mysterious, reflecting the bank's penchant for privacy. Curtains always shrouded its deeply inset windows. As the *Times* said, "The men of the House of Morgan keep in the background as far as possible. They shun the limelight as they would a plague."[1] Whereas the old Drexel building had the firm's name over the doorway, the bank now reverted to London tradition and posted no name.

The interior reflected the layout of London merchant banks, with an open banking floor on the street level. Set off by a marble-and-glass partition, a double row of partners' rolltop desks and brass spitoons stood along the Broad Street side. There were dark wood walls and mosaic panels. Fires blazed at the back of the partners' room, beneath a portrait of Pierpont. Upstairs, each partner had a private office, lined in English oak, and a fireplace. The upper floors housed a private dining room and Jack Morgan's barber shop.

When Jack arrived for his inaugural day as the new Senior, his office was heaped with roses. Now forty-six, he must have taken charge with some trepidation. He was milder, less truculent than his father—he griped and grumbled where his father barked. One journalist wrote that there was in Jack "a suavity . . . that was missing in his father," and Wall Street scuttlebutt compared him with Pierpont unfavorably.[2] As we have seen, his confidence hadn't been bolstered by his father. And for a Morgan partner, he had been mixed up in a surprising number of fiascoes, including the shipping trust. When he solicited a gold loan in Paris during the 1907 panic, the Banque de France rebuffed him—a hard knock for Junius Morgan's grandson. Wall Street wits said that after returning to New York in 1905, Jack's chief innovation at the Corner was introducing English afternoon tea. He was seen as pleasant, friendly, but second-rate.

Jack handled the succession in an intelligent, self-protective way. He did what Pierpont could never do—presided in a relaxed manner, delegating authority to Davison, Lamont, and others. Not hampered by his father's flaming temper or ego, he didn't feel threatened by talented men of his own age and prided himself on his stable of *prima donnas*. The way he restructured the bank suited the needs of the Diplomatic Age, which required a team of strong, independent partners to undertake government missions. The general caliber of the partners would improve measurably under Jack's tutelage.

Decisions were reached by consensus. Where Pierpont held no regular meetings until the 1907 panic, Jack scheduled daily partners' meetings in the informal style of a British merchant bank. No stenographer was present, and no minutes were kept, only lists of attending partners. Where Pierpont preferred subservient partners, Jack would create a bank almost top-heavy with executive talent. Whether from insecurity, shrewdness, tact, or sheer laziness, he put together a symphony orchestra that could, if necessary, play without a conductor.

Even with this looser grip on the business, Jack could still yank the leash and take control. He held $32.3 million in Morgan capital, which was the bank's major cushion. He also reserved his father's extraordinary powers, which included the right to allocate profits among partners, arbitrate disputes, fire partners, and determine a fired partner's departing share of capital. These were the trump cards in a private partnership. So long as he was alive, Jack insisted upon certain central Morgan values—such as conservative management, avoidance of speculation, and loyalty to Britain—that set invisible but real fences around his lieutenants.

Financial partnerships are combustible affairs that frequently blow up as a result of personality clashes and disputes over money. Yet the House of Morgan was always marked by harmony among the partners. If Jack Morgan was devoid of unhealthy egotism and bashful to a fault, his lieutenants, Harry Davison and Tom Lamont, were genial and deferential toward him. A tacit bargain was struck: they would treat Jack with impeccable courtesy, bow to his wishes on important matters, and venerate the Morgan name. In return, they would enjoy day-to-day executive control. Had there been management consultants in those days, they couldn't have devised a better or wiser compromise.

This wasn't a polite charade in which the partners smirked behind the boss's back; they had genuine affection for Jack. Years later, Morgan partner and then chairman George Whitney would say:

> I always find that I have to guard myself because of a fear that I will sound soft and foolish, but he was a great gentleman, a cultured gentleman, if you know what I mean . . . and he'd deny it like hell if he ever heard me say it to anyone. He was a simple and just as sweet a man as you ever saw. . . . As I say, he was never given credit, because he was shy, but he kept that bunch of primadonnas working, the partners, and he was the unquestioned boss and there was never any argument about it. . . . He wasn't a buccaneer like his father, but he was a hell of a guy.[3]

Had there been rebellion in Jack's nature, it would have surfaced after Pierpont's death. Instead, he plunged into a Morgan specialty—father worship. Even after having nursed his mother through her dreadful marriage, he cared for the Hartford grave site of Mimi Sturges Morgan,

Pierpont's first wife. With his New England sense of self-reliance, he didn't think it sporting or fair to blame one's parents for one's troubles; he was no more prone to introversion than Pierpont had been. In 1916, he said of Charles Francis Adams's autobiographical work, "The depressed and gloomy point of view, and the anger at everyone who had anything to do with his bringing up, because he feels himself not a complete success, are rather distressing."[4] And he docilely accepted the dynastic nature of merchant banking, nudging his eldest son, Junius, into the bank just as he was pushed by Pierpont. "Junius is not going into the firm," he told a friend, "but he is coming into the office to see if he is fit to go into the firm later on, which I hope and trust he will be."[5]

In many respects, Jack's life evolved into an eerie act of homage as he tried to metamorphose into his father. If children identify with parents to relieve their fear of them, as some psychologists suggest, then Jack must have had a great deal of fear, for he tried very hard to resemble his father. As a *New Yorker* columnist said, "His similarity to his father in thought and outlook is almost weird."[6] To encourage the confusion, Jack dropped the *Jr.* from his name after Pierpont's death—a common practice—and took to being called Senior—the name that had been Pierpont's. Only Tom Lamont and, later, Russell Leffingwell, called him Jack.

That Jack successfully mimicked Pierpont had much to do with their sheer resemblance. There were differences: Jack's mustache was smaller and trimmer than Pierpont's walrus affair, and his eyes were gentler and less forbidding than the Senior's. Jack also had a peculiar stoop, his shoulders hunching forward as if he were muscle-bound or ducking to pass through a low doorway. But the similarities were more striking. Both were six foot two, broad shouldered, and burly—cartoonists scarcely had to alter their sketches of the pear-shaped, top-hatted tycoon. Jack even wore Pierpont's bloodstone on his watch chain—a favorite touch of the radical caricaturists, who had added it to the iconography of paunchy plutocrats. The strong Morgan nose remained, though without Pierpont's skin disease.

Contemporaries said the two J. P. Morgans even walked and talked alike. Occasionally, one sees a snapshot of "J. P. Morgan" threatening a reporter with his stick and momentarily cannot tell which Morgan it is. Both were high-strung, thin-skinned, moody, and prone to melancholic self-pity. Deeply emotional, they feared their ungovernable passions. A gruff, snappish way of relieving tension and dealing with disappointment was also conspicuous in both.

It is fascinating to follow Jack as he assumed his father's trappings. A sampler: In 1915, he wrote a Piccadilly hat shop for "another hat (felt) of the same shape as those you used to make for the late Mr. Pierpont Morgan."[7] Like his father, he went for his London tailoring to Henry Poole and Company of Savile Row and to Brooks Brothers in New York. He adopted his father's yen for gigantic cigars, ordering five thousand at a time. As his caterer, he retained Louis Sherry, who distributed to favored partners fifty bottles of brandy, one hundred of Musigny, and one hundred of Madeira at a clip. He maintained Pierpont's tradition of sending chests of Chinese tea to friends at Christmastime, wrapped in pretty paper covers. This special Morgan blend, Mandarin Mixture, came from a tiny garden on an inland Chinese plantation. On Christmas Eve, Jack perpetuated the ritual of reading to Morgan children from Dickens's *Christmas Carol*—using the author's own manuscript.

In religion, Jack was pious but less mystical than Pierpont. He, too, became a vestryman of Saint George's Church, sailed with bishops aboard the *Corsair III*, and resumed Morgan patronage of the Episcopal church, financing a revision of the *American Book of Common Prayer.* The New York Yacht Club got a new Commodore J. P. Morgan, while the Harvard Board of Overseers and the Metropolitan Museum of Art also got a new J. P. Morgan. New York City's orphans lost nothing from generational change. Jack made up the annual $100,000 deficit at the New York Lying-In Hospital. (In view of his happy marriage, he was spared the cruel barbs that greeted Pierpont's generosity.) As a philanthropist, Jack permitted small variations, so long as Morgan themes were preserved. Where Pierpont underwrote Egyptian excavations, Jack specialized in Aztec digs for the American Museum of Natural History. More an Anglophile than his father, Jack joined Lamont in an anonymous donation to Britain's National Trust to buy the land surrounding Stonehenge, saving the area from development.

Before Pierpont's death, Jack hadn't shown a particular interest in the library. But soon he developed his father's habit of leafing through its treasures each morning. Jack lacked the capital to mimic Pierpont's sweeping romps through European culture—Pierpont's own collecting had precluded that—so he concentrated instead on books and manuscripts, his specialty being incunabula, books printed before 1500.

Under Pierpont's strict instructions, Jack retained librarian Belle da Costa Greene, who never fully recovered from Pierpont's death; over time, Greene's bright banter would enchant the son as much as it had the father. And over time another amusing generational resemblance between the two became evident—the bullheaded way in which the

Morgan men cornered the market in one artist after another. In 1905, Jack had given his father a manuscript version of Thackeray's *Vanity Fair* and later rounded up remaining Thackerays on the market. Then he marched on Tennyson, eliciting a memorable remark from Greene: "In regard to the Tennyson items which, personally, I loathe, it is a question of perfecting your already very large and fine collection of imbecilities." No less than Pierpont, Jack found the librarian's fresh mouth piquant. He replied, "I reluctantly confirm that we ought to have the Tennyson idiocies."[8]

With less of a gypsy nature than Pierpont, Jack concentrated on creating stately residences. In 1909, he paid $10,000 for barren East Island off the North Shore of Long Island, near Glen Cove. To make the grounds fertile, he had manure shipped in by the bargeload. And after constructing a stone bridge to the mainland, Jack built a $2.5-million red-brick château, modeled after Denham Place, a Buckinghamshire mansion, and called Matinicock Point (sometimes spelled Matinecock). Set on an estate of 250 acres, the mansion was graced with a columned entrance, dormer windows, and high chimneys. It had forty-five rooms in all, including twelve bedrooms, thirteen bathrooms, eighteen marble fireplaces, a sixteen-car garage, and even a small gymnasium.[9] After Jack and Jessie moved there in 1911 (while still retaining their Madison Avenue brownstone), Pierpont had twitted his son about his proximity to Teddy Roosevelt's estate. "I too regret my nearness to Oyster Bay," Jack cabled back, "but expect outlive the troublesome neighbor."[10] Jack commuted to Wall Street by water each morning, pulling up at the New York Yacht Club's pier at East Twentieth Street.

Jack was an inveterate hunter and loved the world of English country houses. With his friend Eric Hambro, Jack bought Gannochy, a shooting lodge with seventeen thousand acres of highland moors in east central Scotland. It was a romantic spot, covered with heather and crossed by deep gorges and salmon-filled streams. Each August, Jack joined the merchant bankers and aristocrats who headed north to Scotland for grouse shooting. His guests sometimes bagged up to a thousand birds a day, while Jack's daughters, watching from an upstairs lodge window, cheered every missed shot. The Gannochy shoots, which later would include King George VI, helped to seal a new intimacy between England and the House of Morgan.

Jack and Jessie Morgan spent up to six months of each year in England. *Fortune* magazine left a portrait of their assimilation into British life, starting with their first stay, from 1898 to 1905: "They lived for eight years in England not as exiled Americans but as all but naturalized

Englishmen. Mrs. Morgan by background and training took easily to English country ways, English houses, English gardens—the whole domestic economy of a life of which the life in Boston was merely a more meager copy. And her husband found . . . that the life of a gentleman and an Episcopalian could be more gracefully and naturally led in London than on Wall Street in New York."[11]

Socially, Jack shared his father's snobbery and disdained the hurly-burly of American life. He never tried to broaden his social sphere or enlarge his sympathies. He might switch from the Union Club to the Union League Club, but that was the extent of his social experimentation. He had a special horror of arrivistes. Summering in Newport might be fine for others, but for Jack the place was "swamped by the horrid vulgar lot who make or rather ruin the reputation of it."[12]

The most conspicuous difference between Jack and his father was in their attitude toward the sexes. Both frowned on divorce among partners or employees and preferred male secretaries in the bank. (Until about the 1940s, women who married had to leave the bank, a regulation that led to several secret marriages.) But Jack was also puritanical in private—it is hard to imagine him swearing or telling off-color stories—and he once blushed to tell his children the facts of life. Perhaps reacting to his father's lechery, he was courtly with women, and he remained absolutely faithful to Jessie, a pretty, somewhat matronly woman.

Jack and Jessie's marriage was almost suffocatingly close. Jessie filled that little spot of doubt inside her husband. Confident and decisive, she propped up his ego, and he relied implicitly on her judgment in many matters. Jessie was strict with the four children and ran the estates with a firm, expert hand. She was cool and businesslike, and her daughters found it easier to take their problems to their father. But to Jack, Jessie was the supportive presence who compensated for his lifelong insecurity and guaranteed he would be spared his father's terribly loveless fate.

A S the new lord of the House of Morgan, Jack instantly faced two crises inherited from Pierpont. Coming on the heels of the Pujo hearings, they would further embitter him toward the public and confirm his sense of national ingratitude toward Morgan bounty. The first crisis involved his father's art collection, whose disposition Pierpont had left to him in his will.

Originally, most of the paintings and decorative objects were housed at Princes Gate, which, for lack of sufficient space, Pierpont had despaired of turning into a museum. (The books and manuscripts had always been under Belle Greene's care in New York.) And until 1909,

American import duties made it prohibitively expensive to bring home this "foreign" wing of the Morgan collection; then Pierpont, who was big enough to move congressional mountains, spurred the enactment of a duty-free exemption for works of art more than one hundred years old. The decision to transport the collection was hastened by another consideration: if it were in London when Pierpont died, his heirs would have to pay heavy death duties. So in 1912, thousands of pieces of art were packed in giant crates and shipped to New York. To please Morgan, U.S. customs inspectors were sent to London to speed the process.

Since Pierpont had expressed a desire to keep his collection together, its eventual destination was a matter of great speculation. At first, he had bequeathed it to the Metropolitan Museum, of which he was president. As a precondition, however, he asked New York City to appropriate money for a special Morgan wing. This was a rich man's way of asking for a token of respect and gratitude. Instead, it provoked a vituperative campaign, spearheaded by the Hearst newspapers and some city officials, who excoriated Pierpont for not providing the funds himself.

In this year of the Money Trust campaign, taxpayers were ripe for Morgan-baiting and prepared to believe that his bank account was bottomless. Stung by the campaign, Pierpont told shocked Metropolitan officials in late 1912 that they might not receive the collection after all. Easily injured, he could be sulky and childish when his pride was hurt. So he left the final decision to Jack. It would be his son's first large posthumous decision. Under a new state law, Jack had two years from the time of Pierpont's death to donate the art if he wished to receive an exemption from the inheritance tax.

While pondering his decision, Jack temporarily permitted the collection to be exhibited at the Metropolitan Museum. It was a breathtaking event that brought together 4,100 works from London and New York—the one time the complete Morgan collection could be viewed in its entirety. America had never seen artistic riches in such profusion. The word *exhibition* didn't capture its scope: it was like the unveiling of a major museum, revealing the fruits of the most frenzied buying spree in art history. There were 550 enamels, 260 Renaissance bronzes, nearly 700 pieces of porcelain from the eighteenth century, 39 tapestries, 900 miniatures, more than 50 European paintings. By glimpsing these treasures, the public developed not only a fuller sense of their worth but a possessive feeling toward them as well.

Now Jack had to weigh the competing claims of his bank and American culture. He and other Morgan partners recalled the unpleasant suspense each year as they wondered whether the Senior's balance would cover the bills pouring in from London and Paris. And now Jack wondered whether he could cover the $3 million in inheritance taxes and the $20 million in individual bequests mandated by Pierpont's will. The approximately $20 million in liquid assets in the estate simply did not match the scale of Pierpont's generosity. While he required liquid capital for bequests, estate taxes, and his business, Jack held, instead, mostly illiquid art masterpieces. What to do?

The answer came in February 1915 and scandalized the art world: Jack decided to dismantle the collection. First he sold the Chinese porcelains for $3 million to Duveen Brothers, who resold them to Henry Clay Frick. Then Fragonard's magnificent *Progress of Love,* four panels executed for Mme du Barry, went for $1.25 million, also to Frick, who adorned a room of his Fifth Avenue mansion with them. Frick's new ascendancy as foremost American collector, heir to Pierpont, evidently pleased Jack, who said he had been kinder to him than any of Pierpont's other business associates. Sugar baron H. O. Havemeyer bought the Vermeer that had captivated Pierpont. "It seems we need the money," Belle Greene sighed.[13]

By the end of this avalanche of sales—during which Greene battled tenaciously for higher prices—$8 million worth of art had changed hands at handsome prices. Pierpont's death hadn't devastated the art market—the new fortunes being amassed by munitions makers in the World War, fortunes often awarded by the Morgan bank itself, picked up the slack. Greene's friend Bernard Berenson commented that Pierpont might be dead, "but his soul goes marching on."[14]

The cognoscenti were horrified by the sale, which they portrayed as a brutal, unfeeling massacre of the world's premiere art collection. Profiting from it, Joseph Duveen nonetheless classified the breakup "with that other great artistic tragedy, the dispersal by the Commonwealth of the carefully chosen treasures of King Charles the First."[15] As a salve for bruised feelings, the Metropolitan was given 40 percent of the collection, a monumental bequest of about seven thousand objects, including Raphael's *Colonna Madonna,* which was the world's most expensive painting when purchased by Pierpont for £100,000. For all the disappointment, this was the biggest windfall in the museum's history, forming the heart of its medieval collection.

Pierpont's literary collection—about twenty thousand items, including Gutenberg Bibles, papyruses, and manuscripts by Keats, Shelley, Swift, and Dr. Johnson—stayed intact at the library, as did many splendid oddities, such as Marie-Antoinette's fan, which Jack would give to the French government in 1925. The other major beneficiary was the

Morgan Memorial at the Wadsworth Atheneum in Hartford, which Pierpont had built in tribute to Junius. (As Pierpont had insisted, portraits of him and Junius hung side by side at the head of the museum's grand staircase.) In 1917, Jack gave the museum such a massive bequest of ancient bronzes and European decorative arts—more than thirteen hundred items—that the Wadsworth at once leapt into fifth place among American museums.

Instead of explaining his decision, Jack sprang it unexpectedly on the public. Then he retreated into a touchy silence, heeding Pierpont's dictum of never answering press attacks. This made him seem guilty and defensive. One can only speculate as to the reasons behind his self-defeating silence. As a private banker, he would have refrained from any statement suggesting a need to shore up the bank's capital—no secret was more closely guarded by merchant bankers than their capital position. At this point, the House of Morgan had never been examined by regulators or revealed a balance sheet; Jack wasn't about to discuss Morgan capital in public. It might have also been hard to explain the urgent need for money without indirectly criticizing his father's prodigality. If blame was to be meted out, it probably should have been directed toward Pierpont, whose collection had outpaced any provision for its storage and display. It was Pierpont, not Jack, who failed to provide for both bank and art collection. Although he did it in boorish, public-be-damned style, Jack may only have been setting things aright.

THE second crisis shadowing Jack's first days at the helm involved the New York, New Haven and Hartford Railroad. Joseph Morgan—Pierpont's grandfather—had sponsored one of its predecessors, giving it a special place in the family. Going on the road's board after 1892, Pierpont came to rule it with a mixture of sentimentality, explosive rage, and willful blindness almost without equal in Morgan annals. In 1903, he had brought in Charles S. Mellen—called "the last of the railway czars"—to run the New Haven. Mellen had a smooth, domed head, white mustache, and a cold, sarcastic manner that made him the most hated man in Boston. The New Haven would be a *folie à deux* for Morgan and Mellen, bringing out the worst in both in their contempt for the public.

The two planned to take over every form of transportation in New England and wantonly usurped steamship lines, interurban electric trolleys, rapid transit systems—anything that threatened their monopoly. The New Haven gobbled up every railroad in Rhode Island, Connecticut, and southern Massachusetts. The centerpiece of their plan was the purchase of the Boston and Maine Railroad in 1907. This was so controversial that Pierpont and Mellen met with President Roosevelt in order to forestall antitrust problems. Though the president offered his tacit consent, he later confessed that he had gone "beyond the verge of propriety in condoning offenses" committed by the New Haven.[16]

The New Haven's expansion was both unwise and unscrupulous. As it paid exorbitant prices to swallow up competitors, its debt load grew crushing. The railroad became a bloated monster of a holding company, with 125,000 employees in 336 subsidiaries. To hide its financial chicanery, it set up hundreds of dummy corporations, some headed by mystified clerks who were periodically called in and told to sign contracts. The House of Morgan made enormous profits from this corporate maze, booking nearly a million dollars in commissions from an incessant flow of stocks and bonds. Meanwhile, the New Haven's real future competitor—the automobile—escaped the wide net that Pierpont had flung over New England transportation.

Unbeknownst to the public, the House of Morgan itself was queasy about Mellen's stewardship. In May 1908, George Perkins wrote to Pierpont, "I still feel, as I have for a couple of years, that Mr. Mellen is getting the New Haven road into considerable of a muddle by his financial methods, and this, I think, is becoming more or less the general opinion."[17] The bank began quietly to sell off its securities in the road.

Unfortunately for Pierpont's image, Mellen was a vocal admirer and later said he never undertook any initiative without first consulting Pierpont. "I wear the Morgan collar," he boasted to reporters, "but I am proud of it. If Mr. Morgan were to order me tomorrow to China or Siberia in his interests, I would pack up and go."[18] He would leave an indelible portrait of Pierpont as an autocratic board member. "It was Mr. Morgan's way, when he wished to cut opposition and discussion short, to fling his box of matches from him, bring his fist down, and say, 'Call a vote. Let's see where these gentlemen stand.' "[19] Other board members, Mellen said, cowered and submitted to him.

The Morgan patronage had definite advantages for the railroad. The New Haven's stock was considered the safest of blue-chip investments and sported a high dividend. And Charles Mellen had redeeming features as a railroad man. For the first time, he enabled passengers to travel from New York to Boston without switching lines. The problem was that Mellen was a thorough rascal. Here was William Allen White's verdict: "Mellen, in the eyes of economic liberals, was the head devil of the plutocracy in Massachusetts and New England. . . . In politics, Mellen walked to his ends directly, justified by the conscience of a plutocrat, which held in contempt the scruples of democracy."[20]

Congressional investigators later revealed that Mellen handed out about a million dollars in bribes on one suburban line alone. Beyond shame, he even suborned a Harvard professor to deliver lectures favoring lenient regulatory treatment for trains and trolleys. So pervasive was New Haven power in New England that it was termed the "invisible government."[21] Mellen's largesse extended right up to the Republican National Committee. When later granted immunity from prosecution, Mellen almost gloried in the vicious squalor, the total absence of business scruples. Testifying about the competition between the New Haven and a rival, he was asked what form it took. "Any form you can imagine—one man cutting the heart out of another, except they were two railroads."[22]

An open scandal, the New Haven attracted the attention of the most cunning and resourceful foe the House of Morgan would ever face— Louis D. Brandeis, now a "people's lawyer" but later a Supreme Court justice. The son of eastern European immigrants, a Harvard Law graduate, Brandeis was already a millionaire lawyer in 1907 when he took on the New Haven as a public-interest cause. That year, he spearheaded the fight against the purchase of the Boston & Maine.

Brandeis conducted a searching critique of the Gentleman Banker's Code—those rituals that governed competition among elite banking houses. He sounded themes of excessive banker influence that would be amplified by the Pujo hearings and echoed in the New Deal, later shaping Securities and Exchange Commission policy. He argued for an arm's-length distance between bankers and companies. For Brandeis, bankers who sat on corporate boards were in a conflict-of-interest situation. Far from being neutral confidants of companies, they were tempted to load up clients with unneeded bonds or charge them inflated commissions. The House of Morgan was his major object lesson; he said it symbolized "a monopolistic and predatory control over the financial and industrial resources of the country."[23] The Brandeis critique was predicated not on government regulation of monopolies but on breaking them up and reverting to a small-scale competitive economy. Over time, this view would prove far more threatening to the House of Morgan than the trust-busting of Teddy Roosevelt and other supporters of large-scale industry.

The New Haven's day of reckoning came in 1911, when its debt burden forced layoffs, pay cuts, and deferral of critical track maintenance. The road piled up a grisly record of train wrecks—four that year, seven the next—that caused dozens of deaths. As the train wrecks mounted in 1912, Brandeis found an ever-wider audience for his attacks on the New Haven, and the Interstate Commerce Commission began to hold hearings on the matter. That summer, Brandeis went to Sea Girt, New Jersey, to consult with Woodrow Wilson, the Democratic presidential nominee. Brandeis advised Wilson on economic matters, wrote speeches, and slipped the Money Trust into his rhetoric, getting Wilson to espouse an end to interlocking directorates between bankers and industrial companies. For Brandeis, the New Haven was an archetypal battle in the eternal war between "the people" and "the interests."

Threatened by Brandeis, Mellen fought back in inimitably dirty style. A Boston publication called *Truth*, subsidized by the New Haven, portrayed Brandeis as an agent of Jacob Schiff and described his campaign as part of the "age-long struggle between Jew and Gentile."[24] In December 1912, Mellen and Morgan issued a stinging press release, accusing Brandeis of trying to destroy confidence in the New Haven. But Brandeis was winning converts, and Mellen was indicted by a federal grand jury on antitrust charges. He waived immunity, apparently hoping to spare Pierpont the strain of a subpoena during the Pujo investigation. The Pujo report further bolstered Brandeis's case against Morgan and the New Haven. And that was where matters stood at Pierpont's death.

That Pierpont's sins would be visited on Jack became evident on June 12, 1913, when a New Haven collision at the Stamford station killed seven passengers. Wilson's new attorney general, James C. McReynolds, already had civil and criminal suits against the New Haven in the works, and the climate was ripe for trustbusters to intensify their campaign. On July 9, the Interstate Commerce Commission published a report criticizing the New Haven's financial management and recommending that the New Haven be stripped of its trolley and steamship holdings. Here came a critical watershed in Morgan history. As a banker of the Baronial Age, Pierpont would have stood obstinately by Mellen, spewing rage. But Jack had replaced his father on the railroad board. Heeding the ICC warning, he ousted Mellen and overrode the rest of the board to do so. It wasn't that Jack had any ideological sympathy with government regulation; he was as rabid on the subject as his father. But as a tactical matter, he was more conciliatory—more a banker of the Diplomatic Age. The New Haven board brought in Howard Elliott of the Northern Pacific to replace Mellen.

The New Haven would always be a touchy subject with the Morgans, who considered themselves benefactors of New England. Pierpont had been the proud president of the New England Society. His grandson Harry Morgan later said that Pierpont "was so loyal to the region" that he had "a blind spot when it came to New England and the New Haven's place in it."[25] Facing a chorus of criticism, Jack tried to defend his deceased father, claiming that in his last years he had spent half his time abroad and couldn't possibly be held responsible for the railroad's excesses. Yet Jack's cables reveal that Pierpont stayed in touch on New Haven matters. He might have been gallivanting on the Riviera or cruising up the Nile, but he followed the railroad's affairs. In 1910, Mellen had wanted to extend the New Haven's territory to the newly completed Pennsylvania Station in Manhattan. Sensing a competitive threat to his other ward, the New York Central, Pierpont threatened to resign if Mellen persisted. All the way from Rome, he bellowed, "You can tell C. S. Mellen with my compliments that if he persists in proposed policy he will, in my opinion, make mistake of his life."[26] Pierpont was remote in body but not in spirit.

Even after Howard Elliott's appointment, horror stories still abounded at the New Haven. In September 1913, another wreck outside New Haven killed twenty-one passengers and trapped forty boys returning from summer camp. An ICC report blamed Morgan and Mellen. Then, in a final humiliation for the bank, the debt-riddled New Haven skipped its dividend in December for the first time in forty years. It was a classic widows-and-orphans stock, and thousands of small investors lost their income before Christmas. Whether from shame, anger, or a desire to avoid blame, both Jack Morgan and George F. Baker missed the meeting at which the historic vote was taken. Attorney General McReynolds still breathed down the necks of the New Haven board, which he thought was dominated by bankers. The Morgan men knew they were outflanked. "Whole situation disgusting," Harry Davison cabled to Jack, "but must recognize that Brandeis et al have ear of President and Attorney General just now."[27] Jack told Davison that he would resign from the New Haven board, except that it might be seen as confirming Brandeis's attacks on him and his father.

During the New Haven controversy, there was an important sideshow that never came to light. During the fall of 1913, Brandeis published his influential series *Other People's Money—and How the Bankers Use It*, in *Harper's Weekly*. His critique of the Gentleman Banker's Code argued that bankers on corporate boards introduced nepotism and double-dealing. As a result of these articles, Tom Lamont decided to put into effect his new public relations policy of meeting privately with bank critics. Through Norman Hapgood, editor of *Harper's Weekly*, he arranged for a private chat with Brandeis in December 1913 at the University Club on Fifth Avenue. A verbatim transcript of the meeting survives.

Let us picture the antagonists as they settled into their armchairs. Speaking with a Kentucky drawl, the young Brandeis had a wide face, large jug ears, powerful shoulders, and flaring eyes. Lamont was short and elegant, had a look of keen, watchful amusement, and was very tough beneath the charm. Confident of his persuasive powers, Lamont was as refined with strangers as Jack was awkward. In his meeting with Brandeis, we see him emerging as the principal image maker and ideologist of the House of Morgan.

Lamont cast Pierpont's faith in Charles Mellen as a virtue: "Mr. Morgan had that large nature which led him almost blindly to have faith in a man when once it was established."[28] He reiterated Morgan dogma that bankers were responsible to investors and had to be on boards to safeguard their interests. Brandeis retorted, "You could be kept precisely as fully in touch and informed off the board as you are on."[29] Lamont seemed caught off guard. Rather than having bankers negotiate private deals with clients, Brandeis espoused open, competitive bidding for securities offerings. Lamont said this worked fine in good times, when investors readily took new issues, but left companies adrift in bad times, when investors became apprehensive. These arguments would reverberate for forty years.

Both Lamont and Brandeis tried to sound friendly, although Brandeis was more dogged, relishing a chance to confront his adversary face-to-face. After a time, it grew clear that both men circled around something unspoken—namely, mythical Morgan power, the belief on Wall Street that if the bank had a single director on a board, he would dictate to all the others. Lamont was exasperated by glancing references to this power and finally confronted it directly:

> *Lamont:* You are picturing our firm . . . as having this gigantic power over men and matters.
> *Brandeis:* But it has that power, Mr. Lamont. You may not realize it, but you are feared, and I believe the effect of your position is toward paralysis rather than expansion.

> *Lamont:* You astonish me beyond measure. How in the world did you
> arrive at the belief that people are afraid of us, or that we have
> this terrific power?
> *Brandeis:* From my own experience.[30]

Brandeis told how he had foreseen the New Haven debacle, had
gone to Boston bankers to complain about the railroad's management,
and was told the road was "Mr. Morgan's particular pet" and that
they feared being excluded from future Morgan bond syndicates if
they offered any protest. This was probably true: any firm that refused to participate on one Morgan issue might be penalized on
others.

In the end, Brandeis scored more points in the debate—one senses
Lamont was unprepared for the attorney's fierce intelligence—but neither side budged in his position. Yet the conversation resonated in
Lamont's mind, particularly Brandeis's charge that Wall Street lacked
interest in small businesses. Years later, when advising Woodrow Wilson at Versailles, Lamont asked the president if he could cite a single
instance of a deserving company being denied credit on Wall Street;
according to Lamont, Wilson could not. The Brandeis encounter started
a lifelong effort by Lamont to present a coherent case for Morgan power.
He needed to make others believe in the bank's virtue. Through him,
Wall Street's most reticent bank would acquire a refined voice and an
explicit ideology.

In the Diplomatic Age, companies remained tied to their Wall Street
bankers, but the strings were already loosening. The Baronial Age was
based on the immaturity of industry. Now large companies were accumulating cash reserves and financing expansion from retained earnings. When private bankers were better known than the companies they
sponsored, exclusive relations with clients guaranteed their access to
scarce capital. But such Morgan offspring as AT&T, U.S. Steel, and
International Harvester were now becoming established companies on
a national and even a global scale, outgrowing the need for banker
protection.

For Pierpont's generation of bankers, membership on the boards of
client companies was an article of faith. But in January 1914, hoping to
placate the Wilson administration, Morgan partners startled Wall Street
by resigning as directors from thirty companies, including banks, railroads, and industrial firms. Jack resigned not only from the New Haven,
but from the New York Central, the National City Bank, the First
National Bank, and the National Bank of Commerce. (By lumping the

New Haven with the others, he didn't give Brandeis the satisfaction of a lone resignation.) He hoped this would stop legislation, supported by Wilson, outlawing bank-company interlocks. The Clayton Antitrust Act of 1914 forbade interlocking boards of competing companies but didn't stop bankers from sitting on the boards of client companies.

Changes in the government-business balance were now occurring with amazing speed. In 1913, the Sixteenth Amendment was ratified; the following year, income taxes soared, and the Federal Trade Commission was created. Jack accepted the changes bitterly. Like Pierpont, he would store up anger silently until it overwhelmed him. Now he stewed inwardly, indulging in jeremiads that prefigure his remorseless hostility toward the New Deal. He inveighed against "destructive elements" that had supposedly controlled the country since Teddy Roosevelt. He wrote a friend in June 1914: "A greater lot of perfectly incompetent and apparently thoroughly crooked people has never, as far as I know, run, or attempted to run, any first-class country. The Mexicans are far better off, because their various bosses only murder and rape, and our bosses run the country and make life intolerable for a much larger number of people."[31]

One final episode in this last flowering of Progressive reform should be noted. On December 23, 1913, President Wilson signed the Federal Reserve Act. Wilson, of course, had insisted on a Federal Reserve Board in Washington under political, not banker, control. "There are only two choices," he said. "Either to give the central control to the bankers or to give it to the government."[32] Earlier in the year, Jack had gone down to Washington with the Morgan plan for a central bank under private control. J. P. Morgan and Company had not only formulated a scheme but had had it beautifully printed up. When Wilson's close adviser, Colonel House, saw what Jack had brought, he hastily told him to present it to Wilson typed on ordinary paper, lest Bryan and the Progressives think the House of Morgan was dropping off a prearranged plan.

The Federal Reserve System that went into operation in November 1914, was, in many ways, a Morgan godsend. It took some political heat off the bank. As Fed historian William Greider has written, "As an economic institution, the Fed inherited the noblesse-oblige role that the House of Morgan could no longer perform—and also some of the resentment."[33] The diminution of Morgan power was less than met the eye. In many ways, the Washington board, which oversaw the twelve regional banks, was toothless. The New York Fed, in contrast, emerged as the focal point for dealing with European central banks and the foreign-exchange markets. So, real financial power remained where it had always resided—on Wall Street.

The critical position in the new system was the governor of the New York Federal Reserve Bank. Its first occupant, Benjamin Strong, had Morgan written all over his résumé. He was a protégé of Harry Davison, who had made him a secretary of Bankers Trust and brought him in as Pierpont's personal auditor during the 1907 panic. There was an emotional bond between the two men. When Strong's wife committed suicide after childbirth and a daughter died a year later, the Davisons took the three surviving Strong children into their home. Strong then married Katherine Converse, daughter of Bankers Trust's president, and had become president himself by 1914.

That year, when the New York Fed job became available, Strong balked at taking it. Not only had he supported the bankers' Aldrich plan, but he had even campaigned against the Federal Reserve Act. Only after spending a long country weekend with Harry Davison and Paul Warburg did he take the job. Strong wanted to endow the New York Fed with the dignity and prestige of the Bank of England. The House of Morgan directed him to Teddy Grenfell for tutorials on how that bank operated. Through Strong's influence, the Federal Reserve System would prove far more of a boon than a threat to Morgans. The New York Fed and the bank would share a sense of purpose such that the House of Morgan would be known on Wall Street as the Fed bank. So, contrary to expectations, frustrated reformers only watched Morgan power grow after 1913.

CHAPTER TEN

WAR

• •
•

E VEN as domestic troubles crowded in upon the House of Morgan, the bank was on the eve of its most spectacular foreign triumph, one that would make Pierpont Morgan look provincial in comparison. During the early summer of 1914, an industrial recession was accompanied by a bear market on Wall Street. Businessmen grumbled that Woodrow Wilson's crusade against the "interests" had chilled the entrepreneurial spirit. In this gloomy frame of mind, American investors panicked when they learned of Austria-Hungary's declaration of war against Serbia on July 28, 1914. Wall Street, which prided itself on its prescience, was once again caught napping by a historic event.

The House of Morgan had closely followed European events. Although later accused of World War I profiteering, it nearly engaged in clandestine diplomacy to stop fighting between the Balkan states and Turkey in 1912. The plan was to have the House of Morgan provide loans to both sides on condition that they submit to American mediation, and President Taft was to have acted as mediator. The scheme was apparently hatched by Herman Harjes, senior partner of Morgan, Harjes in Paris, and U.S. ambassador to France Myron Herrick. Jack Morgan finally vetoed the idea, fearing that the loan money would be used to further the war effort, which the House of Morgan wished to stop.[1] He also refused to proceed without the full cooperation of the European powers.

The hysteria that seized Wall Street in late July 1914 stemmed from a misguided fear that transatlantic trade would collapse and worsen the recession. Americans thought they couldn't survive without European capital and feared that gold would be withdrawn from New York and hoarded in London. After the czar mobilized over a million Russian troops on July 29, all the European markets shut down. As overseas investors rushed to liquidate securities through New York, the Stock Exchange took its steepest one-day dive since the 1907 panic.

By the morning of July 31, 1914, a staggering accumulation of overnight sell orders threatened a thunderous crash. Even though Pierpont Morgan was now dead, his star pupil, Harry Davison, had been well tutored in the 1907 panic. Bankers still instinctively resorted to 23 Wall Street in an emergency. The House of Morgan was more than a man; it had acquired an institutional continuity. Davison summoned Wall Street's bankers to the old Mills Building at 15 Broad Street, the provisional Morgan home while the new headquarters was being readied. Before the start of trading, the Stock Exchange president rushed over for consultation.

Even though Jack was there, Davison presided. Also present was a new Morgan banker, Dwight W. Morrow, a distinguished tax and utility lawyer. Morrow recalled the frantic discussion: "The Stock Exchange authorities wanted to know whether to open or not, and nobody knew what to tell them. It got down to about five minutes of ten, and the President . . . called up the Exchange and told them to announce that the Exchange would be closed." It was a hairbreadth reprieve: the man who rang the opening gong had already assumed his post, and traders shrugged with relief. "It was in my very early days in a banking firm," Morrow added, "and I can remember that I was impressed with how little anybody knew what he was doing."[2] Curiously, Morgan accounts of this meeting omit a 9:30 A.M. phone call that Jack made to Treasury Secretary William G. McAdoo, who advised him, "If you really want my judgment, it is to close the Exchange."[3]

The New York Stock Exchange didn't resume restricted trading until December, and normal trading didn't return until the following spring. A curious fugitive institution sprang up—the so-called gutter market of outlaw brokers, who loitered on the curbs trading stocks. According to Wall Street lore, it started out with "four boys and a dog," but soon a hundred brokerage firms jumped into sidewalk trading on New Street— to the point where the Stock Exchange clamped down. As Alexander Dana Noyes noted, this ragtag band was probably "at the time the only actual stock market in the world."[4]

The war was initially a bleak time for the House of Morgan. Like other banks, it made a great deal of money from broker call loans—loans made to buy stock on margin—and so started the war in low spirits. This despondent mood obscured a momentous shift in world finance: the United States was about to capture financial supremacy from England

and emerge as the leading creditor nation. Although nobody quite realized it at first, the English era was over. After the war, world currency markets would shift from a sterling to a dollar standard.

The news of war was greeted with melodramatic foreboding by Jack Morgan, who foresaw "the most appalling destruction of values in securities which has ever been seen in this country."[5] Later reviled as a "merchant of death" by isolationists, his first reaction, in fact, was spotlessly humane. On July 31, he even issued a rare public appeal for peace: "If the delicate situation can be held in abeyance for a few weeks, I should expect a rising tide of protest from the people who are to pay for war with their blood and their property."[6] Far from rubbing his hands at the prospect of war profits, he scoffed at the notion that New York might supplant London as the world's financial center.

The partner with the best antennae for the seismic shift was Harry Davison. The war would be his glory time. Almost at once, he sensed a Morgan bonanza and immediately dispatched telegrams to Lamont, then trout fishing and horseback riding on a Montana ranch. These telegrams throb with excitement:

> THE CREDIT OF ALL EUROPE HAS BROKEN DOWN ABSOLUTELY SPECIE PAYMENTS SUSPENDED AND MORATORIUM IN FORCE IN FRANCE AND PRACTICALLY IN ALL COUNTRIES THOUGH NOT OFFICIALLY IN ENGLAND. . . .
>
> PROBABLY COULD DO LITTLE IF YOU WERE HERE THE ONLY POINT BEING THAT IS FILLED WITH EXTRA ORDINARY INTEREST AND OF COURSE GREAT POSSIBILITYS. . . . PERHAPS I MIGHT EXPRESS THE SITUATION BY STATING THAT IT IS AS IF WE HAD HAD AN EARTHQUAKE ARE AS YET SOMEWHAT STUNNED BUT WILL SOON GET TO RIGHTING THINGS.[7]

An immediate war casualty was that chronic Morgan stepchild, the city of New York, which had about $80 million in European obligations coming due. As the dollar plunged—making repayment more expensive—and the United States faced a possible standstill in transatlantic trade, sentiment was strong for suspending payment on the debt. Why not exploit the European chaos to save some money? Forming a syndicate to pay off the bonds, the House of Morgan and Kuhn, Loeb organized an impromptu rescue. Gold was shipped to the Bank of England and then credited to Morgan Grenfell, which paid off New York City notes as they matured. The operation was a mark of financial maturity, a signal to the world that New York as a financial center could offer safety comparable to that of London.

For many Americans, the war was at first a distant irrelevance; for isolationists, it provided yet another example of why America should steer clear of foreign imbroglios. Despite his sympathy for the Allies, President Wilson issued a proclamation of neutrality, entreating Americans to be "impartial in thought as well as action." For Morgan partners, this was impossible. As Tom Lamont said, "we wanted the Allies to win, from the outset of the war. We were pro-Ally by inheritance, by instinct, by opinion."[8] As cosmopolitan bankers with London and Paris affiliates, the Morgan partners were deeply enmeshed in European life and had too abiding a faith in Anglo-Saxon civilization to stand on the sidelines. Yet it was also a cardinal rule of the Diplomatic Age not to defy government edicts, and the bank abided by Washington's policy.

In early August, the French, who had appointed J. P. Morgan and Company as their financial agent, sounded out the bank on a possible $100-million loan. The Wilson administration did more than deny this request. The secretary of state, William Jennings Bryan—the toad in the garden of Morgan history—denounced loans to belligerents as "the worst of contrabands."[9] A few days later, he told the press that loans by American bankers to warring nations were "inconsistent with the true spirit of neutrality."[10]

Within six weeks, Bryan's policy on contraband financing was reversed as Wilson tilted—subtly but unmistakably—toward the Allies. Robert Lansing, the State Department counselor and acting secretary of state that fall, figured out a way to sidestep U.S. neutrality through legal legerdemain. He persuaded Wilson to adopt a serviceable distinction between forbidden "loans" made through foreign war bonds and permissible "credits" for Allied purchases of matériel. Why the sudden shift after only two months of war? American exports to Europe had lifted the United States from recession, and even parochial farmers worried that Allied purchases of grain, meat, and cotton might be curtailed for lack of credit. As Davison told Treasury Secretary McAdoo, "to maintain our prosperity we must finance it."[11] The House of Morgan offered a convenient cover for preserving the appearance, while denying the spirit, of neutrality.

With much industrial slack, the United States was an ideal arsenal for the war. But as the Allies bid against each other for American supplies, they drove prices sky-high; even separate departments of the British government ended up in bitter competition. To relieve such price pressure, Lloyd George, then the chancellor of the Exchequer, asked Teddy Grenfell if Morgans in New York could do anything about expanding American rifle production, and Jack Morgan made inquiries at the Remington and Winchester arms companies. But more than expanded production was needed to stop war profiteering. In October 1914, the British Treasury sent over Sir George Paish and Basil Blackett to look into the problem. The most mandarin of Whitehall bureaucracies, the British Treasury needed a Wall Street outpost and found it in their New York agent, the House of Morgan. When the Treasury men returned to London in late November, they had another passenger stowed away on board, Harry Davison. Because Willard Straight was restless, Davison took him and Dorothy along. The Straights' new magazine, *The New Republic,* was already running a letter from Ray Stannard Baker warning American business not to exploit the war "to promote its own business and trade."[12]

Davison had come up with an inspired idea, which Straight claimed was stolen from him. Davison wondered whether the House of Morgan could get rid of plundering middlemen by concentrating Allied purchases in a single agency that would negotiate from a position of strength. He knew the preferred Morgan style was never to grandstand and suggested that Jack Morgan take the boat with the Treasury men. Never one to steal glory, Jack replied, "You jump on the steamer yourself, this is your idea."[13] Jack's friend Sir Cecil Arthur Spring-Rice, the British ambassador in Washington, had lobbied for a similar idea, telling the Foreign Office that it would require a firm of stature in both London and New York. The Anglo-American House of Morgan was the logical choice.

Once Davison was installed at Claridge's, Teddy Grenfell led him on a tour of Bank of England and Whitehall officials. British officials liked the Davison plan, and not only because it would lower prices. Politically, it would convert the House of Morgan into a lightning rod for the inevitable charges of favoritism that go with wartime contracts. The firm's liabilities were also apparent. Some officials feared that British radicals would have a field day with this Wall Street link, and others worried about the bank's unpopularity among certain sectors of American society. The House of Morgan knew its own unpopularity west of the Mississippi. In April 1914, it had considered setting up a rare branch in Chicago to soften midwestern sentiment against it.

On December 16, 1914, Davison lunched with the prime minister, Herbert H. Asquith, and the chancellor, David Lloyd George. He brought along a contract for a proposed Morgan purchasing agency for the Allies. The prime minister reviewed it paragraph by paragraph and said he "approved every word."[14] On January 15, 1915, the House of Morgan signed the Commercial Agreement with the Army Council and the Admiralty. The first purchase was $12 million for horses—then an urgently needed item. In the spring, a similar arrangement was concluded with the French through the senior Morgan partner in Paris, Herman Harjes.

Nobody foresaw the magnitude of the proposed operation. Lord Kitchener, secretary of war, told Davison the purchases might amount to £10 million—and he stressed that he was guessing on the high side. In fact, the purchases came to an astronomical $3 billion—almost half of all American supplies sold to the Allies during the war. Skimming off a 1-percent commission, the House of Morgan booked an astounding $30 million in fees. It was probably the most important deal in its history, not only for the money but for the political and corporate contacts it produced. Jack Morgan had qualms about the bank going into such alien business but feared a political backlash against the United States in Britain if war profiteering continued. At the White House in late January 1915, Jack got Woodrow Wilson's blessing, who said he wouldn't interfere with any action in "furtherance of trade."[15]

The old private banks of Wall Street and the City had a chameleon quality and could quickly adapt to opportunities. To head what became the Export Department, Tom Lamont recruited Edward R. Stettinius, Sr., president of the Diamond Match Company. A former speculator in the Chicago wheat pits, Stettinius had well-brushed silver hair, a mustache, and rimless spectacles. His neat exterior reflected a meticulous, almost obsessive, attention to detail. Later, Secretary of War Newton Baker would refer to his "almost terrifying sense of responsibility."[16] From 9:00 A.M. until midnight daily, he lashed a Morgan staff of 175 known as SOS—Slaves of Stettinius. He didn't simply hire people: he conscripted them, squeezed them, drove them to exhaustion. One drone later said, "If any fellow quit at 9 o'clock at night he was usually congratulated by the others on being about to take a half-holiday."[17]

The purchasing operation reflected the size and the complexity of modern warfare. World War I seemed both primitive and modern, an incongruous mixture of cavalry charges and zeppelin raids, cannon fire and mustard gas. There were endless salvos of deadly projectiles: at the Battle of the Marne alone, two hundred thousand shells were exploded in a day. So the logistical needs were immensely varied and of decisive importance in the war effort.

Stettinius became the single most important consumer on earth, rounding up $10 million in goods per day. He bought, shipped, and insured supplies on an unprecedented scale and stimulated methods of mass production. As word of his operation spread, 23 Wall Street was mobbed by brokers and manufacturers of every description; the bank had to post guards at every door and assign them to partners' homes. Each month, Stettinius presided over purchases equivalent to the world's gross national product a generation before. He bargained hard for corned beef and barbed wire, locomotives and artificial limbs.

The German general staff had never imagined that the United States could switch so quickly to war production. As the capacity of plants became strained, Stettinius promoted the building of new factories. The House of Morgan and Great Britain made loans to Winchester Repeating Arms for new gun capacity and advanced money to many other firms to fulfill their contracts. By war's end, the United States had an arms-making capacity that eclipsed that of England and France combined. For his efforts, Stettinius would bear the unlovely tag of father of the military industrial complex. Even General Erich von Ludendorff was heard to say that Stettinius was worth an army corps to the Allies.[18] He became a czar of American industry. Boris Bakhmeteff, head of a Russian Industrial Mission to the United States, recalled a meeting at which Stettinius assembled the heads of some of America's largest companies and "gave them hell in words that I was ashamed of."[19]

Because Stettinius was the linchpin of the Allied supply operation, his safety became a high priority, especially after Erich von Falkenhayn, chief of Germany's general staff, decided to achieve victory by cutting off the Allied supply line. British intelligence agents informed Stettinius of threats against his life. They told of a "certain lovely lady" in New York who had seen a German agent carrying letters addressed to him. As a security precaution, Stettinius's family was uprooted without warning from their thirteen-acre mansion on Staten Island and relocated on Long Island. Stettinius himself spent the war aboard the cruiser *Margaret,* anchored in New York harbor. His room was tastefully appointed with vases, linen, china, and plated silver, all picked by that well-known decorator Harry Davison.

The Morgan bank also performed intelligence work for the British. When the Morgan partners learned of a plan by German investors to buy up Bethlehem Steel, they met with company officials and had them put their shares in a voting trust, making the defense contractor impregnable to an unwanted takeover. In an extraordinary act of faith, the British exempted the House of Morgan from mail censorship in and out of Britain, allowing it to retain an in-house code developed by Stettinius and his British contact, Charles F. Whigham of Morgan Grenfell. Hence, in wartime cables, Jack retained his code name Chargeless and Lamont, Chalado. Sticking to tradition, the bank wouldn't let any outsider have access to its code book.

Nonetheless, the Export Department wasn't an unqualified success. The French never used it as much as the British did, and the British Admiralty remained cool compared with the War Office—a tension unrelieved by a meeting between Jack and First Lord of the Admiralty Sir Winston Churchill. There were also persistent suspicions that the bank favored friends. Though contracts were distributed to almost one thousand companies, many big winners—General Electric, Bethlehem Steel, Du Pont, and U.S. Steel—were firmly in the Morgan camp.

The war was especially profitable for the Guggenheims. In 1914, the House of Morgan helped them to organize Kennecott Copper, America's biggest copper producer, as a public company; Daniel Guggenheim was a frequent wartime visitor to Morgan partner Thomas Cochran, who sat on Kennecott's board. The Export Department bought up three-quarters of all the electrolytic copper mined in the United States for the British, and the Guggenheims and many others made fortunes from it. Another Guggenheim company, American Smelting and Refining, enjoyed a boom as the Allies bought lead for rifles and bullets. The distribution of billions of dollars in contracts enabled the House of Morgan to win the loyalty of dozens of powerful companies.

Within bounds, the British tried to prevent the bank from abusing its extraordinary powers. To investigate charges of favoritism, Great Britain sent a mission to New York under the Welsh coal magnate David Alfred Thomas, later Lord Rhondda. Staying at the Plaza Hotel for three weeks during the summer of 1915, Thomas hovered around the bank and found Stettinius's work faultless. He did report to England that the bank was buying excessively from Republicans, and Lloyd George advised Davison to spread the wealth around. Davison replied that they would try to distribute contracts geographically.

Thomas's stay in New York had one uneasy moment. One day, he got a call from his secretary at the Plaza, saying a sudden gust of wind had blown some confidential memos out the window; three sheets of top-secret onionskin had fluttered down onto Fifth Avenue. This breach of security was so grave that Lloyd George was notified in London. Through late-afternoon drizzle, Morgan employees scoured the avenue, ducking under parked cars and staring down drains. The sheets were lost. To console Thomas, his staff took three identical sheets, dragged them through bathwater, and showed him how they decomposed.

Notwithstanding Thomas's report, the British remained wary of Morgans and believed it rewarded friendly steel, chemical, and shipping concerns. Asquith consoled himself with the thought that the bank kept its back scratching within tolerable limits. He wrote to Reginald McKenna, who had succeeded Lloyd George as chancellor of the Exchequer: "In regard to Morgan's, while I do not doubt that they have made and will continue to make all that they can out of us, I see no reason to think that they have been acting unfairly, still less treacherously. The original contract with them may or may not have been wise, but it would be bad policy to swop horses now, or to make them suspect that we distrust them."[20]

In fact, the British were never foolishly or blindly in love with the House of Morgan. They welcomed having an Anglo-American listening post on Wall Street, especially as financial power shifted across the Atlantic. But the government's deliberations during the war were veined by a certain cynicism, a belief that Morgan partners drove a hard bargain and needlessly offended people with their arrogance. Relations between the Morgans and the British would always be close but seldom harmonious, a fraternal tension lurking beneath protestations of mutual devotion.

WHERE other partners at 23 Wall Street harbored some secret envy or suspicion of their British brethren, Jack Morgan had no such reservations. He regularly spent up to six months a year in England and was fully bicultural. For him, the war was a holy cause as well as a business opportunity. Even more than Pierpont, Jack was simple and guileless. He inhabited a black-and-white world in which loyalty to England found its equal and opposite emotion in hatred of the Germans. Unstinting in serving England, he donated Dover House, Junius's old country house at Roehampton, as a convalescent home for wounded officers. He instructed his steward at Wall Hall to plough up parkland and plant wheat for the war effort. Once Jack's passions were engaged, his commitment was total. J. P. Morgan and Company even took a stake in Montana wheat fields to supply more war provisions.

With America officially neutral, Stettinius's Export Department exposed the bank to inflammatory criticism. It fanned anti-Morgan sentiment that had existed in the hinterlands ever since William Jennings Bryan's Cross of Gold speech. During rallies at the Corner, agitators would point to 23 Wall and blame Morgan partners for killing thousands of innocents. Senator Robert La Follette echoed small-town sneers when he asked, "What do Morgan and Schwab [head of Bethlehem Steel] care for world peace, when there are big profits in world war?"[21]

Minnesota congressman Charles Lindbergh, who had prompted the Pujo hearings, now condemned the "money interests" for trying to lure the country into war on the side of the Allies. A dual myth was being born—that the Morgans were stooges of the British crown and that their money was drenched in blood. The bank received a flood of hate mail. Lamont received one note that said, "My dear Mr. Lamont—Your death doom is marked by your activity for the British war loan, which will deal death to my brothers on the battlefield in Germany. It shall be a distinct pleasure for me to puncture your black heart with lead some time in the distant future."[22]

Jack tried to avoid publicity that might incite Congress. When Harry Davison and lawyer Paul Cravath wanted to form a political committee to proselytize for the Allies, Jack refused. He also shied away from public appearances with his close friend Sir Cecil Arthur Spring-Rice, the British ambassador. In January 1915, writing about an upcoming trip, Jack told Springy that it might be "wiser for me not to be actually living at your house when I am in Washington. We are endeavouring to conduct this transaction with the British Government as inconspicuously as possible . . . but I must say that I do not see why, when you get away, you should not come and stay with us, which would be more quiet than staying in a hotel."[23]

Jack had always lived with a heightened awareness of danger. While at Harvard, a detective had tagged along behind him. After Jack's younger son, Harry, returned to New York with his British tutor, the boy had become obsessed with fears of kidnapping. While Pierpont was still alive, Jack had experienced a burglary at Madison Avenue that smelled bizarrely of class revenge: the burglar had casually sat around the house, smoking his cigars. Another time, a blackmailer threatened to blow up Jack's house unless money was deposited beneath a bush in Central Park; no money was paid, and no bomb went off.

The House of Morgan was also an irresistible magnet for crackpots, who were attracted by its aura of mystery. Early in the war, a stream of abusive letters arrived from a madman named Schindler, who believed the bank had stolen his interest in an Alaska mine but refused to admit it. Such constant threats stoked Jack's already fertile imagination, and he was wont to see conspirators everywhere.

As it turned out, however, Jack's fears weren't entirely groundless. On the balmy Sunday morning of July 3, 1915, Jack and Jessie were having breakfast at their North Shore estate with Spring-Rice and his wife. They were just finishing the meal when the Morgan butler, Henry Physick, went to answer the door. There wasn't yet a guardhouse at the causeway that connected the island to the Long Island shore, and inter-lopers could walk straight up to the door. A slight, gray-suited stranger greeted Physick and handed him a card saying "SUMMER SOCIETY DIREC-TORY, REPRESENTED BY THOMAS C. LESTER." He asked to see Mr. Morgan.

Physick was a British butler of the old school. He usually wore a dark coat and gray striped trousers and was precise in his manners. Tactful but scenting danger, Physick refused to let the insistent stranger pass. He quickly raced to the library, found Jack and Jessie, and shouted "Upstairs!" Following these cryptic instructions, the Morgans went upstairs and searched the bedrooms, trying to figure out the problem. Then, at the top of the staircase, they saw the gunman, brandishing two pistols and leading the two Morgan daughters up the steps. (Later the gunman confessed that his major mistake was walking in front of the Morgan children, not behind them, thus reducing their value as hos-tages.) Trying to remain calm, the gunman told the Morgans not to be frightened, that he wanted to talk with them.

If the later police depositions are accurate, everyone showed phenom-enal courage. A woman of steely self-control, Jessie Morgan threw her-self at the gunman. Her courage gave the big, burly Jack time enough to wade in and tackle the man; he took two bullets in the groin as he subdued him. While servants pinioned his arms, Jessie and Jack pried loose his two pistols. Then, with timing so exact it resembles Hollywood stagecraft, Physick rushed in and smashed a chunk of coal over the man's head, rendering him unfit for further mischief. (This splendid touch, alas, isn't mentioned in the police depositions.) Only after sub-duing the man did the Morgans see a large stick of dynamite protruding from his pocket. The assassination attempt ended with the Morgan servants submerging the dynamite in water and tightly binding the man in ropes. Dr. James Markoe, the Morgan family physician, was rushed out to Glen Cove to treat Jack's bullet wounds.

At the Nassau County jail, the gunman gave his name as Frank Holt, which turned out to be an alias for Erich Muenter. A man with a shadowy past and a former German instructor at Harvard, Muenter had vanished in 1906 after having been indicted for poisoning his wife with arsenic. Under questioning, he confessed to being a pacifist opposed to American arms exports to Europe. He hadn't planned to kill Jack, he said, only to hold him hostage until munitions shipments were stopped. He possessed a delirious, dreamlike sense of Morgan power. The interro-gator asked, "Do you think that you singlehandedly could arrest the whole trend of the age?" "No, but Mr. Morgan could." "Do you think he could control those countries?" "With his money, if his money didn't flow into their cash drawers, and stop the flow of ammunition."[24] To supplement his attack against Morgan, Muenter had secreted a bomb the day before in the U.S. Senate chambers. Whether Muenter had confederates will never be known. Two weeks later, he committed suicide in the Nassau County jail.

Outwardly, Jack seemed phlegmatic and even clinical about the shooting, as if he had gone through a mildly unpleasant experiment and were jotting down the results. Miraculously, the bullets missed all vital organs, and his wounds healed quickly as he recuperated aboard the *Corsair III.* "It was a most disagreeable experience, though it is not as painful as I imagined it would be to be shot as I was," he said.[25] He credited Jessie's coolness for foiling the plot and said he had done only what any parent would have with an intruder pointing a gun at his family. Dismissive of his own bravery, he was taken aback by the congratulatory messages that swamped the local telegraph office. On August 16, when he emerged from 23 Wall after his first day back at the bank, he was cheered by waiting crowds as he slipped into his limousine. Boyishly surprised, he touched his hat brim and gave a little wave. Unaccustomed to public adulation, he attained a fleeting status as a national hero.

Jack's calm was deceptive, for the shooting had deep effects that he hid beneath an offhanded manner. While a plot was never proved, Jack insisted Muenter was no isolated lunatic but part of a terrorist scheme. At his Adirondack retreat, Camp Uncas, he had the steward "get rid" of Germans and Austrians on the payroll.[26] The shadows suddenly teemed with enemies. From the *Corsair,* Jack wrote Teddy Grenfell that Jessie had "an impression that people are trying to get another shot at me, and I have to look out for this even more than I otherwise would do, in order to satisfy her."[27] There were many reminders that Muenter wasn't a lone Morgan-hater. When news of the 1915 shooting reached Vienna, it was celebrated by fireworks, speeches, and jubilant crowds.

The shooting reinforced Jack's reclusiveness, his penchant for privacy at the retreats of the rich. As a result, he probably spent more time at English country estates or cruising aboard his yacht; it was no coincidence that he recuperated aboard the *Corsair.* The shooting also filled him with a sense of omnipresent danger, playing to a cloak-and-dagger side of his personality. He frequently moved about by stealth. Visiting his older son, Junius, in Baltimore during the war, he wrote a friend about hotel arrangements: "I should greatly prefer that the hotel would not force me to register or to say that I am coming, owing to the fact that, apparently, the Germans are still after me, and I am requested by my family not to state where and when I am going in other towns."[28] After the shooting, Jack would be accompanied by bodyguards, a team of former marines. Such heavy security had the unfortunate effect of further distancing him from ordinary people and making the everyday brands of human misery more remote to him.

Jack's security was also a constant preoccupation of his highly protective partners. He was often unaware of security guards in a crowd. In Paris, senior partner Herman Harjes would notify the *sûreté général* whenever Jack visited. The detectives would stay close but not reveal their presence. Jack moved behind that invisible shield accorded heads of state.

The shooting would be but one in a series of episodes that darkened Jack's view of the world and produced a settled malice toward his enemies. These episodes made him feel frightened and beleaguered and quickened his tendency to lash out against his enemies. For all his wealth and power, Jack felt vulnerable to forces outside his control.

JACK told friends that the shooting had made him more fervently anti-German and more eager to see the United States enter the war on the Allied side. He reviled the Germans as "Huns" and "Teuton savages"—he relished colorful epithets—and exhibited a latent bias against Germany that he had inherited from his father. As partner George Whitney later explained, Pierpont "always accused the Germans of doublecrossing him. . . . So there was an edict put down that we would never do business with the Germans."[29]

World War I was perhaps the last war in which bankers behaved as if they were sovereign states, indulging their biases and waging their own foreign policy. On Wall Street, spoils of war were divided strictly according to political and religious differences among the bankers. The House of Morgan was superbly positioned. Through its London and Paris houses, it had helped France finance the Franco-Prussian War and England the Boer War. Jack even had a soft spot for the czar, to whom he had extended credit.

If a bonanza for Yankee Wall Street, the war was a catastrophe for Jewish firms, which were encumbered by anti-Russian and pro-German sympathies. Jacob Schiff, the autocratic head of Kuhn, Loeb, had been aghast at Russian pogroms, branding the czarist government the "enemy of mankind"; in revenge, he financed Japan in the 1904–5 Russo-Japanese War. Nonetheless, he moderated his German sympathies after 1914, endorsed a negotiated peace, and "dutifully stopped speaking German to his family in public."[30] The less circumspect Henry Goldman of Goldman, Sachs espoused pro-German views, spouting Nietzsche and glorifying Prussian culture—much to the dismay of his partners. The Guggenheims, of German-speaking Swiss ancestry, suppressed any sympathy they might have had for Germany as munitions contracts rolled in.

During the war, Wall Street and the City were full of scurrilous attacks on supposedly disloyal Jews. In 1915, Edward Kraftmeier of the British Nobel Company came to New York to warn the du Ponts that their company, a major Allied manufacturer of smokeless powder, could fall under the share control of "pro-German" Kuhn, Loeb. There were fears that Coleman du Pont might sell his large stake to them. To counter this threat, the du Ponts obtained an $8.5-million loan from Morgans, tightly locking up their shares in a holding company called Du Pont Securities. (When Sir William Wiseman, head of British intelligence in the United States, investigated the warning about Kuhn, Loeb, he found it baseless.) German financial penetration was a concern in the City as well, and the Bank of England "Anglicized" foreign-owned banks; for instance, it brought in the Pearson group to take over Lazard Brothers, fearing the London house might fall into German hands if its Paris affiliate were taken over.

In this highly charged atmosphere, Jack Morgan's pro-British passions and his anti-Semitism began to feed on one another. In September 1914, he complained to Teddy Grenfell that the " 'peace' talk has been fomented and worked up in a large measure by the German Jew element, which is very close to the German Ambassador."[31] Antagonism toward German-Jewish banks sharpened in December, when the House of Morgan extended a $12-million credit to Russia; the next month, Great Britain initiated war purchases for the czar through the House of Morgan. Noting Russia's treatment of Jews, Schiff stiffly protested to Jack, who had to tread gingerly, since the two co-managed big bond issues. The syndicate structure of investment banking made it a world of sharp but sheathed rapiers. Exercising self-control, Jack wrote to Schiff: "I do not think it is for us to endeavor to change the attitude of Russia by applying financial pressure. It seems to me that the question of whether or not Russia is a good and solvent debtor can hardly be mixed up with questions of internal social or policing regulations."[32] Of course, Jack himself didn't regard foreign loans so dispassionately and often mingled his political and financial beliefs.

The friction between Jack and Schiff led to a tense exchange in May 1915, when a German submarine off the Irish coast sank the Cunard's *Lusitania*, one of two lavish ships built in response to Pierpont's shipping trust. Over a thousand people died, including 63 children. Alfred Gwynne Vanderbilt was among the 128 American casualties. There was grief across America. That morning, amid heavy gloom, Schiff suppressed his pride and offered his regrets at the Corner. Haughty and formal, he never made this sort of call. When he entered, he found Jack in the partners' room. Instead of receiving Schiff with courtesy, Jack muttered some angry words and stormed off, leaving Schiff in mystified silence. He shuffled out alone.

The other partners gasped. It was a flagrant breach of the Gentleman Banker's Code, the need to maintain civility on the surface. Jack remarked rather sheepishly, "I suppose I went a little far? I suppose I ought to apologize?" Nobody dared to speak. Then the quick-witted Dwight Morrow scratched a biblical quote on a piece of paper and handed it to Jack. It said, "Not for thy sake, but for thy name's sake, O House of Israel!"[33] Taking the hint, Jack took his hat and went off to Kuhn, Loeb to apologize. The tale vividly captures Jack's contradictory nature—the polite and courtly surface, the mass of churning emotions within—as well as the strains of a highly artificial world that demanded constant civility. With the big syndicated loans, one couldn't antagonize a powerful bank that might be an ally on the next issue.

This muted warfare flared into the open in September 1915, during the creation of the biggest foreign loan in Wall Street history—the $500-million Anglo-French loan. It was five times as big as the previous record holder, the $100-million loan to Great Britain for the Boer War. The Stettinius mill was chewing up £2 million a day and threatened to exhaust British financial resources. As early as April 1, 1915, Jack lunched with Lloyd George and discussed a loan of at least $100 million to prop up the pound. Teddy Grenfell and other directors of the Bank of England were worried about the makeshift war financing.

The financing problem grew acute that July. The British canceled one contract for the Russians in New York for lack of foreign exchange. To meet a dollar deadline at Morgans, Reginald McKenna had to commandeer American securities owned by Prudential Assurance—a piece of *ad hoc* midnight desperation that deeply disturbed Prime Minister Asquith. It was a rickety way to run a war. For the House of Morgan, stymied by the State Department ban on loans, it was an excruciating time. The one riddle Morgans could never resolve was what to do when U.S. and British policy diverged.

Wilson opposed a jumbo Allied loan but was finally persuaded by his cabinet that, without it, U.S. exports would suffer. Treasury Secretary McAdoo argued in late August that U.S. prosperity depended on trade with the Allies. Robert Lansing, who had replaced Bryan as secretary of state, starkly warned that without a loan, "the result would be restriction of outputs, industrial depression, idle capital and idle labor, numerous failures, financial demoralization, and general unrest and suffering among the laboring classes."[34] Wilson was convinced.

In September, the British cabinet dispatched an Anglo-French mission to New York to arrange a huge private loan. The North Atlantic swarmed with submarines, and Grenfell was told not to inform Morgans of the group's membership. The commission was headed by Lord Reading, the lord chief justice, and included Sir Edward Holden, chairman of the Midland Bank, Basil Blackett of the British Treasury, and M. Octave Hombert, the French representative. Harry Davison and Jack went down to the pier to greet the *Lapland* and saw the group settled in at the Biltmore Hotel.

Once again, the Anglo-American Morgan love affair was full of spats and recriminations. Unwavering in support of Britain, Morgan partners felt bruised and demeaned by having to compete for the loan. Nevertheless, they gave the visiting group a red-carpet reception. Lord Reading, *né* Rufus Isaacs, presented a formidable challenge to Jack Morgan's prejudices. Son of a London fruit merchant, he was British, brilliant, titled—and Jewish. He had risen to the position of attorney general, cross-examining witnesses during the British *Titanic* inquiry. Jack and Davison visited Reading at the Biltmore, feted him at the Morgan Library, and entertained him aboard the *Corsair*. Against all odds, personal chemistry between Jack and Reading would help to seal the deal.

The Anglo-French loan tested New York's capacity as a financial market. The victorious Morgans had to contend with broad hostility toward Britain. One in ten Americans was of German ancestry, and many first-generation Irish immigrants opposed the loan. Fantastic numbers were bandied about—up to $1 billion—and skeptics doubted it could be done. Such sums staggered and frightened Americans, much as had the huge trusts a few years before. In retrospect, the Anglo-French loan would mark the rise of America as the world's chief creditor nation. Yet even as the House of Morgan superintended this transfer of financial power, Jack was dubious that it would last, assuring Grenfell that "when the war is over, you will find the United States settling down again into using the European money markets as a clearing house, very much as before."[35] Jack didn't exult over Britain's decline and found it hard to foresee the demotion of his beloved London.

After an honorary dinner at the Morgan Library, Jack invited Reading up to his second-floor study for cigars. He and his partners had to dampen inflated British expectations. Through the haze of cigar smoke, Jack casually knocked several hundred million dollars off the loan. "Reading," Jack said, "I wouldn't ask a billion if I were you. I think you'd be wiser to limit your first large bond issue to half a billion."[36] To Jack's surprise, Reading consented to a $500-million (£100-million) issue. After syndicate charges were factored in, the interest rate was a steep 6 percent. Jack said the House of Morgan would waive any extra compensation as syndicate manager.

Fascinated by Lord Reading, Jack was preoccupied with his religion:

> Lord Reading impressed me enormously. His mind is so clear, and he sees the bearing of each point so quickly that it was a great pleasure to discuss things with him. His only drawback was that he was, and of necessity must be, so much in with the Jews that he takes their point of view to a certain extent. This of course is natural, but seeing that most of the Jews in this country are thoroughly pro-German, and a very large number of them are anti-J. P. Morgan & Co., it would have been desirable if he had not had quite so close affiliations with them.[37]

It was a curious letter. Lord Reading's position as head of the loan mission should have dispelled any doubts as to his loyalty and dashed notions of a monolithic Jewish viewpoint; instead, Jack implausibly perceived some common denominator between Reading and German Jews. In fact, when Reading met Jacob Schiff, the latter laid down a suicidal precondition for Kuhn, Loeb participation in the loan—that not one penny could go to England's ally, Russia. Reading bluntly replied that "no government could accept conditions which discriminated against one of its allies in war."[38] In one stroke, Kuhn, Loeb became *persona non grata* in London finance, further clearing the way for the Morgan triumphal march.

Still more damaging was the controversy at Goldman, Sachs, where partners exercised vetoes in important matters. Loyal to Germany, Henry Goldman refused to share in the Morgan-sponsored issue, provoking a crisis at the firm and causing its voluntary exile from wartime finance on Wall Street. According to Stephen Birmingham, when the "Kleinwort bank in London cabled to New York to say that Goldman, Sachs was in danger of being blacklisted in England," Henry Goldman was forced to resign from the family firm.[39] Feelings ran so high that Goldman and Philip Lehman, dubbed Wall Street's "hottest underwriting team," stopped speaking to each other. For a generation, Jewish banks on Wall Street were handicapped by their affiliation with Germany.

The $500-million Anglo-French loan was far larger than any bond issue orchestrated by Pierpont. Sixty-one underwriters and 1,570 financial institutions marketed the bonds. (The House of Morgan resented not being appointed sole agent responsible for paying the bond's interest.) It was an extremely tough selling job, especially in isolationist sections of the Midwest. To sweeten the deal, participating banks were allowed to keep some of the money that they raised on deposit for a while. It was also widely advertised that the money would be spent only in America. Despite these inducements, only one major bank in Chicago—where pro-German depositors threatened a boycott—joined the syndicate, and there were none from Milwaukee. The Morgan partners signed up many famous individuals, including Andrew Carnegie and even Samuel Untermyer of Pujo fame, as well as suppliers of war matériel such as the Guggenheim brothers and Charles Schwab of Bethlehem Steel, who felt obliged to safeguard their thriving war business. But they couldn't offset the poor midwestern performance, and the syndicate was stuck with $187 million in unsold bonds by year's end.

To raise additional dollars, the British levied a tax on any dividends received from American shares, and British citizens rushed to give their shares to the government. So many securities were tendered that the Bank of England Court Room was heaped high with certificates. Morgans liquidated $3 billion of these securities, delicately feeding them into the New York market so as to prevent a collapse in share prices.

The Anglo-French loan was soon exhausted. Before the war ended, the House of Morgan had arranged over $1.5 billion in Allied credits. The British would lavish many encomia on the Morgan role before U.S. entry into the war. In Morgan Grenfell's Tea Room hangs a Lloyd George letter of 1917 that says, in part, "We were fortunate enough to secure the assistance of a firm which have throughout done everything in its power to protect the interests of the British Government."[40] Visiting the Corner years later, Lord Northcliffe, the British press baron, exclaimed, "The war was won within these walls."[41] Lord Moulton, head of the British Munitions Board, said that Du Pont, Bethlehem Steel, and J. P. Morgan and Company had rescued the French and British armies in 1915.

Yet, as was always true of Morgan relations with Britain, the public embrace concealed a fair degree of tension. The British often felt the bank bungled its political role, however well it handled the financial side. Arthur Willer, the London *Times* correspondent in Washington, described the House of Morgan in 1916: "The most unpopular house in the country, the personification for the radical West of the malign money power of Wall Street, it has done nothing to propitiate either the people or the politicians."[42] That year, Jack campaigned for the Republican presidential candidate, Charles Evans Hughes—which the British thought unwise. Jack and Harry Davison also treated the new Federal Reserve Board in a somewhat high-handed manner. Davison, in particular, seemed to offend the British. He had a brash, decisive manner that inspired subordinates but could be clumsy and arrogant. The Foreign Office called him "injudicious," while Ambassador Spring-Rice said Davison had "all the aggressiveness of the older Morgan without his genius."[43]

Davison either mishandled his relationship with Willard Straight or decided that the romantic, impetuous Straight would just never fit in at Morgans. Straight expected to help negotiate with the Anglo-French loan. "I thought I might have been of service in connection with these negotiations, but I was asked to perform no work, and this rankled," he said.[44] He was given little responsibility, and the august House of Morgan didn't share his interest in poor countries. That September, at age thirty-four, he resigned from the bank. He had never translated his precocious China success into a mundane Wall Street setting and was offended that he hadn't become a Morgan partner. He preferred polo, golf, and his outside literary interests to the consuming dedication that was *de rigueur* at 23 Wall. Shortly after wartime service, in 1918, he died of influenza and pneumonia. His widow, Dorothy, would help to found the New School for Social Research in New York and Dartington Hall, an experimental school in South Devon, England.

By 1917, British credit was practically exhausted. Their salvation was German resumption of unrestricted submarine warfare against American shipping. When the United States entered the war, on April 6, 1917, Washington immediately granted the Allies $1 billion in credit, lifting the onus from J. P. Morgan and Company. After the United States entered the war, the House of Morgan expected to be repaid a $400-million loan to Britain from the proceeds of the first Liberty Loan drive. But Treasury Secretary McAdoo feared Congress would be upset if government money went to that old Democratic bogeyman—the Money Trust. To the amazement of Morgan partners, the British government didn't seem bothered by the double cross. In his journal, Teddy Grenfell noted wounded feelings among the Morgan partners: "Although JPM & Co. had placed all their resources monetary and otherwise at the disposal of the British Government, the ministers especially finance showed little appreciation. . . . The Morgan houses felt very bitterly not only that no appreciation was shown of their services but also that as soon as the Government had got all their monies which Morgan & Co. could lend or borrow from friends for England, that the British Treasury intentionally kept all information from them."[45]

During the summer of 1917, Lord Cunliffe, the abrasive, despotic governor of the Bank of England, argued the Morgan case against the less sympathetic chancellor of the Exchequer, Bonar Law. It formed part of a larger struggle between the bank and the Treasury for control of British financial policy. The row became so vitriolic that Prime Minister Lloyd George threatened to nationalize the Bank of England. On July 4, Grenfell was summoned to a Cabinet meeting at 10 Downing Street, and Lloyd George angrily asked him why the House of Morgan was making such a fuss. (Grenfell referred to Lloyd George as "our little Welsh goat."[46]) In the end, the British Treasury, incensed at Cunliffe's behavior, spiked his reelection as governor in 1918. This paved the way not for a Morgan foe but for Montagu Norman, who took over the bank in 1920 and proved the most influential British ally in Morgan history.

When the United States declared war, Jack was jubilant. With naive, patriotic generosity, he told President Wilson he could transfer the Export Department intact to Washington. He was ready to give Stettinius a leave of absence, cover staff salaries for a time, and forgo commissions. It didn't dawn on him that this was politically impossible. Isolationists continued to accuse the House of Morgan of whipping up pro-war sentiment. And traveling across America, Treasury Secretary McAdoo noted intense ill will toward the house for having profited from the munitions purchases.

To head the powerful new War Industries Board, Wilson chose Daniel Willard of the Baltimore and Ohio Railroad and then Democratic party stalwart, Bernard Baruch; to appease Morgans, he made Stettinius surveyor general of supplies for the U.S. Army. Only half-comically, Baruch confessed relief that Pierpont had spurned his offer of help during the 1907 panic, for had it been accepted, it might have jeopardized his political prospects under Wilson. There was now a political stigma attached to Morgan partners. White House aides noted that President Wilson frowned when he saw Dwight Morrow's name on a list of prospective appointees. Although he did appoint him, to the Allied Maritime Council, he said firmly, "We mustn't have any more of those men."[47] Morrow would, in fact, become an important civilian adviser to General Pershing at Chaumont. Harry Davison, upon being named head of the Red Cross War Council, expected to assume full powers. When he then clashed with Red Cross organizer Mabel Boardman, former president William Howard Taft went to the White House to mediate. Though siding with Davison, Wilson told Taft that "New York bankers liked unrestricted powers, that they had been used to it in their business . . . but that in such a matter it was not wise."[48]

From the standpoint of later Wall Street history, the government's wartime Liberty Loan drives have an important place. The United States sold nearly $17 billion in Liberty Bonds. The spirited promotional campaign brought Charlie Chaplin and Douglas Fairbanks, Sr., to rallies at the Corner. Treasury Secretary McAdoo wanted to reach small farmers, businessmen, and workers and thus created a new generation of American investors. One bureaucratic genius of the campaign was a Wall Street lawyer, Russell C. Leffingwell, who had been a neighbor of Mc-Adoo in Yonkers, New York. McAdoo made him counsel and then assistant treasury secretary in charge of the Liberty Bond drives. He would later be a famous Morgan partner and a critical link with the Democratic party.

The House of Morgan emerged from the war with greatly enlarged power. For Jack Morgan, so widely discounted when he took over in 1913, there was a sense of psychic relief, a knowledge that he had measured up to his father. He told Paris partner Herman Harjes, "I am glad to say that our firm stands, as it always has stood, in the middle of things. . . . I feel that I am able in a measure to take Father's place in the community and help out in many ways."[49] As a young man in London, it had amused him when Lloyd's took out a $2-million insurance policy on Pierpont's life. Now he shattered all records by taking out a $2.5-million policy on his own.

But Jack's hypersensitive nature was such that he seemed more disturbed by criticism than gratified by success. After Wilson rejected this offer of the Export Department, he sulked and licked his wounds. He was a man of fundamentally incompatible desires, who wished to be fabulously rich *and* loved; useful *and* appreciated; not only famous but understood fairly by the masses. He had a way of magnifying enemies. Even as he emerged as the world's best-known banker, he still felt embattled. As he wrote in 1917:

> I have come to the conclusion that the chief reason of the dislike that exists in Washington for J.P. Morgan & Co. . . . originates in the fact that we ask for no favors, that the Democratic party has tried its best to cripple us in every way it could, that they had Steel investigations,

Pujo investigations and Clayton bills and all that sort of thing, devised and directed with the intention of making life impossible for us—and still we have gone ahead and got along pretty well . . . the whole feeling against us is really a political grudge, and they cannot change our feeling, nor can we change theirs.[50]

Another perspective on Morgan power came later from Sir Harold Nicolson in his biography of Dwight Morrow. Nicolson had written that at the outbreak of the war, the House of Morgan "ceased to be a private firm and became almost a Department of government"—which he meant as a mighty compliment.[51] Yet Jack thought it insulting to liken his bank to the government. "I have no right to ask you to alter this," Jack wrote to Nicolson upon reading it in draft form, "but it would be interpreted as if we were reduced to the status of a department subordinate to the Government."[52] The House of Morgan no longer thought itself subordinate to anyone, not even Washington.

1. The inimitable 1903 photo of J. Pierpont Morgan by Edward Steichen. Morgan hated the photo and tore up the first print.

2. George Peabody, the miser-turned-philanthropist who founded the House of Morgan

3. Junius Spencer Morgan, patriarch of the clan, in 1881, at age sixty-eight.

4. 13 Princes Gate, the Morgans' London townhouse and later residence of Ambassador Joseph P. Kennedy and his family

5. *Corsair II.* Pierpont's sumptuous pleasure craft was later conscripted for use as a gunboat in the Spanish-American War.

6. The Morgan family at the Karnak temple, Egypt, 1877. The touring party included a physician, a maid, a nurse, an interpreter, and a French waiter.

7. Pierpont's frail estranged wife, Frances Tracy Morgan, known as Fanny, in 1902

8. Pierpont's mistress, actress Maxine Elliott, as Portia in *The Merchant of Venice* in 1901

9. Pierpont's daughter, Anne, in 1915. Her *ménage à trois* at Versailles with two other women scandalized her father.

10. Pierpont's saucy librarian, Belle da Costa Greene, at a Republican party meeting in 1916

11. Pierpont (second from right on the stairs) at a house party at the Harcourts' Nuneham Park estate. King Edward VII is seated in the center.

12. Pierpont's brownstone at 219 Madison Avenue, later razed to build an annex to the Pierpont Morgan Library

Rare photographs of Pierpont Morgan from the Library of Congress

13. Pierpont gazing ferociously at bystanders at
the funeral of Senator John Fairfield Dryden, 1911

14. Pierpont chatting with a friend in
October 1907, just before the panic. This
unusual photograph shows how his nose
really looked. Most pictures are touched up.

15. Pierpont meting out rough
justice to a photographer, 1910

Four warriors in the Northern Pacific corner, 1901.

16. George W. Perkins, who had
just been made a Morgan partner

17. Robert Bacon, the Greek God
of Wall Street, whose nerves
gave way under the strain

18. Edward H. Harriman, whom Pierpont
sneered at as a "two-dollar broker"

19. Jacob Schiff of Kuhn, Loeb, Pierpont's
formidable Jewish rival on Wall Street

20. Run on the Trust Company of America during the Panic of 1907. The old Drexel building, pre-1913 home of the Morgan bank, is at the right. The successor building dropped the name out front.

21. A grim Pierpont arriving at the Pujo hearings accompanied by daughter Louisa Satterlee and son, Jack, December 1912

The instigators of the Money Trust investigation

22. Louis D. Brandeis, who won national attention with his attacks on Morgan control of the New Haven Railroad

23. Muckraker Lincoln Steffens, who dubbed Pierpont "the boss of the United States"

24. Charles A. Lindbergh, Sr., father of the aviator, who introduced a congressional resolution calling for a Wall Street probe

25. Samuel Untermyer, counsel to the Pujo committee and bogeyman of the Morgan family

26. Willard Straight, Morgan agent in China,
with his heiress wife, the former Dorothy Whitney

27. Straight, in spats, conferring with the American minister
to China, William J. Calhoun, and Colonel Tsat Ting-Kan

28. Official portrait of J. P. ("Jack") Morgan, Jr.

29. Jack's wife, Jane Grew Morgan, known as Jessie, as presented to Queen Victoria in 1898

30. Jack's estate, Matinicock Point, on East Island, off Long Island's North Shore

31. Morgan lieutenant Henry P. Davison, who negotiated the deal by which the bank bought $3 billion in supplies for the Allies

32. Russell C. Leffingwell. As assistant Treasury secretary in 1918, Leffingwell presided over the sale of Liberty bonds.

33. The Paris Peace Conference, 1919. Thomas W. Lamont, standing at the far left, poses with the Reparations Commission. Herbert Hoover sits at the far left, and Bernard Baruch sits second from the right.

34. September 1920 bomb blast outside the House of Morgan. The explosion killed two employees and damaged the building's northern facade.

35. View of 23 Wall Street, right, in the Jazz Age

36. Thomas W. Lamont striking a debonair pose aboard the *S.S. Europa* in 1932

37. Giovanni Fummi, the Morgan agent in Rome, whose arrest Mussolini ordered in September 1940.

38. Benito Mussolini perusing a newspaper. Lamont created a New York publicity bureau to help bolster il Duce's overseas image.

39. Dwight W. Morrow returning from the 1930
London Naval Conference with his wife, Betty

40. Walter Lippmann, lower left, at a Mexican reception with the
Morrows (at head of table) in 1928. Lippmann was on a secret mission
to arbitrate a dispute between Mexico and the Catholic church.

41. Charles A. Lindbergh, Jr., in Mexico in December 1927. The aviator flew there at Morrow's invitation. A Mexican official sits between Lindbergh and Morrow.

42. Charles and Anne Morrow Lindbergh in flying togs, 1931

43. Lindbergh in Nazi Germany in 1937. His admiration for German air power estranged him from the Anglophile Morgan bank.

CHAPTER ELEVEN

EXPLOSION

• •

•

THE United States emerged from the First World War with thriving industries and a record trade surplus, while much of Europe lay in ruins, urgently in need of reconstruction loans. Sovereign states, city governments, and corporations flocked to Wall Street, as they had once courted London's merchant princes. Because of sterling's postwar weakness, the British Treasury had to impose an informal embargo on all foreign loans in the City, leaving wide open the door to traditional British clients. London had surrendered its historic role of financing world trade.

Sunning in postwar glory, the House of Morgan was the world's most influential private bank, able to select the most creditworthy customers and alone capable of handling many huge state loans. Its seal of approval guaranteed a warm reception for bond issues at a time when foreign issues were still new and unfamiliar to American investors. The House of Morgan spoke to foreign governments as the official voice of the American capital markets. Its influence didn't simply stem from money but from intangibles—cachet, political connections, and banking alliances.

With the Jewish banks weakened, the Yankee axis of J. P. Morgan–National City Bank–First National Bank held the keys to the kingdom. For any credit-hungry finance minister, it was a formidable machinery to defy. In October 1919, Baron Emile du Marais, a member of a French financial mission, reported on Morgan power to French president Raymond Poincaré: "I have the impression that Morgan's has put together here a group which includes all the necessary elements for the placement of securities, and that one can in no way manage without their support. It is a fact about which we can do absolutely nothing. In these conditions, wisdom seems to dictate that we accept the fait accompli; and try to give Morgan's the impression that we have full confidence in them."[1] This analysis is reminiscent of Asquith's fatalistic, wartime lament that Britain, willy-nilly, had to reckon with the bank.

Nobody was more emboldened by the new financial power than President Wilson, who was eager to underwrite liberal dreams with Wall Street money. This was the same Woodrow Wilson who had made caustic comments about the Money Trust and snubbed Jack's offer of the Export Department. In December 1918, he set sail for Europe and received a euphoric welcome. He was the man of the hour, and it was thought he could mediate among European powers while rehabilitating Belgium and northern France. At this critical juncture, a metamorphosis took place in the role of the banker. In Pierpont's day, captains of finance had indulged an honest hatred of government. But after World War I, financial diplomacy shifted into a gray area between business and politics, with bankers often functioning as their governments' ambassadors. The advent of the Diplomatic Age was most striking at the House of Morgan, which would evolve into a shadow government and move in tandem with official policy. There would be moments when it acted as a rogue ministry, pursuing its own secret agenda, but for the most part it faithfully followed Washington. As Jack later said, "We were always most scrupulous in our relations with our Government."[2]

During this period, Tom Lamont acquired his keen interest in foreign affairs. In 1917, he was already traveling with Colonel House to Europe to study the European situation. Then Treasury Secretary Carter Glass appointed him as a financial adviser to the U.S. delegation at the Paris Peace Conference. Lamont was horrified by a wartime visit to Flanders and remembered the battlefield as a "Dantaesque inferno," with fires erupting from smoking artillery.[3] The experience made him a convinced advocate of world peace organizations. He developed an ardent faith in Wilson's vision of a League of Nations and funneled large amounts of money into organizations supporting American entry into the League.

Lamont's political beliefs dovetailed with the Morgan bank's financial requirements, for as it expanded its foreign lending, it looked for stable governments, global security, and free trade. The late 1910s would be the heyday of Morgan idealism. In those years, Dwight Morrow penned a brief study, entitled *The Society of Free States,* that examined how nations had negotiated their conflicts in the past. His daughter Anne later recalled, "The talk I heard around the family table in my school years was full of enthusiasm for Woodrow Wilson's Fourteen Points:

'The right of self-determination' for nations and 'a new order of world peace.' "[4]

Against all expectations, the insouciant Lamont dazzled Wilson in Paris. Wilson told him, "I have more and more admired the liberal and public-spirited stand you have taken in all our counsels."[5] A new Morgan partner, George Whitney, said that Wilson seemed to place more trust in Lamont's financial judgment than in that of anybody else.[6] Indeed, Morgan men were so ubiquitous at the Paris Peace Conference in 1919 that Bernard Baruch grumbled that J. P. Morgan and Company was running the show.[7] It is worth stressing that it was a progressive Democratic president who first mobilized the new Wall Street power for political ends (although the exploitation would become more blatant under Wilson's Republican successors). A decade of attacks on the Money Trust seemed to melt into a rapturous embrace.

Tom Lamont found his *métier* in Paris and helped to write the financial clauses of the peace treaty. He developed a vast circle of new friends, including Philip Kerr, later Lord Lothian and then secretary to Lloyd George and a close friend of Nancy Astor, and Jan Smuts of South Africa. Lamont would be the ace financial diplomat of the era. Where Jack Morgan was incapable of guile, Lamont was fast on his feet and ideologically flexible, able to hint to politicians of both parties that he sided with them. He was a man of many masks who played his parts so masterfully that he sometimes fooled himself. He had a gift for straddling political fences. To Wilson, in a typically artful formulation, he labeled himself "a poor Republican . . . who has faith in our present Democratic administration."[8] His tolerance was sometimes indistinguishable from a lack of conviction and his open-mindedness sometimes had a dash of opportunism. On domestic economic issues, he was a conventional Republican. But he espoused enough liberal views on international organizations and civil liberties to make himself uniquely palatable to the Democratic intelligentsia, who marveled at this *rara avis* of Wall Street. By the end of his career, Lamont would count Herbert Hoover *and* Franklin Roosevelt among his close friends.

For a generation, Lamont and the House of Morgan were entangled by the Treaty of Versailles and the problem of German reparations. It was a quagmire from which they could never escape. At the peace conference, Lamont joined a subcommittee studying Germany's capacity to pay war reparations to the Allies. Since much of the war was fought on French soil—northern France was left a lunar landscape of bomb craters—the French were implacable about receiving massive compensation. They had paid reparations to Germany in 1819 and 1871 and wanted their pound of flesh. Compared with the vengeful Allies, Lamont was less hawkish and recommended that Germany pay $40 billion—only one-fifth the French request and one-third the British, but still quite substantial and the highest among the American advisers.

When the Reparations Commission set the burden at $32 billion, its magnitude shocked Ben Strong, who foresaw—prophetically—a weaker German mark and subsequent inflation. Yet Lamont would never renounce his belief that the reparations burden was quite tolerable and that John Maynard Keynes, in his famous polemic *The Economic Consequences of the Peace,* gave the Germans the impression that they had been penalized and thus only fostered their resentment and weakened their resolve to pay. This, he thought, paved the way for Hitler's rise. Lamont belonged to the school of thought that saw the Germans manipulating world opinion into a better postwar financial deal than they deserved. Right through the Second World War, he clung to the belief that the Treaty of Versailles "was more than just to Germany and less than just to the allies."[9]

Whatever the truth of this complex historic debate, Lamont proved prescient in his forecast of lukewarm American support for the League. Sensing mounting isolationism at home, he asked Dwight Morrow to report to him from New York on sentiment toward the League. When he relayed Morrow's pessimistic appraisals, Wilson either pooh-poohed them or seemed puzzled by American doubts. Lamont plied Wilson with memos advocating tactical alterations in the treaty, more consultation with Republican opponents, and even a Washington lobbying effort to pinpoint the position of the dissenting senators and build bipartisan support. Always sensitive to style, Lamont suggested more humor in Wilson's speeches and recommended an "almost childlike language" in explaining the League covenant.[10] Wilson reacted to Morrow's reports in a high-minded but myopic way. "The key to the whole matter is the truth," he told Lamont, "and if we can only get the people at home to see the picture as we see it, I think the difficulties will melt away."[11] By nature a creature of compromise, Lamont watched in horror as Wilson stuck rigidly to his beliefs. They had a last wistful trip across the Atlantic together. By November 1919, the Treaty of Versailles was dead in the Senate, and Wilson was a shattered man. The United States never joined the League of Nations.

Versailles was a formative event for Tom Lamont, his debut on the world stage, from which he took away contradictory lessons. On the one hand, the peace conference left a residual strain of idealism, and Wilson would remain a sacred figure in his memory. He lauded Wilson's "delightful personality" and "ready wit" and his "Scotch mixture of wonderful idealism and stubbornness."[12] Yet he saw that politics was the art of the possible, that Wilson had suffered from excessive purity, and that the world wasn't prepared for Utopia. Of Wilson, he said, "He was a curious character—a great man in so many ways, yet so apt to stand firm at the wrong moments and give in at the right ones."[13] In time, Lamont's own talent for compromise would become pronounced, so that his own political tragedy would be the reverse of Wilson's.

After returning to America, Lamont, imbued with the Wilsonian spirit, proudly hung pictures of the president and Colonel House over his desk at 23 Wall. He had recently become publisher of the *New York Evening Post*, and he departed from a policy of noninterference to insist that the paper adopt a pro–League of Nations stand. As America's premier foreign lender, the House of Morgan also had a certain natural affinity with Wilson's brand of liberal Democratic internationalism. While American industrialists often remained protectionist and provincial in their views, bankers became more cosmopolitan in the 1920s. Only through free trade could countries export and earn foreign exchange to retire their debts. As had happened in the City in the nineteenth century, Wall Street became far more outward-looking than the commercial deposit banks. As exponents of global cooperation, the House of Morgan would often feel uncomfortable with the isolationist Republicans.

Returning home for the Republican National Convention of 1920, Lamont was shocked by its smoke-filled rooms, its arrogant isolationism, and its mean-spirited xenophobia. He saw America suddenly retreating from the world and refusing to take responsibility for postwar European reconstruction. In the election that year, Lamont cast his lone Democratic presidential vote, favoring Governor James M. Cox of Ohio over Warren G. Harding because Cox endorsed the League. Even Jack Morgan supported the League, although with even-handed disgust he boycotted America on Election Day, reviling both the "jellyfish Republican" and the "pro-German Ohio editor."[14] While the bank would have intimate relations with the three Republican administrations of the 1920s, there would always be a tension between its sense of global responsibility and the blinkered vision of the provincial Republicans. Increasingly multinational in scope, the House of

Morgan would fit uneasily into an America that was tired of European entanglements.

WHILE Lamont was negotiating peace at Versailles, Jack was wrestling with his own private demons. He didn't want to negotiate with the Germans but only to see them punished for their "barbarous" misdeeds. In 1917, he wrote a friend that "after the conduct of the Germans during this war, it would be impossible for any civilized nation . . . to have anything to do commercially or financially with people who have shown themselves of such evil character."[15] He said he would rather have General Pershing march on Berlin with half a million men than a merciful peace treaty.[16] Pierpont Morgan could have acted on such spite, but postwar Morgan lending would increasingly reflect U.S. interests rather than partners' whims. Despite Jack's bluster, his bank would sponsor the vast loans that made reparations possible, linking his bank more closely to Germany than he would have ever dreamed possible.

Outwardly, Jack remained the sedate banker, but inside he was fearful and haunted. His insecurity didn't end with the armistice. Even in the postwar atmosphere, it was easy for a prominent banker to feel as if he were a sitting target for terrorists. The rich grew alarmed by events in Russia—the seizure of power by Trotsky and Lenin, the assassination of Czar Nicholas II, and the Bolshevik repudiation of foreign debt. (Barings froze its large Russian deposits after the Bolsheviks tried to transfer them to Guaranty Trust in New York.) During the Mexican Revolution, the Mexican government also defaulted on its foreign debt, and in 1917 it passed a radical constitution that threatened to nationalize American oil interests.

There were predictions that revolution would spread to the shores of North America, and the political air grew thick with talk of class warfare and strikes. During 1919, four million Americans went on strike, with the city of Seattle the scene of a major general strike. Attorney General A. Mitchell Palmer rooted out "Reds" and other foreign agitators in the raids that came to bear his name. The unrest strengthened Jack's suspicion that "destructive elements" wanted to smash the industrial machinery. He applauded Massachusetts governor Calvin Coolidge for suppressing the Boston police strike and Judge Gary for supporting an open shop during a strike at U.S. Steel.

On May Day of 1919, Jack was one of twenty eminent Americans who received identical letter bombs. The intended victims were spared when the packages were intercepted at a New York City post office on account of insufficient postage. Jack and his daughter Jane were also blackmailed by a Michigan janitor named Thorn, who claimed he had poisoned them with slow-acting, secret microbes; he would hand over the antidote for $22,000. Ordinarily, Jack might have shrugged this off, but in the tense atmosphere he thought it advisable to make an example of the black-mailer. Thorn was eventually arrested, convicted, and spent fifteen months in Leavenworth. By 1921, the bank felt so menaced by saboteurs that publicity chief Martin Egan suggested that the bank's private rail-way car, the Peacock Point, be given a nondescript name, lest the associ-ation with Morgan partner Harry Davison's North Shore estate invite trouble.

The incidents that did occur help to explain the factual basis of Jack Morgan's fears, which now drove him to obsessive lengths. Crazy things *were* happening around him. In addition, there was the 1920–21 reces-sion, which was perhaps closer to a depression in its severity. To curb the inflation that followed the war, Ben Strong of the New York Fed raised interest rates sharply. It was the first recession deliberately engi-neered by the Fed to moderate a boom. As unemployment quintupled to 12 percent, four million people were thrown out of work, and over five hundred banks failed in 1921 alone.

By early 1920, Jack Morgan had an almost inverted worldview: the rich struck him as impotent, the masses as all-powerful in the hands of demagogues. In this frightened state of mind, he hired a private detec-tive, William Donovan, a lawyer and a highly decorated officer in World War I. (Later known as Wild Bill Donovan, he would head the Office of Strategic Services, the forerunner of the CIA.) Intelligence work burgeoned with the spread of radicalism around the world. Jack asked Donovan to investigate the Communist International (Comintern), formed in 1919, which had singled out bankers as archenemies of the working class. As a former banker to Czar Nicholas II, Jack was watching the Bolsheviks with extra apprehension. He also asked Donovan to dig up information about the new nations emerging from the old Austro-Hungarian Empire, for it was thought that political chaos in Central Europe could be a breeding ground for communism. Donovan's investi-gation was fairly prosaic—he uncovered only dusty papers and speeches—but the job launched him in high finance and accustomed Jack to a new manner of dealing with his enemies.

Two other events in 1920 contributed to Jack's sense of omnipresent danger. On Sunday morning, April 18, an anarchist and escaped mental patient named Thomas W. Simpkin wandered into Saint George's Church on Stuyvesant Square. The London-born Simpkin had been obsessed with death since the sinking of the *Titanic*. He later said he had come to America to kill Pierpont Morgan, only to discover he was already dead. On this Sunday morning, he was drawn to Saint George's by its beautiful chimes. "The chimes were playing and I was soothed," he said. "Then I went into the church."[17] He knew that it was the church of the Morgan family.

Jack's brother-in-law Herbert Satterlee was there, as was Dr. James Markoe, friend and physician to the Morgans. As Markoe was passing the collection plate, the dingy little Simpkin pulled out a gun and shot him point-blank in the forehead. The collection plate fell to the floor with a noise "like crashing glass."[18] The rector, Karl Reiland, flung his Bible to the pulpit and leapt over the chancel rail. Although the organist stopped playing, the church choir continued to sing angelically as vestrymen in cutaways pursued Simpkin; they caught him in Stuyvesant Square. By coincidence, Dr. Markoe was rushed to the Lying-In Hospital, the hospital he had persuaded Pierpont to endow, and died there a few minutes later. As it turned out, Simpkin had mistaken Dr. Markoe for Jack Morgan. When interrogators asked him why he thought of killing J. P. Morgan, Jr., Simpkin replied that he had heard that Morgan and a Congressman Miller had said that the International Workers of the World ought to be killed.[19]

Then came the blast of September 16, 1920. Shortly after noon, a horse-drawn wagon carrying five hundred pounds of iron sash weights pulled up on Wall Street between Morgans and the U.S. Assay Office across the street. Suddenly it exploded, blowing holes in the pavement, bursting like shrapnel through a terrified lunchtime crowd, killing thirty-eight people and injuring three hundred. Walking by 23 Wall, the young Joseph P. Kennedy was hurled to the ground. Throughout a half-mile radius, the blast punched out windows, including those on the Wall Street side of Morgans. Fire and a weird greenish smoke belched upward, igniting awnings as high as twelve stories above the street. Inside the New York Stock Exchange, panicked traders fled the imploding windows as shattered glass burst through the heavy silk curtains.

In *Once in Golconda*, John Brooks describes the chaos inside the House of Morgan:

> The cavernous interior of J.P. Morgan & Company, the office most
> seriously affected, was a shambles of broken glass, knocked-over

desks, scattered papers, and the twisted remains of some steel-wire screens that the firm had providentially installed over its windows not long before, and that undoubtedly prevented far worse carnage than actually took place. One Morgan employee was dead, another would die of his wounds the next day, and dozens more were seriously injured. Junius Morgan [Jack's older son], sitting at his desk near the north windows on the ground floor, had been pitched forward by the blast and then nicked by falling glass. . . . Another young Morgan man, William Ewing, was knocked unconscious, and awoke a few minutes later to find his head wedged in a wastebasket.[20]

The blast left glass strewn thick as sugar across the main banking floor. Bill Joyce, seated on a high stool, was killed by an iron sash lodged in his body; John Donahue died of burn wounds. A row of pockmarks was engraved deep in the Tennessee marble on the Wall Street side of the building. Whether as a badge of pride or a memorial to its two dead employees, the Morgan bank has never repaired the marble blocks, and they are still clearly visible to pedestrians on Wall Street. One partner later cited the inordinate expense of repairing them but then conceded, "It is right and proper that they should stay there."[21] For a generation, bankers asked, Where were *you* when the blast occurred?

Because the blast occurred in September, Jack was at his Scottish shooting lodge. But other partners were gathered in his office at the time, which, luckily, faced Broad Street. A visiting Frenchman, laughing nervously, said he felt as if he were back in the war. To inspect the carnage, George Whitney went into the street. On the bank's scarred north wall, he saw a macabre sight: "One of those scars had a woman's head and hat plastered up against it. I'll always remember that. It hit her so hard that it just took her head off and it stuck right on the wall."[22]

In another memory from that dreamlike day with its montage of slow-motion horrors, Whitney recalled that Dwight Morrow, a man of legendary absentmindedness, had a noon luncheon appointment with a government official. As the smoke cleared, Whitney saw Morrow trotting punctually downstairs and greeting the official as if it were an ordinary business day. The two strolled off for lunch at the Bankers Club, threading their way among dead bodies, firemen, overturned cars, and craters gouged in the street. "They didn't pay any attention to it, not knowing what they were doing I suppose," said Whitney.[23]

In the weeks ahead, J. P. Morgan and Company muddled through, with canvas sheets draped over its windows and a shaky dome, propped up by scaffolding, above the central banking floor. For this most foppish bank, it was a strange interlude, with many employees wearing slings and bandages to work. Whether Morgans or the Assay Office was the real target of the blast was never known; it went down as a great unsolved crime. It may have been a spontaneous chemical accident, although it coincided with a rash of anarchist acts and has always been attributed to anarchists. The new Stock Exchange building at 11 Wall Street was under construction at the time, which may have accounted for there being explosives in the area. The bank hired the Burns International Detective Agency, which offered a $50,000 reward for information about the incident; nobody ever collected the money.

As soon as the explosion occurred, thirty private detectives took up positions around Jack's brownstone on Madison Avenue. Jack construed the explosion as an attack against Wall Street rather than an attack against the bank. Yet along with the 1915 shooting, the Thorn case, the Markoe shooting, and the million and one crank letters, it must have fed his sense of vulnerability and his growing apprehension of conspiracies.

This period of turbulence provides the backdrop for Jack's deepening anti-Semitism, which played an important part in his outlook and became his shorthand explanation of many incidents, particularly attacks against his family and firm. His anti-Semitism was of a familiar variety. He saw Jews as a global fifth column feigning loyalty to host governments while furtively advancing foreign plots. He generalized the presence of the German-Jewish banks on Wall Street into a broader phenomenon. Like his father, Jack was extremely warm and affectionate toward those within his own circle of intimates, but, again like Pierpont, he often showed coldness and suspicion toward outsiders. In his anti-Semitism, Jack never saw himself as lashing out at the weak; instead, his enemies were more powerful than he, a mere Morgan, and deserved what they got.

In May 1920, serving as an overseer of Harvard University, he rushed to alert President A. Lawrence Lowell of the grave danger posed by a board vacancy:

> I think I ought to say that I believe there is a strong feeling among the Overseers that the nominee should by no means be a Jew or a Roman Catholic, although, naturally, the feeling in regard to the latter is less than in regard to the former. I am afraid you will think

we are a narrow-minded lot, but I would base my personal objection to each of these two for that position on the fact that in both cases there is acknowledgement of interests or political control beyond and, in the minds of these people, superior to the Government of this country—the Jew is always a Jew first and an American second, and the Roman Catholic, I fear, too often a Papist first and an American second.[24]

From this letter, one may discern that Jack had in mind his wartime feud with Kuhn, Loeb, now blown up into a universal theory. It's ironic that he would soon float the biggest German loan in American history and later be decorated by the Vatican for his investment advice.

In 1920, convinced of an anti-Morgan cabal among the German-Jewish bankers, Jack recruited a man named Charles Blumenthal to infiltrate their activities. For two years, Blumenthal reported to Jack periodically. His methods have not been documented, but one target was clearly Samuel Untermyer, whom Jack still planned to punish for his role in the Pujo hearings. Another was the German-born Otto Kahn, the Kuhn, Loeb partner and financial angel behind the Metropolitan Opera. Far more than Jacob Schiff, the ostentatious Kahn mingled with tony society, earning the nickname of the Flyleaf between the Old and the New Testaments.[25] Kahn had subscribed generously to the 1915 Anglo-French loan, and Jack had even praised his patriotic wartime speeches, which were widely circulated by the Allies. Kahn had even been reviled by the kaiser as a traitor to his native country. Then, in 1919, Jack learned about a small loan to several German cities made by Kahn and Kuhn, Loeb early in the war. Kahn was still a naturalized British citizen, and Jack thought the loan *prima facie* evidence of treason. Hopping mad, he wrote Grenfell, "Great Britain cannot shut him in gaol, he now being an American citizen, but it does not strike me as being high-class conduct, and I think it should be known."[26] Kahn's wartime patriotism was forgotten.

Pursuing his quarry, Jack sought proof linking Kahn with the German loan. He apparently got it from Blumenthal in 1920. He wrote Grenfell, "Enclosed is a photographic copy of a letter from Lindheim, who is a Jewish lawyer here in New York with 50 connections with the Untermyer tribe, to Dr. Albert, which, I think, quite sufficiently identifies Mr. Otto Kahn with the proposed German cities loan."[27] It seems both Jack and Teddy Grenfell were swapping intelligence with British authorities, because Grenfell already knew Dr. Albert had spent a lot of German money during the early stages of the war.[28] A couple of years later, the bank got a London source to consult Admiralty records on Samuel Untermyer.

Another possible source of Jack's information was Henry Ford's *Dearborn Independent*, which served as mouthpiece for Ford's bizarre anti-Semitic views and was distributed through Ford dealerships around the country. In 1921, the paper conducted a campaign against "hyphenated Americans"—immigrants of allegedly dubious loyalty to the country. In a warmly fraternal note to the editor, Jack endorsed the campaign: "Owing to the war, I became fully aware of the danger, to the community, of hyphenated Americans; and it seemed to me that the Jews were the only lot of that class of people who had been able to do their work quietly and were steadily working to maintain their hyphenated attitude of mind without calling public attention to it."[29] Jack said he would make information available to the *Independent*. When Charles Blumenthal traveled to Detroit to consult with Henry Ford on the Jewish menace, Jack followed up with a note inviting Ford to visit him in New York.

Jack's confused anti-Semitism was intermingled with business rivalries. The Yankee and Jewish banks still formed warring groups on Wall Street. In 1921, a former Justice Department agent tipped off the bank to a plan by Jewish bankers and German industrialists to restore German fortunes. He told how a Mr. Lehman and a Mr. Rothschild met with Kuhn, Loeb partners in New York to perfect this plot and how they hoped the new combine would drive J. P. Morgan and Company out of business. This may well have happened and been dressed up in alarming, conspiratorial language. Jack had a way of looking at the Yankee-Jewish rivalry on Wall Street and seeing it in conspiratorial and religious terms rather than in the more mundane terms of business.

Relations between Jack and Blumenthal soon deteriorated. Jack advanced him money for a home mortgage, and he failed to make a timely payment. For a banker such as Jack, deadbeats occupied a lower rung in hell than Jews. Relations grew frosty. In 1922, Blumenthal's payments were phased out. Later, when Blumenthal tried to use Morgan's name to raise cash, Jack denied he had ever employed the man. Was this pique—or Jack covering his tracks?

In any event, the hocus-pocus of German plots and Jewish bankers would soon seem silly and irrelevant. No Jew on Wall Street ever did as much for Germany as Jack Morgan would. Even as he terminated relations with Blumenthal in 1922, the State Department was urging him to sit on a committee of bankers who would outline the conditions needed for a massive German loan. After years of doggedly hunting German partisans, Jack Morgan would find himself Germany's master banker. The phantom he had been pursuing all those years turned out to be himself.

DURING the war, Jack had confounded critics who mocked him as a figurehead, a pale, plodding imitation of Pierpont Morgan. His British connections strengthened relations with the Allies, as did the partners he recruited for Morgan Grenfell. Having worked steadily in wartime, he continued to work eight or nine hours a day into the early 1920s. Yet he was a banker *malgré lui,* lacking the giant, locomotive energies that had propelled his father. As he readily acknowledged, he was a loafer, a studious amateur in the style of a British country squire. He loved gardening, yachting, reading detective fiction—activities of a mildly sedative nature. Once, in an indolent mood, he likened his brain to a soft, overboiled cauliflower. Also, he was haunted by his father's breakdowns, illnesses, and death, which he associated with politics and overwork. So he was ready to rely on a strong lieutenant.

Jack was a great fan of Harry Davison, who seemed the clear favorite as Morgan overlord in the postwar period. Davison had natural authority; Paul Warburg of Kuhn, Loeb once said that "men enjoyed following him."[30] His dedication to the bank was exemplary, as is attested by a cable that he sent to Nelson Aldrich after Pierpont died. Davison's house, Peacock Point, had just burned to the ground and he would spend the summer on a houseboat while it was being rebuilt; he cabled Aldrich, "Loss of house mere incident in view of other crushing loss."[31]

Davison's standing was greatly enhanced by the war. As head of the Red Cross War Council, he was elevated in 1919 to the presidency of a global league of Red Cross societies; during his Red Cross tenure, eight million volunteers were signed up. Many stories testify to Davison's massive self-confidence. At one Red Cross rally, he heard former president Taft say, "It gives me great pleasure to introduce to you one of our most distinguished citizens, a man who would rather face a German battery than an audience." Davison was halfway out of his seat when Taft thundered, "General Pershing!"[32]

Another Davison story concerns a trip he made to London in 1918. Upon arriving, he was informed that King George V wished to see him. En route to Buckingham Palace, he was briefed on protocol by the king's equerry and given a short list of royal taboos. He wasn't to cross his legs, offer his hand first, or depart until dismissed by the king. Davison spent a pleasant hour with His Majesty, then, suddenly remembering another appointment, sprang to his feet—a breach of protocol. Who but a Morgan partner would be so blasé about the king or not wish to prolong the experience? Buckingham Palace was just another stop on a busy itinerary; the House of Morgan had become aristocracy in its own right.

After the war, Davison's prestige was such that friends mentioned him as a possible presidential candidate. Davison himself demurred, saying it "could never be," apparently because he had been involved in an extramarital affair that ended tragically in the spring of 1915.[33] He was afraid the story would be dredged up. It turns out to be a grisly one. Davison and his wife, Kate, were close friends of a couple named Boocock, who had been neighbors in Englewood, New Jersey. Howard Boocock was treasurer of the Astor Trust Company. Davison was having an affair with Adele Boocock, a close friend of his wife's, and Howard Boocock was at first unaware of the liaison.

When Howard Boocock did learn of the affair, he became deranged, although in a style appropriate to his position. On March 22, 1915, he came home from the bank early and rather agitated. Yet he and his wife dressed for dinner as usual at their East Seventy-fourth Street townhouse, and the servants noticed nothing untoward during the meal. Afterward, Howard retired briefly to the upstairs library to read his newspaper, while Adele played the piano in the drawing room below. Then Howard joined her. The servants heard the piano music stop abruptly, followed by two pistol reports. When the terrified maids rushed into the room, they discovered that Howard had shot Adele behind the right ear with an old army revolver; then he had shot himself above the left eye. The first person the distraught servants thought to telephone was Adele Boocock's best friend, Kate Davison. It fell to Kate to notify the Boococks' relatives. Kate agreed to take in the two Boocock children—who had slept through the shooting—and the Davisons paid for their education as well. This action was reminiscent of the Davisons' earlier generosity in taking in Ben Strong's children. The double Boocock shooting was one of the sensational "unsolved" crimes of 1915. A coroner's jury concluded that Howard Boocock went haywire from worry over the possibility that he was suffering from intestinal cancer. The truth would remain buried until the present.[34]

In 1920, when Harry Davison returned to the Corner from the Red Cross, he had lost his magnetic, buoyant charm. He complained of queer headaches and sleeplessness and took a year off with his family, which they spent at Magnolia Plantation, his estate in Thomasville, Georgia. A photograph of Davison on a picnic there shows him smoking a blunt cigar and wearing a white shirt and a dark three-piece suit; even in poor health and on a rustic outing, a Morgan man couldn't let his image languish. But the stay didn't put an end to his headaches and dizziness. In August 1921, Davison was diagnosed as having a brain tumor.

He was a manly type who refused to become an invalid. One day at Peacock Point—his sixty-acre Greek-columned estate on Long Island's North Shore that nearly formed a continuous line of property with Jack Morgan's and George Baker's estates—he and Dr. Frederick Tilney were watching a school of porpoises in Oyster Bay. Tilney remarked that he had always wanted a porpoise brain for his research. "Bring me the elephant rifle and tell them to have the motor boat ready for us at once," Davison ordered a servant.[35] Davison went out and shot his porpoise.

Harry Davison died in May 1922, at the age of fifty-four, during an operation to remove the tumor. He left an estate estimated at $10 million, including $4.5 million destined for his son, Frederick Trubee, who had been confined to a wheelchair since his college days. During a summer off from Yale during the war, Trubee and several classmates had formed the first naval reserve air unit, and Davison had bought his son a plane. As Trubee participated in a demonstration show at Peacock Point, the plane's rear engine came loose and hit him in the head, leaving him a paraplegic. His father's special bequest was meant to allow him to pursue a political career without any material distractions. Trubee became an assistant secretary of war for aviation in the Coolidge and Hoover administrations and served as president of the American Museum of Natural History. As indomitable as his father, in spite of his handicap he played tennis and shot big game for display in the museum.

At 23 Wall Street, Davison's death left the path to power unobstructed, and Tom Lamont strolled into a leadership position. Deeply indebted to his mentor, Davison, Lamont perpetuated a Morgan tradition of building monuments to dead kings by writing a hagiographic biography of Davison. Of his other role model, Pierpont, Lamont wrote, "He was not interested in little matters, conducted or proposed by little men." He viewed Pierpont's reign as one of a vanishing gentility—"a kind of golden age of chivalry in affairs."[36] This early exposure to Pierpont and Davison gave Lamont a vision of the banker as statesman and empire builder rather than as bureaucrat or paper pusher.

During the 1920s, Tom Lamont would be the brains of the Morgan bank and the most powerful man on Wall Street. When journalists talked of "prominent banking opinion," they had usually been speaking with Lamont. A Wall Street saying held that "Mr. Morgan speaks to Lamont and Mr. Lamont speaks to the people."[37] In his early banking days, Lamont had been deferential, even obsequious toward his elders, content to play the serviceable courtier. He always knew how to handle the Morgans. Both Pierpont and Jack were brooding loners who liked charming extroverts of an equable disposition. Pierpont had the sociable Bacon and Perkins; Jack, Davison and Lamont. Where the Morgan family was intensely private and domestic, these regents lent the bank a high-society gloss. And Lamont was perceptive enough to give Jack the confidence-bolstering praise that had been withheld by Pierpont.

It is a mystery how Tom Lamont, a poor parson's son, became everybody's image of Wall Street elegance. The first Lamont came to America from Scotland in 1750. Lamont's father was a former Greek professor and a Methodist parson (Tom would later become a Presbyterian). The senior Lamont had an Old Testament face—a broad, square forehead, full beard, and eyes that burned with severity. He banned dancing, cards, and even neighborhood Sabbath strolls for the family; Lamont's mother, luckily, was gentler. Tom spent a thrifty boyhood in upstate Claverack, New York, plotting his escape and devouring novels. He attended both Phillips Exeter Academy and Harvard on scholarship. He admired, but wasn't awed by, the wealthy boys he met. He was a completely self-invented figure and as such would be emblematic of an age based on wild speculation and a frothy optimism. Like Jay Gatsby, he lived in the manner of a poor boy acting out his most lavish fantasies. He was so successful at playing the aristocrat that he passed for the genuine article.

Short and slim with rounded shoulders, smiling eyes, and thinning hair, Lamont was often photographed before his office fireplace, hands in pockets, relaxed, and debonair. Usually he wore an amused, searching expression, as if inviting intimacy yet skeptically probing his guest. He looked at the world closely, as if sizing it up, taking the measure of someone in a glance. He seemed immune to depression, congenitally cheerful, and unflappably poised. His favorite expression was "easy does it" and his son, Corliss, said he never saw his father angry. He had a staggering capacity for work, and his voluminous papers at the Harvard Business School resemble the work of ten busy men. Tom Lamont was a prodigy—in business, finance, and diplomacy—and his career, dazzling in scope, would rival that of Pierpont Morgan himself.

Lamont had a genius for friendship and was irresistible to the literary world. He was a newspaper publisher and a large shareholder in Crowell Publishing, the only Morgan partner drawn to that industry. When British poet John Masefield toured the United States during the war to generate sympathy for England, he became so attached to Lamont that he dedicated his *War and the Future* to him. Lamont also befriended

Walter Lippmann, John Galsworthy, and H. G. Wells. He had a writer's itch to record his thoughts and preserve them for posterity, dashing off hundreds of personal letters monthly.

His conviviality wasn't restricted to celebrities. Each spring, he holed up with three old college chums in Atlantic City, where they fished, played bridge, and talked. He maintained hundreds of relationships—like juggler's balls, he kept them magically aloft—and each acquaintance felt especially singled out by thoughtful gifts, cards, and invitations from 23 Wall.

If Tom Lamont assumed Morgan royalty with such ease, it had much to do with Wall Street's extraordinary self-confidence in the twenties and the banker's new diplomatic role. Lamont was a born politician and meshed exquisitely with his historical moment. In 1928, the Egyptian king said to him, "Mr. Lamont, I will wager I am the only head of a foreign state who has ever received you without asking for a loan for his government."[38] He was probably correct. Later Lamont appeared on a list of sixty-three citizens who ruled America and would certainly have made far shorter lists. In 1937, Ferdinand Lundberg, the radical journalist, would say that Lamont "has exercised more power for 20 years in the western hemisphere, has put into effect more final decisions from which there has been no appeal, than any other person. Lamont, in short, has been the First Consul de facto in the invisible Directory of postwar high finance and politics, a man consulted by presidents, prime ministers, governors of central banks."[39] Overheated prose aside, Lundberg erred in the right direction.

T H A T Lamont had no ordinary dreams can be seen from a 1916 effort to induce Henry Ford to take his car company public. The move was not accomplished until 1956, after Ford's death. The House of Morgan, with its large stake in railroads, had been myopic in recognizing the importance of the automobile industry, and Pierpont had rebuffed an early Ford request for financing. Then George Perkins lost a chance to finance General Motors in 1907, when he sneered at William Crapo Durant's forecast that sales would soar to half a million automobiles per year and cars would someday outnumber horses on America's streets. For turn-of-the-century Wall Street, cars were rich men's toys, plagued by unreliability and poor roads. This attitude rankled Henry Ford and reinforced his contempt for Wall Street bankers.

By 1916, the car companies had acquired new respectability on Wall Street. General Motors declared its first stock dividend—the largest in New York Stock Exchange history—and early skepticism turned to voguish enthusiasm. Henry Ford had introduced the assembly line in his Highland Park plant and in 1914 declared a $5, eight-hour day for his workers—terms generous enough to draw twelve thousand job seekers. Ford now cranked out over half a million Model Ts annually, and Lamont saw the chance for a splashy deal in the Pierpont tradition. That the Senior's ghost hovered in Lamont's mind was clear from a letter he wrote to a Ford associate in which he stated that if Ford took his company public, there would be "nothing just like it since the Steel flotation 15 years ago."[40] As a rule, Ford opposed public ownership and thought shareholders should work for the company. Nevertheless, he invited Lamont to unite the "best ideas" of J. P. Morgan and Ford. What blend of guile and geniality could tame Henry Ford?

In a memo, Lamont flattered but provoked Ford. He began: "You have the premier motor car industry of the country and of the world. . . . From nothing you and your associates have built it up to its present splendid proportions." With Ford softened up, Lamont became shockingly blunt: "The present make-up of your company is your only weakness. So long as the control of the company rests absolutely in your hands, just so long is the future of the business dependent upon the life of one man. . . . There must . . . come to you moments of almost deep oppression for the responsibility that you have to carry day by day." Having expressed sympathy, he stirred up anxiety, pointing to potentially troublesome minority shareholders. Then came the proposal itself, wrapped in a delicate tissue of jargon. Lamont suggested a "large financial operation" that might relieve Ford of burdensome responsibilities—in short, the first public offering of Ford stock.[41]

In a second letter, Lamont drew a parallel between Ford's sale of his company and Carnegie's sale of his steelworks to U.S. Steel. Since Ford was an individualist of the Carnegie type, it was a smart analogy. Lamont proposed that Ford, like Carnegie, retain a substantial interest in the company, holding senior debt "of the highest character, insuring handsome and stable returns to you and your heirs, or nominees, for years to come"—Lamont liked this tony style with fancy clients. But once he had advanced his idea, he backed off and pretended to offer his idea impartially for Ford's consideration. A few weeks later, Ford cordially acknowledged the letters, expressed interest, but let the matter lapse. It was a noble failure, in the end showing only Lamont's fearless ambition and his rare power to manipulate words.

After the Ford proposal was rejected, the House of Morgan stayed on the alert for opportunities in the automobile field. One finally came, through the Morgan link with the du Ponts, whose explosives and chemical business had profited from the Morgan Export Department. The war left the du Ponts awash with cash and with large paint, varnish, and artificial-leather manufacturing plants. They saw a potential market for these products in cars and so accumulated General Motors stock until in 1919 they held a 23-percent stake. They had every spot on the GM finance committee save one, that of founder William Crapo Durant.

A handsome, sporty man with a winsome grin and a flair for invention, Durant had started out as a rich buggy manufacturer. In September 1908, after being turned down by George Perkins, he financed the new General Motors Company himself, merging the car operations of Ransom E. Olds and David Buick and subsequently acquiring Cadillac. Unlike Henry Ford, who stamped out endless Model Ts, Durant favored a diversified product line. He was a persuasive, charming character—he "could coax a bird right out of a tree," Walter Chrysler once said—but a disastrous manager, impetuous and erratic.[42] This son of a failed bank clerk was also an inveterate stock market gambler whose specialty was GM stock itself. Lamont said he tossed around millions as if they were billiard balls.

In 1920, J. P. Morgan and Company sponsored a $64-million stock offering to finance a General Motors expansion. To please the du Ponts, the bank retained a sizable block and privately placed the remaining shares in safe hands. Then Ben Strong at the New York Fed engineered the 1920 recession. Henry Ford slashed car prices, and unsold GM cars piled up at dealerships. As GM stock plummeted, the underwriters—including the House of Morgan, the du Ponts, and Durant himself—struggled with huge losses in unsold shares. Durant had also formed a pool to prop up GM—a stock syndicate kept secret from the du Ponts and J. P. Morgan.

Cool as a flimflam artist, Durant pretended to take the disaster in stride. He didn't slacken his opera attendance, and he affected a cavalier air. Meanwhile, he faced ruin, for he had used his huge holding of GM stock as collateral for loans. If he had to sell stock to pay creditors, he would not only collapse the stock price but panic the Exchange and ruin GM's credit. To make matters worse, he had freely lent GM shares as collateral for other people's borrowings. If he were ruined, he would ruin many others at the same time.

Where the du Ponts trusted Durant, Dwight Morrow and other Morgan partners were suspicious. As GM shares broke below 20, Durant kept trying to hold back the tide by buying up more shares on margin. He continued to deny that there might be a problem. As the stock dropped as low as 12, his losses steadily mounted. By the night of November 18, 1920, Durant needed close to $1 million to meet margin calls before the market opened the next morning. Like Henry Ford, Durant despised bankers, viewing them as complacent men with tunnel vision who plundered the inventions of more original minds. Now he had to phone the House of Morgan and ask whether they would buy his GM stock at the closing price of $12 a share. Pierre du Pont and the Morgan partners, who thought Durant an incompetent, feared a market crash unless he were rescued.

When Dwight Morrow, George Whitney, and Tom Cochran went to Durant's Fifty-seventh Street offices, they found a scene out of a melodrama. His debts had bulged to an extraordinary $38 million, and his anteroom was crowded with creditors demanding repayment. The Morgan partners saw a possible repeat of the 1907 panic, with Durant defaults shutting down a string of brokers. In a frenetic, all-night rescue session, the Morgan men bought up Durant's shares at $9.50 per share—a steep discount from the closing price. The du Ponts put up $7 million, and the House of Morgan raised another $20 million to save Durant from margin calls. By dawn, a new company had been formed to buy Durant's stock. Durant's share of the new company was only 40 percent, while the du Ponts held 40 percent, and the Morgan-led bankers took 20 percent as their commission. Pierre du Pont was ready to deal leniently with Durant, but the pitiless Morgan partners insisted that he resign from GM. Overnight, the du Ponts and J. P. Morgan and Company had kidnapped an industrial empire. Two weeks later, Pierre du Pont emerged from retirement to become president of General Motors, a position he held until Alfred P. Sloan, Jr., replaced him three years later.

It was a double coup in Morgan history, for it confirmed the bank's relationship with General Motors and won the loyalty of the du Ponts. As Pierre du Pont wrote to his brother, Irénée, "Throughout the whole transaction the Morgan partners have appeared to the greatest advantage. They threw themselves into the situation wholeheartedly, stating at the start that they asked no compensation. They have acted with remarkable speed and success, the whole deal involving $60 million or more, having planned and practically completed it in less than 4 days."[43]

What about William Crapo Durant? An unreconstructed plunger, he lost half his net worth in the 1929 crash. In later years, he ran a bowling alley in Flint, Michigan. Poor and almost forgotten, he died in New York in 1947.

DURING the 1920s, a cash-rich America embarked on a binge of buying foreign bonds, a new experience for a country that had long relied on European capital markets to finance its own development. The investing fad had begun when the Treasury sold Liberty and Victory bonds in denominations as small as $50, enticing a public new to buying bonds. After the war, the habit of investing persisted. If Americans traditionally put their money into savings banks, insurance policies, and old mattresses, now they bought bonds *en masse*. Brokerage houses encouraged Americans to think of themselves as potential tycoons, global benefactors, embryonic J. P. Morgans.

The big New York City banks scrambled for the new business. National banks were barred from underwriting and distributing securities, but they could bypass such restrictions by creating separate securities subsidiaries. Chase, National City, and Guaranty Trust opened such affiliates. They sent out thousands of agents across the country, plying investors with a dizzying array of foreign bonds from Brazil and Peru, Cuba and Chile. At the same time, many American banks invaded overseas markets. Before the 1913 Federal Reserve Act, only state-chartered banks could have overseas branches—one reason why J. P. Morgan and Company had an enormous head start with foreign clients. Now nationally chartered banks could do the same. The glad-handing, fast-talking American banker became a figure of folklore around the world.

In a burst of activity, National City went into Russia (where its branches were confiscated by the Bolsheviks), set up a thriving business in China, and established branches in Buenos Aires and Rio de Janeiro. Where Barings had long been dominant in Argentinean business, it was overtaken in the postwar years by National City, J. P. Morgan and Company, and Kuhn, Loeb. At the same time, the City was paralyzed by the Treasury embargo on foreign loans and lost many long-standing sovereign clients. When Argentina invited Barings to share management of a $40-million loan with J. P. Morgan in 1925, the Treasury embargo forced Barings to pass on the large financing.

Washington watched the investing craze with growing fascination and wondered how to exploit it politically. Even after a Republican president, Ohio newspaper publisher Warren Harding, captured the White House in 1920, his *laissez-faire* ideology didn't stop his administration from trying to mobilize the new Wall Street power. The paradox

of the Roaring Twenties was that three free-market Republican administrations would confer new, semiofficial status on foreign lending, assuming the right to veto loans—something no Democratic administration
would have dared to do, lest it be accused of socialist tendencies.

The driving force behind the new loan policy was Secretary of Commerce Herbert Hoover. Hoover saw a precedent in Wilson administration policy toward Russian and Chinese lending, where the government
had maintained a close eye on the bankers. At a White House conference on May 25, 1921, President Harding told Tom Lamont and other
Wall Street bankers that henceforth *all* foreign loans had to be certified
by the State, Treasury, and Commerce departments as being in the
national interest. The secretaries in question—Charles Evans Hughes,
Andrew Mellon, and Hoover—were there to back him up. Morgans had
to notify other banks about the arrangement. Afterward, as spokesman
for the influential private banks and trust companies, Jack Morgan
pledged to Harding that the bankers would "keep the State Department
fully informed of any and all negotiations for loans to foreign governments which may be undertaken by them."[44] For a pro-business administration, it was an astounding extension of governmental power. Carter
Glass, now a Virginia senator, denounced the violation of bankers'
rights.

During the Republican-dominated 1920s, bankers probably attained
their peak of influence in American history. It would be the heyday of
Morgan power. Yet the bank's relations with the White House were
never smooth, however much collusion and back scratching the radical
pamphleteers might have discerned. From the outset, Morgan partners
thought Harding a simpleton, inadequate to the challenge of postwar
reconstruction. Upon Harding, Tom Lamont would later deliver a scathing judgment, seeing him as a "pathetic figure . . . the last man in the
world to lead 120 million people from the darkness and confusion of
World War I out into the light."[45] Even Jack, who was relieved by the
Democratic rout and rushed to offer his services to the president, sniped
at Harding as a "wishy-washy" chauvinist who lacked vision.

The disdain for Harding was more than personal, for the White House
and the House of Morgan represented quite different factions of the
Republican party. By instinct and self-interest, the Morgan bank was
liberal and internationalist on global financial issues. It advocated U.S.
leadership, close consultation with the Allies, and vigorous lending
abroad. On foreign policy issues it felt some kinship with Wilsonian
Democrats. With England handicapped in its resumption of foreign
lending, J. P. Morgan and Company wanted the United States to inherit

British leadership and initiate the rebuilding of Europe. The Harding brand of Republicanism, by contrast, was provincial, protectionist, and wearily contemptuous of European conflicts. These Republicans regarded foreign loans as ways to manipulate foreigners or as wasted welfare payments better spent inside America. Throughout Morgan history, the bank would be strongly drawn to internationalist leaders, not necessarily Republican.

Early in the new administration, the House of Morgan feuded with Harding over some $10 billion that the Allies owed to Washington from wartime loans. (These were the loans extended after the United States entered the war, not those sponsored by J. P. Morgan on Wall Street.) The pro-English House of Morgan argued strenuously to cancel this debt. Jack Morgan said the Allies had sent soldiers against Germany while America was still sending only dollars; decency demanded that the war debt be regarded as a subsidy and not as a loan. For the Harding administration, it was a question of whether Yankees would again be snookered by corrupt, wily Europeans. Collecting war debts was also a way to keep U.S. taxes low. When Lamont went to talk about getting the debt canceled, he found Harding floating in a sea of papers. "Lamont, this job is too much for me," the president said. "Whatever shall I do with all that pile? Well, I suppose I might as well try to learn something about these debts."[46]

Lamont's subsequent meetings weren't any more encouraging. Charles Evans Hughes, the secretary of state, had unsuccessfuly campaigned for U.S. membership in the League of Nations and felt uncomfortable with the insular debt policy. But he cited the lack of a popular mandate to cancel the debt—the same refrain the House of Morgan would hear for a dozen years to come. Lamont loftily suggested to Hughes that the United States take British Honduras in a swap for a piece of the debt—this was thrown out casually! Lamont found the other cabinet members overjoyed at the prospect of squeezing the debtor nations.

The administration adopted a policy of barring Wall Street loans to any foreign government that had not settled its war debts with the United States. After a sobering encounter with Treasury Secretary Andrew Mellon, Lamont reported in horror to Jack: "He is the watchdog of the Treasury and naturally considers it his duty to see that the Treasury gets every penny out of its debtors . . . he seems to think, too, that if we keep alive all these notes owing to us from dinky little countries all over Europe the fact that we are holding the notes will give us a sort of strangle hold politically."[47]

This was an extraordinarily shortsighted attitude that would weigh on world finance for a generation. The mountain of debt would retard world trade, undermine political leadership, and poison relations among the Western nations. Faced with Washington's obstinacy, the House of Morgan and Ben Strong reluctantly advised their British friends to settle the debt with Washington. After meetings between Mellon and Stanley Baldwin, the chancellor of the Exchequer, the British agreed to make payments stretching over sixty-two years. But they didn't accept the bullying cheerfully. When Prime Minister Bonar Law heard the terms from Stanley Baldwin, he fairly howled with rage. The issue would fester throughout the interwar period, placing Morgans in the cross fire between Washington and Whitehall. At the same time, the failure to cancel Allied debt meant that the House of Morgan had to take a tough line toward German reparations. For if the Germans didn't pay reparations to the Allies, how would the Allies pay Washington? This created a destructive merry-go-round of debt that would spin ever faster until the whole system would break down in the 1930s.

If Washington at first demanded control over foreign lending out of concern for the Allied war debt, it soon grew accustomed to exercising its new power. The arrangement took on an unexpected longevity; the procedure became so entrenched that J. P. Morgan and Company would brief the incoming Coolidge and Hoover administrations on how it worked. Later, in remarkable testimony to government-banker ties in the Diplomatic Age, Tom Lamont would state categorically that no sizable loan of the 1920s was made without Washington's tacit approval. The line between politics and finance blurred, then disappeared. The cognoscenti who interpreted Morgan actions as a mirror of official policy were seldom far off the mark.

If this arrangement later collapsed in recriminations, it started in a spirit of mutual convenience. Hiding behind Wall Street banks, the government could disclaim responsibility when countries were approved or rejected for loans. The banks, in turn, saw it as a security treaty, committing the government to protecting loans made under its aegis. It also provided the banks with government intelligence about debtor states. As the United States became a creditor nation, Wall Street confronted that ageless problem of how to enforce payment from sovereign states. Washington seemed to be the answer.

With the Harding review process came a notion—never explicitly stated, but always there—that a government safety net was in place, which would catch investors who fell off the high wire. As Lamont said, the government's stamp of approval "led many American investors into big foreign issues under the impression, whether so stated or not, that the Government had approved the issue or it could not have been made."[48] The arrangement encouraged a lot of wishful thinking and spared bankers unpleasant thoughts about what might happen in the case of default. There was an unspoken invitation to dispense with close examination of debtor nations. In the 1920s, Wall Street operated under an assumption of government protection, a notion that would prove illusory. But while it lasted, it created a mood of intoxication such as the Street had never known before and helped to trigger a decade of dreams that ended in the 1929 crash.

CHAPTER TWELVE

ODYSSEY

. .

.

NOTHING better symbolized the House of Morgan's postwar supremacy or its fusion with American policy in the Diplomatic Age than its new prominence in the Far East. At first, the bank had entered Asia at the government's behest, reluctantly joining the China consortium. Then William Jennings Bryan had condemned such foreign "meddling," and the group was disbanded. But the world war, by strengthening America and weakening Europe in the Pacific, tempted Secretary of State Robert Lansing with new regions. In 1919, rebuffed by his own Treasury Department, he resurrected the China group of private bankers instead. Jack Morgan remarked, "But Mr. Lansing, Mr. Bryan asked us to desist." Lansing, shamefaced, conceded the striking policy reversal.[1]

For this second China consortium, Tom Lamont played the exasperating chairman's role that previously had fallen to Harry Davison. In December 1919, Lamont visited the White House for his marching orders and found his idol, Woodrow Wilson, confined to a wheelchair. In a moving farewell, the president was roiled into the sunshine of a wide bay window. Calm and pensive, even joking about his disability, he hoped Lamont could reconcile differences between the two rival governments struggling to control China. Ever since the 1911 revolution, power had been divided between an official government in Peking and a nationalist one in Canton, with warlords ruling over Manchuria. From a banker's standpoint, this divided China was no less risky than the Manchu dynasty, for there still existed no ultimate guarantor of debt, no government bedrock on which to base loans.

In 1920, Lamont went on a mission to the Far East to see whether the time was ripe for Chinese loans. Coolly watchful, he moved through a China convulsed by strikes and student riots prompted by aggressive Japanese moves in Manchuria. The students were outraged by the Treaty of Versailles, which seemed to ratify Japan's seizure of German possessions in China during the war. Lamont was caught up in the Sino-Japanese rivalry. With diplomatic tact and evenhandedness, he included a side trip to Tokyo on his itinerary. During this 1920 trip, Lamont moved about with royal pomp and a touch of splendor, borrowing a leaf from Pierpont's book. Each morning in Peking, he received local merchants, who brought to his hotel camel caravans laden with costly wares—furs, rugs, silk, jade, and porcelain.

Lamont was pursued by more than just vendors. The Japanese set spies on his trail—such shameless eavesdroppers that they booked rooms on both sides of his hotel room. The insouciant Lamont kept a single item at his side—the code book for deciphering Morgan cables. His secretary lacked such sang froid. Lamont later wrote, "Although I thought it unnecessary precaution, my secretary always took [the code book] to bed with him and insisted upon sleeping with a loaded revolver under his pillow."[2] Afterward, reading a cable on a train, Lamont found a Japanese spy craning to steal a peek over his shoulder. He put the man out of his misery by offhandedly handing him the message.

News reports of Lamont's visit stirred nationalist fears that foreign bankers would try to impose a new financial protectorate over China. His arrival was protested by student demonstrations, which he thought were instigated by the Japanese. He liked to tell of how he had pacified a mob of students in Shanghai. If perhaps slightly embellished, the story testifies to Lamont's belief in reason and refinement as all-purpose weapons:

> One mid-afternoon in Shanghai I was told that a group of a couple of hundred of the Chinese student body were waiting in front of my hotel in order to show their disapproval of the Consortium by stoning me. I sent out word suggesting that the leaders come in for a cup of tea, and talk it all over. A dozen of them turned up at first in rather an ugly mood. But the tea was soothing and as soon as I was able to explain the facts about the Consortium, that it was designed to free China from the worst of her financial difficulties and help put some of her state enterprises on their feet, they readily understood and agreed to cooperate.[3]

Did Lamont believe tea-time chatter had changed the students' minds? Probably not. Yet the story suggests his constant advantage in confrontations. He always sounded so friendly and reasonable that he disarmed his most vocal critics. Nobody could bait him, shake his poise, or make him surrender that casual but impenetrable self-control.

Lamont never warmed to the Chinese and often spoke of them disparagingly. Contrary to his usual reticence in such matters, he retailed stories of Chinese corruption and intolerance. In Shanghai, he wanted to see Dr. Sun Yat-sen, head of the nationalist government in southern China. Because the Chinese leader feared a terrorist attack if he went to Lamont's hotel, Lamont visited him, under a heavy police escort. He saw nothing venerable about Dr. Sun, who had once attended school in Hawaii and had once been an omnivorous reader at the British Museum Library. Repeating Wilson's question of whether peace could be achieved between the two Chinas, Lamont was shocked by the reply. "Peace between the South and North?" Sun echoed. "Why, yes. Just you give me $25 million, Mr. Lamont, and I'll equip a couple of army corps. Then we'll have peace in short order."[4] Lamont was equally disenchanted by his contacts with the Peking government. Over tea, President Hsu suggested that if a government loan fell through, he might be in the market for a $5-million loan for himself.

Reporting back to the American group, Lamont recommended that no Chinese loans be made until north and south were unified, with a parliament that could take responsibility for a loan. It was the same problem faced by the first bankers' consortium—an unstable polity. China never met the group's conditions. By 1922, Lamont was asking Secretary of State Hughes whether the China consortium should be disbanded. An ersatz diplomat, Lamont wished to persevere less for reasons of profit than for reasons of state. But the question was moot: the China group had been stillborn. This didn't upset the House of Morgan, for Japan would be its most profitable customer in the Far East and China only an annoying factor in that relationship. Before long, Morgan involvement in Japan would be so deep as to deprive Tom Lamont of any incentive to renew his Chinese initiatives.

IN contrast with his tumultuous journey through China, the Japanese leg of his 1920 journey was far more congenial, the start of a lasting friendship. Japan was already known as the England of Asia—the highest possible recommendation for a Morgan partner—and with Japan and America ascendant in the Pacific, the time had come for closer financial relations. Like the United States, Japan had prospered during the war by selling ships and supplies to the Allies. Its gold reserves had grown a hundredfold—a war chest likely to impress any banker. And where the United States was already Japan's best customer, Japan was now the fourth best market for U.S. exports.

The political context, too, was auspicious: the Japan that Lamont encountered contained liberal elements eager to cultivate Western bankers and open the country to new influences. For the moment, enlightened aristocrats held the upper hand over militarists, and the cultural mood favored tolerance, openness, even a touch of bohemianism. The Japanese economy was dominated by *zaibatsu*—combination trading houses and industrial conglomerates formed around core banks—and they were fast expanding overseas. So as Britain weakened its long-standing alliance with Japan, Washington moved to fill the vacuum.

Tom Lamont and his wife, Florence, were greeted by Japan's elite: the merchant emperors of the houses of Mitsui and Mitsubishi. Cultured and patrician, these families possessed a natural appeal for someone as ceremonious and attentive to style as Lamont. A friend later remarked that Tom "simply outsmiled the Japanese."[5] Eager to meet Wall Street's newest ambassador, the Japanese business leaders entertained him as a visiting monarch. He marveled at how they produced No dancers at a moment's notice or "bevies of graceful, dancing geisha girls."[6] Florence was taken on a private tour of the twenty-five-acre central Tokyo estate of Baron and Baroness Iwasaki, a maze of lakes, gardens, and secluded courtyards. The Iwasakis were probably Japan's richest family and the founders of the Mitsubishi conglomerate, which owned Japan's largest steamship line.

The power of the House of Morgan in the 1920s owed much to its intimacy with the world's major central bankers, its ability to provide private channels of communication among them. Lamont conferred about the China consortium with Junnosuke Inouye, governor of the Bank of Japan, a gravely erect man with round, black-rimmed glasses and a solemn mien. The towering figure of his generation in Japanese finance, Inouye had served as president of the Yokohama Specie Bank, whose Wall Street office was fiscal agent for the Japanese government. He would twice be governor of the Bank of Japan and three times minister of finance. Like Ben Strong in America, Montagu Norman in England, and, later, Hjalmar Schact in Germany, Inouye made his nation's cental bank a strong, independent voice in the country's affairs. Like so many Lamont meetings, this one was providential. For Wall Streeters eager to believe that justice and decency would prevail over militarism in Japan, Inouye was heaven-sent. He was an apostle of sound currencies and balanced budgets and remained a steadfast, courageous opponent of the militarists.

Lamont established another fateful friendship, with the head of the Mitsui conglomerate, Baron Takuma Dan, a slight, fragile man, with a gentle manner and distinguished gray hair and mustache. His nickname was the Morgan of Japan. Fluent in English, with a mining degree from MIT, he was no less international and cosmopolitan than Tom Lamont. As managing director of the Mitsui conglomerate and chairman of the Mitsui bank, he controlled an empire that extended into every branch of the Japanese economy. It controlled a third of Japanese overseas trade—25 percent of the silk trade, 40 percent of coal exports—and managed a shipping fleet the size of the French merchant marine.

The Mitsui group made the Morgans seem like yesterday's upstarts. For nine consecutive generations, its bank had faced the sacred mountain, Fujisan. The House of Mitsui had become financial agents of the shogunate in the seventeenth century and bankers to the imperial house by 1867. It provided a convenient overseas network for the Japanese government, having more agencies abroad than the government had embassies. At the Mitsui compound in central Tokyo—a fortresslike structure with a huge gate and stone wall bristling with bamboo spikes—Baron Dan entertained Lamont with the same magnificence he later displayed to the Prince of Wales. He showed his guest Gobelin tapestries in his grand salon. Then they strolled by lotus ponds and under pine trees festooned with thousands of paper lanterns. The following year, to promote closer American ties, Dan led a Japanese delegation to Wall Street and dined with the Lamonts at their East Seventieth Street townhouse.

Lamont's success on his 1920 trip bore fruit with amazing speed. On September 1, 1923, an earthquake erupted in the Tokyo-Yokohama vicinity. It was a hot, windy day, and fires fanned over both cities, causing unspeakable damage. It was the century's worst earthquake, and over a hundred thousand people died. More than half of Tokyo and Yokohama was reduced to ashes. The property damage alone wiped out 2 percent of Japan's wealth.

When the news was learned at 23 Wall, Morgan publicity chief Martin Egan paid a condolence call at the Wall Street office of the Yokohama Specie Bank. Dwight Morrow became chairman of the Red Cross Japan Fund, and the Corner was converted into the New York headquarters for relief work. Rumors circulated that Japan planned to float its first bond issue in America since the Russo-Japanese War. Lamont wrote to Inouye, who was now the finance minister, and advised against such an issue. Lamont realized that candor more than greed would pay off in this situation. In his cable he said, "People who are contributing millions of dollars out of pocket for suffering and disaster are a little chary at the same moment of buying bonds for the people whom they are trying to assist."[7]

By late 1923, the Japanese, with their exceptional resilience, had restored Tokyo's electric lights, gas service, and water supply. The Tokyo Stock Exchange was back in service in under three months. The mass destruction had one beneficial side effect: it forced Japan to scrap many old factories and modernize its industrial plants. By declaring a bank holiday that saved many financial institutions, Inouye attained heroic stature in Japan. And when the House of Mitsui rebuilt its bank, the building's white marble facade was designed by Trowbridge and Livingston, the architects of 23 Wall Street. Some saw the House of Mitsui paying tacit homage to the House of Morgan and honoring their new ties.

Once the calamitous mood disappeared, Lamont set about to win the Japanese government as an exclusive Morgan client. The Japanese had found Pierpont rather rough and abrasive—he had offended them by demanding collateral on loans—and preferred doing business with Jacob Schiff of Kuhn, Loeb. For aid provided during the Russo-Japanese War, Schiff was decorated by the mikado with the Order of the Sacred Treasure. On Wall Street in the 1920s, it was a delicate affair to steal away valued business while adhering to the Gentleman Banker's Code. So with guile and subtlety, Lamont had to coach Inouye's emissary, Tatsumi, on Wall Street etiquette. Slyly, he put words in his mouth, tutoring him in the preferred style for an amicable breach. Afterward, Lamont explained how he primed his target:

> However as to the handling of any loan we have told Tatsumi frankly that it appeared to us there were only 2 courses for him to adopt. First to go to Kuhn, Loeb & Co. and state to them that because of the relations existing during the loan operation of the Russian War 20 years ago they desire them now to undertake the projected operation; or second as a complete alternative to go to them and say that because of the national crisis confronting their country; because of the grave necessity they felt themselves under for securing co-operation throughout the entire American investment public; because too of the importance for careful co-operation between the New York and

> London markets they had determined to invite us to make the lead
> in the projected operation and expected their friends Kuhn, Loeb &
> Co. to tell them this course was the wise one.[8]

Kuhn, Loeb was now too small to handle the projected $150-million earthquake loan, which would be the largest long-term foreign loan ever placed in the American market. The firm was also still suffering from the damage done to its standing on account of its supposed German sympathies in the war. When the issue appeared in February 1924, J. P. Morgan and Company brought in its old allies, National City and First National, as syndicate managers. To soothe ruffled feelings, they included Kuhn, Loeb. Whatever the private gloating at Morgans, the firm outwardly respected propriety. There was a twin loan of £25 million in London, and Barings, Schröders, and Rothschilds now had to include Morgan Grenfell in their Japanese financing.

The American loan had a concealed agenda. On two occasions, Lamont had talked with Secretary of State Hughes, who said he would be gratified "to have the Japanese people have clear evidence of the friendly feeling on the part of the two great English speaking nations toward Japan and the Japanese."[9] Once again, Wall Street financing was the visible face of a shift in government policy.

One problem inherent in employing bankers as *de facto* ambassadors was that they might transfer their allegiance to foreign powers. After all, private bankers were schooled in a tradition of absolute loyalty to their clients. A Tom Lamont would feel no less responsible to Japanese bondholders than a Pierpont Morgan would to railroad bondholders. So the House of Morgan believed it had a stake in Japanese success and prosperity and felt obliged to perform political favors for its important new client. Even as the Morgan bank sponsored the big earthquake loan, partners were embroiled in a political controversy on behalf of the Japanese. They protested the Japanese Exclusion Act, which was designed to check Japanese immigration and had a racist tinge. And they complained to the White House about American fleet maneuvers around Hawaii, which were troubling the Japanese. Tokyo and 23 Wall now played a game of mutual adulation. By 1927, the emperor of Japan would invest Jack Morgan with the Order of the Sacred Treasure and Lamont with the Order of the Rising Sun; in 1931, Russell Leffingwell would receive the Second Class Order of the Sacred Treasure. These were rare honors for American bankers.

The tendency to switch loyalties to foreign clients and acquire a strong interest in their survival would have profound consequences for the House of Morgan. For by the mid-1920s, Lamont had recruited three new clients—Japan, Germany, and Italy—whose course would sharply clash with America's. It was strictly by chance that the bank became involved with three future enemies. But over time, these business conquests would create an extraordinary situation in which the true-blue banker of the Allies ended up in the precarious position of banker to the future Axis powers.

IN the new vogue for foreign securities, the major area of attention was Latin America. Bond peddlers from Wall Street banks badgered small investors into buying bonds issued in places they could scarcely pronounce. Few knew the checkered history of Latin American lending or that as early as 1825 nearly every borrower in Latin America had defaulted on interest payments. In the nineteenth century, South America was already known for wild borrowing sprees, followed by waves of default. Now too many bankers again chased too few good deals, and credit standards eroded accordingly. In describing the 1920s, Otto Kahn later said, "A dozen American bankers sat in a half a dozen South and Central American States . . . one outbidding the other foolishly, recklessly, to the detriment of the public."[10] The default of Latin debt in the 1930s would profoundly shake America's faith in Wall Street.

Latin American loans had always been risky because of the region's dependence on fluctuating commodity prices. A dip in copper prices instantly hurt Chile, while lower tin prices could cripple Bolivia. When the price of sugar collapsed in 1920–21, the Cuban economy plunged with it. Faced with many business failures, National City Bank—which held 90 percent of Cuba's deposits and served as the country's national bank—foreclosed on properties and ended up owning a fifth of the island's sugar mills. The Guaranty Trust was also heavily invested in Cuban sugar and had to be rescued by a Morgan-led group of bankers in May 1921. William C. Potter, a manager of the Guggenheims' smelting trust, was brought in as a caretaker executive and loan liquidator for the bank; George Whitney and other Morgan partners went on its board. Devastated by the experience, Guaranty Trust would deteriorate into such a sleepy, stodgy, risk-fearing institution that by 1959 it would be ripe for merger with the far smaller J. P. Morgan and Company.

As the prestige bank of Wall Street, the House of Morgan didn't need to coerce Main Street investors into buying Latin American bonds. It preferred European industrial states, Commonwealth countries (Canada and Australia), and developed states on the periphery (Japan and South

Africa) although it had long shared business in Argentina with Barings. This was the privilege of success: the bank could choose the soundest foreign borrowers, lending its imprimatur only to those countries that probably didn't need it. The only poor country the bank dealt with was Mexico, which had gone from the model Latin American debtor in Pierpont's day to the *bête noire* of global bankers. During the prolonged turmoil of the Mexican Revolution, it had repudiated over $500 million in government and railway debt, an unusual loss of principal on Morgan-sponsored foreign bonds. Adding to the bank's indignation was the fact that the defaulted debt included Pierpont's sacred loan of 1899—the first foreign issue ever floated in London by an American banking house.

Before examining the Mexican debt morass, it is important to note some differences between Latin American debt then and now. During the interwar years, the debt was packaged as bonds and sold to small investors; in our own day, the debt would take the form of bank credits, meaning that the public is not directly at risk. During the 1920s, banks negotiated with Latin American debtors, not on their own account, but as "moral trustees" for small bondholders. Such was the nature of Morgan involvement in Mexico, with Tom Lamont serving as chairman of the International Committee of Bankers on Mexico—the splendidly initialed ICBM. Formed in 1918 with the approval of the State Department and the British Foreign Office, the ICBM negotiated for two hundred thousand small bondholders. In the nineteenth century, Mexican debt talks had been handled by Barings. But citing the Monroe Doctrine, the State Department demanded that the United States have the controlling hand on the committee. With over $1 billion invested in Mexico, the United States behaved like a jealous landlord. Mexico was a resource-rich country that always held out a seductive promise of prosperity, which it never quite fulfilled. And it had a weak political system, always making debt repayment problematic.

Lamont spent so much time wrestling with Mexican debt that a slightly paternal tone crept into his comments, as if Mexico were the backward child of the Morgan brood. Writing a birthday greeting to his son, Corliss, in 1923, he grew mawkish: "Much of my life for 2 years past has been devoted to help poor Mexico to her feet. . . . The accomplishment of that task is one of my daily prayers."[11] Lamont claimed that Mexico was the first thing to occupy him each morning, and he often talked about the widows and orphans who had waited years without receiving interest on their bonds. The Mexican debt crisis demanded saintly patience and something of a romantic's penchant for lost causes. Lamont was ideally suited for the task.

In working with Japan, Lamont had some room in which to maneuver. This wasn't the case with Mexico, where he had close State Department supervision. When it came to Third World countries, Washington more openly exploited American financial power. Secretary of State Hughes opposed diplomatic recognition of Mexico, which had continually threatened powerful U.S. interests there. In 1917, under leftist president Venustiano Carranza, Mexico had enacted a radical constitution, which asserted Mexican ownership of subsoil minerals—a measure denounced as nationalization by American oilmen, who wanted to send in gunboats to repeal it. After Pancho Villa's troops looted his huge cattle ranch in Mexico, William Randolph Hearst began to editorialize in favor of a Mexican invasion in 1916. Hughes was also bothered by Mexico's default on foreign debt and its confiscation of American-owned lands. Until these demands were met, Hughes demanded a credit quarantine around Mexico. The House of Morgan was his main instrument for enforcing it.

Like the China consortium meetings, the ICBM meetings were held at 23 Wall Street. It was the same act of ventriloquism: the State Department talked, and Tom Lamont moved his lips. The Mexicans preferred this charade, for it enabled them to bargain with Washington while being spared the public stigma of negotiating with a *gringo* government. Private banks such as Morgans were perfect channels for frank exchanges between Washington and foreign governments.

But while Lamont was rapturously fascinated by Japan, he knew virtually nothing of Mexico, which was thought too wild for tourism. Hence, Lamont acted as proxy for two hundred thousand bondholders whom he never saw, negotiating with a country he never visited. He became a familiar figure in the Mexican press, the personification of American finance. Interviewing him in 1921, a Mexico City correspondent wrote: "He is not the man behind the throne, he is the man on the throne. He is the most clever, the most listened to, the most powerful of the partners of Morgan."[12]

In 1920, after counterrevolutionaries murdered Carranza, General Álvaro Obregón rose to power. To win recognition from Washington, he embarked on a conciliatory strategy, courting American businessmen, hiring a Washington lobbyist, and distributing favorable literature in the United States. In 1921, when William Randolph Hearst went to tour his vast Mexican properties—which his father had gotten cheaply from the former dictator, Porfirio Díaz—he found Obregón a pleasant surprise. Afterward, he said his properties had been "in continual trouble and turmoil during the several preceding administrations, but have been in complete peace and security during the administration of President Obregón."[13]

Eager to please American bankers and reestablish Mexican credit, Obregón plied Lamont with invitations to visit Mexico. But Secretary of State Hughes wanted a treaty of friendship and commerce from Obregón and insisted that Lamont stall to increase the pressure. When the bank received alarming reports of rebel troop movements against the president, Lamont told Hughes that if he went to Mexico, it might bolster Obregón's standing. Hughes relented. In October 1921, Lamont boarded the bank's private railroad car, Peacock Point, and headed south.

Obregón, a chick-pea farmer from Sonora, was a crafty politician who knew how to temper reforms with authoritarian toughness. To gain peasant support, he would praise revolutionary ideals while scaling back Carranza's reforms. Lamont found the one-armed general a charming host, friendly, expansive, and not without humor. With Prohibition in the United States, Obregón greeted Lamont and gave a brisk summons for some liquor. "At last, Mr. Lamont, you see you are in a free country," he said. One detail of the visit riveted Lamont's attention. Obregón had placed his desk in the middle of a hardwood floor, so he would be able to hear the squeak of an assassin's footsteps.

During his talks with the Mexican president, Lamont confronted the dilemma that accompanies every global debt crisis: the victim threatens to default unless he receives more money. What leverage do bankers ultimately have over a defaulting country if not the prospect of new loans? As Lamont later reported to Secretary of State Hughes, Obregón "could not see the advantage of the government's attempting to live up to its obligations, even in greatly diminished measure, unless, at the same time, it were assured fresh loans upon a large scale."[15] Lamont was saved from this course by a structural obstacle: the debt was in the form of bonded debt, and capital markets wouldn't swallow more Mexican bonds; so the lending had built-in limits. Lamont told Obregón that no new loans would be granted until the old ones were at least partly honored. The Mexican replied that their debt should be proportionate to their ability to pay—an argument that will sound drearily familiar to bankers of a later day—and wanted a 50-percent reduction in principal.

Lamont began to sense that Obregón had a secret agenda. By holding back customs revenues pledged to the defaulted bonds, Mexico drove down the bonds' market price. This was convenient, since the government could then use those revenues to buy back depreciated bonds in the marketplace. Lamont thought this a betrayal of bondholders' trust. At this point, he still insisted that the bonds be redeemed at par. He tried to scare Mexico with arguments that default would make it a pariah in the international marketplace, that it would be unable to secure future loans.

When Lamont left Mexico two days ahead of schedule, he had armed guards posted on the rear platform of his train. It turned out he narrowly escaped harm: when he reached San Antonio, Texas, he learned that his originally scheduled train was attacked by bandits, who planned to kidnap him and demand a half million gold pesos in ransom.[16] Back at 23 Wall Street, Lamont received a wire from Jack Morgan expressing disgust with Mexico. Jack thought it a point of family honor to make sure Mexico repaid his father's 1899 loan: "I did not think any Government of modern times would so frankly proclaim its complete dishonesty or its abandonment of all decent finance or morals. Hope you did not have too trying a time, and congratulate you in getting out before they stole your pocketbook or watch."[17] Again Jack personalized bank policy abroad, while Lamont assumed a diplomat's disinterested professionalism and was thus better attuned to the Diplomatic Age.

There is a tendency to portray Wall Street bankers of the period as reactionary ogres. In Latin America, they certainly had a bias toward strong, authoritarian regimes. But the weakness wasn't for totalitarian or *laissez-faire* regimes so much as for stability, whatever its form. Bankers probably had a higher ethical standard than industrialists of the period, as became evident from the contrasting attitudes taken by the House of Morgan and the oil companies in dealing with Mexico.

Throughout the twenties, American oilmen tried to persuade bankers to protest the hated 1917 Mexican constitution. They also bristled at higher Mexican export taxes and a government requirement that they obtain concessions on land they thought they owned. Both J. P. Morgan and Company and Morgan Grenfell had performed underwriting for Standard Oil of New Jersey, and Lamont was badgered by Standard, the Texas Company, and Sinclair Oil to join their campaign against Mexico. By 1921, Mexico was already the world's biggest oil exporter and a high-priority area for American oilmen.

Lamont didn't want to jeopardize his debt negotiations by entering the murky, often violent strife between the oilmen and Mexico. He performed some perfunctory lobbying for them but generally kept his distance. The oilmen weren't squeamish about their tactics and didn't hesitate to trample governments that defied them. After Lamont returned from Mexico in 1921, Walter Teagle, head of Standard Oil, passed along a memo to him from an unnamed Mexican. In a covering note, Teagle said blithely that it "might be of interest to you in a general way."[18]

Preserved in Lamont's files, the memo is shocking, nothing less than a blueprint for bribing the entire Mexican government. It starts out with a nasty portrayal of the Mexican national character: "The Mexican, and particularly the traditional professional politician of Mexico, after four hundred years of training, is actuated by two dominant motives; one, the fear of force—physical force; the other is the incentive of personal gain. . . . An appeal to patriotism or to idealism is not understood."

The nameless author goes on to say that the use of force would be too costly, leaving only pecuniary gain as a motivating force in Mexico. He contended that Obregón was an unwilling captive to party radicals and could not satisfy the needs of his greedily ambitious lieutenants. How to free him from their influence? "This force can only be removed from and returned to the President himself by putting him in such a financial position as to give him dominance. Money will change his cabinet, make over his congress, give him domination over his governors and allow him to abrogate or modify present unsatisfactory laws."

To provide Obregón with the necessary funds—and this is where the House of Morgan came in—the writer of the memo suggested setting up a Mexican bank that would masquerade as a bank for agricultural development, but would exist to place money at Obregón's personal disposal. The writer concluded that the money, liberally distributed, would achieve miraculous results: "The undesirable elements in his cabinet would be given a certain sum of money and sent to desirable foreign posts. The obstructive radical elements in his congress could be removed. It would soon be seen that the radical *diputado* would become a staid conservative the moment he came into possession of property. . . . Such a bank might well dominate the financial and economic life of Mexico and the American directors of such an institution might well keep in close touch with Washington."[19]

Lamont's file shows no reply or follow-up. Perhaps he responded orally. In all likelihood, he was shocked. He may have regarded silence as the most eloquent expression of scorn, or at least the best way to avoid antagonizing an important client. Lamont was no choirboy in politics, but the House of Morgan shied away from blatant skulduggery. The bank had a strict policy against paying so-called fees or commissions and usually reacted to such requests with frigid New England reserve. The Standard Oil memo provides a benchmark for judging the Morgan bank against the dismal standard of American business conduct in Latin America during the 1920s.

The ensuing Mexican debt talks of the early 1920s can be quickly summarized. There were a few fleeting triumphs, always followed by fresh defaults and despair. Lamont's ingenuity could never win more than a short reprieve. In 1922, he negotiated an agreement with the Mexican finance minister, de la Huerta, that won Obregón the U.S. recognition he had craved. The agreement called for steep concessions by Lamont, including lower interest payments spread over forty-five years. The deal was suspended by early 1924. Among other factors, Mexico was suffering from declining oil production as oil companies vengefully switched to the politically more pliant Venezuela. Another debt agreement was reached in 1925—the initial payment this time was down to a paltry $10.7 million—but it, too, was soon dead. The bankers who had once boldly insisted on full payment had to settle for ever-smaller fractions of the original loans. When final disposition was made of this Mexican debt later in the decade, Lamont would find himself negotiating not with the Mexicans, but with an unexpectedly resourceful adversary: his own former partner, Dwight W. Morrow, recently appointed ambassador to Mexico.

THE Republican evasion of world responsibility presented new opportunities for the House of Morgan. Glorifying entrepreneurs and scorning politicians, the Harding, Coolidge, and Hoover administrations drafted financiers to represent them at economic conferences. This move reflected a 1920s cult in which businessmen were revered as far-sighted problem solvers who could succeed where politicians failed. The new mood suited Morgan partners Tom Lamont, Dwight Morrow, and Russell Leffingwell, who fancied themselves financial diplomats and sometimes joked about their technical ineptitude in more prosaic forms of banking. During the 1920s, Morgan partners spent enormous time at overseas conferences, serving as a legitimate cover for Republican administrations more global-minded than they cared to admit; thus the bank profited from the isolationism it deplored. This was the same use of private proxies that Washington had employed since the days of the first China consortium.

If private bankers enjoyed new stature, they shared it with central bankers, who assumed new power and autonomy. Beneath the euphoria, the Jazz Age was a despairing time. The populace grew disenchanted with politicians who had led them into war and then squabbled over reparations and postwar security. A clique of western central bankers hoped to transcend this political opportunism and forge a banking elite dedicated to sound economic principles. They espoused free trade and an unrestricted flow of capital, balanced budgets and strong currencies. They saw it as their function to maintain financial standards and prod politicians into painful, necessary reforms.

The American representative of this trend was Benjamin Strong of the New York Federal Reserve Bank. When the Harding and Coolidge administrations disclaimed leadership in postwar European reconstruction, the role devolved upon Strong, who was the Fed's contact with the central banks of Europe. Strong was solidly in the Morgan mold—a descendant of seventeenth-century Puritans, counting theologians and bank presidents among his ancestors, and the son of a New York Central superintendent. Like his Morgan friends, Strong matched conservative domestic views with a cosmopolitan receptivity to European thought— so much so that Hoover later chided him as a "mental annex of Europe." Hobbled by a regulation that he couldn't lend directly to foreign governments, Strong needed a private bank as his funding vehicle. He turned to the House of Morgan, which benefited incalculably from his patronage. In fact, the Morgan-Strong friendship would mock any notion of the new Federal Reserve System as a curb on private banking power. In the 1920s, real power in the system resided at the New York Fed's new Florentine palazzo on Liberty Street.

Strong was capable of great warmth and sudden anger. Unlike the smooth Morgan partners, he was a moody and troubled man. He was divorced by his second wife and in 1916 contracted tuberculosis, which would keep him from the bank for several months each year. Perhaps in reaction to his personal disappointments, he became passionately devoted to the Fed. He tried to endow it with the Bank of England's austere, unassailable dignity. A giant presence in American finance, Strong tutored the still green Federal Reserve governors in the art of central banking.

Ben Strong participated in postwar European reconstruction and currency stabilization with his British counterpart, Montagu Norman, governor of the Bank of England after 1920. In Monty, he found a dear friend and alter ego. The divorced Strong and the bachelor Norman plunged into a relationship of such secret intimacy and convoluted intrigue as to arouse fears in both their governments. Taking long vacations together in Bar Harbor, Maine, and southern France, they fortified each other's distrust of politicians. They shared faith in the gold standard and hoped to create autonomous central banks that could conduct global monetary policy free of political tampering. To their two-man cabal, Strong brought the unmatched financial power of Wall Street, while Norman lent British knowledge and professionalism ripened over many generations. The postwar pound was simply too weak for Norman to conduct unilateral financial diplomacy. After the Treasury embargoed foreign loans to shore up the pound, diverting foreign borrowers to New York, Norman desperately needed a Wall Street link to offset the City's weakness. He found it in Ben Strong and the House of Morgan.

For twenty-four years, Monty Norman reigned mysteriously in his mahogany office at the Bank of England. He had been perfectly bred for the job. One of his grandfathers was a long-time bank director, and the other was a governor of the bank. He himself came to the bank via the Anglo-American merchant bank of Brown Shipley and Company (Brown Brothers in New York). Many labels have been applied to Norman—madman, genius, hypochondriac, megalomaniac, conspirator, eccentric, visionary—all of which were true. One banker said he resembled "a painting by Van Dyck—tall, pointed goatee, great hat, like a courtier of the Stuarts."[20] He had a wizard's face—sharp and chiseled, with pointed nose and beard. Despite—or perhaps to counter—rumors of Sephardic Jewish blood, he was viciously anti-Semitic. As he moved about in funereal black beneath a wide-brimmed hat, he retained a touch of Oriental splendor in the emerald that adorned his tie. Sensitive and high-strung, he often suffered breakdowns or lumbago attacks during currency crises. A suppressed hysteric, he would erupt in tantrums that terrified bank employees and made his rule absolute. His thin smile rarely opened into laughter, as if that might shatter his mystique. A proud *prima donna*, he would say he felt "faint" for "want of food" if he didn't eat every two hours.

One of Norman's biographers describes him as giving "the appearance . . . of being engaged in a perpetual conspiracy."[21] This conformed to his sense of central banking, which he approached as a priestly mystery, a rite best conducted in deep shadows. "The Bank of England is my sole mistress," he said; "I think only of her, and I've dedicated my life to her."[22] For Norman, the central banker was answerable only to higher principles, not to any elected representatives. When challenged, he often cited a favorite Arab proverb: "The dogs may bark, but the caravan moves on."[23] He received visitors alone, as if his office were a confessional, and he was privy to the inner thoughts of powerful men. Years later, Franklin Roosevelt unnerved him and stripped him of his wizard's magic by insisting that others be present at their White House meeting. It was Norman who incarnated

Washington fears that British financiers were a sophisticated and treacherous lot who gulled innocent Americans.

Monty Norman was a natural denizen of the secretive Morgan world. Among old friends, he counted his former classmate Teddy Grenfell and Vivian Hugh Smith of Morgan Grenfell. Brooding and melancholy, he liked Grenfell's prankish wit, while he was dedicated to Smith for having helped him to overcome doubts about becoming a director of the Bank of England in 1907. Bucking him up, Smith had written, "Of course you will accept and, when you are on the Court, remember that you are as good as they are."[24] As a solitary bachelor, Norman created a mysterious circle of married female confidantes, including Smith's wife, Lady Sibyl, the beautiful society suffragette. A follower of theosophy and faith healing, she appealed to Norman's kooky side. "Through her influence," says a Norman biographer, "he widened his interest in the esoteric and the occult; for Sybil was emphatic about the crucial importance of religion to a spirit as easily bruised as his."[25] Lady Sybil would disappear for long, platonic weekends with Monty, who became a godfather to the Smith children. Thus, by happenstance, Morgan Grenfell was extremely close to the most influential central banker of the interwar years.

The House of Morgan formed an indispensable part of Norman's strategy for reordering European economies. America had the means to accomplish the task but was still ambivalent about exercising power in Europe. Even among Morgan partners, there was a reservoir of doubt. Russell Leffingwell, a former Treasury official who became a Morgan partner in 1923, told Basil Blackett of the British Treasury, "We feel that we got you out of a pretty pickle [during the war] but we rather think that it is time you were looking out for yourselves. We have never had any taste for world finance and our brief experience has not developed it. We like you and want to see you prosperous and happy and peaceful but we don't like the game you play nor the way you play it and don't want to be forced to sit in it."[26] Norman loved the game. Imperial to the core, he wanted to preserve London as a financial center and the bank as arbiter of the world monetary system. Aided by the House of Morgan, he would manage to exercise a power in the 1920s that far outstripped the meager capital at his disposal.

Norman thought in large, geopolitical terms. He saw the rehabilitation of central Europe as a precondition for restoring prosperity and political order and exempted reconstruction loans from the foreign loan embargo. Through his leadership, Morgans first became involved in Austria. In late 1921, the British sounded out Jack about an Austrian loan, saying its government would furnish Gobelin tapestries as collateral. The next year, Austria's finance minister, Dr. Kienbock, pleaded with Dean Jay of Morgan, Harjes in Paris (now in plush headquarters on the place Vendôme) for a loan. Kienbock cited famine, misery, and a worthless Austrian schilling. He again asked for a loan backed by tapestries and other *objets d'art.* [27] At first, the House of Morgan frowned on this unorthodox request, afraid it would create a "pawn-broking impression" [28]—even beggars had to come suitably attired to Morgans. Lamont—now known as the Morgan empire's secretary of state—wondered whether another bank should undertake the loan. He feared that as former banker to the Allies and fiscal agent for England and France, J. P. Morgan and Company was a poor choice and might even engender hostility in Austria.

The Austrian loan was worked out under the auspices of the League of Nations, which aided Monty Norman's grand design of reconstruction. Impressively wrapped, it was payable in gold coin and backed by Austria's customs and tobacco monopoly. It was issued simultaneously in several capitals. The $25-million New York portion was co-managed by J. P. Morgan and Company and Kuhn, Loeb. In retrospect, the League of Nations cachet perhaps gave a specious air of security to a risky venture.

Austria led to Germany. By early 1922, Germany was already pleading for relief from onerous reparations payments. The British sympathized, but France kept up its grudge, citing extensive war damage on its soil. (The extraordinary Anne Morgan was gathering hundreds of American women to rebuild French villages and raise money for schools, hospitals, and libraries. As a fund-raiser, her American Friends for Devastated France co-sponsored the July 1921 championship fight between Jack Dempsey and Georges Carpentier.) In the most potent form of default imaginable, the Germans expanded their money supply, ran large budget deficits, and depreciated the mark. This had the fatal side effect of unleashing hyperinflation. The Allies felt betrayed as German monetary policy undermined reparations payments. In January 1923, French and Belgian troops occupied the Ruhr. Irate troops ripped German bank notes from the hands of manufacturers and seized the customs machinery.

Monty Norman warned Ben Strong that occupied German soil was the "black spot" of the world and could ignite another war. Germany remained England's main trading partner, and Norman saw its revival as the crux of his master scheme for European prosperity. He was also personally attached to Germany, where he had studied music. Washington similarly placed a high priority on German revival. America had ended the war with vastly expanded factory capacity and needed export markets to absorb its surplus. American corporations were also eager to acquire advanced German technology.

The result was a massive Anglo-American commitment to keeping Germany afloat, with the House of Morgan assigned a central role. As Lamont later wrote, "The British and ourselves regarded Germany as the economic hub of the European universe. We feared that unless Germany were rebuilt and prospered all the surrounding countries of the Continent would likewise languish."[29] Bankers of an earlier generation would probably never have fretted in this way about the fate of the Western world or thought in such explicitly political terms.

The new demands of the Diplomatic Age were graphically seen in Jack Morgan's *volte-face* on Germany. In 1922, Secretary of State Hughes and Commerce Secretary Herbert Hoover asked Jack to participate—allegedly as a "private citizen"—in a global bankers' committee in Paris, which was considering an international loan to Germany. Jack, implacable toward Germany, had sworn after the war that the United States should never trade with that country. He and Blumenthal were then winding up their spying forays against German-Jewish bankers on Wall Street. So Jack's acceptance of Hughes's suggestion must have been disorienting, especially given the outpouring of publicity he received in Paris. The *New York Herald* reported, "Paris dispatches tell us that J.P. Morgan's presence at the international bankers' conference is attracting more attention than has been devoted to any American since President Wilson arrived in the French capital for the Versailles conference. . . . He is a symbol of the tremendous American power that may be used for the rehabilitation of Europe."[30] Jack handled himself ably and raised valid reservations about a German loan but was obliged to suppress his more extreme private opinions of Germany.

From now on, Jack would be the sober financial statesman in public, the confirmed foe of Germany in private. After the Ruhr occupation, he fired off a letter to Hughes condemning it. In eloquent terms, he told Clarence Barron that the Allies shouldn't strip Germany of hope by confiscating all its earnings through reparations. Yet his *personal* correspondence reveals the old demonology of the Hun. To Grenfell, he wrote, "I must say that it begins to look to me as though France is really talking to Germany in the only language that the Germans understand." Of Germany's state of mind, he added, "it calls for the whip and not for conversations."[31]

Meanwhile, German inflation worsened. The government was printing so much money that newspaper presses were commandeered. Thirty paper mills worked around the clock to satisfy the need for bank notes. Prices soared so fast that wives would meet their husbands at factory gates, collect their wages, and then rush off to shop before the next round of price increases. In January 1922, about two hundred marks equaled one dollar. By November 1923, it took over four *billion* marks to buy a dollar. A stamp on a letter to America cost a billion marks. At the end, in a final absurdity, prices doubled hourly.

To restore Germany, a new conference was summoned in early 1924. Again the House of Morgan represented the Coolidge administration, which kept up a bogus air of indifference. In fact, Charles Evans Hughes was very disturbed by reports of starving children and mounting extremism in Germany. As the "private" American representatives to the conference, Hughes chose two people close to J. P. Morgan and Company—Owen Young, chairman of General Electric, and General Charles Gates Dawes, the lone Chicago banker to join the Anglo-French loan of 1915. The German problem was so fraught with risk that upon departing for Europe, Dawes joked, "Oh, well, somebody has to take the garbage or the garlands."[32] The fiction was maintained that these businessmen were just plain private citizens.

This conference generated the Dawes Plan to settle Germany's problems. It was full of financial ingenuity and political hazard. It scaled back reparations and tied them to Germany's capacity to pay. It also stipulated that the Allies would select an agent general to preside over Germany's economy and reparations transfers. This effectively placed Germany in international receivership. (And many reparation payments were funneled through the Morgan bank.) Germany was mortgaged to the Allies, with its railways and central bank subjected to foreign control, a situation that would provide a propaganda bonanza for the Nazis.

Aside from a stipulation ensuring that it would get back the Ruhr, what reconciled Germany to the Dawes Plan was the prospect of a giant loan floated in New York and Europe. Reparations would largely be paid with borrowed money. With Germany now a financial outcast, bankers everywhere were dubious about the loan's chances. Montagu Norman mused, "It can only be accomplished, if at all, through the Bank of England and in New York through J.P.M. & Co."[33] Once again, the State Department was a guiding, if unseen, presence. Hughes told the House of Morgan that it would be a "disaster" and "most unfortunate" if the Dawes Plan miscarried for lack of American participation. Such official wishes were never lightly ignored.

To help along the prospective German loan, Monty Norman arranged a mid-1924 meeting at the Bank of England between Jack Morgan, Tom Lamont, and the new Reichsbank president, Dr. Hjalmar Horace Greeley Schacht (whose father had once worked in a New York brewery and been an admirer of publisher Horace Greeley). To stop the ruinous inflation, Dr. Schacht abolished the old mark and issued a new renten-mark, making him an instant hero in the banking world and winning him the Reichsbank post. On New Year's Eve of 1924, he arrived in London for Bank of England talks. As he disembarked from the train at Liverpool Street Station, he later recalled, "I was not a little surprised to see . . . a tall man with a pointed grayish beard and shrewd, discerning eyes, who introduced himself as Montagu Norman, governor of the Bank of England."[34] This began another of Norman's close, mysterious friendships.

In our narrative, we shall see Schacht playing many different roles—evil genius of Nazi finance, daring plotter against Hitler, boisterously self-righteous defendant at Nuremberg—but we first encounter him at a moment of glory. Under Schacht, the Reichsbank was freed from government control, extending Norman's dream of banker autonomy in Europe. A brilliant, narcissistic windbag prone to extravagant metaphors and bombast, Schacht assured Morgan and Lamont that the Dawes loan would be repaid. He obsequiously remarked that the American offering "would fail completely if it lacked the prestige and moral endorsement of the Morgan bank."[35] For J. P. Morgan and Company, it was critical that the loan take priority over other claims on Germany. The bank had no outstanding German loans and was only being drawn in under politi-cal pressure by Britain and France—a fact that would be loudly repeated when the loan defaulted in the 1930s. Then, in a very different political environment, Lamont would bitterly remind Schacht of his unctuous pledges.

To give the loan international seasoning, half the issue appeared in New York and the other half in London and other European capitals. The $110-million New York portion was enthusiastically received and oversubscribed. By seeming to settle the German question, the loan lifted a weight from financial markets. It electrified Wall Street and spurred foreign lending to Latin America and elsewhere. For Weimar Germany, it was a turning point. It became the decade's largest sover-eign borrower. American capital and companies poured in: Ford, Gen-eral Motors, E. I. Du Pont, General Electric, Standard Oil of New Jersey, and Dow Chemical. Unemployment plunged and Germany's economic slide was reversed into a five-year upturn. This revival would provide Adolf Hitler with a splendid industrial machine and the money to finance massive rearmament. In the meantime, the world was trapped in a circular charade in which American money paid to Germany was handed over as reparations payments to the Allies, who sent it back to the United States as war debt.

Most remarkable in Morgan archives is the partners' skepticism of the Dawes Plan. Russell Leffingwell, now the resident economist, saw the scheme as riddled with dangerous contradictions. Why would investors have faith in a politically neutered Germany? And why did the Allies wish to resurrect their former foe? Prescient, he feared a political backlash, a day of reckoning: "My political doubt about Germany is how long her people will consent to be sweated for the benefit of her former enemies."[36] Montagu Norman and Philip Snowden, chancellor of the Exchequer, also feared Germany had submitted under duress and would later resent its position.

In August 1923, President Warren G. Harding had died of an embolism. His successor, Calvin Coolidge, wasn't any more enlightened about the problem of world debt. He was adamant that the Allies should pay their war debts—"They hired the money, didn't they?" he asked—and kept up the fiction that those debts had nothing to do with reparations.[37] But so long as the United States demanded war-debt payments, the Allies couldn't be flexible on German reparations.

A final aspect of the reparations problem was Morgan involvement in the contest for Germany's new economic czar, the agent general. Amid much hoopla, the press labeled the job the world's most important, since the occupant would supervise the German economy. He would have to extract the last penny from Germany while staving off renewed inflation. Hoping the United States would exert a moderating influence, Germany wanted an American for the post. On Wall Street, a powerful consensus formed behind Morgan partner Dwight Morrow.

An old friend of President Coolidge, Morrow had already been widely touted for numerous government posts. Short, bespectacled, and bookish, he was Morgan's philosopher-king, a man marked for an elusive greatness. Now his moment arrived. He had formidable supporters— Jack Morgan, Charles Dawes, and Owen Young in the private sector; Hughes and Hoover in the cabinet. After a long White House meeting in July 1924, he seemed like a shoo-in. Among other things, the White House thought Morrow's appointment would guarantee the success of the Dawes loan.

The next evening, however, at another White House meeting, the U.S. ambassador to Germany, Alanson Houghton, argued against Morrow's appointment. He said the choice of a Morgan partner would be incendiary in German politics, even fatal to the Dawes Plan. The long, heated meeting ran till midnight. It was difficult for Coolidge to reverse the appointment of a close friend, but the Morrow nomination was nonetheless spiked. As Dawes afterward explained, "Houghton, with great earnestness, pointed out that the appointment of a member of the firm of Morgan & Co. would probably enable the Nationalists in Germany to defeat the Republican Government there by raising the demagogic cry that it was a scheme of the international bankers to crush the life out of Germany instead of helping her. He gave this as the private opinion of the German Government itself."[38]

Other analysts saw less strategic cunning than cowardice behind Coolidge's desertion of his old friend. Because of its wartime role, the House of Morgan was still anathema in German-American communities of the Midwest. Coolidge's aides apparently warned him to avoid any Morrow link. This episode shows that the Morgan bank carried serious political liabilities even in a decade dominated by conservative Republican administrations.

Bitterly disappointed, Lamont and Norman demanded a Morrow clone. The dark horse who emerged victorious was a future Morgan partner, thirty-two-year-old S. Parker Gilbert. Tall and boyish, dubbed the Thinking Machine, he was a protégé of Russell Leffingwell, whom he had replaced as assistant secretary of the Treasury in 1920, becoming the *wunderkind* of the department. At twenty-eight, he was elevated to under secretary, and in the absence of Treasury Secretary Andrew Mellon, he ran the department—the youngest person ever to do so. Paul Warburg described him as a "practical young man with the eyes of a dreamer and the sensitive mouth of a scholar."[39] The Germans would see him far less poetically. Heinrich Köhler, the finance minister, described him thus: "Reserved and taciturn, the tall lanky man with the impenetrable features appeared considerably older than he really was and . . . made an eerie impression."[40]

During his five years in Berlin, Gilbert oversaw the transfer of $2 billion in German reparations. As Germany's economic czar, he was burned in effigy at mock coronations and vilified as a new kaiser. He apparently never learned to speak German and worked compulsively, never attending cultural events or entering into German society. Despite his youth, he was a stern taskmaster, constantly accusing the Germans of fiscal extravagance. He thought they could pay reparations by following sound fiscal policy. Another finance minister, Paul Moldenhauer, noted, "He spoke with a mixture of awkwardness and arrogance, mumbling the words so that one could hardly understand his

English."[41] But Gilbert's reports on Germany's financial conditions would be models of lucidity and precision, winning him a tremendous reputation in Anglo-American financial circles; he would be a figure of worldwide influence in the twenties.

Dwight Morrow didn't long regret his loss and felt that he had been spared a burden. He was soon writing to Hughes and confessing to doubts about the Dawes Plan. Even as the world celebrated the great triumph, there was an undercurrent of deep unease at the House of Morgan. Morrow declared: "It is the foreign control to which Germany is to be subjected that has made us somewhat fearful about the permanent success of the Dawes Plan. . . . It is almost inevitable that this loan will be unpopular in Germany after a few years. The people of Germany, in our opinion, are almost certain, after sufficient time has elapsed, to think not of the release of the Ruhr but of the extent to which what was once a first-class Power has been subjected to foreign control."[42] The fear was prophetic, for it became a cardinal tenet of Nazi propaganda that Germany had been stampeded into the Dawes plan by international bankers. And the House of Morgan would reap the fruits of these mistaken policies of the twenties.

CHAPTER THIRTEEN

JAZZ

• •

•

B Y 1924, the House of Morgan was so influential in American politics that conspiracy buffs couldn't tell which presidential candidate was more beholden to the bank. As far as the partners' support of a candidate was concerned, most backed Calvin Coolidge—out of ideological comfort and respect for his friendship with Dwight Morrow. Coolidge's running mate was Charles Dawes, who had profited from the sudden renown of his plan for Germany's reparations payments. Others might dismiss Coolidge as dour and complacent, but Jack Morgan perceived in him an extraordinary blend of deep thinker and moralist: "In a somewhat long life, I have never seen any President who gives me just the feeling of confidence in the Country and its institutions, and the working out of its problems, that Mr. Coolidge does."[1] He disagreed that Coolidge was a tool of business—sure proof to some that he was. Between the White House and the House of Morgan there existed clear amity, moving *The New Republic*'s TRB to say, "I would rather not have these Morgans boys quite so much at home around the White House."[2]

The bank's peerless renown in the Roaring Twenties was such that the Democratic candidate was the chief Morgan lawyer, John W. Davis. Davis was a backgammon and cribbage partner of Jack Morgan's—they played for a nickel a game—and they both belonged to the Zodiac Club, a secret society in which each member took a different astrological sign. A former solicitor general and ambassador to the Court of Saint James's, Davis was recruited by Allan Wardwell in 1920 to join the law firm that would become Davis, Polk, and Wardwell. They were counsel to both J. P. Morgan and Company and Guaranty Trust. Taking charge of Davis's life in his vigorous style, Harry Davison had whisked him through a weekend of golf at the Piping Rock Country Club on Long Island and convinced him to join Wardwell's firm. In his familiar role as Henry Higgins, Davison even influenced Davis's choice of a home: "We must find the right place in our own island neighborhood."[3] Davis bought a Locust Valley estate right near Jack's and Harry's. He had exactly the right credentials for a Morgan man: debonair and dignified, he favored a larger U.S. role in Europe, supported the League of Nations, and opposed the welfare state and a progressive income tax. He was also a devout Anglophile and one of the duke of Windsor's lawyers. Another friend, King George V, termed him "the most perfect gentleman" he had ever known.[4]

At first, Davis was deterred from seeking the Democratic nomination because of the Morgan handicap. Then he published a cogent letter stating that a lawyer could have rich clients *and* maintain the public trust. His cause was taken up by Walter Lippmann of the *New York World,* who praised his talent and integrity. Davis's Democratic opponent, William McAdoo, drew support from the South and West, always aflame with anti-Morgan sentiment. At the June 1924 national convention, William Jennings Bryan, mustering the strength for one last vendetta against the bank, said, "This convention must not nominate a Wall Street man. Mr. Davis is the lawyer of J.P. Morgan."[5] In fact, the convention was so bitterly and hopelessly divided that Davis received the nomination after a record 103 ballots—by which point the prize was worthless. The Republicans retained power.

One industrialist called Coolidge's 1924 victory a cocktail for financial markets, and the decade now began to bubble and fizz. It was the Gatsby era on Wall Street, with money-making newly glorified. Young Ivy Leaguers turned away from the social protest of the late teens and flocked to Wall Street. In Pierpont's day, the Street had been raw and brawling, no place for the squeamish. Now it became smart and tony, and "many of the old-line brokerage firms were staffed by the sons of the rich—to give them something to do during the mornings."[6] Stockbrokers fancied themselves squires, bred polo ponies, and hunted foxes. Charles E. Mitchell, chairman of National City Bank, traveled about in a special railroad car, complete with kitchen and chef, making business tours as if he were a whistle-stopping president. Corporate directors went to board meetings by private railroad car, the status symbol of the day.

For the House of Morgan, it was a time of unmatched supremacy. The firm attained a pinnacle of success no other American bank would ever match. It stood at the gateway to American capital markets just as the whole world clamored to gain entry. To those who penetrated its tall glass doors, it offered a world of fireplaces and leather armchairs, as sedate and intimate as a British gentleman's club. All the secretaries were male, although their assistants might be female. As one reporter said, "Entering there was like stepping into a page of Dickens."[7] The partners' rolltop desks were apt symbols for the bank. They were made of mahogany or walnut, honeycombed with compartments and closed by sliding down the tambour top; they expressed the private, discreet Morgan style. The employees were as seduced by this atmosphere as the clients. As publicity man Martin Egan once said, "If the firm ever fired me I was lost, having been spoiled for service with any other outfit in the world."[8]

The vast majority of people walking by 23 Wall couldn't bank there. As a wholesale bank, J. P. Morgan and Company would take deposits only from important clients—large corporations, other banks, foreign governments. Like other private New York banks, it rejected deposits from the general public and accepted money only from wealthy people with proper introductions. It paid no interest on deposits of less than $7,500 and held no deposit of less than $1,000.

The bank's power was more than monetary. No other firm had its political links or spoke with its authority. At a time when the Anglo-American axis reigned supreme, it was embedded in the power structure of both Washington and Whitehall. Reporters tried to isolate its essence. "It is not a large bank, as Wall Street banks go," said the *New York Times*. "A dozen other institutions have much larger resources. . . . What really counts is not so much its money as its reputation and brains. . . . It is not a mere bank; it is an institution."[9] Trust, goodwill, integrity—these were the strengths always cited by business clients. This was only part of the story, but it mattered a great deal that the bank always paid its bills promptly, honored its commitments, and stood by its clients during emergencies.

As in Pierpont's day, the bank seemed remarkably small beside the scope of its work. The Morgan houses preferred smallness, which ensured intimate contact among the partners. Harry Davison used to say $400 million was all they could handle without diluting Morgan style. By the end of the 1920s, there would be fourteen partners at 23 Wall, eight at Drexel in Philadelphia, and seven each at the Morgan houses in London and Paris. At these firms, the partners all sat in one big room in the venerable City tradition. Each offered a different secret for the firm's success. George Whitney saw conservative financial management as the critical factor: partners never fooled themselves about the quality of their loans and stayed 80 percent liquid at all times. Lamont had a flywheel theory—the bank thrived because it was cautious in boom times and aggressive in bad times. Jack would later state memorably that the bank did "first-class business in a first-class way."

Wall Street legend accurately claimed that Morgan partners made $1 million a year; with Jack Morgan and Tom Lamont, this figure rose to as much as $5 million by decade's end. A Morgan partnership was the plum of American banking. Many firms chose partners who brought in new capital or new clients, but J. P. Morgan stuck to Pierpont's merito-cratic approach; any white, Christian male might qualify. Many partners had family ties, and new Morgans, Lamonts, and Davisons would join the bank in the 1920s; 23 Wall never had rules against nepotism. But the outstanding partners, those who created the Morgan mystique—Harry Davison, Tom Lamont, Dwight Morrow, and Russell Leffing-well—were chosen strictly on their merits. As much as any other factor, the caliber of the men recruited would explain the extraordinary staying power of the House of Morgan.

The activities of these Jazz Age celebrities were avidly followed in the press. Those partners involved in international finance and diplomacy traveled constantly and spent several months abroad each year. When transatlantic liners left New York, reporters would scan the passenger lists for Morgan partners, hoping to land a shipboard interview. Partners were so prominent that B. C. Forbes even reviewed their golf games, which he found disappointing, as if some chance for perfection had been missed.

From the marble Morgan halls emerged $6 billion in securities under-writings between 1919 and 1933—far more than from any other bank. A third were railroad bonds, another third foreign bonds, and the last third corporate bonds. Like the growing government accounts, the do-mestic roster was matchless—U.S. Steel, General Electric, General Mo-tors, Du Pont, AT&T, IT&T, Montgomery Ward, Kennecott Copper, American Can, Con Edison, and the New York Central. By managing securities issues for these companies and assigning syndicate places to other banks, the House of Morgan defined the pyramid of Wall Street power. It also performed humdrum services—foreign exchange, banker's acceptances, and commercial credits—that were the bread-and-butter of merchant banking. Not every partner enjoyed the fantasy life of a Tom Lamont or a Dwight Morrow.

The Gentleman Banker's Code was alive and well on Wall Street in the 1920s. The House of Morgan didn't advertise or post a nameplate. It didn't chase customers or open branches; clients still paid Morgan partners the ancient tribute of traveling to see them. Competition was elegant and masked behind elaborate courtesies. Clients were mortgaged to one bank and needed permission to switch to another. As Otto Kahn explained, "Kuhn, Loeb & Co. and firms of similar standing would not even touch any new business, on any terms, if the corporation concerned was already a regular client of another banker, and had not definitely broken off relations."[10] From the outside, it resembled polite collusion; underneath, it could be vicious. Far from objecting to exclusive relations, businessmen boasted about their bankers and considered a Morgan account a hallmark of success.

Morgan partners still sat on boards of favored companies but were more selective than in the days when Charles Coster kept abreast of fifty-nine companies. Partners didn't descend lightly from Olympus. Martin Egan remarked that "there is a constant plea to get Morgan partners on all manner of committees and into all sorts of organizations. The process is diffusive and cheapening."[11] Although the Morgan bank took stakes in its companies, partners agreed in the 1920s not to get involved in outside enterprises. Gradually, if imperceptibly, the banker was becoming less a corporate partner and more a professional, a disinterested intermediary. This was the transition favored by Louis Brandeis, and it would be markedly speeded up by New Deal reformers. In Pierpont's day, weak companies needed to lean on strong bankers. But by the 1920s, a Standard Oil of New Jersey or a U.S. Steel had a stability comparable to that of the House of Morgan itself.

Who were the other Morgan partners? They fit a rough profile— white, male, Republican, Episcopalian, and Anglophile, with an Ivy League education and eastern seaboard antecedents. Harvard was the alma mater of Jack Morgan and his sons and was clearly the preferred school. The bank was perhaps most selective about religion—race wasn't even an issue then, so remote were blacks from the world of banking. Jews were definitely forbidden but had opportunities elsewhere on Wall Street. Private Jewish banks continued to win business, such as retail underwriting, thought vulgar by the blue-blooded Yankee banks. Lehman Brothers had both R. H. Macy and Gimbel Brothers among its clients. Some Jewish bankers lived in an opulent style surpassed only by the Morgans. Otto Kahn of Kuhn, Loeb built a Norman castle on Long Island's North Shore that had 170 rooms, 11 reflecting pools, a zoo complete with lions, an 18-hole golf course with a resident pro, a Georgian dining room that seated 200, and a staff of 125 servants. It would later be the set for *Citizen Kane*. But until after the Second World War, no Jew would penetrate the House of Morgan.

On the Wall Street of the 1920s, Catholics were borderline cases and often found it harder than Jews to enter high finance. Snubbed by Protestants, they turned to stock market speculation by default, and Jazz Age plungers were disproportionately Irish. Armed with ticker tape and telephones at the Waldorf-Astoria Hotel, Joe Kennedy made a fortune in stock pools but still found Morgan acceptance elusive. One day, he decided to break the ice with the bank. He marched into 23 Wall and asked for Jack Morgan. He was curtly told Mr. Morgan was too busy to see him. Before the Morgan gates, he bore the double stigma of being a Catholic and a stock market operator.

The best-known Morgan Catholic was certainly Edward Stettinius, yet even he switched to his wife's more acceptable Episcopalianism and became a vestryman of Saint James Episcopal Church. Settling his spiritual accounts in 1921, Stettinius reverted to Catholicism and wrote Saint James a guilt-ridden letter of resignation: "I have come to feel strongly that a Vestryman should not only be a regular attendant at your services, but also a communicant and an ardent and consistent supporter of the Episcopal faith. Unfortunately, however, I find myself steadily drawing away from, rather than toward, the Episcopal Church."[12]

A compulsive record keeper, Stettinius has left us a detailed inventory of a partner's life in the twenties. He entertained magnificently at his Park Avenue mansion. For the debutante ball of their daughter Betty, the Stettiniuses invited three hundred guests, including dancers and musicians from Tokyo's Royal Theater. (Betty later married Juan Trippe, founder of Pan American Airways.) In the cellar of Stettinius's mansion was enough liquor to float a battleship: 336 bottles of gin, 196 of sauterne, 79 of sherry, 60 of champagne, 114 of vermouth, 40 of Haig and Haig Scotch, 88 of claret, 32 of port, 53 of amontillado, 26 of Park and Tilford Topaz—over a thousand bottles of fine liquor.[13] From a Broad Street tobacconist, he would order six thousand Havana cigars at a time and then draw down his "balance." With six cars and several houses to maintain, it cost Stettinius $250,000 a year just to cover basic living expenses—perhaps the reason why he approached his work with such famous thoroughness.

In 1922, he bought a thirty-four-acre estate overlooking Long Island Sound and was among those partners who lived close to Jack's Glen Cove mansion, like medieval vassals biding near their lord. A meticulous man who left nothing to chance, Stettinius decided to create a Morgan cemetery at Locust Valley. The local church, Saint John's of Lattingtown, provided spiritual solace to many tycoons and was called the millionaire's church. On Sunday mornings, the collection plate was passed around by Jack Morgan himself—surely a heavenly treat. Jack was so fond of the church that he redecorated its interior in carved oak brought over from a small Scottish church. Stettinius's plan was to buy up property beside the church burial ground on which to create a cemetery.

The one obstacle was a New York State law forbidding cemetery expansion. So in April 1923, Stettinius lobbied state lawmakers for special legislation. Then he plotted a takeover of the Locust Valley Cemetery. On June 1, 1925, the cemetery's annual board meeting was packed with Morgan luminaries, including Jack's son-in-law Paul G. Pennoyer, Harry Davison's son, Trubee, and Stettinius. It was perhaps the greatest show of financial strength in cemetery history. After winning control, they hired architects and landscape gardeners to spruce up the shrubbery and install fancy wrought-iron gates. What resulted was a double cemetery: "The older, open section of small plots continued very much as it had been, while the new sections of woods and spacious glades became a Valhalla for Morgan partners and their friends."[14] Having made these arrangements, Stettinius took a well-earned rest in plot number 7. Many blamed his wartime labors for his death. In any case, he perpetuated the Morgan tradition, started by Charles Coster, of heroic exertion and premature death.

The partner who most typified the Jazz Age was that small miracle of sophistication, Tom Lamont. Socialite and sportsman, he loved to camp in the High Sierras or fish for Canadian salmon. To the bank's image he added an urbane 1920s gloss, a shade literary. If a Morgan partner suggested a stylish, well-rounded Anglophile, a Republican who could travel in Democratic circles, a liberal internationalist orthodox in domestic affairs, then Lamont was surely his prototype. Yet this figure who symbolized the 1920s on Wall Street harbored a secret ambivalence toward it. "That decade, with its exotic exuberance of prosperity and its speculative excesses in almost every phase of economic life . . . was for America a decadent one," he later wrote.[15]

Lamont became the richest Morgan partner, his wealth matched by a progression of stately homes. First he and his wife, Florence, lived in Englewood, New Jersey—so thickly populated with Morgan partners it was called the bank's branch office. They joined the Dwight Morrows in the local Shakespeare club, where they all took parts and read plays aloud. From 1915 to 1921, the Lamonts rented Franklin Roosevelt's house on East Sixty-fifth Street while its owner served as assistant secretary of the navy. Then, in 1921, Lamont bought the townhouse at 107 East Seventieth Street that would become a stopping place for visiting politicians, writers, and socialites; it featured everything from a British butler to a solarium. The Lamonts were terribly ambitious, determined to know everybody of importance in New York and to snare every celebrity who passed through town. To a remarkable extent, they succeeded.

For recreation, they bought Sky Farm, an island retreat off the Maine coast with a panoramic view of Penobscot Bay. In 1928, they purchased Torrey Cliff, a hundred-acre estate on the Palisades that formerly was owned by a well-known botanist, John Torrey, and later would be donated to Columbia University for its geological observatory. The property encompassed cliffs and woodlands, brooks, flowers, and spectacular vistas of the Hudson River. Finally, Lamont and John Davis regularly stayed at Yeamans Hall in South Carolina, a millionaires' development with over a thousand acres of golf courses, forest paths, and giant moss-covered oaks.

Florence Lamont was a short, bright, pleasant-looking woman with a thoughtful stare. She took herself seriously, both as a hostess determined to snare celebrities and as an intellectual. A graduate of Smith with a master's degree in philosophy from Columbia, she supported numerous causes, including birth control and women's trade unions. Earnest, a trifle tedious, always craving intellectual companionship and stimulating company, she sometimes had a bluestocking intensity. Anne Morrow Lindbergh, after hearing Florence make grandiloquent speeches about pacifism at a social gathering, noted in her diary: "Mrs. Lamont distrusts all informal, feminine discussion, thinking it gossip. Is it because she can't do it very well?"[16]

High-spirited and sociable, the Lamonts were on everybody's party list in the Jazz Age, and they knew dozens of celebrities. When their son Corliss went to Oxford in 1924, he lived with the Julian Huxleys, lunched with Lord and Lady Astor at Cliveden, and took a weekend with H. G. Wells—such was the range of his parents' friends. The Lamonts' East Seventieth Street townhouse echoed with laughter and ideas, as their children Corliss, Tommy (later a Morgan partner), and Margaret turned it into an exuberant debating society. Again, Anne Morrow Lindbergh has left a vivid impression of this animated household: "To the Lamonts' for dinner. . . . We had decided before we got there that we would *not* argue. Instead we let the Lamonts argue among themselves. Tommy and Corliss, Mrs. Lamont and Mr. Lamont, Margaret and Tommy, Margaret and Mrs. Lamont, back and forth across the table. Tommy, loudly and platformly; Corliss, lightly, nervously, and humorously. Margaret, of course, dead serious. Mr. Lamont suavely and Mrs.

Lamont petulantly. We all sat back quite happily . . . and listened. It was great fun."[17]

If Florence sometimes took herself too seriously, Tom, with his genial energy, roused her from it. He could never have enough friends, enough dinners, or enough lively chatter. He had a marvelous sense of humor, which surprised many people who imagined that Morgan bankers must be dour and self-important. He once said of an enemy that if he had ordered a trainload of sons of bitches and received only that man, he would consider the order amply filled. Once, Tom Lamont and Betty Morrow wanted the two couples to throw a party together—they were the good dancers—but Florence and Dwight balked. So guests received the following invitation:

Mrs. Dwight Morrow and
Mr. Thomas Lamont
Request the honor of your company
at a dance given in honor of
Mrs. Thomas Lamont and Mr. Dwight Morrow.[18]

JACK Morgan moved through the twenties like a monarch. One journalist described him embarking from his limousine at 23 Wall: "I saw two other men inconspicuously draw themselves up in an attitude of attention, like soldiers in mufti, acting on their instincts or through force of habit. . . . The great doors with their huge panes of spotless glass and their polished brass swung open and shut."[19] He enjoyed his spot at the top of the Morgan empire. About to present Pope Pius XI with restored Coptic texts in 1922, he made this observation: "My special job is the most interesting I know of anywhere. More fun than being King, Pope, or Prime Minister anywhere—for no one can turn me out of it and I don't have to make any compromises with principles."[20]

Jack lived regally at his 250-acre island estate, Matinicock Point, off the North Shore. Visitors passed through enormous wrought-iron gates and down an endless drive shaded by linden trees; in season bloomed several thousand tulips and daffodils under the direction of Jessie Morgan. The estate required several dozen full-time gardeners. There were also cows, horses, greenhouses, boxwood and rose gardens, cottages for the staff, and a dock down at the Sound.

Amid open lawns and high trees, the red-brick mansion was grander than any of Pierpont's residences. It was designed by Grant La Farge with an imposing columned entrance. Inside, three famous ladies—Rubens's Anne of Austria, Gainsborough's Lady Gideon, and Sir Thomas Lawrence's countess of Derby—stared down from the walls of a house specially fireproofed for them. The majestic stairway of the forty-five-room house was lined with beautiful floral arrangements.

Jack liked quiet, domestic pleasures. Delicate and sedentary, a born dabbler, he enjoyed detective novels and crossword puzzles. His literary hero was Rudyard Kipling. He disapproved of contact sports, and when his two sons, Junius and Harry, went to Groton, he protested the introduction of football, calling it immoral, dangerous, and brutal.[21] He loved taking drives in his chauffeured cars and had four of them—two Rolls-Royces, a Lincoln, and a Buick roadster.

He was fanatical about his privacy and hostile to the press. The Morgans always kept their daughters and granddaughters off the society pages. Like his father, Jack often threatened intrusive photographers and would screen his face with his Panama hat as he left church on Sunday mornings. Because he commuted to Wall Street by water, photographers awaited him on boats in the Sound. To foil them, he constructed a flowery archway that curved down to the dock and obscured his movements. The only problem was the gangplank. For the final seconds it took to board the boat, his butler, Henry Physick, would remove his coat and hold it up to shield his master from the press. Sailing home from work, Jack would take afternoon tea on board.

Only once did Jack submit willingly to press photographs. One day, as a motorboat was taking him out to the *Corsair* the photographers were in their usual hot pursuit, when Jack's Panama hat blew into the Sound. A photographer fished it from the water and gave it to Jack's boatswain, saying, "Your boss hasn't treated me with much courtesy, but I am glad to do him a favor."[22] Like Pierpont, Jack was sentimental and could be disarmed by a gallant gesture. When he heard the story, he ordered the photographer up on deck and posed for twenty minutes of pictures.

Both Jack and Jessie loved England, which they visited each spring and summer. When the London *Times* tagged him an English squire, Jack was thrilled.[23] He had a London townhouse at 12 Grosvenor Square and bequeathed Princes Gate, the old family townhouse, to the U.S. government as a residence for the American ambassador. Just as George Peabody had hosted annual Fourth of July dinners, Jack hoped future ambassadors would "live like gentlemen and have their Fourth of July receptions in adequate surroundings."[24] Later on, Princes Gate would be the wartime residence of Ambassador Joe Kennedy, who finally slipped into the House of Morgan through a back door. It was the house opposite Hyde Park fondly remembered by the Kennedy sons.

Jack's major British residence was Wall Hall, his three-hundred-acre estate north of London with artificial lakes and gardens. He ruled the village like a whimsical Prospero. He didn't simply live in the village; he owned it. As *Fortune* magazine explained, "At Wall Hall he is a Tory squire with the whole of Aldenham Village as his property except the ancient church, and with all the villagers in his employ, each supplied with a rent-free house and registered milk and free medical treatment and an old-age pension and membership in the Aldenham Parish Social Club."[25]

A paternalistic landlord, he fretted about his villagers. So that they wouldn't loaf, he provided them with cricket grounds, tennis courts, and bowling greens. He was afraid that the village tavern, the Chequers, might be bought by a brewer. So he dispatched Teddy Grenfell on a secret mission to buy it at any price. This high-level corporate raid occasioned some drollery between them. "It is a new kind of business for me altogether," Jack said, "as I have owned many kinds of property, but never a public house before, and I am quite excited at the investment."[26] Rather old-maidish, Jack considered taking away the tavern's liquor license. But the problems that accompanied Prohibition in America persuaded him to retain the pub license. He even added a hall for movies and dancing, saying, "It's really going to make a difference to a good number of honest, hard working and powerfully dull men and women."[27]

To an extraordinary degree, he was a creature of custom and comfort. So that he could drive without removing his plug hat, he had an English firm design a car with a special high top. He corresponded with a haberdasher about socks that didn't slide smoothly enough over his heel. Perhaps fearing his own emotions—or else in homage to his Yankee-trading ancestors—he always wanted things around him to proceed tidily. He was obsessed with punctuality. At Wall Hall, he had so many clocks that someone came in weekly just to rewind them. For gifts, he often gave his partners rare gold watches.

The year had its unchanging rhythms for Jack. The high spot was August 12—the Glorious Twelfth that launched the Scottish grouse-hunting season. "Nearly everybody I know has started for shooting in Scotland," he once wrote a partner in early August.[28] Who else in America could make such a statement? After 1913, Eric Hambro and Jack jointly owned Gannochy Lodge near Edzell, in Scotland. They and their eminent guests bagged up to ten thousand birds a year, and each hunter was attended by a butler. In honor of Jack, the Scottish retainers even put together a "Morgan tartan."

For his Manhattan residence, Jack retained the townhouse at Madison Avenue and Thirty-seventh Street that his father had bought for him. Somber and brooding outside, it was light and airy within. It had white marble fireplaces, French revival furniture, and crystal chandeliers. When staying there, Jack would visit the library next door each day. He added four thousand books and manuscripts to his father's nineteen thousand and continued his raid on illuminated books and British literature. A tip from Tory leader Stanley Baldwin brought him the manuscript of Sir James Barrie's *Shall We Join the Ladies?* "I hate manuscripts leaving the country," Baldwin confessed to Jack. "But if they have to go, I would far rather they found a home with you than anybody else!"[29]

After his father's death, Jack hadn't been able to pursue collecting and was preoccupied with settling the estate. Now, in another parallel to Pierpont's life, Jack widened his collecting as he moved into his midfifties. Once again, Belle Greene went on buying trips to Europe, and Jack regarded her with affection and slightly fearful awe. When four rare manuscripts owned by the earl of Leicester came on the market, Greene was afraid to commit so much money on her own. She asked Jack to negotiate. He went to Europe and after a sleepless night bought them for an estimated $500,000. Jack told the seller: "My librarian told me she wouldn't dare spend so much of my money. But just the same, I wouldn't dare face her if I went home without the manuscripts."[30]

Jack hadn't yet erected the sort of monument to Pierpont that Pierpont had to Junius. In 1924, he incorporated the Pierpont Morgan Library in his father's memory, with Belle Greene as the first director; he provided a $1.5-million endowment. Perhaps recalling the brouhaha over the art collection's breakup, he summoned reporters for a wistful interview. Seated in the West Room, where Pierpont had worked and Junius stared down from above the mantel, Jack said, "This is the room where my father literally lived. I think it is probably the most peaceful room in New York. You never hear a thing here except occasionally a bad automobile horn."[31]

As he took reporters around the library, he snatched up interesting items and talked about them. Taking up a Dickens manuscript, he said, "Scrooge and all the rest of them are there. Isn't that nice?" In his remarks may be heard the plaintive note of a man seeking public love—love that he felt he deserved but was always denied. At the end of his tour, he asked, "Now what do you think of it? Have I done a good thing in making this gift?"[32]

In 1928, Pierpont's brownstone mansion next to the library was torn down and replaced by an annex, designed by Benjamin Wistar Morris, to provide exhibition facilities and more space for scholars. (One now enters the library through the annex.) Under the imperious sway of Belle Greene, the library remained a jewel-box institution with a tiny staff. Belle could be curt with dilettantes, voyeurs, and just plain fools, but her stature in the museum world was mythical on account of her devotion to genuine scholars.

While Jack was paying tribute to his father, he tried to groom his two sons to take over the bank. His eldest, Junius Spencer, Jr., graduated from Harvard in 1914. He served as a junior officer on a destroyer off the English coast in the war, an experience that left him with shattered nerves. Tall and extraordinarily handsome, with the face of a sensitive actor, he became a Morgan partner in 1919. Warmly approachable and possessed of a dry sense of humor, Junius was probably the nicest Morgan—but the most dismal businessman. Jack tried to fool himself that Junius was cut out for banking and sent him to Morgan Grenfell for a two-year apprenticeship in 1922. Jack wrote to Grenfell, "I cannot tell you how glad I am to have him go over and learn London methods, and the London outlook of business, under your careful eye."[33] Junius went through the motions of being a banker and served as a director of U.S. Steel and General Motors. But his real dream was to be a marine architect. His would be a sad, wasted business life, showing the limited options open to sons in a banking dynasty. Like his father and grandfather and brother, Junius became a commodore of the New York Yacht Club—the only certifiable Morgan activity that really fit him.

Jack's younger son, Harry Sturgis, looked more promising as a businessman. Born in London in 1900, he was short and stocky, with a more aggressive and temperamental air than Junius. If Junius looked friendly and rather languid, Harry was all thrusting energy, his chin assertive, his lips tightly compressed, his gaze fiery. In 1923, one week after graduating from Harvard, he married Catherine Francis Adams, daughter of Charles Francis Adams, secretary of the navy under Herbert Hoover. That year, Harry started as a $15-a-week Morgan messenger and ran securities around Wall Street. As a Christmas present in December 1928, Harry received his $1-million-a-year Morgan partnership.

During this period, Jack suffered two emotional blows from which he never recovered. In 1924, he lost his mother, who was still living in the original Madison Avenue mansion; it was torn down only after her death. She had survived into her eighties, by then a stone-deaf old woman. Jack, as a boy, had gravitated toward his mother's warmth and gentleness. His own close marriage to Jessie probably recapitulated the earlier relationship.

Like Fanny, Jessie Morgan became somewhat weak and sickly, but there were major differences. Jessie was a natural executive and extremely efficient in running four giant households, supervising butlers, footmen, and housekeepers. She had a shy, matronly look that hid steely discipline. Feminine on the outside, she was tough at the core—as when she lashed out at the would-be assassin in 1915. Neither she nor Jack believed that women should be emancipated, and she tended her gardens, collected lace, and gathered drawings of flowers. She had no interest in politics or lunching with other women. Beneath the frills, she was determined and even slightly fearsome.

Jack Morgan's happiness revolved around her and his children. In April 1925, he told Grenfell, "The only excitement in the family—and it is real excitement—has been the arrival in this woeful world of Frances' twins, running the number of my grandchildren up from nine to eleven in twenty minutes. This satisfies even my most ambitious aspirations."[34] What didn't jibe with this picture of family harmony was that Jack and Jessie were so engrossed with one another that their children felt excluded. Jessie served Jack, adored him, and advised him in every aspect of his life. She was the invisible safety net that stopped him from falling, and he relied on her judgment implicitly.

Then, in the summer of 1925, Jessie contracted a sleeping sickness— an inflammation of the brain—then prevalent in the United States. It was thought to derive from the influenza pandemic of 1917–18. Jessie fell into a coma and had to be fed through a tube. Antibiotics weren't yet available, and eminent physicians could only counsel patience. They told Jack the disease was running its course and that Jessie would eventually wake up. A trusting person, Jack waited and prayed. Afraid of submitting to melancholy, he put on a brave front and reported to 23 Wall every day, taking comfort from Jessie's smallest stirrings and from the fact that, as she slept, she was well nourished and gaining weight. He wrote: "Jessie is getting on well, the doctors assure me, and they all assure me that the recovery, though very slow, will ultimately be complete. Though she is still wholly unconscious, there are little almost imperceptible signs that she will eventually emerge from that state."[35] And: "Of course no one can tell how long she must sleep, but while she sleeps she is not conscious of any pain or discomfort, and the cure is proceeding all the time."[36]

How to reconcile this tender Jack Morgan with the stern anti-Semite of earlier pages? He was a true Morgan. His humanity was deep but narrow, his world divided between those who counted and those who did not. With his family, he was capable of total love. By mid-summer, Jessie had slowly improved, and Jack was buoyed by reports that her condition was better than at any time since the onset of the illness. Doctors assured Jack he could go to work without fear. On August 14, 1925, he went to the office only to receive a late-morning call to return home at once. By the time he arrived, Jessie was dead. Her heart had stopped from what doctors thought was an embolism. They were stunned by the sudden reversal.

Still recovering from his mother's death, Jack was distraught, inconsolable. He mourned deeply and reverently, much as Pierpont had mourned the sainted Mimi. In a moving outburst of grief and affection, he told Lamont, "Well, I have all these years to look back upon, everything to remember and nothing to forget."[37] In a letter to a partner, Lamont described Jack during Jessie's illness: "[He] had felt perfectly confident the last few weeks that his wife was going to come out all right. He was determined that she should. He thought of nothing else day and night. He was looking forward to the time when she would emerge from her sleep. He was most anxious to be with her at that time, thinking that his presence might be an aid to her in regaining her normality . . . he had been wonderful, courageous, and perfect throughout it all."[38]

In her will, Jessie left the bulk of her property to her two sons and two daughters. She included an oddly touching tribute to her husband—one can almost see the ironic twinkle in her eye as she wrote, "I feel sure that if, through any unforeseen circumstances, my dear husband should ever be in need, my children will share with him the property derived from me."[39]

After his wife's death, Jack became more withdrawn. At Matinicock Point, he left her bedroom as she had left it and tended her tulips and English rose garden. (Becoming a dedicated gardener, he entered dahlias in a Nassau County show and won the J. P. Morgan Prize!) Well drilled by Jessie, the servants ran the estates without her. Although now alone, Jack closed no houses and sold no boats or cars. In some ways, he refused to acknowledge the change in his life. Many of his friends testified to the eerie sense that Jessie still was present—not a superstitious feeling so much as one of Jack refusing to let her rituals die. In 1927, Jack bought up waterfront property in Glen Cove to dedicate a $3-million Morgan Memorial Park to his wife. From its quaint clubhouse with its fluted eaves, Jack embarked on his Mediterranean cruises each year.

Solitary, clad in tweeds, and smoking his meerschaum pipe, Jack wandered about his formal gardens, a melancholy widower. His partners noticed his loneliness. Easily wounded, he had had a tendency toward melodrama and self-pity, both of which now became pronounced. Writing of his fourteen grandchildren in 1928, he told a friend, "It makes a great difference to me in my life, which is necessarily very lonely."[40] Sometimes he asked his chauffeur of twenty-five years, Charles Robertson, to drive him down to the Morgan Memorial Park. He would sit beside the chauffeur and stare silently at the water. For all his money, he now thought himself the loneliest of men.

CHAPTER FOURTEEN

GOLDEN

. .
.

B Y the mid-1920s, the Morgan story had come full circle. Where
George Peabody and Pierpont and Junius Morgan had attained
power by tapping the flow of British capital to America, the relationship
was now fully reversed. London's merchant banks, hobbled by the postwar embargo on foreign loans, had to act on a smaller stage, their overseas lending largely limited to British dominions or colonies and
reconstruction loans. Meanwhile, Wall Street thrived, and J. P. Morgan
and Company far surpassed Morgan Grenfell in power. Managing the
British portion of the international loans sponsored by 23 Wall, Morgan
Grenfell was somewhat buffered from the general London decline.

In early 1927, Morgan Grenfell left 22 Old Broad Street and took up
residence at 23 Great Winchester Street. The new headquarters stood
at the angle of a small, L-shaped street around the corner from Liverpool
Street Station. As former home to the British India Steam Navigation
Company, its exterior was adorned with exotic tropical motifs—cor-
nucopias and vines. The firm had these stripped away, to create an
unmarked townhouse with a tall City doorway that dwarfed visitors. It
was a posh, leisurely place with butlers. A 1926 photograph of Morgan
Grenfell's cricket team shows what looks like a set of pipe-smoking
aristocrats—yet some of these young men were clerks or messengers.

The resident partners at Morgan Grenfell were handpicked power
brokers. Though their names aren't conspicuous in history books, they
mediated dealings between the British and American financial establish-
ments. J. P. Morgan and Company and Morgan Grenfell always enjoyed
intimate relations. They swapped young apprentices, visited regularly,
and kept up a vast correspondence that provides a comprehensive portrait of Anglo-American finance between the wars. Within the Morgan

empire, however, the British house was subservient. And though the two houses collaborated on many deals, they also did much separate business.

If Lamont set the tone in New York, the London grandee was Teddy Grenfell, later Lord Saint Just. Fastidious and dashing, with pocket handkerchief, trim mustache, and smooth, glossy hair, he had a smart air and a brittle wit. His keen eyes sloped down in a penetrating stare that spied out people's thoughts; Grenfell had the clear vision of the coldly unsentimental. Outwardly, he was neat and formal and correct in his behavior. But his judgments, expressed in a torrent of letters to 23 Wall and to his close friend, Jack Morgan, were funny, unsparing, and fiercely opinionated. Nobody in the House of Morgan was more prescient about people and affairs than Teddy Grenfell. He especially delighted in exposing the folly of social reformers. In his sneering but incisive way, he exhibited much racial and religious bigotry and poured buckets of scorn on his targets. This probably appealed to Jack, who shared Grenfell's prejudices but was more reticent about expressing them. By 1922, Grenfell was not only a Bank of England director, but a conservative member of Parliament for the City.

The slim, handsome Grenfell remained an eligible bachelor until the age of forty-three, when he married twenty-three-year-old Florence Henderson. Florence's father was a director of the Bank of England and chairman of the Borneo Company, a Far East trading concern. At the wedding, legend has it, the church was crammed with women weeping at their loss. With the exception of Virginia Woolf, who found Florrie "dulled" and "coarsened" by wealth, everybody seemed enchanted by Grenfell's bride.[1] She was tall, beautiful, and distinguished-looking, with a deep, fascinating voice. Anne Morrow Lindbergh found her "fawnlike and fragile" and picked up a certain gamine quality about her, a feeling she was "incorrigibly young . . . and likes to be teased."[2] She likened Florrie to Virginia Woolf's Mrs. Dalloway—a sociable woman who knew everybody and loved to organize events.

It proved a difficult marriage. Florrie had an unconventional streak. She danced, took voice lessons, and became an early patron of Diaghilev's Ballets Russes. The impresario referred to her as his *fidèle amie* and invited her to rehearsals. But she was more than just a society patroness plowing Morgan Grenfell money into dance. She was a woman of sophistication and flair who went to the theater every night and wrote penetrating blurbs on what she saw. All this was lost on the brilliant but limited Grenfell, who golfed and sailed and had no time for the artistic modernism that entranced his young wife. He would come home to their townhouse at 4 Cavendish Square and find partly clad Russian dancers and musicians strewn about the place. The famous ballerina Markova attended parties there, and Florrie also befriended Lydia Lopokova, later the wife of John Maynard Keynes. Snobbish and aloof, settled in his ways, Grenfell was jarred by the bohemian activity, despite his affection for Florrie. His wife, in turn, wasn't ready to submit to the stuffy pleasures of the countinghouse crowd. The marriage lasted, but more through friendship than love.

The other reigning partner at Morgan Grenfell was the tall, redheaded Vivian Hugh Smith, later the first Lord Bicester. He had a broad, open face and handlebar mustache and a nature more equable than Grenfell's. In early pictures, he sucks on a pipe and smiles like the cat who swallowed the canary, as if he knew many City secrets but wouldn't tell. He seldom got depressed, loved to tell shocking stories in deadpan style, and had unshakable composure. He was a country squire, with a mad passion for horses and steeplechase contests—while still at Eton, he was disciplined for sneaking off to Ascot. He occupied strategic posts—governor of the Royal Exchange Assurance Company, chairman of the City's Conservative party, and a director of Associated Electrical Industries. His family connections ramified everywhere, and among his five brothers were bankers, admirals, and businessmen. (His brother Lancelot, senior partner with stock brokers Rowe and Pitman, executed many Morgan Grenfell deals.) Family scuttlebutt claimed Smith was envious of his cousin Ted Grenfell, whom, he felt, stole too much of the glory.

In aristocratic circles, Smith was known as the establishmentarian with the outrageous wife. Slim and very Irish, with pale gold hair, Lady Sybil Smith brought seven more City Smiths into the world. She combined great charm and conviviality with deep political commitment. Beyond her interest in theosophy, which she shared with Monty Norman, she was a dedicated suffragette. As treasurer of the Women's Social and Political Union in 1913, she was its chief fund-raiser in Mayfair drawing rooms; with her delightful voice, she interspersed her pitch with musical interludes. The daughter of her great friend, Emmeline Pankhurst, remembered Lady Sybil singing "in her long straight gown, like a nymph from a Greek vase."[3]

Vivian Smith was very amused by Lady Sybil, and they teased each other mercilessly. Yet tolerance had its limits. One day, Vivian picked up the newspaper and read the headline "LADY SYBIL SMITH ADOPTS CHILD." Vivian quickly unadopted the child, a waif Sybil had picked up. In July 1913, came the great test of his composure. Sybil joined a delegation of militant suffragettes who invaded the House of Commons to oppose the Male Suffrage Bill. After an unsatisfactory interview with Reginald McKenna, then the home secretary, some of the women began making speeches; scuffles and arrests ensued. Lady Sybil pushed a constable who had taken a suffragette into custody and was sentenced to fourteen days. She insisted upon going to prison in solidarity with her sisters. Once in prison she gaily launched a hunger strike, as if it were a lark. Cool as a cocktail-party hostess, she wore a "tea-gown and golden slippers," as another suffragette recalled.[4] But the government didn't like having an earl's daughter in prison, and Lady Sybil's sentence was commuted to only four days. Still, McKenna swore no favoritism was shown. During her prison stint, Grenfell cabled Jack that Vivian was trying to be a good sport, apparently with difficulty: "V.H.S. distressed, but as usual considerate and dignified."[5]

The Smiths were as odd a couple as the Grenfells. Sylvia Pankhurst, Emmeline's daughter, saw Vivian as a "very dull foil" to Sybil, who managed a day nursery for destitute mothers and their babies in London's East End. Sybil exhibited an idealism never apparent in her husband. As Pankhurst wrote of her, "She possessed a rare absence of class consciousness, a sensitive perception of the good qualities in other people and the precious ability to perceive that, at bottom, we most of us have the same needs."[6] Lady Sybil naturally became friends with her New York counterpart in the Morgan universe, the activist Dorothy Whitney Straight.

MORGAN Grenfell emerged as an important conduit between the City and Wall Street at a time when U.S.-British rivalry threatened to overwhelm friendship. As American exports boomed under the tutelage of Herbert Hoover's aggressive Commerce Department, British heavy industry languished. Britain felt threatened by America's new industrial strength and marketing talent. There was a fad for American movies and cosmetics in Britain, an Anglo-American battle for raw materials, and a first wave of investment in Britain by American industry, symbolized by Ford's new factory at Dagenham on the Thames and General Electric's assault on the British electric industry.

Montagu Norman, who would enjoy an extraordinary reign as governor of the Bank of England from 1920 to 1944, wished to reestablish London financial preeminence in the 1920s and reverse the decline in British industry. To do this, he needed Wall Street money and connections. He found both in the House of Morgan, giving him power fantastically disproportionate to Britain's postwar wealth. The Morgan partners in New York shared his vision of transatlantic cooperation and Anglo-

American partnership, resisting the insular American mood of the 1920s.

In 1919, Britain was forced off the gold standard. Restoring the link between sterling and gold became an indispensable first step in restoring the City's status as a world financial center. London's strength in foreign lending had always been premised on a stable pound. Like king and country, the gold standard was an abstraction that made British bankers feel snug and cosy. Norman thought it the best means by which to stop fluctuating exchange rates, and he wanted England to lead in restoring this monetary discipline.

The American Morgan partners were instrumental in putting England back on gold. It was their holy cause. As early as September 1923, Russell Leffingwell told Jack in Scotland that after the grouse season he wanted to speak to him about "this dream of mine"—that England go back on gold. New to the firm, Leffingwell said he would "sell his shirt to help England out of this mess" and asked, "Could anything be more heartening than for England and America to lock arms for honest money?"[7]

Like Monty Norman, the Morgan partners feared that if exchange rates weren't tied to gold, they would be managed by politicians. Sober finance might then be held hostage to political expediency, giving a bias toward inflation and paper money. Keynes was already advancing such heretical ideas. Leffingwell warned Morgan: "Keynes . . . is flirting with strange gods and proposing to abandon the gold standard forever and to substitute a 'managed' currency . . . it is better to have some standard than to turn our affairs over to the wisdom of the publicist-economists for management."[8]

Teddy Grenfell was Monty Norman's intermediary between the Bank of England and Wall Street. He briefed the New York partners about Norman's strange temperament and fragile nerves: "Norman elaborates his own schemes by himself and does not take anyone into his counsel unless he is obliged to do so in order to combat opposition. . . . As I have explained to you before, our dear friend Monty works in his own peculiar way. He is masterful and very secretive."[9] As a Bank of England director, Grenfell also alerted New York partners to impending changes in Bank of England interest rates—priceless information—just as Herman Harjes reported on upcoming gold movements by the Banque de France.

In late 1924, Norman got cold feet about gold. To bolster his confidence, he went to New York to see Jack and Ben Strong. For Jack, the return to gold was gospel. Hadn't his father saved America's gold standard in 1895? He fervently told Norman that if Britain failed to return to gold, centuries of goodwill and moral authority would have been squandered. And Treasury Secretary Andrew Mellon told Norman that Washington approved of J. P. Morgan and the New York Fed helping Britain to go back on gold.

Morgan cooperation was vital. For the pound to maintain its new, higher value in currency markets, the dollar couldn't pose too strong a competitive threat. Otherwise, speculators would sell pounds and buy dollars, driving the pound back down. Either Norman had to maintain high interest rates in London—drawing money into the pound—or Strong had to keep rates low in New York—making dollar investments less attractive. The House of Morgan insisted on higher British interest rates as the answer. Instead, Monty's loyal friend, Ben Strong, depressed American interest rates. This was no small technical matter: it would be blamed by some for causing the 1929 crash on Wall Street.

Strong was always sensitive to insinuations of his being in league with Norman and wanted to involve the House of Morgan in the gold opera- tion as political cover. J. P. Morgan and Company could be useful in another way as well. The British needed a large credit to defend the pound against any speculative attacks that might occur. Under the law, Strong could make loans to other central banks, such as the Bank of England, but not to other governments—for instance, the British Trea- sury. So it would take Strong and J. P. Morgan together to provide money to the bank and the Treasury.

Norman had already manipulated a series of short-lived chancellors of the Exchequer. In 1925, the chancellor was Winston Churchill, who would later regard the gold decision as possibly his worst political mis- take. At sea in finance, he privately confessed to feeling inadequate in that area and was easy prey for the devious Norman. Churchill's son recalled that Norman would appear at Chartwell and mesmerize Win- ston by intoning, "I will make you the golden Chancellor."[10]

Grenfell disliked Churchill and privately criticized him as "still at heart a cheeky, over confident boy."[11] Both Norman and Grenfell wanted pliant politicians who would relegate financial decisions to the merchant bankers, for in the twenties the merchant bankers still domi- nated the Court of the Bank of England. (The five large commercial, or "clearing," banks still didn't have power commensurate with their re- sources, which grew fantastically through mergers in the 1920s.) Before announcing the gold decision in April 1925, Grenfell watched Chur- chill as if he were an unpredictable truant who might do something stupidly independent: "We, and especially Norman, feel that the new

Chancellor's cleverness, his almost uncanny brilliance, is a danger. At present he is a willing pupil but the moment he thinks he can stand on his own legs and believes that he understands economic questions he may, by some indiscretion, land us in trouble."[12]

As an attempt to restore the old imperial pound, the 1925 gold-standard decision was a colossal miscalculation, a nostalgic attempt to restore Britain's former power. It was so lethal because Norman wished to return to gold at the lofty prewar rate of £1 to $4.86. At that rate, British industry couldn't compete with world exports; even Russell Leffingwell thought Norman too heedless of the British employment situation.

Not everybody cheered the plan. Keynes thought it would weaken British industry and force a sharp decline in wages to offset the stronger currency. (Perhaps in retaliation, the merciless Grenfell took to describing Keynes's new bride, Lydia Lopokova, as the "little ballet girl.") Many British industrialists echoed this alarm, and the jittery Norman almost backed down. One last boost was needed. Grenfell cabled Jack, "I think the Governor would like me to give him assurance that you personally still approve of his course of action in this whole matter."[13] Jack did.

On April 28, 1925, in the House of Commons, with Norman in the distinguished-visitors' gallery, Churchill announced Britain's return to gold. Fearing a runaway chancellor, Grenfell was relieved that the chancellor didn't depart from his prepared text. The New York Fed provided a $200-million credit to the Bank of England, and J. P. Morgan and Company a $100-million credit to the British Treasury. Because the pound soared and speculative attacks didn't materialize, the credits weren't needed. By November, Churchill announced that the embargo on foreign loans was lifted.

The architects were in a self-congratulatory mood. Jack's friend Prime Minister Stanley Baldwin praised Strong and the House of Morgan as "men than whom there are none in the world who stand higher for financial ability and moral rectitude."[14] The left wing, however, was up in arms about the threat to British industry and the more than 1-percent commission J. P. Morgan charged for keeping the unused credit ready. Grenfell itched to counterattack but was dissuaded by Churchill: "As we are paying a commission to Messrs Morgan, it would obviously be unsuitable for you to speak in the debate and it would I'm sure expose you to annoyance at the hand of the Socialists."[15] Grenfell withdrew to that natural habitat of Morgan men—the shadows.

Before long, Keynes's worst fears were vindicated, and British coal, textiles, and steel lost their competitiveness in world markets. Far from revivifying Britain, the gold standard seemed to accelerate its decline. There arose the predicted pressures for lower wages to counterbalance a higher pound. But it was impossible for wages and retail prices to adjust to the world price level. By late spring 1926, England had suffered a coal strike and a general strike with venomous overtones of class warfare. (During the strikes, Grenfell joked that he was glad to be relieved of the roar of motor buses and found the office pleasantly devoid of business.) When Ben Strong visited London during the strike, he met with Churchill and Norman. They managed to avoid talk of the gold standard altogether. Stanley Baldwin and Monty Norman didn't mention the big blunder either. They forgot their troubles by playing duets together—Baldwin at the piano, Norman singing. It was a curiously civilized form of escape as strikers and policemen clashed in the streets.

A S the House of Morgan moved from sterling to stabilize other currencies, it drew closer to the Italian government, which was alarmed by a sudden fall in the lira in 1925. The fascist government of Benito Mussolini had been in power for three years, and Wall Street bankers were comforted by the Italian's macho pride in the lira's strength. Ben Strong and Monty Norman favored a loan to stabilize Italy's currency but had qualms about il Duce himself. Shocked by a 1926 visit to Italy, Strong said of the dictator: "I should imagine that he would not hesitate to cut off a man's head instantly if he failed to deliver what was expected of him."[16] And Norman was dismayed by political meddling at the Banca d'Italia—an affront to the chastity of a central bank.

Tom Lamont, however, viewed Mussolini in a rosier light. In New York political circles, Lamont enjoyed the reputation of a liberal. His son Corliss, a socialist and later a professor of philosophy at Columbia, saw his father's foreign-policy views as spotless: "Although my father was a successful banker, and a Republican in politics, he was in essence a liberal, particularly in international affairs."[17] Corliss praised the tolerant atmosphere of the Lamont household, dubbed the International Inn for its many visiting celebrities and intellectuals. One visitor, H. G. Wells, interested Corliss in socialism, and the two would team up in arguments against the *paterfamilias*. To his credit, Lamont handled Corliss's radical politics with admirable tact. Corliss would view his own politics not as a negation of his parents' views but as an extension of their liberalism.

Always proud of his work for Woodrow Wilson, Lamont seemed to stand out as the great exception, refuting, in Corliss's words, the "stereotype of rich people and Republicans as conservative or reactionary plutocrats opposed to all forms of progress and liberalism."[18] Nor was this just a loving son's bias; such accolades tumbled in upon Lamont. To poet John Masefield, the Lamonts were an exemplary couple, representing everything civilized: "Their political views, national and international, were ever generous and liberal. They always seemed to be in touch with the generous and the liberal of every country."[19] Even General Smuts of South Africa told Lamont, "There is no doubt that your house is an international meeting place, and an influence for good . . . second to none in the world."[20]

Why should they have thought otherwise? Reasonable and fond of discourse, an engaging letter writer, Lamont lacked the smug conservatism of many on Wall Street. He was one of the major contributors to the League of Nations Association and the Foreign Policy Association. For many years, he was financial angel of the *Saturday Review of Literature* and knew poets ranging from Robert Frost to Stephen Vincent Benét. He was that rare banker with an appreciation for words, a zest for ideas. Because Lamont was a partner in a mysterious, private bank, his admirers couldn't compare his stated beliefs with his business behavior. That he served as banker to Italy during its Fascist period apparently didn't faze them. They doubtless imagined that he kept a businesslike distance from Mussolini and served his client with thinly disguised distaste.

But Lamont could do nothing halfway. As a Morgan man, he had to render those thousand and one special touches that made a client feel pampered. As with Pierpont, unvarnished banking lacked some final satisfaction for Lamont. His elaborate letters and memorandums seem almost a substitute for the writing career he never had. He always wanted to go beyond mere dollars and invest his deals with some larger meaning. He tried to make loans a total experience, by immersing himself in the politics and culture of client countries. In Italy, he would meet with Mussolini one day, then picnic in the Roman *campagna* the next. Despite the Fascist regime, he saw an Italy touched with poetry and romance. As president of the Italy-America Society, he hosted meetings of its Dante Committee at his East Seventieth Street townhouse and once screened a Florentine film on Dante and Beatrice. At the office, he worked at a beautiful Italian refectory table. Yes, his life would be all of a piece, a fusion of business and pleasure.

The Morgan agent in Rome was Giovanni Fummi, whom Lamont had met at the Paris Peace Conference. Fummi was a former stockbroker with an American wife, a charming, extroverted man with a trim mustache and laughing eyes. He lived well at the Hotel Excelsior and was tanned both summer and winter. He was typical of the powerful but discreet lobbyists the bank employed in foreign capitals. He was rich in contacts, both in the government and in the Vatican. Lamont would boast of Fummi's high standing with Mussolini yet insist he was free of Fascist taint. Fummi was perhaps less a Fascist than a conformist willing to sacrifice his principles for *la dolce vita.* He was an expert rationalizer and even when faced with Italian atrocities would contend that criticism might only polarize the Fascist party and bring more extreme elements to the fore. Funny, charming, and sentimental, Fummi made a curious match with the cool, patrician House of Morgan.

After the war, J. P. Morgan and Company sparred with Dillon, Read for business with the Italian government. Lamont wanted an exclusive relationship, as understood by the Gentleman Banker's Code. In 1923, six months after taking power, Mussolini first met with Lamont to discuss how to restore Italian credit. Initially Wall Street viewed il Duce benignly, as the man who had saved strike-torn Italy from Bolshevik hands. The Blackshirt terror that killed a hundred people in the 1921 elections was conveniently overlooked. Traveling through Italy, Jack Morgan reported to a friend, "We had the great satisfaction of seeing Mr. Mussolini's Revolution."[21] In the early days, Mussolini stuck to conservative financial policies and kept flunkies from the key financial posts. Italian financial policy was something of a showcase for the outer world.

During their fifteen-year relationship, Lamont and Mussolini would form an implausible pair. Lamont was stylish and natty with wonderful manners, scores of friends, and a refined sense of beauty. Mussolini was sloppy and unshaven, an insecure, misanthropic loner with a megaphonic voice and a black view of human affairs. Their relationship had a Beauty and the Beast quality that hid one likeness: both men were former journalists and newspaper owners and were fascinated by the art of public relations. Both had the knack of giving a pretty verbal gloss to ugly things, and much of their relationship revolved around the manipulation of words.

Lamont didn't start out an apologist for Mussolini. As usual, the path to perdition comprised a series of small steps. In the summer of 1923, Italian troops occupied the Greek island of Corfu, and their bombing of civilians outraged world opinion. If the League of Nations thwarted him, Mussolini promised to destroy it. Appalled, Lamont told Fummi, "I think you ought to know direct from me that the action of Mr.

Mussolini in the Grecian affair has given us all a tremendous jolt here." The fact of the occupation bothered Lamont less than the manner: "There was no reason in the world why he shouldn't have been able to occupy it peacefully instead of shooting up and killing several innocent civilians, including children."[22] The indignation wasn't simply humanitarian, for Lamont realized that Corfu would make impossible the financing he had discussed with Mussolini the previous May.

The following year, Blackshirt violence intensified. Hundreds were murdered or wounded during the rigged 1924 elections, scores of judges were later dismissed, and Italian democracy was dismantled. Mussolini now controlled six of the thirteen cabinet departments and the three armed services. For the first time, a conflict arose between Lamont's business commitment to Italy and the humane indignation of some important friends, most notably Walter Lippmann, who attacked the Corfu invasion in the *New York World.* When Lippmann returned from Rome in 1924, he had dinner with Lamont and told him il Duce needed these violent antics to stay in power. Lamont didn't disagree.

How would Lamont deal with the growing strain between his liberalism and his desire to expand Morgan business in Italy? He would paper it over with words. He had a politician's talent for speaking in different voices to different people. He never exactly lied but shaded the truth and pretended to side with everyone. Only Lamont was bright enough to keep all his stories straight and wrap them up in outward consistency. After the dinner with Lippmann, he wrote to Prince Gelasio Caetani, the Italian ambassador in Washington, about the chat: "This all sounds to me like silly gossip; nevertheless I had to keep within bounds because I was the host."[23] This was a more cynical voice than the one Lippmann heard. Through nods, winks, and pats on the back, Lamont would keep everyone happy.

A certain convenience of vision, a selective filtering out of details, began to accompany the verbal touch-ups. Mussolini's henchmen had now killed Giacomo Matteotti, the regime's eminent foe, causing Socialist deputies to boycott Parliament. Yet when Lamont visited Italy in April 1925 to meet with Mussolini, he seemed oblivious to these grisly developments. Bonaldo Stringher, the governor of the Banca d'Italia, assured Lamont that il Duce resorted to strong-arm tactics only when absolutely necessary. With Corliss, the Lamonts motored through Italian hill towns and stopped by Bernard Berenson's villa, I Tatti, for tea and a chat about Italian Renaissance art. Afterward, Lamont wrote this paean: "The Italy through which I traveled seemed to be industrious and prosperous. The newspaper headlines in the New York and even

London papers seemed to me exaggerated. Everybody, both in and out of the Government, laughed at these stories of street fights, unrest upsetting the Government etc.''[24] Back at 23 Wall, Lamont received an autographed photograph from Mussolini, which was now featured as prominently on his wall as the earlier picture of Woodrow Wilson had been.

In reviewing Lamont's files, one gets the impression that in 1925 he made a moral leap and cast his lot with Mussolini. The year was rife with rumors, encouraged by Lamont's trip, of a $100-million Morgan emergency loan. In part, Mussolini wanted Morgan money to rebuild Rome as a monument to his own maniacal splendor. The new secretary of state, Frank Kellogg, made it clear that no loan would be forthcoming unless Rome settled more than $2 billion in war debts with Washington. In October 1925, Mussolini sent a mission to Washington, headed by his finance minister, Count Giuseppe Volpi, to negotiate the debt.

As the big $100-million loan hung in the balance, Lamont made his most startling shift with Mussolini, one that went far beyond basic banking requirements. This former champion of the League of Nations began to coach the Italian dictator on how to appeal to Anglo-American opinion. He fed him sugared phrases, language that would make reprehensible policies palatable abroad. A modern man, Lamont knew that any product, if attractively packaged, could be marketed to the public. The Italian problem was redefined as one of public relations. After Mussolini suspended town councils and bullied Parliament into passing 2,364 decrees at once, Lamont sent fresh publicity angles to Fummi for il Duce's consideration:

If Mr. Mussolini declares that parliamentary government is at an end in Italy such a declaration comes as a shock to Anglo-Saxons. If, on the contrary, Mr. Mussolini had explained that the old forms of parliamentary government in Italy had proved futile and had led to inefficient government and chaos; therefore they had to be temporarily suspended and generally reformed; then Anglo-Saxons would understand.

Again, when Mr. Mussolini announces that the mayors of interior cities will be appointed by the Fascista government, Anglo-Saxons jump to the natural conclusion that such a step means that the interior cities are to be deprived of all local self-government. If, at the time of such announcement, Mr. Mussolini had explained that in most cases the mayors of the interior cities were simply the appointees and tools of local deputies, and were conducting the affairs of the municipalities so badly that, for the time being, the central government had to intervene, then again such an explanation would have seemed reasonable.[25]

In public appearances, Lamont tried to deflect attention from Mussolini's politics to his economic record. Wall Street enjoyed pretending that there were two Mussolinis—the sound economic leader and the tough politician—who could be treated separately. Mussolini spouted the predictable litany of promises—balanced budgets, low inflation, and sound money—that bankers adored. Resorting to sophistry, Lamont said he was only praising the Italian economy, not Mussolini or fascism. In a January 1926 speech before the Foreign Policy Association, Lamont extolled Italy's record in lowering inflation, stopping strikes, and reducing unemployment. He even endorsed Mussolini's highway and public works projects—measures that would be roundly denounced by Morgan partners during the Roosevelt administration. Lamont's trump card was his claim that the Italians supported Mussolini: "At this gathering to-day, we all count ourselves liberals, I suppose. Are we sure that we are liberal enough to be willing for the Italian people to have the sort of government which they apparently want?"[26]

Lamont's efforts were crowned with success: in early 1926, Washington reached a lenient settlement of Italy's war debt, paving the way for a Morgan operation. Treasury Secretary Andrew Mellon had already advised President Coolidge that without a conciliatory debt settlement, Wall Street might lose the Italian loan to Britain. So Coolidge was pleased when, a week later, Lamont announced the $100-million Morgan loan. It triggered a vituperative debate in Congress, with critics such as Representative Henry Rainey, Democrat of Illinois, calling Mussolini a murderous dictator and protesting the favoritism shown toward the Fascist regime. As with the Dawes Loan to Germany, the Morgan loan to Italy proved a catalyst for further American investment. The bank itself went on to provide loans to Rome and to two industrial clients, Fiat and Pirelli. In December 1927, J. P. Morgan again joined with Ben Strong and established a credit for the Banca d'Italia that permitted a return to the gold standard.

On a Wall Street disturbed by European radicalism and worshipful of economic progress, Lamont wasn't the only Mussolini supporter. Jack Morgan and George Whitney both hailed him as a great patriot. Otto Kahn of Kuhn, Loeb likened his iron rule to that of a tough receiver straightening out a bankrupt company. With a poetic flourish, Willis

Booth of Guaranty Trust said Mussolini lifted Italy "out of the slough of despair into the bright realm of promise."[27] Judge Elbert Gary of U.S. Steel and publicist Ivy Lee joined the fan club. As a self-professed "missionary" for Mussolini, Lamont's contribution was singular. One scholar has noted, "Of all the American business leaders, the one who most vigorously patronized the cause of Fascism was Thomas W. Lamont. . . . Though not the most voluble business spokesman for the Italian government, Lamont was clearly the most valuable. For it was he who translated verbal apologetics into hard cash, securing for Mussolini a $100 million loan."[28]

Was Lamont ignorant of events inside Italy? Not likely. As lender to sovereign states, the bank maintained thick clipping files and received abundant intelligence from around the world. (It was partly the excellence of Lamont's files that enabled him to keep abreast of an extraordinary range of clients.) In January 1926, publicity man Martin Egan passed on to Lamont an anguished letter from a friend in Anticoli, Italy:

> I wonder if you all in New York know just what you are doing in backing Fascistism in Italy. We had a taste of it last night here. A party of Fascists motored up from Rome armed with revolvers, rapiers and loaded whips, arrived at nine and proceeded to beat up with fierce brutality the peasants who could not produce a Fascisti card. . . . If any peasant objects he is shot. This is happening all over the place. It seems funny for American money to be perpetuating it.

On top of this, Lamont scribbled, "Pretty terrible, I must say."[29] In addition, an Italian opposition leader reported to him how his house in Rome was plundered by Blackshirts; he passed along a sheaf of bellicose speeches in which Mussolini boasted of his readiness for war. These speeches occasionally upset Lamont, but he always ended up recasting the problem as public relations.

At the same time, Lamont was plied with constant requests from a new Italian ambassador, Giacomo de Martino, whom he used to put up at the University Club in New York. Most of de Martino's requests were for more sympathetic press treatment of Mussolini. To this end, Lamont lined up favorable editorials in the New York *Sun*, protested dispatches of an "anti-Fascist" correspondent in the *World*, and arranged for de Martino to plead with Walter Lippmann at his home. Mussolini took a personal interest in winning over Lippmann and even sent him a personal photograph with a tribute to Lippmann's "wisdom" scribbled across it.[30] (Lippmann worked in a penthouse under signed photos of the British ambassador and Morgan partner Thomas Cochran.) Lippmann's antagonism toward Mussolini only deepened, however, confirmed by Italian press censorship, which he saw as symptomatic of weakness. "As long as the censorship lasts, I shall remain persuaded that the Mussolini Government is not certain of its hold on the Italian people," he told Lamont. "If the opposition to it inside of Italy were as negligible as Fascists like the Ambassador make out, there would be no occasion for a censorship of this character."[31]

Mussolini stamped out all press freedoms in Italy. He was so preoccupied by his image that he would examine in advance front-page layouts of national newspapers. By 1930, half of his ministers were recruited from the press corps, and he decreed that all journalists be Fascists. Dissenting editors were jailed, and many foreign journalists were mugged by street toughs. Hence, Mussolini's only fear of press exposure was from abroad.

At the time of the $100-million loan, Lamont and Martin Egan convinced Ambassador de Martino to suggest an American press service to Mussolini. Its purpose, Lamont said, would be to "acquaint our financial community more faithfully with the proper situation in Italy."[32] Mussolini was excited by the idea, and the secret operation went into effect in 1927. Paid for by Italy, it would write up favorable press releases and bring over speakers. There was some difficulty in finding an appropriate American journalist to head the operation. The first choice was Associated Press correspondent Percy Winner, who once wrote of Mussolini, "An artist in the use of millions of human beings as tools and a nation as a canvas, the Duce rises so far above the typical politician or even dictator as to defy definition."[33] Even de Martino was relieved when Winner's name was dropped for a less slavish admirer. Early preparations for the press bureau were cleared with Lamont, and it eventually operated under the aegis of his Italy-America Society.

How did Lamont, a Woodrow Wilson protégé, end up an accomplice of Benito Mussolini? The answer is partly personal. He had a romantic attachment to Italy and a proprietary feeling toward the Italian account, which he had won. His training as a Morgan banker taught him to transcend the mundane and to move mountains for important clients. This personal approach to business suited him, for he had varied and contradictory ambitions. He yearned to be a sleuth, a statesman, a political fixer, and a *bon vivant.* He loved politics, not so much as an ideological contest, but for the intrigue and the high-stakes gambling with fate. As a result, he could cooperate with politicians of many stripes. Washington's tacit support for Italian loans perhaps also removed any inhibitions that might otherwise have existed.

Lamont's Italian adventure exposed other problems. The highly intimate style of "relationship banking" meant that bankers came to share their clients' interests and identify with them. They felt almost too responsible for the success of their issues. As Lamont once said, when the House of Morgan undertook to market a block of common shares, it assumed responsibility. not simply for the solvency of the corporation involved but for its brilliant, successful management. This was the old London tradition upheld by Pierpont in dealing with bankrupt, profligate railroads. Now that tradition was being transposed into a policy of backing dictators whose bonds were floated by the House of Morgan. Although lending to sovereign states had political overtones and moral imperatives quite absent from conventional business banking, the style of "relationship banking" was transferred intact.

There was another factor of paramount importance in Morgan's growing involvement in Italy—the Vatican. Earlier, Pope Pius X had grown wistful and regretted not having requested investment tips from Pierpont. This papal prayer was belatedly answered in the late 1920s, during the reign of Pius XI. The new relationship owed something to the friendship between Jack Morgan and the pope. In his earlier incarnation as Monsignor Ratti, prefect of the Vatican Library, the pope had restored the Morgan collection of sixty Coptic texts dug up from an old stone well in an Egyptian monastery. As an expert on early Christian documents, he had hardened the parchments until they became legible. The task consumed twelve years before the texts were finally returned to the Pierpont Morgan Library.

Even more important to the future Morgan relationship with the Vatican was the 1929 Lateran Treaty, which resolved a fifty-eight-year dispute between Italy and the papacy. Back in 1871, Italy had taken control of the Papal States, which included much of southern Italy and had provided the Vatican with enormous revenues. In 1929, Mussolini not only recognized the Vatican's sovereignty but paid almost $90 million in compensation for the seized lands. This vast sum was paid in the form of Italian treasury bonds worth 1.5 billion lira.

Before this, the Vatican had managed money in a conservative and rather primitive way. At the turn of the century, Pope Leo XIII had simply filled a trunk with gold coins and stored it under his bed. But with his good Milanese business head, Pius XI wanted to manage the Vatican's assets in a modern, secular manner. On June 2, 1929, he met with Bernardino Nogara of the Banca Commerciale Italiana, one of the rare meetings in papal history not recorded on the Vatican calendar. Nogara was not only a highly experienced banker but had so many priests and nuns among his siblings as to make him an acceptable layman for confidential Vatican work.

The Pope asked Nogara to create the Special Administration of the Holy See and convert the Italian treasury bonds into a diversified stock portfolio. The operation was so secret that only one report was produced each year. Nogara would hand-deliver it to the pope, who would inspect it and then place it in his personal safe. Pius XI put no restrictions on Nogara's investments, and the banker was given full power to invest in stocks, gold, and real estate and even take equity stakes in different companies. Nogara decided to select the best investment advisers in a number of foreign financial centers and was perhaps swayed by his friendship with Giovanni Fummi. In New York, he chose J. P. Morgan and Company; in London, Morgan Grenfell; in Paris, Morgan et Compagnie (the new name given to the Paris house in the late 1920s); in Holland, Mees and Hope; in Sweden, the Wallenbergs' Enskilda Bank of Stockholm; and the Union Bank of Switzerland.

The Vatican would be very grateful for the investment advice provided by the House of Morgan. Jack Morgan, who had once lobbied to keep a Catholic off the Harvard board, would become a favorite in Vatican City. For investment advice, Pope Pius XI would confer upon both Jack and Tom Lamont the Grand Cross of Saint Gregory the Great. As an account of both Morgan Grenfell's and J. P. Morgan's, the Vatican is an important explanation of some of the alacrity with which Lamont performed services for Mussolini. After all, the devil's work was now sprinkled with holy water.

CHAPTER FIFTEEN

SAINT

• •

•

D WIGHT Whitney Morrow vied with Tom Lamont for honors as the chief Morgan statesman and theoretician. His twenties celebrity owed much to his friendship with the president. When Coolidge took office, reporters flocked to Morrow for comments and speculated on which high post he would occupy. The two had been close friends in Amherst's class of 1895, boarding together for a year. They both remembered the day when they sat on a hilltop and fantasized about their future. According to legend, in their senior class everybody voted Morrow the Most Likely to Succeed—except Morrow, who voted for Coolidge. "Coolidge in college was a quiet, unassuming man," Morrow later said, and he was one of the few to penetrate the president's reserve.[1]

As a student of ancient civilizations, Morrow wanted to clothe the mundane, often sordid world of the twenties in some larger classical dimension. Spearheading the Amherst College Coolidge-for-President Committee in 1920, Morrow viewed his old friend in grandiose terms: "Coolidge is a very unusual man and a strange combination of a transcendental philosopher and a practical politician."[2] With similar hyperbole, Morrow confided to Lamont, "I think it is a miracle that a man of Coolidge's type has been produced for this emergency."[3] Coolidge talked of Morrow no less reverently. Morrow had been a brilliant student, Coolidge said, but without the usual bookworm qualities. "While he was . . . friendly and sympathetic, he was always dignified. . . . He had no element of selfishness. He never strove to excel anyone or defeat anyone."[4]

One suspects that Coolidge cleverly presented Morrow with the scholarly image the latter wanted to see. During the 1920 presidential race,

Morrow sent four volumes by the Yale economist William Graham Sumner to Coolidge, who replied, implausibly, from the campaign trail that he had almost finished all four! "I regard his arguments on the whole as sound," Coolidge said, but added, "I do not think that human existence is quite so much on the basis of dollars and cents as he puts it."[5] Coolidge, as they say, had Morrow's number. While Morrow addressed him as "Dear Calvin," Coolidge usually responded with "Mr. Morrow," as if he were writing not to an old school pal but to an elderly sage.

Along with Lamont and Russell Leffingwell, Morrow gave the House of Morgan its patina of culture, its reputation as a home to bankers who wrote essays, gave speeches, joined foreign policy councils, and served on foundation boards. He belonged to a 1920s cult that believed in the wisdom of businessmen as managers of America's political affairs. Witty, bristling with ideas, the pint-sized Morrow had a professorial air. With penetrating blue eyes and a faraway look, he wore pince-nez and baggy trousers and never fit into the foppish Morgan world. The bank used to post a page at the men's room door just to remind him to pull up his suspenders when he left. Attending the wedding of Harry Davison's daughter, he smelled so badly of mothballs that the other partners made him don a fur coat to mask the odor. His sartorial deficiencies, it seems, symbolized a deeper unease in the posh Morgan world of tall, rich, self-confident men.

Like many bright, obsessive people, Morrow was notoriously absent-minded. He once spent a dinner at the Lamonts gesturing with a partially eaten olive until Metcalf, the Lamont butler, offered a plate for the well-chewed pit. Everybody at J. P. Morgan told the story about Morrow's riding the train. When the conductor asked for his ticket, Dwight couldn't find it and with his hands restlessly searched every pocket. The ticket, it seems, was clenched between his teeth. "I bet you thought I didn't know it was there," Morrow said to the conductor. "Actually, I was just chewing off the date." Once, while taking a bath, he called out to his valet for soap that lathered better; the problem turned out to be not the soap but that he was still wearing his pajamas.

Like Lamont, Morrow craved something finer than mere banking. He professed ignorance of the business's technical side and styled himself "a lawyer in a banking firm."[6] A banker of the Diplomatic Age, he was as much at home in Washington as on Wall Street. He clung to his intellectual ambitions, reading Bryce and Thucydides and writing essays, studded with recondite references, in favor of the League of Nations. He plied Coolidge with books such as Hallam's *Constitutional*

History of England. What makes Morrow's story unique in Morgan annals is that he never entirely renounced his youthful goals or political ambitions and saw his partnership as a springboard.

There is pathos in Dwight Morrow's journey from a poor Pittsburgh home to the summit of world finance, and the story of his boyhood makes for uncomfortable reading. His father was a high-school principal and supported the family with difficulty. Pale and sickly, Dwight inherited both his father's reverence for education and his fear of poverty. After he graduated from high school, at fourteen, he worked as an errand boy for four years until he was old enough to go to college. He attended Amherst with the aid of a student loan and wore hand-me-down shirts given him by Jacob Schiff's son Mortimer. To make ends meet, he tutored other students. He practiced such austerity that he shared a pipe with a roommate to save money. After graduating from Columbia Law School, he landed a job at the Wall Street firm of Reed, Simpson, Thacher, and Barnum, which specialized in utility law. Within seven years he was a partner in the firm, now called Simpson, Thacher, and Bartlett. Living in Englewood, New Jersey, he locked umbrellas with Harry Davison in the rain one day and befriended Tom Lamont along the way. The two Morgan partners recruited him in 1914.

To become a Morgan partner was then a national event, and Morrow's mother was mobbed by well-wishers in the Pittsburgh streets. But after his first day, Dwight admitted to his wife, Betty, that he felt "pretty lonely and blue all day." To a friend he confessed that he felt "like a cat in a strange garret."[7] This was partly beginner's jitters, but the uneasiness never entirely deserted him.

Morrow performed spectacularly at 23 Wall and mastered every subject through sheer diligence. He mutualized the Equitable Life Assurance Society and oversaw Morgan lending to Cuba. He also masterminded Kennecott Copper, a public company formed around the Morgan-Guggenheim syndicate in Alaska and other properties. Daniel Guggenheim was awed by Morrow's retentive brain and said that "six months after Morrow had started upon his investigation, he knew more about copper than I or any of my six brothers."[8] In his absentminded way, however, Dwight neglected one detail of the Kennecott operation: "You have forgotten to provide for our commission," Davison gently chided him.[9]

Morrow was always torn between idealism and materialism. One life couldn't encompass his dreams, and he was tormented and made extremely nervous by the choices he faced. He and his wife traveled in monied circles and were frequent guests of Pierre du Pont at Longwood in Pennsylvania, with its fountains, conservatories, and ten-thousand-pipe organ. Yet they felt misplaced in this rich world. While still at Simpson, Thacher, Dwight would have pangs of Puritan guilt and say, "This, Betsey, is not the life for you or me."[10] Together they day-dreamed of how they would save up $100,000, and Dwight would then teach history and Betty write poetry—Betty Morrow was a Smith gradu-ate and a poet whose work appeared in *Harper's* and *Scribner's Maga-zine*. They could never acknowledge their overpowering ambition.

Morrow's conflicts gnawed at him even in his sleep. One night, he bolted up in terror from a nightmare. "I dreamt, Betsey, that we had become rich," he explained. "But *enormously* rich."[11] Offered a Mor-gan partnership, he went through "weeks of acute spiritual crisis," according to his biographer, Sir Harold Nicolson. While pondering his choice in Bermuda, Morrow saw a malicious cartoon that showed a vulturelike Jack Morgan feasting upon the innards of New Haven share-holders. This libel persuaded him to take the Morgan job, he said, and the bank's defense of its New Haven financing was his first assignment. Morrow used lofty rhetoric to justify actions prompted by lesser mo-tives. After accepting the Morgan partnership, he told an old Amherst professor that service—not the prospect of a $1-million-a-year income—drew him to the House of Morgan.

Morrow always flirted with the idea of retreating to the cloistered university world. He spent so much time on Amherst matters that Jack Morgan reportedly said one day, "Dwight, if you will get off that Am-herst Board of Trustees I'll make a present of a hundred thousand dollars."[12] In 1921, his bluff was called: he was approached with a tentative offer to become president of Yale. He turned it down, saying he wasn't a Yale alumnus and lacked special training. The excuse was flimsy, and for months afterward Dwight was depressed. Amherst and the University of Chicago also pursued him in vain.

Morrow's real passion was politics. He balked at the Morgan partner-ship lest it prove a political handicap—an accurate fear, as it turned out. The British press baron Lord Beaverbrook once told him that if he were an Englishman, he would already be a cabinet minister. The remark haunted and distressed him.[13] At first, Calvin Coolidge's election seemed a godsend, and Morrow was touted for Treasury secretary and other positions that never materialized. "My mother was upset and felt rather bitterly about it," said his daughter. "She felt that my father didn't ask for things."[14] Morrow used to tell his children to obey "Rule 6—Don't take yourself too seriously!"[15] Yet the Morrows took every setback in earnest.

One suspects that Coolidge kept a self-protective distance from Morrow. "Ever since Mr. Coolidge became President Mr. Morrow has, of course, been a frequent guest at the White House," wrote Ivy Lee, who was a publicity consultant for the Morgan bank as well as for the Rockefellers. "It is an open secret that the President has consulted with him on numerous occasions."[16] Harold Nicolson, by contrast, claimed that Coolidge telephoned Morrow only once between 1923 and 1929. Morrow's files suggest that the truth lay in between, with Nicolson's comment nearer the mark. Coolidge had wanted to make Morrow, not Parker Gilbert, agent general for Germany and only capitulated after warnings from the U.S. ambassador to Germany. Clearly, some Coolidge advisers feared the stigma of associating with a Morgan partner.

Perhaps to soften up public opinion for an appointment, Coolidge assigned Morrow in 1925 to chair a board studying the application of airplanes to national defense. Coolidge first mentioned it in a letter to Morrow a few days after his 1925 inauguration, but Morrow learned about it officially from the Sunday papers that September. The Morrow board drew up plans for army and navy use of airplanes. In 1925, Daniel and Harry Guggenheim—old friends of Dwight's from his Kennecott Copper days—set up a special $3-million fund to advance aviation. Through Morrow, they got Coolidge to accept the money on behalf of the government to speed up airplane development.

Through his stint on the Aviation Board, Dwight Morrow became friends with the young Charles Lindbergh. In fact, Morrow's files show that the Morgan partners ended up paying for Lindbergh's historic flight to Paris aboard *The Spirit of St. Louis.* Under the original scheme, Lindbergh had planned to compete for the $25,000 Orteig Prize, set up to reward the first nonstop flight between New York and Paris. The trip was thus supposed to be self-financing. Lindbergh contributed $2,000, and a number of other Saint Louis sponsors added $1,000 or $500 apiece. Altogether, they raised $8,500 in subscriptions against a loan of $15,000 from a Saint Louis bank. Then, in his rush to be first across the Atlantic, Lindbergh decided that he couldn't afford certain delays demanded by the Orteig Prize and so forfeited his chance. In June 1927, one St. Louis sponsor, broker Harry F. Knight, told Morrow that the historic flight had actually cost between $16,000 and $17,000. The Morgan partners pitched in $10,500, not only repaying the bank loan, but permitting Lindbergh to retrieve his own $2,000 investment.

When Lindbergh made a triumphant trip to Washington, Coolidge invited him to stay as his guest at the temporary White House on Du Pont Circle. The president saw that Lindbergh's celebrity would make him a major force in the budding airline industry and so he invited the Morrows as guests as well. Morrow and Lindbergh liked each other immediately. As a trustee of the Daniel Guggenheim Foundation for the Promotion of Aeronautics, Morrow steered Lindbergh to Harry Guggenheim, who sponsored Lindbergh's three-month tour in *The Spirit of St. Louis.* And Morrow became Lindbergh's personal financial adviser.

While the Morrows were staying at the temporary White House, Coolidge sounded out Dwight about becoming ambassador to Mexico. Dwight had been restless at 23 Wall and apparently told Coolidge of his willingness to leave. The offer of the ambassadorship was formalized a month later. This position wasn't just a bone tossed belatedly to an old friend, but an extremely sensitive appointment. As Coolidge later said, "It would be difficult to imagine a harder assignment. But Mr. Morrow never had any taste for sham battle."[17]

American Catholics and oilmen were agitating to break diplomatic relations with Mexico, and some called for a military invasion. Secretary of State Kellogg had already condemned the regime of President Plutarco Elías Calles as a "Bolshevik threat."[18] In American eyes, Mexico had committed multiple sins. It had nationalized church property and closed Catholic schools, defaulted on foreign debt, insisted that oil companies trade in property titles for government concessions, and confiscated American-owned land without compensation. Newspapers were calling Mexico America's foremost foreign-policy problem.

The Morrow appointment was an inspired choice. Coolidge was under pressure to do something dramatic, and he did it. Walter Lippmann hailed it as the "most extraordinary appointment made in recent years" and helped to shepherd it through the Senate Foreign Relations Committee.[19] As a specialist in Latin American loans and an opponent of dollar diplomacy, Morrow had moderated Wall Street's often truculent attitude toward Latin American debtors. When Cuba threatened to default on foreign bonds during the 1921 sugar debacle that nearly collapsed Guaranty Trust, Morrow was credited with keeping out the marines. "Is there any one who thinks that if a man owes him money and cannot pay it, there is profit in going out and killing him?" he wrote.[20] Morrow favored diplomacy over armed intervention, an enlightened attitude for the time.

Betty Morrow expressed both elation and bitterness at the appointment. The Morrows had just decided to build a new home in Englewood, and she didn't want their lives disrupted. *She* didn't see Coolidge as a transcendental philosopher: "The blow has fallen! President Coolidge wrote to Dwight today asking him to be Ambassador to Mexico and Dwight is going to do it. It is a hard job, and not much honor, and it comes late. . . . Coolidge won't run again, but Dwight goes and does a hard job for him when there is no chance of reward. How characteristic![21] Betty sarcastically told friends that Coolidge was like a father who had given away valuable gifts and thrown Dwight a little tin whistle at the end.

Morrow was sufficiently pessimistic about Mexico to say privately that the best he could do was get Mexico off the front page. Lamont advised him against taking the post, saying the turmoil of a pending presidential campaign made it an inauspicious time for action. Friends concurred and were aghast that Dwight would surrender a Morgan partnership for such a risky position. Even Lindbergh was dubious: "From what little I have seen at our border stops, I am afraid that the position will be a difficult one."[22]

The Mexicans were also wary of Morrow, believing he would function as a collection agent for the New York banks. They chanted, "First Morrow, then the marines." The fear was unjustified. The Lamont-led bankers' committee for Mexico was less interested in military action than in peaceful negotiations to get Mexico to resume debt repayment. They wanted stability, not further turmoil, in Mexico. In the end, it would be the Mexicans who would be pleasantly surprised by Dwight Morrow and the House of Morgan that would feel embittered and betrayed.

A S ambassador to Mexico, Dwight Morrow patented a new style for a *gringo* emissary in Latin America—warm and voluble, treating Mexicans as peers, not wayward children. Soon after his arrival, he told the local U.S. Chamber of Commerce that it should respect Mexican sovereignty. (With slight embarrassment, he had to write the White House and ask for a photograph of Coolidge to hang above his desk—another telltale sign of the distance between the two.) Morrow developed a close rapport with President Calles and would casually drop in on him, like an old friend. They would breakfast at Calles's ranch or tour Mexican dams and irrigation works together. Morrow's friendly, trusting manner contrasted with that of his predecessor, James R. Sheffield, who had treated nonwhites patronizingly, taken a pro-invasion stand toward Mexico, and studiously served the interests of American oil companies.

Morrow not only respected Mexican culture but liked the easygoing informality of the people. He and Betty spent weekends at Casa Mañana, a villa in the semitropical town of Cuernavaca. It overlooked two volcanoes and overflowed with Mexican pottery and Indian handicrafts.

Morrow commissioned Diego Rivera, the left-wing Mexican muralist, to paint frescoes at the Cortés Palace, including one that depicted the revolutionist Zapata. To improve U.S.-Mexican relations, he even brought down Will Rogers to tour with him and Calles. While Rogers was there, Morrow threw a banquet complete with Mexican songs and dance. At one point, the ebullient Morrow said to Rogers with a smile, "Imagine going to war with a people like this!"[23]

Sometimes Morrow seemed more popular among Mexicans than in the American colony. The public debate about Mexico in the United States became more inflammatory in late 1927. William Randolph Hearst nursed a grudge against President Calles after the latter appropriated sections of his gigantic Babicora Ranch. That November, the Hearst newspapers ran sensational articles purportedly showing Mexican plots against the United States. Some observers thought Hearst was not only expressing pique against Calles but was deliberately fomenting trouble for Dwight Morrow; the isolationist Hearst had always disliked the Anglophile House of Morgan. On December 9, 1927, the twenty-six Hearst papers published documents that supposedly outlined a Mexican plot to bribe four U.S. senators with over $1 million. These documents were later exposed as forgeries, but in the meantime they damaged relations with Mexico.

BEFORE leaving for Mexico, Morrow had invited Charles Lindbergh to his East Sixty-sixth Street apartment. Acting on a suggestion from Walter Lippmann, Morrow proposed that the young aviator pilot *The Spirit of St. Louis* to Mexico as a goodwill gesture. Lindbergh liked the idea. He had flown to Paris on a spring day, and before donating his plane to a museum, he wanted to prove the practicality of night and winter flights. To strengthen the political message, Lindbergh suggested a flight linking Washington and Mexico City.

So on December 14, 1927, with rifle, machete, and tropical medicine on board, Lindbergh took off through stormy night skies. It was a few days after the Hearst "exposé" and a perilous moment in U.S.-Mexican relations. When the sun rose the next morning, Lindbergh sailed through a cloudless Mexican morning but couldn't figure out where he was. He dipped low enough to read the names of a hotel and train stations and briefly thought all Mexican towns were named Caballeros, because he kept seeing that sign at the stations. Then he spotted a sign for Toluca, a town about fifty miles from Mexico City.

Sharing picnic sandwiches and lemonade, Morrow and President Calles awaited Lindbergh in sweltering heat at Valbuena Airport, where a special grandstand was set up for dignitaries. Morrow nervously paced up and down. When Lindbergh landed—six hours late—a crowd of Mexicans estimated at 150,000 rushed exuberantly across the field. As Lindbergh accompanied Morrow and Calles to their car, they were thronged by shouting, delirious spectators. They rode to the embassy in triumph, horns blaring, horses rearing, and crowds posted "on trees, on telegraph poles, tops of cars, roofs, even the towers of the Cathedral," as Betty Morrow recalled. "Flowers and confetti were flung every moment."[24]

Lindbergh spent Christmas at the embassy with the Morrows and took Calles on his first plane ride. He also took notice of Dwight's daughter, Anne, on vacation from her senior year at Smith College. She was a shy, pretty poetess, as slight of build as Charles was rangy and with Betty's heavy eyebrows. Lindbergh liked the fact that when he first sat next to her, she didn't ask any questions. Theirs was the strong bond of two shy people who had found each other.

Morrow hadn't especially liked the young men his daughters dated— Anne and Elisabeth having gone out with Corliss Lamont, among others. He approved of Charles Lindbergh as a "nice clean boy" who didn't drink, smoke, or see girls.[25] But when Anne announced that she and Charles wanted to get married, Morrow seemed flabbergasted. "He's going to marry Anne? What do we know about this young man?" he asked.[26] He insisted they be engaged first and get to know each other better. Despite his flustered reaction, Morrow was very fond of Charles and would beam with gee-whiz delight when he narrated his aviation adventures.

On May 27, 1929, Anne and Charles were married at the Morrows' new Georgian mansion in Englewood, called Next Day Hill. It was an event of such fascination worldwide that the Morrows had to fool the press and bill it as a prewedding party. Even the guests were told only to drop by for lunch and a bridge game. Then Anne suddenly appeared in a white chiffon wedding gown, and a brisk ceremony took place. Only after Anne and Charles had changed clothes and escaped through the back door did Dwight and Betty broadcast the news to reporters. The young couple briefly stayed at the Leffingwell house in Oyster Bay during their secretive honeymoon, and the servants were threatened with dismissal if they mentioned the couple's presence to tradespeople in town.

It was a strong, intense match but one riddled with contradictions. Anne was the daughter of a former Morgan partner and had imbibed her father's idealism and internationalism. Charles's father, who had died in 1924, was the populist Minnesota congressman who had instigated the Pujo hearings, fulminated against the Money Trust and the Morgan cabal with the Federal Reserve Bank, and castigated the bankers who dragged America into the war. The congressman's son inherited his father's suspicion of eastern bankers and would never entirely slough it off. In the late 1930s, his isolationism would place him at odds with the House of Morgan and create a painful dilemma for Anne. But in the late 1920s, he socialized with the Morrows and Guggenheims and thrilled the Davisons by taking their beach-party guests at Peacock Point for seaplane rides.

THOSE who saw Ambassador Morrow as a proxy for the House of Morgan in Mexico were in for a rude shock. The ambassador already had a separate political agenda, Morrow having confided to Walter Lippmann that he coveted a seat in the U.S. Senate. Hence, he needed to distance himself from the bank. During the 1928 presidential campaign, he was already being toasted as a potential senatorial candidate at Republican dinners. It was now in Morrow's political interest to function as a sensitive, fair-minded arbiter in settling Mexican disputes.

Morrow had quick success with the long-running oil controversy. He developed an ingenious scheme of "perpetual concessions" for American oil companies. It gave them new concessions on pre-1917 wells, while Mexico saved face and retained theoretical ownership. This rational statesmanship delighted Walter Lippmann, who told Morrow afterward, "There is a disposition in some quarters to ascribe it to some kind of private magic which you have at your disposal."[27] For Lippmann, Morrow qualified as the most talented public man of his generation, far beyond the common run of politicians.

Another major dispute involved the Catholic church. Calles had tried to nationalize church lands, and the violent Cristeros movement had arisen in protest. A state of war existed in parts of Mexico, with thousands of men marching under the church's banner. Morrow smuggled Walter Lippmann into the country on a secret diplomatic mission. They negotiated a compromise under which Calles agreed not to interfere with the church while Mexican priests agreed to call off their protest strike. Morrow and Lippmann sold the deal to the Vatican, and the settlement reopened the churches. One morning in Cuernavaca, Betty and Dwight were awakened by the ringing of church bells. "Betty, I have opened the churches," Dwight said, laughing. "Now perhaps you will wish me to close them again."[28]

The most frustrating area for Morrow was, ironically, the foreign debt.

By 1928, Mexico had been in default for fourteen years, and its budgetary situation worsened with the lower oil revenues. In a desperate mood, bankers didn't see how Mexico could satisfy all its creditors. The country owed money to the foreign bondholders represented by Lamont as well as to western U.S. railroads and domestic lenders. Lamont thought the two hundred thousand bondholders he represented should have first claim. He argued that they had patiently waited many years for payment. Morrow, in contrast, favored a comprehensive settlement for all creditors, on the model of a bankruptcy settlement. He feared that if Mexico struck a series of separate deals, it would promise more money than it could deliver. To Lamont, the notion of one big settlement was an impractical dream that would only penalize his bondholders. And it would be so cumbersome that nobody would ever get paid.

A heated feud arose between Morrow and Lamont. Although he would never admit it, Lamont had secret reservations about Morrow. He would later eulogize him as "sparkling, brilliant, whimsical, lovable," yet he thought Morrow had an unearned reputation for sainthood. There was perhaps envy here, a feeling that Morrow threatened his own image as the leading liberal banker. Posing as Morrow's friend, Lamont gave Harold Nicolson a 125-page critique of a draft of Nicolson's biography of Morrow and reproached him for idealizing his subject. Morrow and Lamont were perhaps too much alike to be completely fooled by one another. Each was more worldly and ambitious than he cared to admit.

It's hard to know whether Lamont found Morrow's position on Mexican debt a political ploy to separate himself from 23 Wall or a quixotic plan that only an absentminded professor could espouse. In any event, by 1929 Lamont decided to break with the Morrow-inspired State Department plan for a comprehensive debt settlement. He circulated bitter memos at 23 Wall Street, sarcastically referring to Morrow as the ambassador. The ICBM, he warned, "will be by no means content to stand by idly for a year while the ambassador is perfecting his Government claims." A few days later, Lamont informed his partners that he planned to cut a separate bargain with Mexico "despite Ambassador's attitude."[29] George Rublee, the legal adviser to the U.S. embassy in Mexico and a close friend of Morrow's, later said, "Mr. Lamont would rather take his chances and get what he could ahead of somebody else than to cooperate in a general settlement."[30]

For all his charm, Lamont could play rough when crossed. He tried to figure out an elegant way to get rid of Morrow while appearing to help him. In November 1929, he had Martin Egan hand a letter to President Hoover that recommended Morrow as secretary of war. Lamont stressed that Morrow knew nothing of the request—implying that Hoover should keep the suggestion confidential. He doubted his stratagem would work, however, owing to Hoover's insecurity in the face of Morrow's massive intellect. "Dwight was so brilliant that he would talk around [the president] in circles," Lamont said.[31] Hoover had already rebuffed an earlier request from Calvin Coolidge to appoint Morrow as his secretary of state. Hoover didn't rise to Lamont's bait. Close to Morrow—they spoke several times weekly—the president wasn't eager to advance a potential political competitor.

That month, two events made Lamont's exertions unnecessary. On November 12, Hoover appointed Morrow to represent the United States at the upcoming Naval Conference in London. Later in the month, New Jersey governor Larson asked Morrow if he would fill the brief time remaining in the unexpired term of Senator Walter E. Edge, who had just been appointed ambassador to France. A deal was struck whereby David Baird would occupy the Senate seat with the understanding that he would step aside if Morrow wanted to campaign for the Republican nomination in the spring. This provided Morrow with further incentives to oppose Lamont on the debt issue and eliminate his former Morgan partnership as a potential campaign issue.

In December, the simmering political dispute between Morrow and Lamont boiled over. By this point, Morrow, the liberal do-gooder, had moved into the position of self-appointed overlord of Mexico's finances. The man who had held back the marines now minutely reviewed Mexico's budget. When Lamont's assistant, Vernon Munroe, met with Morrow, he was shocked by the extent to which the ambassador wanted to dictate Mexican financial policy. According to Munroe, Morrow wanted to cut the Mexican budget by "eliminating the courthouse entirely, cutting 2.5 million off the education appropriation, one million pesos off the public health, 2.5 million pesos off statistics and some 4 million pesos off communications."[32] Under the guise of helping his Mexican brothers, Dwight seemed to succumb to delusions of grandeur.

During the May-June campaign for the Republican Senate nomination in New Jersey, Morrow was still serving as Mexican ambassador, and as such he followed the debt situation. Then a campaign blunder drastically reduced his influence in that post. While he was at the London Naval Conference, his military attaché in Mexico, Colonel Alexander J. MacNab, made a speech in which he extravagantly praised Morrow's role in Mexican reform. He actually made Lamont's point— that Morrow was intruding more in Mexican domestic affairs than any Wall Street banker. "There is no department of government in Mexico which he has not advised and directed," MacNab said of Morrow. "He took the Secretary of Finance under his wing and taught him finance."[33] The Mexican press treated the speech as a scandal. It made Mexican officials look as if they were the ambassador's puppets, and Morrow never again had the same influence in Mexico. Nevertheless, he won the Republican nomination.

During the summer of 1930, Morrow kept flying down to Mexico to advise on the debt. The Morrow-Lamont dispute resulted in some blistering exchanges. Morrow kept urging Lamont to lecture the finance minister about the growing Mexican budget; Lamont did this, then regretted it. In a July 24 letter, his pent-up contempt for Morrow surfaced: "I have a feeling that you are a bit disgusted with our mental processes up here and are genuinely upset that we are unable to adopt in toto your point of view." He referred to a talk with the finance minister: "He retorted by telling me politely that it was really none of my business. . . . Now, my dear Dwight, you may have some means of compelling the Finance Minister to give you precise information as to his budget plans for several years ahead, but I must confess that in any such effort I, myself, am powerless." In the end, Lamont bluntly warned Morrow to stay away from his debt settlement with Mexico: "I hope you can see your way clear to letting the matter rest where it is rather than feeling called upon to defeat this plan."[34] In a cool reply, Morrow repeated that Mexico was bankrupt and should treat creditors equally. He warned Lamont that if he persisted in his course, he would ultimately have to deal with the State Department.[35]

The day after Lamont wrote Morrow—without awaiting a reply—he signed a separate accord at 23 Wall with a representative of Mexico's Chamber of Commerce. It nearly halved Mexico's debt, reducing it from $508 million to $267 million, in one stroke. True to his threats, Morrow advised Mexico to delay ratification, but his influence with President Pascual Ortiz Rubio, Calles's successor, was much diminished. As it turned out, the feud between the two Morgan men was for naught. Mexico kept postponing the date of debt repayment, and the whole farce would collapse by 1932. The outcome would have been laughable had it not consumed so much of Lamont's life and impoverished small Mexican bondholders. By 1941, Mexican debt had shrunk to $49.6 million, or a tenth of the original amount.

Although Morrow's break with the House of Morgan was now complete, the association haunted him in the Senate race that fall. As one New Jersey paper described his opponent's strategy: "The Ambassador was to be pictured to New Jersey voters as the tool and puppet of Big

Business interests, and his candidacy as a Wall Street conspiracy to capture the Presidency via the U.S. Senate route."[36]

Morrow was exhausted and dispirited. He suffered from insomnia and headaches and ran a lackluster campaign. Nicolson suggests he had a serious drinking problem. Coincidentally, Prohibition became a central topic in the campaign. Not ducking the issue, Morrow became the first federal official to favor outright repeal of the Eighteenth Amendment.

Again, he seemed driven by his ambition, and the Senate campaign produced more anxiety. Betty recorded in her diary that "Dwight is so tired; so discouraged; so *wild* that he has been trapped into this Senatorial campaign. He is exhausted, does not want it, would be glad to lose."[37] Fate, devising new ways to punish him, produced a landslide victory in November.

As senator, Morrow seemed worn from the immense burdens he had carried over the years. He immediately disappointed liberal admirers. Despite the Depression, he voted against food relief, the soldiers' bonus bill, and tougher utility regulation. This prompted one journalist to declare that in three months he had wiped away the liberal reputation of a lifetime.[38] Such remarks stung Morrow. He approached problems in his thorough, dogged way but got mired in their complexity. He passed sleepless nights reading tomes on unemployment, and Betty warned him that he was getting too little sleep. "That's nonsense," he replied. "Most people have exaggerated ideas about sleep. If I can get two solid hours I'm all right."[39] At the family Fourth of July celebration in 1931, Morrow stared sadly at the lawn of his Englewood home and said to his son-in-law, "Charles, never let yourself worry. It is bad for the mind."[40]

In September, Morrow had a minor stroke while he and Betty lunched with newspaper publisher Roy Howard on a yacht in Maine. Yet he couldn't stop his compulsive activity or moderate his exhausting pace. On October 2, 1931, after spending a sleepless night on a train from Washington to New York, he told a passenger, "I kept waking up thinking what a hell of a mess the world is in."[41] That day he attended a political reception at his Englewood home. He shook hands with four thousand people; his right hand became blistered, and he had to use his left. Three days later, then in his late fifties, Dwight Morrow died in his sleep of a cerebral hemorrhage. The man once unsettled by his dream of great wealth left a million dollars in charitable bequests alone.

And Harold Nicolson left an appropriately ambiguous epitaph: "There was about him a touch of madness or epilepsy, or something unhuman and abnormal. . . . He had the mind of a super-criminal and the character of a saint. There is no doubt at all that he was a very great man."[42] Yet Nicolson tempered this judgment with a far less generous one: "Morrow was a shrewd and selfish little arriviste who drank himself to death."[43]

In one respect, fate proved merciful to Dwight Morrow. Five months after Morrow died, his grandson, Charles Lindbergh, Jr., was kidnapped from his family's home near Hopewell, New Jersey. The House of Morgan tried to help solve the famous case. Jack Morgan sounded out an underworld contact, and the bank fielded tips from several sources, including a palmist. It also bundled and numbered the ransom money that Lindbergh's associate, Dr. John F. Condon, passed across a dark cemetery wall to the kidnapper. When the baby's body was discovered in a wood two months later, Anne and Charles moved to Next Day Hill, the Morrow house in Englewood. Haunted by the press and bad memories, they left the United States for England in 1935. There they lived at Long Barn, a thatched Kentish house owned by Harold Nicolson, Anne's father's biographer.

The Lindbergh kidnapping also spread fear through the House of Morgan. Afterward, an army of 250 bodyguards protected the families of Morgan partners, and many of their grandchildren would remember growing up surrounded by opulence and armed guards.

CHAPTER SIXTEEN

CRASH

• •
•

W E picture the bull market of the twenties as spanning the entire decade, when in fact it was compressed into the second half. It was largely a Wall Street phenomenon, not matched by other stock markets around the world. Germany's market had peaked in 1927, Britain's in 1928, and France's in early 1929. Why the enormous burst of Wall Street optimism? It was partly a reaction to the unsettled postwar years, with their inflation and labor strife, their bitter Red-baiting and anarchist turmoil. Financial history teaches us that the desire for oblivion is the necessary precondition for mayhem.

The euphoria was also generated by a liquidity boom of historic proportions. Cash was everywhere. In 1920, Ben Strong sharply raised interest rates to cool off an inflationary commodity boom. This created not only a recession but disinflationary conditions that lasted for several years. Money fled hard assets. As commodity bubbles burst—ranging from Texas oil to Florida land—the money poured into financial markets. Stocks and bonds floated up on a tremendous wave.

With Europe devastated by war, America's economy outpaced competitors and created a large trade surplus. The economic boom was lopsided. Commentators spoke of "sick sectors" in farming, oil, and textiles. With half of America still living in rural areas, the Wall Street rally seemed unreal and irrelevant to farmers. Nor did all banks prosper. Weakened by farming and oil loans, small-town banks failed at the rate of two a day, a fact not noticed in urban areas, where finance and real estate thrived together. For instance, in late 1928, John J. Raskob, Democratic national chairman, started plans to build the Empire State Building as a monument to "the American way of life that allowed a poor boy to make his fortune on Wall Street."[1]

Raskob and other prophets of the age espoused an ideology of endless prosperity and talked of a new economic era. Their shibboleths were readily believed by the large number of young, inexperienced people recruited by Wall Street. As the *Wall Street Journal* said after October 1929's Black Thursday, "There are people trading in Wall Street and many over the country who have never seen a real bear market."[2] If many on Wall Street were determined to forget past panics, most were too young to have ever known about them.

For many pundits, the sheer abundance of cash precluded any crash. A big worry of the late 1920s was that America might run short of stocks. The day before the 1929 crash, the *Wall Street Journal* reported, "There is a vast amount of money awaiting investment. Thousands of traders and investors have been waiting for an opportunity to buy stocks on just such a break as has occurred over the last several weeks."[3] The excess cash was viewed as a sign of wealth, not as an omen of dwindling opportunities for productive investment.

Riding this cash boom, the American financial services industry grew explosively. Before the war, there were 250 securities dealers; by 1929, an astounding 6,500. A critical shift in the popular attitude toward stocks occurred. Bonds had always dwarfed stocks in importance on the New York Stock Exchange. Before the war, banks and insurance companies might trade stocks, but not small investors. We recall Pierpont Morgan's steady disdain for stocks. When asked why the market went down, he would say dismissively, "Stocks will fluctuate," or "There were more sellers than buyers," as if the subject weren't worthy of analysis.[4]

In the 1920s, small investors leapt giddily into the stock market in large numbers. They frequently bought on a 10-percent margin, putting only $1,000 down to buy $10,000 worth of stock. Of a total American population of 120 million, only 1.5 to 3 million played the stock market, but their slick, easy winnings captured the national spotlight. The 1929 market disaster would be heavily concentrated among the 600,000 margin accounts.

With active securities markets, it was cheaper for big corporations to raise money by issuing securities than it was for them to raise money by paying for short-term bank credit. Many companies also financed expansion from retained earnings, continuing to wean themselves away from the banker dominance of the Baronial Age. In fact, some businesses had so much surplus cash that they engaged in stock speculation and margin lending—much as Japanese companies in the 1980s would use spare cash for *zai-tech* investment—so that the Federal Reserve's pressure on banks to stop margin lending was offset by unregulated industrial lenders.

In this pre-Glass-Steagall era, corporate preference for securities issues posed no threat to Wall Street. The big New York banks profited through their new securities affiliates, which could also bypass limits on interstate banking. Guaranty Trust opened offices in Saint Louis, Chicago, Philadelphia, Boston, and even Montreal. The securities unit of the Chase National Bank not only operated coast-to-coast but set up offices in Paris and Rome. The world of integrated global markets was thus already foreshadowed by the 1929 crash. In 1927, Guaranty Trust invented American depositary receipts (ADRs), enabling Americans to buy overseas stocks without currency problems. This would be an extremely lucrative business for J. P. Morgan and Company when it later took over Guaranty Trust.

There were now two securities worlds on Wall Street. One was retail-oriented and pedestrian and was typified by the National City Company, the affiliate of the bank. National City chairman Charles Mitchell lent a carnival tone to securities marketing. He would organize contests and pep talks for his nearly two thousand brokers, spurring them on to higher sales. Bankers took on the image of garrulous hucksters. Among these men, there was a fad for foreign bonds, especially from Latin America, with small investors assured of their safety. The pitfalls were not exposed until later on, when it became known that Wall Street banks had taken their bad Latin American debt and packaged it in bonds that were sold through their securities affiliates. This would be a major motivating factor behind the Glass-Steagall Act's separation of the banking and securities businesses.

By the 1929 crash, large deposit banks had vanquished many old partnerships in the securities business and originated a startling 45 percent of all new issues. The National City Bank Company sponsored more securities than J. P. Morgan and Kuhn, Loeb combined. Nevertheless, elite Wall Street survived, typified by the august House of Morgan. The bulk of prime securities business remained with the prestigious, old-line, wholesale houses. J. P. Morgan had no distribution network but originated issues distributed by as many as twelve hundred retail houses; still distant from markets, the bank allocated shares to "selling groups." It co-managed issues with its Money Trust allies—National City, First National, and Guaranty Trust—while Morgan Grenfell worked with the Houses of Baring, Rothschild, Hambro, and Lazard.

As in the days of the Pujo hearings, big bond issues were still conducted according to fixed rituals. AT&T provides an excellent example.

At the Morgan Library in 1920, Jack Morgan, Harry Davison, and Robert Winsor of Kidder, Peabody worked out a secret deal to divide American Telephone and Telegraph issues. They kept identical participations throughout the decade: Kidder, Peabody, 30 percent; J. P. Morgan, 20 percent; First National Bank, 10 percent; National City Bank, 10 percent; and so on. The Gentleman Banker's Code prohibited the raiding of customers. It was thought not only bad form, but dangerous. J. P. Morgan and Kuhn, Loeb feared that if they competed for each other's clients, they would destroy each other in bloody, internecine battles.

On its marble pedestal, the wholesale House of Morgan didn't need to twist the arms of small investors. As *The New Yorker* said in 1929, "It is doubtful whether any private banker ever enjoyed the individual prestige of Morgan senior, but the firm now is vastly more powerful than it was in his day."[5] By decade's end, it would have less to repent than many other banks. Some of this was the result of tradition, as the bank profited from its Victorian disdain for the stock market—as Pierpont once told Bernard Baruch, "I never gamble."[6] Jack Morgan had held a Stock Exchange seat since 1894 but never conducted a transaction. Only once, during a Liberty Bond rally, did he appear on the Exchange floor. He kept the seat only to reduce commissions from the thirty-odd brokers the bank used. In addition, common stock issues accounted for a mere 3 percent of Morgan-sponsored securities. Since the chief damage of the 1920s would be done by stock manipulation, the House of Morgan was spared involvement in some of the worst excesses.

J. P. Morgan and Company engaged almost solely in a wholesale bond and banking business. With glaring exceptions, it refused to water down standards. It recommended conservative investments, such as railroad bonds, but shied away from the tipster's art of plugging stocks. On the notable occasion when this Morgan policy was violated, the bank was deeply embarrassed. In July 1926, Morgan partner Thomas Cochran, setting sail for Europe, entertained a reporter aboard the liner *Olympic*. (In the Roaring Twenties, even luxury liners had brokerage offices.) When Cochran was at sea, the Dow Jones ticker quoted him as saying that General Motors would eventually sell at 100 points higher than its current price. Aware of the Morgan–Du Pont interest in the company, traders drove up GM stock by 25 points in two days. Aghast at this proof of its power, the bank made sure such incidents didn't recur.

Although the Morgan bank, as an institution, was distant from the stock market, its partners weren't averse to speculation. They were in an excellent position to take advantage of insider trading, which was a common vice of the 1920s, and not illegal. Not only did Jazz Age Wall Street echo with rumors, but being in a position to plant false reports was considered a mark of financial maturity. Lax Stock Exchange rules and meager corporate reports made inside information more valuable, and investors milked their Wall Street friends for news. Inside tips didn't guarantee success—many investors perished on Black Thursday clutching them—yet they were profitable enough to be considered a major perk of Wall Street employment.

In the 1930s, Morgan partners joined those favoring an end to insider trading. Lamont would say flatly, "This is a simple and unanswerable proposition in business ethics."[7] Some had had the courage to take this stand earlier. Judge Elbert Gary, chairman of U.S. Steel, used to hold board meetings each day after the stock market closed; following these meetings, he would brief the press, denying directors an exclusive opportunity to benefit from his news. By and large, however, Morgan partners, like others on Wall Street, did benefit from insider trading, not so much on pending deals as on routine corporate information.

Edward Stettinius was a loquacious director of both General Motors and General Electric. In 1922, Harry Davison asked whether he should buy GM preferred stock for his wife. Stettinius replied: "I hesitate . . . about buying any common stock until after the statement has been published showing the results of last year's operations. This statement, which is now in the course of preparation, will probably show a total debit against Surplus Account of about $58 million as indicated in the memo attached hereto. I think it possible that this statement may have a depressing effect on the stock and would not favor purchases of the stock until after the statement shall have been published."[8] Stettinius handled GM purchases for both Jack Morgan's and Tom Lamont's personal accounts.[9] We might call this the shooting-fish-in-a-barrel school of finance.

In passing tips, Stettinius displayed a vague sense of the impropriety of doing so. In 1923, Morgan partner Herman Harjes in Paris asked about buying General Electric shares. Note how Stettinius hesitates before spilling the news:

> I would much prefer to buy than to sell the stock of the General Electric Co. at present prices, say 196. I do not feel that I can properly tell you what information has come to me as a member of the Executive Committee and Board of Directors of the Co., but I do think that I can say to you (to be treated confidentially) that it is my guess that some action will be taken within the next 6 months to still further

enhance the value of the company's shares. I shall be surprised if the shares do not sell on a basis of 225 or 230 per share, within the next six or nine months. The Co. is doing a wonderful business—and this again in confidence—profits for 11 months of 1923 show an increase of 50% over the profits for the corresponding period of 1922.[10]

If Stettinius displayed scruples, it was less about revealing corporate information than in having it leak out to those beyond the inner circle of J. P. Morgan partners.

The House of Morgan was involved in another period phenomenon that belied its well-advertised repugnance toward common stock. Between 1927 and 1931, the bank participated in more than fifty stock pools, which weren't outlawed until the New Deal. They were regarded as racy and glamorous, attracting cocktail party sophisticates, and their progress was reported in the press. These syndicates blatantly manipulated stock prices. Some would hire publicity agents or even bribe reporters to "talk up" a stock. Pools made Joe Kennedy's reputation after he was enlisted in 1924 to defend John D. Hertz's Yellow Cab Company against a bear raid; afterward, Hertz suspected Kennedy of carrying out such a raid against the stock himself. By October 1929, over one hundred stocks were being openly rigged by market operators. So while Morgan partners claimed they preferred sound long-term investments, they were far from immune to the speculative atmosphere.

The 1920s were also a time of manic deal making. As Otto Kahn recalled, there was "a perfect mania of everybody trying to buy everybody else's property. . . . New organizations sprang up. Money was so easy to get. The public was so eager to buy equities and pieces of paper, that money was . . . pressed upon domestic corporations as upon foreign governments."[11] Although J. P. Morgan had no formal merger department, it informally spun many webs. It specialized in deals of strategic import, requiring sensitive contacts abroad or covert government support. Many of its deals were directed against British interests; first and foremost, 23 Wall operated as an arm of Washington.

Consider telecommunications. After the war, the United States feared the British military monopoly of undersea cable communications, which had yielded invaluable wartime intelligence. The U.S. Navy favored the use of a new private corporation, supported by Washington, to battle Britain in the emerging field of radio technology. Privately, President Wilson notified General Electric that he wanted to counter Britain's cable monopoly with an American radio monopoly. Morgan money helped GE to buy out British interests in American Marconi, which became the core of Radio Corporation of America. Washington stayed on RCA's board as a nonvoting observer.

During the 1920s, the House of Morgan also helped Sosthenes Behn to launch his worldwide empire of International Telephone and Telegraph. Again the bank's role wasn't raiding but arbitrating. A historic truce was hatched at 23 Wall, whereby AT&T ceded overseas markets to Behn, who promised, in turn, that ITT wouldn't build telephone plants in the United States. The deal, amazingly, lasted sixty years. This cartel arrangement showed that the Morgan bank still preferred collusion among big industrialists to the competitive economy of *laissez-faire* ideologues.

With his taste for political intrigue, Behn and the House of Morgan were a natural match. Through Morgan partner Herman Harjes in Paris, Behn took over the Spanish telephone system, which became the crown jewel in his international empire. In the mid-1920s, J. P. Morgan and Company helped Behn to take over telephone systems in Brazil, Argentina, Chile, and Uruguay, ousting the British from their former preeminence. The bank championed Behn's cause in numberless ways. When it learned during Austrian loan negotiations that the government planned to buy telephone equipment from Siemens, it mentioned that ITT was eager to tender bids. Lamont sometimes functioned as Behn's secret plenipotentiary. In 1930, he had an audience with Mussolini solely to advance Behn's desire to build a factory in Italy. Deal making in this era was always a discreet, behind-the-scenes operation and had none of the flamboyance associated with the stock market raiders of a later day.

IN early 1929, a sure sign of impending disaster occurred when the House of Morgan cast aside its traditional aversion and joined the flurry of stock promotion. Wall Street was being swept by new forms of leveraging. Borrowing a British concept, many brokerage houses, including Goldman, Sachs, introduced leveraged mutual funds, called "investment trusts." A second favorite device was the holding company. Holding companies would take over many small operating companies and use their dividends to pay off their own bondholders, who had financed the takeovers in the first place. This permitted an infinite chain of acquisitions.

Adopting the vogue for utility holding companies, the House of Morgan in 1929 sponsored the United Corporation, which took over Mohawk-Hudson, the Public Service Corporation of New Jersey, Columbia

Gas and Electric, and other companies that controlled more than a third of the electric power production in twelve eastern states. It was a throwback to the days when Pierpont promoted trusts, kept a large block of stock for himself, and appointed the directors. The United Corporation's books were kept at 23 Wall, and its board was filled with Morgan friends and partners. The bank also sponsored Standard Brands, an amalgam of food-product companies that included Fleischmann, Royal Baking Powder, Chase and Sanborn, and E. W. Gillette.

The master boondoggle of 1929 was the Morgan-sponsored Alleghany Corporation, a holding company for the railroad and real estate empire of Cleveland's Van Sweringen brothers. Oris P. and Mantis J. Van Sweringen were a queer, taciturn pair who lacked much formal education. Short, dumpy, and round-faced, they seemed as inseparable as Siamese twins. Living at Daisy Hill, their seven-hundred-acre Swiss chalet farm outside Cleveland, the bachelor brothers ate together, shared a bedroom, seldom socialized, avoided alcohol and tobacco, and dispensed with chauffeurs, valets, and other trappings of wealth. On the eve of the crash, they were worth over $100 million.

Beginning with their development of suburban Shaker Heights, the brothers had learned the art of using other people's money. They got into railroads when they built a line from downtown Cleveland to the development. They whirled into the Morgan orbit in 1916 when the Justice Department pressured the New York Central into divesting the "Nickel Plate" railroad, which ran into Cleveland; the Van Sweringens arose as the friendly party who would take the road off New York Central's hands for a mere $500,000 cash. Alfred Smith, president of the New York Central, took the boys into 23 Wall, threw his arms around them, and told Lamont, "I have had many experiences with these two boys. They are very capable. . . . I want you to cooperate with them in any way you legitimately can."[12] Lamont complied.

The House of Morgan and Guaranty Trust orchestrated financing for the brothers' railroad and real estate takeovers. As masters of leverage, the Van Sweringens used each new purchase as collateral for the next. Their holding companies took control of other holding companies in an endless hall of mirrors, all supported by little cash but powerful Morgan connections. By 1929, the Van Sweringen railroads ruled America's fifth largest railroad system from atop a forty-story Cleveland tower and controlled trackage equal in length to all of Britain's railroads.

Issued by J. P. Morgan and Company in January 1929, the stock of the Alleghany Corporation was meant to be a summary achievement for the brothers—the super holding company atop their pyramid of debt.

In the words of the *New York Times*, it was "the holding-company device pushed to its uttermost limits."[13] The association with the Van Sweringen brothers showed how the recklessness of the 1920s had at last infected the citadel of respectability itself—the Morgan bank. Even the mystical Morgan name couldn't hold together a pyramid built of nothing but faith. It would be four years before the public finally knew the questionable circumstances under which the Alleghany shares had been floated. In early 1929, however, the issue looked like the best buy in town.

FOR much of 1929, Jack Morgan and Tom Lamont were distracted from the coming storm by the thorny problem of Germany's reparations. They had continually warned against excess German borrowing only to find themselves subsequently making the loans. In this twilight of the businessman-diplomat, an admiring America still looked to Morgan bankers for guidance. GE chairman Owen Young and Jack Morgan were chosen as American delegates to a Paris conference that was supposed to devise an ultimate solution to the reparations issue; Tom Lamont and Boston lawyer Thomas W. Perkins were alternates. The group was technically unofficial although again in close touch with Washington. In February, they set sail on the *Aquitania*. Upon landing at Cherbourg, they were greeted by French officials, who quickly transferred them to a private railroad car for the trip to Paris.

Chaired by Owen Young, the conference took place at the plush new Hôtel George V. Once again the sticking point was Germany's capacity to make reparations. As usual, the French, represented by Emile Moreau of the Banque de France, were obstinate in their opposition to lower reparations. And the U.S. refused to lower war debts. Believing reparations financially insupportable, the Reichsbank president, Dr. Schacht, disrupted the conference several times, flying into a rage and storming from the room. One of the British delegates, Lord Revelstoke, noted that with "his hatchet, Teuton face and burly neck and badly fitting collar . . . he reminds me of a sealion at the Zoo."[14]

At this conference, Jack Morgan had difficulty hiding his intense dislike of the Germans. Dr. Schacht made the mistake of buttonholing him about the House of Morgan's financing of Germany's railways. Jack was scornful. "From what I see of the Germans they are 2nd-rate people," he cabled New York, "and I would rather have their business done for them by somebody else."[15] He grumbled about how the conference was ruining his plans for a *Corsair* cruise on the Mediterranean, not to mention those for shooting in Scotland; Dr. Schacht noted Morgan was the first to slip away. This was a rare occasion when Jack let his feelings surface in public, and Lord Revelstoke compared him to "a wild bison in a shop that sells Dresden china."[16]

In Paris, Dr. Schacht hoped to win substantial decreases in reparations and was irate at French intransigence. He shocked the Allies, in turn, by proposing that Germany get back the Polish corridor and take overseas colonies in exchange for the high cost of reparations. To help break a diplomatic logjam, Owen Young responded to a suggestion by his young assistant, David Sarnoff, shortly to be president of RCA, that he attempt informal negotiations with Schacht. Lamont told Sarnoff, "Good luck. If anyone can do this job, you can."[17] On May 1, the Russian-Jewish immigrant and the German Hjalmar Schacht had their first dinner at Schacht's room at the Hôtel Royal Monceau. There was instant rapport. Schacht had once studied Hebrew, a language Sarnoff learned while studying for the rabbinate, and they ended up talking about everything from German opera to the Old Testament. They also discussed reparations, and the first dinner turned into a marathon, eighteen-hour negotiating session. Sarnoff later took credit for selling a "safeguard clause" to Schacht that related reparations to German economic performance. This idea reconciled Schacht, however briefly, to the plan.[18]

Jack was so delighted by Sarnoff's initiative that he brought him a big bunch of ripe French strawberries. He also told Sarnoff, "David, if you actually bring back a signed agreement, you can have anything you ask for that is within my gift."[19] After another lengthy bargaining session in late May, Sarnoff brought an agreement back to the Ritz Hotel. Jack, amazed, tipped his black homburg to Sarnoff. "I doff my hat to you," he said with a bow. "And I propose to stick to my promise. Ask for anything you want, and it will be yours."[20] Sarnoff asked for a meerschaum pipe of the sort Jack smoked. It was made by an elderly London pipemaker, who first made Pierpont's. Jack chartered a plane so someone could fly to London and fetch the pipe for Sarnoff.

The Young Plan reduced the schedule of reparations payments from that designated by the earlier Dawes Plan, stretching them over a fifty-nine-year period. It also attempted to depoliticize German debt by converting it into tradable bonds. Instead of paying the Allies directly, Germany would pay bondholders through a new Bank for International Settlements. This would free Germany from political interference and lift the yoke of the hated agent general's office. The boyish Parker Gilbert left Berlin to become a J. P. Morgan partner, a move that didn't surprise the Germans. When Gilbert warned the Germans against seeking any foreign loan beyond the Young loan, Karl von Schubert of the German Foreign Office spied an ulterior motive. J. P. Morgan was about to float a big loan for France, and a German loan "would be seen [by Gilbert] as a disagreeable competitor for the project of the House of Morgan, to which he is known to be close," said von Schubert.[21]

Set up in a hotel off the main square of Basel, Switzerland, the new Bank for International Settlements fulfilled Montagu Norman's dream of a place where central bankers could forge international monetary policy without political interference. Norman lovingly called it a confessional. A provincial U.S. Congress didn't like the word *international* and refused to let the Federal Reserve join, although several private American banks bought shares in it. The BIS would outlast the Young Plan and develop into a central bank for central bankers, just as Monty Norman had envisioned.

In June 1929, the German debt settlement was announced. Newspapers showed Dr. Schacht leaning across Owen Young to shake hands with Emile Moreau of France's central bank. No sooner were the documents signed than a window curtain caught fire and burst into flames—a lurid omen suggesting the Young Plan's fate in Germany, where it would prove no more popular than the Dawes plan. Dr. Schacht signed the document with strongly felt ambivalence, insisting that the German Cabinet take responsibility. Before long, he would denounce it and become a Nazi favorite. The $100-million portion of the Young loan, sponsored by the House of Morgan in June 1930, would be its second and final effort for Germany. Unlike the robust reception given to the Dawes loan, the Young loan aroused scant enthusiasm. Nevertheless, in 1929 the Paris conference gave a sense of closure to the era's most intractable problem and helped spur the final upward rise of the stock market in New York City. Owen Young was even mentioned as a possible presidential candidate.

WHILE Jack stayed behind for the grouse season, Lamont returned to New York. As a rule, Morgan partners didn't belong to the select group of financiers who could later point out their apocalyptic warnings about the stock market. (Joe Kennedy later said he sold stocks after hearing his bootblack touting them.) Lamont was an exponent of the new economic era and thought only a business downturn could derail stocks. George Whitney thought the Federal Reserve Board a "set of damn fools" for tightening credit in 1929. The only Morgan seer was Russell Leffingwell, the former assistant Treasury secretary who had come to the Corner in 1923 from the law firm of Cravath, Henderson, Leffingwell, and de Gersdorff. An entertaining and courtly man, Leffingwell had a long pointed nose and a shock of premature white hair that gave him an air of wisdom. He was a liberal and sometime Democrat. In his combative, curmudgeonly intellectual style, he pilloried ideologues of both the left and the right. A perpetual worrier, he was withering in his view of the optimistic Andrew Mellon: "Meanwhile, the greatest Secretary of the Treasury since Alexander Hamilton grows richer on paper and thinks that all is for the best possible in the best of possible worlds."[22]

Leffingwell subscribed to the cheap-money theory of the crash; that is, he blamed excessively low interest rates for the speculation in stock. In 1927, Monty Norman had visited New York and asked Ben Strong for lower interest rates to take pressure off the pound. Strong obliged by lowering his discount rate. Leffingwell believed this had triggered the stock market boom. In early March 1929, when Leffingwell heard reports that Monty was getting "panicky" about the frothy conditions on Wall Street, he impatiently told Lamont, "Monty and Ben sowed the wind. I expect we shall all have to reap the whirlwind. . . . I think we are going to have a world credit crisis."[23] Later he held the two directly responsible for the Depression. It may be recalled that Jack Morgan and others at 23 Wall had favored England's return to gold in 1925, but only with the proviso that Monty raise rates, not that Ben lower them.

Benjamin Strong didn't live to see the crash. He went through a hellish series of illnesses—tuberculosis, influenza, pneumonia, and shingles—and was shot full of morphine when he died, at age fifty-five, in October 1928; Montagu Norman, disconsolate, mourned Strong's death for years. During the spring and summer of 1929, Strong's hand-picked successor, George Harrison, pleaded with the Federal Reserve Board in Washington to increase interest rates. Instead, the board vetoed rate hikes in New York. Russell Leffingwell saw a Greek tragedy unfolding. He feared that Harrison had inherited the antagonism left by Strong and that "the immense resistance offered by the Washington Board may be partly the result of ten years of bottled up bitterness against poor Ben's domination."[24] At the worst possible moment, the system was undercut by bureaucratic feuding. When the discount rate was belatedly raised in August 1929 from 5 to 6 percent, it was too late to cool off the boom.

On September 5, 1929, the tragedy of that Black Thursday was foreshadowed when an obscure economist named Babson repeated a warning he had been making for years: "Sooner or later a crash is coming, and it may be terrific."[25] In ordinary times, the remark would have been ignored. Instead, circulated on news wires, it briefly cracked the stock market. Professor Irving Fisher of Yale, high priest of academic hope, rallied the faithful: "Stock prices have reached what looks like a permanently high plateau."[26] But the American economy had peaked in August and was falling even as Fisher spoke.

By mid-October, the stock market gyrations so worried Hoover that he sent an emissary, Harry Robinson, to consult Lamont, his chief adviser on Wall Street. Hoover, the first president with a telephone on his desk, frequently rang Lamont before breakfast. Despite Hoover's closeness to the House of Morgan, many partners secretly ridiculed him as cold, pompous, and pigheaded. Parker Gilbert once called him "Secretary of Commerce and Under-Secretary of all the other departments."[27] During the 1928 campaign, the Democrats had released a memo written by Leffingwell in his Treasury days that said, "Hoover knows nothing about finance, nothing about exchange and nothing about economics."[28] Hoover was petulant because the bank hadn't done more to aid his reelection. Before the primary, he sent a threatening note to Lamont, accusing him of working for Charles Dawes.

To his credit, however, the president wasn't heedless of the Wall Street peril. In early 1928, while commerce secretary, he was flabbergasted by Coolidge's cavalier lack of concern about the stock market. And in March 1929, as president, he summoned to the White House Richard Whitney, vice-president of the New York Stock Exchange and brother of Morgan partner George Whitney. Hoover wanted the Exchange to curb speculation—a plea that was ignored. Hoover also blamed the Fed for low interest rates and providing banks with ample reserves, which were then used to finance buying on margin.

Now Hoover's messenger, Harry Robinson, wished to know the answers to two questions: Were the increasing number of stock mergers grounds for concern? And should the federal government take action to stop speculation on Wall Street? Five days before Black Thursday, Lamont wrote Hoover a memo in which he whitewashed the practices of an era. He blandly waved away Hoover's well-founded worries: "First we must remember that there is a great deal of exaggeration in current gossip about speculation. . . ." He paid tribute to the self-correcting forces of the marketplace. Citing industries that had lagged in the rally—automobiles, lumber, oil, paper, sugar, and cement—he declared that the market hadn't overheated. With a nod to United Corporation and Alleghany, he praised the new holding companies that now dominated railroads and public utilities. His rousing peroration set all fears to rest: "Since the war the country has embarked on a remarkable period of healthy prosperity. . . . The future appears brilliant."[29] The only fault he found was with the Federal Reserve Board in Washington—for blocking higher interest rates at the regional reserve banks.

Martin Egan brought the memo to the White House. The president was so eager to hear Lamont's report that he held up a parade for ten or fifteen minutes in order to talk to Egan, who found him generally confident about his presidency, if edgy about Wall Street. The satisfaction didn't last long. On October 22, the president sent a frantic messenger to Lamont expressing concern about the "speculative situation which seemed to him to be running very wild," as Lamont relayed the message to Jack.[30] Hoover was correct—if a little late. The next day, panic selling hit selected blue chips, with Westinghouse dropping 35 points and General Electric 20. The balloon was about to burst.

The following morning, Winston Churchill stood in the visitors' gallery of the New York Stock Exchange. Two weeks earlier, he had lunched with the Morgan partners who had helped him to restore England to the gold standard in 1925. Now he looked down on a scene that many would circuitously trace to that 1925 decision, with its need for lower U.S. interest rates. Within the first two hours of trading, almost $10 billion was lost on paper. The drops posted were so sharp and the resulting shrieks so fearful that the gallery was closed by late morning.

As in 1907, desperate men stood on the steps of Federal Hall, hands in their pockets, their hats pulled low, staring grimly ahead. Their shocked silence is almost palpable in the photographs taken that day. They stood six deep outside the Stock Exchange. Having bought on margin, many investors were ruined outright. Newspapers noted a strange noise filtering through the canyons of the Street—a roar, a hum, a murmur. It was the cumulative sound of thousands of stunned people giving vent to their feelings. Violence was in the air. When a workman appeared atop a building, the crowd assumed he wanted to leap and was impatient with his hesitation. A dozen suicides were reported, some poetically apt. "Two men jumped hand-in-hand from a high window in the Ritz," Galbraith noted. "They had a joint account."[31] Only the Stock Exchange pages, who lacked investments, savored the ruin of their bosses.

Around noon, the master bankers of Wall Street marched briskly up the steps of 23 Wall. These were the men whose exploits had thrilled America—Charles Mitchell of National City, Albert Wiggin of Chase, Seward Prosser of Bankers Trust, William Potter of Guaranty Trust. They represented $6 billion in assets, perhaps the world's greatest pool of wealth. For the last time, they enjoyed the heroic stature that the Jazz

Age had conferred upon them. To Street veterans, it came as no surprise that the meeting was chaired by fifty-eight-year-old Tom Lamont. The Morgan role in rescues was now automatic. Whatever its flaws, it was the banker's bank, the arbiter of disputes, the statesmanlike firm that offered confidentiality no other house could match. In the words of B. C. Forbes, "Thomas W. Lamont, foremost Morgan partner, stepped into a role on Thursday which the original J. P. Morgan used to take in past panics."[32]

Even in a crisis, Lamont was debonair, his sangfroid now legendary. He was Wall Street's mystery man, and Black Thursday would be his celebrated moment. He was a strange candidate for the part. In his youth, he had lost a year's salary by selling short and thereafter forswore stock speculation. He was also the banker who had advised a skittish Hoover to take a posture of benign indifference toward Wall Street.

The bankers' rescue on Black Thursday proved longer on symbolism than on substance. The men knew they couldn't prop up a collapsing stock market, so they tried to introduce liquidity and engineer an orderly decline. There had been terrifying moments that morning when no buyers appeared. So they pledged $240 million to buy up assorted stocks and stabilize the market. (The Guggenheims joined this pool.) It was just a finger in the dike, but it was the best they could manage.

Because the president of the Stock Exchange was in Honolulu, the acting president, Richard Whitney, was agent for the bankers' rescue. He seemed an ideal choice because his brother was a Morgan partner and his own firm was a Morgan bond broker. Richard Whitney was also a great pretender, and his cool demeanor masked the fact that he and his wife, an heiress, were absorbing stock losses that would amount to $2 million.[33] So when he took his jaunty stroll across the Exchange floor at 1:30 P.M., it was an extraordinary performance. He went to the trading booth for U.S. Steel and bid 205 for twenty thousand shares—topping the previous bid by several points. As news of his purchase spread, the market seemed to steady for a time.

The choice of U.S. Steel, a Morgan ward, was no accident: as gentleman bankers, Lamont and the others felt they should support companies they had sponsored. It later turned out Whitney had bought only two hundred shares of Steel and pulled his order when others jumped in. At another fifteen or twenty trading posts, he repeated his bidding, placing almost $20 million in orders. By day's end, only half the bankers' money was actually spent. Yet their lingering magic was such that the market briefly rallied that afternoon. It was the last conjuring trick of the 1920s.

At the end of the trading day, the bankers regrouped for a second meeting and designated Lamont their spokesman. He was mobbed by newsmen shouting questions. Dangling his pince-nez, he came up with the most memorable understatement in American financial history: "There has been a little distress selling on the Stock Exchange."[34] Although often mocked, the line was actually a reply to a sarcastic reporter who asked whether Lamont had noticed the selling on the Exchange that day. Lamont blandly blamed the decline on a "technical condition" and spoke of "air pockets" in the market. In a phrase of incomparable ambiguity, he said the market was "susceptible to betterment."[35] These hand-holding sessions with reporters continued for weeks and made Lamont a celebrity. He leapt to the cover of *Time* magazine.

Almost at once, Wall Street began to issue bravely hopeful statements. The silver-lining specialists appeared in force. That night, the retail brokers met at the brokerage house of Hornblower and Weeks and pronounced the market "technically in better condition than it has been in months."[36] The headline in the *Wall Street Journal* the next morning featured not the crash but the rescue: "BANKERS HALT STOCK DEBACLE: 2-HOUR SELLING DELUGE STOPPED AFTER CONFERENCE AT MORGAN'S OFFICE: $1,000,000,000 FOR SUPPORT."[37] The bankers asked Hoover to plug stocks as a cheap buy. Instead, he disgorged his well-known platitude: "The fundamental business of the country, that is production and distribution of commodities, is on a sound and prosperous basis."[38] The market staggered through Friday and Saturday morning trading without a fresh crisis.

The 1929 crash unfolded in two stages, with a weekend in between. On Sunday, the mood was grim as tourist buses made ghoulish swings through Wall Street to see where the crash had occurred. Those who pondered Hoover's statement over the weekend apparently rushed to sell on Monday. American Telephone and Telegraph dropped 34 points, and General Electric 47 points. Both the market and public faith in bankers were collapsing.

On Tragic Tuesday, October 29, investors looked back on Black Thursday as a halcyon time. On this worst day in market history, the ticker lagged two and a half hours behind. More than sixteen million shares changed hands—a record that would stand for forty years. By day's end, the two-day damage had dragged share prices down by nearly 25 percent. Buying didn't dry up this time: it simply disappeared. At the rally's peak, White Sewing Machine sold for 48, then slumped to 11 on Monday. On Tuesday, when no buyers surfaced, an alert messenger bought shares at $1 apiece. When commuters entered Grand Central Terminal that evening, newsboys hawking papers shouted, "Read 'em and weep!"

Unlike Black Thursday, Tragic Tuesday exposed the bankers' frailty. They were little men standing before a tidal wave. The *New York Times* wrote, "Banking support, which would have been impressive and successful under ordinary circumstances, was swept violently aside, as block after block of stock, tremendous in proportions, deluged the market."[39] Where rumors on Black Thursday were hopeful—men winked and talked of the "organized support" taking control—Tragic Tuesday was marked by reports of bankers dumping stocks to save themselves.

Lamont now faced a more hostile group of reporters. He had to deny reports that his group was sabotaging the market for profit. "The group has continued and will continue in a cooperative way to support the market and has not been a seller of stocks."[40] With his usual cunning phraseology, he said the situation "retained hopeful features."[41] In a vain effort to bolster confidence, U.S. Steel and American Can declared extra dividends.

As if expressing a new bunker mentality, the Stock Exchange governors met on Tragic Tuesday in a basement room under the Exchange floor. When Lamont and George Whitney tried to slip in unnoticed, they were briefly detained by guards. The main topic was whether to shut the market. Richard Whitney thought a closing would unsettle the public and create a black market on the curb, as happened at the outbreak of World War I. He also feared it would create chaos among banks with heavy call loans to brokers. At various points in 1929, Morgans had $100 million outstanding in such loans, with stocks pledged as collateral. How would Wall Street banks and brokers function with stock collateral frozen?

As in 1987, the group decided to shorten Exchange hours instead. An excuse was at hand: overworked clerks were haggard from lack of sleep; shorter hours would let them catch up on paperwork. Instead of ringing at ten o'clock, the opening gong would sound at noon on Thursday, and the Exchange would be shut Friday and Saturday. Richard Whitney left a graphic impression of the basement meeting: "The office they met in was never designed for large meetings of this sort, with the result that most of the governors were compelled to stand or to sit on tables. As the meeting progressed, panic was raging overhead on the floor. . . . The feelings of those present were revealed by their habit of continually lighting cigarettes, taking a puff or two, putting them out and lighting new ones—a practice which soon made the narrow room blue with smoke."[42]

In the weeks after Tragic Tuesday, rumor mills produced tales of clandestine lunchtime meetings in the Stock Exchange basement. One version had Lamont and Richard Whitney spying on traders through a periscope. Whitney continued to walk about with a rakish air, exuding confidence, although he later spoke of the "war atmosphere" of those days. Before emerging into public, he would exhort his associates, "Now get your smiles on boys!"[43] As it happens, the real remedial action that was taken came not from the old Wall Street club but by a force new to financial panics—the Federal Reserve.

In late October, Jack, back from Europe, chaired a meeting at the Morgan Library with George Harrison, Ben Strong's successor at the New York Fed. Son of an army officer, a graduate of Yale and Harvard Law School, Harrison was a handsome, pipe-smoking man who limped as a result of a boyhood accident. An activist in the Strong mold, Harrison lowered interest rates and pumped in billions of dollars in credit to buoy banks with heavy loans to brokers. "The Stock Exchange should stay open at all costs," Harrison announced. "Gentlemen, I am ready to provide all the reserve funds that may be needed."[44] Rebuked by Fed governor Roy A. Young in Washington, Harrison courageously replied that the world was "on fire" and that his actions were "done and can't be undone." He bought up to $100 million in government bonds per day and made sure Wall Street banks had adequate reserves with which to deal with the emergency. In scale and sophistication, his postcrash actions made Pierpont's in 1907 look antediluvian in comparison, for he could expand credit as needed. Harrison confirmed the principle of government responsibility in financial panics.

The days after the crash were a great time for pep talks and false bravado. The redoubtable Irving Fisher found it consoling that weak investors were shaken from the market and that stocks now rested in stronger hands. He described the postcrash market as a bargain counter for shrewd investors.[45] From the fastness of his Pocantico Hills estate, John D. Rockefeller issued an oracular statement: "Believing that fundamental conditions of the country are sound . . . my son and I have for some days been purchasing sound common stocks."[46] Rockefeller's words were relayed to Eddie Cantor, then starring in *Whoopee* on Broadway and a victim of the collapse of the Goldman Sachs Trading Corporation. Cantor replied, "Sure, who else had any money left?"[47]

Eddie Cantor later filed a $100-million suit against Goldman, Sachs.

This was probably less damaging to the firm's future than his new vaudeville routine. In it, a stooge walked out on stage violently wringing a lemon. "Who are you?" Cantor asked. "I'm the margin clerk for Goldman, Sachs," the stooge replied. So many suits were filed against Goldman, Sachs that during listless Depression days brokers with a taste for black humor would call up the firm and ask for the Litigation Department. From now on, even humor would puncture Wall Street's pretensions. The age had come to an abrupt, calamitous end. The crash was a blow to Wall Street's pride and its profits. As Bernard Baruch later said, "The stereotype of bankers as conservative, careful, prudent individuals was shattered in 1929."[48]

CHAPTER SEVENTEEN

DEPRESSION

• •

•

A FTER the crash, Herbert Hoover wasn't quite as passive or impotent as legend suggests. He announced tax cuts and public works programs and asked utilities to embark on new construction. Bringing business leaders to the White House, he extracted pledges to maintain wages and thus avert an erosion of purchasing power. Henry Ford cut car prices and boosted workers' wages to $7 a day. Meanwhile, the New York Fed orchestrated a swift series of interest-rate cuts that more than halved its discount rate, to 2½ percent, by June of 1930. Clearly, the principle of government action to ease economic misfortune was enshrined before the New Deal.

Wall Street tried to face the crash with stoic fortitude and treat it as a stern but salutary lesson. Everybody sounded philosophical. In late 1929, Lamont described the crash as an unpleasant warning of no lasting harm: "I cannot but feel that it may after all be a valuable lesson and the experience gained may be turned to our future advantage. . . . There has never been a time when business as a whole was on a sounder basis."[1] This reasonable approach reflected a belief that the financial trouble had ended; in fact, it had just begun.

Never entirely comfortable with the radical, tax-cutting Republicanism of the twenties, Morgan partners hoped the crash presaged a return to more conservative economics. They had been uneasy with the speculative debauch of the twenties and welcomed a return to thrift and hard work. Dwight Morrow, then a New Jersey senator, agreed that "there is something about too much prosperity that ruins the fiber of the people."[2] Russell Leffingwell viewed the slowdown as a "healthy purge" after a seven-year bacchanalia: "The remedy is for people to stop watching the ticker, listening to the radio, drinking bootleg gin, and dancing to jazz . . . and return to the old economics and prosperity based upon saving and working."[3] Such comments savored of puritans punishing the wicked. Treasury Secretary Andrew Mellon, who had ducked a leadership role after the crash, now said of the downturn, "It will purge the rottenness out of the system. People will work harder, live a more moral life."[4] Keynes, however warned that such austerity would only deepen the Depression.

Many of the people who voiced these soothing statements were living off the riches of the 1920s. Although Morgan partners suffered huge losses, they still boasted wealth of embarrassing proportions. At Christmas 1928, each partner had received a bonus of $1 million. In 1929, Jack's son Junius moved into Salutation, a forty-room stone mansion on an island beside his father's island estate. Even as stock brokers jumped from building ledges in October, workmen in Bath, Maine, rushed to complete *Corsair IV*, a six-thousand-horsepower yacht, 343 feet long, with gross tonnage of 2,181. Reputed to be the biggest private yacht of all time, a floating palace with elevators, beamed ceilings, India teak paneling, mahogany armchairs, and fireplaces, it required a crew of over fifty and cost Jack an estimated $2.5 million. If the price tag was stupendous, it amounted to only about half the annual income that Jack took from the bank in the late 1920s.

Jack Morgan spent the Christmas of 1929 with his fifteen grandchildren at Matinicock Point, and it was a warm, happy time. "It really resembled nothing so much as some of the families of pigs I have seen on the farm," he said.[5] In the new year, he looked forward to a cruise to Palestine with his friend Dr. Cosmo Lang, the archbishop of Canterbury.

What made the postcrash lull tolerable on Wall Street was that a political backlash hadn't yet gathered force. Nobody yet demanded radical overhauls of the system. That December, learning of proposed staff cuts at the American Museum of Natural History, Jack covered the budget shortfall; the munificence of rich men still meant something. Soon, though, the Depression would unleash a popular fury against bankers that would rage for years.

Wall Street perhaps had better excuses for postcrash complacency in 1929 than in 1987. America boasted a trade and budget surplus and was finishing the most triumphant economic decade in its history. In the world economy, it was the ascendant power and the leading creditor nation. J. P. Morgan and Company was so flush with cash that it was giving large gifts to its less fortunate London and Paris partners in the late 1920s. The age can be forgiven some of its hubris.

The speculative mood didn't immediately disappear. Those with money who rushed in to buy stocks were at first vindicated: by early 1930, the market had regained much lost ground. People chattered about a little bull market. Business investment rose, accompanied by an upturn in car and home sales. On March 7, 1930, President Hoover proclaimed: "All the evidence indicates that the worst effects of the Crash upon unemployment will have passed during the next sixty days."[6]

In April, however, the stock market began to slide, then dropped in May and June with each new Hoover expression of hope. Unlike the spectacular downward swoops of the previous October, the deterioration in prices was small and steady but unrelenting. In mid-1932, the market would bottom out at one-tenth of its September 1929 peak. So the yokels who sold in terror after the Crash fared better, in the long run, than the canny traders who scouted for bargains.

We shall never know whether wise economic management might have averted the Great Depression. But two events led to a frightful, downward momentum. On June 17, 1930, ignoring the pleas of over a thousand American economists, President Hoover took up six gold pens and signed the Hawley-Smoot Tariff Act. Its heavy tariffs would account for more than half the price of some imports. The day before Hoover signed the bill, the stock market, in nervous anticipation, suffered its worst day since Tragic Tuesday.

As a major sponsor of foreign loans, the House of Morgan was naturally dismayed. If debtors couldn't export goods to the United States, how would they ever earn foreign exchange and pay off loans? "I almost went down on my knees to beg Herbert Hoover to veto the asinine Hawley-Smoot tariff," Lamont declared.[7] He soon referred to the world trading system as an insane asylum.[8] Apprehensively, America's most international bank watched the rise of a new economic nationalism. It would dismantle the structure of free trade and free flow of capital that the House of Morgan, along with Montagu Norman and Ben Strong, had struggled to create in the twenties. Within two years, two dozen countries would retaliate against the Hawley-Smoot tariff by raising their own tariffs and slashing U.S. imports. The age of "beggar thy neighbor" economics had begun.

The second great mid-1930 blunder was made by the Federal Reserve Board in Washington: it ended the liberal provision of credit and shrank the money supply. This was part of an attempt to rein in the New York Fed and end its backdoor diplomacy with European ministries. Treasury Secretary Andrew Mellon wanted higher interest rates to stop the flow of gold to Europe. Many at the Fed saw austerity as a bitter but necessary medicine. "The consequences of such an economic debauch are inevitable," said the Philadelphia Fed governor. "Can they be corrected and removed by cheap money? We do not believe that they can."[9] By the second half of 1930, the postcrash calm was gone. That fall, Hoover complained to Lamont about bear raids, short selling, and other unpatriotic assaults against national pride. The following year would be the worst in stock market history.

While the Fed had assumed responsibility for the health of the entire financial system after the 1929 crash, the House of Morgan still played a part in specific, smaller crises. The Fed had no obligation to rescue individuals, banks, or companies; its concerns were more general. The crash's aftermath revealed much about Morgan priorities. While claiming to represent the public interest, the firm actually represented its clients, cronies, and fellow bankers. Part of its power had always stemmed from its fidelity to Wall Street friends, its generosity in making loans to bankers and other financial houses. This was strikingly demonstrated after the crash.

Take, for instance, the case of Charles E. Mitchell, chairman of the National City Bank. Right before the crash, Mitchell had put together a deal to merge with the Corn Exchange; if he had succeeded, he would have produced the world's largest bank, surpassing even the Midland Bank in London. Since the deal was to be effected with National City shares, Mitchell needed to maintain their price at $450. During the crash, the price plunged through this floor, and even furious buying by the National City Company, the bank's securities affiliate, couldn't sustain it. On his way to work, Mitchell stopped by 23 Wall and walked out with a $12-million personal loan, secured by his own National City stock. When he later failed to meet payments, the House of Morgan temporarily became the second largest stockholder in National City. Later Mitchell said of Morgans, "That firm stood at the very peak as to ethics, understanding, and leadership."[10] Yet however laudable in terms of loyalty, it was a reckless loan from a financial standpoint.

Loyalty to clients was always the vice of the House of Morgan. Sometimes it got in so deep it couldn't get out. After the crash, the Van Sweringen brothers, those financial acrobats of the 1920s, suddenly lost their balance. Their overly indebted railroads were among the worst crash performers. Much like William C. Durant with General Motors in 1920, the Van Sweringens kept buying Alleghany stock on its way down. Using borrowed money, they only augmented their losses. They ignored polite warnings from Morgans to stop their rash purchase of more railroads, including the huge Missouri Pacific. Buying on credit had become a Van Sweringen habit.

The Alleghany shares feverishly bid up in the frothy days of early 1929 now led the market down in the autumn of 1930. They fell from 56 to 10 in just two months. On the evening of October 23, 1930, Oris and Mantis Van Sweringen met at Tom Lamont's East Seventieth Street townhouse along with representatives of Guaranty Trust. The short, moon-faced brothers were $40 million in hock to their broker. Having sponsored $200 million in securities in their behalf, Morgans and Guaranty felt bound to prop them up. Lamont was pessimistic about the prospects of railroads. He was already telling Hoover how two hundred affluent passengers were arriving daily by air in New York City. Yet he also feared a domino effect among Wall Street brokers who dealt with the brothers.

The two banks led a syndicate that furnished a $40-million rescue loan for the Van Sweringens. The rescue was handled with a delicacy and secrecy that seldom accompanies personal bankruptcy. The Van Sweringens would remain as figureheads so that nobody would suspect their true plight. They were rewarded for their profligacy with a personal allowance of $100,000 a year. In the words of Matthew Josephson, "The Van Sweringens' personal insolvency during 5 years was one of the best kept secrets in Wall Street."[11] The following year, when the brothers missed payments on their loans, Morgans and Guaranty Trust foreclosed on their Alleghany Railroad empire. Ultimately Alleghany stock would fall to 37½ cents per share.

As a lender of last resort, the House of Morgan favored like-minded institutions of similar character and background. Kidder, Peabody was just such a firm. It didn't hustle business or steal clients and always played by Morgan rules. In 1930, it was hit by multiple blows. The Italian government removed $8 million in deposits, and the new Bank for International Settlements instructed Kidder to switch big sums to a Swiss bank. This led to another rescue at Jack Morgan's home, chaired by George Whitney, who had started his career as a Kidder clerk. The House of Morgan arranged a $10-million line of credit. Under Whitney's tutelage, the old Kidder, Peabody was folded. Whitney brought in his friends Edwin Webster, Chandler Hovey, and Albert H. Gordon to take over the company's name and goodwill. "Incidentally, we are slowly making the grade socially," Gordon reported to the elder Webster. "Yesterday for the first time Morgan invited us to tea on our way out from the almost daily conference."[12]

Unstinting in serving its friends, the House of Morgan could be heartless to those whose image didn't fit the preferred profile. This became apparent with the failure of the Bank of United States on December 11, 1930. With 450,000 depositors, it was New York's fourth largest deposit bank. In general, the crash and subsequent deflation had damaged the collateral behind bank loans. From a rate of 60 bank failures a month in early 1930, the figure snowballed to 254 in November and 344 in December of 1930. There were over a thousand bank failures for the year. The failure of the Bank of United States was the largest thus far and threatened more general ruin.

But this bank wasn't a high-class operation. Its Jewish owners had chosen its grand name in an effort to fool its Jewish immigrant customers into thinking it had government support. In the lobby hung a large oil portrait of the U.S. Capitol, reinforcing the misleading message. A proposed rescue plan for the Bank of United States got a cool reception on Wall Street, even after Lieutenant Governor Herbert H. Lehman, the state banking authorities, and the New York Fed all pleaded for it. The regulators wanted to merge the Bank of United States with three other banks, backed by a $30-million loan from the Wall Street banks.

At an emotional meeting, Joseph A. Broderick, the state banking chief, warned that if the bankers rejected the rescue plan, it might drag down ten other banks. One in ten New York families using bank accounts would be stranded. As the Wall Street bankers sat stony-faced, Broderick reminded them how they had just rescued Kidder, Peabody and how they had banded together years before to save Guaranty Trust. But they refused to save the Jewish bank, pulling out of their $30-million commitment at the last minute. "I asked them if their decision to drop the plan was still final," Broderick recalled. "They told me it was. Then I warned them they were making the most colossal mistake in the banking history of New York."[13] The biggest bank failure in American history, the Bank of United States bankruptcy fed a psychology of fear that already gripped depositors across the country.

The failure of the Bank of United States has been attributed to anti-Semitism among Wall Street bankers. At the time, there were few commercial banks owned by Jews, Manufacturers Trust being the only other important one in New York. It is impossible to verify whether anti-Semitism stopped the bankers from rescuing the Bank of United States. But Morgan records show that its clientele's Judaism was very much in the partners' minds. When informing Morgan Grenfell of events in New York, Lamont's son Tommy noted that it was patronized largely by foreigners and Jews.[14] Russell Leffingwell described it as "an uptown bank with many branches and a large clientele among our Jewish population of small merchants, and persons of small means and small education, from whom all its management was drawn."[15] Their attitude was shortsighted, for the bank's failure shook confidence across America. It was a failure that could have been easily avoided by the proposed merger.

Had it not been for the large number of depositors, the Bank of United States would not have deserved to survive. Its securities affiliate had sponsored shoddy stocks and issued misleading prospectuses, and had been manipulated by the bank's own offices. Two of its owners were jailed for loose banking practices. One, bank president Bernard K. Marcus, was the uncle of Roy Cohn, who always blamed the bank's failure on an anti-Semitic plot. Even banking superintendent Broderick was indicted for not having shut the bank sooner. (He was acquitted, after two trials.) To have to bail out such a bank undoubtedly grated on the patrician bankers. But with so many Morgan rescues occurring in those years, all backed up with high-flown rhetoric about saving the banking system, it's hard to believe religion wasn't a major factor behind Wall Street's refusal to act. Hundreds of thousands of Jewish depositors were not worth one Charles Mitchell. Jews were always a blind spot in the Morgan vision, no less than in the days when Pierpont Morgan had vied with Jacob Schiff.

T H E City of London had reacted to the New York crash with alarm, but also with some quiet satisfaction and *schadenfreude*. After Black Thursday, the *New York Times* reported that the "selling left London's 'City' in a comfortable position saying 'I told you so.' It had been expected for a long time."[16] In many ways, London profited from the crash as investors switched funds from New York, easing the strain on British gold reserves. In 1930, there was even a brief spurt in foreign lending as London became a safe haven for investors. At the same time, the deeper prognosis for Britain remained grim. Its industry languished, its unemployment rose, and London's port was vulnerable to spreading protectionism. Several Commonwealth countries dependent on agricultural exports—Australia, Canada, and India—were hit early by the Depression, and this hurt the City.

England's real crisis, however, originated in Central Europe, just as Montagu Norman had always suspected it would. Reparations continued to burden Germany's economy and polarize its politics. In March 1930, Dr. Schacht submitted his resignation as Reichsbank president to protest additional German debt mandated by the Young Plan. Germany's day of reckoning—so feared and so long predicted—was at hand.

In the elections of September 1930, the National Socialists and the Communists scored sizable gains, and Chancellor Heinrich Brüning adopted an antireparations policy. The right wing capitalized on the reparations issue. On January 5, 1931, Dr. Schacht attended a dinner party thrown by Hermann Göring. For his tough stand on reparations, Schacht had become a great favorite of the National Socialists. At the dinner, he met Hitler and Joseph Goebbels and became a critical link between the Nazis and German big business. That spring, as political street fights broke out in Germany, pressure mounted to cast off the Versailles burden.

Into this already volatile situation came the powerful jolt of a major bank failure. On May 11, 1931, the Credit Anstalt failed. It was not only Austria's largest bank but probably the most important bank in Central Europe. A rescue plan announced by the Austrian National Bank and Rothschilds only served to alert the world to trouble and brought on a run. The disaster spread through Central Europe, collapsing Austrian and German banks. In June, Norman gave emergency credit to Austria's central bank to prop up the schilling—his swan song as a global lender of last resort. Along with an emergency loan to Germany, it marked the end of British financial leadership in the 1930s.

It was against this backdrop that Lamont telephoned Hoover on June 5, 1931, to propose a holiday on payment of war debts and reparations. Without it, he warned, there might be a European crash that could prolong America's Depression. As Lamont's files show, Hoover reacted in a grumpily defensive manner: "I will think about the matter, but politically it is quite impossible. Sitting in New York, as you do, you have no idea what the sentiment of the country at large is on these inter-governmental debts." A banker of the Diplomatic Age, Lamont didn't merely couch his argument in economic terms: he made an unashamedly political appeal. "These days you hear a lot of people whispering about sidetracking the Administration in the 1932 Convention," Lamont told Hoover. "If you were to come out with such a plan as this, these whisperings would be silenced overnight."[17] In closing, Lamont said that if the plan ever reached fruition, the bank would hide its role and let Hoover take the credit: "This is your plan and nobody else's." What a cunning fellow Lamont was when he whispered in Hoover's ear!

Treasury Secretary Mellon tried to spike the idea and dismiss the debt as Europe's mess, but Hoover had now had enough with myopic isolationism. On the evening of June 20, 1931, he telephoned Lamont at Torrey Cliff, his home on the Palisades, to say that he had just announced a one-year moratorium on war debt and reparations payments.

He knew France would be indignant at the mercy shown toward Germany and asked whether Lamont could sell the plan to the French. Lamont expressed sympathy for the French position but also reminded Hoover that they were the world's most difficult people to deal with—a recurring theme in his letters. Finally, though, he agreed to lobby the French government through the Banque de France. True to Hoover's predictions, the French thought the moratorium an Anglo-American plot to let Germany escape reparations.

The Hoover moratorium was a belated response to a crumbling world financial system. The Danat Bank, one of Germany's largest, failed on July 13, 1931. A teary-eyed Chancellor Brüning rejected a New York rescue out of fear that a bad loan to President Hindenburg's son Oskar might surface in such an operation. After the Danat failure, Germany had to shut the Berlin bourse and the city's banks. Around the world, creditors were calling in German loans. The Morgan-led bond issues for Germany and Austria, heralded with trumpet peals in the 1920s, plummeted with frightening speed. All the laborious work of that decade was coming apart.

Now the crisis shifted to London, as investors traced financial ties between Germany and England. During the summer of 1931, investors dumped sterling in massive amounts. Even without Germany, the pound was already in a parlous state. In late July 1931, a committee of bankers and economists, the May Committee, had predicted that Britain's budget deficit would widen to £120 million, with no end of red ink in sight. The committee recommended higher taxes and a 10-percent cut in the dole. A few days later, sterling cracked on world markets. The Bank of England told Philip Snowden, the chancellor of the Exchequer, that Britain had almost exhausted its foreign exchange. Despite the need for stringency, Ramsay MacDonald's Labour government was stymied in coping with the problem. With 2.5 million unemployed, the unions wouldn't surrender unemployment benefits.

A few days before the May report was published, Monty Norman left the bank "feeling queer." A year before, tired and wrung out, he had taken a two-month vacation in South America. Now haggard from overwork, the high-strung Norman was ordered to bed by doctors. When he was again ambulatory, it was recommended that he travel abroad to recover from his nervous collapse. Norman was temporarily replaced by his deputy governor, Sir Ernest Harvey. As a sterling crisis loomed, Jack Morgan and Teddy Grenfell decided to smuggle Norman out of England. Fearing he might break, the House of Morgan plotted with British authorities to place him in temporary exile. After clearing Norman's removal with Edward Peacock, a Bank of England director, Grenfell reported to New York, "M.N. has not made any progress and it has been intimated to him that he should keep away and leave No. 2 to run the show."[18] It is unclear whether the doctors were part of this scheme or whether they were invoked as a cover for the operation.

One marvels at both Morgan's imperial hauteur and the tender solicitude for Norman. The bank wished to banish him with dignity. Jack telegrammed with a gesture of royal magnanimity: if he wished, Norman could take the *Corsair IV* anywhere in Europe, North Africa, or the Far East, attended by a doctor of his own choosing. "There are rooms for six beside himself," Jack told Grenfell, "and for all the servants he could want."[19] Norman was steaming to Quebec when Jack's message came by radio, and he declined the "glorious offer." To scotch rumors of a bankers' cabal, he wanted to avoid the United States altogether. He recuperated at the Château Frontenac, where he also conferred with George Harrison. In exile, Monty was spared the need to take the ax to his beloved gold standard, and Grenfell said afterward he wouldn't have been able to withstand the strain.

The House of Morgan had helped Britain back onto the gold standard in 1925 and now underwrote a last-ditch effort to save it. Prime Minister Ramsay MacDonald and Philip Snowden knew the pound couldn't be defended without a foreign loan. New York and Paris owned most of the world's gold, and George Harrison suggested a joint U.S.-French loan. It fell to 23 Wall to keep MacDonald informed of Wall Street opinion *vis-à-vis* British chances for a credit. The messenger was Teddy Grenfell, who had triple authority—as a Bank of England director, a Conservative member of Parliament from the City, and the senior Morgan Grenfell partner. Pitiless toward Labour politicians and staunchly opposed to their program of nationalizing industry, he had a scathing opinion of MacDonald, whom he found coarse and gutless. "The only white thing about him is his liver, and the only portion of him that is not red is his blood."[20] In early August, Grenfell warned MacDonald that halfway measures wouldn't do and that a British loan from Wall Street would be dimly received unless he took courageous action and cut the budget deficit. Sensing a crisis in the offing, Grenfell tracked down the Conservative leader, Stanley Baldwin, then in France, and suggested he return to England at once.

Depending on one's viewpoint, Ramsay MacDonald's story in 1931 is either that of a farsighted prime minister who nobly sacrificed ideology to the national good or that of a blackguard who betrayed his party and platform to satisfy the foreign bankers. (There are striking parallels between MacDonald's actions and Grover Cleveland's alienation from his Democratic followers during the 1895 gold crisis.) A fiery, opinionated socialist, MacDonald had taken office in 1929 promising to fight unemployment, and he enacted unemployment benefits that became sacred to the trade unions. For all his rabble-rousing, however, he had a true-blue Englishman's faith in sterling as the medium of world finance. So his dilemma was stark in August 1931. Foreign bankers insisted that he close the budget gap as the precondition for a loan. But any such austerity talk brought outcries from Labour ministers, who saw it as a betrayal of their followers to appease rich bankers.

Speaking for Wall Street, Grenfell talked bluntly to MacDonald. "We are all getting tired of promises," he warned in mid-August."[21] Grenfell watched MacDonald warily, suspecting he would opt for expediency. As with Churchill in 1925, the Morgan partner took a rather mordant view of his target: "The P.M. is at last alarmed but he is so conceited and fluffy headed that it will be difficult to keep him up to the scratch."[22] He greatly underestimated MacDonald. When trade unions proved intransigent about cuts in unemployment benefits, MacDonald, angered by their obstinacy, was converted to Grenfell's cause. Many of his own ministers dug in their heels and resisted cuts in the dole.

The next steps in the crisis were intricate. The Bank of England sounded out the New York Fed on whether Chancellor Snowden's compromise plan for budget cuts would guarantee a Wall Street loan. MacDonald was afraid his cabinet would be offended by the idea of consulting New York bankers and wanted to test opinion covertly. George Harrison of the New York Fed referred the Bank of England to Morgans.

Throughout the crisis, J. P. Morgan and Morgan Grenfell had a secret back channel with the Bank of England. As Grenfell explained, "If the Prime Minister were to tell his Cabinet that he had already exposed his plan to foreign bankers and asked for a loan his Cabinet would be much incensed. . . . You must understand that neither Prime Minister nor his Cabinet have ever seen any of the cables between J.P. Morgan & Co. and Morgan Grenfell though many of them have been shown to Governor Norman and Deputy Governor."[23] On August 22, 1931, Harrison received a cable from the Bank of England outlining the new compromise budget that MacDonald would discuss with his cabinet on Sunday, August 23. The prime minister wished to know whether they could be sure of a New York loan if the cabinet adopted it. Harrison showed the cable to George Whitney and other Morgan partners, who had gathered at the Glen Cove home of partner Frank D. Bartow.

This backdoor intrigue set the stage for a showdown between Mac-Donald and his cabinet. That Sunday evening, the cabinet ministers paced through a warm twilight in the garden of 10 Downing Street. They had awaited New York's verdict since noon. Morgan partners pored over figures calling for £70 million in budget cuts—including a 10-percent dole cut—and an extra £60 million in taxes. Finally, at 8:45 P.M., Sir Ernest Harvey at the Bank of England called Downing Street to announce a telephone message from New York. He offered to carry it right over.

For MacDonald, the suspense must have been excruciating: his political career hinged on the message. When Harvey arrived, MacDonald tore the cable from his hand and rushed back to the cabinet. This split-second action was fraught with historic consequence, for Mac-Donald didn't stop to screen the contents of the message or even ascertain the sender's identity. He introduced it as being from nameless New York bankers. The cabinet ministers assumed, wrongly, that the message came from the New York Fed. It actually came from George Whitney and was addressed to the Bank of England, not to the cabinet.

Coming upon the cable in Morgan Grenfell's files, it is disappointing to see the blandness of this government-toppling document. It briefly expresses sympathy for a British credit but stipulates no specific budget cuts. It's a sterile document, as if the bankers who penned it were being extremely cautious. But the cabinet ministers were hot and tired, and their nerves were frayed from debate. They spied sinister meaning behind its final lines: "In the foregoing we have as always given you the precise trend of our thought. Let us know promptly as indicated above what the Government's desires are and within 24 hours we shall be able to give you our final judgment. Are we right in assuming that the programme under consideration will have the sincere approval and support of the Bank of England and the City generally and thus go a long way toward restoring international confidence in Great Britain?"[24]

When MacDonald read these words aloud, there was such a commotion in the cabinet room that Sir Ernest Harvey heard it outside, and he later recalled that "pandemonium had broken loose."[25] This last paragraph, clearly, was intended for the Bank of England alone. To those present, it awakened old fears of dark dealings between private banks in London and New York. The other stumbling block was MacDonald's apparent mention of a 10-percent dole cut. This wasn't mentioned by Morgans. Later, in reconstructing events, Grenfell told Lamont that "the Cabinet have gone on repeating . . . that the American Bankers insisted on a 10% cut. . . . If he made mention of a 10% cut as a condition MacDonald must have invented it as it does not appear in your cable."[26] The cable supports Grenfell.

MacDonald felt that he lacked the cabinet mandate to proceed with the emergency budget cuts required to restore foreign confidence in sterling. The bickering grew so fierce that at 10:20 P.M. he arrived at Buckingham Palace and laid his resignation before King George V. Looking wild and distracted, he told the king that "all was up."[27] In insisting upon the budget cuts, MacDonald set himself against powerful segments of his own party, and he now knew he had crossed some personal Rubicon. The king asked him to return to Buckingham Palace the next morning along with the opposition leaders—Stanley Baldwin of the Conservatives and Sir Herbert Samuel of the Liberals. To spread political risks and ensure passage of the cut in unemployment benefits, the king invited the three to form a coalition government. MacDonald would remain prime minister of a government that was Tory at heart.

The new government cut the budget deficit with higher taxes on gasoline, beer, tobacco, and income and lower salaries for civil servants. J. P. Morgan and Company provided a $200-million revolving line of credit, and another $200 million came from France. Unfortunately, it proved impossible to restore confidence in the pound. Many Labourites now regarded MacDonald as a traitor and were vitriolic in their criticism of him. In September, the Communists marched on Parliament and insisted that a cold-blooded bankers' "ramp," or conspiracy, had imposed unfair hardship on British workers. Unemployed workers rioted in Battersea and mounted police charged demonstrators on Oxford Street. It was widely believed that the New York Fed had brought down the government. London's *Daily Herald* featured a photograph of George Harrison on the front page, charging that a New York–led conspiracy had plotted against the British welfare state. "The *Daily Herald* to-day discloses a startling and apparently successful attempt by US bankers to dictate the internal policy of Great Britain," the headline read.[28]

One can picture Grenfell's sardonic smile as he followed this misunderstanding. To operate in the political shadows, to pass wraithlike through a crisis and exert an unseen influence on large events—for Grenfell, these were the perfections of his art. When he was pumped for information in Parliament, he played the "village idiot," he said. He confided to Lamont, "I believe it is the opinion of the late Cabinet that

George Whitney's long telephone message. . . . was a message from the Federal Reserve Bank. For the present, therefore, the fall of Ramsay MacDonald will be put down to the domineering action of poor George Harrison, who will not I imagine lose his sleep in consequence."[29]

Did the House of Morgan bring down the Labour government? MacDonald himself exonerated the bankers and stressed the need to maintain the place of sterling in world finance. Morgan records confirm that the bank refrained from recommending specific budget cuts. Yet it was no secret that Wall Street wanted the dole cuts. And the broad body of American bankers had a veto over any big British loan on Wall Street. There was no hidden Morgan agenda, only the usual bankers' mentality of favoring austerity and cuts in spending. It was Britain's choice to defend the gold standard, which placed it in the thrall of foreign investors. Morgans merely expressed the consensus among bankers.

A few days after the Sunday cabinet meeting, Lamont spoke by phone with Hoover, who gave qualified approval to the British credit. Since the large credit would enlist 110 American banks, Hoover warned that Wall Street would be accused of funneling money to Britain at a time of American distress.[30] Not for the first time, small-town America looked askance at Morgan assistance to Britain, even as Britain's left accused American bankers of treacherous interference.

The *coup de grâce* to Britain's gold standard came in September 1931, when naval units at Invergordon, Scotland, struck against proposed pay cuts. This little mutiny terrified foreign investors, who saw it as proof that the British public would never accept an austerity budget. Sterling crashed again. Monty Norman was sailing home from Canada on September 21, 1931, when England went off gold. Hence, it would no longer redeem sterling for gold at a fixed rate: the old imperial fantasy was dead, and the pound fell a shocking 30 percent. Keynes exulted over gold's demise: "There are few Englishmen who do not rejoice at the breaking of our gold fetters."[31] But Monty Norman, arriving at Liverpool, was stunned that the edifice he built was shattered. He took the train down to Euston Station and had a temper tantrum when he arrived at the bank. Yet his associates, Harvey and Peacock, believed that he would have done the same thing had he been in charge. Twenty-five countries followed Britain off gold in a rush of competitive devaluations.

In an Associated Press interview from London, Jack Morgan applauded Britain's departure from gold. When Lamont read this in New York, he was thunderstruck. Hadn't they just enlisted over one hundred banks to save that gold standard? And wouldn't those banks now feel betrayed? Lamont, who almost never got angry, was beside himself.

Now came the moment that was destined to occur—when the power relationship at the bank was revealed and even Jack Morgan would feel the sting of Lamont's pen. They had for some time a tacit deal: Jack would be semiretired figurehead, and Lamont would retain executive control. Now in his early sixties, Jack was an absentee boss who preferred golfing and yachting; he was aging and no longer traveled on the *Corsair* without a surgeon aboard. In most banking matters, control had slipped from his grasp.

Lamont had never challenged Jack openly. Now, in his fury, he confronted him directly. So unprecedented was the accusatory letter he sent that he cosigned it with Charles Steele, the other major partner in terms of capital share and an old-timer from Pierpont's days. Steele was a friend of Jack's and was regarded around the bank as a pleasant, wise old man.

It may be said that this letter of September 25, 1931, marks the moment when the House of Morgan ceased operating as a family bank. Lamont wrote: "The point that we must make to you—a point that we fear you little realize—is to have you know fully the uncomfortable position in which the New York firm has been placed before the whole American world and the public generally. What the banks here, without exception, fail to understand, is why this enormous credit operation should have been permitted to blow up in our faces over night so to speak."

Lamont reminded Jack of the solemn pledges to preserve the gold standard that were made to participating banks:

> It was upon that prophecy, made wreckage in just three weeks to the day, that we were able to complete the group for the credit. There was, as we told you at the time, great reluctance upon the part of many banks to join in the credit. . . . Now the outcome has manifestly and inevitably diminished our prestige, not only publicly but with the American banking community which has for years so largely supported us in our efforts for the preservation here of British credit. And this is a fact that every partner of the firm, which (under you and your Father before you) has built up its American reputation upon careful judgment and prudent dealing, must keep in the forefront of his mind for a long time to come. . . .
>
> Now, we have said our say about the situation over here, and will

try not to allude to the subject again. But with you so far away, it has been we have thought, quite important to acquaint you with the unpleasant facts which have come to us all.[32]

Ten years before, Lamont would never have dared this. He had always dealt with Jack gingerly so that he would never lose face. Now, however, Lamont's money and position gave him incontestable power. Still, nobody confronted a Morgan without grave anxiety. At one point in the letter, Lamont gave Jack an out: he hinted that the AP quote must have come at the end of a long interview and he closed the letter "with much love from us all," signing it "Faithfully." Lamont knew the letter was uniquely candid and bare-knuckled. After posting it, he telephoned Jack to say no blame was intended and that he, Lamont, would have acted the same under the circumstances. Yet the letter showed that a palace revolution had taken place at the House of Morgan and that the Morgan family had surrendered its absolute power. From that time onward, the influence of the Morgan family would steadily diminish within the House of Morgan and then all but disappear.

A S the political skies darkened in 1931, Tom Lamont seemed blind to the spread of political extremism and militarism around the world. This was partly a reflection of his innate optimism, his almost instinctive faith in the future. He kept thinking the Depression couldn't get any worse, that the world would suddenly return to its senses, that the dictators would be held in check. The gregarious Lamont often found it hard to credit people's malevolence and was reluctant to probe beneath their reassuring smiles.

This blind spot was especially apparent with sovereign clients, where a banker's self-interest bolstered his preference for looking on the bright side of things. Partisan in behalf of clients, he tried to keep their reputations as unblemished as that of the House of Morgan itself. Their good name was especially vital in the Depression's volatile market for foreign bonds. Unfortunately, a concern with the financial standing of foreign states could slip over into questionable dealings with them. In extreme cases in the 1930s, the House of Morgan would function as an unfettered government in its own right, conducting a secret foreign policy at odds with that of Washington.

As fiscal agent for the imperial Japanese government in the late 1920s, Lamont had devotedly served his client. For a Western banker, he had achieved remarkable, unheard-of triumphs. After the mammoth earthquake loan, he had floated loans for Tokyo, Yokohama, and Ōsaka, advised on a merger between Tokyo Electric Power and Tokyo Electric Light, mediated between the Bank of Japan and the New York Fed, and extended a $25-million credit that restored Japan to the gold standard in January 1930. On the eve of the crash, the House of Morgan was exploring a possible working link with the House of Mitsui, talks that enjoyed official Japanese patronage. When it came to Japanese business, Lamont took great pride in his accomplishments.

His early faith in Japan was understandable. When he first visited in 1920, Japan stood on the brink of more than ten years of liberal, pro-Western party rule. He developed distinguished and cultured friends, especially Junnosuke Inouye, the commanding figure of Japanese finance, with whom he corresponded frequently. Inouye was finance minister for a third time after 1929. Humane and courageous, he was known for his conciliatory views on foreign affairs and was often at loggerheads with the army. He represented the enlightened antimilitarist forces in Japan. At Inouye's request, Lamont would lobby the New York press and argue Japan's case. In 1928, after meeting with editors of the *New York Times,* he told his friend, "I also told them of the patient and tolerant attitude of your people toward China and the Chinese. . . . It therefore is a matter of satisfaction to me to see how fair and sound the *Times* has been."[33]

The House of Morgan attained peak involvement in Japan just as that nation's experiment with liberal rule began to crumble. Following a wave of bank failures and the stock market closing in 1927, it slipped into a depression before most Western countries. That year, Japan was enraged by China's boycott of its goods in protest of foreign encroachment—a slap at national pride that Japan would invoke during the Manchurian invasion. In 1930, the Morgan-assisted restoration of the gold standard, under Inouye's aegis, proved a masterpiece of bad timing. It made exports expensive just as world trade contracted. When Depression-plagued America economized on luxury clothes, Japanese silk exports plunged. Silk was still a staple of Japan's economy, with two of every five families drawing income from it. Poverty spread throughout the countryside, breeding a vicious new strain of rural nationalism. Rice prices also tumbled. The budding Japanese export boom was blighted by Western protectionism, feeding xenophobia. These economic setbacks enhanced the power of the militarists, who blamed foreign powers for Japan's troubles. Militarism would be bloodily manifested in Manchuria.

The Japanese had long coveted Manchuria, that resource-rich northeastern corner of China. Whenever problems beset Japanese society—whether overpopulation, too great a reliance on foreign raw materials, or the need for new export markets—militarists saw China as the solution. They claimed Manchuria almost as a matter of divine right. China was still fragmented and chaotic, with warlords ruling parts of the country, and it appeared to be easy prey for aggressors. It was weakened by a civil war that had culminated in 1927 with Chiang Kai-shek's defeat of the Communist rebels under Mao Tse-tung. By treaty with China, Japan controlled the South Manchuria Railway and even stationed a garrison in the region. This treaty gave the Japanese militarists a legitimate cover behind which to carry out their plunder. Japan's Kwantung army plotted to use Manchuria as the base for military expansion in China.

In many ways, the House of Morgan shared Japan's jaundiced view of the Chinese, a common one in Western financial circles. China was unpopular on Wall Street and in the City. It was prone to default and adept at playing foreign bankers off against each other. Ever since the abortive China consortium under Woodrow Wilson, Lamont had looked upon the Chinese as wily and duplicitous. He perceived them less as victims of foreign intruders than as two-faced opportunists.

It was an easy attitude to assume. Japan was a major Morgan client, and no business came from China, which was still in default on a substantial portion of its foreign debt. (National City Bank, on the other hand, did a thriving business in China, which generated almost one-third of the bank's profits in 1930.) So Lamont was quick to find merit in Japanese claims that Manchuria was economically indispensable, lay well within her sphere of influence, provided a buffer against bolshevism, and had been won with Japanese blood and treasure in the Russo-Japanese War of 1905. With billions of yen invested in Manchuria and millions of Japanese living there, some nationalists saw the region as a simple extension of Japan.

In mid-1931, while the West was distracted by the Credit Anstalt failure and the sterling crisis, the Kwantung army set in motion a plot to seize Mukden and other Manchurian towns. On September 18, it launched a surprise raid against Chinese barracks in Mukden; by the next day, the city had fallen to the Japanese. As a pretext for this aggression, the Japanese military manufactured stories of Chinese assaults against the Japanese-controlled South Manchuria Railway—stories that were later exposed as fraudulent or exaggerated. Emboldened by popular support in Japan, the military flouted civilian officials, such as Inouye and Foreign Minister Kijuro Shidehara, who opposed the use of force. Japan's Foreign Office was afraid that if it tried to rein in the Kwantung Army, it might face an armed revolt in the ranks. As fifteen thousand Japanese troops swarmed across Manchuria, diplomats lamely said that the moves were temporary and that the troops would be evacuated shortly. As historian Richard Storry said, these were "weeks of public embarrassment and secret humiliation for the Wakatsuki government."[34]

Stunned by the Mukden raid, Secretary of State Henry L. Stimson swiftly protested to Japan, and Hoover later called it "an act of rank aggression."[35] Financial markets clamored for an explanation. As finance minister, the proud, dignified Inouye had to issue a statement. He was in a precarious spot, for he had spearheaded cabinet opposition to reinforcing troops in Manchuria. He was also identified with demands for cuts in the defense budget, which earned him the lasting enmity of the military (much as Dr. Hjalmar Schacht's faith in old-fashioned balanced budgets would finally doom him with the Nazis).

Inouye consoled financial markets with an amazingly artful statement about Mukden. The *New York Times* printed it verbatim on October 22 in a dispatch with a Tokyo dateline. Entitled "INOUYE SAYS JAPAN IS EAGER TO RETIRE," it became the statement that defined Japan's position for Western financial markets. Observant readers must have been struck by its clever analogies to the Panama Canal, its quoting of Daniel Webster, and its sure feel for American sensibilities:

A clear understanding of the present state of affairs in Manchuria shows that the question is simply one of self defense. A long, narrow strip of territory, along which runs the vital nerve called the South Manchuria Railway, is and has been by treaty arrangements since the Russo-Japanese War of 1904–5 under the complete administration of Japan. By treaty with Russia, duly recognized and adopted by China, Japan administers this "South Manchuria Railway Zone"—polices and protects it much as the United States Government polices and protects the Panama Canal Zone.

On the 18th of September last, a night attack was made on this zone by regular Chinese troops, and the railway line was destroyed. It was evidently necessary for Japan to take strong and immediate steps. When points under the protection of one's army are invaded by regular troops, and the extent of the threatened invasion is utterly unknown, the obvious means of self defense is to proceed at once to the headquarters of the offending troops. The emergency was one which, in Mr. Webster's classic words, was 'instant, overwhelming, leaving no choice of means, and no moment for deliberation.'

The middle section of the statement portrays Japan as saving Manchuria from anarchy. It brushes aside as "minor military measures" the actions taken at Mukden. The closing is forceful:

> In the final analysis, there is nothing in the situation that should create a war and the whole affair has been magnified beyond reason in being deemed an actual danger to the peace of the world. The Japanese, as repeatedly stated, have no intention whatsoever of making war on China. On the contrary, the Japanese Government and people entertain the friendliest feelings towards the Chinese. They are probably more anxious than any other nation of the earth could possibly be, to maintain friendly relations with the Chinese.[36]

The press release was actually drafted by Tom Lamont. It was issued, with only cosmetic changes, by Japan's Ministry of Finance. (The preceding is quoted from the original in Lamont's files.) The Japanese wanted Lamont to release the statement himself, but he replied that Morgans would be thought biased and might offend the Chinese—an understatement. Perhaps he also feared his reputation among American liberals would be blackened by any revelation of his authorship; as a former champion of the League of Nations, he probably didn't want to side publicly with an aggressor. To assuage the Japanese, he explained that if Inouye "will let me know what day he plans to issue the statement, I will arrange to have it gain extra publicity here."[37]

Lamont now found himself in stark opposition to Washington's policy and faced the dilemma always latent in his role as a banker *cum* diplomat. Why did he conspire with a foreign power in a military action condemned by the U.S. government and the League of Nations? Could he have accepted, at face value, Japan's story about Manchuria? Reporters in China pointed out that versions of the Mukden incident originated with Japan's military and were suspect. There were also widespread suspicions of a staged incident, a premeditated invasion. As the London *Times* said on September 21, the Japanese army, three days before taking Mukden, had conducted "something like a dress rehearsal" for the invasion, and "though it is reported that the incident of the South Manchuria Railway was the cause of the developments, the truth is that the whole movement was on foot before the alleged incident occurred."[38] There was, in short, plenty of evidence to give a reasonable man pause. Add to this the clear public impression that the cabinet was being duped by the army, and Lamont's alacrity is puzzling.

Cynicism toward China certainly explains much of the Morgan sympathy for the Mukden attack. Russell Leffingwell, in a hot-blooded letter to Walter Lippmann, said the indignation over Mukden was entirely misplaced. "It is grotesque for the League or for America to interfere on the side of Chinese raiders and revolutionaries, who have kept their people in war and fear and misery all these long years; and on the side of red Russia; and against the side of Japan, who in pursuance of her treaty rights has been keeping order in Manchuria and maintaining the only safe-asylum open to the fear-ridden Chinese." He hoped the Japanese would "thumb their noses" at any League of Nations or U.S. protest against its action.[39]

Along with his secret work for Mussolini, the Mukden incident is probably the most disturbing episode in Lamont's career (although nobody knew about it then). Was he trying to impress the Japanese with elite Morgan services? Or was he simply trying to maintain the value of Japanese securities? He undoubtedly wanted to shore up Inouye's tenuous position in the government. The finance minister had to demonstrate to the military that he wouldn't betray or work against it. In fact, in November, Lamont warned the Japanese that if Inouye were expelled from the cabinet—as the military favored—there would be a "distinct chill" on Wall Street and in the City.[40] But if Inouye felt a need to appease the military, why did Lamont join him?

As with Mussolini, Lamont was going beyond public relations to something approaching propaganda for a foreign power. It was a strange new application of the Gentleman Banker's Code of absolute loyalty to one's clients. Any banker could underwrite securities, but only Lamont could lobby politicians, shape newspaper editorials, and sway public opinion. The Mukden press release exposed the dangers in having bankers act like politicians and adopt the same proprietary feeling toward foreign governments as toward industrial concerns. It pointed up the perils of blurring politics and finance in the Diplomatic Age.

If Lamont were truly taken in by Mukden, then he was soon rudely stripped of his illusions. In December 1931, a less liberal Japanese cabinet took power, and Inouye was replaced by Korekiyo Takahashi, who promptly took Japan off the gold standard. In late January 1932, the world was horrified by Japanese bombing of Chinese civilians in thickly populated suburbs of Shanghai. Once again, the Japanese blamed Chinese provocation. The terrorist tactics were far more naked than those used in Mukden, and the evidence of brutality more graphic and abundant. Newsreels brought shocking pictures of the carnage into American movie theaters. Lamont was so dismayed he told his friend Saburo Sonoda of the Yokohama Specie Bank that Japan could no longer raise money in American markets—so ghastly was the impression left by Shanghai.[41] For the House of Morgan, Shanghai initiated a slow process of disenchantment. A chastened Leffingwell wrote to Teddy Grenfell, "I confess to having had a good deal of sympathy with the Japanese in Manchuria, though none at all with the Japanese at Shanghai."[42]

Now Lamont was to absorb one stunning blow after another. Rightwing terrorism—which had already claimed the life of Prime Minister Hamaguchi in a 1930 shooting—turned on the world of finance. One by one, Lamont's Japanese friends were killed. During the Shanghai fighting in February, he received a telegram from Sonoda that said: "WITH SORROWING HEART INFORM YOU OF ASSASSINATION AND DEATH OF MR. J. INOUYE. . . . IT SEEMS [AS] IF A GREAT LIGHT HAS BEEN EXTINGUISHED AND MY DEAR COUNTRY IS FALLING INTO DARK DAYS."[43]

Inouye, sixty-three, was in the midst of a general-election campaign. As leader of the Minseito, he was expected to become the next prime minister. As he stepped from his car at a suburban Tokyo school, a twenty-two-year-old rural youth stepped from the shadows in a tattered kimono and black felt hat. He shot Inouye in the chest. The assassin was a member of the secretive, superpatriotic Blood Brotherhood, a group of fanatic young nationalists. At the police station, he boasted of his deed and blamed rural poverty on Inouye's deflationary policies. Speaking to reporters at the Imperial University Hospital, Inouye's somber, dry-eyed widow explained that she had readied herself for this moment while her husband was in the cabinet.

Lamont was profoundly upset; after all, it was Inouye who gave him hope that the old illustrious families and their liberal allies could keep militarism at bay. He wrote a touching letter of condolence to his friend Sonoda: "Such a gentle soul he was—it seems the more inexplicable that his end should be like this."[44]

The more Lamont resisted the truth about Japan, the more forcibly it intruded. A few weeks after Inouye's assassination came the murder of Lamont's other major Japanese friend, Baron Takuma Dan, the MIT-trained mining engineer and chief executive of Mitsui, who had hosted him at his villa in 1920. Baron Dan was shot as he emerged from his car at the white marble Mitsui Bank. Again the assassin was a rural youth and was apparently also a member of the Blood Brotherhood. Lamont wrote to Baron Dan's family, recalling the 1920 trip: "I had thought at times of him as a poet in business and this impression came to me as he showed me his house and garden and we stood together looking at Fujiyama, a majestic picture towering above a superb landscape."[45]

Baron Dan's killing was an act of revenge against the House of Mitsui, which rightists had accused of treacherous profiteering in the so-called dollar-buying scandal. After England left the gold standard in September 1931, Mitsui and other *zaibatsu* banks expected the yen to be forced off gold, too, an effective devaluation. So they furiously sold yen and bought dollars. These foreign-exchange transactions netted Mitsui an estimated $50 million. But they also triggered a patriotic uproar about banks speculating against their country's currency. The issue proved an emotional one during the 1932 election. In the growing atmosphere of political extremism, many Japanese sympathized with Inouye's and Baron Dan's assassins, who received lenient sentences. Both were released from prison within a few years.

Lamont didn't readily admit error and didn't know how to abandon clients. By now, the strong rightward shift of Japanese politics was evident. The Kwantung army had overrun Manchuria, creating the puppet state of Manchukuo in March and installing Pu Yi, the last Manchu emperor, as its pliant figurehead. The incident at Mukden, the bombing of Shanghai, the murders of Inouye and Baron Dan—these events should have opened Lamont's eyes. He could no longer plead ignorance. His files from early 1932 do reveal a deep displeasure with the Japanese as he warned them not to repeat the Shanghai error, which had destroyed any sympathy they still had on Wall Street.

Nevertheless, that spring, in a bizarre turn, Lamont and Martin Egan drifted back to a pro-Japanese stance. The two had become close friends with Count Aisuke Kabayama, who had been educated at Princeton, was married on Long Island, and was close to Emperor Hirohito. Kabayama's grandfather had been an admiral and a governor of Taiwan. Lamont and Egan encouraged him to set up a Japanese information bureau in America on the Mussolini model and proudly briefed him on their Italian work. In the late spring, Egan went to Japan for talks about Manchuria. When he returned talking about "banditry and disorder in Manchuria" and blaming China for hostilities, he sounded like a Japanese militarist.[46]

The House of Morgan no longer knew which master it served—America or Japan. A few days later, on May 15, 1932, another political murder blackened Japan's image: the aging prime minister, Tsuyoshi Inukai, was gunned down in his official residence by nine young army officers, probably because he wanted to curb the military. He was replaced by Admiral Makoto Saitō. It would be the end of party government in Japan until after World War II.

In the fall of 1932, Lamont had to confront the unpleasant truth about Mukden, the knowledge that his press release for Inouye had been a hollow piece of propaganda. The League of Nations had dispatched an investigative commission to the Far East under Lord Lytton. Even before the Lytton report was endorsed by the League, Lamont's assistant, Vernon Munroe, dined one evening with General Frank McCoy, the commission's American member. The next morning, Munroe told Lamont, "The General said there was a grave question as to whether there was any explosion, that the Japanese had never been able to explain how the regular trains continued to run immediately after the explosion was supposed to have taken place and the more they had explained the more of a contradiction they had gotten into."[47] A month later, the Lytton report condemned Japanese aggression as violating the League's Covenant and branded Manchukuo a puppet state. Although the report was critical of Chinese provocations, Japan walked out of the Assembly of the League and brazenly tightened its grip on Manchuria.

By this point, Lamont was in a quandary. He wanted to maintain a belief in Japan's good intentions amid overwhelming, contradictory evidence. To sort out his feelings, he sat down and wrote a memo marked "Secret and Strictly Confidential." Whether he ever circulated it is uncertain, but it shows a man fleeing reality. "These are entirely my private thoughts," it starts out, then continues, "American suspicions as to Japan's motives are essentially these: that Japan has aggressive designs on the Asiatic Continent and that Japan may even be courting war with the United States—which are not true." To correct such misconceptions, he recommends a joint U.S.-Japanese declaration on trade and peaceful relations. The conclusion is a desperate pipe dream: "If such a joint declaration can be made, all war talk will immediately be silenced, the psychology of men will undergo a change and whatever question may arise between our two countries will become capable of an easy solution."[48]

It became progressively more difficult for Lamont to sustain any belief in Japan's imminent return to civil government. As lords of Manchukuo, the army built huge dams and industries to strengthen the nation's preparedness for war. The new finance minister, Takahashi, known as the Japanese Keynes, boosted military spending to almost half the Japanese budget. The liberalism of the twenties, along with its foremost exponents, was dead.

In 1934, Lamont underwent a sudden change of heart. Once his eyes were open, he felt fooled, and his trust turned to bitterness. He cut off subscriptions to Japanese cultural groups, snubbed visiting Japanese dignitaries, and warned Japan's consul general that the Japanese should not mistake America's peaceful spirit for cowardice. When he heard rumors that the British cabinet might renew an alliance with Japan, he lobbied against the move. He sent an impassioned letter to Grenfell, which he expected to be passed around Whitehall: "In place of the fair liberal government that existed in the first twenty years of this century there has arisen a military clique which . . . if accounts from the liberal elements in Japan are true, have been conducting itself a good deal as a lot of the young German Nazis have been conducting themselves."[49]

The Japanese army would continue to annex parts of northern China, a campaign that in 1937 would culminate in the Sino-Japanese War and the butchering of tens of thousands of Chinese civilians in the rape of Nanking. It was a dismal, ironic denouement to Morgan involvement in China, which began with Willard Straight's dream of America acting as a buffer against Japanese encroachment in Manchuria and ended with a senior Morgan partner serving as apologist for that very action.

CHAPTER EIGHTEEN

MIDGET

• •

•

THE Wall Street of 1932 was a dismal ghost town. Securities firms declared "apple days"—unpaid vacation days each month that enabled destitute brokers to go out and supplement their income by selling apples on the sidewalk. Apple vendors appeared at the Corner. Downtown real estate was so depressed that building companies defaulted; astute investors who bought their bonds became the future owners of Wall Street. The misery extended everywhere. Riverside Park was lined with Hoovervilles, and sylvan retreats in Central Park looked like ragged hillbilly hollows. On Park Avenue, ten-room apartments that had been occupied by financiers of the twenties now lacked tenants. The new, half-occupied Empire State Building was mocked as the "Empty State Building."

For aristocrats in private clubs, it was a time of often macabre mirth. The Union League Club had a room wallpapered with stock certificates that were rendered worthless by the crash. (They were peeled off by itchy fingers when the market recovered.) After falling for over two straight years, the stock market hit bottom on July 8, 1932. By that point, two thousand investment houses had failed, and new underwritings stood at 10 percent of their 1929 peak volume. On the Stock Exchange floor, listless traders invented games to kill time. Big Board seats that fetched $550,000 before the crash now sold for as little as $68,000. The major financial work was refunding old bonds at lower interest rates.

In 1932, almost thirteen million of America's 125 million people were unemployed. Two million roamed America searching for work, boarding boxcars and sleeping in hobo camps. Hoover refused to renounce economic orthodoxy and mount a vigorous attack on the Depression. Sometimes he flirted with fanciful solutions to America's despondency. At various times, he thought America needed a good laugh, a good poem, a good song. He even approached Will Rogers about writing a good joke to end panic hoarding. Hoover himself wore a funereal expression. Of a White House meeting with him, Secretary of State Henry Stimson said, "It was like sitting in a bath of ink." And sculptor Gutzon Borglum remarked, "If you put a rose in Hoover's hand it would wilt."[1] Hoover had a way of minimizing the nation's suffering. In 1932, he insisted "Nobody is actually starving. The hoboes, for example, are better fed than they have ever been. One hobo in New York got ten meals in one day "[2]

That spring, Jack Morgan was briefly roused to a rare act of public activism. A believer in self-reliance, he cited as his favorite biblical text Ezekiel 2:1: "And he said unto me, Son of man, stand upon thy feet, and I will speak it unto thee."[3] Jack construed this as God clucking his tongue at the welfare state. He preached the old-time religion, telling the marquess of Linlithgow that honesty, integrity, and economy were "the real solution of our troubles, most of which, in my opinion, come from greed."[4] He rallied to Hoover's plea for private benevolence instead of government intervention. In March 1932, he participated in a fundraiser for the Block Community Organization of New York. Dressed in dinner jacket at his Murray Hill mansion—with butler Henry Physick and other servants listening at a rear-hall receiver—he broadcast a radio appeal for help. "We must all do our bit," he said, endorsing a plan by which workers contributed small weekly sums to a fund for the jobless. A shy man who dreaded public appearances, Jack's cooperation reflected a fearful mood among the rich. Lamont, meanwhile, helped the Red Cross raise money for farmers victimized by the Midwest drought.

An outdated allegiance to classical economics tipped a postcrash recession into seemingly insoluble depression. In late 1931, Federal Reserve Banks hiked up their discount rate by 2 percentage points in two weeks. To balance the budget, the Federal Revenue Act of 1932 almost doubled tax rates—again, the perfect medicine to kill the patient. Not everyone at Morgans automatically resisted experimentation. Throughout 1932, Russell Leffingwell, the resident Democratic iconoclast and self-styled curmudgeon, laughed at those who feared inflationary spending as "people who in an Arctic winter worry about the heat of the tropics."[5] Yet Leffingwell's own views spun like a weathervane in a high gust, and at moments he reverted to budget-balancing orthodoxy. He told Walter Lippmann that a public works program would only prolong the Depression, and he doggedly maintained the need for the gold standard.

The major Hoover policy initiative of 1932, the Reconstruction Finance Corporation, was a major boon to Morgan interests. It was set up to make loans to banks, railroads, and other hard-pressed businesses. The previous year, Lamont had told Hoover that the plight of America's railroads was "the principle impediment to domestic recovery." The railroads were burdened with debt from the twenties and couldn't service their bonds. When the Van Sweringens defaulted on their secret rescue loan in 1931, Morgans and Guaranty Trust invited the brothers in for a frank chat, telling them that "we are, in effect, the owners of all of their properties."[6] So the bank dropped its usual objections to government bailouts when it came to railroads. Oris Van Sweringen said that he and Mantis were "on the doorstep waiting for them [the RFC] to open."[7] The Van Sweringens borrowed $75 million from the RFC, strengthening the case of those who saw it as a welfare agency for the rich.

Hard times didn't touch the splendor of top-drawer Morgan partners. If their drawing rights from the bank—that is, their annual percentage take as partners—were halved, they still had wealth left from the twenties. The main problem was enjoying it free of guilt. What would Jack do with his new *Corsair*, big enough to house a small village of hoboes? He decided, for decency's sake, to mothball it for a while, telling Cosmo Lang, the archbishop of Canterbury, "It seems very unwise to let the 'Corsair' come out this summer. There are so many suffering from lack of work, and even from actual hunger, that it is both wiser and kinder not to flaunt such luxurious amusement in the face of the public."[8] He offered to charter the boat to John D. Rockefeller, Jr.

With over $20 million in his partnership account, Tom Lamont had time to catch up on travel. Where Jack liked to sail with bishops and surgeons, Lamont preferred the company of writers, intellectuals, and socialites. In the spring of 1931, he and Florence went on a leisurely Aegean cruise with Walter Lippmann and his wife, and classics scholar Gilbert Murray. They were joined in Athens by the John Masefields. There are photos of this Depression party aboard the *Saturnia*. One shows Lamont in a double-breasted suit with pocket handkerchief and a jaunty striped vest. His shrewd eyes crease into crow's-feet as he gazes into the camera. Small and balding, he has appraising eyes, sympathetic but vigilant, that seem to take in everything. In another photograph, taken at the captain's table, the group is elegantly erect. Walter Lippmann looks dashing, while Lamont peers attentively down the table. Dining in this wood-paneled interior, with its fresh table linen, the group has a glitter that is remote from the American dreariness of the moment.

The Lamonts arrived at Patras with forty-two pieces of luggage. The Greeks treated them as visiting foreign dignitaries and followed protocol carefully. The provincial governor carried Florence's hatbox ashore while a Greek cabinet representative (probably wondering to what depths he had sunk) inspected every toilet on their hotel floor. Tom and Florence Lamont liked to affect a bohemian innocence. During this idyllic trip, Florence reported, "We almost always have a picnic luncheon because the hotels are most of them so bad. We sit in the sun and read poems about Greece after luncheon."[9]

If the Morgan world seemed to survive the Depression intact, the surface was deceptive. Between 1929 and 1932, the bank saw its net worth—its basic capital cushion—drop with frightening speed, from $118 million to half that before Hoover left office. Total assets plunged from $704 million to $425 million. Even for the House of Morgan, these were staggering blows. The real casualties were junior partners, who shared in the losses without having reaped the spectacular bull market profits. The bank still recruited based on talent. As an official Morgan history says, "The alternative of seeking additional capital by recruiting new partners with more money than talent, thereby diluting the quality of the firm, was deemed unacceptable."[10]

The House of Morgan retained Pierpont's paternalism. When salaries were slashed by as much as 20 percent, the staff was told these cuts would be restored before partners resumed full drawing rights from their capital accounts. When the bank closed its employee dining room, it distributed cash allowances for lunch. Staff families also got two free weeks each year at a rustic Morgan camp in Maine. For the Morgan Grenfell staff, the Depression *ennui* was partly lifted by Jack's gift of a sports ground in Beckenham, with a cricket pitch, hard tennis courts, trimmed lawns, and a tea pavilion. These touches inspired fierce loyalty and a cultlike intimacy among employees. Their Depression suffering, if real, was extremely modest compared with the unspeakable suffering beyond the marble walls.

LET us consider 1932 politics, for the events that led to the Glass-Steagall Act—the Banking Act of 1933—and the division of the House of Morgan were rooted in that year. It was Herbert Hoover who first waged war on Wall Street and prompted hearings that led to new banking legislation. There had always been a slightly paranoid edge to Hoover's dealings with his Morgan friends. After staying at the White House in the summer of 1931, Dwight Morrow told Lamont that Hoover was blue and felt "he had been trying to carry out the views of the banks here in New York and yet had got rather cold comfort from them."[11] Lamont sent Hoover a note to cheer him up, yet there was an undercurrent of uneasiness in his relations with the president.

Hoover's relationship with the House of Morgan dated back to his days as a mining engineer. In 1917, he acted as intermediary between Sir Ernest Oppenheimer, who wanted to take public his Johannesburg gold-mining group, and Morgans. To consolidate his new Wall Street tie, Oppenheimer insisted on the word *American* appearing in the new company's name. Thus was born the Anglo-American Corporation, afterward Africa's richest company. Evidently Lamont thought this would inaugurate a series of mining ventures tapping Hoover's talents. As he told Morgan Grenfell, the Anglo-American deal was "part of a comprehensive plan involving association with Mr. Hoover in mining ventures generally."[12] But Hoover reneged on the deal, and Lamont later applauded Oppenheimer for ousting Hoover and engineer William Honnold. "We never shall have any quarrel with [Oppenheimer] in regard to his feeling about Honnold and/or Hoover," Lamont informed London.[13]

Beyond this history, Morgans and Hoover were doomed to have policy quarrels. Hoover felt straitjacketed by a Congress that cared little for Europe's troubles, favored buy-America campaigns, and lacked interest in inheriting economic leadership from Britain. The House of Morgan, in turn, had European clients to protect, and its internationalism was no less problematic for Hoover than for his Republican predecessors. There were also clashing personal styles: Hoover was brusque and humorless, while Morgan partners were silky aristocrats.

In July of 1932, it looked as if the world economy might finally cast off the twin burdens of German reparations and Allied war debt. At Lausanne, European leaders reached a gentleman's agreement that effectively ended the debt charade; if they could stop paying off war debts, they would stop asking for reparations. Lamont was jubilant, seeing this as an end to the economic warfare that had been waged since Versailles. He dispatched Martin Egan to the White House, not to advise Hoover to cancel the war debts outright but simply to reexamine them.

Returning from Washington, Egan said he had never seen the president so emotional about an issue. He had made a speech full of anger, self-pity, and impotent frustration. "Lamont has this matter all wrong," Hoover had insisted, echoing widespread public sentiment. "If there is one thing the American people do not like and will not stand for it is a combination of this kind against them. . . . Lamont cannot appreciate the rising tide of resentment that is sweeping over the country. . . . They are trying to 'gang' us. . . . Maybe they have settled German reparations but they did it the worst damned way they could."[14] He wouldn't extend his one-year debt moratorium and rejected French and British proposals for deferring upcoming payments; he forced France to default. So on the eve of Hitler's advent, the Allies were squabbling over moldy financial issues that had bedeviled them for years.

The Morgan-Hoover feud over debt was mild compared with their debate over short selling on Wall Street. Moody and isolated, taciturn and stony-faced, Hoover now shared the average American's view of Wall Street as a giant casino rigged by professionals. He saw the stock market as a report card on his performance, and it showed consistently failing grades. He came to believe in a Democratic conspiracy to drive down stocks by selling them short—that is, by selling borrowed shares in the hope of buying them back later at a cheaper price.

The "bear raiders" first achieved notoriety in the 1930 suicide market. The master was Bernard E. "Sell-'Em Ben" Smith, a twenties pool speculator who was trounced by rising prices in 1929. That October, he suddenly came into his own and whooped it up on the day of the crash, shouting "Sell 'em all! They're not worth anything."[15] Such tales convinced Hoover of malevolent forces at work in the market. He began to compile lists of people in the bear cabal and even claimed to know they met every Sunday afternoon to plot the week's destruction![16] Hoover's obsession was fed by confidants. Senator Frederick Walcott of Connecticut told Hoover that Bernard Baruch, John J. Raskob, and other Wall Street Democrats were planning bear raids to defeat his reelection.

Hoover thought Stock Exchange officials should openly denounce the culprits. In January 1932, he called Stock Exchange president Richard Whitney to the White House for a verbal drubbing. He said short sellers were preventing an economic rebound and warned that unless Whitney curbed them, he would ask Congress to investigate the Exchange and possibly impose Federal regulation. Whitney refused to admit any danger in short selling. Privately Morgan partners mocked Hoover's obsession as absurd and fantastic, but they couldn't dissuade him from his vendetta.

Although fearing that public hearings would dredge up "discouraging filth" and sabotage recovery efforts, in 1932 Hoover asked the Senate Banking and Currency Committee to start an inquiry into short selling. Wall Street bankers were so upset that Lamont lunched at the White House with Hoover and Secretary of State Stimson, trying to spike the inquiry. Hoover said destructive short sellers had offset his beneficial measures, a remark that led to a heated exchange about the hearings. "I tried to make clear to the President that if such an enquiry was encouraged to run riot it would create nothing but uneasiness through-out the country and would help to defeat the very constructive ends to which he was leading us," Lamont said.[17]

In April, the first witness was Richard Whitney, who called Hoover's charges "purely ridiculous." Even as the hearings commenced, Hoover and Lamont were secretly trading barbed remarks about short selling. Hoover blamed the bears for everything—low public confidence, busi-ness stagnation, and falling prices. Lamont's reply was candid to the point of comic cruelty. Responding to Hoover's contention that "real values" were being destroyed by bear raids, he asked, "But what can be called 'real value' if a security has no earnings and pays no dividends?"[18] He blamed 99 percent of the market's decline on poor business.

The press had a dandy time ridiculing the Senate bear hunt, which never unearthed a Democratic conspiracy. Nevertheless, at the end of April, a subcommittee broadened the hearings to include pools and market manipulations of the 1920s. The machinations of the RCA pool were unfolded before the public. Walter E. Sachs of Goldman, Sachs had to explain the losses of Eddie Cantor and forty thousand other investors in the Goldman Sachs Trading Corporation. Something curious now happened: as the hearings shifted from present to past, memories of the crash grew in the public mind. At first, Main Street smirked at the crash as a Calvinist thunderbolt hurled at big-city sinners. Only now, when the crash was seen as a forerunner of depression, did public rage against the bankers crystallize.

Amid the controversy, Hoover had to deal with a serious slump in the bond market—where short selling was prohibited. Corporate America couldn't cope with the debt accumulated in the 1920s, much of it to finance takeovers. Many bonds defaulted and in extreme cases dropped 10, 20, or 30 points between sales, threatening the banking system. If savings banks couldn't cash in bonds, they might have no money to pay off depositors, possibly causing runs and failures. The upshot was a Morgan-led operation to halt the bond market slide. Thirty-five banks pledged $100 million to buy high-quality bonds in a pool nicknamed the Stars and Stripes Forever. It was chaired by Lamont, who sported more titles than the mikado during this period. The bank touted the patriotic nature of the venture, but it was again that Morgan specialty— public service for profit. The bank considered bonds seriously under-valued and had excess cash on hand during the Depression. "If the organization of the Corporation . . . should have any degree of reassuring effect upon the public so much the better," J.P. Morgan and Company told the Paris partners.[19]

Lamont kept Hoover posted on the pool. In the bond market opera-tion, some cynics spied a move to improve Republican prospects in the fall election—as if Hoover would field his own hard-charging bulls against the bears. If so, the strategy almost backfired on Hoover. Lamont used the pool as a bargaining chip and threatened to disband it unless the short-selling hearings were canceled. In the end, the pool went ahead and made a tidy profit. The hearings would drag on and eventu-ally assume dimensions unforeseen in early 1932. They would finally take their name from a new subcommittee counsel, Ferdinand Pecora, appointed in January 1933. The Pecora hearings would lead straight to Glass-Steagall and the dismemberment of the House of Morgan.

I N the autumn of 1932, Hoover presided over one last humiliation—a nationwide banking crisis. Three years of deflation had eroded the col-lateral behind many loans. As banks called them in, the business slump worsened and produced more bank runs and failures. Before 1932, the thousands of bank closings were mostly confined to small rural banks. Then, that October, Nevada's governor shut the state's banks. There followed a frightening crescendo of state bank closings—euphemisti-cally called holidays—climaxed by an eight-day closing of Michigan banks in February. The contagion spread so fast that thirty-eight states had shut their banks by Roosevelt's inauguration.

Between the November election and the March 1933 inauguration was a time of paralysis and glowering hostility between Hoover and Roosevelt. Irritated, beleaguered, and resentful, the president refused to undertake new initiatives without Roosevelt's cooperation; Roosevelt, on the other hand, wanted to wait until he assumed full power. For the House of Morgan, it was a season of peril. Through three consecutive Republican terms, it had probably enjoyed better access to Washington than any other bankers in American history. Under Hoover, the presi-dent was a telephone call away. Sometimes Morgan power had seemed as awesome as crude left-wing propaganda would have it. Now the bank combated threats to its survival as the political wheel came full circle.

As early as 1929, Hoover advanced the idea of separating commercial and investment banking, a notion that now took hold. It appeared in a banking bill introduced by Senator Carter Glass as early as 1930 and formed part of the Democratic party platform in 1932. During the campaign, Roosevelt blamed Hoover for the speculative binge of 1929 and the spate of foreign loans that left a bloody trail of defaults. After Bolivia became the first Latin American debtor to default in 1931, nearly every Latin American government followed suit.

After Hoover's "bear raid" crusade, the president's departure wasn't mourned at the Corner. Russell Leffingwell and Parker Gilbert formed a Morgan minority that voted for Roosevelt. "The truth is," Leffingwell confessed to Walter Lippmann, "I can't bring myself to vote for a desperate man who wishes to continue desperate remedies for a desperate situation."[20] Nor was it self-evident that FDR would emerge as an enemy. Genial and aristocratic, he chastised Hoover as a big spender and advocated balanced budgets; he looked more bland than bold. Leffingwell almost patronized Roosevelt, calling him "a pleasant, kindly, well-meaning chap with a pleasing smile."[21]

Socially, FDR fit the Morgan mold far more than Hoover. Leffingwell—who knew Roosevelt from his own Treasury days, when Roosevelt was in the Navy Department—excitedly set down his pedigree for Vivian Smith of Morgan Grenfell. He noted Roosevelt's Groton and Harvard education, his Hudson River upbringing and old New York Dutch ancestry, and his employment at the Wall Street firm of Carter, Ledyard, and Milburn, which defended corporate clients against antitrust actions. Leffingwell ended sarcastically, "All that is the background of the man who is a peril to American institutions according to Hoover the foreign mining engineer."[22] Lamont also knew Roosevelt, having rented his East Sixty-fifth Street house. Before the inauguration, he phoned him and busily dashed off "Dear Frank" letters.

If the winter interregnum suggested possible good relations, there were also warning signs. Late in the summer of 1932, Leffingwell and Roosevelt had an exchange that previewed, in miniature, the titanic feud to come. In August, Leffingwell sent "Frank" a note deriding the banking reforms being advanced by Carter Glass; in it, he tried to strike a note of camaraderie and shared values: "You and I know that we cannot cure the present deflation and depression by punishing the villains, real or imaginary, of the first post-war decade, and that when it comes down to the day of reckoning nobody gets very far with all this prohibition and regulation stuff."[23] Far from indulging Leffingwell, Roosevelt threw cold water in his face: "I wish we could get from the bankers themselves an admission that in the 1927 to 1929 period there were grave abuses and that the bankers themselves now support whole-heartedly methods to prevent recurrence thereof. Can't bankers see their own advantage in such a course?"[24] It would be the tragedy of the House of Morgan that it couldn't see the advantage in such a course. The public demanded a *mea culpa* for 1929, which the bankers wouldn't provide. As Leffingwell told Roosevelt, "The bankers were not in fact responsible for 1927–29 and the politicians were. Why then should the bankers make a false confession?"[25] Yet such was Leffing-well's disgust with Hoover's tariffs, isolationism, and reparations policy that he gladly voted for FDR.

The bank campaigned to slip Leffingwell into a Treasury post, which became a litmus test of Roosevelt's financial soundness. All aflutter, Monty Norman told Lamont, "I shall wait to hear that R.C.L. is estab-lished before I can rest happily."[26] When Senator Carter Glass was approached about taking the Treasury secretary job again, he said he would want to hire two Morgan men and former deputies: Leffingwell and Parker Gilbert.[27] Walter Lippmann joined the bandwagon, but Roosevelt cringed: "We simply can't tie up with 23."[28] The shorthand betrayed a knowingness that would work to the bank's disadvantage. Despite his failure to get a Treasury post, Leffingwell would remain a trusted friend and adviser of Roosevelt's and something of a black sheep on Wall Street for his partial support of the administration.

The person who probably shot down Leffingwell's trial balloon was Ferdinand Pecora, the fifty-three-year-old former assistant district attor-ney from New York, who took over the Senate's Wall Street probe in January 1933. Smoking a blunt cigar, his shirtsleeves rolled up, the hard-bitten Pecora captured the public's attention. For six months, the hearings had been stalled. Republicans and Democrats, with fine impar-tiality, had feared fat cats of both parties might be named and united in a conspiracy of silence. With Pecora as counsel, the hearings acquired a new, irresistible momentum. They would afford a secret history of the crash, a sobering postmortem of the twenties that would blacken the name of bankers for a generation. From now on, they would be called banksters.

Even before Roosevelt's inauguration, Pecora turned his investigative spotlight on the National City Bank, showing eminent bankers in sordid poses, particularly the bank's head, Charles E. Mitchell, a member of the Black Thursday rescue squad. Through Pecora, the public got a view of bankers scheming while supposedly protecting the public. Pecora revealed that the $12-million Morgan loan to preserve National City's merger with the Corn Exchange Bank had represented more than 5 percent of Morgans' net worth, sticking the bank with a substantial loss. It was also disclosed that to buffer crash losses at National City, one hundred top officers had borrowed $2.4 million, interest free, from a special morale loan fund—loans never repaid.

Pecora also studied the operations of the National City Company, whose 1900 salesmen had unloaded risky Latin American bonds on the masses. It emerged that in touting bonds from Brazil, Peru, Chile, and Cuba to investors, the bank had hushed up internal reports on problems in these countries. After bank examiners criticized sugar loans made by the parent bank, the securities affiliate sold them as bonds to investors, an example of how commercial banks might palm off bad loans through securities affiliates. Pecora cited the case of an Edgar D. Brown of Pottsville, Pennsylvania, whose National City salesman had pushed him into "a bewildering array of Viennese, German, Peruvian, Chilean, Rhenish, Hungarian, and Irish government obligations."[29]

Another supposed hero of Black Thursday was Albert H. Wiggin of Chase, a poker-playing clergyman's son who sat on fifty-nine corporate boards. He was also exposed as being up to his ears in mischief. For six weeks in 1929, he had shorted shares of Chase stock and earned several million dollars; the speculation was backed by an $8-million loan from Chase itself. For good measure, Wiggin had set up a Canadian securities company to avoid federal taxes. The stories of Chase and National City showed the extent to which the traditional distinction between savings and speculation had disappeared in the 1920s—a distinction the Glass-Steagall Act would seek to restore.

The Pecora findings created a tidal wave of anger against Wall Street, and against this backdrop Roosevelt vetoed the Leffingwell nomination. As people followed the hearings on their farms and in their offices, on soup lines and in Hoovervilles, they became convinced that they'd been conned in the 1920s. Yesterday's gods were no more than greedy little devils. Even most of Wall Street was shocked by this phase of the hearings. Senator Burton Wheeler of Montana said, "The best way to restore confidence in the banks would be to take these crooked presidents out of the banks and treat them the same way we treated Al Capone when he failed to pay his income tax." Even Carter Glass, a staunch Morgan friend, joked nastily, "One banker in my state attempted to marry a white woman and they lynched him."[30]

When Roosevelt took office on March 4, 1933, he ran up a flag of independence from Wall Street. That morning, Governor Herbert Lehman shut New York's banks, and Richard Whitney mounted the podium to close the Stock Exchange. The financial massacre was complete: of twenty-five thousand banks in 1929, some seven thousand had now failed. Amid this atmosphere of financial ruin, a grim Roosevelt delivered a stinging indictment of the bankers: "The money changers have fled from their high seats in the temple of our civilization. We may now restore that temple to the ancient truths."[31]

To offer advice on the banking crisis, Lamont had telephoned Roosevelt and urged him to avoid drastic measures. This counsel reflected a faith not only in market mechanisms but in political expediency. As J. P. Morgan and Company cabled London: "There is great reluctance to contemplate any form of federal action which it might be difficult later on to get rid of"[32] Roosevelt brushed aside Lamont's tepid remedies and announced a sweeping week-long bank holiday; over five hundred banks never reopened. Along with an emergency bank bill, this tough action restored public confidence and revealed a new public receptivity to emergency measures. Throughout the New Deal, the House of Morgan would repeat the same political error: it would advocate marginal reforms, which would be dismissed as self-serving. Instead of devising its own alternative reform package, it settled for scare tactics.

Despite these early Roosevelt rebuffs, Hoover's bleak record made even Morgan bankers ripe for experimentation. Jack Morgan was at first ecstatic about FDR. "Of course, it is quite possible that some of his cures may be wrong ones, but, on the whole, things were so bad that almost any cure may do some good."[33] In correspondence from the Morgan files of March 1933, the partners sound remarkably like other frightened Americans: they, too, needed a savior. Hadn't they seen their own prescriptions fail? After Roosevelt's March 12 fireside chat and the reopening of the banks, 23 Wall reported with relief to Morgan Grenfell: "The whole country is filled with admiration for President Roosevelt's actions. The record of his accomplishment in just one week seems incredible because we have never experienced anything like it before."[34] The Stock Exchange soared and posted a 54-percent gain for 1933.

The House of Morgan couldn't see that, like a black speck on the horizon, the Pecora hearings were a hurricane heading in its direction. During this false honeymoon, the House of Morgan committed a famous act of apostasy: it applauded Roosevelt for taking America off the gold standard in April. It was hoped this would devalue the dollar, raise commodity prices, and reverse the lethal deflation. A radical measure in ordinary times, it was less controversial in 1933. Harking back to greenback currency (currency with no metal backing) and free-silver coinage, farmers and other debtors were reviving old inflationary nostrums from the days of William Jennings Bryan. Roosevelt was under pressure to choose *some* inflationary expedient. Gold was moving abroad in large quantities, and there was fear it would contract the monetary base, feeding deflation.

The House of Morgan provided intellectual support for leaving gold. Russell Leffingwell lunched with Walter Lippmann and advised him on a newspaper column favoring an end to a rigid gold standard. Leffingwell saw the need for higher commodity prices. He also felt the downward drift of European currencies had led to an overvalued dollar, hurting U.S. exports. After lunch, Leffingwell said, "Walter, you've got to explain to the people why we can no longer afford to chain ourselves to the gold standard. Then maybe Roosevelt, who I'm sure agrees, will be able to act."[35] Lippmann let Leffingwell vet the article and sharpen its fine points.

Leffingwell had great intellectual stature among the New Dealers. When Roosevelt later accused Treasury Secretary Henry Morgenthau, Jr., of sounding like Leffingwell, Morgenthau retorted, "I wish I had half his brains."[36] One of the more radical brain trusters, Columbia professor Rexford G. Tugwell, noted Leffingwell's influence on Roosevelt in the gold decision. "Consulting widely among New York acquaintances he regarded as public-minded—Russell Leffingwell of the House of Morgan was perhaps the most trusted—he had concluded that gold must be sequestered entirely, hoarding forbidden, and shipment abroad prohibited."[37] The day after Walter Lippmann's column appeared, Roosevelt publicly advocated an end to gold. Through a series of executive orders, he prohibited gold exports and hoarding. Congress in June abrogated the clause in bond issues that mandated compulsory payment in gold coin. Even Jack Morgan smilingly applauded the move. For those who remembered Pierpont's 1895 rescue of the gold standard and Morgan efforts to put countries back on gold throughout the twenties, such statements were wondrous to behold, proof that the safe nineteenth-century world of neoclassic economics had been turned topsy-turvy.

Many financial experts were in a state of shock, as if the ship of state's rudder had been violently torn off. Budget Director Lewis Douglas intoned, "This is the end of Western civilization."[38] Bernard Baruch felt a similar alarm at this sudden turn in financial policy: "It can't be defended except as mob rule. Maybe the country doesn't know it yet, but I think we may find that we've been in a revolution more drastic than the French Revolution."[39] The perplexity was greater in Europe, where bankers wondered why the United States had cheapened its currency despite a trade surplus and an adequate gold store. When informed that Monty Norman thought the move would plunge the world into bankruptcy, Roosevelt—who called him Old Pink Whiskers—just laughed. The gold embargo showed that both the United States and England had renounced world leadership in favor of domestic ends. The world was adrift in a full-blown war of economic nationalism, fought with competitive currency devaluations.

For people schooled in the old economic verities, it was a disorienting new world. Bernard S. Carter, a Morgan et Compagnie partner in Paris, told J. P. Morgan partners how a Romanian banker walked into Morgans' place Vendôme office and launched into the following diatribe:

> Here are the 3 great financial countries of the world, who have been preaching the sanctity of contracts to us ever since the war, and who have now all resorted to repudiation of one kind or another in their turn. First England goes off the gold standard, then France refuses to pay her debts to America, and now America goes off the gold standard. I guess we Roumanians are not such crooks after all![40]

By summer, Roosevelt was chiding the gold standard and other "old fetishes of so-called international bankers" and praising the brave new world of managed national currencies.[41] Although by background an internationalist and a strong supporter of the League of Nations, FDR pursued domestic recovery at the expense of global economic leadership. More cosmopolitan than Hoover, he had a vestigial fear of British finance. He ended British war-debt payments, as Leffingwell had advised, but couldn't suppress a view of British bankers as a devious bunch out to trick the Yanks. "The trouble is that when you sit around the table with a Britisher he usually gets 80% of the deal and you get what's left," Roosevelt explained.[42]

So the early New Deal threatened the House of Morgan in two ways: the Pecora hearings were exposing practices that could bring fresh regulation to Wall Street. And the White House attitude toward European finance augured an end to the House of Morgan's special diplomatic role of the 1920s. After an incestuous relationship with Washington in the twenties, the bank would suffer the curse of eternal banishment.

THAT spring, FDR urged the Senate Banking Committee to adopt a broader, more amorphous mandate to investigate "all the ramifications of bad banking." It was nothing less than a license for a comprehensive inquest into Wall Street. The committee turned to private bankers—whom Pecora defined as men "who make their own rules and are not subject to examination"—with J. P. Morgan and Company topping the list. It was too much to expect America's richest bankers to get off scot-free. What retrospective of the twenties would be complete without the bank that epitomized the decade's power? As a former Republican party chairman said, "Never before in the history of the world has there been such a powerful centralized control over finance, industrial production, credit, and wages as is at this time vested in the Morgan group."[43] It was time for Washington to storm the Bastille of Wall Street.

In Ferdinand Pecora, the committee's $255-a-month counsel, history provided a perfect foil for Morgan bankers. A Sicilian-born, anti-Tammany Democrat, he had thick, wavy black hair mixed with gray, a jaunty grin, and an assertive chin. A devoted Bull Mooser in 1912, he had switched to Wilson's progressive Democrats in 1916. As assistant district attorney in New York, he took on tough assignments—from bucket shops to crooked banks, the Police Department to bail bondsmen—posting an 80-percent conviction rate. Even when his prosecutorial manner was mild, he had a talent for taunts and withering asides. He was also fearless and incorruptible and had rejected several offers from Wall Street law firms. When he took over the Senate probe, he thought he would be through before Roosevelt took office. Instead, the investigation went on until May 1934, producing ten thousand pages of testimony that filled up eight fat tomes.

At first, the House of Morgan snickered at the Pecora hearings, seeing them as a circus. Lamont thought they were a political ploy "designed to acquaint a curiosity-loving public with the nature and extent of our own banking institutions."[44] With its fetish for secrecy, the bank tried to limit the inquiry's scope. On March 22, 1933, Lamont and counsel John W. Davis—the 1924 Democratic presidential candidate, dubbed the Morgan prosecuting attorney—visited Pecora at his shabby, temporary offices at 285 Madison Avenue. Davis had assiduously protected the House of Morgan's rights as a private bank and had written a New York State statute that exempted private banks from state inspection. Pecora was striking at an ancient privilege of gentleman bankers—keeping their capital position secret. On Davis's advice, Lamont refused to give a statement of Morgan capital, opposed examination of the bank's records, and insisted on the confidentiality of client accounts. As a close friend and near-neighbor of Jack Morgan's and a fellow vestryman of

Saint John's of Lattingtown, Davis was in high dudgeon at any insinuation of Morgan dishonesty. He quickly elevated the affair into a matter of honor and constitutional rights. Two days later, he told Pecora he was "very chilly" to his request for five years of J. P. Morgan and Company balance sheets.

Along with Parker Gilbert, Lamont visited George Harrison of the New York Fed and tried to enlist his influence for withholding the annual statements. Not only did Harrison refuse, but in his diary he registered shock at the request. Pecora interpreted the Morgan refusal to answer his questions as barefaced defiance and waged war against the bank in the press and on Capitol Hill. He got the Senate to pass a resolution enabling the committee to investigate private banking—a timely reminder to Morgans that it remained unregulated only at government sufferance. Pecora had won. For over six weeks, his sleuths worked in a room at 23 Wall, sifting through records no outsider had ever before seen. In the sole concession to Morgan eminence, investigators stopped at six each evening, while their colleagues worked until midnight elsewhere on the Street.

As bank image maker, Lamont tried to soften any impression that he was obstructing the investigation. On April 11, he wrote a clever letter to Roosevelt vowing cooperation; the bank would make political hay by yielding to the inevitable: "So far as this particular item is concerned, we haven't the slightest hesitation at any time in showing our balance sheet to members of the Committee, and I may add that I think you would regard it as a highly satisfactory one."[45] This last remark alluded to shared values, as if Lamont were reminding Roosevelt of his patrician background.

Jack Morgan was especially enraged by Pecora. He believed implicitly in Morgan integrity and interpreted any investigation, by definition, as a vendetta. He unpacked a colorful array of ethnic epithets; at age sixty-six, he wasn't about to learn tolerance. Pecora was degraded to a "dirty little wop," "a sharp little criminal lawyer," and "a 2nd-rate criminal lawyer."[46] It never occurred to Jack that Pecora might uncover anything amiss; he, too, thought the hearings were cooked up to pander to public voyeurism. He told the marquess of Linlithgow: "The risk of finding anything crooked in our affairs, honestly looked at, is nil; but it is taking a large part of the time of all the partners, and one whole firm of lawyers, to go through all the bank history and get ready to answer [the committee's questions]."[47] Lamont told his friend Lady Astor that he deplored the "Spanish Inquisition" in Washington and the conduct of the "young native Sicilian counsel, Ferdinand Pecora."[48] With such an inflated sense of virtue, the Morgan partners marched blindly into the hearings.

As the partners prepared for their May appearance, the hearings took on a new urgency. Sponsored by Senator Carter Glass of Virginia and Representative Henry Steagall of Alabama, a bill was working its way through Congress to separate commercial and investment banking. This would force large commercial banks to give up their securities affiliates; deposit-and-loan business would be severed from securities work. The political movement to punish Wall Street was becoming a juggernaut. Nobody had expected securities reform to dominate the early New Deal. But Pecora's sensational findings pressured the Roosevelt administration to take action against Wall Street.

Amid an upsurge of populist feeling in 1933, demagogues of the left and right found the House of Morgan a convenient idol to smash. Responding to the Pecora inquiry, Louisiana's Huey P. Long gave a speech entitled "Our Constant Rulers." In it, he argued, against all evidence, that Roosevelt had stacked the Treasury Department with Morgan men. Roosevelt, claimed Long, was no less beholden to 23 Wall than Hoover: "Parker Gilbert from Morgan & Company, Leffingwell . . . what is the use of hemming and hawing? We know who is running the thing."[49]

Threats to the bank went far beyond redneck demagogues or professors in Roosevelt's brain trust: they came from the banking community itself. In 1930, the Chase bank had merged with the Equitable Trust to form the world's largest bank of its time. Winthrop W. Aldrich, a brother-in-law of John D. Rockefeller, Jr., had succeeded the disgraced Albert Wiggin as Chase president in early 1933 and wanted to refurbish the bank's image. To this end, he got behind the push to divide commercial and investment banking. In March 1933, he took steps to spin off the Chase securities affiliate, Chase Harris Forbes. Similarly, James Perkins, who succeeded Charles Mitchell at National City, believed that its reckless stock affiliate had nearly ruined the bank, and he, too, favored a sequestration of financial functions. The bankers' unity of the 1920s was breaking down into furious backbiting and jockeying for advantage. According to Arthur Schlesinger, Jr., "Aldrich's action was interpreted as a Rockefeller assault on the House of Morgan; and for a time he achieved almost the dignity of a traitor to his class." The counterattack came from William Potter of Guaranty Trust, who criticized Aldrich's proposals as "quite the most disastrous . . . ever heard from a member of the financial community."[50] This division within the realm of banking sped the passage of the Glass-Steagall Act.

The House of Morgan was the first private bank investigated by Pecora. After three months of nonstop preparation, the Morgan entourage swept into a $2,000-a-day suite of rooms at the Carlton Hotel attended by a small army of Davis, Polk lawyers. Jack was to be the first witness. The night before, John Davis rehearsed him with biting questions. Believing that Pierpont's arrogance before the Pujo Committee had harmed the House of Morgan, Davis advised the men not to be coy, argumentative, or defensive. "I lined up the partners and held school every day," he later recalled.[51] As star witness, Jack was awaited with feverish anticipation. That morning, crowds ringed Capitol Hill to get seats in a sweltering, overflowing Senate Caucus Room. On the way, Jack confided to his chauffeur that he was afraid he would lose his temper. Charles Robertson sniffed, "Oh, you would not lose your temper with the likes of them."[52] Restored to his senses, Jack decided not to stoop to their level. No, he would conduct himself with honor. He entered the Capitol accompanied by several tough-looking bodyguards.

Shortly before ten o'clock on Tuesday morning, May 23, guards cleared the way for Jack Morgan to enter the hearing room; he was flanked by Tom Lamont and John Davis. Flashbulbs exploded and spectators buzzed as the world's most famous private banker stepped beneath the chandeliers and Corinthian pilasters. Despite his legendary name, Jack, age sixty-six, was a mystery man to most Americans, ghostly and insubstantial. He didn't look fearsome. Over six feet two with broad shoulders and an egg-shaped head, he was a balding, white-haired old man with dark eyebrows. Within himself he might feel sheepish, but he had a kindly smile and radiated a well-tailored poise in his three-piece suit and gold watch chain. He and Pecora typified contrasting images— the imperturbable Bourbon and the assertive immigrant.

Nobody was less eager than Jack to be dragged from his semiretirement. At this moment of crisis, he reverted to the tradition upheld by three generations of Morgans, the Gentleman Banker's Code, first pounded into Pierpont's head by Junius sixty years before. Jack's opening statement harked back to Pierpont's statement at the Pujo hearings, that character was the basis of credit:

> The private banker is a member of a profession which has been practiced since the middle ages. In the process of time there has grown up a code of professional ethics and customs, on the observance of which depend his reputation, his force and his usefulness to

the community in which he works . . . if, in the exercise of his profession, the private banker disregards this code, which could never be expressed in any legislation, but has a force far greater than any law, he will sacrifice his credit. This credit is his most valuable possession; it is the result of years of faith and honorable dealing and, while it may be quickly lost, once lost cannot be restored for a long time, if ever.

If I may be permitted to speak of the firm, of which I have the honour to be the senior partner, I should state that at all times the idea of doing only first class business, and that in a first class way, has been before our minds.[53]

This was as clear a statement of principles as Jack could muster: this was his birthright, what it meant to be a Morgan banker. Yet his attempt at candor sounded strangely anachronistic to American ears. Jack was an old-school banker, as out of place as an alchemist in the atomic age. Historian William E. Leuchtenburg has said, "On the witness stand, Morgan appeared to have been resurrected from some Dickensian counting-house."[54] This was literally true, for Jack was trained in late Victorian London and never abandoned its banking folkways.

His black hair swept up in a pompadour, his chin jutting, Pecora jabbed the air and posed aggressive questions; sometimes he even pointed his cigar at Jack. Abiding by Davis's advice, Jack didn't joust with the attorney. He smiled nervously, called Pecora "Sir," and hardly seemed a world-devouring tycoon. He breathed no fire, hurled no thunderbolts. The public saw the figure well-known to friends and associates but seldom, if ever, seen in public—the bluff, genial, but shy and vulnerable banker. "I should like it if the stuttering part were cut out of my answer to that question," Jack asked at one point. "I am not used to this form of examination, Mr. Pecora, and I do not get my words quite straight always."[55]

Like Samuel Untermyer at the Pujo hearings, Ferdinand Pecora focused on the House of Morgan's standing as the banker's bank. Jack saw nothing wrong with Morgan partners sitting on the boards of Guaranty Trust and Bankers Trust. Nor was he ashamed of the Morgan bank making loans to sixty officers and directors of other banks, including Charles Mitchell of National City, Seward Prosser of Bankers Trust, and William Potter of Guaranty Trust. Denying that this afforded any special advantages, Jack said, "They are friends of ours, and we know that they are good, sound, straight fellows."[56] Far from regretting the Morgan role as the Wall Street clubhouse, Jack boasted that a private bank offered neutral territory, where incorporated banks might "meet and discuss the general problems without rivalry or competition."[57]

Jack's testimony exposed Depression America to a form of wholesale, private banking that it had never known existed. When Pecora asked for the firm's partnership agreement, John Davis protested such public revelation. So in executive session, Pecora unrolled the agreement: a magnificently hand-lettered scroll that even some Morgan partners had never seen. It disclosed Jack's absolute powers to arbitrate disputes, allocate undivided profits, and even dissolve the bank. Jack was proud of the bank's secrecy. "Our relations with our clients are much more confidential, in my opinion, than the relations with an incorporated bank can be," he said.[58]

In a culture that worshiped the hard sell, the reticent J. P. Morgan and Company was a puzzling curiosity. As a private New York bank, it couldn't advertise, solicit deposits from the general public, or pay interest on deposits of less than $7,500. Apparently, getting a Morgan account was like being accepted at an exclusive country club. Even Senator Duncan U. Fletcher of Florida, the Chairman of the Senate Banking and Currency Committee, was perplexed by this:

> *Fletcher:* But you are serving the public?
> *Morgan:* Yes; but we are serving only our own clients who are our clients by our own choice.
> *Fletcher:* But you do not turn a man down; you do not select your clients; you do not give them tickets and pass on them?
> *Morgan:* Yes; we do.
> *Fletcher:* You do?
> *Morgan:* Yes, indeed; we do.
> *Fletcher:* I suppose if I went there, even though I had never [seen] any member of the firm, and had $100,000 I wanted to leave with the bank, you would take it, wouldn't you?
> *Morgan:* No; we should not do it.
> *Fletcher:* You would not?
> *Morgan:* No.
> *Fletcher:* I'm quite sure then you would not . . .
> *Morgan:* Not unless you came in with some introduction, Senator.[59]

Then who banked at this place? Pecora outlined a list of companies that kept million-dollar balances at Morgans—AT&T, Celanese, Du

Pont, General Electric, General Mills, Ingersoll-Rand, ITT, Johns-Manville, Kennecott Copper, Montgomery Ward, New York Central, Northern Pacific, Standard Brands, Standard Oil of New Jersey, Texas Gulf Sulphur, and U.S. Steel. Their executives often chose J. P. Morgan for their personal bank accounts as well. Pecora had charts showing that Morgan partners held 126 directorships in 89 corporations with $20 billion in assets. He later called this "incomparably the greatest reach of power in private hands in our entire history."[60] He seemed incredulous when Jack said partners went on boards only at the "earnest request" of a company.

If Jack entered the hearings with serene confidence, he was soon engulfed in an issue that would shadow him throughout the New Deal—income taxes. Pecora revealed that Jack had paid no income tax for 1930, 1931, and 1932, and all twenty Morgan partners paid nothing for 1931 and 1932. (Jack had paid taxes in England for these years.) Pecora also showed that by making Parker Gilbert a partner on January 2, 1931—instead of December 31, 1930, as would have been customary—the firm claimed a $31-million capital loss for 1931. Bumbling and flustered, Jack couldn't recall the details of his tax picture; such vagueness was plausible to his associates, suspicious to the public. Although Jack and most of the partners hadn't violated the law and had simply taken sizable write-offs from stock losses, their failure to pay taxes was politically explosive in the Depression. Tax shelters had not yet become a favorite American pastime, and the government desperately needed money. The next day, headlines trumpeted the Morgan partners' "tax evasion."

There were further embarrassing disclosures. Lamont's son Tommy, now a Morgan partner, had created a $114,000 capital loss by selling depressed shares to his wife, then buying them back three months later—a practice known as a wash sale. The young Lamont had to pay $3,949 in back taxes to remedy the problem. It turned out that the Internal Revenue Service had been curiously lax in examining Morgan tax returns; so sterling was the bank's reputation—or so feared was its power—that agents never closely inspected tax returns prepared there. As Pecora later said: "The Bible tells us that a good name is rather to be chosen than great riches. But it was vouchsafed to the members of J. P. Morgan and Company to enjoy both."[61]

As Jack's testimony took on a carnival atmosphere, Kentucky senator Alben W. Barkley told the doorkeeper to shut the rear door and asked photographers to stop setting off the blinding flashbulbs. The cacophony from voices and chairs scraping in the gallery sometimes drowned out Jack's soft voice. The pugnacious Carter Glass—who considered it a waste of time to interrogate upstanding Morgan partners—experienced mounting indignation. A small man with a shock of disheveled hair and a spare face, he thought the hearings a "Roman holiday" that were distracting attention from his banking bill. He sniped at Pecora for his treatment of the Morgan partners. "I do not intend to see any injustice done to the House of Morgan," he said, reddening with anger. "That is my attitude."[62] Fed up with the commotion over Jack's appearance at the hearings, he blurted out, "We are having a circus, and the only things lacking now are peanuts and colored lemonade."[63]

This gibe would change Jack Morgan's life. Overnight it echoed in the mind of Charles Leef, a Ringling Brothers press agent. The next morning, he brought to Capitol Hill a thirty-two-year-old midget named Lya Graf. She wore a blue satin dress and red straw hat. Only twenty-seven inches tall, she had a Kewpie-doll face with bright eyes and round cheeks. To enliven a delayed start to the hearings, Ray Tucker, a Scripps-Howard newsman, went out into the corridor and shepherded Leef and Lya into the Senate Caucus Room to meet the celebrated banker. "Mr. Morgan, this is Miss Graf," Tucker said. "She works for the circus." Graf blanched, but Jack stood and shook her hand with instinctive ceremony. When he sat down, Leef, emboldened, plunked Graf on his lap, to the horror of Morgan partners and lawyers. Jack apparently thought at first she was a child.

"I have a grandson bigger than you," Jack said in the sudden glow of dozens of flashbulbs.

"But I'm older."

"How old are you?"

"Thirty-two," interjected Leef.

"I'm not," Graf protested. "Only twenty."

"Well, you certainly don't look it," Jack replied. "Where do you live?"

"In a tent, sir."

"Lya," said Leef, "take off your hat."

"No, no," she said.

"Don't take it off," Jack said. "It's pretty."[64]

The most powerful men on Wall Street—Tom Lamont, John Davis, Richard Whitney—bitterly watched what they saw as a vulgar stunt, even a cruel attempt to embarrass Jack. When the senators filed in, they were outraged by what had happened and appealed to the press not to print the pictures, a request honored only by the *New York Times*. The next day, pictures of Jack and Lya Graf appeared on front pages across

America. They would rank as some of the best-known of all Depression photographs.

They are actually lovely shots, bright with whimsy, and they probably accomplished more for Jack's image than anything since the 1915 shooting. Between the portly businessman and the ringleted midget on his knee, there was an electric chemistry. While Graf steadied herself, Jack watched with fascinated amusement; he was tender with the midget and resembled a proud grandfather. For a generation of Americans, this would be their indelible image of Jack Morgan. The pictures were widely credited with starting a new age in financial public relations.

When his testimony was over, Jack dozed through the appearances of the other Morgan partners. At one point, he awoke abruptly to ask what year it was. In the sultry hearing room, a senator suggested they take off their coats. The old-fashioned Jack balked prudishly, then slipped off his light gray jacket, showing his white suspenders. He laughed and joked with guards and asked one if he needed his gun as protection against the senators. He showed reporters the famous bloodstone Pierpont had worn. Yet he was not nearly as calm or relaxed as he appeared. When a newsman told him he hadn't seen such hoopla since the Lindbergh kidnapping, Jack said privately that he "felt quite sick" at the comment.[65] His seeming aplomb contrasted with his deep mortification at being held up to public scrutiny.

Jack could have used the episode with Lya Graf to capitalize on goodwill. Instead, he was embittered by the hearings and sulked over the incident. His New England pride wouldn't let him admit what the photographs suggest—that he had enjoyed the impromptu encounter. He didn't want to be made human in such a sordid way and said the incident had been "very unusual and somewhat unpleasant."[66] With the press, he tried to react to the episode with faint sarcasm. When asked why he hadn't removed the woman from his lap, he replied, "Well, you see, I didn't know but what she might be a member of the Brain Trust or one of the Cabinet."[67]

Everyone noted the uncanny parallels between the Pujo and Pecora hearings. Newspaper commentary favorably contrasted Jack's cooperation with Pierpont's truculence and Will Rogers even forecast a brilliant career for Jack. In milder moments, Jack conceded that Pecora hadn't been as taxing as Untermyer. But he was still unforgiving in his general appraisal. "Pecora has the manners of a prosecuting attorney who is trying to convict a horse thief. Some of these senators remind me of sex suppressed old maids who think everybody is trying to seduce them."[68]

For someone as bashful as Jack, a public grilling was a gruesome affair. He declared, "To have stood before a crowd of people and attempt by straight answers to crooked questions, to convince the world that one is honest, is a form of insult that I do not think would be possible in any civilized country."[69]

Sometimes Jack could laugh about the experience. One day on the golf fairway, he was lining up a shot when his caddy, Frank Colby, said he should think of the ball as Pecora's head. When Jack hit a splendid shot, they both laughed appreciatively.[70] But most of the time, Jack brooded about the hearings, which ended up alienating him from the New Deal. Afterward, he got a visit from William Jay Schieffelin, son-in-law of Dr. Markoe, who was trying to win support for a scheme enabling poor people to buy life insurance from savings banks. Jack not only refused to help, but made a revealing comment: "I only wish I had the capacity you have, a capacity for indignation at outrages. I've been so outraged that it leaves me cold when I hear of somebody else being outraged."[71] This sense of his own victimization would close Jack's mind toward the Roosevelt programs. More and more, he would feel a revulsion from America, a sense of being abandoned by his own country, and profound anger at the tarnishing of his bank's reputation.

The story of Lya Graf ends sadly. As sensitive as Jack, she was traumatized by the endless jokes about the episode—so much so that in 1935 she decided to return to her native Germany, even though she was half Jewish: her real name was Lia Schwarz. Two years later, she was arrested by the Nazis as a "useless person" and sent to Auschwitz, where she died in the gas chambers. All this was learned only after the war when Nate Eagle, the Ringling Brothers manager who cared for the midgets, traced her history. Jack Morgan never knew what became of her, nor that her extreme distress over their brief encounter set in motion events that led, ultimately, to her death.

AS Pecora adroitly exposed their subterfuges, the other partners fared no better than Jack. When George Whitney read a statement favoring disclosure of commissions in security offerings, Pecora sarcastically noted that the legislation had just been passed. Returning in his questioning to 1929, Pecora lobbed another grenade over to the Morgan side. That year, the bank had joined the craze for creating new holding companies and had sponsored Alleghany Corporation as a vehicle for the railroad and real estate interests of the Van Sweringen brothers; United Corporation, an electric-utility holding company; and Standard Brands, a merger of four food and consumer-products companies.

Instead of placing shares only with dealers, Morgans borrowed a British precedent and placed shares with scores of friendly individuals. These shares came from a block of stock the bank kept as its underwriting fee. On Wall Street in the 1920s, it wasn't uncommon to have company officers or well-heeled individuals serve as underwriters. By allocating shares of the three holding companies to rich investors, Morgans claimed, it had tried to strike a compromise with its usual policy of not enticing individuals into risky stock transactions. As George Whitney said, they chose only those customers whom they knew were "competent financially and mentally to undertake the risks, whatever the risk may be."[72]

Such self-serving descriptions didn't capture the reality of 1929. In the souped-up bull market, shares offered to Morgan intimates before the public issue were already selling on a when-issued basis at a steep premium. (When-issued sales occur before a public offering and anticipate the price that will prevail when trading begins.) Between the Morgan price for lucky friends and this provisional market price lay a wide gap, an instant windfall. For instance, the bank was giving Alleghany shares to friends at $20 apiece; these could soon be cashed in for $35; United shares at $75 would soon go for $99; and Standard Brands shares bought at $32 could be redeemed just sixty days later at $41. In the soaring 1929 market, there was no great risk in carrying these shares before public issue, and the potential rewards were colossal. The shares seemed almost to be outright gifts—the sort of royal bequest only the House of Morgan could bestow. In Alleghany stock alone, the bank had over $8 million in profits to distribute. The setup was dubbed the gravy train.

The revelation of the House of Morgan's so-called preferred list of friends confirmed Main Street's cynicism of Wall Street as a place of easy riches and loose morals. For Morgan critics, this was at last the smoking gun, the tangible proof of corruption. The stunning list of recipients encompassed the American business and political elite. It started at the very top. After leaving the White House, Calvin Coolidge had been advised on finances by Morgan partner Tom Cochran and received three thousand shares of Standard Brands; somewhat ashamed at this revelation, he told friends that it saddened him to appear on the preferred list while they were on the welfare list.[73] Other Republican beneficiaries included Charles O. Hilles, chairman of the Republican National Committee, and Charles Francis Adams, Hoover's secretary of the navy and the father-in-law of Jack's younger son, Harry.

Hedging its bets, Morgans also cultivated Democrats. This side of the ledger was even more embarrassing to its recipients, among them William G. McAdoo, the former Treasury secretary, a mentor of Russell Leffingwell. What made McAdoo's plight especially mortifying was that as a senator, he now sat on the Pecora committee. Also on the list was John J. Raskob, chairman of the Democratic National Committee. The list reached straight into the New Deal itself. When he was president of American Car and Foundry Company in 1929, William H. Woodin, now FDR's Treasury secretary, had taken up Morgans on an offer.

Beyond politics, the preferred list exposed an astonishing range of Morgan corporate contacts. There were business chieftains—Owen Young of General Electric, Myron Taylor of U.S. Steel, Walter Teagle of Standard Oil of New Jersey, Walter Gifford of AT&T, and Sosthenes Behn of ITT; financiers—Albert Wiggin of Chase, George F. Baker of First National, Richard Whitney of the New York Stock Exchange, and Bernard Baruch; a war hero—General John Pershing; a national hero—Charles Lindbergh; distinguished lawyers—John W. Davis and Albert G. Milbank; and distinguished families—Guggenheims, Drexels, Biddles, and Berwinds.

The House of Morgan was shaken by the disclosures and the imputation of dishonesty. When hiring partners, both Pierpont and Jack had always made the same statement; they would say, "I want my business done up there"—holding their hands in the air—"and not down here"—pointing to the ground.[74] Jack would tell people that at the first sign of unethical conduct, they should come straight to him. Now the bank had to face charges that it had unscrupulously curried favor with a broad spectrum of business and political leaders. How to defend the indefensible?

The task fell to George Whitney, whose Brahmin good looks and lacquered black hair made him the prototypically handsome Morgan partner of his generation. He had enjoyed Alleghany bounty himself, netting $229,000 on the sale of eight thousand shares. A tough, unyielding witness, Whitney stuck to the line that the bank was shielding small investors from risk. "They took a risk of profit," Whitney said of the preferred customers; "they took a risk of loss." Pecora later rejoined: "Many there were who would gladly have helped them share that appalling peril!"[75] At moments, even the self-assured Whitney seemed confused, stammering at one point, "I don't know, Senator Couzens. It is hard to say why we did things. It is even harder to say why we didn't."[76]

Even as Morgan partners denied that shares were distributed to influence people, Pecora released subpoenaed bank records that confirmed a less than angelic intent. In 1929, Morgan partner William Ewing had written to William Woodin coyly acknowledging the bonanza being offered:

> I believe that the stock is selling in the market around $35 to $37 a share, which means very little, except that people wish to speculate. We are reserving for you 1,000 shares at $20 a share, if you would like to have it. There are no strings tied to this stock, and you can sell it whenever you wish. . . . We just want you to know that we were thinking of you in this connection and thought you might like to have a little of the stock at the same price we are paying for it.[77]

Other documents suggested that the operation was conducted secretly. Partner Arthur Anderson told lawyer Albert Milbank, "It probably is unnecessary for me to add that I hope you will not make any mention of this operation."[78] Some correspondence resorted to sly hints. Golfing in Palm Beach, John J. Raskob, a former Du Pont treasurer and General Motors director, thanked George Whitney for his shares with the sincere hope that "the future holds opportunities for me to reciprocate."[79]

Lamont was indignant at charges of influence peddling. Yet his own files contain a February 1929 memo that may be the most damaging of all. In a postscript written to Arthur Anderson, it shows how the distributed shares were discussed internally: "It occurred to me this morning to make inquiry from you whether in our distribution of Alleghany common we had allotted anything to Frederick Strauss. He was so exceedingly helpful and at considerable sacrifice to himself in going over to Washington to testify in the matter of the stock issues, that I am not at all sure that we ought not to try to do something for him even at a date as late as this."[80] Clearly, the preferred list had less to do with protecting small investors than with rewarding important friends.

The preferred list came at a particularly inopportune time both for the Roosevelt administration and the Morgan bank. High finance was on trial, and congressional hoppers bulged with securities-reform bills. The cabinet spent an hour deciding whether Woodin should remain in his post as Treasury secretary. Vice-President John Nance Garner favored his resignation to establish that the administration was free of Morgan influence, but Roosevelt feared abandoning a friend under fire. "The

President took the position that many of us did things prior to 1929 that we wouldn't think of doing now; that our code of ethics had radically changed," Interior Secretary Harold Ickes wrote in his diary.[81] Woodin remained in the cabinet until November 1933, when, gravely ill, he was replaced by Morgenthau. The cabinet was also disturbed by the appearance of Norman Davis, its roving ambassador, on the preferred list. Some feared that if the Roosevelt administration moved closer to the League of Nations or the British government, the public would impute the action to Morgan influence over Davis. Despite this, Davis represented Washington at several high-level European conferences in the 1930s.

The public reacted to the preferred list scandal with extreme disillusionment: the brightest angel on Wall Street had fallen. The bank had avoided the flagrant abuses of other banks—even Pecora called Morgans a "conservative" firm—but the preferred list cast it in the mud with other banks. A stunned Walter Lippmann told Morgan friends that no group of men should have such private power without public accountability. It was a bitter pill for Lippmann, who had often dined at Lamont's table. His biographer, Ronald Steel, suggests that he and other journalists were lulled to sleep by Lamont, whose "charm and familiarity with the trade enabled him to persuade many journalists to look upon the activities of the Morgan firm no more critically than he did himself."[82]

Lippmann wasn't the only shocked journalist. As if some mighty public trust had been betrayed, the *New York Times* wrote an elegiac editorial: "Here was a firm of bankers, perhaps the most famous and powerful in the whole world, which was certainly under no necessity of practicing the small arts of petty traders. Yet it failed under a test of its pride and prestige. . . . They have given their warmest friends cause for feeling that somehow the whole community, along with numbers of men whom all had delighted to honor, has been involved in a sort of public misfortune."[83]

Reading this, Lamont became distraught. Of the Morgan partners, he had the most personal need for admiration. He wrote his friend Adolph Ochs, publisher of the *Times,* trying to extenuate the scandal. He said Morgans hadn't expected people on the list to serve in public office again. He cited the risks of owning common stock and made it sound as if the list were made up only of family and friends. The explanations sounded strained: "We naturally turned in part to individuals who had ample means and who understand the nature of common stock—men who are prepared to take a chance with their money."[84] All his arts couldn't hide what had become a certifiable scandal, setting the stage for the bill that would dismember the House of Morgan.

THE Glass-Steagall Act was sponsored by a Virginia senator who felt more warmly toward 23 Wall than any of his Senate Banking Committee colleagues. Small and peppery, Carter Glass was a former Lynchburg newspaper editor with little formal education. As a congressman, he had helped to write the Federal Reserve Act and had espoused strong banker control. As Wilson's Treasury secretary, he had been Russell Leffingwell's boss. In early 1933, he was a mass of contradictions. After supporting Roosevelt's election, he quickly emerged as an articulate critic of FDR. He rebuffed the president's offer to become Treasury secretary and attacked New Deal activism from a Jeffersonian standpoint; he was the sole Democratic senator to oppose the gold devaluation. Glass sponsored his famous bill with no personal animus toward Wall Street. In fact, he and Leffingwell often exchanged nostalgic, syrupy notes about their years in the Treasury Department. Although Leffingwell described their friendship as one of his most cherished, he was frustrated in his efforts to capitalize on it that spring: when subcommittee members working on the bank-reform bill swore not to talk to outsiders about it, Glass had to abide by the decision.

Glass-Steagall evolved in a way that owed much to fate. Huey Long and other congressional populists wanted federal deposit insurance in the bill, as well as restrictions on interstate branching. Both features were anathema to Roosevelt, who favored a national banking system that would put small-town Republican bankers out of business, not prop them up. Like Hoover, he feared that deposit insurance would pull strong banks down with the weak and thought it "puts a premium on sloppy banking and penalizes good banking."[85]

Roosevelt kept the press guessing whether he would support Glass-Steagall. The Pecora hearings certainly contributed to public support of the bill. But what sealed its fate was the flood of mail to Congress favoring deposit insurance. The inclusion of deposit insurance was also important because nobody wanted to insure the securities affiliates of banks; if they had federal insurance, they would be obliged to stick to conservative loan-and-deposit banking. Finally, the bill set ceilings on savings interest rates. The Glass-Steagall Act was signed on June 16, 1933, by a president who didn't even think the public was particularly eager for banking reform. From now on, banks would either take deposits and make loans or merchandise securities—but not both.

A surprise last-minute insertion in the bill was a provision endorsed by Chase president Winthrop Aldrich that forced private banks to choose between deposit and securities businesses. This was the *coup de grâce* for the House of Morgan. Later Carter Glass told Leffingwell that Aldrich drafted this provision and that Roosevelt foisted it on him. Pecora's disclosure about the Morgan partners' avoidance of income taxes made it impossible to delete this provision, so strong was public wrath.[86] Adding to the pressure was Chase's decision to disband its securities affiliate, whose refugees joined with renegades from the First National Bank of Boston to form First Boston, the first modern American investment bank.

The Glass-Steagall Act took dead aim at the House of Morgan. After all, it was the bank that had most spectacularly fused the two forms of banking. It had, ironically, proved that the two types of services could be successfully combined; Kuhn, Loeb and Lehman Brothers did less deposit business, while National City and Chase had scandal-ridden securities affiliates. The House of Morgan was the active double threat, with its million-dollar corporate balances and blue-ribbon underwriting business.

What was the theory behind the Glass-Steagall Act? Foremost, it was meant to restore a certain sobriety to American finance. In the 1920s, the banker had gone from a person of sober rectitude to a huckster who encouraged people to gamble on risky stocks and bonds. As Pecora noted, small investors identified commercial banks with security, so that National City stock salesmen "came to them clothed with all the authority and prestige of the magic name 'National City.'"[87] It was also argued that the union of deposit and securities banking created potential conflicts of interest. Banks could take bad loans, repackage them as bonds, and fob them off on investors, as National City had done with Latin American loans. They could even lend investors the money to buy the bonds. A final problem with the banks' brokerage affiliates was that they forced the Federal Reserve System to stand behind both depositors and speculators. If a securities affiliate failed, the Fed might need to rescue it to protect the parent bank. In other words, the government might have to protect speculators to save depositors.

Ultimately, Glass-Steagall was as much an attempt to punish the banking industry as it was a measure to reform it. It was Main Street striking back at Wall Street, rounding out the 1929 disaster. The bill also had supporters among small investment banks eager to exclude large commercial banks from their domain. Many economic historians have pointed out the tenuous links between the crash and the subsequent bank failures. Bank failures were concentrated among thousands of country banks across America, while big Wall Street banks with securities affiliates withstood the Depression relatively well. Yet Glass-Steagall and other New Deal reform acts were directed at Wall Street and insulated little crossroads banks from big-city competition. This made political, but not economic, sense. The speculative fever of the 1920s had infected *all* securities houses, whether or not they were subsidiaries of deposit banks. The Jazz Age on Wall Street might have been no less effervescent if a Glass-Steagall arrangement had already been in place.

The House of Morgan had trenchant arguments to make against the bill, but nobody listened. After the Pecora hearings, even well-reasoned arguments by the financial elite resembled self-serving blather. Lamont pointed out that the flagrant scandals of the 1920s had involved retail-investment affiliates. Why, then, couldn't wholesale banks, such as J. P. Morgan, distribute securities not to individuals but to dealers and large institutions? The Morgan partners also argued that disclosure requirements in the new Securities Act of 1933 would force banks to identify any loans outstanding to countries or companies whose bonds they issued—safeguards for bond investors lacking in the 1920s.

Lamont contended that size wasn't to blame for America's fragile banking system so much as fragmentation. The country had over twenty thousand banking institutions, resulting in a financial history peculiarly checkered with panics, failures, and runs. England, France, and Canada, by contrast, had a small number of large national banks, and these had passed through the Depression in far better shape. Then why not bigger, better-capitalized banks? To free banks from reliance on a single industry—whether Texas oil or Kansas farming—Lamont favored interstate banking. Russell Leffingwell contended as well that removing big commercial banks from underwriting work would produce capital-short investment banks—a prophecy not fully appreciated until decades later.

In 1933, however, such a perspective was bootless. The public wanted to see the giants slain and didn't care about the dusty little banks that had faltered from bad luck or mismanagement. America's atomized banking system might have contributed to its stormy financial history, but the political response was always to segment it further. With the Glass-Steagall Act, America experienced the catharsis awaited since Black Thursday. As Leffingwell said, "There is so much hunger and distress that it is only too natural for the people to blame the bankers and to visit their wrath on the greatest name in American banking."[88] All the while, Morgan partners felt that they suffered for sins committed by others. George Whitney later remarked that "we never retailed while I was in our office, but that's where the trouble started, and the New Deal was smart enough to realize that if they could cut the security business up in pieces, they would take this power away and they did."[89]

CHAPTER NINETEEN

CRACK-UP

. .
.

A FTER passage of the Glass-Steagall Act, there was a grace period, during which the House of Morgan had to choose between deposit and investment banking. The partners still hoped the measure would be repealed. But after its unrivaled political influence in the 1920s, the bank seemed paralyzed, unable to exercise influence. As Arthur Schlesinger, Jr., has noted, no group lost more in public esteem, or more keenly lamented its exclusion from Washington, than the bankers. They became a caste of untouchables right at the start of the New Deal. For the House of Morgan, there were moments when the rout by enemy troops seemed terrifyingly complete. Its old foes were entrenched in Washington. For the new securities-disclosure law, the White House had asked Samuel Untermyer, of Pujo fame, to prepare a draft. Untermyer lost standing with Roosevelt, however, when he bragged too much about his supposed intimacy with the president.

The intellectual mentor of much legislation was that scourge of the New Haven Railroad, Louis Brandeis, now a Supreme Court justice. In May 1933, the precepts he had expounded to Lamont at the University Club twenty years before became law in the Securities Act. This truth-in-securities law required the registration of new securities and full disclosure of information about companies and underwriters. *Caveat vendor* replaced *caveat emptor* as the regulatory philosophy. When FDR spoke in favor of the bill, he alluded to Brandeis's book about the New Haven railroad, *Other People's Money;* the law, said Roosevelt, would embody "the ancient truth that those who manage banks, corporations, and other agencies handling or using other people's money are trustees acting for others."[1]

For the House of Morgan, Louis Brandeis was more than just a critic;

he was an adversary of almost mythical proportions. In early 1934, Leffingwell told Lamont he should read a new edition of *Other People's Money* and blamed Brandeis for the Glass-Steagall provision pertaining to private banks: "I have little doubt that he inspired it, or even drafted it. The Jews do not forget. They are relentless. . . . The reason why I make so much of this is that I think you underestimate the forces we are antagonizing. . . . I believe that we are confronted with the profound politico-economic philosophy, matured in the wood for twenty years, of the finest brain and the most powerful personality in the Democratic party, who happens to be a Justice of the Supreme Court."[2] Despite the separation of powers, Brandeis advised Roosevelt through an emissary— his daughter, Elizabeth Raushenbush. Roosevelt referred to Brandeis by the code name Isaiah.

In 1934, the House of Morgan joined with New York Stock Exchange president Richard Whitney in a zealous lobbying effort to defeat the Securities Exchange Act. Operating from a Georgetown townhouse nicknamed the Wall Street Embassy, they warned that federal regulation would convert the Street into "a deserted village."[3] It was a campaign of such harrowing intensity that despite the anti–Wall Street mood, the bill's authors were surprised by their victory. One of them, Thomas G. Corcoran, exulted, "Rayburn and I stood alone against all the batteries of lawyers sent by Morgan's and the Stock Exchange—and we won out!"[4] Another Morgan hobgoblin, Joseph Kennedy, snubbed by Jack before the crash, became the Securities and Exchange Commission's first chairman. Ferdinand Pecora, who worked on the bill, was named a commissioner. The money changers had indeed been chased from the Temple, by the Irish, the Italians, and the Jews—the groups excluded from Wasp Wall Street in the 1920s.

The Morgan partners resorted to hyperbolic criticism when they should have been conciliatory. Jack Morgan inveighed against "absurd" federal deposit insurance and warned of dying capital markets if securities laws were enacted. Faced with the decline of the bank's power, he emitted an air of subdued defeat. He complained to friends that he was a punching bag for every political propagandist. Like other partners, he felt muzzled in contesting the New Deal—perhaps the reason why he didn't join his friend and lawyer John Davis in forming the anti–New Deal Liberty League in 1934. "If anybody lifts his voice in protest . . . he is at once held up to public scorn as a totally selfish, grasping individual, wholly unresponsive to the new thought,"[5] he declared. He was an easy butt for critics. He often antagonized reporters by curtly refusing interviews: "I do not think my opinion is worth a damn."

Other times, he would talk and denounce progressive income taxes or take other inflammatory stands. Either way, his popularity declined.

Teddy Roosevelt had been Pierpont's tormenter, and now another Roosevelt served the same role for Jack. At moments, the Roosevelt family seemed one big throng of Morgan-hating harpies. When somebody mentioned TR, Jack spluttered: "God damn all Roosevelts!"[6] He was fond of quoting Richard Hooker, the English Renaissance divine, that to live by one man's will was every man's misery. For Jack, that man was FDR, whom he saw as a frightening left-wing charlatan out to destroy his own class. In 1934, he said, "I am gradually coming to the opinion, which I did not have at first, that the United States will probably outlive even the attacks upon it by Franklin Roosevelt and I am particularly satisfied to see the rising tide of opposition to his fierce methods and his wholesale slaughter of reputations."[7] The Roosevelt hatred became obsessive. When Jack developed a heart condition, his grandchildren were instructed not to mention the president's name in his presence. Other accounts tell of retainers snipping Roosevelt photos from Jack's morning paper, in deference to the master's high blood pressure.

Rather than bending with the time, Jack's conservatism grew crustily defensive. The old swipes at Congress lapsed into ugly diatribes against democracy and universal suffrage. Congressmen were "wild men" who controlled his destiny, while the intelligent, propertied class were subjected to the whims of a fickle, emotional majority. He regarded the New Deal less as a set of economic reforms than as a direct, malicious assault on the social order, aimed at the "extinction of all wealth and earning power."[8] Notwithstanding a 25-percent jobless rate, he wanted balanced budgets and low taxes. "The more I see of the New Deal," he said, "the more I realize that there is nothing new about it except its name."[9]

As chief bank lobbyist, Lamont wasn't reflexively antagonistic to the New Deal and applauded measures to combat deflation, such as open-market operations (the purchase and sale of government securities) by the Fed. At moments in the 1930s, Morgans supported easy-money policies while hidebound Wall Street fretted about inflation. But even Lamont never presented a reform program that would steal the bank critics' thunder; Wall Street let its enemies write the new laws.

As was his wont, Lamont used different voices as he spoke to different people. At a private dinner in 1934, he told relief administrator Harry Hopkins, "Well, if the country was willing to spend thirty billion dollars in a year's time to try to lick the Germans, I don't see why people should complain about its spending five or six billion dollars to keep people from starving."[10] Here he sounded like a free-spending liberal. Yet in chatting with Chancellor of the Exchequer Neville Chamberlain that year, he praised Britain for overcoming the Depression through sound, old-fashioned policies, not deficit spending. He joked, "I suppose I mustn't hold you personally responsible for having sent Keynes over and to have made our President spend another ½ billion dollars in public works."[11]

The best weapon the Morgan bank had for changing New Deal policy was Russell Leffingwell. With his pure white hair and Pinocchio nose, he looked like a sage or an elder statesman. He was an omnivorous reader, a man of wide vision who could offer cogent opinions on any subject. Leffingwell had the most balanced view of the New Deal and often told friends Roosevelt had saved America from revolution in 1933. He wasn't afraid to scandalize Wall Street by consorting with the president. Sometimes he used his friend Morris Ernst, a liberal lawyer, as an intermediary to the White House, so that Walter Winchell and other columnists wouldn't get wind of his influence. Yet even Leffingwell couldn't make the intellectual adjustment required by the economic emergency. When Roosevelt brought him to the White House in October 1934 to discuss a new public works program, Leffingwell rejected the plan with ritual assertions that it would cause inflation and crowd out private capital from financial markets. Yet deflation was the major problem, and far from being overcrowded, capital markets were empty. Leffingwell was a nineteenth-century liberal and found it hard to approve of many forms of government intervention in the economy.

In many ways, the House of Morgan was a muscle-bound giant, afraid its lobbying efforts would be twisted by opponents into proof of insidious power. By late 1933, the airwaves were filled with demagogic voices that ascribed the Depression to Wall Street–inspired monetary policy. Father Charles E. Coughlin, the radio priest, stoked the old prairie fires once lighted by William Jennings Bryan. From his Shrine of the Little Flower near Detroit, he incited his nationwide audience with tales of a bank that had enslaved America to the gold standard, had long colluded with the British crown, and had forced debt and deflation on farmers. That the same bank had hailed Britain and America's departure from gold mattered not a whit. In a November 1933 broadcast entitled "Thus Goeth the Battle!" Coughlin dredged up old myths about the House of Morgan: "Who in God's name ever accused the Morgans of having patriotism to this country? Who doesn't know that they have been playing the British game for years; that they pay taxes to England and none to America?''

He then evoked a football team of politicians—Morgan stooges all—who had pushed America into the Depression:

> And on the sidelines there sits J. Pierpont Morgan—the Knute Rockne of the grand old guard—the scout in the pay of England, the master mind of tax-dodging, the strategist of the financial huddle.
> . . .
>
> There are two powerful generations of Morgans—the elder who sold guns to the Civil War soldiers—guns that couldn't shoot—and the younger who arranged money for more guns that shot to no avail in the last war. . . . Now where do you stand? Choose between Roosevelt and Morgans! Choose between these anointed racketeers of Wall Street . . . and the "new deal"![12]

Father Coughlin would ask his listeners to mail in dollar bills. It later was revealed that he used some of the money to speculate in silver futures through a personal account at Paine Webber.

In these scurrilous attacks by Coughlin, the Hearst press, and other isolationist organs, a powerful theme emerged—that World War I and the Depression had been instigated by the same Wall Street bankers. The argument was that the bankers drew America into the war to safeguard their Allied loans and that the debts and reparations produced by the war led to the Depression; *ergo,* Morgans and other international bankers were to blame for American participation in the war and for the Depression. For Anglophobic populists, this was a convenient equation. They could exploit discontent with Wall Street to argue against closer ties with Britain, and they could tap isolationist sentiment to press for tougher bank controls. The House of Morgan was the natural target for this attack.

ROOSEVELT was as perplexed and annoyed with the Wall Street bankers as they were with him. He saw himself as saving the patient with radical surgery, not killing him. His talent for experimentation, for latching onto new ideas, was profoundly disturbing to bankers who had lived by sacred, immutable laws. To try to patch up relations, FDR invited Morgan loyalist George Harrison, Ben Strong's successor at the New York Fed, for a weekend cruise aboard his yacht, the *Sequoia.*

Commenting on the bankers' mistrust, Roosevelt said ruefully, "They oppose everything I do, even though it is with the intention of helping them."[13]

Eager to mediate, Harrison arranged for FDR to address a meeting of the American Bankers Association in Washington. Lamont and Parker Gilbert attended, the first time Morgan partners ever graced an ABA meeting. The effort at mediation only worsened matters. Jackson Reynolds of the First National Bank of New York delivered a keynote speech lauding FDR. But when it was discovered that Roosevelt himself had vetted the speech, the bankers felt cheated, and the New Deal–bankers truce was ended. Both sides retreated into a bitter standoff.

Perhaps the most sophisticated foray against the House of Morgan came from those who sought changes in the Federal Reserve System. A little-noticed provision of the Glass-Steagall Act forbade the New York Fed to conduct negotiations with foreign banks. This was Washington's response to the elaborate connivance between Ben Strong and Monty Norman—a relationship so important for the House of Morgan. The seemingly innocuous measure was one of Washington's canniest moves against the bank.

Then in 1934, a young Utah banker, Marriner Stoddard Eccles, advised the Roosevelt administration on revisions to the Federal Reserve Act. Eccles wanted to emasculate the New York Fed and shift power to the Federal Reserve Board in Washington so as to purge the influence of Wall Street bankers from the system. Leffingwell was especially incensed at this move because he blamed the 1929 crash on the Washington board's interference with the New York Fed, which had wanted to raise interest rates and arrest speculation. George Harrison tried to marshal enough conservative senators to defeat the Banking Act of 1935, but his efforts were in vain. Under the Eccles legislation, the district banks lost much of their autonomy; power was now lodged in the seven-member Washington board. In two symbolic steps underscoring the Fed's new independence, the Treasury secretary was removed from the board, and the Fed, which had operated from Treasury premises, got its own building.

Later Eccles tried to put Parker Gilbert on the reorganized Fed board, but Morgan partners dismissed the move as a sop, knowing that the Fed now responded to new political masters. In many ways, the Eccles reforms belatedly accomplished the aims of the Fed's progressive supporters, who had wanted an American central bank to curb Wall Street power. The 1920s Republican abdication of an international role had permitted Ben Strong and the House of Morgan to subvert that intention. Now, over twenty years later, the ghost of the Money Trust was finally exorcised.

AMONG Wall Street banks, none agonized more than the House of Morgan over whether to choose deposit or investment banking. It postponed a final decision until the summer of 1935. By that point, it had been legally barred from securities work for a year. Disturbed by the paucity of industrial issues on Wall Street, Carter Glass inserted an amendment into the proposed Banking Act of 1935 that restored limited securities powers to deposit banks. The partners rested their final hopes on this peg.

George Whitney, as head of corporate underwriting, was under mounting pressure to inform Morgan clients of the bank's decision. With interest rates down, many companies wanted to refund maturing bonds at lower rates. They kept asking Whitney what to do. In late July, Charles Mitchell, former chairman of the National City Bank and now a partner in Blyth and Company, found Whitney still hoping for a last-minute reversal of Glass-Steagall. "I think they are waiting . . . to see if the underwriting amendment in the banking bill will pass," Mitchell told a partner, "and regarding this they are more optimistic than they have been."[14] In late August, the banking amendment reached a House-Senate conference committee. But President Roosevelt—bringing down his fist in one last blow to the House of Morgan—interceded to kill the amendment. He refused to consider any modification of Glass-Steagall.

As if too depressed to face the truth, Jack had kept assuring Teddy Grenfell that the amendment would pass. Yet mysterious doings in the art market of early 1935 betrayed his underlying pessimism. Citing inheritance taxes and a desire to put his estate in order, Jack sold six magnificent paintings for $1.5 million. To Fritz Thyssen, the German steel magnate, went Domenico Ghirlandajo's portrait of Giovanna Tornabuoni while the Metropolitan Museum got a Fra Filippo Lippi triptych and Rubens's Anne of Austria. Through Christie's in London, Jack auctioned seven cases of coveted miniatures amassed over thirty years. In oppressive July heat, with a nurse in attendance in case anyone fainted, Christie's sold a portrait by Hans Holbein the Younger, a gold pendant with Queen Elizabeth's profile, and other rarities. Only astute press commentators connected this sudden need for cash with a pending decision about the House of Morgan. As he had demonstrated after his father's death, Jack was ready to pare his art collection ruthlessly if he needed to conserve the bank's capital.

Before J. P. Morgan and Company made its decision, a new arrangement was devised with Morgan Grenfell in June 1934 to comply with Glass-Steagall. The British house became a limited company in which the New York firm held a one-third stake. This was designed to buffer the new commercial bank, J. P. Morgan and Company, from British securities work, a structure preferred by the Bank of England as well. New York would now be a passive investor. "It was definitely a hands-off situation," noted Tim Collins, a later Morgan Grenfell chairman.[15] There remained a close, familial feeling between 23 Wall and 23 Great Winchester, and the London *Times* called it only a "slight technical alteration."[16] Yet for a firm that had always been subordinate to New York, the change represented a new level of British autonomy. It also occurred at a time when the City could no longer float huge foreign loans, as it had before the war, except for the British Empire. Morgan Grenfell and London's other merchant banks concentrated instead upon securities and merger work for domestic companies.

In August 1935, Tom Lamont gathered the J. P. Morgan chieftains at his island farm off the Maine coast. The group included Morgan partners Leffingwell, Whitney, S. Parker Gilbert, and Harold Stanley, and Lansing Reed of Davis, Polk, and Wardwell. At this secret meeting, the House of Morgan decided irrevocably to remain a deposit bank and spin off an investment bank called Morgan Stanley. No minutes survive from this summit, thus leaving unanswered several essential questions. Why did Morgans—nonpareil of underwriters—opt for "commercial" rather than "investment" banking? Why the preference for deposits and loans rather than securities and brokering? Why an action that, in retrospect, seems a failure of vision?

Fifty years later, the choice seems strange. Between 1919 and the Pecora hearings, Morgans had sponsored $6 billion in securities for blue-chip companies and foreign governments. The Morgan cachet on bond issues brought in collateral banking business, such as the payment of dividends on bonds. As Russell Leffingwell had told Lamont, "I believe further that our securities business is a necessary feeder to our banking business, and that without it the banking business would in time dry up."[17] Except for Brown Brothers Harriman, most distinguished partnerships—Kuhn, Loeb; Goldman, Sachs; and Lehman Brothers—opted for "investment banking" (a misnomer for the securities business the term denotes). The world of commercial banking— with its letters of credit, loans, foreign exchange, and stock-transfer work—seemed prosaic for a bank of such rarefied tastes and as active in secret diplomacy as J. P. Morgan and Company.

The choice was heavily influenced by the moribund state of the securities markets. Securities underwriting had become the firm's least profitable activity, and new securities laws strapped underwriters with large potential liabilities. Stung by the preferred-list scandal, perhaps Jack Morgan favored commercial banking as more stable and consistently profitable than investment banking. In urging repeal of Glass-Steagall, Leffingwell wrote a letter to Roosevelt that shows the way in which securities work was regarded during the Depression:

> The business of underwriting capital issues is and should be a byproduct business. It is occasional and sporadic. Nobody can afford to be in the business unless he has a good bread and butter business to live on. A house exclusively in the underwriting business is under too much pressure to pay overhead and living expenses to pick and choose the issues it will underwrite.
>
> One reason why our record is so good . . . may be . . . that we have no salesmen, very little overhead attributable to the underwriting business and that we have a good bread and butter banking business. So we could and did say no to half of Europe and of South America.[18]

This approach of keeping overhead low, not having salesmen, and selecting only prime clients would shape Morgan Stanley's philosophy for the next forty-five years.

The human factor was undoubtedly also significant in choosing commercial banking. In 1935, about 20 percent of American workers were unemployed. It would have been hard to renounce the labor-intensive activities on the commercial-banking side. To have entered investment banking would have meant wholesale firings—an egregious betrayal for a paternalistic firm. Says an official Morgan history: "At the time of that decision the partnership, J.P. Morgan & Co., had a staff of about 425 people. If the firm had chosen to remain solely in the securities business, a large part of this staff probably would have become surplus. . . . Approximately 400 people were busy in commercial banking and other activities and remained with the firm; about twenty left to form Morgan Stanley & Co."[19]

There were also less benign motives. Morgan partners wanted to retain the option of someday recreating the House of Morgan without losing its clients. In late 1934, Lamont wrote to his partner Charles Steele: "We all feel, I think, that ways and means will be found to get us back into the securities business, either through the amendment of the existing laws or through *some separate corporate plan* or otherwise. We are considering all these matters now, but have by no means accepted the idea that . . . we are to be eliminated from the security business''[20] (italics added). The reference to a separate corporate plan hints at Morgan Stanley's genesis. Lamont, it seems, believed they could stay in securities without changes in Glass-Steagall, suggesting he had a trick or two up his sleeve.

Both at 23 Wall and elsewhere, Morgan Stanley was regarded as a branch of the main trunk, a successor firm. As a cable to Morgan Grenfell explained, ''The fact it is a segregation is apparently well understood. At the same time, everyone looks to the new company to carry on the traditions of the firm.''[21] The House of Morgan probably wanted to create a firm that later, under a friendly Republican administration, could be cleanly folded back into J. P. Morgan and Company. Lamont may have recalled the birth of Bankers Trust as a ''captive'' bank, one that would politely return customers referred to them for trust business. If Morgans had chosen investment banking and released 90 percent of its staff, it would have been impossible to rebuild the House of Morgan if Glass-Steagall were rescinded.

At four o'clock on the afternoon of September 5, 1935, the eve of Jack Morgan's sixty-eighth birthday, the House of Morgan was officially divided. Lamont, Whitney, and Stanley stood before the fireplace at the end of the long narrow partners' room, below the oil portrait of Pierpont. They announced to two dozen newsmen that several people from the Morgan Bond Department would leave to form Morgan Stanley. The new firm would have three J. P. Morgan partners—Harold Stanley, who had joined the firm in late 1927, after Dwight Morrow was appointed ambassador to Mexico; Jack's younger son, Harry; and William Ewing— and two Drexel partners, Perry Hall and Edward H. York. Lamont said the new firm would conduct a securities business ''of the character formerly handled by our firm.''[22]

Jack and Harry Morgan were absent from the conference, refusing to forgo the pleasures of grouse shooting, even on this historic occasion. It was a mournful moment. One reporter, noting the solemn faces, observed, ''The segregation of the old firm was taken as seriously as a separation of any private family.''[23] Yet however lugubrious for Morgans, the new Morgan Stanley was cheered as a sign of returning prosperity, a tonic to Wall Street's mood.

Morgan Stanley looked less a distant cousin than a richly endowed stepson of J. P. Morgan and Company, which financed it almost fully. Morgan Stanley officers owned virtually all the $500,000 of common stock, and they retained voting control. But the real start-up capital was $7 million in nonvoting preferred stock, $6.6 million of it held by J. P. Morgan partners. Jack and his family held about 50 percent of the preferred shares; Tom Lamont and his family, over 40 percent. Small wonder the new offshoot caused grumbling from some competitors, a feeling that J. P. Morgan and Company had honored the letter, but violated the spirit, of Glass-Steagall.

On September 16, 1935, Morgan Stanley opened for business at 2 Wall Street, about a hundred yards from 23 Wall. The office of this splendid bastard had a view of the Trinity Church steeple and its decor evoked its blue-blooded parentage. Prints of old New York adorned the walls, and signature rolltop desks were lined up in the manner of 23 Wall. It had something of the mood of a J. P. Morgan branch office. "My first job in the bank was going to Morgan Stanley," recalled Ellmore C. Patterson, later chairman of Morgan Guaranty. "They were short-handed. It got very busy and they borrowed two of us for about a year."[24]

September 16 was one of the most bizarre opening days in American business history: it didn't resemble that of a new business. The night before, Perry Hall asked the janitor to set out a table in case anybody sent flowers. When he reported to work, he found two hundred floral displays. "In fact, the entire length of our office was just one row after another of these magnificent flowers in vases. . . . Nearly every one of them was from our competitors and associates on the Street."[25] One reporter said it resembled a flower show. The *New York Times* noted the eerie sense of continuity: "The inauguration of business proceeded as if it were just the beginning of another week in any old-established firm."[26] One Morgan Stanley legend, perhaps apocryphal, claims that so many companies came for business the first week that when one utility chairman arrived to discuss financing, Stanley said, "Tell him to come back next week."[27]

At the new firm, the leading personalities were recognizable Morgan types. The press, as if covering the debut of a new country club, showed them golfing or emerging from the surf. Harold Stanley, a utility-bond expert, was handsome and distinguished looking with thick, prema-turely gray hair, a long face, and steady eyes. Now nearly fifty, he was president and senior statesman of the firm and a figure of enormous stature on Wall Street.

Son of a General Electric engineer—the inventor of the Thermos bottle—Stanley had a very Morgan pedigree: he was a Massachusetts Episcopalian, a star hockey and baseball player at Yale, and a Skull and

Bones member. He owned a home in Greenwich, Connecticut, and an apartment on Sutton Place. As a negotiator, he was tough and stubborn but honest. "While others banged conference tables he sat shyly by; but he seldom budged in an argument," reported *Newsweek*. [28] Coolly diplomatic, he was well suited for the political attacks that would shadow Morgan Stanley for twenty years.

Absent from the opening-day festivities was the firm's new treasurer, Harry Morgan, thirty-five, then returning from England aboard a cruise ship. Harry's aloofness from the affairs of the firm foreshadowed later developments. Yet it would be important for the new firm to have not only the Morgan name and money, but a real, breathing Morgan on the premises.

Harry Morgan had shiny, pomaded hair, a sharp chin, and electrically intense eyes. He was brusque and aggressive like his grandfather and with some of Pierpont's flamboyance. He bought up the Eaton's Neck peninsula on the North Shore and commuted by seaplane to Wall Street. As had happened with Jack in relation to Pierpont during the Pujo hearings, Harry became deeply embittered by the Pecora hearings' treatment of his father. It would be the formative event of his life, making him fanatically private and aloof from any public role other than in the world of yachting. It would likewise make Morgan Stanley far less prone than the old House of Morgan to dabble in politics or seek publicity. In 1935, the press portrayed Harry as the real heir to the Morgan business talents, and he shone in comparison with his more languid, gentle older brother, Junius, who remained with J. P. Morgan and Company. Harry would function more as the conscience of Morgan Stanley, the custodian of its traditions, than as a day-to-day executive. He also had important business contacts through his friendship with European banking families, including the Wallenbergs and the Hambros. He explained his role thus: "My father, as my grandfather got older, brought into his firm some very brilliant and desirable new partners. He built a team, and he was immensely successful in doing that and in acting as a moderator and team captain. In many ways when this firm was started, I thought that there was a place for me to act in such a capacity." [29]

The founders of Morgan Stanley romanticized their early days, stressing the perils they braved. "We were going out into a rough sea in a little tiny rowboat," said Perry Hall. "We didn't know how we would be received." [30] They were, in fact, received like members of a Renaissance court in exile. There were many links between J. P. Morgan and the new firm. Morgan Stanley closings—that is, payments for and deliveries of securities—took place at 23 Wall. And George Whitney, acting as "family physician" to clients, steered them to Morgan Stanley. Morgan Stanley started out with only a few spillover deals from the Corner—but what deals! George Whitney steered such clients as Wendell Willkie, chairman of Consumers Power, to Harold Stanley; before September 1935 was over, Morgan Stanley had its first big electric utility issue. Early in the summer, Walter Gifford of AT&T had asked Stanley about rumors that Morgan partners would form a securities firm. When Stanley confirmed this, Gifford said, "That solves my problem." He then put on his hat and left.[31] AT&T needed to do some new financing, and the Securities and Exchange Commission was eager for AT&T to return to capital markets to prove their health under the new regulations. In a historic issue for Illinois Bell Telephone, Morgan Stanley published the first newspaper prospectus conforming to New Deal securities laws, following consultations in Washington between Stanley and SEC chairman Joseph P. Kennedy.

Despite predictions from the House of Morgan that the New Deal would kill capital markets, they boomed in 1935, and underwritings jumped fourfold. In its first year of operation, Morgan Stanley handled an astounding $1 billion in issues, sweeping a quarter of the market. *Forbes* hailed a wonder: "Most firms, institutions and companies start off modestly. Unique is the record of Morgan Stanley & Co. . . . never remotely approached by any other newly created organization."[32] The firm originated issues but generally wouldn't participate in others' issues. SEC rules limited the size of underwriting stakes relative to a firm's capital, and so syndicates grew huge. On telephone issues, Morgan Stanley might marshal up to one hundred underwriters and five hundred or six hundred distributors. Its power to exclude firms from issues made it feared. Gradually much of J. P. Morgan's clientele—lovingly referred to as the Franchise—shifted to the new firm. By the late 1930s, New York Central, AT&T, General Motors, Johns-Manville, Du Pont, U.S. Steel, and Standard Oil of New Jersey, as well as the governments of Argentina and Canada, had come for securities work. Morgan Stanley was strong in the same areas as the pre-Glass-Steagall unified bank—utilities, telephone companies, railroads, heavy industry, mining, and foreign governments.

The rest of Wall Street assumed that Morgan Stanley had inherited its parent's mantle of authority. Charles Blyth and his partner, Charles Mitchell, sought to ingratiate themselves with the new leaders. "Our main job is to get under the covers and as close to them as possible," Blyth told Mitchell.[33] To cultivate Morgan Stanley, he suggested opening an account at J. P. Morgan and Company. "It is true our account won't be very important," he told Blyth, ". . . but it would show that our hearts are in the right place."[34] Such was the persisting faith in any firm bearing the Morgan name.

For New Deal reformers, it was also hard to believe that J. P. Morgan and Company didn't lurk somewhere in the shadows. That Morgan Stanley assumed so many former J. P. Morgan clients bred suspicion. One powerful enemy who resolutely tracked Morgan Stanley conquests was Interior Secretary Harold L. Ickes. After the firm's formation, he wrote in his diary, "Meanwhile, taking advantage of the depression, the Morgan people have extended their financial domination. Ordered to put a stop to the underwriting business of their bank, they have organized a separate company which is doing even more business than was done by the bank itself along this line."[35] Ickes and other enemies bided their time. But they would soon strike back in a sustained attack, through Congress and the courts.

For J. P. Morgan partners down the street, the sudden boom in the securities market was bitterly ironic, for the parent firm was sleepy in the late 1930s. Almost the entire bank was squeezed into 23 Wall, with some scattered offices in 15 Broad Street, next door. With $430 million in total resources, J. P. Morgan and Company still ranked as the biggest private bank in the world. But Glass-Steagall had meant more than a loss of business, money, and power. It robbed the bank of some ineffable mystery that had surrounded it. With the Pecora hearings, the bank had published a balance sheet for the first time. Now the firm had to publish statements and submit to government examination. Likewise in London, Monty Norman asked Teddy Grenfell for the firm's balance sheet for the first time in 1936. Slowly, gradually, the gentleman bankers' world was being bureaucratized, and the financiers were emerging, dazed and blinking, into unaccustomed sunlight.

CHAPTER TWENTY

WIZARD

. .
.

IT was now the twilight of the Diplomatic Age for the House of Morgan. Far from enjoying privileged access to the White House as it had in the twenties, it bore a special stigma. This new detachment from Washington was most apparent as the bank wrestled with the fate of the huge German loans from the 1920s—the celebrated 1924 Dawes loan and 1930 Young loan. Although these appeared under quasi-governmental auspices, Washington now dodged responsibility for their repayment and even showed a cavalier indifference. The New Dealers didn't want to jeopardize trade and security interests to enforce debt repayment, and the Morgan partners felt cheated. After all, dating back to the first China consortium, they had cooperated with the government on the assumption that they would receive official support in negotiating with defaulting debtors. That was the *quid pro quo.* Now the House of Morgan, after carrying out the bidding of its political masters, felt abandoned as Germany threatened default with Hitler's advent as chancellor in 1933.

To follow the saga of the Morgan involvement with the German reparations payments, it is helpful to retrace the odyssey of Dr. Hjalmar Schacht, who alternately posed as friend and foe of the House of Morgan. In 1930, he had resigned from the Reichsbank to protest the final terms of the Young Plan. After the Nazi election success in 1932, he sided with that party and prodded fellow bankers at the Deutsche and Dresdner banks to lend financial support. Among the German industrial class, Dr. Schacht conferred legitimacy on Hitler's thugs. At Hermann Göring's home in early 1933, he helped Hitler raise M 3 million from businessmen, a meeting climaxed by Gustav Krupp von Bohlen und

Halbach's pledge, on behalf of the rich guests, to give staunch support to the Nazis. Schacht even consented to a request from Hitler that he administer the new campaign fund.

Hindenburg, yielding to Hitler's wishes, restored Schacht to his post as Reichsbank president. After 1934, Schacht was also the minister of economics. As financial overlord of the Third Reich, Schacht would supervise public works, including construction of the Autobahn, his services winning him a reputation as the evil wizard of Nazi finance, the mountebank who could make financial magic for the Führer. According to William Shirer, "No single person was as responsible as Schacht for Germany's *economic* preparation for the war which Hitler provoked in 1939."[1] In one panegyric, Hitler said that Schacht had accomplished more in a three-year period than had the entire Nazi party combined.

As a Nuremberg war criminal, Schacht would portray himself as an early foe of Hitler's, a beleaguered man trying to stop the mad progress of the war machine. He never joined the Nazi party and claimed that he had opposed the persecution of the Jews. But there was a great deal of humbug about Schacht, who liked to pretend his pure intentions were being subverted by unscrupulous German politicians. In his duplicitous style, he would tell Jewish bankers that Hitler was a temporary evil needed to restore order, and he would vocally oppose persecution of the Jews. (He feared that such persecution would tarnish Germany's image in overseas banking circles.) Then he would boast privately to Hitler that he had blocked Jewish bank accounts and channeled the money into German rearmament. Because there was some truth to his self-defense, his story is more complex than that of his unreservedly diabolic associates. In the words of Nuremberg prosecutor Telford Taylor, "This self-righteous and stiff-necked individual was and remains the most enigmatic and controversial person of the pre-war years."[2]

Dr. Schacht was an anomaly among high German officials. He remained a gentleman banker of the old school, giving Nazi finance a patina of dignity. Sporting rimless spectacles, parting his fine, white hair down the middle, smoking cigars, and wearing pinstripes and suspenders, he was indispensable to Hitler, not only for the ingenious way in which he harnessed German banking to a war economy, but for the respectability he won abroad. Having slain the 1923 hyperinflation, Schacht could fool international bankers into thinking they had a friend in Berlin who adhered to their own financial standards. And he had already won the lasting friendship of Montagu Norman. Where others saw a Nazi collaborator, Norman saw a courageous central banker fighting inflation and combating German rearmament for its incompatibility with sound finance. Schacht once told Hitler, "Only two things can bring about the downfall of the National-Socialist regime, war and inflation."[3] This was the Hjalmar Schacht that Monty Norman preferred to see. The Morgan partners were more quickly disillusioned, believing that Schacht never wanted to pay reparations and had misled them into thinking he did.

Unlike the many flunkies who surrounded Hitler, the arrogant Schacht exercised real power; finance was an area beyond the pale of the Führer's obsessions. At first, he gave Schacht *carte blanche* in running the Reichsbank. "He understood nothing whatever about economics," Schacht later explained. "So long as I maintained the balance of trade and kept him supplied with foreign exchange he didn't bother about how I managed it."[4] Bullheaded and conceited, Schacht wouldn't hesitate to yell at Hitler and took liberties that would have cost others their heads. Once the Führer gave him a painting as a gift; Schacht returned it, saying it was a forgery. Nothing fazed him, and the cocksure banker had Hitler a bit bamboozled. Albert Speer noted of Hitler, "All his life he respected but distrusted professionals such as . . . Schacht."[5]

From a political standpoint, no instant alarm sounded at the House of Morgan when Hitler took office in 1933 and gained the power to rule by decree. Jack Morgan still nursed the old grudges against the Hun, but his reservations about Hitler were less moral than nationalistic. As he told his friend the Countess Buxton, "If I could feel more easy about your friends, the Boche, I should feel myself that we were all going to get along pretty well; but, except for his attitude toward the Jews, which I consider wholesome, the new Dictator of Germany seems to me very much like the old Kaiser."[6]

Nevertheless, a shift in Germany's policy toward foreign debt appeared quickly. In May 1933, Hitler dispatched Schacht to Washington for eight days of talks. To divert him on his transatlantic crossing, Lamont sent biographies of Napoléon and Marie-Antoinette—volumes that perhaps contained their own tacit message about the corruption of absolute power. Meeting with Roosevelt and Secretary of State Cordell Hull, Schacht boisterously insisted that stories about the harassment of Jews were grossly exaggerated and said that foreign protest would only backfire. He also warned that Germany was running short of foreign exchange to service the $2 billion in debt held by American investors.

This White House meeting occurred during the Pecora hearings, and Schacht recorded this curious reaction from the president: "Roosevelt gave his thigh a resounding smack and exclaimed with a laugh: 'Serves the Wall Street bankers right!' "[7] Afraid that Schacht might take this literally, Roosevelt's advisers warned the president of the potential damage of his little jest. The next day, Hull rushed to tell Schacht that Roosevelt was actually shocked by the default threat. "It occurred to me that the President had not expressed any shock until twenty-four hours had elapsed," observed Schacht.[8] Roosevelt's attitude may well have emboldened Schacht in his determination to repudiate German debt held in America.

That June, Schacht announced a moratorium on long-term overseas debt. The big German loans had been multinational—the Young loan, for instance, had appeared in nine markets and currencies—but the various creditor countries didn't mount a united defense. Rather, they behaved like panicky creditors in a crowded bankruptcy court, each trying to get Germany to pay off his own bonds first. Articles appeared in the U.S. press reporting that European creditors wanted to strike separate deals with the Nazis. As a lever to pry open foreign markets to German goods, Schacht favored deals with countries running trade surpluses with Germany. The implicit message was buy more from us, and we might look more favorably upon your bonds. It was a policy of selective default, a clever divide-and-conquer strategy that broke down creditors' unity and set them against each other. Schacht hoped that by stalling the creditors and driving down the price of the German bonds, he could buy them back at a price significantly lower than their face value—a tactic that apparently pleased Hitler.

When Lamont learned that Schacht was contemplating selective repudiation in 1934, he reminded him that Morgans had supplied over half the Dawes funds and a third of the Young funds. With pardonable overstatement, he said the bank had always advocated moderation toward Germany. Most of all, Lamont appealed loftily to international law, promises made to investors that these loans superseded all others and enjoyed special political protection. Lamont was speaking reasonably to a man already hip-deep in diabolic machinations: "Of course, we expect to see the Reich obligations on [the Young Loan], as on the Dawes loan, carried out. Otherwise all international agreements might as well be torn up."[9]

From Dr. Schacht's reply, it was clear that the usual norms of business behavior no longer applied in Germany. Written in an extravagant, hysterical style, it was not the sort of letter people usually sent to the sedate precincts of 23 Wall. Schacht began by saying Germany's problem was not default but a transfer difficulty resulting from a lack of foreign exchange. Then he veered off into bombast and mad whimsy:

> Whether you may threaten me with death or not will not alter the situation because here is the plain fact that I have no foreign valuta [foreign exchange], and whether you may call me immoral or stupid or whatever you like it is beyond my power to create dollars and pounds because you would not like falsified banknotes but good currency. . . .
>
> I would be willing to sell my brain and my body if any foreigner would pay for it and would place the proceeds into the hands of the Loan Trustees, but I am afraid that even the proceeds of such a sale would not be sufficient to cover the existing liabilities.[10]

Schacht may have wanted to drive a wedge between England and America, perpetuating tensions over war debts and reparations. By threatening to strike a separate bargain by which British bondholders received some payments (albeit at lower interest rates) and Americans didn't, he delivered a blow to Anglo-American amity. (Schacht argued that Germany's trade surplus with England allowed it to make the interest payments.)The fight over unequal treatment, first with German, then with Austrian, debt, would prove the most divisive issue ever between J. P. Morgan and Company and Morgan Grenfell.

There had always been a latent contradiction at the heart of the Anglo-American Morgan empire. So long as U.S. and British interests coincided, it could be straddled. When those interests diverged, however, British and American partners were obliged to follow the wishes of their respective governments. They were too deep in politics to do otherwise. With J. P. Morgan and Company now a minority stockholder rather than a partner in Morgan Grenfell, there was also a new structural distance between the two firms.

For more than twenty years, Teddy Grenfell had been the Morgan ambassador to the British government. Now, somewhat unwillingly, he conveyed stiff protests from his New York partners to Whitehall. With rumours of a separate German deal with England swirling around Wall Street, Lamont drafted a letter to the British government, demanding that it take responsibility for American bondholders of German debt. Morgan Grenfell partners argued against its testy wording, but Lamont and Leffingwell refused to back down. Biting his tongue, Grenfell duly delivered the cable to Prime Minister Ramsay MacDonald. For a letter to a chief of state, it struck a faintly arrogant chord, a tone of mild menace:

> Prior to the issue of the External Loan of 1924, we had not been associated with German finance, public or private, and we venture most respectfully to remind you that in your then capacity as Prime Minister you did us the honor of addressing our firm . . . by which you conveyed to us the requests of His Majesty's Government that we should undertake the placing of the Dawes Loan in this country. . . . Meanwhile, however, for the reasons indicated above, we believe that His Majesty's Government . . . will wish to use its good offices in every way possible for the protection of interests of all holders of these loans irrespective of nationality. . . .[11]

Two weeks later, Lamont followed this up by meeting with Neville Chamberlain, then chancellor of the Exchequer. It was a vintage Lamont performance—tough resolve beneath suave civility. He said Morgans had become involved with Germany only because the Bank of England wanted to put Weimar Germany back on its feet and enable it to make reparations. Affable and noncommittal, Chamberlain asked what he would recommend. Lamont asked whether Chamberlain would scuttle a separate accord with Germany if no justice were done to American investors.

> *Chamberlain:* I should not feel justified in going so far as to cancel my British arrangements if they fail to accede to my request re U.S.A.
> *Lamont:* No, I agree, nor should I expect you to do so. I believe that the representations you make will be so clear and strong as to go far toward getting similar treatment accorded to us.[12]

The British never rode to the rescue. What made this so galling to Lamont was that he always believed Britain had initiated the side deal with Schacht. Morgan partners were thunderstruck by what they saw as British cynicism and the end of financial leadership they had always associated with the City. Schacht himself didn't seem to dispute Lamont's version of events. When George Harrison went to Germany with

Roosevelt's encouragement, Schacht professed dismay over discrimination against American bondholders. He said the British had blackmailed him into their deal and kept telling Harrison "God bless you!" for protesting to the foreign minister. Harrison came back to New York very disturbed. "He utterly disagrees with Monty about Hitler and Hitlerism," Leffingwell told Lamont about Harrison's visit. "He didn't see a smile on any face in Germany in two days."[13]

To press his case, Lamont got Secretary of State Cordell Hull worked up about the discriminatory treatment of American bondholders. As he told Grenfell, "The American Government feels very strongly that the American investment community was had."[14] Jack Morgan appealed to Monty Norman, whom he believed to be the one person outside Germany with any influence over Schacht.

Norman wasn't so upset by the German actions and was willing to make allowances for the Nazis. He continued to harbor more hostility toward France than toward Germany. In July 1934, he arrived in New York looking sickly and dispirited. He immediately telephoned Russell Leffingwell and took a cab down to 23 Wall. Leffingwell summarized their meeting for Lamont: "Monty says that Hitler and Schacht are the bulwarks of civilization in Germany and the only friends we have. They are fighting the war of our system of society against communism. If they fail, communism will follow in Germany, and anything may follow in Europe."[15] This high regard for German culture had led Norman to back the 1924 Dawes loan in the first place. But the admiration now persisted under altered circumstances. As we shall see, most Morgan partners took a relatively benign view of German intentions, although there were skeptics from the start. The cynically acute Grenfell first penetrated Schacht's disguises, already believing in 1934 that he was building up stocks of raw materials with which to prepare Germany for war.

Meeting with Schacht at Baden-Baden in 1935, Lamont worked out a debt settlement that provided about 70 percent of the interest due on the two large German loans. After this meeting, Lamont and Schacht continued to perform a strange duet by mail. They pretended to be normal bankers in normal times, although Schacht's behavior seemed increasingly erratic. In 1936, Morgan Grenfell partner Francis Rodd visited Schacht in Berlin and found him in a crazily jocular mood. He rather giddily instructed Rodd to "send his love" to Lamont and praised Morgans as the world's premier bank. Schacht even invited Lamont to attend the Olympic Games, held that year in Berlin.

In a power struggle, Schacht finally lost out to his arch rival, Göring. His downfall began when he balked at buying foreign exchange for Nazi propaganda efforts abroad and tried to limit military imports of raw materials to what could be obtained by barter arrangements. In the last analysis, Schacht was too orthodox a banker, favoring slower growth and civilian production rather than a permanent war economy. In 1936, sitting on the terrace at Berchtesgaden, Albert Speer overheard Schacht arguing with Hitler in his office. As Speer recalled: "Some time around 1936 Schacht had come to the salon of the Berghof to report. . . . Hitler was shouting at his Finance Minister, evidently in extreme excitement. We heard Schacht replying firmly in a loud voice. The dialogue grew increasingly heated on both sides and then ceased abruptly. Furious, Hitler came out on the terrace and ranted on about this disobliging, limited minister who was holding up the rearmament program.[16]

Göring was put in charge of raw materials and foreign exchange. Although Schacht soon relinquished the economics ministry to Göring, he retained the Reichsbank presidency until January 1939.

Schacht will reappear in the Morgan saga at the time of the Austrian Anschluss. At this point, however, suffice it to say that the German debt quarrel left deep wounds on both sides of the Atlantic and dredged up the old issue of war debts. The British felt the United States should have canceled old war debts; Americans, even Morgan partners, believed Britain could have made a more determined effort to pay. Now that the Depression had finally retired lingering issues of debt and reparations, a new set of issues over the settlement of default debt would tear at Anglo-American financial harmony. The tension would last right up until the war.

T H E mid-1930s resounded with charges that to protect Allied loans the House of Morgan had led America into the First World War. Isolationists exploited this canard to try to ensure American neutrality in any future European war. They rallied the country against Wall Street, propounding a simplistic view of history that equated big business with bloodlust for war profits. A Wisconsin congressman, Thomas O'Malley, introduced a bill requiring the richest Americans to be drafted first—a foolproof way, he thought, to end wars. "It will be Privates Ford, Rockefeller, and Morgan in the next war," he said.[17]

Portents of war were visible everywhere—for those who cared to see them. In March 1935, Hitler tore up the Versailles treaty and reintroduced obligatory military service. He boasted to Sir John Simon, the British foreign secretary, that the Luftwaffe had attained parity with the Royal Air Force. A year later, the Führer occupied the Rhineland without any military rebuke from the Allies. Yet Sir Anthony Eden, secretary of state for foreign affairs, thought the best way to keep Germany from war was to strengthen Hitler's economy. In 1936, Charles Lindbergh, at the invitation of Hermann Göring, toured Germany and marveled at its aircraft factories and technology, later urging Britain and France to retreat in self-defense behind a string of British dreadnoughts and the Maginot Line.

Isolationists might portray the Morgan partners as warmongers, but they weren't alarmed by developments in Germany. In fact, they were strangely sanguine. After the Rhineland occupation, Lamont told Dr. Schacht, "The American public has to a considerable extent gotten the idea that Europe is about to plunge into the midst of another general war. . . . I may be too much of an optimist, but I do not share this view."[18] Even while espousing cooperation with England, the bank steadfastly refused to interpret Axis rearmament as the prelude to a new European conflict. For all the rhetoric about mercenary bankers, the Morgan partners were more prone to appeasement than hawkishness.

In early 1936, the ghost of World War I was revived by a Senate munitions investigation chaired by Senator Gerald P. Nye, a North Dakota Republican and adherent of Father Coughlin. With his pugnacious face and thrusting chin, Nye, like Pecora, formed a picturesque contrast to the stately Morgan partners he subpoenaed. He set out to prove that J. P. Morgan and other banks had dragooned America into war to safeguard loans and perpetuate a booming munitions business. Once again, the timid Jack Morgan was transmogrified into a venal, snarling monster. As *Time* magazine said, "Before the Committee for settlement was a scandalous question: should J. P. Morgan be hated as a war-monger second only to Kaiser Wilhelm?"[19] For Jack, who so earnestly hated the Germans, it was a mortifying comparison.

Once again, a Morgan retinue departed for Washington, occupying an entire eighth-floor wing of the Shoreham Hotel and remaining barricaded behind a phalanx of plainclothes guards. (That same year, Polaroid founder Edwin H. Land visited Jack at 23 Wall and found him guarded by men with machine guns.) As if to show their sublime contempt for the hearings and disdain for the follies of petty men, the partners dressed in dinner jackets for their nightly meal. Newspapers showed George Whitney, legs folded, elegantly reading a newspaper in a smoking jacket, bedroom slippers, and bow tie before retiring for the night. Once again, Morgan staffers were sidetracked by a government inquiry. From a Brooklyn warehouse, they disinterred the bank's wartime documents—twelve million of them, enough to fill up forty trucks.

The Nye hearings were a flop. Unlike the Pecora hearings, where partners were defensive and stammered their way through sometimes incoherent answers, the Nye committee invited them to relive their proudest hour. "We were pro-ally by inheritance, by instinct, by opinion," Lamont boasted, admitting that partners were glad to see America enter the war.[20] At that dawn of the Diplomatic Age, he contended, the bank had scrupulously heeded Washington's wishes, waiting until Robert Lansing had replaced William Jennings Bryan and approved Allied credits.

Far from seeming bellicose, Jack looked like a sleepy, avuncular old man. When Lamont said money was the root of all evil, Jack slyly interrupted: "The Bible doesn't say 'money,' " he grinned. "It says, 'The *love* of money is the root of all evil.' "[21] And while Lamont parried questions, Jack dozed or chatted with newsmen during breaks. Indeed, he had been appalled by the outbreak of war and had issued appeals to belligerents in 1914 to stop the combat. When it came to supporting the Allies, he was proudly secure in his position. "The fact that the Allies found us useful and valued our assistance in their task is the fact of which I am most proud in all my business life of more than 45 years."[22] His personal defense was bluntly effective: "Do you suppose that because business was good I wanted my son to go to war? He did, though."[23]

The hearings had as much to do with the Depression as with the war, and there was an uproar over Jack's classic blooper: "If you destroy the leisure class, you destroy civilization." Asked by reporters to define this class, Jack stumbled: "By the leisure class I mean the families who employ one servant, 25 million or 30 million families."[24] Critics from the Housewives League of America gleefully pointed out to newspaper editors that there were fewer than thirty million families in the United States, and only two million of them had cooks or servants. As an amateur sociologist, Jack left something to be desired.

Although Morgan partners considered the controversy a sideshow, it had an enduring influence, helping to muzzle their pro-Allied views and making them gun-shy of political controversy as World War II approached. In 1934, California senator Hiram W. Johnson, an isolationist, had sponsored the Johnson Act, which forbade loans to foreign governments that were in default on their dollar obligations. Neutrality Acts were also passed that blocked warring countries from purchasing arms or raising loans in the United States. This was part of an attempt to forestall any repetition of the Morgan Export Department or the Anglo-French loan in the event of war and to induce a steady American disengagement from Europe's affairs.

Even as America debated its position in a hypothetical European war, Mussolini launched a full-scale invasion of Ethiopia in October 1935. Il Duce had a megalomaniac vision of merging this territory with the colonies of Eritrea, Italian Somaliland, and Libya to forge an East African empire. Some five hundred thousand Ethiopians were sacrificed in a campaign infamous for its savage use of mustard gas. Like the Japanese in Manchuria, Mussolini's army pretended to act in self-defense and had the effrontery to denounce Ethiopian aggression. Fifty League of Nations states condemned the violation of Ethiopian sovereignty and voted economic sanctions. Relying on voluntary compliance by American business, Secretary of State Cordell Hull asked for a "moral" embargo on sales of war matériel to Italy—shipments of oil, metal, and machinery. These exhortations were often ignored by American industry. Although Britain went along with the League's economic sanctions, it stopped short of more extreme measures, such as cutting off all supplies of oil. Prime Minister Stanley Baldwin instructed his foreign secretary, Sir Samuel Hoare, "Keep us out of the war, Sam. We are not ready for it."[25]

By the mid-1930s, the House of Morgan's enthusiasm for il Duce had cooled, as had Wall Street's in general. One student of U.S. business support for Mussolini describes the post-1934 attitude as one of "a clamorous repudiation of the whole Fascist experiment."[26] Not only did the Johnson Act block new Italian loans, but Mussolini's behavior scared away American investors. There was apprehension about the dictator in high Anglo-American circles. Visiting Stanley Baldwin at 10 Downing Street in July 1935, Jack Morgan found him "terribly disturbed and apprehensive, as all are here, about Mussolini and Abyssinia."[27] Lamont warned the bank's Roman agent, Giovanni Fummi, that the rumored African campaign would jeopardize any renewal of credits to the Banca d'Italia.

As before, the Morgan bank portrayed Giovanni Fummi as a non-Fascist who happened to have extraordinary access to Mussolini. They paid him handsomely for his services—some $50,000 a year, or the same salary Parker Gilbert received as agent general for Germany. But Fummi wasn't upset by the Ethiopian bloodshed and praised the country's economic potential. He relayed a message to 23 Wall saying that Mussolini hoped U.S. capital could be funneled into the area. To dim such expectations, Lamont replied that Ethiopia would hurt Italy's financial prospects abroad for a long time. In 1936, Mussolini sent a new Italian ambassador, Fulvio Suvich, to New York to drum up support for an Italian loan. When Italy sent troops to fight alongside Franco's insurgents in the Spanish Civil War that summer, the effort was doomed (though Lamont supported Franco—and had heated quarrels with his son Corliss about the war). That fall, Hitler and Mussolini joined together in a Rome-Berlin Axis.

After Ethiopia, relations between Mussolini and Lamont remained in abeyance for a time. In April 1937, Lamont visited Rome, ostensibly on a pleasure trip. There was a hidden agenda behind the holiday, however. Lamont had contacted British officials, who expressed hope that Mussolini could be weaned from Hitler. He also conferred with Cordell Hull about the latter's program of lower global tariffs. In 1934, Congress had passed the Reciprocal Trade Agreements Act, an attempt to end the economic nationalism of the Depression by cutting tariffs to half their 1930 levels so long as other governments reciprocated with U.S. exports. Along with Germany, Italy was now on the road to autarky—that is, economic self-sufficiency—and Hull was alarmed by its retreat from the world economy. He thought that if the United States could conclude trade agreements with Axis powers, it might avert war. Lamont promised that in his talks with England, France, and Italy, he would promote Hull's pet notion of lower tariffs. For Lamont, it was a momentary reversion to his heady Republican missions of the 1920s.

Operating behind veils of mystery, Tom Lamont often had several reasons for his actions. He undoubtedly wanted to prevent a war and destroy the beggar-thy-neighbor spirit symbolized by the Hawley-Smoot Tariff Act of 1930. But he was also ready to forgive Mussolini his violent excesses and return to the *status quo ante.* Recently he had begun to meditate on ways of rehabilitating Mussolini in Anglo-Saxon eyes, telling a correspondent two weeks before his April trip to Italy, "I must say I prefer, of two foul evils, the fascists who make war, to the communists who seek to overthrow our governments. . . . The Duce should be presented to the public not as a warrior or in warlike attitudes, but in pastoral, agricultural, friendly, domestic and peaceful attitudes."[28] This would have been news to the half a million Ethiopian dead.

Soon after Lamont arrived in Rome, Vincenzo Azzolini, governor of the Banca d'Italia, learned of his visit. Il Duce—ever eager to flaunt his popularity with world business leaders—then invited Lamont and Fummi in for a private audience. It occurred amid press reports that Mussolini would visit Hitler in late summer or early fall. It was Lamont's first chat with the Italian leader since 1930. A transcript of the April 16, 1937, meeting has survived in Lamont's papers. Mussolini began by spouting hysterical pleas for sympathy:

> *Duce:* We have made a great conquest in Africa—that is finished
> now—I am for Peace, I am for World Peace—I am very strong for
> Peace. I need Peace—I need Peace—I am very strong for Peace.
> We are satisfied.
>
> *Lamont:* I believe you, Excellency, when you say that; I know it must
> be so, but the impression in America is very different. There you
> are pictured as a man who wants war rather than peace; that
> impression should be corrected. It is very important that in
> America your real attitude should be understood.[29]

As he had promised Hull, Lamont touted free-trade policies, and
Mussolini hinted he would like a generous helping of American money
in exchange: "America, Mr. Lamont, holds the key to economic cooperation. You see, Mr. Lamont, America has enormous quantities of gold,
too much gold for the world's good."[30] Mussolini also expressed a wish
for better relations with Britain, toward whom his policy had been
wildly contradictory. He would talk about new agreements one day,
then broadcast anti-British radio propaganda the next. In fact, the
month before, he had secretly informed his army officers that he
planned to destroy Britain. (Later it turned out he kept posted on British
diplomacy by having his aids sift through the wastebaskets at the British
embassy in Rome.) Mussolini's plea for improved Anglo-Italian relations was marred by a comic slip:

> *Duce:* I am doing everything I can to increase the friendship with
> Great Britain, everything, but Great Britain is always suspicious
> of what we say or do, and attributes wrong reasons to our speech
> and actions.
>
> *Lamont:* It pleases me immensely to have you say you are doing all
> you can to increase the friendship with England. In London last
> July I heard important expressions along the same line. It hap-
> pened that when there I dined with the then King Edward VIII,
> and he said to me "now that sanctions are to be ended we must
> get back to the basis of our traditional friendship with Italy." Mr.
> Neville Chamberlain, the Chancellor of the Exchequer, who is
> to succeed Mr. Stanley Baldwin as Prime Minister voiced to me
> the same sentiments. (For a moment the Duce seemed to think
> that I alluded to the late Sir Austen Chamberlain whose friend-
> ship for Italy was well-known, but he remembered, and corrected
> himself with "Oh yes, I know that Mr. Neville Chamberlain is
> well disposed toward us.)"[31]

The interview had started uneasily, as if Lamont wished to register his moral disapproval for the record. Then he warmed appreciably and resorted to the old courtier's mode, saying that Italians and Americans shared traits of industry, thrift, and imagination. He extolled Rome's tuberculosis sanatorium and regretted that Americans missed such wonders. "We spend too much time gazing at what the Romans were doing in 100 A.D., and not enough time in looking at what the Romans are doing in 1937 A.D."[32] In a vaguely surreal moment, he told Mussolini that tourism to post-Ethiopia Italy could be tremendously expanded. In a telling reminder of the old days, Lamont said he had jotted down fresh points on how Mussolini might handle public opinion. "Ah yes," said Mussolini, "I am very grateful for your counsel . . . do not hesitate to advise me direct in regard to these matters. One of my mottoes is 'advice from everyone, collaboration by many, decision and responsibility by a few.' "[33] Lamont and Fummi applauded this formulation.

Toward the close, perhaps afraid that things had gotten too friendly, Lamont returned to American fears of Italian aggression. He said—with perhaps an icy smile—"The American people, Excellency, have unbounded admiration for the marvellous achievements you have accomplished for Italy since 1922, unbounded admiration for these great material developments, but as regards yourself, Excellency . . . they are really afraid of you."[34] Smiling, Mussolini said the impression must be corrected. He urged Lamont to make a statement to the Italian press—which Lamont declined to do. Afterward, Lamont briefed William Phillips, the American ambassador in Rome, who seemed delighted by the talk.

Clearly, part of Lamont's Italian agenda was to curb Mussolini's war-like tendencies and nudge him closer to the United States and Britain. His visit enjoyed official encouragement. Yet soon afterward, Lamont reverted to propaganda work that could hardly have been sanctioned by Washington and was reminiscent of his relationship with il Duce in the twenties. True to his pledge, Lamont forwarded a memo designed to help Mussolini "enlighten American and British opinion" about his peaceful intentions. It paralleled the memo drafted for Junnosuke Inouye after Japan's 1931 invasion of Manchuria, drawing specious analogies between Mussolini's actions and American history, trying to convert the story of Ethiopian slaughter into a comforting tale of Italians conquering a wilderness. How should Mussolini quiet concern? By likening the Ethiopian campaign to America's westward expansion: "In previous speeches in the last few months the Duce has spoken of the growth of new empire in Africa. His Government's ends have been achieved. There now remains the task of agricultural and economic development in Ethiopia. There is a vast and fertile region as yet largely uninhabited and uncultivated. It would yield to the hard work and intelligent cultivation of Italian emigrants, just as a half century or more ago the vast resources of Western America were developed by American emigrants."[35]

What exactly was Lamont's purpose here? Was he trying to push Mussolini toward a new policy, or merely generating clever lines to hoodwink English and American opinion? Did he have any qualms about equating pioneers settling the American West with Italian troops hurling mustard gas? It is hard to imagine that the State Department or the British Foreign Office would have condoned this, notwithstanding *pro forma* lines about the need for world economic cooperation. After Libya, Corfu, Ethiopia, and Spain, these attempts at coaching Mussolini seem terribly misplaced. Lamont's slick publicity lines were now as empty as the dictator's own speeches:

> It is true that each of the great nations of the world must have adequate defences. But preparation to that end is approaching completion on every side, including Italy's own defences; so that now the primary end today and tomorrow must be the maintenance of world peace. . . . Italy was immeasurably the leader of the Renaissance, that great revival of the arts and learning that set the whole world upon a new path of enlightenment and progress. It is that same eager vitality that marks the Italian race today. . . . Italy welcomes the study of its past and is aware what attractions its galleries, its monuments, its cities, have for friends from abroad. They should study also the modern Italy, the material development of the past fifteen years, the public works, the reclamation projects, the industrial and agricultural policies, and perhaps above all the social and welfare system with its wonderful work as shown in hospitals, sanatoria, etc. Then indeed would Italy's friends be impressed with what has been accomplished here.[36]

Lamont's last fling with Mussolini again reveals his willingness to renounce principle for convenience. The most polished man on Wall Street, known for his thoughtful gifts and exquisite courtesies, was now a victim of his own disguises. Nothing mattered any longer but surfaces; his moral center had eroded and slipped away over the years. The bullying dictator and the eloquent banker no longer seemed as antithetical a pair as they had at the start of their friendship, when Lamont was fresh from his tutelage under Woodrow Wilson. The *New York Times* once said that Lamont "was a man who hated to see a friendship come to an end."[37] His relationship with Mussolini perversely confirmed that insight.

There was, however, yet another ongoing aspect of Morgan involvement in Italy—the Vatican account, which prospered even as government business stagnated. Lamont and other Morgan partners fed portfolio advice to Fummi, who in turn advised the Vatican on American securities holdings. The bank held papal securities in custody. (Fummi occasionally bungled the signals from Wall Street, advising the Vatican in 1938 to sell American stocks just as Lamont sent an updated report urging purchases. The Vatican then loaded up on American stocks, expecting that the Neutrality Act would be repealed, triggering a bull market on Wall Street.) Morgan judgments were always respectfully considered. As Fummi once told Lamont, "I hope you will approve of my above line of reasoning for there is no doubt that it has influenced the decision taken by the Amministrazione Speciale della Santa Sede a good deal."[38]

Lamont conducted his own personal diplomacy to restore traditional Anglo-Italian amity. Through his friend Lady Astor, he lobbied Lord Halifax, the foreign secretary, in April 1938 and argued the need to recognize the Ethiopian conquest as a *fait accompli.*[39] He apparently didn't worry that tossing Ethiopia to Mussolini might embolden him. Meanwhile, Neville Chamberlain dispatched his sister-in-law Ivy—the widow of Sir Austen Chamberlain—to Rome to speak with her friend Mussolini in the hopes of drawing him away from Hitler. In early 1938, the British recognized Italy's Ethiopian conquest in exchange for Italian troop withdrawals from the Spanish Civil War. Russell Leffingwell, who had denounced the Ethiopian invasion as a "predatory war," told Lamont he thought Britain was "throwing Ethiopia to the wolves."[40] The British diplomatic triumph was fleeting: in 1939, Mussolini would seize Albania and sign a "pact of steel" with the Nazis.

CHAPTER TWENTY-ONE

EMBEZZLER

. .

.

EMBITTERED by the New Deal, Jack Morgan didn't age gracefully or happily and divided his time between apathy and rage. He was a lonely man who had never recuperated from his wife's death. He didn't remarry and continued to tend Jessie's gardens. At his Gannochy Lodge shooting parties, he would invite the Queen Mother's sister or some comparable dowager to serve as hostess. Whether attending Yale-Harvard regattas in his boater or browsing in the Morgan Library, he gave off a solitary air. This sense of loneliness was accentuated by the grandeur of his surroundings. At Matinicock Point, he lived alone in a forty-five room house. Although a widower for nearly ten years, he refused to shut his English or American estates or vary the annual ritual that called for Camp Uncas in the Adirondacks in the spring or Gannochy Lodge in August. At exorbitant expense, he maintained butlers, housekeepers, and gardeners, as well as the fifty-man crew of *Corsair IV*. This unchanging structure provided emotional solace and support but also frittered away much of the fortune that would have gone to his heirs.

Jack took inordinate pride in his grandchildren, sixteen strong by 1935. When a four-year-old grandson asked why locomotive engineers blew whistles at grade crossings, Jack assigned high-priced Davis, Polk lawyers to find the answer. Yet he often seemed closed and aloof to his grandchildren. Once a week, he hosted a black-tie dinner for the entire family at Matinicock Point. Extremely punctual, he would stand at the door checking his watch and start exactly on time. Everybody lived in fear of being late. When he took five of his grandchildren across the Atlantic on the *Corsair*, he allowed them to read or play solitaire but not to enjoy deck games. If sensitive within, he seemed cold and distant without.

Jack still reported regularly to the Corner, taking his spot at the far end of the double row of rolltop desks, beneath Pierpont's portrait. He was an archaic figure in a world mad with reform. Change and experimentation were so alien to his nature that the crash and Depression produced no evolution in his philosophy. In 1936, he enunciated his business creed this way: "Do your work; be honest; keep your word; help when you can; be fair."[1] Another favorite saying was "Keep your mouth shut and your eyes and ears open."[2] His philosophy showed no scuff marks of the time, only a somber faith that with sufficient patience and fortitude traditional values would prevail.

Jack didn't travel in circles likely to challenge his views. He told U.S. Steel chairman Myron Taylor that he knew nobody in favor of the 1935 Wagner Act, which sanctioned collective bargaining; and he probably didn't. Never attempting to broaden his outlook, he came to typify the New Deal stereotype of the "economic royalist." In 1935, for the first time, he instituted personal economies. He trimmed living expenses to $60,000 annually and halved his contributions to Saint John's of Lattingtown, the millionaire's church whose burial ground was so liberally graced with Morgan partners. Such economies, if arduous for Jack, still left him with a life style inconceivably majestic to ordinary citizens.

The Nye "merchants of death" hearings in early 1936 confirmed Jack's suspicion that he was the eternal target of demagogues and left him feeling depressed. During the hearings, his friend King George V died. He wrote a British friend: "the death of the King has caused a great feeling of sadness in this country as well as in yours."[3] As if they were the unconquerable curses of his house, the combined strain and fatigue of Pecora and Nye had the same effect on Jack as the Pujo hearings had on Pierpont. In mid-June 1936, while visiting Jessie's sister, Mrs. Stephen Crosby, in Massachusetts, he had his first heart attack, complicated by a severe neuritis attack, which made it difficult for him to walk.

The Morgan family wanted to transport him back to Glen Cove with minimal publicity, and he was moved by stretcher to a private railroad car. His sons, Junius and Harry, waited for him at the Mill Neck Station on Long Island. They paced the platform anxiously, smoking pipes, their hats pulled low, trying to dissuade photographers from taking pictures. As the train pulled in, Jack, in blue silk robe and white scarf, saw the photographers and lowered his window shade, his old disgust for the press welling up. An ambulance hidden in the bushes moved toward the train, and four men lifted Jack in a chair to the ground. A photographer rushed to the ambulance window for a last shot of Jack inside and Harry went white with fury. A less inhibited Morgan guard smashed the photographer in the jaw.

That winter, Jack spent two weeks cruising the South Seas, convalescing with a heart specialist on board. By now, his views of the world were etched with a corrosive anger. In late 1936, King Edward VIII abdicated, and Jack saw nothing romantic or pitiable in his plight, merely a betrayal of trust. He told Lord Linlithgow: "What a pity that the little king had not the guts enough to do his job."[4] The gutless action would prove highly advantageous for the House of Morgan. Only a year earlier, Jack had entertained the duke and duchess of York—now to be King George VI and Queen Elizabeth—at Gannochy for the Glorious Twelfth. They would continue to be guests at Gannochy and aboard the *Corsair*. In late April 1937, Jack sailed for Plymouth *en route* to the coronation, bearing a special invitation to sit in the royal family's box. As the squire of Wall Hall, he invited two thousand guests, mostly local farmers, to celebrate the occasion at his estate. But he suffered a second heart attack and missed the Westminster Abbey coronation. He had to listen to the ceremonies over the radio.

When he returned to America aboard the *Queen Mary*, his physician advised him not to talk to reporters, lest his blood pressure rise again. (Trying to be more affable, Jack had taken to granting shipboard interviews.) As the ship docked in a thick Manhattan fog, reporters dashed all over the ship trying to find Jack. They finally tracked him down in a stuffy little room and got him talking on the subject that was his invariable downfall during the New Deal—taxes. He had already inflamed public opinion in 1935 by saying that "everybody who makes any money in the United States actually is working eight months of the year for the government."[5] When he said this, a fifth of the work force was idle and many people relied on relief or public works programs for survival. Now Jack put his foot in his mouth once again. While he was in England, Roosevelt and Treasury Secretary Morgenthau had started a campaign against tax evasion by the rich to reverse declining federal revenues. Jack didn't know how incendiary the topic had become. He told reporters: "Congress should know how to levy taxes, and if it doesn't know how to collect them, then a man is a fool to pay the taxes. If stupid mistakes are made, it is up to Congress to rectify them and not for us taxpayers to do so."[6]

Once again, Jack was flabbergasted by the public outrage that ensued; he never ceased to be a political naïf. Lamont had to explain to him patiently how inflammatory such remarks might sound in the current political atmosphere. Lamont said of Jack to Walter Lippmann's wife, Faye, "You see, as a matter of fact, he is as simple as a child, and when he once gets started with newspaper men he talks with them just as carelessly as he would with his own partners."[7] Even though Jack rushed to retract his statement, stressing that he had no sympathy for tax dodgers, the damage was already done. Two weeks later, the Treasury released the names of sixty-seven wealthy taxpayers who had used legal schemes to avoid taxes. Jack's name didn't appear on this list, but Lamont's did.

For New Dealers, Jack Morgan symbolized the self-destructive complacency of America's rich, those unable to adjust to changing times. Reading Jack's shipboard comments, Felix Frankfurter seized on them as proof of the decadence of business leaders who couldn't see that their real self-interest lay in New Deal reform. "What a temper of mind J.P. Morgan revealed in this morning's press," Frankfurter wrote to President Roosevelt. "I nearly exploded. . . . When the most esteemed of financiers discloses such a morally obtuse, anti-social attitude, one realizes anew that the real enemy of capital is not Communism but capitalists and their retinue of scribes and lawyers."[8]

Jack was far more affected by criticism than politicians realized. The public assumed that all tycoons were crusty, unemotional, and immune to public wrath. J. P. Morgan had become less a person than a political symbol for the rich and reactionary who opposed social justice. Yet Jack had been emotionally unhinged since Jessie's death, and he remained terribly shy and unsure of himself. This tended to make him gruff, aloof, and elusive. Unsophisticated, he could be easily baited by clever reporters. A lonely widower in retirement, he poured out his grief to assorted duchesses, old college chums, and selected archbishops. He still found it hard to cope without Jessie's emotional support.

Over time, Jack had come to see the Roosevelt administration as one giant conspiracy out to hound him. Gnashing his teeth, he told Monty Norman, "The state of affairs might be so satisfactory and helpful so easily if we did not have a crazy man in charge and my chief feeling is one of resentment at what he is putting us through."[9] To Owen Young of General Electric, we owe a startling vignette that shows how dangerously frayed Jack's nerves were in early 1938. The two men were chatting at 23 Wall when Jack erupted into a tirade. He lost all control of his emotions. Young was so thunderstruck that he recorded his impressions immediately afterward, together with strict instructions not to publish them until both were dead. Young recalled Jack saying:

"I just want you to know, Owen Young, that I don't care a damn what happens to you or anybody else. I don't care what happens to the country. All I care about"—and he became vehement, almost passionate—"all I care about is this business! If I could help it by going out of this country and establishing myself somewhere else I'd do it—I'd do anything. In all honesty I want you to know exactly how I feel. And if things go on this way much longer I won't put up with 'em. I'll take the business and get out." His hand trembling—under great emotional strain.

Attempting to calm him, Young put his arm around Jack and reminded him gently of Pierpont's faith in America, the talents the Morgans had contributed to their bank. Then he tried to rouse his spirits: "You'll stay right here and outface these passing discouragements, because if you ran away you wouldn't be Jack Morgan. You owe it to the future and you owe it to yourself.' When I was finished," Young wrote, "he was silent, and I was startled to find that his eyes had filled. 'Well, Owen,' he said, 'I guess I needed some one to talk to me like that. And I guess you're the only one who could have done it.' "[10]

Jack never found peace under Franklin Roosevelt, at least not until the Second World War dissolved the feuds of the 1930s in a warm bath of patriotic fervor. Only when the focus of national attention switched from the Depression and domestic economic inequities to foreign menace did the Morgan bank and the New Deal again find any common ground.

EVEN as the House of Morgan fended off assaults from Franklin Roosevelt, it experienced the ire of his successor, Senator Harry S. Truman of Missouri. In his first Senate term, Truman later said, he spent more time on railroad finance than any other single subject. This led to a collision with the House of Morgan, which, with Kuhn, Loeb, still dominated railroad issues in the 1930s. Struggling to compete with new truck and air traffic, the railroads were an intractable Depression problem, with bankers blamed for their mismanagement. In 1935, Truman joined a subcommittee chaired by Burton K. Wheeler, a progressive Montana Democrat, investigating banker influence over railroads. The Wheeler hearings studied the manacles that bound railroads to exclusive relations with traditional bankers. From the time of Louis Brandeis's campaign against Morgan domination of the New Haven Railroad, reformers had urged an arm's-length distance between bankers and clients. Now they again espoused competitive bidding to allow all bankers to compete for a given issue.

By a curious historical freak, Max Lowenthal, counsel to the Wheeler subcommittee, introduced Truman to that ubiquitous Morgan demon, Louis Brandeis, who was now a Supreme Court justice. In the late 1930s, justices still received visitors for tea one afternoon a week. At teas held at his California Street home, Brandeis would leave other visitors and buttonhole Truman for hours, quizzing him on the hearings and arguing for stricter regulation of railroads and a severing of their Wall Street links. Truman was converted to Brandeis's gospel of a competitive economy based on small business and zealous antitrust regulation. This philosophy exerted a powerful hold during Roosevelt's second term and naturally exacerbated the clash with that apostle of big-business planning and economic concentration, the House of Morgan.

Anticipating the onslaught of Senator Wheeler and his committee, the Morgan partners in 1935 acted to jettison that great embarrassment from the Jazz Age—the bankrupt Van Sweringen brothers. For five years, Morgans had secretly propped them up with a $40-million "rescue" loan, even though they owed $8 million in back interest charges. When the brothers again defaulted in May 1935, the bank decided it would be political suicide to take control of their collateral—the vast Alleghany railroad and their real estate empire. Political expediency demanded they cut their losses and sell off Alleghany stock. This need to propitiate Washington was a striking sign of diminished Morgan power and prestige. The bank placed a small newspaper ad announcing plans to sell off the collateral at an auction. It was a shabby anticlimax to the bank's once-glamorous relationship with the Van Sweringens.

On September 30, 1935, the remnants of the Van Sweringen empire went under the gavel at the securities auction room of Adrian H. Muller and Sons. Mullers was known as the securities graveyard, and its offices had an appropriate view of the cemetery of Saint Paul's churchyard. Beneath bare electric bulbs, in a drab room strewn with dusty paintings and worthless junk, George Whitney sat with legs crossed on a cheap folding chair. Smart and well tailored, he smiled blandly and tried to look blasé at this moment of Morgan disgrace. The House of Morgan's handsome, blond attorney, Frederick A.O. Schwarz of Davis, Polk, and Wardwell, brought along the Alleghany securities in two rich-looking leather portfolios. It was a packed house. In the rear, like a resurrected ghost of the 1929 crash, a tense, pale Oris Van Sweringen flitted about. With twenty-eight thousand miles of track, or a tenth of the entire American railroad system, Alleghany fetched only $3 million, exposing a loss of $9 million apiece for both Morgans and Guaranty Trust. And it turned out that the indestructible Van Sweringens had repurchased the railroads by creating one last holding company and getting two associates to advance the cash.

Afterward, George Whitney—with a tight-lipped smile—shook hands with a happy, flushed Oris Van Sweringen. "I would rather have paid the bill," Oris whispered to Whitney. The funereal auction room provided a fitting end to the fiasco. But following the strange copycat pattern of their lives, the Van Sweringens died in quick succession. Mantis died that December. Eleven months later, Oris arrived in Hoboken for a meeting at Morgans and died of a coronary thrombosis while still in his private sleeping car. He left an estate consisting of hardly much more than Mantis's life insurance. The Van Sweringen railroads, meanwhile, remained heavily in hock to the banks.

The auction didn't pacify the Wheeler investigators. Even Glass-Steagall and the creation of Morgan Stanley hadn't modified Senator Wheeler's belief that J. P. Morgan and Company controlled the railroad securities business. He asked one witness, "But generally in the Street is it not conceded that Morgan Stanley & Co. is the same thing, or is just as much dominated by Morgan, as before?"[11]

For six months in 1936, Wheeler investigators pored over records at 23 Wall Street: once sacred, confidential documents were becoming increasingly smudged with the fingerprints of government investigators. Committee counsel Max Lowenthal became the new Morgan bogeyman, and George Whitney complained to Jack about the "Jewish lawyer element" behind the investigation.[12] Whitney thought the Van Sweringens the real object of their investigation, with the bank serving as their proxy after they died. In 1937, Senator Wheeler, distracted by the battle over Supreme Court reform, appointed Truman as acting chairman of the railroad investigation. At this point, the committee turned to the Van Sweringen's 1930 purchase of Missouri Pacific, bought with proceeds from the Alleghany underwriting of 1929, made notorious by the preferred list.

A future president was now educated in the Wall Street plunder of the 1920s. As Margaret Truman recalled, "It was my father's investigation of the Missouri Pacific that really enraged him and convinced him for all time that 'the wrecking crew,' as he called Wall Street financiers, were a special interest group constantly ready to sacrifice the welfare of millions for the profits of a few."[13] Under Alleghany—and ultimately Morgan control—the Missouri Pacific had become an open scandal. The railroad was milked for dividends while management fired thousands of workers, abandoned improvements, and made no provision for an emergency fund. There were also malodorous political dealings with Missouri legislators, one state senator having received $1,000, which he itemized as "covering services in the Alleghany–Missouri Pacific matter."[14]

The feisty Truman dug in his heels against tremendous Wall Street pressure to desist from the investigation. He blamed the House of Morgan for his troubles. As he wrote his wife, Bess, "It is a mess and has created a terrible furor in New York. Guaranty Trust and J. P. Morgan have used every means available to make me quit. I'm going to finish the job or die in the attempt."[15] Truman saw himself as the upright country boy who wouldn't be hoodwinked by smart-alecky New York types, and he had a cultural as well as a political aversion to the bank. Even as a young man, he had considered Pierpont a snob who consorted with decadent European royalty, and he was quick to pick up on George Whitney's air of superiority, his disdain for little midwestern senators. "Mr. Whitney is very much inclined to feel his position," he told Bess. "He came to my office at about a quarter to ten and told me what he was going to do. I simply asked him who the chairman of the committee happened to be and he immediately dismounted and went along like a gentleman."[16] Truman's experience left him with an enduring view of Wall Street bankers as smart, greedy, and oblivious to the hazards of concentrated wealth. The ordinary government bureaucrat, he declared, was no more a match for Wall Street lawyers than a lamb for a butcher.

The Wheeler hearings spawned a Morgan enemy who would plague both J. P. Morgan and Company and Morgan Stanley for twenty years. Robert Young was a self-styled Texas populist who had worked for General Motors in New York and made a fortune selling short in the 1929 crash. He left to form his own investment firm, buying for himself, GM president Alfred P. Sloan, Jr., and other auto company executives. After buying a major block of Alleghany stock in the early 1930s, he and his clients were rebuffed by Morgans and Guaranty Trust in securing a board seat. Young would never forget this insult.

After the Van Sweringens died, Young and his associate, Allen Kirby, an heir to the Woolworth fortune, bought control of the bankrupt Alleghany empire, still heavily mortgaged to J. P. Morgan and Company and Guaranty Trust. But rather than being a pliant client, Young decided to use Alleghany as a springboard for an assault on the House of Morgan itself. While other businessmen bucked the New Deal, Young cleverly mouthed its slogans and cast himself as a plucky outsider, proclaiming his mission as "saving capitalism from the capitalists." He said he wanted to diffuse the power of Morgans and its associates. Lamont was outraged by Young's testimony before the Truman subcommittee and called him on the carpet at 23 Wall. It was a dressing down that stung for the rest of Young's life. When he told Lamont that he intended to keep him informed about his Alleghany rehabilitation plans, Lamont replied, "You don't understand me. I want not only to be informed, but I want to help guide you in your policies."[17]

For Young, all was revealed in a flash of light. He often repeated the story, the way sinners retell their moments of conversion. Lamont had made him feel "just like a country boy" and had "literally put me on the carpet, spanked me and raked me over the coals for having the temerity to be developing a . . . plan without discussing it with Morgan's."[18]

Inflamed by Lamont's high-handed manner and emboldened by the Wheeler hearings, Young led a revolt against Morgan hegemony in railroad finance. His main target was the exclusive relations that gentleman bankers demanded from clients. The House of Morgan had managed issues for the C&O railroad, which was part of the Alleghany empire. Young and his banking associates, Harold Stuart of Halsey, Stuart in Chicago and Cyrus Eaton of Otis and Company in Cleveland, laid a trap for the Morgan interests in November 1938. Young traveled out to Cleveland in a private railroad car with Harold Stanley of Morgan Stanley and Elisha Walker of Kuhn, Loeb for a meeting of the C&O finance committee. The New York bankers expected to negotiate a new $30-million bond issue in private.

Stanley and Walker must have known something was afoot, for they had been asked to submit sealed bids for the issue. It was unprecedented for a Morgan Stanley partner to travel to a board meeting in this way. In what he doubtless thought a great concession, Stanley told the meeting that he would allow Kuhn, Loeb's name to appear alongside Morgan Stanley's as co-manager. At this point, Young delivered his bombshell: "Mr. Stanley, we are not interested in the advertising, or whose name appears above whose. . . . What we are interested in is what C&O is to get for the bonds."[19] Young suddenly disclosed that he had brought a competitive bid from Otis and Halsey, Stuart that would net the C&O $3.5 million more than the terms proposed by Morgans and Kuhn, Loeb. Some old Van Sweringen loyalists on the board still wanted to accept the traditional Wall Street bankers. Young threw them into confusion by threatening to sue them if they rejected the lower bid. He pranced about the room singing, "Morgan will not get this business! Morgan will not get this business!"[20] The flustered directors recessed, conferred with lawyers, then came back and accepted the lower bid.

Young's palace coup inaugurated a brand-new era on Wall Street. Instead of having gentleman bankers privately negotiate issues with clients, more issues would be opened up to competitive bids. This typically meant smaller "spreads" between the price paid to the company and the price at which the issues were resold to the public. With smaller profit margins for the investment bankers, more money, in theory, would remain for the issuer.

During the next two years, the *troika* of Young, Eaton, and Stuart got two other railroads to accept competitive bids. In 1941, the SEC promulgated Rule U-50, mandating competitive bidding for public utility holding company issues. In 1944, the Interstate Commerce Commission enacted a similar ruling for railroads. However notable these victories for anti–Wall Street forces, they didn't touch the far more lucrative industrial issues outside of railroads and utilities. The major proponents of old-fashioned banking would be Harold Stanley and his firm. Stanley would argue against the "casual intermittent connections" between bankers and issuers produced by competitive bidding, warning that companies would receive poor advice and sell issues at improper prices. If the argument were transparently self-serving, industrial America would willingly submit to its logic. For another forty years, blue-chip America would agree to exclusive relations with Morgan Stanley, an alliance unbroken until IBM rebelled in 1979.

CLEARLY, if there were going to be a rapprochement between the House of Morgan and the New Deal, it wouldn't come from Jack Morgan, whose implacable bitterness made him politically valueless. It also wouldn't come from George Whitney, the very model of the patrician banker that the reformers abhorred. Any new approach to the White House would have to involve Tom Lamont, who yearned to return to the political game and chafed under his Washington exile.

The turbulent year of 1937 presented a possible opening for the bank. After drifting from spring to late summer, the economy and the stock market nose-dived in September. So steep was the fall in stock and commodity markets that October 19 was dubbed Black Tuesday. Markets slumped almost halfway to their 1932 lows. Investment banks took such a severe beating on two issues—Bethlehem Steel bonds and Pure Oil preferred stock—that there was talk of closing the Stock Exchange. Assuming the Morgan role of Wall Street leadership, Harold Stanley called in the heads of several investment banks and took an informal survey of their condition. In return, he offered them a rare, confidential look at Morgan Stanley's books. Glass-Steagall had left an investment banking field of small, poorly capitalized banks, and the inevitable shakeout now began. Suffering heavy underwriting losses, the firm of Edward B. Smith and Company—the successor to Guaranty Trust's securities affiliate—merged with Charles D. Barney and Company to form Smith, Barney, a firm that fell into the Morgan group. The confidence of the New Deal was shaken by this sudden reversion to the unsettled financial markets of the early 1930s.

The industrial sector was also in turmoil. In January and February of 1937, the fledgling United Auto Workers paralyzed General Motors with sit-down strikes. In Flint, Michigan, police fired on strikers armed only with slingshots. From 14 percent in 1937, unemployment would zoom to 19 percent the following year. These events not only created a sense that the New Deal had stalled, but they intensified conflicts between the two chief administration factions. One group—inspired by Louis Brandeis and identified with Felix Frankfurter, Thomas G. Corcoran, and Benjamin V. Cohen—blamed big business for America's failure to shake off the Depression and advocated more competitive markets. Their ally, Robert H. Jackson, chief of the Justice Department's antitrust division, argued that monopolists had "priced themselves out of the market, and priced themselves into a slump."[21] Echoing this theme, Interior Secretary Harold Ickes warned of the pernicious influence of America's sixty ruling families. Roosevelt was fond of experimentation, and his political church had many pews. For the moment, he favored the antitrust faction and told brain truster Rexford G. Tugwell that it might "scare these people [i.e., business] into doing something."[22]

There was another wing of brain trusters who had been influential during the so-called First New Deal, from 1933 to 1935. They admired the technological efficiency of big business and regarded the Brandeis view of a small-scale, competitive economy as a fanciful wish for a bygone America. They accepted the inevitability of economic concentration and advocated public control of the large economic units rather than vainly trying to break them up. They denounced the Jackson-Ickes speeches as demagogic and counterproductive. By late 1937, they were emboldened to mount a counterattack when FDR told Tugwell that "perhaps a message addressed to him by a mixed group of labor and business leaders would be one way in which he could find means for retreat and a change of policy."[23]

In fashioning their group, these left-wing New Dealers found common cause with Morgans. This wasn't as contradictory as it sounded. From Pierpont's day, the House of Morgan had supported industrial planning, albeit under private control. What were the railway associations and U.S. Steel if not planned economic systems? (We recall the covert ideological link between the bank and the Progressives, epitomized by the friendship between Teddy Roosevelt and George Perkins.) At the same time, the partners were by no means hostile to all federal intervention to stop the Depression. If they hewed to the balanced-budget dogma and opposed higher taxes, Lamont, Leffingwell, and Parker Gilbert also advocated cheaper money to combat deflation. By contrast, the American Bankers Association attacked Roosevelt's policy of low interest rates. The obscurantism of their fellow bankers sometimes bothered the Morgan men. "I sometimes wonder whether we ought to continue to give our silent sanction to the American Bankers Association by continuing our membership in it," Leffingwell said, blaming tight Fed policy in 1936–37 for that year's downturn.[24] In modern parlance, the Morgan partners were sympathetic to macroeconomic management of the overall economy, even if they deplored microeconomic regulation of specific industries.

Adolf A. Berle was an important theoretician of government planning, and in 1932, with economist Gardiner Means, he co-authored a classic text, *The Modern Corporation and Private Property.* Berle and Means insisted that the large corporation was an ineradicable fact of modern economic life and that government had to adjust to it. Disturbed by Robert Jackson's speeches, Berle started to correspond with Lamont, who, of course, spoke kindly about big business, which he asserted had higher ethical standards than small business. He also stressed his allegiance to Roosevelt's foreign policy and a good portion of his domestic policy as well. There was considerable poetic embellishment here. Not long before, Lamont had complained to his close friend Lady Astor about the "extravagance, waste, and loose administration" of Roosevelt's White House.[25] But whatever license he took, Lamont was at least willing to talk and bargain with the New Dealers—a vast improvement over the fruitless rage of Jack Morgan and the rest of diehard Wall Street. Lamont struck a deal with Berle: he would support relief payments and deficit spending in exchange for a repeal of the surplus profits and capital gains taxes. At the same time, political attacks against business, especially utilities, had to end. This was the sort of political horse-trading so conspicuously absent from previous Morgan efforts to affect the New Deal.

On the afternoon of December 22, 1937, eight members of a new

Advisory Group met at New York's Century Club, with Berle as chairman. Lamont and Owen Young of General Electric represented big business; Rexford Tugwell and Charles Taussig spoke for the New Deal; and Philip Murray, president of the steelworkers' union, John L. Lewis of the Congress of Industrial Organizations, and CIO counsel Lee Pressman were there for the labor movement. In a decade badly polarized by class conflict, it was a unique moment. The eight men jointly opposed the antitrust prosecutions of Robert Jackson and endorsed the broad outlines of an agreement that had already been worked out by Berle and Lamont. At the end, Tugwell promised to set up a meeting with Roosevelt to discuss the pact.

As a creature of the shadows, Lamont imagined the meeting with Roosevelt on January 14, 1938, would be a private, discreet affair. Instead, the participants had to run a gauntlet of photographers and reporters. There were press gibes about "Mr. Berle's economic zoo" and front-page coverage supplied by unsympathetic White House leaks.[26] Nevertheless, it was a productive meeting, with the conferees approving expanded purchasing power through federal spending rather than the old deflationary shaving-wages approach to hard times. Despite Roosevelt's desire for more meetings, the experiment was stillborn. Brandeis-influenced regulators in the administration—such as Thomas Corcoran and Ben Cohen, who drafted the securities law—opposed such overtures to business. And a far-left faction in the CIO was equally bent on spiking this nascent business-labor-government triumvirate.

For his part, Lamont regretted that the White House meeting had degenerated into cheap political theater and that the cooperation offered by him and Owen Young "had been used to make third rate politics."[27] At a time of political invective, it was a missed opportunity that demonstrated the potential benefit of practical discussions between business and labor. For the House of Morgan, it was an especially irretrievable chance, because the White House meeting occurred on the eve of a Morgan scandal that would turn the clock back to the dark days of 1933, calling into question the partners' view of themselves as enlightened, public-spirited financiers.

FOR the House of Morgan, the winter of 1937–38 turned into a time of debacle and mourning. In February 1938, worn by responsibility and the labors of a precocious early adulthood, forty-five-year-old S. Parker Gilbert died. The prodigy who ran the Mellon Treasury Department in his twenties had suffered from hypertension; his death was caused by heart and kidney problems, but many thought he had worked himself to death. The years of staying till two in the morning at the Treasury and the years in Weimar Berlin, where the Germans noted his unrelenting devotion to work, had taken their toll. Earlier, Gilbert and his bride, Louise, a Kentucky belle whose racy sayings were repeated around Wall Street, had postponed their honeymoon for five years. After joining the bank in 1931—Parker hadn't asked for a set salary, waving it aside as a detail—the Morgan partners protected him, always urging him to vacation and conserve his strength. His prodigious work and dedication earned him decorations from France, Belgium, and Italy and honorary degrees from Harvard and Columbia. A year after he died, the pretty, round-faced Louise married Harold Stanley, whose first wife had died in 1934. This not only created a novel link between J. P. Morgan and Morgan Stanley but meant that Louise's son, S. Parker Gilbert, Jr., Morgan Stanley chairman in the 1980s, would claim a unique Morgan lineage.

Parker Gilbert's death came two weeks before scandal broke. If the House of Morgan lost its investment banking business with Glass-Steagall, it perhaps lost its honor in the Richard Whitney case. Where Ferdinand Pecora had exposed questionable practices—things legitimate but of dubious wisdom—the Whitney scandal was for the House of Morgan a closer brush with the law. The case became a morality play of old versus new Wall Street, of private versus public trust. It would do more than just scotch Lamont's attempt to ingratiate himself with the New Deal. It would also speed reforms of the New York Stock Exchange.

As president of the Exchange from 1930 to 1935, Richard Whitney had been the most arrogant Wall Street foe of federal securities regulation. For New Dealers, he personified the smug insolence of the *ancien régime* on Wall Street. When he testified about securities reform before the Senate Banking and Currency Committee in 1932, he lectured the senators on the need for a senatorial pay cut. Opposing creation of the SEC, he told Pecora's investigators, "You gentlemen are making a great mistake. The Exchange is a perfect institution," and he wouldn't let brokers answer the Pecora questionnaires.[28] In 1937, he met his match in SEC chairman William O. Douglas, who succeeded Joe Kennedy that year. Douglas had engaged in talks with Stock Exchange president Charles R. Gay about Exchange reform, and Whitney led a board faction opposed to such efforts. In the autumn of 1937, Douglas gave the Stock Exchange leaders a stern tongue-lashing: "The job of regulation's got to be done. It isn't being done now, and, damn it, you're going to do it or we are."[29] Resigned to the need for change, Gay appointed a committee under Carle C. Conway of Continental Can to study reforms. In January 1938 it recommended a complete revamping of the Exchange, including a full-time paid president, a professional staff, and nonmember governors. It was amid such rancorous skirmishing that the Richard Whitney scandal would unfold.

George and Richard Whitney were both tall, impressive, and patrician. Sons of a bank president, they had a Boston Brahmin upbringing and had attended Groton and Harvard. People would notice the gold watch chain with the Porcellian pig that Richard wore from his Harvard days. Morgan partner George had developed a dislike of his Groton classmate Franklin Roosevelt that he never shed. "My brother and I went to college, and we were always comfortable," he said. "There was no poor-boy stuff about this."[30] George came to Morgans via Kidder, Peabody, becoming a partner in 1919.

With a ruggedly handsome face, solid jaw, and elegant hauteur, George was emblematic of the Morgan bank in those years. A British visitor later commented, "George Whitney—tall, slim, iron gray head, very goodlooking and altogether charming—Miss Macey regards him as dangerous both to men and women!"[31] He perpetuated the Morgan tradition of fashion-plate partners. By a splendid coincidence, he had married Martha Bacon, daughter of Robert, the Greek God of Wall Street who had so entranced Pierpont.

By the late 1930s, George Whitney ran the Morgan bank and was a director of Kennecott Copper, Texas Gulf Sulphur, Johns-Manville, and Guaranty Trust. As the head of domestic underwriting, he suffered more than other Morgan partners from Glass-Steagall and watched his business pass into Harold Stanley's hands. He was greatly respected on Wall Street and, despite his reserve, very popular in the bank. Of the Morgan partners who trooped to Washington to answer questions, George Whitney often seemed the most snobbishly indignant, as if unwilling to concede the legitimacy of the proceedings. Just when it looked as if New Deal attacks might relent, the scandal that broke meant more government inquisitors trying to penetrate his polished defenses.

George grew up in the shadow of his older brother, Richard, the star of the family. Richard's early career on Wall Street seemed to live up to his family's high expectations. On Black Thursday in 1929, as vice-president of the Stock Exchange, he had taken the fabled stroll, placing the bid for U.S. Steel and other stocks; the following spring he was elevated to president of the Exchange, the youngest person in history to hold the position. He became popularly known as the man who halted the panic of 1929 and emerged as something of a folk hero.[32] Cold and pompous, he was Mr. Wall Street, presiding in a black cutaway in his palatial suite on the Exchange's top floor. In the private-club atmosphere, he represented the reactionary elements, the floor traders and specialists who resisted federal regulation, against the relatively more liberal retail brokers.

Richard's association with J. P. Morgan went beyond his brother. His firm, Richard Whitney and Company, was the major broker handling gilt-edged bonds for the bank. Even if nobody at Morgans had been involved in the scandal, it would have reflected on the bank. As journalist John Brooks has said, "When the gods of 23 Wall materialized on the earthly market across the street, the bodily form they took was that of Dick Whitney."[33] The bank generally stayed aloof, not involving itself in disputes at the Exchange, and was dismayed by the popular impression that Richard Whitney represented its views. By the time the scandal broke, it was too late to correct that impression.

Richard Whitney led a double life in the 1930s. As he defended pools, short sales, and other speculation from Washington attacks, he was struggling with an addiction to gambling. He was a sucker for fast-buck artists. He bought stock in a Florida fertilizer company right before that state's economy collapsed and invested in a bootleg applejack called Jersey Lightning. All the while, he lived like a country squire. Married to the heiress daughter of a former president of the Union League Club, he bred thoroughbreds at a five-hundred-acre New Jersey estate, presided over the Essex Fox Hounds, owned a Fifth Avenue townhouse, and swaggered about like a tycoon.

Chronically indebted, Richard was always borrowing and enlisting people in joint investment schemes. In 1929, he tried to lure his distant cousin, Jock Whitney, into an investment partnership. But by then Richard's reputation was already sufficiently murky that lawyer Lewis Cass Ledyard talked Jock out of it. (Later, with his friend David O. Selznick, Jock would buy the movie rights to *The Story of Richard Whitney*.) The remarkably faithful George kept Richard solvent and indulged his fantasies of financial glory. Before the crash, George lent Richard $500,000 to buy a Stock Exchange seat. After that, the loans grew more frequent, and Richard ran up a staggering $3-million debt to his brother. These loans permitted others; as Richard panhandled on Wall Street, people assumed George stood behind him. The fear and respect accorded the House of Morgan was such that throughout Richard's protracted financial crisis, nobody ever demanded repayment.

In 1931, the Morgan bank made a $500,000 loan to Richard that had to be continually renewed. The partners professed to like Richard's roguish style, but with deep, unspoken reservations. At one point, they tried to get a veteran Stock Exchange governor to merge his firm with Richard's in order to curb the latter's excesses. Several times, Lamont warned George that Richard's shrilly condescending attacks against securities reform were counterproductive. George himself knew Richard was being reckless. And when Morgans underwent its first inspection by state bank examiners in 1934, George had to supply his own securities as collateral for Richard's loan.

By the mid-1930s, in a sure sign of desperation, Richard was approaching Jewish Exchange members for loans, even though he had blackballed them from the Exchange's upper echelons. In 1936, George asked partner Henry P. Davison, Jr., Harry's son, to inspect Richard's finances. While quizzing Richard in a polite, offhand manner, Davison noticed that his loans lacked sufficient collateral. Worse, Richard was using borrowed securities as collateral for more loans—the broad and open highway to financial ruin so memorably paved by William Crapo Durant a generation before.

At this point, Richard graduated from poor judgment to outright crime and began to loot two blue-blooded institutions. The Stock Exchange had a $2.5-million Gratuity Fund, which provided death benefits to members' families; Richard helped himself to $1 million of its securities as collateral for loans to himself and his firm. As treasurer of the New York Yacht Club, he misappropriated $150,000 in securities. The scandal was uncovered when Richard Whitney skipped a meeting of the Gratuity Fund trustees and a meek clerk divulged the missing securities. Suddenly Richard had to replace the "borrowed" shares. Among others, he tapped Averell Harriman for $50,000 but needed bigger money. On November 23, 1937, he went to George for a $1-million emergency loan. The bank's formal culpability began here, because Richard admitted his criminal acts to his brother. It must have been a nightmare for George, who had spent years in Washington hotly defending the House of Morgan against insinuations of impropriety. As Richard said of George, "He was terribly disturbed and aghast that it could have been done and asked me many, many times why I had done it, and just couldn't understand it--thunderstruck, as he had reason to be."[34]

Lacking ready cash, George went to Lamont and told him Richard was in a "very serious jam." ("Jam" would be the all-purpose euphemism of the scandal.) He admitted the misappropriation of Stock Exchange securities and said they had to be replaced the next day. Cool but sympathetic, Lamont said, "Well, that is a devil of a note, George. Why,

Dick Whitney is all right; how could he mishandle securities even for a moment, no matter what the jam?"[35] The next day, in an extraordinary act of fear or friendship, Lamont sat down and wrote out a personal check for $1 million; George then made it over to Richard. Two weeks later, after repaying Lamont, George asked Jack Morgan if he could withdraw money from his partnership capital, vaguely referring to Richard's being in an "awful jam." Jack didn't inquire as to the reason. He later said he assumed the money was for a business matter.

Because Lamont and George didn't report Richard's crime, they were guilty of misprision of a felony. For three months, they knew Richard was a crook but told nobody at the Stock Exchange and handled the embezzlement as a matter best settled privately among gentlemen. They faced an excruciating dilemma. The Morgan partners never paid bribes and prided themselves on their integrity, but now there were strong temptations to hush up the scandal. George was naturally reluctant to expose his brother's crimes. And the bank knew the New Dealers would gladly exploit a scandal to impose further reforms on Wall Street. They didn't want to throw Richard to the liberal Democratic wolves, especially to William O. Douglas, who was ready to pounce on the House of Morgan and the Stock Exchange.

A zealous regulator with a bottomless hatred of Wall Street, Douglas was a certified Morgan-hater. He had labeled the "Morgan influence . . . the most pernicious one in industry and finance today."[36] He loathed the "goddamn bankers" and castigated the "financial termites" driven by a thirst for immediate profit. He continually plied Roosevelt with memos about the need for new regional industrial banks to "displace the Morgan influence in the various regions [with] a new and enlightened leadership in the business."[37] Douglas was also conducting his crusade against the New York Stock Exchange, which he regarded as an archaic private club. In fact, he threatened to take over the Exchange the same month Richard went to George for his emergency loan.

It is apt at this point, before examining the final act of the Whitney scandal, to relate a small anecdote that deserves a place in the Morgan annals. In February 1938, Richard took a $100,000 loan from a Walter T. Rosen. Evidently Rosen was well versed in Morgan lore, for in agreeing to the loan, he told Richard, "I have always been much impressed by the attitude of the elder Mr. Morgan who held the view that the personal integrity of the borrower was of far greater value than his collateral." With a straight face, Richard replied, "Mr. Morgan was entirely right."[38] By this point, Richard had racked up $27 million in loans.

On March 5, 1938, while George was recuperating from an illness in Florida, Richard suddenly appeared at the Links Club. He interrupted Morgan partner Frank Bartow at a bridge game. "I am in a jam," he blurted out and asked Bartow for a loan. He admitted that he had embezzled shares from the New York Yacht Club. Bartow said, "This is serious." Richard replied, "This is criminal."[39] Richard was about to appear before a Stock Exchange investigative committee and desperately needed money. Bartow refused to make a move before consulting a lawyer. The next day, he and Jack Morgan met with John Davis, who warned that any attempt to lend money to Richard could ruin the House of Morgan.[40] Their refusal to help sealed Richard's fate. When they telephoned George in Florida and told him of his brother's impending downfall, George simply gasped, "My God!"[41]

On March 7, 1938, the board of governors of the Stock Exchange voted misconduct charges against Richard Whitney. The next morning, an Exchange representative sounded the gong on the trading floor and announced the suspension of Richard Whitney and Company for insolvency. Pandemonium followed, and share prices plunged. Soon afterward, New York County district attorney Thomas E. Dewey indicted Whitney for grand larceny and securities theft, including a $100,000 theft from his wife. It came as a great shock to America's aristocracy, including President Roosevelt. With old class loyalty surfacing, the president sat teary-eyed when William O. Douglas brought him the news as he breakfasted in bed. "Not Dick Whitney!" the president cried; "Dick Whitney—Dick Whitney. I can't believe it!"[42] For a moment, the economic royalists seemed as unconscionable as New Deal slogans claimed.

The House of Morgan was outraged by the hastily arranged SEC investigation into the Whitney scandal. The crowded New York hearings took place at 120 Broadway, right near the Corner. Dean Acheson of Covington, Burling represented the Stock Exchange, while a young SEC lawyer named Gerhard A. Gesell led the questioning. When Gesell asked Jack Morgan whether he thought he had responsibilities to the Exchange in the matter, Jack replied, "No, none at all."[43] When Gesell asked why Morgans had lent money to Richard, Jack replied that he had never inquired as to the reason. "Well, you didn't think it was wine and women and horses, did you?" Gesell asked. When Jack said no, the sum was too large for that, everybody laughed.[44] Tired and defeated, Jack sat with eyes shut through much of the testimony, as if it were a bad dream from which he would soon thankfully

awake. Gesell later praised him as a "perfectly delightful old gentleman . . . mellow and always truthful."[45]

Lamont's usual sangfroid deserted him. At the hearings, he admitted
that it hadn't occurred to him that Richard was a thief, that he lent the
money to George, and that he assumed Stock Exchange officials knew
of the share dealings. He indignantly asked, "Would you expect me, Mr.
Gesell, to say to Mr. George Whitney, 'Yes, George, I will help you out
to cure this default, which you believe is a perfectly isolated thing, but
I must trot down to the district attorney's office and denounce your
brother forthwith?'"[46] Lamont said he had done what any friend would
do. Similarly, George Whitney said he had done what any brother
would do.

Lamont's papers confirm his sense of bafflement. Even to his friend
Lady Astor, he felt obliged to plead his innocence:

> It is all a bit like Alice in Wonderland to me. Ought we all to forget
> the principles on which we were trained to help one another, to try
> to forgive and to try to give the fellow another chance? . . .
>
> Of course, as the evidence proved, Dick was a thoroughgoing
> crook. He lied to George up to the last moment, he falsified his books,
> he deceived his wife and children, etc. etc. But all this was unknown
> to George last November at the time that he tried to help Dick undo
> the wrong that he had done.[47]

Although Richard Whitney pleaded guilty to grand larceny, George
and Lamont escaped punishment. Prosecutor Dewey perhaps thought
the rich had suffered enough. But the SEC report harshly criticized the
pair and said they had known of Richard's criminal conduct and financial difficulties. (Even before seeing the report, Jack told Lamont and
George it would be another "poisonous" SEC document.[48]) Hard and
relentless, William O. Douglas wanted Morgan blood. During the hearings, he summoned Gesell to his office and said, "The press tells me
you're being soft on George Whitney." Gesell shot back, "Bill, that's
beneath you. I've been bringing out the facts, but I'm not going to rub
George Whitney's face in the dirt simply because he helped his brother.
And I'm not being soft on him."[49] Whitney respected Gesell and later
encouraged Covington, Burling to hire him. "But you'd better get rid of
this fellow Acheson," he told Harry Covington. "He's no good."[50]

Douglas asked the Justice Department to review George Whitney's and Lamont's conduct for possible misprision of a felony. When Justice Department attorney Brien McMahon refused to prosecute them, Douglas saw a malign conspiracy at work. He later said McMahon would "cast our reports into the dustbin. . . . Somewhere in the background was a powerful figure with money and political connections."[51] When he tried to get the Exchange to pursue the Morgan partners, only University of Chicago president Robert Hutchins voted for censure.

Douglas capitalized on the scandal to push through a new constitution and reform slate at the Exchange. The embezzlement demonstrated the need for greater openness at the Stock Exchange. By mid-May, the reforms recommended by the Conway committee were enacted. The board of governors was broadened to include public members, and the thirty-four-year-old secretary of the Conway committee, William McChesney Martin of Saint Louis, was elected the first salaried president of the Exchange. Douglas thus converted the Exchange from a private club into a body responsive to SEC dictates. He also pushed another reform agenda—competitive bidding for securities issues. In December 1938, he won a partial victory when the SEC ruled that investment banks couldn't collect underwriting fees from public utilities unless they engaged in arm's-length bargaining. Other financial crusaders also took heart from Whitney's disgrace. Railroadman Robert Young later said he had the courage to persist against Lamont's opposition after reading about Whitney's arrest, which he saw as proof of decaying Morgan power.

And what happened to Richard Whitney? After his arrest he behaved like a French nobleman being dragged off to the guillotine. Determined to face down his executioners, he berated Gerhard Gesell for being five minutes late to one interrogation. He objected to being described as insolvent, saying in a huff, "I still can borrow money from my friends."[52] Meanwhile wealthy sympathizers stacked up floral wreaths in front of his East Seventy-third Street townhouse. After he was convicted of grand larceny, a circus atmosphere attended his departure for a five- to ten-year prison term at Sing Sing. Five thousand spectators at Grand Central Terminal saw a tall bowler-hatted man being led to the train by police. He was shackled to two other prisoners—an extortionist and a man convicted of assault. Unlike these two criminals, the impassive Whitney made no attempt to hide his face from photographers. He became inmate number 94835 at Sing Sing, and the first Stock Exchange president ever to serve time there.

In the long run, the scandal's real beneficiary may have been George Whitney. For years, he profited from comparison with Richard and became the Nice Honest Whitney Brother, softening his image as a defender of privilege. His loyalty to Richard stirred even the New Dealers. Over the years, Gerhard Gesell would be touched by news photographs of George taking a glove or a bat to Richard so he could play on the prison baseball team. (Richard was also visited by his old Groton headmaster, the Reverend Endicott Peabody.) By August 1941, Richard was eligible for parole, and George drove up to meet him at the prison gate. Richard then served as superintendent of a dairy farm in Barnstable, Massachusetts. He never again entered the world of finance or public life.

APPEASEMENT

· ·
·

FROM its inception, the House of Morgan had been Anglo-American in spirit and character. The Great War, in particular, fused the London and New York banks in a belief in Anglo-American responsibility for world peace and prosperity. Morgan partners subscribed to an idea expressed by Walter Lippmann in 1915 that U.S. foreign policy would experience a "crowning disaster" if uninformed by "a vision of the Anglo-American future."[1] That vision was Morgan dogma, the bedrock of partners' political beliefs. Yet the Second World War—both its prelude and the early stages, before Pearl Harbor—would prove a divisive experience, exposing tensions between New York and London that had been unacknowledged or long suppressed.

The Anglo-American comradeship had always been a bit one-sided. The Wall Street partners were ardent Anglophiles who celebrated British culture and made annual trips to London. Whether renting a Scottish castle or buying Sir Joshua Reynolds paintings, they identified with the British and affected their manners. This pro-British sentiment owed much to the fact that during most partners' early adulthood, London stood supreme in world banking. The partners at 23 Wall belonged to a generation that had eagerly boarded transatlantic luxury liners in the early 1900s to partake of British sophistication. Of his first visit to London, Lamont recalled, "For me London was the most thrilling spot that I had ever known or could imagine existed."[2] The test of a true J. P. Morgan partner was whether he saw the City as his ancestral home.

Jack Morgan preferred to be in England, where he wasn't caricatured as an uncaring plutocrat. He enjoyed the secluded privacy of Wall Hall outside London and had a wood-paneled office at 23 Great Winchester Street. England respected his privacy and was an ideal sanctuary from the strident New Deal denunciations. While Franklin Roosevelt hounded him, British royalty lionized him. George V said he felt comfortable with only two Americans—Jack Morgan and Ambassador Walter Hines Page. (Jack's granddaughter Jane married Walter Page's grandson, who bore the ambassador's name and became a postwar Morgan Guaranty chairman.) After shooting at Gannochy as Jack's guest, George VI told Sir Gerald Campbell, "I consider Mr. Morgan the world's greatest gentleman. Whenever he comes into the room, I instinctively feel that I must arise."[3] When Lamont reported this, Jack blushingly said it made him feel "a little shy; but it is naturally very pleasant to me to hear of such nice things being said by a man whom I have known for a considerable number of years."[4] Jack bounced the king's daughter, the future Queen Elizabeth, on his knee, and his friendship with the royal family was a factor in Morgan Grenfell's later handling of a significant share of Elizabeth II's personal wealth.

Morgan Grenfell partners never fully reciprocated this admiration. Despite their real affection for the New York partners, they weren't enthralled by American history and probably found the country charming but provincial. By the late 1930s, several of the London partners were exalted personages, peers of the realm—Grenfell (Lord Saint Just), Smith (Lord Bicester), and Tom Catto (Lord Catto). Their institutional ties bound them as strongly to the British power structure as to their New York brethren. Smith was governor of the Royal Exchange Assurance Company and chaired the City of London Conservative and Unionist Association. Grenfell—now suffering from heart and lung problems and laid up with a patch on his lung—was a member of Parliament and a Bank of England director and had worked a Bank of England symbol into his coat of arms.

J. P. Morgan and Company had always hired gifted outsiders—Perkins, Davison, Morrow, Lamont, and Leffingwell—who rose on the strength of their intelligence. Morgan Grenfell recruited from a smaller circle of family members and friends. This would give the firm an inbred feeling, a genteel hothouse atmosphere, and a stuffy complacency that would make it dangerously ossified by the 1950s. Lord Bicester's son Rufus became a partner, and Francis Rodd, the son of a former British ambassador to Rome, was married to Rufus's sister. Morgan Grenfell partners displayed an upper-crust insularity. The first Lord Bicester, Vivian Hugh Smith, is the best example. As squire of Tusmore Park in Oxfordshire, he indulged a mad passion for steeplechase horses. Every year he went to Ireland to buy them and was frustrated in his great ambition of winning the Grand National. In a remark that some might have deemed insulting—but Bicester doubtless treasured—Lamont told him, "It is a great life you lead. You are my ideal of the English gentleman of the Victorian Age."[5] These weren't the sort of people to be enamored of American culture.

After Glass-Steagall, J. P. Morgan and Company not only became a minority shareholder in Morgan Grenfell but became more distanced from its affairs. As Lamont explained, "Morgan Grenfell & Co. considers that business done through them is their business."[6] After J. P. Morgan chose commercial banking, New York and London couldn't issue securities together, as they had in the 1920s. And foreign lending was down throughout the Depression. Hobbled by a weak pound and government restrictions on overseas lending, the City's merchant banks, tired and unimaginative, entered a deep sleep from which they wouldn't awaken until the aluminium war of the late 1950s.

The most serious threat to J. P. Morgan–Morgan Grenfell unity was over foreign debt, which, like a bad hangover, remained from the 1920s lending binge. The first split had occurred with German debt. The Nazi policy of selective defaults generated ill will between the Morgan houses in London and New York. Then in March 1938, it looked as if history would repeat itself. Hitler ordered his troops into Austria and made a triumphant entry into Vienna, cheered by ecstatic crowds. Fulfilling his *Mein Kampf* prophecy, he reduced Austria to a German province while the Gestapo unleashed a wave of violence against Jews and other undesirables.

The J. P. Morgan and Company partners immediately feared default on a huge 1930 Austrian reconstruction loan. No less than in Pierpont's day, the bank had a fanatic sense of responsibility toward bonds it had issued. The British portion of the loan had been managed by several London banks, including Morgan Grenfell. Would the Nazis honor Austrian debt? Or would they classify it with German reparations loans and claim it was foisted upon Austria by the Allies? Most important, would Germany again cut a separate deal with England?

Hjalmar Schacht's power had continued to wane. Increasingly disgruntled with the Nazis, he feared the inflationary consequences of Germany's military buildup: he had defiantly told his arch rival, Göring, "Your foreign-exchange policy, your policy regarding production, and your financial policy [are] unsound."[7]

After the Austrian Anschluss, Schacht said, he secretly lost all sympathy with Hitler and began to contemplate his overthrow. But his apostasy was carefully disguised. Schacht was charged with running Austria's National Bank and subordinating its financial system to German monetary policy. Two weeks after the bloodless invasion, he assembled the staff of the central bank and delivered a terrifying speech: "Not a single person will find a future with us who is not wholeheartedly for Adolph Hitler. . . . The Reichsbank will always be nothing but National Socialist or I shall cease to be its manager." After administering a loyalty oath to the Führer, he led the bank staff in a brisk chanting of *"Sieg Heil!"*[8] Schacht fired Dr. Kienbock, the Austrian banker who had offered Gobelin tapestries to Morgans as loan collateral in the early 1920s. With his usual self-congratulatory bent, Schacht later explained, "I saw to it that he was able to retire on a full pension and with flying colors though he was known to be of partly Jewish extraction."[9] The old Jewish Viennese banks were torn asunder. Baron Louis von Rothschild was arrested, jailed, and released only after signing over all Rothschild assets in Austria to the state.

The House of Morgan closely monitored German speeches about Austrian debt. Before long, Walther Funk, who had replaced Göring as economics minister just before the Anschluss, was making statements that equated Austrian loans with German loans and claiming that they, too, were made by the Allies merely to ensure reparations. He ranted about scheming bankers and craven politicians who had conspired to draw Germany into "debt and interest slavery." In New York, Lamont watched nervously for signs of a deal between England and the Nazis. On April 25, 1938, his son, Tommy, spotted an item in the London financial press that alerted them to an impending settlement. "In other words," Tommy said, ". . . our good friends in the Bank of England and the City are contemplating pulling a fast one to the disadvantage of the American holders of Austrian bonds."[10]

Lamont was furious: the man who never got angry flew into a rage. To Sir Frederick Leith-Ross, the reparations expert at the British Treasury, he wrote a letter in stiletto-sharp prose. Recalling the 1934 British deal with Germany, he said:

> I am recalling all this not in a spirit, my dear Leith, of anything except good will in pointing out to you the advantage of considering American interests in connection with the 1930 Austrian loan. The new fashion in the world is that every country should develop its own nationalism to the nth degree. But over here when our people listen to polite inquiries from our British friends as to what America's attitude might be in the case of Britain's becoming involved in a general war, the inclination is to wonder a little why the British sometimes overlook these matters (like the Dawes and Young loan

matter) which are small in themselves, but which constitute an un-
ceasing cause of irritation.

Lamont ended by alluding to the State Department's "deep interest" in
the Austrian loan.[11]

While Lamont's exquisite courtesy toward the British now turned
into elegant taunts and insults, his warnings proved fruitless. Schacht
and Monty Norman kept up their mysterious dialogue, meeting
monthly at the Bank for International Settlements in Basel. In June, an
Anglo-German debt settlement was announced in Parliament, and
professions of British-American financial solidarity yielded to brazen
opportunism. It is interesting to note that Neville Chamberlain, in his
desire to appease Germany, was indifferent to reports of Schacht's secret
defection from Hitler. That summer in Basel, Schacht told Norman of
his decision to abandon Hitler and work for his overthrow. When Norman repeated this to Chamberlain, the prime minister retorted, "Who
is Schacht? I have to deal with Hitler."[12]

How did Britain justify its deal? Norman told Lamont that Britain
tried to settle Austrian debt on a nonpartisan international basis but
that the Nazis insisted on discriminatory treatment. At the same
time, the British—echoing Schacht's viewpoint—said they were running a trade deficit with Germany and that Austrian debt repayments
would recycle to Britain some of the money they were paying for
German goods. It was a depressing reversal from the Diplomatic Age
of the 1920s. Monty Norman—the man who wanted to lift finance
above the muddy realm of politics and into the clear air—now submitted to nationalistic pressures. With his usual theatrics, he wrote
Lamont a lachrymose explanation: "For few debtor countries nowadays are willing to treat debts from the standpoint of ethics and equity and not from the standpoint of politics and convenience. . . .
You cannot answer this because I am going away for a long time
to heal my wound and I only write to clear your views and my
conscience!"[13]

The feud between J. P. Morgan and Morgan Grenfell lingered; that
the latter had placed British interests ahead of joint Morgan interests
could not be lightly dismissed. In a tone he usually reserved for the
browbeating of debtors, Lamont warned the London partners not to take
Anglo-American cooperation for granted in the event of war—a shockingly grave threat. He wrote, "Must we accept that the high sanction
of Great Britain is to be given to the growing habit of ignoring interna-

tional connections and the rights of property?"[14] This sort of reprimand would have surprised isolationists, who saw only collusion between the House of Morgan and England.

Apparently fearing the Austrian feud would imperil Anglo-American financial relations, Francis Rodd circulated Lamont's letter at the British Treasury—without consulting New York. When Lamont learned of this, he exploded, believing his letter had been sent in strict confidence and could damage Morgan relations with the Treasury and the Bank of England. He sent a stinging rebuke to 23 Great Winchester Street:

> You are aware that for generations past the partners of our house have always felt it to the great advantage of both our countries that the friendliest possible relations should exist between them. . . . As you know now we never meant our letter to be filed with the British Treasury. . . . There are lots of things one can say to a man that he cannot write to him, and that is a thousand times more true with regard to governments. The priceless value of Morgan Grenfell & Co. to us . . . has been precisely in the ability of the partners of Morgan Grenfell & Co. to interpret us to the British Treasury and the British Treasury to us. We have never thought of Morgan Grenfell & Co. as a post office for the transmission of our letters to the British Government.[15]

The pitfalls of the Anglo-American Morgan relationship were here apparent: did Morgan Grenfell represent the British government to J. P. Morgan or J. P. Morgan to the British government? How could New York partners expect Morgan Grenfell to be so intimate with Whitehall yet detached at the same time? These question had never been adequately posed, much less answered, because no serious conflict had arisen during the 1920s, the heyday of financial internationalism. Now the nationalistic squabbling of the 1930s destroyed many illusions about the supposed allegiance of the London partners to J. P. Morgan and Company. The "Trojan horse" strategy followed since the early 1900s—of giving the London house a British complexion and character—had, in the last analysis, backfired on the New York house.

THE New York partners traveled in aristocratic British circles and were frequent visitors at the Astor estate at Cliveden. No less than the House of Morgan itself, Nancy Astor represented a marriage of American capital and British aristocracy. Born Nancy Langhorne in Virginia, she ended up as the first woman to hold a seat in the House of Commons (having campaigned for office in pearls and accompanied by a liveried coachman). A stylish, pretty woman with a sharp tongue and a zest for political rows, she liked to heckle, tease, and argue. Once, while visiting her adversary Winston Churchill at Blenheim, Astor said, "If I were married to you, I would put poison in your coffee." Churchill replied, "And if I were married to you, I would drink it."[16]

Nancy was married to the rich but feckless Waldorf Astor, second viscount and the grandson of John Jacob Astor III. Waldorf drew the bulk of his income from rentals of his Manhattan real estate holdings, so the transatlantic structure of the House of Morgan perfectly suited his business needs. Waldorf also consulted Tom Lamont about his personal finances, and Lamont had switched him out of American securities and into Canadian municipal bonds after the 1929 crash. The Lamonts and the Astors socialized and even vacationed together.

Lady Astor bewitched Tom Lamont, and for twenty years they kept up an abundant correspondence. There was a likeness between them. Both were romantics with a taste for *noblesse oblige,* self-invented aristocrats who had acted out extravagant dreams and confidently inhabited their stations. From government offices, Cunard staterooms, hotel rooms—even once while Astor set her hair—the two exchanged long, often effusive letters. They traded gossip, personal confessions, and political intelligence. After the Richard Whitney scandal, Lamont sent her clippings to establish his innocence and Astor replied, "Dearest Tom, I don't have to read your cuttings, or anything else for that matter, to know that you would never do wrong. Such is my affection for you!"[17]

Their correspondence had a vaguely romantic cast. Lamont termed Lady Astor "the kindest-hearted and best friend in the world" and called her "the girl I love most."[18] In his inimitable fashion, he showered her with gifts and favors. He could break down anybody's resistance, conquer anyone with charm, such was his genius for cultivating friends. Golfing with him at Cliveden in 1930, she had admired a set of clubs owned by another guest, Frank Kellogg, until recently the U.S. secretary of state. Back on Wall Street, Lamont tracked down the original manufacturer and had identical clubs made for her. "I am really ridiculously excited and grateful," she wrote back.[19] Another time, Lamont slipped away from 23 Wall, went uptown, and bought her two frocks at Saks Fifth Avenue. It was a warm friendship, indeed.

On the eve of World War II, Lamont's friendship with the Astors took on important political dimensions. Cliveden, the Astor estate on the

Thames, had become a gathering place for politicians and intellectuals who favored appeasement of the Nazis. They thought England could coexist with Hitler, feared a war would shatter the British Empire, and supported the appeasement policies of Stanley Baldwin and Neville Chamberlain. In time, the name Cliveden became synonymous with a phobic hatred of Russia, a benign or even admiring view of Fascist intentions, and a rejection of Churchill's warnings about German rearmament.

Like his Cliveden friends, Lamont believed that Europe's dictators could be held at bay through diplomacy and that war could be avoided. He also thought Britain and France were woefully unprepared for war. To some extent, Lamont and his partners were still cowed by the Nye committee charges that they had been "merchants of death" in World War I. They weren't eager to stick their necks out in support of another war. "As for our dictators, Hitler and Mussolini," Lamont wrote Lady Astor in 1937, "they don't seem to have changed their spots very much, but I seem to think that raging at them will do no good, and if there is a possibility of methods of appeasement, these are our only chance."[20] Earlier, Lamont had asked Lady Astor to lobby the Foreign Office in support of its recognizing Mussolini's conquest in Ethiopia. When Hitler took over Austria, Lamont assured her that his Italian friends were "aghast" at the coup and said their view must surely reflect il Duce's own horror. Right up to the war, he believed that Italy had sided with the Germans only under extreme duress.

Lamont took a more alarmist view of events in the Pacific. He had never fully recovered from his sense of betrayal by the Japanese militarists, and this only deepened his sense of their malevolence. During Japan's fierce aggression against China in July 1937 and the slaughter of thousands of Chinese civilians in the rape of Nanking, he spied a design to subdue all of East Asia. He didn't mince words with Japanese businessmen who made overtures to the bank. In September 1937, he assured the Japanese consul general that he would not "find one American in one hundred thousand who is not shocked and distressed beyond measure" by Japanese military operations in and around Shanghai.[21] (In fact, a few weeks later Russell Leffingwell told Lamont that China would fare better under Japanese domination.[22]) In contrast with his gullible acceptance of the Mukden incident of 1931, an irate Lamont now protested to the Bank of Japan that "faked stories" about China were being circulated by Japan all over the world.[23]

In September 1938, Neville Chamberlain flew to Munich and capitulated to Hitler's demand for the Sudetenland. Hitler forswore further territorial ambitions, and Chamberlain hoped that the partition of Czechoslovakia would sate the dictator's appetite for conquest. In accepting the Munich Pact, the British cabinet wasn't completely naive about Hitler's intentions: many thought England needed time to mount an expensive rearmament program and that war with Germany would be suicidal. Returning to Downing Street talking of "peace with honour," Chamberlain received a tumultuous welcome. The London *Times* said, "No conqueror returning from a victory on the battlefield has come adorned with nobler laurels."[24] Amid a rapturous greeting in the House of Commons, Churchill was the sour, lonely voice of dissent, branding Munich a "total and unmitigated defeat." He was predictably heckled by Nancy Astor.[25]

The House of Morgan stoutly supported Munich. In a flight of fancy, Lamont predicted a new German regime within two years. Jack Morgan was sure that in the end Hitler would have to be stopped forcibly. In the meantime, he thought his friend Chamberlain had bought valuable time. "What an achievement!" he wrote to the prime minister in breathless tones. "I little thought when you were at Gannochy at tea and I said I had a hunch that there would be no war and you said hunches were the only thing to go on, and that you had the same hunch as I did, that you were going to be the one to have the imagination and courage to make that hunch come true! It never occurred to me that a single man could do so much by sheer force of courage, fairness and reasonableness."[26] With rather heavy snickering, Jack said that if Churchill or Lloyd George were in charge, the world would have been at war long ago.[27] Vivian Smith, now Lord Bicester, was more muted in his support of Munich, warning that Hitler was a "fanatic" and that Göring and Goebbels were "gangsters" using the Nazis as a cloak for their evildoing.[28] While congratulating the Morgan Grenfell partners that Chamberlain had averted war, Russell Leffingwell privately lamented to Lamont that Britain had submitted to blackmail.[29]

Hitler was puffed up with the success of his blackmail. In March 1939, he devoured the rest of Czechoslovakia, and the German army marched into Prague. Czechoslovakia's extinction shattered the appeasement movement. Nancy Astor's intimate friend Lord Lothian sent a despondent note to Lamont saying he had abandoned hope of decent behavior from that gangster, Hitler. Two days later, Lady Astor herself urged Chamberlain to condemn Germany. By the end of the month, Chamberlain reversed his course and guaranteed Poland's independence.[30]

The British public dealt harshly with the complacency Baldwin and

Chamberlain had shown in the face of the German threat. Political adulation turned into vitriolic abuse as the British solidly closed ranks behind a determined response to Hitler. In America, however, the division of public opinion toward the European turmoil only grew more contentious. For Morgan partners in New York, it was an especially problematic dispute. As Lamont had warned Morgan Grenfell and the British Treasury, there was a residue of pent-up American hostility left over from the financial disputes of the 1930s. And the power of American isolationists was such that the bank couldn't immediately proclaim the proud, unalloyed support for Britain that it had in 1914. J. P. Morgan and Company would find itself in the uncomfortable position of antagonizing the isolationists for doing too much for Britain while disappointing the British for not doing enough.

An indirect casualty of Munich was Hjalmar Schacht, who had joined in the secret generals' plot of September 1938 to overthrow Hitler. He later claimed the conspirators were disheartened by the Allies' cowardice at Munich. Schacht's standing in Nazi Germany had grown precarious in late 1938. At the Reichsbank Christmas party, held several weeks after the burning of Jewish shops and synagogues on Kristallnacht, he deplored such actions. In early 1939, the deluded Schacht still churned out Reichsbank memos on the need to cut inflationary arms expenditures, as if Hitler cared about neoclassical economics. In London that December, he presented a plan for the emigration of fifty thousand Jews from Germany—to be paid for with all their belongings and ransom payments from the world Jewish community. In the first week of January, Monty Norman made a last trip to Germany, to attend the christening of his godson—Schacht's grandson Norman Hjalmar—named in tribute to him. When Hitler fired Schacht from the Reichsbank on January 20, Norman belatedly awoke to the full horror of the Nazi menace.

RIGHT before the outbreak of World War II came the first state visit by a British monarch to the United States—a piece of pageantry and propaganda in which the House of Morgan participated. The trip was inspired by Joseph Kennedy, who became ambassador to the Court of Saint James's in 1938. Like many Roosevelt appointments, this one infuriated 23 Wall. Several of his biases simultaneously aroused, Jack Morgan told Monty Norman, "I share your wonder that an Irish Papist and a Wall Street punter should have been selected for the London Embassy. Of course you must expect him to have to be a New Dealer, because Franklin would not appoint anyone else."[31] Although Norman patronized Kennedy as a social climber of inferior Irish stock, they met weekly, and Norman shared his pessimistic views about England's prospects in a war against Germany.

What made Kennedy's appointment doubly galling for Jack was that as ambassador the Irishman was living at Princes Gate, which Jack had given to the State Department as an ambassador's residence in the 1920s. (Joe Kennedy had his revenge on Morgan snubs: today the blue marker outside the house commemorates John F. Kennedy's brief residence there and says nothing of the Morgans' original ownership of the property.) Princes Gate would enjoy only a fleeting existence as an official residence, however. After the war, Barbara Hutton, the Woolworth heiress, donated her Winfield House in Regent's Park, and that became the new residence of American ambassadors.

The 1939 visit came about when Queen Elizabeth one day said to Kennedy, "I only know 3 Americans—you, Fred Astaire, and J. P. Morgan—and I would like to know more."[32] To remedy this, Kennedy suggested a goodwill trip to the United States. Through their private secretary, the royal couple sounded out Jack Morgan and John Davis, who agreed that a visit would indeed be timely. When the king and queen came to the United States in June 1939, Joe Kennedy was pointedly snubbed and excluded from attending their party.

As planned, the American trip elicited a tremendous outpouring of pro-British sympathy. The royal couple enjoyed hot dogs at Hyde Park, and Roosevelt outlined limited naval steps he could take to support Britain in case of war. But it didn't help the House of Morgan, for it reinforced the old stereotype of the firm's being in league with the British crown. At a garden party at the British embassy in Washington, the king and queen sat up on the porch in remote splendor with several private citizens—Jack Morgan, John D. Rockefeller, Jr., and Mrs. Cornelius Vanderbilt. Only two New Dealers, James Farley and Cordell Hull, were allowed to join them. Stranded down on the lawn with other commoners, the saturnine Harold Ickes enviously watched Morgan and the other economic royalists up on the porch and felt demeaned. He wasn't mollified when the king and queen descended to mingle with the "common herd."[33]

In late August 1939, Jack Morgan and King George VI were shooting together at Balmoral in Scotland, complaining about the bird shortage, when Europe suddenly mobilized for war. Like sovereigns retreating to their respective capitals, the king returned to London and Jack to Wall Street. On September 1, Germany invaded Poland. Soon Neville Chamberlain, his voice shaking, announced that Britain was at war with

Germany. The New York Stock Exchange reacted with its best session in two years, and the bond market leaped upward with the heaviest one-day volume in history. Unlike the outbreak of World War I, American investors weren't fooled as to who would profit from the conflict and foresaw an economic boom. It was the Second World War—not the New Deal—that would wipe away the vestiges of the Depression.

It dawned on the House of Morgan that the firm might dust off the World War I purchasing-agency concept. Might not the bank again aid the Allies behind a shield of neutrality? After pondering such a move, the bank informed the British, French, and U.S. governments that it wouldn't try to repeat the experience. After so many years of hearings, the bank felt politically vulnerable and feared a revival of war-profiteering charges.

The bank also contended with an anti-Wall Street faction in Washington, which was determined to block any Morgan role. This opposition was apparent when Roosevelt created a short-lived War Resources Board. In an amazing coincidence, he chose as chairman Edward R. Stettinius, Jr., son of the Morgan genius of the Export Department in World War I. A handsome man with prematurely silver hair, Stettinius had risen through the ranks of two Morgan clients, General Motors and U.S. Steel, ending up chairman of the latter. The war board included another Morgan favorite, Walter Gifford of AT&T. Roosevelt wanted to counteract charges of being an enemy of business, but his liberal subordinates smelled extreme danger in this tactical retreat. Hugh Johnson, former head of the National Recovery Administration, told Assistant Secretary of War Louis Johnson that the government did not "intend to let Morgan and DuPont men run the war."[34] Henry Wallace, then FDR's secretary of agriculture, also warned against bringing Wall Street bankers to Washington.

The assiduous Harold Ickes quickly gathered his cabal of Brandeis men, Tom Corcoran and Bob Jackson. He noted, "We wondered how far the President would go or would permit others to go in abdicating in favor of big business, as Wilson did at the time of the First World War."[35] Ickes thought Wilson's liberal credentials were tarnished by his wartime closeness to Wall Street and he hoped Roosevelt could avoid such a fate. His efforts to keep the Morgan bank out of war work dovetailed with his friend Cyrus Eaton's efforts to break up Morgan power in the financial world. In late 1939 and early 1940, the Temporary National Economic Committee investigated an alleged monopoly in the investment banking field, with Morgan Stanley its prime suspect.

These anti-Morgan maneuvers, coming from several directions, prevented the bank from resuming its World War I role, as did earlier U.S. entry into the war. In the Second World War, Washington would take charge of industrial mobilization through the War Production Board and other agencies. The federal government was vastly more powerful now than it had been in Woodrow Wilson's day, and it didn't hesitate to intervene in the economy for political ends. In fact, government resources now eclipsed those of private banking houses. By World War II, banks were no longer large enough to bankroll wars, as Barings, Rothschilds, and Morgans had done in their heydays. With their large budgets, central banks, and taxing powers, the modern nation-states no longer needed to rely on the good offices of private bankers.

The House of Morgan championed economic support for Great Britain. As a belligerent, Britain was covered by the arms embargo of the Neutrality Act (passed, *inter alia,* to prevent a recurrence of the House of Morgan's role in World War I). Lamont lobbied Roosevelt to repeal it, contending that it not only favored but emboldened Germany. In November 1939, Congress did repeal the embargo, permitting arms exports to countries at war on a "cash and carry basis": that is, they could purchase U.S. supplies so long as they paid for and transported them. Under this arrangement, American planes would fly to the U.S.-Canadian border, and Canadian pilots would then fly them to Britain.

The cash-and-carry decision created an urgent need for gold or dollars for the massive purchases. As in World War I, Britain raised money by commandeering American securities held by its nationals. The House of Morgan was charged with selling these securities in New York without triggering sharp price declines. It handled the British operation alone but shared a comparable French operation with Lazard Frères. Only a few people in each brokerage house knew the seller's identity, and Morgans warned brokers that if any information leaked out, their services would be terminated within twenty-four hours. To oversee the operation, the British Treasury sent T. J. Carlyle Gifford to 23 Wall. He was already known to Morgans as chairman of the Scottish Investment Trust of Edinburgh, which used J. P. Morgan as custodian for U.S. securities. Impressed by the House of Morgan's performance, Gifford nonetheless agreed with Roosevelt's assessment that the bank's participation was a severe political liability: "It seems the President and [Treasury Secretary] Morgenthau would much have preferred us not to go to J.P. Morgan & Co. and so have probably resented that and are now afraid it may cause difficulties when they appear [before] Congress," he reported back to London.[36]

Both for Nancy Astor's and Britain's sakes, Lamont assisted Lady Astor's great spiritual companion, Lord Lothian, who was sent to Washington as British ambassador in April 1939. A former secretary of the Rhodes Trust and a founder of the Royal Institute of International Affairs, Lothian was shy, professorial, and, like Lady Astor, a devout Christian Scientist. Immediately after his appointment, he cabled Lamont, "Shall want all your advice and help."[37] In Washington, Lord Lothian found the mood very much opposed to Hitler but, at the same time, resolutely opposed to war. Drawing on his Wall Street ally, he would fly up to New York on a late-afternoon flight, speak to a dinner assembled by Lamont, then take a night train back to Washington. Lothian, repenting of his Cliveden appeasement period, would prove a superbly eloquent spokesman in enlisting support for Britain.

In 1939, the most vociferous opposition to U.S. entry into the war came from the German and Italian immigrants, midwestern farmers, and labor unions. The isolationist agenda didn't change from World War I: there was the same disgust with European broils and the same suspicion that Britain would dupe the United States into saving its own empire. Complicating matters was the still fresh memory of the Great War.

The Morgan partners flatly opposed U.S. entry into the war and were dubious about the Allies' chances of beating Germany. As Russell Leffingwell said right before the war's outbreak, the British and French "cannot subjugate the Germans. There are too many of the devils, and they are too competent."[38] In May 1940, Lamont joined William Allen White in forming the Committee to Defend America by Aiding the Allies, whose outlook perfectly reflected the Morgan position. The group assailed the same nemeses—the Hearst newspapers and Senators Wheeler and Nye—that had hounded the House of Morgan for years. While fervently attacking the isolationists, it parted company from a kindred group, Fight for Freedom, which endorsed U.S. entry into the war; instead, it heeded FDR's call for all aid short of war. (At this time, Jack's sister Anne formed the American Friends of France and by June 1940 was sailing to that country to evacuate refugees and head an ambulance unit. She would have a special plaque dedicated to her memory in Les Invalides, the Paris war memorial, after she died in 1952.)

One of Lamont's special committee assignments was to neutralize Herbert Hoover's Anglophobia. Still bruised from his presidency and wishing to repeat his wartime triumph with European food relief, Hoover favored a scheme for feeding Nazi-occupied countries; Lamont supported Britain's blockade against such activity. When Lamont and White visited Hoover, they couldn't change his mind and vowed to fight him. Afterward, a press account popped up describing Hoover truculently pacing the room and swearing that he would tour the country and fight Britain on the issue. Lamont assured Hoover that *he* hadn't talked to a newsman and said the account must have been a misrepresentation. Even at the end, the Lamont-Hoover relationship—once seen as a Faustian pact between Wall Street and Washington—was tense and querulous.

The House of Morgan's pro-British views brought it into conflict with the nation's most visible isolationist, Charles Lindbergh. In late 1935, the Lindberghs had moved to England, hoping to find a tranquillity denied them in America after their son's kidnapping. At the prompting of the U.S. military, Lindbergh visited Nazi Germany in 1936 to tour German aircraft factories. He made subsequent trips in 1937 and 1938 and developed a growing admiration for German air power—admiration that he expressed to Stanley Baldwin at Downing Street and in the drawing rooms of Cliveden. Lindbergh insisted that a war against Germany was unwinnable, would destroy American democracy, and would open the way for Communist infiltration. When he accepted a decoration from Hermann Göring at a reception, it added to suspicion in some quarters that Lindbergh was not only awed by the Nazis but sympathetic to them.

By the time the Lindberghs returned to America in April 1939, Charles had a settled belief in German invincibility and French and British decadence. That fall, he began making radio speeches urging U.S. neutrality and arguing against repeal of the arms embargo. His remarks were sometimes laced with racist innuendos. On October 13, 1939, he said, "If the white race is ever seriously threatened, it may then be time for us to take our part for its protection, to fight side by side with the English, French, and Germans. But not with one against the other for our mutual destruction."[39] Whether consciously or not, Lindbergh had absorbed many Nazi doctrines. In the *Atlantic Monthly* of March 1940, he cynically saw England and France as fighting for their possessions and ethics, whereas the Germans claimed "the right of an able and virile nation to expand—to conquer territory and influence by force of arms as other nations have done at one time or another throughout history."[40]

During the debate over the war, Lindbergh increasingly reverted to his father's midwestern populism, with its reflexive hatred of the Money Trust and its dark vision of Anglo-American finance. While the younger

Lindbergh might have taken comfort from following in his father's footsteps, the situation was more complicated for his wife. Anne Morrow Lindbergh was torn between her isolationist husband and the memory of her late internationalist father. She had always admired the Morgan partners, a type she saw as "keen man-of-the-world, discreet, kindly and cultured."[41] She once talked of the "whole warm rich world of my father and mother" and remembered idealistic talk over breakfast between her father and Jean Monnet, a French economist and diplomat. She cherished memories of her father, and after reading Harold Nicolson's biography of him, she wrote, "I suddenly feel my heritage, feel him in me. It is mine."[42]

Now Anne was in an excruciating situation. Her mother felt strongly that Dwight would have favored aid for the Allies. Most of the Lindberghs' friends on Long Island held similar views. The Lindberghs also had many French and British friends, and as soon as Germany began mobilizing for war in 1938, Anne imagined Florrie Grenfell, Lady Astor, and the rest wiped out by air raids.[43] Yet Anne shared Charles's simplistic views of European politics, albeit without the nasty overlay of racism. In 1940, she published a book called *The Wave of the Future* in which she saw the war not as a contest between good and evil but as one between the "Forces of the Past" (the Allies) and the "Forces of tne Future" (Germany).

If Charles felt buoyed by his identification with his father, Anne was tormented by the ghost of hers. She told herself that Charles was as idealistic as her father but that it was the idealism of a later age. After William Allen White formed the Committee for Defending America by Aiding the Allies, Anne asked herself, "I wonder where Daddy would stand? Probably behind the committee *et al.* And yet he was among those idealists, very practical, intensely practical—that was his great gift."[44] Nevertheless, as the Lindberghs were socially ostracized by old friends—including Harry Guggenheim, who had sponsored Charles's three-month tour following the solo flight—Anne was haunted by her father's specter. She lamented that "Charles . . . has the memory of his father with him," but "I'm entirely alone."[45]

Anne's dilemma was sharpened on May 19, 1940, when Charles made a radio speech entitled "The Air Defense of America." By then, the Nazis had conquered Denmark and were overrunning Holland and Belgium. Lindbergh's speech made menacing reference to "powerful elements in America" who controlled the "machinery of influence and propaganda." These elements, he said, wanted to push America into war for profit and to serve their foreign allies.[46] The Morgan bank wasn't named, but Lindbergh's language echoed that used in attacks on the bank ever since the Nye hearings. President Roosevelt told Treasury Secretary Henry Morgenthau the next day, "I am absolutely convinced that Lindbergh is a Nazi."[47]

Betty Morrow, now acting president of Smith College (having attained the academic distinction denied Dwight), was disturbed by Charles's insinuations. Five days after the radio speech, she had an emotional lunch with Anne at the Cosmopolitan Club. Betty felt ashamed that America hadn't rushed to join England and said in anguish to Anne, "How they will *hate* us—oh, how they will *hate* us."[48] Yet despite her candor with her daughter, Morrow felt constrained in challenging her son-in-law. The day after the lunch, she secretly wrote to Lamont asking him to reason with Lindbergh: "I am in a difficult position just now . . . but my chief worry is over Anne. She is torn in spirit and it is telling on her health."[49]

Taking the tone of a concerned uncle, Lamont wrote to the rather aloof Charles Lindbergh. He said he had hesitated to contact him and cited his affection for the Morrow family. Then he asked point-blank who those nameless conspirators in his speech were. He added that he didn't know of any such elements. Trying to recapture the personal warmth of earlier years, Lamont admonished him tactfully: "Dear Charles—It is so important that we shall have unity in our country that we must not broadcast suspicions and accusations unless we have complete basis for the charges."[50]

The return letter must have chilled Lamont. It wasn't hostile so much as cool and correct, as if Lindbergh had turned into a stranger. "I intentionally did not specify individuals, groups, or organizations in my address because I still hope that it will not be necessary to do this," Lindbergh said, claiming that to do so would only stir up dangerous class antagonisms. He warned that U.S. entry into the war would cause "chaotic conditions" and destroy American moderation. He concluded, "I have great respect for your judgment, but I am afraid that our viewpoints differ in regard to the attitude this country should take toward the war in Europe."[51] Later, when a reporter asked Lamont why he didn't visit the Lindberghs, he snapped, "I have nothing to do with them."[52]

Her secret overture through Lamont having failed, Betty Morrow decided to make public her opposition to her son-in-law. During the Dunkirk evacuation in June, she made a speech for the William Allen White committee rebutting Charles's views. She telephoned Anne first to soften the blow. "Your father would have wanted me to do it," she told Anne, who thought her mother was being exploited for the purposes of publicity.[53] Betty came to agree with this appraisal after White made a speech boasting of his "smart trick" in setting her against Charles. After that, Betty Morrow was "very humanly, unwilling to appear again in a public clash with Lindbergh," as Russell Leffingwell informed Roosevelt.[54]

THERE was a moment in the spring of 1940 when it seemed the House of Morgan might simultaneously defeat the New Deal and advance the British cause. The long-awaited middle path opened up in the Republican party. Along with the British ambassador, Lord Lothian, Lamont attended a dinner at the home of publisher Ogden M. Reid, who presented two would-be Republican presidential candidates. Robert A. Taft, son of the former president and a Republican senator from Ohio, was predictably anti-internationalist. But the other aspirant, Wendell Willkie, was a revelation. As president of the giant utility holding company Commonwealth and Southern Corporation, he had clashed with FDR over the Tennessee Valley Authority's takeover of his generating plants. At the dinner, Willkie came out in favor of unqualified support for Britain, including the provisioning of planes and naval equipment. On the spot, Lamont and Reid championed his candidacy, and Lamont was instrumental in getting him to run. Willkie then repeated his pro-British pep talk before a dinner at Lamont's house, a gathering credited with enlisting Wall Street support for his run for the presidency.

For Morgan partners, Willkie was tailor-made. Ever since McKinley, the bank had been baffled by a Hobson's choice in American politics. It could side either with Democrats, who were too interventionist at home, or with Republicans, who were too isolationist abroad. As a major foreign lender, it favored free trade and free flow of capital at a time when big business was still mostly protectionist. On balance, the bank had opted for Republicans, but not without considerable discomfort on foreign issues.

Willkie was decidedly in the Morgan grain. A former Democrat, he was an outward-looking Anglophile, a supporter of reciprocal trade agreements, and generally attuned to FDR's foreign policy. At the same time, he was a supporter of domestic free markets and wished for a midcourse correction in New Deal policies and a more favorable environment for investment. He had plenty of Wall Street friends, including

Perry Hall of Morgan Stanley (where Willkie was one of Harold Stanley's first clients in 1935), and provided a version of Republicanism they could unreservedly support.

With his broad, open face, big grin, and Indiana twang, Willkie was folksy and sophisticated and uniquely able to advance Wall Street's cause without seeming like an ambassador for the rich. *Fortune* called him a "clever bumpkin," and Harold Ickes memorably mocked him as "a simple barefoot Wall Street lawyer."[55] The verdict was too harsh, for Willkie wanted to retain many New Deal innovations—collective bargaining, minimum wages, and maximum hours—that were anathema to Wall Street bankers. Though Willkie declared his candidacy only seven weeks before the Republican National Convention in June 1940, his dark-horse candidacy galloped fast. He had to soft-pedal his Morgan support so as not to alarm the small-town, anti–Wall Street wing of the party. To foster a down-home image, he took a modest two-room suite at the Benjamin Franklin Hotel in Philadelphia, site of the convention, and Tom Lamont was expressly instructed to avoid his headquarters.

Despite this sanitary distance, the anti-Willkie troops wasted no time in fastening onto his Wall Street links in order to discredit him. Representative Usher L. Burdick of North Dakota circulated an alarmist tract to delegates that said, "I believe I am serving the best interests of the Republican Party by protesting in advance and exposing the machinations and attempts of J.P. Morgan and the other New York City bankers in forcing Wendell Willkie on the Republican Party. Money, I know, talks."[56]

The Republicans were famished for new leaders and finally chose Willkie on the sixth ballot over prosecutor Thomas Dewey (who had indicted Richard Whitney) and Senator Taft. The following month, FDR was nominated for a third term in Chicago, with Henry A. Wallace of Iowa as his running mate. Willkie tried gamely to forge a compromise between support for FDR's foreign policy during the war emergency and moderate reform of New Deal policy. He even sounded out Roosevelt about a deal in which the president would consult him on foreign policy in exchange for a pledge to keep the war out of the campaign. Roosevelt didn't trust the Republicans enough to accede to this and was loath to confer the prestige of such a deal upon Willkie.

In November, Roosevelt won by over five million votes. Willkie's defeat didn't end charges of Wall Street machinations but only strengthened the conviction of those who saw wily bankers as having foisted him upon the party. As historian Harry Elmer Barnes afterward charged: "It is doubtful if any man was ever nominated for the Presidency on the basis of less popular knowledge and approval. There were at least a dozen or more persons in the famous 'smoke-filled room' in the Chicago hotel where Warren G. Harding was chosen for the nomination in 1920. Two men decided that Mr. Willkie should be the Republican nominee. . . . These men were Ogden Mills Reid . . . and Thomas W. Lamont."[57]

As it turned out, the House of Morgan didn't suffer as much from Willkie's defeat as might have been expected. Bolstered by his election victory, Roosevelt moved more vigorously to support Britain, and in this effort he needed the Morgan bank. With marvelous suddenness, the chill in Morgan-Roosevelt relations thawed and was replaced by cordiality from the White House of a sort that 23 Wall hadn't known since the twenties. As America's attention shifted from blistering debates over domestic policy to ways in which to deal with Europe's dictators, the power of the House of Morgan surged accordingly.

HOSTAGES

• •
•

O N June 22, 1940, the new French Premier, Marshal Henri Philippe
Pétain, submitted to the Nazi *blitzkrieg* and signed an armistice
with Hitler, leaving Britain to fight alone against the Axis powers. This
left Morgan et Compagnie in a vulnerable situation. The stately *Banque
Morgan*, as the French termed it, occupied an imposing mansion at 14
place Vendôme, its marble banking floor illuminated by a huge skylight.
Established by the Drexels in 1868, the firm had an illustrious heritage,
having stayed open during the Franco-Prussian War and World War I.
It was known as Morgan, Harjes until 1926, when partner Herman
Harjes died in a Deauville polo accident and the name was changed to
Morgan et Compagnie. Under the interlocking partnership structure of
the pre-Glass-Steagall Morgan empire, Jack Morgan was senior partner,
and New York had provided most of the bank's capital.

If Morgan et Compagnie never achieved quite the renown of the New
York and London banks, it still ranked as one of the largest foreign
financial institutions in Paris even in the 1980s. It was a conduit for
dealings between the French government and J. P. Morgan and Company and was very close to the Banque de France. Its French officers had
often held high government posts. Morgan et Compagnie served the
subsidiaries of most American companies in France, provided traveler's
checks and letters of credit for rich American tourists, handled currency
transactions for Americans in France, and had vaults brimming with
securities owned by Americans and Frenchmen. It exchanged young
apprentices with Morgan Grenfell and J. P. Morgan. Yet in the last
analysis, the French house was always stymied by Morgan intimacy with
Great Britain and France's nationalistic resistance to American business
penetration.

So total was the wartime news blackout that an account of what happened to Morgan et Compagnie during the Nazi occupation wasn't known until September 1944; it can now be reconstructed from unpublished memoirs at Morgan Guaranty. The story begins with the Banque de France, which didn't trust the phony peace promulgated by the Munich Pact and in 1938 began making plans to protect its gold. It shipped gold to New York as a fund for future war purchases and took gold bullion stored at its vaults on the rue de la Vrillière and distributed it to fifty-one strategic sites around the country.

Many Parisian banks made similar contingency plans. Morgan et Compagnie bought a run-down hotel in Niort, a town southeast of Nantes. It was redesigned as a self-sufficient unit for protecting securities, with safes in the basement and sleeping quarters upstairs for staff. After war was declared, the French government advised Morgans to set up an office in Châtel-Guyon, in unoccupied France, to protect its exchange dealings with the Banque de France. Several weeks before the Nazis stormed Paris, Morgans and other banks shipped out securities to these safe houses in south-central France and left behind skeleton staffs in Paris. Then, five days before France fell, two American partners of Morgan et Compagnie, Bernard S. Carter and Julian Allen, fled Paris along roads swollen with refugees and clogged with horse-drawn carts and bicycles. All of these acts proved wise precautions.

During the German occupation, the Nazi flag flew over the Justice Ministry and the Ritz Hôtel, Morgan et Compagnie's neighbors on the place Vendôme. Three of the American banks with Paris branches—J. P. Morgan, Guaranty Trust, and Chase National—stayed open, while the fourth—National City—shut down. In late June 1940, Leonard Rist of Morgan et Compagnie was arrested and dispatched to a German prison camp in the Sudetenland. Rist was the son of an eminent French economist, Charles Rist, and had been personally recruited by Jack Morgan. When Leonard was in New York in 1928, he recalled, Jack "asked me what the hell I was doing in any other place than Morgan's in exactly those words; whereupon I decided to apply for a job at Morgan's in Paris."[1]

Rist ended up spending eighteen months behind barbed wire while his parents worked out emergency plans to secure a Wall Street job for their younger son through Russell Leffingwell. The House of Morgan finally sprang Leonard through their old Vatican friend, Bernardino Nogara, the treasurer of the Special Administration of the Holy See. Nogara somehow convinced the Germans that Rist's release was needed to maintain French financial health. The combined force of the Morgan mystique and Rist's reputation was such that the argument worked. After the war, the French Treasury assigned Leonard Rist to the World Bank, and he ended up as head of its Economic Department.

For the rest of the war, executive control of Morgan et Compagnie fell to two stubborn, courageous Frenchmen—the elegant Maurice Pesson-Didion, a veteran wounded in the Battle of the Marne, and Louis Tuteleers, chief of the Credit Department, who limped from a wartime injury suffered while serving in the Belgian army. The two bankers had to contend with constant, hovering Nazi interference and menacing surveillance of their activities. To finance his conquests, Hitler set a policy of plundering gold and foreign currency from banks in occupied territories. As part of his revenge for Versailles, he chose to extort money from France. Like other banks, Morgan et Compagnie could conduct business in franc accounts, but foreign-exchange transactions were outlawed. The bank had to apprise the Germans of any foreign currency it held as well as any property in safe deposit boxes.

The House of Morgan has always been proud that it operated in Nazi-occupied Paris without compromising its principles. Yet the bank may have had a secret patron: Marshal Pétain, head of the collaborationist Vichy government. As a celebrated war hero in 1917, Pétain had associated with many fund-raising society ladies, including Herman Harjes's wife and Anne Morgan. It was perhaps through such meetings that he came to have an account at Morgan et Compagnie. This embarrassing account was disclosed in November 1941, during a boisterous debate in the British House of Commons. It came out that Pétain had signed an annuity plan with a Canadian company in 1937; even after the fall of France and the British blockade, the Canadian company duly paid £600 annually to Morgan Grenfell, which then credited Pétain's account at Morgan et Compagnie. The transfers were sanctioned by a British Treasury license.

In the House of Commons, Dr. Russell Thomas protested to Chancellor of the Exchequer Kingsley Wood, "Will the right honorable gentleman consider that the payment tends to irritate the public temper, lowers the prestige of the Government, and opens up avenues of suspicion at a time when national unity is essential?"[2] In defending the transfers, Kingsley Wood noted that Canada had maintained diplomatic relations with Vichy France and that Pétain was a head of state. Nevertheless, at some point, the transfers were stopped.

After Pearl Harbor, Morgan et Compagnie was branded an enemy bank and assigned a special German overseer, Herr Caesar, who operated out of 18 place Vendôme. He insisted that the firm accept accounts from

Nazi banks and businesses. To avoid this indignity, Pesson-Didion informed the Nazis that J. P. Morgan and Company had instructed him not to accept new accounts or expand old ones; if forced to break this rule, he said bluntly, he would have to liquidate the bank. This prearranged strategy worked, and the bank took no Nazi deposits.

With Jewish accounts, Morgan et Compagnie had less success. The Nazis had assembled a special administrative team to ransack Jewish securities and accounts. At Morgans and other Paris banks, they emptied the accounts and safety deposit boxes of Jewish clients and looted Fr 11.5 million in all. Morgans lodged protests to no avail. It seems doubtful whether any bank could have operated during the occupation if it had resisted these efforts too strenuously.

The most dramatic encounter with the Nazis occurred in 1944, when a Defense Corps—SS—officer marched into the bank and demanded money kept by a certain depositor. When the redoubtable Tuteleers resisted, the officer drew a gun and shoved it in his back, forcing him to limp out into the street. Tuteleers and Leonard Rist were taken to SS headquarters on the rue des Saussaies and informed that unless the depositor's money were promptly handed over, they would be sent to a German prison camp. Prodded with gun butts and sequestered for an hour or two in a dark broom closet, the two were released when the $8,000 ransom was paid.

On another occasion, defying threats of prison or deportation, Maurice Pesson-Didion refused to hand over some French Treasury bills. A Gestapo officer then demanded to see a list of securities owned by Morgan et Compagnie and was incredulous that aside from government securities, the bank owned so little. Evidently imbued with a sense of mythical Morgan power, he swore that Pesson-Didion must be mocking him and the Reich. Citing supposed Morgan influence over other French firms, the officer expected to find lists of huge holdings of Crédit Lyonnais and other bank stocks. He wouldn't abandon the belief that the House of Morgan held reams of French bank shares. Lamont later retold the story of what the German officer had said: " 'If they did not, how in the world were they able to control all the banks?' Pesson-Didion replied they held none. Then the German official asked him to explain 'the immense influence which the Morgan firms seemed to have all over the Continent and everywhere.' Pesson-Didion replied quietly that he could think of no explanation unless it lay in the character of the men who made up the Morgan institutions."[3] Lamont may have embellished the tale, but Morgan et Compagnie doubtless exercised less influence in reality than in the overheated minds of Nazi officialdom. There was always a mistaken sense that the House of Morgan principally exerted power through direct-share ownership in companies rather than through exclusive banking and advisory relations. With the full panoply of J. P. Morgan and Company power behind it, Morgan et Compagnie didn't need vast capital resources.

Morgan et Compagnie was the sole American bank in Paris to stay open throughout the war. It even turned a small profit. Leonard Rist was smart enough to see that such success might smack of collaboration, or at least of moral corner cutting. Perhaps as a result, he frequently cited his décoration from General Eisenhower for "gallant service in assisting the escape of Allied soldiers from the enemy."[4] That the U.S. government approved Morgan et Compagnie's wartime conduct was confirmed in late 1944 when the Treasury and War departments asked J. P. Morgan and Company to send senior Paris partner Dean Jay and other Americans back to the place Vendôme to restore a semblance of normality. Of the small, white-haired Dean Jay, it was said that American businessmen in France seldom made a major move without consulting him, and so his return carried symbolic weight. In the highest tribute of all, Morgan et Compagnie was assigned to handle deposits for American troops in liberated France.

A S the lights went out across Europe in 1940, Tom Lamont made a last-ditch effort to steer Benito Mussolini away from Adolf Hitler. His faith in Mussolini had survived many atrocities. In January 1939, after Mussolini gassed villages in Libya and Ethiopia, Lamont was still reassuring the Morgan agent in Rome, Giovanni Fummi, of his "genuine admiration for the Duce's extraordinary domestic achievements in behalf of his people."[5] He clung to the fiction prevalent on Wall Street in the 1920s that there were two Mussolinis—the good domestic manager and the bad foreign adventurer—who somehow coinhabited the same stocky body.

By the spring of 1939, Lamont's overtures to Mussolini were inextricably intertwined with U.S. government policy. In his last mission of the Diplomatic Age, he operated as a private diplomat for Roosevelt as he tried to pull Italy back from war. In serving the White House, Lamont had to overcome a hurdle—how to explain to FDR Fummi's matchless access to Mussolini? However much the bank might cast Fummi as a neutral agent, for twenty years he had fulsomely praised il Duce. Fummi had predicted that Mussolini would make Italy a great Mediterranean power. Now Lamont trotted out the standard formula regarding Fummi: "While he is loyal to his Government, he is not a fascist."[6] Whether

Roosevelt believed this or not, Lamont was an uncommonly handy intermediary between the United States and Italy.

That spring, Lamont toyed with the idea of traveling to Rome and picknicking *alfresco* in the countryside. "I have every now and then a sort of longing or a nostalgia for the sunshine and brightness of Italy," he told Fummi.[7] But he canceled a proposed trip, fearing a reporter might spot his name on a steamship list. He jovially told Joe Kennedy that "the Duce's antics in Albania"—Italy's April 1939 conquest of Albania—lay behind his cancellation of a scheduled stay at the American Academy in Rome, an institution subsidized by Morgan partners since Pierpont's days.[8]

Instead of visiting, Lamont addressed a letter to the Italian government, warning that the United States would staunchly resist German—and, by implication, Italian—aggression. In the intricate ways of Morgan secret diplomacy, Fummi passed the letter to Bernardino Nogara, the Vatican's financial secretary, who passed it to Azzolini at the Banca d'Italia. It thus arrived on Mussolini's desk with the incontestable authority of God and money behind it.

The Vatican figured importantly in both Lamont's and Roosevelt's efforts to sway Mussolini. In February 1939, Roosevelt had sent Joe Kennedy to the funeral of Pope Pius XI as a way of currying favor with the Vatican. A year later, he became the first president to assign a personal representative to the Vatican—Myron Taylor, former head of U.S. Steel and, in earlier years, an admirer of Mussolini. The Vatican feared its own political isolation if Hitler and Mussolini made an alliance, so it welcomed the Roosevelt opening, which aroused intense opposition from American Protestants.

In the spring of 1940, Lamont made a final approach to Mussolini. He sent a letter that he cleared first over the telephone with Roosevelt and that Tom Catto also showed to the British foreign secretary, Lord Halifax. Lamont tried to puncture Mussolini's delusion that in the event of war, he could count on faithful support from Italian-Americans. Lamont said that Italian-Americans were rabidly anti-Hitler and that Italy shouldn't be fooled by American isolationists. He warned against a Nazi *blitzkrieg.* Once again, Fummi handed the message to Nogara at the Vatican, who promised to transmit its contents to Mussolini. Not only did the mission fail, but it perhaps backfired, planting the notion in Mussolini's mind that Fummi, as a Morgan courier, could function as an Anglo-American spy. Lamont's maneuvers coincided with a mission to Mussolini undertaken by Undersecretary of State Sumner Welles for FDR. After a rather frigid interview with Welles, Mussolini told his son-in-law Galeazzo Ciano, "Between us and the Americans any kind of understanding is impossible because they judge problems on the surface while we go deeply into them."[9] Mussolini also rebuffed a mission undertaken by Francis Rodd of Morgan Grenfell, who believed that the British War Office was bungling the chance to co-opt il Duce. Shortly after the June 1940 evacuation of the British Expeditionary Force at Dunkirk, Mussolini permanently locked arms with Hitler.

In September 1940, Mussolini ordered the arrest of Giovanni Fummi—his way of rewarding the House of Morgan for its years of thankless loyalty. According to Morgan records, Fummi was abducted from his Roman hotel and held incommunicado at the Regina Coeli prison. Mussolini was now a financial as well as a political renegade and no longer had to flatter Lamont. Two months before, Italy had defaulted on its municipal and government loans. Officially, Fummi was charged with expressing pro-British sentiments through the mail. This was a specious, legalistic indictment that thinly veiled a political vendetta. For Fummi, it was a crushing end to twenty years of selling Mussolini to Wall Street's most powerful bankers. It was also an unmerited slap, for even after Mussolini embraced Hitler, Fummi still rationalized it as the only course left. Up until the war, both Lamont and Fummi had contended that Mussolini was driven into Hitler's arms not by madness or megalomania, but by Western diplomatic ineptitude.

Lamont, stunned and blindsided, felt personally responsible for securing Fummi's release. The two men had had a close, if curiously unequal, relationship. Fummi would address him as Mr. Lamont, while Lamont would reply using the diminutive Nino. A professional hand-wringer, the sentimental, hypochondriacal Fummi had shared many trials with Lamont—his first wife's death from cancer in 1930, several breakdowns from overwork, and arthritis. In Morgan annals of crisp business letters, Fummi's notes stand apart as the musings of a tender, melancholic man who bared his grief in a most un-Morgan-like manner.

Whether operating from the Via Veneto in Rome or a Saint-Tropez villa—made possible by his ample Morgan retainer—Fummi was always vulnerable to charges of his being a foreign agent. For twenty years, he had performed a tightrope act, balancing patriotism with professional necessity. Most of the time, he could serve both his Wall Street masters and Mussolini. But what if their interests clashed? Fummi often told Lamont that if a conflict ever arose, the bank would take precedence over Italy. Then, in 1939, he conceded that if war came, he would serve in the Italian army. He never resolved the confusion over his national identity.

Compounding Fummi's trouble was that in 1934 he had married Lady Anne Crawford, daughter of the Earl of Crawford and Balcarres and niece of Sir Ronald Lindsay, the British ambassador in Washington. This English veneer must have excited Mussolini's suspicions. For Fummi's wedding, the House of Morgan sent the couple a pair of George II silver mugs. In 1938, Fummi chattered happily about how Anglicized he had become, with "an English wife, an English secretary and an English nannie!"[10] When war came, however, he knew he was in a ticklish situation and packed off his English wife, children, and nannie to Scotland while he stayed behind in Rome. Perhaps the arrest came as less than a total surprise.

Lamont orchestrated Fummi's release in a masterful way. First he got the State Department involved. Then, through Myron Taylor, he sent confidential messages to the papal secretary. There was good reason to expect Vatican sympathy: Fummi was a close confidant of Nogara, who headed the Vatican's investment arm, the Special Administration of the Holy See. While Pope Piux XI was alive, it had even been assumed that Fummi would someday replace Nogara as the Vatican's chief portfolio manager. It is also likely that Nogara was secretly hostile to the Germans, for neither before nor after the war would he invest Vatican funds in German securities. In addition, Lamont had once lunched with the new pope, Pius XII, in New York. Responding to Lamont's pleas, the Vatican cabled back that they were doing "utmost privately and officially in order to obtain release friend." The papacy underscored Mussolini's personal involvement in the affair: "We understand ultimate decision has to be taken by Government chief."[11]

In the end, only a personal appeal to Mussolini by Lamont would work. It was as if the sadistic Duce wanted to extract one last tribute, one last insufferable humiliation, from his banker. Lamont had to check his anger and argue that Fummi had represented Italy to the House of Morgan and not the reverse. If there were more truth to this than Lamont would ever care to admit, it now had to be grossly overstated. He wrote:

> It was Fummi, and Fummi alone, who urged my original visit to Rome in 1923 and the subsequent visits which resulted in these favorable loan operations for your Government. On every occasion he was active in the negotiation and zealous to advance the good name of his Government and to protect it at every point. While it is true that Fummi was our own representative in Italy, yet it is even truer, so to

speak, that he acted broadly and wisely as a financial ambassador for
your Government.

Far from evading the subject of Fummi's marriage to an English-
woman, Lamont rather brazenly advanced it as an extra guarantee of
Fummi's patriotism: "As time went on, we became more and more
impressed with the fidelity which he did show and was bound to show
towards his own Government and people. The fact of his having married
Lady Anne Crawford only served to make him more meticulous in the
manner in which he handled himself and in the correctness of his
attitude toward his own Government."

It is noticeable that Lamont never directly accused Mussolini of ar-
resting Fummi or of having prior knowledge. He wrote as if he were
entreating a wise, neutral, and all-powerful arbiter. In the end, Lamont
groveled one last time: "Finally, it is because of your kindly and generous attitude towards me personally in all our interviews, and perhaps
especially because of the charming sense of proportion that you have
always shown in such interviews, that I have ventured to address you
this urgent personal appeal in Fummi's behalf."[12]

About ten days after Fummi's arrest, a cable arrived at Morgans from
Vatican City. It reported that Fummi had been safely released and would
be exiled to Switzerland. For Lamont, it was an ironic end to seventeen
years of having scraped and bowed and hoped that Mussolini could be
reformed. He wasn't left with the dignity of any comforting illusions.
As he wrote in a somber letter to Fummi in Saint-Moritz, Switzerland,
"Some time or other, dear Nino, a new day will dawn and America and
Italy will once more be friends. But before that day comes there will be
fire and flame and sword, grief for us all."[13]

In February 1941, the Morgan office in Rome was closed. Two
weeks later, the irrepressible Fummi popped up in London to supervise
a secret transfer of Vatican gold bullion stored in a basement room at
Morgan Grenfell. Throughout the 1930s, the Vatican had bought the
gold at the fixed price of $35 an ounce, never selling any. Fummi
would discreetly refer to it as the "special commodity." For security
reasons, the Vatican now decided to ship the gold to New York. The
wartime transfer was carried out under the official aegis of Lord Halifax, until recently Britain's foreign secretary. The gold ended up at the
Federal Reserve Bank of New York. There it would dizzily appreciate
in the postwar years.

In 1942, Bernardino Nogara tried to call in his IOU for his help in the
release of Leonard Rist and Giovanni Fummi. The Vatican held a large

stake in a South American banking group, Sudameris, which was head-quartered in Paris but had branches in Argentina, Brazil, and other Latin American countries. America's wartime blacklist had produced heavy losses for the Brazilian bank, and it faced possible liquidation; Nogara wanted to get Sudameris off the list. To this end, he proposed that Morgans buy half of the company. In exchange, he said the House of Morgan would have final approval over its actions. Although Fummi was ready to go to New York to negotiate and Nogara promised to "guarantee the fullest respect of the Allied interests in the management of the South American branches of Sudameris," Lamont explained the political and legal impossibility of buying shares in foreign banks that had French and Italian backing.[14] Vatican appeals to the State Department bore no fruit, either. But the discussion reveals an interesting example of the Vatican's diplomatic independence in Axis Italy.

IN May of 1940, Neville Chamberlain resigned in favor of Winston Churchill, a man with whom the House of Morgan had always had a peevish, family quarrel. Teddy Grenfell had been blind to Churchill's merits, saying of him after the crash, "His record for thirty years has shown him to be the most unreliable of statesmen as well as the most unstable of friends . . . I wish he would change his party for the third time and go over to Ramsay MacDonald, or even further to the left."[15] During the summer of 1940, Nancy Astor grudgingly conceded to Tom Lamont that Churchill was doing a good job but regretted Lloyd George's absence from the cabinet.

In August 1940, the Battle of Britain began. Reported vividly to America by Edward R. Murrow's broadcasts, the nightly blitz drove Londoners into the Underground. Morgan Grenfell had girded for war, adding air-raid shelters and gas-proof access to street and stairways. Although 23 Great Winchester escaped a direct hit, the square mile of the City was badly bombed, and the Dutch Church across the narrow lane from Morgan Grenfell was destroyed. When a parachute mine in its rubble exploded, the blast stripped wood panels from the Morgan partners' room and blew out several doors. A nearby conflagration at Carpenters' Hall was extinguished in time to save 23 Great Winchester. Later on, a V-1 missile fell in Old Broad Street, where George Peabody and Junius Morgan had once worked. After each such pounding of London, Harold Nicolson would send Charles Lindbergh a needling postcard, saying, "Do you still think we are soft?"[16]

As British children were evacuated from London, the House of Morgan proudly did its duty. No cause warmed Jack Morgan's blood more than England at war. Gray and tired, he went to a West Fourteenth Street pier for the arrival of almost four hundred British children aboard two ocean liners. There he met the eleven-year-old Lord Primrose and two of Lord Bicester's grandchildren, all with governesses and nurses in tow. They would be his wartime guests at Matinicock Point, along with three other City Smith offspring. "Jack Morgan lived in considerable Victorian splendor, with armed guards all over the place," recalled Charles E. A. Hambro, who spent part of the war with the Harry Morgans in New York before rushing back to play on Eton's cricket team in 1943, "and there was Lord Primrose in isolation with the old boy."[17] In a further caretaker service for Britain, the vaults of J. P. Morgan and Company received British government rowing trophies, along with two Gutenberg Bibles.

Chartering George Whitney's old boat, the *Wanderer*, Jack transferred *Corsair IV* to Britain for war service. He donated many of its interior decorations, from a blue rug to wicker deck chairs, to a "Bundles for Britain" benefit at Gimbel's, and Harry Morgan sold his Grumman amphibian plane to the Canadian government for use in coastal patrols. After France fell, a British visitor at 23 Wall expressed fear for the future. "Our turn is next," he told Jack. "The Huns will let loose on us a blitz that will be hard to withstand." Jack brimmed with emotion. "My good friend," he said, "you need not be downcast for a single moment. I tell you, Britain will never give in, never, never, never!"[18] His fecund imagination now had fresh cause to picture pursuing Germans. In escaping from London raids, young Luftwaffe pilots would empty surplus bombs over Wall Hall, and in October a load blew out the mansion's windows. For safekeeping, his silver collection was brought into the 23 Great Winchester vaults that housed the Vatican gold.

Morgan Grenfell was depopulated as partners entered government service, a logical culmination of the firm's activities during the Diplomatic Age. It was already something of a branch office for the Bank of England, the Treasury, and the Foreign Office. Francis Rodd, who had explored the southern Sahara in the 1920s and won a medal from the Royal Geographic Society, was posted to Africa, while Willy Hill-Wood spent much of the war in Washington as a U.K. censor. Lord Bicester and Lady Sybil converted their Oxfordshire estate, Tusmore, into a fifty-bed convalescent home, as other British country houses were turned into barracks or troop hospitals.

Monty Norman recommended Tom Catto for a new, unpaid position as financial adviser to the chancellor of the Exchequer, Kingsley Wood.

A short, shrewd, dignified Scot of humble background, Catto had been a Morgan Grenfell partner since 1928. Before that, he had managed the large Indian merchant house of Andrew Yule and Company, owned by Morgan partners in London and New York. He had the exotic, global connections of an empire-building entrepreneur, having done deals with Vivian Smith in the Middle East and Russia. He and John Maynard Keynes were assigned rooms on opposite sides of the chancellor's office; Keynes to represent the independent, theoretical view; Catto, the practical, banking side. They were soon dubbed Catto and Doggo, and Lord Bicester, with muted glee, reported to 23 Wall that Catto was liberally throwing out many of Doggo's impractical ideas. Monty Norman preferred dealing with Catto, who would succeed him as governor, perpetuating Morgan Grenfell's charmed access to the Bank of England.

With much of Europe under Nazi control, Churchill knew he had to woo America with all the wit, charm, and energy at his disposal. He faced a new opponent, an organization equally determined to keep America out of the war—America First. Formed by two Yale graduate students, R. Douglas Stuart, Jr., and Kingman Brewster, it was a response to the William Allen White committee and promptly recruited Charles Lindbergh. Through his America First speeches, Lindbergh destroyed the last remnants of the hero worship he once aroused. Stumping the country, he would claim that "the three most important groups which have been pressing this country toward war are the British, the Jewish and the Roosevelt administration."[19] He talked of insidious Jewish influence in the American government and media.

Despite the impact of Lindbergh's speeches, the nightly terror in London engendered a wave of sympathy for Britain. Strengthened by his November 1940 reelection, Roosevelt stepped up efforts to aid England. He and Churchill negotiated an exchange of fifty old U.S. destroyers for eight British air bases in the West Indies. By late November 1940, Lord Lothian sounded the alert regarding a looming British cash crisis, and in early December, Churchill told Roosevelt the time was coming when England would "no longer be able to pay cash."[20]

During this desperate autumn in Britain, the House of Morgan and the Roosevelt administration were reunited in a campaign to provide all aid short of war. This rapprochement produced a sense of mutual relief. After chatting with Roosevelt at the White House, Leffingwell told him on December 24, 1940, that "whatever differences there may have been about domestic affairs, I and my colleagues are heart and soul with you for unlimited material aid to Britain and for national defense."[21] That weekend, Roosevelt was broadcasting a fireside chat in support of Britain, and Leffingwell offered some pointers. "When you say 'give,' you mean give or lend goods, guns, ships, planes, munitions and whatnot . . . you are not interested in giving England a bank account, but in giving her the things she needs."[22] In his radio address, Roosevelt exhorted Americans to make the United States "the great arsenal of democracy," and a week later he asked Congress to enact a lend-lease program that would let Washington guarantee payment for British war orders in the United States and lease supplies indefinitely. There would be no immediate cost to the Allies. Roosevelt hoped that the Lend-Lease Act would avert another war debts/reparations mess after the war. Churchill called it "the most unsordid act in the history of any nation."[23] Morgan support of the plan is notable in that it precluded any repetition of the bank's financing role in World War I.

As Lindbergh and other isolationists testified against the Lend-Lease Act, Roosevelt and Treasury Secretary Morgenthau sought a dramatic way to rebut charges that Britain had billions of dollars in idle assets salted away around the world. They decided to ask for an act of bloody public self-sacrifice—nothing less than the sale of a major British industrial holding in America to show that Britain had exhausted all options before pleading for aid. In March 1941, on the eve of congressional passage of lend-lease, Roosevelt and Morgenthau notified Whitehall that it would have to consummate an important sale at once. The White House itself selected Britain's single most valuable industrial possession in America—the American Viscose Company, a subsidiary of the Courtaulds' textile empire. With seven plants and eighteen thousand employees, it was probably the world's largest rayon producer. Washington urged extreme haste and imposed a seventy-two-hour deadline for announcing the sale.

The British found this need to demonstrate faith to an old friend degrading. A somber delegation, including Tom Catto, broke the news to chairman Samuel Courtauld, who reacted in exemplary fashion. He asked only one question: "Was the sale essential in the national interest, whatever the hardship on him and his company?"[24] When Catto replied that it was required by the essential interests of wartime finance, the patriotic Courtauld fell on his sword. The Courtaulds' board was given thirty-six hours to make arrangements—surely the fastest such major divestment in history.

To sell American Viscose to American investors, J. P. Morgan and Company recommended to the British Treasury that Morgan Stanley and Dillon, Read manage the sale, with 23 Wall providing the necessary bank loans. The handling of the sale rankled the British for years. In unsettled, wartime conditions, it was hard to know what price might attract American investors. Textile shares had been fluctuating wildly, and underwriting tasks that normally took weeks were compressed into days. While Britain received $54 million, the seventeen-firm syndicate headed by Morgan Stanley and Dillon, Read resold the shares publicly for $62 million, pocketing the difference. Some Britons—most notably Winston Churchill—thought they had been fleeced by the bankers. At the time, the Courtaulds' directors claimed the company's tangible assets alone were worth $128 million. Obviously, there was a fantastic discrepancy.

After the war, Churchill described the sale in dryly cynical terms: "The great British business of Courtaulds in America was sold by us at the request of the United States Government at a comparatively low figure, and then resold through the markets at a much higher price from which we did not benefit."[25] When Harold Stanley read this description in a 1949 newspaper excerpt of Churchill's memoirs, he was shocked. Through Lord Harcourt of Morgan Grenfell, he made extensive efforts to get Churchill to modify it. He even tried to draw on Churchill's old friendship with his wife, Louise (formerly Mrs. Parker Gilbert), who had aided Churchill when he had an accident in New York years before. In revising his book, Churchill agreed to delete the impression that the bankers were too richly rewarded for their services. But he wouldn't budge in his opinion that American Viscose had fetched far less than its intrinsic worth. At the time of the sale, it was agreed that the matter would be referred to a three-man arbitration tribunal. In bitter postwar litigation, Courtaulds received additional compensation from the British government.

After congressional passage of Lend-Lease on March 11, 1941, Roosevelt approved a long list of supplies to be shipped to England. The progressive wing of the isolationist movement resented not only its defeat on Lend-Lease but also Roosevelt's about-face in his attitude toward Wall Street and the House of Morgan. That April, Senator Burton Wheeler of Montana, who had pursued Morgans in the railroad hearings, castigated Roosevelt for inviting the "money changers" and "Wall Street lawyers" into his camp. He angrily noted that people such as Willkie and Lamont were suddenly portrayed as "liberals," while progressives were being styled as "Tories, Nazi sympathizers, or anti-Semites" because of their opposition to U.S. participation in the war.[26]

While attacked by progressives as warmongers, the House of Morgan was actually engaged in a hidden feud with its British friends for taking the opposite position. Tom Lamont had helped Roosevelt lobby for

Lend-Lease yet insisted that the United States not enter the war. Ostensibly, this was so America could remain an arsenal for England, but there were also festering sores from the 1930s feuds. Lamont and Catto at the British Treasury shared their own diplomatic back channel, and Lamont's letters became increasingly petulant. In May 1941, he wrote a remarkable letter to Catto, full of bile and defending the U.S. failure to go to war:

> If the American people have seemed sluggish in coming to Britain's aid, nevertheless, it must be acknowledged that the U.S.A. is the first nation to go all-out in their opposition to Hitler without having faced an immediate, desperate threat to its existence. On that point does not America deserve praise for such progress rather than implied criticism for its slowness? Every country in Europe, including Britain, waited almost until Hitler had his thumb on its windpipe before it waked up and got started.
>
> Most English people look upon America, because it was (150 years ago) a British colony, as simply a younger, perhaps more vigorous, less polished England. That picture is emphasized by our former habit of calling England 'the Mother Country.'

At this point in the letter, Lamont dredged up the quarrels of the 1930s. He recalled Britain's double cross on German debt and its unwillingness to make payments on the World War I debt, which might have won American sympathy. He recalled how in 1935 he had begged Neville Chamberlain to consider a commercial treaty with the United States to create goodwill for England in America, saying it might be needed in some future crisis. "Mr. Chamberlain smiled an icy smile and was not interested in American good will."

The letter ended by implying that British snobbery toward America was no less galling to Lamont than were the financial betrayals of the 1930s. He referred to an inequality behind the fraternal Anglo-American facade: "Meanwhile, Britain, with the exception of a few of us, has, as I have intimated, never shown any great interest in America unless or until she needed America's help desperately. Tens of thousands of Americans would journey annually to the other side. But I can number on the fingers of less than my two hands the number of eminent British persons who have ever been interested to visit America."[27]

It seemed a strange time to kick the British, who had suffered the winter bombings in London, Coventry, and Plymouth. Those radical

American pamphleteers who had portrayed the House of Morgan as fawning, uncritical Anglophiles—how startled they would have been by this letter from Lamont. He showed it to Leffingwell, who actually thought it sounded too apologetic. "If I were talking to Americans, I might be saying the same things," Leffingwell confessed, "but talking to Britishers I think it unduly encourages their sense of superiority to colonials and Americans."[28]

Tom Catto replied with gallantry. To be sure, he was a high Treasury adviser and afraid to alienate an influential American. But Catto also had considerable personal skill in handling delicate matters. He wrote a letter of such dignity that it perhaps reminded the J. P. Morgan partners of why Britain's restoration as a world financial center had for decades been such an emotional issue with them:

> I was much interested in your letter and you must never think that hitting straight from the shoulder on such matters upsets me in any way. We have known each other too many years for that. . . . Whatever our shortcomings and however short our memory may be, we are cheered and encouraged by the knowledge that your great country is with us in our struggle. We have entire confidence that in the end that will mean victory! . . . It is a long road that has no turning. When we reach that turning, I believe Hitler and his gangsters will get a surprise. . . . Do not worry about us. We are all cheerful. We have had a few knocks but we can take them; indeed one hears less of the proverbial British grousing in these times than in days of peace.[29]

L A T E R Lamont would tell of the time when a "heavy fire curtain" fell between J. P. Morgan and Morgan Grenfell, and the House of Morgan was internally divided.[30] One partner didn't live to see the curtain rise. Teddy Grenfell—Lord Saint Just—died ten days before Pearl Harbor. In the late 1930s, he'd had heart and lung problems and was frail and bedridden for months at a time. Doctors recommended golf at Sandwich or West Indian cruises with his wife to restore his health.

Grenfell belonged to a vanishing species—the diplomatic banker. His work was often an inseparable blend of private and public purpose. Cool and dapper, he had been a Morgan sphinx, cloaked in mystery, working unseen in the top echelons of government and finance. "English Bankers and Houses are very much more secretive than those in New York," he told Lamont, and secrecy was his unchanging creed.[31] He believed implicitly in the wisdom of his class, country, and profession and had no patience with reformers. His mind was acute, his predictions unerring, his tailoring immaculate, and his pose debonair. But his sympathies were limited and his tolerance dim. He saw bankers defending immutable truths against political folly and public ignorance. He would have been misplaced in the coming Casino Age, when governments, not private bankers, would assume financial leadership. So strong was Grenfell's friendship with Jack Morgan that his death would weaken the tie between the New York and London houses.

E V E N with Europe at war, Tom Lamont didn't shed his Panglossian tendency to predict favorable outcomes in world affairs. He expected Japan to refrain from war against the Allies, not from any scruples, but because self-interest dictated that it be on the winning side. Three weeks before Pearl Harbor, he told Walter Lippmann that if Japan "were on the losing side she would lose complete influence in the whole Pacific region and would sink there to the status of a second or third rate power. . . . I may be 100% mistaken, but I am really not worried at all about the Far East for the moment."[32] On December 7, 1941, Japan attacked Pearl Harbor, and yet another Lamont illusion was shattered. In the most eloquent expression of disgust with Japan, Lamont joined that year with Henry Luce in merging eight China aid groups into United China Relief. The Japanese presence on Wall Street was abolished as the New York State superintendent of banks seized the assets of the Yokohama Specie Bank, Japan's fiscal agent before the war.

U.S. entry into the war in 1941 repaired the breach within the House of Morgan. With the United States and Britain fighting side by side, Morgan partners revived the belief that their countries were destined to rule the world jointly. In a new spirit of forgiveness, Lamont took to citing English, Scottish, and Irish blood in American veins as the country's real source of strength. Vindictive toward Britain two years before, Russell Leffingwell said warmly, "To my mind the only thing worth fighting for is to save England and the British Empire. For that I would shed every drop of blood in my own veins, and let many millions of Americans shed theirs too."[33]

J. P. Morgan and Company resumed its customary role of defending the mother country. When *Life* magazine published an open letter saying the war shouldn't be fought so Britain could keep her empire, Lamont sparred with Henry Luce. The bank had known Luce well ever since his Yale classmate Henry P. Davison, Jr., became the first investor in *Time* magazine and a company director. Lamont now told him that America had its own imperialism and backed its own Latin American dictators: "Why do we yell about 'imperialism' when we are busy day and night scheming to get the whole Caribbean under our control and sweeping all of Latin America into our orbit by lavish loans and diplomatic manoeuvres?"[34]

A new rapport between Roosevelt and Jack Morgan was evident in November 1941, when labor leader John L. Lewis ordered a strike against captive coal mines owned by the steel companies. When Roosevelt appealed for patriotic restraint, Lewis said his adversary should also be restrained. "My adversary is a rich man named Morgan, who lives in New York," he declared.[35] To Roosevelt, Lamont protested this insinuation that U.S. Steel was just a tool of Jack's. Not only did Roosevelt side with Jack—a novelty in itself—but he did so with a new geniality. A class traitor no more, he told Lamont: "I was really angry at Lewis' unwarranted, untrue, and demagogic statement about Jack. . . . When you see Jack, tell him for me not to concern himself any more about Lewis' attack, for after many years of observation, I have come reluctantly to the conclusion that Lewis' is a psychopathic condition."[36]

Able to slough off divisive, prewar domestic issues, FDR and the Morgan partners became fast friends. After Lamont congratulated him for declaring war, Roosevelt wired back, "Generous words of approval from an old friend like you are heartening."[37] They swapped jokes, anecdotes, and amusing press clips, including one citing Communist leader Earl Browder's accusation that Roosevelt had prevailed upon Lamont and Walter Lippmann to engineer Willkie's nomination. In early 1942, Lamont spent almost an hour at the White House speculating as to how the U.S. might use Fort Knox gold in the postwar world to stabilize currencies. Roosevelt said America was trusted more in continental Europe than was Britain. This was the relationship Lamont had craved—full of secrets, confidences, and back scratching. Turning to the subject of Churchill, FDR confided to Lamont that Winston didn't have the economic mind they had.[38] (Yet in 1939, the British embassy in Washington filed this tart appraisal of Roosevelt: "His knowledge of certain subjects, particularly finance and economics, is superficial."[39]) At Roosevelt's request, Lamont appeared at a Madison Square Garden rally for Soviet-American friendship—the one time Tom appeared politically with his left-wing son, Corliss.

What strengthened ties between Roosevelt and the House of Morgan was that both felt beleaguered by the same isolationist forces. In the spring of 1942, Leffingwell told the president that the war effort required more parades, brass bands, and flag-waving. Agreeing, Roosevelt added that "the real trouble is not in the people or the leaders, but in a gang which unfortunately survives—made up mostly of those who were isolationists before December seventh and who are actuated today by various motives in their effort to instill disunity in the country."[40] So the new concord between Roosevelt and Morgans corresponded to the old political axiom that the enemy of my enemy is my friend. War had finally made peace between the White House and the House of Morgan.

PASSAGES

• •
•

T HE early war years saw the final transformation of J. P. Morgan and Company from a private partnership to a corporation. This momentous step in Morgan history was taken only after extensive deliberations at the Pierpont Morgan Library. In announcing the transformation in February 1940, Jack made an unprecedented appearance at the press conference. He would be board chairman, George Whitney chief executive, and Lamont head of the executive committee. In dropping the partnership form, Jack had to sell the New York Stock Exchange seat bought by Pierpont in 1895. As a private bank, partners had been exposed to the full risk of loss. But they had gladly accepted this risk in order to keep their capital position secret and their books free from inspection. This tradition had contributed immeasurably to the firm's mystery and power.

Why, then, the change? The bank feared rapid capital depletion as the three richest partners aged: Tom Lamont, Charles Steele, and Jack Morgan. Steele had died in Westbury, New York, in mid-1939, after spending his last years watching his grandsons play polo. If either Jack Morgan or Lamont died soon, too, there could be a serious drain on capital. A combination of the Depression and inheritance and income taxes had whittled the bank's assets down from $119 million in 1929 to only $39 million in 1940. By converting to share ownership, heirs could sell their stakes without disrupting the bank's capital. There was also a wish to enter the trust business, which was closed to partnerships. In 1927, American Telephone and Telegraph had funded the first big corporate retirement plan, and Morgans wanted to capture similar huge pools of capital.

There were other blows to Morgans' traditional aloofness as well. In

1942, it joined the Federal Reserve System—having been the largest holdout—in a move related to its heavy purchase of government bonds, which was Wall Street's principal wartime activity: the Corner witnessed Victory Loan rallies for which huge throngs turned out before a flag-draped Stock Exchange. Now for the first time, the House of Morgan's nearly $700 million in deposits became subject to federal deposit insurance. Also in 1942, ownership of Morgan shares spread beyond the eighty or ninety people, mostly family and friends, who had controlled it before. A syndicate led by Smith, Barney offered 8 percent of Morgan shares to the public—the first time ordinary mortals could buy a piece of a Morgan bank. This both broadened ownership and assigned value to closely held shares. In a final affront to tradition, J. P. Morgan and Company disclosed its earnings in a prospectus.

In this period of transition, the Morgan link with its Philadelphia affiliate, Drexel and Company, also ended. The Philadelphia firm had brought the Drexels, Biddles, Berwinds, and other Main Line families into the Morgan fold. As Pierpont had told Arsene Pujo, "It only has a different name, owing to my desire to keep Mr. Drexel's name in Philadelphia."[1] In 1940, 23 Wall took over Drexel's deposits, shut the Philadelphia office, and sold the name to some Philadelphia partners who were forming an investment bank. Later on, I. W. "Tubby" Burnham merged his Burnham and Company with the reincarnated Drexel, so that the famous name would later grace the junk-bond operation of Drexel Burnham Lambert.

To qualify for Stock Exchange membership, Morgan Stanley became a partnership in 1941. It was now harried by the Brandeisian trustbusters who had pursued J. P. Morgan and Company and saw Morgan Stanley as simply a retooled version of the original company. Morgan Stanley's instant success had aroused suspicion, for it had managed a quarter of all negotiated bond issues since Glass-Steagall. During the Temporary National Economic Committee hearings in 1939 and 1940, the committee's chairman, Senator Joseph O'Mahoney of Wyoming, refused to believe J. P. Morgan had withdrawn from investment banking: "Now that the Banking Act has separated two functions that were formerly merged, Morgan Stanley in the investment field has succeeded to a similar dominant position that J.P. Morgan formerly held."[2] SEC counsel John Hauser advanced a conspiracy theory that dismissed Morgan Stanley as a "legal fiction" set up by J. P. Morgan partners to bypass Glass-Steagall. An exasperated Harold Stanley was repeatedly asked whether he took orders from 23 Wall after Glass-Steagall. "We were a separate, split-off organization," he insisted. "We owned and ran the business. Our money had been risked in the common stock."[3] Notwithstanding his denials, the SEC charged that J. P. Morgan and Company had used its influence over Dayton Power to obtain business for Morgan Stanley.

What weakened Morgan Stanley's claim to autonomy was that most of its preferred stock was owned by J. P. Morgan and Company officers. The SEC asserted this created "an identity of pecuniary interest" between the two Morgan houses and an "emotional" and "psychological" affiliation.[4] So Morgan Stanley began buying the preferred stock, and J. P. Morgan executives sold it to their wives, sons, grandchildren, and so forth—a transparent ruse that didn't fool anybody. To retire the bogey of J. P. Morgan control once and for all, Morgan Stanley redeemed and canceled its preferred shares on December 5, 1941. This ended any formal link between the two firms, although a multitude of intangible links would weave them together for decades.

At this point, the campaign against Wall Street shifted to a lower gear. The investment banking business was moribund during the war as the Treasury Department asked underwriters to desist from new bond issues so as not to compete with government war-bond drives. Therefore, the drive to reform investment banking was stalled until the Medina trial of the early postwar years. In the meantime, by switching to a partnership form, Morgan Stanley retreated into the world of "mystery and dignity," as Judge Medina later labeled it, just as J. P. Morgan was emerging into the sunlight.

AFTER initial grumbling, Jack Morgan settled amiably into his new role as board chairman. "What he had looked forward to with distaste he found not at all disagreeable," said Russell Leffingwell.[5] On January 31, 1943, Jack presided over the first public shareholders meeting of J. P. Morgan and Company, Inc. It was a pleasant, autumnal time for him: the war had silenced New Deal charges of villainy, and everybody was saying that Jack hadn't seemed so happy since before Jessie's death, eighteen years before. He enjoyed serving as nanny to his English war babies and went duck shooting nearly every weekend that fall. There were gentler pursuits as well, including the new hobby of taking color photographs of cherry blossoms and other flowers.

The soft-shoe, avuncular Jack was much more in evidence. Every evening, he stopped to chat with the Pinkerton guards at Matinicock Point, thanking them as they opened the gates that guarded the estate. Playing backgammon with John Davis for a nickel a game, he had a winning streak and teased Davis's butler that he was about to lose his wages. He observed life's smaller details. Each morning, at the same bend in the road, he passed a young neighbor driving to work in the opposite direction; when the young man overslept one morning and they passed further down the road than usual, Jack wagged a satirical finger of rebuke.

In late February, doctors gave Jack a clean bill of health before he left for a Florida holiday, a quiet fishing trip on the Gulf of Mexico. On the train to Boca Grande, he had heart trouble, however, followed by a cerebral stroke. His steadfast valet of twenty-eight years, Bernard Stewart, managed to get him to his rented cottage at the Gasparilla Inn, a winter resort on a barrier island, and his New York heart specialist, Dr. Henry S. Patterson, came down to look after him. Jack survived less than two weeks. He died in a coma on March 13, 1943, and his body was brought north in a special Pullman car attached to the Seaboard Line.

Even in death, there were eerie parallels between Jack and Pierpont Morgan. Both died at the age of seventy-five, and again news of the death was withheld until after the stock market closed, so as not to disturb share prices. The voluminous obituaries that followed were of the full-page variety reserved for heads of state. The *New York Times* commented, "The private banking house of J.P. Morgan & Co. . . . gained a position of world-wide importance and a place in international financial affairs that not even the house of Rothschild attained in the period of its greatest power."[6] The paper called Jack the last financial titan—they had said the same thing of Pierpont—noting that for the first time since George Peabody's retirement, the Morgan bank was not headed by a Morgan. Tom Lamont ascended to board chairman.

Jack's funeral service, too, was reminiscent of Pierpont's. He lay in state at the Pierpont Morgan Library before a funeral at Saint George's Church on Stuyvesant Square. The service featured the black baritone Harry Burleigh, who had sung at the 1913 funeral. Again flags flew at half-mast over the New York Stock Exchange and the Corner. One difference was subtly apparent to the twelve hundred mourners who arrived in a heavy downpour: they were solemnly escorted to their seats by the directors of *two* banking houses—J. P. Morgan and Company and Morgan Stanley. After cremation, Jack's ashes were sent to Hartford for burial at Cedar Hill Cemetery, alongside the graves of Pierpont and Junius.

In his will, Jack perpetuated Pierpont's tradition of flamboyant generosity, including a $1-million trust fund for his elderly domestic employees. Henry Physick, Jack's butler of thirty-four years and the man who was so resourceful during the 1915 assassination attempt, received $25,-

000. His secretary of forty years, John Axten, hired as a boy of nineteen, got $50,000, as did Belle da Costa Greene. With a paternalistic flourish in the style of Pierpont, Jack gave six months' wages to long-time bank employees and three months' to those hired more recently.

As they had been at his father's death, everybody was surprised by the relative modesty of Jack's estate—only $16 million before taxes and expenses, $4.6 million afterward. Following merchant-banking tradition, he left the bulk of his estate to his sons, Junius and Harry. His daughters' families, the Nichols and the Pennoyers, would enjoy the prestige but less of the fortune associated with the Morgan name. During his lifetime, Jack gave away an estimated $35 million, including $15 million to the Pierpont Morgan Library and $9 million to the Metropolitan Museum of Art. His fortune wasn't frittered away only by philanthropy. After Jessie's death, he had maintained the fantastic indulgence of the colossal yachts and the regal estates.

Opinion of Jack's place in history was immediately divided. Clearly, his business career had been a personal triumph. When he took over the bank, Wall Street rumor mills had patronized him as a bungler. Yet under him, the House of Morgan had amassed power beyond that of the bank under Junius or even under Pierpont. It had taken on extraordinary international breadth, winning many governments, finance ministries, and central banks as clients and capitalizing on the merger of politics and finance in the Diplomatic Age. The building at 23 Wall now seemed less a smoky clubhouse of banking cronies than a gathering place for the world's financial elite. With some glaring exceptions— such as the Van Sweringen escapade and the Richard Whitney scandal— Jack had preserved the bank's reputation for fair, conservative dealings.

He had also put in place a superlative team and allowed its members to employ the full scope of their energies. He was a good "successor" figure who knew how to delegate power and take disinterested pleasure in his partners' feats. If the Morgan bank moved like a well-oiled machine and was free of internal warfare, it had something to do with Jack's reputable stewardship. A more self-centered boss might have regretted his own absence during the 1929 crash, yet Jack took fatherly pride in his partners' behavior: "I . . . was made very happy by the absolutely magnificent conduct of all my partners during the 'late unpleasantness' in Wall Street. The Firm showed that it could behave just as well when I was not there, as it could have done had I been there."[7] Unlike his father, he was never a prisoner of his ego.

Of Jack's public role, a far less flattering judgment must be rendered. The *New Republic* acidly observed that Jack had "added nothing creative or humanizing to American life, and . . . his passing subtracts nothing."[8] In the Victorian age, he would have been a model banker, cherishing honor, integrity, and Christianity. Such values, however, were inadequate during the worldwide Depression, when many people went hungry while still abiding by them. It was a harsh Providence that dropped such a hidebound, frightened man into an age of radical upheaval and experimentation. He asked for privacy in an era that demanded accountability. Increasingly the Morgan bank operated as an adjunct of government. It couldn't accept the benefits of public service without also accepting its burdens. Fleeing his political troubles, Jack kept aloof from his countrymen and never understood plain Americans the way he did English aristocrats. The *New Yorker* once said with justice, "One feels he could both teach and learn if he would cross the Mississippi frequently and meet the people that largely make up America."[9]

At a time that demanded fresh thinking, Jack could only reiterate ancient economic verities and brood over affronts to his dignity. Rather than giving new ideologies a fair hearing, he found them evil and insidious. For a man of such delicacy, who reported late to work so he could watch the tulips bloom, he could be heartless with his supposed enemies—Jews, Catholics, Germans, liberals, reformers, and intellectuals—whom he lumped together into a single nefarious plot. "The world knew him only as a somewhat mysterious colossus of finance," said The *New York Herald Tribune*.[10] If the world saw remarkably little of his compassion, he had himself to blame for it. He never gave of himself freely to the public. At bottom, he didn't believe in common humanity and imagined his foes driven by motives unlike his own. Instead of accepting change as a fact of life, he raged against his moment in history and suffered in the process.

That Jack Morgan was an anachronism could be seen by the fate of his possessions: only institutions could afford his boats and residences. *Corsair IV* was bought by Pacific Cruise Lines and converted into a cruise ship for eighty-five passengers. His Georgian brick mansion on Long Island was rented to the Soviet UN delegation in 1949. Soviet diplomats and their families played volleyball on a lawn that once had been owned by the czar's banker; in the mansion, they installed seventy-one beds, sixty-seven canvas chairs, and eight big cafeteria tables. The town of Glen Cove objected to this use of the property, and the Russians had to depart. For many years afterward, the estate served as a convent for the Sisters of Saint John the Baptist, who built a chapel in the courtyard between the main house and Jack's sixteen-car garage. The mansion was later torn down, and one hundred suburban houses were put up on the old estate grounds. The fifteen-hundred-acre Camp Uncas in the Adirondacks was bought by the Boy Scouts, while the United Lutheran Church paid a scant $245,000 in 1949 for Jack's forty-five-room Madison Avenue townhouse. In 1988, when the Lutherans decamped for Chicago, they sold it back to the Pierpont Morgan Library for $15 million. Wall Hall was acquired by the county council for a green belt around London. Princes Gate, once among the finest private homes in London, became headquarters of the Independent Television Authority in the 1950s (and in 1980 had as its neighbor just a few doors away the Iranian embassy, which in that year was the scene of a violent siege). The world of the grandees was over. In the post–World War II era the Wall Street and City banks would grow into vast, global institutions of a hitherto unimaginable size. But the bankers inhabiting them would, paradoxically, seem that much smaller.

FOR central bankers of the Diplomatic Age, the war proved a time of melancholy reflection. Monty Norman bemoaned the curse of modern democracy, of making decisions by "counting noses," as he scornfully phrased it. He blamed politicians for destroying the rational system of gold-linked currencies that he and his Morgan friends had created in the 1920s. All had foundered on the rocks of nationalism and politics. Finance, it turned out, wasn't a sterile laboratory that could be run by scientific bankers in white coats. Nor could it be left to a mysterious, self-appointed priesthood. In the Casino Age, central and private banks would no longer function as sovereign states but would be linked to government entities, both national and multilateral.

Throughout the war, Russell Leffingwell sent food packages to Monty Norman. A rattled man wanting reassurance, Norman asked Leffingwell whether he was wrong about the gold standard and his attempts to refurbish the old imperial pound. Any other course of action, Norman pleaded, would "have shaken the confidence in Europe, and have produced a feeling of uncertainty, which seemed the one thing to be avoided."[11] Leffingwell agreed that only gold formed a bulwark against the modern plagues of managed currencies, budget deficits, and bloated welfare states. He, too, recognized the futility of their labors: "How we labored together, you and Ben, my partners and I, to rebuild the world after the last war—and look at the d—— thing now!"[12] Monty was equally despondent: "As I look back, it now seems that, with all the thought and work and good intentions which we provided, we achieved *absolutely* nothing. . . . I think we should have done just as much good if we had been able to collect the money and pour it down the drain."[13]

There would be a day of reckoning for Monty Norman no less than there had been for Ben Strong. The Labour party had never forgiven him for his tough attitude toward the first Labour government in the 1920s, nor for the austerity imposed in 1925 on behalf of the gold standard. When the government abandoned gold in 1931, it only reinforced suspicions that financial "rules" were ruses to intimidate recalcitrant left-wing governments. The bitter 1931 gibe of Labour party veteran Beatrice Webb—"Nobody told us we could do it"—still reverberated. Now Norman's autocratic twenty-four year reign at the Bank of England would belatedly produce new government controls over British finance.

Norman's health declined in 1943 and 1944 and he was diagnosed as having pneumonia and then meningitis. Fragile and broken in his seventies, he heeded doctors' advice that he resign. For several years, Tom Catto had been mentioned as a successor, and his conscientious work at the wartime Treasury impressed Norman. Although Catto had been the sole liberal at the solidly Tory Morgan Grenfell, the Labour party feared he would perpetuate City rule at the Bank of England. As early as 1940, Hugh Dalton, minister of economic warfare, warned Chancellor of the Exchequer Kingsley Wood that "there will be much feeling against Catto as successor. He comes from the most reactionary firm in the City, Morgan Grenfell, who, I say, have a notorious record as partisan Tories."[14]

Chosen governor in 1944, Catto made a wistful pilgrimage to Norman's country house to receive the older man's blessing. "My dear, Catto," Norman said, "I had been my own first choice for re-election as Governor of the Bank of England, but the doctors say 'No.' You are my second choice. God bless you."[15] Touched by this gesture, Catto broke down and paced the garden with Norman's wife before he could regain his composure. Catto's appointment was interpreted as underscoring the need for close postwar cooperation with the United States.

After the surprise defeat of Churchill's government in the 1945 elections, Clement Attlee's Labour government put nationalization of the bank at the top of its parliamentary agenda. Although the bank had long handled national debt, currency issues, and foreign exchange, it was privately owned by seventeen thousand stockholders. Now the central bankers were to be driven from the shadows in which they had operated. For Labour partisans, it was a long overdue act of revenge against Norman.

Die-hards in the City thought Catto should resign as a matter of honor rather than supervise a bank under government control. Monty Norman never quite overcame the feeling that Catto should have been wily enough to defeat nationalization. Catto, in fact, proved a perfect transitional figure and probably secured a better deal for the bank than Norman could have. He wasn't regarded as a City figure hostile to Whitehall and was a shrewd, conciliatory man. He recognized that Norman's dictum, "Never excuse, never explain," wouldn't suffice in the new age. Central banks could no longer be priestly or hermetic, and Catto thought it best for a sound banker to manage the transition. To preserve the bank's independence, he won agreement that the governor be appointed for five-year renewable terms and dismissed only by act of Parliament.

In March 1946, after more than 250 years of independence, the Bank of England became a public institution. It would now be less influenced by merchant bankers, and more industrialists and union leaders would be appointed as its postwar directors. Catto told Lamont with relief, "The ship had to be steered between Scylla and Charybdis but we managed somehow!"[16] After serving as governor until his seventieth birthday, Catto in 1949 took a desk again at Morgan Grenfell but didn't resume formal duties at the firm. His son Stephen, however, would be a postwar Morgan Grenfell chairman.

For Monty Norman, the new world embodied everything he despised. Lamenting the "socialisation at a gallop" overtaking England, he told Leffingwell that he seldom went into the City anymore and found it a sad place, reduced to refunding bonds at lower interest rates. The man who had devoted his life to maintaining London as a world financial center now saw it as a place of faded glory: "I fear that the various ancient businesses of London have practically come to an end, or continue perhaps as shadows."[17] As foreign business shifted more decisively to New York than it had after World War I, leaving little room for London leadership, Norman seemed lost, unhinged, distraught. "I wonder what old Ben would think of all this," he said.[18] On February 4, 1950, Montagu Norman died, having suffered a stroke the year before.

AFTER the war, a hearty survivor, Dr. Hjalmar Horace Greeley Schacht, had resumed his correspondence with Monty Norman. Arrested by the Gestapo in July 1944 after participating in another plot against Hitler, he was sent to the Ravensbrueck concentration camp and ultimately passed through thirty-two prisons, including the death camp at Dachau. He formed part of a distinguished group of prisoners that included the former Austrian chancellor Kurt von Schuschnigg and Léon Blum. In the last stages of war, their captors hurried them south-east to escape the advancing American troops. On May 4, 1945, Schacht and the others were about to be executed by the Gestapo, under express orders from Hitler, when they were liberated by Allied troops in the south Tirol.

Schacht tried to visit the ailing Norman, but he hadn't been officially de-Nazified and was denied an English visa. He was a shameless, bull-headed man whose sheer arrogance seemed to preserve him in adversity. After being indicted as a war criminal by the Nuremberg tribunal, he was placed under arrest by General Lucius Clay, commander of the U.S. Army of Occupation in Germany. When Clay went to Schacht's chalet outside Berlin to take him into custody, Schacht resisted the notion that he was anti-American. As proof, he told Clay, "Look at the picture on the wall." It was a signed photograph that David Sarnoff had given him at the Young Plan conference in Paris in 1929.[19]

Awaiting the Nuremberg war trials at a prison camp, Schacht continued to behave in a bizarrely unpredictable manner. Albert Speer, Hitler's architect and minister of armaments, recalled how Schacht delivered dramatic poetry readings to pass the time. When American military psychologists delivered IQ tests to the war criminals, Schacht scored first in the group. There were many strange reunions at Nuremberg. Schacht hadn't seen Hermann Göring since losing out in the power struggle to him in 1937. "Our next meeting was in prison at Nuremberg when we were taken to a cell with 2 bathtubs where—I in one and Goering in the other—we each proceeded to soap ourselves all over," Schacht wrote. "Sic transit gloria mundi!"[20]

At Nuremberg, Schacht refused to admit responsibility for Hitler's success and denied he had made a unique contribution to the Nazi cause. He said of Hitler, "He would have found other methods and other assistance; he was not the man to give up."[21] Schacht could document enough resistance in the late 1930s to offset the impression of collaboration with the Nazis. He cast himself as a solitary critic of the regime who was appalled by the cowardice of workers, liberals, churchmen, and scientists. So the man who rallied Krupp, Thyssen, and other German industrialists around Adolf Hitler and helped mold the robust German war economy was one of only three Nazis acquitted at Nuremberg. A German de-Nazification court afterward convicted him as a major Nazi offender, and he was sentenced to eight years in a labor camp, although he appealed and was released after a year. In the 1950s, he wrote a long-winded, self-adoring autobiography that was conspicuously short on contrition for his role in Nazi finance. He died unrepentant in 1970, at the age of ninety-three, of complications resulting from a fall.

STARTING in 1943, Tom Lamont had heart trouble and no longer reported regularly to the bank. Toward the end of the war, his handsome grandson Thomas W. Lamont II, died aboard the submarine *Snook* in the Pacific. Now in his seventies and nostalgic with age, Lamont composed a charming volume of memoirs about his boyhood in a country parsonage. His romantic nature never flagged. Throughout the war, he had sent food parcels to Nancy Astor, who even in her sixties was energetic enough to perform cartwheels in the air-raid shelters. In 1945, after she had retired from twenty-five years in Parliament, Lamont paid $3,000 in expenses for her to visit the United States. On the eve of her visit, he wrote her, "And meantime with your war cares largely removed I shall find you I know looking younger and lovelier than ever before." Then he added, forgetfully, "How proud you must be that it was Britain who in 1940 stood all alone against the entire world of barbarism and saved civilization."[22]

Unpleasant reminders of the past would intrude. In 1944, the Italian government dispatched a financial mission to Lamont. Some of the old gang wanted to crank up the Italy-America Society, but Lamont suggested that maybe they should wait awhile. When news came of Mussolini's death in 1945, Lamont said its "indecent" manner upset him but that otherwise nobody regretted it. With a new anti-Fascist mood in postwar Italy, Lamont took pains to rewrite history. In 1946, he told Count Giuseppe Volpi, the former finance minister, that the $100-million loan to Italy in 1926 was made under duress. He implied that he had frowned upon it: "I hardly have to say that the loan was not one that we were eager to arrange, nor was it sought by us. On the contrary, it was a part of the series of post-war reconstruction operations encouraged by our own Government."[23]

By war's end, Lamont came to the bank only for short periods each week. He continued to make the grandly liberal gestures that had marked his extraordinary tenure at 23 Wall. For $2 million, he endowed an undergraduate library at Harvard—appropriately, it would be for government documents—and sent what Norman called a "whomping" check for restoring Canterbury Cathedral. He ended his banking career with a Pierpontian act of munificence: in the lean year of 1947, the firm had skipped bonus payments; Lamont decided to compensate by giving every staff member a Christmas gift equal to 5 percent of his or her salary.

Lamont had time to wonder about the hopefulness that had buoyed him between the wars, making him susceptible to the false allure of appeasement. He now saw Americans as too self-absorbed by materialism and too coddled by peace to brace for violence. In a 1945 essay, "Germany's Heartbreak House," he tried to figure out why the Allies were deaf to Churchill's pleas regarding Hitler. He wrote:

> The truth is that the British and French, like us Americans, are so peace-loving that it has always been hard for them to realize that there are gangster peoples going about the world seeking whom they may devour. We have all refused to believe until the last moment that there were Dillinger nations prowling about with completely laid plans of evil portent. . . . For in the makeup of the Anglo-Saxon peoples there is . . . that extreme of humaneness that abhors cruelty and will have naught of it.[24]

The explanation omits the large measure of self-interest that had led Lamont to cling first to Japan, then to Italy.

On February 3, 1948, Tom Lamont died at his home in Boca Grande, Florida, at age seventy-seven, and Russell Leffingwell became chairman of the House of Morgan. So many friends flocked to Lamont's funeral at the Brick Presbyterian Church on Park Avenue that folding chairs were hastily arranged in the side aisles and balcony. Two veterans of Black Thursday—William Potter of Guaranty Trust and Albert Wiggin of Chase—were in evidence. Whereas at Jack's funeral the mourners sang "Onward Christian Soldiers," at Tom's passages from Milton's *Samson Agonistes* were read against a brilliant backdrop of white flowers.

Lamont's estate was so enormous that the charitable and educational bequests came to $9.5 million, including $5 million to Harvard and $2 million to Phillips Exeter Academy. Through a syndicate managed by Morgan Stanley, his estate sold off his twenty-five-thousand-share block of J. P. Morgan stock. It was the largest block in existence, with an estimated market value of nearly $6 million.

Lamont was a man of prodigious gifts, the real J. P. Morgan behind J. P. Morgan and Company. Had he lived in Pierpont's day, he might have summoned steel mills or transcontinental railroads into being. Instead, as a man of the Diplomatic Age, he was the architect of huge state loans in the 1920s. As they defaulted in the 1930s, he had to devote his time to fruitless salvage operations, and his gifts were squandered in the general wreckage. For all his power, he seems in retrospect a tiny figure bobbing atop a gigantic tidal wave. His story is a sobering tale of human limitations.

In its front-page obituary, the *Times* said that the driving force of Lamont's life "was an unremitting search for the good, the full and the gracious life."[25] Indeed, one admires his ambition to lead a beautiful, rounded life and bring poetry into the straitlaced world of banking. He gave a literary gloss and an intellectual richness to the House of Morgan, stretching the sense of what it means to be a banker. He was a man who dealt with the large issues of the day, saw the strategic significance of his actions, and transcended a provincial concern with profit. His vision of banking was remarkably spacious.

Yet he resorted to moral shortcuts and political compromises. He was too quick to paper over conflicts with rhetoric and to settle arguments with smiles. The optimism that made him an inspiring leader also contained an element of pure opportunism. He refused to terminate business relationships until *force majeure* supervened, and his complicity with Japanese militarists and Mussolini are black marks on his record. By the end, he could no longer distinguish policy from public relations or separate means from ends. In trying to please too many people, he lost the habit of truth—a habit, once lost, that can never be regained. Perhaps the most extraordinary figure in Morgan history, Lamont was a dreamer whose reach exceeded his grasp. He fell short of the ideals that he himself articulated. After his death, Wall Street would seem grayer and more bureaucratic. As a confidant of presidents, prime ministers, and kings, he was the last great banker of the Diplomatic Age.

PART THREE

The Casino Age
1948-1989

• •
•

METHUSELAH

. .

.

A FTER Tom Lamont's death, Russell Leffingwell served as chairman of J. P. Morgan from 1948 to 1950. Sucking on a long, straight pipe, he had an air of Methuselah-like wisdom, with his large pointed nose and white hair. As chairman of the Council on Foreign Relations from 1946 to 1953, he would stop by its offices on his way home to East Sixty-Ninth Street. Bookish and witty, a masterly rhetorician, he could write a trenchant essay or speak extemporaneously on any subject. His mind was promiscuously rich. Once, after delivering a fiery opinion at a board meeting, he asked, "Does anyone disagree?" Tom Lamont replied softly, "Would anyone dare, Russell?" He had a gift for comebacks. When his daughter went on her first cruise, she asked how many people she could tip. "Well," he said dryly, "if you have enough money, you can go right up to the captain."[1] The writer Edna Ferber left this impression of Leffingwell at a dinner party: "He seemed to me to be wise, tolerant, sound, liberal; and, combined with these qualities, he has, astoundingly enough, humor."[2] She couldn't imagine a Scrooge behind his "florid rather Puckish face."[3]

Leffingwell was the last of the handpicked thinkers that Morgans bred prolifically between the wars, when Wall Street still produced Renaissance men. As members of small partnerships, the elite financiers straddled all aspects of business. They had time to read, to ponder, to enter politics: the gray era of specialization hadn't dawned. Leffingwell thought that Glass-Steagall, by segmenting banking, had destroyed the most interesting jobs on the Street.

After World War II, the Morgan bank was upstaged by a new set of multilateral institutions. Between the wars, the mysterious *troika* of the Bank of England, the New York Fed, and Morgans had largely governed the international monetary order. At Bretton Woods, New Hampshire, in 1944, they were superseded by a proposed World Bank and International Monetary Fund. These twin bodies would try to lift currency stabilization and European reconstruction to a supranational plane. In the postwar era, there would also be greater collaboration among central banks and finance ministries of the major industrial countries. The upshot was that financial tasks entrusted to private bankers in the 1920s were placed irretrievably in public hands. Bankers were distanced from politicians by a new sense of public propriety, with secret collaboration regarded as corrupting by government. The Diplomatic Age was dead.

In the new Casino Age, as we shall call it, banks would operate in a broader competitive sphere. The banker had grown powerful when capital markets were limited, with few financial intermediaries to tap them. In the post–World War II period, however, capital markets would burgeon and become globally integrated. At the same time, the financial field would grow crowded with commercial banks, investment banks, insurance companies, brokerage houses, foreign banks, government lending programs, multilateral organizations, and myriad other lenders. Gradually Wall Street bankers would lose their unique place in world finance. Never again would a private bank such as J. P. Morgan be the most powerful financial agency on earth. Far from standing guard over scarce resources, bankers would evolve into glad-handing salesmen, almost pushing the bountiful stuff on customers.

The new Bretton Woods bodies were shaped by the interwar lending disaster. The memories of the 1920s were fresh, with over a third of foreign government securities still in default. The World Bank's decision to finance only meticulously conceived projects was a reaction to this loose sovereign lending. Even so scrupulous a lender as Morgans smarted from a flood of outstanding defaulted bonds—$197 million in Japanese debt, $20 million from Austria, $151 million from Germany. No banker was foolish enough to assert that countries never went bust or that government loans were less risky than commerical loans. Since the World Bank had to tap U.S. capital markets—only the United States had spare cash—it needed to please Wall Street and erase the stigma of foreign lending.

The World Bank's second president, John J. McCloy, had to safeguard the new institution's credit and consulted Leffingwell about Morgan's interwar experience. With his usual style of passionate urgency, Leffingwell told McCloy about the bank's sense of betrayal over foreign loans that had enjoyed phantom government guarantees—most notably the German loans. McCloy concurred in Leffingwell's critique of 1920s lending—that politics had gotten confused with finance, encouraging debtors to regard loans as disguised foreign aid. This destroyed discipline and invited excessive borrowing, followed by default.

Considering the defaults on Latin American loans, McCloy asked whether the bank should lend to the region. Leffingwell shot back, "Except for the Argentine, I do not think of any Central or South American country that hasn't got a contemptible, discreditable record of default to American investors."[4] (Argentina was always a special case: when Juan Perón came to power in 1946, the country boasted a large supply of gold amassed from food exports to wartime Europe; Perón even favored paying off foreign debt to avert bondage to foreign bankers.) If the World Bank made Latin American loans, Leffingwell warned McCloy, it might tarnish the World Bank's own bonds with American investors. McCloy had greater sympathy for the Latin Americans than Leffingwell did, arguing that bankers had tempted the region into over-borrowing. "The competition that went on in Europe and in Latin America for loans was something to see," he told Leffingwell. "I know because I was a part of it."[5] Although the World Bank made Latin American loans, it insisted that Peru and other nations first settle outstanding debt with private bondholders. This shored up creditors and prevented Latin American debt from contaminating the bank's own credit.

Leffingwell thought private lending to Europe couldn't resume until political turmoil in the area ended. In 1946, Churchill sounded the alarm with his "Iron Curtain" speech in Fulton, Missouri. His fears of European disintegration were spookily analogous to those following World War I, especially with food shortages and poor crops in early 1947. As Under Secretary of State Robert Lovett had warned Lamont, "At no time in my recollection have I seen a world situation which was so rapidly moving toward real trouble."[6] Leffingwell feared a stingy, punitive approach to rebuilding Europe, reminiscent of Versailles. He, in turn, warned Lovett, his friend and Locust Valley neighbor: "Western Europe is drifting toward catastrophe. Penny-wise and pound-foolish, we dribble out little loans and grants, too little and too late, meeting a crisis here or there . . . while we neglect to deal constructively on a great scale with the problem of the reconstruction of western Europe"[7] He stressed aid to Britain and France, without strings: "The British and French are not infants nor aborigines to be dictated to by the nouveaux riches Americans."[8]

With U.S. investors still skittish about foreign bonds, the World Bank couldn't cope with the Western European crisis. In December 1947,

Truman presented Congress with plans for the multibillion-dollar Marshall Plan to raise Europe from wartime rubble behind a NATO defense shield. "What took place after World War I was the forerunner of the Marshall Plan," noted McCloy, who had worked on the Dawes loan in the 1920s. "But back then the rehabilitation of Europe was done in a private capacity."[9] The scope of the Marshall Plan—$5 billion for the first year alone—far exceeded Wall Street's meager resources, still depleted by the Depression, war, and Glass-Steagall.

The internationalism that had always ostracized the House of Morgan in the hinterlands was now irrevocably established in Washington. The war, television, and foreign travel all acted to reduce American parochialism. As the Republicans shed their traditional isolationism, the bank had a party in which it could place implicit faith. No longer would Morgans rise as an alien institution, conspiratorially aligned with foreign powers. If this increased the bank's political comfort, it also reduced its influence. Foreign governments with better entrée in Washington had less need of a Wall Street agent to conduct their diplomacy.

During the early summer of 1947, the Truman administration was in a quandary over whether to include the Soviets in the Marshall Plan. George F. Kennan wanted to invite the Soviets to participate because he assumed they would spurn the offer and get blamed for partitioning Europe. Lovett wasn't convinced and received permission from Truman to sound out Leffingwell at 23 Wall. According to his son-in-law, after pondering whether to invite the Soviets, Leffingwell told Lovett, "Bob, the answer is very simple. If you don't ask Soviet Russia, there will be hell to pay. If you do ask them, they'll tell *you* to go to hell."[10] Leffingwell managed to convince Lovett where Kennan had failed. As Kennan and Leffingwell predicted, the Soviets later rebuffed the overture.

In the late 1940s, it looked as if Morgan political influence would be limited to such sophisticated advisory roles. As an investment bank before Glass-Steagall, it had floated many government bond issues. As a commercial bank lending its own money, it strained just to eke out postwar loans to England and France. When J. P. Morgan and Company and Chase co-managed two French loans totalling $225 million in 1950, they nearly exhausted Morgan resources. Leffingwell wanted to aid France despite his rather harsh view of de Gaulle: "There is no place in modern France for the general on horseback. De Gaulle can be and is I think a disturbing influence. . . . He has never shown statesmanship, judgment or common sense. In a way it was the very lack of these qualities which made him a great war leader of the resistance."[11]

The capital-short House of Morgan had to neglect many former foreign clients and was powerless to help devastated Japan. Clinging to a dated view of England and America as coequal partners, Leffingwell couldn't fathom Britain's demotion to a second-class power. In 1947, he wrote his friend T. J. Carlyle Gifford of the British Treasury, "However bungling we may think the governments of the West, it is plain that there can be no hope for democracy and a world of free men except that England be restored and aided to take her place again in the world."[12] To his friend Lady Layton he said, "Nothing matters as much as the British empire and the United States of America and their collaboration."[13] Britain's diminished place in world affairs would lessen the value of Morgan ties to the British Treasury and the Bank of England. Unlike the 1920s, after World War II the United States no longer deferred to Britain's financial leadership. When John Maynard Keynes proposed that the World Bank and the International Monetary Fund be based in London or New York, the United States, in a symbolic act, placed its Bretton Woods wards a short walk from the White House.

For Leffingwell, the touchstone of any policy was how it would affect both America and Britain. Like others at Morgans, he was violently anti-Zionist, imagining that agitation for a Jewish homeland would stir up the Moslem world against the British Empire. J. P. Morgan and Company was still a Wasp, homogeneous bank, drawing a large fraction of its people from Ivy League schools and prominent families. Leffingwell championed minority rights but was impatient with minorities who asserted those rights too aggressively. In 1946, his close friend Morris Ernst, a Jewish lawyer active in civil liberties causes, chided Morgans for having no Jewish directors. Leffingwell fairly breathed fire in defense: "Why not be just citizens and Americans and drop all this talk about the rights of Jews. . . . So long as some Jews regard themselves as a racial and religious minority in other people's countries, and agitate for their rights, I fear they will be disliked."[14] After delivering this churlish judgment, Leffingwell ended with a tribute to Ernst's own brilliance. Ernst, in turn, urged Truman to consult Leffingwell as an adviser, assuring the president he wasn't a publicity monger like Tom Lamont.[15]

If there was a bilious quality to Leffingwell's thoughts in later years, it probably came from too many political disappointments. Known around Wall Street as the resident Morgan liberal, he was less of a dreamer than a hard, practical man. And he loved the cut and thrust of debate. He thought the League of Nations was a sad mistake, a cover for taking territory from Germany and Austria. He once told Lamont, "The truth of the matter is that this is a predatory world in which some if not all nations go out to take what they want sooner or later by force."[16] In the early 1950s, he believed the Soviets were hellbent on world domination and cited Berlin, the Balkans, Iran, Yugoslavia, and Korea as examples.[17] He had little use for disarmament and talked unapologetically about the United States serving as the world's policeman. He had seen too many dictators.

While deploring McCarthyism, Leffingwell wanted to root out subversives and argued that schools and governments should have a free hand to fire such persons. Later appointed by Truman to an internal security commission headed by Admiral Chester W. Nimitz, he thought civil liberties should yield priority to national security: "I think employee tenure and civil rights generally have to be subordinated to the rights of the nation to defend itself against Russia, which is the enemy of all civil rights and all the freedoms."[18]

At the start of the Korean War, during the summer of 1950, George Whitney wrote to Truman pledging the bank's support. While the two had had a testy exchange during the Wheeler railroad hearings years before, Truman now recognized the need for national harmony. The president told Whitney rather shamelessly that his letter had "brought back pleasant memories of our meeting so many years ago."[19]

Despite their support for the Korean War, the Morgan officials grew alarmed in the fall of 1950 when South Korean troops reached the Chinese border and General Douglas MacArthur seemed to yearn for a showdown with the Chinese Communists. This brought out an old Morgan bias against China as well as a fear that the United States would save Asia at the expense of Western Europe. Leffingwell warned Truman that the country shouldn't go to war "with those miserable 400 million Chinamen. They have been the victims of their own war lords, and of their own misgovernment, and of their Japanese conquerors, and now of their Communist conquerors. We have no mission to kill Chinamen; and to get involved with them will leave us defenseless at home and in Europe."[20] Truman agreed. In April 1951, he relieved MacArthur of his duties after the latter urged the United States to emphasize Asia instead of Europe and take the war to the Chinese mainland.

The House of Morgan shared Truman's cold war liberalism yet differed with him on economics, where the president reverted to his earlier cynicism about Wall Street. This became clear when Leffingwell met with Truman at the White House in early 1951 to make a plea for market-based interest rates. Since early in the Second World War, the Federal Reserve had pegged long-term rates at 2.5 percent, a policy prolonged after the war with Truman's blessing. In the early 1920s,

Truman had been dumbfounded when his government bond dropped in price after Ben Strong raised interest rates. He didn't see this as bad luck but as a sinister betrayal of the bondholder, and it made him disposed to fix interest rates. The Fed was now spending billions of dollars to keep prices high and yields low on Treasury bonds. Along with Allen Sproul of the New York Fed, Leffingwell thought this a waste of money and wanted to return to free market interest rates.

Treasury Secretary John Snyder spied in Sproul and Wall Street a cabal intent on returning to the good old days, when the New York Fed and Morgans dictated monetary policy. Truman was eager to stifle inflation jitters during the Korean War and was irritated by what he saw as the bankers' patent selfishness. He gave Leffingwell a tongue-lashing reminiscent of the earlier New Deal diatribes:

> I appreciate your interest in this matter but it seems to me that an emergency is a very poor time for bankers to try to upset the financial apple cart of the nation. The stability and confidence of the nation are entirely wrapped up in the two hundred and fifty-seven billion dollar debt that is now outstanding. . . . For my part I can't understand why the bankers would want to upset the credit of the nation in the midst of a terrible emergency. It seems to be what they want to do and if I can prevent it they are not going to do it.[21]

There was something strained in Truman's cordiality toward the House of Morgan, and at moments his real but usually carefully guarded feelings would flare up again.

WHEN George Whitney became Morgan chairman in 1950—leaving Russell Leffingwell to hover as a wise man during the decade, firing off position papers—J. P. Morgan and Company was a hothouse bank surpassed in size by ten other New York banks alone. It was compactly squeezed into 23 Wall, with Whitney seated at a rolltop desk at the end of the glass-enclosed room along Broad Street, his white hair well-brushed, his elegance unbending, and his tailoring faultless. As publicity man James Brugger recalled, he was "patrician, reserved, terse in speech and blunt in comment, [his] countenance cool but capable of crinkling with a mischievous grin."[22] The elegance was sometimes belied by a booming voice and a gruff manner.

Whitney was always haunted by his brother's embezzlement scandal and vowed to pay back every penny, even though doing so markedly thinned his own fortune and that of his heirs. "It was emotionally debilitating to him," said his grandson George Whitney Rowe. "The reputational disaster was even harder than the money. It cost him a tremendous amount of money near the end of his earning power, but he made every penny good."[23] He was forced to sign away easy, pretax money of the 1920s. Worried about his grandchildren, he asked John M. Meyer, Jr., a later chairman, to watch out for their interests. In the Morgan tradition of nepotism, several Whitney heirs ended up working at the bank. The Whitneys tried not to treat Richard like a pariah, but the subject was so touchy and explosive that family members came to blows over it. Barred from finance, Richard performed odd jobs—he imported Florida oranges at one point—but was mostly supported by his heiress wife, Gertrude.

Perhaps as a result of his brother's crimes, George Whitney made a fetish of honesty. In 1955, J. P. Morgan and Company and Morgan Stanley teamed up on a General Motors "rights issue"—new shares offered at a discount to existing shareholders. The company wanted to raise $325 million for retooling in order to produce cars with power steering, power brakes, and V-8 engines. Morgan Stanley handled the financial end and J. P. Morgan the clerical end—the typical arrangement of the day. In a massive team effort, Whitney pitched in to deal with crowds. A *New Yorker* reporter recorded a telling vignette of J. P. Morgan's Boston Brahmin as recounted by a broker:

> While [Whitney] was on duty, a lady stockholder came in to exercise her rights for two shares and handed him a stack of bills that supposedly totalled a hundred and fifty dollars. Whitney, it seems, was too polite to count them in her presence, so he just took them, smiled, shook her hand, and gave her a receipt. Well, after she had left, he counted the money and was flabbergasted to find that it came to a hundred and *seventy* dollars. Everybody was in a terrible tizzy until it was discovered that the papers hadn't yet disappeared into the files, so they knew who the stockholder was and could send the overpayment back to her, along with her stock.[24]

The 1950s would expose the extreme damage done to the House of Morgan by Glass-Steagall in a way not clear during the Depression, when nobody needed loans anyway. As an investment bank, J. P. Morgan and Company had towered over its rivals, while as a commercial bank it couldn't match the more plebeian banks that courted retail deposits. Nationally it fluctuated in size somewhere between twentieth and thirtieth. It was hard to believe that this small, genteel, somewhat stuffy bank had been the glowering red-eyed dragon of American finance.

Even in its reduced state, the House of Morgan still fancied itself Wall Street nobility. Employing seven hundred people, it retained the gentlemanly mood of an old Wall Street partnership. It was so tiny that to celebrate staff members who were returning from the service in 1947, the entire staff was able to fit into a dinner dance at the Waldorf-Astoria. George Whitney did the hiring himself, mostly bringing in men with prep-school and Ivy League backgrounds; everybody started in the mail room and rotated upward. Once a year, Whitney would stroll over to Davis, Polk, ask for the year's legal bill, go back to his desk, and write out a check. Morgan style was simple, British and informal. The bank of the fifties would have still been recognizable to partners of the twenties. At 10:30 A.M., the top twenty officers met around a large table to comment on world affairs and swap news, an exchange that continued over free lunches.

The paternalistic Morgans pampered its people. Employees lived in a warm cocoon and received better pay and longer vacations than anyone else on Wall Street. The bank had a plantation atmosphere. Its dining room was staffed by white-gloved black waiters who ladled out soup from beautiful metal tureens. One newcomer nearly protested when a waiter seemed to drop dirty ice cubes into his iced tea. Then he realized that the cubes were *made* from tea, so that they wouldn't dilute the drink. It was that kind of place.

The bank lovingly tended its image, the glamorous *23* on its door. Its phone number was Hanover 5-2323, the license plate on its black company Cadillac G-2323. As banker to old money and high society, it obeyed strict etiquette. When calling, young bankers wore hats, and in the office risked irreparable career damage if they removed their jackets *en route* to the men's room. In this prudish place, the ladies' room of the Trust Department was left unmarked because red-faced bankers couldn't agree on the sign's proper wording. The preferred style was low profile. Clients were never mentioned to outsiders, annual reports contained no pictures, and advertising was strictly forbidden. When one new arrival asked the publicist his job, he was told, "I'm the guy paid to keep the bank out of the press."[25] With client relations still close and raiding the business of competitors taboo, there was no particular need for self-promotion.

Even as the Morgan bank exploited its mystique, a lot of bluffing was going on. "The reputation of doing business only with the biggest of the big, the image of aloofness, could be off-putting to a new generation of entrepreneurs and corporate executives," remarked Jim Brugger, the bank's publicist. "Without enunciating it in so many words, the bank in this period worked to shed some elements of the mythology that clung to it."[26] The Gentleman Banker's Code dictated that clients come to bankers. Yet Morgans could no longer afford such imperial passivity, and Whitney dispatched young "bird dogs" across the country to scout up business. He wanted greater geographic breadth in the client base. Without putting too fine a point on it, the mighty Morgans was begging for new clients, which offended some old-timers. As Longstreet Hinton of the Trust Department later wrote, "A few people within the organization believed that potential customers should take the initiative to do business with the bank and some even had the strange notion that no existing clients would ever even dream of taking their business elsewhere."[27]

An enduring Morgan myth was that the bank required a $1-million balance for personal checking accounts. These rare Morgan checks were cashed on sight anywhere in the world and were good for cultivating executives. At a Bond Club spoof in the 1950s, a vaudeville team satirized the Morgan approach, singing "Our tellers have a million-dollar smile. They only smile at people with a million dollars."[28] This exclusivity could be self-defeating. At one annual meeting, George Whitney created a sensation by denying the $1-million minimum. "WHITNEY EXPLODES 'MORGAN MYTH'" ran the the incredulous *New York Times* headline; "LESS THAN MILLION DEPOSIT TAKEN."[29] But further down in the article, Whitney seemed to waver, saying the bank wasn't "geared physically" to small accounts. He finally left the impression that perhaps there was a $1-million minimum for personal deposits after all.

THIS posturing hid problems at the House of Morgan that would intensify through the decade. They stemmed from the way Wall Street banks financed their operations—especially a practice called compensating balances. In exchange for a loan, companies would leave up to 20 percent of the money behind in interest-free deposits. By paying such tribute, the borrowers preserved the banking relationship and received free services, such as the right to consult the bank economist or have a merger arranged. Compensating balances also guaranteed credit during times of scarcity, an assurance that reflected historic corporate anxiety about maintaining a constant flow of capital. This setup bound Wall Street banks to their customers in an intimate relationship and gave banks free cash to lend at high spreads. It was a wonderful racket. In these fading days of relationship banking, profits seemed almost guaranteed, producing a pleasant but stolid generation of bankers.

In retrospect, it may seem peculiar that companies should have left so much idle money with their banks. But while inflation and interest rates were low, they really sacrificed little. Leffingwell was in the forefront of those arguing for free-market interest rates. The bank knew that the easy days of compensating balances were numbered. Nevertheless, it got a jolt in September 1949, when it found itself the unexpected victim of a sensational crime—a tabloid story that didn't make the financial pages but had a profound impact at the bank.

A French-Canadian jeweler known as J. Albert Guay had an illicit passion for a nineteen-year-old waitress named Marie-Ange. Determined to get rid of his interfering wife, Guay tucked a bomb into her suitcase just before she boarded a Quebec Airways flight. He wanted not only to indulge his illicit ardor but to collect his wife's $10,000 in life insurance as well. Fifty miles northeast of Quebec, the plane exploded, incinerating Quay's wife and twenty-two other passengers. The scheming jeweler collected neither cash nor mistress, but ended up condemned to death by hanging.

Such melodrama seemed worlds away from the sedate J. P. Morgan and Company. Yet the plane victims included E. Tappan Stannard, head of Kennecott Copper. Stannard belonged to Kennecott back when Dwight Morrow helped the Guggenheims to organize it during World War I. In 1942, soon after Morgan's incorporation, he became the first "outside" director on the bank's board. Now Stannard's mystified successor asked his chief financial officer about a $60-million deposit the copper company kept at Morgans. The flustered CFO said the company always kept big balances there. Not schooled in such absurdities, the new president asked, why not leave $10 million and invest the other $50 million? This bright idea shocked 23 Wall: Kennecott was withdrawing 10 percent of the bank, despite the fact that George Whitney was a Kennecott director. (According to other versions of the story, Morgans actually encouraged Kennecott to spread its deposits among several banks for reasons of safety.) The move foreshadowed a central feature of the Casino Age—the death of relationship banking, which had been characterized by exclusive ties that bound major companies to the House of Morgan and other Wall Street banks.

Morgans needed these big cash balances to survive. Under legal lending limits, it couldn't commit more than 10 percent of its working capital to a single customer. (Bank capital was actually smaller than deposits—essentially, what would remain after the bank had paid off all its debts.) This meant it could provide only a piddling $5 million or $6 million to a General Motors, a U.S. Steel, or a General Electric. With directors on these companies' boards, Morgan still had an inside edge, but its shortage of capital threatened to rob it of major business. As Leonard McCollom of Continental Oil (afterward Conoco) told George S. Moore of National City, "J.P. Morgan's not big enough to be an oil bank, but you are, and you should gear up for it."[30] Continental, it may be noted, was formed by a Morgan-arranged merger back in the 1920s, and McCollom was even a J. P. Morgan director. If they had to, companies would bolt traditional bankers and no longer feared antagonizing Wall Street. Their options in the Casino Age were far more diversified than they had been in the old days of captivity.

The House of Morgan wrestled with the unpleasant fact that it was too small to survive as a major financial institution and that only a merger could restore its former power. In 1953, John J. McCloy, the former World Bank president who was now chairman of the Chase Bank, made a merger overture to Whitney. Chase was now a colossus beside Morgans; its vast assets put it third in size nationwide. Yet the House of Morgan believed unquestioningly in its special destiny. When Whitney explored the possible merger with McCloy, he bargained as if J. P. Morgan were the bigger bank. Whitney inquired who would control the merged bank and extracted a surprise concession from McCloy: "I am quite prepared to step aside if, as a result of . . . analysis, it would seem that others should conduct the affairs of this bank."[31] When Whitney pursued this extraordinarily generous offer with his colleagues, he found no jubilation. Rather, he faced intransigent opposition from two sons of famous partners—Henry P. Davison and Tommy S. Lamont—who refused to merge with anyone, let alone Chase. They didn't want to adulterate the purebred Morgan culture. By decade's end, this clannishness would belatedly force the Morgan bank into a lifesaving merger. McCloy, meanwhile, resumed talks with the Bank of the Manhattan and consummated a merger that turned Chase from a wholesale bank into the leading retail bank, Chase Manhattan.

DURING the Truman years, the Morgan bank was still subject to political attacks that echoed the New Deal. It was now accused of the old political crimes without having actually enjoyed committing them. Yet reformers couldn't believe the House of Morgan had been emasculated. In 1950, Representative Emmanuel Celler of New York showed that J. P. Morgan directors sat on the boards of companies whose assets totaled over $25 billion, which he called a "breath-taking figure." Similarly, during a brief brouhaha about Morgan power, U.S. Steel chairman Irving S. Olds reassured an annual meeting with these words: "It happens that a member of J.P. Morgan & Co. is on this board. I say that J.P. Morgan & Co. or no other financial interest or group controls U.S. Steel."[32] The imagery suggested here, borrowed from Money Trust days, now seemed anachronistic. The giant American corporations, multinational in scope, were no longer beholden to a single Wall Street bank.

By the early 1950s, the anti–Wall Street vendetta that had raged for twenty years was petering out, and Morgan executives could again function as political allies. Yet the political involvement was of a different nature. George Whitney and others felt the bank had gotten burned by fooling around in politics. Gun-shy, they shrank from the power-broker role that Tom Lamont had played in the Republican party. Although a lifelong Republican, Whitney had no stomach for public fights and associated politics with public exposure, scandal, and demeaning interrogation. His influence would be more personal than institutional in nature and so discreet as to be invisible to the general public.

Whitney had a close relationship with Dwight D. Eisenhower, which came about almost by chance. Whitney's son Robert had served on Eisenhower's staff during the war and worked in his presidential campaign; he introduced his father to Ike, who lunched with the Whitneys in Old Westbury when he was president of Columbia. In 1951, George Whitney helped bankroll the volunteer group Citizens for Eisenhower, which encouraged Ike Clubs to sprout across America.

When Eisenhower went to Paris in 1951 as the military commander of SHAPE (Supreme Headquarters Allied Powers Europe), he invited Whitney to draft weekly or monthly letters outlining his views on topical issues at home. Whitney obliged with long, opinionated letters that were acerbic in their judgments of most politicians, labor leaders, and businessmen but deferential and affectionate toward Eisenhower. Ike felt at sea on economic and financial issues and welcomed these lectures. "Your letters are one of the brightest things in my office life," he told Whitney.[33]

Whitney's letters reflect a frustration with the contemporary economy that says much about the fallen state of bankers in the new age. By his own admission, his favorite bugbear was organized labor, yet he was no less reluctant to chastise management for caving in to labor's demands. Although he had sat on the General Motors board for twenty-seven years, he took more pot shots at GM president Charles E. Wilson than anybody else. He was especially irate that Wilson had negotiated a cost-of-living allowance with the United Auto Workers, which he thought would foster inflation, even if it might benefit the company. At one point, Whitney mockingly sent Ike a Wilson speech about stopping inflation, pointing out the incongruity between author and subject. The days when the House of Morgan dictated to its industrial clients were over.

Whitney loathed the Truman administration, which he saw as perpetuating the worst New Deal tendencies—a welfare-state mentality that encouraged people to expect support from government, imposition of federal controls over business, and a bias toward fighting unemployment rather than inflation. He thought Truman scapegoated the rich and exploited class divisions. Yet he was no less fearful of the Republican candidacy of Senator Robert Taft of Ohio, whom Lamont had rejected in favor of Wendell Willkie a decade earlier. In late 1951, Ike was still evading any commitment to run for president, citing the nonpartisan requirements of his position at SHAPE. But when Whitney heard that Taft had announced his candidacy in October 1951, he went beyond gentle prodding and made a strong plea for Eisenhower to get into the race: "It is quite clear that the work you are now carrying on would be put in jeopardy if Taft's candidacy succeeded because his strongest backers represent the strongest isolationist movement in this country. . . . I see little comfort in a Republican Administration headed by Taft."[34] Ike's election confirmed the ascendancy of the internationalists in the postwar Republican party.

Only a month after Eisenhower's election, Whitney's pleasure in the victory was cut short. His thirty-six-year-old son, Robert, an assistant VP at the bank in charge of Southwest business and a ruggedly handsome, athletic man, was hit by a car one evening in late December 1952 and was killed instantly. Robert Whitney left behind a wife and four children.

For a man whose early life had suggested easy prosperity, George had led a life full of trouble. Dwight and Mamie Eisenhower sent a handwritten note of condolence: "We can find no words to express the shock and grief we suffer from the news we have just received of Bobby's tragic accident."[35]

In Eisenhower, the Morgan bank had a nearly perfect ally—conservative on economic issues yet opposed to economic nationalism and political isolationism. Not since Hoover had the bank enjoyed such a neat fit. Calling Whitney his Wall Street "listening post," Eisenhower invited him to his White House "stag dinners" for business friends—occasions that produced charges of Ike's being corrupted by rich friends. The president clearly heeded Whitney's advice. In the early 1950s, there was a movement to unfix the price of gold. Some wanted higher, other lower, gold prices. Whitney and Leffingwell convinced Eisenhower to keep the gold price at $35 an ounce, where it had stood since 1934. Ike thought Leffingwell's memo on the gold question the best he had read.

The early Eisenhower years certified that the long-standing Morgan preference for international economic cooperation was firmly entrenched in Washington. The historic split that had so bedeviled Morgans—between rural isolationists, who favored inflation, and eastern-seaboard bankers, who favored hard money and had financial ties to Europe—had become a thing of the past, a topic for history students. American companies were going abroad, farmers were cultivating export markets, and Washington was operating military bases around the world. America no longer seemed so distant from the rest of the world and was explicitly tied to Europe through the Atlantic alliance. The House of Morgan had ceased to be an alien presence in America's political culture.

MAVERICKS

. .
.

IF the Wall Street of the 1950s was a closed, privileged club, the trend-setting firm and social arbiter was Morgan Stanley. It was a remarkably small place, with fewer than twenty partners, a hundred staffers, and a paltry $3 million in capital. Nonetheless, it was the paragon of investment banking and exerted enormous influence. Its one office at 2 Wall Street, with green carpets and white walls, overlooked Trinity Church. In an elevated area called the platform—analogous to the partners' room at Morgan Grenfell—stood a double row of mahogany rolltop desks, exact replicas of those at 23 Wall. Like a twin separated at birth, it showed common ancestry with J. P. Morgan and Company down the block.

Morgan Stanley boasted a matchless list of Fortune 500 clients and had tight handcuffs on many old House of Morgan stalwarts, including General Motors, U.S. Steel, Du Pont, General Electric, and Standard Oil of New Jersey. In the late 1940s, it added Mobil, Shell Oil, Standard Oil of Indiana, Bendix, H. J. Heinz, and numerous others. It represented six of the seven-sister oil companies and pumped out more bonds than any other firm. As confidants of the mighty, Morgan Stanley partners dealt mostly with chief executives and were privy to their secret long-range plans. They monopolized the stock and bond issues of client companies. Nobody tried to steal Morgan Stanley clients, which was considered bad form and fruitless to boot.

A palpable warmth still existed among the Morgan firms, many senior people having worked together at J. P. Morgan and Company or Guaranty Trust in the 1920s and 1930s. They might be divided by the Glass-Steagall wall, but they sent a thick trail of vines snaking over the top. J. P. Morgan and Morgan Stanley encouraged their employees to fraternize and referred business to each other. Each year, they hosted an honorary dinner, assigning ten promising young people in each firm to attend; like doting parents, they pushed the children together. Morgan Stanley shared a cafeteria with J. P. Morgan and Company at 120 Wall Street. Morgan Stanley partners had personal accounts at 23 Wall and were among the few mortals to possess J. P. Morgan home mortgages.

Wherever possible, the two Morgan firms cooperated on business. J. P. Morgan managed Morgan Stanley's pension fund and profit-sharing plan, while Morgan Stanley sponsored J. P. Morgan securities issues. If Morgan Stanley floated a bond, J.P. Morgan paid out the dividends. They were wedded by a special bookkeeping arrangement that dated from the Depression, when Morgan Stanley feared cyclical fluctuations in securities work and wanted to keep overhead low. Morgan Stanley had no clerical or back-office staff, and the "closing" on bond issues— the physical exchange of checks and securities—still took place at 23 Wall. At this point, however, the fraternal Morgan relationship was highly unequal. Morgan Stanley was now the uncontested leader in investment banking, while J. P. Morgan was a shabby genteel aristocrat in commercial banking, backed by a great deal of tradition, but without comparable contemporary power. As partners in their firm, Morgan Stanley people made far more money than their 23 Wall counterparts. During these community-of-interest days, Morgan Grenfell people also apprenticed at both J. P. Morgan and Morgan Stanley. Despite Glass-Steagall, it was still a happy Morgan family.

Far more than J. P. Morgan and Company, Morgan Stanley shrank from political involvement and never displayed an equivalent sense of either public service or *noblesse oblige.* Harold Stanley was all business, and Harry Morgan shared his father's distaste for politicians. As mostly an issuer of blue-chip bonds, Morgan Stanley seldom dealt with the SEC and had little need to lobby Washington on industry issues. At one point in the 1950s, Eugene Rotberg (later World Bank treasurer) and Fred Moss of the SEC visited Morgan Stanley to study "hot issues"— new stock offerings that soared and gyrated wildly after issue. The SEC visit was unprecedented, even an occasion for mirth at 2 Wall Street. The two SEC men were greeted by a man in livery—a red jacket with white bands across the chest—who escorted them to the platform. At a desk in the middle stood Perry Hall, the funny, fiery managing partner, who introduced himself by saying "My name is Perry Hall—partner, Morgan Stanley, Princeton." Fred Moss retorted, "My name is Fred Moss—SEC, Brooklyn College. Before my name was Moss it was Moscowitz. And before that it was Morgan, but I changed it in 1933."[1] Following an old House of Morgan custom, Morgan Stanley didn't sell, trade, or distribute securities but allocated them to other firms; its partners worked far from the vulgar din of the Stock Exchange and wouldn't stoop to sponsor new companies. It turned out that Morgan Stanley partners didn't know what "hot issues" were.

In the Truman years, there was still a lingering New Deal suspicion of Wall Street which culminated in one last cannonade against the Morgan interests. In October 1947, the Justice Department filed suit against seventeen investment banks and their trade group, the Investment Bankers Association, charging them with conspiracy to monopolize underwriting in violation of antitrust laws. The suit, *U.S. v. Henry S. Morgan et al.*, designated Morgan Stanley the leader of the plot and Harold Stanley its devious mastermind. Now in his sixties, the very proper Stanley—nobody's idea of a conspirator—gruffly dismissed the case as "utter nonsense." He thought the instigator of the suit was Cleveland financier Cyrus Eaton, the head of Otis and Company, who had tried to make a financial comeback after the collapse of his investment trust in the 1929 crash. In a thinly veiled reference to Eaton, Stanley said that "someone, for whatever reasons, has misled the Department of Justice."[2]

Dubbed the Club of Seventeen, these swank gangsters handled 70 percent of Wall Street underwritings. The rich procession of suspects included Kuhn, Loeb; Goldman, Sachs; Lehman Brothers; First Boston; Smith, Barney; Kidder Peabody; Dillon, Read; and Drexel and Company. Such firms as Lazard Frères, Merrill Lynch, and Salomon Brothers (which sympathized with the government's case), weren't yet influential enough to be suspected of gross criminality. Some, however, were secretly heartsick at being excluded from this band of class martyrs. As defense lawyer Arthur Dean of Sullivan and Cromwell said of those snubbed by the government, "It made them feel like second-class citizens."[3]

The suit extended charges raised in the late 1930s by the Temporary National Economic Committee. The chief instigators were vocal Morgan critics who had then advocated competitive bidding for railroads and public utility issues—Cyrus Eaton; maverick railroad man Robert Young, chairman of the Alleghany and C&O railroads, who had ambushed Harold Stanley by demanding competitive bids at a C&O board meeting in 1938; and Harold Stuart of Halsey, Stuart and Company, formerly banker to utility mogul Samuel Insull. Although larger than some Club of Seventeen firms, Halsey, Stuart and Eaton's Otis and

Company were excluded from the suit, confirming suspicions that those firms had provoked it. Toward the end of World War II, Stuart and Eaton held dozens of briefings with the Justice Department. Their efforts got a fillip when Truman became president: Truman, a disciple of Brandeis, favored compulsory bidding for securities to drive a wedge between companies and their customary bankers.

When the Justice Department first lodged its suit, in 1947, some pundits saw an attempt by Truman to resurrect FDR's crusade against the "money changers." If so, Truman quickly lost interest, for there was no longer a public clamor to slay the bankers, who now looked more like dwarfs in giants' robes. The suit came at a time of meager earnings, and the Money Trust had never looked less forbidding. The New Deal had chased the real financial giants—the old House of Morgan, National City, and Chase—out of the securities business. Ten members of the Club of Seventeen couldn't even muster $5 million in capital. If one added up the combined capital of Morgan Stanley and the next seven investment banks, together they were only a third the size of the Chase and National City securities affiliates of 1929. Investment banks were populated by genteel, graying men in their fifties and sixties; younger men still shied away from a stodgy Wall Street that had never fully recuperated from the damage of 1929.

The case was assigned to Judge Harold Medina, who would monopolize it like a stand-up comic working a nightclub audience. With clipped mustache and glasses, bow tie and furrowed brow, the cigar-smoking Medina sat through the interminable trial like a frazzled Groucho Marx, murdering the self-confidence of the prosecution. Appointed to the bench by Truman in 1947, Medina had sacrificed a lucrative law practice. He specialized in real "stinkers," as he called them—long, tough, complex cases. After presiding over a stormy trial of eleven Communist party officials charged with conspiracy to overthrow the government, he won the nickname of the Patient Judge. But his patience flagged during the juryless trial against the Club of Seventeen. As the case dragged on for more than six years, producing a thirty-two-thousand-page transcript, Medina turned it into a comic purgatory, from which he delivered occasional howls of pain.

The trial itself began on November 28, 1950. The government's case was fine sociology but inept prosecution. It mistook a club for a conspiracy and a highly ritualized form of competition for oligopoly. Prosecutors got the externals of investment banking right, showing a white-glove world governed by gentleman's agreements, back scratching, and tacit understandings—the Gentleman Banker's Code. These practices were unquestionably clubby and unfair and worked to exclude outsiders. They just weren't illegal.

The case hinged on something called the triple concept. This said that blue-chip companies possessed "traditional bankers," who retained exclusive rights to manage their issues. When these bankers formed syndicates to float a company's securities, the rules of the game required that they assign the same "historical position" to participating firms—that is, the same allotment as on previous issues. Finally, by the rule of "reciprocity," investment banks would swap places in each other's syndicates. The triple concept captured the collusive form but missed the cutthroat spirit of Wall Street. The rules didn't civilize the sharks but kept them from devouring each other in vicious feeding frenzies. Any firm would happily steal away another's client—*if they could*—but most of the territory was pretty well carved up. Even Morgan Stanley never chased department-store business, which was locked up by Jewish houses.

At first, the government traced the conspiracy to Morgan's $500-million Anglo-French loan of 1915. While this added a little wartime drama, it also introduced a problem: how did the conspiracy survive Glass-Steagall and the breakup of so many banks? To solve this, the government devised the notion of "successor" firms—that is, J. P. Morgan had metamorphosed into Morgan Stanley, Guaranty Trust into Smith, Barney, and so on. Although Harold Stanley dismissed this as "farfetched" and "silly," it had a rough plausibility. Old-timers still called First Boston "First of Boston," which was an echo of its derivation from the First National Bank of Boston. To keep the trial's length manageable, Medina cut off the successor issue. So the government revised the conspiracy to date from Jack Morgan's 1933 statement before Ferdinand Pecora. Why Jack would have broadcast the new conspiracy to a nationwide audience before a hostile investigating committee wasn't clear.

Swamped with thousands of documents, Medina ordered an intricate, custom-made cabinet to manage the flow of paper. To learn more about underwriting, he followed a syndicate put together for a Con Edison issue at Halsey, Stuart's Wall Street office. Yet the trial nearly brought him to a nervous collapse, a strain relieved only by doomsday humor. Bemoaning the suit's slowness, he said, "I guess I was never supposed to have been a judge."[4] At one point, he counted six children born to lawyers during the trial. When a government attorney suggested a recess, his face brightened. "It's wonderful to see that little glimpse of paradise," he said.[5] Coming back from one summer recess, he said bluntly that he "hated to get back to the trial."[6] At another point, the tension became so great that he leaned across the bench and whispered to the opposing lawyers, "How about a ball game?"[7] They recessed to attend a Dodgers-Giants baseball game. When it came to gallows humor, Medina vied with Morgan Stanley's lawyer, Ralph M. Carson of Davis, Polk, who described the proceedings as an "endless sandy waste" and "a Sahara of words."[8]

As a legal duel, the trial was highly uneven—three or four government prosecutors lined up against thirty-five of the highest-priced attorneys in New York. The courtroom crackled with sophisticated repartee. Terrified of losing, Morgan Stanley thought the suit was too important to be left only to lawyers. Young associates dredged up soot-blackened syndicate records from 23 Wall's basement, and Perry Hall proofread the trial transcript daily. The partners only reluctantly opened their files to competitors and spent a lot of time studying other firms' documents. As letters and memos were made public, clients were also examining them in what turned into a great game of rampant voyeurism. Some at Morgan Stanley thought that Con Edison was never again as close to the firm after certain documents were made public.

As managing partner until 1951, Harold Stanley was most directly involved. Unlike the feisty, red-blooded Perry Hall, Stanley was austere and remote and, to young associates, seemed older than God. He was so aloof from everyday affairs that at one syndicate meeting at 2 Wall, he was asked for his name by a young Morgan clerk. When he said, "Harold Stanley," the young man replied, "And the name of your firm?"[9] He was prepped for the trial by two young assistants, Alexander Tomlinson and Sheppard Poor. One day, Poor was waiting for a cab when Stanley appeared on the same corner, and the assistant graciously yielded to the older man. As Poor held the door open for him, Stanley said, "Thank you, Tomlinson."[10] Clerks were indistinguishable. But Stanley's depositions proved a major factor in the trial.

At first, Medina was impressed by the plethora of government documents. Yet in scanning charts of the Club of Seventeen's performance, he noticed that while Morgan Stanley always stood at or near the top, telltale shifts occurred down below. First Boston zoomed up from number-ten underwriter during World War II to second place behind Morgan Stanley by the time of the trial. If the defendants were united by a deep, dark pact, why these striking shifts? Medina was also struck by the fact that no Morgan Stanley letter or memo even vaguely referred to the conspiracy. What sort of conspiracy lasted for decades but left no fingerprints? Without a documented agreement, Medina refused to apply the antitrust provisions of the Sherman Act.

By the time Medina published his landmark 212-page opinion in February 1954, he believed he was chasing a phantom conspiracy constructed from flimsy circumstantial evidence. Where the government saw collusion, Medina saw "a constantly changing panorama of competition among the seventeen defendant firms."[11] He noted that when companies switched bankers, the winning firm gladly accepted the new client—a violation according to the rules of a conspiracy. Firms didn't hustle Morgan Stanley's august clients, he said, because "there was no point in running around, wasting one's time, in a patently futile attempt to get business, where a competitor was on good terms with an issuer and doing a good job."[12]

Medina's opinion was a paean to Morgan Stanley and probably the best advertising the firm ever got. He was amused by its policy of appearing alone atop syndicate mastheads or not at all, which reminded him of Hollywood starlets fussing over their marquee billing. He was enormously impressed with Harold Stanley. He praised Stanley's "absolute integrity" and said Morgan Stanley's entire history would have been different without him. Then he added, "The fact that Stanley denied the existence of any such conspiracy as charged . . . is one of the significant facts of the case."[13] This was a very peculiar statement: Medina was saying that a defendant's mere assertion of his own innocence was somehow proof of that innocence.

The Medina trial would soon seem an almost nostalgic glance at a rapidly fading Wall Street. "Banker domination" wouldn't be the problem of the Casino Age, and even dedicated trustbusters at the Justice Department thought the suit about fifteen years too late. The cozy banker-company ties would finally end, not through judicial ruling or executive fiat but by structural changes in the marketplace. Over the next generation, the entire system that the Justice Department exposed would be rudely torn apart, and the firm most directly threatened would be the one with the most loyal clients to lose—Morgan Stanley.

IN the last stages of a trial conducted by depositions, Judge Medina yearned to question a live witness—someone he could "look in the eye," as he said eagerly. The government obliged with Robert Young, chairman of the Chesapeake and Ohio Railroad and certifiably America's most rabid Morgan-hater. He was the man who smarted after being rebuked by Tom Lamont for his testimony at the Wheeler railroad hearings in the late 1930s. Touted by the press as the Justice Department's "anti-Morgan machine gun," he so ardently supported the suit that Davis, Polk's Ralph Carson suggested it be renamed *Young v. Morgan.* [14] Sounding his favorite theme of Morgan and Kuhn, Loeb domination of the railroads, Young fired broadsides from the witness stand until Medina glared at him. "This is a courtroom and there will be no appealing here to the public over the head of the judge," Medina snapped.[15] He criticized Young's "hell raising propensities" and mocked the notion that any banker could control Robert Young.[16] When Young stepped down from the stand, he extended his hand to Medina, who just gave it a withering look.

A dapper, pint-sized Texan, Young could seem boyish, with his bulbous nose, pink cheeks, and dimples. Then his face would tighten, his blue eyes would blaze, and he would stare with icy fury. His lifelong Morgan obsession bespoke secret envy. He told Medina that as a young man, he felt "in banking all roads led to Rome and to me the Corner was Rome."[17] He rose through the Morgan universe, first as a worker at a Du Pont plant during World War I, then as a General Motors assistant treasurer in the 1920s. Before the 1929 crash, he advised Pierre du Pont to switch from stocks to bonds and won a following as an investment adviser among rich executives. And in 1937, Young and his sidekick, Allen P. Kirby, had bought control of the bankrupt Alleghany empire, still heavily indebted to J. P. Morgan and Guaranty Trust. The House of Morgan always suspected that he espoused competitive bidding to camouflage the fact that, by controlling six railroads, he was a monopolist himself.

Robert Young was a prototypical man of the new age, a publicity monger adept at courting public opinion. In the early 1950s, he seemed to grin from every magazine cover, deriding the sleeping cars he called rolling tenements and blaming "Wall Street banker control" for decaying railroads. In one celebrated ad, he showed a happy hog riding in style in a cross-country cattle car; the caption read, "A HOG CAN CROSS THE U.S. WITHOUT CHANGING TRAINS—BUT YOU CAN'T."[18] He even had a magazine moniker dreamed up by his publicists—the Daring Young Man of Wall Street. This exponent of people's capitalism lived like a mogul, buying a forty-room Tudor mansion in Newport from a Drexel family member. He had a cream-colored Spanish villa in Palm Beach and a sumptuous apartment at Manhattan's Waldorf Towers.

For a man of such ambition, the giant C&O—a dusty, coal-carrying railroad—lacked suitable cachet. Instead, he craved the glamorous New York Central, America's second-biggest railroad, which ran sleek passenger trains, such as the Twentieth Century Limited from Chicago. For a century, it was known as the Vanderbilt road or the Morgan road. It still boasted two authentic Vanderbilts on its board, plus George Whitney and five other Wall Street bankers. For a Texas insurgent like Young, the New York Central epitomized the eastern financial establishment. It was the final inner sanctum that he longed to enter. By 1947, Young, with four hundred thousand shares of the railroad, was its largest stockholder. But feeling threatened, the board refused to grant him more than two seats, and even these were then withheld by the Interstate Commerce Commission on antitrust grounds.

By late 1953, Young and his troops amassed one million shares of New York Central stock, or nearly 20 percent of the total. Ordinarily this would translate into control, but the railroad wouldn't submit gracefully to its fate. In February 1954, its blue-ribbon board met at the University Club and adamantly refused to put Young on the board or make him chairman, as he demanded. It was a pompous, hidebound reaction of people who were clinging to outdated prerogatives. Perhaps to forestall charges of Vanderbilt-Morgan control, one Vanderbilt and George Whitney skipped the critical meeting. A humiliated, vengeful Young launched a proxy battle that would turn into the decade's most bellicose corporate skirmish, prefiguring takeover wars of a generation later. To avoid antitrust problems, he resigned from the C&O board and sold its New York Central stake to a friend, Cleveland financier Cyrus Eaton. Now he could storm the Central.

Though Young mouthed old Money Trust clichés, the financial landscape had changed markedly. Family ownership was a disappearing force in the American economy. Where William Vanderbilt had once inherited 87 percent of the New York Central from Commodore Vanderbilt and hired Pierpont Morgan to disperse the shares, his descendant, Harold Vanderbilt, now owned less than 1 percent of outstanding shares. The "banker-dominated" board held less than 2 percent of all shares. After Glass-Steagall, Morgans, Chase, National City, and the rest couldn't hold large equity stakes in companies, further eroding their influence. So the glue that compressed companies, banks, and rich families into a coherent financial class was coming unstuck. Meanwhile, New York Central stock was dispersed among forty thousand small shareholders, whom Young called Aunt Janes and assiduously courted. However much he railed against the "interests," Young knew that financial power was becoming more pluralistic in the new age. The real threat to the House of Morgan would come, not from Washington, but from new financial powers beyond the control of the old eastern elite. The short Texas raider was a portent of later raiders and mavericks, many from the old populist strongholds of the South and West, who would take pleasure in taunting the Wall Street establishment.

A proxy fight, an attempt to elect a dissident slate of directors, was the favorite takeover device of the 1950s. It stacked the cards in favor of management, which could usually marshal more resources and out-gun the opposition. As a rich outsider, however, Young waged a campaign in the style of a national election, producing a flurry of press releases, newspaper ads, and even direct-mail pleas. The new age would witness many such loud, brassy, vituperative campaigns. Pierpont Morgan and Tom Lamont had waged their corporate struggles behind closed doors, dealing with like-minded bankers. In the New York Central battle, Young forced the sedate clubmen of Wall Street to fight in the open—where they felt naked and profoundly uncomfortable. Both sides spent over $1 million and grew so paranoid that they swept their respective headquarters in search of hidden microphones.

Robert Young did everything that gentlemen bankers thought undig-nified. He appeared on *Meet the Press* and promised to triple the rail-road's profits, evoking a vision of high-speed, futuristic train service. He hired a small army of three hundred vacuum-cleaner salesmen to tele-phone shareholders and even sued directors on the New York Central board, including George Whitney. Despite his own tremendous wealth and railroad empire, he managed to portray himself as a doughty little David combating the Goliath of the New York Central's board.

Although it seemed tangential, Young spent much of the campaign assailing the House of Morgan. He urged companies to renounce their exclusive relations with Morgan Stanley and solicit competitive bids from other bankers. He blurred the identities of J. P. Morgan and Com-pany and Morgan Stanley and lumped them together as the "Morgan crowd." "He assumed that fighting one meant fighting both, plus Guar-anty Trust and other banks," said Clifford H. Ramsdell, then an Allegh-any vice-president.[19] Young revived ancient myths that a single Morgan director on a board could bully the rest, claiming the "real issue" was whether the railroad would "continue to submit to a Morgan non-ownership board with countless conflicting interests."[20] The Brandei-sian rhetoric is less notable than its application by a millionaire corporate raider in the middle of a takeover battle. The New Deal had only wanted to curb Morgan power; Robert Young wished to appropriate it.

There was an element of bear baiting in Young's attacks on the Mor-gan interests. He must have known these proper gentlemen wouldn't emerge from their clubs, roll up their sleeves, and resort to fisticuffs;

they had no tactical repertoire for street fights, which they considered ill-bred and highly offensive. Morgan Stanley lacked any publicity apparatus and so found itself contending in a strange, alien world. "Young was beneath our respect," said Perry Hall. "Why get into a public fight with a person like that?"[21] In an unprecedented move, Morgan Stanley ran a large advertisement attacking Young and denouncing government-stipulated competitive bidding. However strong this seemed to Morgan Stanley partners, it was tame stuff compared with Young's merciless guerrilla warfare.

J. P. Morgan and Company was no less baffled in countering Young. Like Saint Sebastian, it stood still taking the arrows. The bank dispatched an emissary to Allen Kirby and asked whether Young could please stop making such nasty statements in public. "Publicity is the only effective weapon we have and we are going to use it," Kirby replied.[22] In April 1954, the Morgan bank published an open letter from president Henry Clay Alexander denying Morgan control of the New York Central. Alexander noted that the bank couldn't own stock and competed with several other banks on the railroad's board. "You are wrong and I have a deep suspicion you know it," Alexander lectured Young. "You think, no doubt, it is good propaganda in seeking stock-holders' votes . . . we welcome the opportunity to demonstrate once again that the theory of Morgan banker domination is a fantasy and a myth."[23] He called Young a Little Caesar setting up straw men. This was the closest 23 Wall ever came to invective.

Two months later, Young startled Wall Street when he won the proxy battle by more than a million votes. The speculators backed Young, as did the big retail houses, such as Merrill Lynch and Bache, whose margin accounts went for Young. Lifting his hands like a boxing champ—he didn't mind rubbing it in—Young strode into the New York Central headquarters at 230 Park Avenue and sat down beneath a portrait of Commodore Vanderbilt. When the board met in June, no Morgan banker or Vanderbilt sat on it for the first time since the nineteenth century. The Visigoths had sacked the Holy City. Young's board included Lila Acheson Wallace of the *Reader's Digest* and Indianapolis publisher Eugene C. Pulliam—businesspeople from beyond the Wall Street pale. Ever since the 1930s, economists had commented on the separation of management from ownership in the modern corporation. Now a corporate raider had acted on that momentous shift.

On Wall Street, crestfallen financiers wondered why the Morgan houses hadn't mounted a more spirited defense or formed an informal syndicate to keep the road in friendly hands. *Fortune* asked, almost plaintively, "Why did Morgan not use its prestige?"[24] The answer was partly that the Morgan houses were still smarting from the New Deal controversies. As president Henry Alexander said, "We don't try to run other people's business and there have been so many charges in the past that we want to avoid the appearance of doing so."[25] While Young played on old associations, J. P. Morgan power stood at its modern nadir. Young's success had proved, paradoxically, that bankers didn't control the railroads. The lack of a more tenacious banker defense also reflected the decaying fortunes of the roads. Morgan Stanley hadn't handled a major public offering for the New York Central since 1936. There just wasn't that much business at stake.

The Morgan houses had one last sour laugh on Robert Young. Like many hostile raiders, he was ignorant of the true state of his target. And the New York Central was bankrupt. All those slick passenger trains that had dazzled Young were losing money, and freight traffic was being siphoned off by trucks and planes. Young appointed Alfred E. Perlman as the railroad's president, the first Jew to hold that position. When they first examined the Central's books, Young said, "Al, aren't you afraid?" Perlman replied, "No, but we'd better get to work."[26]

During the 1957 recession, the New York Central, battered by heavy losses, opened merger talks with its historic rival, the Pennsylvania Railroad. In January 1958, the Central skipped its dividend payment, which plunged Young into a terrible state of depression. For a long time, he had struggled with deep psychological problems, veering between brisk optimism and deep melancholia. A close friend, Edward Stettinius, Jr., son of the late Morgan partner, had once found him sitting alone in his Newport library, staring absently into space while a gun lay on his desk. Perhaps after so much brave talk, his failure with the New York Central was too shameful for him to face. On January 25, 1958, he went into the billiard room of his Palm Beach mansion, the Towers, picked up a shotgun, and shot himself to death.

THE chummy world of Wall Street bankers and corporate executives that so enraged Robert Young reached its peak in the 1950s and began to slip. In this high noon of industrial power, before the European economies rebounded or the Pacific rim threatened, the United States dominated automobiles, steel, oil, aluminum, and other heavy industries. As investment banker to big smokestack firms, Morgan Stanley was in an enviable position. Like a caretaker of a cache of crown jewels, it didn't need to scout out new wealth. The sole objective was to stand guard over the franchise—the superb client list inherited from the old

House of Morgan. As the firm's William Black later said, "All you needed to do in the 1950s was to execute superbly on client business."[27]

In pleasing clients, a smooth golf swing or a convivial party style was the standard weapon in the investment banker's arsenal. By modern standards, it was a very sociable, leisurely world, with two-hour lunches at the Bond Club still in fashion. The master at entertaining clients was Perry Hall, the managing partner from 1951 to 1961. Where Harold Stanley was gray and austere, Hall was pleasantly brash and garrulous, blessed with a salesman's patter. Freckled and chunky, he had a broad face and penetrating eyes. He terrified subordinates, charmed women, and lorded it over corporate chieftains. He could sell refrigerators to Eskimos. Like André Meyer of Lazard Frères or Sid Weinberg of Goldman, Sachs, he was on a first-name basis with every American CEO. "He would shout at presidents and thump the table and tell them what he thought," said one person who observed him in those years. "His relationship with all those tycoons was unique."

Hall had emerged from an F. Scott Fitzgerald world where Princeton eating clubs and Yale secret societies were the passports to Wall Street success. A 1917 Princeton graduate, he had sat next to Fitzgerald in many classes, due to the alphabetical proximity of their names. (Hall was unimpressed by Fitzgerald's prose and insisted that several forgotten classmates were superior stylists.) For Hall, Ivy League sports provided his all-purpose pantheon of heroes. Whatever his partner's business accomplishments, for example, Harold Stanley remained for him captain of the Yale baseball and hockey teams. Hall hired his own successor, Bob Baldwin, two weeks after watching him play baseball for Princeton. A varsity letter was perhaps the most eloquent letter of introduction at Morgan Stanley.

As the last managing partner from the old House of Morgan, Hall never modified his conviction that FDR was the "worst enemy the U.S. ever had."[28] Hall had worked at the Guaranty Company, survived the 1920 bomb blast, and become a bond manager at J. P. Morgan and Company in 1925. After the 1929 crash, Jack Morgan separately summoned Hall and Charles Dickey. He asked Dickey to become a J. P. Morgan partner and Hall to become a Drexel partner in Philadelphia. Jack, it seems, had bungled his instructions to offer both young men Drexel partnerships. The error deeply wounded Hall and led to a Morgan Stanley tradition of having two people present at important announcements. In 1935, Hall moved over to the new Morgan Stanley, which he liked to regard as his personal creation. He was boastful, but invested his vanity with considerable charm. "We were the *crème de la crème*," Hall remarked. "Everybody was jealous of us."[29]

Hall was perfectly suited to the relationship banking of the 1950s. He would entertain clients while shooting wild turkeys in South Carolina or fishing near his house in Woods Hole, Massachusetts. (At age seventy-three, he was still powerful enough to harpoon a 552-pound swordfish.) An amateur golf and tennis champ, he attracted corporate executives who wanted to test their game. Hall would perform elite missions for clients and behaved like a member of their family. When a General Motors chairman was upset by his daughter's plans to marry a Pakistani, Uncle Perry went to reason with the young woman. He asked whether her children would get into the right schools, have the right friends, and so on. She was persuaded. Such services made General Motors an untouchable Morgan Stanley client in the 1950s.

Hall admired Tom Lamont and his prankish spirit. Once, at an all-night party on Gramercy Park, Hall got separated from his wife. Wandering about, he came upon Marlene Dietrich and Salvador Dali in a doorway. Hall told the actress that he had idolized her ever since *The Blue Angel.* His wife, Alice, then appeared, and Hall pretended not to know her. "Hey, blondie," he called to her. "Wanna try this bed?" Alice sat down, pretended to test the bed. "This feels pretty good," she replied. Later Dietrich cornered Hall. "Did you know that woman?" "I never saw her before in my life," Hall replied. "You're the freshest man I ever met," said Dietrich and stormed off. Hall treasured this anecdote more than he did the biggest General Motors or U.S. Steel underwriting.

Morgan Stanley people were extremely bright—like the old House of Morgan, the firm rewarded intelligence—but investment banking didn't require an enormous amount of financial ingenuity. Inflation was low, currencies were stable, and the securities business was relatively straightforward—if you had the right clients. Underwriting spreads were fat in industrial issues. Right off the bat, Hall told his young recruits from Princeton and the other Ivy League schools to coddle their clients and study their needs. "I'm interested in the man who can bring the business in," he said. "Leave the rest to the business school students. Once you do the deal, put on your hat and go home."[30] With securities issues pretty standardized, companies had little incentive to shop around among investment banks; the astrophysicists had not yet arrived on Wall Street. That Morgan Stanley offered an extra, indefinable mystique was all the inducement most clients needed to remain loyal.

After the New Deal, it was vital to prepare a good securities prospectus and comply with the new legislation. Investment bankers had to exercise "due diligence" and testify to the accuracy of offering documents. Wall Street feared the legal liability that came with the securities laws. Here the firm's secret weapon was the profane, irreverent Allen Northey Jones, who had headed the J. P. Morgan bond department. A Trinity College alumnus, Jones enjoyed tweaking his partners and would grouse within earshot of Hall about "those goddamn stupid Princeton bastards."[31] Son of an impoverished Episcopal minister, bald, and moon-faced with bulging eyes, Jones would chug around the office in red suspenders, smoking a pipe.

He enjoyed shocking people. Once, when the partners were interviewing a new recruit, he bellowed at the nervous young man, "Are you spoiled?" When the interviewee said he had been lucky in life and was indeed spoiled, Jones jumped up, barked "Hire him and send him to me," and walked out.[32] In new recruits, he inculcated a meticulous attention to detail. He would dump a thick prospectus in a rookie's lap and tell him there was a single error and the young man had until the next morning to find it. He wanted Morgan Stanley to produce the best prospectuses, and corporations counted on the firm to shield them from legal problems. This led to such manic perfectionism at Morgan Stanley that Harvard MBAs proofread every SEC submission. If the old Wall Street was a restricted club, it had the luxury of exercising extreme care in the kind of business it did.

Northey Jones trained a generation of Morgan Stanley partners. If a trainee wished to learn railroad finance, Jones would sit with him late at night, poring over maps of a railroad's tracks and unlocking the company's secret business strategies. His dedication was total, almost monastic. A perennial bachelor, he glanced at his watch one Saturday and sprang to his feet. "I've got an appointment in half an hour," he said. The appointment was for his wedding. Jones did as much as anyone to ensure Morgan Stanley's reputation for excellence.

The influence of Harry S. Morgan, Jack's younger son, was more elusive. He probably stayed at Morgan Stanley out of a sense of family duty and actually spent more time yachting than issuing securities. He worked beneath a framed certificate of U.S. Steel shares from Pierpont's 1901 issue. Harry had a classic Morgan resume—commodore of the New York Yacht Club, trustee of the Metropolitan Museum of Art, General Electric director, Harvard overseer. His North Shore estate at Eaton's Neck, near Huntington, included a manor house, cottages for butler, chauffeur, and gardener, a swimming pool, and an eight-car garage.

Sometimes crusty, he was also kindly and gentlemanly and fairly popular at the firm—with reservations.

Like his father, Harry was wary of the public and obsessively private. In the 1960s, Princeton made a pitch to house the Morgan papers and sent several distinguished scholars to lobby him over lunch. When they had finished their presentation, Harry startled them by saying, "I'm sorry to tell you gentlemen, there *are* no Morgan papers." Faces dropped. Arthur Link, a noted Woodrow Wilson scholar, stammered, "But there *must* be Morgan papers." Harry said his father had warned him to scatter or destroy any papers, lest the government get hold of them and again harass the Morgan family as Pujo and Pecora had. In fact, there were papers, a rich collection, which Harry eventually left with the Pierpont Morgan Library.

Perry Hall was somewhat disdainful of Harry Morgan, whom he felt occasionally got in the way. "The other partners were jealous and annoyed at the continued presence of an older man who contributed nothing in their view but yet held the reins in his hand," said someone close to the firm. "This got more and more true as time went on." In 1956, there was a bruising fight over whether Harry's son Charles F. Morgan would be made a partner. Harry had retained legal title to the Morgan name, which he threatened to withdraw unless his son were brought into the firm. To other partners, it seemed that Charlie was a pleasant fellow with little interest in, or special aptitude for, banking. After some testy exchanges, Harry traded his rights to the Morgan name for Charlie's partnership.

Charlie Morgan would be the only partner in Wall Street history to serve primarily as office manager—he often sat behind heaps of construction blueprints. Years later, when a new partner arrived for his first day, he was told that the man down on his knees fixing his doorknob with a screwdriver was his new partner Charlie Morgan. "If ever two people, father and son, were miscast in life, it was Harry and Charlie Morgan," sighed an ex-partner. When Morgan Stanley moved uptown to the Exxon Building, Charlie supervised the installation of the new telephone system.

After the Charlie Morgan feud, so much residual anger remained that when Harry's younger son, John, was proposed as a partner, an antinepotism rule was invoked. (The rule was passed after one partner, the son-in-law of a prominent partner, proved to be an alcoholic.) Morgan Stanley now rebelled against the Morgans. Thus John Adams Morgan, who even bore his great-grandfather's bulbous nose, was blackballed. "Harry Morgan was told, 'You've got Charlie, that's enough,'" said an ex-partner. The irony was that John A. Morgan proved the son most interested in finance and later headed the corporate finance departments at both Dominick and Dominick and Smith, Barney.

In his time, Harry Morgan tried to set the tone and uphold standards at Morgan Stanley. Following family tradition, he gave everyone in the firm a bonus on his twenty-fifth anniversary there, in 1960. "Harry stood for the gentlemanly, principled way of doing business that we felt in those days Morgan Stanley and J. P. Morgan epitomized," said a former Morgan Stanley partner, Sheppard Poor. At the annual partners' dinner at the Union Club, he would say, "Gentlemen, the hardest ship to sail is a partnership."[33] In an often greedy business, he presented himself as "brakeman on the Morgan Stanley express train." Harry prevented the place from degenerating into a haven of the Social Register and perpetuated the Morgan tradition of taking smart, ambitious people from modest backgrounds and turning them into aristocrats. He would say, "We recruit and hire in accord with Morgan tradition—which is to hire people who are brighter than the partners." Each year, he visited the Harvard Business School and spoke with finance professors about their most promising pupils; he would often conduct initial job interviews himself. Because Harry Morgan also lent money to young people to become partners, he had more than his nominal $2 million in the firm, giving him veto power.

Though the world's prestige investment bank, Morgan Stanley seldom appeared in the press. It didn't promote itself and conscientiously avoided publicity. "It was like a doctor not advertising," said Perry Hall. To advertise would be "kind of cheap."[34] Investment bankers subordinated themselves to clients and tried to keep their profiles low. There was a huge internal row about whether to put the partners' pictures into a promotional booklet—an agony resolved in the affirmative after GM chairman Fred Donner said they were all so ugly they would probably scare clients off anyhow. This aversion to publicity was related to the restrained style of competition: if you couldn't raid other firms' clients, why bother to advertise? Morgan Stanley's goal was to freeze the status quo.

Morgan Stanley did have one form of advertising, however—the tombstone ads listing the members of underwriting syndicates. All Morgan-sponsored issues were printed in Ronaldson Slope typeface. Sometimes, when traveling, Morgan people stuffed Ronaldson Slope type into their pockets, in case local printers lacked the numerical fractions. Prospectuses were always done in royal-blue type. The great Morgan Stanley hobbyhorse was that its name stand alone atop tombstone ads and that the firm single-handedly manage issues. This enabled it to price issues and allocate shares among participating firms; it also didn't have to split lucrative management fees with a co-manager. On the rare occasions when Morgan Stanley deigned to join somebody else's syndicate, it asked that its name be omitted. By managing the huge industrial syndicates, Morgan Stanley shaped the Wall Street pyramid and decreed the relative standing of firms. This produced a self-assurance that partners would describe as pride but competitors would see as arrogance.

As the Justice Department noted in the Medina suit, syndicate rankings seldom changed for a particular company. If Morgan Stanley expelled a firm from a syndicate, the firm might not regain admittance for a long time. Risks were widely distributed in the 1950s, so firms didn't need much capital. On big industrial issues, Morgan Stanley might enlist three hundred underwriters and eight hundred dealers, endowing itself with godlike powers. The firm had virtually nothing to do with selling securities and was strictly a wholesale outfit. It had a clerk on hand to sell unsold syndicate shares around the Street, usually at a loss. This was as close as it ventured into the world of trading.

Nobody could afford to alienate Morgan Stanley, which presided over most of the decade's record issues, such as the General Motors $300-million debt issue of 1953 and its $328-million stock issue of 1957, the $231-million IBM stock offering of 1957, and the $300-million U.S. Steel debt issue of 1958. These securities didn't finance speculation or line the pockets of a self-serving management. They went for new V-8 auto engines or a steel plant on the Delaware River or IBM's expansion into the computer business. At this point, investment banking still functioned according to a textbook model in which capital was tapped for investment, not financial manipulation. Investment bankers were still intermediaries between providers and users of capital, and they considered it unprofessional to function as the "principal" in a transaction. The age of financial engineering hadn't yet dawned.

Morgan Stanley's monopoly of so much of America's industry made the firm far less adventurous than J. P. Morgan and Company in exploring foreign markets. In the early postwar years, its few foreign financings had a distinctly Anglo-Saxon or European bias. It sponsored large issues for Australia and Canada, smaller ones for France and Italy. During the 1950s, Morgan Stanley made only one exception to its sole-manager policy, and that was for the World Bank, where it co-managed issues with First Boston. The names of the two firms alternated in the top-left corner of the prospectuses. Through the World Bank, Morgan Stanley

partners believed that they made their contribution to European reconstruction and the Atlantic alliance.

In the early days, the World Bank was a highly conservative institution. The International Monetary Fund, however—and contrary to its
later image—was then feared as a hotbed of left-wing activism. Russell
Leffingwell derided it as a "dream child" that would prop up overvalued
currencies, and the American Bankers Association lobbied vigorously
against its creation. But the World Bank seemed a pillar of sound finance
and was congenial to Morgan Stanley. Because the bank depended on
U.S. capital markets for money, early World Bank presidents were chosen from Wall Street. In 1949, Eugene Black, formerly a senior vice-
president at Chase, replaced John J. McCloy as president. After a brief
experiment with competitive bidding, Black (whose son Bill was later
a Morgan Stanley executive) chose Morgan Stanley and First Boston as
a permanent team to market the Bank's triple-A-rated issues in 1952.
Black later explained his choice: "Morgan Stanley has a close connection with Morgan Grenfell in London, and with the old firm of Morgan
in Paris. They had a very fine reputation in Europe."[35]

In selling the World Bank to investors, Morgan Stanley and First
Boston faced a formidable job. Its very name—the International Bank
for Reconstruction and Development—was a mouthful. There were
fears—noted earlier—that it might repeat the foreign lending disasters
of the 1920s. To promote the bank, Morgan Stanley and First Boston
organized huge syndicates of up to 175 underwriters, put on road shows,
published booklets, and even seconded people for brief stints at the
bank. Morgan Stanley got a critical guarantee that World Bank bonds
were backed by America's capital contribution and were therefore as
good as obligations of the U.S. Treasury itself. Morgan Stanley partners
always took immense pride in the World Bank account, which marked
the summit of the firm's success: they were banker to the world's bank,
a big enough honor to satisfy even the most swollen Morgan ego.

I N the 1950s, the City of London hadn't yet awakened from its Depression slumber. It was stuffy, inbred, and unimaginative, feeding off past
glory. England had lost a quarter of its national wealth in defeating
Germany and couldn't function as a world banker. It had lost Italy to
the Marshall Plan and China and Eastern Europe to the Communists. Its
old foreign clients were fair game to be picked off by Wall Street firms:
in 1946, Dudley Schoales of Morgan Stanley snared the first postwar
loan to Australia—already a J. P. Morgan client in the 1920s—and the
firm sponsored Qantas Airlines two years later.

The City was hobbled by exchange controls and a weak pound. Under the postwar Anglo-American Loan Agreement, the United States lent Britain $3.75 billion to cover its payments deficit. In exchange, Britain was supposed to make sterling convertible to other currencies by July 15, 1947. The attempt failed abysmally as investors rushed to dump pounds for dollars. Speaking at the Lord Mayor's Dinner in October 1947, Lord Catto, governor of the Bank of England, ruefully reviewed this blow to British pride: "Confidence was returning; sterling balances were being more and more freely held in London as in the days before the war. . . . At any rate, we were obliged to try."[36] The sterling market was largely shut to foreigners until Margaret Thatcher dismantled exchange controls in 1979. In its century-long contest with the City, Wall Street had won hands down.

Like most places of obsolete splendor, the City was full of charming eccentricities. At one merchant bank, incoming mail was laid on a table each morning so partners could scan each other's correspondence. At N. M. Rothschild's townhouse, partners shook little bells marked "butler" when they sought refreshment. At the manorial Hambros, senior people were called Mr. Olaf or Mr. Charles. Self-respecting merchant bankers still wore bowler hats and carried furled umbrellas; their reading glasses were always crescent-shaped. Junior men wore stiff collars and were considered dangerously uppity if they let them soften. In this conformist world, when a Lloyds Bank chairman appeared in black suede shoes, people buzzed for days about the frightful lapse in taste.

With slightly over one hundred employees, Morgan Grenfell emerged from the war in relatively strong shape. In U.S. banking terminology, it was a cross between a commercial and an investment bank, underwriting bond issues but also managing pension funds and making loans. Like Morgan Stanley, it seemed to have a monopoly on major industrial accounts. In 1945, it sponsored the first postwar share issue and floated debt for virtually every British electric company, including Associated Electrical Industries and British General Electric. It also handled denationalization of steel companies—the legacy of Teddy Grenfell's work with Monty Norman to rationalize the industry in the 1930s—and participated in World Bank issues. But the firm was softened by prewar success. The partners (technically directors) had a lazy, custodial attitude toward accounts and wouldn't dig up new business or stir from their chairs. When they disappeared to Boodle's or Brooks's for lunch, they might return—or they might call it a day. Rod Lindsay, a later Morgan Guaranty president who apprenticed at Morgan Grenfell, recalled the somnolent mood: "By Thursday afternoon at four, one of the senior partners would come across to the juniors and say, 'Why are we all still here? It's almost the weekend.' "[37]

J. P. Morgan and Company still held a passive, one-third share in Morgan Grenfell. It was the only foreign bank with a sizable stake in a merchant bank on the elite Accepting Houses Committee. Lacking a London office, J. P. Morgan and Company used the firm as its U.K. branch equivalent, and the two houses traded apprentices and clients. When Esso mapped out big postwar expansion plans for refineries in Western Europe, 23 Wall Street steered the company to Morgan Grenfell. Ditto for Procter and Gamble, Monsanto, Inco, Alcan, and General Foods. After stepping down as Bank of England governor in 1949, Tom Catto took a desk back at Morgan Grenfell (though he didn't resume his partnership) and extended the special access of both J. P. Morgan and Morgan Grenfell to the Bank of England.

Morgan Grenfell was so heavy with peers that it was derided as the House of Lords (in sometimes sniggering tones) by its J. P. Morgan counterparts. In a caste system common in the City, partners were drawn largely from family members, with only Sir George Erskine, a brilliant, driving Scots banker, rising from the managerial ranks to become a partner. (By no coincidence, he was the best banker.) The aging Lord Bicester—Vivian Hugh Smith—reigned, somewhat terrifyingly, as senior partner, and his authority was unquestioned until his death, in 1956. He treated other partners like errand boys as they rushed in and out to get his approval. Everybody called him the Old Man. He was a sphinx who kept his own counsel and never tipped his hand. During eighteen years in the House of Lords, he never delivered a speech. Once, on a deadlocked charity board, he was asked whether he favored a proposed measure. "No," he said, then added, "Or have I said too much?"[38] To be interviewed for a job by Bicester was to endure an array of skeptical snorts, grunts, and harrumphs.

Even when he was in his late seventies, Vivian Smith wouldn't pass the reins to his son, Rufus, who had patrolled on the roof of 23 Great Winchester Street during the wartime buzz-bomb raids. Rufie was relegated to a sad Prince of Wales role. A portly man with a jolly well-fed look, round-faced and mustachioed, he acted the grandee: he was the sort of large, stately man who would rap on doors with the knob of his cane. He loved steeplechase horses and hunting and tossed off whiskey by the tumblerful. Like his father, he had connections everywhere. He served as a director of Shell, Vickers, and AEI and also sat on the Court of the Bank of England. His wife, Lady Helen, was a daughter of the earl of Rosebery.

Rufie was cowed by the thunderous presence of the Old Man and patiently suffered a marathon apprenticeship lasting well into late middle age. In the late 1940s, Sir Edward Peacock, the senior partner of Barings, told Russell Leffingwell how the Old Man was pleased that Rufie had taken the lead in a Shell financing and proven himself as a good, sound fellow.[39] Yet Rufie had already been through two world wars! In 1949, Lord Bicester relented and let his son take part in a major steel business. "Oh well, the boy's got to learn sometime," he sighed.[40] The boy was then fifty-one and had been a partner for almost twenty years.

In the City of the 1950s, with most business revolving around relationships, Morgan Grenfell was hard to match. It was the City's major portfolio manager for the Vatican, thanks partly to the flamboyant, multilingual Francis Rodd (the second Baron Rennell), son of a former ambassador to Italy. A portly, snuff-taking man who blew his nose into a big red handkerchief, Rodd was a protégé of Monty Norman's and a former British manager of the Bank for International Settlements in Basel. As a close friend of T. E. Lawrence (Lawrence of Arabia), he was once asked by Monty Norman to recruit Lawrence as secretary of the Bank of England. (Lawrence declined.) Rodd himself was spirited away to Morgan Grenfell by his father-in-law, Vivian Smith, in 1933.

Assigned to Harold Macmillan's wartime staff in 1943, Rodd was made chief civilian aide to Sir Harold Alexander, who administered occupied territory in Italy. Left-wing commentators criticized the choice, noting that Morgan loans had propped up Italian fascism and warning that Rodd might help to give former fascist finance officials a voice in postwar Italy. Nevertheless, Rodd acted ably to alleviate hunger and sickness in liberated Naples. Macmillan thought Rodd a *prima donna* and an intriguer but also praised him as "quick, intelligent and persistent."[41] So long as Rodd was around, the Vatican business stayed in Morgan Grenfell's hands.

The chief partner for portfolio management was Wilfred William Hill Hill-Wood, who provided Morgan Grenfell with entrée to Buckingham Palace. A shrewd, entertaining fellow and a brilliant cricketer, Hill-Wood had served as intermediary between Morgan Grenfell and 23 Wall. Like Jack Morgan, he was a close friend of George VI. "Uncle Willy became friends with George VI at Trinity College, Cambridge, and the king asked him to look after some of his personal finances," said his nephew Sir David Basil Hill-Wood.[42] Hill-Wood reported regularly to the king on his finances, keeping details of the account to himself. His friendship with George VI guaranteed that when Elizabeth became queen in the early 1950s, Morgan Grenfell would manage a significant portion of her wealth as well. The queen was amused by Willy and apparently on easy terms with him. When she knighted him at Buckingham Palace, she took the sword from behind the curtain, tapped him, and then whispered slyly, "You can get up now, Willie."[43]

Rich in memorabilia, Morgan Grenfell's atmosphere in the 1950s was antiquated. Partners sipped sherry by coal fires while young clerks on tall stools copied accounts into large bound books. These victims of the "fagging system" didn't emerge into adulthood until about age forty, by which point many were thought brain dead. Sexual segregation at Morgan Grenfell was strict. To mask their sexuality "tea ladies" were required to wear linen dusters around the office and leave their jobs when they married. Nomenclature was highly revealing: the firm called itself a countinghouse and directors were partners; it was listed under "merchants" in the London telephone directory.

The thunderclap that roused the City from this profound torpor was Siegmund Warburg's first hostile raid in the famous aluminium war of 1958–59. To understand the furor, it is necessary to note the City's cultural homogeneity. It was a hermetic world of men who had passed through Eton and Oxford, Cambridge, or the Guards and met at Lord's or Wimbledon on weekends. Shot through with class barriers, the City made upward mobility all but impossible for foreigners. From an eminent Hamburg banking family, Siegmund Warburg had fled Hitler in the 1930s and started a merchant bank in 1946. As a Sephardic Jew with a German name and a German accent, bored by shooting and yachting, he seemed to grate on City bankers. One merchant banker admitted, "Siegmund's Jewishness was a problem. He was a little *too* Jewish, as they say in the City."

Warburg was an unlikely revolutionary who followed all the old merchant-banking folkways. He posted no nameplate, opened no branch offices, and valued personal contacts. But he was always an activist, an innovator, and he would quote Dwight Morrow, whom he had met as a young man in the 1920s. "The world is divided into people who do things and people who get the credit. Try if you can to belong to the first class; there is far less competition."[44] In his Belgravia apartment were books in six languages, and he said he would rather hire someone steeped in George Eliot than someone steeped in banking. His use of handwriting analysis for recruiting employees added to his eccentric image.

While Morgan Grenfell floated through long, pleasant lunches, Warburg ran a firm disciplined in Prussian punctuality. Some Warburg people sat through two lunches—one at 12:30, one at 1:30—to maximize the business they conducted. Young recruits arrived early, stayed late, and worked weekends, while young Morgan Grenfell men were out shooting blizzards of birds from the sky. Warburgs, significantly, was the first firm to scrap the bowler-hat-and-umbrella costume in favor of modern dress.

With a cool outsider's perspicacity, Siegmund Warburg saw that the City disliked unpleasantness and would tolerate mediocrity just to avoid a row. This wasn't surprising, with so many family-run banks and such extensive intermarriage in the City. Warburg also saw that merchant banks no longer had the capital to finance industry or government on a large scale. In the advisory area, by contrast, small capital was no handicap. "In the sense that bankers provide money for industry, they're becoming less important," he said; "but in the sense of being consultants—what I call 'financial engineers'—they're becoming much more important."[45] This was the critical insight of the Casino Age, the idea that would push merchant bankers from the staid world of securities issues into the piratical world of takeovers. The merchant bankers would no longer hand out free merger advice to preserve underwriting relationships. Before Siegmund Warburg was through, the "stuffy" City would be rife with marauders.

In 1958, Warburg mounted the first major hostile takeover in postwar Britain. Takeovers had existed there for decades—they had formed Imperial Chemical Industries, Unilever, Shell, and the big deposit banks. As early as 1925, Morgan Grenfell had negotiated General Motors' investment in Vauxhall Motors. But these were genteel affairs, consummated over sherry. By mid-1958, Warburg had persuaded Reynolds Metal of Virginia to launch a hostile bid for British Aluminium. To give the move a British veneer, Reynolds allied itself with Tube Investments, a Midlands engineering group. Moving stealthily, Warburgs had bought more than 10 percent of British Aluminium by October 1958. Siegmund Warburg would shift the City battleground from contacts to capital and introduce an unsettling new form of democracy.

When British Aluminium learned of Warburg's scheme, management summoned Olaf Hambro and Lord Kindersley of Lazard Brothers. (Lazards was close to Morgan Grenfell in the 1950s, with the two firms even sharing a box at Covent Garden.) In comparison with the upstart raiders, British Aluminium had a true-blue patriotic image. The managing director, Geoffrey Cunliffe, was a son of the World War I Bank of England governor. Its chairman was the bemedaled Lord Portal of Hungerford, a wartime hero as chief of air staff and a president of the

Marylebone Cricket Club. Although the firm was already negotiating a partnership deal with the American colossus Alcoa, the Hambro-Lazard defense rested on a bogus threat to national sovereignty. "One day, a party consisting of Olaf Hambro and other senior figures paid a state visit to the partners' room at Morgan Grenfell," recalled Tim Collins, a later Morgan Grenfell chairman. "They said, 'This is a patriotic duty and the City is going to collapse otherwise.' The Morgan Grenfell partners joined in without a fight."[46]

In November, Sir Ivan Stedeford, the self-made chairman of Tube Investments, presented a proposal to Lord Portal by which Tube and Reynolds would buy a majority stake in British Aluminium for a generous 78 shillings per share. Lord Portal curtly refused, made veiled references to talks in progress, and brazenly withheld Stedeford's plans from shareholders. Later he issued the following mystifying statement: "Those familiar with negotiations between great companies will realize that such a course would have been impracticable."[47] Although its defense was predicated on scare talk about a Yankee invasion—Tube was dismissed as Reynolds's "window dressing"—British Aluminium continued talks with its "white knight," Alcoa. Within a week, it negotiated a deal that allowed Alcoa to buy one-third of the company at a miserly 60 shillings a share. The institutional investors—the new powers of the age—were inflamed by this wanton disregard for shareholders. And they became a key constituency in Warburg's camp.

In the popular mind, it was still axiomatic that nobody could prevail against the unified power of the merchant banks. Schroders and Helbert Wagg sided with Warburgs. Otherwise, the City closed ranks behind British Aluminium in a seemingly invincible phalanx, including Hambros, Lazards, Morgan Grenfell, Flemings, Samuel Montagu, and Brown Shipley. From an *aide-mémoire* prepared by Hambros and Lazards, it's clear that Warburg's ungentlemanly method upset the group far more than the noisily trumpeted demerits of the Reynolds-Tube proposal. This internal document conceded the offer's soundness, only inveighing against its irresponsible manner. It was clear that Warburg himself, not some alleged American invasion, was the real issue. The City establishment thought he had failed to play by accepted rules. Members of the establishment either had to join forces to defeat him, or he would wreck British industry.[48]

The next day, these City men, who ordinarily negotiated unseen in their clubs, published the first defensive advertisement that had ever been used in a hostile takeover. The game was no longer being played in their preferred cloakroom style. In late December 1958, fourteen City institutions created a war chest of £7 million, with Morgan Grenfell chipping in £500,000. Where Lord Portal had been prepared to sell his company for 60 shillings a share, the City consortium now made a partial bid for British Aluminium at 82 shillings a share. This not only topped the Tube-Reynolds offer by 4 shillings but indirectly exposed the cheapness of the earlier deal.

Awed by this strength, the London *Times* referred to "an array of City institutions on a scale never before seen in a take-over battle."[49] The *Daily Express* likewise trembled before the heroic show of firepower: "Lined up on the City side supporting British Aluminium are such famed financiers as Lords Bicester, Harcourt, Rennell, Astor, Glenconner, Kindersley, Cowdray, Poole, and Brand. . . . But as history has seen in the past when the big battalions of the City unite, they can almost be sure of victory."[50] One paper toted up twenty-seven titles on the British Aluminium–Alcoa side, including a marquess, sixteen lords, ten knights, and—as if tossed in for good measure—the queen's uncle.

By New Year's Eve, the British Aluminium side had two million shares and felt confident of victory. Lord Cobbold, governor of the Bank of England, and D. Heathcoat Amory, chancellor of the Exchequer, asked Warburg to desist, noting that Prime Minister Harold Macmillan concurred. But Warburg had coldly analyzed the situation and later said, "It was not a deed of genius at all; I had just mobilized big amounts of money for the cash purchases of my clients."[51] Defying government pressure, Warburgs lifted its bid to 85 shillings a share and began huge share sweeps on the Stock Exchange, sometimes buying hundreds of thousands of shares per day. By January 9, 1959, Tube-Reynolds obtained over 50 percent of British Aluminium and declared victory.

The City was stunned. It was an apocalyptic moment. At first, the merchant bankers refused to alter their style or acknowledge that things had changed. Lord Kindersley of Lazard said flatly, "I will not talk to that fellow" and would cross the street to avoid Warburg. The dazed elite couldn't comprehend why the press and investors had lionized the outcast Warburg. Like Robert Young in his battle for the New York Central, Warburg realized the need to court public opinion as share ownership became dispersed. Henceforth, the City would shift from its opaque, secretive style to greater visibility. As one banker commented prophetically, "No company [head] whose shares are publicly quoted could sleep well from now on, because he must always wake up in the middle of the night and wonder who will make a raid on the company."[52]

After a period of estrangement, Olaf Hambro went around to see

Siegmund Warburg. Embracing him, Hambro cried out, "Siegmund, haven't we been awful fools?"[53] The bitterness persisted much longer at Morgan Grenfell, which had thought Warburg's behavior monstrous and unforgivable. After all, if capital and cunning counted for more than contacts, what would happen to Morgan Grenfell? For an astonishing fifteen years, the firm refused to deal with Warburgs, even as the latter became London's most innovative firm in the Euromarkets. Warburg made peace overtures and even asked Morgan Grenfell to share in a deal for Associated Electrical Industries. Morgan Grenfell refused and, far from appreciating the gesture, haughtily said it wanted to do the deal alone.

It's tempting to say Morgan Grenfell's fate was decided by the aluminium war. For beneath the indignation flowed new subterranean currents. A group of Young Turks, notably Stephen Catto (son of Tom) and Tim Collins, son-in-law of Rufus Smith, felt the firm was stuck in suicidal snobbery. In many ways, they wanted to ape Warburg, not condemn him. "The aluminium war showed that Morgan Grenfell wasn't aggressive enough," said Stephen Catto. "It came as quite a shock here. We were outmaneuvered and demoralized. It was almost the first time and it had a marked effect."[54]

Within a decade, Morgan Grenfell would not only undertake but specialize in flamboyant takeovers and flaunt its transformation. It would learn to beat Warburg at his game and come to symbolize the new, aggressive way of doing business. Like Morgan Stanley in New York, Morgan Grenfell would show in bold relief the death of the sleepy old world of high finance and the dangerous birth of the new. As the firms that had profited most from old-fashioned relationship banking, the Morgan houses had the most to lose and would react to the threat in an unaccustomed, bare-knuckle style.

JONAH

. .

.

I N the late 1950s, it seemed the parade had passed J. P. Morgan and Company by and that the name would take on a venerable but slightly antiquated ring, as Rothschild and Baring had. It seemed to be a banking dynasty in terminal decline. While Morgan bankers stuck to their wholesale formula, the competition took banking to the masses. Such large commercial rivals as National City and Chase were raking in consumer deposits, invading shopping centers, and appealing to the new suburban middle class of the Eisenhower era. Bankers Trust, which had insisted on a $5,000 minimum account, dropped the rule and went retail, too.

Henry Clay Alexander, who succeeded George Whitney as chairman in 1955, saved Morgans from genteel oblivion. Despite a shared sense of the essence of banking, the two men were very different. Whitney was the East Coast patrician, while Alexander "was graced with an easy Southern affability, relaxed in conversation, intense and enthusiastic at business—Hollywood handsome with an unruly forelock," recalled Jim Brugger, then the bank's publicist.[1] Both Whitney and Alexander were so handsome that when they appeared in public, women chased them down the block.

Henry Alexander was probably Wall Street's most popular banker in the fifties. He appeared on the cover of *Time,* and his winning personality took some starch from the Morgan image. As a young Davis, Polk lawyer, he had been assigned to Jack Morgan during the Nye "merchants-of-death" hearings. "I like that young man," Jack had said. Those five words secured Alexander's fortune. On Christmas Eve 1938, Jack invited him to become the first new partner since the Pecora hearings. "Think about it," Jack said. "We will have a talk a month hence."[2]

Alexander agonized over whether to be a Morgan or a Davis, Polk partner. "You have been dealt two straight flushes," a law partner said, "and you've got to pick between them."[3] He chose Morgans and performed legal work for the bank's incorporation. He was a protégé of Lamont, who thought him precociously wise, and of Whitney, who said, "Henry's so remarkably able."[4]

Like Lamont, Alexander was a self-invented figure whose elegance appeared hereditary. Tall and slim with wavy hair and a weak chin, his dapper look was sometimes accentuated by a pocket handkerchief and homburg. Yet he was from Murfreesboro, Tennessee, the son of a grain-and-feed merchant. He attended public high school, Vanderbilt University, and Yale Law; he first learned law hanging about a sleepy southern courthouse. He had a politician's versatility. Once on a visit to Tennessee, he chatted with a mule farmer who said afterward, "He is the nicest mule trader I ever met."[5]

Alexander projected contradictory images. He was a Jacksonian Democrat by birthright, he said, yet a registered Republican. He favored sound, orthodox financial policy—as well as tax cuts to spur growth. As a Methodist with an Episcopalian wife (who was a former Powers model), he would say, "I'm a Methodist in town and an Episcopalian in the country."[6] This kept everyone thoroughly confused about his identity. Tutored in secrecy, Alexander wouldn't name clients and once told a reporter, with excruciating circumlocution, that the number of Morgan clients was "more than half-way up to 10,000."[7]

Alexander relaxed the bank's pontifical image. He sailed a ten-foot dinghy, drove a Chevrolet station wagon, and bought suits off the rack. As American business power shifted toward the South and the West, the home base of many oil companies and defense contractors, it helped to have a chairman with a southern accent who could drum up business in Texas, California, and other places so long *terra incognita* for the bank. Alexander played the smart hick superbly. His occasional corn-pone patter—his sly, down-home aw-shucks manner—belied real sophistication. "When and if you decide you would like to borrow a little money," he would tell corporate executives, "I hope you will not forget your country cousin at 23 Wall Street."[8] It was a shrewd way to disguise the fact that the bank badly needed new business.

During Eisenhower's second term, the Morgan bank had excellent access to the White House. In early March 1956, Ike had wrestled with the decision of whether to keep Richard Nixon as his vice-president. A flurry of rumors reported that he would dump Nixon, who prepared to announce his retirement. Eisenhower made it the subject of a "stag dinner" and invited George Whitney to attend. Whitney recommended that Ike choose the older and more experienced Christian Herter as his running mate. Nixon, he said in a subsequent letter, could be better groomed as a future Republican leader in a high-appointed post—a tactful way of shoving him aside. In a reply marked "personal and confidential," the president agreed, but added resignedly, "The attitude [among politicians] seems to be 'do the thing that seems most popular at this moment.' "[9]

Henry Alexander was so popular at the White House that the press dubbed him "Ike's banker." Although Alexander was the most domestically oriented chairman in Morgan history—he came in after the foreign loans of the twenties and never lived abroad—he fully internalized the Morgan identification with Britain. This was patent during the Suez affair. On July 26, 1956, Egypt's prime minister Gamal Abdel Nasser nationalized the Suez Canal. The next day, the British prime minister, Sir Anthony Eden, informed Eisenhower that Britain was drawing up military contingency plans to reclaim the canal. By early November, Britain, France, and Israel invaded Egypt, to the great dismay of Eisenhower and his secretary of state, John Foster Dulles.

The Suez affair produced a deep rift in the Atlantic alliance—always painful for the House of Morgan—and the bank tried to win back U.S. support for Britain. Speaking at the Executive's Club of Chicago on December 7, Henry Alexander, in a rare bit of verbal pyrotechnics, conjured up a Nasser who "stirs the Arab world and breathes fire and damnation." He argued that the Soviet Union planned to join with Nasser in strangling NATO through their joint control of Middle East oil. Alexander proposed an American doctrine for the Middle East like that which the United States had extended to protect Greece, Turkey, and Formosa. In his peroration, he urged that the United States get back on "speaking terms" with Great Britain and France. He said, "We must save our alliances. They are mainstays of our defense, the floodgates holding back the Communist tide."[10]

George Whitney, meanwhile, had always refrained from exploiting his friendship with Eisenhower; this modesty had enhanced his credibility. But on December 26, 1956, in an unusual step, he sent Ike a grave letter bluntly advocating a tougher approach toward Nasser:

> At some point somebody has got to tell [Nasser] where he gets off in no uncertain terms, taking the calculated risk of what this may blow up. Probably you have already done so; if not, I am afraid you

might. Every day that goes by without some forward motion carries with it more serious risks. It is not only the financial plight of Western Europe, it is the injury to the prestige of the Western powers that to me is the most unfortunate repercussion. I am ready to assume the United States' position has been improved with a good many people in Asia and Africa, but I am afraid that this may have been attained at an unprecedented cost to the Western world.[11]

Eisenhower showed the letter to Dulles, who knew Whitney well. The secretary of state reminded Eisenhower that the Morgan bank was the fiscal agent for the British government and submitted that Whitney's sources were "somewhat biased."[12] Ike sidestepped Whitney's letter. By the time he replied, he reported that he had just heard of Anthony Eden's resignation as a result of England and France's lack of success in the Suez affair. Then he abruptly turned to personal pleasantries.

Unlike the situation of the 1920s, the Morgan influence at the White House was vastly disproportionate to the bank's slender resources. During the fifties, the bank seemed to shrink, if only because its rivals grew so rapidly. It had to cobble together syndicates to serve large clients, such as France. Nevertheless, Alexander stayed aloof from branch banking and the spree of banking mergers. The old Wall Street vanished as musty, dignified old banks were snapped up by hungry retail giants. The First National Bank of New York—the bank of Pierpont's pal George F. Baker—was illustrative of the situation. Refusing to hustle for business and demanding client introductions, it was dying with dignity, like a fussy old dowager, and was acquired by National City. Spurned by Morgans, Chase took over the Bank of the Manhattan Company; Chemical acquired New York Trust; and Manufacturers Trust later merged with Hanover Bank. Over a third of New York's banks vanished. They had to merge if they were to grow to a size commensurate with their multinational clients.

It was a brand-new age of banking, one with a less austere image. The stereotypical banker had been a grumpy Scrooge who closely scrutinized loan applications and was congenitally biased toward rejecting them. That befit a historic situation of scarce capital rationed by bankers. But the situation was reversed in the Casino Age, which was characterized by new financial intermediaries and superabundant capital. The banker now evolved into an amiable salesman who belonged to the Rotary Club, played golf, and smiled in television ads. Where banks once resembled forbidding fortresses or courthouses flanked by Corinthian columns, they switched now to inviting exteriors. In 1954, Manufacturers Trust opened a Fifth Avenue branch that wooed pedestrians. Its thirty-ton safe sat behind the bank's plate-glass window so that strollers could peer through its open door. Inside the new banks, marble corridors and tellers' cages gave way to soothing pastel shades, open counters, and soft furniture. Chase launched its advertising campaign with the slogan "You Have a Friend at Chase Manhattan." For elitist Morgan bankers, this was too much. "You can't provide custom tailoring to a mass market," sniffed Henry Alexander.

Showing their new subordination to corporate clients, many Wall Street banks moved their headquarters to midtown. Now past were the days when supercilious bankers expected company chairmen to troop to them. Between 1950 and 1965, hardly any new construction occurred on Wall Street. Chase, a large downtown landlord, feared property values might fall. To protect the bank's interests and restore faith in Wall Street, John J. McCloy and David Rockefeller worked out a deal with real estate mogul William Zeckendorf to create Chase Manhattan Plaza, one block from Wall Street.

As part of this package, Chase had to find a buyer for its thirty-eight-story tower at 15 Broad Street. The natural buyer was the adjoining House of Morgan. When Zeckendorf broached the subject with Alexander in 1954, they had a highly revealing conversation:

> "We're not real-estate people," Alexander said. "We already have this beautiful little corner here. We play a special role in finance; we are not big, but we are powerful and influential, we have relationships. Furthermore, we don't want to be big and don't need the space."
>
> "Henry," said Zeckendorf, "you're going to get married."
>
> "What?"
>
> "Someday you are going to merge with another bank, a big one. When you do, this property will be in the nature of a dowry coming with a bride; you will be able to make a better deal with your partner."
>
> "Morgan will never merge."
>
> "Well, that's just my prediction."[13]

Zeckendorf would later remind Alexander of this talk.

Bankers who had survived the Depression shied away from property speculation, and Alexander bargained fiercely for 15 Broad. He got it for

$21.25 million with a 3½-percent mortgage—terms so unfavorable for Chase that it later bought out the mortgage. Fifteen Broad was then joined internally to 23 Wall, which became the larger building's triumphal entryway. The flamboyant Zeckendorf used the deal to conquer Morgan's aversion to real estate lending and ended up getting loans from the bank. He later told of how a journalist he met while flying back to New York from a trip had coaxed him into stopping *en route* to attend a wedding at a nudist camp. By the time he arrived at a 23 Wall meeting, press photos had appeared of him with the wedding revelers. He thought this publicity might end his relationship with the decorous Morgans. Instead, every high officer, including Henry Alexander and George Whitney, turned out to hear the juicy details.

Many Morgan people opposed a merger because they liked working in a small, paternalistic bank with terrific perks; they thought a merger would cheapen the genuine article. There was a deeper dilemma: if the bank merged with a bigger bank to increase capital—the only sensible reason for doing so—it would become the junior partner, and J. P. Morgan and Company would effectively cease to exist. Finally, though, a decision would have to be reached. But even in late 1958, Alexander was still bluffing about the bank's self-sufficiency: "Some mergers are a good thing. But while I wouldn't say it can't happen here, we have no desire to merge. We've been doing very well, thank you, sticking to our last."[14] He told people, "We don't have the urge to merge."

Henry Alexander solved the problem with brilliance and extraordinary luck. Around the corner at 140 Broadway stood the fat, sleepy, dowdy Guaranty Trust. Long on capital and short on talent, it was the mirror image of Morgans. Its huge lending limit was larger than that of all the Chicago Loop banks combined. A former Money Truster, it had been a Morgan ward after its disastrous sugar lending in the early 1920s. After merging in 1929 with the National Bank of Commerce—once known as Pierpont Morgan's bank—it became New York's second largest bank. In the 1930s, George Whitney chaired its trust committee and Tom Lamont its executive committee. It was a blue-chip bank with almost all of America's top-one-hundred companies as customers. "We used to think of Morgans as a nice small bank," remarked Guido Verbeck, then a Guaranty officer. "Because of their lending limits, when they participated in large loans, they could only take a small share and they were very worried about it."[15]

Guaranty's chairman was J. Luther Cleveland. An old-school banker, he had rimless spectacles, neatly brushed hair, and a somber mien. Curt and humorless, he tried to run the whole bank, and his autocratic style prompted an exodus of talented people. He was the imperious Mr. Cleveland to subordinates, and grown men quailed in his presence. His own son would pop up like a jack-in-the-box when he entered the room. Cleveland would let visitors wait in his outer office, then grill them when they came inside. Despite shareholder discontent and sluggish business, he snorted at the idea of branch offices and small checking accounts.

J. Luther Cleveland was an expert practitioner of relationship banking. He sat in a gloomy office, a dark, sleep-inducing room, attending to a single document on his desk. "It was a list of ten names," recalled A. Bruce Brackenridge, then with Guaranty and later a group executive at Morgan Guaranty. "These were ten very important clients to the bank. He made sure that he called them periodically to let them know he was interested in their business."[16] A former Oklahoma oil banker, Cleveland had a powerful array of oil clients, including Cities Service and Aramco, the four-member consortium (today's Exxon, Mobil, Texaco, and Chevron) with exclusive rights to pump Saudi Arabian oil on very sweet terms. To stay on good terms with his board, he played poker with the directors. One oil director even packed a rare $10-thousand bill in his wallet, always ready for a quick game. The whole operation, ex-employees allege, was riddled with cronyism. "The only loan I ever saw Cleveland approve was a stock option loan to a crony of his," said a Guaranty banker. "It was later criticized by bank examiners." Adding to Guaranty's troubles was a paralyzing conservatism left over from the sugar debacle. "It was more important not to lose money than to make money," remarked Frank Rosenbach, then a Guaranty credit analyst.[17]

Eventually Cleveland's monstrous ego precipitated a board rebellion. When a director asked who could replace him, Cleveland thundered, "Nobody!" So the board opened merger talks with Henry Alexander in order to dump Cleveland. The last straw came when Ford Motor, dismayed by Guaranty's handling of its pension fund, switched the fund to Morgans. The board told Cleveland he couldn't be doing a very good job if he couldn't keep his largest account. At first, Guaranty's board came to 23 Wall with a proposal for a new bank called Guaranty Morgan—an insufferable thought to Alexander. A year later, in December 1958, with mounting frustration over Cleveland, the board swallowed hard and consented to Morgan Guaranty. When the autocratic Cleveland assembled his vice-presidents to break the news, it was the only meeting of the bank's officers anyone could remember having ever taken place.

In taking over a bank four times the size of J. P. Morgan and Company, the press likened Morgans to Jonah swallowing the whale. Alexander had engineered the dream deal. Guaranty was strong in railroads and public utilities. While J. P. Morgan was the lead bank for U.S. Steel, Guaranty had Bethlehem Steel. While Morgan had Kennecott Copper, Guaranty had Anaconda. While Morgan was peerless in the northeastern United States and Western Europe, Guaranty was well-connected in the South, the oil patch, the Middle East, and Eastern Europe. It had historic branches in London, Paris, and Brussels, having been the U.S. Treasury's agent in Europe during World War I. Guaranty had provided financing for Thomas Watson's IBM in the 1920s, and several of its executives had grown rich investing in the company. It held more American Express deposits than any other bank. And it claimed the account of Huntington Hartford and the A&P. What a prize!

On Wall Street, people said that Guaranty had really merged with Henry Alexander. When Bill Zeckendorf came to congratulate him, Alexander said, "You know, I've often thought of that conversation we had and how right you were." "I wasn't right, Henry," Zeckendorf replied; "I was wrong." "How so?" asked Alexander. "You're not the bride," Zeckendorf answered.[18]

Alexander chaired the merged bank while Luther Cleveland played almost no part, retiring after a year. Tommy S. Lamont and Henry P. Davison, Jr., became vice-chairmen, with Dale Sharp as president—the sole Guaranty person to retain a top post. While 23 Wall and 15 Broad were refurbished for the merged bank, Alexander and the others temporarily moved into Guaranty's offices at 140 Broadway. Far from feeling defeated or humiliated, the Guaranty troops in the trenches felt liberated by the advancing Morgan army. The one grievous error Alexander made was not notifying Morgan Grenfell of the merger until an hour before it was publicly announced. It was a terrible blow to the London bank, especially since Guaranty had a large, competitive London office.

After the merger was consummated on April 24, 1959, Alexander summoned the combined staff and indoctrinated its members with Morgan groupthink: "I want all of you to know—as the relatively fewer Morgan people here know—that an important element of your career path will be how well you train the people underneath you to replace you."[19] This close-knit corporate culture, which stressed the group over the individual, would distinguish Morgan Guaranty from other Wall

Street banks, which functioned as collections of contending egos.

Even with swollen ranks, Alexander kept up the traditional meetings with department heads. Although Morgans had been stingy with titles, Alexander liberally handed out promotions in order to smooth relations with Guaranty officers. In merging the two banks, petty problems of style proved most intractable. There was prolonged squabbling about a typographical style for the stationery. Since both banks used monogrammed silver in their dining room, weighty talks occurred over silverware and matchbook covers.

In April 1960, Junius S. Morgan celebrated the merger with a luncheon for eight hundred people at his North Shore mansion, catered by Louis Sherry's. Jack's elder son was even less suited for banking than his brother, Harry, and had remained in the business out of family loyalty. The colossal Morgan energies had petered out in this pleasant but somewhat ineffectual generation. Junius, a commodore of the New York Yacht Club, had yearned to be a marine architect, and his home was full of model ships in glass. Generous, charming, but lacking ambition, he'd become another Morgan male lashed to the wheel of the family dynasty. Though he put on pinstripes and fedora each morning, he never quite looked the part. "Junius was the nicest man you've ever known," a colleague remembered. "But he should have been in the Navy. He didn't know anything about banking and it was pitiful to watch him."

That luncheon would be Junius's farewell to the bank. Tall, and handsome in an old patched jacket, he greeted his guests in the doorway of his forty-room stone mansion, Salutation, a place of faded elegance and English furnishings. Seven massive glazed Ming pottery figures stood in the main hall's niches. Shaking hands, Junius stood by his wife, Louise, whose cardigan had a hole in it. Described by some family members as artistic and eccentric—by others as pushy and spoiled— Louise yearned to "touch up" John Singer Sargent's portrait of Jessie Morgan. She bred golden Labradors, and dozens of them ran about the tents and tables, the twenty acres of gardens, the tennis courts, and the swimming pool. Six months later, at age sixty-eight, Junius died from a sudden attack of ulcers while on a hunting trip in Ontario.

By merging with Guaranty, the House of Morgan regained its status as the world's largest wholesale bank. Suddenly flush, with over $4 billion in deposits, it now stood fourth in size behind First National City, Chase Manhattan, and Bank of America. But this didn't tell the whole story of its corporate strength. It had an unmatched number of corporate accounts, ten thousand including ninety-seven of the hundred biggest U.S. companies. By the mid-1960s, the newly merged bank would do more corporate lending yearly than the next five competitors combined.

The new bank produced fears of a sort missing since the New Deal. But they were expressed by other banks, not by Washington. Twenty years before, a Morgan-Guaranty merger would have raised impassioned shouts of protest in the populist heartland. Now there were only mild peeps, notably from Texas Congressman Wright Patman, who wanted to stop the merger on antitrust grounds. Approving it, New York State banking authorities noted certain altered facts of the Casino Age: corporations could now bypass banks and turn to life-insurance companies for capital, raise money through bond issues, or finance expansion from retained earnings. As banks lost their special position as providers of capital, the old fears of excessive bank power disappeared as a major issue in American politics.

At first, the Kennedy years looked auspicious for Morgans. Although his father had been snubbed by Jack Morgan and the financial establishment, President John F. Kennedy wanted to court Wall Street to counteract his slim victory over Nixon. "He was also financially conservative," remarked C. Douglas Dillon. "A lot of people didn't realize that. I think it was the influence of his father."[20] He turned to Robert Lovett, then of Brown Brothers Harriman, for advice on cabinet selections. Lovett suggested John J. McCloy, Douglas Dillon, or Henry Alexander for Treasury secretary. Apparently Alexander had the appointment sewn up but then made a strategic blunder. After Kennedy spent an hour with him during the campaign, Alexander declared his support for Nixon. "I don't think there is any question that the head of the Morgan bank . . . would have received the job," said Robert Kennedy of Alexander's faux pas. "Jack felt that this was a personal insult."[21] Dillon won the job. Alexander probably wouldn't have fit into the Kennedy cabinet anyhow. Even as cabinet selections were being considered, he was telling bankers, apropos of Nixon's defeat, "Let's not, as businessmen, wall ourselves off or sulk in our tents."[22]

Alexander was drawn into one historic episode in the Kennedy White House, however—JFK's confrontation with U.S. Steel chairman Roger M. Blough over a steel-price increase in 1962. The administration had applied pressure to the steelworkers' union to accede to a moderate wage settlement in exchange for price restraint by management. So Kennedy felt double-crossed when Blough came to him on April 10, and informed him of a 3.5-percent price increase. This was the betrayal that prompted

Kennedy's famous outburst: "My father always told me that all businessmen were sons of bitches, but I never believed it until now."[23]

While Kennedy started a campaign against the price increase and resorted to harsh invective against businessmen, the administration cast about for more discreet ways to influence U.S. Steel. Henry Alexander was on the company's board, and John M. Meyer, Jr., of Morgans was on its executive committee. Robert V. Roosa, under secretary of the Treasury and former Brown Brothers Harriman partner, telephoned Alexander and asked him to appeal to Blough. The House of Morgan no longer had the mythical power to rescind a U.S. Steel increase, but Alexander might have gotten Blough to soften his anti-administration rhetoric at a news conference during the standoff. After Blough finally responded to Kennedy's pressure and rolled back the increase on April 16, Alexander accompanied Blough on a series of meetings to repair relations with the White House.

Still, the Kennedy years provided a politically friendly environment for bankers, who were no longer the bogeymen, as they had been in the 1930s. The Morgan bank even got giddy and overreached itself. In 1961, finally catching deposit fever, Alexander decided to drop Morgan's ancient aversion to retail business. By affiliating with six large upstate banks, he hoped to create America's biggest bank, a holding company monstrosity called Morgan New York State. "The basic idea was that the bank would have a Cadillac division and a Chevrolet division," explained Bruce Nichols, a partner with Davis, Polk, and Wardwell. The stately Morgans would suddenly have 144 offices in places like Oneida and Binghamton. It turned out there was some vestigial fear of bankers among the populace, and Morgans had awakened it. James J. Saxon, JFK's comptroller of the currency, torpedoed the move on antitrust grounds. Some believed the bank had bungled things by proposing an overly grandiose plan. Afterward, Alexander sighed to colleagues, "Well, we'll just have to stick to wholesale banking." Later the bank would feel that Saxon had saved it from a ghastly mistake.

When the Morgan Guaranty entourage swept back into the renovated Corner, the building's interior mirrored a new era of banking. Everything was open: the glass-and-marble enclosures had been torn down. The signature rolltops, with their secret cubbyholes, were traded for flat, leather-topped mahogany desks. An enormous Louis XV chandelier, of a sort found in old German and Austrian palaces, now shed a rich glow over the room; the old mosaic panels were covered with apple-green fabric. The grandeur remained, but the old mystery had vanished. The most important change was that this banking floor—once the entire

bank—was now just a gorgeous anteroom for the 15 Broad Street skyscraper, although top officials kept their offices on the second floor of
23 Wall. As if showing off its disregard for mundane concerns of cost,
the bank rejected proposals to expand its short landmark building.
Standing in the perpetual shade of skyscrapers, 23 Wall probably remained the least cost-effective use of real estate in the world.

SHORTLY after the merger, American banking began to wriggle free
from its regulatory confines. Under Eisenhower, bankers had dreamed
of deposits: in pursuit of billions in beautiful deposits, Henry Alexander
had wooed Guaranty. But as interest rates floated up to a heady 4.5
percent by the late 1950s, corporate treasurers were loath to leave behind interest-free deposits ("compensating balances") in exchange for
loans. In what some bankers thought heresy, Morgans helped clients
move their deposits into higher-yielding money market instruments. As
George Whitney told critics, "My customers are not stupid."[24]

The prospect was for a progressive erosion of the free balances. For the
House of Morgan, without a cushion of consumer deposits, the specter
of losing corporate deposits was especially ominous. Some inside the
bank saw the dismal future of wholesale banking with remarkable clarity. Thomas S. Gates, Jr., who would succeed Alexander as chairman,
used to say to him kiddingly, "You know, this isn't a very good business
to be in."[25]

Emancipation was at hand. In 1961, George Moore and Walter Wriston of First National City figured out how to circumvent the regulatory
cap on interest rates. By law, banks couldn't pay interest on deposits
held under thirty days. But by selling "negotiable certificates of deposits" that matured in more than thirty days, banks *could* pay interest.
These CDs could also be traded (hence, the "negotiable" in their name).
Their use sparked a revolution in the way commercial banks operated,
freeing them from reliance on deposits. Bankers no longer had to wait
for deposits and were liberated from both companies and consumers.
Now they could roam the world and raise money by selling CDs in
overseas wholesale markets. The new system was known as managed
liabilities. (In banking parlance, loans are assets and deposits, liabilities.) So relationship banking was crumbling on two sides—that of the
restless corporate treasurers, who demanded yields from their deposits,
and that of the freewheeling bankers, who could dispense with deposits
and turn to money markets.

The Morgan innovator was the tall, florid Ralph Leach. A University of Chicago graduate and a disciple of Milton Friedman, he started out as a Federal Reserve Board staffer and tennis partner of Fed chairman William McChesney Martin: the two would dash from morning meetings of the Federal Open Market Committee to grab the Fed's court by noon. When Leach left for Guaranty Trust in the early 1950s, Martin, who'd been the first salaried president of the New York Stock Exchange, told him, "Don't forget, Ralph, your associates in the next year or two will be people we could have put in jail fifteen or twenty years ago."[26] As Morgan Guaranty's treasurer, Leach still advised the Fed and coached its board of governors and staff on money market operations. In the new era, Morgans' intimacy with the Fed would come not through lending, as in the Twenties, but through its Treasury operation. It would act as the Fed's eyes and ears in the marketplace and sometimes receive central-bank intelligence in return. It would now have better connections at the Washington Fed than it did during the New Deal. In the 1950s, Morgans had hired Arthur Burns as a consulting economist, and he would follow Martin at the Fed.

At Guaranty Trust, Leach had peppered Cleveland with memos showing how the bank could manage its capital more aggressively. The patronizing Cleveland would reply, "Young man, go upstairs and run the portfolio and we'll run the bank."[27] After the merger, Leach got to pursue his experiments and pioneered in the Federal funds market. Fed funds were reserves that commercial banks deposited with the Fed. Some banks would temporarily have "surplus" Fed funds—that is, reserves beyond their legal requirements. Morgans began to take the temporary, unused reserves from small interior banks and either use them or lend them to other banks on an overnight basis. The size of these short-term loans rose spectacularly, to $1 billion or $2 billion a day. Some banks believed the new market shouldn't be used for trading profits. Leach, however, a born trader, viewed the Fed funds market as a source of profit.

For commercial bankers, the world of negotiable CDs and Fed funds signified a dramatic change. As banking switched from a deposit to a money-purchase business, the center of gravity shifted from the banking floor to the trading room. The business acquired a new speculative cast as banks built up huge, diversified investment portfolios. Banking became not only riskier but more impersonal. The old-fashioned banker lunched with corporate treasurers to make sure they kept deposits at the bank. But traders were a lean, hyperthyroid breed who spent days on the telephone, riveted to the changing prices; they didn't need to be particu-

larly polite or cultured. The leisurely pace of deposit banking was replaced by the traders' snap judgments.

The Fed saw perils in this volatile new form of banking. Would
savings and speculation become jumbled, as they had in the 1920s?
Hadn't Glass-Steagall shielded banks from such fast-moving markets?
Morgans handled its trading operation with great panache, and its trading desk would be a postwar strength. But how would the new system
work in clumsier hands? Would it turn into a dangerous instrument?
"The Fed would say to us, 'It's all right for Morgan to do it, but what
if Bank of America or City did it?'" recalled Leach. "Their feeling, in
many cases, was, 'It's good for you guys, but bad for the country.' When
they asked how other banks would fare, I would duck it by saying that
I wasn't arrogant enough to answer."[28]

Gradually the House of Morgan drifted back into capital and money
markets. Banned from corporate securities by Glass-Steagall, it became
the most active dealer in Treasury and municipal securities in the 1960s.
Unlike the straitlaced bankers of old, Leach would place large bets on
the direction of interest rates. Now a commonplace banking practice,
this was a frighteningly novel departure for conservative souls at 23
Wall. In 1960, Leach saw an excellent chance to speculate on one-year
Treasury notes being auctioned by the Fed. When he calmly proposed
a huge bet to the Morgan board, Henry P. Davison, the vice-chairman,
asked, "Ralph, what kind of numbers are we talking about?" Leach said
airily, "Oh, $800 million to $1 billion." Swallowing hard, Davison
replied, "This is going to take us time to digest, Ralph. That was the size
of our entire bank a year ago."[29]

This new banking would wake up the drowsy Wall Street of the
1950s. Soon the tenth floor of Morgan's building at 15 Broad Street had
scores of frenetic young traders taking positions in T-bills, negotiable
CDs, foreign exchange, and Fed funds. Before long, Leach oversaw $1
billion of market transactions daily. In 1966, *Fortune* claimed that
Leach "very likely handles more money in the course of a year than any
other man in private industry."[30]

At one point, Leach became too assertive, and the government
stepped in. In August 1962, the Treasury auctioned $1.3 billion in bills
maturing in three months. Leach placed a shockingly large bid—$650
million, then the largest bid ever submitted for T-bills. Wall Street saw
an attempt to corner the market. Although Leach blandly denied any
sinister intent, Treasury Secretary C. Douglas Dillon promulgated a new
policy, courtesy of the Morgan bank. Henceforth, no single bidder

would be awarded more than a quarter of the bills offered at any weekly auction. The Morgan allotment was halved to $325 million.

It would take the general public many years to catch on to these changes. The rise of bought money, negotiable CDs, and daring trading would have an enduring effect on banking. Bankers formerly had been preoccupied with the "asset" side of the business—that is, making loans. Now the liability side—the money on which loans were based—took on equal importance. Profits could be expanded in two ways—by securing higher interest rates on loans or by buying money more cheaply in the marketplace. In this new environment, that bastion of conservatism, the House of Morgan, elevated the trader to unaccustomed eminence.

Unfortunately for the banks, this new world of wholesale money markets also worked to the advantage of their corporate customers. Just as the Morgan bank could sell its CDs around the world, so a General Motors or a U.S. Steel could circumvent the bank and sell promissory notes called commercial paper at interest rates lower than those they would pay for a bank loan. In the wholesale corporate world in which Morgans operated, the banker was shedding his unique place as an intermediary between the providers and the users of capital. In the Casino Age, large corporations would increasingly serve as their own bankers, creating a crisis in the wholesale lending business, which had seemed so safe to the J. P. Morgan partners back in 1935.

THE rise of the Euromarkets accelerated the banking revolution of the early 1960s. With scarcely a whisper of public protest, these unregulated overseas markets subverted the spirit of Glass-Steagall. In the 1950s, so long as America was rich and other countries poor, bright young Morgan bankers avoided international banking. Henry Alexander's career was emblematic: he lacked the ties to foreign ministers that were symbolic of the careers of Tom Lamont and Russell Leffingwell. Yet he foresaw foreign trade and investment as the next phase of American economic life. American companies were expanding overseas at a rapid clip. Soon after the Morgan-Guaranty merger, Alexander and Walter Page went abroad to set up Morgan offices in Frankfurt, Rome, and Tokyo, resurrecting the old international network. Morgans used the 1919 Edge Act, which allowed American banks to take equity stakes in foreign banks if a country didn't allow U.S. bank branches. By 1962, the House of Morgan had interests in eleven financial houses from Australia to Peru to Morocco. Once again, in the Casino Age, American banks were trailing after their multinational customers, not leading them.

To round out the foreign side, Henry Alexander recruited Thomas Sovereign Gates, Jr., Eisenhower's last defense secretary. They had complementary contacts: Alexander knew the corporate heads and central bankers, Gates the prime ministers and foreign secretaries. It was also hoped Gates would use his administrative talents to organize the larger, more bureaucratic bank produced by the merger.

Gates seemed a rare lateral entrant into the Morgan hierarchy but really had true-blue Morgan roots. His father was a Drexel and Company partner and president of the University of Pennsylvania. As a Drexel bond salesman in the 1930s, Tom, Jr., had apprenticed at J. P. Morgan and Company. Drawn to intrigue, he served with Naval Air Intelligence in World War II. Starting his Washington career in 1953, he served as under secretary and secretary of the navy and finally succeeded Neil McElroy as defense secretary.

Rich and affable, a cowboy in well-tailored suits, Gates gave off an easy air of authority, an engaging conviviality. A macho hero to subordinates, he loved wine, women, and warplanes. "Gates liked living and liquor better than anybody I knew," recalled an admiring associate. At the Pentagon, he was a blunt, no-nonsense manager. After receiving a bulky study arguing for the retention of a troublesome traffic light that caused congestion near a Virginia navy arsenal, Gates scrawled across the top, "Turn off the damn light."[31] He took flak as navy secretary by closing useless bases. When he closed one in Texas before consulting Lyndon B. Johnson, the future president never forgave him and later harassed him with an FBI investigation.

As defense secretary, Gates loved covert activity. Through the National Security Council, he contributed to a four-point plan to topple Fidel Castro, an early blueprint for the Bay of Pigs disaster. He revered Secretary of State John Foster Dulles, a frequent dinner guest at the Gates household. Gates was closely involved with the U-2 spy plane and authorized its final flight, even though Ike told the CIA to stop such activity. "It was just an unbelievable thing, that U-2," he said nostalgically while Morgan chairman. "I often dream about the U-2."[32] When the plane was shot down, just before Ike's summit in Paris with Nikita Khrushchev, Gates advised the president to take responsibility. He also added to the controversy by putting U.S. forces on alert during the tense summit. "The timing of the exercise was just a shade worse than sending off the U-2 on its perilous mission two weeks before the Summit," noted Walter Lippmann.[33]

The day before his inauguration, John Kennedy was briefed by Gates, who painted an alarming picture of the imminent fall of Laos to the Communists and advocated limited American military involvement. He said it would take a couple of weeks to get American troops into Laos. An early plan had Gates being reappointed as defense secretary, with Bobby Kennedy his under secretary, and a year later Bobby would succeed him. This scheme ran into trouble when JFK's advisers pointed out an embarrassing discrepancy between Kennedy's campaign rhetoric about a U.S.-Soviet "missile gap" and a Gates reappointment. When Robert S. McNamara, president of Ford Motor, got the job instead, Henry Ford II proposed a "swap"—Gates as president of Ford and McNamara as defense secretary. Gates was also asked to head General Electric. Nonetheless, he chose Morgans. "He said he was always a banker and didn't want to learn how to make toasters," said his son-in-law Joe Ponce.[34]

Gates brought an easygoing style to the bank. One subordinate remembered a meeting between Gates and Jimmy Ling, head of Ling-Temco-Vought, the acquisitive aerospace and electronics conglomerate. Gates was bubbling over in his enthusiasm for a favorite warplane, while Ling kept asking whether Morgan would finance his acquisition of Wilson Sporting Goods. "No problem, Jimmy," Gates said, then returned to his beloved warplane. When Gates at last dispatched a subordinate to Stuart Cragin, head of the Credit Policy Committee, the latter flatly turned down Ling's request and overrode the casual Gates. Morgans thus became the first Wall Street bank to stop Ling's acquisitions binge.

Gates never fully recovered from Potomac fever. He was a good friend not only of Eisenhower, who volunteered to back him for a Senate seat, but of two later Republican presidents, as well, Richard Nixon and Gerald Ford. (His subordinates speculated as to whether the second phone on Gates's desk was a hot line to the White House.) His connections extended everywhere. He belonged to an exclusive group formed by Stephen Bechtel, Sr., of the secretive San Francisco–based construction firm and an active Morgan director after 1954. At the Carlyle Hotel, Bechtel regularly convened a study group that included Pan Am founder Juan Trippe, Texaco chairman Augustus Long, General Lucius Clay, and Gates. These brandy-and-cigar discussions might feature Bechtel on Saudi Arabia, Long on oil-price trends, and Gates on NATO and the Russian threat.[35] Gates would exploit his numerous contacts to spread Morgan influence around the globe.

WHEN Kennedy first took office, nobody could have foreseen the international thrust of banking in the 1960s. What was apparent was that the president had to staunch a massive outflow of American capital. In early 1962, Eisenhower convened a meeting of his old cabinet and Republican leaders. Tom Gates was impressed by a talk by Arthur Burns, who warned that a continuing drain of U.S. dollars and gold abroad would so badly damage the country's balance of payments that JFK would have to resort to extreme measures. Burns "believes the only thing left will be some direct controls," Gates warned Alexander. "The Administration does not wish such controls, but is drifting into a situation where they will probably be the only answer."[36] The House of Morgan braced for a new era in which American multinationals would get their financing abroad. As Alexander said, "As business goes, so goes banking."

In late 1962, Alexander, presiding over a turbulent meeting, asked a question that had not been heard for thirty years: should the House of Morgan return to underwriting, this time in Paris? In a decision that produced mild wonder at 23 Wall—wonder that the bankers kept to themselves—the Fed had passed a tentative ruling that Glass-Steagall would pose no obstacle outside the United States. But would it withstand a legal challenge? People were wary. "There was reluctance on the part of the other senior people to do something that could be seen as skating close to the edge of legality," recalled Evan Galbraith, then with the bank and later ambassador to France. "But Henry was quite visionary about it." Alexander went around the room listening to antagonistic opinions. At last, overriding objections, he said, " 'Well, I think this will be what you call a business decision.' "[37] The plan called for a new Parisian underwriting subsidiary, Morgan et Compagnie, Société Anonyme, with Morgan Grenfell and Mees and Hope of Holland as passive, minority shareholders. (The name Morgan et Compagnie had been dormant since the Guaranty merger.) Content with its American business, Morgan Stanley spurned this first invitation to enter Europe.

On July 18, 1963, Kennedy proposed an Interest Equalization Tax to throttle the dollar outflow. By penalizing the sale of some foreign securities to American investors, it provided incentives for banks to flock abroad. Hearing the news, Alexander divined a watershed. Assembling Morgan officers that afternoon, he made a quick, prescient judgment: "This is a day that you will all remember forever. It will change the face of American banking and force all the business off to London. It will take years to get rid of this legislation."[38] Two years later, Lyndon B. Johnson imposed voluntary restraints on lending to foreign borrowers and personally stressed their importance in White House meetings with Gates.[39] Suddenly overseas banking became the preferred career path for the ambitious.

Luckily, dollars abounded outside the United States—in part from the payments deficit itself—forming a pool of stateless money. The first Eurodollars had come into being after World War II, when the Soviet Union, wary of reprisals by American authorities, deposited its dollars at the Banque Commerciale pour l'Europe du Nord in Paris and in London's Moscow Narodny Bank. In time, *Euro* came to signify any currency held outside its country of origin. In other words, Eurodollars are dollars held outside the United States, Euroyen are yen held outside Japan, and so on. By the mid-1980s, this free-floating unregulated market—a free marketeer's pipe dream—would swell to $2.5 trillion in deposits.

A wholesale world catering to big business, governments, and institutions, the Euromarkets were immediately congenial to the House of Morgan. Here banks didn't pay deposit-insurance premiums on dollar deposits or set aside mandatory reserves against deposits; they could lend dollars as freely as they pleased. Conditioned by New Deal legislation, American bankers were initially edgy about this freedom but soon adapted. Along with the new trend of buying money instead of gathering deposits, the creation of the Euromarkets lifted restrictions on growth. If the Fed tightened credit in the United States, banks could sell large CDs in London and use Eurodollars to finance their domestic lending.

The New York banks doggedly fought to retain these privileges. At one point early in the Johnson administration, Washington tried to stop American banks from keeping Eurodollar accounts in branches abroad. An assistant Treasury secretary named Paul Volcker invited Morgan's head of international banking, Walter Page, and others to Washington for comment. The bankers delivered a stern warning. "We said it was the end of the American banking system," recalled Page. "You will throw us out of Europe and Singapore and Japan. And, my God, Paul that evening rewrote the whole basis with me. He got it all done before you could say Jack Robinson."[40] The regulation was dropped. In Volcker, Morgans had its paladin for the next twenty-five years.

While Morgan Grenfell dozed, that perennial London iconoclast, Siegmund Warburg, sponsored the first Eurobond issue for the Italian *Autostrade* in 1963. Morgan's new Paris subsidiary was an early star in this market. Since the Guaranty merger provided duplicate Paris offices and an embarrassing surplus of mansions, Morgan kept its place Vendôme branch, while the new Morgan et Compagnie, S.A., moved into the chandeliered Guaranty branch at 4 place de la Concorde near

Maxim's. Once called the Hôtel de Coislin, the building was a national monument. In it, Benjamin Franklin signed the treaty with France recognizing U.S. independence, and Chateaubriand wrote his romances. During World War II, it was occupied by the Gestapo. From its glittering interior, the House of Morgan would launch its assault on global securities markets.

Besides opening up the Paris operation, the new Euromarkets provided a chance for the Morgan banks to expand their relationship with the Vatican. During the 1950s, almost all Vatican funds in New York were managed by the J. P. Morgan Trust Department, just as almost all Vatican funds in London were under Morgan Grenfell's supervision. In the late 1950s, after the retirement of Bernardino Nogara—the mysterious, powerful creator of the Special Administration of the Holy See—the House of Morgan lost its foremost papal ally. To fortify the relationship, Morgan Guaranty, Morgan Grenfell, and Morgan Stanley joined with the Vatican in 1963 to form a Rome investment bank called Euramerica. The Vatican was financially rich and innovative in the 1960s—it controlled Immobiliare Roma, which built the Watergate Hotel in Washington—and Euramerica was supposed to be the first American-style investment bank in Italy.

The new operation was managed by Dr. Nicola Caiola, whose father headed a prewar Vatican trade department and who himself grew up in Vatican City. After working as a junior stock analyst under Nogara in the late 1940s, he got a Banca d'Italia fellowship and apprenticed at J. P. Morgan and Company and Morgan Stanley in the early 1950s. While Caiola was visiting Rome in the early 1960s, the Vatican expressed interest in sharing an investment bank with the Morgans; Caiola returned to the United States to prepare a blueprint. Morgan Guaranty and Morgan Grenfell leapt at the chance, but Morgan Stanley, which then had a curiously provincial and complacent attitude toward the outer world, joined in only reluctantly. On the eve of Caiola's departure for Rome, Harry Morgan summoned him and said, "Remember, it took us a long time to establish our name. Our name is now in your hands."[41]

The Vatican took a one-third interest, and the Morgan houses another third, while the remainder was divided among Italian companies. Despite its weighty Vatican patronage, Euramerica was a swinging operation, a Euromarket pioneer. Although based in Rome, it did dollar financing and challenged the investment banking monopoly of Italy's omnipotent Mediobanca. It was profitable every year until 1971, when the Morgans bowed out because they faced a conflict of interest with their thriving Paris operation.

Meanwhile, in Paris, Morgan et Compagnie, S.A., made what looked like an extremely auspicious debut. In February 1963, it launched a Euroequity (stock) issue for Germany's largest mail-order house, Neckermann, which owned twenty-three department stores. In taking his company public, founder Josef Neckermann planned to retain a majority interest. Friedrich Flick, possibly Germany's richest man, the scion of a steel family and a convicted war criminal, wished to sell his Neckermann stake. Neckermann feared that these shares would fall into the hands of German banks, which are permitted to hold industrial stakes. He was particularly eager to bypass Deutsche Bank, Germany's largest, which controlled a veritable industrial empire. Neckermann favored global syndication, with only a small portion of the shares allotted to Germany.

For the new Paris operation, the Neckermann issue seemed a smashing success. Morgans bought the $30-million issue, then turned around and resold it to Belgian, Swiss, and Dutch banks. In London, where Morgan Grenfell led a large purchasing group, the issue shot up to a premium. Said Evan Galbraith, then a leading Morgan man in Paris: "It was the first internationally marketed issue. People saw you could distribute something on an international basis."[42] There was one telltale hint of trouble, however. When Morgans sent out the offering by telex, German banks didn't answer. When Deutsche Bank then complained about the issue's being sold outside Germany, Galbraith said Morgans was simply heeding the client's wishes. He didn't quite fathom the depth of anger he had aroused or how deeply he had offended tradition. Deutsche Bank would bide its time and get even in extremely dramatic fashion.

Though extraterritorial in nature, the early Euromarkets were riled by fierce nationalistic clashes. Except in the Eurodollar market, banks expected to lead issues denominated in their own currencies. (The U.S. Treasury even briefly insisted that American firms lead Eurodollar issues.) The now-swaggering Morgans came up against this parochialism when it tried to invade the most sacred banking monopoly of all—that of Switzerland. Crédit Suisse, Swiss Bank Corporation, and Union Bank of Switzerland formed a cartel that dominated Swiss franc issues, and outside banks defied them at their own peril. The Morgan Paris operation did just that in September 1963, when the city of Copenhagen wished to raise money and its treasurer consulted friends at Morgan

Grenfell. As Tim Collins of Morgan Grenfell, recalled, "Somebody had the bright idea that since interest rates were low in Switzerland, why not denominate the issue in Swiss francs?"[43]

This time, Galbraith warned 23 Wall Street to expect an angry response, though nobody quite expected the furor that erupted. "The Swiss banks went bananas," said Galbraith. "They called up Henry Alexander and said, 'You can't do this. Swiss francs are *not* an international currency. They should be controlled by the Swiss. . . . Henry was swamped with phone calls, threatening all sorts of things.'"[44] The Swiss government told Washington that if further flotations occurred, they would convert dollars into gold and sink the dollar. They refused to let their money function as an international currency. They also pressured the Bank of England. "There was a *froideur* between the Bank of England and the Swiss central bank for some time," recalled Collins.[45] The ill-fated Copenhagen issue was both the first and the last Swiss-franc Euroissue for a generation.

Meanwhile, the Germans still smarted from the Neckermann issue and awaited a chance to retaliate. When Morgan et Compagnie, S.A., announced an issue for another German mail-order house, Friedrich Schwab and Company, Deutsche Bank saw its golden opportunity for revenge. Instead of obtaining written contracts from underwriters, Morgans proceeded with far more tenuous "indications of interest." This would prove a fatal mistake. The firm also enlisted a small German trade-union bank that would prove too weak to stop the coming onslaught. Once the issue was announced, Deutsche Bank sprang its power play, putting intense pressure on banks around the world not to participate. It was a full-scale disaster for Morgans, which had to swallow $9 million worth of the $13-million stock issue, a huge amount for those days. The New York office was stunned.

The passive partner, Morgan Grenfell, was very upset by the brash "American" way in which the Morgan Guaranty people had conducted themselves. Under U.S. law, 23 Wall couldn't pump in more capital, and Morgan Grenfell had to organize a temporary rescue among London's merchant banks—an act for which it felt itself insufficiently appreciated by its American cousins. The Paris operation was later bailed out when Singer Company chairman Donald Kircher, who sat on Morgan Guaranty's board, bought Schwab for $16 million.

In the meantime, another complication arose, deepening the sense of disaster in Paris. The SEC ruled that Morgans couldn't both act as a trustee for companies in New York and underwrite for them in Paris. This was the last straw: Morgan Guaranty withdrew from running the

Paris operation. "John Meyer, head of international operations, was very downhearted as a result of the Schwab deal," recalled Galbraith.[46] Shattered by the Schwab affair, Morgan Guaranty wouldn't return to Euromarket issues for more than a decade. For a bank so surefooted in foreign markets in the 1920s, it was a crushing defeat and left a legacy of self-doubt in securities work.

Enter Morgan Stanley, then a bit belatedly discovering the Euromarkets. While Henry Alexander had busily set up operations around the world, Morgan Stanley still lacked a single European office. It began to shed its insularity in 1966, when Bill Sword and Frank A. Petito made a secret trip to Rome and met with Guido Carli, head of the Banca d'Italia. Petito, born in Trenton, New Jersey, was the first Italian-American partner at Morgan Stanley and had always been a potential secret weapon in Italy. But he didn't speak Italian, and the aging, aristocratic Giovanni Fummi, who still advised the Morgan houses in the 1950s, scoffed at him as a peasant.

The imaginative Petito had an inspiration. From Italian exports and overseas remittances, Carli had stored up $4 billion in excess dollars. Petito suggested that Morgan Stanley's big clients in Italy—Exxon, General Motors, and Du Pont—could borrow in liras and convert them into dollars the same day, relieving Carli of his excess. Carli was delighted and swore Morgan Stanley to silence about this exclusive deal. In two whirlwind months, Morgan Stanley did $600 million worth of the secret lira loans, whetting the firm's appetite for European work and building its reputation for finding pockets of money buried around the world.

In January 1967, Morgan Guaranty brought in Morgan Stanley to run the ailing Paris operation, selling it two-thirds of the business; it retained a one-third share with Morgan Grenfell, the Dutch firm of Mees and Hope, and the Wallenberg family's Enskilda Bank of Stockholm. The one-third stake was patterned after Morgan Guaranty's one-third stake in Morgan Grenfell. Petito was willing to give Morgan Guaranty half the Paris operation, but the bank's confidence was shattered after the Schwab debacle, and it preferred a minority share.

For this new Morgan et Compagnie International, the old crew was pushed out and a more seasoned Morgan Stanley group under Sheppard Poor came in to run it. Their advent coincided with a Eurobond boom. Once Morgan Stanley shook off its insularity and discovered the outside world, it made a spectacular success in Paris, financing Standard Oil of New Jersey, U.S. Steel, Eastman Kodak, Texaco, American Tobacco, Procter & Gamble, Amoco, and so on. As the lugubrious atmosphere waned, the Paris venture surpassed all rivals. By 1975, it would issue $5 billion in yearly offerings.

With Morgan et Compagnie International, the Morgan community of interest evolved into a more direct fusion of overseas securities work. Without fanfare, the House of Morgan was being welded back together. It was a loose partnership. Morgan Guaranty's involvement in Paris was passive, one of many minority stakes it held, and John Meyer, Jr., saw it mostly as a way to avoid having to refer clients to Chase or First National City for Eurobusiness. Yet whatever its limitations, Morgan et Compagnie International represented partial repeal of Glass-Steagall.

At 23 Wall, it hurt Morgan Guaranty to hand over the Paris reins to Morgan Stanley. The Morgan Stanley people felt Morgan Guaranty never delivered the promised clients, while Morgan Guaranty always sensed inadequate gratitude for having launched Morgan Stanley abroad. (The Morgan houses were always amazingly thin-skinned with each other.) It was a turning point for Morgan Stanley, which gained a critical foothold in Europe. It sent "revolvers" to Paris, who got international seasoning. Morgan Stanley proudly applied its new Morgan et Compagnie label to all overseas issues except those of Australia. In those days, it never dawned on Morgan Guaranty that it was breeding a competitor or that it would emerge as a rival investment bank of Morgan Stanley in the 1980s.

Morgan Guaranty kept one piece of European business all to itself. In 1968, it started Euro-clear in Brussels, the largest clearing system for Eurosecurities and the first to automate the market. Initially it aroused powerful, paranoid resistance from European banks, which thought their inner secrets would be divulged to the House of Morgan. The genius of Euro-clear, in fact, lay elsewhere. It became enormously lucrative because traders left in the system money that could be lent to other participants, who used their Eurobonds as collateral. Morgan Stanley was never invited to share in the Brussels operation. The community of interest among the Morgan banks was always a community of convenience. Whenever one bank dug up buried treasure, it hoarded it and tried to keep it from its Morgan brethren. Hence, this era of collaboration among the Morgan banks, far from bringing them closer together, would eventually drive them apart, breeding mutual suspicions and accusations of double-dealing. Their relations would end up having the special rancor of a family feud.

JAPAN was the country that produced the most persistent friction between Morgan Guaranty and Morgan Stanley. Outside Europe and

North America, finance ministers frequently assumed Morgan houses were closely affiliated and constituted a *de facto* House of Morgan. This confusion was most pronounced in Japan, which had its own conglomerates, or *zaibatsu,* organized around core banks. "Every time they wrote about us in the Japanese newspapers," recalled Jack Loughran of Morgan Guaranty, "they would refer to the Morgan *zaibatsu* that controls General Motors and U.S. Steel."[47]

For a long time after the war, the problem seemed academic as Japan emerged slowly from its defeat. When Tokyo's stock exchange reopened in 1949, it was a small, provincial affair. During the occupation, General Douglas MacArthur reformed Japanese finance along American lines and even authorized a Glass-Steagall equivalent, Article 65, separating banking and securities work. MacArthur wanted to splinter and neutralize the *zaibatsu* that had dominated interwar Japan and cooperated with the military in their East Asian conquests. Briefly, Japanese banks took on neutral occupation names. When the Americans left, Mitsubishi, Sumitomo, and the others reverted to their traditional names. During the occupation, four American banks—National City, Bank of America, Chase, and Manufacturers—set up branches to serve military personnel. After admitting American Express for traveler's checks, the Ministry of Finance halted further foreign penetration, and the "bamboo curtain" descended.

As their economy rebounded in the early 1950s, the Japanese wanted to reinstate their spotless credit reputation and make good on old Morgan-sponsored debt—the 1923 earthquake loan and the 1930 gold-standard loan—on which they had stopped payment after Pearl Harbor. Boasting that they hadn't defaulted in two thousand years, they made a great ceremony of resuming payment and refurbishing their Morgan ties. After Japan signed the peace treaty with the United States in 1951, a Ministry of Finance official came to 23 Wall saying, "I have come to honor my signature."[48] With help from Smith, Barney and Guaranty Trust, Japan serviced its bonds in full, and two Smith, Barney officials were decorated by the emperor.

J. P. Morgan and Company had always been proud of its preeminence in Japan. The bank would cite decorations bestowed by Emperor Hirohito upon Jack Morgan, Tom Lamont, and Russell Leffingwell. But in the 1950s, its scant resources were exhausted by England and France, and it couldn't re-create its special relationship with Japan. This began to change after the merger with Guaranty, which had been a major trustee for Japanese government and electric-utility bonds. It was also a Wall Street training ground for many Japanese bankers, who went home and copied its forms for their own banks.

The two banks had another advantage in pursuing Japanese business—a virtual monopoly in American depositary receipts or ADRs, which were invented by Guaranty Trust back in 1927. ADRs permitted American investors to buy foreign stocks in the United States with a minimum of difficulty. They would actually buy receipts against shares held in a foreign bank vault. The cooperating American bank would convert dividends into dollars and spare the investor foreign-exchange problems. In the spring of 1960, Regis Moxley of Morgan Guaranty, an evangelist for ADRs, visited Japan to preach their virtues. Afraid ADRs would breach the nation's capital controls, the Ministry of Finance warily consented to an ADR for Sony, the first ever for a Japanese stock. Setsuya Tabuchi, chairman of Nomura Securities, later said, "If there was a single milestone in the internationalization of the Japanese financial market, it came in 1961 when Sony issued American depositary receipts in the U.S."[49]

As with Schwab, Morgan Guaranty, long absent from foreign markets, inadvertently stirred up local ire. With ADRs, Morgans had to assign a foreign bank to hold the actual shares while it issued tradable receipts in New York. Naively hoping to spread business democratically among Japanese banks, Moxley tapped the Bank of Tokyo as custodian for Sony's ADR. He didn't realize that as Sony's principal banker, Mitsui would resent encroachment on its territory. An incensed Mitsui delegation appeared at Morgan's doorstep to protest this serious violation of protocol. "They almost chopped my head off," declared Bob Wynn of Morgan Guaranty. When the bank issued ADRs for Toshiba, Hitachi, and Fuji Iron and Steel, it didn't repeat the error.

In the 1960s, Morgan Guaranty decided to pierce the bamboo curtain and upgrade its representative office into a Japanese branch—extremely difficult at the time. It faced a terrible handicap because of Morgan Stanley's attitude toward the country. Morgan Stanley had mostly confined its foreign dealings to tried-and-true Western clients—Canada, Australia, France, and Italy. Spoiled by its rich American clientele, it was more ambivalent about foreign markets than was Morgan Guaranty. The problem was compounded by the fact that several partners were war veterans and openly antagonistic toward Japan. This attitude didn't matter in the 1950s, when Japan was still poor and borrowed heavily from the World Bank. Later in the decade, however, World Bank president Eugene Black told two Ministry of Finance representatives that a rejuvenated Japan had outgrown the World Bank and should tap Wall

Street on its own. When they asked Black whom they should see, he handed them—just by coincidence—a World Bank prospectus with First Boston and Morgan Stanley on the top.

Preparing for a large metropolis of Tokyo issue, the Japanese went first to First Boston and were so impressed that they accepted them as co-managers. Expecting equally considerate treatment at Morgan Stanley— wasn't the House of Morgan Japan's honored friend?—they were coldly and uncivilly rebuffed. "The old-timers in the Ministry of Finance were really horrified," said Morgan Guaranty's Loughran, who had to deal with the unpleasant consequences for 23 Wall.[50]

Why did Morgan Stanley spurn Japan? The decision contained elements of both business calculation and xenophobia. Morgan Stanley still held to an unswerving policy of managing securities issues alone or not at all, a lucrative form of snobbery that allowed the firm to pocket all management fees. Barging in blindly, the Japanese didn't realize that their casual decision to accept First Boston first made it impossible for Morgan Stanley to participate without violating its cardinal rule. The sole exception it had made was for the World Bank itself, which doubtless misled the Japanese.

Why didn't it make another exception? "The prestige of being banker to the World Bank was regarded as greater than being banker to a defeated country," explained former Morgan Stanley partner Alexander Tomlinson. "The Japanese didn't realize what a sensitive subject it was for us. The partners involved in the war weren't enthusiastic about doing business in Japan anyway. And the older partners had deeply resented the attack on Pearl Harbor. They had a personal relationship with Japan that they felt had been offended."[51] Also, in Western eyes, Japan seemed less of a full-fledged industrial power than a superior version of a developing country. In the early 1960s, it was still the second most heavily indebted country in the world, after India.

Whatever the business rationale, the Morgan Stanley decision was laced with a subtle racism, for similar objections never stopped the firm from doing business with Italy or Germany. "The Germans somehow converted themselves into nice guys," an ex-partner said cynically. "All the Nazis seemed to have been purged." At the time, a single Morgan Stanley partner could blackball a major decision. One partner who was a former fighter pilot made rabble-rousing patriotic speeches invoking Hirohito, Pearl Harbor, the sale of war bonds, and so on. To this day, Perry Hall is unrepentant about the decision: "I wouldn't do business with the Japanese even now."[52] Although younger partners thought the older ones a bunch of stubborn fools, the latter wouldn't budge.

This intransigence was a big problem for J. P. Morgan and Company, which was then trying to wrest big balances from Japan's Ministry of Finance. Fearing fallout from Morgan Stanley's insult, international chief John Meyer had long, angry talks with his close friend John Young, who was Morgan Stanley's senior partner for foreign business. The problem acquired new urgency for Morgan Guaranty after a September 1964 meeting in Tokyo. Morgan Guaranty director, Steve Bechtel, Sr., and his friend General Lucius Clay, former military governor of Germany, prevailed on Meyer to try to open a Japanese branch. Bechtel said Tokyo was becoming a world information capital. More to the point, his own firm planned to open an office there—always strong inducement for Morgans to follow. A decision was made to open a Japanese branch as part of Morgan's strategic blueprint to establish branches in major world markets and end its Eurocentric bias.

Japan was then far more closed than it is today, and no bureaucrat cared to accept the political stigma of admitting Morgans. The government felt there were enough foreign banks; approving more was extremely sensitive business. In 1965, Tom Gates, who had fought at Iwo Jima and Okinawa, made an initial presentation for a branch license to Michio Mizuta, Japan's foreign minister. Even with the Japanese, Gates had a straightforward style; skipping ceremony, he bluntly asked for a branch. Far from settling anything, this meeting was the opening round of a long, dreary battle. For all the bowing and deference to the Morgan name, the Japanese made the bank grovel for twenty-nine months. The Finance Ministry laid down two rules: Morgans couldn't discuss the negotiations with the U.S. embassy (honored) or with a lawyer (flouted). The talks sometimes seemed to be endurance contests, conducted by the Japanese in an elaborate language of shrugs, sighs, and veiled allusions to nameless difficulties.

The bank deployed many emissaries and sent international head John Meyer, Jr., for early talks. Meyer, who would follow Gates as Morgan Guaranty chairman in 1969, was the most austere and humorless of the postwar bank chairmen. Tall and granite-hard, he had a bald domed head and huge bushy eyebrows, which the Japanese interpreted as the sign of a great samurai spirit. He seldom smiled as he puffed watchfully, enigmatically, on his pipe. With his elephantine memory and vast experience, he always seemed several steps ahead of everybody else, and his thoroughness at the House of Morgan was legendary. Having started at the Guaranty Company in 1927, he could remember obscure details of railroad bonds from forty years before.

Unlike the charming Henry Alexander and Tom Gates, Meyer made subordinates feel uneasy. Borrowing an old trick from FDR, he would assign more than one person to the same task, although he often knew the answer in advance. He would pretend to defer to the judgment of some young banker on a giant loan, then watch the young person squirm. He had an incomparable mastery of detail that some colleagues found counterproductive. "He would read every last word of a credit report on a tiny $9-million loan to Ireland," said a former colleague.

Meyer carried Morgan secrecy and discretion to new lengths. Despite a vast awareness of political developments, he had the lowest public profile of any Morgan chairman. Constantly absorbing financial intelligence from around the world, he was thick as thieves with Arthur Burns, Fed chairman after William McChesney Martin, and they had long phone talks each Sunday. "Meyer should have been in the CIA," remarked an admiring former associate; "he was a real inside man, with a style of quiet influence." With Meyer, the Morgan bank would no longer exercise the visible Wall Street leadership that had come so naturally to his predecessors.

A man of legendary strength, Meyer's idea of a happy weekend in Tokyo was climbing Fujisan. He was capable of outlasting even the Japanese. Each time that Meyer in New York would ask Loughran in Tokyo what he needed, Loughran would cable back, "Patience, patience, patience."[53] The patience would be rewarded: Morgan Guaranty became the first American bank since 1952 to win branch approval and penetrate the bamboo curtain.

In breaking through Japan's *cordon sanitaire,* Morgan negotiators profited unexpectedly from history. Some Finance Ministry old-timers remembered Tom Lamont. Of even greater help was the memory of a beautiful, fated *geisha.* In 1904, Pierpont Morgan's nephew George Morgan, living in Yokohama and collecting Japanese art, married Yuki Kato. Although George's friends told reporters, "I understand that the young lady he has married comes of an excellent family," George had actually bought out the contract of a young *geisha.*[54] During their honeymoon in Newport and on Long Island, Yuki Morgan was ostracized by George's family, and the couple ended up living in Paris. When George died, in Spain in 1915, his wife inherited his wealth.

Yuki's trust fund was administered by J. P. Morgan and Company, which was unable to send her payments during World War II. Afterward, Henry Alexander went to Cologne as vice chairman of the U.S. Strategic Bombing Survey Committee. He tracked her down and gave her not only the accumulated interest but interest on the interest as well. When Yuki later moved back to Kyōto, she told her neighbor, "You always must trust the Morgans."[55]

On March 24, 1969, the day the Morgan branch finally opened in Tokyo, one of Yuki's Kyōto neighbors traveled in to deposit her life savings of Y 8 million (by this point, Yuki was dead); the neighbor was gently told that Morgans wasn't that kind of bank. Adding to Yuki's fame was a musical based on her life, which depicted her pining for a young student as she was signed over to George Morgan. When Morgan negotiators made the rounds in Tokyo, staid bureaucrats would stop to ask about Yuki Morgan. "The Japanese are very sentimental," explained Morgan's Loughran, "and everybody over forty knows the story."[56]

Another arrow in the Morgan quiver was Aisuke Kabayama. As the prewar Count Kabayama, he had squired Tom and Florence Lamont around Tokyo and in the 1930s had helped Lamont set up an information bureau. After the occupation, he had to renounce his title; now he would be an elite Morgan adviser. Employed by the new Morgan branch, he could perform no prosaic mortal labors but only advise. Even without his title, his noble identity was well-known, and he could get an appointment with anybody from Emperor Hirohito on down.

In its quest for a branch, the House of Morgan had had one last weapon, a man of indeterminate nationality known as both Satoshi Sugiyama and David Phillips. In the 1950s, John Phillips, an American professor working with the U.S. Air Force in Japan, befriended a Mr. Sugiyama of the Asahi newspapers, who wanted an American education for his son Satoshi. (An American education then inspired veneration in Japan.) Phillips adopted the boy; rechristened David Phillips, he lived for thirteen years with the Phillips family in Long Beach, California. He studied Japanese daily. After graduating from Berkeley, he worked in New York for Morgan Guaranty's stock-transfer unit. Then the Immigration and Naturalization Service challenged his adoption and threatened to deport him; Davis, Polk lawyers contested in vain. So in 1964, David Phillips, né Sugiyama, was posted to Morgan's representative office in Tokyo.

The deportation had unexpected consequences within the Morgan empire. While Phillips started as office manager, he was soon caught up in the secret lobbying for the Morgan branch. As he said, "Because of my Japanese face, the Japanese press would never question why I was going into the Ministry of Finance all the time."[57] With no real bank training, he was good at scouting out new business and didn't mind going out nightly on the Ginza, Tokyo's main commercial district. He was a perfect Morgan hybrid—a fully bilingual, bicultural man who

44. Jack Morgan dandling circus midget Lya Graf during the 1933 Pecora hearings. The stunt humanized Jack's image but deeply scarred him.

45. Russell C. Leffingwell hunting on the Devonshire moors
with his wife and daughter, 1927. Leffingwell was the lone
Morgan partner to foresee a financial crisis in 1929.

46. The 1929 crash at Broad and Wall streets. This photo
reveals several flappers and a surprising number of young people.

47. The dapper Edward C. ("Teddy") Grenfell with Jessie Morgan and her two daughters, Jane and Frances

48. Jack Morgan and Captain Porter aboard the *Corsair* off Nassau in the Bahamas

49. Jack and Jessie Morgan (at Jack's right) and Teddy Grenfell aboard the *Corsair* with a Mr. Gardiner and a Miss Williams. The House of Morgan was known as a white-shoe bank.

50. The bearded Montagu Norman of the Bank of England
greeting Dr. Hjalmar Schacht of the Reichsbank at Liverpool Street
Station, December 1938. Hitler fired Schacht a month later.

51. Junnosuke Inouye, governor of the
Bank of Japan and finance minister.
Inouye was murdered by a nationalist
fanatic in February 1932.

52. Teddy Grenfell, who became
a Bank of England director a year
after he became a Morgan partner

53. Counsel Ferdinand Pecora (left) eyeing his quarry, Jack Morgan. Senator Carter Glass, in hat, scoots between them.

54. Tom Lamont, George Whitney (center), and Jack Morgan huddling during the Nye "merchant-of-death" hearings on Morgan involvement in World War I, January 1936

55. S. Parker Gilbert returning from Berlin in 1930 after retiring as agent general for Germany, with his wife, Louise, who later married Harold Stanley. Their son, S. Parker, Jr., chaired Morgan Stanley in the 1980s.

56. Lady Nancy Astor, right, and her son William Waldorf entertain the Henry Fords at Cliveden. Several Morgan partners sympathized with the Appeasement sentiments of the Cliveden set.

57. Jack Morgan at the 1939 Harvard commencement
exercises with his sons. Junius (left) remained with J. P. Morgan
and Company; Harry was a founder of Morgan Stanley.

58. Harold Stanley (left), George Whitney, and Russell
Leffingwell (right) at congressional monopoly hearings in 1939.
Whitney's hair has turned white since his brother's scandal.

59. Richard's wife, Gertrude, at the Whitneys' New Jersey estate during a hunt of the Essex Fox Hounds.

60. George Whitney, who survived his brother's embezzlement to become chairman of the Morgan bank in 1950

61. Richard Whitney entering Sing-Sing to serve a five- to ten-year sentence for grand larceny. Note Whitney's pocket handkerchief.

62. King George VI and Jack Morgan sip tea at the
embassy garden party in Washington, June 1939.

63. Jack Morgan greets "war babies" at a Manhattan pier
in July 1940. Beside him are eleven-year-old Lord Primrose and
six-year-old George Vivian Smith, grandson of Morgan Grenfell's Lord
Bicester. The two boys spent the early war years at Jack's estate.

64. Judge Harold Medina, who supervised the antitrust trial against seventeen leading investment banks. The judge's humor enlivened a dreary ordeal.

65. Perry Hall, the towering figure at Morgan Stanley in the 1950s

66. Texan Robert Young lifting his arms in victory after his successful 1954 fight for the New York Central. He is seen here with Lila Acheson Wallace of the *Reader's Digest*, whom he made a director of the railroad.

67. A 1955 dinner in New York. Vice-President Richard M. Nixon chats with Fed chairman William M. Martin (second from right) and Viscount William Harcourt (far right), a Morgan Grenfell partner then serving as British economics minister in Washington. At far left is Rudolph Smutny of the Investment Bankers Association.

68. Morgan Guaranty chairman Henry Clay Alexander (left) as he tried to mediate the 1962 dispute between President Kennedy and U.S. Steel chairman Roger M. Blough (center) after the latter raised steel prices

69. Frustrated by his slow rise at Morgan Stanley, Robert Baldwin (right) served as navy under secretary from 1965 to 1967. He is sworn in by Rear Admiral Wilfred A. Hearn and Navy Secretary Paul H. Nitze (center).

70. Bob Greenhill of Morgan Stanley, the first takeover star of the new Wall Street, wearing his trademark suspenders.

71. Antonio Gebauer, head of Morgan Guaranty's Latin American lending in the early 1980s and later at the center of an embarrassing scandal

72. The partners' room of Morgan Grenfell. In this pre-Guinness photograph, Lord Stephen Catto, chairman of the holding company, sits between joint chairmen Christopher R. Reeves (right) and Charles F. M. Rawlinson.

73. 23 Great Winchester Street, home of Morgan Grenfell since the 1920s

74. As chief adviser to Guinness, Roger Seelig led Morgan Grenfell into the worst scandal in the firm's history.

75. Chairman Bill Mackworth-Young, whose untimely death, in 1984, set Morgan Grenfell up for the scandal

76, 77. Margaret Thatcher demanded the heads of Christopher Reeves (left), chief executive, and Graham Walsh, corporate finance chief.

78. White House meeting on the New York City fiscal crisis in 1975. From left to right: L. William Seidman, President Ford's economic assistant; Ellmore C. Patterson, Morgan chairman; Walter Wriston, Citicorp chairman; Treasury Secretary William Simon; President Gerald R. Ford; Chase chairman David Rockefeller; and Fed chairman Arthur Burns

79. Dennis Weatherstone, the London transport-worker's son who rose to the top of the House of Morgan

80. Lewis T. Preston, the tough, witty ex-marine who steered the Morgan bank back toward investment banking

81. 60 Wall Street, the new Morgan bank headquarters;
more space and computers, but less poetry and mystery

wore expensively tailored suits and cuff links and smoked Dunhills.

The advent of Phillips helped Morgan Guaranty solve its Morgan Stanley problem. To overcome any lingering Japanese doubts about the Morgan banks, John Meyer kept urging John Young of Morgan Stanley to open a Tokyo office. With the imposition of U.S. capital controls, Morgan Stanley needed to find money around the world for its clients, and Japan was becoming too big to ignore. So in 1970, Morgan Stanley agreed to set up a Tokyo representative office on two conditions—that it get space adjoining a new World Bank liaison office in Tokyo and that David Phillips head the office. Morgan Guaranty obliged on both counts.

So remarkable was Phillips's work for Morgan Stanley that in 1977 he became its first nonwhite managing director. He always surprised new clients. "I've been with David a few times when we are meeting clients," said Morgan Stanley's Bob Greenhill, "and you can just see their jaws drop."[58] Phillips signed up Hitachi, Mitsubishi, Industrial Bank of Japan, and Nippon Steel. He won a large private placement from Sony despite competition so feverish that Goldman, Sachs reportedly asked Henry Kissinger to talk with Sony chairman Akio Morita. Yet as much as Morgan Guaranty people admired Phillips, they watched with dismay as he exploited the old confusion about the Morgan *zaibatsu*. Morgan Guaranty, for instance, had floated a convertible Eurobond issue for Takeda, a Japanese pharmaceutical company. Yet after the senior Takeda died, his son took a bond issue to Morgan Stanley, thinking he was rewarding an old friend. David Phillips, thought the Morgan Guaranty people, didn't always clear up such misconceptions.

Business for the new Morgan Guaranty branch was extremely profitable, with huge profit margins on loans. The bank made yen loans to American multinationals in Japan and dollar loans to Japanese companies, including Hitachi, Toshiba, Nippon Steel, Honda, and Nippon Tel and Tel. Both Morgan houses targeted the Mitsubishi group, which stressed shipping and heavy industry and meshed with Morgan's smokestack orientation. As a purveyor of clothing and other army provisions, the Morgan bank's prewar favorite *zaibatsu*, Mitsui, hadn't fared as well after the armistice.

What made Japanese business irresistible was that dollar loans to companies were guaranteed by their Japanese bankers. In 1976, Ataka and Company, Japan's third largest trading house, failed after taking losses on a Newfoundland refinery; Morgans had a loan outstanding to Ataka. The morning he received the news, Bob Wynn called Lew Preston, head of international banking, and said, "Lew, it looks like you've got your first loss in Japan." Before the day was over, however, the Bank of Japan stepped in and ordered Ataka's principal banker, Sumitomo Bank, to bail the company out. That afternoon, an astonished Wynn called Preston back to say their unsecured loan would be honored after all. "Why the hell are they doing that?" asked a bewildered Preston. "They've got their marching orders from the government," Wynn replied.[59] In this banker's paradise, Morgan Guaranty would steadily expand its country lending limit. Nobody ever regretted the marathon ordeal of acquiring the Tokyo branch.

TABLOID

· ·

·

A LTHOUGH Glass-Steagall had supposedly banished banks from the securities markets, the House of Morgan and other Wall Street banking firms exerted a major impact on the stock market through their trust departments. Despite their unequal size, J. P. Morgan and Company and Guaranty Trust brought $3 billion apiece in trust assets to their merger, forming America's biggest trust operation. Morgan's money was mostly in pension funds and Guaranty's in personal trusts. The merged bank also provided "corporate trust" services that formed the infrastructure for much stock trading on Wall Street. As transfer agent for nearly six hundred companies, it received over twenty-five thousand certificates daily and sometimes handled a quarter of all shares traded on the New York and American stock exchanges. It mailed out twelve million dividend checks a year and maintained updated shareholder lists for many companies.

The old House of Morgan had commanded a sizable portfolio for its own account, but it was a less-than-scientific operation. Allied with the Guggenheims and the Oppenheimers, it gambled 30 percent of its entire portfolio on copper stocks in the early 1930s. Before 1940, the bank offered investment advice informally to wealthy individuals and old families. Partners managed money for their pet institutions, such as Dwight Morrow for Amherst College, Tom Lamont for Phillips Exeter Academy, and Russell Leffingwell for the Carnegie Corporation. The House of Morgan was always a magnet for ecclesiastical institutions, which shared its discretion and somber dignity. In 1917, Jack Morgan contributed start-up money for the Episcopal church's pension fund, and the bank always handled part of that money. Under Henry Alexander, the Presbyterians also switched their money to the Morgan Trust Department.

Eligible for trust work after the 1940 incorporation, the bank converted Jack Morgan's mirrored, marble-walled barber shop into a waiting room for patrons. The first objective was to snare estates of the rich and recently dead. This required patience, waiting until a sufficient number of clients had died. After a dinner spent wearily sifting through names of potential chieftains, George Whitney turned to a young associate, Longstreet Hinton, and said apologetically, "Street, I guess you're it."[1] It was then considered quite daring and unorthodox for a nonlawyer to run a trust department, which was always entangled in legal estate questions.

Street Hinton was from Vicksburg, Mississippi, and reminded everybody of a Southern cavalry general. He was tall and spare, ramrod straight, somewhat curmudgeonly, with a long face and prominent ears. His father had ended up as minister of Saint John's of Lattingtown in Locust Valley, the "millionaire's church" so dear to Jack Morgan. Hinton's formative experience was in settling Jack Morgan's estate. He drew upon the art expertise of Belle da Costa Greene. "She told me that Fifty-seventh Street was the crookedest place in the world and not to trust anyone," recalled Hinton of his first foray into the world of art dealers.[2] A tough customer, he quickly took control after the merger, telling the people who had run the Guaranty Trust Department: "What makes you think you know how to run a trust department?" He reminded them that they had lost their largest account, Ford Motor, to J. P. Morgan. Hinton ran the combined show.[3]

Trust departments had been regarded as loss leaders. Hinton thought they should make money. Most trust managers were sober men with iron-gray hair who put money into government bonds and they weren't notable for their imagination. When the Morgan Trust Department made its first common-stock purchase, in 1949, it was thought so audacious that Hinton had to telephone Russell Leffingwell, on vacation in Lake George, New York, to clear the purchase. After 1950, changes in tax laws and collective bargaining prompted an explosion in pension funds, and much of this money gravitated to commercial banks. After General Motors designated Morgans as one of its pension-fund managers and allowed investment of up to 50 percent in stocks, the business boomed. "What made us was the General Motors fund," said Hinton. "When we led the parade there, then everybody else wanted us."[4]

In the early 1960s, the Morgan Trust Department operated from a wood-paneled room with antique furniture, facing the New York Stock Exchange. Forty impeccably dressed managers in dark suits and black shoes sat in leather armchairs before glossy rolltop desks. Invoking Pierpont Morgan's philosophy, Hinton initiated the gospel of buy and hold. When a corporate director asked for a policy statement, he replied, "It's easy. We don't have one. We never sell stocks."[5]

Hinton had more flexibility than he conceded and was a cagey manager. At meetings with portfolio managers, he would call on Peter Vermilye, the resident bull, if he wished to buy stocks; if he wished to sell, he favored Homer Cochran, a durable bear. During the Kennedy bull market, the Morgan Trust Department became a trendy place. Young Ivy League portfolio managers loaded up with the glamorous growth stocks of the day—the so-called nifty fifty that so mesmerized money managers. Hinton's young highfliers bought Schlumberger before people could pronounce the name and were early buyers of Xerox, which multiplied a hundredfold. Symbolic of the new style was Carl Hathaway, who drove a fire-engine-red sports car and issued solemn dicta, such as "Never invest in companies run by fat men." "Lazy people bore me," he said. "The most successful of my friends remind me of a 727 at takeoff: full throttle and straight up."[6]

By the mid-1960s, Morgan was managing an incomparable $15 billion in assets, yet trouble lurked ahead. Control of such gigantic sums invited new public scrutiny, especially from Representative Wright Patman, the bullnecked populist chairman of the House Banking Committee. Like Louis Brandeis, Patman saw bankers' possible abuse of "other people's money" and feared that banks would use trust assets to exercise influence over business. In 1966, he issued a report that accused big commercial banks of dangerously "snowballing economic power" over large chunks of U.S. industry.[7]

The Patman report disclosed how banks had hijacked the new pools of investment capital. Of more than $1 trillion in assets held by U.S. institutional investors, 60 percent resided in commercial banks' trust departments. Because of the Wall Street merger wave, most of these assets were now concentrated in the hands of Morgans and four other banks. There were eye-popping figures on Morgan holdings. It held gargantuan stakes in two old Guggenheim standbys: 17.5 percent of Kennecott Copper and 15.5 percent of American Smelting and Refining; and it could have bossed around the entire airline industry, with a 7.4-percent stake in Trans World Airlines, 7.5 percent in American Airlines, and 8.2 percent in United. The danger was more latent than actual, for the conservative Morgan bank usually sided with management in disputes and didn't try to substitute its own judgment. But since a 5-percent holding could now control most companies in an age of dispersed share ownership, the numbers were disturbing.

There were also new fears about insider trading of a sort that took the banks by surprise. In the twenties, fortunes had been made through whispered tips and sly winks. The public tolerated this because only a tiny percentage of them owned stock. As personal investing grew in the 1950s and early 1960s, the public didn't wish to take part in a rigged game. It took time for the banks to perceive the danger, or at least the new public apprehension. In the 1960s, trust departments weren't yet segregated from other departments. At Morgans, senior bank officers—many of them directors of five or ten companies—sat on the Trust Committee, which also had as members outside directors of the bank, including, at various times, people such as Alfred P. Sloan of General Motors and Henry Wingate of International Nickel. These men were expected to bring their specialized knowledge to bear in picking stocks. At that point, banks didn't worry that they might misuse confidential information from the lending side in making investment decisions; there weren't yet legal barriers, or "Chinese walls," between the commercial and the trust departments.

It was amid new concerns that the SEC in April 1965 charged thirteen people associated with Texas Gulf Sulphur of profiting from inside information about an Ontario ore bonanza. One illustrious name leapt from the headlines—Tommy S. Lamont, son of the famous partner and only recently retired as Morgan Guaranty's vice-chairman. Lamont was accused of relaying information to Longstreet Hinton, who had bought Texas Gulf for Morgan trust accounts. It was a shocking charge, for since the 1930s the bank had been obsessed with its integrity and was undoubtedly one of the world's most reputable banks. Street Hinton worshiped George Whitney and had watched his anguish over his brother's scandal. Tommy Lamont had gone through the Pecora hearings, in which he was charged with making "wash sales" to his wife—an experience he didn't care to repeat—and he had cherished a reputation as a highly principled banker.

Thomas Stillwell Lamont resembled his father. Perhaps the face was rounder, the neck a shade fuller, but he had the same strong voice that emerged surprisingly from a slight build. Like many at Morgans, he patterned himself after a sainted father, adopting his interests. He became president of the Phillips Exeter board and a member of both the Harvard Corporation and the Council on Foreign Relations. Adopting his father's literary bent, he mailed birthday verses and sentimental greetings to friends and proudly chronicled the Lamont family history. Yet despite certain outward similarities, Tommy Lamont was more proper, more remote, and certainly more private than his famously gregarious father.

Tommy Lamont had been the House of Morgan's ambassador to the mining world, joining the Texas Gulf board in 1927. He had helped install Claude Stephens as company president and rated him so highly that he recommended the stock to Street Hinton for the Trust Department in the early 1960s. When the company cut its dividend, an already skeptical Hinton soured on the stock, and there matters stood for a while.

In November 1963, Texas Gulf drilled a secret hole at Timmins, Ontario, that flabbergasted its chief mining engineer: it was richer than anything he had seen, richer than anything ever reported in the technical literature. This mother lode of copper, zinc, silver, and lead was later valued at up to $2 billion; it was rich enough to supply 10 percent of Canada's need for copper, 25 percent of its zinc. It was a vein so fabled that the ore sat right on the surface and could be "scooped up like gobs of caviar," as one miner said.[8] As Texas Gulf ran tests that winter, its stock doubled, based on rumors of feverish miners mortgaging their houses to buy more shares in the company. Texas Gulf withheld an official announcement of the strike, fearing it would drive up the cost of surrounding property.

How to hush up reports of El Dorado? On April 10, 1964, Claude Stephens telephoned Tommy Lamont and asked whether he had heard the rumor. Lamont said he had. "Is there any truth in it?" Lamont inquired. "We don't know," Stephens replied. "We need a little time to evaluate our program in this particular area."[9] Lamont advised him to delay any statement, suggesting that he wait for the April 23 annual meeting in New York to make a formal press announcement.

The next morning, the *New York Herald Tribune* reported the biggest strike since Yukon days, a legendary bed of copper six hundred feet thick. On April 12, prodded by the SEC, Texas Gulf issued a statement of such cool understatement that the government later condemned it as false and misleading. Even though it knew it had at least ten million tons of copper and zinc, the company blandly described Timmins as a "prospect" that required more drilling for "proper evaluation."[10] Texas Gulf scheduled a board meeting and press conference at the Pan Am Building in New York for April 16. Street Hinton had taken notice of the wildly gyrating stock and asked Lamont to report to him after the meeting.

April 16, 1964 would be a day nightmarishly imprinted on the memories of both Hinton and Lamont. The Texas Gulf meeting began at nine sharp, with a full complement of fifteen directors. At about ten o'clock, twenty reporters were herded in for a press conference. It was "a New York corporate version of the old days when the old prospector rushed into the saloon to announce he had struck it rich," said Jerry E. Bishop, who was there for the *Wall Street Journal*.[11] The company wanted to keep all reporters in the room until the press conference was over. But once Claude Stephens finished his announcement, Norma Walter, covering her first spot news story for Merrill Lynch's monthly magazine, managed to slip out a side door. She got the news on the firm's in-house network at 10:29 A.M. A reporter for a Canadian wire service got out another door. Meanwhile, the other reporters stayed put, forced to watch color slides of the ore deposit. At the first moment of freedom, they dashed to the telephones to report the sensational news. Jerry Bishop's dispatch appeared on the Dow Jones "broad tape" of market news at 10:55 A.M.

After the meeting, Lamont mingled with reporters, viewing core samples and color slides of Timmins. About 10:40 A.M., he phoned Hinton from the Texas Gulf offices. "Take a look at the ticker," Lamont said. "There is an interesting announcement coming over about Texas Gulf." "Is it good?" Hinton asked. "Yes, it's good," Lamont said.[12] Later Hinton would testify to a curious sense of having seen the news flash over the broad tape. In fact, he failed to verify that it had appeared. Hinton then was treasurer of the Nassau Hospital Association and personally ran its portfolio. He at once telephoned the trading desk and bought three thousand Texas Gulf shares for the hospital. Then he advised Peter Vermilye to add the stock to a Morgan Guaranty profit-sharing plan and a mixed fund that invested for two hundred pension plans; Vermilye bought one thousand and six thousand shares respectively. All the while, the story hadn't shown up on the Dow Jones broad tape, even though it had been flashed to 159 Merrill Lynch branches.

Unaware of having committed any crime, Lamont returned to his office at 15 Broad Street and at 12:33 P.M. bought three thousand Texas Gulf shares for himself and his family. Now the news had been on the Dow Jones wire for over an hour and a half. The stock market had reacted deliriously. Driven by a 7-point rise in Texas Gulf stock, by day's end the New York Stock Exchange smashed all previous volume records. Far from feeling guilty, Hinton was disappointed the next day to learn how modestly Vermilye had bought. Only twelve days later did Lamont learn of the Trust Department purchases triggered by his call. He hadn't advised Hinton to buy. He later claimed he was discharging a duty and not phoning in a hot tip.

A year later, Texas Gulf directors were planning a reunion to savor their Timmins triumph. Though still a Morgan director, Tommy Lamont had now taken his mandatory retirement at age sixty-five. On the eve of the Texas Gulf meeting, a reporter reached him at home to say that the SEC had just charged him with "tipping off other bank officials" about the Timmins strike. Lamont was stunned. "I did not tip off other bank officials," he shot back.[13] The publicity value of his golden name was such that it dominated a front-page headline in the *Times* the next morning. He was tossed in with Texas Gulf executives and geologists who had blatantly traded on the inside information—a bit of editorializing that deeply embittered him. The *Times* sent a reporter to eighty-three-year-old Judge Ferdinand Pecora, now an elderly New York Supreme Court justice. Leaning back in his large red-leather chair on East Seventieth Street, Pecora marveled at the "extraordinary coincidence" that Thomas W. Lamont's son was involved in the insider trading scandal: "It's history repeating itself. It's symptomatic of the temptations of Wall Street."[14]

That Lamont was a member of the Morgan Trust Committee allowed the SEC to spotlight a broader problem of institutional investing. It branded the entire department an inside trader. Although not directly charged, Hinton was crushed, thunderstruck. Inside the bank, he had a reputation for sometimes ferocious independence and for telling the rich and powerful where to go. Peter Vermilye, now head of Baring America Asset Management, recalled:

> At one point, AT&T came to Hinton and said, "We want to make you a major pension fund manager for AT&T, but we'll only pay you quite a low fee." Hinton said he couldn't charge them less than any other client and refused to do business with them. Exxon said to Hinton, "We want to do business with you, but we want to direct the brokerage fee." Hinton thought the Exxon treasurer wanted to make a big figure with his brokerage friends out in the Hamptons and said, "No way." Another time, Meshulam Riklis bought control of a company that was a Morgan client and wanted to use its pension funds for his own machinations. Hinton threw him out of the office.[15]

What made the affair so devastating for Hinton was that Lamont blamed him for making the purchases. (Perhaps the most convincing proof of Lamont's innocence.) "He never forgave me," recalled Hinton emotionally. "All the other Morgan officers tried to tell him he was wrong, but he never forgave me."[16] Lamont was haunted by the case and treated it as a personal crusade. Insisting upon his innocence, he ran up enormous legal bills with Davis, Polk and fought in both the legal and the political arenas. Stung by the *Times* coverage, he typed up a twelve-page critique and handed it to executive editor Turner Catledge over lunch. It said the paper had "over and over again given special emphasis to me in its stories dealing with the Texas Gulf case. . . . I am bothered by this record of inaccurate reporting and careless editing."[17] Ducking the issue, Catledge said that headlines by their very nature were cryptic.

Some people charged by the SEC were clearly guilty of insider trading. One geophysicist had bought shares the day before the news conference; another company official, the previous night. Ordinarily, insider prohibitions disappeared once news was publicly disclosed. Now the SEC promulgated a new standard, arguing that news had to be released *and* digested by the public before insiders could trade—a hazy definition that would prohibit buying for minutes or days afterwards. At first, the SEC identified 10:55 as the moment the legal embargo ended, when the Timmins news moved on the Dow Jones tape. A year later, it arbitrarily stretched the period to encompass Tommy Lamont's purchase at the office at 12:33 P.M.—an outrageously long time after the news conference was disbanded. As Hinton said hotly, "If the SEC intends to make a new rule on that point, well and good . . . but it is not fair to write a rule retroactively."[18]

Lamont's defense team dwelled upon a supposed twenty-minute delay before Jerry Bishop's report ran on the Dow Jones broad tape. Lamont was alleged to be the victim of a technical glitch. But Bishop and his editors didn't think there was any delay at all. A year or two after the trial, Bishop figured out why there appeared to be a delay. Lamont's lawyers had assumed that Norma Walter had filed her Merrill Lynch report after the news conference; in fact, she had filed her story twenty minutes before the other reporters. Whether or not Bishop is correct doesn't affect the guilt or innocence of Tommy Lamont, who instructed Hinton to watch the tape. But if he is correct, Lamont must have gone to the phone almost immediately.

In December 1966, District Judge Dudley J. Bonsal exonerated eleven of the thirteen defendants, including Lamont. He said the facts were public information once relayed to reporters on August 16, 1964, and that Lamont and Hinton had acted entirely properly. While the SEC appealed, Lamont's health took a turn for the worse. He had a heart condition and suffered from fibrillations exacerbated by tension and depression. In April 1967, he checked into Columbia-Presbyterian Medical Center; he never regained consciousness after undergoing open-heart surgery. As soon as the SEC heard the news, they called S. Hazard Gillespie, Lamont's lawyer at Davis, Polk, and said they were dropping their appeal. Perhaps in atonement, the *Times* ran a fulsome, three-column obituary of Lamont that was disproportionate in length to his historical importance. It was a recurrence of an old Morgan condition—public exposure and political harassment leading to death.

However misguided in its pursuit of Lamont, the SEC in the Texas Gulf case drew attention to the growing dangers of financial conglomeration in the Casino Age. As both commercial and investment banks developed huge, diversified operations, it would be increasingly difficult for them to segregate diverse and often legally incompatible operations. A few years later, the Morgan bank was accused of selling stock in the failing Penn Central based on information passed to the Trust Department by a lending officer—charges the bank always denied and that were never conclusively settled. Its Trust Department was finally moved to Fifty-seventh Street so that it would be physically separate from the rest of the bank. Years later, the problem posed by conglomeration would reappear for Morgans as it entered merger work, and it would generally shadow the burgeoning Wall Street banks and brokerage houses throughout the postwar years.

IN London, meanwhile, the City had sloughed off its sleepy atmosphere. By the mid-1960s, there were now two Cities. One was a clubby, bowler-hatted core that dealt in sterling and was protected from foreigners by the Bank of England. Here whispered references to Grandma meant the governor of the Bank of England. This world required attendance at good schools and the right contacts for success and was ruled by patrician families.

The second City was a rich colony of foreigners trading in the new Euromarkets, and it would eventually surpass the domestic City in size. As if deploying an army for battle, Morgan Guaranty sent its crack young executives to London. So many Americans flocked to the City that the British press muttered about "Yank banks" and dubbed Moorgate the Avenue of the Americas. Starting with a Bankers Trust issue for Austria in 1967, these foreign bankers put together large syndicated loans for many countries, paving the way for massive Latin American lending in the 1970s. In this more egalitarian City, capital, not contacts, determined success.

With the Guaranty merger, Morgans inherited a full-fledged London branch on Lombard Street, a short walk from Morgan Grenfell. This sharpened an old dilemma: were Morgan Grenfell and Morgan Guaranty partners or competitors? Protestations of fraternal warmth were often clouded by mutual suspicion. Morgan Guaranty's London staff thought Morgan Grenfell "didn't help them any more than any other merchant bank and, in fact, were inclined to be a little more suspicious of them," declared Rod Lindsay, later a Morgan Guaranty president.[19] When Lew Preston managed the London branch in the late 1960s, he found Morgan Grenfell opportunistic, quick to share bad deals but tending to hoard the good business. "Lew perceived the one-way-street nature of things," remarked an associate. "The benefits were flowing in one direction." Preston found it hard to convince his troops that Morgan Grenfell wasn't a competitor.

There was cultural friction, too. Junior Morgan Guaranty people were excluded from the partners' room at 23 Great Winchester Street when seniors went inside. Especially infuriating was Morgan Grenfell's condescending treatment of a young British foreign-exchange trader, Dennis Weatherstone, son of a London transport worker. In 1946, Weatherstone, at the age of sixteen, had started as a bookkeeper at Guaranty's London branch while attending night school. With his quick mind for figures, he excelled in the lightning-fast trading that was now transforming banking. In the mid-1960s, he was spotted by Lew Preston, who noticed that people kept stopping by his desk to ask questions; Preston promoted him to deputy general manager in London. The short, wiry Weatherstone was a local hero for working-class recruits to the City. Some of Morgan Grenfell's aristocrats found no romance in this proletarian success story and snubbed Weatherstone, who later ended up president of the House of Morgan: he would decide that his career opportunities in New York were wider than those in the class-bound City.

Morgan Grenfell was an inbred, marginally profitable firm that was being strangled by its own pomposity, as the acrimonious aluminium war had shown. Its stagnation spawned gloomy humor. One City journalist, Christopher Fildes, recalled his editor keeping a headline in standing type: "FIRST WIN FOR MORGAN GRENFELL"; the editor joked he might need it some day.[20] Morgan Grenfell directors stuck to their old, informal style of doing business. They wouldn't advertise, seldom held formal meetings, and made decisions informally in their partners' room.

Entering the 1960s, the firm was owned by a tight-knit cluster of families—Grenfells, Smiths, Harcourts, and Cattos—and by Morgan Guaranty, which held a one-third share. To create incentives for its young executives, the bank issued new shares, which would gradually dilute the power of the old families. Morgan Grenfell also created new "assistant directors"—a seemingly petty organizational detail that for the first time allowed commoners to ascend into the formerly closed caste of directors: the senior partner, Viscount Harcourt, wanted to end the rigor mortis. In 1967, right before the second Lord Bicester—the jolly Rufie—died in a road accident, Harcourt recruited the virile Sir John Stevens, executive director of the Bank of England, to open up overseas outposts.

Among its young professionals, Morgan Grenfell's stodgy reputation bred an exaggerated thirst for freedom. In 1967, Stephen Catto, the former partner's son, invited film producer Dimitri de Grunwald for lunch at 23 Great Winchester. De Grunwald had a brainstorm: if distributors could finance film production through a global consortium, they could shatter America's monopoly in filmmaking; he denied that only Americans could make westerns. Eager to show it could move with the times, Morgan Grenfell decided to back the venture.

To prove his point, de Grunwald signed up Sean Connery and Brigitte Bardot for *Shalako*, a film about an aristocratic safari of Europeans deep in Apache territory; it was an instant success. The idea of a staid old merchant bank financing Brigitte Bardot was symptomatic of Morgan Grenfell's inner ferment, its itch for experimentation. Elated, de Grunwald talked of his dreams for developing film talent. "He believes the secret of success is not to play safe," noted the London *Times*. These famous last words set him up for the catastrophic *Murphy's War* (Murphy's Law might have been more apt), on which Morgan Grenfell took such a bath that the Bank of England intervened; Grandma placed a man at 23 Great Winchester to straighten the mess out. "At least it kept us out of the shipping and property disasters of the early 1970s," said Lord Catto philosophically.[21]

But the firm was shedding its past caution too quickly. The man who accelerated the process was Lord William Harcourt, a great-grandson of Junius Morgan's. With trim mustache and narrow face, round spectacles, and a bow tie, Bill Harcourt was a funny, snobbish man who wouldn't deign to shake hands with a junior member of the firm. Behind the imperious air, he hid a wicked wit, an acute sense of the ridiculous. He had served as British economics minister in Washington and U.K. executive director at the IMF–World Bank and was known as Morgan Grenfell's political fixer.

The son of a colonial secretary and grandson of a chancellor of the Exchequer, Harcourt graduated from Eton and Oxford and married the only daughter of Baron Ebury. Harcourt and his wife lived in splendor at Stanton Harcourt, a family estate with several acres of gardens behind high walls. A visitor, Danny Davison of Morgan Guaranty, recalls gaping at its magnificence. "Gee, this is a magnificent place you have here," he boyishly told Harcourt. "When did you get it?" "Ten-eighty," was Harcourt's crisp retort.

The contradictory Harcourt piloted the firm into the treacherous waters of controversial takeovers. They were common in the City by the mid-1960s, driven by a new management creed that only multinational corporations could survive in the new age. By 1968, seventy of Britain's one hundred largest companies had been involved in takeovers in just two years. Where Morgan Grenfell had indignantly protested Siegmund Warburg's tactics in the aluminium war, it was now determined that the firm would surpass him in verve and even ruthlessness.

The takeover that revealed this shift was the battle for Gallaher, the manufacturer of Benson and Hedges cigarettes. In May of 1968, Morgan Grenfell and Cazenove, the blue-blooded stock broker, helped Imperial Tobacco sell off a 36.5-percent stake in Gallaher; Imperial had to divest it on antitrust grounds. The underwriting was a fiasco that left the underwriters with a third of the slumping shares and made Gallaher feel vulnerable to unwanted suitors. Indeed, by June, Philip Morris, backed by that Morgan Grenfell nemesis, Warburgs, began to close in on its prey.

Following these events in New York, Barney Walker of American Tobacco told Bill Sword and Jack Evans of Morgan Stanley that he wanted to expand his Gallaher stake and rescue the company from Philip Morris. Sword called Ken Barrington of Morgan Grenfell, who had just returned to his flat after a summer lawn party with the queen at Buckingham Palace. Barrington and his colleague George Law promptly flew to New York. In American Tobacco's boardroom, Barney Walker—a red-faced Irishman with no college degree—gave Sword and Barrington their marching orders. "Look, I wanna win," he said. "I want an absolute guarantee that we will win. What will it take?" "I suppose it depends on the size of your purse," said Barrington. "What'd he say?" grumbled Walker. "It depends how much money we're prepared to pay," an aide translated. Walker barked that money was no object. At this pivotal moment, it was industry, not the bankers, who demanded a new red-blooded, cutthroat style of business. Both Morgan Grenfell and Morgan Stanley would later plead, with some justice, that they were provoked into aggressive takeovers by their clients and that their metamorphosis into merger artists didn't occur in a financial vacuum. In the 1960s, the bankers were still more the instruments than the engines of takeovers.

The Morgan Stanley–Morgan Grenfell team flew off to the City to mount the most vigorous operation in London Stock Exchange history, fortified by a $150-million credit led by Morgan Guaranty. Stymied by LBJ's capital controls, American Tobacco could afford only a partial bid, and this enforced economy led to the controversy. All over the City, insurance companies, pension funds, and other underwriters sat with unwanted, depressed Gallaher shares, gnashing their teeth at Morgan Grenfell. At a Sunday night meeting, the takeover team plotted its strategy with Sir Antony Hornby, senior partner of Cazenove and Company, who was assigned to handle the Stock Exchange operation. They decided to go into the Exchange the next morning and buy the shares from the May underwriters. This controversial tactic—which would redeem Morgan Grenfell in the eyes of the underwriters—also guaranteed that the takeover would enrich a handful of institutions while small shareholders wouldn't learn about it until afterward.

Lately there had been many questions raised about the City. As takeovers grew bloody and unscrupulous, the Labour government threatened to impose strict regulations. To avert that, the Bank of England had created a committee, chaired by Morgan Grenfell's Ken Barrington, to strengthen the Takeover Code. To enforce it, Sir Leslie O'Brien, the Bank of England governor, had set up a Takeover Panel with offices in the bank itself. Lacking statutory powers, the panel was criticized as unhealthily close to the people it oversaw. Yet despite Barrington's role in devising the new code, Morgan Grenfell posed the first and stiffest challenge. Article 7 of the Takeover Code said no shareholder in a target company should receive an offer "more favorable than a general offer to be made thereafter to the other shareholders."[22] This principle was challenged by the American Tobacco takeover, which was a so-called "street sweep"—a huge share purchase without a tender offer.

On Monday morning, Hornby began whirlwind buying such as London had never seen. He went to the May underwriters and paid 35 shillings for Gallaher shares that had slumped to 18 shillings; he was instructed to purchase about five million shares that day. Instead, he was engulfed by a tidal wave of twelve million shares by morning's end. Most small shareholders didn't hear about the sudden windfall until lunchtime, by which point it was too late. They could get 35 shillings for only *half* of their holdings and were outraged by the apparent collusion between big institutions and merchant banks.

Morgan Grenfell had always cooperated with the Bank of England instinctively and sided with the financial authorities. Now it was acting more like a cheeky, defiant outsider, bent on stirring things up and testing the rules of the new Takeover Panel. Suddenly it resembled the assertive, iconoclastic Warburgs that had so offended its sense of propriety a decade before. In an amazing transformation, it had turned into its own worst enemy.

The Takeover Panel censured both Morgan Grenfell and Cazenoves. To the astonishment of the press, Harcourt and Hornby, those City demigods, didn't beat their breast in atonement. Within an hour of the panel's ruling, they simply rejected it out of hand! Here were Sir Antony Hornby, on the board of the Savoy Hotel and Claridge's, and Lord William Harcourt, with his huge estate, thumbing their noses at authority and rebuffing a panel clothed with the prestige of the Bank of England. Hornby sounded like a ruffian: "There's a certain cut and thrust in the market that is the essence of City dealing. If you're going to wait for the amateurs then business will stop."[23]

Bill Harcourt's hauteur was memorable. He came up with a classic retort that expressed both his mischievous humor and magnificent contempt: "Can't a man go in on Monday morning and buy a few shares?" He finished by telling a startled news conference that he would entertain no questions. "I am totally confident that the purchases are in fully conformity with the City code."[24] Bill Sword later claimed that the American Tobacco team had secured approval of the Takeover Panel for its action but that Harcourt courageously withheld this information, lest the panel's authority be weakened. But his initial manner seemed far more defiant than respectful toward the panel and was so reported in the press.

The public was in an uproar. Not only did the press back the panel, but the increasingly powerful institutional investors displayed almost unanimous support for censure. Three-quarters even favored further action. These institutions were the new countervailing powers; merchant banks no longer held all the cards. As would happen on Wall

Street, the providers of capital—the mutual funds, pension funds, insurance companies and so on—were growing powerful at the expense of capital-short merchant banks in London and investment banks in New York.

In a carefully staged reconciliation, Lord Harcourt, a humble, hairshirted suppliant, told the panel, "I should like to assure the committee that it was never my firm's intention to show any lack of respect for the authority of the panel."[25] The Takeover Panel allowed that perhaps he and Hornsby had misunderstood the rules. Although Morgan Grenfell emerged unscathed and banked a gigantic $1-million fee, the damage to its reputation was severe. As London's *Sunday Telegraph* said, "The days when Morgans spoke only to Cazenoves and Cazenoves spoke only to God were clearly at an end."[26]

For Morgan Grenfell, the American Tobacco takeover showed that merchant banks with modest capital and large client lists could make a fortune in the new takeover game—precisely what Siegmund Warburg had seen. Here they could capitalize on old-school ties while both lending and securities work became commodity businesses, dominated by the biggest and strongest. At first, the old financial aristocracy was squeamish about performing hostile takeovers, giving Warburg his head start. But now, only ten years later, the old guard had already lost its compunctions, proving that it could behave with a ferocity ordinarily not associated with the country-house set.

SEVERAL months after the American Tobacco takeover of Gallaher, Morgan Grenfell entered a publishing battle that confirmed its new zest for controversy. In this case, it assisted Rupert Murdoch in his purchase of the *News of the World,* a London tabloid. The paper was a trashy mix of sports, pinups, Tory editorials, and royal gossip. Its major coup was the 1964 purchase of Christine Keeler's memoirs recounting her dalliance with Secretary of State for War John Profumo and a Russian military attaché. The paper sold six million copies every Sunday, topping all English-language newspapers. Half the British adult population loyally enjoyed its salacious pages.

Breaking into British newspapers was then exceedingly difficult: Fleet Street was the preserve of family fiefdoms, and major papers seldom came up for sale. "They were almost looked down upon as toy things by the proprietors," said Lord Stephen Catto, who was to advise Murdoch.[27] Since the nineteenth century, the *News of the World* had been controlled by the Carr family, with Sir William Carr alone holding a

30-percent share. He was oblivious to the paper's declining performance, said one observer, "because he was invariably drunk by half-past ten every morning, a habit which had earned him the popular alias 'Pissing Billy.' "[28]

When Murdoch, Australia's third-largest publisher, began scouting British newspapers in 1967, the objective was less to buy at rock-bottom prices than to crash the Fleet Street gates. He had already befriended Lord Catto, who was married to an Australian and, as a director of the Hongkong and Shanghai Banking Corporation, would stop by to see Murdoch on his Asian tours. Easygoing and convivial, Stephen Catto was less starchy and rigidly upright than his father, the former Bank of England governor. But his breezy manner and quick smile hid a shrewd detachment. Educated at Eton and Cambridge, Catto had trained at Morgan Stanley and J. P. Morgan and was good with "colonials."

Catto was emblematic of his era, just as his father had symbolized the City's solemn prewar rectitude. Catto *fils* didn't shrink from publicity and liked the fact that Murdoch was on call, day or night, in pursuit of a hot deal. In 1967, Murdoch visited Catto, saying he wanted to expand beyond Australia. "Much to my surprise, he sat down and said, 'I want to buy the *Daily Mirror*,' " recalled Catto, who patiently explained that Murdoch would have to pry it loose from the formidable International Publishing Corp. "Then let's start buying IPC," said Murdoch.[29] Catto liked Murdoch's confident, forthright style and had a premonition of bigger things ahead.

Accumulating a small stake in London's *Daily Mirror*, Catto and Murdoch spotted a more promising opportunity when Derek Johnson, a cousin of Sir William Carr, decided to sell his 26-percent stake in *News of the World*. Residing in France and Switzerland, Johnson had variously been a pilot, a steeplechase rider, and an Oxford spectroscopy professor. He wanted to spare his sixth wife onerous inheritance taxes by selling off the stake. Yet he had enough reservations about the Carr family that he didn't automatically sell them the shares.

Carr knew that by controlling the shares, he would possess a solid majority holding in the tabloid and so offered 28 shillings per share for the stake. This was a foolishly stingy offer that fell a shilling short of the stock's current price on the London Stock Exchange. Not bothering to reply, Johnson's London banker, Jacob Rothschild, peddled the block at 37 shillings a share to Robert Maxwell, the publisher of Pergamon Press, the largest scientific and technical publisher in the country. Labeling the move "cheeky," Carr had *his* banker, Hambros, begin buying shares in *News of the World*.

Maxwell wasn't yet the world-devouring mogul of the *Daily Mirror*. Like Murdoch, he saw the Carr tabloid, for all its peephole proclivities, as his entrée into the upper echelon of publishing. Born into a Czechoslovakian peasant family as Jan Ludwig Hoch, Maxwell emigrated to Britain in 1940, changed his name, served in the British army, and took over Pergamon Press after the war. Massive, brawny, and smart, he had a prickly style that scared the daylights out of respectable folk. He was a self-made man who had been elected to Parliament as an avowed socialist. Recalling the episode, Catto stressed Maxwell's somewhat murky business reputation at the time: "Pergamon Press had the hard sell with their encyclopedias. They were virtually forcing them on poor people. There were also doubts about the way he managed his financing. He mixed his own private company with publicly quoted companies in a way that made one uneasy."[30] Nevertheless, Maxwell made a tender offer of over 37 shillings per share for *News of the World*, making Carr's bid look cheap and unsporting in comparison.

To the Carrs, Maxwell was a foreigner unfit to run their Tory paper. This set them up for the blandishments of Rupert Murdoch. One morning in the fall of 1968, Catto's wife heard on the news that the *News of the World* stake was up for sale. "Why don't you get your friend Murdoch to buy it?" she asked Stephen. He soon cabled Murdoch that he had spoken with Sir William Carr's bankers, Hambros, which had expressed interest in his support against Maxwell. Murdoch needed no coaxing.

On Saturday, October 19, Catto summoned Murdoch to come to London at once, tracking him down at a sporting event in Melbourne. Murdoch jumped on a plane to Sydney, where his wife, Anna, handed him a suitcase and his passport. Then he jumped on a Lufthansa plane for Frankfurt, where he switched to a flight for London. Landing at Heathrow's Terminal 2, he evaded reporters thronging Terminal 3. London was by now rife with rumors about Murdoch's arrival, and the press hunted for him relentlessly. Murdoch thought his room at the Savoy might be bugged. So Catto put him up at his country place, where he paced up and down, jotting notes on backs of envelopes. The looming battle gave Morgan Grenfell another chance to shuck its musty image. As the London *Observer* said, "Morgan Grenfell, having been for long regarded as a grouse-moor bank, with a record of unsuccessful defensive battles, is nowadays determined to show it can be as aggressive as the rest of 'em."[31]

Despite the strident denunciations of Maxwell by the Carr forces, Murdoch resembled his competitor in many ways. Both were loners who hated committees and enjoyed a scrapping good fight. Even their politics weren't so dissimilar. As an Oxford student, Murdoch had flirted with political radicalism, and his supposed anti-British sympathies were cited as reasons to oppose his ownership of the *News of the World.* Like Siegmund Warburg, Murdoch thought the British upper class weak and effete, and this emboldened him in his maneuvering. Murdoch's output was already mixed. Though he published the staid *Australian,* he also put out a racy weekly called *Truth.* Nonetheless, Sir William Carr would embrace Murdoch as an unblemished white knight.

During their country-house weekend, Catto outlined to Murdoch a three-pronged strategy that called for securing Carr's support, beating Maxwell, then taking full control of *News of the World.* (Events would unfold in that precise order.) Carr wanted to use Murdoch to destroy Maxwell but without ceding full power to him. As Murdoch later said, "I was expected not as a white knight, but as a Sancho Panza to Carr's Don Quixote."[32] Catto laid out a plan to turn the tables on Carr. After buying a small stake in the *News of the World,* they would take advantage of Carr's vulnerability to gain control of the tabloid. Catto's guile was a revelation to Murdoch, who had equated the City with gentility, said one biographer; "yet here was Lord Catto, a principal in one of the City's most celebrated banks, proposing a strategy that bordered on the Machiavellian in its slyness—perhaps even of the deceptive and fraudulent, as Sir William Carr, its victim, would later claim."[33]

Coached by Catto, Murdoch then had breakfast with Carr at his Cliveden Place residence on Tuesday morning, October 22. Murdoch brashly said that he would buy a majority stake in *News of the World* but that he wanted Carr to step aside as top executive. When Carr balked, Murdoch got up to leave. "I'm here to help you if you want it," said Murdoch. "But I don't like to waste time on dither." "Sit down, Mr. Murdoch," Carr replied.[34] In a complicated deal, they agreed that Murdoch would buy more *News of the World* shares and secure their combined majority. In exchange, Murdoch would get a 40-percent stake in the paper through newly issued shares. They would jointly manage the paper, but Carr would remain as chairman. Murdoch chafed at these terms, but Catto assured him it was the "foot in the door" he needed.[35]

The first phase of the tabloid battle resembled a straight bidding war. Maxwell put together a 30-percent stake by buying the original Derek Johnson block plus additional purchases. The Murdoch forces adopted more controversial tactics. Carr's banker, Hambros, bought *News of the World* shares in apparent violation of the Takeover Code, which forbade companies to buy their own shares. And through a Morgan Grenfell account, Catto bought a 3.5-percent stake in the paper that would be set aside for Murdoch.

In the American Tobacco–Gallaher affair, Lord Harcourt had arrogantly dismissed the press at his peril. Now, in announcing his pact with Carr, Murdoch hired a publicist. Catto found this departure exciting—while his father would doubtless have found it abhorrent and beneath a banker's dignity. At a press conference on Wednesday, October 23, Murdoch, age thirty-seven, made his debut on the British stage. He was tagged the "quiet Australian" by the London press, which knew little about him. At first relaxed and grinning, he tried to answer questions frankly, but he was stunned by a barrage of hostile questions accusing him of violating the Takeover Code. Catto sat quietly by his side, a contemplative finger at his lips.

Robert Maxwell protested to the Takeover Panel what he saw as a side deal between management and Murdoch not in the best interests of shareholders. He also claimed that the Carrs were violating the code by buying their own shares through a surrogate, Hambros. Maxwell had boosted his bid to a hefty 50 shillings per share, but was thwarted by the pact negotiated at breakfast at Cliveden Place. The panel found enough merit in the charges and countercharges to suspend trading in *News of the World* stock for two months. At the time of the standstill, neither side had a 51-percent stake. The panel turned the battle into a proxy fight to be decided at a general shareholders' meeting on January 2, 1969. Catto rallied Murdoch's spirits, saying the decision enhanced their chances for victory. Shortly before the meeting, the panel said neither side could cast votes obtained before Maxwell's first tender offer.

Sir Leslie O'Brien, the Bank of England's governor, fretted that the angry contest would wreck the code. Voluntary self-regulation seemed a feeble way to restrain the mercenary tendencies of the Casino Age. At the Lord Mayor's banquet on November 11, Prime Minister Harold Wilson had reiterated his dislike of the new marauding style in the City, exhorting merchant bankers to police their own behavior. Once again, Morgan Grenfell, long part of the City establishment, openly sparred with City authorities.

When the Carr-Murdoch deal was voted on at the Extraordinary General Meeting held on January 2, the atmosphere was ugly and xenophobic. The Great Queen Street hall was packed with ringers. Murdoch later admitted that some pro-Carr shareholders who couldn't attend had temporarily signed over their shares to *News of the World* staffers. When Sir William Carr marched in like a benevolent patriarch, he was lustily cheered. Dressed in a flashy blue suit, Maxwell was hooted and booed by a chorus shouting "Shame!" "Withdraw!" and "Go home!"[36]

Although Maxwell's standing offer of 50 shillings was the financially superior one, the discussion pivoted on his fitness to run the paper. While Murdoch pretended that he would retain Carr as chairman, Maxwell candidly said he would replace him, telling the paper's publisher, "Every time I have a haircut at the Savoy late in the afternoon, around 4 P.M., I find you and your *News of the World* cronies still drinking Martinis and I don't think that is suitable training for any chairman of mine."[37] Maxwell's combative style didn't work nearly as well as Murdoch's crafty, self-effacing manner. In the final vote, the Carr-Murdoch group got 4.5 million shares, and Maxwell, 3.2 million. Murdoch celebrated with a party at his Embankment flat that night. For Morgan Grenfell, it started a long relationship with the world's most powerful publisher. As an influential board member of Murdoch's News International board, Catto would negotiate his future U.K. newspaper purchases, including that of the London *Times.* Yet the relationship between Murdoch and Morgan Grenfell would have a curious ambivalence, for the banking side of the firm wouldn't lend to Murdoch, believing his operations too dangerously leveraged.

By mid-1969, Sir William Carr saw that with Murdoch he had admitted a Trojan horse. The Australian continued to buy shares after the meeting, so he would safely control more than 50 percent of the paper. He fired Carr's jingoistic editor, Stafford Somerfield. Then he demoted Carr to president and took the chairmanship himself. Murdoch was launched in Britain. That December, he bought the London *Sun,* which would prove his real profit maker. Loading it with pinups, he soon doubled its circulation, to two million, and established it as Britain's biggest daily paper.

The American Tobacco–Gallaher affair and the Murdoch-Maxwell brawl prompted reform of the Takeover Panel, which got a full-time chairman in Lord Hartley William Shawcross, a Morgan Guaranty adviser and a director of Morgan et Compagnie International. The code was revised to forbid partial bids of the American Tobacco variety, and new sanctions were introduced. In a single tumultuous year, Morgan Grenfell's character had changed almost beyond recognition. Mergers were suddenly pitching in a third of the firm's profits. It was operating publicly and flouting authority in a way that would have been inconceivable a decade earlier. Though the firm still issued securities and managed money, it increasingly would take its tone from the piratical world of mergers. This change would also affect the firm's sociology; now a premium would be placed on intellect and experience; Morgan Grenfell would attract a new breed of talented, well-trained lawyers and accountants who could master the intricacies of the complex deals. The new City would be more ruthless but also more democratic, and it would look much more like the Warburgs of the 1950s than the Morgan Grenfell of the 1950s.

SAMURAI

. .
.

Like Morgan Grenfell, Morgan Stanley entered the 1960s a model of civility, then turned itself inside out. In the early 1960s, it radiated a winner's confidence. Nearly two dozen partners in Brooks Brothers suits and monogrammed shirts sat behind rolltop desks at 2 Wall Street. Decorated with English hunting prints, this platform area was a sanctum of mystical power. As one partner said, "It's one of the few places where a single phone call can raise $100 million."[1] Morgan Stanley partners didn't raid, compete, or crudely solicit business and had exclusive relations with their clients. If they hired somebody from another firm, they politely asked that firm's permission.

As befit a firm of illustrious heritage, tradition was venerated. The old House of Morgan had encouraged attendance at partners' meetings by handing out gold coins. In a modern variant, Morgan Stanley gave out ten- or twenty-dollar bills to partners when they entered a meeting. They also got to divide the booty left by absentees. The only unanimous attendance occurred once, in a snowstorm, when everybody planned to make a killing.

As students protested the Vietnam War in the 1960s, it was hard to lure graduates to Wall Street. When Frank A. Petito went to the Harvard Business School to try to recruit students, he ended up sitting alone in a classroom until a professor took pity on him and stopped by to chat. Although they had mostly gone to Princeton, Yale, or Harvard, Morgan Stanley partners came from diverse backgrounds. Like the old Morgan bank, Morgan Stanley was receptive to talented poor boys, even though it was unfairly stereotyped as a Social Register firm. Dick Fisher, a future president, was discouraged from applying for a job by a Harvard Business

School professor who said Morgan Stanley required "blood, brains, and money" and that Fisher failed on two counts.

Nevertheless, the hauteur of the senior partners *could* be oppressive. Once at the firm, Fisher drove up to Canada with one of the partners to work on the Churchill Falls hydroelectric project. At the border, an immigration official, peering at Fisher in the backseat, asked the partner, "Who's that in the back with you?" "I'm traveling by myself," the partner answered. When the officer gestured toward the person sitting in the backseat, the partner said gruffly, "It's no one. It's a statistician."[2]

By the 1960s, Wall Street's religious segregation was crumbling. Many Jewish firms had Protestant partners, especially in syndication, where they had to truckle to Morgan Stanley and First Boston. In 1963, Morgan Stanley hired its first Jew, Lewis W. Bernard, who had roomed at Princeton with Frank Petito's son and frequently stayed at the Petito home. "When Bernard was interviewed, everybody was in favor of hiring him," recalled a former partner. "But it was very hard for some older partners to overcome their ancient prejudice." One Morgan Stanley partner even rushed over to Standard Oil of New Jersey to sound out an official: if Morgan Stanley ever sent over a Jewish employee, would the company be upset? "I think you ought to know, if you don't," the official bristled, "that our chief executive officer is Jewish."[3] The partner slunk away. In 1973, at age thirty-one, Bernard became the youngest partner in Morgan Stanley history (except for the special case of Charlie Morgan), and he would develop into an important strategic thinker.

Entering the 1960s, Morgan Stanley seemed secure, almost invulnerable, in its supremacy. The nonpareil of American investment banking, it counted as clients fifteen of the world's twenty-five largest industrial companies, as well as Australia, Canada, Egypt, Venezuela, and Austria. These were comprehensive, exclusive relationships, a relic of the days when clients needed to wrap themselves in the aura of powerful banks. Morgan Stanley served its clients diligently and was always dreaming up new ways to finance AT&T or General Motors. As the Casino Age progressed, however, and capital was no longer so rare a resource, the traditional ties would erode.

Morgan Stanley would go to any length to serve a faithful client. During the 1950s, it managed securities issues for J. I. Case, a farm-equipment manufacturer. In 1961, when Case faced bankruptcy and bankers threatened to pull their loans, Samuel B. Payne of Morgan Stanley became temporary chairman of the company. For six months, Payne spent three or four days a week at Case headquarters in Racine,

Wisconsin, turning the company around. Later, a rehabilitated Case was sold to Tenneco. Similarly, Morgan Stanley undertook a record financing for the billion-dollar Churchill Falls hydroelectric project in Labrador, Newfoundland, twice the size of Grand Coulee Dam. Some Morgan Stanley partners worked on it daily for eight straight years. In 1969, when the chairman of the Churchill Falls Corporation was killed in a plane crash, partner William D. Mulholland stepped in and ran the company.

The Morgan Stanley partner who first saw the cracks in this immaculate world of loyal bankers and loyal clients was Robert H. B. Baldwin, a protégé of Perry Hall, who had retired in 1961. Baldwin was a man who sharply polarized opinion and was later seen as either the savior or the ruination of the firm. For better or worse, he would sweep away the cobwebs and drag Morgan Stanley into the modern era. At a place of proper gentlemen, Baldwin had a high energy level, fanatic drive, and a tremendous desire to manage people. Tall and athletic with cold piercing eyes and a brusque, humorless manner, he was the opposite of the archetypal Morgan man. His partners found him cold and awkward, a man who had trouble relaxing or making small talk, and he seemed misplaced in Wall Street's most elegant firm. Yet that was perhaps an advantage, for he wasn't shy about assuming power, as were the gentlemen.

Opinion divides on the question of Baldwin's intelligence. He had an outstanding academic record: a triple threat in sports at Princeton— football, baseball, and basketball—he also received a *summa cum laude* degree in economics. Yet his intelligence wasn't subtle or reflective but obsessive and suggestive of an implacable will. In his office, he had a needlepoint pillow on which was stitched, "The harder I work, the luckier I get."[4] At a notably discreet firm, Baldwin would abruptly inform people that they were overweight or smoking too much. Entertaining clients, he would suddenly launch into extended monologues on his own achievements.

Bob Baldwin would develop into a classic hell-on-wheels boss who would dominate Morgan Stanley for years, making life memorably miserable for his subordinates. "He could be a real bastard in the supercilious way that he would exercise his power with subordinates," said one ex-partner. "And he sometimes made a terrible fool of himself in the process of trying to be a big wheel." Said another: "He lacks humility, he's self-centered and insecure and quite humorless. You don't want to have a drink with Bob Baldwin." Yet he was also honest and forgiving.

More to the point, he was extremely perceptive about the strategic direction of investment banking.

Baldwin was relentless in pushing an idea. He once harangued legislators during testimony in Washington, then harangued his companion in a cab; when his companion got off, he harangued the driver. His hero was no dreamy poet or thinker, but Admiral Chester Nimitz. When his son was at Phillips Exeter Academy in the early 1970s, Baldwin, an unabashed defense hawk, addressed the student body on "the other side of the military-industrial society that was in such disrepute."[5]

Much like the Young Turks at Morgan Grenfell, Baldwin was maddened by what he called the white-shoe thing—the notion that Morgan Stanley partners were inept stuffed shirts who succeeded because of blood ties and social contacts. "My grandfather was a conductor on the Pennsylvania Railroad," he pleaded. "My yacht is a 13-foot Sunfish."[6] Or: "I get wild when they talk about that white-shoe thing. Why are we number one? Because we are nice people? Because we play golf? I stand on our record."[7] As at Morgan Grenfell, this discomfort with a sedate past sparked revolt among younger partners and enabled Baldwin to push for sweeping changes in the firm's *modus operandi*.

Baldwin was also perceptive about Morgan Stanley's defects in the mid-1960s. It was poorly managed and becoming too big for the old consensual style. There were no budgets, no planning, and no modern management—just endless collegial discussions. Bookkeeping was still done by clerks on high stools, who copied entries into leather-bound ledgers on tilt-top tables. All the while, the firm was growing and bursting in its small headquarters. In 1967, it vacated its cramped offices at 2 Wall Street. It was still unthinkable that Morgan Stanley would lack a Wall Street address. Harry Morgan was afraid that if the firm had a Broadway address, London friends might think him a theatrical producer. He was only reconciled to a new office building at 140 Broadway because it was the former Guaranty Trust address.

During the 1960s, Baldwin made repeated efforts to run the firm but was rebuffed. Stymied by his slow advancement, he went down to Washington from 1965 to 1967 and served as under secretary of the navy. In these years, Baldwin was always promoting schemes to proselytize for the war on college campuses. Partners who found him pushy hoped he wouldn't return. When he did, they again spurned his demand to take charge of daily operations, and he again decided to leave.

He nearly escaped to the giant Hartford Insurance Company. Felix Rohatyn of Lazard Frères was playing matchmaker between ITT chairman Harold Geneen and the Hartford board. As Hartford's investment banker, Baldwin frostily rejected an overture from Rohatyn. The Hartford board decided to bring in Baldwin as a one-man "white knight" to ward off ITT's advances. In December 1968, Baldwin was set to become Hartford's chief executive when Geneen, enraged by reports of his move, launched a hostile tender and forced Baldwin to retreat back to Morgan Stanley. Now it was a no-exit situation: Baldwin and Morgan Stanley had to come to terms. With his enormous frustration and bottled-up energy, Baldwin resumed his campaign to shake up the firm and in 1969 got it to call a rare planning session. Outvoted, he later conceded it was a "god-damned disaster."[8] What saved him was partly a generational change. As older, Depression-era partners retired, they were slowly being replaced by a new group recruited in the early 1960s. In 1970, the firm's twenty-eight partners admitted six young men, including Dick Fisher and Bob Greenhill. They were known as the "irreverent group of six," and eventually they would tip the power balance toward Baldwin, giving him the votes to launch change. But at first, they wanted the nice, tight, rich Morgan Stanley of old.

Contrary to the views of more myopic partners, Bob Baldwin saw Morgan Stanley as fighting for its life. He queasily noted the rise of Salomon Brothers and Goldman, Sachs, which were using their trading skills to chip away at the four dominant firms—Morgan Stanley, First Boston, Kuhn, Loeb, and Dillon, Read. At this point, Morgan Stanley still exhibited vintage snobbery about "traders" being socially inferior to "bankers"—a tradition dating back to Pierpont Morgan. This was also true at First Boston, which would call its underwriting wing the House of Lords and its trading room the House of Commons. Trading was still thought a coarse commodity business best left to Jewish firms such as Salomon and Goldman, Sachs. In the Salomon Brothers culture, in contrast, traders stigmatized corporate finance people as "light-bulb changers" or "order takers."[9]

John Gutfreund of Salomon Brothers was using the firm's trading prowess to win new business and secure a better spot in syndicates. "Salomon and the rest were besieging chief financial officers with suggestions and ideas that we couldn't match," said Sheppard Poor, a former Morgan Stanley partner. "There was a proliferation of different financing vehicles."[10] Morgan Stanley had always cultivated the big corporations, the users of capital. Salomon and Goldman, in contrast, had close relations with the suppliers of capital, the institutional investors who now accounted for three-quarters of the New York Stock

Exchange trading. And power was now tilting toward these providers of capital.

In the volatile 1960s, with inflation induced by Vietnam spending, pension funds, insurance companies, and so on were managing their portfolios more actively. Instead of buying large blocks of bonds and holding them until maturity, they wanted to swap new blocks for old ones. This was impossible for an underwriter like Morgan Stanley, which had no trading operation. Large investors had other specialized needs. Trading big cumbersome blocks of stocks, they needed intermediaries to do "block positioning"—that is, temporarily taking the block off their hands and selling it whole or piecemeal. Salomon Brothers had the capital and trading strength to perform such intricate feats and used these services to expand its underwriting business. As an outsider, John Gutfreund had no scruples about raiding clients or doing other things anathema to the Wall Street club. He was the first to show that "the power to distribute securities would become the power to underwrite them."[11]

Gutfreund seemed to enjoy tweaking Morgan Stanley. When former defense secretary Robert McNamara became World Bank president in 1968—the bank's first non–Wall Street president—he wanted to stimulate competition among underwriters and brought in Salomon Brothers along with Morgan Stanley and First Boston. In a tough bargaining session with the three firms, McNamara demanded a better price. Larry Parker of Morgan Stanley got up and said, "Well, I've got to go and consult my partner." In a puckish mood—but also telegraphing that he would compete on price—Gutfreund rose to consult *his* partner. Then he suddenly sat back down. "Well," he said slyly, "she's always said yes to whatever I want to do." This put pressure on Morgan Stanley and First Boston to follow his lead.[12]

To maintain syndicate leadership, Baldwin saw that Morgan Stanley would have to admit people long shunned as the rabble of the business—salesmen and traders. This move toward trading and distributing securities—and not simply allocating them to other firms to sell—would explode the small, posh Morgan Stanley, which then had about 250 people. The firm could no longer monitor securities markets from a lordly distance. At a 1971 planning session, Bob Baldwin finally got a decision to develop a sales and trading operation, and Morgan Stanley ceased to be the stately underwriting house created in 1935. It would develop relationships with institutional investors by trading and distributing stocks and bonds. "We made one decision," said Dick Fisher later, "and that simple decision led to all the subsequent growth of our firm."[13] The changes were implemented piecemeal, with Fisher put in charge of corporate bond trading. Later, Archie Cox, Jr., son of the Watergate special prosecutor, presided over equity trading.

Trading meant risk and required more than the $7.5 million in capital that Morgan Stanley had in 1970. The younger partners had long feared that the firm's precious capital might be depleted by the death of its aging partners. To preserve capital, Morgan Stanley switched in 1970 from a partnership to a partially incorporated firm. This also allowed dividends to flow in from Morgan et Compagnie International in Paris without punitive taxes.

As Morgan Stanley expanded into a full-service firm, the corporate culture changed. For almost forty years, Morgan Stanley men had traveled in a sedate, elite world, dealing only with chief executives. Traders inhabited a rougher world. "It was a different kind of culture," said one trader. "Instead of the low-key, white-shoe style, this group was the raucous, tough-minded, four-letter-word kind of crowd that you get in a high-pressure situation." Many older partners wrinkled their noses at the traders. "There were also young partners who looked down on us as if we had dirt under our fingernails and were an inferior breed," recalled a former trader. Tastes changed: Morgan Stanley suddenly had a Sky Box at Madison Square Garden. A former partner noted that "Morgan Stanley partners didn't go to basketball games up till then."

At first, it was difficult to recruit people: nobody believed the august Morgans was serious about trading. Traders lived in a world of split-second, high-pressure decisions. Where corporate finance people ambled in at 9:30 or 10:00, traders were at their desks by 8:00. When Fisher tried to ban employees from eating lunch at their desks, he couldn't enforce the rule. In the superhuman effort to recreate the firm, some people worked all night. "I can remember someone asking me early one morning whether I was coming or going," recalled Frederick H. Scholtz, who came in from General Foods to oversee planning.[14] His secretary would surreptitiously change her dress to hide that she had stayed all night.

The trading operation was built from scratch. Morgan Stanley hadn't had its own floor trader at the New York Stock Exchange. Partners had feared, rather vainly, that if the Morgan trader sold General Motors or AT&T, it would precipitate an avalanche of selling. Now traders were installed without setting off any market crashes.

This helter-skelter expansion had healthy side effects—especially an end to the firm's homogeneity. Before long, the Wasp citadel had "partners" with strange ethnic names. In 1975, Luis Mendez, a Cuban refugee with a distinctly Spanish accent, who had once wrapped packages in B. Altman's basement, was made a partner from the bond-trading desk. His success reflected a new stress on performance. This trend was strikingly revealed when Robert McNamara visited the firm. At a luncheon with Morgan Stanley executives, McNamara ignored more senior figures to question Mendez, who sat in the rear and could clarify pricing mysteries about World Bank issues. The blunt, streetwise Mendez told McNamara that the World Bank was overpricing its issues and alienating customers. Afterward, McNamara said to his companion, Eugene Rotberg, "This firm isn't as stuffy as I thought it was."[15]

Morgan Stanley tossed many traditions out the window. It no longer had the luxury of growing its own people and inculcating them with Morgan style. In recruiting traders, it had to favor those with youth, nerve, and stamina; almost half the managing directors enlisted after 1970 were under thirty-five. To attract traders, the firm introduced production-oriented compensation, which eroded collegiality and generated new rivalries and tensions. Baldwin gloried in this rough world of sharp elbows. Where Morgan men had disdained competition, he said approvingly, "The only way to make investment banking more competitive would be to gouge eyes out."[16] As the firm increased tenfold in a decade, it suffered terrible growing pains and throbbed with new tensions.

To woo institutional investors, Morgan Stanley established a Stock Research Department. In April 1973, Frank Petito called in Barton Biggs, a Yale man and an ex-marine, who had managed a hedge fund in Greenwich, Connecticut. Biggs had been a go-go "gunslinger" portfolio manager of the late 1960s, but a respectable version of the breed. As *Institutional Investor* said, "Biggs was definitely the kind of gunslinger you could introduce to your daughter."[17] Petito offered Biggs a partnership, which he accepted on the spot. It was one of the rare times in Morgan Stanley history that anybody was brought in as a partner.

The stock-research decision was controversial. Perry Hall and other senior people opposed it, claiming it might threaten their blue-chip franchise and open up conflicts of interest with clients. As partner Larry Parker said, when Morgan Stanley started equity research, "We took a very deep breath." To establish his autonomy, Biggs fired salvos at IBM in a 1974 piece in *Barron's*. Scrapping an old Wall Street taboo, Morgan Stanley raided other firms, hiring analysts with such abandon that Baldwin was besieged with angry calls. "I've had a number of good friends call up and be damned mad at me," he said. "I've promised we'd take no more."[18]

In rapid succession, major elements of the Gentleman Banker's Code were breaking down. Like Morgan Grenfell, Morgan Stanley kept up its gentlemanly aura only so long as nobody poached on its territory; once threatened, it retaliated with a vengeance. Both on Wall Street and in the City, the graceful, leisurely world of securities syndicates was being replaced by the predatory world of mergers and the freewheeling, irreverent world of traders. Form was simply following function.

During this transition, Harry Morgan continued to represent standards in a firm that was easily tempted to forget them. Although he became a limited partner in 1970 and technically lacked a vote, he still made his influence felt. Shortly after Morgan Stanley was incorporated, American Express tried to acquire it. Opinion was divided, some older partners favoring the acquisition, many younger ones dead set against it. Harry Morgan, in an emotional speech, said he wouldn't sell his birthright for a mess of porridge. "You can do what you want, but the name Morgan is not for sale." American Express was sent packing.

Similarly in 1969, the firm entered into a new venture with Brooks, Harvey and Company to finance and invest in real estate. This real estate offshoot got off to a shaky start. At one point, the Teamsters came along with an irresistible proposal: they wanted Morgan Stanley to manage all their properties in the United States. Almost everyone favored the move except Harry Morgan, who sat silently through the discussion. "Young fellows," he said at last, "as long as I'm alive, this firm is not going to do business with the Teamsters."[19] The discussion ended.

By 1973, the burgeoning Morgan Stanley was surveying both uptown and downtown sites for new offices. Many partners refused to abandon Wall Street to follow corporate clients to midtown. Baldwin disagreed but couldn't budge them. Then he lunched with André Meyer of Lazard Frères, which had moved up to Rockefeller Center. He told Meyer about the controversy. "Fine," said Meyer, laughing, "I'll be having lunch uptown with your clients while you're having lunch downtown with your competitors." Baldwin went back downtown all fired up. He prevailed upon his colleagues to look at three floors available in the Exxon Building on Sixth Avenue.

Baldwin took them uptown via the Sixth Avenue subway, changing at West Fourth Street, rather than by way of the Seventh Avenue line, whose nearest stop, at Fiftieth Street and Seventh Avenue, was a popular spot for streetwalkers. The manipulation worked. In August 1973, Morgan Stanley, the very symbol of Wall Street, moved to the Exxon Building in midtown. The move underscored that paramount reality of the Casino Age—that once-proud and all but omnipotent bankers were now subservient to their corporate clients.

BOB Baldwin's palace coup at Morgan Stanley coincided with a top-secret attempt to recreate the old House of Morgan abroad. As finance became more global, the Morgan houses were colliding in obscure places and casting confusion. The problem was typified by Japan's stubborn belief that Morgan Guaranty and Morgan Stanley—whatever their mischievous, self-serving denials—belonged to the same *zaibatsu*. The situation was endowed with comic-opera complexity on account of Morgan Grenfell's global expansion in the late 1960s.

In the dozy 1950s, Morgan Grenfell was boxed into Britain by exchange controls and the fear of clashes abroad with Morgan Guaranty. In 1967, to jolt Morgan Grenfell from lethargy, Lord Harcourt had drafted his friend Sir John Stevens as the new chief executive. Like Harcourt, Stevens had been British economics minister in Washington and U.K. executive director of the IMF–World Bank. During his six-year tenure, Stevens would exert a pervasive influence on Morgan Grenfell. At a firm weak in broad strategic thinkers, his vision of a global future was exceptional. He also brought an air of adventure to the stodgy old bank. During World War II, he had parachuted into Italy as a member of the Special Operations Executive, Britain's secret dirty-tricks intelligence unit, to finance the underground Piedmont Liberation Committee. He infiltrated occupied territory in Greece and France and in 1945 accepted the surrender of German divisions in northern Italy, receiving the freedom of the city of Turin for his work with Italian partisans. Fluent in six or seven languages, he became a roving emissary for the Bank of England and, in 1957, executive director. The next year, chattering in Russian and dazzling Muscovites, he made the initial contact between the Bank of England and the Soviet State Bank, later giving Morgan Grenfell a financial edge with the Soviets. By the early 1960s, Stevens was on the short list to be governor of the Bank of England. When he lost out, he accepted Harcourt's offer to come to Morgan Grenfell.

As Stevens toured the world opening up new Morgan Grenfell offices with Foreign Office recruits, the firm happily exploited 23 Wall's fame. Morgan Grenfell's overseas clients tended to be American companies who banked with Morgan Guaranty. As David Bendall, one of Stevens's

Foreign Office recruits, said, "As Morgan Grenfell went abroad, nobody knew the firm. But they did know J. P. Morgan and Company, and we used the name."[20] "They were known worldwide as the number-one American bank," conceded Stephen Catto, "and so the Morgan Guaranty stake was very helpful in our establishing business abroad."[21] Of course, as Morgan Stanley and Morgan Grenfell traded on the name, Morgan Guaranty's difficulties increased geometrically.

Morgan Grenfell was growing restless with Morgan Guaranty, which prevented it from entering the vital, lucrative U.S. market. Under Glass-Steagall, Morgan Grenfell couldn't function as an investment bank in New York. "And I'm sure that from the viewpoint of the older, more senior Morgan Grenfell people, we were American upstarts anyway—second-class citizens and clearing-bank types," said Rod Lindsay.

Morgan Guaranty, meanwhile, was going like gangbusters in the Euromarkets and by the early 1970s had nearly six hundred people based in London—nearly the size of the entire bank in the 1950s. Companies that used Morgan Guaranty in home markets, such as Michelin and Siemens, flocked to it in London. When Danny Davison became Morgan Guaranty's London manager in the late 1960s, he found Morgan Grenfell such a dry, sleepy place that he preferred doing business with Lazards or even Warburgs—a sore point at Morgan Grenfell. As liaison with 23 Great Winchester Street, Davison imagined he was entitled to share trade secrets. Early in his tour, he attended a partners' meeting but found that confidential sections were neatly snipped from his briefing book. Insulted, he swore never to return. It was the same old confusion bred by the bizarre situation in which Morgan Guaranty held a giant stake in Morgan Grenfell, but was supposed to remain passive. If this appeased the Bank of England and the Federal Reserve, it went counter to logic and human nature.

Around the same time, Lew Preston sent Sir John Stevens a letter protesting Morgan Grenfell's mounting foreign-exchange dealings. As its New York banker, he was disturbed by excessively large open positions Morgan Guaranty had to cover. "From then on, there was a perceptible cooling off, although in the most friendly way," recalled one ex-Morgan Grenfell executive. And as banker to Morgan Stanley's new trading operation, Morgan Guaranty was also intermittently disturbed by *its* overdrafts.

As shown by American Tobacco's electrifying dash at Gallaher, Morgan Grenfell and Morgan Stanley had been drawn together by merger work. Sir John Stevens of Morgan Grenfell and Bill Sword of Morgan Stanley now contemplated a scheme for closer global cooperation. But they couldn't proceed without Morgan Guaranty, which owned a third of Morgan Grenfell and shared in Morgan et Compagnie International, the Paris underwriting operation Morgan Stanley had inherited. (The latter now handled at least twice the Eurodollar financing of any other U.S. investment bank.) Morgan Guaranty was indeed intrigued by the notion of a foreign merger after a Morgan Grenfell delegation broached the idea at a confidential New York meeting in August, 1972. Disputes over the Morgan name, especially in Japan and the Middle East, had caused unending friction. Since some foreign customers would never fathom the whole Byzantine Morgan history, why not make an advantage of necessity? Paris had already shown the fantastic power latent in combined effort.

So on June 20, 1973, exactly forty years after Pecora's thunderous denunciations, members of the three Morgan houses journeyed to the Grotto Bay Hotel in Bermuda, a honeymoon hideaway, for a secret meeting. Its purpose—to resurrect the House of Morgan beyond U.S. regulatory reach. The precautions for secrecy were extraordinary. The operation had taken the code name Triangle and was so hush-hush that only the most senior people knew of the meeting. (Over sixteen years later, when Ralph Leach, then chairman of Morgan Guaranty's Executive Committee, was asked about the Bermuda meeting, he replied, "What Bermuda meeting?" When it was described to him, he said bitterly, "Gee, it must be nice to be a Morgan insider."[22]) For older Morgan people, the proposed reunion seemed to be a chance to relive glory days. The plan called for the three houses to pool their overseas securities business in something called Morgan International. Morgan Guaranty and Morgan Stanley would each have a 45 percent stake and Morgan Grenfell the remaining 10 percent. The new entity, in turn, would own half of Morgan Grenfell. In foreign outposts where they had sparred, the three houses would cooperate instead. It would be an elegant solution to the chronic identity problem.

Important to these discussions was a momentous development that had taken place at Morgan Guaranty. In 1969, the firm created a one-bank holding company called J. P. Morgan and Company, reviving a name dormant since the Guaranty merger in 1959. "There was controversy about dropping the Guaranty name for the holding company," explained Guido Verbeck. "But we just wanted to keep pushing that Morgan name. It was magical."[23] At first, Morgan Guaranty constituted virtually all of J. P. Morgan and Company, but it would gradually shrink as Morgans became a diversified, financial conglomerate. Such one-bank holding companies allowed banks to expand into leasing and other fields and issue commercial paper exempt from Federal Reserve interest-rate ceilings. Along with CDs, commercial paper, and Eurodollar deposits, they helped to liberate 23 Wall from the constraints of Glass-Steagall. This new freedom perhaps made the bank more skeptical of any alliance.

For all its imaginative appeal and historic resonance, the Bermuda meeting was a fiasco. A major obstacle was political: if banks no longer operated under direct political supervision, as they had with the 1920s foreign loans, they still behaved in a manner broadly consonant with national interests. They instinctively sought government protection for foreign loans and couldn't casually defy the State Department or Foreign Office. As in the 1930s, geopolitical divergences in U.S. and British policy made cooperation difficult. "Morgan Grenfell was lending money to our friend Castro in Havana," said Walter Page, then Morgan Guaranty president. "They were also lending money to North Korea. We couldn't do that and Morgan Stanley couldn't either. That kind of thing made it almost impossible."[24] The Cuban and North Korean loans were, in fact, guaranteed by the British government. Thanks to Sir John Stevens, Morgan Grenfell was also strong in export credits to Iron Curtain countries.

For Morgan Grenfell, the meeting brought out an old ambivalence toward "big brother" in the proudly sensitive junior partner. As the smallest of the three Morgan houses, the British firm feared that it would be overpowered by the bigger Americans. This sentiment was especially prevalent in the Corporate Finance Department, which threatened a revolt if the deal went through. Great Britain was about to enter the Common Market. On that basis, David Bendall of Morgan Grenfell pleaded for a special British role, arguing that his firm had the best access to Commonwealth countries and should "lead" the new joint venture into Europe. "I guess I was the one who put his foot in the plate," said Bendall. "The Americans said it was the most chauvinistic thing they had ever heard. But we felt we were being fitted into somebody else's structure."[25] Lewis Preston and the Morgan Guaranty people felt they had been grossly misled as to the level of Morgan Grenfell enthusiasm. They had been prodded into the meeting in the belief of an imminent Morgan Grenfell–Morgan Stanley deal. The two American houses were also deeply offended by Bendall's insinuation that Americans were disliked in Europe. Preston was so incensed that he threatened to sell Morgan Guaranty's one-third stake, although he was soon calmed down by Morgan chairman Ellmore C. Patterson.

The Baldwin coup at Morgan Stanley added complications. It had installed a new generation whose brusque, thrusting energy and irreverent style offended Morgan Grenfell sensibilities. "The Morgan Stanley boys were the real go-ahead graspers," recalled a Morgan Grenfell official. "You could see a mile off they were just there for the grab. They were assuming they would be entitled to boss the thing and lead it." Many Morgan Stanley naysayers, in turn, thought Morgan Grenfell a morguelike merchant bank full of lazy, pompous dukes and earls employing anachronistic methods. They were not about to play second fiddle to the Brits.

The Morgan Guaranty people had secret reservations about the new venture with Morgan Stanley. As a former official at 23 Wall noted, 'There was always a feeling at the bank that Wall Street [i.e., Morgan Stanley] was full of get-rich people." The salary differential had always been a sore point: a Morgan Stanley partner might earn $150,000 in a bad year, $500,000 in a good year, so that even a junior partner might earn more than Morgan Guaranty's chairman. Anybody who stayed at Morgan Guaranty had to believe it represented something superior. Otherwise why not jump ship and go to the more lucrative Morgan Stanley?

Morgan Guaranty also jealously treasured the fruits of a spectacular decade of building up overseas branches and taking equity stakes in foreign banks. Of the three firms, it had experienced the most robust growth, traveling far beyond the little hothouse bank that stood in Morgan Stanley's shadow in the 1950s. "By Bermuda, Morgan Guaranty was a real entity in this world and had more feet in a lot of places than any of the others," Walter Page explained. "We would have been giving up a hell of a lot that we had accomplished already in Japan, Australia, Singapore, and Hong Kong."[26] By 1972, a third of J. P. Morgan and Company's profits were coming from abroad, a figure that would soar to over 50 percent within a few years. It had moved furthest and fastest toward globalization and didn't want to share its booty with others.

The final set of reservations in this complicated game came from Morgan Stanley. Buoyed by its success in Paris, the firm felt understandably brash and confident and willing to go it alone abroad. "They thought they were big, independent, and successful and didn't need nannies," recalled an observer. Yet not everybody was opposed. Sheppard Poor later said, "The internationalists thought it would be beneficial to expand our ties overseas. The domestic people thought we would be giving away more than we were getting."[27] Worried about Morgan Stanley's limited capital, Frank Petito felt strongly about his firm's need for Morgan Guaranty's deep pockets. (The visionaries at all three firms were always obsessed with capital.) But Baldwin, suspicious of foreign business, which he often saw as a waste of time and money, didn't provide the necessary push, despite his sentimental attachment to the Morgan name and history.

At the Bermuda meeting, the House of Morgan—as a dream, a possibility, a will-o'-the-wisp—ceased to be. Afterward, the three firms largely went their own ways and evolved into separate and quite combative competitors. The age of interlocking partnerships, of spheres of interest and mysterious interplay among financial powers, was over. In 1974, Morgan Grenfell set up a New York representative office, the first beachhead of a counterinvasion. Far more than the two other firms, it would suffer from Bermuda's failure, which might have given it a strong, early presence in global securities markets, albeit at the cost of its identity. A minority, led by Lord Catto, presciently believed that it was better to be a major player in global markets, even if in a junior role, than to be doomed to second-rate autonomy. In 1976, Morgan Stanley bought up the remaining one-third interest of the Paris operation, renamed it Morgan Stanley International, and packed it off to London under Archie Cox, Jr. In 1979, Morgan Guaranty, having at last recovered from the Schwab trauma, set up Morgan Guaranty Limited in London for Euromarket underwriting, facing off against the Cox venture. Both times Morgan Grenfell spurned invitations to participate, afraid of being swallowed up. Now the three Morgan houses would fight each other without quarter.

At Bermuda, the House of Morgan died a quiet death. In characteristic Morgan style, the funeral itself was unknown to the outside world. No obituaries appeared in the press; it died in secrecy.

WHILE Morgan Guaranty retained a tweedy, well-bred style of banking in the mid-1970s, Morgan Stanley experimented with a more muscular approach to business. It faced competitive threats that didn't permit the old mannerly Morgan style. For all its braggadocio and chest-thumping swagger, the firm was very vulnerable, as Bob Baldwin realized when he campaigned for a new trading operation in stocks and bonds. As his chief visual aid, Baldwin would hold up an old tombstone ad and point out the legions of competitors who had perished. Morgan Stanley now faced a host of brawny rivals, trading powers such as Salomon Brothers and Goldman, Sachs, and that retail behemoth, Merrill Lynch. The gentlemanly way of doing business was becoming a privilege the firm could no longer afford.

Morgan Stanley betrayed no mood of crisis. With clients such as

General Motors, Exxon, General Electric, AT&T, and Texaco, it didn't exactly panic. As *Business Week* said in 1974, "It is still the most prestigious of the investment banking houses, and its name still opens doors everywhere."[28] Even in appearance, Morgan Stanley partners seemed immune to the relaxed look of the times. Of a photograph of two dozen somber partners that illustrated the 1974 *Business Week* article, one writer noted, "The picture looked as though it might have been posed for at a mortician's convention."[29]

Nevertheless, a crisis lurked below the surface. The investment banker's historic role as middleman and gatekeeper of capital markets was being devalued. Mature companies could now sell commercial paper or place debt privately with institutions. Some companies had grown so rich—Ford; Sears, Roebuck; and General Electric—that they would serve as banks themselves. Lewis Bernard of Morgan Stanley accurately predicted: "Clients will try to do more for themselves. Our principal competition is our clients."[30]

The new trading and distribution wing shored up Morgan Stanley's underwriting business. At the same time, it highlighted the fact that underwriting was becoming a humdrum commodity business. Morgan Stanley needed another main event, not just new sideshows. It found the answer in the predatory world of mergers and acquisitions, setting up Wall Street's first M&A department in the early 1970s. As Morgan Grenfell had already discovered, it was an ideal business for posh but capital-poor firms.

Merger work was no novelty to the firm. In the 1950s, Northey Jones had consolidated several carpet companies into Mohasco Corporation. Alex Tomlinson had been a matchmaker for British Petroleum in its purchase of a large stake in Standard Oil of Ohio. (Morgan Stanley's role was hidden to avoid angering its seven-sister clients, who might not warm to a new oil giant in the U.S. market.) And Bill Sword aided Morgan Grenfell in the American Tobacco takeover of Gallaher. In the past, Morgan Stanley had collected a modest fee for such work or used it as a free loss leader to generate underwriting business. Merger work formed part of a total advisory relationship with clients. Some Morgan Stanley partners now objected to marketing it as a discrete service. This segmentation of the business, known as transactional banking, would gradually supplant the earlier system of comprehensive dealings with clients, or relationship banking.

For the most part, Morgan Stanley had sat out the conglomerate wave of the 1960s. This movement attempted to reduce diverse companies to a common calculus of profit and loss. Conglomerates threw together scores of unrelated businesses to bypass antitrust restrictions that might block intra-industry mergers. The craze remade the corporate landscape, creating eighteen of America's one hundred largest companies; twenty-five thousand businesses vanished in the 1960s. Many takeovers were financed by inflated share prices of the conglomerates themselves—financial hocus-pocus that made Morgan Stanley nervous. The firm wasn't really pressed to participate in the craze. Most conglomerates were acquisitive upstarts and not the staid, blue-chip firms on the Morgan Stanley client roster.

Corporate restructuring was still curbed by Wall Street etiquette, which frowned on unsolicited takeovers. Afraid of conflicts with clients, Morgan Stanley had a rule against hostile takeovers. In 1970, it nearly engaged in its first hostile bid when Warner-Lambert decided to take over part of Eversharp's shaving business; in that case, the mere threat of a hostile takeover made the target submit. So Morgan Stanley's taboo-breaking hostile raid was postponed until 1974, when International Nickel (Inco) pursued the Philadelphia-based ESB, formerly called Electric Storage Battery.

By this point, an ambitious young partner named Bob Greenhill headed the four-man M&A Department. He had reluctantly entered the takeover area, regarding it as a slow track to the top. Then he saw there was money—lots of money—to be made. As Wall Street's first takeover star, Greenhill would rewrite the rules of the game. He wanted the work to be tough, professional, and extremely disciplined. Most of all, he wanted it to be profitable and not a lagniappe thrown to a favored client. While some older partners still wanted to offer merger service free, Greenhill, Yerger Johnstone, and Bill Sword devised a fee schedule that took a percentage of the money involved in a takeover. From now on, the firm would ask for retainers just to scout mergers, a process in which employees sat around fantasizing matchups.

When merger work was a free service designed to preserve an underwriting relationship with a client, the investment banker had no incentive to approve or reject a takeover, thus guaranteeing his objectivity. Now the incentive system was quite heavily loaded toward advocating takeovers. The bigger and more frequent the takeover, the more profit for Morgan Stanley. The new fee-for-service mentality directly related to the declining importance of underwriting. If blue-chip clients brought in less bond business, why pamper them with extras? "We charge for the services we provide," Lewis Bernard explained. "When a client asks us to take on an assignment, we expect to get paid for it."[31]

Son of a Swedish immigrant and Baltimore clothing-company owner,

Bob Greenhill came to Morgan Stanley via Yale, Harvard Business School, and the U.S. Navy. He was one of the "irreverent six" who participated in Bob Baldwin's bloodless coup. In the navy, he was called Greenie, and he remained so called at Morgan Stanley, a firm with a preppy relish for nicknames. (Baldwin was Baldy.) Short and trim with curly hair, powerful shoulders, and a narrow waist, he had a boyish grin that masked an obsessive intensity.

Greenhill personified the rock-'em, sock-'em style that would characterize Wall Street in the 1980s. He came alive in combat, and his stamina in all-night bargaining sessions was mythical. He was tailor-made for financial warfare. A former partner declared: "Bob is smart and completely insensitive. He couldn't care less what you think and he has no need for peer acceptance or approval. He marches to his own drummer. He's very rational, very focused. On the wall of his office, he has an Al Capp cartoon showing Fearless Fosdick riddled with bullets. The caption is 'MERE FLESH WOUNDS.' That's how Bob sees himself." Once called the "ultimate samurai," Greenhill had qualities that made him a formidable negotiator but a trying person. Another former partner remarked, "Bob knows he's good and he talks down to clients. But CEOs can't afford not to use the best. So they just decide to stomach him because he's so good."

Greenhill was that Morgan rarity—a partner who emerges as a distinct personality in the public mind. Publicity accompanied transactional banking as naturally as secrecy did relationship banking. Where Morgan style of dress had been aloof and understated, Greenhill wore suspenders monogrammed with dollar bills. (Surely Harold Stanley would have cringed!) He resembled a commando more than the martini-drinking Morgan banker of yesteryear. He was a resourceful, derring-do character. Once in Saudi Arabia, after missing a scheduled commercial flight, he hired a private plane just so that he and two other partners could make a dinner appointment in another Saudi city.

Instead of tennis or golf, Greenhill liked solitary sports that tested endurance. Early each morning, he jogged near his Greenwich, Connecticut, home. He was also a motorcycle enthusiast. Once on a vacation, a bush pilot dropped him and several fellow canoeists into an icy river within the Arctic Circle. A month and five hundred miles later, the pilot rendezvoused with these wilderness explorers in the Atlantic. Greenhill's takeovers resembled such holidays. As a friend told the writer David Halberstam, "Bob regards these battles as miniature Okinawas."[32] Greenhill savored a new rhetoric of corporate battle: "It's important to know about a chief executive, whether he has the stomach for a fight.

You see people with the veneer stripped away, in their elemental form."[33] The world of investment banking, once attractive for its leisurely elegance, was now a cockpit for pin-striped combatants.

In 1974, Greenhill was field marshal for Morgan Stanley's first hostile takeover—International Nickel's raid on ESB, the world's largest maker of batteries. It wasn't the first unsolicited takeover in Wall Street history: what was the 1901 Northern Pacific corner if not a raid by Edward H. Harriman? But the auspices shocked Wall Street, for Inco was a conservative, blue-chip firm and Morgan Stanley was the official custodian of the Gentleman Banker's Code.

The old House of Morgan had long dominated mining, having financed Anglo-American; Kennecott; Anaconda; Newmont Mining; Phelps, Dodge; and Texas Gulf Sulphur. Inco's plight typified that of Morgan Stanley's mature mining clients. In the 1950s, the Canadian company had controlled an astonishing 85 percent of Western nickel output. By the 1970s, its monopoly was slipping. Buffeted by fluctuations in nickel and copper prices, management decided to diversify. After the 1973 Arab oil embargo, Inco was tantalized by Philadelphia-based ESB, and there was fanciful talk about electric cars powered by ESB car batteries, with Inco nickel powder in those batteries.

It is important to note that the impetus for this landmark takeover originated not with Morgan Stanley but with Inco. Inco's chief financial officer, Chuck Baird, had worked under Bob Baldwin as assistant navy secretary. It was Baird who convinced his superiors to undertake the ESB attack—with or without Morgan Stanley. By conducting such a raid, a new Inco management team wanted to shed the company's stolid image. So the proposal came from a trusted client, putting Morgan Stanley on the spot.

The merger business had boomed during the bear market of 1973–74. Hundreds of brokerage firms left the business, limousines disappeared from the canyons, and downtown rents plummeted. The Coachman Restaurant, a favorite luncheon spot, sported a sign that said "ALL THE SALAD YOU CAN EAT" and "FREE FLOWING WINE."[34] Old-timers said the Street hadn't been so cheerless since the 1930s. Yet for the investment banks, there were hopeful signs in the new *stagflation*—the combination of inflation and economic stagnation. Stagflation suddenly made it cheaper to buy companies on Wall Street than to invest in bricks and mortar. The age of "paper entrepreneurialism," to use Harvard economist Robert Reich's term, had arrived.

The nearly forty Morgan Stanley partners (technically directors after the 1970 partial incorporation) debated whether to spurn Inco or defy a code that had governed the world of high finance for almost 150 years. The firm still moved by consensus in major matters. Against more squeamish souls, Greenhill had lined up Baldwin and chairman Frank A. Petito. Petito's role was curious. Although nominally the firm's chairman, Petito, shy and introverted, shrank from administration, ceding the task to Baldwin. Yet on important policy matters, his vote carried tremendous weight. He was very much the statesman and the conscience of the firm, inheriting the Harry Morgan role. Petito recognized the need for a new pugnacity. A revealing term had slipped into the Morgan Stanley lexicon: when Greenhill's squad needed to prod a reluctant senior man into aggressive action, they said he needed to be *fapped*—a reference to *Frank A. Petito*.

Greenhill made a pitch for hostile takeovers as an irresistible trend that was fair to shareholders, if not always to management. The argument of inevitability was probably the decisive one. As one partner recalls, "The debate was, if we don't do what our clients want, somebody else will." The partners were more receptive to this argument after Morgan Stanley's work with Morgan Grenfell, and Yerger Johnstone cited unsolicited raids in London as a precedent for America. Bob Baldwin agreed: "We did a lot of mental gymnastics about it. . . . When the water rises in London, it will soon flood New York."[35]

Frank Petito figured out how to twist the desecration of tradition into seeming veneration: in obliging Inco, the firm would simply be honoring an old Morgan tradition of serving faithful clients. But Petito had enough qualms about what they were doing to cast the upcoming Inco raid as an exception. A compromise was forged: the bank, in future, would engineer hostile raids only for existing clients and would fully warn them of unpleasant consequences. This, of course, didn't rule out much business. Morgan Stanley's large clients were just the sort that would now want to conduct raids, and they would know all about the unpleasant consequences. The compromise mostly reassured the firm's clients that it wouldn't be coming after *them*.

At this juncture, Morgan Stanley made another unorthodox decision. Like Morgan Guaranty, the firm had long relied on the Wasp white-glove law firm of Davis, Polk, and Wardwell, which had looked on takeover work as vulgar and had avoided it. With Morgan Stanley partners terrified of lawsuits ensuing from takeover work, they now wanted a tough, seasoned specialist. Greenhill insisted on hiring the experienced Joe Flom of Skadden, Arps, Slate, Meagher, and Flom, whom he had met through Bill Sword. Flom was a short, friendly man in glasses who had attended Manhattan's tuition-free City College, then Harvard

Law. He pioneered in hostile takeovers in the 1950s, when Skadden, Arps was still a humble, four-man operation. For twenty years, he thrived on the scraps from law firms that were too haughty or too dignified to conduct hostile raids.

When Flom was made a special counsel to Morgan Stanley, there were stormy scenes with Davis, Polk partners, who were deeply offended by the decision. Whatever its other consequences, the trend in hostile takeovers democratized the New York legal world and provided an opening in Wall Street for Jewish lawyers. Both Joe Flom and Marty Lipton of Wachtell, Lipton, Rosen, and Katz profited from the early refusal of old-line Wasp firms to sully their hands with takeovers. In time, Flom would earn $3 million to $5 million a year, and his law firm would end up as New York's largest, with nine hundred lawyers. Flom would be integral to Morgan Stanley's takeover machine. Greenhill later said, "we know each other's jobs so well that we're almost interchangeable."[36] In 1975, Morgan Stanley completed the incorporation process, not wanting to have unlimited liability with the risky Greenhill operation underway.

As for the Inco raid—on July 17, 1974, Bob Greenhill called Fred Port of ESB to say that he and Inco representatives wanted to visit him in Philadelphia the next day. Port was about to depart for a Kenyan safari. Stunned, he privately dismissed Greenhill as a whippersnapper but canceled his plans. Inco's outside directors didn't learn about the imminent move until the next morning, when Chuck Baird and Greenhill briefed them. Approval was nearly unanimous; the sole holdout was Ellmore Patterson of Morgan Guaranty, who cited his board seat at Union Carbide, an ESB rival, as his reason for abstaining.

The raiders then flew off to Philadelphia by helicopter. Their attack would be vintage Flom-Greenhill—a *blitzkrieg* that gave them the advantage of surprise, a tactic that worked wonders in the early days when they faced inexperienced executives. ESB's Fred Port was shocked when told that Inco wanted to buy his company for $28 a share—a substantial premium over its $19 market price. When Baird added that they would proceed whether ESB liked it or not, Port flushed deeply.

Enlisting the aid of Steve Friedman of Goldman, Sachs, Port issued a letter denouncing such ungracious behavior. Friedman, suspecting shame was now obsolete on Wall Street, advised Port either to fight on antitrust grounds or find a "white knight." All at once, Morgan Stanley and Goldman, Sachs had settled into their respective slots in the takeover world. Representing the restless, mature giants who wished to diversify into other fields, Morgan Stanley took the offense. Associated with the more medium-sized and retail firms likely to be prey, Goldman, Sachs found its *métier* in defense. Billing itself the Robin Hood of Wall Street, Goldman, Sachs would refuse to represent aggressors, although it would sometimes offer them advice. Gradually Wall Street divided into two camps—the offensive (Morgan Stanley, First Boston, Drexel Burnham, Merrill Lynch, and Lazard Frères) and the defensive (Goldman, Sachs; Kidder, Peabody; Salomon Brothers; Dillon, Read; and Smith, Barney). And Joe Flom would consistently square off against defense specialist Marty Lipton.

ESB did bring in a white knight—Harry Gray of United Aircraft (later United Technologies), who leapt into a bidding war that sent the battery maker's price far above the initial bid. Spurred on by Greenhill, Inco delivered a knockout blow, boosting its final bid from $38 to a victorious $41 a share in a day. Inco was suddenly worth more than twice as much as before the frenetic bidding began.

Greenhill would remember Inco nostalgically, whereas Frank Petito would prove more sober and ambivalent about the hostile raids legitimated by Morgan Stanley. "Many did not work out," he later said. "But you've got to remember what the times were like. And it was always management that wanted to do them."[37] This was Morgan Stanley gospel in the 1970s—that the firm was a passive instrument of its clients, even a somewhat unwilling party. Greenhill insisted, "Wall Street had not created the merger trend. . . . We get the transactions done."[38] If this deterministic view spared the firm responsibility, it also betrayed some unspoken uneasiness. Greenhill could never quite mouth the words *hostile* or *unfriendly*. "We prefer not to call them unfriendly takeovers," he told *Business Week* in 1974. "Just because the management doesn't go along doesn't mean that the deal isn't in the best interest of the stockholders, and Morgan Stanley would never allow itself to get so involved in a deal that wasn't."[39]

Like Robert Young's New York Central raid, Inco-ESB would show the shot-in-the-dark quality of hostile takeovers. When Greenhill swooped down on Fred Port, the company had just registered record earnings of over $300 million for its fiscal year. For all its promises, Inco couldn't improve on that. ESB slipped in its rivalry with Duracell batteries and the Delco-Sears maintenance-free car battery. By 1980, it was losing money, and its new chairman, Chuck Baird, put ESB up for sale, professing discomfort with its retail-oriented business. That Bob Greenhill was later wistful about Inco-ESB says much about the way in which investment banking was becoming disconnected from the economic realities of jobs, factories, and people. By what logic could the takeover be construed as a victory? Investment bankers were beginning to take a shorter-term view of their clients' businesses.

Once Morgan Stanley sanctioned hostile takeovers, competitors jumped in. A year later, George Shinn of First Boston paired up Bruce Wasserstein and Joe Perella to launch a separate M&A operation. In 1974, $100 million was still considered a big deal. By 1978, over eighty deals exceeded that amount, with a $500- to $600-million range already commonplace. Unlike the conglomerate takeovers of the 1960s, which were financed with the shares of the acquiring company, the new takeovers were largely effected with cash. Because Morgan Stanley booked fees as a percentage of the total, its profits soared.

Like the trading operation, takeover work helped to diversify the firm. Three female professionals were assigned to the M&A Department. Yet Greenhill and his male colleagues erected a wall around the women and segregated them as "statisticians." Their wives also conspired to relegate the women to second-class status: when the unmarried Morgan Stanley women were about to travel to London and Cleveland on takeover business, two irate wives called, squawking about the arrangement. No Morgan Stanley woman would make managing director until the mid-1980s.

The Wall Street move into merger work accelerated into a stampede after May 1, 1975, when the SEC abolished fixed commissions on stock trades. This stripped away an easy, dependable flow of revenue and forced securities houses to forage for new business. Morgan Stanley, which now executed block trades for institutions, lobbied hard against the measure. Borrowing a term from his navy days, Bob Baldwin warned that "Mayday" might prompt the failure of 150 to 200 regional firms—an alarming forecast that proved on the low side. Morgan Stanley regarded these regional firms as possible buffers against retail giants like Merrill Lynch. As head of a wholesale firm long reliant on regional brokers, Baldwin was reluctant to see the demise of his cherished world of syndicates.

When "Mayday" arrived, in 1975, Morgan Stanley tried to buck the tide and cling to old rates. Unsubstantiated rumors spread through Wall Street that the firm might blackball from its syndicates any firms that stooped to price cutting—a charge Baldwin labeled an "outrageous lie." It was impossible, however, to hold back a sea of change, and commission rates plunged 40 percent for institutional investors. From these ashes arose the new, piratical Wall Street. Even conservative firms began adopting tactics once considered suitable only to disgruntled outsiders. In the Inco-ESB takeover, it was Morgan Stanley, the flagship of Wall Street, that first unfurled the Jolly Roger, and it would sail it through increasingly troubled seas.

CHAPTER THIRTY

SHEIKS

. .
.

For Morgan Guaranty, too, the recession of 1973–74 disclosed a turbulent new world. The Arab oil embargo and consequent jump in world oil prices produced inflation and skidding financial markets. With an end to fixed exchange rates in the early 1970s, foreign-exchange trading became a wild poker game. In November 1973, Morgan president Walter Hines Page warned friends at Franklin National Bank against excessive foreign-exchange gambling and quietly alerted the New York Fed to the problem. In May 1974, Franklin's foreign-exchange losses led to the first major bank run since the Depression and the biggest bank failure in U.S. history. When Bankhaus Herstatt, West Germany's biggest private bank, mysteriously failed in June, it saddled Morgan Guaranty with a $13-million loss. That fall, *Fortune* warned, "The nation's financial system is facing its gravest crisis since the Bank Holiday of 1933. The crisis is one of confidence. The public has become increasingly worried about the solvency of even the most profitable banks."[1]

With this thick pall hanging over the banking world, the banks were suddenly tempted by Arab petrodollars. If the Arabs caused the financial crisis, they also presented an apparent cure. For Morgan Guaranty, which had struggled to retain balances, the shower of petrodollars had a surreal beauty, like a rainbow in a storm. "We were so worried about dollars," said Walter Page. "Then here came the Saudis with more dollars than we knew how to keep. You almost had to become Saudi Arabians—quickly."[2] The petrodollars flowed mostly into four U.S. banks—Morgan Guaranty, Chase, Citibank, and the Bank of America. Thoroughgoing snobs, the Arabs preferred conservative blue-ribbon banks and prized Morgan's old-money aura, its discreet style, and its resolutely Christian past (the bank had no high-ranking Jewish officer until the 1980s).

As bankers swarmed across the Middle East groveling before Saudi sheiks, Morgan Guaranty enjoyed access no carpetbagger could duplicate. The secretive Morgan-Saudi relationship dated back to Ibn Saud's forging of the Saudi kingdom in the early 1930s, when money-changing shops with mud floors served as makeshift banks. In April 1933, Standard Oil of California (Socal) negotiated the first oil concession with the Saudi finance minister, Abdullah Sulaiman. They agreed to an initial £30,000 gold loan, plus the first year's rent of £5,000 in gold. Making payment posed a riddle, for the antediluvian Saudi monetary system employed only chunky metal coins; the kingdom wouldn't adopt paper money for another twenty years. So gold—massive heaps of it—was shipped in to make the payments.

The deal was nearly scuttled when FDR, heeding the advice of Walter Lippmann and Russell Leffingwell, embargoed U.S. gold exports. As an American company, Socal required U.S. Treasury permission to ship gold to Saudi Arabia. As it awaited the official go-ahead, its Saudi Arabian future seemed to ride on that one gold shipment. On July 26, 1933, Dean Acheson, then Treasury under secretary, turned down Socal's request. So the panicky oil company bought thirty-five thousand gold sovereigns from a Guaranty Trust branch in London, flouting the new regulations.

In early August 1933, this black-market gold sailed for the Persian Gulf aboard a P&O liner. When it arrived, a Socal representative counted out thirty-five thousand coins under Sulaiman's vigilant gaze. When the Saudis asked what they should do with the money, Socal recommended Guaranty Trust. For years, American oilmen shipped millions of British gold sovereigns to the Saudis by boat or plane. By the 1940s, Socal had taken Texaco, Standard Oil of New Jersey, and Mobil into its desert oil kingdom in a new operation christened the Arabian-American Oil Company, or Aramco. Aramco erected structures ranging from hospitals to camel troughs, exerting an influence in the kingdom rivaling that of the Saudi royal family itself. By importing a great deal of material, Aramco had a constant need for letters of credit and other old-fashioned banking services. And its stalwart banker was Guaranty Trust.

Guaranty's Harold Anderson was probably the only American banker who traveled regularly to Saudi Arabia after World War II, although the Dutch and French were well entrenched there. (The Netherlands Trading Society serviced Indonesian pilgrims to Mecca.) As long-time camel

traders, the Arabs valued personal relationships, and the genial, easygoing Anderson brought them colorful gifts, like studded saddles, to win
their friendship. Guaranty made loans to Saudi Arabia against oil revenues (possibly including small personal loans to King Saud) and also
managed dollar accounts for leading Saudis. As Aramco's banker, Guaranty also managed Saudi oil revenues in dollars.

Although J. P. Morgan and Company had no dealings with Saudi
Arabia in the 1950s, it was banker to that other ubiquitous giant in the
Arabian Peninsula, Bechtel, the shadowy global construction giant that
did the actual building for Aramco. Bechtel formed a close partnership
with Saudi entrepreneur Suliman Olayan, a once penniless Aramco
dispatcher who ended up with over $1 billion and a 50-percent stake in
Saudi Arabian Bechtel Company. As a member of Morgan Guaranty's
International Council, Olayan would form part of a dense, impenetrable
web whose strands bound Morgan Guaranty, Bechtel, the Saudi royal
family, and American oil companies.

Like a storybook miser, Finance Minister Suliman was often said to
hoard the nation's wealth—silver riyals and gold sovereigns—in a chest
tucked under his bed. It was one of the world's few portable central
banks. After 1950, as the Saudis split royalties with Aramco on the more
equitable fifty-fifty basis, the coins came to fill a vault seventy feet long,
seventy feet wide, and eight feet high. The old medieval finances would
no longer suffice. Yet any attempt to modernize the monetary system ran up against the Islamic injunction against paying or receiving
interest.

In 1952, when the Saudis created a central bank, they shrank from
so labeling it, in order to avoid inflaming the faithful. Instead, they
cunningly anointed it the Saudi Arabian Monetary Agency or SAMA,
which started out with about $15 million. It issued Saudi gold coins and
the kingdom's first paper money for use by pilgrims to Mecca. This
gradually replaced the weighty coin of the realm. But many desert
warriors and kingdom retainers preferred solid, precious metals, and
King Faisal himself would keep bags of silver in the basement of the
Netherlands Trading Society.

Morgan Guaranty helped reform Saudi finance through a remarkable
man named Anwar Ali, a Pakistani who first went to Saudi Arabia on
a two-week tour of duty as head of the IMF's Middle East department.
In 1958, the Saudis drafted him to be SAMA's governor. His mission
was to straighten out the kingdom's finances, then in critical disarray
as a result of corruption, inflation, and extravagant spending. (The
Saudi royal palace had the world's second largest air-conditioning sys-

tem after that of the Pentagon.) Ali was gentle and scholarly, a devout Muslim in silver-rimmed glasses and urbane Western suits. He became personal financial adviser to King Faisal. As SAMA governor, he commanded more petrodollars than anyone on earth, more gold than Midas. As journalist Tad Szulc wrote in 1974, "Not many kings and presidents held such personal power."[3] With nice semantic juggling, he turned *interest* into *return on investment*, permitting SAMA to amass a modern securities portfolio without offending Allah. "One of the first things Anwar told me about the messy finances he faced was that he had discovered to his dismay that many Saudi accounts in New York were not drawing any interest," recalled William D. Toomey, then with the U.S. embassy in Saudi Arabia. "He found it touching that the banks were so sensitive to the Saudis' religious scruples against acceptance of interest."[4]

To map portfolio strategy, Ali recruited a tiny group of Western bankers, sometimes called the White Fathers or the Three Wise Men in this myth-shrouded operation. Among them was the tall, beetle-browed John M. Meyer, Jr., then head of Morgan's International Division and later chairman. Ali favored such conservative investments as Treasury securities, and Meyer was just the old-school type to appeal to him. (Inside the bank, he was nicknamed Moody Meyer because he remembered in excruciating detail *Moody's* entry on every security, down to the smallest indenture.) Meyer was also secretive, inscrutable, and trusted for his plain truthfulness. He, in turn, admired Ali's incorruptibility in a land rife with corruption. (Harold Anderson's assistant, John Bochow, would tell colleagues sarcastically, "Never do business in a country where they don't wear overcoats part of the year.") Diverting SAMA deposits to Morgan Guaranty, Ali made it the major Saudi depository. The bank, in turn, hired Ali's son Pasha, a Yale graduate.

For several years, Morgan Guaranty provided SAMA with investment counseling. In the 1960s, however, the American bank became a casualty of its own success. As government adviser, it couldn't solicit Saudi business without encountering a conflict of interest. Morgans needed to open some breathing space between itself and the Saudis. "You couldn't have advisers in a government agency and deal with it at the same time," explained an ex-Morgan executive. So Morgans bowed out and brought in White, Weld of New York and Baring Brothers and Richard Fleming of London.

When the petrodollar gusher erupted, Morgan Guaranty was beautifully positioned. It could pose as protector of the defenseless Saudis against rapacious, self-serving bankers. Recognizing a need for new

Saudi financial expertise, Ali toyed with the idea of an international merchant bank. In 1973, SAMA still operated out of a ramshackle building near the Riyadh airport and lacked telex machines. It was moving tens of billions of dollars in deposits around the world with a slim staff of only ten professionals.

At a 1973 IMF meeting in Nairobi, Meyer, Walter Page, and Lew Preston cornered Ali with a plan for a London-based Saudi merchant bank to be the kingdom's Euromarket outlet. Page recalled, "We told him, 'You have to have a window on the world of finance. You have to invest in the right way and keep current with what's going on in the world.' "[5] The Eurodollar market was then moving into high gear in London, and the timing seemed auspicious.

At first, the Saudis wanted to share this largesse in a consortium arrangement with their five principal bankers in Europe and Japan. Instead, Morgans deprecated the voguish consortium concept. "We told the Saudis that they had to tie someone with a bigger share to make it work," said Page.[6] And who, pray, would that responsible party be? When the Saudi International Bank was announced in 1975, SAMA owned 50 percent and Morgan Guaranty 20 percent, with 5-percent shares distributed to other banks. Edgar Felton of Morgans was dispatched to London to manage the new bank. This seemed an inimitable coup for Morgan Guaranty—a partnership with the Saudi central bank.

News of the SIB deal, secretly crafted by Morgan Guaranty, dealt the *coup de grâce* to the special relationship with Morgan Stanley. These were the waning days of the Paris partnership, and Morgan Stanley, learning the news only shortly before its public announcement, was stunned. A SAMA board member, Ali Alireza, told his nephew Hisham, then at Morgan Stanley, about the deal. The firm couldn't believe its total ignorance of the negotiations. According to a former Morgan Stanley partner, "It was a big disappointment to Morgan Stanley and Morgan Grenfell. The lure of the vast Saudi Arabian fortune and all the money to be made was too much for Morgan Guaranty. There wasn't an alliance any longer. Morgan Guaranty had clearly made its mind up to go its own way at the Bermuda meeting." A former Morgan Guaranty official concurs: "When the petrodollars came along, we no longer needed Morgan Stanley."

The Saudi International Bank was a fertile source of fantasies at 23 Wall. Some thought the Saudis might funnel all their export-import financing through the bank; others thought the SIB might have a big account at 23 Wall. The most specific expectation was that the SIB would train Saudi Arabia's future financial elite, allowing Morgans to seed loyal people throughout the Saudi power hierarchy. The country desperately needed a stratum of competent financiers, and the SIB promised to deliver them. The House of Morgan thus looked to be the one bank that would profit from a stress on Saudiizing Saudi finance.

In practice, the SIB never retained the rich young Saudis sent to train there. The explosion of oil prices in late 1973 and early 1974 put too much wealth at the disposal of young Saudis; business opportunities at home beckoned. These Bedouin Arabs were also too attached to culture and family to remain in London for an extended period. "There were never enough Saudis," said one Morgan person. "They all wanted to make their name in Saudi Arabia or peddle influence. Banking was too boring. We ended up dealing with the technocrats, not the royal family." Some Morgan people argue that the Saudi royal family never put its full weight and prestige behind the bank. It took small pieces of sovereign loans but never really blossomed. So its main utility to 23 Wall was simply in preserving the SAMA relationship.

Morgan Guaranty was protective of Saudi Arabia in U.S. politics. In early 1975, Senator Frank Church tried to extract figures on petrodollar deposits. He feared that by threatening to pull out their short-term deposits, the Arabs could blackmail the U.S. government. Morgans and other banks wouldn't divulge the information. Morgan chairman Ellmore Patterson declared: "Much of the information you request would involve a breach of our obligation to keep confidential the affairs of particular clients." Morgans was petrified that the Swiss banks would steal away the deposits. Fed chairman Arthur Burns brokered a deal with the banks, releasing aggregate deposit figures for Middle East states. Of $14.5 billion in deposits by the OPEC states, 78 percent resided in six banks—Morgan Guaranty, Bank of America, Citibank, Chase, Manufacturers Hanover, and Chemical.

Senator Church proved correct in worrying that petrodollars would enlist the political allegiance of bankers in disturbing ways. The sheiks wanted to use letters of credit as a way of enforcing compliance with the Arab boycott of Israel. Under this arrangement, banks had to certify that goods being exported to the Middle East didn't originate in Israel or with blacklisted American companies, didn't bear the Star of David, and wouldn't travel aboard Israeli planes or ships. In 1976, the American Jewish Congress singled out Morgan Guaranty and Citibank for loyally executing this dirty work and cited their "pivotal role in the implementation of the Arab boycott."[7] Morgan Guaranty executed 824 letters of credit including the language of the boycott although they protested and successfully expunged the offensive language in two dozen cases. While some banks welcomed tough anti-boycott legislation, Chemical Bank and Morgans testified against it; it was finally enacted in 1977.

As a general rule, the postwar Morgan bank had avoided the sort of political lobbying or proselytizing for foreign governments in which Tom Lamont had specialized. Yet in the case of the Saudis, the bank seemed to hark back to the old days. Along with Bechtel, GM, GE, Ford Motor, and the oil companies, Morgan Guaranty contributed to Georgetown University's Center for Contemporary Arab Studies. "Violent criticism of Israel and American support for Israel are the single most dominant themes of the center's extremely active program," explained one observer.[8] In 1980, the august Morgans also made an uncharacteristic foray into public television, after the broadcast of a British television movie, *Death of a Princess*. This controversial documentary told the story of a Saudi prince who ordered the execution of his own granddaughter after she balked at an arranged marriage. The woman was shot while the husband she had chosen instead watched; he was then beheaded. The Saudis were outraged, and the State Department tried to mollify them. So Morgans joined with Texas Instruments, the Harris Corporation, and Ford Motor to sponsor a glossy, benign three-part series on Saudi Arabia designed to counteract the movie.[9]

UNLIKE Morgan Guaranty, Morgan Stanley had no experience in the Middle East. In its clumsy, often farcical rush to woo Arabs, it ended up in bed with the shady Adnan Khashoggi, then commonly billed as the world's richest businessman. The son of a court physician to King Saud, Khashoggi brokered billions of dollars in arms deals with Saudi Arabia and skimmed off fees from over three-quarters of all defense contracts. He kept palatial homes in ten cities, had his own DC-8 and a yacht fitted with gold fixtures. In 1974, the Saudi ambassador to the U.N. steered Khashoggi to Morgan Stanley. Allegedly worried about a two-tier Arab world in which Saudi sheiks drove Cadillacs while the masses starved, Khashoggi told the Saudi royal family that they couldn't live so luxuriously while the Sudan lay poverty stricken. The conservative oil states feared Sudan's flirtation with socialism. To correct this, Khashoggi wanted to introduce agribusiness into the region. With the blessings of Egyptian president Anwar Sadat, he planned to create a seventeen-thousand-acre dairy farm near the Suez Canal and a million-acre cattle ranch near the Blue Nile in Sudan. Needing the appropriate technology, Khashoggi eyed an American company called Arizona-Colorado Land and Cattle, which had huge property tracts and cattle herds out West. But the company wouldn't sell until Morgan Stanley came in and negotiated a $9-million stake for him.

In pursuing his vision, Khashoggi was often accompanied by Jan Stenbeck, a handsome blond bachelor from one of Sweden's richest families who was affiliated with Morgan Stanley. Stenbeck seemed to thrive on intrigue and entertained friends with stories about sitting on the tarmac at Khartoum with Sudan's president while the sand swirled around them. Khashoggi would spout a thousand inventive ideas about irrigation and agricultural development but then quickly lose interest and turn to other matters. Mostly he delighted in playing pranks on Stenbeck. Once arriving late at a Cairo hotel for a rendezvous with the Arab, an exhausted Stenbeck told the desk clerk not to disturb him with phone calls. After midnight, when Khashoggi arrived, he was told of Stenbeck's instructions, which suggested to him a practical joke. Mimicking an operator's voice, he dialed the sleeping Stenbeck's room and said his Morgan Stanley boss would soon come on the line from New York. As Stenbeck fought to stay awake, Khashoggi enjoyed his dinner. Periodically, he would pick up the phone to reiterate that Stenbeck's boss would soon be on the line and he must hold on. Stenbeck held on in desperation until he finally succumbed to sleep.

The clever, babbling Khashoggi tempted Morgan Stanley with another mesmerizing vision of riches. He said that his friend Crown Prince Fahd, having lost a reported $6 million while gambling in Monaco, was in hot water with King Faisal; to improve his image, the prince planned to set up a $1-billion foundation to perform good works, possibly with Morgan Stanley as its financial adviser. Would Morgan Stanley be interested in pursuing this with Prince Fahd at Deauville, in northwest France? Stenbeck, S. Parker Gilbert, and Bill Sword took a suite of rooms at a Deauville hotel. Khashoggi was a floor below, Fahd a floor above.

At 8:30 one evening, Khashoggi ushered the trio into his suite to meet the prince. There were over a dozen chairs set up in a circle, with a stool beside each. The prince entered ceremoniously, sat beside Sword, and expressed a noble wish to do great things for humanity. At one point, when a gorgeous woman in an evening dress walked in, Khashoggi came over and whispered to Sword, "Do you mind if my secretary sits next to Prince Fahd?" Sword, a short, church-going Presbyterian, said no and slid over a seat, wondering at this beautiful secretary. Soon after, a somewhat older, but no less attractive, lady in her forties came in and sat down on Fahd's other side. "We have here the wife of the editor of *Paris Match*," Khashoggi whispered to Sword. "She's doing a feature story on the prince." Now every few minutes another beautiful young woman entered and sat down on a stool until there was one beside each man. When the room was full, Fahd announced that he had booked a Trouville restaurant for the evening. As the meeting ended, Sword went over and chatted earnestly with the *Paris Match* woman about Henry Luce, Axel Springer, and other publishers; he was surprised by how little she knew about publishing.

Back at the hotel, with the door shut, Gilbert and Stenbeck burst out laughing. They had caught on sooner than Sword to Khashoggi's game: he had flown in "models" from Paris for a party. Stenbeck kidded Sword: "The Prince and all the girls were very impressed that you had picked out the lead woman, the 'editor from *Paris Match.*' She was the biggest hooker of them all."[10] What Khashoggi's biographer concluded of Stenbeck might be an epitaph for Morgan Stanley's early efforts to drum up Saudi business: "He traveled with [Khashoggi] to see heads of state about projects to turn deserts into Gardens of Eden. But when the trips were over and the glitter gone, there was little to show for it."[11]

FOR Morgan Grenfell, the petrodollar boom was providential, taking up slack as the late 1960s takeover boom wound down. Although it arranged the first Eurosterling issue, in 1972, it lacked the capital to be a top-flight Euromarket competitor and needed a new act in order to survive. It was a pretty dismal time. British exports flagged badly as a near-depression atmosphere overtook the nation's industry. Amid rising interest rates, the City was rocked by a bust in the property market and a secondary banking crisis in 1973–74. When Lord Poole of Lazards was asked how he survived the debacle, he replied: "Quite simple: I only lent money to people who had been at Eton."[12]

At Morgan Grenfell, the Arabs would temporarily answer the firm's problems. With their penchant for secrecy and their appreciation of the confidential style of British merchant banks, the Arabs were naturally drawn to the mysterious maze of the City. They loved the cachet of old stately houses. Also, sympathy for the Arab cause was far more prevalent in the Foreign Office than in the State Department. "In the Mideast, Morgan Grenfell could take advantage of the U.S. inability to act," declared Christopher Whittington, the firm's deputy chairman. "We could sell them Tornado fighter planes, while the U.S. couldn't because of Congress."[13] Morgan Grenfell had another edge: many London merchant banks were tainted by their Jewish ancestry. So 23 Great Winchester Street became the City firm most immersed in Middle East business. At its peak in the seventies, Arab business contributed up to 70 percent of the bank's revenues.

At first, the man leading the charge was Sir John Stevens, the inveterate traveler and former polyglot Bank of England executive who had advised Iran's central bank. By then he had planted the Morgan flag in old imperial outposts of Hong Kong, Singapore, Australia, and New Zealand and got a Morgan office going in Moscow. David Bendall, brought in from the Foreign Office, did the same in Latin America.

As at previous times in Morgan Grenfell history, stepped-up foreign business forged deeper links with Whitehall. Morgan Grenfell now specialized in arranging government-guaranteed export credits, which Britain was then using to win goodwill abroad. These credits led Morgan Grenfell to finance arms exports to Oman and Jordan as well as power plants, refineries, and other capital projects in the region. Through export credits, the bank also became more involved with Eastern Europe. In 1975, Morgan Grenfell became the first merchant bank to win the Queen's Award for Export Achievement, for managing over a quarter of the government-guaranteed credits. Through all the vagaries of merger work, the firm's rock-solid export credits and impressive portfolio management would lend strength to its balance sheet. In the last analysis, the dull, solid stuff would be its salvation.

Aside from Saudi Arabia, most Arab states before 1973 were too impoverished to be considered good credit risks. The sudden, almost overnight, revolution in their financial status was revealed in a controversial loan that Sir John Stevens secretly negotiated during the Yom Kippur War, in the fall of 1973. On October 6, Egypt, Syria, and Iraq attacked Israel. On October 20, during a fierce, bloody phase of fighting, news leaked out of a Morgan-led loan to Abu Dhabi. Israeli tanks had just advanced fifteen miles beyond the Suez Canal, knocking out Egypt's surface-to-air missile batteries. Disclosure of the loan sent up an uproar, especially among Jewish firms in the City. Official British policy was neutral. Then as now, Morgan Grenfell insisted on the loan's peaceful nature. According to Chris Whittington, "The Abu Dhabi loan was already in the works before the fighting began. We just didn't cancel it."[14]

It was the bank's most controversial loan of the postwar era, sparking heated debate. With each new report, this mystery loan seemed to expand. First announced as a £40-million loan ($100 million), it suspiciously mushroomed to $200 million within three days. Even as Stevens talked of its use for hospitals or budgetary purposes, it sounded patently suspicious. Awash with oil money, the seventy thousand privileged residents of Abu Dhabi might have enjoyed the world's highest per-capita income. In those years, $200 million was an enormous Eurodollar loan, representing nearly $3,000 for each Abu Dhabi resident—absurdly wasteful and unnecessary borrowing for a tiny oil sheikdom under ordinary circumstances.

Also heightening suspicion was the fact that on October 20, the London *Times* reported that the loan negotiations had just begun—suggesting that its origins hadn't antedated the war after all. Even the loan's dollar denomination raised eyebrows. All summer, the Soviets had sent weapons to Egypt and Syria and were now strapped for foreign exchange. It was known in diplomatic circles that in exchange for weaponry, they were demanding hard currency from the Arabs—in other words, dollars. Adding piquancy to the speculation was the fact that two of Morgan Grenfell's Middle East specialists were the sons of cabinet ministers—David Douglas-Home, son of Foreign Secretary Alexander Douglas-Home, and Rupert F. J. Carrington, son of Defense Secretary Peter A. R. Carrington.

With Abu Dhabi having just slapped an oil embargo on the United States, American banks reacted skittishly to a loan that, if problematic in the City, was plain anathema on Wall Street. Morgan Guaranty and First National City quietly bowed out of the syndicate—the more striking in Morgan's case in that it advised the small sheikdom on its $2.5-billion portfolio. The Japanese had no qualms about joining, however. In fact, Japan's government wanted to cultivate Abu Dhabi through direct oil purchases and thus bypass major oil companies. It saw a chance to buy friendship, and the Tokai Bank syndicated a $30- to $50-million piece of the loan among Japanese banks.

Admitting that money was fungible, even Sir John Stevens couldn't vouch categorically for the ultimate destination of the jumbo loan. Others involved no longer pretend about it. One claimed:

> It was certainly a war loan. Eurodollar loans at that level were very few and far between. The loan was prepaid in a matter of weeks. In fact, it did Morgan Grenfell no good whatsoever. As soon as oil prices quadrupled, Abu Dhabi's credit rating went from okay to extra special. So it was hard to explain to Abu Dhabi why the interest rate was so high. It seemed like pure usury to them. The reason the rates were high was because it was a war loan.

On October 27, 1973, after six years at Morgan Grenfell, Sir John Stevens died at the age of 59. He had already recruited his wife's cousin Bill Mackworth-Young, from the corporate stock-brokerage firm of

Rowe and Pitman. Mackworth-Young was the leading new issue broker in the City, a man of acute intellect who would succeed Stevens as chief executive and figure importantly in the firm's future. In retrospect, Stevens's death deprived the firm of a figure who might have propelled it into a global powerhouse, like the rival Warburgs. But he had already injected some dynamism into the firm and set it on an upward international course, restoring it to the front ranks of London merchant banking. Bolstered by lucrative Arab business, Morgan Grenfell would chalk up record profits in a recessionary environment.

With the chameleonlike adaptability of a merchant bank, Morgan Grenfell took on Arab colors with remarkable speed. To please the Middle Easterners, it adopted a policy of not hiring Jews, at least not on the international side. The firm would resort to euphemisms to describe this rule—saying it was "Arab-oriented" or "non-Israel-oriented"—but it boiled down to blackballing Jewish employees and Israeli business. The newly Arabized Morgan Grenfell advised Qatar and Dubai on investment strategy, entered into a joint venture with Jordan's Arab Bank, opened offices in Egypt and Iran, and formed a link with France's Compagnie Financière de Suez, whose subsidiary, Banque de l'Indochine, had branches throughout the Middle East.

As its Middle East fame spread, Morgan Grenfell found at its doorstep people who required inside knowledge of Arab finance or introductions into Persian Gulf diplomatic circles. In 1975, it drew a suitor who demanded an ironclad guarantee of confidentiality—Henry Ford II. Emissaries from Ford Motor posed a maddening riddle: how could the company, blacklisted by the Arab boycott, operate in both Israel and Egypt? This seemed the political equivalent of squaring the circle.

Ford Motor was a pariah in the Middle East. From 1950 to 1966, it had operated an assembly plant in Alexandria, Egypt. Then an Israeli Ford dealer got permission to assemble Fords in Israel from imported parts. Despite the absence of direct Ford investment or personnel in Israel, the Arab League threatened a regional boycott of Ford cars if the Israeli deal weren't scuttled. For Henry Ford, the decision was sensitive because of embarrassment about his grandfather's anti-Semitism. So the grandson refused to renounce his principles or submit to Arab pressure, and the Israeli operation proceeded unhindered. "It was just a pragmatic business procedure," he later said. "I don't mind saying I was influenced by the fact that the company still suffers from a resentment against the anti-Semitism of the past. We want to overcome that."[15] Some observers also credited Ford with a shrewd public relations maneuver.

When Ford Motor appeared on the Arab blacklist in 1966, its Alexandrian operation was shut down, starting Ford's exile from the Muslim world. Despite the loss of Arab business, Henry Ford never wavered in his decision. As he flatly told his close friend Max Fisher, a top American fund-raiser for Israel, "Nobody's gonna tell me what to do."[16] In 1972, Fisher accompanied Ford on a tour of Israel, where they were received by Prime Minister Golda Meir, Moshe Dayan, and Shimon Peres. Ford seemed quite comfortable with his decision.

What Henry Ford never told Max Fisher was that he undertook secret efforts through Morgan Grenfell to reintroduce his company into the Arab world. He wanted to reopen the Alexandria plant as a joint venture with Egypt to manufacture diesel engines, tractors, and trucks. There was a high-level political agenda. Ford thought his company's presence in Egypt might erode Arab resistance, dissolving the sharp distinction between pro-Israeli and pro-Arab American companies. Egypt was more relaxed about the boycott than other Arab countries, although it still put up formidable obstacles. The Ford people had picked up encouraging hints in Washington and the Arab world that the company might soon come off the blacklist.

Ford came to Morgan Grenfell circuitously, after sounding out Morgan Guaranty and other banks as to who had the best Middle East connections. In the early postwar years, Ford Motor had viewed the House of Morgan warily because of its historic association with General Motors. Over the years, however, Morgan Grenfell had handled a remarkable variety of Ford business. It supervised the final sale of Ford U.K. to the Detroit parent company (which then held only a partial interest), introduced Ford stock on the London exchange with Lazards, and managed Ford U.K.'s pension fund. As added incentives to Henry Ford II, Morgan Grenfell had been commissioned by Egypt's central bank to study its nation's foreign-investment law and had even entered into a joint venture with the speaker of Egypt's Parliament.

In 1975, Morgan Grenfell outlined a precise sequence of steps to circumvent the Arab blacklist. The firm knew exactly which sheiks could fix things so that behind a facade of Arab militance, business could proceed unimpeded by religious or political zeal. Morgan Grenfell suggested selling equity stakes in the Alexandria operation to influential bankers, families, and institutions across the Arab world, not just in Egypt. This would build a powerful Arab constituency for getting Ford off the blacklist and would also help to line up cheap Middle East financing. This last was crucial, for Ford believed that only cheap financing could offset prohibitive operating costs in Egypt.

President Anwar Sadat took a personal interest in furthering the project. He was sympathetic to removing American companies from the blacklist if they made investments in the Arab world comparable to those they had in Israel. He insisted that Ford be removed from the Arab blacklist as a precondition for operating in Alexandria but also intimated that he might just go ahead and unilaterally strike Ford from the Egyptian blacklist. It was never entirely clear whether in the end he would courageously defy his Arab brethren or back off.

For two years, Morgan Grenfell and Ford Motor tried to seduce various sheiks. They played on the willingness of royal Arab families to exploit their positions for personal gain. The Morgan Grenfell strategy accurately gauged the depth of Arab cynicism. Some shieks wanted exclusive Ford dealerships before participating. Some bankers wanted a personal share of Ford's Egyptian plant in exchange for loans. In Saudi Arabia, Morgan Grenfell had targeted Khalid Alireza, a shareholder in Morgan Grenfell and the Egyptian Finance Company. The Alirezas were a powerful, highly respected merchant family and importing agents for many American, British, and German companies. They had even held the Ford dealership before the Arab boycott. Nevertheless, as strict Muslims and uncompromising anti-Zionists, they finally refused to participate. In general, the Kuwaitis were more receptive than the more militant, hard-line Saudis.

This clandestine lobbying continued during the 1976 presidential campaign, when Henry Ford II was a leading business fund-raiser for Jimmy Carter. During the fall campaign, Morgan Grenfell shepherded Ford people around the Gulf states, a mission requiring airtight secrecy, given Ford's link with Carter and the potential for political embarrassment among Jewish voters. In February 1977, promoting his proposed Egyptian operation, Ford met privately with President Sadat for several hours. Sadat saw the Ford plant as a magnet that might draw other companies into an Alexandrian industrial zone. To Ford Motor, Coca-Cola, Xerox, and other American companies barred from the Arab world, he wanted to offer a deal—invest in Egypt, and he would work to delete them from the blacklist.

In May 1977, Morgan Grenfell nearly pulled off the supreme trick of Middle East politics: Egypt announced a joint venture with Ford to assemble trucks and diesel engines; Egypt's approval was contingent on Ford's securing the removal of its name from the pan-Arab blacklist. Egypt was to contribute 40 percent of the capital, and Ford Motor 30 percent, with the remaining 30 percent parceled out to the Arab friends Morgan Grenfell had rounded up. In October 1977, after Egypt removed Ford from its own blacklist, the agreement was signed.

In the end, the project was stillborn, apparently for a variety of reasons. There was thunderous Arab opposition: the lobbying effort hadn't silenced Arab militance or purchased the necessary high-level cooperation. Mohammed Mahgoub, Sudanese head of the Arab boycott, bitterly denounced Ford and threatened to boycott products made in the Alexandrian plant. And since the plant was to produce for export as well as domestic consumption, this would reduce its value to Ford. Perhaps the greatest sticking point was that the Egyptians, after endless haggling with Morgan Grenfell, refused to modify their Public Law 43, which set tough conditions on foreign investment. Without such changes, Ford felt that it couldn't operate at a profit.

The Egyptian initiative would disappear, despite public announcement of the deal in 1977 and more meetings that year between Ford officials and Anwar Sadat. It was almost as if it had never happened, so completely was it buried and forgotten. When approached about it, Ford Motor wouldn't comment, saying the information was "legally privileged." And when Henry Ford's close friend Max Fisher was asked, he said, "Frankly, I have never heard of any of this before."[17] It was a Morgan operation in the classic style of Teddy Grenfell: it left no footprints behind.

T H E exorbitant oil prices and interest rates that followed the Arab oil embargo produced many bankruptcies, and Morgan Guaranty spent much of 1975 desperately plugging fingers into dikes. It was lead banker to W. T. Grant, America's third largest variety-store chain, which foundered that year in history's largest retail failure. The House of Morgan took a $50-million write-off. "We don't make many mistakes," said Morgan's Rod Lindsay, "but when we do make one, it's a beaut."[18]

However grand its global operations, the House of Morgan remained a New York City bank. It had always regarded the city's credit as a proxy for America. To that end, it had saved New York in the 1907 panic, in August 1914, and in 1933. These earlier crises illustrated the strength of the Morgan bank. But by 1975, New York had a population the size of Sweden's and a budget as big as India's. During the city's fiscal crisis that year, the Morgan role would seem marginal compared with that of the three earlier rescues.

Starting with the administration of Mayor John V. Lindsay (brother of Morgan Guaranty's Rod) in the 1960s, New York City had borrowed heavily for expanded social welfare programs. By late 1974, city paper saturated the markets, driving up interest rates and causing steep losses for underwriters, including Morgans. (Commercial banks could underwrite municipal issues backed by taxing power.) That December, Mayor Abraham Beame held an emergency breakfast with bankers at Gracie Mansion. There an advisory group of three influential bank chairmen was formed—David Rockefeller of Chase, Walter Wriston of First National City, and Ellmore C. Patterson of Morgans. Patterson became the leader, because Wriston was ideologically hostile to government and Rockefeller's brother, Nelson, was then the nation's vice-president.

Ellmore ("Pat") Patterson was very midwestern, with a relaxed manner and a slow drawl. His description of the Morgan staff might apply as well to himself: "We're not known for geniuses charging around, but for good solid people with a strong feeling toward the bank."[19] Tall and straight, with a friendly grin, he wasn't a brainy executive, but he was popular and unpretentious. After Nixon devalued the dollar and imposed an import surcharge, Patterson lunched with the head of the Sumitomo bank, who wanted to know how Patterson could let Nixon take steps harming Japan. "I don't know the president," Patterson said breezily. "I never met him." His luncheon guest was shocked. "You— the head of Morgan Guaranty—don't know the president of the United States?" Patterson, smiling, said no. If the story says something about Japan, it also says something about Patterson's candor. He would express no fake altruism about the New York City rescue: "I just didn't want to have that much debt going bust—just protecting my own hide, so to speak. I sure didn't want to write off all those investments we had."[20] His Financial Community Liaison Group held its (mostly unpublicized) meetings at 23 Wall.

In early 1975, when financial markets wouldn't swallow more city paper, the Patterson group began to function as a *de facto* government. However Beame might bluster in public, he had to submit to the bankers' coup. There was a transfer of power from the city's highest elected official to a new, unelected mayor, Pat Patterson. The humiliated Beame would badger Patterson for news, sometimes telephoning him after midnight. When Patterson went golfing, he would see a golf cart speeding toward him and know it carried a message from the mayor. "He kept calling me and he'd say, 'What's going on?' " Patterson recalled. "As Beame lost more control, we gradually had to tell him what he could and couldn't do."[21]

Despite such seeming banker omnipotence, 1975 would actually demonstrate reduced banker influence. Unlike earlier Morgan-led rescues of the city, the bankers were as vulnerable as the city itself. They had granted multibillion-dollar credits to the city and held its paper; at one point, Morgan Guaranty alone had an estimated $300 million of city notes and bonds in its portfolio. By May, trading in New York City debt wound to an eerie halt. Along with a balanced budget and a commission to review city finances, the Patterson group wanted federal guarantees to pry open the closing market. From now on, their "rescue" would involve lobbying Washington and Albany. They were appealing to the government to rescue *them* and not just the city.

Patterson set up a White House appointment with President Ford, against whom he'd played college football. Accompanied by Rockefeller and Wriston, Patterson argued in the Oval Office that a New York City default would trigger general damage, depressing all municipal bonds. President Ford, thanking the group for coming, offered nothing in return. Long afterward, Beame would stand in Patterson's office staring at a photograph taken during the Oval Office meeting. "If Ford had said yes that day," sighed Beame, "he would have been president today."[22]

The New York City crisis presented an ideological clash among conservative businessmen. Said Treasury Secretary William Simon: "It was one of the saddest days of my life when financial giants like Pat Patterson of Morgan Guaranty and Walter Wriston . . . caved in and finally joined the others in asking Washington for federal aid."[23] Yet the House of Morgan had never adhered to extreme *laissez-faire* Republicanism. Much like Pierpont Morgan, it placed a premium on financial order. It was close to the Federal Reserve and favored government action to avoid financial disruption. It would never produce as ideological a hawk as Walter Wriston.

On May 26, 1975, Dick Shinn, head of Metropolitan Life, hosted a meeting at his home with Felix Rohatyn of Lazard Frères and other representatives of New York governor Hugh Carey. They worked out a plan for a Municipal Assistance Corporation ("Big MAC") to issue, under state auspices, bonds backed by city sales taxes. This permitted banks to exchange $1 billion in shaky city paper for new debt with an A rating. It was Carey's involvement, not the banks', that was the critical turning point. With the city again facing default in September, Carey created an Emergency Financial Control Board to assume budgetary powers from the city.

In mid-October 1975, world financial markets experienced one of those queer moments of falling pressure that sometimes presage storms. Amid fears of a New York City default, Patterson, Wriston, and Rockefeller pleaded for federal help before the Senate Banking Committee. Patterson warned that they were drifting into an unpredictable no-man's-land that could create an "economic downpull of general economic activity."[24] The three bankers asked for a direct federal loan or loan guarantee to prevent otherwise certain default.

In November, New York State announced a moratorium on $1.6 billion of short-term debt. Now fearing a generalized crisis, President Ford got spooked and had Congress approve a $2.3-billion line of credit to the city. Much as the state had put the city in its power, so the federal government put New York State under its control. Patterson felt vindicated: "There were a lot of people who would just as soon have seen New York go bankrupt. They thought it was a good thing to clean it out and get rid of the labor contracts. But our committee, fortunately, stuck with it."[25] Patterson was praised by labor leaders and government officials for his constructive, conciliatory approach.

In the end, the bankers exchanged their risky short-term paper for safe long-term MAC bonds. It had proven necessary to enlist state and federal help. The House of Morgan no longer presided over financial crises. As banks dwindled in power, they could cooperate with government-sponsored rescues instead of leading them. Even the largest could no more control the vast financial markets than they could bid the Red Sea part. The days when a Pierpont Morgan could sit down and extemporaneously write out a single sheet of paper to save the city were long gone.

TOMBSTONES

• •

•

To the outside world, Morgan Stanley still presented a debonair facade in the late 1970s. An *Atlantic Monthly* reporter, visiting its six floors atop the Exxon Building, marveled at its aplomb, its artfully modulated decor in brown and ocher. "To stroll through the hallways of Morgan Stanley is to move through a landscape of rolltop desks and Brooks Brothers suits," the reporter declared.[1] If it stumbled in the Middle East, it profited handily from the oil boom, arranging an astounding 40 percent of the money raised by the big oil companies. As investment banker to Standard Oil of Ohio, it did a record $1.75-billion private placement for the Trans Alaska Pipeline. In 1977, it supervised Wall Street's end of a $1-billion offering of British Petroleum shares owned by the British government, the largest stock offering in history. Right through the mid-1970s, it ranked first in the stock and bond offerings it managed.

It didn't seem a place in ferment, yet it was. Each year, it sprouted a new wing: portfolio management (1975), government bond trading and automated brokerage for institutions (1976), and retail brokerage for rich investors through its purchase of Shuman Agnew and Company in San Francisco (1977). The pride, even smugness, of the old Morgan Stanley stemmed from its extreme selectivity in hiring. Now, in a decade, the firm grew from about two hundred to seventeen hundred employees, with capital soaring from $7.5 million to $118 million. It was growing too fast to preserve a homogeneous culture.

As architect of this brave new world, Bob Baldwin often seemed disoriented by the range of new businesses. He had instinctively understood the need to trade and distribute securities yet never quite mastered these alien operations. He found it hard to adjust to a bizarre new world of fluctuating market signals and elevated risk. Risk, after all, had been foreign to the old Morgan Stanley, which only wanted sure things. When a $20-million bet on long Treasury bonds went the wrong way, Baldwin, in a sweat, summoned a meeting of all the senior partners. Another time, when bad news from Washington sent the market tumbling, Baldwin appeared on the floor insisting, "The market should go up. The market's wrong!" This world couldn't be controlled, even by somebody as strong and willful as Bob Baldwin.

Bob Baldwin probably saved the firm and destroyed its soul. This new Morgan Stanley was a monument to his force and clear vision, a brilliant adaptation to altered circumstances. Yet he badly politicized a firm long unified by a special *esprit de corps.* His management philosophy played people off against each other. If meant to improve performance, it pro-
duced a tense, unpleasant atmosphere. For the first time in the firm's history, senior partners defected for other firms. To some extent, turf fights were inevitable in a larger, richer firm. Baldwin, however, exacerbated the tensions. One example involved extremely close friends, Luis Mendez and Damon Mezzacappa, the two stars of the new trading operation. Yet Baldwin gave Mendez a $25,000 bonus, then went out of his way to tell Mezzacappa about it, saying Mendez was doing a better job. This was either obtuse or insensitive. As Baldwin became more abrasive and difficult, Bill Black, son of the former World Bank president, functioned as the great mediator, pleading for those who found it hard to deal directly with the difficult Baldwin. By softening Baldwin's rough edges, Black held the firm together and prevented an outright split between bankers and traders, such as would later shatter Lehman Brothers.

The major threat to Morgan Stanley's preeminence was its celebrated but increasingly tenuous policy of appearing as sole manager atop tombstone ads, those black-bordered boxes of underwriters' names that appear in newspapers. Tombstone positions were a life-and-death matter for Wall Street firms. Those in higher layers, or brackets, received larger share allotments, while the smaller firms tried to struggle their way upward. Within brackets, firms were listed alphabetically. During the Great Alphabet War of 1976, Halsey, Stuart adopted its parent's name, Bache, just to bootstrap up a few lines in tombstones. This was no joking matter. On May 13, 1964, Walston and Company had been demoted from a top bracket in a Comsat offering; the next day its managing director, Vernon Walston, shot himself, giving a macabre new aptness to the term describing the ad.

In the late 1960s and early 1970s, the top tier—called the bulge bracket—consisted of Morgan Stanley; First Boston; Kuhn, Loeb; and Dillon, Read. The first two originated most business, and Morgan Stanley was reluctant to relinquish the undivided profits of sole managership. A former managing director explained, "When I first went to Morgan Stanley, a senior person laughed and said to me, We only have to scare people into using us as sole manager 50 percent of the time and we're still better off." There was a touch of narcissism in wanting to appear alone in the top left corner of tombstones. There was also an unstated agenda: before the 1970s, Morgan Stanley lacked selling power and disguised this weakness by leading syndicates and having other firms do the selling. As Lewis Bernard later said, the firm "had to keep the Street from realizing the emperor had no clothes."[2] While other firms tried to ape the sole-manager strategy, none succeeded nearly as often as Morgan Stanley.

In order to make the policy stick, Morgan Stanley had to sacrifice even powerful clients who demanded co-managers on issues. (The Japanese rebuff was an early and notorious example of this.) It skipped one underwriting after Houston Industries insisted on rotating lead managers. It skipped another when Singer wanted to reward Goldman, Sachs for some merger work by appointing it co-manager. But such was Morgan Stanley's evergreen mystique that many firms, from Du Pont to J. P. Morgan and Company itself, still submitted to its golden chains on all their underwritings.

Because up to two hundred firms participated in Morgan Stanley syndicates, they feared its displeasure. Before 1975, Morgan's syndicate manager was Fred Whittemore. Bright, sardonic, and voluble, an avid collector of Pierpont Morgan memorabilia, he was called the Godfather or Father Fred. He had a pervasive power on Wall Street. When William Simon wished to return to Salomon Brothers after serving as treasury secretary, it was Father Fred who interceded with John Gutfreund. In the early 1970s, many attributed E. F. Hutton's stunning rise to Father Fred's patronage, and he didn't hesitate to thwart competitors, such as Lehman Brothers. After each issue, Father Fred filled out large yellow cards listing each firm's performance. Sometimes participants lied or took losses just to look good.

There was always suspicion that Morgan Stanley exploited its sole-manager power to fend off competitive threats. "We could be talking to their clients about an investment banking relationship, and if Morgan saw this, instead of giving us half-a-million shares, they might hold back on us," one rival told the *New York Times* in 1975.[3] Morgan Stanley bristled at these anonymous snipes in the press, which appeared periodically. Father Fred created the modern Wall Street lineup. He kicked out the fading Kuhn, Loeb and Dillon, Read from the bulge bracket and brought in Merrill Lynch, Salomon Brothers, and Goldman, Sachs. After Kuhn, Loeb—historically the most redoubtable Morgan adversary—was absorbed by Lehman Brothers in 1977, senior partner John Schiff met Harry Morgan at a board meeting of the Metropolitan Museum of Art. When Morgan asked how this had happened, Schiff replied, "Henry, you chose your partners better than I did."[4] Schiff's remark pointed to a continuing strength of the Morgan houses—the sheer excellence of their people.

But by the late 1970s, Morgan Stanley's sole-manager policy was a gilded anachronism. How could you handcuff clients in global financial markets when corporate treasurers enjoyed so many options, so much room in which to maneuver? The firm, significantly, had never made the sole-manager policy stick at its Paris joint venture with Morgan Guaranty. A loyal home client like General Motors Acceptance Corporation openly used other bankers abroad. In April 1977, in a final break with 23 Wall, Morgan Stanley closed up shop in Paris and set up Morgan Stanley International in London, linchpin of its Euromarket operations. The new operation had a rude shock when Australia, a faithful client since 1946, jumped to that old Morgan nemesis, Deutsche Bank. The event underscored not only the new power of global distribution, but the far more anonymous world of interlinked financial markets.

Even at home, there were new forces corroding the chains that bound companies to bankers. Since the days of Louis Brandeis, political reformers had advocated an arm's-length relationship between companies and investment bankers. It was the theme broadcast by Robert Young during his testimony before Judge Medina and in his fight for the New York Central. The system had survived, however, because companies craved the association with the august House of Morgan, a vestige of the days when capital was scarce. But how could bankers still lord it over companies when capital was no longer rationed—when it was available in many markets in many forms? What leverage did they have as new financial intermediaries sprang up? From the clients' standpoint, was there any longer a rationale for having an exclusive banker relationship? The answer was no.

So corporate America now did the work that was once solely the cause of reformers. One by one, corporate treasurers broke the links in the bankers' chains. In the 1970s, Texaco, Mobil, International Harvester, and other clients circumvented Morgan Stanley and placed their debt directly with institutional investors. Other companies used dividend-reinvestment plans or employee stock purchase plans to raise capital. Having to cope with inflation and unstable exchange rates, corporate treasurers were receptive to bright ideas thought up by competing banks to deal with the new volatility. Jack Bennett of Exxon delighted in making Morgan Stanley spar with other firms. "We decided that any time a banker came up with a good idea, we'd talk to him," said Bennett. When he set up "Dutch auctions" for issues, encouraging several competing syndicates, Morgan Stanley began to sense that its sole manager policy faced a mortal threat.

For Morgan Stanley, the doomsday trumpet sounded in 1979. That year, IBM asked the firm to accept Salomon Brothers as co-manager on a $1-billion debt issue needed for a new generation of computers. It was a telling sign of corporate autonomy in the Casino Age that IBM had a $6-billion pile of cash on hand. It had never needed a public debt offering. (Some Morgan people say the IBM relationship—nominally Bob Greenhill's account—was mishandled because nobody ever expected the company to require money.) In applying its sole-manager policy, Morgan Stanley had never before been obliged to turn down a client of such stature. Now here was one of the world's largest corporations, a twenty-year client with a triple-A rating, undertaking the largest industrial borrowing in history.

Morgan Stanley directors had an emotional, protracted debate about whether to reject the IBM offer and miss a fee of approximately $1 million. The meeting was filled with high-flown rhetoric about upholding tradition. Bob Baldwin and Fred Whittemore were among the hawks who feared an IBM exception would embolden the other slaves to cast off their chains. After much resounding talk, nearly everybody voted to defy IBM and demand sole management. Morgan Stanley was shocked when word came back that IBM hadn't budged in its demand: Salomon Brothers would head the issue, as planned. It was a landmark in Wall Street history: the golden chains were smashed.

Before long, investment banks were raiding other Morgan Stanley clients with abandon, destroying the Gentleman Banker's Code. A competitor observed cheerily, "Once the client list starts unwinding, it's going to unwind all the way. It's just a matter of time."[5] Afterward, most of IBM's business went to Salomon. Swallowing its pride, Morgan Stanley agreed to share issues for General Electric Credit, Du Pont, and Tenneco. It even began to participate in syndicates below the level of manager—a sight as shocking to old-timers as that of a master suddenly donning the livery of his footman. The age of relationship banking was dead.

Snubbed by its blue-chip clients, Morgan Stanley displayed a new receptivity to emerging-growth companies. It had long been chary of lending its imprimatur to untested companies—the name Morgan was synonymous with *established*—and had refrained from initial public offerings of stock. This squeamishness dated back at least to the pre-ferred-list disaster of 1929. In 1980, perhaps taking a swipe at IBM, Morgan Stanley introduced rival Apple Computer to the stock market. (It also bought Hitachi computers for the office, something it wouldn't have done before 1979.) For a long time, the firm had resisted high-tech start-ups. Now Morgan Stanley would lend its name to new ventures. Much like the indigent aristocrat who rents his castle to tourists, the firm would shamelessly trade on its class.

A S underwriting became a more mundane, impersonal business, Morgan Stanley relied more on its takeover department, which boomed under Bob Greenhill's tutelage. Already in the late 1970s, merger work was being hailed as the last gold mine by investment bankers who assumed that Glass-Steagall would someday collapse and lead to a securities business overrun by commercial banks.

Takeovers transformed Morgan Stanley's ethos. As a sponsor of securities, the old Morgan Stanley had fashioned a stately, incorruptible image. Emerging from the fury of Ferdinand Pecora, early partners took fright at the first breath of scandal. This culture was now tested by the more lucrative takeover work. By the late 1970s, the four-man M&A Department had expanded to a crack squad of fifty. Just five years after the watershed Inco-ESB raid, the firm was handling deals worth $10 billion yearly, with a hundred potential deals in the hopper at any time. M&A was now the firm's major source of profits. At the same time, takeover work had become divorced from the old seamless relationship with faithful clients. It was a giant, disciplined machine separated from the rest of the firm.

Greenhill's brawny raids didn't fit easily into the old collegial firm, especially with his department contributing so disproportionately to profits. As one former partner recalls, "Greenhill was making a hell of a lot of money, and he was lording it over everybody." Opposition, predictably, emerged from the syndicate side. Thomas A. Saunders III, who replaced Father Fred as syndicate chief, issued truculent warnings: "Greenhill should remember that whatever success he has comes from the franchise."[6]

By now, Morgan Stanley had left the white-shoe stereotype far behind, as the brash style of corporate marauders replaced the sedate style of underwriters. The old leisurely syndicate pace gave way to the fast, staccato beat of takeovers, with their weeks of frenetic activity. People now wore beepers, worked ninety-hour weeks, and remained on call over weekends, restricting their outside cultural and political activities—hallmarks of partners in the old House of Morgan. As the corps of managing directors ballooned in size, decisions were no longer made by milling around, and the firm was run in a more autocratic, from-the-top-down style.

Expanding swiftly, Morgan Stanley found it harder to screen people or instill the old culture. As happened in the 1920s, a burgeoning financial industry rapidly attracted a new generation of young people. Untested college graduates were slipped into positions of great responsibility, with almost instant access to information worth millions. The demographic accent tilted to youth.

As questions of possible conflicts of interest in merger work surfaced, Bob Baldwin would quote Jack Morgan's dictum of doing first-class business in a first-class way: "Nobody's perfect, but we think we have the highest ethical standards in the industry."[7] In 1973, the *New York Times* ran an article on insider trading with this caption below Baldwin's photo: "ROBERT H. B. BALDWIN OF MORGAN STANLEY THINKS THE PRACTICE IS PASSÉ." "Maybe I'm naive," he said, "but I think the day of partners swapping that kind of information is long gone."[8] Baldwin wasn't cavalier about ethics, but he placed extraordinary faith in the power of so-called Chinese walls to insulate Greenhill's operation from the rest of the firm.

Morgan Stanley tried to throw the fear of God into merger specialists and monitored their activities closely. Briefed on legal and ethical issues, young professionals had to sign statements that they understood house rules. To foster a healthy paranoia about using inside information for personal gain, scare memos listing grounds for dismissal were circulated periodically. Oil analyst Barry Good remarked, "I have visions of someone stalking into my office to rip the epaulettes off my shoulders, break my calculator over his knee and drum me right out of the corps."[9] Every fortnight, security officers conducted electronic sweeps, and projects were camouflaged with the names of English kings or Greek philosophers. Staff members weren't permitted to discuss them in halls or elevators and weren't supposed to know each other's deals. Stock-research people couldn't even browse in the library's corporate-finance section.

These safeguards grew more important as more major deals churned through the Greenhill mill. The deals—and the fees—were growing astronomically. In a 1977 milestone, Morgan Stanley got a $2.7-million fee for representing Babcock and Wilcox against a takeover by McDermott, advised by John A. Morgan (Harry Morgan's bulbous-nosed, ruddy son, rejected by Morgan Stanley after the Charlie Morgan controversy) of Smith, Barney. Babcock demolished the myth that billion-dollar companies were immune to takeovers. Because its stock doubled during the bid—way above the usual 40-percent premium—it attracted a new breed of professional arbitrageurs. These speculators swept up the outstanding stock of takeover candidates, concentrating it in fewer hands, thus setting the stage for merger mania.

In the fall of 1977, Morgan Stanley became involved in an ethical tangle from which it never fully extricated itself. Like other big, Morgan-financed mining firms, Kennecott Copper wanted to diversify, and it turned to Greenhill as adviser. Among the prospects he scouted was a Louisiana forest-products concern, Olinkraft. While a friendly bid still seemed possible, Olinkraft provided Kennecott with confidential earnings estimates. Then Kennecott's attention was distracted by a company named Carborundum, which it finally bought. Losing interest in Olinkraft, it returned the confidential data. Morgan Stanley apparently did not.

In early 1978, another Morgan-organized mining conglomerate, Johns-Manville, showed up for diversification advice and was assigned to Greenhill's sidekick, Yerger Johnstone. When talk turned to Olinkraft, Morgan Stanley mentioned earlier talks with the company but didn't divulge the valuable data. By late June, Johns-Manville had decided not to pursue Olinkraft. Two weeks later, Texas Eastern made a $51-a-share offer for Olinkraft, which the latter's board approved. Now, having seen confidential projections that Olinkraft would earn over $8 a share by 1981, Morgan Stanley knew the company was selling out very cheap. So it shared the data with Johns-Manville, which reversed its decision, stepped straight into a bidding war with Texas Eastern, and won with a top bid of $65 a share. As the dust settled, the question arose: had Morgan Stanley betrayed Olinkraft?

According to its later defense, Morgan Stanley consulted Davis, Polk, and Wardwell and Joe Flom's law firm of Skadden, Arps before making a move. Both approved disclosing data to Johns-Manville provided the confidential estimates appeared in an SEC filing connected with the bid. This was duly done. Yet when published in September 1978, the filing caused shock, since Morgan Stanley hadn't received Olinkraft's permission to share such internal information. It seemed that client-banker trust—the bedrock of merchant banking for a century—was being violated in an opportunistic way. When the *Wall Street Journal* broke the story on October 26, it saw the flap as betokening larger problems: "No one is accusing Morgan Stanley of any wrongdoing, but some close observers of the firm, including some clients, lately have grown uneasy about what they see as mounting aggressiveness at Morgan Stanley as it scrambles for sizable takeover-bid advisory fees."[10]

At first, Morgan Stanley couldn't produce a coherent defense. After its managing directors met for several hours, a spokesman said lamely, "I'm afraid we've decided we can't comment."[11] While some Morgan people reacted angrily toward the press, others, troubled by Greenhill's bravado, welcomed what they saw as a salutary rebuke. Petito and Baldwin published a nine-paragraph defense in the *Wall Street Journal,* which asserted that the firm had "acted with the highest standard of professional responsibility" in showing the Olinkraft data to Johns-Manville.[12] They pointed out that Morgan Stanley's action had benefited Olinkraft shareholders, who reaped a 25-percent premium over the Texas Eastern bid. True enough. But was such bidding fair to Texas Eastern? Greenhill argued that the withholding of vital information from Johns-Manville might have posed questions, too. "If someone tried to stir up trouble, he might come in and say, 'Hey, these guys are trying to buy a company with undisclosed, secret information.' "[13] This was a valid point—and a perfectly good argument for bowing out of the deal altogether.

Morgan Stanley's attempts at explanation only worsened matters. Speaking to *Institutional Investor,* Greenhill and Dick Fisher said the firm had neither a verbal nor a written agreement with Olinkraft that enforced confidentiality. For the House of Morgan—the historic custodian of the "my word is my bond" approach to business—this defense seemed a betrayal of the Morgan tradition. As *Institutional Investor* said, "Morgan Stanley appeared to be enunciating a new investment banking doctrine: that any information a corporation provides to an investment banker will not necessarily be kept in complete and lasting confidence unless that corporation obtains either a written or oral promise from the investment banker to keep the information confidential."[14]

There was more bad news. About two years before, Morgan Stanley had set up a "risk arbitrage" department to speculate in takeover targets. As would become clear during the insider trading scandals of the 1980s, such operations were incompatible with M&A work. How could one side of a firm execute takeovers while another side was betting on them? Again Morgan Stanley extolled its Chinese wall, insisting its arbitrageurs existed in a sealed universe apart from Greenhill's group. Then, a second *Wall Street Journal* story disclosed that the Arbitrage Department had taken a 150,000-share position in Olinkraft in mid-July, soon after the original Olinkraft–Texas Eastern discussions were revealed. This $7-million stake was unusually large. Only two months later did Johns-Manville learn that one wing of Morgan Stanley had a huge vested interest in seeing it pay top dollar for Olinkraft.

Bob Baldwin refused to concede any lapse in the firm's vaunted integrity: "If you ask any 50 investment bankers on Wall Street which firm has the highest standards of ethics, I can assure you that Morgan Stanley will be the firm that is most often mentioned."[15] Elsewhere in Wall Street, the Olinkraft episode produced deep uneasiness. Morgan Stanley was the flagship of Wall Street and its troubles tarred everyone. "The Morgan Stanley situation is going to hurt all of us," said a rival. "For years we have all been cloaked in the integrity Morgan Stanley has shown in the corporate world."[16]

Olinkraft showed that as Wall Street firms grew and diversified, there were myriad opportunities for cheating and cutting corners. For some ex-partners who had grimly watched the firm evolve over the previous ten years, Olinkraft confirmed their fears. Some had thought it a matter of time before "accidents" occurred. One former partner said:

> Morgan Stanley took on jobs that visibly represented conflicts of interest and sooner or later they got into trouble. Before, the attitude was that if you saw a conflict of interest, you said "no" right away. There was no idea that you had to go for the last nickel. And you never looked at an individual buck outside of its effect on that basic business of preserving client relationships. That's what Morgan Stanley slipped away from for quite awhile. I always felt they lost their soul.

By now, the merger business had acquired an irresistible momentum. In 1979, Morgan Stanley earned a stratospheric $14.3-million fee for advising Belridge Oil on its sale to Shell Oil—then history's largest takeover. Among the losing auction bidders were two furious Morgan Stanley clients—Mobil and Texaco. The irate Mobil gradually shifted business to Merrill Lynch, while Greenhill pretended to be blasé: "We'll always do our best for a client, and Belridge was the client."[17] Unlike syndicate work, takeover business required antagonizing some clients to please others. It therefore eroded historic ties on Wall Street.

This was again revealed in August 1981, when Du Pont bought Conoco for $7.8 billion. Advised by Morgan Stanley, Conoco turned to Du Pont as a white knight to ward off Seagram's advances. Because Greenhill and Flom were already teamed up with Conoco, Du Pont—a House of Morgan mainstay from the World War I Export Department and the 1920 General Motors takeover—had to drop Morgan Stanley and turn to the surging First Boston team of Joe Perella and Bruce Wasserstein. The three-month battle netted Morgan Stanley $15 million. Afterward, Morgan Stanley found itself sharing Du Pont underwritings with First Boston. The new banker ties developed through takeovers translated into less loyalty in underwriting as well.

In 1981, Morgan Stanley was destined to suffer an embarrassment greater than that precipitated by the Olinkraft takeover. The case would darkly foreshadow later Wall Street scandals. It started with the hiring of Adrian Antoniu, a Romanian refugee whose family settled in New York in the 1960s. The Antonius had no money and spoke no English; Adrian's would be a classic success story: after his father died, he supported his mother, worked his way through NYU, and in 1972 graduated from the Harvard Business School. Hired as a Morgan Stanley associate that year, he worried about money. He fretted about his mother's failing fabric business in Queens and was concerned about making payments on his student loan.

Bright and sociable, Antoniu was mesmerized by the new wealth around him and took up a trendy lifestyle, complete with BMW and Park Avenue apartment. He belonged to a tony club called Doubles, frequented smart restaurants, and hung out at the Hamptons. The more perceptive wondered what lay below the aura of sophistication. "He just looked too good, too well-pressed and too well-groomed," said an acquaintance.[18] Starting in corporate finance, Antoniu was soon drawn into Greenhill's growing merger operation, where a newcomer could quickly lay his hands on valuable information.

In 1973, Antoniu hatched a deal with a former N.Y.U. classmate, James Newman, who worked in a brokerage house. Antoniu would feed names of takeover candidates to Newman, who put up the money to buy the stocks; profits were to be shared equally. He cut similar deals with two other graduates from his business-school class. At first, the bets were touchingly modest. In the first of eighteen deals, Antoniu told Newman that Morgan Stanley was defending CertainTeed in a tender offer by Compagnie de Saint-Gobain-Pont-à-Mousson. Their CertainTeed purchases netted $1,375. In a second deal—Newman had now moved to Miami and taken another brokerage job—Antoniu revealed that Ciba-Geigy, advised by Morgan Stanley, would soon launch a bid for Funk Seeds. Soon they were placing bigger bets. For instance, when Morgan Stanley helped North American Philips in its bid for Magnavox, Antoniu and Newman bought 17,600 shares of Magnavox. Starting to show real flair, the young men took to using offshore Bahama bank accounts.

They grew strangely heedless of danger. Later on, they read a newspaper account of an insider trading case against three people at Sorg Printing who used inside information from tender-offer documents they were printing. "Look what happened to these people at Sorg," said Antoniu, briefly dismayed. "Well, you see the worst that could happen in a case like this," Newman replied. "They ask for your money back, and they give you a slap on the hand. People have to steal or kill to get this kind of money, but you don't have to go to jail for it."[19]

In early 1975, the conspiracy nearly ended when Antoniu was edged out of Morgan Stanley and hired for M&A work by Kuhn, Loeb, soon to merge with Lehman Brothers. Luckily, he found a new Morgan Stanley confederate in yet a fifth member of the Harvard Business School class of 1972. Unlike the free-and-easy Antoniu, the French-Canadian E. Jacques Courtois had an intense, tight-lipped expression. His father, a rich Montreal lawyer who headed a group that owned the Montreal Canadiens, sat on a bank board. Over chess at the Harvard Club, Antoniu drew Courtois into his scheme. Courtois promptly repaid his confidence with a tip—that Pan Ocean Oil, a Morgan Stanley client, was involved in merger talks with Marathon Oil. They made a quick killing of $119,000. Between 1973 and 1978, they would earn $800,000.

It took time before the authorities zeroed in on Antoniu. Meanwhile, he had fallen in love with Francesca Stanfill, daughter of Dennis Stanfill, the powerful chairman of Twentieth Century Fox. By the spring of 1978, when the government targeted him as a prime suspect, Antoniu was engaged to Francesca, who wrote about fashion for the Sunday magazine of the *New York Times*. He somehow neglected to tell Eric Gleacher, his boss at the M&A Department of Lehman Brothers Kuhn Loeb, that he was being investigated. Learning of this fact on the eve of Antoniu's wedding, Gleacher saw double disaster: not only was Antoniu his employee but Twentieth Century Fox was a major Lehman client.

He insisted to Antoniu, "If there is nothing to the charges and you want to have the Stanfills stand by you in defending against them, you really ought to tell them."[20]

On June 28, 1978, Antoniu married Stanfill at a civil ceremony in Venice, neglecting to tell her family about the federal probe. Discovering this, Gleacher roared into the telephone from New York: "Unless you tell Mr. Stanfill before the church wedding, I will!"[21] On July 1, the church wedding took place at the Basilica di San Pietro di Castello in Venice, with Albino Cardinal Luciani, about to become Pope John Paul I, bestowing his blessing on the couple in a written message. Adrian delivered a poetic toast: "Here's to the longest run Twentieth Century Fox will ever have."[22] As guests waved good-bye, the newlyweds drifted off in a white gondola. Back in New York, Gleacher cleared out Antoniu's desk. Within a month, the wedding was annulled, presumably because the Stanfills learned of the investigation.

E. Jacques Courtois's voluntary departure from Morgan Stanley in 1979 caused great anguish. "Morgan Stanley was rocked at the time," said a colleague. "They had lost 3 people, including Jacques, in something like 3 weeks. They had a series of meetings to make sure they were hanging on to the rest of us."[23] Courtois said he might go into computer software or manage his investments. Marrying the niece of Colombia's president, he moved to Bogotá. Courtois was fingered by government investigators because he alone in the M&A Department *hadn't* worked on the takeovers in question. This raised questions about Morgan Stanley's claim that their people never discussed takeovers with others.

The criminal indictments handed down in February 1981 were the first such ever brought against investment bankers. Newman got a one-year prison sentence, while Antoniu's plea bargaining got him a suspended sentence. Antoniu said, "Anyone familiar with the securities markets knows these circumstances are not uncommon."[24] Courtois spent a year in prison and paid $150,000 in fines.

Morgan Stanley cooperated with the government and contacted clients to reaffirm its integrity. Lewis Bernard was chosen to inform the firm's managing directors. He recalled, "People in that room cried. They cried out of anger. We have the feeling of being violated."[25] Although the overwhelming majority of inside tips came from Morgan Stanley, Bob Baldwin complained that Lehman Brothers received less publicity: "What do the headlines say? Morgan. We make the headlines in these darned situations . . . we had people practically crying around here, they work so hard to do a first-class job in a first-class way."[26]

Public reaction to this insider trading ring distinctly echoed that to the 1933 preferred-list scandal and the Richard Whitney affair. People unconnected to Morgan Stanley felt as if a public trust had been violated. "I've always thought of Morgan Stanley as the *crème de la crème*," said Benedict T. Haber, dean of Fordham's Graduate School of Business. "It's like an icon has been knocked down."

SAMBA

. .

.

B Y the mid-1970s, J. P. Morgan and Company—the holding company of Morgan Guaranty—was drawing half its profits from more than twenty offices abroad. By a minor miracle, the bank's pell-mell global expansion didn't dilute staff cohesion. As Pat Patterson said, "Our operation is worldwide in a compact way."[1] The bank used various devices— from providing free lunches at its dining rooms to rotating executives—to preserve an inbred feeling. The refusal to open branch networks in foreign countries concentrated personnel, furthering intimacy. "It would be a little like a fish out of water for us to run a system of branches in Germany or England when we don't have it here," said the avuncular, balding Walter Page, who succeeded Patterson as chairman in 1978.[2]

When Morgans started underwriting in Paris in the early 1960s, it wasn't clear where the Euromarkets would settle; even Geneva and Zurich were in the running. During the oil boom of the 1970s, however, London emerged as the clear winner, recycling OPEC surpluses at a furious rate to debtor countries. The City of London suddenly had more American banks than Wall Street! They leapt into syndicated Eurodollar loans, which formed the genesis of the Latin American debt crisis. Latin American governments paid much higher interest rates on loans than corporations back home. And in the Casino Age, those corporations were bypassing banks to borrow in securities markets. Thus, the lemming rush into Latin American lending was symptomatic of the deterioration of the banks' commercial lending business. Foreign borrowing now expanded beyond the industrial countries that had received the bulk of cross-border lending in the 1950s and 1960s.

Previous cycles of Latin American lending and default dated back at least to the 1820s. During the Great Depression, every Latin American country save Argentina had defaulted on its foreign debt. The nations had been sternly lectured by the bankers that they would be forever barred from future lending. Yet this history was conveniently forgotten by the young bankers on the swank London party circuit, who booked huge loans to those same countries. As members of a venerable old bank, Morgan people should have had a better memory, and to some extent they did. "Lew Preston and I spent a lot of time talking about the parallels," recalled A. Bruce Brackenridge, the senior credit officer in the late 1970s. "We used to refer to the loans that the British made here to our railroads. The money that J. P. Morgan and Peabody raised to build America—that was the sort of loans we made to the Itaípu Dam in Brazil. There's a very clear analogy there."[3] It was, alas, the wrong analogy, skipping over all the disastrous Latin American precedents. It also overlooked the fact that many American state and railroad loans in the nineteenth century had defaulted—a history that haunted George Peabody and subsequently made the Morgan imprimatur so sacred to European creditors.

In earlier generations, Rothschilds, Barings, and Morgans made Latin American loans through large bond issues that distributed risk among thousands of small investors. (An estimated half-million Americans were stuck with largely worthless foreign bonds during the 1930s.) Modern Latin American loans, in contrast, took the form of bank debt, concentrating the risk in the banking system. Large syndicate managers, such as Morgan Guaranty and Citibank, would unite up to two hundred banks for a loan. If this spread risk, it perhaps also created an illusory sense of safety in numbers.

Why didn't banks sell Latin American bonds? "Because you wouldn't have been able to sell the bonds," explained Brackenridge. This should have been a tip-off of high risk.[4] Since only a handful of developing countries were eligible to sell bonds, Morgan Stanley and other investment banks were mostly spared the Latin American debt crisis. (Both a commercial and an investment bank in American terms, Morgan Grenfell participated in some export credits and syndicated loans to Brazil and elsewhere.) So banks rushed in where investors feared to tread. This spared the "little people" the bloodshed of the earlier debt crisis but also introduced the potential for large disruptions in the global financial system.

Because the Latin American debt crisis originated with the recycling of Arab petrodollar deposits, the banks would later cite official approval of such lending. Indeed, Washington and the other Western governments cravenly ceded responsibility for the problem to the private banks. But as shown by the experience with German reparations and Allied war debt in the 1920s, even explicit official approval of loans didn't guarantee government support in case of trouble. There would always be popular cynicism about spendthrift foreign debtors—not to mention an assumption of banker greed—that would arise to hobble governments in solving the problem. Ironically, the petrodollar blackmail so feared by Senator Church wasn't the real problem. By *keeping* petrodollars and lending them out to Latin America, banks damaged themselves and the world economy.

Morgan Guaranty was a good bellwether of changing American attitudes toward Latin American lending. In the 1920s, the bank had proudly boasted of the number of South American governments it had turned down. In the 1940s, Tom Lamont was aghast when Franklin Roosevelt advocated postwar lending to Brazil, and Russell Leffingwell urged World Bank president John J. McCloy not to lend to the region. In the 1950s, the Eurocentric Morgans largely limited foreign lending to England and France. But with its core lending business eroded in the Casino Age, it suddenly emerged in the 1970s and 1980s as an "MBA bank"—so-called after the first initials of the three largest Latin American debtors: it made $1.2 billion in loans to Mexico, $1.8 billion to Brazil, and $750 million to Argentina. For Wall Street's most conservative bank to have its largest foreign stake in Brazil showed its reliance on progressively riskier loans for profitability.

Several overriding illusions clouded judgment. One was that countries didn't go bankrupt—a canard associated with Citicorp's Walter Wriston. This almost inverted historic truth. Default on sovereign debt had been commonplace for 150 years. Even the discriminating old House of Morgan ended up with massive defaults on Austrian, German, and Japanese loans by World War II. There were more recent cases of debt repudiation as well, including China in 1949, Cuba in 1961, and North Korea in 1974. Banks could foreclose on companies but not on countries, making the latter more careless about repaying loans. And political risk was always piled atop economic risk.

Another factor of comfort to the bankers was the International Monetary Fund. By the 1970s, gunboat diplomacy was passé. For reasons of foreign policy, Washington was often more eager to appease Latin American governments than bully them about loans. Bankers didn't like meddling in foreign countries, especially now that they had branches abroad. In 1976, when Peru was nearly bankrupt, Citibank, Morgans, and other banks imposed an austerity plan in exchange for a $400-

million loan. Requiring a steep rise in food and gas prices, it provoked riots in Lima and new charges of dollar diplomacy. The banks were appalled by the backlash. "It doesn't take much to whip up the peasantry with stories about the House of Morgan and U.S. imperialism to explain why there's no food," said a congressional staffer.[5] Stung by bad publicity, the banks turned to the IMF as a surrogate that could withstand political criticism in debtor countries. It seemed a useful shield behind which to effect painful economic reforms.

The IMF laid down strict conditions for loans. As banks made their loans contingent on agreement to the IMF austerity programs, the fund's power soared. The problem was that the fund was set up to handle temporary payment imbalances, not protracted debt problems. Nobody knew whether its orthodox prescriptions—cutting spending, ending subsidies, and deflating economies—revived economies or simply squeezed them to pay off bankers. There was the further problem that strong Third World countries, such as Brazil, bypassed the fund altogether and borrowed only from commercial banks. Yet whatever the fund's limitations, it encouraged bankers to believe that they had some control over errant debtors, forcing them to undertake sound policies. And during the Latin debt crisis, the fund would indeed provide forms of control over debtor countries unknown to earlier generations of bankers.

The structure of syndicated loans invited banks to abdicate responsibility and coast along with the others. Some fifteen hundred banks worldwide piggybacked onto the expertise of a Morgans or a Citibank, especially in Brazil. Often new to foreign lending, small banks left the scrutiny of loans to the larger banks. In a world of telex-driven anonymity, banks would receive cursory "offering memorandums" of mostly boilerplate language. Tens of billions of dollars in loans were assembled through $10-million participations. By the late 1970s, a fierce price war cut profit margins on loans until they no longer reflected the gargantuan risks involved. Said one Morgan banker involved: "By the mid-1970s, it was very clear that things were getting out of control, with crazy lenders and crazy borrowers." It was a giant mechanism gone mad.

Somewhat more than most, Morgans tried to resist the wild grab bag. In 1979, its London syndicate operation was run by a young Smith graduate, Mary Gibbons, known for her toughness. "At 31, wielding all the power that Morgan Guaranty's position in the Eurocurrency market commands, Gibbons is unquestionably the most influential female decision maker in the City, if not in the entire world of international banking," said *Institutional Investor.*[6] She balked at credits even for

Britain, Sweden, and Canada, fearing watered-down standards. In general, however, Morgans was swept up in the bankers' suicide dash. One ex-Morgan banker recalled, "There was a lot of unscrupulous lending and forcing loans down the throat of these countries. Anything to get a loan to a government."

The most convoluted, baffling Morgan relationship was with Brazil, a newcomer among its clients. Even as the House of Morgan advised the country, Brazil balked at granting it a branch, which rankled at 23 Wall. "They said that if Morgan got a branch, they would be dominant and then the government would have to let in forty other banks," said an ex-Morgan official. "It was a real sore point." The Morgan people were proud of their Brazil loans, which went to seemingly well-managed mining and electric enterprises. Recipients included the vast Itaípu hydroelectric project, with its World Bank patronage. The bank also boasted that Brazil had a good credit profile—that is, its loans matured at nicely spaced intervals. Sometimes Morgan people sounded as if history had cheated them, making their splendid Brazilian portfolio look miserable.

As a latecomer to Latin America, Morgan's position as chief adviser to Brazil was a startling achievement. It was accomplished through the virtuosity of an engaging young banker of mixed nationality named Antonio Gebauer. Born in Colombia to a wealthy Venezuelan brewer of German birth, Gebauer had been educated at Columbia University's Graduate School of Business and was married to a Brazilian. He retained his Venezuelan citizenship while at Morgans. Short, with horn-rimmed glasses and sandy hair, he was fluent in Spanish, Portuguese, German, and other languages. He was both charming and impatient, bright but prone to a brusque arrogance. When he started at Morgans in the 1960s, domestic bankers were kings, and he seemed to have a slim chance for advancement. Then, as Latin American lending surged in the 1970s, the Anglophile Morgan bank, with its European bias, found Gebauer providential in catching up with Chase and Citibank in Latin America. His delighted bosses gave him a wide berth.

Tony Gebauer spectacularly developed new business and was trusted by Brazilian officials. He socialized in elite circles and was probably on a first-name basis with every Latin finance minister and central banker. In the heady world of petrodollar recycling in the 1970s, Gebauer was a jet-setting star, a frequent guest at Brazilian coffee plantations, his doings covered by Rio de Janeiro gossip columnists. He appeared on Brazilian television, landed on the cover of the country's top news magazine, *Veja,* and became president of the Brazilian-American Chamber of Commerce. It was highly unusual for the Morgan bank to tolerate such a high-profile approach to banking. Other bankers watched in wonder. At home, Gebauer threw flashy parties in his East Side apartment and at his East Hampton weekend home, which was called Samambaia, or "fern" in Portuguese. Carlos Langoni, Brazil's young central bank president, spent weekends there. All the while, Gebauer was booking Brazilian loans 2 percentage points above Morgan's own costs—spreads so profitable as to ease doubts about their soundness.

Occasionally there were fleeting concerns at high levels about this lending binge. At one point, Chairman Pat Patterson received an award from Brazil declaring him the country's best banker. He was slightly jarred and confided to President Walter Page that it was perhaps a dubious achievement. "Maybe we better not get another award and be busted," Patterson told Page.[7] But such doubts were momentary. By pushing back the exposure limits in each borrowing country by small increments, bankers averted their eyes from the developing danger. Brackenridge recalled, "We didn't say, 'How much of our capital should be in these loans?' We played with it, but we really didn't say, 'Hey, we really shouldn't have more than 50 percent of our capital in loans to Brazil just out of a spread of risk.' "[8]

Despite Gebauer's virtuosity, the Morgan bank had limited power to force Brazil to curb its prodigal, inflationary spending. In 1980, it vainly badgered the country to go to the IMF. When the bank went to the IMF instead to get its perspective on Brazil—an exercise meant to instill market confidence—Delfim Netto, Brazil's short, squat, bespectacled planning minister, got very angry. He thought Morgans was going behind the country's back to check up on it. So the banks found it hard to police sovereign clients without antagonizing them. They began slipping into a situation in which they were hostages to their large debtors. The full extent of this bondage wouldn't become apparent until the fall of 1982. Then everyone would rediscover the old adage that if a debtor is big enough, he controls the bank.

THE April 1982 war over the Falkland Islands cast a black cloud over Latin American lending, projecting a view of the whole region as unstable. After Argentina invaded the islands, Britain retaliated by freezing its London-based assets. When hostilities ended, the House of Morgan undertook secret diplomacy to patch up relations between the two countries. The central banks of England and Argentina didn't know how to resume relations without losing face. Who would initiate talks? Tony Gebauer, now the senior vice-president for Latin America, acted as matchmaker. Representatives from the two central banks flew to New York and were closeted in a conference room at 23 Wall—the ice-breaking contact between them.

After the war, it grew harder for bankers to make nice distinctions among Latin American debtors. Regional banks were less disposed to share Morgan's view of Brazil as a textbook Third World country investing in sound infrastructure. Rather, they saw a nation grotesquely burdened with a $90-billion debt—the world's biggest—borrowing a stupendous $1.5 billion monthly to stay afloat. Morgans urged Carlos Langoni to come to New York to make reassuring speeches. In a rare coup, it even got Secretary of State George Shultz—as Bechtel president, a Morgan director in the 1970s—to accept an award from the Brazilian-American Chamber of Commerce along with Ernane Galveas, Brazil's finance minister; Shultz seldom consented to such mingling of private and public purpose.

When Mexico startled the world in August 1982 by announcing that it could no longer service its $87-billion foreign debt, it blackened the image of all Latin American debtors. They were being drowned in a common economic deluge of rising interest rates, global recession, and steeply falling commodity prices. On September 21, 1982, Langhorne Motley, the U.S. ambassador to Brazil, told the State Department that Mexico's troubles were sparking flight from Brazilian debt: "Japanese banks are out of the market, European banks are scared, regional U.S. banks don't want to hear about Brazil, and major U.S. banks are proceeding with extreme caution."[9]

In October 1982, under cover of a UN speech made by Brazil's president, Netto and Galveas visited 23 Wall for clandestine talks. Frightened by Mexico, banks had pulled up to $3 billion in short-term Brazilian loans. Netto and Galveas didn't see how Brazil could escape default without an emergency loan of $2.5 to $3 billion, plus a rescheduling to reduce interest and stretch out payments of principal. In the protocol of such crises, the bank with the largest debt exposure ordinarily managed the rescheduling. But the Brazilians' faith in Tony Gebauer was such that they wanted Morgans to preside over this mammoth rescue, even though four other American banks had larger stakes. With $4.6 billion in loans to Brazil, Citibank was the natural leader. To avoid bruised feelings, Gebauer suggested that Citi co-chair the committee. "You have to go and do proper protocol," he told the Brazilians, to whom Citibank acquiesced. Gerard Finneran would be the Citibank representative.

The choice of Morgans and Citi had an intricate political backdrop. Some on Wall Street thought Morgans grabbed at the co-chairmanship in its frustrated quest for a Brazilian branch—a view that infuriated the bank. Perhaps more pertinent was the extremely intimate relationship between Fed chairman Paul Volcker and Lewis T. Preston, Walter Page's successor as Morgan chairman in 1980. This hidden relationship never surfaced in the press. Yet behind Preston's moves during financial crises, the cognoscenti sometimes discerned the fine hand of Paul Volcker. In 1980, Preston led a $1-billion rescue for the Hunt brothers when their attempt to corner the silver market collapsed, nearly dragging down Bache and other brokerage houses. The Hunts were hardly typical Morgan clients, yet the bank performed the rescue at the behest of Volcker.

With Brazil, Volcker apparently again used Preston as his proxy. Just as the House of Morgan in the 1920s provided a convenient back channel for government action, so Volcker could direct bailouts through Preston without advertising his presence. Morgan's smaller lending to Brazil was advantageous. A Preston confidant explained: "In the fall of 1982, Volcker told Lew that Morgan had to be in charge of the committee. He wanted Morgan to take on the Brazilian loan because we had far less exposure than other banks on Wall Street. We could, if necessary, take on more Brazilian debt without getting screwed up." (Other bankers, it should be said, pooh-pooh this story, stressing the Gebauer link.) More than any chairman since Henry Alexander, Preston was imbued with a Morgan sense of *noblesse oblige* and Wall Street statesmanship. "Lew has been thinking more and more of the system, even to the detriment of the bank," said the confidant. He tended to gripe at Citibank, which he often saw as acting selfishly and unilaterally without consulting the general good.

As in interwar days, the debt crisis produced bad blood between American and European bankers. More than half of Brazil's debt was held by non-American banks, yet Morgans and Citibank alone ran the show, as they had many of the earlier syndicated loans. Some in the City suspected that Brazil had groomed Morgans as its pet banker to secure lenient treatment. Guy Huntrods of Lloyds International Bank feared Brazil's strategy was to cook up a sweetheart deal with New York bankers, then foist it on the Europeans. That October, he turned down Brazil's request for an emergency loan unless accompanied by an IMF loan and stiff emergency measures. So the all-American team of Morgans and Citi led the first phase of Brazil's rescue.

The debt rescues of the 1980s reflected global political realities as well as financial stakes. Again and again, steering-committee banks were predominantly American. Japan was second to the United States in Third World lending, yet in the early rescues it typically settled for a single, token representative from the Bank of Tokyo, which had the largest Latin exposure. Much as the rising financial power—the United States—had deferred to Monty Norman's intellectual leadership in the 1920s, so the Japanese, even while starting to overtake Wall Street, bowed to Paul Volcker's authority. Not until the late 1980s would Japan begin to demand a voice at the IMF and the World Bank fully commensurate with its new financial power.

Back in the 1920s, Tom Lamont had represented two hundred thousand Mexican bondholders worldwide. In the unwieldy modern debt crisis, Morgans and Citibank had to deal with a bureaucratic monstrosity—some seven hundred banks with large and small loans to Brazil. After secretly hatching a rescue plan with Brazil and the IMF, the two banks summoned Brazil's creditors to New York's Plaza Hotel on December 20, 1982. Carlos Langoni shocked them by stating that Brazil couldn't service debt coming due in 1983. Jacques de la Rosière, the IMF's managing director, unveiled a complex, four-part Morgan-Citi plan for saving Brazil. Citibank would reschedule $4 billion in principal; Chase would maintain trade credits; and Bankers Trust would restore short-term "interbank" lines to Brazil. The linchpin was a Morgan-led effort to raise a new $4.4-billion loan for Brazil, the biggest in Morgan history.

The plan set a fateful precedent of "curing" the debt crisis by heaping on more debt. In this charade, bankers would lend more to Brazil with one hand, then take it back with the other. This preserved the fictitious book value of loans on bank balance sheets. Approaching the rescue as a grand new syndication, the bankers piled on high interest rates and rescheduling fees. It was hard to stop the greed so prevalent for so many years. The Europeans watched sourly from the sidelines. "It was very much an American party," said Guy Huntrods, a dogged, balding, talkative banker who became British point man on Latin American debt. "The Brazilians had taken no advice from anybody except Citi and Morgan Guaranty. We were told to go home and do what we were instructed. This created the most awful impression among us."[10]

Tensions rose between Wall Street banks, with their huge and irrevocable commitments to Brazil, and regional banks, which wanted to cut their smaller losses and run. One German banker observed, "I come into these sessions and I find all these hillbillies. The big American banks have made the loans and sold part of them to the little ones. And these fellows, who don't know the Baltic from the Barents Sea, were all crying, 'I want my money back.' "[11] This split produced bitterness between the large and small banks and poisoned the atmosphere of the first rescue.

In early 1983, Morgan credit officers worked around the clock to raise the $4.4 billion. Although the megaloan was assembled in a remarkable two months, it left a residue of ill will toward Tony Gebauer, who embodied the big-stick approach of the Wall Street banks. The smaller banks felt they had been browbeaten into participating, and some, piqued by Gebauer's high-handed manner, balked at providing new money.[12] But afraid of antagonizing the Fed and the Wall Street banks, they grudgingly abided by the plan.

On February, 24, 1983, Brazil hosted a dinner at the Waldorf-Astoria to thank their bankers for the rescue loans. Over dessert, the Brazilians let slip that they might not make timely payments on these new loans either. Nevertheless, the next day, several hundred bankers, bruised and battered, signed copies of the loan agreement that Morgans and Citi laid out for their signature at the Plaza Hotel. The IMF chipped in a $5-billion loan for Brazil in what appeared a successful finale.

This success was illusory. While the banks had committed $4.4 billion for the Morgan-led loan, they had also drained off a corresponding amount in short-term credit lines to Brazil. Thus some banks got their secret revenge. This financial legerdemain neutralized the loan's effect. Gebauer was furious as he saw banks sabotaging the agreement. The whole sham got him hopping mad because among the banks he suspected of bad faith was Citibank—his co-chair in the rescue operation. By the spring of 1983, Brazil was missing its IMF economic-reform targets, and the fund and the banks halted their emergency payments. The Fed was alarmed by Brazil's eroding short-term credit lines. On May 31, Volcker called in Preston and other chairmen to discuss the rescue. The Fed was disturbed by reports of Gebauer's treatment of the regional banks, and Preston feared that he was alienating the British bankers. Gebauer was squabbling openly at meetings with Citibank's Finneran, demoralizing the bankers further. A decision was made to replace Gebauer with William Rhodes of Citibank, who had headed the effort to rescue Mexico.

This came as a blow to Morgan pride, especially in view of the Morgan-Citi rivalry. "The Morgan bank was very high on Brazil and I think they were a little unhappy that the chairmanship had to be taken away," remarked Anthony M. Solomon, then New York Fed chief.[13] Some

Morgan people grumbled about a power-hungry Citibank bringing Brazil into its fold along with Mexico and Argentina. Yet it was Preston who urged Citibank chairman Walter Wriston to relieve Morgan of the leadership burden. And there was secret relief at 23 Wall, which was uncomfortable with its unaccustomed high-profile role in the debt talks. Said one former Morgan official, "People had never identified Morgan that much with Latin America, and it suddenly became a liability." Gebauer's role drew attention to the bank's embarrassingly huge Latin American exposure.

In a second Brazil rescue, Bill Rhodes didn't want to work with Gebauer, whom he saw as tainted. To appease the bank, he brought in Leighton Coleman of Morgans as deputy chairman; to appease the British, he brought in Guy Huntrods of Lloyds as the other deputy chairman. The reschedulings became more global, creating tremendous creditor unity and averting the internecine feuds among nations that had so weakened the banks in the 1930s. Instead of the largely private bank solution of phase 1, Rhodes wanted to get creditor governments more involved and touched base with the IMF, the World Bank, the U.S. Treasury, the Fed, and the State Department. His actions confirmed the intrinsically political nature of sovereign lending—an old story.

The specter of Tony Gebauer wasn't yet banished. As Brazil's economy deteriorated during the summer of 1983, Rhodes opted for secret talks, hoping that blunt language would shock the Brazilians into strong action. On August 16, 1983, Rhodes, Huntrods, and Coleman flew to Brazil in a private plane. Rhodes and Huntrods were faintly nervous about having Coleman along, not on a personal level, but because they feared he might have shared information with Gebauer. In Brasília, they believed their worst fears had been confirmed. Meeting with Netto, Langoni, and other powers at the home of Finance Minister Galveas, they delivered a stern warning. Rhodes began: "We can't keep the banks on board much longer." Coleman chimed in: "You've got to speak with one voice." Huntrods delivered a dramatic peroration: "There is a smell of defeat around the streets of Brasília that reminds me of France before Dunkirk."[14] Because Netto had never heard of Dunkirk, a short lesson in history ensued.

Huntrods felt they had lost the critical element of surprise: he believed somebody had tipped off the Brazilians. "We had absolute certain proof that Gebauer, who was Coleman's boss, had already telephoned the Brazilians what our game plan was," said Huntrods adamantly. "*That* we knew beyond a shadow of a doubt." He thought that Gebauer was either ingratiating himself with the Brazilians or, motivated by envy, was trying to sabotage phase 2. In the end, Gebauer never got back into the game and some say that his career at Morgans stalled afterward. Among bankers, the new Rhodes team would be credited with creating a more cooperative atmosphere and a spirit of shared sacrifice among the banks.

In the last analysis, phase 2 was simply a more workable way of muddling through the debt crisis and postponing the inevitable. The collective power of the commercial banks kept the lid on the pressure cooker in a way impossible in earlier times. These giant global banks had many more levers than the investment banks of the 1920s with which to keep debtors from outright repudiation. Among other things, they could cancel the trade credits of defaulting countries or reduce their overnight "interbank" credit lines. In consequence, as the 1980s progressed the banks were able to boost their loan-loss reserves and weather the crisis, while living standards tumbled in indebted Latin American countries. For most of the 1980s, the Baker Plan—the principle of lending new debt in exchange for economic reforms—was enshrined as the solution to the crisis, and it enjoyed the support of Lew Preston. But the promised economic growth never appeared. Instead, oppressed by interest payments and despite a prolonged boom in the industrial countries, Latin America suffered through a severe depression. How Latin American debtors could withstand the next global recession without widespread default was unclear as the 1980s came to an end.

In February 1987, Brazil, stifled by a $121-billion debt, which had grown monstrously through the reschedulings, declared a moratorium on repayment that lasted for a year and a half. The country seen as the model debtor in the 1970s had rudely disappointed the House of Morgan. In early 1988, Argentina stopped payment on its debt and fell billions of dollars into arrears. For all the power and ingenuity of the banks in dealing with the debt crisis of the 1980s, the upshot appeared frustratingly similar to that of earlier waves of default. In 1989, the new administration of President George Bush conceded that the only real solution was debt forgiveness. By that point, mobs were ransacking supermarkets in Argentina, as they had earlier in Brazil. In September, 1989, the Morgan bank acknowledged that its Latin debt was a hopeless fiasco by adding $2 billion to its loan loss reserves, fully covering its longer maturity loans. The Morgan fling with the Third World was temporarily over.

THERE was another coda to the Brazilian debt crisis that tattered the image of Morgan invincibility and belied any notion that it alone was immune to the corruptions of the Casino Age. Even as he chaired Brazil's rescue, Tony Gebauer was leading a secret, illicit life as an embezzler—a term everyone later danced around in embarrassment, for it savored of small-time crooks and greasy hands in the till, not of the world's toniest bank. Embezzlement was rare in the world of high-finance for obvious reasons: people made stupendous amounts of money, and if they wanted more, there were legal ways to get it.

At 23 Wall, there had been a curious negligence about Gebauer, a tendency to look the other way. He enjoyed an entrepreneurial freedom that was rare at Morgans. Later people would recall the fruits of his suspiciously profligate spending—a $5-million Manhattan duplex co-op, two homes in East Hampton worth a combined $2 million, an apartment in France, and a share in a Brazilian coffee farm. This didn't square with a $150,000-a-year salary. With mild shock, Walter Page learned of a yacht that Gebauer had bought from a wealthy friend on Long Island's Shelter Island. Only later did such details cohere into a telltale picture.

There were two reasons why no one examined Gebauer critically. Everybody had a vague, somewhat correct notion that he came from a wealthy Venezuelan family. More significantly, he had reaped tens of millions in profit for the bank, compensating for its late start and patrician discomfort in Latin America. From 1981 to 1984, as senior vice-president for Latin America, Gebauer controlled most of Morgan's Western Hemisphere lending outside North America. He was one of the few irreplaceable stars at a bank with a chronic glut of talented young executives.

Along with the big loans, Gebauer supervised the accounts of several hundred Latin American businessmen. Technically, they weren't personal accounts but belonged to executives with whom the bank had commercial dealings—an honored Morgan technique to please and befriend the influential. In 1976, Gebauer had started to divert money from some Brazilian accounts in order to furnish his duplex apartment. In the end, he would dip into four accounts, including those of a landowner and a construction mogul. The money mostly resided in six Panamanian holding companies from which he issued cashier's checks to himself. These illegal diversions lasted over nine years and amounted to $6 million—this at a bank that prided itself on tight internal controls. The thefts, remarkably, persisted right through the Brazilian debt rescue.

This was more than a straight embezzlement case, for Gebauer apparently drew on some form of "flight capital"—money smuggled from Latin America to evade taxes or exchange controls. Even as he withdrew the money, there was discussion of how such capital was jeopardizing the debt-rescue effort headed by him and the Morgan bank. As Brazil, Mexico, and Argentina raised billions of dollars in new loans, their disloyal, unethical nationals were stuffing suitcases with bills and flying north to open bank accounts. The big Wall Street banks making the Latin American loans wooed the flight capital and ended up taking as deposits money they had recently lent out.

Behind the title of international private banking, Morgans and other banks helped wealthy Latin Americans to invest in offshore trusts and investment companies. These devices could aid the unscrupulous in dodging taxes. In the 1970s, Morgan Guaranty and other banks also opened Miami subsidiaries to tap the personal wealth of visiting Latin Americans. In the wrong hands, confidential Morgan accounts could serve as excellent cover for illegal activity. All the Wall Street banks had mysterious Latin American depositors who seldom appeared in person. "They particularly don't want monthly statements or any other mail sent to their home countries," noted *Fortune* in 1982. "Their accounts at places like Morgan are labeled 'hold mail.' They drop by in person from time to time to look at the statements."[15]

By extreme estimates, commercial banks were booking more in deposits of flight capital than they extended in new Latin American loans, making them net borrowers from the region. Flight capital siphoned off an estimated one-half of Mexico's borrowed money, one-third of Argentina's. Among those bemoaning the problem was Morgan economist Rimmer de Vries. "Capital flight accelerates, enhances, and aggravates a problem that exists," he stated.[16] Morgan chairman Lew Preston was no less disturbed, telling one annual meeting, "It's a terrible problem for the banks. If the amount of Mexican investment abroad—if that interest—were brought back into Mexico, it would cover their debt service."[17] Even though American banks could legally accept flight capital, Morgans had a stated policy of questioning depositors about the origin and purpose of any suspect accounts. Yet Gebauer was apparently plundering "hold mail" checking accounts. Otherwise, why did years elapse before depositors detected the theft? Why weren't they monitoring their accounts more closely? One raided Brazilian depositor reportedly hadn't shown up in five years.

Prohibited from maintaining dollar deposits in the United States, Brazilians customarily gave their Wall Street bankers wide latitude in managing their investments. It was later unclear whether Gebauer had permission to withdraw money from some clients' accounts—something to which his lawyer would make cryptic allusion. Yet this couldn't have been uniformly true, for Gebauer manufactured bogus statements on Morgan stationery, then mailed them to clients. To plug holes in the accounts, he secured Morgan loans of about $2.9 million. Why would he have resorted to these extraordinary measures if he were acting with the consent of his depositors?

In 1982, even as Brazil teetered on the edge, Gebauer took $1.5 million from the account of a Brazilian named Francisco Catao. This money represented a "commission" Catao received from an arms dealer in exchange for the dealer's being introduced to Gebauer. This, in turn, led to a $35-million Morgan loan to the arms merchant. Might Gebauer have had a proprietary feeling toward that particular $1.5 million? In an equally bizarre twist, he diverted embezzled money into his own Latin American business, using it to make loans at low interest rates—as if he were entering the banking field as a minicompetitor to the Morgan bank itself.

Tony Gebauer lacked any of the standard motivations for committing a crime. Unlike the routine cases, his crime coincided not with failure but with stunning success in the sphere of international banking. He had no reason whatever to resent the bank or wish to embarrass it. In fact, he had a deep, abiding love for Morgan traditions, lining his bookshelf with Morgan history and taking great pride in his association with the bank. At tremendous sacrifice to his personal wealth, he remained there when he could have parlayed his connections into a $1-million-a-year income at an investment bank. It's even conceivable that he resorted to crime so he could remain at the bank yet live in a style befitting his fantasies. He apparently let months pass without touching the Brazilian accounts and wasn't consumed by his crime. It was more tangential, gratifying some psychic need left unsatisfied even by his exceptional career.

Like many embezzlers, Gebauer planned to make restitution someday. Much like the Brazilians he rescued, he was defeated by the interest, not the principal, accumulating on his burdensome debt—$2 million of it. Late in the summer of 1985, after a twenty-four-year Morgan career, he left for Drexel Burnham Lambert, to work with Michael Milken on a special project to repackage Third World debt into junk bonds (the 1920s solution). Some at Morgans thought his career had been derailed by the controversial Brazilian debt rescheduling. Shortly after he left, the bank was alerted to his crime by a puzzled

Brazilian client whose money supposedly on deposit in New York was wired from Venezuela. The timing seemed coincidental: neither Brazil nor the bank needed Tony Gebauer any longer. He was found out when nobody but he would suffer from exposure of the crime. The House of Morgan sent Price Waterhouse auditors and trusty Davis, Polk lawyers to Brazil to investigate. They netted an accomplice to Gebauer—Keith McDermott, a vice-president who allegedly received $200,000 in kick-backs for Morgan work on behalf of two clients. The bank's investigators passed on their information to the Fed and the U.S. district attorney's office. When confronted with the charges by Drexel Burnham officials, Gebauer resigned on the spot.

When the affair hit the news in 1986, it made headlines in Brazil as well as in New York. How had the world's best-run bank missed the scandal for nine years? Gebauer reportedly believed the millions were too trivial to warrant the attention of a bank grappling with billion-dollar debts. After the scandal broke, the bank was in a sticky situation, guilty of either incompetence or complicity. It portrayed Gebauer as a lone culprit and swore that no customer lost a penny in the end. "Our investigation convinces us that the responsibility for wrongdoing lies with one person. . . . We think it's unfair that other people be implicated," declared a spokesman.[18] Gebauer quickly became a taboo subject at 23 Wall. Morgan officials still find it hard to utter his name and often refer to him as "that fellow," as if they had never known him very well.

Gebauer didn't contest the charges. To avoid the stigma of embezzlement, he pleaded guilty to bank fraud, tax evasion, and doctoring statements. Because he had submitted some surreal tax returns—one year he banked over $1 million in taxable income but reported only $21,000—he owed the Internal Revenue several million dollars in back taxes and penalties. He also paid back $8 million in principal and interest to the bank. His clever lawyer, Stanley Arkin, referred obliquely to flight capital and hinted that Gebauer might have had authority to use some Brazilian money: "That authority was premised on the unusual and Byzantine relationships that often exist between bankers and flight capitalists."[19] Such loose talk made Morgans jittery and eager to strike a deal.

In February 1987, a contrite Tony Gebauer stood in a blue pin-striped suit before Judge Robert W. Sweet for sentencing. The judge saw a large dimension of fantasy in Gebauer's life, a venal excess characteristic of the age. "You are indeed a Lucifer, a fallen angel of the banking world," he told him. "Although your employment at the top of your profession provided you with a princely income, you spent like an emperor."[20] Gebauer received a three-and-a-half-year prison sentence but served only half that time.

The Gebauer affair left behind red faces and personal wreckage in the corporate suites at Morgans. Half a dozen executives were shifted about. In a sad conclusion, Tony Gebauer, so proud of his Morgan employment, ended up disgracing the bank.

TRADERS

• •

•

I N the early 1980s, as the final vestiges of fraternity among the Morgan houses disappeared and Morgan Guaranty abandoned wholesale lending to enter global investment banking, it ran into Morgan Stanley. It was also on a convergence path with Morgan Grenfell. When Morgan Guaranty occupied a sleek building of brown granite and smoked glass near the Bank of England—snobbishly named the Morgan Bank, disregarding poor Morgan Grenfell some blocks away—the ancient Anglo-American link, too, was threatened. Starting in 1979, the London-based Morgan Guaranty Ltd. became a major underwriter in the Euromarkets. How could Morgan Guaranty retain a one-third stake in Morgan Grenfell as they clashed in foreign outposts and invaded each other's home turf? As Bill Mackworth-Young of Morgan Grenfell said, "It doesn't make sense to be 33% owned by one of your competitors."[1]

Morgan Grenfell needed expansion capital but couldn't pry it loose from 23 Wall. The London bank's home success had bred hopes for bigger things abroad, especially in New York, where it had had a small office since 1974. To transcend that token presence was impossible so long as Morgan Guaranty owned a one-third stake. So in 1981, the Morgan chairman, Lew Preston, and president, Robert V. "Rod" Lindsay, flew to London to inform Lord Stephen Catto, over dinner, that 23 Wall had decided to sell its stake. The House of Morgan petered out, mourned by few. "It was a bit of a twinge for me and a few seniors at Morgan Grenfell and a few others around here," recalled Lindsay. "But it became clear to everybody that they needed more freedom to go their own way."[2] Lew Preston had grown uncomfortable with Morgan Grenfell as the old, aristocratic families faded from the scene, people who had all trained at 23 Wall. He explained, "The Bank of England expected us to share one-third of every loss, but there was a management evolution where we didn't know the people who were running the firm."[3] The new breed was typified by chief executive Christopher Reeves, a former assistant personnel manager at Hill Samuel, who had never passed through the Morgan Guaranty training program.

Thus ended a transatlantic axis more than a century old, the armature on which the House of Morgan had been built. Catto said, "I had seen it coming with regret. We had one request: that they not sell it all at once, which would look like a loss of confidence in us. They agreed to sell it piecemeal."[4] Within a year, the bank took its stake below 4 percent, pocketing $40 million and leaving the Lloyd's insurance broker Willis Faber as chief shareholder, with 24 percent. In a declaration of freedom in 1981, Morgan Grenfell set up an investment banking subsidiary in New York, expanding its money management and international M&A businesses. By 1985, it belonged to the New York Stock Exchange. The pretense of brotherhood had given way to raw competition.

A creature of markets, J. P. Morgan and Company—the parent company of Morgan Guaranty—now operated by new principles. It raised billions of dollars daily in the money markets and was emancipated from dependence on loan spreads and deposits. Though the bank still had no retail branches, Morgan people joked that they *had* a retail bank— Merrill Lynch, whose money market fund bought Morgan CDs. The House of Morgan had all but given up on wholesale lending as an anachronistic business for a bank whose blue-chip clients could raise money more cheaply in the marketplace, as they increasingly did in the early 1980s. In 1983, international bond offerings, for the first time, passed global bank lending in scope. Lew Preston didn't want to join an extinct breed. "Basic lending is never going to return to the profitability that existed in the Fifties and Sixties," he predicted.[5] Foreign bank competition also thinned loan spreads.

The upshot was that the Morgan bank began making more money from investment banking fees and trading income. The future bank took shape in London, where Morgan Guaranty had become the top Eurobond underwriter among American commercial banks, with clients including Exxon, IBM, Du Pont, and even Citicorp. From number forty-six in 1980, it zoomed to second place in Eurobonds four years later. It also accelerated trading in gold bullion, foreign exchange, and financial futures.

The locomotive behind these changes was Lew Preston, who embodied the bank's old silken charm but imbued it with a new, sometimes fierce energy. A Harvard graduate from a rich Westchester family, he had started in the Morgan mailroom (as everybody did) in the early 1950s. He was first viewed by elders as a playboy, socialite, and jock. Tall and broad-shouldered, he played semipro ice hockey with the Long Island Ducks until he came home one night with six stitches in his head. "You damned fool," his wife said, "why don't you grow up."[6] His second wife, Patsy, was a granddaughter of newspaper publisher Joseph Pulitzer and mixed with Brooke Astor, Jane Engelhardt, and other socialites.

This Lew Preston seemed all tradition. Among the antique furnishings in his office were an oil portrait of Jack Morgan, a rolltop desk, and a photograph of Pierpont and Jack striding manfully into the Pujo hearings. Wearing half-moon glasses and red suspenders and smoking Don Diego cigars, he could effect an extremely dignified presence. Once, after making a presentation to Noboru Takeshita, then Japan's finance minister and later prime minister, the dignitary breathed with admiration. "You were prime ministerial in your presentation," he said. "I am stunned."

The elegant manner and dryly mischievous wit covered early scars. When Lew was a boy, his father died of tuberculosis. He also struggled with dyslexia. ("It's very fashionable now," he remarked. "Everybody seems to have it."[7]) At seventeen, he enlisted in the Marine Corps and was sent to China. He ended up as a bodyguard to James Forrestal, later Truman's secretary of defense and a close family friend. Demobilized, Preston attended Harvard, from which he graduated in 1951. He would always be a cross between a Harvard socialite and a tough marine. Curt with fools, sometimes abrupt at meetings, he would show exemplary kindness to someone who was hospitalized, bereaved, or recently divorced. Some at 23 Wall revered Lew Preston, some were slightly afraid of him, and some both revered and feared him.

This dual personality mirrored the Morgan transition. Preston tried to perpetuate the old Morgan culture of teamwork and subordination of the individual to the group: "I want people who want to do something rather than be someone." With department heads, he held the traditional weekly meetings and encouraged senior people to lunch together in the executive dining rooms. This Preston conceded that "a little bit of conservatism in a bank is not a bad thing" and said rather loftily of Citicorp's Walter Wriston, "He's running a financial conglomerate and we're running a bank."[8] He tended the bank's image as if it were a stage set. "We spend an extraordinary amount of time just worrying about the environment," he said.[9]

At the same time, an avuncular style no longer worked completely in a bank with over fifteen thousand employees. Morgan elders had taken a fatherly interest in their staff, with talk of one's being "brought up" at 23 Wall. Now in a vastly speeded up bank, there wasn't time for prep-school camaraderie. Preston had to retrain masses of old-time commercial bankers and credit analysts, making them into risk-taking market whizzes. This meant encouraging aggressiveness and imagination, not just politeness and caution. Competing with investment banks, Preston had to pay huge bonuses and use other compensation methods that fostered divisiveness. By the 1987 crash, some Morgan traders earned more than Preston's own $1.3-million salary. As the eighties progressed, many people left the bank or were gently nudged out. Even among those who stayed, there was a bittersweet sense that the bank was less fun and caring than in the old days. It was also a far more diversified firm. In 1984, for instance, Boris S. Berkovitch became vice-chairman of the bank—the first Jew ever to rise to the top of Morgan officialdom.

A major protagonist in this shifting drama was Preston's protégé, Dennis Weatherstone, the foreign-exchange wizard from London. A short, trim Englishman with crinkly hair and a quick smile, Weatherstone never lost his working-class accent. He had a natural grace and friendliness, not the cultivated polish of his Morgan colleagues. He joked about his early bookkeeping days as the time he had "no shoes." During a brief Royal Air Force stint, he had scanned radar screens in simulated air flights, computing fuel usage for planes—an experience, he said, that sharpened his mind for foreign-exchange trading. Weatherstone was the quintessential Casino Age banker—a man versed in new financial instruments, interest swaps, and currency swaps. Early on, he saw the impact of "securitization"—the packaging of loans as tradable securities—on the traditional lending business. In 1980, he became chairman of the bank's executive committee, right under the blue-blooded president, Rod Lindsay, and then succeeded Lindsay in 1987.

Preston and Weatherstone were complementary and inseparable. "They spoke in a patois," recalled a colleague. "They were like Siamese twins. One would start a sentence and the other would finish. They were very unlike, but they thought the same." Since much Morgan influence with central banks derived from its Treasury operation, Weatherstone fit handily into the special relationship with the Fed. "Both he and Preston probably have more credibility with Washington policy makers and regulators than any other bankers I can think of," said Anthony Solomon, former president of the New York Fed.[10] The Preston-Weatherstone team was therefore, predictably, at the center of the 1984 rescue of Continental Illinois Bank and Trust Company.

The Morgan role had some irony to it. The Chicago bank was a stiff competitor of Morgans and so similar in style and structure that it was called the Morgan of the Midwest. A prestigious, old-line wholesale bank, it had courted rich families and financed much American auto and steel business from its stately, pillared building on South LaSalle Street. In the early 1980s, it vied with Morgans for the title of premier corporate lender. Like Morgans, it had plunged into the roulette world of "liability management"—that is, it financed its operation from the money markets rather than by deposits. Rounding up $8 billion daily, it borrowed overnight Fed funds, sold CDs, or issued commercial paper. The House of Morgan had played this game with such panache since the days of Ralph Leach that its risks were often obscured. Continental's collapse would show the extraordinary perils inherent in the new banking.

Morgans had long suspected that Continental's success was a mirage. It undercut competitors too vigorously on real estate, agriculture, and energy loans and rather cavalierly made loans to Chrysler, International Harvester, and other troubled firms. One Morgan official recalled, "All our younger bankers were saying, 'How do these guys do it? They must be doing it with mirrors.' They were making loans that any number of banks had shied away from." Continental was also paying exorbitant interest rates for its $8 billion. It relied mostly on "hot money"—large, volatile deposits from foreign and domestic institutions. Such jumbo deposits ran anywhere from $5 million to $200 million and far exceeded the $100,000 lid covered by deposit insurance. Managers of such deposits were skittish and apt to pull funds at the first hint of trouble. Yet even so conservative a bank as Morgan Guaranty drew 75 percent of its deposits from "hot money."

Continental began to unravel during the Fourth of July weekend of 1982 with the failure of the Penn Square Bank. This was the notorious Oklahoma shopping-center bank that had booked and resold to Continental $1 billion in bum energy loans. (One picturesquely modern aspect of Penn Square's downfall was a run at its drive-in window.) To reassure institutions holding its paper, Continental began to pay higher rates on its CDs. When domestic money managers balked, the bank relied more on Japanese and European funds and sent its financial evangelists abroad to preach calm. "We had the Continental Illinois Reassurance Brigade and we fanned out all around the world," said David Taylor, Continental's chairman in 1984.[11]

The bank never fully recuperated from Penn Square, which led to the first global electronic bank run in May 1984. It began with a fugitive rumor floating around Tokyo that an American investment bank was shopping Continental to possible buyers. This triggered the sale of up to $1 billion in Continental CDs in the Far East, spilling over into panicky European selling the next day. The Continental run was like some modernistic fantasy: there were no throngs of hysterical depositors, just cool nightmare flashes on computer screens.

The bank's new chairman, David Taylor, pencil-slim, aristocratic, and with a grave voice, struggled to contain the damage. To spike rumors, he sent what he thought was a reassuring telex to two hundred banks around the world. By spotlighting Continental's troubles, however, it only intensified fears. The next day, Paul Volcker was on the phone with Lew Preston, who expressed skepticism about a private safety net. But in Washington, there was hope that a private credit raised by big banks could restore confidence in Continental. It was a political preference: Reagan administration ideologues were tantalized by a "market solution." Bankers also thought they could more legitimately claim expanded securities powers if they didn't always beg for federal protection. Even as the private credit was being organized that Friday, Continental borrowed $4 billion from the Chicago Fed. During the next week, the "private rescue" would have a slightly fictitious flavor, masking the federal government's far deeper and more critical involvement.

Why did Continental choose Morgan to lead the rescue—a choice so reminiscent of 1907 and 1929? "Morgan Guaranty was the obvious choice," explained a former high Continental official. "It had the strongest financial situation and an unquestioned reputation." Morgans was also Continental's twin. "We felt Morgan was a similar institution that didn't have the problems we had, but was similarly funded," Taylor recalled.[12] Morgans also got the job by default. Citibank had earlier tried to invade Continental's Illinois turf, leaving behind acrimonious feelings.

Through a Mother's Day weekend, with telephone circuits jammed, Preston and Taylor assembled a $4.5-billion credit line from sixteen banks. These sophisticated bankers relied on primitive methods. Often, they simply called banks, got the security guards on duty, and had them track down their chairmen. Amazingly, the Federal Reserve Board didn't possess emergency home phone numbers of America's most powerful bankers. Security Pacific's chief credit officer was found windsurfing. While bankers haggled over their credit shares, they all knew the gravity of the crisis. As a Continental official said, "They knew that Continental's problems could spill over into a couple of other banks." There was a fear that Continental would focus unwelcome attention on Manufacturers Hanover's Third World debt or the Bank of America's bad real estate loans. "There were also fifty-odd Midwestern banks that had more than their entire bank capital on deposit at Continental," said Preston. "*That*'s why it was worth saving."[13] By Sunday night, the $4.5-billion credit line was ready.

On Monday morning, global markets yawned at this show of strength by America's richest banks. A Pierpont Morgan might have commanded the gold market, but private resources now paled in global markets. The runs continued amid telephone calls between Volcker and Preston. "That Monday, Volcker didn't call anybody else but Preston, not even the administration," recalled Irvine Sprague of the Federal Deposit Insurance Corporation. "It became clear the bankers' rescue plan was not going to work. Obviously, the government would have to step in the next day."[14]

The stakes were tremendous: Continental was larger than all the banks that failed during the Depression *combined*. As a "hot money" bank, it was insured for only about 10 percent of its $40 billion in "deposits." Could the world really cope with $36 billion in losses? Nobody wanted to find out. At a meeting on Tuesday morning, May 15, Volcker, Comptroller of the Currency Todd Conover, and William Isaac and Irving Sprague of the FDIC agreed that a Continental failure would be cataclysmal and decided on an FDIC capital infusion.

They sold this idea to Treasury Secretary Donald T. Regan, who wanted to keep alive the private rescue. The banks were to put up a portion of the money. After lunch, Volcker phoned Preston and asked him to set up a summit of seven bank chairmen in New York the next morning. They met in secrecy at Morgan Guaranty's offices at Fifth Avenue and Forty-fourth Street, an assemblage including the chairmen of Morgans, Chase, Citibank, Bank of America, Chemical, Bankers Trust, and Manufacturers Hanover and the top bank regulators, including Volcker. Chaired by Lew Preston, the meeting had both a sentimental and a combative mood. Some bankers made resounding speeches about past days of Wall Street glory, when the House of Morgan managed private rescues. John McGillicuddy of Manufacturers Hanover argued that the bankers should go it alone. Preston, low-key and conciliatory, let the more vehement bankers talk themselves out. "His style was quite cool," recalled Irvine Sprague. "He lay back and sort of nudged people. I thought he was very skillful."[15]

There was an element of make-believe in this "bankers' rescue," for they pretended to mount a rescue without the necessary resources. Some bank regulators saw the bankers trying to grab credit but pushing the real risk and responsibility onto the government. Citi vice-chair Thomas C. Theobald (later Continental's chairman) laid down especially stringent conditions for his bank's participation, asking for absolute government guarantees against risk. As Sprague later wrote, "They wanted it to look as if they were putting money in but, at the same time, wanted to be absolutely sure they were not risking anything. I said I would not vote for such a sham."[16]

That day and the next, restless regulators invited the bankers to provide $500 million of a $2 billion capital injection. At the last minute, Citi tried to insert language protecting the bankers from losses. Only a call from Volcker to Citi chairman Walter Wriston in California ended the impasse. It was largely sham heroics by the bankers: after agreeing to their $500 million, they sat around arguing about how to "lay off" the risk on other banks. William Isaac of the FDIC has said flatly: "The bankers lost no money, and in hindsight their participation was unnecessary."[17]

In the end, the FDIC effectively nationalized Continental, taking an 80-percent ownership stake. Setting a breathtaking precedent, it decreed that *all* depositors were insured; it had never before given such a blanket insurance for small bank failures. Washington was now saying that some banks were too big to fail. Yet even the full faith and credit of the U.S. government couldn't immediately stem the bank run. "Bankers around the world said, 'So what?' " recalled Preston. "They weren't impressed that the deposits were guaranteed by the U.S. government. *That* surprised me."[18] Continental Illinois's aftermath was ironic: although the affair exposed the unacceptable peril of large bank failures in modern financial markets, the government had created new incentives to bypass small banks and keep deposits at large ones.

Continental Illinois served as a warning about the state of commercial banking in the 1980s. As banks lost their core lending business and tried to maintain profits, they ran into a lengthening list of disasters—in shipping, real estate investment trusts, energy loans, farm loans, and Latin American lending. The Glass-Steagall Act had attempted to insulate commercial banks from risk by separating them from securities work. Instead, it had confined them to a dying business and starved them of profits that might have kept them sane and healthy. By 1984, bank failures were running at a post-Depression high. During the 1980s, the commercial banks faced chronic instability while securities houses raked in record profits. This reversed Glass-Steagall's intentions and confirmed J. P. Morgan and Company in its decision to move further in the direction of becoming a global investment bank. By the 1987 crash, it would be earning more money from such fee business than from standard loan spreads.

FUNERAL rites for the old Wall Street were held in March of 1982, when the SEC enacted Rule 415, which provided for "shelf registration." This bland technical name masked a bold revolution. Instead of registering each new security issue separately, blue-chip companies could register a large block of stock and sell it off piecemeal on short notice over two years. Thus corporate treasurers could capitalize on sudden dips in interest rates. Rule 415 converted underwriting into a world of fast trades and split-second decisions rather than the old Morgan Stanley world of elegant syndicates formed over several weeks. Companies could even dispense with investment banks and sell straight to institutions. As one Dillon, Read executive gloated, "A lot of Morgan's biggest clients are the most sophisticated ones. They're more likely to say, 'Take a walk, pal.' "[19]

For Morgan Stanley syndicate chief Thomas A. Saunders III, a sinewy Virginian with thin lips and a wide mouth, the potential of Rule 415 hit him while out jogging one day. Staggered by the implications, he came into work the next morning and spluttered, "Hold it, fellers, this thing is *unbelievable*." Before long, he was phoning around the Street, telling people, "Holy God, this is insane."[20] As with the Mayday end to fixed commissions in 1975, Bob Baldwin led the effort to quash the ruling, again dressing up the effort as a crusade to save the regional firms. He hand-delivered a protest letter to the SEC: "The rule may produce fundamental changes in the capital-raising process . . . with undesirable consequences that have not been explored."[21] His warnings that Rule 415 would damage smaller firms and lead to a Wall Street monopolized by a few large, well-capitalized firms duly materialized.

Though Morgan Stanley claimed twenty-eight of America's one hundred largest corporations as clients, many of them favored Rule 415. Exxon, U.S. Steel, and Du Pont even plied the SEC with supporting letters. These rich captives were finally shrugging off their chains. Some critics feared 415 would sweep away fifty years of "due diligence," with investment banks vouching for the soundness of issues. A Morgan Stanley stamp of approval had always reassured investors. In the Casino Age, however, blue-chip firms no longer needed bankers to certify their health. They often had better credit ratings than their bankers.

The force of 415 was swiftly revealed in its trial usage by AT&T in 1982. A year earlier, Morgan Stanley had mustered a traditional AT&T syndicate of 255 houses. Now, for a $100-million shelf issue, AT&T

invited bids from twenty-one underwriters. Instead of syndicates, Rule 415 operated through "bought deals" in which a firm or group of firms bought the whole issue and quickly resold it. Salomon Brothers and First Boston had been doing such deals for years. Morgan Stanley felt itself under excruciating pressure to win the open contest. "We had been AT&T's banker previously for all of their equity, as well as much of their debt, and we needed to show that we still were," said Saunders.[22] An internal memo warned of "reputation risk" on the AT&T deal: "We don't *need* to be first, but it will help establish our role."[23] This set the stage for a rash attempt by Morgan Stanley to show it could measure up in the savagely competitive new environment. That the crazy stunt succeeded didn't detract from its folly.

On May 6, 1982, Morgan Stanley agreed to buy two million shares of AT&T stock at $55.40 a share, $.15 above the current market price. It hoped to resell the entire parcel the next day. This "bought deal" was really a block trade from AT&T to Morgan Stanley with no syndicate to cushion the risk. Morgan's chief equity trader, Anson Beard, passed a miserable, sleepless night and later admitted that it was a reckless deal done "for the bragging rights."[24] Luckily, he disposed of the two million shares the next day, mostly at $55.65 or a $.25 profit over cost. If clever advertising, the maneuver exposed the risks associated with 415. For carrying a $100-million exposure overnight, Morgan Stanley netted a paltry $400,000. Later in the year, when AT&T raised $1 billion through a traditional syndicate, Morgan Stanley suddenly had to tolerate four co-managers. Corporate treasurers were the new potentates, and soon even General Motors relied on four investment banks, including Morgan Stanley.

In 1981, Morgan Stanley reigned as number one in underwriting, as it mostly had since 1935. By 1983—after the 415 shake-up—it plummeted to sixth place, with the trading-oriented Salomon Brothers arising as the new leader. Underwriting was now a banal commodity business in which capital and trading prowess counted for far more than did contacts with companies. In a stunning rout, trading firms that were once the outcasts of Wall Street high society toppled the patricians. Morgan Stanley was hardly impoverished: it remained first in stock underwriting and second in the Euromarkets, but it had slipped in relative position and lost its special halo of success. It sometimes seemed to resent this new world. As syndicate chief Saunders griped: "But corporate treasurers are the same as you and me. They want to be innovative, they want to tell the board, 'Look what I did! I created this competitive situation, I got those five banks beating a path to our door, and wasn't it wonderful? I've taken the shackles off. The issuer is now in control of the world, and here I come.' "[25]

The arm's-length relationship between companies and bankers advocated by Louis Brandeis now evolved in response to market forces and at the behest of corporate America. Far from democratizing Wall Street, this market-based reform merely led to reshuffling among the top firms. Only the Wall Street powerhouses—Morgan Stanley; Goldman, Sachs; First Boston; Merrill Lynch; Salomon Brothers; and Shearson Lehman— had the capital to take big blocks of shares and unload them quickly. Where the six major firms handled a quarter of new debt before 415, they underwrote almost half of it afterward. So the demise of relationship banking didn't open the doors to scrappy newcomers, as reformers had hoped, but only strengthened the position of those firms that were already dominant.

Rule 415 came near the end of Bob Baldwin's tenure at Morgan Stanley, bringing down the curtain on his world of syndication. He once said that if Glass-Steagall were repealed, he would be first on line at Morgan Guaranty's doorstep the next morning. Yet as chairman of the Securities Industry Association in 1977–78, he had vigorously contested expanded underwriting powers for the commercial banks. "He dealt us a couple of mortal blows," said Jack Loughran, then Morgan Guaranty's lobbyist.[26] After his SIA stint, Baldwin returned to a Morgan Stanley he understood less and less well. Colleagues thought him lost in a new world of trading and risk that he himself had created.

One ex-partner observed, "When Baldwin came back from the SIA, he became an obstacle. He had lost control of the firm and only made more enemies. He treated everybody like a kid. He would start making a speech and nobody could talk. He was always trying to relive his days of glory as Under Secretary of the Navy. He wouldn't listen. At the end, nobody wanted him around." Said another: "He talked at people, he postured, he always liked to be the lordly guy from Morgan Stanley. He was always talking about himself, telling stories where he was the hero."

To the last, Baldwin remained hypercompetitive and bent on having his way. Yet for all his flaws, the tough, tactless Baldwin had emerged as the most important person in modern Morgan Stanley history, giving the firm the market skills to compete in a world no longer based on old-school ties. He had saved it from genteel obscurity, a languid demise. As the Baldwin era ended in late 1983 without an obvious successor, there was nervous jockeying among three prime contenders—Bob Greenhill, Dick Fisher, and Lewis Bernard. Much was at stake. In a decade, Morgan Stanley had grown tenfold. It now employed about three thousand people and had about $300 million in capital. Although there was no black or female managing director, the ethnic mix among its eighty managing directors was otherwise surprisingly diverse. But it was more tense and confrontational than in the old days, full of ambitious overachievers.

To prevent squabbling, Baldwin was replaced by a surprise choice: forty-nine-year-old Yale-educated S. Parker Gilbert, who claimed a unique Morgan lineage. His *wunderkind* father was the agent general of Germany in the 1920s and a J. P. Morgan partner in the 1930s. Tall and polished, with a wide face, aquiline nose, and urbane manner, Gilbert had his father's boyish smile but the reserve of Harold Stanley, his stepfather. "Parker was a compromise who wouldn't piss off Greenhill, Fisher, or Bernard," explained one former partner. Among the hard-charging deal makers, he had a light touch in arbitrating disputes. According to Robert A. Gerard, a former managing director, "Parker has two things going for him. He has a tremendous instinct for minimizing awkward situations and getting people to work together. Everybody respects his integrity. He really is the glue that holds the firm together."[27]

Gilbert was the most international of the top executives, having done tours in Paris and handled Middle East business. As one would expect, he was close to Morgan Guaranty and specialized in preserving old clients. One Morgan Guaranty vice-president called Parker "the old breed. It was the barracudas down below who had no sense of the relationship." He was meant to connote tradition at a time of rapid change. Said a former colleague: "Parker is where he is because his father and stepfather were where they were. He's a symbolic figure, like Harry Morgan." According to another ex-partner: "The general fiction that people lived by at Morgan Stanley was that he wanted to prove that he was getting ahead for reasons other than being Harold Stanley's stepson. Then he would go off and play golf." In fact, whatever the original plans, Gilbert turned into more than a figurehead and became an unexpectedly strong-willed chairman. His caution would be credited with sparing Morgan Stanley some of the ravages of the 1987 crash.

The real heir to Bob Baldwin was probably Dick Fisher. A polio victim who was paralyzed from the hip down and walked with a cane, Fisher applied for a job at Morgan Stanley upon graduating from Harvard Business School, but first he needed to conquer his own doubts about his ability to perform. Partners also had wondered how a handicapped person could take business trips and move around freely. Bright, sociable, and popular, he would prove a master politician and an adept handler of people. "Dick is tough underneath but doesn't appear so," remarked a former colleague. "He can be a ruthless man with velvet gloves."

Fisher found the answer to his handicap in the sedentary world of trading. Working out of a soundproof glass box, the so-called lean-to on the trading floor, he organized the new bond trading operation in the 1970s. (With nice symmetry, his brother David would head J. P. Morgan Securities.) It was a lucky choice. Like Dennis Weatherstone at Morgan Guaranty, Fisher's stock rose at Morgan Stanley in direct proportion to the growing vogue for trading on Wall Street.

Another critical figure was Lewis Bernard, nicknamed Brainy Bernard, the first Jewish partner and probably the best strategic thinker in the firm. He chaired a 1979 task force to devise a ten-year plan for Morgan Stanley. It was Bernard who introduced the computerized, multicurrency system for global trading that would make Morgan Stanley a trendsetter. In 1983, he headed a new fixed-income division that belatedly led the firm into the trading of gold, precious metals, and foreign exchange and the issuing and trading of commercial paper, municipal bonds, and mortgage-backed securities—all tools to please increasingly demanding corporate customers. These activities also required more traders and salespeople, further transforming Morgan Stanley into an anonymous global financial conglomerate.

In a critical strategic step, Morgan Stanley, so averse to foreign markets in the early post-war era, made a major commitment to trade and distribute securities overseas. It wisely abolished all managerial distinctions between its domestic and international operations. As trading and mergers superseded underwriting at Morgan Stanley, elegance was out and brashness was in—a jarring experience for its once sedate culture. As the *New York Times* said in 1984, "Morgan executives, who for generations have seemingly enjoyed their reputation for being the aristocrats of investment banking, seem confused these days about their image."[28] As its exclusive ties with clients lapsed, it had to hustle for business and encourage aggression. As at Morgan Grenfell, a firm once mocked for stuffiness proved it could be ruthless if necessary in preserving its privileges.

In the takeover area, Morgan Stanley shed all pretense of passivity. In 1978, merger specialist R. Bradford Evans had said, "We don't pester our clients and say, 'Why don't you accept this company, or that company, anything to get a deal.' "[29] In 1981, Morgan Stanley still led Wall Street with $40 million in merger fees, doing a third of all deals. Then Goldman, Sachs, First Boston, and Lehman Brothers leapt ahead. By

1983, under intense competitive pressure, Morgan's takeover department of seventy-five professionals was scouring the landscape in search of target companies. They started banging on doors, using the hard sell. "In the past there was a reluctance to call people," said Bob Greenhill. "It was the culture to let the client call you."[30] Now Morgan Stanley would increasingly serve as an engine of the takeover boom.

As its underwriting business declined, Morgan Stanley turned to businesses it once would have rejected haughtily, entering the netherworld of junk bonds. These high-risk high-yield bonds were often issued to support takeovers by companies of questionable solidity. The new junk bond department coincided with Morgan Stanley's sudden interest in small start-up companies. As Bob Greenhill explained, "Morgan was building a high-technology effort at that time, and I said, 'How can we not be in a business that is so necessary for so many of our growing clients?'"[31]

Junk bonds revolutionized Wall Street by magnifying the money available to corporate raiders. Where conglomerate takeovers in the 1960s used share exchanges, and cash was the method of choice in the 1970s, the junk bond market let corporate raiders flout the Wall Street establishment and finance their incursions by selling bonds to investors. The merger frenzy was also fueled by abundant money from commercial banks, whose dwindling prospects in wholesale lending attracted them to the financing of takeovers. Thus both sides of Wall Street—commercial and investment banking—found takeover work a salvation from the fundamental crises in their core lending and underwriting business. The razzle-dazzle of Wall Street in the Reagan years would obscure this underlying fragility, the irreversible decline of traditional businesses, the obsolescence of the traditional banker.

With considerable hoopla, Morgan Stanley talked about gentrifying junk bonds, but self-congratulation proved premature. In mid-1982, Morgan Stanley joined with Hambrecht and Quist to sponsor the first public offerings of People Express, the pioneering no-frills discount airline. Buying up used Lufthansa planes and ripping out their first-class sections, People founder Donald C. Burr wanted to create cheap air travel for the masses; his feisty, hustling airline was the antithesis of a classic Morgan client. Between 1983 and 1986, Morgan Stanley underwrote more than $500 million in junk bonds for People. As if still leary of its junk bond departure, the firm overruled custom and let Charles G. Phillips, head of its junk bond department, take a seat on People's five-member board.

From modest beginnings at Newark International Airport, People rocketed to the top rank of American airlines. In the end, Burr was victimized by his own ambition, making an ill-fated purchase of Frontier Airlines and trying to beat the major carriers on their own turf. He financed his frantic expansion by a staggering accumulation of debt. Later it was alleged in lawsuits that Phillips egged on Burr to borrow and expand too quickly. Whatever the truth, when crisis struck People Express, some bondholders felt betrayed by Morgan Stanley. They not only suffered serious losses, with some paper trading as low as 35 percent of the original issue price, but accused Morgan Stanley of failing to maintain a market during the turbulence. By one account, Morgan Stanley bought People bonds until it had $40 million worth in its inventory.

There was a second dimension to the controversy. For two and a half months, as bondholders suffered, Morgan's M&A Department shopped People to potential customers, exposing the firm to a possible conflict of interest. Honoring the Chinese wall, Charles Phillips kept the merger talks secret and didn't notify the bond traders of these efforts. Yet bondholders felt deprived of information that should have been provided by Morgan Stanley as the bond underwriter. The problem here was not that Morgan Stanley neglected its duties. The problem was that the conglomerate structure of modern Wall Street presented Morgan Stanley with incompatible duties. For People investors, the end was short, nasty, and brutish. When Frank Lorenzo of Texas Air bought People Express, he paid 75 percent on the face value of unsecured bonds and 95 percent on secured bonds.

In the early takeover days, there had existed a clear-cut distinction for Morgan Stanley between its stalwart clients and their takeover targets. It would never represent a raider against a client because it then might sacrifice that client's lucrative underwriting fees. But as underwriting ties with blue-chip companies decayed, there was no reason why the firm shouldn't represent raiders as well. The very notion of a client list—a sacred group of companies—broke down. In the new transactional environment, Morgan Stanley might represent a raider one year, then defend another client against that same raider the next. So many deals were germinating in the big merger departments that shifting loyalties and conflicts of interest were inevitable.

The inescapable danger was illustrated by Morgan Stanley's relationship with T. Boone Pickens of Mesa Petroleum. Back in the 1970s, Morgan Stanley couldn't have dealt with a corporate predator like Pickens, because he menaced its seven-sister clients. But as the big oil companies grew less loyal to Morgan Stanley, so the firm gladly dealt with other energy firms. In 1982, T. Boone Pickens enlisted Morgan Stanley to raid the Dallas-based General American Oil. "They were delighted to get the business," recalled Pickens, "for GAO was not part of the establishment that Morgan caters to."[32] On January 6, 1983, Pickens signed a standstill agreement with GAO stipulating that he wouldn't buy stock or try to gain control of the firm; it was bought the next day by Phillips Petroleum. Morgan brokered a deal by which Phillips Pete bought 38 percent of Mesa's shares and even picked up its $15 million in fees to the bankers and lawyers. During the summer of 1983, Morgan Stanley and Pickens briefly thought of teaming up to bust up a major oil company. The deal fell through, Pickens thought, when Morgan decided not to "alienate some of their clients—the Good Ol' Boys in spades."[33]

In December 1984, Pickens tried to swallow Phillips Pete, now represented by Morgan Stanley's Joseph G. Fogg III, a young, prematurely balding man who wore clear-framed glasses and had a cool, precise, intellectual look. As with Greenhill, clients found him abrasive but tolerated him for his brilliance. He was a whirling dervish in the non-stop oil takeovers. In 1984, he advised Standard Oil of California in its $13.4-billion takeover of Gulf Oil, the largest on record. Morgan Stanley banked a royal fee of $16.5 million for its work, even though it had committed no capital and used perhaps a dozen people.

The 1984 battle for Phillips Petroleum ended up pivoting on the standstill agreement of early 1983. It was a ticklish situation. Fogg and Pickens, who were then partners, were now opponents, and their recollections of the agreement were different. Fogg said he and Joe Flom had told Pickens the agreement would apply to Phillips as well as GAO. Pickens had "recognized the fact, expressed lack of concern and proceeded to execute the agreement," contended Fogg.[34] "Other people involved in the GAO deal remembered it differently," replied Pickens, who claimed that the deal applied only to GAO. And it was Pickens who won a favorable court ruling. He observed, "Since Fogg was working for us at the time, it cost him and Morgan credibility on Wall Street."[35]

Just as it seemed that Rule 415 had liberated companies from their Wall Street bankers and opened up a permanent distance between them, a new trend, called merchant banking, arose to obliterate the trend. Morgan Stanley had always been a service outfit, never compromising its objectivity by acting as an investor as well. Bob Baldwin had said in 1980, "We're so client-oriented and so busy that most of us have done very poor jobs of investing our money. That would not be the case with some firms, which have had all kinds of entrepreneurial investments."[36] That year, the firm conquered its prudery. It took a share in an Exxon oil-shale project in Australia, scouted timber investments, expanded its real-estate portfolio, and started to invest in high-tech start-ups. For the first time, Morgan Stanley was acting as a principal (investing its own money) and not just as an agent (advising clients on investing their money.) These investments foreshadowed a Wall Street fad that would entail a retrogression to some of the worst excesses of the robber baron era.

In 1982, to inaugurate the new merchant-banking operation, Morgan Stanley hired Donald P. Brennan, a former vice-chairman and fifteen-year veteran of International Paper. It was rare for an industrialist to work on Wall Street. The tough, fierce-willed Brennan would bring unique management skills, for he thought like a corporate executive. The firm set up a short-lived leveraged buyout fund with CIGNA Insurance, which reaped twenty-five times its original investment and whetted its appetite for more. Nobody envisioned how central the small merchant-banking group would eventually become to Morgan Stanley.

Breaking with another tradition, Morgan Stanley in 1980 began managing money for individuals and institutions. Another Chinese wall went up around another department. Some Wall Street firms balked at entering the business, fearing possible conflicts as they invested money in companies that were also takeover or underwriting clients. Once again, Morgan Stanley's decision conferred legitimacy on a dubious practice. As money manager Sanford Bernstein said, "If Morgan Stanley is in it, that means we're kosher."[37] In 1980, the firm had less than $1 billion under management, an amount that swelled to $10 billion by 1985. After details appeared in the press about Citibank's management of Kuwait's money, the sheikdom switched over about $4 billion in securities to Morgan Stanley's money managers. In the days of Harry Morgan, the firm had refused to do business with the Teamsters. Now it beat out twelve other firms for a contract to manage America's largest and most controversial pension fund, the $4.7-billion Teamsters Central States fund.

Morgan Stanley's new wing caused a small revival of the relationship with Morgan Guaranty. The Morgan bank was still legally barred from distributing mutual funds but could offer investment advice. So it agreed with Morgan Stanley in 1982 to create the first Pierpont Fund, with Morgan Stanley managing and Morgan Guaranty advising it. This family of funds would attract $2 billion through a time-honored Morgan formula of scorning the vulgar herd. They had a $25,000 minimum, versus the standard $1,000, and unlike other mutual funds, they didn't report their daily results in the newspapers. In the words of Morgan Stanley's Matthew Healey, "We didn't want to take the Pierpont funds into the competitive arena."[38] Everywhere else, however, Morgan Stanley was right smack in the middle of competition for the first time and was playing as rough as anybody.

BANG

• •

•

I N late 1986, Morgan Grenfell presented a curious study in contrasts. Outwardly it maintained a sedate air. Upholding a tradition of nearly 150 years, the bank posted no nameplate outside—the old brass plaques hung in the reception area—and the interior paid homage to the past. In the thickly carpeted, arched hallways, there were prints of Saint Paul's and the Bank of England, of hansom cabs rolling through gaslit streets in a *fin de siècle* City. Morgan Grenfell was said to have the last man in the City to wear a bowler hat—one Julian Stamford. It still seemed a civilized place.

But the calm was deceptive. Morgan Grenfell had charted a course roughly parallel to Morgan Stanley's, dispensing with politeness and becoming a tough, aggressive firm. For twenty years, it had revolted against its sleepy past. Starting with the American Tobacco fight for Gallaher in the late 1960s, it had enjoyed testing the rules. "They liked the image of being the most buccaneering firm in the City, of pushing out the boundaries," observed an ex-merger specialist with the firm. "Every deal was a little more provocative and cheeky and less British than the one before."

Morgan Grenfell's two leaders in the early 1980s reflected both the old and the new City. Chairman Bill Mackworth-Young had spent twenty-one years with the aristocratic brokerage firm of Rowe and Pitman, second in prestige only to Cazenove. If Morgan Grenfell wasn't particularly well known for brilliant executives, the bookish Mackworth-Young gave the firm intellectual cachet. He had been a star Eton pupil, along with his classmate Robin Leigh-Pemberton, later governor of the Bank of England. The son of an English civil servant and archaeologist in India and married to an earl's daughter, Mackworth-Young was a good salesman and a charming after-dinner speaker. He was especially adroit with Americans, having gone yearly to Bohemian Grove in California, the rustic stag camp for American power brokers. A warm, stocky man with a ready, avuncular smile, he lacked malevolence and was universally popular.

A heavy smoker, Mackworth-Young died abruptly of lung cancer in 1984. Later, the City would ritually repeat that had he lived, Morgan Grenfell would have been spared the Guinness scandal. According to a rival executive, "Mackworth-Young would have given free rein to the takeover *prima donnas,* but he would have been quite aware of what was happening. He would have taken a longer term view of how the business should be conducted." When things later went awry at Morgan Grenfell, Mackworth-Young only grew more saintly in memory.

Morgan Grenfell's chief executive and deputy chairman was Christopher R. Reeves, who epitomized the new, self-made City executive. A graduate of Malvern College, he worked at the Bank of England and the merchant bank of Hill Samuel before Sir John Stevens recruited him to Morgan Grenfell in 1968. He belonged to the first generation of Morgan Grenfell executives who didn't come from the old families and hadn't apprenticed at the Morgan bank in New York. Slim and blond with a chiseled, angular face, he had a photogenic grin and a look of gritty determination. In a firm once faintly embarrassed about seeking new business, Reeves didn't mind the hard sell. Tough and adept, he was enigmatic to his subordinates. "He was a superb presence but a bit of a sphinx," a former corporate finance director recalled. "Silence was his partner." He was drawn to the tough tactics of "corporate finance"—a term that in England signifies takeover work.

Neither Reeves nor Mackworth-Young was a master strategist. Unlike Morgan Guaranty or Morgan Stanley, Morgan Grenfell never operated by a blueprint or comprehensive vision of the financial future. Its history was devoid of planning conferences or retreats during which the firm could strategically reorient. Its postwar history had no Bob Baldwins or Lewis Bernards, no Henry Alexanders or Lew Prestons, and certainly no Siegmund Warburgs. Its moves seemed improvised, a snatching at sudden opportunities. To paraphrase Winston Churchill, it was a pudding without a theme, and this absence of a clear design would be its downfall. Both Reeves and Mackworth-Young ran a series of successful, often unrelated businesses without any single thread binding them together. By comparison, Morgan Guaranty and Morgan Stanley had a seamless quality, a smoothly coordinated approach to business that seemed to anticipate changes in financial markets.

Morgan Grenfell had enjoyed some remarkable successes, which masked long-term problems. It managed money for the world's two richest people—the sultan of Brunei and Queen Elizabeth II—and surpassed all other British banks in handling American pension funds. It specialized in international portfolios when many short-sighted asset managers were still mired in local markets. After years of torrid growth, by the 1987 crash it managed $25 billion. This dwarfed America's top asset manager among wholesale firms, Morgan Stanley, with its meager $11 billion. At 23 Great Winchester, pension money for San Francisco, the state of California, Fort Worth, and the Rockefeller Foundation was handled.

It was also distinguished in trade and project financing. Morgan Grenfell had led in financing North Sea oil and chalked up several energy triumphs, including the record $1.6-billion financing for Woodside Petroleum's natural gas project in Australia, the biggest such loan ever to hit the Euromarkets. It was also active in financing projects in the Soviet Union. And when other banks wrote off Africa in the 1970s as poor and hopelessly indebted, Morgan Grenfell established a business advising black African states. To please black Africa, it even ended most of its dealings with South Africa. Among the forty countries it advised outside of Europe were Sudan, Uganda, Tanzania, and Zambia.

Yet despite these accomplishments, Morgan Grenfell was vulnerable. Like other capital-short merchant banks, it was somewhat anachronistic in modern, global markets. Unlike Warburgs, it never graduated into the front ranks of the City's Eurobond and foreign-exchange markets. In that larger City, capital was decisive, with cosy ties counting for little— the reason takeover work had been such a godsend to Morgan Grenfell. The firm had thrived only in the insular City of British work, which would be a dangerous shortcoming as the decade progressed.

The so-called Big Bang deregulation of October 1986 tore down the walls that had divided the two Cities since the Euromarkets emerged in the early 1960s. To guarantee London's survival as a financial center, the Thatcher government decided to stop cosseting London banks and expose them to more domestic and foreign competition. Despite their evocative names, British merchant banks were tiny beside the new global conglomerates. Japan's Nomura Securities, with a $20-billion capitalization, was *forty times* the size of Morgan Grenfell. It could swallow all the merchant banks for breakfast. By opening the City's gates to foreign firms, the British government ensured London's survival as a financial center but not the survival of individual London houses. They would have to compete against American commercial banks, which wanted to build investment banking operations in London that they could then repatriate to the United States after Glass-Steagall tumbled. At the same time, the big British clearing banks—National Westminster, Midland, Barclays, and Lloyds—had begun to encroach on the traditional turf of the merchant banks.

In its specifics, Big Bang sounded innocuous. It ended the City's antiquated fragmentation into bankers, brokers, and market makers, let foreign firms enter these areas, and scuttled fixed brokerage commissions. These measures collectively threw the formerly closed City wide open to competition. Christopher Reeves was aware of the carnage on Wall Street after fixed commissions ended in May 1975. He warned, "Greater risks will be run by those firms which do not adjust their business to exploiting the new opportunities."[1] Oddly, Morgan Grenfell would be just such a laggard and would figure as a major casualty of Big Bang. In a failure of vision, it would move too gingerly, too indecisively, and would squander its chance to translate its eminence to an international sphere.

The little cottage industries of the City were swept away by Big Bang. Scores of small private partnerships, which had given the City its pleasantly Dickensian flavor, were taken over by world-devouring giants. At the same time, banker-company relations grew looser, more impersonal. As British corporate treasurers were besieged by foreign bankers, they got a new sense of what could be accomplished in global markets and were less content to rely on a single banker. Consolidations also meant sudden wealth for young deal makers and traders, whose salaries jumped as much as tenfold in a few years. Young bond traders were suddenly driving Ferraris and making six-figure salaries.

The elite world of merchant banking faded as the rhythms of the trader speeded up City life. Long lunches at Boodle's or White's gave way to twelve-hour days. It was impossible to equip all the trading desks with old Etonians, and so the City became a more egalitarian place. Some people, of course, resisted the new ways. When the *Economist* tried to track down City executives, it discovered several absentees: "Many were sighted at the Wimbledon tennis tournament, the Henley regatta and the Ascot horse races."[2] For the most part, however, the City was now a more hectic, grueling place, with people grabbing lunches at the fast-food restaurants and crowded sandwich shops scattered among the Wren churches and new office blocks. It grew in such helter-skelter style that it almost made Wall Street seem gracious by comparison.

Along with Warburgs and Kleinwort Benson, Morgan Grenfell had a chance to parlay past glory into modern power. Christopher Reeves welcomed Big Bang as an opportunity to form an integrated securities firm that could compete in world markets. This was a radical shift for Morgan Grenfell which had always shied away from the risks and capital investment associated with securities trading. Like Morgan Stanley in the 1950s, it had maintained an aristocratic distance from markets, drawing on brokers to price the securities it issued. Under the British underwriting system, the august "houses of issue," such as Morgan Grenfell, didn't put their capital directly at risk. They placed the issues with institutional underwriters, who provided a contingency backing for issues. Big Bang elicited predictions that "bought deals" would revolutionize London as they had New York after Rule 415. This meant that underwriting would suddenly require enormous piles of capital. Of the merchant banks, Warburgs responded with great clarity to Big Bang, while Morgan Grenfell vacillated and lagged fatally behind.

Morgan Grenfell's bungling of Big Bang would do more lasting damage than the Guinness scandal. Early on, a split developed, mostly between the younger directors, who favored audacious, far-reaching action in response to the challenge, and the traditional directors, who were fearful of venturing into risky new businesses. In 1984, Morgan Grenfell was approached by the brokerage house of Rowe and Pitman, Mackworth-Young's old firm, about a possible alliance. Afraid it would cost too much, 23 Great Winchester dithered and lost its chance; later Warburgs grabbed the firm, helping to make it preeminent among merchant banks in international markets. The most insistent foe of the Rowe and Pitman deal was evidently Graham Walsh, the takeover chief. "Walsh was *very* adamant against it," a former colleague recalled angrily. "He said, 'We're doing beautifully as we are, we're on the top of the pile, and it's risky to do this.'" So the easy, seductive profits of takeovers clouded the firm's strategic vision at a critical moment.

Morgan Grenfell frittered away other chances: it passed up the opportunity to buy Phillips and Drew and Wood Mackenzie; fumbled a chance to merge with Hoare, Govett by demanding majority control; and was blocked from taking over Exco, a financial services group, first by a Bank of England veto, then by its own indecision. It ended up doing Big Bang on the cheap, buying two firms that many thought booby prizes—the antiquated Pember and Boyle (a broker) and Pinchin Denny (a jobber, or market maker). Expressing a common judgment, an indignant former director said, "They hemmed and hawed and finally bought a cheap jobber and a cheap broker. They got the worst of all worlds." As time has confirmed, the new financial order would tolerate global

firms offering a comprehensive package of services or domestic bou-
tiques specializing in a few functions. It would be pitiless toward those,
such as Morgan Grenfell, stuck in the middle bracket.

Right before Big Bang, in June 1986, Morgans overcame historic reservations and sold shares to the public to amass capital for trading. It
raised £154 million ($229 million) and borrowed another £140 million
($200 million). Although some jowly die-hards were petrified that
shareholders might demand shorter lunches or even interfere with
weekend shooting (God forbid), most accepted the grim necessity. The
Bank of England had just chastised the firm for having inadequate
capital to back its share purchases during the Guinness takeover of
Distillers, and raiding was becoming a more capital-intensive art. Like
its Wall Street counterparts, Morgan Grenfell might someday have to
provide temporary "mezzanine" financing or even issue junk bonds in
takeovers.

There were also unspoken reasons for going public. A former corporate finance director explained: "A principal reason was to have publicly
quoted shares as acquisition currency. It didn't work out that way."
Another speculated that it was a way to appease the firm's takeover stars,
Roger Seelig and George Magan: "I suspect they weren't making enough
money and needed an equity hit. They both had standing offers from
American investment banks to pay them $1 million to go to them—
much more than they were getting from Morgan Grenfell."

The confused and halfhearted way that Morgan Grenfell reacted to
Big Bang reflected an unhealthy dependence on takeover work. The firm
might boast that it offered thirty-two services, and it could point to
twenty-two overseas offices, yet the heart of the operation was mergers.
By Big Bang, the 120-person takeover unit was reportedly chipping in
almost half the pretax profits in a firm of 2,000 people. As London's
premier takeover house, it was handling an awesome volume of business—some fifty-one deals in 1986 valued at almost £14 billion.

Like Morgan Stanley, Morgan Grenfell usually took the offensive,
earning a reputation as "the most aggressive agent in the City for the
hostile bidder," in *Euromoney*'s words.[3] As a blue-blooded firm, it
legitimated a new, swashbuckling style of finance. On Wall Street and
in the City, traditionalists were appeased when a Morgan firm validated
controversial practices. Aware of the mounting takeover frenzy in the
United States, Morgan Grenfell was determined to show it could slug
it out with any Yanks that came to London.

Mackworth-Young and Reeves presided with a light hand over their
circus of takeover *prima donnas.* The Seeligs and the Magans had great

power in the firm, for they captured new clients; the old taboo about poaching clients was fading. Morgan Grenfell had an individualistic culture very unlike the team spirit drilled into recruits at Morgan Guaranty, S. G. Warburg, and Goldman, Sachs. Not surprisingly, it encouraged a flamboyant, free-wheeling star system among its young professionals, who became recognizable figures in London, like pop stars. But such freedom, if conducive to inventive takeover work, could also induce a perilous euphoria, a giddy sense of invulnerability.

The group's superstar was Roger Seelig. In a more innocent age, his background might have fitted him for tamer pursuits. In 1971, after taking a degree from the London School of Economics and working at Esso, Seelig joined Morgan Grenfell. (That he was Jewish apparently mattered less in those days before the petrodollar boom.) He and his mother shared a three-story Gloucestershire mansion—a very grand, formal place topped by a row of balusters. It wasn't far from the Prince and Princess of Wales's Highgrove House. The bachelor Seelig's girlfriend lived with him at his Marble Arch apartment, but he professed to be "too busy" to marry, as if matrimony might cost a valuable deal or two. He rode with the Beaufort hunt, belonged to the Royal Society of Arts, and was partial to official balls—not your usual corporate stalker.

At Morgan Grenfell, Seelig ran his own show and Reeves proudly touted him to clients as the most "entrepreneurial" of the takeover stars. Seelig made his own hours and served as his own boss. Carrying a mobile telephone, he would pop up at theaters or expensive nightclubs, Annabel's in Berkeley Square being a favorite spot. He was a high-tech dandy, financial impresario, and gentleman masher. Speaking in a clipped, affected manner, he had a smugly theatrical smile, with lips pursed and corners drawn down, like a rogue in a Restoration comedy. His debonair ascot-and-handkerchief style transported a country-house ethos into the cutthroat takeover world.

One former corporate finance director remembers him thus: "Roger loved to fly his spinnaker. He wore suits nipped heavily at the waist and had a Beau Brummel stride, with his chest thrown out. It was a metaphor for his personality. He liked to 'mingle' with grand people, like Jacob Rothschild or Henry Kravis. He was a talented banker, but his manner masked an inferiority complex." Earning £250,000 annually for snuffing out targets, Seelig was London's top deal maker. He was especially good at latching onto acquisition-hungry firms, such as the giant retailer Storehouse PLC, which owned the Habitat home-furnishing stores in England and Conran's in the United States; Storehouse was

chaired by Seelig's friend Sir Terence Conran. With sixteen professionals in Morgan Grenfell's takeover department, Seelig reportedly hauled
in a quarter of the profits, encouraging management to view his tactics
benignly and allow him considerable leeway. He developed an attitude
that takeover rules were silly hindrances to be tested by clever financiers. In 1985, he boasted that rivals "may just be reading the rules. We
changed most of the rules."[4]

Mirroring Morgan Grenfell's split personality, the other takeover star
was George Magan, a short, sharp-faced man with glasses. His manner
was entirely different from Seelig's. The offspring of an old Irish family,
an accomplished pianist with a dry, delightful wit, Magan was popular
with his colleagues. He was nicknamed Teddy, short for teddy boy,
because of his slicked-back hair and slick suits. Though unlike Seelig in
other ways, Magan also gloried in aggressive tactics and talked of "using
every inch of the playing surface."[5] Ubiquitous on London's takeover
scene, he was involved in six of Britain's top ten deals in 1985.

There was a lot of jockeying and rivalry among the *prima donnas,* and
Morgan Grenfell created an unstructured environment that allowed
them to wheel and deal without bumping into each other. This required
a conciliatory figurehead to oversee the Corporate Finance Department.
His name was Graham Walsh. An accountant and former director general of the Takeover Panel, Walsh was a shy, neat, introverted man who
never quite made eye contact with other people. Known as a hypochondriac, he would shuffle about shutting windows in winter. Walsh feuded
with Seelig, and they ended up scarcely on speaking terms. As he kept
his department humming tidily along, Graham Walsh little dreamed
that Margaret Thatcher would someday take a personal interest in his
job.

Such an operation required a strong chief executive to curb the ani-
mal spirits of Walsh's takeover professionals. Yet Christopher Reeves
accentuated the impetuosity of the takeover team. He sometimes made
rules sound optional: "Merchant banking is all about innovation. . . .
We must not believe that rules are written in tablets of stone."[6] As one
former Morgan Grenfell official said bitterly, "He was imbued with this
win-at-any-cost or by-any-means attitude. And it communicated itself
down to the operatives in the Corporate Finance Department." From
1980 to 1984, a healthy equilibrium existed between Reeves's red-
blooded dynamism and Mackworth-Young's wise discretion. An outside
adviser recalled, "Christopher Reeves had tremendous thrusting ability,
but he needed the balancing factor of Mackworth-Young's slightly
wider and more public-spirited view. Christopher Reeves was all acceler-

ator and no brake." In 1984, when Mackworth-Young suddenly died, it robbed Morgan Grenfell of this temperate influence.

The dazzling team of Seelig and Magan made Morgan Grenfell untouchable in takeover work, with only second-place Warburgs remotely approaching it. Between 1982 and 1987, Morgan Grenfell ranked number one in mergers and acquisitions year after year. It was on such an intoxicating ride—in 1985, directors received twice the pay of the year before—that the gray old men of Morgan Grenfell tolerated the antics of the young hotshots. As the scale of the takeover wars escalated crazily, the temptation to break the rules heightened. Before 1985, London had never seen a £1-billion takeover bid; there were four on the table by year's end. Much to the British Treasury's annoyance, 23 Great Winchester blithely refused to work on Margaret Thatcher's privatization boom. Why? Because corporate finance people thought the fees trivial and didn't want to pull stars off the glitzy merger carousel.

The momentum was pushing Morgan Grenfell toward ever more hazardous enterprise. "Merchant banks tend to attract business by their reputation," explained a former corporate finance director. "And Morgan Grenfell was being approached by more racy people because they were doing racier things." The press noted this vicious circle. As London's *Business* magazine said in 1986, "The mention of Morgan Grenfell in some banking circles gets the sort of reaction the sight of Attila the Hun must have provoked in Rome."[7] One observer remarked, "They are trotting into action with all the arrogance of a crack Polish cavalry regiment in 1939."[8] These would be prophetic judgments.

Morgan Grenfell's balloon was finally punctured by the Guinness scandal, which convulsed Britain and focused more anger against the City than had any scandal since the "rascally stock jobbers" of the eighteenth century. It started with an exceptionally aggressive client— Guinness chairman Ernest Saunders. As his most famous product, black Irish stout, lost favor with wine-tippling yuppies, Saunders wanted to diversify his huge conglomerate. Like Robert Maxwell, Saunders was an immigrant who craved acceptance by the British establishment. His Jewish parents had fled Nazi-controlled Austria in 1938 and settled in London. The Jewish-born Ernst Schleyer was re-invented as the Anglican Ernest Saunders. He would acquire all the trappings of upper class success, including a Buckinghamshire mansion.

At the start of his buying spree, Saunders booted out Guinness's old adviser, N. M. Rothschild, and brought in Morgan Grenfell. At a dinner at the Connaught hotel in early 1985, Christopher Reeves advised Saunders to expand aggressively, lest Guinness itself be a takeover target. In June 1985, advised by Tony Richmond-Watson of Morgan Grenfell, Saunders launched a £330-million hostile bid for the Scotch whisky and hotel company, Arthur Bell and Sons. Bell's chairman, Raymond Miquel, was flabbergasted, because Morgan Grenfell had represented his firm for twenty years, assisting in its purchase of the Gleneagles Hotel Group and even handling its public offering in 1971. When Miquel complained to the Takeover Panel, Morgan Grenfell countered with evidence that Bells had terminated its services in November 1984; Miquel cited more recent links.

Whatever the exact truth, Morgan Grenfell had twenty years' worth of intimate knowledge about Bells and thus subverted a tradition of merchant banker confidentiality. (This was the rationale for having traditional bankers: a company's innermost secrets were safe from competitors.) At first, the panel mildly rebuked Morgan Grenfell, then retracted even that. Some attributed its leniency to Christopher Reeves's informing the panel that Morgan Grenfell had booked only £20,000 in fees from Bells versus £6 million from Guinness in the previous two years. Such an argument, it was thought, swayed the banker-oriented panel.

There was no outright illegality in the Bell's takeover, but things were skirting the edge. Apparently a Guinness employee, pretending to be a Scottish reporter, questioned Raymond Miquel.[9] Also, Saunders had assured Bell's shareholders that he might sell the Piccadilly Hotel in London but keep the rest. Then through Morgan Grenfell's property arm, he set up a Dutch auction for the Caledonian and North British hotels in Edinburgh. The winning bidder, Norfolk Capital, came as a shock, because its chairman was none other than Tony Richmond-Watson of Morgan Grenfell. There were, predictably, accusations of favoritism and double-dealing. By this point, both Guinness and Morgan Grenfell seemed ripe for trouble. Christopher Reeves, meanwhile, kept telling Saunders that Guinness would have to digest another company if it wished to stay independent.

In January 1986, Saunders entered into a more massive takeover whose record size would make the city tremble. A supermarket chain, Argyll, had made a bid for the far larger Scottish brewer, Distillers. This David assault on Goliath—a new City phenomenon—had clear class overtones. Argyll's James Gulliver was a husky, rough-hewn grocer's son, while Distillers was an aristocratic Scottish firm. From plush headquarters on London's St. James's Square, Distillers marketed drinks with a classy ring—Johnnie Walker, Haig and Haig, and White Horse scotch,

Booth's and Gordon's gin. Behind the tony facade, however, the poorly run company was losing ground in the scotch market. And it had never completely overcome its infamy as the manufacturer of thalidomide, a sedative that when taken by pregnant women apparently caused cruel deformations in the developing fetus.

Distillers scoffed at the Scottish commoner Gulliver. "Gulliver deals in potatoes and cans of beans," said a deputy chairman of Distillers. "We are not selling brown water in cheap bottles. We are selling Scotch."[10] The Gulliver people exhibited their own class bias. Hoping to swoop down on Distillers by surprise, they favored an August raid, saying, "Let's shoot them up the backside while they're out on the grouse moor."[11]

So along came Ernest Saunders in January 1986, volunteering to be the "white knight" who would save Distillers from that coarse ruffian, Jimmy Gulliver. There was more than altruism here: Saunders was already considering pouncing on Distillers, anyway. If he could make a ceremonial entrance through the front door, well, so much the better. He even secured an agreement by which Distillers would defray Guinness's fees for taking it over—a highly unusual measure.

Saunders liberally distributed promises to win Distillers' support. Chairman John Connell was apparently led to believe he would chair the merged entity. Ditto for Sir Thomas Risk, governor of the Bank of Scotland. The duping of Risk would be one of the most disgraceful parts of the Guinness affair. The Guinness forces needed to placate Scottish nationalists, who would protest the loss of Distillers' autonomy. Charles Fraser, an Edinburgh lawyer and chairman of Morgan Grenfell, Scotland, was among those pressing for a Scottish non-executive chairman. To this end, Saunders and Seelig cajoled the respected Risk into agreeing to take such a post in the new firm, which would have its headquarters in Scotland. This promise was incorporated into takeover documents, and the Distillers board made it a precondition of the "friendly" bid; many institutional investors backed Guinness on its strength. Nevertheless, Guinness later reneged on its pledge, claiming that the two-tier structure was unworkable from a commercial standpoint. It even circulated rumors to blacken Risk's reputation, claiming that he was unduly concerned with retaining Guinness business for his bank. Morgan Grenfell protested the treatment of Risk but didn't resign. After an extraordinary general meeting, Risk was dropped by Guinness without legal repercussions. But the lingering resentment over the dispute would add extraordinary venom to the Guinness affair.

Tony Richmond-Watson should have been Morgan Grenfell's point man in the Guinness takeover. But he was busy helping United Biscuit complete a £1-billion merger with Imperial Group, so he bowed out. Roger Seelig took his place. (Some accounts say Saunders demanded the more aggressive Seelig.) According to Saunders, Reeves warned him that Seelig was a "very powerful personality and will want to do things his way."[12] As a member of the so-called Guinness war cabinet, Seelig sat by Saunders at meetings and was integral to everything that happened. Even before the later disclosure of share manipulation, it seemed a nasty campaign. Both sides stooped to such scurrilous ads that the Takeover Panel had to curb their use.

The essence of the Guinness scandal involved manipulation of share prices. The Lilliputian grocer, Jimmy Gulliver, was trying to take over a liquor company three times his company's size. Where a comparable bid in the United States would have been financed with cash and junk bonds, Gulliver hoped to pay primarily with shares of his own company, much as American conglomerates did in the 1960s. As it started bidding against Gulliver, Guinness also relied on a swap of its own shares and cash. So the decisive factor would be the price of Argyll and Guinness stock; the more they rose, the more their individual bids would be worth.

Guinness embarked on a campaign to pump up its own share price and thus enhance its bid. It wasn't illegal for people to buy Guinness stock, nor for Morgan Grenfell to tout it. Roger Seelig got his friend, the beefy, bespectacled Lord Spens—formerly of Morgan Grenfell but now a corporate finance director with Henry Ansbacher—to coax his clients into buying two million shares. Jacob Rothschild bought. Robert Maxwell reportedly picked up two million shares. L. F. Rothschild Unterberg Towbin bought a six-million-share Guinness block, which it sold back to Morgan Grenfell when the battle was over. The illegality would arise only if Guinness underwrote share purchases or guaranteed buyers against loss by doing so. That would violate the Companies Act of 1985, which prohibited companies from buying their own shares or assisting others in doing so. Whether or not criminal acts took place in connection with the Guinness "affair" will, of course, be resolved in criminal proceedings to be commenced in 1991, in which the defendants denied all charges.

Despite the law, Seelig, Saunders, and Guinness finance director Olivier Roux allegedly orchestrated what is called a concert party, or a fan club, to inflate the Guinness share price while deflating Argyll stock. They are said to have conducted their secret work on such a large and brazen scale that one wonders how, in the long run, they hoped to escape detection. The list of deals cut by the Guinness war cabinet makes for sobering reading. British businessman Gerald Ronson, chairman of Heron Corporation, had introduced Seelig to the notorious American arbitrageur, Ivan Boesky. At Seelig's urging, Boesky poured £100 million into Guinness and, for good measure, "shorted" Argyll stock to depress it. The Boesky link would later clarify a mystery of the Guinness takeover: why Argyll shares dipped each afternoon in London, just about the time New York trading opened. The American company, Schenley Industries, bought £60 million of Guinness stock. By coincidence, it received an extended contract afterward to market Dewar's whiskey in the United States. The biggest stake was taken by the venerable Bank Leu, Switzerland's oldest bank, which bought tens of millions of shares and was allegedly indemnified against any losses.

As Guinness's share prices spiraled wildly skyward, buoyed by the coordinated buying, Gulliver complained to the Takeover Panel about the share levitation. As it had since 1968, Britain still relied on the private panel to enforce the Takeover Code. This self-regulatory body seemed too genteel to deal with the harsh tactics and mercenary culture of the modern City. Much to its later embarrassment, the Takeover Panel failed to act on Argyll's complaint. Morgan Grenfell also accused Argyll of inflating *its* share price. A 25-percent jump in Guinness's share price finally tipped the scales in the takeover. On April 18, 1986, Ernest Saunders declared victory over Argyll, claiming to have more than 50 percent of Distillers' shares in a bid valued at £2.53 billion. Morgan Grenfell had won the biggest, ugliest, most searing takeover of the decade and basked in dubious glory.

Ethics aside, Guinness involved some risky financial footwork for Morgan Grenfell, providing further proof of its win-at-any-cost mentality. It had bought £180 million of Distillers shares, straining its capital resources of only £170 million—to say the least. This behavior was deemed so irresponsible by the Bank of England that it promptly issued new rules, limiting such share buying by a bank to 25 percent of its capital—an implicit rebuke of Morgan Grenfell. Once again, the firm that was the Bank of England's staunchest ally in Teddy Grenfell's day now seemed its chief nemesis.

As in any share-rigging scheme, there was a critical weakness: what would happen to artificially elevated share prices when the secret props were removed? Apparently Roger Seelig feared that friendly parties might suddenly dump up to 20 percent of Guinness's shares on the market. And the price indeed began to slide sharply from the 355-pence takeover price. If, as alleged, Guinness had promised to insure the concert party against losses, its liability could be tremendous if the share price plummeted. Seelig appealed to institutions to hold their shares until autumn. Mayhew of Cazenove, Guinness's broker, also worked out a plan for Guinness to buy back Morgan Grenfell's stake in Distillers, which would be converted into Guinness shares after the takeover.

More direct measures were taken to stop selling. Lord Spens had a two-million-share block for which Guinness allegedly paid him £7.6 million. Seelig and Oliver Roux, Saunders's financial adviser, are said to have characterized the £7.6 million as an interest-free deposit in order to dissuade Spens from selling. It was hard to see what the difference would be between such a *de facto* guarantee and an outright purchase. It is also alleged that Bank Leu in Switzerland also got a £50-million "deposit" from Guinness to ensure that it wouldn't liquidate its shareholding. During the summer of 1986, Guinness transferred £69 million to a venture fund managed by Ivan Boesky, who had invested so heavily in Guinness shares. It was this aspect that later outraged the Guinness board and precipitated the dismissal of Ernest Saunders. When all the deals finally surfaced in the press, share manipulation apparently added up to a staggering £200 million.

To understand the fierce public outcry that greeted the exposure of the Guinness scandal, one must note several factors. Billion-pound hostile deals were becoming common for the first time. And during the Thatcher years, the number of shareholders in Britain had more than tripled, to nine million. Never before had so many people been riveted on the doings of the City. Big Bang was accompanied by a numbing barrage of publicity. And at least part of the populace revered the new money makers. At the time of Guinness, the white-hot Morgan Grenfell was receiving about fifteen hundred job applications yearly from university graduates, half from Oxford and Cambridge, for thirty places. So some of the public disenchantment reflected the earlier worship of new idols.

Among other factors was a growing sense that the City was corrupting the general culture and harming the economy. The *New Statesman* called the City "an unpatriotic casino which pays itself obscenely high salaries for dancing on the grave of British industry."[13] Sir Claus Moser of N. M. Rothschild warned, "the City is absorbing too many of our ablest people. If I were a dictator over Britain, I'd move 9/10 of them into manufacturing, industry and teaching."[14] As on Wall Street, high finance was no longer principally involved in financing the operations of industry. Instead, it was financing changes in the ownership of industry, to the stunning benefit of bankers and raiders. Add to this the sheer envy of ordinary Britons at the stratospheric salaries in the City, and one can understand the incendiary public reaction to Guinness.

The year 1986 was one of double scandal for Morgan Grenfell. Right after Big Bang and before the Guinness revelations surfaced, the firm was tarred by an insider trading scandal. Its new chief securities trader, thirty-five-year-old Geoffrey Collier, had been hired for Big Bang at a salary of $284,000. He had joined the firm the year before after setting up a New York office for Vickers da Costa, a broker later taken over by Citicorp. In the past, British authorities had taken a relaxed attitude toward insider trading, which wasn't even a criminal offense until 1980. This *laissez-faire* attitude was incompatible with the new conglomerates encouraged by Big Bang. There were now fears that traders would abuse information from their mergers departments. In global financial markets, there was also a need for higher universal standards—a particular concern of the Thatcher government in its quest to insure the City's worldwide standing. Right before Big Bang, Morgan Grenfell distributed a little in-house manual in which it stated that any staff purchases of shares had to be channeled through Morgan Grenfell's own brokers. The penalty for violating the rule was summary dismissal.

Collier made illegal purchases through his old firm, now Scrimgeour Vickers. He made small profits on a sixty-thousand-share purchase of Associated Engineering after he learned that Hollis, a Morgan client, was about to acquire it. He almost made a killing on his purchase of call options on Cadbury Schweppes, then being acquired by General Cinema, another Morgan Grenfell client. But his trade in Associated Engineering led to suspicions and forced him to sell the Cadbury options prematurely, at a loss. After Scrimgeour Vickers tipped off Morgan Grenfell about Collier's trading, the firm forced his resignation, on November 10, 1986, shocking the City. Collier got a one-year suspended sentence and £25,000 ($44,250) fine. The case fortified the resolve of those who wanted stricter regulation as firms turned into conglomerates fraught with potential conflicts of interest.

The Collier scandal was a mere curtain raiser for the next act in the drama. In late 1986, Morgan Grenfell was winding up a superlative year, bolstered by $833 million in capital, double the year before. Then Ivan Boesky pleaded guilty in November to one felony charge and agreed to pay a $100-million penalty for insider trading. Nobody yet dreamed of any Morgan Grenfell connection. But in the Collier investigation, the SEC had already shared information with Britain's Department of Trade and Industry under a new, bilateral pact. It was information from Boesky, relayed by American authorities to the British, that provoked the Guinness investigation. The suspicious stock gyrations during the takeover had not in themselves produced a full-blown probe.

Equipped with new Big Bang powers, investigators from the Department of Trade and Industry moved into action. In early December, three weeks after the Collier affair, they staged simultaneous morning raids on Guinness headquarters in Portman Square and on Morgan Grenfell to round up records. Then a month of revelations flooded London's press, drawing to the surface the latent public resentment of the City. Nobody at 23 Great Winchester quite saw the gathering storm. Seelig himself thought the firm would stand behind him. When a journalist said, "Mr. Seelig, your colleagues are going to throw you to the wolves," he was incredulous. "Now you're making me very angry," he replied. "We're very solid here."[15] But under intense pressure, Morgan Grenfell told Seelig he was drawing too much publicity and had to be sacrificed. In a tumultuous series of late-December decisions, Morgan Grenfell resigned as Guinness's merchant banker and fired its brightest star, Roger Seelig. Since the Guinness board had already brought in Lazard Brothers as their new adviser, some observers saw an empty public relations gesture in Morgan Grenfell's resignation.

Morgan Grenfell hoped this would cleanse the firm and close the scandal. It circulated a reassuring letter to shareholders to that effect. But the public pressure to go further was unrelenting. Even within the City, there was thinly veiled satisfaction at seeing Morgan Grenfell punished. "When a firm has been so outstandingly successful on the back of very aggressive people and go no distance out of their way to be popular or help other firms—then the absence of friends shows up at once when they trip up," said a rival executive. "It was very noticeable that people didn't jump to their rescue."

Inside the firm, the shifting ground suddenly turned to quicksand. A former staffer recalled, "The first reaction was absolute shock and horror. It didn't happen as one big announcement. It was like a faucet dripping lousy water. It kept on coming. It was a real horror that tore the guts out of the firm." On January 9, 1987, Ernest Saunders stepped down as Guinness's chairman. A week later, Price Waterhouse outlined the £200-million share-support operation, mapping out links across several countries. They reported to the Guinness board the existence of £25 million in mysterious invoices. The operation seemed almost inconceivably vast.

Once Morgan Grenfell could have counted on the Bank of England's goodwill, but it had let that historic relationship lapse. Since the death of Sir John Stevens, in 1973, Morgan Grenfell hadn't had a director on the Court of the Bank of England. Some saw this as reflecting official displeasure; for others, it simply betokened an absence of executives of real stature at Morgan Grenfell. The bank's deputy governor, George Blunden, wasn't appeased by Seelig's removal and thought Reeves and Walsh were either knaves or fools. As late as January 18, 1987, Reeves, earning £300,000 a year, and Walsh, earning £200,000 a year, felt secure and insisted they would stay. They saw no systematic corruption that merited further action and so informed the staff. "They called together everyone in corporate finance," said an ex-director. "They said management had done an exhaustive, internal look at the big deals and not to worry. They said, 'We'll be sticking here; there'll be no resignations.' "

This wishful thinking was exploded within forty-eight hours. Expecting a general election in the near future, the Tories feared retribution if they seemed to coddle the City. Presumably, Margaret Thatcher saw a chance to steal the thunder of the Labour Party by seeming tough in disciplining her own kind. Many in the City also feared that the spreading scandal would bring calls for statutory regulation of a sort that was always abhorrent to the City. Robin Leigh-Pemberton, Governor of the Bank of England, told a dinner audience that Guinness was "a threat to the entire basis of trust which still predominates in our business life and in the City of London in particular."[16] So great was the fear of seeming soft on the financiers that John Wakeham, chief Tory whip and close Margaret Thatcher adviser, was heard to say, "We've got to get the handcuffs on quick."[17] *Handcuffs* became a metaphor that thrilled the public, with its suggestion of rough justice and a leveling of the mighty. It worked its way into several anonymous newspaper threats leaked by government officials.

Blunden called in Sir Leslie O'Brien, the former Bank of England governor who had set up the Takeover Panel and, ironically, chastised Morgan Grenfell a generation earlier for its behavior in Gallaher–American Tobacco and *News of the World* battles. In an odd turnaround, O'Brien was now on Morgan Grenfell's International Advisory Council. Blunden laid down the law, citing Section 17 of the Banking Act, which gave the Bank of England authority to oust officials for imprudently managing a bank. This apparently didn't have the desired effect on Reeves and Walsh. The firm issued a statement denying any further dismissals.

Now Thatcher began to pressure Nigel Lawson, chancellor of the Exchequer, to draw more blood from the Guinness affair. In an extraordinary intervention, she reportedly told Lawson, "I want Reeves and Walsh out today, not next week or next month, but by lunchtime today." This was duly communicated to the Bank of England and transmitted, in turn, to a Morgan Grenfell delegation led by Lord Catto. In the office of Robin Leigh-Pemberton, governer of the Bank of England, the Morgan men were bluntly warned that if certain actions weren't taken, Lawson would appear before the House of Commons to announce that the government was selecting a new Morgan Grenfell management. Afterwards, Catto and Sir Peter Carey, a Morgan director, met with Reeves and Walsh who were, as a Morgan Grenfell official phrased it, "politely forced out."[18] As Thatcher had demanded, the heads rolled by lunchtime. It was a breathtaking reversal: the free-market prime minister striking down the City's most entrepreneurial firm in the worst disaster to hit a City firm in many years. A columnist for London's *Financial Times*, reflecting on the double disaster of the Collier and Guinness scandals, said, "It seems that there can be no end to the disasters that the market can dream up (or wish upon) Morgan."[19]

The Guinness scandal had broad repercussions for the City. There were parliamentary calls to crack down on the bankers. As part of Big Bang, the government had set up a new Securities and Investment Board to oversee a cluster of self-regulatory groups. After Guinness, reformers wanted to toughen up the SIB, making it more like the SEC and less of a City-dominated body. There were proposals to outlaw guarantees for third parties who bought shares during a takeover (the "Seelig clause") and to avert share buying by companies with a commercial stake in the outcome (the "Riklis clause," after Meshulam Riklis of Schenley Industries). The City shifted further from the old-boy network to a strictly policed financial center.

Awaiting the outcome of the interminable government investigations, Morgan Grenfell found itself in a terrible limbo. In May 1987, Ernest Saunders was arrested for allegedly destroying and fabricating Guinness documents. Later that year, Roger Seelig was arrested and charged with faking £2.5 million in invoices that were used, at least in part, as covers to indemnify members of the "fan club." Seelig was further charged with conspiring to create a false market and stealing £1 million from Guinness two weeks after the Department of Trade and Industry's first raid on Morgan Grenfell in early December, 1986. Five other prominent City figures were arrested.

That year, the Takeover Panel ruled that Guinness had violated the code in the Distillers battle. This later made Guinness liable for compensatory payments of £85 million to former Distillers shareholders.

Guinness could survive such a blow. But if the company turned around and filed a counterclaim against Morgan Grenfell, the smaller bank would clearly stagger. Throughout the DTI investigations, Morgan Grenfell officials lived with this constant nightmare; it was feasible that Guinness could deliver a mortal blow.

Short of such an outcome, however, it didn't seem that Guinness would do lethal damage. The firm's long-time rival, Warburgs, stepped briskly over its bleeding body to gain the number-one takeover spot, but Morgan Grenfell clung to second place in 1987. Looking only at publicly quoted companies, it actually remained in first place that year. Clients generally stuck by the firm, and there was no mass defection of staff. Perhaps most upset were the Third World countries that dealt with Morgan Grenfell for its classy aura and now had a tainted banker.

For several months in early 1987, Morgan Grenfell remained a ward of the Bank of England, which installed Sir Peter Carey—a short, mustachioed, highly respected former civil servant—as chairman. The firm could no longer indulge its takeover stars and give them free rein. Committees, bureaucracy, regimentation—these were the necessary correctives. Guinness exposed an absence of strong leadership and the managerial defects of an "oligarchy" that ran the firm like a private partnership. These older executives seemed a universe apart from the young takeover artists. As merger specialists were now subordinated to more organizational discipline, some people quit, notably George ("Teddy") Magan and much of the takeover team in New York.

"They were putting a saddle on a horse that never had one," said one departing star. "It had been an organic, free-wheeling organization of entrepreneurial spirit. People had booked into that. The most buccaneering of merchant banks started forming committees. But it was a franchise that hadn't been built on caution and procedures and checks and balances. Reeves and Walsh had created a magic bubble, a hothouse, and there wasn't the opportunity to do that anymore." Many people in Britain would have said "Amen."

Shortly after the takeover, a Morgan Grenfell official had told the press, "No man of the calibre of Ernest Saunders is going to employ Morgan Grenfell if we just tell him that Takeover Panel rules suggest that something can't be done."[20] This habit of bending or rewriting the rules had been growing remorselessly for twenty years. Now it had led Morgan Grenfell straight over the precipice. The Morgan name had always been synonymous with integrity and trust. Now, with Guinness, it became a byword for scandal in the modern City.

BULL

• •

•

WALL Street in the Reagan era self-consciously retraced the experience of the 1920s. Commentators noted eerie parallels between
the decades—a booming stock market, Republican tax cuts, a Latin
American debt crisis, fluctuating currencies, a merger wave, trade wars,
farm and energy slumps. Fed chairman Paul Volcker served up the
disinflation tonic, much as Ben Strong had in the 1920s, and the world
suddenly swam in cash. Newspapers superimposed stock market graphs
from the Coolidge and Hoover days onto those of the Reagan years,
comforting bulls and bears alike. As in the 1920s, sages said old value
measures were outdated and again worried about a shortage of common
stock. The speculative froth on Wall Street was again regarded as a sign
of economic dynamism.

In the 1920s, the United States was the world's chief creditor, a rising
power with a bulging trade surplus. Armed with superior technology,
American companies expanded around the globe. But the heady Wall
Street of the 1980s masked America's declining economic position relative to that of Japan and Europe. Thanks to Reagan's tax cuts and budget
deficits, the United States became a net borrower from the world. The
stock market frenzy neither enhanced American competitiveness nor
trimmed the trade deficits, which had been persistent since the early
1970s. Morning headlines screamed of billion-dollar deals that were
supposed to improve the economy, but they never seemed to strengthen
America's position in world markets.

As Wall Street returned to favor, America's youth flocked to the
casino. By 1986, one of every ten Yale College graduates applied for a
job at First Boston and over 30 percent of Harvard Business School
graduates ended up at Morgan Stanley; Goldman, Sachs; Merrill Lynch;

or First Boston. They came to a world that had little in common with the sedate, gentlemanly Wall Street of the early postwar years. Even the name now seemed a misnomer. "Except for Brown Brothers Harriman," said Martin Turchin of Edward S. Gordon Company, "I can't think of a major investment banking firm that has its headquarters on Wall Street."[1] They had all trailed their clients uptown.

The Reagan years saw the demise of relationship banking and with it the end of grace and civility on Wall Street. Wall Street was tougher, meaner, smarter, and more macho than ever before. The leisurely syndicate world faded after Rule 415, and the Gentleman Banker's Code was fully obsolete. As the taboo against raiding clients and making cold calls broke down, investment bankers clashed with one another. There was no longer any agreed-upon etiquette to temper the greedy impulses that always existed in finance. Wall Street was run by bright, young executives who seemed curiously devoid of larger political or social concerns in their narrow pursuit of profits.

In 1985, Morgan Stanley named Eric Gleacher to succeed Joe Fogg as head of Mergers and Acquisitions; at Lehman Brothers Kuhn Loeb, Gleacher had been Adrian Antoniu's boss. A short, trim former marine commander of a rifle platoon, he had an MBA from the University of Chicago, believed in a gung-ho takeover style, and ran his department with martial discipline. Called a "steel wall" at the bargaining table, he had tremendous stamina and skied, golfed, and ran marathons in his spare time. Through Gleacher, Morgan Stanley would branch out from takeovers in behalf of blue-chip corporations to more direct involvement with corporate raiders. For example, Gleacher recruited as a Morgan Stanley client the cigar-smoking Ronald O. Perelman, who acquired Revlon Incorporated in a bitter 1985 fight.

In his merger factory, Gleacher had a team of ten bright young people who did nothing but cook up deals for the firm to sell to clients. In 1978, Bob Greenhill had said that Morgan Stanley was simply executing clients' deals, not iniating them.[2] Now passivity was scrapped: every deal announced in the morning newspaper was studied for a profit angle. Each morning, the ten high-priced well-educated dreamers lined up outside Gleacher's office to pitch their ideas in rapid-fire style. When a subordinate brought a three-inch-thick notebook full of figures for a possible deal, Gleacher dropped it in the wastebasket. "Come back when you know what you're talking about," he said.[3]

Wall Street no longer seemed subservient to corporate clients or simply the executor of their wishes; it had assumed a disturbing life of its own. Far from taking his cues from clients, Gleacher believed "deal makers should never take no for an answer," asserted *Fortune*.[4] The magazine told how he had badgered Robert Cizik of Cooper Industries in Houston into buying McGraw Edison. "Let me fly down and talk to you," Gleacher had said on a cold call. "It's my nickel."[5] His persuasive presentation the next day convinced Cooper Industries to make the $1-billion acquisition, netting Morgan Stanley $4 million. Gleacher also convinced Pantry Pride to take over Revlon, bringing in $30 million in fees in a Ronald O. Perelman raid financed by a flood of junk bonds. A decade earlier, naive bankers had trembled to ask for a $1-million fee.

The portion of corporate America now passing through the merger mills was staggering. Morgan Stanley handled $8.5 billion in merger transactions in 1982. Within two years, that figure zoomed to a record $52 billion. After some backsliding under Fogg, Morgan Stanley nosed out the First Boston team of Bruce Wasserstein and Joe Perella in 1985 to recover first place in merger work, booking an awesome $82 million in fees and giving Morgan Stanley Wall Street's highest return on equity. In the four years leading up to the 1987 crash, Morgan Stanley was involved in $238 billion worth of mergers and acquisitions. As Joe Flom would say in 1989, "We've gone through the most massive corporate restructuring in history over a period of 15 years."[6] The figures were now so fantastic that they seemed to have dazed and stupefied the public.

Many deals were spurred by needed change. At a time of technological flux, mature companies had to transfer money from dying industries to thriving ones. Foreign competition and deregulation were stimulating radical shifts in hitherto protected industries, including airlines, telecommunications, energy, media, and finance itself. Investment banks were the agents for the global integration of markets, much as they had welded together national markets in the era of Pierpont Morgan.

But too many deals seemed to be hatched by investment banks and corporate raiders merely for self-enrichment. The prototypical 1980s raiders—Boone Pickens, Carl Icahn, and Sir James Goldsmith—talked self-righteously about "cleansing" or "liberating" companies from "entrenched management." They claimed target companies were the victims of a harsh, Darwinian necessity, implying that they were invariably poorly run companies. Yet in 1978, before this became the party line, Bob Greenhill had said, "The acquiring companies are not simply looking for bargains, or corporations in trouble. Typically, they are interested in well-managed companies."[7] This was often the case.

Aside from the painful dislocations suffered by towns and workers, as a result of mergers, the takeover flurry penalized companies with clean balance sheets, little debt, and lots of cash. To stay independent, they had to cripple themselves by loading up on debt. The old Morgan Stanley had favored sound, conservative finance and was protective of the credit ratings of clients. The new Morgan Stanley stampeded companies into taking on debt, whether to conduct raids or to ward them off.

The firm's M&A people dismissed the existence of any problem. In 1986, with nationwide takeovers running at a robust $200 billion a year, Eric Gleacher said, "When you look at the debt of the world, the debt of the country, and the debt of the private sector, you can't with a straight face tell me that a few speculative merger deals are going to tip the balance and create disaster?"[8] Note that Gleacher doesn't praise the debt: it's more of a defensive everybody-is-doing-it kind of argument. There were also now more than "a few speculative merger deals." In 1970, only 10 takeover deals passed the million-dollar mark; by 1986, the figure had surged to 346 in a wave of consolidations that engulfed the economy.

Joe Fogg similarly had dismissed any problem. When asked whether the debt binge wasn't draining capital from productive uses, he called that notion "very silly and superficial. . . . The fact is, acquisition transactions merely reflect a change in ownership of capital assets. The money does not disappear. It is then used for other investments."[9] This was surely true of money changing hands in a takeover. But how was that additional takeover money raised in the first place? Typically by bank loans or junk bonds whose interest payments then siphoned off money from productive investment. This bias in favor of debt was strikingly at odds with the old Morgan Stanley, whose culture Bob Baldwin had described as "risk-averse" as recently as 1980.

Merger mania on Wall Street produced a stunning paradox in the 1980s: corporations grew financially weaker during the sustained Reagan boom. By the 1987 crash, nonfinancial corporate debt stood at a record $1.8 trillion, with companies diverting fifty cents of every dollar of earnings to pay off creditors—a far greater percentage than in earlier years. It was hard to see how corporate America could weather a severe recession without unspeakable destruction. As in the Jazz Age, much of the era's financial prestidigitation seemed premised on an unspoken assumption of perpetual prosperity, an end to cyclical economic fluctuations, and a curious faith in the Federal Reserve Board's ability to avert disaster.

Not surprisingly, Morgan Stanley was drawn to that most lucrative of 1980s fads—the leveraged buyout, or LBO. As a dangerous form of leverage, LBOs rivaled the pyramidal holding companies of the 1920s.

In a basic LBO, a company's managers and a group of outside investors borrow money to acquire a company and take it private; the company's own assets are used as collateral for the loans, which are repaid from future earnings or asset sales. (Interest payments, significantly, are tax deductible.) In the 1970s, they were called "bootstrap financings" and seldom exceeded $100,000. André Meyer of Lazard Frères had taken equity stakes for years, but Wall Street didn't take notice until 1979, when First Boston did an LBO for a conglomerate called Congoleum. LBOs became popular as the conglomerates of the 1960s were dismantled and managers took over pieces of them. They became rampant as a byproduct of takeovers, with managers resorting to them to fend off raiders or even flush them out. The LBO was thus a natural sequel to the merger wave.

With its unerring instinct for profitable activities, Morgan Stanley noted the LBO profits at First Boston and Merrill Lynch. In 1985, it joined with CIGNA Insurance to create a leveraged buyout fund. It struck spectacular deals that made merger profits look like small change in comparison. In 1986, it joined with an Irish paperboard concern, Jefferson Smurfit, to purchase Container Corporation of America from Mobil for $1.2 billion. Morgan and Jefferson put up only $10 million apiece, borrowing the rest. Morgan Stanley pocketed a fast $32.4 million: $11 million for arranging the buyout, $20.4 million for underwriting nearly $700 million in junk bonds to effect the purchase, and a $1-million advisory fee. Such fees recalled investment banks feasting on new trust issues at the turn of the century. In LBOs, the target company suffered the pain and carried the risk, having to sell assets and cut costs to pay off the debt. Meanwhile, as a limited partnership, the Morgan Stanley buyout fund couldn't lose more than its tiny, original $10-million investment. The risks were remarkably limited in view of the enormous potential profits. And only three years later, Morgan's $10 million stake was worth $140 million.

Soon afterward, Morgan Stanley helped Kohlberg Kravis Roberts, the leading LBO firm, take over Owens-Illinois for $4.2 billion. Again it scored triple fees, this time of $54 million. Even though it had only $1.5 billion in capital, Morgan Stanley made a temporary $600-million bridge loan to effect the deal. (What bank would have gotten away with *that?* Yet investment banks could bypass SEC safeguards by issuing bridge loans through their holding companies.) Where the old Morgan Stanley minimized its capital risk and remained a financial intermediary, the new Morgan Stanley was gambling more of its capital in a new push into "merchant banking." Although Wall Street relished the historical associations of the term, it bore little resemblance to the mercantile financing engaged in by George Peabody and Junius Morgan. It simply referred to management buyouts, taking equity stakes in takeovers, or making temporary bridge loans to finance takeovers.

In 1986, to raise capital for these new activities and strengthen its position in world capital markets, Morgan Stanley sold 20 percent of its shares to the public. There was a wonderful irony here: it went public so it could take other companies private. To give these shares global distribution, a third of them were sold to buyers outside North America. The shares were offered in-house at $15.33, with the allotted number per person determined by a complex formula based partly on the amount an employee already had invested in the firm. On its inaugural day, the Morgan Stanley stock jumped from $56.50 a share to $71.25. This netted over $250 million for the firm and created instant fortunes for those irrevent young men who had transformed the firm in the early 1970s. Parker Gilbert had 772,133 shares worth $57.3 million by day's end (a rich reward for a compromise chairman); Dick Fisher had 729,-574 shares ($54.1 million); Bob Greenhill, 710,275 ($52.7 million); and Lewis Bernard, 673,521 ($50 million). With its public offering, Morgan Stanley lost one of its last links to the past. It was now a vast, publicly traded company, with 114 managing directors (including its first female), 148 limited partners, and 4,000 employees worldwide. The firm now employed an astonishing number of multimillionaires. Only Goldman, Sachs remained an old-fashioned Wall Street partnership, and even it sold a stake to Sumitomo of Japan.

Bolstered by its public offering, Morgan Stanley pushed ahead with merchant banking. The next year, it launched the Morgan Stanley Leveraged Equity Fund II, with Tom Saunders eventually rounding up a $2.2 billion war chest, the largest ever assembled by a major investment bank and second in the world after that of Kohlberg Kravis Roberts. In its new dual role, Morgan Stanley would both manage the fund and invest $225 million of its own capital in it. As with hostile takeovers and junk bonds, Morgan Stanley took an activity of questionable benefit and made it acceptable in elite circles. It enlisted sixty institutions for its fund, including the General Motors and AT&T pension funds, Japanese trust companies, Middle East government agencies, Volvo, Barclays Bank, and several American commercial banks. Not only would Morgan Stanley receive about a third of the capital gains from the fund, but it would also skim off a 2-percent fee for managing the money. This was only the beginning, as the huge leveraged buyout of Burlington Industries would show.

In early April 1987, reports surfaced that raider Asher B. Edelman was accumulating stock in Burlington, the largest textile company in America, based in Greensboro, North Carolina. Frank Greenberg, Burlington's chief executive, cast about for a "white knight" to ward off Edelman and his partner, Dominion Textile of Canada. In a meticulous reconstruction of events published in an August 1987 issue of *Barron's*, Benjamin J. Stein chronicled what happened next. On April 15, thirty-two-year-old Alan E. Goldberg of Morgan Stanley telephoned Greenberg and said Morgan would be interested in buying Burlington while retaining current management. In a follow-up letter of April 21, Bob Greenhill reinforced the naked appeal to Greenberg's self-interest, saying, "We would have no interest in proceeding except upon a basis agreed to by your management."[10] At an April 29 meeting with Greenberg, Morgan Stanley laid out plans to give management a 10-percent stake in the buyout, plus another 10 percent if certain performance standards were met.

Facing a clear-cut choice between a hostile raider, who threatened his livelihood, and the Morgan LBO fund, enticing him with lucrative incentives, could Frank Greenberg render a fair, impartial judgment for his shareholders? As Benjamin Stein noted, Morgan Stanley customarily dangled before management promises of salary increases ranging from 50 percent to 125 percent after a buyout. In this tempting situation, Greenberg granted some exceptional concessions to Morgan Stanley. He agreed to give Morgan a $24-million "break-up" fee in the event it failed to acquire Burlington. Morgan Stanley justified this princely fee by citing interest it would allegedly forgo by locking up capital during the talks. Yet, as Stein noted, Morgan Stanley had no capital at risk until the takeover's completion—and then only $125 million of its own money. The break-up fee, however, worked out to interest that would have accrued on *$7 billion* over a two-week period. As Stein concluded, "The 'breakup' fee could be understood only as a form of payoff to Morgan from its *partners* on the Burlington board for being included in the deal in the unlikely event that the deal cratered. It simply made no sense otherwise."[11] Greenberg waited until mid-May before disclosing his secret talks with Morgan Stanley, which was privy to company secrets denied Asher Edelman and Dominion. It was hard to see how both bidder groups were being accorded equal treatment.

In late June, the Morgan Stanley group made a bid of $78 a share, or about $2.4 billion, for Burlington, defeating the Edelman raid. It got about a third of America's largest textile company for only $125 million and even most of that came from Bankers Trust and Equitable Life

Assurance. It also earned $80 million in fees, including profits from underwriting almost $2 billion in junk bonds to finance the deal. Did Burlington profit equally with Morgan Stanley from this financial alchemy? Before the buyout, the firm had a clean balance sheet, with debt less than half the value of common shareholders' equity. When the LBO went through, the company suddenly struggled with over $3 billion in debt, or *thirty times* as much debt as equity. It subsequently had to fire hundreds of middle-level managers, sell off the most advanced denim factory in the world (ironically, to Dominion Textile), close its research and development center, and starve its capital budget to $50 million for a five-year period. All this not only upset the lives of Burlington employees, but drastically weakened the firm's ability to compete in global markets.

By the last quarter of 1987, Burlington Industries was losing money despite higher earnings from operations. Why? It had to pay $66 million in interest for the quarter. LBO defenders praised these high levels of debt as stimulating management to greater effort—an argument reminiscent of Dr. Johnson's observation that hanging wonderfully concentrates the mind. Did companies have to stare at the gallows to perform better? Most cost cutting and asset sales that followed LBOs weren't designed to improve company performance; they were just steps to pay for the LBOs and were often unnecessary without them. Many LBOs were quick bets on the bust-up values of firms rather than serious attempts to run a company for many years.

LBO supporters claimed that owners were more enterprising than managers and didn't have to attend slavishly to their stock prices. The claim was parroted at every turn. "An enormous amount of management time in this country is devoted to managing the market price of the shares," said Tom Saunders of Morgan Stanley. Yet for years, Bob Greenhill, Joe Fogg, and Eric Gleacher had warned companies to get up their share prices—or else. Who created that preoccupation with share prices and quarterly earnings from which companies were now being rescued? Ironically, many LBO specialists were being transferred over from merger work, where they suddenly had to adopt a long-term perspective. This defense also sounded odd coming from a firm that had managed the initial public offering of several companies in the 1980s. Finally, it ignored the simple fact that the objective of taking companies private was to take them public at a later date and reap a quick killing. Presumably, the firms would then tout the benefits of public ownership.

There were profound political and social issues at stake in the LBO fad. Participants hailed the trend as a return to the "good old days" when bankers put their own capital at risk. They didn't look closely at that history and the conflicts of interest that had resulted from excessive cosiness between bankers and the companies they financed. As we have seen, it took decades of agitation and reform to fulfill Louis Brandeis's vision of investment bankers' having an arm's-length relationship with companies. This had been the purpose of endless investigations—Pujo, Pecora, and Wheeler—as well as the purpose of the Medina suit and various government measures to mandate competitive bidding in railroads and utilities. Just when the 1982 Rule 415 had seemed to end the problem of banker-company collusion, investment banks reinvented it with merchant banking. It was no coincidence that Morgan Stanley's entry into merchant banking occurred after the advent of Rule 415, for through LBOs it could restore the exclusive relationships lost in the transactional age. What better hold to have on a company than to own a large piece of it? Three of the five Burlington board members were suddenly Morgan Stanley managing directors.

The merger of industry and finance had made some sense in the Baronial Age and had given some stability to the American economy. Companies were then weak and had difficulty tapping capital markets, especially abroad. Only the banker's reputation could reassure skittish creditors. That was no longer the case in the Casino Age, when companies were often better known than bankers. Burlington Industries needed no introduction to investors. The new merchant banking also differed from the old-fashioned relationship banking of the 1950s, when Wall Street firms had a purely advisory role and could provide objective advice. If the old Morgan Stanley had a firm grip on its clients, it also had no built-in temptation to mislead or abuse them.

The LBO trend ensnared investment banks in another set of potential conflicts of interest. Were they now advisers or investors? Were the roles of principal and agent compatible? LBOs put investment banks into the position of competing against their underwriting clients. After Morgan Stanley added Fort Howard Paper to a portfolio that already included the Container Corporation of America, its paper-industry clients were aghast. David J. McKittrick, the chief financial officer of James River, had used Morgan Stanley to manage a number of stock offerings. "We have looked with concern at Morgan Stanley's increasing equity position in the paper industry," he said.[12] There were similar problems with takeover clients. If Morgan Stanley's merger people spied an undervalued company, should they take it to a client or keep it for the firm? And if they recommended an LBO to a company, could they claim objectivity when the firm stood to make windfall profits in advisory fees and junk bond underwritings? According to one report, CIGNA insurance stayed away from the second Morgan Stanley LBO fund from a belief that the firm was chasing "elephant" deals that would generate giant fees.

People at Morgan Stanley recognized the potential problem but too quickly waved it away. "Our business is full of conflicts," said Dick Fisher. "In an industry as integrated as ours, I don't see how they can be avoided."[13] He noted that if Morgan Stanley scouted a company for a client, that client had first crack. But what if the firm spied an opportunity on its own initiative? Was its first loyalty to its clients? Or to its shareholders? Bob Greenhill replied, "The first party that steps forward is the client; we talked to several companies about Burlington, but none were interested. The point is, because of our tradition, we bend over backwards to accommodate our traditional clients."[14] So Morgan Stanley would save the scraps for itself and only take deals rejected by everybody else? Wall Street was now tangled so deep in ethical thickets that it could no longer fight its way out.

THE parallel with the 1920s had its inevitable sequel on October 19, 1987, when the Dow Jones industrial average fell 508 points. Some $500 billion in paper value—equal to the gross national product of France—vanished, though there were no untoward scenes at the Corner or mobs of ruined investors. No stock brokers executed swan dives from high ledges. Seventy percent of stock trading was now done by institutions—mutual funds, pension funds, and the like—which were averse to theatrics and tracked the market on computer screens. Depression, migraine headaches, even sexual impotence were later reported among investors, but no aerial artistry as in 1929. Aside from a somewhat longer visitors' queue at the New York Stock Exchange, the Corner betrayed little sense of calamity on this Black Monday.

The Morgan houses were actually less remote from the 1987 crash than they'd been from the one in 1929. All the banks and brokerage houses were now trading operations. And Morgan Stanley was a major practitioner of stock-index arbitrage—computer-driven trades that exploited small price discrepancies between stocks in New York and stock-index futures in Chicago. Such transactions were blamed for wild market gyrations and even, unfairly, for the crash itself. In a secret, restricted computer room known as the Black Box for its sophisticated software—some programs forced traders to don 3-D glasses— fifty Morgan Stanley traders and analysts pored over information and scanned arbitrage opportunities. They took risks that would have harrowed Harold Stanley's soul. On September 11, 1986, after the market suffered a steep drop, Morgan Stanley, gambling on an upturn, had bought *$1 billion* in stock futures and suffered enormous losses. Such futures-related trading reintroduced leverage into the market that the government thought it had stamped out with stiffer margin requirements in the 1930s.

From 1984 to 1987, stock prices had risen without a 10-percent correction. This cheered bulls, muzzled bears, and blinded people to warning signals. Following exactly the 1929 pattern, the bond market slumped in the spring of 1987, and the Federal Reserve raised the discount rate in September. In early October, Morgan Stanley, fearing clients would miss the next leg of the bull market, exhorted them to be *100-percent* invested in common stock. Later, when it sent financial commentator Adam Smith an exuberant buy recommendation, he mused, "You had me one hundred percent invested in October and I lost half my money. How am I supposed to buy something now?"[15]

Where 1929 was a home-grown American crash, 1987 was a global panic. Around the world, stocks rose, crashed, then rebounded together. The same financial deregulation that had interlaced markets led to synchronized drops in Tokyo, Hong Kong, New York, London, Paris, and Zurich. "For days everyone just kept passing the bear market around the time clock," said Barton Biggs of Morgan Stanley. New links among world stock markets seemed to exaggerate movements in both directions, accentuating the instability of the world financial system instead of ironing out fluctuations.

From the standpoint of Morgan history, the significant aspect of Black Monday was the lack of any overt role in a rescue. *That* was the big script difference from 1929—the absence of a bankers' rescue. President Reagan, eager to echo Hoover, said, "the underlying economy remains sound."[16] John Phelan, the New York Stock Exchange chairman, played the Richard Whitney role, debating with advisers about whether to close the Exchange. There were again stock buybacks and early Exchange closings to deal with paperwork. But no bankers marched up the steps of 23 Wall. Phelan consulted mostly with William Schreyer of Merrill Lynch and John Gutfreund of Salomon Brothers—not with Morgan Stanley—reflecting the new importance of trading and retail houses, rank outsiders to the club in 1929.

The Federal Reserve moved with a dispatch that left no doubt as to its resolve. On October 20, Alan Greenspan issued a tersely effective statement affirming the Fed's "readiness to serve as a source of liquidity to support the economic and financial system."[17] The Fed bought dollars and engineered a sharp drop in interest rates. E. Gerald Corrigan, president of the New York Fed, personally pleaded with banks to continue lending to sound securities firms. Some New York Stock Exchange specialists ended Black Monday with bloated stock inventories as they tried to stem the decline, and they were floated by their chief lenders, including Morgan Guaranty, Manufacturers Hanover, and the Bank of New York. The Fed acted admirably; Wall Street no longer needed a House of Morgan, which couldn't have coped with a crisis of such magnitude. As Continental Illinois had showed, private rescues were passé in huge, unfettered global markets. There would never be another financier who bulked as large as Pierpont Morgan or Tom Lamont.

The crash exposed underwriting hazards of a sort forgotten during the bull market. In November 1987, when the British government sold its 32-percent stake in British Petroleum, investors couldn't absorb this mammoth $13.2-billion issue so soon after Black Monday. Four U.S. underwriters—Morgan Stanley; Goldman, Sachs; Salomon Brothers; and Shearson Lehman—stared at $350 million in paper losses. Disaster was averted when the Bank of England agreed to buy back shares at 70 pence per share. Higher oil prices and a Kuwaiti purchase of a 20-percent BP stake then rescued the Bank of England.

After the crash, Main Street again prayed that Wall Street had learned its lesson and gloated over its misery. "It's been a nice week for the have-nots of the world," said a GM auto worker. Stock brokers retired the haloes they had worn for several years. "Before the Crash," bemoaned one broker, "everyone wanted you to meet their daughter. Now we're the scum of the earth."[18] But the hobgoblins of sustained prosperity—consumerism, greed, and speculation—weren't to be slain so quickly. When a *Newsweek* cover asked, "IS THE PARTY OVER?" the unrepentant young staffers at Morgan Stanley used a copy of the glossy page as an invitation to a big bash, with the letters *NFW*—no fucking way—scrawled defiantly across the top.[19] Eric Gleacher, whose merger mill was grinding through two hundred deals at a time, asked, "Why shouldn't it go on?"[20] Morgan Stanley was proudly unscathed by the crash—it even offered to extend credit to one thunderstruck commercial bank—but the staff was shaken by a nearly 20-point drop in the firm's own newly issued stock.

Because the crash didn't usher in a recession, the public wasn't immediately galvanized into reform. Yet financial reform had lagged behind the 1929 crash by three to four years, arising only after prolonged Depression exposed the full economic consequences of the 1920s speculation. The closest analogy to the post-1929 outcry over pools and short selling was the controversy over computerized program trading. Once again there was a tendency to trace the crash to the internal mechanics of the market itself. In January 1988, Merrill Lynch, Shearson Lehman Hutton, and Goldman, Sachs suspended index arbitrage trading for their own accounts. But Morgan Stanley didn't need to worry about angry small investors and exhibited its new renegade stance, despite the fact that Parker Gilbert was a governor of the New York Stock Exchange. It suspended its own "proprietary" program trading only after pressure from Congressman Edward J. Markey's Subcommittee on Telecommunications and Finance. It was also notified by Maurice R. Greenberg, chief executive of the American International Group, a New York insurer, that his firm would cease business with houses that persisted in stock-index arbitrage for their own accounts.

On May 10, 1988, in a splashy coordinated effort, Morgan Stanley, Salomon Brothers, Bear Stearns, Paine Webber, and Kidder, Peabody announced they would stop the practice. Morgan Stanley had apparently orchestrated the move by alerting the others to its plans. Blocked from program trading in the United States, Morgan Stanley then went to Japan that December and caused a furor by introducing the practice there, spurring the Tokyo exchange to a record high. In 1989, it unabashedly led the resumption of program trading among the major firms after only a nine-month hiatus. The question of whether program trading increases volatility is complex and unresolved. What is worth noting is Morgan Stanley's apparent disregard of public opinion and greater willingness to defy financial authorities—behavior conspicuously at odds with Morgan Guaranty's strong sense of corporate citizenship.

If Main Street hoped that Black Monday would throw a cautionary fear into Wall Street, it was dead wrong. It only prodded the Street into more assertive, reckless behavior. Securities firms had already lost many safe, reliable businesses. Brokerage commissions dropped after Mayday in 1975 and underwriting margins shrank after Rule 415 in 1982. Now trading profits plunged with the crash, creating a large contraction in Wall Street and City employment. Mergers already accounted for half of Wall Street's profits, and with the decline of other opportunities, the attraction to such business became irresistible. To help things along, the crash and a weaker dollar created bargain prices for takeovers. And if raiders didn't materialize, Wall Street was prepared to do the raids itself through its new merchant-banking departments and junk bond syndicates.

So many companies had already passed through the merger mill that it was becoming harder to find suitable candidates. Everybody was scrutinizing the same lists, often with the same techniques. One solution was to target industries that by law or custom had been immune to hostile takeovers. Eric Gleacher, and all of Morgan Stanley, now overturned a sacred financial taboo: thou shalt not mount a hostile raid against a bank. It was always thought such raids might shake depositor confidence or jeopardize the dividends of the proverbial widows and orphans who held bank stock. So in the past, bank mergers were either friendly or forced on troubled banks by regulatory authorities.

Shortly before the crash, this etiquette was shattered when the Bank of New York launched a $1-billion raid against Irving Trust. It was a clash of two hoary institutions steeped in history. The Bank of New York was founded by Alexander Hamilton and his associates in 1784—no other bank had operated so long with the same name—while Irving was named after Washington Irving and dated from the mid-nineteenth century. The Bank of New York was advised by Eric Gleacher of Morgan Stanley and H. Rodgin Cohen of Sullivan and Cromwell and Irving Trust by Goldman, Sachs and Morgan Guaranty.

The year-long battle showed just how vicious and merciless Wall Street had become. These were genteel, old-line banks, the sort that pampered rich, elderly clients. Irving was so sleepy that it had sat out the trend for foreign-exchange trading that was a boon to other commercial banks. It seldom fired people and usually gave everybody a fat Christmas bonus equal to 15 percent of salary.

Bank of New York chairman J. Carter Bacot initiated the Irving raid because he feared his own bank would be swallowed by another firm. In their gorgeous art deco headquarters at 1 Wall Street, Irving executives first scoffed at the bid, sure the Fed would never countenance a hostile bank takeover. Gleacher and Cohen correctly predicted that Fed chairman Alan Greenspan would break the precedent. The Bank of New York stalked Irving with lawsuits, proxy fights, and strident exchanges of press releases. After the Bank of New York won, Gleacher quickly threw fear across the economic landscape, telling the press the hostile fight was "a precursor of things to come."[21] The Bank of New York had promised to pay for the takeover through normal attrition. By early 1989, it had begun to fire one hundred people from the foreign side. As an Irving executive said: "The bloodbath has begun."[22] No form of financial marauding was any longer off-limits to Morgan Stanley.

IN the wake of Black Monday, a new spirit was also blowing through 23 Wall. As it evolved from a purely commercial bank into a novel hybrid with many investment banking activities, its character changed.

At an opulent postcrash Christmas party, Lew Preston said he was pleased to see so many spouses present, because now they would know that their husbands and wives would be working late over the coming year. At a second reception the next evening, he said he wanted to make sure everyone could hear him because the night before "some people didn't hear me and went home happy."[23] As if to underscore new perils facing the bank, Moody's Investors Service dropped its triple-A rating for J. P. Morgan and Company, the holding company of Morgan Guaranty. Standard and Poor's kept its triple-A rating for the holding company, and both still honored Morgan Guaranty Trust with the only triple-A rating for a large American bank. Moody's action was a small, but noticeable dent in Morgan's shining armor.

As J. P. Morgan and Company grew into a fifteen-thousand-person conglomerate, it tried to preserve the old partnership flavor. New management trainees underwent a rigorous six-month training program meant to acculturate them to the bank. Rarely did 23 Wall recruit from outside, and it spent millions annually on free lunches to promote camaraderie. There remained an ethic of not stealing credit or upstaging colleagues. "The Morgan feeling of collegiality is the most important thing we've got," said former Morgan president Rod Lindsay. Preston regularly sent memos admonishing employees that they worked for clients and the bank, not for themselves. In Lindsay's words, "We don't want people if they're going to be by themselves at the top of the list all the time."[24]

Morgan Guaranty had been much more respectful of tradition than Morgan Stanley or Morgan Grenfell and was recognizably the heir of the old, aristocratic House of Morgan. Yet its unique civility was threatened. The bank was engaged in a full dress rehearsal for the day when it would again be a "universal" bank, like the old House of Morgan. At home, it fused commercial lending and capital market activities into a corporate finance group that was an embryonic investment bank. It specialized in "deals that are sufficiently complex that they don't lend themselves to the commercial paper market," according to Preston.[25] It milked every legal securities business. It dealt in Treasury bonds, underwrote municipal bonds, advised cities, provided stock research and brokerage, and traded in gold bullion, silver, and foreign exchange. It continued to have the fanciest private banking operation, wooing rich customers with ads that promised to relieve their anxiety about possessing $50-million portfolios.

Abroad, Morgans stepped up capital market activity, specializing in interest-rate swaps, currency swaps, and other financial esoterica. It had merchant banks in Japan, Hong Kong, Belgium, and Germany. In London, the headquarters of its global capital markets operation, it spent $500 million to outfit two historic buildings near the Thames—the vacant Guildhall School of Music and Drama and the City of London School for Girls—with vast trading floors. Eventually fifteen hundred employees would work beneath stained-glass windows and timbered ceilings, flanked by busts of Shakespeare and Milton. As Preston noted ruefully, "We may be in the ironic position of becoming a global securities firm without being able to underwrite in our own market."[26]

To mark its emancipation from commercial banking, the House of Morgan increasingly substituted J. P. Morgan in its advertising for Morgan Guaranty, the old—and now shrinking—bank core. Morgan Guaranty Limited in London was rechristened J. P. Morgan Securities. Morgans had to reconstitute commercial bankers as deal makers and market men. It probably spent more on educating employees than any other bank. "We run almost a small university here," said group executive Robert Engel.[27] The bank hoped to maintain its gentlemanly culture by being brainy and innovative. Yet it wasn't clear that new products could be peddled with the old style. A lending officer could be a gentleman or a lady. But what about a currency trader? A takeover artist?

Takeover work was the acid test of the new Morgans. Until the late 1960s, it had provided such advice *gratis* as part of a total package. This informal operation—just a file on buyers and sellers—was offered to clients in exchange for million-dollar deposits. As early as 1973, Morgans had tried to systematize this and even picked up a $600,000 fee for arranging the takeover of Gimbel Brothers by British-American Tobacco. But the operation never got off the ground. As with Morgan Stanley, the bank was hampered by its long client list and found it hard to represent one client without injuring another. As a commercial bank, it still wanted to please everybody.

The problem was glaringly exposed in 1979, when American Express attempted to take over the McGraw-Hill publishing empire. AmEx chairman James D. Robinson III—a Morgan alumnus who'd been an assistant to Tom Gates when he was chairman in the 1960s—turned to the bank to finance the takeover. At first, Robinson thought he could arrange a friendly merger. Instead, he touched off a furious reaction from Harold W. McGraw, Jr., who called in Yerger Johnstone of Morgan Stanley and defense lawyer Martin Lipton and unleashed a blistering counterattack.

McGraw picked up any brickbat at hand. He sued American Express for libel, said it cooperated with the Arab boycott of Israel, asked the Federal Communications Commission and the Federal Trade Commission to study antitrust problems, chastised American Express as a menace to the First Amendment, and raised a dozen other issues, bogus and legitimate. In the ultimate slap, McGraw chided American Express for not paying interest on the float from its traveler's checks.

American Express had planned to borrow $700 million for the merger, with Morgan Guaranty as lead banker. This outraged McGraw, who considered himself a faithful Morgan client. In 1977, Morgan chairman Pat Patterson had thrown a lunch for McGraw to commemorate the fiftieth anniversary of the publisher's relationship with the bank. In his desk drawer, McGraw still kept a sterling silver cigar box he had received on that occasion.

Now McGraw wondered aloud whether Robinson had deliberately chosen Morgans to rob him of his banker and whether Morgans had leaked confidential information to Robinson. He denounced AmEx for using "its financial power to cause a bank to violate its relationship with a client."[28] It turned out the Morgan Trust Department held up to 1.8 million shares of McGraw-Hill stock in fiduciary accounts. To vote—or not to vote—the shares would hopelessly enmesh the bank in a conflict of interest. The proposed merger degenerated into such a noisy, unseemly squabble that American Express decided to quit, while Morgan Stanley collected a $1.5-million fee. It was hard to see how the omnipresent Morgan Guaranty could perform hostile takeovers without constantly stirring up a hornet's nest of lawsuits and client conflicts. At the same time, the bank's close relations with corporate clients created the potential for a formidable merger department.

In 1985, the Morgan bank formed a separate merger and acquisitions group, piloted by the Cuban-born, Yale-educated Roberto Mendoza. A big, brooding man with a slightly hooded gaze, he looked tougher and more determined than the average Morgan banker. He was more reminiscent of Morgan Stanley deal makers than of the sedate Morgan Guaranty bankers of old. A high-adrenaline type, he liked furious games of midnight tennis and drove his young charges to devise unorthodox deals. Mendoza thought investment banks were gouging clients and was willing to compete with them on price—perhaps the one taboo Wall Street still held sacred. He also thought high fees sometimes warped the judgment of investment bankers. Morgan Guaranty ran ads for its takeover group that needled the Street: "In M&A, clients who require totally objective advice, research free from conflict of interest . . . can rely on one firm. J. P. Morgan."[29] One ad showed an empty tombstone and said pointedly: "We don't promote M&A deals just to generate fees."[30] It would soon pay a price for these holier-than-thou ads.

The bank knew its genteel image hurt in the slash-and-burn takeover game. As Bob Engel said, "When a chairman wakes up in the middle of the night with a phone call from someone saying, 'We want to buy your company,' he thinks of Morgan Stanley instead of Morgan Guaranty. It's going to be a selling job, no question."[31] Besides the image problem, Morgans faced the reluctance of companies to share secrets with large lending institutions, which might have trouble preserving secrecy or might use information to deny future loans.

By the late 1980s, Preston and Mendoza stated publicly that Morgans would not only back unfriendly raids but might even finance both sides in a takeover, setting up opposing teams. Once J. P. Morgan and Company placed its authority behind hostile raids, Wall Street's transformation seemed complete. The situation was not unlike 1929, when the bank submitted to the fad of forming holding companies with the Alleghany and United Corporation promotions.

Before the crash, Mendoza's department scored small victories but no big, attention-getting deals. Then, in January 1988, Morgans became the first commercial bank to counsel a hostile raider in a billion-dollar deal, advising F. Hoffman–La Roche on its $4.2-billion tender offer for Sterling Drug. The Swiss pharmaceutical company, F. Hoffman–La Roche, did a $6-billion-a-year business. After its Valium patent expired in 1985, it needed new products in order to fill the sales pipeline. Sterling made Bayer aspirin, Phillips milk of magnesia, and many other products. With its cartellike cosiness, the pharmaceutical industry had been ruled by gentleman's agreements and spared bloody takeover wars. This was the first time a large pharmaceutical firm had made a hostile assault against a healthy competitor. Adding to the shock was that J. P. Morgan and Company had been a banker to Sterling Drug for more than fifty years.

Advised by Mendoza, Hoffman–La Roche followed a frenzied raiding strategy known as a bear hug. It made an opening bid of $72 a share for Sterling, then twice stepped up the bid in rapid succession without any formal rejection of the earlier offers. Sterling chairman John M. Pietruski had jolted his firm from its former lethargy and lifted its earnings to healthy double-digit levels. He was consequently irate at Hoffman–La Roche's overture and called in Joe Fogg of Morgan Stanley and Joe Flom of Skadden, Arps as advisers.

Taking a leaf from Harold McGraw, Pietruski let loose a blast that Morgan Guaranty wouldn't soon forget. In an open letter, he said he was "shocked and dismayed by what I consider to be Morgan bank's unethical conduct in aiding and abetting a surprise raid on one of its longtime clients." The bank, he said, was "privy to our most confidential financial information."[32] He laid out their ties of recent years, including borrowing, Morgan work as Sterling's registrar and transfer agent, and Morgan's management of Euromarket issues for Sterling. It was a clever broadside, for Pietruski echoed the language of the old Wall Street, as if shaming the bank with recollection: "How many relationships of trust and confidence do you have to have with a client before you consider not embarking on a course of action that could be detrimental to [his] best interest?"[33]

In an unusual public rejoinder, Lew Preston hinted that the letter was hypocritical bluster crafted by a publicist. "It's kind of interesting that we're still their transfer agent," he said afterward. When the battle was over, Preston elaborated: "That wasn't a letter from the chairman of Sterling. That was a letter written by the investment bankers to embarrass this firm."[34] He disputed the notion that Morgan betrayed a deeply loyal client, noting that Sterling's principal banker was Irving Trust and that 23 Wall had only performed "mechanical functions" for Sterling. For Preston, the surprise was less in the raising of the betrayal issue—obviously anticipated in planning for the takeover—than in the way that Wall Street ganged up to bad-mouth Morgan's handling of the deal.

Indeed, investment bankers believed that Hoffman had made too low an initial bid and only ended up drawing other sharks into the water. Morgan Stanley brought in Kodak as a friendly suitor, and it snatched Sterling away for $89.50 a share. Although Wall Street crowed that Morgan Guaranty had bungled the deal—the glee was scarcely disguised—the bank hinted that Kodak had overpaid. The price was high—twenty-two times Sterling's estimated 1988 earnings. The investment banks, of course, had a vested interest in denigrating the performance of Morgan Guaranty, which was poaching on their territory. They were especially incensed when Mendoza charged a paltry $1 million for the losing effort, surely the most unforgivable sin of all.

Clearly, Morgans considered Hoffman–La Roche a much closer and more profitable client than Sterling Drug. But was this to be the new standard for choosing targets? Would the bank feed off stronger clients at the expense of weaker ones? Would it sacrifice those deemed less important? Then who would trust the bank in the future? The controversy also highlighted the multiple possibilities for conflicts of interest as big banks conducted raids. For instance, as transfer agent for Sterling Drug, Morgan Guaranty held its confidential shareholder list—information invaluable to any raider. (Later that year, the Morgan bank sold its shareholder service operation to First Chicago, terminating a corporate trust business over a century old. Preston denied a Sterling link, although such shareholder work was clearly incompatible with merger activity.) Even as the bank invoked its internal controls for protecting confidential information, it was encouraging loan officers to pass along ideas to the Mendoza team in its "one bank" concept of teamwork.

Lest McGraw-Hill or Sterling seem a freak, the bank again ran into trouble in April 1988. James R. Houghton, chairman of Corning Glass, announced an agreement to acquire International Clinical Labs, Incorporated, for $26 a share. A stout opponent of hostile deals, Houghton thought this deal was done and used Morgan Guaranty as his depository and lender. Then Smithkline Beckman unveiled a surprise bid, quickly kicking up the price to a winning $37 a share. The defeated Houghton was stunned: Smithkline's adviser was his own stalwart banker, Morgan Guaranty. More shocking was that Houghton sat on the Morgan board! On the eve of Morgan's annual meeting, Houghton threatened to resign and was pacified only after a talk with Lew Preston. Again, Morgan earned more by advising Smithkline than by being depository for Corning. But was this short-term calculus to be the new operating standard? Would the bank auction itself off to the highest bidder? It was moving toward a two-tier structure in which it coddled the larger clients and sacrificed the smaller. And in this, it was beginning—just beginning—to resemble the rest of Wall Street, which had now operated that way for many years.

SKYSCRAPER

• •

•

IN 1989, Morgan Stanley, with sixty-four hundred employees, occupied seventeen floors of the Exxon Building on Sixth Avenue—more than Exxon itself. The building was now owned by a Mitsui unit. Stepping off the elevator into the thirtieth-floor reception area, one was greeted by a portrait of Jack Morgan and glimpses of old rolltop desks salvaged by now-retired partners. In the posh dining room, with its well-spaced tables and leather armchairs, uniformed waiters served Madeira or dry sherry, but (by Morgan tradition) no hard liquor. Such touches aside, the new Morgan Stanley—bold, rich, swaggering—had little in common with the mandarin firm that started life in September 1935 in a flower-banked room at 2 Wall Street.

Instead of underwriting, Morgan Stanley now stressed takeovers and merchant banking. After the crash, it de-emphasized securities distribution and edged out dozens of managing directors, largely from the sales and trading side. In 1988, Merrill Lynch, once scorned as plebeian, led domestic underwriters for the first time as Morgan Stanley slumped to sixth place. Morgan mostly pursued junk bonds, now the most profitable form of underwriting and an indispensable adjunct to takeover work. When Drexel Burnham lost ground with the investigation into junk bond king Michael Milken, Morgan Stanley briefly emerged as the top junk bond firm in America! Did the ghosts of Pierpont, Jack, and Harry Morgan shudder?

Morgan Stanley was an undoubted success story, an awesome performer. For over fifty years, it had stood at or near the peak of investment banking—a claim no other firm except First Boston could make. It had survived every competitive threat. Smart, with an uncanny surefire strategic sense, it alone seemed immune to the postcrash blues on

Wall Street. In 1987, it was the one publicly traded securities house to boost earnings. As if invincible, it lifted the pay of its five top executives to about the $3-million mark, so that each made more than the chairmen at rival firms; Parker Gilbert was paid $4.4 million in salary and bonus. It registered $395 million in profits for 1988—an extraordinary 71-percent rise in a sluggish trading environment. At the same time, it had avoided the chronic dissension that debilitated many rivals.

Yet for all its astounding success, the Morgan Stanley story was profoundly troubling. It had followed a flawless instinct for profit into ever-riskier activities with greater potential hazard for the nation's economy. As the 1980s ended, it resembled an industrial holding company more than a financial services firm. It had stakes in forty companies with over $7 billion in assets and seventy-two thousand employees. Morgan Stanley was suddenly a part owner of food chains and paper mills, textile plants and airplane-engine makers. These investments were reaping 40-percent returns and foreshadowed an even stronger tilt toward merchant banking and away from the trading and distribution of securities in New York, London, and Tokyo that had been the firm's salvation in the 1980s.

In the 1970s, LBOs had been small, largely friendly deals involving stable, recession-proof companies. Now the sheer scale of institutional money mustered by LBO funds—$25 billion in 1988, or enough to acquire $250 billion worth of companies—created irresistible pressure to take over all kinds of companies. In striking testimony to the speculative bent of American finance, 40 percent of the loan portfolios at large Wall Street banks were going to LBOs. Through pension fund stakes in such activity, corporate America was cannibalizing itself. With so much easy money at their disposal, LBO funds turned to hostile raids and now operated by the same ruthless logic as merger work.

The *reductio ad absurdum* was the $25 billion RJR Nabisco deal, the largest LBO ever. In 1985, Morgan Stanley had represented Nabisco Brands when it was being acquired by R. J. Reynolds; everybody lauded the diversification. Now, three years later, the same people spotted hidden values in busting it up. Along with Drexel Burnham, Merrill Lynch, and Wasserstein, Perella, Eric Gleacher of Morgan Stanley advised Henry Kravis, who defeated an investor group led by RJR Nabisco chief executive F. Ross Johnson and his investment banker, Shearson Lehman.

For a takeover that promised no economic benefit for the company, the RJR Nabisco deal showered bankers with huge rewards—almost $1 billion in fees and expenses. Morgan Stanley came away with a cool $25 million. Like most LBOs, it was executed almost entirely with borrowed money. In return, RJR Nabisco was burdened with over $20 billion in debt. Before it sold a cigarette or a biscuit each year, it was already in the hole for $3 billion in interest payments. It was forced to shoulder debt equal to the combined national debt of Bolivia, Jamaica, Uruguay, Costa Rica, and Honduras. Only ten countries in the world were more indebted. In more innocent days, investment bankers had put companies on a sound footing and jealously guarded their credit rating. Now, even as the Kravis forces toasted their victory, RJR Nabisco bondholders saw their A-rated bonds deteriorate into junk bonds, with $1 billion in value wiped out overnight. And by the summer of 1989, the company had announced plans to fire 1,640 workers as a way to save money to service the oppressive debt burden. That fall, a collapse in the junk bond market suggested that RJR Nabisco had indeed been the era's crowning folly.

In Morgan Stanley's high-risk, high-reward LBO strategy, some observers saw the prelude to a final deal—the firm would sell out to the highest bidder. Its executives had already profited royally from the 1986 public offering, earning tens of millions of dollars apiece; now they would gain a second bonanza. According to one theory, this ultimate deal would await S. Parker Gilbert's stepping down as chairman. As son of a J. P. Morgan partner and stepson of Harold Stanley, the prediction went, he didn't want to be Morgan Stanley's last chairman. The firm was also being rent by turf battles, especially between Dick Fisher and Bob Greenhill, and top people wearied of the infighting.

In another sign of the times, Morgan Stanley ended up in an insider trading scandal second in size only to Ivan Boesky's. In June 1986, Morgan Stanley hired Stephen Sui-Kuan Wang, Jr., who had recently left the University of Illinois, evidently without graduating. Wang, twenty-four, was first assigned to the LBO division, then in March 1987 was moved over to mergers.

In mid-1987, Wang was coaxed into an insider trading scheme by a Taiwanese investor named Fred Lee. From July 1987 to April 1988—undeterred by the crash—Wang fed Lee tips on twenty-five pending deals in exchange for a modest $250,000. Within a year, Wang—young and green—had obtained information on twenty-five proposed takeovers despite his personal lack of involvement in many of them. He started his criminal career right after the extensive publicity generated by the Dennis Levine and Ivan Boesky insider trading scandals. Armed with Wang's tips, Lee earned $16.5 million in ten months—while Boesky had taken five years to earn $50 million and Levine had taken five years to make a scant $12.6 million.

Though Morgan Stanley had no criminal involvement, it didn't escape criticism. U.S. District Attorney Rudolph Giuliani said, "You would think there would have been better controls, better procedures."[1] According to affidavits, junior analysts sat in a big space called the bull pen, where they openly discussed their deals. More embarrassing, the brazen Fred Lee had five trading accounts at Morgan Stanley and routed many trades through the firm itself. His account there showed over $2 million in profit. He frequently visited Morgan Stanley and had even developed an in-house reputation for pestering LBO fund analysts with calls. Morgan Stanley's computers had flagged Lee's trades, but when investigators challenged him on nine of them, he attributed his extraordinary luck to rumors and newspaper stories. The Morgan Stanley investigators swallowed this story, even though the trades occurred right before public announcements and tallied with Morgan Stanley's own deals. Among others, SEC commissioner David Ruder was puzzled by the firm's failure to detect such shameless operators.

In October 1988, Stephen Wang was sentenced to three years in federal prison, Federal District Judge Kevin T. Duffy telling him, "You had a brilliant future and you blew it on greed. . . . The first time you could have been a crook, you were."[2] Lee remained a fugitive from justice. Public reaction to the Wang case differed markedly from that to the Adrian Antoniu case early in the decade. Once again, the press noted the prestige of Morgan Stanley, but without the same sense of disbelief, the mournful sense of a smashed idol, that accompanied the earlier news. The firm had squandered its moral franchise. Morgan Stanley was now another big, wealthy Wall Street house out to make a buck and was distinguished only by the fact that it did so better than anybody else.

INSIDE 23 Great Winchester Street, Morgan Grenfell hardly seemed in ferment. With its green carpets and ornately framed portraits on pale yellow walls, it maintained its aristocratic dignity. Yet Morgan Grenfell was fighting for its future. After Guinness, it hired John Craven as chief executive, buying his boutique firm, Phoenix Securities, for $25 million and giving him a 5-percent stake in Morgan Grenfell. He already had several ports of call on his crowded résumé. A protégé of Sir Siegmund Warburg, he had been chairman of Crédit Suisse White Weld and Merrill Lynch International. He had quit Merrill after confronting then-chairman Don Regan over what he saw as meddling from New York.

Creating and operating Phoenix Securities from his Chelsea home, he engineered two dozen Big Bang mergers and emerged as the deal maker's deal maker. Handsome, demanding, and restless, he didn't pass a full week in England in 1986 and crisscrossed the Atlantic forty times.

Although Craven envisioned Morgan Grenfell as a global investment bank on the American model, the firm wouldn't fulfill his goals. Unlike Morgan Stanley and Morgan Guaranty, 23 Great Winchester had gone too long without a carefully conceived strategy. The world of securities trading had been too alien to its former leadership. It hadn't anticipated change or focused the scattered energies of the firm. In retrospect, it had erred fatally by spurning its Morgan brethren at Bermuda in the early 1970s. It had sacrificed that one inestimable advantage—its association with the American House of Morgan.

Worst of all, distracted by the casual riches of takeovers, it had moved gingerly in preparing for Big Bang and gotten stuck with bit players. It never established a major presence in trading gilts (British government bonds) or equities. The firm's takeover clients never broadened their business to the firm's weak securities side. Craven himself had sounded warnings of disaster in the overcrowded London markets after the drop in share volume that followed Black Monday. Morgan Grenfell's trading rooms were bleeding the firm.

On December 6, 1988, Morgan Grenfell abruptly shut its securities operation, ending its chances of becoming an integrated global investment bank. There was a wholesale firing of 450 people, or a quarter of its entire payroll—one of the biggest sackings in City history. Some traders had earned £200,000 a year (about $370,000), and their fate underscored the City's transient wealth. Even the method of their dismissal was emblematic: by an accidental leak, the news first appeared on their trading screens. To offset the leak, the firm rushed out an announcement as people arrived for work. In this confused situation, some gilt traders continued dealing for an hour, unaware that they were jobless. Though Craven handled the massacre with commendable tact, arranging generous severance packages, it was a terrible blow to Morgan Grenfell. For the City, this biggest firing since Big Bang was a thunderclap that symbolically closed the frantic 1980s. In March 1989, John Craven announced a loss for 1988—perhaps the first in Morgan Grenfell's 151-year history.

The modern world wasn't charitable to capital-short banks, and Morgan Grenfell was stuck in that perilous middle rut. It still had a collection of choice businesses, especially the booming merger and global-asset-management departments. It had bought C. J. Lawrence in New York, an excellent institutional research and brokerage firm, which it merged with its American operation. Thanks to strength in export and project finance, it had over $600 million in government-guaranteed loans to strengthen its balance sheet. Finally, as a specialist in financing trade with the Soviet Union, it was the merchant bank best poised to capitalize on *perestroika.* And Craven moved aggressively to capitalize on such assets. Yet without a securities operation, these strengths didn't coalesce into a modern global bank.

Sheared of its money-losing securities business, Morgan Grenfell suddenly looked like a takeover target. Many City cynics suspected that Craven, an inveterate job hopper and shrewd deal maker, had a mandate to make the investment bank's strategy work or else auction off the firm. "I think John's goal is to turn Morgan Grenfell around, get it in shape, and then sell it, probably to Deutsche Bank," a friend remarked. (Deutsche Bank had bought a 4.9-percent stake in 1984.) "He's a bulldog—he won't let anything slip out of his bite." Morgan Grenfell had long been protected by loyal institutional shareholders. Yet the day after the crash, insurance broker Willis Faber said its one-fifth stake was up for sale. Morgan Grenfell was joining the faithless, rootless world of modern finance.

By 1989, Morgan Grenfell seemed ripe for the taking by bigger rivals. In shedding the bank's securities business and swiftly restoring profitability, Craven only added to its allure as a takeover target. And so the bank that had specialized in hostile takeovers found itself in November the object of an unwelcome embrace from Banque Indosuez of France. Craven brought in Deutsche Bank as a white knight and extracted a rich price for the firm: over $1.4 billion, or more than twice its book value. This breathtaking bid settled the contest. Craven, the consummate negotiator, became the first foreigner invited onto the Deutsche Bank board. The hoopla was spiked by the grisly slaying of Deutsche Bank head Alfred Herrhausen by terrorists. The generous settlement also obscured the fact that 151 years of noble independence had been suddenly swept away.

OVER fifty years later, J. P. Morgan and Company appeared to have erred in its choice of commercial banking in 1935. If it saved Depression-era jobs, it also burdened the House of Morgan with what proved to be a dying business—wholesale lending. Large companies no longer turned to banks for short-term credit or seasonal lending—activities now relegated to the commercial paper market. So Morgans had gradually undone its history and grown into a hybrid investment bank, much like its rival down the block, Bankers Trust.

The House of Morgan led the fight to repeal Glass-Steagall. Like other banks, it tried to scramble into so many investment bank activities that Congress would have to rubber-stamp the marketplace reality. Lew Preston also believed in making an intellectual case for change, and in 1984 the bank produced a treatise called *Rethinking Glass-Steagall.* One patron was Alan Greenspan, then a Morgan director, who followed Paul Volcker as Fed chairman. "As a director, Greenspan was very instrumental in getting that document out," said a Morgan insider.

Lew Preston knew that after Rule 415, straight blue-chip underwriting was a less lucrative auction business. The Morgan bank wanted to underwrite corporate bonds mainly to offer customers a full line of financial services. It was also necessary to finance takeovers. Although Morgans was dubbed the Fed's bank, Preston could never budge Paul Volcker on Glass-Steagall. Still worried about banks performing "risky" securities work, Volcker would reply that he didn't worry about Morgans, but about three or four other banks. Morgans was also reaping the highest return on equity and assets of any American bank during the Volcker years. "Unfortunately, we were having some pretty good earnings," Preston conceded, "and so there was skepticism on the part of the Fed chairman."[3]

Having helped Volcker at least three times—with the Hunt brothers, Continental Illinois, and the Brazil debt rescheduling—Preston fretted about the lack of a *quid pro quo.* A friend of Preston's noted that "Lew was very close to Volcker in pulling acorns out of the firm. He had broken his back on those three cases. I remember Lew saying, 'I had a lot of chits on Paul, and yet Paul is still against banks going into the debt markets.' I'm absolutely positive that Preston felt somewhat betrayed by Volcker." Other Morgan officials felt they had gained little for being such a model of obedience. As one Morgan insider said bitterly, "I'm tired of being the Fed's pet."

As recently as 1984, the *New York Times* had said it would be "a matter of seconds" before Morgan Guaranty and Morgan Stanley got back together if Glass-Steagall fell.[4] Twenty years before, this was indisputable. But as the 1980s progressed, the warmth between the Morgan brethren waned. Young hotshots at Morgan Stanley felt more kinship with the flamboyant Bankers Trust, which specialized in risky trading and merchant banking, than with the austere, circumspect Morgan Guaranty. One could more readily imagine Morgan Guaranty teamed up with Goldman, Sachs than with Morgan Stanley. The two Morgan houses no longer made a natural match and were especially keen adversaries in Tokyo and London.

Investment bankers were fatalistic about Glass-Steagall's fall. As Fred Whittemore said of Morgan Stanley's decision to go public in 1986, "We are taking advantage of a 3-to-5 year window, before the banks become full-fledged competitors, to become as large and powerful as quickly as we can."[5] Morgan Stanley's LBO war chest and large capital freed it from reliance on commercial banks in financing takeovers. With its new merchant-banking orientation, Morgan Stanley didn't much care about Glass-Steagall's demise, which would affect only a small, declining part of its operations. Morgan Stanley managing director Robert A. Gerard warned Congress, in strangely populist tones, that if Glass-Steagall fell, "there will be a vast increase in the concentration of economic power in large banking organizations."[6] But his firm made only perfunctory moves against what it saw as a largely irrelevant law.

For commercial banks, exasperation over Glass-Steagall mounted as everything from car loans to mortgages was packaged as securities and placed beyond their reach. Preston quietly chafed at Volcker's obstinacy. In a *Fortune* article in April 1986, he made a shocking admission: the Morgan bank had considered surrendering its commercial bank charter and simply becoming an investment bank. This would have sacrificed perhaps 20 percent of its business, forcing it to forgo checking accounts and deposit insurance. Although the statement apparently wasn't a case of clever premeditation, Preston didn't mind the uproar. Bob Engel reiterated the point: "If we became convinced that we would never get full expanded securities power, we would owe it to our shareholders to reconsider whether we still wanted to be a bank. We could still become a private bank—drop out of the Fed and the payments system."[7] Some of this was tactical bluster, but it revealed the impatience at 23 Wall.

The 1929 crash had led straight to Glass-Steagall. Ironically, the 1987 crash would prove its undoing, as Black Monday deepened national discontent with Wall Street. Morgan Stanley and the other big securities houses looked increasingly like a cosy cartel protected by Glass-Steagall —an outcome quite different from that expected by the New Deal reformers, who wanted to bust up concentrated Wall Street power. Meanwhile, commercial banks were the clear casualties of the 1980s. The Latin American debt crisis showed that lending was now far riskier than trading. The crisis mocked the spirit of Glass-Steagall, which had tried to guarantee the stability of deposit banks. With foreign banks able to underwrite securities in the United States, Glass-Steagall seemed only to penalize American banks and invite them to make rash decisions. With Japan now claiming seven of the world's ten largest banks, this competitive disadvantage was no small matter.

In Senator William Proxmire, chairman of the Senate Banking Committee, the banks found an unexpected ally. He was willing to grant them power to underwrite stocks and bonds provided big commercial and investment banks didn't merge. "Washington does not like the thought of Morgan Guaranty and Morgan Stanley making up after all those years," said the *Economist*. [8] As a J. P. Morgan director for ten years, Alan Greenspan had promised to excuse himself as Fed chairman from decisions affecting the bank. Yet Greenspan was the tutelary spirit behind a partial Glass-Steagall repeal. The banks had already secured permission to underwrite commercial paper and municipal revenue bonds. In January 1989, the Fed added limited powers to float corporate bonds. Among the first five banks streaming through the open gates was J. P. Morgan Securities—easily the largest such operation, with $400 million in capital and seven hundred employees. And in October 1989, it became the first American commercial bank since the Depression to float a corporate debt issue, managing a $30 million bond issue for the Savannah Electric and Power Company.

There was a disquieting side to all this. Would banks soon underwrite corporate raids with junk bonds? Would they palm off Latin American debt on bondholders, as they had in the 1920s? And how would banks insulate depositors from any future risks in securities work? The concerns were genuine. But such problems would have to be dealt with by Congress and the wisdom of bank regulators, for the status quo had become more dangerous to the commercial banks than any risks introduced by expanded securities powers.

The years ahead promise to witness the rise of vast universal banks at home and abroad, the Morgan bank certainly among them. In the view of *Institutional Investor*, commercial banks had "grandiose plans" to become "shimmering financial institutions as omnipotent as the old House of Morgan was prior to Glass-Steagall."[9] J. P. Morgan and Company was now a global entity, not just an American bank operating abroad. Three of its six top executives were non-American, as were half the people in its management-training program in New York. Every high official had served a tour of duty abroad.

By 1989, the bank had outgrown its shrine at 23 Wall. Lew Preston wanted a personal computer on every banker's desk, and trading desks required an exotic jungle of electric wiring. To accommodate a high-tech bank, Morgans bought a new forty-seven-story glass-and-stone tower at 60 Wall Street that was designed by Kevin Roche. It wasn't custom-made for the House of Morgan, as 23 Wall had been. To save time and money, the bank bought a real estate package assembled by developer George Klein. First budgeted at $530 million, the cost overruns at 60 Wall pushed the price up to $830 million. In 1988, the Morgan bank borrowed $400 million from the Dai-Ichi Mutual Life Insurance Company to help finance the new tower. Preston said that he hadn't picked the furnishings for his new office because Dennis Weatherstone might not like them. He thus mischievously telegraphed the message that Weatherstone, self-made son of a London transport worker, would succeed him as the first foreign-born bank chairman on Wall Street. On the eve of the bank's departure for 60 Wall in the summer of 1989, reports circulated that the bank would have to cut ten percent of its work force, or about fifteen hundred people. It was another reminder that the days of paternalism and coddled, lifelong employment were long gone.

T W E N T Y - T H R E E Wall had always reflected the House of Morgan. From the moment you stepped through the doors and stood beneath the radiant Louis XV chandelier, with its nineteen hundred crystal pieces, you could feel the self-confidence of the place, the massive weight of tradition. It had a splendid touch of theater about it. As the bank transferred to 60 Wall Street, there was talk of selling 23 Wall, which Lew Preston denied. "It's a monument," he said wistfully. "It's really got no value to anybody except us."[10] The little temple of finance, which had witnessed more history than any American banking house, was now a costly relic from a vanished world of civility.

Would any banking house ever again have the mystery of the old House of Morgan? Probably not. The Morgan partners were adornments of a world too closed and too collusive by today's more egalitarian standards. The spacious vision and cultivation of Tom Lamont, Dwight Morrow, and Russell Leffingwell sprang from a world of small partnerships and few competing sources of financial power. They worked on a quieter, slower Wall Street and could afford to be gentlemen and scholars.

Much of the bank's special flavor derived from its global outlook. As a conduit for capital transfers between America and Europe, the old House of Morgan had naturally looked abroad and was uniquely cosmopolitan at a time when America was still provincial and isolationist. Now the rest of the country had caught up. The Morgan bank's foreign connections, once incomparable, might today be matched by those of many foreign ministries, central banks, or even multinational corporations. Financial power has become widely dispersed among American, European, and Japanese firms. No single firm will ever again be as lordly or preeminent as the House of Pierpont and Jack Morgan.

The old House of Morgan's power stemmed from the immature state of government treasuries, companies, and capital markets. It stood sentinel over capital markets that were relatively small and primitive. Today, money has become a commonplace commodity. A company in need of capital can turn to investment banks, commercial banks, or insurance companies; it can raise it through bank loans, bond issues, private placements, or commercial paper; it can draw upon many currencies, many countries, many markets. Money has lost its mystique, and banking, therefore, has lost a bit of its magic.

The Morgan story is the story of modern finance itself. A Pierpont Morgan exercised powers that today are dispersed among vast global banking conglomerates. The activities once performed by a knot of side-whiskered men in mahogany parlors are now spread across trading rooms around the world. We live in a larger, faster, more anonymous age. There will be more deals done and more fortunes made, but there will never be another barony like the House of Morgan.

ACKNOWLEDGMENTS

Although I didn't realize it at first, this was a propitious time in which to write a history of the House of Morgan, perhaps the first time anyone could do it justice. Secrecy has always been a Morgan fetish, and almost all earlier works were based on secondary sources and some guesswork. In recent years, however, new archives have opened up, offering a clear glimpse into the shrouded Morgan world and allowing a more authoritative account. As members of a private bank before 1940, Morgan partners had a proprietary feeling toward their papers and freely donated them to educational institutions. Consequently, the bank has lost control over much of its own records for the pre–World War II period—a curious and, I suspect, uncomfortable situation for such a secretive institution.

The life of Pierpont Morgan has inspired about ten books—and merits the attention. He is a figure of inexhaustible fascination. But the post-1913 history of the bank has remained virgin territory, even though it was the heyday of global Morgan power. Only a thin, academic volume, published in 1984, chronicles the life of J. P. Morgan, Jr., and I wanted to remedy that extraordinary omission. So while I have done some fresh research on nineteenth-century Morgan history, I have strongly emphasized the bank's twentieth-century history. The post–World War II story of the three Morgan houses was, mysteriously, a total blank. Hence, this is the first all-inclusive history of the Morgan empire ever to appear.

Luckily, the new archives dovetailed with my emphases. After years of vacillation, Harry S. Morgan finally donated a rich trove of family and business papers to the Pierpont Morgan Library before he died in 1982. Though sketchy in the George Peabody–Junius Morgan–Pierpont Morgan era, it contains a comprehensive set of Jack Morgan's papers. To this the library has added the papers of Martin Egan, bank publicist of the interwar period. I would like to thank the indispensable David W. Wright, as well as Inge du Pont and Elisabeth Agro of the library for steering me through these materials. And I warmly applaud John P. Morgan II and the Morgan family for allowing me to quote generously from the papers, despite their reservations about my use of some controversial material.

I have drawn heavily on the voluminous Thomas W. Lamont papers at Harvard and the Russell C. Leffingwell papers at Yale. Thanks to the courtesy of his grandson, Daniel P. Davison, I had access to Harry Davison's cable book. To a lesser extent, I have used the George W. Perkins papers at Columbia, the Edward R. Stettinius papers at the University of Virginia, and the Dwight W. Morrow papers at Amherst College. I also quote from several oral histories collected at Columbia University, most notably that of George Whitney. I would like to thank the staff members of all these institutions, especially Florence Lathrop at Harvard; Judith Schiff and William Massa at Yale; and Ronald Grele at Columbia. For the post–World War II period, I drew on materials from the Harry S. Truman Library, the Dwight D. Eisenhower Library, the John Fitzgerald Kennedy Library, the Lyndon B. Johnson Library, the Gerald R. Ford Library, and the Jimmy Carter Library.

Together, these unpublished papers offer a vast record of the bank's intrigue over many decades. Delving into such archives, I felt as if I were an explorer hacking his way through a lost continent and uncovering majestic, moss-covered ruins. I hope I have communicated a fraction of my daily excitement. These records do more than merely supply fresh details about familiar events. In many instances, they write brand-new chapters in our history, especially about the bank's dealings with Italy, Germany, Mexico, and Japan. My research strongly convinced me that financial history is a sadly neglected stepchild of the history profession.

Two of the three Morgan banks were receptive to my project. I received the contract for this book right before the Guinness scandal, which threatened to complicate access to Morgan Grenfell people. But when I spent two months in London in 1987, the firm did something extraordinary: they threw open their files to me without restriction. They installed me in a conference room and brought me soot-blackened files from a warehouse near the Thames. I examined records touching on controversies from the early 1900s right up through the 1960s and 1970s. Whether the firm's intention was to show confidence in its integrity after the Guinness scandal or to emphasize its scandal-free years, I do not know. But I was touched and impressed by its generosity. I would especially like to thank Desmond Harney for squiring me about 23 Great Winchester and Kathleen Burk, the Morgan Grenfell historian, who showed a true collegial spirit and sent me three chapters of her official history in galleys. I regret that their late arrival did not permit me to acknowledge her contribution in my footnotes.

J. P. Morgan and Company reacted with some ambivalence to my first appearance, fearing association with the suddenly notorious Morgan Grenfell. Yet here, too, timing worked in my favor, for in shifting toward investment banking, the Morgan bank has adopted a higher profile. Despite an initial reluctance, the bank ended up handling the book with customary polish and set up many appointments, including interviews with every living chairman, past and present. I treasured the bribery of the Morgan lunches, the best publicity weapon ever devised. Fred Allen and Jack Morris were consistently courteous, intelligent, and professional in rendering assistance. They are a class act. I would also like to thank Melanie Smith for arranging access to the bank's in-house library, which has some fine unpublished memoirs.

Alone among the Morgan banks, Morgan Stanley refused cooperation and wouldn't consent to a single interview. The decision surprised me less than the way it was handled. Both management and publicity man Peter Roche tried to lower an iron curtain around the firm. They discouraged people, current and retired, from talking to me. When I wrote to Parker Gilbert and Dick Fisher deploring this adversarial atmosphere and asking for an explanation, I didn't receive a reply.

I am most grateful to those former Morgan Stanley partners who did cooperate. They were a tremendously impressive group—pound for pound, the most informative and perceptive people I talked to. Many of the interviews lasted several hours and more than compensated for the lack of official cooperation. Far from being disloyal, they performed a real service and enhanced my appreciation of the firm. Their enthusiasm made me doubly regretful of the current leadership's intransigence.

In writing the section on the Casino Age, I performed over a hundred interviews to get an "inside" feel comparable to that of the two earlier sections, which were based on hundreds of books and tens of thousands of unpublished documents. Since Morgan bankers would sooner swallow cyanide tablets than name clients, this was no small feat. A mute breed schooled in confidentiality, they weren't accustomed to talking openly about their business. This makes me especially grateful to the people I interviewed. Some patiently sat through talks that started in the morning and ended at dusk. Others typed out page after page of impressions. I am humbled by their generosity, which I cannot adequately repay. The pleasure of their company was one of the real pleasures of writing the book. I felt privileged to share their reminiscences.

Lest anyone take offense at a misplaced emphasis, I will simply list all those who answered questions in person, by phone, or by mail. My special thanks to the descendants of Jack and Pierpont Morgan, Dwight Morrow, Tom Lamont, George W. Perkins, Harry Davison, Russell Leffingwell, George Whitney, Vivian H. Smith, Teddy Grenfell, Thomas S. Gates, Jr., Montagu Norman, Nancy Astor, and Charles Lindbergh for permitting me to quote from their unpublished papers. I owe a special debt to Edward Pulling, Paul and Cecily Pennoyer, and Laura Phillips, who not only answered questions, but permitted me to reprint photographs from their family albums. I especially thank those whose situation required that their names be omitted from the following list of acknowledgments: David Band, John Baylis, David Bendall, Jerry E. Bishop, H. P. K. den Boesterd, A. Bruce Brackenridge, William D. Brewer, James R. Brugger, Dr. Nicola Caiola, Rupert F. J. Carrington, Robert Carswell, Lord Stephen G. Catto, Randall Caudill, Dorothy B. Colby, Frank W. Colby, J. E. H. ("Tim") Collins, Edward Costikyan, Daniel P. Davison, Harry Davison II, C. Douglas Dillon, David Douglas-Home, Robert G. Engel, Edgar Felton, Max M. Fisher, John Douglas Forbes, George S. Franklin, Helena Franklin, John B. Fraser, Evan Galbraith, Robert A. Gerard, Jackson B. Gilbert, S. Hazard Gillespie, Victor Gotbaum, Raphael de la Guerronnière, Perry E. Hall, Charles E. A. Hambro, Keith R. Harris, Carl Hathaway, Robert K. Heimann, Robert A. Henderson, Michael Hildesley, Sir David Basil Hill-Wood, Longstreet Hinton, Guy Huntrods, Shiro Inoue, William M. Isaac, Robert Isom, Sir Martin Jacomb, Lord Roy Jenkins, Fred W. Kirby, Corliss Lamont, Edward M. Lamont, Ralph F. Leach, Jerome Levinson, Anne Morrow Lindbergh, Robert V. Lindsay, Jack Loughran, John McDaniels, Luis S. Mendez, John M. Meyer, Jr., Damon Mezzacappa, George

S. Moore, Catherine Adams Morgan, Constance Morrow Morgan, Sir Jeremy Morse, Bruce Nichols, Sir Leslie O'Brien, Jane Nichols Page, Walter H. Page, Ellmore C. Patterson, the late Frances Tracy Pennoyer, Joseph L. Ponce, Sheppard Poor, Lewis T. Preston, Thomas L. Pulling, Clifford H. Ramsdell, Charles Rawlinson, Judson P. Reis, William Rhodes, Frank Rosenbach, Eugene Rotberg, George W. Rowe, Charles Ryskamp, William Salomon, David T. Schiff, Frederick H. Scholtz, Anthony M. Solomon, Andrew Spindler, Irvine Sprague, William Sword, David Taylor, Fred Tetzeli, Alexander C. Tomlinson, William D. Toomey, Guido Verbeck, Peter Vermilye, Fred Vinton, Norma Walter, Anthony Weighill, John Weinberg, Christopher Whittington, and Robert J. Wynn.

On the publishing end, I would like to thank my London agent, Deborah Rogers, for her able handling of the manuscript and Nicholas Brealey, editorial director of Simon and Schuster, Limited, for his astute readings of the manuscript. At home, I have enjoyed the steady support of a marvelous group of people. My agent, Melanie Jackson, is the sort writers dream of but seldom find. She has been a Rock of Gibraltar in support, a prodigiously hard worker, and a joy to work with. The book would not have appeared without her. My editor, Morgan Entrekin, had a clear vision of the story from the start and never wavered in his enthusiasm or generosity. He delivered excellent advice and timely shots of adrenaline that sustained me through a long, complicated task. I couldn't have asked for stronger faith. My parents, Ruth and Israel, provided my only research assistance in the final stages of the book and helped with the mammoth task of collecting photographs. They proved ideally loving, self-sacrificing parents—which I already knew. I owe the largest debt to my saintly wife and lovely muse, Valerie. She had to make room for this sacred monster, the House of Morgan, that suddenly loomed in our midst. She was wise, tender, loving, and solicitous in nursing me through my obsession. Perhaps in the end, the monster devoured us both.

ABBREVIATIONS

AL	*American Lawyer*
AM	*Atlantic Monthly*
B	(London) *Business*
BA	*Barron's*
BE	*Brooklyn Eagle*
BM	*Bankers Magazine*
BW	*Business Week*
CB	*Current Biography*
CH	*Current History*
CUOH	Columbia University Oral History Collection, New York
CUOH-BB	Columbia University Oral History Collection, Boris Bakhmeteff
CUOH-EB	Columbia University Oral History Collection, Eugene Black
CUOH-GR	Columbia University Oral History Collection, George Rublee
CUOH-GW	Columbia University Oral History Collection, George Whitney
CUOH-LR	Columbia University Oral History Collection, Leonard Rist
CUOH-WJS	Columbia University Oral History Collection, William J. Schieffelin
DDE	Dwight D. Eisenhower Library, Abilene, Kansas
DE	(London) *Daily Express*
DH	(London) *Daily Herald*
DT	(London) *Daily Telegraph*
DWM	Dwight W. Morrow Papers, Amherst College Library, Amherst, Massachusetts
E	*Economist*
ERS	Edward R. Stettinius, Sr., Papers, Aldenham Library, University of Virginia, Charlottesville
EU	*Euromoney*
FA	*Foreign Affairs*
FB	*Forbes*
FD	(Hartford) *Financial Digest*
FO	*Fortune*
FT	*Financial Times*
GWP	George W. Perkins Papers, Butler Library, Columbia University
HFJ	*Hartford Financial Journal*
HLS	Herbert L. Satterlee Papers, Pierpont Morgan Library, New York
HPD	Henry P. Davison Cable Book, courtesy of Daniel P. Davison
HST	Harry S. Truman Library, Independence, Missouri
II	*Institutional Investor*
J	(New York) *Journal*

JPMJ	J. P. Morgan, Jr., Papers, Pierpont Morgan Library
JPMS	J. P. Morgan, Sr., Papers, Pierpont Morgan Library
JSM	J. S. Morgan & Co. and George Peabody & Co. Papers, Guildhall Library, London
LBJ	Lyndon Baines Johnson Library, Austin, Texas
ME	Martin Egan Papers, Pierpont Morgan Library
MGR	Morgan Grenfell Papers (1910 to the present)
N	*Newsweek*
NFP	*Newark Free Press*
NY	*New York*
NYDN	(New York) *Daily News*
NYH	*New York Herald*
NYHT	*New York Herald Tribune*
NYK	*New Yorker*
NYT	*New York Times*
NYTR	*New York Tribune*
NYWT	*New York World Telegram*
O	*Observer*
RCL	Russell C. Leffingwell Papers, Sterling Memorial Library, Yale University, New Haven, Connecticut
SEP	*Saturday Evening Post*
ST	(London) *Sunday Telegraph*
T	(London) *Times*
TI	*Time*
TSG	Thomas S. Gates, Jr., Papers, Van Pelt Library, University of Pennsylvania, Philadelphia
TWL	Thomas W. Lamont Papers, Baker Library, Harvard University, Cambridge, Massachusetts
WP	*Washington Post*
WSJ	*Wall Street Journal*

NOTES

PROLOGUE

1. *FB*, May 20, 1985; Hamilton, *Financial Revolution*, p. 80.
2. *II*, July 1976.
3. S. Parker Gilbert, comments made at Morgan Stanley Annual Meeting, May 5, 1988.
4. Hoffman, *Deal Makers*, p. 34.

CHAPTER ONE: SCROOGE

1. Wechsberg, *Merchant Bankers*, p. 14.
2. Hoyt, *Peabody Influence*, p. 106.
3. Chapple, *George Peabody*, p. 26.
4. Sobel, *Panic on Wall Street*, p. 41.
5. Hidy, *George Peabody*, p. 360.
6. Ibid., p. 40.
7. Birmingham, *"Our Crowd,"* p. 73.
8. Sampson, *Money Lenders*, p. 61.
9. Makin, *Global Debt Crisis*, p. 41.
10. Hidy, *House of Baring*, p. 309.
11. Hidy, *George Peabody*, p. 264.
12. Ziegler, *Sixth Great Power*, p. 155.
13. Ibid., pp. 154–55.
14. Hidy, *House of Baring*, pp. 326–27; Hidy, *George Peabody*, p. 273.
15. Hidy, *George Peabody*, p. 306.
16. Lamont, *Across World Frontiers*, p. 19.
17. Chapple, *George Peabody*, pp. 22–23.
18. Parker, *George Peabody*, p. 14.
19. JPMS, letter from Charles C. Gooch to George Peabody, October 31, 1856.
20. JPMJ, Reminiscences of J. P. Morgan, Jr., pp. 9–10, Insert A.
21. JPMS, Diary, October 2, 1854.
22. JPMJ, Reminiscences of J. P. Morgan, Jr., pp. 4–5.
23. Carosso, *Morgans*, p. 64.
24. Chapple, *George Peabody*, p. 21.
25. Carosso, *Morgans*, p. 64.
26. Ibid., p. 110.
27. Carter, *Cyrus Field*, p. 162.

28. *NYT*, October 21, 1987.

29. Parker, *George Peabody*, p. 93.

30. Chapple, *George Peabody*, p. 24.

31. Morgan Grenfell, *George Peabody & Co.; J. S. Morgan & Co.; Morgan Grenfell & Co.*, p. 5.

32. Parker, *George Peabody*, p. 8.

33. Chapple, *George Peabody*, p. 43.

34. Morgan Grenfell, *George Peabody & Co.; J. S. Morgan & Co; Morgan Grenfell & Co.*, p. 4.

35. JPMJ, Reminiscences of J. P. Morgan, Jr., p. 7.

36. Ibid., p. 12.

37. Carnegie, *Autobiography*, p. 270.

38. TWL, Box 112, Folder 13, letter from Vivian Hugh Smith, December 17, 1946.

CHAPTER TWO: POLONIUS

1. Moody and Turner, "Masters of Capital in America," p. 7.

2. Smalley, *Anglo-American Memories*, p. 219.

3. Wheeler, *Pierpont Morgan & Friends*, pp. 62–63.

4. Carosso, *Morgans*, p. 29.

5. Wechsberg, *Merchant Bankers*, p. 33.

6. *B*, April 1986.

7. Hughes, *Vital Few*, p. 410.

8. Jean Strouse, lecture, Pierpont Morgan Library.

9. Carosso, *Morgans*, p. 84.

10. Young, *Merchant Banking*, p. 25.

11. Sinclair, *Corsair*, p. 17.

12. Ziegler, *Sixth Great Power*, pp. 138–39.

13. Wechsberg, *Merchant Bankers*, p. 9.

14. Ibid., p. 197.

15. *FO*, February 1930.

16. Ziegler, *Sixth Great Power*, p. 85.

17. Carosso, *Morgans*, p. 84.

18. Hinton, Meyer, and Rodd, *Comments about the Morgan Bank*, p. 16.

19. Smalley, *Anglo-American Memories*, p. 216.

CHAPTER THREE: PRINCE

1. Josephson, *Robber Barons*, p. 24.

2. Sinclair, *Corsair*, p. 58.

3. Josephson, *Robber Barons*, p. 75.

4. Wheeler, *Pierpont Morgan & Friends*, pp. 96–97, 102–3.

5. Gordon, *Scarlet Woman of Wall Street*, p. 240.

6. Carosso, *Morgans*, p. 142.

7. Wheeler, *Pierpont Morgan & Friends*, p. 122.

8. JPMS, Letter Press Book, 1873–1880, letter to Junius S. Morgan, August 5, 1879.

9. Birmingham, *"Our Crowd,"* p. 143.

10. Carosso, *Morgans*, p. 144.

11. Sobel, *Panic on Wall Street*, p. 167.

12. Ibid., p. 172.

13. Ibid., p. 185.

14. Carosso, *Morgans*, p. 175.

15. Noyes, *Market Place*, p. 17.

16. Carosso, *Morgans*, p. 175.

17. Moody and Turner, "Masters of Capital in America," p. 16.

18. JPMS, Letter Press Book, 1873–1880, letter to Junius S. Morgan, April 29, 1874.

19. Ibid., letter to Junius S. Morgan, April 1873.

20. Carosso, *Morgans*, p. 225.

21. Ibid., p. 280.

22. Ibid., p. 163.

23. Black, *King of Fifth Avenue*, p. 658.

24. Carnegie, *Autobiography*, pp. 165–66.

25. JPMS, Letter Press Book, 1873–1880, letter to Walter Hayes Burns, January 2, 1879.

26. Black, *King of Fifth Avenue*, p. 567.

27. Sinclair, *Corsair*, p. 243.

28. Carosso, *Morgans*, p. 274.

29. JPMS, Letter Press Book, 1873–1880, letter to Junius S. Morgan, July 24, 1873.

30. *Dictionary of American Biography*, s.v. Morgan, Junius S.

31. Sinclair, *Corsair*, p. 114.

32. Josephson, *Robber Barons*, p. 170.

33. Ibid., p. 87.

34. New York Central and Hudson River Railroad, "Prospectus."

35. Carosso, *Morgans*, p. 225.

36. Sinclair, *Corsair*, p. 53.

37. Allen, *Great Pierpont Morgan*, p. 36.

38. JPMS, Letter Press Book, 1873–1880, letter to James J. Goodwin, February 24, 1880.

CHAPTER FOUR: CORSAIR

1. Allen, *Great Pierpont Morgan*, p. 52.

2. Josephson, *Robber Barons*, p. 338.

3. Sinclair, *Corsair*, p. 111.

4. Noyes, *Market Place*, p. 182.

5. Ibid., p. 53.

6. Moody and Turner, "Masters of Capital in America," p. 20.

7. Sinclair, *Corsair*, p. 189.

8. U.K. Parliament, Committee to Review the Functionings of Financial Institutions, *Evidence Given by the Accepting Houses Committee*, p. 84.

9. Jackson, *J. P. Morgan*, p. 69.

10. Moulton, *St. George's Church New York*, p. 112.

11. Sinclair, *Corsair*, p. 16.

12. Wheeler, *Pierpont Morgan & Friends*, p. 158.

13. Moulton, *St. George's Church New York*, p. 68.

14. Ibid., p. 79.

15. Ibid., p. 80.

16. Sinclair, *Corsair*, p. 69.

17. Ibid.

18. Josephson, *Robber Barons*, p. 293.

19. Carosso, *Morgans*, p. 254.

20. Wheeler, *Pierpont Morgan & Friends*, pp. 162–63.

21. Ibid., p. 174.

22. Moody and Turner, "Masters of Capital in America," p. 20.

23. Weller, *New Haven Railroad*, p. 19.

24. Hughes, *Vital Few*, p. 422.

25. Sinclair, *Corsair*, p. 76.

26. Wheeler, *Pierpont Morgan & Friends*, p. 188.

27. Sinclair, *Corsair*, p. 146.

28. Wheeler, *Pierpont Morgan & Friends*, pp. 178–79.

29. Klein, *Life and Legend of Jay Gould*, p. 439.

30. Wheeler, *Pierpont Morgan & Friends*, p. 180.

31. Klein, *Life and Legend of Jay Gould*, pp. 460–61.

32. Carosso, *Morgans*, p. 265.

33. *T*, April 9, 1890.

34. JPMJ, Box 3, Folder 1, letter to Frances Tracy Morgan, July 12, 1887.

35. Carosso, *Morgans*, p. 274.

36. *T*, April 9, 1890.

37. Jackson, *J. P. Morgan*, p. 281.

38. JPMJ, Box 1, Folder 3, letter to Frances Tracy Morgan, March 10, 1881.

39. Ibid., letter to Frances Tracy Morgan, March 27, 1881.

40. Ibid., letter to Frances Tracy Morgan, February 27, 1881.

41. JPMJ, Box 2, Folder 2, letter to Frances Tracy Morgan, October 23, 1885.

42. JPMJ, Box 2, Folder 1, letter to Frances Tracy Morgan, November 19, 1884.

43. JPMJ, Box 3, Folder 3, letter to Frances Tracy Morgan, February 8, 1889.

44. JPMJ, Box 2, Folder 2, letter to Frances Tracy Morgan, November 16, 1885.

45. Forbes, *J. P. Morgan, Jr.*, p. 16.

46. Ibid., p. 22.

47. Hovey, *Life Story of J. Pierpont Morgan*, p. 318.

48. JPMJ, Box 3, Folder 3, letter to Frances Tracy Morgan, March 18, 1889.
49. Ibid., letter to Frances Tracy Morgan, March ?, 1889.
50. Paul G. Pennoyer and Frances Tracy Pennoyer, interview with author.
51. Sinclair, *Corsair*, p. 115.
52. Ibid., p. 22.
53. Smalley, *Anglo-American Memories*, p. 230.
54. Josephson, *Money Lords*, p. 15.
55. Sinclair, *Corsair*, p. 22.
56. Smalley, *Anglo-American Memories*, p. 230.
57. *NYT*, February 19, 1964.
58. TWL, Box 110, Folder 3, memorandum to Robert Gordon Wasson, March 27, 1939.
59. Carosso, *Morgans*, p. 465.
60. Schacht, *Confessions of the Old Wizard*, pp. 97–98.
61. Carosso, *Morgans*, p. 366.
62. Ibid., p. 365
63. Winkler, *Morgan the Magnificent*, p. 116.
64. Moody, *Masters of Capital*, p. 29.
65. Leffingwell, *Memorial of Charles Steele*.
66. *SEP*, March 12, 1927.

CHAPTER FIVE: CORNER

1. Sampson, *Money Lenders*, p. 60.
2. *WSJ*, April 18, 1988.
3. Nevins, *Grover Cleveland*, p. 657.
4. Sinclair, *Corsair*, p. 98.
5. JSM, HC 3.1.1, telegram from J. P. Morgan, Sr., to J. S. Morgan & Co., February 1, 1895.
6. Nevins, *Grover Cleveland*, pp. 659–60.
7. Wheeler, *Pierpont Morgan & Friends*, p. 30.
8. Allen, *Great Pierpont Morgan*, p. 90.
9. Winkler, *Morgan the Magnificent*, p. 19.
10. Satterlee, *J. Pierpont Morgan*, p. 289.
11. JSM, HC 3.2.2.2 (1), telegram from J.P. Morgan, Sr., to J. S. Morgan & Co., February 5, 1895.
12. Carosso, *Morgans*, p. 333.
13. Hale, *Britain and Japan and the Financial Bogeymen*, p. 10.
14. Glad, *McKinley, Bryan, and the People*, p. 177.
15. Scott, *Robert Bacon*, p. 78; Sinclair, *Corsair*, p. 96.
16. Hale, *Britain and Japan and the Financial Bogeymen*, epigraph.
17. Allen, *Great Pierpont Morgan*, p. 145.
18. Ibid.
19. Daniel, *Chronicle of the 20th Century*, p. 25.
20. Garraty, *Right-Hand Man*, p. 84.

21. JPMJ, Box 7, Folder 1, letter to Frances Tracy Morgan, June 21, 1901.
22. Satterlee, *J. Pierpont Morgan*, p. 430.
23. Jackson, *J. P. Morgan*, p. 253.
24. Wheeler, *Pierpont Morgan & Friends* p. 196.
25. JPMJ, Box 4, Folder 3, letter to Frances Tracy Morgan, April 20, 1898.
26. Ibid., letter to Frances Tracy Morgan, March 28, 1898.
27. Ziegler, *Sixth Great Power*, p. 286.
28. Weller, *New Haven Railroad*, p. 17.
29. Pringle, *Theodore Roosevelt*, p. 227.
30. Hendrick, *Life of Andrew Carnegie*, p. 131.
31. Carosso, *Morgans*, p. 467.
32. Ibid., p. 466.
33. Allen, *Great Pierpont Morgan*, p. 140.
34. Satterlee, *J. Pierpont Morgan*, p. 346.
35. Scott, *Robert Bacon*, p. 83.
36. Josephson, *Robber Barons*, p. 425.
37. Carosso, *Morgans*, p. 84.
38. Sinclair, *Corsair*, p. 129.
39. Weller, *New Haven Railroad*, p. 148.
40. *WSJ*, November 15, 1988.
41. Cashman, *America in the Gilded Age*, p. 76.
42. Wheeler, *Pierpont Morgan & Friends*, p. 61.
43. Wecter, *Saga of American Society*, p. 124.
44. Nicolson, *Portrait of a Marriage*, pp. 59–60.
45. Jackson, *J. P. Morgan*, p. 295.
46. Wecter, *Saga of American Society*, p. 124.
47. Sinclair, *Corsair*, p. 192.
48. Ibid., p. 69.
49. Scott, *Robert Bacon*, p. 71.
50. Wheeler, *Pierpont Morgan & Friends*, p. 27.
51. Scott, *Robert Bacon*, p. 70.
52. Sinclair, *Corsair*, p. 206.
53. Scott, *Robert Bacon*, p. 70.
54. Kobler, *Otto the Magnificent*, pp. 23–24.
55. Birmingham, *"Our Crowd,"* p. 19.
56. Auletta, *Greed and Glory on Wall Street*, p. 27.
57. Kobler, *Otto the Magnificent*, p. 23.
58. Adler, *Jacob H. Schiff*, p. 176.
59. Winkler, *Morgan the Magnificent*, p. 10.
60. Birmingham, *"Our Crowd,"* p. 147.
61. Scott, *Robert Bacon*, p. 91.
62. *NYT*, May 9, 1901.
63. *NYH*, May 9, 1901.
64. *NYT*, May 9, 1901.
65. Borkin, *Robert R. Young*, p. 21.
66. Winkler, *Morgan the Magnificent*, p. 190.

67. Johns, *The Man Who Shot McKinley*, pp. 126–27.
68. *JPMJ*, Box 7, Folder 1, letter to Frances Tracy Morgan, April 20, 1901.
69. *J*, November 14, 1901.

CHAPTER SIX: TRUST

1. *JPMJ*, Box 6, Folder 1, letter to Frances Tracy Morgan, February 21, 1899.
2. Forbes, *J. P. Morgan, Jr.*, p. 41.
3. Ibid., p. 52.
4. Ibid.
5. JPMJ, Box 6, Folder 1, letter to Frances Tracy Morgan, March 3, 1899.
6. JPMJ, Box 4, Folder 2, letter to Frances Tracy Morgan, February 8, 1898.
7. JPMJ, Box 6, Folder 2, letter to Frances Tracy Morgan, April 20, 1899.
8. Forbes, *J. P. Morgan, Jr.*, p. 24.
9. JPMJ, Box 4, Folder 2, letter to Frances Tracy Morgan, February 25, 1898.
10. JPMJ, Box 6, Folder 3, letter to Frances Tracy Morgan, March 9, 1900.
11. Hovey, *Life Story of J. Pierpont Morgan*, p. 332.
12. Ziegler, *Sixth Great Power*, p. 292.
13. Ibid., p. 291.
14. Wheeler, *Pierpont Morgan & Friends*, p. 228.
15. Allen, *Great Pierpont Morgan*, p. 178.
16. *NYT*, August 11, 1963.
17. Forbes, *J. P. Morgan, Jr.*, p. 49.
18. Wade, *Titanic*, p. 33.
19. Hulderman, *Albert Ballin*, pp. 49–50.
20. *NYT*, April 29, 1902.
21. *NYT*, April 20, 1902.
22. Cecil, *Albert Ballin*, p. 57.
23. Ziegler, *Sixth Great Power*, p. 296.
24. Ibid., p. 298.
25. Wecter, *Saga of American Society*, p. 123.
26. GWP, Box 5, cable to Theodore Roosevelt, September 14, 1901.
27. Pringle, *Theodore Roosevelt*, p. 245.
28. Ibid., p. 256.
29. Ibid.
30. Ibid.
31. Ibid., p. 272.
32. Ibid., p. 277.
33. Ibid.
34. Ibid., p. 264.
35. Garraty, *Right-Hand Man*, p. 84.
36. Ibid., p. 89.
37. Carosso, *Morgans*, p. 479.
38. GWP, Box 6, letter to J. P. Morgan, Sr., July 30, 1902.
39. Garraty, *Right-Hand Man*, p. 141.

40. GWP, Box 9, letter to J. P. Morgan, Sr., June 10, 1908.

41. CUOH-WJS, pp. 28–29.

42. White, *Autobiography,* pp. 459, 484, 490.

43. Garraty, *Right-Hand Man,* p. 219.

44. Schlesinger, *Crisis of the Old Order,* p. 21.

45. Winkler, *Morgan the Magnificent,* p. 284.

46. Sinclair, *Corsair,* p. 169.

47. Ibid., p. 162.

48. Satterlee, *J. Pierpont Morgan,* p. 437.

49. Carosso, *Morgans,* p. 645.

50. JPMJ, Box 6, Folder 3, letter to Frances Tracy Morgan, January 2, 1900.

51. JPMJ, Box 7, Folder 1, letter to Frances Tracy Morgan, April 3, 1901.

52. Smalley, *Anglo-American Memories,* p. 226.

53. Beebe, *Big Spenders,* pp. 285–86.

54. Ibid.

55. Winkler, *Morgan the Magnificent,* p. 10.

56. Josephson, *Robber Barons,* p. 293.

57. Kobler, *Otto the Magnificent,* pp. 72–73.

58. Winkler, *Morgan the Magnificent,* p. 7.

59. Allen, *Great Pierpont Morgan,* p. 4.

60. Cashman, *America in the Gilded Age,* p. 38.

61. Winkler, *Morgan the Magnificent,* p. 136.

62. Robertson, *My Aunt Maxine,* pp. 200–201.

63. Nicolson, *Portrait of a Marriage,* p. 59.

64. Jackson, *J. P. Morgan,* p. 293.

65. Ibid.

66. Ibid., p. 312.

67. Sampson, *Money Lenders,* p. 65.

68. Jackson, *J. P. Morgan,* p. 249.

69. Sinclair, *Corsair,* p. 205.

70. JPMJ, Box 32, cable to J. P. Morgan, Sr., June 23, 1911.

71. *SEP,* August 26, 1922.

72. *NYT,* December 16, 1956. Sinclair, *Corsair,* p. 207.

73. JSM, Extracts of Correspondence—Edward C. Grenfell—Count Maurice de Bosdari, p. 88.

74. RCL, Group 1030, Series I, Box 7, Folder 169, memorandum to Robert Gordon Wasson, February 23, 1945.

CHAPTER SEVEN: PANIC

1. JPMJ, Box 31, cable to J. P. Morgan, Sr., March 25, 1907.

2. Ibid., cable from J. P. Morgan, Sr., March 25, 1907.

3. Pringle, *Theodore Roosevelt,* p. 436.

4. Garraty, *Right-Hand Man,* p. 206.

5. Chandler, *Benjamin Strong,* p. 28.

6. Sinclair, *Corsair*, p. 179.

7. HLS, Folder 2, notes of Ben Strong about Henry P. Davison.

8. Ibid., memorandum from George W. Perkins about the Panic of 1907, p. 6.

9. Allen, *Great Pierpont Morgan*, p. 202.

10. Satterlee, *J. Pierpont Morgan*, p. 474.

11. Ibid., p. 479.

12. Sinclair, *Corsair*, p. 189.

13. Lamont, *Across World Frontiers*, p. 37.

14. Allen, *Great Pierpont Morgan*, p. 207.

15. Allen, *Lords of Creation*, p. 139.

16. Ibid., p. 142.

17. Link, *Road to the White House*, p. 116.

18. Sinclair, *Corsair*, p. 226.

19. GWP, Box 9, cable to J. P. Morgan, Sr., July 23, 1908.

20. *BM*, July/August 1984.

21. Kolko, *Railroads and Regulations*, p. 179.

22. GWP, Box 9, letter to J. P. Morgan, Sr., February 29, 1909.

23. Attali, p. 57.

24. JPMJ, Box 32, cable to J. S. Morgan & Co., October 25, 1909.

25. Croly, *Willard Straight*, p. 339.

26. JPMJ, Box 32, cable from J. P. Morgan, Sr., June 3, 1909.

27. Carosso, *Morgans*, p. 553.

28. Ibid.

29. Swanberg, *Whitney Father, Whitney Heiress*, p. 257.

30. Croly, *Willard Straight*, p. 381.

31. Swanberg, *Whitney Father, Whitney Heiress*, p. 271.

32. Ibid., p. 299.

33. Ibid.

34. Ibid., p. 310.

35. Croly, *Willard Straight*, pp. 394, 399.

36. Swanberg, *Whitney Father, Whitney Heiress*, p. 309.

37. Croly, *Willard Straight*, p. 397.

38. Ibid., p. 418.

39. Ibid., pp. 436–38.

40. Ibid.

41. Carosso, *Morgans*, p. 574.

42. Swanberg, *Whitney Father, Whitney Heiress*, pp. 337–38.

43. Carosso, *Morgans*, p. 561.

44. JPMJ, Box 32, cable to Edward C. Grenfell, February 19, 1912.

CHAPTER EIGHT: TITANIC

1. Wheeler, *Pierpont Morgan & Friends*, p. 134.

2. Hovey, *Life Story of J. Pierpont Morgan*, p. 313.

3. Wheeler, *Pierpont Morgan & Friends,* p. 132.

4. Ibid.

5. Jackson, *J. P. Morgan,* p. 237.

6. Steffens, *Autobiography,* p. 694.

7. Marbury, *My Crystal Ball,* p. 153.

8. Ibid., p. 152.

9. Barron, *They Told Barron,* p. 34.

10. GWP, Box 10, letter to J. P. Morgan, Sr., May 10, 1910.

11. Garraty, *Right-Hand Man,* p. 234.

12. *BM,* July/August 1984.

13. Ibid.

14. Lamont, *Henry P. Davison,* p. 121.

15. Ibid., p. 232.

16. Lamont, *Across World Frontiers,* p. 58.

17. *NYT,* February 3, 1948.

18. Lamont, *Across World Frontiers,* p. 40.

19. Ibid., p. 46.

20. JPMJ, Reminiscences of J. P. Morgan, Jr., p. 11.

21. JPMJ, Box 32, cable from J. P. Morgan, Sr., April 15, 1912.

22. Wade, *Titanic,* p. 448.

23. JPMJ, Box 32, cable to J. P. Morgan, Sr., April 19, 1912.

24. *NYT.* August 11, 1963, showing cartoon from *Philadelphia Public Ledger,* 1912.

25. Link, *Road to the White House,* pp. 128–29.

26. HPD, letter to Morgan Grenfell & Co., October 26, 1911.

27. Ibid., letter to J. P. Morgan, Jr., October 30, 1911.

28. Pringle, *Theodore Roosevelt,* p. 552.

29. Garraty, *Right-Hand Man,* p. 265.

30. Davis, *Hero,* p. 46.

31. Link, *Road to the White House,* p. 443.

32. Greider, *Secrets of the Temple,* p. 275.

33. JPMJ, Box 7, Folder 8, letter to Vivian Hugh Smith, July 27, 1911.

34. Ibid., letter to Edward C. Grenfell, August 9, 1911.

35. Ibid., Box 32, cable to J. P. Morgan, Sr., April 25, 1912.

36. HPD, cable from J. P. Morgan, Jr., October 27, 1913.

37. Cruikshank, *A Delicate Experiment,* p. 100.

38. JPMJ, Box 32, cables from Thomas W. Lamont to Henry P. Davison, May 3, 1912, and from Henry P. Davison to J. P. Morgan, Jr., and Thomas W. Lamont, May 4, 1912.

39. TWL, Box 91, Folder 1, letter to Henry P. Davison, June 1, 1911.

40. Carosso, *Morgans,* p. 620.

41. JPMJ, Box 32, cable to J. P. Morgan, Sr., February 2, 1911.

42. Allen, *Great Pierpont Morgan,* p. 8.

43. Carosso, *Morgans,* p. 633.

44. U.S. Congress, House, Testimony before the Money Trust Investigation, p. 92.

45. Ibid., p. 21.
46. Ibid., p. 67.
47. Ibid., p. 57.
48. Harbaugh, *Lawyer's Lawyer*, p. 320.
49. Birmingham, *"Our Crowd,"* p. 343.
50. JPMJ, Box 32, cable to J. P. Morgan, Sr., December 20, 1912.
51. Forbes, *J. P. Morgan, Jr.*, p. 71.
52. Hinton, Meyer, and Rodd, *Comments about the Morgan Bank*, p. 25.
53. Satterlee, *J. Pierpont Morgan*, p. 569.
54. JPMJ, Box 32, cable from Louisa Satterlee, February 13, 1913.
55. Ibid., cable from Louisa Satterlee, February 16, 1913.
56. *NYT*, December 16, 1956.
57. Satterlee, *J. Pierpont Morgan*, p. 583.
58. Ibid., p. 416.
59. Carosso, *Morgans*, p. 642.
60. JPMJ, Letter Press Book 14, Box 10, letter to ?, March 14, 1914.
61. Carosso, *Morgans*, p. 644.
62. JPMJ, Box 32, cable to Louisa Satterlee, April 9, 1913.
63. *ME*, Morgan Firm, Folder 5.
64. Hughes, *Vital Few*, p. 404.
65. Greider, *Secrets of the Temple*, pp. 268–69.

CHAPTER NINE: METAMORPHOSIS

1. *FD*, May 1926.
2. Ibid.
3. CUOH-GW, p. 33.
4. JPMJ, Letter Press Book 12, Box 18, letter to Mrs. William Hooper, May 26, 1916.
5. JPMJ, Box 147, letter to Eliot Tuckerman, July 12, 1915.
6. *NYK*, February 2, 1929.
7. JPMJ, Letter Press Book 16, Box 11, letter to Messrs. Lincoln Bennett & Co., February 3, 1915.
8. Forbes, *J. P. Morgan, Jr.*, p. 137.
9. *NYT*, August 11, 1950.
10. JPMJ, Box 32, cable to J. P. Morgan, Sr., June 24, 1912.
11. *FO*, August 1933.
12. Forbes, *J. P. Morgan, Jr.*, p. 45.
13. *NYT*, December 16, 1956.
14. Samuels, *Bernard Berenson*, p. 158.
15. Sinclair, *Corsair*, p. 232.
16. Kolko, *Railroads and Regulations*, pp. 156, 160.
17. GWP, Box 9, letter to J. P. Morgan, Sr., May 15, 1908.
18. Allen, *Great Pierpont Morgan*, p. 187.
19. Weller, *New Haven Railroad*, p. 51.

20. White, *Puritan in Babylon*, p. 97.
21. Weller, *New Haven Railroad*, p. 3.
22. Ibid., p. 46.
23. Ibid., p. 7.
24. Ibid., p. 149.
25. Carosso, *Morgans*, p. 607.
26. JPMJ, Box 32, cable from J. P. Morgan, Sr., March 24, 1910.
27. HPD, cable from J. P. Morgan & Co. to J. P. Morgan, Jr., December 11, 1913.
28. TWL, Box 84, Folder 16, Transcript of Meeting at University Club, December 2, 1913.
29. Ibid.
30. Ibid.
31. JPMJ, Letter Press Book 14, Box 10, letter to Hon. Henry White, June 5, 1914.
32. Kettl, *Leadership at the Fed*, pp. 20–21.
33. *NYK*, November 16, 1987, p. 81.

CHAPTER TEN: WAR

1. HPD, cable from J. P. Morgan, Jr., to Herman Harjes, October 30, 1912.
2. Nicolson, *Dwight Morrow*, p. 166.
3. McAdoo, *Crowded Years*, p. 290.
4. Noyes, *Market Place*, p. 249.
5. JPMJ, Letter Press Book 15, Box 11, letter to ?, September 14, 1914.
6. ME, Morgan Firm, Folders 4 and 5, Statement before Senate Munitions Committee, January 7, 1936.
7. TWL, Box 91, Folder 2, cables from Henry P. Davison, August 4 and 7, 1914.
8. *NYT*, October 14, 1935.
9. Cherny, *Righteous Cause*, p. 46.
10. Link, *Wilson*, p. 64.
11. Colby, *DuPont Dynasty*, p. 187.
12. Swanberg, *Whitney Father, Whitney Heiress*, p. 348.
13. Lamont, *Henry P. Davison*, p. 6.
14. Burk, *Britain*, p. 19.
15. Ibid., p. 21.
16. Forbes, *Stettinius, Sr.*, p. 74.
17. Ibid., p. 49.
18. Seymour, *Intimate Papers of Colonel House*, p. 98.
19. CUOH-BB, p. 160.
20. Hyde, *Lord Reading*, p. 185
21. Colby, *DuPont Dynasty*, p. 186.
22. JPMJ, Box 147, letter from Thomas W. Lamont, July 1, 1915.

23. JPMJ, Letter Press Book 16, Box 11, letter to Sir Cecil Arthur Spring-Rice, January 6, 1915.

24. Notes of Examination of Frank Holt, by Charles MacDonald, M.D., in the Nassau County Jail, July 6, 1915, Pierpont Morgan Library.

25. JPMJ, Letter Press Book 12, Box 17, letter to F. W. Stevens, August 19, 1915.

26. Ibid., letter to John Callahan, August 9, 1915.

27. Ibid., Box 147, letter to Edward C. Grenfell, July 28, 1915.

28. Ibid., Letter Press Book 14, Box 21, letter to Morris Whitridge, August 13, 1917.

29. CUOH-GW, p. 81.

30. Birmingham, "Our Crowd," p. 344.

31. JPMJ, Letter Press Book 15, Box 11, letter to Edward C. Grenfell, September 20, 1914.

32. JPMJ, Letter Press Book 16, Box 11, to Jacob Schiff, February 3, 1915.

33. Nicolson, Dwight Morrow, pp. 188–89.

34. JPMJ, Box Cabinet 3, Drawer 2.1, memorandum from Ray Stannard Baker about foreign affairs, p. 13; letter from Robert Lansing to Woodrow Wilson, September 6, 1915.

35. JPMJ, Letter Press Book 15, Box 11, letter to Edward C. Grenfell, September 5, 1914.

36. NYK, February 9, 1929.

37. JPMJ, Letter Press Book 12, Box 17, letter to Edward C. Grenfell, November 15, 1915.

38. Birmingham, "Our Crowd," p. 344.

39. Ibid., p. 363.

40. MGR, letter from David Lloyd George, December 10, 1917.

41. J. P. Morgan & Co., America and Munitions, p. 15.

42. Burk, Britain, America, and the Sinews of War, 1914–1918, pp. 88–89.

43. Ibid., p. 89.

44. Swanberg, Whitney Father, p. 355.

45. JSM, Extracts of Correspondence, Edward C. Grenfell, Great War, 1914–15, pp. 101–2.

46. JPMJ, Edward C. Grenfell File, letter from Edward C. Grenfell, April 29, 1920.

47. CUOH-GR, pp. 165–66.

48. BM, July/August 1984.

49. JPMJ, Letter Press Book 15, Box 11, letter to Herman Harjes, September 20, 1914.

50. JPMJ, Edward C. Grenfell File, letter to Edward C. Grenfell, August 9, 1917.

51. Nicolson, Diaries & Letters, p. 76.

52. Ibid.

CHAPTER ELEVEN: EXPLOSION

1. Burk, "House of Morgan in Financial Diplomacy," p. 4.

2. JPMJ, Box Cabinet 3, Drawer 2.2., digest of Nye Hearings, p. 4.

3. Lamont, *Across World Frontiers*, p. 80.

4. Lindbergh, *Flower and the Nettle*, p. xxv.

5. Lamont, *Across World Frontiers*, p. 193.

6. ME, Morgan Firm, Folder 37, letter from George Whitney, June 2, 1919.

7. ME, Edward R. Stettinius Folder, letter from Edward R. Stettinius, May 6, 1919.

8. TWL, Box 171, Folder 28, letter to Woodrow Wilson, June 13, 1919.

9. Lamont, *Across World Frontiers*, p. 126.

10. TWL, Box 171, Folder 28, memorandum to Woodrow Wilson about treaty ratification, June 13, 1919.

11. Ibid., letter from Woodrow Wilson, June 7, 1919.

12. Lamont, *Across World Frontiers*, p. 158.

13. TWL, Box 115, Folder 19, letter to Robert A. Lovett, November 21, 1932.

14. JPMJ, Letter Press Book 17, Box 28, letter to Henry P. Davison, August 12, 1920.

15. Ibid., Letter Press Book 14, Box 22, Letter to Morris Whitridge, November 26, 1917.

16. Ibid., Letter Press Book 16, Box 26, letter to Franklin D. Locke, February 2, 1920.

17. *NYT*, April 20, 1920.

18. Ibid.

19. Ibid.

20. Brooks, *Once in Golconda*, p. 6.

21. Ibid., p. 20.

22. CUOH-GW, p. 59.

23. Ibid., p. 60.

24. JPMJ, Letter Press Book 17, Box 27, letter to A. Lawrence Lowell, March 2, 1920.

25. Wecter, *Saga of American Society*, p. 155.

26. JPMJ, Letter Press Book 16, Box 25, letter to Edward C. Grenfell, April 9, 1919.

27. Ibid., Letter Press Book 17, Box 27, letter to Edward C. Grenfell, March 3, 1920.

28. Ibid., Edward C. Grenfell File, letter from Edward C. Grenfell, April 22, 1920.

29. Ibid., Letter Press Book 18, Box 29, letter to Paul Tynes.

30. *BM*, July/August 1984.

31. HPD, cable to Nelson W. Aldrich, April 7, 1913.

32. Lamont, *Henry P. Davison*, p. 298.

33. *BM*, July/August 1984.

34. *NYT*, March 23 and 24, April 18, 1915.

35. Lamont, *Henry P. Davison*, p. 325.
36. Lamont, *Across World Frontiers*, pp. 45–46.
37. Brooks, *Once in Golconda*, p. 47.
38. Lamont, ed., *Thomas Lamonts*, p. 119.
39. Lundberg, *America's 60 Families*, p. 33.
40. TWL, Box 94, Folder 16, letter to Jack Prentiss, February 24, 1916.
41. TWL Box 94, Folder 16, letter to Henry Ford, June 19, 1916.
42. *BW*, December 10, 1979.
43. Sloan, *My Years with General Motors*, p. 43.
44. JPMJ, Letter Press Book 18, Box 29, letter to Warren G. Harding, June 6, 1921.
45. Lamont, *Across World Frontiers*, p. 219.
46. Ibid., p. 218.
47. TWL, Box 108, Folder 13, letter to J. P. Morgan, Jr., October 6, 1922.
48. Ibid., Box 127, Folder 29, memorandum of March 24, 1933, p. 10.

CHAPTER TWELVE: ODYSSEY

1. RCL, Group 1030, Series I, Box 4, Folder 97, memorandum to Thomas W. Lamont, May 5, 1939.
2. Lamont, *Across World Frontiers*, p. 242.
3. Lamont, ed., *Thomas Lamonts*, p. 116.
4. Lamont, *Across World Frontiers*, p. 238.
5. Lamont, ed., *Thomas Lamonts*, p. 111.
6. Lamont, *Across World Frontiers*, p. 231.
7. MGR, File, Japan Government Loan, 1924, telegram from Thomas W. Lamont to Junnosuke Inouye, October 10, 1923.
8. Ibid., File 1, Japan Government Loan, 1924, telegram from J. P. Morgan & Co. to Edward C. Grenfell, January, 1924.
9. Ibid, File 27, Japan Government Loan, 1924, telegram from Thomas W. Lamont to Edward C. Grenfell, January 28, 1924.
10. Carosso, *Investment Banking in America*, p. 257.
11. Lamont, *Yes to Life*, p. 18.
12. *El Universal*, August 5, 1921.
13. Swanberg, *Citizen Hearst*, p. 339.
14. Lamont, ed., *Thomas Lamonts*, p. 118.
15. TWL, Box 197, Folder 19, letter to Charles Evans Hughes, April 18, 1924.
16. Lamont, ed., *Thomas Lamonts*, p. 118.
17. TWL, Box 192, Folder 7, cable from J. P. Morgan, Jr., October 25, 1921.
18. Ibid., letter from Walter C. Teagle, December 15, 1921.
19. Ibid., Anonymous memo, December 14, 1921, attached to letter from Walter C. Teagle, December 15, 1921.
20. Chandler, *Benjamin Strong*, p. 260.
21. Clay, *Lord Norman*, p. 487.

22. Boyle, *Montagu Norman*, p. 198.

23. Clay, *Lord Norman*, p. 482.

24. Ibid., p. 55.

25. Boyle, *Montagu Norman*, p. 86.

26. RCL, Group 1030, Series I, Box 1, Folder 9, letter to Basil P. Blackett, March 2, 1920.

27. Jay, Morgan & Cie., p. 24.

28. Burk, "House of Morgan in Financial Diplomacy," p. 29.

29. TWL, Box 182, Folder 27, "Heartbreak House," April 18, 1945.

30. *NYH*, May 25, 1922.

31. JPMJ, Letter Press Book 19, Box 32, letter to Edward C. Grenfell, March 10, 1923.

32. Forbes, *J. P. Morgan, Jr.*, p. 277.

33. Sayers, *Bank of England*, p. 81.

34. Schacht, *Confessions of the Old Wizard*, p. 179.

35. TWL, Box 182, Folder 2, letter to Dr. Hjalmar Schacht, April 7, 1934.

36. RCL, Group 1030, Series I, Box 3, Folder 62, letter to S. Parker Gilbert, February 2, 1928.

37. Case and Case, *Owen Young and American Enterprise*, p. 280.

38. Ibid., p. 300.

39. J.P. Morgan & Co., News Report on the Death of S. Parker Gilbert.

40. McNeil, *American Money and the Weimar Republic*, p. 30.

41. Ibid.

42. Nicolson, *Dwight Morrow*, p. 276.

CHAPTER THIRTEEN: JAZZ

1. JPMJ, Letter Press Book 24, Box 41, letter to Charles C. Hilles, May 28, 1928.

2. TWL, Box 115, Folder 17, letter to Bruce Bliven, no date.

3. Harbaugh, *Lawyer's Lawyer*, p. 184.

4. JWD, 1873–1955 (?).

5. Harbaugh, *Lawyer's Lawyer*, p. 211.

6. Josephson, *Money Lords*, p. 21.

7. *NYWT*, March 13, 1943.

8. ME, Dwight W. Morrow Folder, letter to Dwight W. Morrow, April 28, 1927.

9. Lamont, ed., *Thomas Lamonts*, p. 385.

10. Pecora, *Wall Street under Oath*, p. 45.

11. ME, Russell C. Leffingwell Folder, letter to Russell C. Leffingwell, July 31, 1924.

12. Forbes, *Stettinius, Sr.*, p. 207.

13. Ibid., p. 106.

14. Ibid., p. 199.

15. Lamont, *Across World Frontiers*, p. 216.

16. Lindbergh, *Flower and the Nettle,* p. 199.

17. Ibid., p. 207.

18. Lamont, ed., *Thomas Lamonts,* p. 107.

19. *HFJ,* May 1926.

20. Forbes, *J. P. Morgan, Jr.,* p. 126.

21. Ibid., p. 67.

22. *NYK,* February 2, 1929.

23. *N,* February 9, 1935.

24. JPMJ, Letter Press Book 24, Box 42, letter to Charles G. Dawes, July 15, 1929.

25. *FO,* August 1933.

26. JPMJ, Edward C. Grenfell Folder, letter to Edward C. Grenfell, April 12, 1920.

27. Forbes, *J. P. Morgan, Jr.,* p. 113.

28. JPMJ, Charles Steele Folder.

29. *NYT,* September 4, 1967.

30. Ibid.

31. Forbes, *J. P. Morgan, Jr.,* p. 138.

32. Ibid., p. 140.

33. JPMJ, Edward C. Grenfell Folder, letter to Edward C. Grenfell, January 19, 1922.

34. Ibid., Letter Press Book 21, Box 36, letter to Edward C. Grenfell, April 17, 1925.

35. Ibid., Letter Press Book 22, Box 37, letter to Louisa Lee Schuyler, July 23, 1925.

36. Ibid., letter to Mrs. J. Kearny Warren, July 14, 1925.

37. TWL, Box 191, Folder 1, letter to Giovanni Fummi, July 10, 1930.

38. Ibid., letter to Charles Steele, August 17, 1925.

39. *NYK,* February 9, 1929.

40. JPMJ, Letter Press Book 24, Box 41, no date.

CHAPTER FOURTEEN: GOLDEN

1. Woolf, *Diary,* p. 210.

2. Lindbergh, *Flower and the Nettle,* pp. 64–65.

3. Pankhurst, *Suffragette Movement,* p. 393.

4. Ibid., p. 484.

5. JPMJ, Box 32, cable from Edward C. Grenfell, July 26, 1913.

6. Pankhurst, *Home Front,* p. 71.

7. Burk, "House of Morgan in Financial Diplomacy," p. 12.

8. RCL, Group 1030, Series I, Box 6, letter to J. P. Morgan, Jr., September 10, 1923.

9. JPMJ, Edward C. Grenfell Folder, letter from Edward C. Grenfell, March 23, 1925.

10. Boyle, *Montagu Norman,* p. 189.

11. JPMJ, Edward C. Grenfell Folder, letter from Edward C. Grenfell, June 24, 1926.

12. Ibid., letter from Edward C. Grenfell, March 23, 1925.

13. MGR, File 5, British Gold Loan, cable from Edward C. Grenfell to J. P. Morgan, Jr., April 3, 1925.

14. *DT*, May 5, 1925.

15. MGR, File 5, British Gold Loan, letter from Winston Churchill to Edward C. Grenfell, May 1, 1925.

16. Chandler, *Benjamin Strong*, p. 384.

17. Lamont, *Yes to Life*, p. 22.

18. Ibid.

19. Lamont, ed., *Thomas Lamonts*, p. 139.

20. Ibid., p. 95.

21. Forbes, *J. P. Morgan, Jr.*, p. 125.

22. TWL, Box 190, Folder 13, letter to Giovanni Fummi, October 5, 1923.

23. Ibid., Box 190, Folder 14, letter to Prince Gelasio Caetani, April 21, 1924.

24. Ibid., Box 103, Folder 11, letter to Russell C. Leffingwell, April 20, 1925.

25. Ibid., Box 190, Folder 17, letter to Giovanni Fummi, December 11, 1925.

26. Thomas W. Lamont, speech before the Foreign Policy Association Luncheon, New York City, January 23, 1926.

27. Diggins, *Mussolini and Fascism*, p. 145.

28. Ibid., pp. 147–49.

29. ME, Thomas W. Lamont Folder, memorandum to Thomas W. Lamont, January 7, 1926.

30. Diggins, *Mussolini and Fascism*, p. 50.

31. Lippmann, *Public Philosopher*, p. 214.

32. TWL, Box 190, Folder 22, letter to Giacomo de Martino, April 6, 1927.

33. *CH*, 28, July 1928.

CHAPTER FIFTEEN: SAINT

1. DWM, Calvin Coolidge File (1922–31), letter to James R. Sheffield, June 1, 1920.

2. TWL, Box 113, Folder 4, letter from Dwight W. Morrow to Howard C. Robbins, January 16, 1920.

3. Nicolson, *Dwight Morrow*, p. 229.

4. Howland, *Morrow*, p. vi.

5. DWM, Calvin Coolidge File (1922–31), letter from Calvin Coolidge, March 10, 1920.

6. Nicolson, *Dwight Morrow*, p. 140.

7. Ibid., p. 136.

8. Ibid., p. 148.

9. Ibid., p. 149.
10. Ibid., p. 103.
11. Ibid., p. 124.
12. Howland, *Morrow*, p. 67.
13. Nicolson, *Dwight Morrow*, p. 246.
14. Anne Morrow Lindbergh, interview with author.
15. Constance Morrow Morgan, letter to author, April 19, 1989.
16. *NYHT*, October 9, 1927.
17. Howland, *Morrow*, p. xi.
18. Davis, *Hero*, p. 253.
19. Steel, *Walter Lippmann and the American Century*, p. 238.
20. *FA*, January, 1927.
21. Nicolson, *Dwight Morrow*, p. 291.
22. DWM, Charles A. Lindbergh Folder, letter from Charles A. Lindbergh, September 29, 1927.
23. Lindbergh, *Hour of Gold, Hour of Lead*, p. 128.
24. Nicolson, *Dwight Morrow*, p. 313.
25. Lindbergh, *Hour of Gold, Hour of Lead*, p. 20.
26. Anne Morrow Lindbergh, interview with author.
27. Lippmann, *Public Philosopher*, p. 211.
28. CUOH-GR, p. 223.
29. TWL, Box 192, Folder 15, cable to J. P. Morgan partners, March 2, 1929; cable to J. P. Morgan & Co., March 5, 1929.
30. CUOH-GR, p. 215.
31. TWL, Box 114, Folder 4, letter to Harold Nicolson, May 17, 1935.
32. Ibid., memorandum from Vernon Munroe, December 11, 1929.
33. Nicolson, *Dwight Morrow*, p. 382.
34. TWL, Box 192, Folder 18, letter to Dwight W. Morrow, July 24, 1930.
35. Ibid., Box 197, Folder 21, letter from Dwight W. Morrow, August 18, 1930.
36. *NFP*, August 13, 1930.
37. Nicolson, *Dwight Morrow*, p. 379.
38. Ibid., p. 388.
39. Davis, *Hero*, p. 295.
40. Ibid., p. 291.
41. Nicolson, *Dwight Morrow*, p. 399.
42. Nicolson, *Diaries and Letters*, p. 71.
43. Brooks, *Once in Golconda*, p. 49.

CHAPTER SIXTEEN: CRASH

1. *WSJ*, May 1, 1989.
2. Wendt, *Wall Street Journal*, p. 203.
3. Ibid., p. 201.
4. Mayer, *Markets*, pp. 50, 272.

5. *NYK*, February 2, 1929.

6. Fogarty, *The Story of Texasgulf*, p. 11.

7. TWL, Box 127, Folder 29, memorandum of March 24, 1933, p. 17.

8. ERS, Box 8, Folder 154, letter to Henry P. Davison, February 4, 1922.

9. Ibid., Box 11, Folder 200, letter to Thomas W. Lamont, August 21, 1924.

10. Ibid., Box 11, Folder 187, letter to Herman Harjes, December 19, 1923.

11. Josephson, *Money Lords*, p. 48.

12. TWL, Box 126, Folder 12, private memorandum about Oris P. and Mantis J. Van Sweringen, July 6, 1928.

13. Brooks, *Seven Fat Years*, p. 221.

14. Ziegler, *Sixth Great Power*, p. 356.

15. JPMJ, Box 38, cables 1929–35, cable to J. P. Morgan & Co., August 30, 1929.

16. Ziegler, *Sixth Great Power*, pp. 356–57.

17. Lyons, *David Sarnoff*, p. 150.

18. Bilby, *David Sarnoff and the Rise of the Communications Industry*, pp. 96–98.

19. Lyons, *David Sarnoff*, p. 153.

20. Ibid., pp. 153–54.

21. McNeil, *American Money and the Weimar Republic*, p. 261.

22. TWL, Box 103, Folder 13, letter from Russell C. Leffingwell, March 8, 1929.

23. Ibid.

24. Ibid., letter from Russell C. Leffingwell, April 16, 1929.

25. *TI*, November 2, 1987.

26. Galbraith, *Great Crash*, p. 71.

27. Schlesinger, *Crisis of the Old Order*, p. 84.

28. *NYT*, August 1, 1928.

29. TWL, Box 98, Folder 15, letter to Herbert Hoover, October 19, 1929.

30. Ibid., Box 108, Folder 14, letter to J. P. Morgan, Jr., October 22, 1929.

31. Galbraith, *Great Crash*, p. 132.

32. Ibid.

33. Josephson, *Money Lords*, p. 102.

34. Brooks, *Once in Golconda*, p. 124.

35. *NYT*, October 25, 1929.

36. Galbraith, *Great Crash*, p. 109.

37. *WSJ*, October 25, 1929.

38. Galbraith, *Great Crash*, p. 109.

39. *NYT*, October 30, 1929.

40. Ibid.

41. Galbraith, *Great Crash*, p. 114.

42. *TI*, November 2, 1987.

43. Josephson, *Money Lords*, p. 102.

44. Ibid., p. 100.

45. *NYTR*, November 3, 1929.

46. *TI*, November 2, 1987.

47. Galbraith, *Great Crash*, p. 21.

48. Sampson, *Money Lenders*, p. 77.

CHAPTER SEVENTEEN: DEPRESSION

1. TWL, Box 131, Folder 26, notes on the stock market debacle, n.d.

2. Davis, *The Hero*, p. 290.

3. TWL, Box 103, Folder 14, letter from Russell C. Leffingwell, August 14, 1930.

4. *NYK*, November 16, 1987, p. 91.

5. JPMJ, Letter Press Book 24, Box 42, letter to Edward C. Grenfell, December 26, 1929.

6. Sobel, *ITT*, p. 67.

7. Burner, *Herbert Hoover*, p. 298.

8. TWL, Box 111, Folder 23, letter to Edward C. Grenfell, October 30, 1931.

9. Kettl, *Leadership at the Fed*, p. 37.

10. U.S. Congress, Temporary National Economic Committee, *Investigation of Concentration of Economic Power*, p. 11552.

11. Josephson, *Money Lords*, pp. 97–98.

12. Carosso, *Investment Banking in America*, p. 315.

13. Friedman and Friedman, *Free to Choose*, pp. 81–82.

14. MGR, Box 264, J. P. Morgan & Co., Miscellaneous File, U.S. Financial Affairs, letters from Thomas S. Lamont to Edward C. Grenfell, December 13 and 30, 1930.

15. RCL, Group 1030, Series I, Box 4, Folder ?, letter to Benjamin Joy, January 23, 1931.

16. *NYT*, October 30, 1929.

17. TWL, Box 98, Folder 18, memorandum to Russell C. Leffingwell, Debt Suspension Matter, June 5, 1931.

18. MGR, Box 1087, 1931 Loan, letter from Edward C. Grenfell to J. P. Morgan, Jr., August 12, 1931.

19. Ibid., letter from J. P. Morgan, Jr., to Edward C. Grenfell, August 12, 1931; telegram from Edward C. Grenfell to Montagu Norman, August 18, 1931.

20. TWL, Box 111, Folder 16, letter from Edward C. Grenfell to Thomas W. Lamont, October 25, 1924.

21. MGR, Box 1087, 1931 Loan, letter from Edward C. Grenfell to J. P. Morgan, Jr., August 14, 1931.

22. Ibid., letter from Edward C. Grenfell to J. P. Morgan, Jr., August 12, 1931.

23. Ibid., Cable 4929, from Edward C. Grenfell to J. P. Morgan & Co., August 23, 1931.

24. Ibid., Cable 2383, from J. P. Morgan & Co. to Morgan Grenfell, August 23, 1931.

25. Boyle, *Montagu Norman*, p. 272.

26. MGR, Box 1087, 1931 Loan, letter from Edward C. Grenfell to Thomas W. Lamont, n.d.

27. Boyle, *Montagu Norman*, p. 273.

28. *DH*, August 25, 1931.

29. MGR, Box 1087, 1931 Loan, letter from Edward C. Grenfell to Thomas W. Lamont, August 27, 1931.

30. Ibid., Cable 2401–27, from J. P. Morgan & Co. to J. P. Morgan, Jr., August 27, 1931.

31. Medlicott, *Contemporary England*, pp. 264–65.

32. TWL, Box 108, Folder 15, letter from Charles Steele and Thomas W. Lamont to J. P. Morgan, Jr., September 25, 1931.

33. TWL, Box 186, Folder 28, letter to Junnosuke Inouye, June 11, 1928.

34. Storry, *History of Modern Japan*, p. 188.

35. Hoover, *Memoirs*, vol. 2, p. 365.

36. TWL, Box 187, Folder 11, Junnosuke Inouye's statement on Manchuria situation, n.d.

37. TWL, Box 187, Folder 11, letter to Kakutaro Suzuki, October 17, 1931.

38. *T*, September 21, 1931.

39. RCL, Group 1030, Series I, Box 5, Folder 108, letter to Walter Lippmann, October 23, 1931.

40. TWL, Box 187, Folder 12, letter to Saburo Sonoda, November 23, 1931.

41. Ibid., Box 187, Folder 14, letter to Saburo Sonoda, March 10, 1932.

42. RCL, Group 1030, Series I, Box 3, letter to Edward C. Grenfell, February 18, 1932.

43. TWL, Box 187, Folder 13, telegram from Saburo Sonoda, February 9, 1932.

44. Ibid., letter to Saburo Sonoda, February 10, 1932.

45. Ibid., Box 188, Folder 15, letter to Ino Dan, September 14, 1932.

46. ME, Japan Folder, memorandum to Thomas W. Lamont, May 12, 1932.

47. TWL, Box 187, Folder 20, memorandum from Vernon Munroe, February 3, 1933.

48. Ibid., Box 184, Folder 9, internal memorandum, marked "Secret and Strictly Confidential," either late 1932 or early 1933.

49. Ibid., Box 122, Folder 6, letter to Edward C. Grenfell, October 11, 1934.

CHAPTER EIGHTEEN: MIDGET

1. Leuchtenburg, *Franklin D. Roosevelt and the New Deal*, p. 11.

2. Schlesinger, *Crisis of the Old Order*, p. 242.

3. TWL, Box 112, Folder 13, letter to Vivian Hugh Smith, December 14, 1943.

4. JPMJ, Letter Press Book 25, Box 43, letter to the marquess of Linlithgow (Victor Hope), January 4, 1932.

5. RCL, Group 1030, Series I, Box 1, Folder 17, letter to Bernard S. Carter, January 30, 1932.

6. Borkin, *Robert R. Young,* p. 31.

7. Ibid., p. 32.

8. JPMJ, Letter Press Book 25, Box 43, letter to the Lord Archbishop of Canterbury (Dr. Cosmo Lang), March 16, 1932.

9. Lamont, ed., *Thomas Lamonts,* p. 98.

10. Hinton, Meyer, and Rodd, *Comments about the Morgan Bank,* p. 35.

11. TWL, Box 108, Folder 15, letter to J. P. Morgan, Jr., July 28, 1931.

12. MGR, Anglo-American File 1, cable from J. P. Morgan & Co., October 18, 1919.

13. Ibid., Anglo-American File 2, letter from Thomas W. Lamont to Vivian Hugh Smith, November 7, 1922.

14. TWL, Box 98, Folder 22, memorandum from Martin Egan, July 14, 1932.

15. Whalen, *Founding Father,* p. 106.

16. TWL, Box 98, Folder 17, memorandum, October 10, 1930.

17. Ibid., Box 98, Folder 21, Memorandum for Partners Alone, April 15, 1932.

18. Ibid., Box 116, Folder 7, letter to Herbert Hoover, April 8, 1932.

19. MGR, Box 264, J. P. Morgan & Co. Miscellaneous File, U.S. Financial Affairs, letter from J. P. Morgan & Co. to Morgan & Cie., April 6, 1932.

20. RCL, Group 1030, Series I, Box 5, Folder 109, letter to Walter Lippmann, October 25, 1932.

21. Leffingwell, *Selected Letters,* p. 93.

22. RCL, Group 1030, Series I, Box 7, Folder 155, letter to Vivian Hugh Smith, November 11, 1932.

23. Leffingwell, *Selected Letters,* p. 78.

24. Ibid., p. 81.

25. Ibid., pp. 80–81.

26. TWL, Box 122, Folder 1, letter from Montagu Norman, February 26, 1933.

27. *BW,* June 7, 1933.

28. Brooks, *Once in Golconda,* p. 156.

29. Pecora, *Wall Street under Oath,* p. 85.

30. Leuchtenburg, *Franklin D. Roosevelt and the New Deal,* p. 22.

31. Ibid., p. 41.

32. MGR, Box 264, J. P. Morgan & Co. Miscellaneous File, U.S. Financial Affairs, cable from J. P. Morgan & Co., March 2, 1933.

33. Forbes, *J. P. Morgan, Jr.,* p. 175.

34. MGR, Box 264, J. P. Morgan & Co. Miscellaneous File, U.S. Financial Affairs, cable to J. P. Morgan & Co., March 15, 1933.

35. Steel, *Walter Lippmann and the American Century,* pp. 302–3.

36. Morgenthau, *From the Morgenthau Diaries,* p. 236.

37. Tugwell, *Roosevelt's Revolution,* p. 22.

38. Kindleberger, *World in Depression,* p. 202.

39. Schlesinger, *Coming of the New Deal,* p. 202.

40. RCL, Group 1030, Series I, Box 1, Folder 17, letter from Bernard S. Carter, April 26, 1933.

41. Kindleberger, *World in Depression,* p. 219.

42. Ibid., p. 231.

43. *FO,* August, 1933.

44. TWL, Box 82, Folder 3, letter to Lady Nancy Astor, June 5, 1933.

45. Carosso, *Investment Banking in America,* pp. 336–37.

46. Forbes, *J. P. Morgan, Jr.,* p. 155; JPMJ, Letter Press Book 25, Box 44, letters to the marquess of Linlithgow (Victor Hope), April 24, 1933, and Morris Whitridge, May 16, 1933.

47. JPMJ, Letter Press Book 25, Box 44, letter to the marquess of Linlithgow (Victor Hope), April 24, 1933.

48. TWL, Box 82, Folder 3, letter to Lady Nancy Astor, June 5, 1933.

49. Schlesinger, *Politics of Upheaval,* pp. 54–55.

50. Schlesinger, *Coming of the New Deal,* p. 443.

51. Harbaugh, *Lawyer's Lawyer,* p. 324.

52. JPMJ, Letter Press Book 25, Box 44, letter to Morris Whitridge, June 23, 1933.

53. U.S. Congress, Senate Committee on Banking and Currency, *Stock Exchange Practices,* J. P. Morgan, Jr., opening statement, May 23, 1933.

54. Leuchtenburg, *Franklin D. Roosevelt and the New Deal,* p. 59.

55. Harbaugh, *Lawyer's Lawyer,* p. 325.

56. U.S. Congress, Senate Committee on Banking and Currency, *Stock Exchange Practices,* p. 60.

57. Ibid., J. P. Morgan, Jr., opening statement, May 23, 1933.

58. Ibid.

59. U.S. Congress, Senate Committee on Banking and Currency, *Stock Exchange Practices,* p. 105.

60. Pecora, *Wall Street under Oath,* p. 36.

61. Ibid., p. 199.

62. Harbaugh, *Lawyer's Lawyer,* p. 326.

63. Forbes, *J. P. Morgan, Jr.,* p. 177.

64. *BE,* March 13, 1943.

65. JPMJ, Letter Press Book 25, Box 44, letter to William Duane, July 5, 1933.

66. Brooks, *Once in Golconda,* p. 180.

67. *N,* February 9, 1935.

68. Leuchtenburg, *Franklin D. Roosevelt and the New Deal,* p. 59.

69. Brooks, *Once in Golconda,* p. 180.

70. Frank W. Colby, interview with author.

71. CUOH-WJS, p. 62.

72. Carosso, *Investment Banking in America,* p. 340.

73. White, *Puritan in Babylon,* p. 428.

74. Lamont, *Henry P. Davison,* p. xviii.

75. Pecora, *Wall Street under Oath,* p. 32.

76. Schlesinger, *Coming of the New Deal,* p. 437.

77. U.S. Congress, Senate Committee on Banking and Currency, *Stock Exchange Practices*, p. 143.

78. Ibid., p. 216.

79. Ibid., p. 173.

80. TWL, Box 190, Folder 28, letter to the partners of J. P. Morgan & Co., with P.S. for Arthur M. Anderson, February 13, 1929.

81. Ickes, *Secret Diary: First Thousand Days*, p. 45.

82. Steel, *Walter Lippmann and the American Century*, p. 250.

83. *NYT*, May 27, 1933.

84. TWL, Box 112, Folder 3, letter to Adolph Ochs, May 27, 1933.

85. *BW*, May 24, 1933.

86. RCL, Group 1030, Series I, Box 3, Folder 67, letter from Carter Glass, July 12, 1933.

87. Pecora, *Wall Street under Oath*, p. 89.

88. RCL, Group 1030, Series I, Box 4, Folder 83, letter to Dean Jay, February 17, 1934.

89. CUOH-GW, p. 44.

CHAPTER NINETEEN: CRACK-UP

1. Carosso, *Investment Banking in America*, p. 353.

2. RCL, Group 1030, Series I, Box 5, memorandum to Thomas W. Lamont, January 2, 1934.

3. Beschloss, *Kennedy & Roosevelt*, p. 84.

4. Josephson, *Money Lords*, p. 172.

5. JPMJ, Letter Press Book 25, Box 44, letter to F. W. Muth, April 2, 1935.

6. Schlesinger, *Coming of the New Deal*, p. 567.

7. Forbes, *J. P. Morgan, Jr.*, p. 179.

8. JPMJ, Letter Press Book 25, Box 44, letter to Rt. Rev. William T. Manning, May 3, 1935.

9. Ibid., letter to Morris Whitridge, March 12, 1935.

10. Schlesinger, *Coming of the New Deal*, p. 498.

11. TWL, Box 182, Folder 4, interview with Neville Chamberlain, June 29, 1934.

12. Charles E. Coughlin, "Thus Goeth the Battle!" radio address delivered November 19, 1933.

13. Josephson, *Money Lords*, p. 164.

14. U.S. Congress, Temporary National Economic Committee, *Investigation of Concentration of Economic Power*, p. 83.

15. Tim Collins, interview with author.

16. *T*, June 18, 1934.

17. RCL, Group 1030, Series I, Box 4, memorandum to Thomas W. Lamont, January 2, 1934.

18. Ibid., Group 1030, Series I, Box 7, Folder 146, letter to Franklin D. Roosevelt, January 4, 1934.

19. Hinton, Meyer, and Rodd, *Comments about the Morgan Bank*, p. 29.

20. TWL, Box 131, Folder 21, letter to Charles Steele, November 15, 1934.

21. MGR, Bundle 187, File 6, Change of Firm, cable from J. P. Morgan & Co. to Henry S. Morgan, September 7, 1935.

22. *TI*, September 16, 1935.

23. *FT*, September 6, 1935.

24. Ellmore C. Patterson, interview with author.

25. Morgan Stanley, *Fiftieth Anniversary Review*, p. 13.

26. *NYT*, September 17, 1935.

27. Alexander C. Tomlinson, interview with author.

28. *N*, September 14, 1935.

29. Morgan Stanley, *Fiftieth Anniversary Review*, p. 111.

30. Perry E. Hall, interview with author.

31. Medina, *Corrected Opinion*, p. 250.

32. *FB*, May 1, 1936.

33. U.S. Congress, Temporary National Economic Committee, *Investigation of Concentration of Economic Power*, p. 83.

34. Ibid., p. 92.

35. Ickes, *Secret Diary: Inside Struggle*, p. 384.

CHAPTER TWENTY: WIZARD

1. Shirer, *Rise and Fall of the Third Reich*, p. 260.

2. Taylor, *Sword and Swastika*, p. 124.

3. Boyle, *Montagu Norman*, p. 304.

4. Schacht, *Confessions of the Old Wizard*, pp. 301-2.

5. Speer, *Inside the Third Reich*, p. 197.

6. JPMJ, Letter Press Book 25, Box 44, March 23, 1933.

7. Schacht, *Confessions of the Old Wizard*, p. 283.

8. Ibid.

9. TWL, Box 182, Folder 2, letter to Dr. Hjalmar Schacht, April 7, 1934.

10. Ibid., Box 182, Folder 3, letter from Dr. Hjalmar Schacht, April 20, 1934.

11. Ibid., draft of letter to J. Ramsay MacDonald, June 15, 1934.

12. Ibid., Box 182, Folder 4, interview with Neville Chamberlain, June 29, 1934.

13. RCL, Group 1030, Series I, Box 4, memorandum to Thomas W. Lamont, July 25, 1934.

14. TWL, Box 182, Folder 9, letter to Edward C. Grenfell, May 23, 1935.

15. RCL, Group 1030, Series I, Box 4, Folder 96, memorandum to Thomas W. Lamont, July 25, 1934.

16. Speer, *Inside the Third Reich*, p. 97.

17. *N*, January 19, 1935.

18. TWL, Box 182, Folder 16, letter to Dr. Hjalmar Schacht, September 25, 1936.

19. *TI*, January 20, 1936.

20. Ibid.

21. Ibid.

22. U.S. Congress, Senate Special Committee Investigating the Munitions Industry, *World War Financing*, p. 7485.

23. *TI*, January 20, 1936.

24. Wecter, *Saga of American Society*, p. 458.

25. Thomson, *Prime Ministers*, p. 203.

26. Diggins, *Mussolini and Fascism*, pp. 166–67.

27. TWL, Box 83, Folder 15, letter from J. P. Morgan, Jr., July 30, 1935.

28. Ibid., Box 83, Folder 25, memorandum to T. H. Beck, April 2, 1937.

29. Ibid., Box 191, Folder 13, memo of interview with il Duce (Benito Mussolini), April 16, 1937, p. 1.

30. Ibid.

31. Ibid., p. 3.

32. Ibid., p. 5.

33. Ibid., p. 4.

34. Ibid., p. 6.

35. Ibid., letter to Giovanni Fummi, April 19, 1937.

36. Ibid., memorandum to Giovanni Fummi, April 19, 1937.

37. *NYT*, February 3, 1948.

38. TWL, Box 191, Folder 7, letter from Giovanni Fummi, June 15, 1938.

39. Ibid., Box 82, Folder 5, memorandum to Lady Nancy Astor, received April 5, 1938.

40. Leffingwell, *Selected Letters*, p. 99.

CHAPTER TWENTY-ONE: EMBEZZLER

1. Forbes, *J. P. Morgan, Jr.*, p. 186.

2. Frank W. Colby, interview with author.

3. Forbes, *J. P. Morgan, Jr.*, p. 185.

4. Ibid., p. 187.

5. *NYHT*, March 13, 1943.

6. Forbes, *J. P. Morgan, Jr.*, p. 187.

7. TWL, Box 105, Folder 3, letter to Faye Lippmann, June 10, 1937.

8. Freedman, *Roosevelt and Frankfurter*, p. 425.

9. Forbes, *J. P. Morgan, Jr.*, p. 189.

10. Case and Case, *Owen Young and American Enterprise*, p. 702.

11. U.S. Congress, Senate Committee on Interstate Commerce, *Investigation of Railroads, Holding Companies, and Affiliated Companies*, p. 1863.

12. JPMJ, George Whitney File, letter from George Whitney, October 7, 1936.

13. Truman, *Harry Truman*, pp. 105–6.
14. Ibid.
15. Truman, *Dear Bess*, p. 404.
16. Ibid.
17. Borkin, *Robert R. Young*, pp. 44–45.
18. Ibid., p. 43.
19. *AM*, December 1947.
20. Hoffman, *Deal Makers*, pp. 22–23.
21. Lash, *Dealers and Dreamers*, pp. 324–27.
22. Ibid.
23. Schwartz, *Liberal* p. 111.
24. RCL, Group 1030, Series I, Box 3, Folder 63, memorandum to S. Parker Gilbert and Thomas S. Lamont, June 8, 1936.
25. TWL, Box 82, Folder 5, letter to Lady Nancy Astor, April 6, 1936.
26. Lash, *Dealers and Dreamers*, pp. 326–27.
27. Schwartz, *Liberal*, p. 113.
28. Carosso, *Investment Banking in America*, p. 376.
29. Mayer, *Markets*, pp. 217–18.
30. CUOH-GW, p. 2.
31. Gifford, *Letters from America*, p. 24.
32. Josephson, *Money Lords*, p. 91.
33. Brooks, *Once in Golconda*, p. 61.
34. United States Securities and Exchange Commission, *In the Matter of Richard Whitney, Edwin D. Morgan, Jr., and Others*, p. 142.
35. Ibid.
36. Seligman, *Transformation of Wall Street*, pp. 156–57.
37. Ibid., pp. 202–3.
38. Brooks, *Once in Golconda*, p. 260.
39. United States Securities and Exchange Commission, *In the Matter of Richard Whitney, Edwin D. Morgan, Jr., and Others*, p. 153.
40. Louchheim, ed., *Making of the New Deal*, p. 133.
41. United States Securities and Exchange Commission, *In the Matter of Richard Whitney, Edwin D. Morgan, Jr., and Others*, p. 155.
42. Seligman, *The Transformation of Wall Street*, p. 169.
43. Forbes, *J. P. Morgan, Jr.*, p. 190.
44. Louchheim, ed., *Making of the New Deal*, pp. 132–33.
45. Ibid.
46. Brooks, *Once in Golconda*, pp. 284–85.
47. TWL, Box 82, Folder 5, letter to Lady Nancy Astor, May 16, 1938.
48. JPMJ, Box 40, Cables 1938–43, cable to Thomas W. Lamont and George Whitney, November 2, 1938.
49. Louchheim, ed., *Making of the New Deal*, p. 135.
50. Ibid., p. 134.
51. Seligman, *Transformation of Wall Street*, p. 172.
52. Louchheim ed., *Making of the New Deal*, p. 132.

CHAPTER TWENTY-TWO: APPEASEMENT

1. Steel, *Walter Lippmann and the American Century*, p. 93.
2. Lamont, *Across World Frontiers*, p. 12.
3. Forbes, *J. P. Morgan, Jr.*, p. 191.
4. TWL, Box 108, Folder 16, letter from J. P. Morgan, Jr., October 14, 1936.
5. Ibid., Box 112, Folder 13, letter to Vivian Hugh Smith, December 10, 1946.
6. Ibid., Box 191, Folder 11, letter to Giovanni Fummi, September 12, 1940.
7. Taylor, *Sword and Swastika*, p. 127.
8. Shirer, *Rise and Fall of the Third Reich*, p. 352.
9. Schacht, *Confessions of the Old Wizard*, p. 354.
10. TWL, Box 182, Folder 18, memorandum from Thomas S. Lamont, April 25, 1938.
11. TWL, Box 182, Folder 18, letter to Sir Frederick Leith-Ross, May 5, 1938.
12. Schacht, *Confessions of the Old Wizard*, p. 353.
13. Clay, *Lord Norman*, p. 453.
14. TWL, Box 182, Folder 21, letter to Morgan Grenfell, July 22, 1938.
15. Ibid., Box 112, Folder 10, letter to Francis Rodd, September 14, 1938.
16. Cowles, *Astors*, p. 202.
17. TWL, Box 82, Folder 5, letter from Lady Nancy Astor, May 26, 1938.
18. Ibid., Box 191, Folder 8, letters to Giovanni Fummi, February 21, 1929, and Lady Nancy Astor, May 22, 1945.
19. Ibid., Box 82, Folder 3, letter from Lady Nancy Astor, July 14, 1930.
20. Ibid., Box 82, Folder 5, letter to Lady Nancy Astor, June 4, 1937.
21. Ibid., Box 188, Folder 4, letter to K. Wakasugi, September 17, 1937.
22. RCL, Group 1030, Series I, Box 4, Folder 97, memo to Thomas W. Lamont, October 19, 1937.
23. TWL, Box 188, Folder 5, letter to E. Araki, September 28, 1937.
24. Thomson, *Prime Ministers*, pp. 215–16.
25. Medlicott, *Contemporary England*, p. 391.
26. Forbes, *J. P. Morgan, Jr.*, pp. 191–92.
27. Ibid., p. 192.
28. RCL, Group 1030, Series I, Box 7, Folder 155, letter from Vivian Hugh Smith, October 6, 1938.
29. Leffingwell, *Selected Letters*, p. 100.
30. Beschloss, *Kennedy & Roosevelt*, p. 186.
31. Forbes, *J. P. Morgan, Jr.*, p. 189.
32. Beschloss, *Kennedy & Roosevelt*, p. 187.
33. Ickes, *Secret Diary: Inside Struggle*, p. 644.
34. Cochran, *Harry Truman and the Crisis Presidency*, p. 11.
35. Ickes, *Secret Diary: Inside Struggle*, p. 716.
36. Gifford, *Letters from America*, p. 67.
37. TWL, Box 105, Folder 11, radiogram from Lord Lothian, April 29, 1939.

38. RCL, Group 1030, Series I, Box 4, Folder 97, memorandum to Thomas W. Lamont, April 7, 1939.

39. Davis, *Hero*, p. 391.

40. Ibid., p. 392.

41. Lindbergh, *Hour of Gold, Hour of Lead*, p. 58.

42. Lindbergh, *Locked Rooms and Open Doors*, p. 288.

43. Lindbergh, *Flower and the Nettle*, p. 418.

44. Lindbergh, *War within and Without*, pp. 97–98.

45. Davis, *Hero*, p. 409.

46. Charles E. Lindbergh, "The Air Defense of America," radio address delivered May 19, 1940.

47. Cole, *Roosevelt and the Isolationists*, p. 460.

48. Lindbergh, *War within and Without*, pp. 86–87.

49. TWL, Box 104, Folder 24, letter from Betty Morrow, May 25, 1940.

50. Ibid., letter to Charles E. Lindbergh, May 29, 1940.

51. Ibid., letter from Charles E. Lindbergh, June 7, 1940.

52. Davis, *Hero*, pp. 406–7.

53. Lindbergh, *War within and Without*, p. 97.

54. RCL, Group 1030, Series I, Box 7, Folder 147, letter to Franklin D. Roosevelt, January 9, 1941.

55. *CB*, 1940.

56. Johnson, *Wendell Willkie*, p. 76.

57. Ibid., p. 105.

CHAPTER TWENTY-THREE: HOSTAGES

1. CUOH-LR, p. 1.

2. *T*, December 10, 1941.

3. TWL, Box 111, Folder 1, memorandum about Maurice Pesson-Didion, December 12, 1945.

4. Rist, Recollections of Morgan & Cie.

5. TWL, Box 191, Folder 8, letter to Giovanni Fummi, January 19, 1939.

6. Ibid., Box 191, Folder 10, letter to Franklin D. Roosevelt, May 17, 1939.

7. Ibid., Box 191, Folder 9, letter to Giovanni Fummi, April 4, 1939.

8. Ibid., Box 101, Folder 9, letter to Joseph P. Kennedy, June 13, 1939.

9. Ciano, *Diaries*, entry for February 26, 1940.

10. TWL, Box 191, Folder 8, letter from Giovanni Fummi, October 13, 1938.

11. TWL, cable from the Amministrazione Speciale della Santa Sede, Vatican City, September 25, 1940.

12. Ibid., Messages to the Italian Official Authorities, September 20, 1940, signed J. P. Morgan & Co., Inc.

13. Ibid., Box 191, Folder 12, letter to Giovanni Fummi, February 3, 1942.

14. Ibid., Box 133, Folder 11, memorandum from Bernardino Nogara, August 2, 1944.

15. Ibid., Box 111, Folder 21, letter from Edward C. Grenfell, November 19, 1929.

16. Davis, *Hero,* p. 407.

17. Charles E. A. Hambro, interview with author.

18. TWL, Box 82, Folder 7, letter to Lady Nancy Astor, October 29, 1943.

19. Davis, *Hero,* p. 410.

20. Cole, *Roosevelt and the Isolationists,* p. 41.

21. Leffingwell, *Selected Letters,* p. 85.

22. Ibid., p. 86.

23. Boyle, *Montagu Norman,* p. 316.

24. Catto, *Personal Memoir,* p. 95.

25. MGR, American Viscose, Box P-467, letter from T. J. Carlyle Gifford to Lord William Harcourt, August 29, 1949.

26. Cole, *Roosevelt and the Isolationists,* p. 468.

27. TWL, Box 112, Folder 12, letter to Lord Thomas Sivewright Catto, May 23, 1941.

28. Ibid., memorandum from Russell C. Leffingwell, May 26, 1941.

29. Ibid., Box 112, Folder 2, letter from Lord Thomas Sivewright Catto, July 25, 1941.

30. Ibid., Box 112, Folder 11, letter to Lord Thomas Sivewright Catto, n.d.

31. Ibid., Box 111, Folder 23, letter from Edward C. Grenfell, July 18, 1931.

32. Ibid., Box 105, Folder 3, memorandum to Walter Lippmann, November 13, 1941.

33. TWL, Box 103, Folder 24, letter to Thomas W. Lamont, November 24, 1941.

34. TWL, Box 49, Folder 10, private memorandum to Henry Luce, October 20, 1942.

35. Alinsky, *John L. Lewis,* pp. 240–41.

36. TWL, Box 127, Folder 26, letter from Franklin D. Roosevelt, November 10, 1941.

37. Ibid., letter from Franklin D. Roosevelt, December 17, 1941.

38. Ibid., Box 127, Folder 27, memorandum, about conversation with the president, February 5, 1942.

39. *NYT,* January 1, 1970.

40. RCL, Group 1030, Series I, Box 7, Folder 147, letter from Franklin D. Roosevelt, March 16, 1942.

CHAPTER TWENTY-FOUR: PASSAGES

1. U.S. Congress, House Committee on Banking and Currency, Testimony before the Money Trust Investigation, p. 2.

2. U.S. Congress, Temporary National Economic Committee, *Investigation of Concentration of Economic Power,* p. 249.

3. *NYT,* January 26, 1940.

4. Kneisel, *Morgan Stanley,* p. 21.

5. RCL, Group 1030, Series I, Box 2, Folder 47, letter to T. J. Carlyle Gifford, March 31, 1943.

6. *NYT*, March 13, 1943.

7. Forbes, *J. P. Morgan, Jr.*, p. 167.

8. Ibid., p. 205.

9. *NYK*, February 2, 1929.

10. *NYHT*, March 13, 1943.

11. RCL, Group 1030, Series I, Box 6, letter from Montagu Norman, June 6, 1943.

12. Ibid., letter to Montagu Norman, July 2, 1943.

13. Boyle, *Montagu Norman*, p. 327.

14. Dalton, *Second World War Diary*, p. 54.

15. Catto, *Personal Memoir*, p. 89.

16. TWL, Box 83, Folder 16, letter from Lord Thomas Sivewright Catto, June 11, 1946.

17. RCL, Group 1030, Series I, Box 6, Folder 133, letter from Montagu Norman, September 1, 1947.

18. Ibid., letter from Montagu Norman, November 14, 1945.

19. Lyons, *David Sarnoff*, pp. 152–53.

20. Schacht, *Confessions of the Old Wizard*, p. 345.

21. Ibid., p. 278.

22. TWL, Box 82, Folder 8, letter to Lady Nancy Astor, May 22, 1945.

23. Ibid., Box 191, Folder 12, letter to Count Volpi, May 2, 1946.

24. Ibid., article entitled "Germany's Heartbreak House or Germany in Chaos," April 18, 1945.

25. *NYT*, February 4, 1948.

CHAPTER TWENTY-FIVE: METHUSELAH

1. Edward Pulling, interview with author.

2. Leffingwell, *Selected Letters*, p. 15.

3. Ibid.

4. RCL, Group 1030, Series I, Box 6, Folder 121, letter to John J. McCloy, May 29, 1947.

5. *Ibid.*, letter from John J. McCloy, February 21, 1949.

6. Isaacson and Thomas, *Wise Men*, p. 419.

7. RCL, Group 1030, Series I, Box 5, Folder 117, letter to Robert A. Lovett, May 15, 1947.

8. Ibid., Group 1030, Series I, Box 1, Folder 2, memorandum to Henry Clay Alexander, August 11, 1947.

9. Isaacson and Thomas, *Wise Men*, p. 122.

10. Edward Pulling, interview with author.

11. Leffingwell, *Selected Letters*, p. 116.

12. Ibid., p. 123.

13. Ibid., p. 115.

14. Ibid., p. 146.

15. HST, letter from Morris L. Ernst, December 2, 1948.

16. Leffingwell, *Selected Letters*, p. 108.

17. RCL, Group 1030, Series I, Box 4, Folder 91, memo to Thomas W. Lamont, July 7, 1950.

18. Leffingwell, *Selected Letters*, p. 141.

19. HST, letter to George Whitney, August 24, 1950.

20. RCL, Group 1030, Series I, Box 7, Folder 165, letter to Harry S. Truman, November 27, 1950.

21. Ibid., letter from Harry S. Truman, February 10, 1951.

22. James R. Brugger, letter to author, November 21, 1988.

23. George W. Rowe, interview with author.

24. *NYK*, April 23, 1955.

25. Robert G. Engel, interview with author.

26. James R. Brugger, letter to author, November 21, 1988.

27. Hinton, Meyer, and Rodd, *Comments about the Morgan Bank*, p. 37.

28. *FB*, December 15, 1958.

29. *NYT*, January 19, 1950.

30. Moore, *Banker's Life*, p. 157.

31. Wilson, *Chase*, p. 57.

32. *NYT*, May 2, 1950.

33. DDE, letter to George Whitney, June 14, 1951.

34. DDE, letter from George Whitney, October 16, 1951.

35. DDE, Box 34, George Whitney Folder, telegram from Mamie and Dwight D. Eisenhower to George Whitney, December 26, 1952.

CHAPTER TWENTY-SIX: MAVERICKS

1. Eugene Rotberg, interview with author.

2. Gleisser, *World of Cyrus Eaton*, p. 156.

3. Carosso, *Investment Banking in America*, pp. 464–65.

4. *NYT*, April 9, 1952.

5. Ibid., October 28, 1952.

6. Ibid., October 1, 1952.

7. Ibid., May 2, 1952.

8. Ibid., April 10, 1953.

9. Alexander C. Tomlinson, interview with author.

10. Ibid.

11. Ferris, *Master Bankers*, p. 96–97.

12. Medina, *Corrected Opinion*, p. 248.

13. Ibid., p. 238.

14. *NYT*, April 17, 1953.

15. Ibid., December 8, 1951.

16. Ibid., December 14, 1951.

17. Ibid., December 5, 1951.

18. Ibid., February 13, 1954.
19. Clifford H. Ramsdell, letter to author, November 21, 1988.
20. *NYT,* February 11, 1954.
21. Perry E. Hall, interview with author.
22. Josephson, *Money Lords,* p. 240.
23. *NYT,* April 19, 1954.
24. *FO,* August 1955.
25. Ibid.
26. Borkin, *Robert R. Young,* p. 217.
27. *EU,* March 1982.
28. Perry E. Hall, interview with author.
29. Ibid.
30. Ferris, *Master Bankers,* p. 94.
31. William Sword, interview with author.
32. Ibid.
33. Sheppard Poor, interview with author.
34. Perry E. Hall, interview with author.
35. CUOH-EB, pp. 13–14.
36. Gardner, *Sterling Dollar Diplomacy,* pp. 318–19.
37. Robert V. Lindsay, interview with author.
38. Anthony Weighill, interview with author.
39. RCL, Group 1030, Series I, Box 6, Folder 138, letter from Sir Edward
R. Peacock, December 15, 1947.
40. Tim Collins, interview with author.
41. Macmillan, *War Diaries,* p. 190.
42. Sir David Basil Hill-Wood, interview with author.
43. Ibid.
44. *II,* March 1980.
45. Sampson, *Anatomy of Britain,* pp. 390–91.
46. Tim Collins, interview with author.
47. Wechsberg, *Merchant Bankers,* p. 204.
48. MGR, British Aluminium *aide-mémoire,* December 15, 1958.
49. *FT,* January 8, 1959.
50. *DE,* December 31, 1958.
51. *II,* March 1980.
52. Ibid.
53. Ferris, *Master Bankers,* p. 60.
54. Lord Stephen G. Catto, interview with author.

CHAPTER TWENTY-SEVEN: JONAH

1. James R. Brugger, letter to author, November 21, 1988.
2. *FO,* August 1955.
3. Ibid.
4. Ibid.

5. *TI,* November 2, 1959.
6. Ibid.
7. *FB,* December 15, 1958.
8. *FO,* August 1955.
9. DDE, Box 34, George Whitney Folder, letter to George Whitney, March 12, 1956.
10. Henry Clay Alexander, speech before the Executive's Club of Chicago, December 7, 1956.
11. DDE, Box 34, George Whitney Folder, letter from George Whitney, December 26, 1956.
12. Ibid., memorandum from John Foster Dulles, January 4, 1957.
13. Zeckendorf, *Zeckendorf,* pp. 269–70.
14. *FB,* December 15, 1958.
15. Guido Verbeck, interview with author.
16. A. Bruce Brackenridge, interview with author.
17. Frank Rosenbach, interview with author.
18. Zeckendorf, *Zeckendorf,* pp. 269–70.
19. Robert V. Lindsay, interview with author.
20. C. Douglas Dillon, interview with author.
21. Schlesinger, *Robert Kennedy and His Times,* vol. 1, p. 235.
22. *NYT,* December 15, 1969.
23. Hoopes, *Steel Crisis,* p. 21.
24. Mayer, *Bankers,* p. 199.
25. Bruce Nichols, interview with author.
26. Ralph F. Leach, interview with author.
27. Ibid.
28. Ibid.
29. Ibid.
30. *FO,* December 1966.
31. *NYT,* November 29, 1959.
32. TSG, Oral History Project, p. 33.
33. Beschloss, *May-Day,* p. 281.
34. Joseph L. Ponce, interview with author.
35. McCartney, *Friends in High Places,* p. 138.
36. TSG, Box 12, memorandum to Henry Clay Alexander, June 4, 1962.
37. Evan Galbraith, interview with author.
38. A. Bruce Brackenridge, interview with author.
39. LBJ, letter from Thomas S. Gates, February 25, 1965.
40. Walter H. Page, interview with author.
41. Dr. Nicola Caiola, interview with author.
42. Evan Galbraith, interview with author.
43. Tim Collins, interview with author.
44. Institutional Investor, *Way It Was,* p. 339; Evan Galbraith, interview with author.
45. Tim Collins, interview with author.
46. Evan Galbraith, interview with author.

47. Jack Loughran, interview with author.
48. Ibid.
49. Institutional Investor, *Way It Was*, p. 806.
50. Jack Loughran, interview with author.
51. Alexander C. Tomlinson, interview with author.
52. Perry E. Hall, interview with author.
53. Jack Loughran, interview with author.
54. *NYT*, February 2, 1904.
55. Jack Loughran, interview with author.
56. Ibid.
57. *NYT*, March 30, 1982.
58. Ibid.
59. Robert J. Wynn, interview with author.

CHAPTER TWENTY-EIGHT: TABLOID

1. Hinton, Meyer, Rodd, *Comments about the Morgan Bank*, pp. 46–47.
2. Longstreet Hinton, interview with author.
3. Peter Vermilye, interview with author.
4. Longstreet Hinton, interview with author.
5. Ibid.
6. Kaplan and Welles, *Money Managers*, p. 157.
7. *NYT*, July 9, 1968.
8. *BW*, November 26, 1966.
9. Shulman, *Billion Dollar Windfall*, pp. 137–38.
10. Ibid., p. 156.
11. Jerry E. Bishop, letter to author, March 7, 1989.
12. U.S. Securities and Exchange Commission, *In the Matter of Texas Gulf Sulphur Co.*, p. 5.
13. *NYT*, April 20, 1965.
14. Ibid., April 25, 1965.
15. Peter Vermilye, interview with author.
16. Longstreet Hinton, interview with author.
17. Patrick, *Perpetual Jeopardy*, p. 110.
18. *NYT*, April 21, 1965.
19. Robert V. Lindsay, interview with author.
20. Fallon and Srodes, *Takeovers*, p. 169.
21. Lord Stephen G. Catto, interview with author.
22. Sampson, *New Anatomy of Britain*, p. 549.
23. BBC-2 TV, July 18, 1968.
24. *T*, July 17, 1968.
25. *FT*, August 24, 1968.
26. *ST*, July 28, 1968.
27. Lord Stephen G. Catto, interview with author.
28. Bower, *Maxwell*, p. 126.

29. Lord Stephen G. Catto, interview with author.
30. Ibid.
31. *O,* January 5, 1969.
32. Kiernan, *Citizen Murdoch,* p. 94.
33. Ibid., p. 96.
34. Ibid.
35. Ibid., p. 97.
36. Haines, *Maxwell,* p. 361; *O,* January 5, 1969.
37. Haines, *Maxwell,* p. 360.

CHAPTER TWENTY-NINE: SAMURAI

1. *BW,* December 13, 1969.
2. *EU,* March 1982.
3. Alexander C. Tomlinson, interview with author.
4. *FO,* February 27, 1978.
5. *NY,* November 12, 1979.
6. *BW,* January 19, 1974.
7. Hoffman, *Deal Makers,* pp. 36–37.
8. *FO,* February 27, 1978.
9. *BW,* December 9, 1985.
10. Sheppard Poor, interview with author.
11. *BW,* December 9, 1985.
12. Institutional Investor, *Way It Was,* p. 101.
13. Morgan Stanley, *Fiftieth Anniversary Review,* p. 20.
14. Frederick H. Scholtz, interview with author.
15. Eugene Rotberg, interview with author.
16. *BW,* January 19, 1974.
17. *II,* June 1974.
18. Ibid.
19. Luis S. Mendez, interview with author.
20. David Bendall, interview with author.
21. Lord Stephen G. Catto, interview with author.
22. Ralph F. Leach, interview with author.
23. Guido Verbeck, interview with author.
24. Walter H. Page, interview with author.
25. David Bendall, interview with author.
26. Walter H. Page, interview with author.
27. Sheppard Poor, interview with author.
28. *BW,* January 19, 1974.
29. Jensen, *Financiers,* p. 21.
30. *FO,* February 27, 1978.
31. *II,* May 1979.
32. Halberstam, *Reckoning,* pp. 675–76.
33. Ferris, *Master Bankers,* p. 111.

34. *NYT,* August 28, 1974.
35. Brooks, *Takeover Game,* p. 4.
36. *AL,* November 1981.
37. Madrick, *Taking America,* p. 24.
38. *NYT,* May 17, 1978.
39. *BW,* December 14, 1974.

CHAPTER THIRTY: SHEIKS

1. *FO,* October, 1974.
2. Walter H. Page, interview with author.
3. *WP,* November 16, 1974.
4. William D. Toomey, letter to author, March 16, 1989.
5. Walter H. Page, interview with author.
6. Ibid.
7. *NYT,* September 12, 1976.
8. Emerson, *House of Saud,* p. 306.
9. Ibid., p. 308.
10. William H. Sword, interview with author.
11. Kessler, *Richest Man in the World,* p. 91.
12. Sampson, *Changing Anatomy of Britain,* p. 278.
13. Christopher Whittington, interview with author.
14. Ibid.
15. Herndon, *Ford,* pp. 238–39.
16. Ibid.
17. Max M. Fisher, letter to author, December 20, 1988.
18. *FO,* July 13, 1981.
19. Ellmore C. Patterson, interview with author.
20. Ibid.
21. Ibid.
22. Ibid.
23. Simon, *Time for Truth,* p. 159.
24. U.S. Congress, Senate Committee on Banking, Housing, and Urban Affairs, *New York City Fiscal Crisis,* p. 644.
25. Ellmore C. Patterson, interview with author.

CHAPTER THIRTY-ONE: TOMBSTONES

1. *AM,* July 1979.
2. *WSJ,* June 27, 1985.
3. *NYT,* May 25, 1975.
4. *EU,* March 1982.
5. *NYT,* October 8, 1979.
6. *WSJ,* July 17, 1980.

7. Ibid.
8. *NYT,* May 14, 1973.
9. *II,* June 1974.
10. *WSJ,* October 26, 1978.
11. Ibid.
12. *WSJ,* October 26, 1978.
13. *II,* February 1979.
14. Ibid.
15. Ibid.
16. Ibid.
17. *WSJ,* July 17, 1980.
18. *WSJ,* February 13, 1981.
19. Hoffman, *Deal Makers,* p. 165.
20. Ibid., p. 173.
21. Ibid.
22. Ibid.
23. *WSJ,* February 13, 1981.
24. Hoffman, *Deal Makers,* p. 176.
25. *WSJ,* February 13, 1981.
26. *EU,* March 1982.

CHAPTER THIRTY-TWO: SAMBA

1. *BW,* November 3, 1975.
2. Ibid.
3. A. Bruce Brackenridge, interview with author.
4. Ibid.
5. *II,* October 10, 1976.
6. *II,* March 1979.
7. Walter H. Page, interview with author.
8. A. Bruce Brackenridge, interview with author.
9. *WSJ,* August 30, 1983.
10. Guy Huntrods, interview with author.
11. *TI,* January 10, 1983.
12. *BW,* June 2, 1986.
13. Anthony M. Solomon, interview with author.
14. Lampert, *Behind Closed Doors,* p. 176.
15. *FO,* November 1, 1982.
16. *BW,* October 3, 1983.
17. Lewis T. Preston, comments made at J. P. Morgan & Co. Annual Meeting, April 12, 1989.
18. *WSJ,* October 10, 1986.
19. *NYT,* October 9, 1986.
20. *WSJ,* February 2, 1987.

CHAPTER THIRTY-THREE: TRADERS

1. *NYT*, September 15, 1981.
2. Robert V. Lindsay, interview with author.
3. Lewis T. Preston, interview with author.
4. Lord Stephen G. Catto, interview with author.
5. *FO*, April 28, 1986.
6. *II*, January 1980.
7. Lewis T. Preston, interview with author.
8. *NYT*, April 10, 1983.
9. Ibid.
10. *BW*, October 20, 1986.
11. David Taylor, interview with author.
12. Ibid.
13. Lewis T. Preston, interview with author.
14. Irvine Sprague, interview with author.
15. Ibid.
16. Sprague, *Bailout*, p. 158.
17. William M. Isaac, interview with author.
18. Lewis T. Preston, interview with author.
19. *WSJ*, June 21, 1982.
20. Ferris, *Master Bankers*, p. 154.
21. *II*, June 1982.
22. Brooks, *Takeover Game*, p. 115.
23. Ibid.
24. *WSJ*, June 27, 1989.
25. Ferris, *Master Bankers*, p. 155.
26. Jack Loughran, interview with author.
27. Robert A. Gerard, interview with author.
28. *NYT*, April 1, 1984.
29. *II*, December 1978.
30. *WSJ*, June 27, 1985.
31. *II*, November 1987.
32. Pickens, *Boone*, p. 172.
33. Ibid., p. 186.
34. *NYT*, December 7, 1984.
35. Pickens, *Boone*, p. 225.
36. *II*, August 1980.
37. Ibid., September 1980.
38. *WSJ*, May 31, 1988.

CHAPTER THIRTY-FOUR: BANG

1. *FT*, October 22, 1986.
2. *E*, July 4, 1987.

3. *EU*, February, 1987.
4. Fallon and Srodes, *Takeovers*, p. 169.
5. Ibid.
6. Pugh, *Is Guinness Good for You?* p. 149.
7. *B*, July 1986.
8. Ibid.
9. *BW*, August 14, 1989.
10. Kochan and Pym, *Guinness Affair*, pp. 65–66.
11. Fallon and Srodes, *Takeovers*, p. 180.
12. Saunders, *Nightmare*, p. 142.
13. *NYT*, October 28, 1986.
14. *E*, February 21, 1987.
15. Pugh, *Is Guinness Good for You?* p. 138.
16. *FT*, January 27, 1987.
17. *B*, June 1987.
18. *WSJ*, January 21, 1987.
19. *FT*, December 4, 1986.
20. *B*, May 1986.

CHAPTER THIRTY-FIVE: BULL

1. Institutional Investor, *Way It Was*, p. 604.
2. *NYT*, May 17, 1978.
3. *FO*, February 17, 1986.
4. Ibid.
5. Ibid.
6. *WSJ*, June 8, 1989.
7. *II*, November 1987.
8. *FO*, February 17, 1986.
9. *NYT*, July 3, 1984.
10. *BA*, August 3, 1987.
11. Ibid.
12. *NYT*, May 18, 1989.
13. *II*, November 1987.
14. Ibid.
15. Mayer, *Markets*, p. 60.
16. *TI*, November 2, 1987.
17. *WSJ*, November 20, 1987.
18. Ibid., October 7, 1988.
19. Ibid., October 26, 1987.
20. *NYT*, September 28, 1988.
21. Ibid., May 1, 1988.
22. *WSJ*, February 2, 1989.
23. Ibid., March 22, 1988.
24. Robert V. Lindsay, interview with author.

25. Lewis T. Preston, interview with author.
26. *FO,* April 28, 1986.
27. Robert G. Engel, interview with author.
28. *NYT,* January 23, 1979.
29. *WSJ,* March 6, 1989.
30. *NYT,* February 7, 1988.
31. Robert G. Engel, interview with author.
32. *WSJ,* January 7, 1988.
33. Ibid.
34. Lewis T. Preston, interview with author.

CHAPTER THIRTY-SIX: SKYSCRAPER

1. *NYDN,* September 8, 1988.
2. *NYT,* October 27, 1988.
3. Lewis T. Preston, interview with author.
4. *NYT,* April 15, 1984.
5. Patrick and Tachi, *Japan and the United States Today,* p. 146.
6. *NYT,* September 15, 1988.
7. Robert G. Engel, interview with author.
8. *E,* December 5, 1987.
9. *II,* February 1982.
10. Lewis T. Preston, interview with author.

BIBLIOGRAPHY

BOOKS AND ARTICLES

Adams, Frederick B., Jr. *An Introduction to the Pierpont Morgan Library.* New York: Pierpont Morgan Library, 1964.

Adler, Cyrus. *Jacob H. Schiff: His Life and Letters.* Vol. 1. Freeport, N.Y.: Books for Libraries Press, 1928.

Alinsky, Saul. *John L. Lewis.* New York: G. P. Putnam's Sons, 1949.

Allen, Frederick Lewis. *The Great Pierpont Morgan.* 1949. Reprint. New York: Harper & Row, Perennial Library, 1965.

———. *The Lords of Creation.* New York and London: Harper & Brothers, 1935.

Andrews, Wayne. *Mr. Morgan and His Architect.* New York: Pierpont Morgan Library, 1957.

Attali, Jacques. *A Man of Influence: Sir Siegmund Warburg, 1902–82.* Translated by Barbara Ellis. London: Weidenfeld & Nicolson, 1986.

Auletta, Ken. *Greed and Glory on Wall Street: The Fall of the House of Lehman.* New York: Random House, 1986.

Barron, Clarence W. *They Told Barron: Conversations and Revelations of an American Pepys in Wall Street.* Edited by Arthur Pound and Samuel Taylor Moore. New York and London: Harper & Brothers, 1930.

Baruch, Bernard M. *Baruch: My Own Story.* New York: Henry Holt, 1957.

Beebe, Lucius. *The Big Spenders.* Garden City, N.Y.: Doubleday, 1966.

Beschloss, Michael R. *Kennedy & Roosevelt: The Uneasy Alliance.* New York: W. W. Norton, 1980.

———. *May-Day: Eisenhower, Khrushchev, and the U-2 Affair.* New York: Harper & Row, 1986.

Bilby, Kenneth. *David Sarnoff and the Rise of the Communications Industry.* New York: Harper & Row, 1986.

Birmingham, Stephen. *"Our Crowd": The Great Jewish Families of New York.* New York, Evanston, and London: Harper & Row, 1967.

Black, David. *The King of Fifth Avenue.* New York: Dial Press, 1981.

Borkin, Joseph. *Robert R. Young: The Populist of Wall Street.* New York, Evanston, and London: Harper & Row. 1947.

Bower, Tom. *Maxwell: The Outsider.* London: Aurum Press, 1988.

Boyle, Andrew. *Montagu Norman.* London: Cassell, 1967.

Bramsen, Bo, and Kathleen Wain. *The Hambros, 1779–1979.* London: Michael Joseph, 1979.

Brooks, John. *Once in Golconda: A True Drama of Wall Street, 1920–1938.* 1969. Reprint. New York: E. P. Dutton, Truman Talley Books, 1985.

————. *The Seven Fat Years.* New York: Harper & Row, 1954.

————. *The Takeover Game.* New York: E. P. Dutton, Truman Talley Books, 1987.

Bryant, J. S. *The Life of the Late George Peabody.* Westminster: 1914.

Burk, Kathleen. "The House of Morgan in Financial Diplomacy—1920–1930." In *The Struggle for Supremacy: Anglo-American Relations in the 1920s,* edited by B. J. McKercher. London: Macmillan, 1987.

————. *Britain, America and the Sinews of War, 1914–1918.* London: G. Allen & Unwin, 1985.

Burner, David. *Herbert Hoover: A Public Life.* New York: Alfred Knopf, 1979.

Carnegie, Andrew. *The Autobiography of Andrew Carnegie.* Boston: Houghton Mifflin, 1920.

Carosso, Vincent P. *Investment Banking in America: A History.* Cambridge, Mass., and London: Harvard University Press, 1970.

————. *The Morgans: Private International Bankers, 1854–1913.* Cambridge, Mass., and London: Harvard University Press, 1987.

Carter, Samuel, III. *Cyrus Field.* New York: G. P. Putnam's Sons, 1968.

Case, Josephine Young, and Everett Needham Case. *Owen Young and American Enterprise.* Boston: David R. Godine, 1982.

Cashman, Sean Dennis. *America in the Gilded Age.* New York: New York University Press, 1984.

Catto, Thomas Sivewright. *A Personal Memoir and a Biographical Note.* Edinburgh: T. & A. Constable, 1962. Privately printed.

Cecil, Lamar. *Albert Ballin.* Princeton, N.J.: Princeton University Press, 1967.

Chandler, Lester V. *Benjamin Strong: Central Banker.* Washington, D.C.: Brookings Institution, 1958.

Chapple, William Dismore. *George Peabody: An Address.* Salem, Mass.: Peabody Museum of Salem, 1933.

Cherny, Robert W. *A Righteous Cause: The Life of William Jennings Bryan.* Boston and Toronto: Little, Brown, 1985.

Ciano, Galeazzo. *The Ciano Diaries.* Garden City, N.Y.: Doubleday, 1946.

Clarke, Stephen V. O. *Central Bank Cooperation—1924–31.* New York: Federal Reserve Bank of New York, 1967.

Clay, Sir Henry. *Lord Norman.* London: Macmillan, 1957.

Clews, Henry. *Twenty-Eight Years in Wall Street.* New York: J. S. Ogilvie, 1887.

Cochran, Bert. *Harry Truman and the Crisis Presidency.* New York: Funk & Wagnalls, 1973.

Colby, Gerald. *DuPont Dynasty.* 1974. Reprint. Secaucus, N.J.: Lyle Stuart, 1984.

Cole, Wayne S. *Charles A. Lindbergh and the Battle against American Intervention in World War II.* New York: Harcourt Brace Jovanovich, 1974.

————. *Roosevelt and the Isolationists, 1932–45.* Lincoln and London: University of Nebraska Press, 1983.

Cowles, Virginia. *The Astors: The Story of a Transatlantic Family.* London: Weidenfeld & Nicolson, 1979.

Corey, Lewis. *The House of Morgan: A Social Biography of the Masters of Money*. New York: G. Howard Watt, 1930.

Cray, Ed. *Chrome Colossus: General Motors and Its Times*. New York: McGraw-Hill, 1980.

Croly, Herbert. *Willard Straight*. New York: Macmillan, 1924.

Cruikshank, Jeffrey L. *A Delicate Experiment*. Boston: Harvard Business School Press, 1987.

Dalton, Hugh. *The Second World War Diary of Hugh Dalton, 1940–45*. Edited by Ben Pimlott. London: Jonathan Cape, 1986.

Daniel, Clifton. *Chronicle of the 20th Century*. Mount Kisco, N.Y.: Chronicle Publications, 1987.

Davie, Michael. *Titanic: The Death and Life of a Legend*. New York: Alfred A. Knopf, 1987.

Davis, Kenneth S. *The Hero: Charles A. Lindbergh and the American Dream*. Garden City, N.Y.: Doubleday, 1959.

Davis, L. J. *Bad Money*. 1982. Reprint. New York and Scarborough, Ontario: New American Library, A Mentor Book, 1983.

Diggins, John P. *Mussolini and Fascism: The View from America*. Princeton: Princeton University Press, 1972.

Donovan, Robert J. *Tumultuous Years: The Presidency of Harry S. Truman, 1949–53*. New York: W. W. Norton, 1982.

Egan, Edward W., Constance B. Hintz, and L. F. Wise, eds. *Kings, Rulers and Statesmen*. New York: Sterling, 1976.

Emerson, Stephen. *The House of Saud*. New York: Franklin Watts, 1985.

Fairbank, John King. *The Great Chinese Revolution—1800–1985*. 1986. Reprint. New York: Harper & Row, Perennial Library, 1987.

Fallon, Ivan, and James Srodes. *Takeovers*. London: Hamish Hamilton, 1987.

Fay, Stephen. *Portrait of an Old Lady: Turmoil at the Bank of England*. New York: Viking Penguin, 1987.

Ferretti, Fred. *The Year the Big Apple Went Bust*. New York: G. P. Putnam's Sons, 1976.

Ferris, Paul. *The Master Bankers*. 1984. Reprint. New York and Scarborough, Ontario: New American Library, A Plume Book, 1984.

Fogarty, Charles F. *The Story of Texasgulf*. New York: Newcomen Society in North America, 1976.

Forbes, John Douglas. *J. P. Morgan, Jr., 1867–1943*. Charlottesville: University Press of Virginia, 1981.

———. *Stettinius, Sr.: Portrait of a Morgan Partner*. Charlottesville: University Press of Virginia, 1974.

Ford, Gerald. *A Time to Heal*. New York: Harper & Row and Reader's Digest, 1979.

Freedman, Max, ed. *Roosevelt and Frankfurter: Their Correspondence, 1928–1945*. Boston: Little, Brown, 1967.

Friedman, Milton, and Rose Friedman. *Free to Choose: A Personal Statement*. New York: Harcourt Brace Jovanovich, 1980.

Galbraith, John Kenneth. *The Great Crash*. Boston: Houghton Mifflin, 1972.

Gardner, Richard N. *Sterling Dollar Diplomacy in Current Perspective.* New York: Columbia University Press, 1980.

Garraty, John A. *Right-Hand Man: The Life of George W. Perkins.* New York: Harper & Brothers, 1957.

Gifford, T. J. *Letters from America, 1939–41.* Edinburgh: T. & A. Constable, 1969.

Glad, Paul W. *McKinley, Bryan, and the People.* Philadelphia and New York: J. P. Lippincott, 1964.

Gleisser, Marcus. *The World of Cyrus Eaton.* New York: A. S. Barnes, 1965.

Gordon, John Steele. *The Scarlet Woman of Wall Street.* New York: Weidenfeld & Nicolson, 1988.

Greider, William. *Secrets of the Temple: How the Federal Reserve Runs the Country.* New York and London: Simon & Schuster, 1987.

Guaranty Trust Company of New York. *Employee Handbook.* New York: Guaranty Trust, n.d. Morgan Guaranty Trust Library, New York.

Haines, Joe. *Maxwell.* Boston: Houghton Mifflin, 1988.

Halberstam, David. *The Reckoning.* New York: William Morrow, 1986.

Hale, David H. *Britain and Japan as the Financial Bogeymen of U.S. Politics, or Comparison between the Presidential Elections of 1896 and 1988.* Chicago: Kemper Financial Services, 1987.

Hamilton, Adrian. *The Financial Revolution.* New York: The Free Press, 1986.

Harbaugh, William H. *Lawyer's Lawyer: The Life of John W. Davis.* New York: Oxford University Press, 1973.

Hendrick, Burton J. *The Life of Andrew Carnegie.* 2 vols. Garden City, N.Y.: Doubleday, Doran, 1932.

Herndon, Booton. *Ford.* New York: Weybright & Talley, 1969.

Hidy, Muriel. *George Peabody: Merchant and Financier, 1829–1854.* New York: Arno Press, 1978.

Hidy, Ralph W. *The House of Baring in American Trade and Finance.* Cambridge, Mass.: Harvard University Press, 1949.

Hinton, Longstreet, John M. Meyer, Jr., and Thomas Rodd. *Some Comments about the Morgan Bank.* 1979. Reprint. New York: Morgan Guaranty Trust, 1985.

Hocking, Anthony. *Oppenheimer and Son.* Johannesburg: McGraw-Hill, 1973.

Hoffman, Paul. *The Deal Makers: Inside the World of Investment Banking.* Garden City, N.Y.: Doubleday, 1984.

Hoopes, Roy. *The Steel Crisis.* New York: John Day, 1963.

Hoover, Herbert. *The Memoirs of Herbert Hoover.* Vol. 2, *The Cabinet and the Presidency, 1920–1933.* New York: Macmillan, 1952.

Hovey, Carl. *The Life Story of J. Pierpont Morgan.* New York: Sturgis & Walton, 1912.

Howland, Hewitt H. *Dwight Whitney Morrow.* New York: Century, 1930.

Hoyt, Edwin P., Jr. *The House of Morgan.* New York: Dodd, Mead, 1966.

———. *The Peabody Influence.* New York: Dodd, Mead, 1968.

Hughes, Jonathan. *The Vital Few: American Economic Progress and Its Protagonists.* Boston: Houghton Mifflin, Riverside Press Cambridge, 1966.

Hulderman, Bernhard. *Albert Ballin.* London, Cassell, 1922.

Hyde, H. Montgomery. *Lord Reading: The Life of Rufus Isaacs, First Marquess of Reading.* New York: Farrar, Straus & Giroux, 1967.

Ickes, Harold L. *The Secret Diary of Harold L. Ickes: The First Thousand Days, 1933–1936.* New York: Simon & Schuster, 1953.

———. *The Secret Diary of Harold L. Ickes: The Inside Struggle, 1936–1939.* New York: Simon & Schuster, 1954.

Institutional Investor. *The Way It Was: An Oral History of Finance: 1967–87.* New York: William Morrow, 1988.

Isaacson, Walter, and Evan Thomas. *The Wise Men: Six Friends and the World They Made.* New York: Simon & Schuster, Touchstone Books, 1986.

Jackson, Stanley. *J. P. Morgan: The Rise and Fall of a Banker.* London: William Heinemann, 1983.

Jay, N. D. *Morgan & Cie.* 1968. Morgan Guaranty Trust Library, New York.

Jensen, Michael C. *The Financiers.* New York: Weybright & Talley, 1976.

Johns, A. Wesley. *The Man Who Shot McKinley.* South Brunswick and New York: A. S. Barnes, 1970.

Johnson, Chalmers. *MITI and the Japanese Miracle: The Growth of Industrial Policy, 1925–1975.* Stanford, Calif.: Stanford University Press, 1982.

Johnson, Donald Bruce. *Wendell Willkie and the Republican Party.* Urbana: University of Illinois Press, 1960.

Johnston, Moira. *Takeover: The New Wall Street Warriors.* New York: Arbor House, A Belvedere Book, 1986.

Josephson, Matthew. *The Money Lords: The Great Finance Capitalists, 1925–1950.* New York: Weybright & Talley, 1972.

———. *The Robber Barons: The Great American Capitalists, 1861–1901.* New York: Harcourt, Brace, 1934.

Kaplan, Gilbert E., and Chris Welles. *The Money Managers.* New York: Random House, 1969.

Kellett, Richard. *The Merchant Banking Arena.* New York: St. Martin's Press, 1967.

Kessler, Ronald. *The Richest Man in the World: The Story of Adnan Khashoggi.* New York: Warner Books, 1986.

Kettl, Donald. *Leadership at the Fed.* New Haven, Conn.: Yale University Press, 1986.

Kiernan, Thomas. *Citizen Murdoch.* New York: Dodd, Mead, 1986.

Kindleberger, Charles P. *The World in Depression, 1929–1939.* Berkeley and Los Angeles: University of California Press, 1973.

Klein, Maury. *The Life and Legend of Jay Gould.* Baltimore: Johns Hopkins University Press, 1986.

Kneisel, William J. *Morgan Stanley & Co., Inc: A Brief History.* New York: Morgan Stanley, 1977.

Kobler, John. *Otto the Magnificent.* New York: Charles Scribner's Sons, 1988.

Kochan, Nick, and Hugh Pym. *The Guinness Affair: Anatomy of a Scandal.* London: Christopher Helm, 1987.

Kolko, Gabriel. *Railroads and Regulation, 1877–1916.* New York: W. W. Norton, 1965.

Kraft, Joseph L. *The Mexican Rescue.* New York: Group of Twenty, n.d.

Lamont, Corliss. *Yes to Life: Memoirs of Corliss Lamont.* New York: Horizon Press, 1981.

————, ed. *The Thomas Lamonts in America.* South Brunswick and New York: A. S. Barnes, 1962.

Lamont, Thomas W. *Across World Frontiers.* New York: Harcourt, Brace, 1951.

————. *Henry P. Davison: The Record of a Useful Life.* New York and London: Harper & Brothers, 1933.

Lampert, Hope. *Behind Closed Doors: Wheeling and Dealing in the Banking World.* New York: Atheneum, 1986.

Lash, Joseph P. *Dealers and Dreamers.* New York: Doubleday, 1988.

Leffingwell, Russell C. *Memorial of Charles Steele.* New York: Association of the Bar of New York, 1940.

————. *Selected Letters of R. C. Leffingwell.* Edited by Edward Pulling. Hicksville, N.Y.: Exposition Press, 1980. Privately printed.

Leuchtenburg, William E. *Franklin D. Roosevelt and the New Deal.* New York: Harper & Row, 1963.

Lindbergh, Anne Morrow. *The Flower and the Nettle: Diaries and Letters 1936–1939.* New York and London: Harcourt Brace Jovanovich, 1976.

————. *Hour of Gold, Hour of Lead: Diaries and Letters 1929–1932.* New York and London: Harcourt Brace Jovanovich, 1973.

————. *Locked Rooms and Open Doors: Diaries and Letters 1933–1935.* New York and London: Harcourt Brace Jovanovich, 1974.

————. *War within and Without: Diaries and Letters 1939–1944.* New York and London: Harcourt Brace Jovanovich, 1980.

Lindbergh, Charles A. *Autobiography of Values.* New York and London: Harcourt Brace Jovanovich, 1976.

Link, Arthur S. *The Road to the White House.* Princeton, N.J.: Princeton University Press, 1947.

————. *Wilson.* Vol. 3, *The Struggle for Neutrality—1914–15.* Princeton, N.J.: Princeton University Press, 1947.

Lippmann, Walter. *Public Philosopher: Selected Letters of Walter Lippmann.* Edited by John Morton Blum. New York: Ticknor & Fields, 1985.

Louchheim, Katie, ed. *The Making of the New Deal.* Cambridge, Mass., and London: Harvard University Press, 1983.

Lundberg, Ferdinand. *America's 60 Families.* 1937. Reprint. New York: Citadel Press, 1946.

————. *The Rich and the Super-Rich.* 1968. Reprint. Toronto, New York, and London: Bantam Books, 1969.

Lyon, Peter. *Eisenhower: Portrait of the Hero.* Boston and Toronto: Little, Brown, 1974.

Lyons, Eugene. *David Sarnoff.* New York: Harper & Row, 1966.

McAdoo, William Gibbs. *Crowded Years.* Port Washington, N.Y.: Kennikat Press, 1931.

McCartney, Laton. *Friends in High Places: The Bechtel Story.* New York and London: Simon & Schuster, 1988.

Macmillan, Harold. *War Diaries: Politics and War in the Mediterranean.* London: Macmillan, 1984.

McNeil, William C. *American Money and the Weimar Republic.* New York: Columbia University Press, 1986.

McRae, Hamish, and Frances Cairncross. *Capital City: London as a Financial Centre.* 1973. Reprint. London: Methuen, 1985.

Madrick, Jeff. *Taking America: How We Got from the First Hostile Takeovers to Megamergers, Corporate Raiding and Scandal.* Toronto, New York, and London: Bantam Books, 1987.

Makin, John H. *The Global Debt Crisis.* New York: Basic Books, 1984.

Marbury, Elisabeth. *My Crystal Ball.* New York: Boni & Liveright, 1923.

Mayer, Martin. *The Bankers.* 1974. Reprint. New York: Ballantine Books, 1976.

———. *Markets.* New York and London: W. W. Norton, 1988.

———. *The Money Bazaars: Understanding the Banking Revolution Around Us.* New York: E. P. Dutton, A Truman Talley Book, 1984.

———. *Wall Street: Men and Money.* New York: Harper & Brothers, 1955.

Medlicott, W. N. *Contemporary England, 1914–1964.* London: Longmans, 1967.

Moody, John. *The Masters of Capital.* New Haven: Yale University Press, 1919.

Moody, John, and George Kibbe Turner. "Masters of Capital in America," *McClure's,* November 1910 and months following. Bound copy in Pierpont Morgan Library, New York.

Moore, George S. *The Banker's Life.* New York and London: W. W. Norton, 1987.

Morgan, J. P., and Company. *America and Munitions: The Work of Messrs. J. P. Morgan & Co. in the World War.* 2 vols. New York: J. P. Morgan, 1923. Privately printed.

Morgan Grenfell and Company. *George Peabody & Co.; J. S. Morgan & Co.; Morgan Grenfell & Co.; Morgan Grenfell Co. Ltd; 1838–1958.* Oxford: Oxford University Press, 1958. Privately printed.

Morgan Guaranty Trust Company. News Release on the Death of Russell C. Leffingwell. 1960. Morgan Guaranty Trust Library, New York.

Morgan Guaranty Trust Company. News Report on the Death of S. Parker Gilbert, 1892–1938. 1938. Morgan Guaranty Trust Library, New York.

Morgan Stanley, *Morgan Stanley Fiftieth Anniversary Review.* New York: Morgan Stanley, 1985.

Morgenthau, Henry. *From the Morgenthau Diaries.* Edited by John Morton Blum. Boston: Houghton Mifflin, 1959.

Morton, Frederic. *The Rothschilds: A Family Portrait.* New York: Atheneum, 1962.

Moulton, Elizabeth. *St. George's Church New York.* New York: Saint George's Church, 1964.

Nevins, Allan. *Grover Cleveland.* New York: Dodd, Mead, 1933.

New York Central and Hudson River Railroad. "Prospectus for New York Central and Hudson River Railroad, January 19, 1880." New York: New York Central and Hudson River Railroad, 1880. Pierpont Morgan Library, New York.

Nicolson, Harold. *Diaries & Letters 1930–1964.* Edited by Stanley Olson. New York: Atheneum, 1980.

———. *Dwight Morrow.* New York: Harcourt, Brace, 1935.

Nicolson, Nigel, *Portrait of a Marriage.* New York: Atheneum, 1973.

Noyes, Alexander Dana. *The Market Place.* New York: Greenwood Press, 1938.

Pankhurst, E. Sylvia. *The Home Front.* 1932. Reprint. London: Cresset Library, 1987.

———. *The Suffragette Movement.* London, New York, and Toronto: Longmans, Green, 1931.

Parker, Franklin. *George Peabody—1795–1869: Founder of Modern Philanthropy.* Nashville: George Peabody College for Teachers, 1955.

Patrick, Hugh T., and Ryuichiro Tachi, eds. *Japan and the United States Today.* New York: Center on Japanese Economy and Business, Columbia University, 1986.

Patrick, Kenneth G. *Perpetual Jeopardy.* New York: Macmillan, Arkville Press Book, 1972.

Pecora, Ferdinand. *Wall Street under Oath: The Story of Our Modern Money Changers.* New York: Simon & Schuster, 1939.

Pickens, T. Boone, Jr. *Boone.* Boston: Houghton Mifflin, 1987.

Plender, John, and Paul Wallace. *The Square Mile: A Guide to the New City of London.* London: Century, 1985.

Pringle, Henry F. *Theodore Roosevelt: A Biography.* New York: Harcourt, Brace, 1931.

Pugh, Peter. *Is Guinness Good for You?* London: Financial Training Publications, 1987.

Rist, Leonard. Recollections of Morgan & Cie. during World War II. N.d. Morgan Guaranty Trust Library, New York.

Robertson, Diana Forbes. *My Aunt Maxine: The Story of Maxine Elliott.* New York: Viking Press, 1964.

Roth, Linda Horvitz, ed. *J. Pierpont Morgan, Collector: European Decorative Arts from the Wadsworth Atheneum.* Hartford: Wadsworth Atheneum, 1987.

Rousmaniere, John. *The Golden Pastime: A New History of Yachting.* New York: W. W. Norton, 1986.

Sampson, Anthony. *Anatomy of Britain.* New York and Evanston, Ill.: Harper & Row, 1962.

———. *Black and Gold: Tycoons, Revolutionaries, and Apartheid.* New York: Pantheon Books, 1987.

———. *The Changing Anatomy of Britain.* New York: Random House, 1982.

———. *The Money Lenders: The People and Politics of the World Banking Crisis.* 1981. Reprint. Harmondsworth, England, and New York: Penguin Books, 1983.

———. *The New Anatomy of Britain.* New York: Stein & Day, 1972.

Samuels, Ernest. *Bernard Berenson: The Making of a Legend.* Cambridge, Mass., and London: Harvard University Press, Belknap Press, 1987.

Satterlee, Herbert L. *J. Pierpont Morgan: An Intimate Portrait.* New York: Macmillan, 1939.

Saunders, James. *Nightmare: The Ernest Saunders Story.* London: Hutchinson, 1989.

Sayers, R. S. *The Bank of England, 1891–1944.* Cambridge: Cambridge University Press, 1976.

Schacht, Hjalmar. *The Confessions of the Old Wizard.* Boston: Houghton Mifflin, 1956.

Schlesinger, Arthur M., Jr. *The Coming of the New Deal.* Boston: Houghton Mifflin, Riverside Press Cambridge, 1959.

———. *The Crisis of the Old Order, 1919–1933.* Boston: Houghton Mifflin Company, Riverside Press Cambridge, 1957.

———. *The Politics of Upheaval.* Boston: Houghton Mifflin, Riverside Press Cambridge, 1960.

———. *Robert Kennedy and His Times.* Vol. 1. Boston: Houghton Mifflin Company, 1978.

Schwartz, Jordan. *Liberal: Adolf A. Berle and the Vision of an America Era.* New York: Free Press, 1987.

Scott, James Brown. *Robert Bacon: Life and Letters.* Garden City, N.Y.: Doubleday, Page, 1923.

Seaman, L. C. B. *Post-Victorian Britain—1902–1951.* London: Methuen, 1966.

Seligman, Joel. *The Transformation of Wall Street: A History of the Securities and Exchange Commission and Modern Corporate Finance.* Boston: Houghton Mifflin, 1982.

Seymour, Charles, ed. *Summary of the Intimate Papers of Colonel House.* Boston: Houghton Mifflin, 1926.

Shirer, William L. *The Rise and Fall of the Third Reich: A History of Nazi Germany.* New York: Simon & Schuster, 1960.

Shulman, Morton. *The Billion Dollar Windfall.* New York: William Morrow, 1970.

Silver, Nathan. *Lost New York.* New York: Weathervane Books, 1967.

Simon, William. *A Time for Truth.* New York and Chicago: Reader's Digest Press and McGraw-Hill, 1978.

Sinclair, Andrew. *Corsair: The Life of J. Pierpont Morgan.* Boston and Toronto: Little, Brown, 1981.

Slater, Robert. *The Titans of Takeover.* Englewood Cliffs, N.J.: Prentice-Hall, 1987.

Sloan, Alfred P., Jr. *My Years With General Motors.* Edited by John McDonald with Catharine Stevens. 1963. Reprint. Garden City, N.Y.: Doubleday, Anchor Books, 1972.

Smalley, George Washburn. *Anglo-American Memories.* London: Duckworth, 1912.

Smith, Denis Mack. *Mussolini: A Biography.* 1982. Reprint. New York: Random House, Vintage Books, 1983.

Smith, Jane S. *Elsie de Wolfe: A Life in the High Style.* New York: Atheneum, 1982.

Sobel, Robert. *Inside Wall Street: Continuity and Change in the Financial District.* New York and London: W. W. Norton, 1982.

———. *ITT: The Management of Opportunity.* New York: Times Books, Truman Talley Books, 1982.

———. *Panic on Wall Street: A Classic History of America's Financial Disasters—with a New Exploration of the Crash of 1987.* 1968. Reprint. New York: E. P. Dutton, Truman Talley Books, 1988.

Speer, Albert. *Inside the Third Reich: Memoirs.* New York: Macmillan, 1970.

Sprague, Irvine. *Bailout: An Insider's Account of Bank Failures and Rescues.* New York: Basic Books, 1986.

Steel, Ronald. *Walter Lippmann and the American Century.* Boston and Toronto: Little, Brown, 1980.

Steffens, Lincoln. *The Autobiography of Lincoln Steffens.* New York: Harcourt, Brace & World, 1931.

Stewart, James B. *The Partners.* New York: Simon & Schuster, 1983.

———. *The Prosecutors.* 1987. Reprint. New York and London: Simon & Schuster, A Touchstone Book, 1988.

Storry, Richard. *A History of Modern Japan.* 1960. Reprint. Harmondsworth, England, and New York: Penguin Books, 1987.

Swanberg, W. A. *Citizen Hearst.* New York: Charles Scribner's Sons, 1961.

———. *Whitney Father, Whitney Heiress.* New York: Charles Scribner's Sons, 1980.

Taylor, Telford. *Sword and Swastika: Generals and Nazis in the Third Reich.* Chicago: Quadrangle Paperbacks, 1952.

Thomson, George Malcolm. *The Prime Ministers: From Robert Walpole to Margaret Thatcher.* New York: William Morrow, 1981.

Truman, Harry. *Dear Bess—The Letters from Harry to Bess Truman.* New York: W. W. Norton, 1983.

Truman, Margaret. *Harry Truman.* New York: William Morrow, 1973.

Tugwell, Rexford G. *Roosevelt's Revolution.* New York: Macmillan, 1977.

Vazquez, Josefina Zoraida, and Lorenzo Meyer. *The United States and Mexico.* Chicago and London: University of Chicago Press, 1985.

Wade, Wyn Craig. *The Titanic: End of a Dream.* New York: Penguin Books, 1979.

Wechsberg, Joseph. *The Merchant Bankers.* Boston and Toronto: Little, Brown, 1966.

Wecter, Dixon. *The Saga of American Society: A Record of Social Aspiration, 1607–1937.* 1937. Reprint. New York: Charles Scribner's Sons, 1970.

Weller, John L. *The New Haven Railroad: Its Rise and Fall.* New York: Hastings House, 1969.

Welles, Chris. *The Last Days of the Club.* New York: E. P. Dutton, 1975.

Welsh, Frank. *Uneasy City: An Insider's View of the City of London.* London: Weidenfeld & Nicolson, 1986.

Wendt, Lloyd. *The Wall Street Journal.* Chicago, New York, and San Francisco: Rand McNally, 1982.

Whalen, Richard J. *The Founding Father: The Story of Joseph P. Kennedy.* New York: New American Library, World Book, 1961.

Wheeler, George. *Pierpont Morgan & Friends: The Anatomy of a Myth.* Englewood Cliffs, N.J.: Prentice-Hall, 1973.

White, William Allen. *The Autobiography of William Allen White.* New York: Macmillan, 1946.

———. *A Puritan in Babylon: The Story of Calvin Coolidge.* New York: Capricorn Books, 1965.

Williams, Marcia. *Inside Number 10.* London: Weidenfeld & Nicolson, 1972.

Williams, T. Harry. *Huey Long.* New York: Alfred A. Knopf, 1970.

Wilson, John Donald. *The Chase.* Boston: Harvard Business School Press, 1986.

Winkler, John K. *Morgan the Magnificent: The Life of J. Pierpont Morgan (1837–1913).* New York: Vanguard Press, 1930.

Woolf, Virginia. *The Diary of Virginia Woolf.* Vol. 3, *1925–1930.* New York and London: Harcourt Brace Jovanovich, 1980.

Young, George K. *Merchant Banking: Practice and Prospects.* London: Weidenfeld & Nicolson, 1966.

Zeckendorf, William. *Zeckendorf: The Autobiography of William Zeckendorf.* With Edward McCreary. New York: Holt, Rinehart & Winston, 1970.

Ziegler, Philip. *The Sixth Great Power: A History of One of the Greatest of All Banking Families, the House of Barings, 1762–1929.* New York: Alfred A. Knopf, 1988.

GOVERNMENT DOCUMENTS

Medina, Harold R. *The Corrected Opinion of Harold R. Medina, United States Circuit Judge, in United States of America, Plaintiff, v. Henry S. Morgan, Harold Stanley, et al., Defendants.* New York: Record Press, Inc., 1954.

U.K. Parliament. Committee to Review the Functioning of Financial Institutions [Wilson Committee]. *Transcript of the Oral Evidence Given by the Accepting Houses Committee.* December 6, 1977.

U.S. Congress. House. Committee on Banking and Currency. *Commercial Banks and Their Trust Activities.* Staff Report. Vols. 1–2, 1968.

U.S. Congress. House. Committee on Banking and Currency. Testimony of Mr. J. Pierpont Morgan and Mr. Henry P. Davison before the Money Trust Investigation, 1913. Morgan Guaranty Library, New York.

U.S. Congress. Senate. Committee on Banking and Currency. *Stock Exchange Practices: Hearings.* 72nd Cong., 1933–34.

U.S. Congress. Senate. Committee on Banking, Housing and Urban Affairs. *Legislation Concerning Foreign Investment and the Arab Boycott: Hear-*

ings before the Subcommittee on International Finance. 94th Cong., 1st sess., 1975.

U.S. Congress. Senate. Committee on Banking, Housing, and Urban Affairs. *New York City Fiscal Crisis: Hearings.* 94th Cong. 1st sess., 1975.

U.S. Congress. Senate Committee on Interstate Commerce, *Investigation of Railroads, Holding Companies, and Affiliated Companies: Hearings,* 74th Cong., 2d Sess., 1937.

U.S. Congress. Senate. Special Committee Investigating the Munitions Industry. *World War Financing and U.S. Industrial Expansion 1914–15.* Part 25, *Hearings.* 74th Cong., 1936.

U.S. Congress. Temporary National Economic Committee. *Investigation of Concentration of Economic Power: Hearings.* 76th Cong., 2nd sess., part 22, 1939–41.

U.S. Securities and Exchange Commission. *The Financial Collapse of the Penn Central Company.* Staff Report. Presented to the Special Subcommittee on Investigations of the Committee on Interstate and Foreign Commerce, Hon. Harley O. Staggers, chairman, August 1972.

U.S. Securities and Exchange Commission. *In the Matter of Richard Whitney, Edwin D. Morgan, Jr., and Others.* Vol. 1, *Report on Investigation.*

U.S. Securities and Exchange Commission. *Major Issues Confronting the Nation's Financial Institutions and Markets in the 1980s: Transcript of an SEC Conference at the Sheraton Hotel in Washington, D.C., October 7 and 8, 1982.* Chicago: Commerce Clearing House Inc., 1982.

U.S. Securities and Exchange Commission. *Official Transcript of Proceedings before the SEC in the Matter of Texas Gulf Sulphur Co.* Examination of Longstreet Hinton in New York, July 16, 1964.

PHOTO CREDITS

INDEX

M

S